THE LONGMAN
ANTHOLOGY OF
AMERICAN
DRAMA

Longman English and Humanities Series
Series Editor: Lee A. Jacobus

THE LONGMAN ANTHOLOGY OF

AMERICAN DRAMA

Edited by
LEE A. JACOBUS
University of Connecticut, Storrs

Longman
New York & London

THE LONGMAN ANTHOLOGY OF AMERICAN DRAMA

Longman Inc., 95 Church Street, White Plains, N.Y. 10601
Associated companies, branches, and representatives
throughout the world.

Developmental Editor: Gordon T. R. Anderson
Editorial and Design Supervisor: Joan Matthews
Interior Design: Angela Foote
Manufacturing and Production Supervisor: Anne Musso

Library of Congress Cataloging in Publication Data

Main entry under title:

The Longman anthology of American drama.

    (Longman English and humanities series)
    1. American drama.   I. Jacobus, Lee A.
II. Series.
PS625.L66   822'.008   80–21895
ISBN 0–582–28242–X (paper)
ISBN 0–582–28348–5 (cased)

Manufactured in the United States of America
9 8 7 6 5 4

Acknowledgments

Contents

For Joanna, Sharon, and Jamie,
who love the theater

Introduction

All the plays in this collection are remarkable; they read well and they play well. Even the earliest plays contain valuable insights for a contemporary reader. The contrast between innocence and experience in Royall Tyler's play reappears in one form or another throughout the history of American drama, although it is clear that America's anxiety about Europe's influence comes and goes in steady rhythms (whether this influence is in the fashions and manners the Americans try to emulate or in the literature and drama American playwrights learned from). Tyler's play is prophetic because it clarifies the struggle Americans have, even today, in establishing an identity separate from that of Europe. In Lorraine Hansberry's *A Raisin in the Sun*, we find this anxiety extended to the African legacy of black Americans. The American experience has developed in contrast with other nations, but even within our own nation, as Arthur Kopit's *Indians* begins to show us, there are also contrasts to be drawn.

There is more than contrast present in these plays, however. They represent a remarkable portrait of a nation, showing us what our people could face in themselves and what they could not face, what they thought important enough to discuss in a public forum devoted to entertainment and what they felt was unnecessary. The American world view has been dominated by hopefulness, the sense of the possible, and the ideals of equality and law, and it is evident in these plays in many ways. For instance, the plays are largely melodramas or tragi-comedies. This collection has no genuine tragedy, unless we regard *The Basic Training of Pavlo Hummel* as one, or the "tragi-comical farce" of Kopit's *Indians*. Arthur Miller's *Death of a Salesman*, not reprinted here, has usually been regarded as the one legitimate tragedy of the American stage, but since tragedy depends on fate, the forces of gods that lie without our control, and the inherent flaw of character that drags a hero down to his doom, we might be able to see tragedy in a number of important American plays, perhaps even in O'Neill's *Emperor Jones*.

Comedy is a more comfortable genre for American drama, it would seem. Tyler's play depends on it, although not quite to the extent that Neil Simon's *The Sunshine Boys* does; both plays, however, do also contain a deeper, more serious note. This collection has, in actuality, precious little laughter. We find some humor in *The Skin of Our Teeth*, *The Green Pastures*, *A Raisin in the Sun*, and *Suppressed Desires*. But we must always observe closely what it is we find amusing; the reasons why we laugh are as important as the fact that we laugh.

The serious side of American drama is more fully represented here, even in those plays in which we laugh most vigorously. The social problems that lie behind such plays as *Uncle Tom's Cabin*, *The Octoroon*, *The Adding Machine*, *Waiting for Lefty*, *TV*, and *No Place To Be Somebody* show a constant awareness of the elements of our society, our way of life. The theme of blackness, although rarely examined carefully before the current generation of black playwrights, has been with American drama since its beginnings. Black characters and black issues figure in at least half these plays, and if I could have included Edward Albee's *The Death of Bessie Smith* and Imamu Amiri Baraka's *The Dutchman*, the theme would have been even more fully represented. Alas, high permissions fees and technical restrictions put me in the position of Yeats, who once apologized for excluding Kipling from an anthology on the same grounds.

Others have written extensively on the dominant concerns of American drama in its different historical epochs. I wish only to point out that the plays selected come from a repository of immense richness. One cannot read through them without a sense of wonder that our literature is so strong, so powerful in its willingness to strike at the truth of our own nature. There is also a sense of walking through a picture gallery wherein we view what we were like as a nation; with drama, there is a more important sense in which these "pictures" are active participants in our own life now—they speak to us, exhort us, amuse us, instruct us, and allow us to revivify them. We participate with them even on the printed page—and how much more impressively on the stage itself—to such an extent that we realize there is nothing musty about them. They are not items in a museum; they are, instead, a living literature of which we are a part.

One cannot read or see these plays without asking some questions about their import. For instance, it is clear they show us a view of a nation absorbed for a time with its own identity, then with its mission. We cannot ask drama for answers on these issues, but we can look to it for ways in which the questions are posed. For example, the question of innocence is prominent in *The Contrast,* just as almost two hundred years later it is prominent in Ed Bullins' *Clara's Ole Man.* However, the concept of innocence has changed so much that we are forced to see just how much our society itself has changed. The value of work is treated in *The Adding Machine* and *TV* and many plays in between. *The Little Foxes* explores the rapacity that is also implied in a number of these plays. They all raise the question of what the rewards for honest labor might be; in a sense, they ask the ultimate question of integrity: in a world in which people are grasping, dishonest, and in collusion, can the honest man or woman succeed? And success, we know, is an ingrained American concept. The criminality of the late plays, such as *A View from the Bridge, Clara's Ole Man, The Basic Training of Pavlo Hummel,* and *No Place To Be Somebody* is something of a novelty, but only in certain ways. The language is often overtly that of the criminal, with expletives that our forebears (only a generation ago!) would not have tolerated and which only a few years ago could not have been spoken on the stage or even published. Before the turn of the century, plays showed a curious mix of quaint innocence, as in *Fashion* and *The Contrast,* with deeper implications that can only be termed criminal, as, for example, in *The Octoroon,* in which the camera "catches" a murderer whose entire mode of life must be seen as criminal in nature. Perhaps *Shenandoah* and *Uncle Tom's Cabin* can be interpreted as having criminality, in one form or another, at their roots, but there is no denying that they cannot be as direct, as overt, as shocking as some dramas of our most recent decades. Our modern plays do not imply; they state directly, and they force us to confront the fact that in some ways the style of life in America is criminal. Many of the values important characters reveal in some of these plays are unabashedly criminal, and to ignore those values, to pretend they do not exist, that they do not permeate all levels of society, and to deny that they are often taken for granted is to wish destruction on oneself. The despair such a revelation may engender is caught in Charles Gordone's *No Place To Be Somebody.* These plays, when seen in overview, seem to imply that the criminality we fear when we view it in the Mafia, in Gordone's or Arthur Miller's play, or in the black street gang thugs in Bullins' play, may be rooted in the deepest recesses of our character. So many of the plays deal with the theme of the criminal that we may be forced to face ourselves and see something we do not want to see. Yet, that is sometimes the function of drama.

This collection, arbitrary as all anthologies must be, is still a monument to talent and greatness. In some ways the finest service of literature is forcing us to face ourselves; these plays do that unflinchingly, despite all the cautionary notes about the stage serving as a place for tired business executives and people who simply want to be taken out of the miseries of everyday life and transported by some kind of magic into a never-never land. These plays do not bear witness to that need; they instead acknowledge a toughness and resilience that is admirable.

Thanks are always due to innumerable people on a project of this sort. The three thousand teachers of drama who were polled about this book and who were asked to react to this table of contents were remarkable in their generosity. Their enthusiasm buoyed the project. Most were positive and expressed a desire for the book almost immediately; some wanted plays we could not obtain; one denounced the project. This book is intended to help those who would like in one volume a selection of plays that covers the range of American drama since its beginnings, that brings together most of our best playwrights, and that offers direction for further reading. I have tried to remain unobtrusive while introducing each play, providing only what I felt was the most important information. I would like to thank those who helped with the project: Kathi Walsh, Sharon Jacobus, and particularly Pat Terry, who helped with bibliography, research, and a good critical eye. Perhaps I should thank most of all Gordon T. R. Anderson of Longman, who suggested I do this project in the first place.

Storrs, Connecticut

Lee A. Jacobus

Royall Tyler: *The Contrast* (1787)

Born in Boston in 1757, Royall Tyler prepared at Harvard to become a lawyer. After graduation in the class of 1776, he served as an aide to General Sullivan in the American Revolution, attaining the rank of Major. He saw action in the battle of Newport. After the war he practiced law in several states and settled in Vermont, where he suffered an indefinable psychological depression for many years. His introduction to the theater came when he was again on military duty, this time with General Benjamin Lincoln, in New York, suppressing the Shays Rebellion. He stayed long enough to see Richard Brinsley Sheridan's *School for Scandal* in 1787. Three weeks later, he had written his own play and showed it to the character actor, Thomas Wignell, who played Jonathan in the first production and helped get the play published.

Much of what Tyler wrote, both legal material and the more exciting fiction of *The Algerine Captive,* a novel, was rather serious in tone. But *The Contrast* shows that he had a remarkable comic gift. The play lays claim to being the first professionally produced native American drama, and it can still be successfully performed.

The theme of the play is the contrast between European sophistication and American innocence. As Dimple puts it in his exit line near the end of the play, "I take my leave, and you will please to observe, in the case of my deportment, the contrast between a gentleman, who has read Chesterfield and received the polish of Europe, and an unpolished, untravelled American." The play emphasizes that we must look beneath the polished surface of manners and into the hearts of people if we are to live well and fully. Van Rough, father of the heroine, Mary, is a fine example of a sensible American businessman who wants to know how things truly are. His ruse of hiding to hear Mary and Colonel Manly in order to evaluate their relationship is typical of the English Restoration stage, but it deepens the theme of the play and intensifies the contrast between him and Dimple.

Jonathan, "a true born Yankee American son of liberty," tells about his visit to *The School for Scandalization* in *The Contrast's* most memorable scene. He asked for his money back because the play disappointed him—all it did was show him people like those he already knew, doing things they usually did, whereas he expected some "sights" of the sort he'd never seen before. Jonathan's innocence begot many imitations, and he quickly became a stereotype; "Jonathans" were to be seen on the stage for more than a generation to come.

Royall Tyler eventually became Chief Justice of the Vermont Supreme Court and died in 1826. He did write other plays, some of which have been lost, but none were close to the quality of *The Contrast*. The energies a successful playwright of later years might have put into writing for the stage were obviously put into his profession, since there could have been no hope in 1787—and for many decades to come—of making a respectable living from his pen. Nonetheless, *The Contrast* stands as a worthy beginning for our literature, with themes that recur in later plays, with a growing national self-awareness, and with a clear analysis of the deceit of the old European world in contact with the shrewdness and honesty of the new world. Like the plays of Sheridan and Molière, *The Contrast* is lively, comic, and a careful evaluation of the manners and the mores of its society. We cannot read it or watch it on stage without being aware of how young and vital our country was then, and of how many traits it still maintains from that time.

Selected Readings

Arthur Hobson Quinn, *A History of the American Drama, from the Beginning to The Civil War* (New York: Harper Bros., 1923). See entry for Tyler.

Royall Tyler, *The Prose of Royall Tyler,* ed. Marius B. Peladeau (Montpelier: The Vermont Historical Society, 1972).

Royall Tyler, *The Verse of Royall Tyler,* ed. Marius B. Peladeau (Charlottesville: University Press of Virginia, 1968).

The Contrast

Royall Tyler

CHARACTERS

COL. MANLY	CHARLOTTE
DIMPLE	MARIA
VAN ROUGH	LETITIA
JESSAMY	JENNY
JONATHAN	SERVANTS

SCENE: New York

PROLOGUE

Written by a young gentleman of New-York, and spoken by Mr. Wignell

EXULT, each patriot heart!—this night is shewn
A piece, which we may fairly call our own;
Where the proud titles of "My Lord! Your
    Grace!"
To humble *Mr.* and plain *Sir* give place.
Our Author pictures not from foreign climes
The fashions or the follies of the times;
But has confin'd the subject of his work
To the gay scenes—the circles of New-York.
On native themes his Muse displays her pow'rs;
If ours the faults, the virtues too are ours.
Why should our thoughts to distant countries
    roam,
When each refinement may be found at home?
Who travels now to ape the rich or great,
To deck an equipage and roll in state;
To court the graces, or to dance with ease,
Or by hypocrisy to strive to please?
Our free-born ancestors such arts despis'd;
Genuine sincerity alone they priz'd;
Their minds, with honest emulation fir'd;
To solid good—not ornament—aspir'd;
Or, if ambition rous'd a bolder flame,
Stern virtue throve, where indolence was shame.

But modern youths, with imitative sense,
Deem taste in dress the proof of excellence;
And spurn the meanness of your homespun arts,
Since homespun habits would obscure their parts;
Whilst all, which aims at splendour and parade,
Must come from Europe, *and be ready made.*
Strange! we should thus our native worth
    disclaim,
And check the progress of our rising fame.
Yet *one,* whilst imitation bears the sway,
Aspires to nobler heights, and points the way.
Be rous'd, my friends! his bold example view;
Let your own Bards be proud to copy *you!*
Should rigid critics reprobate our play,
At least the patriotic heart will say,
"Glorious our fall, since in a noble cause.
"The bold *attempt alone* demands applause."
Still may the wisdom of the Comic Muse
Exalt your merits, or your faults accuse.
But think not, 't is her aim to be severe;—
We all are mortals, and as mortals err.
If candour pleases, we are truly blest;
Vice trembles, when compell'd to stand confess'd.
Let not light Censure on your faults offend,
Which aims not to expose them, but amend.
Thus does our Author to your candour trust;
Conscious, the *free* are generous, as just.

ACT I

SCENE. *An Apartment at* CHARLOTTE'S.

(CHARLOTTE *and* LETITIA *discovered.*)

LETITIA: And so, Charlotte, you really think the pocket-hoop unbecoming.

CHARLOTTE: No, I don't say so. It may be very becoming to saunter round the house of a rainy day; to visit my grand-mamma, or to go to Quakers' meeting: but to swim in a minuet, with the eyes of fifty well-dressed beaux upon me, to trip it in the Mall, or walk on the battery, give me the luxurious, jaunty, flowing, bell-hoop. It would have delighted you to have seen me the last evening, my charming girl! I was dangling o'er the battery with Billy Dimple; a knot of young fellows were upon the platform; as I passed them I faultered with one of the most bewitching false steps you ever saw, and then recovered myself with such a pretty confusion, flirting my hoop to discover a jet black shoe and brilliant buckle. Gad! how my little heart thrilled to hear the confused raptures of—*"Demme, Jack, what a delicate foot!" "Ha! General, what a well-turned—"*

LETITIA: Fie! fie! Charlotte (*stopping her mouth*), I protest you are quite a libertine.

CHARLOTTE: Why, my dear little prude, are we not all such libertines? Do you think, when I sat tortured two hours under the hands of my friseur, and an hour more at my toilet, that I had any thoughts of my aunt Susan, or my cousin Betsey? though they are both allowed to be critical judges of dress.

LETITIA: Why, who should we dress to please, but those who are judges of its merit?

CHARLOTTE: Why, a creature who does not know *Buffon* from *Souflée*—Man!—my Letitia—Man! for whom we dress, walk, dance, talk, lisp, languish, and smile. Does not the grave Spectator assure us that even our much bepraised diffidence, modesty, and blushes are all directed to make ourselves good wives and mothers as fast as we can? Why, I'll undertake with one flirt of this hoop to bring more beaux to my feet in one week than the grave Maria, and her sentimental circle, can do, by sighing sentiment till their hairs are grey.

LETITIA: Well, I won't argue with you; you always out-talk me; let us change the subject. I hear that Mr. Dimple and Maria are soon to be married.

CHARLOTTE: You hear true. I was consulted in the choice of the wedding clothes. She is to be married in a delicate white sattin, and has a monstrous pretty brocaded lutestring for the second day. It would have done you good to have seen with what an affected indifference the dear sentimentalist turned over a thousand pretty things, just as if her heart did not palpitate with her approaching happiness, and at last made her choice and arranged her dress with such apathy as if she did not know that plain white sattin and a simple blond lace would shew her clear skin and dark hair to the greatest advantage.

LETITIA: But they say her indifference to dress, and even to the gentleman himself, is not entirely affected.

CHARLOTTE: How?

LETITIA: It is whispered that if Maria gives her hand to Mr. Dimple, it will be without her heart.

CHARLOTTE: Though the giving the heart is one of the last of all laughable considerations in the marriage of a girl of spirit, yet I should like to hear what antiquated notions the dear little piece of old-fashioned prudery has got in her head.

LETITIA: Why, you know that old Mr. John-Richard-Robert-Jacob-Isaac-Abraham-Cornelius Van Dumpling, Billy Dimple's father (for he has thought fit to soften his name, as well as manners, during his English tour), was the most intimate friend of Maria's father. The old folks, about a year before Mr. Van Dumpling's death, proposed this match: the young folks were accordingly introduced, and told they must love one another. Billy was then a good-natured, decent-dressing young fellow, with a little dash of the coxcomb, such as our young fellows of fortune usually have. At this time, I really believe she thought she loved him; and had they then been married, I doubt not they might have jogged on, to the end of the chapter, a good kind of a sing-song lack-a-daysaical life, as other honest married folks do.

CHARLOTTE: Why did they not then marry?

LETITIA: Upon the death of his father, Billy went to England to see the world and rub off a little of the patroon rust. During his absence, Maria, like a good girl, to keep herself constant to her *nown true-love*, avoided company, and betook herself, for her amusement, to her books, and her dear Billy's letters. But, alas! how many ways has the mischievous demon of inconstancy of stealing into a woman's heart! Her love was destroyed by the very means she took to support it.

CHARLOTTE: How?—Oh! I have it—some likely young beau found the way to her study.

LETITIA: Be patient, Charlotte; your head so runs upon beaux. Why, she read Sir Charles

Grandison, Clarissa Harlow, Shenstone, and the Sentimental Journey; and between whiles, as I said, Billy's letters. But, as her taste improved, her love declined. The contrast was so striking betwixt the good sense of her books and the flimsiness of her love-letters, that she discovered she had unthinkingly engaged her hand without her heart; and then the whole transaction, managed by the old folks, now appeared so unsentimental, and looked so like bargaining for a bale of goods, that she found she ought to have rejected, according to every rule of romance, even the man of her choice, if imposed upon her in that manner. Clary Harlow would have scorned such a match.

CHARLOTTE: Well, how was it on Mr. Dimple's return? Did he meet a more favourable reception than his letters?

LETITIA: Much the same. She spoke of him with respect abroad, and with contempt in her closet. She watched his conduct and conversation, and found that he had by travelling acquired the wickedness of Lovelace without his wit, and the politeness of Sir Charles Grandison without his generosity. The ruddy youth, who washed his face at the cistern every morning, and swore and looked eternal love and constancy, was now metamorphosed into a flippant, palid, polite beau, who devotes the morning to his toilet, reads a few pages of Chesterfield's letters, and then minces out, to put the infamous principles in practice upon every woman he meets.

CHARLOTTE: But, if she is so apt at conjuring up these sentimental bugbears, why does she not discard him at once?

LETITIA: Why, she thinks her word too sacred to be trifled with. Besides, her father, who has a great respect for the memory of his deceased friend, is ever telling her how he shall renew his years in their union, and repeating the dying injunctions of old Van Dumpling.

CHARLOTTE: A mighty pretty story! And so you would make me believe that the sensible Maria would give up Dumpling manor, and the all-accomplished Dimple as a husband, for the absurd, ridiculous reason, forsooth, because she despises and abhors him. Just as if a lady could not be privileged to spend a man's fortune, ride in his carriage, be called after his name, and call him her *nown dear lovee* when she wants money, without loving and respecting the great he-creature. Oh! my dear girl, you are a monstrous prude.

LETITIA: I don't say what I would do; I only intimate how I suppose she wishes to act.

CHARLOTTE: No, no, no! A fig for sentiment. If she breaks, or wishes to break, with Mr. Dimple, depend upon it, she has some other man in her eye. A woman rarely discards one lover until she is sure of another. Letitia little thinks what a clue I have to Dimple's conduct. The generous man submits to render himself disgusting to Maria, in order that she may leave him at liberty to address me. I must change the subject. (*Aside, and rings a bell.*)

(*Enter* SERVANT.)

Frank, order the horses to.—Talking of marriage, did you hear that Sally Bloomsbury is going to be married next week to Mr. Indigo, the rich Carolinian?

LETITIA: Sally Bloomsbury married!—why, she is not yet in her teens.

CHARLOTTE: I do not know how that is, but you may depend upon it, 'tis a done affair. I have it from the best authority. There is my aunt Wyerly's Hannah. You know Hannah; though a black, she is a wench that was never caught in a lie in her life. Now, Hannah has a brother who courts Sarah, Mrs. Catgut the milliner's girl, and she told Hannah's brother, and Hannah, who, as I said before, is a girl of undoubted veracity, told it directly to me, that Mrs. Catgut was making a new cap for Miss Bloomsbury, which, as it was very dressy, it is very probable is designed for a wedding cap. Now, as she is to be married, who can it be but to Mr. Indigo? Why, there is no other gentleman that visits at her papa's.

LETITIA: Say not a word more, Charlotte. Your intelligence is so direct and well grounded, it is almost a pity that it is not a piece of scandal.

CHARLOTTE: Oh! I am the pink of prudence. Though I cannot charge myself with ever having discredited a tea-party by my silence, yet I take care never to report anything of my acquaintance, especially if it is to their credit,—*discredit*, I mean,—until I have searched to the bottom of it. It is true, there is infinite pleasure in this charitable pursuit. Oh! how delicious to go and condole with the friends of some backsliding sister, or to retire with some old dowager or maiden aunt of the family, who love scandal so well that they cannot forbear gratifying their appetite at the expense of the reputation of their nearest relations! And then to return full fraught with a rich collection of circumstances, to retail to the next circle of our acquaintance under the strongest injunctions of secrecy,—ha, ha, ha! —interlarding the melancholy tale with so many doleful shakes of the head, and more doleful "Ah!

who would have thought it! so amiable, so prudent a young lady, as we all thought her, what a monstrous pity! well, I have nothing to charge myself with; I acted the part of a friend, I warned her of the principles of that rake, I told her what would be the consequence; I told her so, I told her so."—Ha, ha, ha!

LETITIA: Ha, ha, ha! Well, but, Charlotte, you don't tell me what you think of Miss Bloomsbury's match.

CHARLOTTE: Think! why I think it is probable she cried for a plaything, and they have given her a husband. Well, well, well, the puling chit shall not be deprived of her plaything: 'tis only exchanging London dolls for American babies. —Apropos, of babies, have you heard what Mrs. Affable's high-flying notions of delicacy have come to?

LETITIA: Who, she that was Miss Lovely?

CHARLOTTE: The same; she married Bob Affable of Schenectady. Don't you remember?

(*Enter* SERVANT.)

SERVANT: Madam, the carriage is ready.

LETITIA: Shall we go to the stores first, or visiting?

CHARLOTTE: I should think it rather too early to visit, especially Mrs. Prim; you know she is so particular.

LETITIA: Well, but what of Mrs. Affable?

CHARLOTTE: Oh, I'll tell you as we go; come, come, let us hasten. I hear Mrs. Catgut has some of the prettiest caps arrived you ever saw. I shall die if I have not the first sight of them. (*Exeunt.*)

SCENE 2. *A Room in* VAN ROUGH's *House.*

(MARIA *sitting disconsolate at a Table, with Books, Etc.*)

SONG

I

The sun sets in night, and the stars shun the day;
But glory remains when their lights fade away!
Begin, ye tormentors! your threats are in vain,
For the son of Alknomook shall never complain.

II

Remember the arrows he shot from his bow;
Remember your chiefs by his hatchet laid low:
Why so slow?—do you wait till I shrink from the pain?
No—the son of Alknomook will never complain.

III

Remember the wood where in ambush we lay,
And the scalps which we bore from your nation away:
Now the flame rises fast, you exult in my pain;
But the son of Alknomook can never complain.

IV

I go to the land where my father is gone;
His ghost shall rejoice in the fame of his son:
Death comes like a friend, he relieves me from pain;
And thy son, Oh Alknomook! has scorn'd to complain.

There is something in this song which ever calls forth my affections. The manly virtue of courage, that fortitude which steels the heart against the keenest misfortunes, which interweaves the laurel of glory amidst the instruments of torture and death, displays something so noble, so exalted, that in despite of the prejudices of education I cannot but admire it, even in a savage. The prepossession which our sex is supposed to entertain for the character of a soldier is, I know, a standing piece of raillery among the wits. A cockade, a lapell'd coat, and a feather, they will tell you, are irresistible by a female heart. Let it be so. Who is it that considers the helpless situation of our sex, that does not see that we each moment stand in need of a protector, and that a brave one too? Formed of the more delicate materials of nature, endowed only with the softer passions, incapable, from our ignorance of the world, to guard against the wiles of mankind, our security for happiness often depends upon their generosity and courage. Alas! how little of the former do we find! How inconsistent! that man should be leagued to destroy that honour upon which solely rests his respect and esteem. Ten thousand temptations allure us, ten thousand passions betray us; yet the smallest deviation from the path of rectitude is followed by the contempt and insult of man, and the more remorseless pity of woman; years of penitence and tears cannot wash away the stain, nor a life of virtue obliterate its remembrance. Reputation is the life of woman; yet courage to protect it is masculine and disgusting; and the only safe asylum a woman of delicacy can find is in the arms of a man of honour. How naturally, then, should we love the brave and the generous; how gratefully should we bless the arm raised for our protection, when nerv'd by virtue and directed by honour! Heaven grant that the man with whom I may be connected—may be connected! Whither has my imagination transported me—whither does it now lead me? Am I not indissolubly engaged, "by every obligation of honour which my own consent and my father's approbation can give," to a man who can never share my affections, and whom a few days hence it will be criminal for me to disapprove—to disapprove! would to heaven that were all—to despise. For, can the most frivolous manners, actuated by the most depraved heart, meet, or merit, anything but contempt from every woman of delicacy and sentiment?

(VAN ROUGH *without*. Mary!)

Ha! my father's voice—Sir!———

(*Enter* VAN ROUGH.)

VAN ROUGH: What, Mary, always singing doleful ditties, and moping over these plaguy books.

MARIA: I hope, Sir, that it is not criminal to improve my mind with books, or to divert my melancholy with singing, at my leisure hours.

VAN ROUGH: Why, I don't know that, child; I don't know that. They us'd to say, when I was a young man, that if a woman knew how to make a pudding, and to keep herself out of fire and water, she knew enough for a wife. Now, what good have these books done you? have they not made you melancholy? as you call it. Pray, what right has a girl of your age to be in the dumps? haven't you everything your heart can wish; an't you going to be married to a young man of great fortune; an't you going to have the quit-rent of twenty miles square?

MARIA: One hundredth part of the land, and a lease for life of the heart of a man I could love, would satisfy me.

VAN ROUGH: Pho, pho! child; nonsense, downright nonsense, child. This comes of your reading your story-books; your Charles Grandisons, your Sentimental Journals, and your Robinson Crusoes, and such other trumpery. No, no, no! child; it is money makes the mare go; keep your eye upon the main chance, Mary.

MARIA: Marriage, Sir, is, indeed, a very serious affair.

VAN ROUGH: You are right, you are right. I am sure I found it so, to my cost.

MARIA: I mean, Sir, that as marriage is a portion for life, and so intimately involves our happiness, we cannot be too considerate in the choice of our companion.

VAN ROUGH: Right, child; very right. A young woman should be very sober when she is making her choice, but when she has once made it, as you have done, I don't see why she should not be as merry as a grig; I am sure she has reason enough to be so. Solomon says that "there is a time to laugh, and a time to weep." Now, a time for a young woman to laugh is when she has made sure of a good rich husband. Now, a time to cry, according to you, Mary, is when she is making choice of him; but I should think that a young woman's time to cry was when she despaired of *getting* one. Why, there was your mother, now: to be sure, when I popp'd the question to her she did look a little silly; but when she had once looked down on her apron-strings, as all modest young women us'd to do, and drawled out ye-s, she was as brisk and as merry as a bee.

MARIA: My honoured mother, Sir, had no motive to melancholy; she married the man of her choice.

VAN ROUGH: The man of her choice! And pray, Mary, an't you going to marry the man of your choice—what trumpery notion is this? It is these vile books (*throwing them away*). I'd have you to know, Mary, if you won't make young Van Dumpling the man of *your* choice, you shall marry him as the man of *my* choice.

MARIA: You terrify me, Sir. Indeed, Sir, I am all submission. My will is yours.

VAN ROUGH: Why, that is the way your mother us'd to talk. "My will is yours, my dear Mr. Van Rough, my will is yours"; but she took special care to have her own way, though, for all that.

MARIA: Do not reflect upon my mother's memory, Sir———

VAN ROUGH: Why not, Mary, why not? She kept me from speaking my mind all her *life*, and do you think she shall henpeck me now she is *dead* too? Come, come; don't go to sniveling; be a good girl, and mind the main chance. I'll see you well settled in the world.

MARIA: I do not doubt your love, Sir, and it is my duty to obey you. I will endeavour to make my duty and inclination go hand in hand.

VAN ROUGH: Well, well, Mary; do you be a good girl, mind the main chance, and never mind inclination. Why, do you know that I have been down in the cellar this very morning to examine a pipe of Madeira which I purchased the week you were born, and mean to tap on your wedding day?—That pipe cost me fifty pounds sterling. It was well worth sixty pounds; but I overreach'd Ben Bulkhead, the supercargo. I'll tell you the whole story. You must know that———

(*Enter* SERVANT.)

SERVANT: Sir, Mr. Transfer, the broker, is below. (*Exit.*)

VAN ROUGH: Well, Mary, I must go. Remember, and be a good girl, and mind the main chance. (*Exit.*)

MARIA (*alone*): How deplorable is my situation! How distressing for a daughter to find her heart militating with her filial duty! I know my father loves me tenderly; why then do I reluctantly obey him? Heaven knows! with what reluctance I should oppose the will of a parent, or set an example of filial disobedience; at a parent's command, I could wed awkwardness and deformity. Were the heart of my husband good, I would so magnify his good qualities with the eye of conjugal affection, that the defects of his person and manners should be lost in the emanation of his virtues. At a father's command, I could embrace poverty. Were the poor man my husband, I would learn resignation to my lot; I would enliven our frugal meal with good humour, and chase away misfortune from our cottage with a smile. At a father's command, I could almost submit to what every female heart knows to be the most mortifying, to marry a weak man, and blush at my husband's folly in every company I visited. But to marry a depraved wretch, whose only virtue is a polished exterior; who is actuated by the unmanly ambition of conquering the defenceless; whose heart, insensible to the emotions of patriotism, dilates at the plaudits of every unthinking girl; whose laurels are the sighs and tears of the miserable victims of his specious behaviour,—can he, who has no regard for the peace and happiness of other families, ever have a due regard for the peace and happiness of his own? Would to heaven that my father were not so hasty in his temper? Surely, if I were to state my reasons for declining this match, he would not compel me to marry a man, whom, though my lips may solemnly promise to honour, I find my heart must ever despise. (*Exit.*)

ACT II

SCENE 1. *Enter* CHARLOTTE *and* LETITIA.

CHARLOTTE (*at entering*): Betty, take those things out of the carriage and carry them to my chamber; see that you don't tumble them. My dear, I protest, I think it was the homeliest of the whole. I declare I was almost tempted to return and change it.

LETITIA: Why would you take it?

CHARLOTTE: Didn't Mrs. Catgut say it was the most fashionable?

LETITIA: But, my dear, it will never fit becomingly on you.

CHARLOTTE: I know that; but did not you hear Mrs. Catgut say it was fashionable?

LETITIA: Did you see that sweet airy cap with the white sprig?

CHARLOTTE: Yes, and I longed to take it; but, my dear, what could I do? Did not Mrs. Catgut say it was the most fashionable; and if I had not taken it, was not that awkward gawky, Sally Slender, ready to purchase it immediately?

LETITIA: Did you observe how she tumbled over the things at the next shop, and then went off without purchasing anything, nor even thanking the poor man for his trouble? But, of all the awkward creatures, did you see Miss Blouze endeavouring to thrust her unmerciful arm into those small kid gloves?

CHARLOTTE: Ha, ha, ha, ha!

LETITIA: Then did you take notice with what an affected warmth of friendship she and Miss Wasp met? when all their acquaintance know how much pleasure they take in abusing each other in every company.

CHARLOTTE: Lud! Letitia, is that so extraordinary? Why, my dear, I hope you are not going to turn sentimentalist. Scandal, you know, is but amusing ourselves wiith the faults, foibles, follies, and reputations of our friends; indeed, I don't know why we should have friends, if we are not at liberty to make use of them. But no person is so ignorant of the world as to suppose, because I amuse myself with a lady's faults, that I am obliged to quarrel with her person every time we meet: believe me, my dear, we should have very few acquaintance at that rate.

(SERVANT *enters and delivers a letter to* CHARLOTTE. *Exit.*)

CHARLOTTE: You'll excuse me, my dear. (*Opens and reads to herself.*)

LETITIA: Oh, quite excusable.

CHARLOTTE: As I hope to be married, my brother Henry is in the city.

LETITIA: What, your brother, Colonel Manly?

CHARLOTTE: Yes, my dear; the only brother I have in the world.

LETITIA: Was he never in this city?

CHARLOTTE: Never nearer than Harlem

Heights, where he lay with his regiment.

LETITIA: What sort of a being is this brother of yours? If he is as chatty, as pretty, as sprightly as you, half the belles in the city will be pulling caps for him.

CHARLOTTE: My brother is the very counterpart and reverse of me: I am gay, he is grave; I am airy, he is solid; I am ever selecting the most pleasing objects for my laughter, he has a tear for every pitiful one. And thus, whilst he is plucking the briars and thorns from the path of the unfortunate, I am strewing my own path with roses.

LETITIA: My sweet friend, not quite so poetical, and a little more particular.

CHARLOTTE: Hands off, Letitia. I feel the rage of simile upon me; I can't talk to you in any other way. My brother has a heart replete with the noblest sentiments, but then, it is like—it is like—Oh! you provoking girl, you have deranged all my ideas—it is like—Oh! I have it—his heart is like an old maiden lady's bandbox; it contains many costly things, arranged with the most scrupulous nicety, yet the misfortune is that they are too delicate, costly, and antiquated for common use.

LETITIA: By what I can pick out of your flowery description, your brother is no beau.

CHARLOTTE: No, indeed; he makes no pretension to the character. He'd ride, or rather fly, an hundred miles to relieve a distressed object, or to do a gallant act in the service of his country; but should you drop your fan or bouquet in his presence, it is ten to one that some beau at the farther end of the room would have the honour of presenting it to you before he had observed that it fell. I'll tell you one of his antiquated, antigallant notions. He said once in my presence, in a room full of company,—would you believe it?—in a large circle of ladies, that the best evidence a gentleman could give a young lady of his respect and affection was to endeavour in a friendly manner to rectify her foibles. I protest I was crimson to the eyes, upon reflecting that I was known as his sister.

LETITIA: Insupportable creature! tell a lady of her faults! if he is so grave, I fear I have no chance of captivating him.

CHARLOTTE: His conversation is like a rich, old-fashioned brocade,—it will stand alone; every sentence is a sentiment. Now you may judge what a time I had with him, in my twelve months' visit to my father. He read me such lectures, out of pure brotherly affection, against the extremes of fashion, dress, flirting, and coquetry, and all the other dear things which he knows I doat upon,

that I protest his conversation made me as melancholy as if I had been at church; and heaven knows, though I never prayed to go there but on one occasion, yet I would have exchanged his conversation for a psalm and a sermon. Church is rather melancholy, to be sure; but then I can ogle the beaux, and be regaled with "here endeth the first lesson," but his brotherly *here*, you would think had no end. You captivate him! Why, my dear, he would as soon fall in love with a box of Italian flowers. There is Maria, now, if she were not engaged, she might do something. Oh! how I should like to see that pair of pensorosos together, looking as grave as two sailors' wives of a stormy night, with a flow of sentiment meandering through their conversation like purling streams in modern poetry.

LETITIA: Oh! my dear fanciful——

CHARLOTTE: Hush! I hear some person coming through the entry.

(*Enter* SERVANT.)

SERVANT: Madam, there's a gentleman below who calls himself Colonel Manly; do you chuse to be at home?

CHARLOTTE: Shew him in. (*Exit* SERVANT.) Now for a sober face.

(*Enter* COLONEL MANLY.)

MANLY: My dear Charlotte, I am happy that I once more enfold you within the arms of fraternal affection. I know you are going to ask (amiable impatience!) how our parents do,—the venerable pair transmit you their blessing by me. They totter on the verge of a well-spent life, and wish only to see their children settled in the world, to depart in peace.

CHARLOTTE: I am very happy to hear that they are well. (*Coolly.*) Brother, will you give me leave to introduce you to our uncle's ward, one of my most intimate friends?

MANLY (*saluting* LETITIA): I ought to regard your friends as my own.

CHARLOTTE: Come, Letitia, do give us a little dash of your vivacity; my brother is so sentimental and so grave, that I protest he'll give us the vapours.

MANLY: Though sentiment and gravity, I know, are banished the polite world, yet I hoped they might find some countenance in the meeting of such near connections as brother and sister.

CHARLOTTE: Positively, brother, if you go one step further in this strain, you will set me crying, and that, you know, would spoil my eyes; and then I should never get the husband which our good papa and mamma have so kindly wished me—never be established in the world.

MANLY: Forgive me, my sister,—I am no enemy to mirth; I love your sprightliness; and I hope it will one day enliven the hours of some worthy man; but when I mention the respectable authors of my existence,—the cherishers and protectors of my helpless infancy, whose hearts glow with such fondness and attachment that they would willingly lay down their lives for my welfare,—you will excuse me if I am so unfashionable as to speak of them with some degree of respect and reverence.

CHARLOTTE: Well, well, brother; if you won't be gay, we'll not differ; I will be as grave as you wish. (*Affects gravity*.) And so, brother, you have come to the city to exchange some of your commutation notes for a little pleasure?

MANLY: Indeed you are mistaken; my errand is not of amusement, but business; and as I neither drink nor game, my expenses will be so trivial, I shall have no occasion to sell my notes.

CHARLOTTE: Then you won't have occasion to do a very good thing. Why, here was the Vermont General—he came down some time since, sold all his musty notes at one stroke, and then laid the cash out in trinkets for his dear Fanny. I want a dozen pretty things myself; have you got the notes with you?

MANLY: I shall be ever willing to contribute, as far as it is in my power, to adorn or in any way to please my sister; yet I hope I shall never be obliged for this to sell my notes. I may be romantic, but I preserve them as a sacred deposit. Their full amount is justly due to me, but as embarrassments, the natural consequences of a long war, disable my country from supporting its credit, I shall wait with patience until it is rich enough to discharge them. If that is not in my day, they shall be transmitted as an honourable certificate to posterity, that I have humbly imitated our illustrious WASHINGTON, in having exposed my health and life in the service of my country, without reaping any other reward than the glory of conquering in so arduous a contest.

CHARLOTTE: Well said heroics. Why, my dear Henry, you have such a lofty way of saying things, that I protest I almost tremble at the thought of introducing you to the polite circles in the city. The belles would think you were a player run mad, with your head filled with old scraps of tragedy; and as to the beaux, they might admire, because they would not understand you. But, however, I must, I believe, introduce you to two

or three ladies of my acquaintance.

LETITIA: And that will make him acquainted with thirty or forty beaux.

CHARLOTTE: Oh! brother, you don't know what a fund of happiness you have in store.

MANLY: I fear, sister, I have not refinement sufficient to enjoy it.

CHARLOTTE: Oh! you cannot fail being pleased.

LETITIA: Our ladies are so delicate and dressy.

CHARLOTTE: And our beaux so dressy and delicate.

LETITIA: Our ladies chat and flirt so agreeably.

CHARLOTTE: And our beaux simper and bow so gracefully.

LETITIA: With their hair so trim and neat.

CHARLOTTE: And their faces so soft and sleek.

LETITIA: Their buckles so tonish and bright.

CHARLOTTE: And their hands so slender and white.

LETITIA: I vow, Charlotte, we are quite poetical.

CHARLOTTE: And then, brother, the faces of the beaux are of such a lily-white hue! None of that horrid robustness of constitution, that vulgar cornfed glow of health, which can only serve to alarm an unmarried lady with apprehension, and prove a melancholy memento to a married one, that she can never hope for the happiness of being a widow. I will say this to the credit of our city beaux, that such is the delicacy of their complexion, dress, and address, that, even had I no reliance upon the honour of the dear Adonises, I would trust myself in any possible situation with them, without the least apprehensions of rudeness.

MANLY: Sister Charlotte!

CHARLOTTE: Now, now, now, brother (*interrupting him*), now don't go to spoil my mirth with a dash of your gravity; I am so glad to see you, I am in tip-top spirits. Oh! that you could be with us at a little snug party. There is Billy Simper, Jack Chaffé, and Colonel Van Titter, Miss Promonade, and the two Miss Tambours, sometimes make a party, with some other ladies, in a sidebox at the play. Everything is conducted with such decorum. First we bow round to the company in general, then to each one in particular, then we have so many inquiries after each other's health, and we are so happy to meet each other, and it is so many ages since we last had that pleasure, and if a married lady is in company, we have such a sweet dissertation upon her son Bobby's chin-cough; then the curtain rises, then our sensibility is all awake, and then, by the mere force of apprehension, we torture some harmless expression into a double meaning, which the poor author never dreamt of, and then we have recourse to our fans, and then we blush, and then the gentlemen jog one another, peep under the fan, and make the prettiest remarks; and then we giggle and they simper, and they giggle and we simper, and then the curtain drops, and then for nuts and oranges, and then we bow, and it's pray, Ma'am, take it, and pray, Sir, keep it, and oh! not for the world, Sir; and then the curtain rises again, and then we blush and giggle and simper and bow all over again. Oh! the sentimental charms of a side-box conversation! (*All laugh.*)

MANLY: Well, sister, I join heartily with you in the laugh; for, in my opinion, it is as justifiable to laugh at folly as it is reprehensible to ridicule misfortune.

CHARLOTTE: Well, but, brother, positively I can't introduce you in these clothes: why, your coat looks as if it were calculated for the vulgar purpose of keeping yourself comfortable.

MANLY: This coat was my regimental coat in the late war. The public tumults of our state have induced me to buckle on the sword in support of that government which I once fought to establish. I can only say, sister, that there was a time when this coat was respectable, and some people even thought that those men who had endured so many winter campaigns in the service of their country, without bread, clothing, or pay, at least deserved that the poverty of their appearance should not be ridiculed.

CHARLOTTE: We agree in opinion entirely, brother, though it would not have done for me to have said it: it is the coat makes the man respectable. In the time of the war, when we were almost frightened to death, why, your coat was respectable, that is, fashionable; now another kind of coat is fashionable, that is, respectable. And pray direct the taylor to make yours the height of the fashion.

MANLY: Though it is of little consequence to me of what shape my coat is, yet, as to the height of the fashion, there you will please to excuse me, sister. You know my sentiments on that subject. I have often lamented the advantage which the French have over us in that particular. In Paris, the fashions have their dawnings, their routine, and declensions, and depend as much upon the caprice of the day as in other countries; but there every lady assumes a right to deviate from the general *ton* as far as will be of advantage to her own appearance. In America, the cry is, what is the fashion? and we follow it indiscriminately,

because it is so.

CHARLOTTE: Therefore it is, that when large hoops are in fashion, we often see many a plump girl lost in the immensity of a hoop-petticoat, whose want of height and *en-bon-point* would never have been remarked in any other dress. When the high headdress is the mode, how then do we see a lofty cushion, with a profusion of gauze, feathers, and ribband, supported by a face no bigger than an apple! whilst a broad full-faced lady, who really would have appeared tolerably handsome in a large head-dress, looks with her smart chapeau as masculine as a soldier.

MANLY: But remember, my dear sister, and I wish all my fair country-women would recollect, that the only excuse a young lady can have for going extravagantly into a fashion is because it makes her look extravagantly handsome.—Ladies, I must wish you a good morning.

CHARLOTTE: But, brother, you are going to make home with us.

MANLY: Indeed I cannot. I have seen my uncle and explained that matter.

CHARLOTTE: Come and dine with us, then. We have a family dinner about half-past four o'clock.

MANLY: I am engaged to dine with the Spanish ambassador. I was introduced to him by an old brother officer; and instead of freezing me with a cold card of compliment to dine with him ten days hence, he, with the true old Castilian frankness, in a friendly manner, asked me to dine with him to-day—an honour I could not refuse. Sister, adieu—Madam, your most obedient——— (*Exit.*)

CHARLOTTE: I will wait upon you to the door, brother; I have something particular to say to you. (*Exit.*)

LETITIA (*alone*): What a pair!—She the pink of flirtation, he the essence of everything that is *outré* and gloomy.—I think I have completely deceived Charlotte by my manner of speaking of Mr. Dimple; she's too much the friend of Maria to be confided in. He is certainly rendering himself disagreeable to Maria, in order to break with her and proffer his hand to me. This is what the delicate fellow hinted in our last conversation. (*Exit.*)

SCENE 2. *The Mall.*

(*Enter* JESSAMY.)

JESSAMY: Positively this Mall is a very pretty place. I hope the cits won't ruin it by repairs. To be sure, it won't do to speak of in the same day with Raneleghor Vauxhall; however, it's a fine place for a young fellow to display his person to advantage. Indeed, nothing is lost here; the girls have taste, and I am very happy to find they have adopted the elegant London fashion of looking back, after a genteel fellow like me has passed them.—Ah! who comes here? This, by his awkwardness, must be the Yankee colonel's servant. I'll accost him.

(*Enter* JONATHAN.)

Votre très-humble serviteur, Monsieur. I understand Colonel Manly, the Yankee officer, has the honour of your services.

JONATHAN: Sir! ———

JESSAMY: I say, Sir, I understand that Colonel Manly has the honour of having you for a servant.

JONATHAN: Servant! Sir, do you take me for a neger,—I am Colonel Manly's waiter.

JESSAMY: A true Yankee distinction, egad, without a difference. Why, Sir, do you not perform all the offices of a servant? do you not even blacken his boots?

JONATHAN: Yes; I do grease them a bit sometimes; but I am a true blue son of liberty, for all that. Father said I should come as Colonel Manly's waiter, to see the world, and all that; but no man shall master me. My father has as good a farm as the colonel.

JESSAMY: Well, Sir, we will not quarrel about terms upon the eve of an acquaintance from which I promise myself so much satisfaction;—therefore, sans ceremonie———

JONATHAN: What?———

JESSAMY: I say I am extremely happy to see Colonel Manly's waiter.

JONATHAN: Well, and I vow, too, I am pretty considerably glad to see you; but what the dogs need of all this outlandish lingo? Who may you be, Sir, if I may be so bold?

JESSAMY: I have the honour to be Mr. Dimple's servant, or, if you please, waiter. We lodge under the same roof, and should be glad of the honour of your acquaintance.

JONATHAN: You a waiter! by the living jingo, you look so topping, I took you for one of the agents to Congress.

JESSAMY: The brute has discernment, notwithstanding his appearance.—Give me leave to say I wonder then at your familiarity.

JONATHAN: Why, as to the matter of that, Mr.———; pray, what's your name?

JESSAMY: Jessamy, at your service.

JONATHAN: Why, I swear we don't make any great matter of distinction in our state between quality and other folks.

JESSAMY: This is, indeed, a levelling principle.—I hope, Mr. Jonathan, you have not taken part with the insurgents.

JONATHAN: Why, since General Shays has sneaked off and given us the bag to hold, I don't care to give my opinion; but you'll promise not to tell—put your ear this way—you won't tell?—I vow I did think the sturgeons were right.

JESSAMY: I thought, Mr. Jonathan, you Massachusetts men always argued with a gun in your hand. Why didn't you join them?

JONATHAN: Why, the colonel is one of those folks called the Shin—Shin—dang it all, I can't speak them lignum vitæ words—you know who I mean—there is a company of them—they wear a china goose at their button-hole—a kind of gilt thing.—Now the colonel told father and brother, —you must know there are, let me see—there is Elnathan, Silas, and Barnabas, Tabitha—no, no, she's a she—tarnation, now I have it—there's Elnathan, Silas, Barnabas, Jonathan, that's I— seven of us, six went into the wars, and I staid at home to take care of mother. Colonel said that it was a burning shame for the true blue Bunker Hill sons of liberty, who had fought Governor Hutchinson, Lord North, and the Devil, to have any hand in kicking up a cursed dust against a government which we had, every mother's son of us, a hand in making.

JESSAMY: Bravo!—Well, have you been abroad in the city since your arrival? What have you seen that is curious and entertaining?

JONATHAN: Oh! I have seen a power of fine sights. I went to see two marble-stone men and a leaden horse that stands out in doors in all weathers; and when I came where they was, one had got no head, and t'other wern't there. They said as how the leaden man was a damn'd tory, and that he took wit in his anger and rode off in the time of the troubles.

JESSAMY: But this was not the end of your excursion?

JONATHAN: Oh, no; I went to a place they call Holy Ground. Now I counted this was a place where folks go to meeting; so I put my hymn-book in my pocket, and walked softly and grave as a minister; and when I came there, the dogs a bit of a meeting-house could I see. At last I spied a young gentlewoman standing by one of the seats which they have here at the doors. I took her to be the deacon's daughter, and she looked so kind, and so obliging, that I thought I would go and ask her the way to lecture, and—would you think it?—she called me dear, and sweeting, and honey, just as if we were married: by the living jingo, I had a month's mind to buss her.

JESSAMY: Well, but how did it end?

JONATHAN: Why, as I was standing talking with her, a parcel of sailor men and boys got round me, the snarl-headed curs fell a-kicking and cursing of me at such a tarnal rate, that I vow I was glad to take· to my heels and split home, right off, tail on end, like a stream of chalk.

JESSAMY: Why, my dear friend, you are not acquainted with the city; that girl you saw was a———(*Whispers.*)

JONATHAN: Mercy on my soul! was that young woman a harlot!—Well! if this is New-York Holy Ground, what must the Holy-day Ground be!

JESSAMY: Well, you should not judge of the city too rashly. We have a number of elegant, fine girls here that make a man's leisure hours pass very agreeably. I would esteem it an honour to announce you to some of them.—Gad! that announce is a select word; I wonder where I picked it up.

JONATHAN: I don't want to know them.

JESSAMY: Come, come, my dear friend, I see that I must assume the honour of being the director of your amusements. Nature has given us passions, and youth and opportunity stimulate to gratify them. It is no shame, my dear Blueskin, for a man to assume himself with a little gallantry.

JONATHAN: Girl huntry! I don't altogether understand. I never played at that game. I know how to play hunt the squirrel, but I can't play anything with the girls; I am as good as married.

JESSAMY: Vulgar, horrid brute! Married, and above a hundred miles from his wife, and thinks that an objection to his making love to every woman he meets! He never can have read, no, he never can have been in a room with a volume of the divine Chesterfield.—So you are married?

JONATHAN: No, I don't say so; I said I was as good as married, a kind of promise.

JESSAMY: As good as married!———

JONATHAN: Why, yes; there's Tabitha Wymen, the deacon's daughter, at home; she and I have been courting a great while, and folks say as how we are to be married; and so I broke a piece of money with her when we parted, and she promised not to spark it with Solomon Dyer while I am gone. You wou'dn't have me false to my true-love, would you?

JESSAMY: May be you have another reason for constancy; possibly the young lady has a fortune? Ha! Mr. Jonathan, the solid charms: the chains of love are never so binding as when the links are made of gold.

JONATHAN: Why, as to fortune, I must needs say her father is pretty dumb rich; he went representative for our town last year. He will give her—let me see—four times seven is—seven times four—nought and carry one,—he will give her twenty acres of land—somewhat rocky though—a Bible, and a cow.

JESSAMY: Twenty acres of rock, a Bible, and a cow! Why, my dear Mr. Jonathan, we have servant-maids, or, as you would more elegantly express it, waitresses, in this city, who collect more in one year from their mistresses' cast clothes.

JONATHAN: You don't say so!———

JESSAMY: Yes, and I'll introduce you to one of them. There is a little lump of flesh and delicacy that lives at next door, waitress to Miss Maria; we often see her on the stoop.

JONATHAN: But are you sure she would be courted by me?

JESSAMY: Never doubt it; remember a faint heart never—blisters on my tongue—I was going to be guilty of a vile proverb; flat against the authority of Chesterfield. I say there can be no doubt that the brilliancy of your merit will secure you a favourable reception.

JONATHAN: Well, but what must I say to her?

JESSAMY: Say to her! why, my dear friend, though I admire your profound knowledge on every other subject, yet, you will pardon my saying that your want of opportunity has made the female heart escape the poignancy of your penetration. Say to her! Why, when a man goes a-courting, and hopes for success, he must begin with doing, and not saying.

JONATHAN: Well, what must I do?

JESSAMY: Why, when you are introduced you must make five or six elegant bows.

JONATHAN: Six elegant bows! I understand that; six, you say? Well———

JESSAMY: Then you must press and kiss her hand; then press and kiss, and so on to her lips and cheeks; then talk as much as you can about hearts, darts, flames, nectar and ambrosia—the more incoherent the better.

JONATHAN: Well, but suppose she should be angry with I?

JESSAMY: Why, if she should pretend—please to observe, Mr. Jonathan—if she should pretend to be offended, you must———But I'll tell you how my master acted in such a case: He was seated by a young lady of eighteen upon a sofa, plucking with a wanton hand the blooming sweets of youth and beauty. When the lady thought it necessary to check his ardour, she called up a frown upon her lovely face, so irresistibly alluring, that it would have warmed the frozen bosom of age; remember, said she, putting her delicate arm upon his, remember your character and my honour. My master instantly dropped upon his knees, with eyes swimming with love, cheeks glowing with desire, and in the gentlest modulation of voice he said: My dear Caroline, in a few months our hands will be indissolubly united at the altar; our hearts I feel are already so; the favours you now grant as evidence of your affection are favours indeed; yet, when the ceremony is once past, what will now be received with rapture will then be attributed to duty.

JONATHAN: Well, and what was the consequence?

JESSAMY: The consequence!—Ah! forgive me, my dear friend, but you New England gentlemen have such a laudable curiosity of seeing the bottom of everything;—why, to be honest, I confess I saw the blooming cherub of a consequence smiling in its angelic mother's arms, about ten months afterwards.

JONATHAN: Well, if I follow all your plans, make them six bows, and all that, shall I have such little cherubim consequences?

JESSAMY: Undoubtedly.—What are you musing upon?

JONATHAN: You say you'll certainly make me acquainted?—Why, I was thinking then how I should contrive to pass this broken piece of silver —won't it buy a sugar-dram?

JESSAMY: What is that, the love-token from the deacon's daughter?—You come on bravely. But I must hasten to my master. Adieu, my dear friend.

JONATHAN: Stay, Mr. Jessamy—must I buss her when I am introduced to her?

JESSAMY: I told you, you must kiss her.

JONATHAN: Well, but must I buss her?

JESSAMY: Why kiss and buss, and buss and kiss, is all one.

JONATHAN: Oh! my dear friend, though you have a profound knowledge of all, a pugnency of tribulation, you don't know everything. (*Exit.*)

JESSAMY (*alone*): Well, certainly I improve; my master could not have insinuated himself with more address into the heart of a man he despised. Now will this blundering dog sicken Jenny with his nauseous pawings, until she flies into my arms for very ease. How sweet will the contrast be between the blundering Jonathan and the courtly and accomplished Jessamy!

ACT III

SCENE 1. DIMPLE's *Room.*

(DIMPLE *discovered at a Toilet.*)

DIMPLE (*reading*): "Women have in general but one object, which is their beauty." Very true, my lord; positively very true. "Nature has hardly formed a woman ugly enough to be insensible to flattery upon her person." Extremely just, my lord; every day's delightful experience confirms this. "If her face is so shocking that she must, in some degree, be conscious of it, her figure and air, she thinks, make ample amends for it." The sallow Miss Wan is a proof of this. Upon my telling the distasteful wretch, the other day, that her countenance spoke the pensive language of sentiment, and that Lady Wortley Montagu declared that if the ladies were arrayed in the garb of innocence, the face would be the last part which would be admired, as Monsieur Milton expresses it, she grinn'd horribly a ghastly smile. "If her figure is deformed, she thinks her face counterbalances it."

(*Enter* JESSAMY *with letters.*)

Where got you these, Jessamy?

JESSAMY: Sir, the English packet is arrived.

DIMPLE (*opens and reads a letter enclosing notes*):

"Sir,
"I have drawn bills on you in favour of Messrs. Van Cash and Co. as per margin. I have taken up your note to Col. Piquet, and discharged your debts to my Lord Lurcher and Sir Harry Rook. I herewith enclose you copies of the bills, which I have no doubt will be immediately honoured. On failure, I shall empower some lawyer in your country to recover the amounts.
"I am, Sir,
"Your most humble servant,
"JOHN HAZARD."

Now, did not my lord expressly say that it was unbecoming a well-bred man to be in a passion, I confess I should be ruffled. (*Reads.*) "There is no accident so unfortunate, which a wise man may not turn to his advantage; nor any accident so fortunate, which a fool will not turn to his disadvantage." True, my lord; but how advantage can be derived from this I can't see. Chesterfield himself, who made, however, the worst practice of the most excellent precepts, was never in so embarrassing a situation. I love the person of

Charlotte, and it is necessary I should command the fortune of Letitia. As to Maria!—I doubt not by my *sang-froid* behaviour I shall compel her to decline the match; but the blame must not fall upon me. A prudent man, as my lord says, should take all the credit of a good action to himself, and throw the discredit of a bad one upon others. I must break with Maria, marry Letitia, and as for Charlotte—why, Charlotte must be a companion to my wife.—Here, Jessamy!

(*Enter* JESSAMY. DIMPLE *folds and seals two letters.*)

DIMPLE: Here, Jessamy, take this letter to my love. (*Gives one.*)

JESSAMY: To which of your honour's loves?— Oh! (*reading*) to Miss Letitia, your honour's rich love.

DIMPLE: And this (*delivers another*) to Miss Charlotte Manly. See that you deliver them privately.

JESSAMY: Yes, your honour. (*Going.*)

DIMPLE: Jessamy, who are these strange lodgers that came to the house last night?

JESSAMY: Why, the master is a Yankee colonel; I have not seen much of him; but the man is the most unpolished animal your honour ever disgraced your eyes by looking upon. I have had one of the most *outré* conversations with him!—He really has a most prodigious effect upon my risibility.

DIMPLE: I ought, according to every rule of Chesterfield, to wait on him and insinuate myself into his good graces.————Jessamy, wait on the colonel with my compliments, and if he is disengaged I will do myself the honour of paying him my respects.—Some ignorant, unpolished boor————

(JESSAMY *goes off and returns.*)

JESSAMY: Sir, the colonel is gone out, and Jonathan his servant says that he is gone to stretch his legs upon the Mall.—Stretch his legs! what an indelicacy of diction!

DIMPLE. Very well. Reach me my hat and sword. I'll accost him there, in my way to Letitia's, as by accident; pretend to be struck by his person and address, and endeavour to steal into his confidence. Jessamy, I have no business for you at present. (*Exit.*)

JESSAMY (*taking up the book*): My master and I obtain our knowledge from the same source;— though, gad! I think myself much the prettier fellow of the two. (*Surveying himself in the glass.*) That was a brilliant thought, to insinuate that I

folded my master's letters for him; the folding is so neat, that it does honour to the operator. I once intended to have insinuated that I wrote his letters too; but that was before I saw them; it won't do now; no honour there, positively.—"Nothing looks more vulgar, (*reading affectedly*) ordinary, and illiberal than ugly, uneven, and ragged nails; the ends of which should be kept even and clean, not tipped with black, and cut in small segments of circles."—Segments of circles! surely my lord did not consider that he wrote for the beaux. Segments of circles; what a crabbed term! Now I dare answer that my master, with all his learning, does not know that this means, according to the present mode, let the nails grow long, and then cut them off even at top. (*Laughing without.*) Ha! that's Jenny's titter. I protest I despair of ever teaching that girl to laugh; she has something so execrably natural in her laugh, that I declare it absolutely discomposes my nerves. How came she into our House! (*Calls.*) Jenny!

(*Enter* JENNY.)

Prythee, Jenny, don't spoil your fine face with laughing.

JENNY: Why, mustn't I laugh, Mr. Jessamy?

JESSAMY: You may smile, but, as my lord says, nothing can authorise a laugh.

JENNY: Well, but I can't help laughing.— Have you seen him, Mr. Jessamy? ha, ha, ha!

JESSAMY: Seen whom?

JENNY: Why, Jonathan, the New England colonel's servant. Do you know he was at the play last night, and the stupid creature don't know where he has been. He would not go to a play for the world; he thinks it was a show, as he calls it.

JESSAMY: As ignorant and unpolished as he is, do you know, Miss Jenny, that I propose to introduce him to the honour of your acquaintance?

JENNY: Introduce him to me! for what?

JESSAMY: Why, my lovely girl, that you may take him under your protection, as Madame Rambouillet did young Stanhope; that you may, by your plastic hand, mould this uncouth cub into a gentleman. He is to make love to you.

JENNY: Make love to me!————

JESSAMY: Yes, Mistress Jenny, make love to you; and, I doubt not, when he shall become *domesticated* in your kitchen, that this boor, under your auspices, will soon become *un amiable petit Jonathan*.

JENNY: I must say, Mr. Jessamy, if he copies after me, he will be vastly, monstrously polite.

JESSAMY: Stay here one moment, and I will

call him.—Jonathan!—Mr. Jonathan!—(*Calls.*)

JONATHAN (*within*): Holla! there.—(*Enters.*) You promise to stand by me—six bows you say. (*Bows.*)

JESSAMY: Mrs. Jenny, I have the honour of presenting Mr. Jonathan, Colonel Manly's waiter, to you. I am extremely happy that I have it in my power to make two worthy people acquainted with each other's merits.

JENNY: So, Mr. Jonathan, I hear you were at the play last night.

JONATHAN: At the play! why, did you think I went to the devil's drawing-room?

JENNY: The devil's drawing-room!

JONATHAN: Yes; why an't cards and dice the devil's device, and the play-house the shop where the devil hangs out the vanities of the world upon the tenter-hooks of temptation? I believe you have not heard how they were acting the old boy one night, and the wicked one came among them sure enough, and went right off in a storm, and carried one quarter of the play-house with him. Oh! no, no, no! you won't catch me at a play-house, I warrant you.

JENNY: Well, Mr. Jonathan, though I don't scruple your veracity, I have some reasons for believing you were there: pray, where were you about six o'clock?

JONATHAN: Why, I went to see one Mr. Morrison, the *hocus pocus* man; they said as how he could eat a case knife.

JENNY: Well, and how did you find the place?

JONATHAN: As I was going about here and there, to and again, to find it, I saw a great crowd of folks going into a long entry that had lantherns over the door; so I asked a man whether that was not the place where they played *hocus pocus?* He was a very civil, kind man, though he did speak like the Hessians; he lifted up his eyes and said, "They play *hocus pocus* tricks enough there, Got knows, mine friend."

JENNY: Well—

JONATHAN: So I went right in, and they shewed me away, clean up to the garret, just like meeting-house gallery. And so I saw a power of topping folks, all sitting round in little cabbins, "just like father's corn-cribs"; and then there was such a squeaking with the fiddles, and such a tarnal blaze with the lights, my head was near turned. At last the people that sat near me set up such a hissing—hiss—like so many mad cats; and then they went thump, thump, thump, just like our Peleg threshing wheat, and stampt away, just like the nation; and called out for one Mr. Langolee,—I suppose he helps act the tricks.

JENNY: Well, and what did you do all this time?

JONATHAN: Gor, I—I liked the fun, and so I thumpt away, and hiss'd as lustily as the best of 'em. One sailor-looking man that sat by me, seeing me stamp, and knowing I was a cute fellow, because I could make a roaring noise, clapt me on the shoulder and said, "You are a d——d hearty cock, smite my timbers!" I told him so I was, but I thought he need not swear so, and make use of such naughty words.

JESSAMY: The savage!—Well, and did you see the man with his tricks?

JONATHAN: Why, I vow, as I was looking out for him, they lifted up a great green cloth and let us look right into the next neighbour's house. Have you a good many houses in New-York made so in that 'ere way?

JENNY: Not many; but did you see the family?

JONATHAN: Yes, swamp it; I see'd the family.

JENNY: Well, and how did you like them?

JONATHAN: Why, I vow they were pretty much like other families;—there was a poor, good-natured, curse of a husband, and a sad rantipole of a wife.

JENNY: But did you see no other folks?

JONATHAN: Yes. There was one youngster; they called him Mr. Joseph; he talked as sober and as pious as a minister; but, like some ministers that I know, he was a sly tike in his heart for all that. He was going to ask a young woman to spark it with him, and—the Lord have mercy on my soul!—she was another man's wife.

JESSAMY: The Wabash!

JENNY: And did you see any more folks?

JONATHAN: Why, they came on as thick as mustard. For my part, I thought the house was haunted. There was a soldier fellow, who talked about his row de dow, dow, and courted a young woman; but, of all the cute folk I saw, I liked one little fellow——

JENNY: Aye! who was he?

JONATHAN: Why, he had red hair, and a little round plump face like mine, only not altogether so handsome. His name was—Darby;—that was his baptizing name; his other name I forgot. Oh! it was Wig—Wag—Wag-all, Darby Wag-all,—pray, do you know him?—I should like to take a sling with him, or a drap of cyder with a pepper-pod in it, to make it warm and comfortable.

JENNY: I can't say I have that pleasure.

JONATHAN: I wish you did; he is a cute fellow. But there was one thing I didn't like in that Mr. Darby; and that was, he was afraid of some of them 'ere shooting irons, such as your troopers wear on training days. Now, I'm a true born Yankee American son of liberty, and I never was afraid of a gun yet in all my life.

JENNY: Well, Mr. Jonathan, you were certainly at the play-house.

JONATHAN: I at the play-house!—Why didn't I see the play then?

JENNY: Why, the people you saw were players.

JONATHAN: Mercy on my soul! did I see the wicked players?—Mayhap that 'ere Darby that I liked so was the old serpent himself, and had his cloven foot in his pocket. Why, I vow, now I come to think on't, the candles seemed to burn blue, and I am sure where I sat it smelt tarnally of brimstone.

JESSAMY: Well, Mr. Jonathan, from your account, which I confess is very accurate, you must have been at the play-house.

JONATHAN: Why, I vow, I began to smell a rat. When I came away, I went to the man for my money again; you want your money? says he; yes, says I; for what? says he; why, says I, no man shall jocky me out of my money; I paid my money to see sights, and the dogs a bit of a sight have I seen, unless you call listening to people's private business a sight. Why, says he, it is the School for Scandalization.—The School for Scandalization! —Oh! ho! no wonder you New-York folks are so cute at it, when you go to school to learn it; and so I jogged off.

JESSAMY: My dear Jenny, my master's business drags me from you; would to heaven I knew no other servitude than to your charms.

JONATHAN: Well, but don't go; you won't leave me so———

JESSAMY: Excuse me.—Remember the cash. (Aside to him, and—Exit.)

JENNY: Mr. Jonathan, won't you please to sit down? Mr. Jessamy tells me you wanted to have some conversation with me.

(Having brought forward two chairs, they sit.)

JONATHAN: Ma'am!———
JENNY: Sir!———
JONATHAN: Ma'am!———
JENNY: Pray, how do you like the city, Sir?
JONATHAN: Ma'am!———
JENNY: I say, Sir, how do you like New-York?
JONATHAN: Ma'am!———
JENNY: The stupid creature! but I must pass some little time with him, if it is only to endeavour to learn whether it was his master that made such an abrupt entrance into our house, and my young mistress's heart, this morning. (Aside.)

As you don't seem to like to talk, Mr. Jonathan —do you sing?

JONATHAN: Gor, I—I am glad she asked that, for I forgot what Mr. Jessamy bid me say, and I dare as well be hanged as act what he bid me do, I'm so ashamed. (Aside.) Yes, Ma'am, I can sing —I can sing Mear, Old Hundred, and Bangor.

JENNY: Oh! I don't mean psalm tunes. Have you no little song to please the ladies, such as Roslin Castle, or the Maid of the Mill?

JONATHAN: Why, all my tunes go to meeting tunes, save one, and I count you won't altogether like that 'ere.

JENNY: What is it called?

JONATHAN: I am sure you have heard folks talk about it; it is called Yankee Doodle.

JENNY: Oh! it is the tune I am fond of; and if I know anything of my mistress, she would be glad to dance to it. Pray, sing!

JONATHAN (sings):

Father and I went up to camp,
Along with Captain Goodwin;
And there we saw the men and boys,
As thick as hasty-pudding.
        Yankee doodle do, etc.

And there we saw a swamping gun,
Big as log of maple,
On a little deuced cart,
A load for father's cattle.
        Yankee doodle do, etc.

And every time they fired it off
It took a horn of powder,
It made a noise—like father's gun,
Only a nation louder.
        Yankee doodle do, etc.

There was a man in our town,
His name was———

No, no, that won't do. Now, if I was with Tabitha Wymen and Jemima Cawley down at father Chase's, I shouldn't mind singing this all out before them—you would be affronted if I was to sing that, though that's a lucky thought; if you should be affronted, I have something dang'd cute, which Jessamy told me to say to you.

JENNY: Is that all! I assure you I like it of all things.

JONATHAN: No, no; I can sing more; some other time, when you and I are better acquainted, I'll sing the whole of it—no, no—that's a fib—I can't sing but a hundred and ninety verses; our Tabitha at home can sing it all.——— (Sings.)

Marblehead's a rocky place,
And Cape-Cod is sandy;
Charlestown is burnt down,
Boston is the dandy.
                    Yankee doodle, doodle do, etc.

I vow, my own town song has put me into such topping spirits that I believe I'll begin to do a little, as Jessamy says we must when we go a-courting—(*Runs and kisses her.*) Burning rivers! cooling flames! red-hot roses! pig-nuts! hasty-pudding and ambrosia!

JENNY: What means this freedom? you insulting wretch. (*Strikes him.*)

JONATHAN: Are you affronted?

JENNY: Affronted! with what looks shall I express my anger?

JONATHAN: Looks! why as to the matter of looks, you look as cross as a witch.

JENNY: Have you no feeling for the delicacy of my sex?

JONATHAN: Feeling! Gor, I—I feel the delicacy of your sex pretty smartly (*rubbing his cheek*), though, I vow, I thought when you city ladies courted and married, and all that, you put feeling out of the question. But I want to know whether you are really affronted, or only pretend to be so? 'Cause, if you are certainly right down affronted, I am at the end of my tether; Jessamy didn't tell me what to say to you.

JENNY: Pretend to be affronted!

JONATHAN: Aye aye, if you only pretend, you shall hear how I'll go to work to make cherubim consequences. (*Runs up to her.*)

JENNY: Begone, you brute!

JONATHAN: That looks like mad; but I won't lose my speech. My dearest Jenny—your name is Jenny, I think?—My dearest Jenny, though I have the highest esteem for the sweet favours you have just now granted me—Gor, that's a fib, though; but Jessamy says it is not wicked to tell lies to the women. (*Aside.*) I say, though I have the highest esteem for the favours you have just now granted me, yet you will consider that, as soon as the dissolvable knot is tied, they will no longer be favours, but only matters of duty and matters of course.

JENNY: Marry you! you audacious monster! get out of my sight, or, rather, let me fly from you. (*Exit hastily.*)

JONATHAN: Gor! she's gone off in a swinging passion, before I had time to think of consequences. If this is the way with your city ladies, give me the twenty acres of rock, the Bible, the cow, and Tabitha, and a little peaceable bundling.

SCENE 2. *The Mall.*

(*Enter* MANLY.)

MANLY: It must be so, Montague! and it is not all the tribe of Mandevilles that shall convince me that a nation, to become great, must first become dissipated. Luxury is surely the bane of a nation: Luxury! which enervates both soul and body, by opening a thousand new sources of enjoyment, opens, also, a thousand new sources of contention and want: Luxury! which renders a people weak at home, and accessible to bribery, corruption, and force from abroad. When the Grecian states knew no other tools than the axe and the saw, the Grecians were a great, a free, and a happy people. The kings of Greece devoted their lives to the service of their country, and her senators knew no other superiority over their fellow-citizens than a glorious pre-eminence in danger and virtue. They exhibited to the world a noble spectacle,—a number of independent states united by a similarity of language, sentiment, manners, common interest, and common consent in one grand mutual league of protection. And, thus united, long might they have continued the cherishers of arts and sciences, the protectors of the oppressed, the scourge of tyrants, and the safe asylum of liberty. But when foreign gold, and still more pernicious foreign luxury, had crept among them, they sapped the vitals of their virtue. The virtues of their ancestors were only found in their writings. Envy and suspicion, the vices of little minds, possessed them. The various states engendered jealousies of each other; and, more unfortunately, growing jealous of their great federal council, the Amphictyons, they forgot that their common safety had existed, and would exist, in giving them an honourable extensive prerogative. The common good was lost in the pursuit of private interest; and that people who, by uniting, might have stood against the world in arms, by dividing, crumbled into ruin;—their name is now only known in the page of the historian, and what they once were is all we have left to admire. Oh! that America! Oh! that my country, would, in this her day, learn the things which belong to her peace!

(*Enter* DIMPLE.)

DIMPLE: You are Colonel Manly, I presume?

MANLY: At your service, Sir.

DIMPLE: My name is Dimple, Sir. I have the honour to be a lodger in the same house with you, and, hearing you were in the Mall, came hither to take the liberty of joining you.

MANLY: You are very obliging, Sir.

DIMPLE: As I understand you are a stranger here, Sir, I have taken the liberty to introduce myself to your acquaintance, as possibly I may have it in my power to point out some things in this city worthy your notice.

MANLY: An attention to strangers is worthy a liberal mind, and must ever be gratefully received. But to a soldier, who has no fixed abode, such attentions are particularly pleasing.

DIMPLE: Sir, there is no character so respectable as that of a soldier. And, indeed, when we reflect how much we owe to those brave men who have suffered so much in the service of their country, and secured to us those inestimable blessings that we now enjoy, our liberty and independence, they demand every attention which gratitude can pay. For my own part, I never meet an officer, but I embrace him as my friend, nor a private in distress, but I insensibly extend my charity to him.————I have hit the Bumkin off very tolerably. (*Aside.*)

MANLY: Give me your hand, Sir! I do not proffer this hand to everybody; but you steal into my heart. I hope I am as insensible to flattery as most men; but I declare (it may be my weak side) that I never hear the name of soldier mentioned with respect, but I experience a thrill of pleasure which I never feel on any other occasion.

DIMPLE: Will you give me leave, my dear Colonel, to confer an obligation on myself, by shewing you some civilities during your stay here, and giving a similar opportunity to some of my friends?

MANLY: Sir, I thank you; but I believe my stay in this city will be very short.

DIMPLE: I can introduce you to some men of excellent sense, in whose company you will esteem yourself happy; and, by way of amusement, to some fine girls, who will listen to your soft things with pleasure.

MANLY: Sir, I should be proud of the honour of being acquainted with those gentlemen;—but, as for the ladies, I don't understand you.

DIMPLE: Why, Sir, I need not tell you, that when a young gentleman is alone with a young lady he must say some soft things to her fair cheek—indeed, the lady will expect it. To be sure, there is not much pleasure when a man of the world and a finished coquette meet, who perfectly know each other; but how delicious is it to excite the emotions of joy, hope, expectation, and delight in the bosom of a lovely girl who believes every tittle of what you say to be serious!

MANLY: Serious, Sir! In my opinion, the man who, under pretensions of marriage, can plant thorns in the bosom of an innocent, unsuspecting girl is more detestable than a common robber, in the same proportion as private violence is more despicable than open force, and money of less value than happiness.

DIMPLE: How he awes me by the superiority of his sentiments. (*Aside.*) As you say, Sir, a gentleman should be cautious how he mentions marriage.

MANLY: Cautious, Sir! No person more approves of an intercourse between the sexes than I do. Female conversation softens our manners, whilst our discourse, from the superiority of our literary advantages, improves their minds. But, in our young country, where there is no such thing as gallantry, when a gentleman speaks of love to a lady, whether he mentions marriage or not, she ought to conclude either that he meant to insult her or that his intentions are the most serious and honourable. How mean, how cruel, is it, by a thousand tender assiduities, to win the affections of an amiable girl, and, though you leave her virtue unspotted, to betray her into the appearance of so many tender partialities, that every man of delicacy would suppress his inclination towards her, by supposing her heart engaged! Can any man, for the trivial gratification of his leisure hours, affect the happiness of a whole life! His not having spoken of marriage may add to his perfidy, but can be no excuse for his conduct.

DIMPLE: Sir, I admire your sentiments;—they are mine. The light observations that fell from me were only a principle of the tongue; they came not from the heart; my practice has ever disapproved these principles.

MANLY: I believe you, sir. I should with reluctance suppose that those pernicious sentiments could find admittance into the heart of a gentleman.

DIMPLE: I am now, Sir, going to visit a family, where, if you please, I will have the honour of introducing you. Mr. Manly's ward, Miss Letitia, is a young lady of immense fortune; and his niece, Miss Charlotte Manly, is a young lady of great sprightliness and beauty.

MANLY: That gentleman, Sir, is my uncle, and Miss Manly my sister.

DIMPLE: The devil she is! (*Aside.*) Miss Manly your sister, Sir? I rejoice to hear it, and feel a double pleasure in being known to you.———Plague on him! I wish he was at Boston again, with all my soul. (*Aside.*)

MANLY: Come, Sir, will you go?

DIMPLE: I will follow you in a moment, Sir. (*Exit* MANLY.) Plague on it! this is unlucky. A fighting brother is a cursed appendage to a fine girl. Egad! I just stopped in time; had he not discovered himself, in two minutes more I should have told him how well I was with his sister. Indeed, I cannot see the satisfaction of an intrigue, if one can't have the pleasure of communicating it to our friends. (*Exit.*)

ACT IV

SCENE 1. CHARLOTTE's *Apartment.*

(CHARLOTTE *leading in* MARIA.)

CHARLOTTE: This is so kind, my sweet friend, to come to see me at this moment. I declare, if I were going to be married in a few days, as you are, I should scarce have found time to visit my friends.

MARIA: Do you think, then, that there is an impropriety in it?—How should you dispose of your time?

CHARLOTTE: Why, I should be shut up in my chamber; and my head would so run upon—upon —upon the solemn ceremony that I was to pass through!—I declare, it would take me above two hours merely to learn that little monosyllable— *Yes*. Ah! my dear, your sentimental imagination does not conceive what that little tiny word implies.

MARIA: Spare me your raillery, my sweet friend; I should love your agreeable vivacity at any other time.

CHARLOTTE: Why, this is the very time to amuse you. You grieve me to see you look so unhappy.

MARIA: Have I not reason to look so?

CHARLOTTE: What new grief distresses you?

MARIA: Oh! how sweet it is, when the heart is borne down with misfortune, to recline and repose on the bosom of friendship! Heaven knows that, although it is improper for a young lady to praise a gentleman, yet I have ever concealed Mr. Dimple's foibles, and spoke of him as of one whose reputation I expected would be linked with mine; but his late conduct towards me has turned my coolness into contempt. He behaves as if he meant to insult and disgust me; whilst my father, in the last conversation on the subject of our marriage, spoke of it as a matter which lay near his

heart, and in which he would not bear contradiction.

CHARLOTTE: This works well; oh! the generous Dimple. I'll endeavour to excite her to discharge him. (*Aside.*) But, my dear friend, your happiness depends on yourself. Why don't you discard him? Though the match has been of long standing, I would not be forced to make myself miserable: no parent in the world should oblige me to marry the man I did not like.

MARIA: Oh! my dear, you never lived with your parents, and do not know what influence a father's frowns have upon a daughter's heart. Besides, what have I to alledge against Mr. Dimple, to justify myself to the world? He carries himself so smoothly, that every one would impute the blame to me, and call me capricious.

CHARLOTTE: And call her capricious! Did ever such an objection start into the heart of woman? For my part, I wish I had fifty lovers to discard, for no other reason than because I did not fancy them. My dear Maria, you will forgive me; I know your candour and confidence in me; but I have at times, I confess, been led to suppose that some other gentleman was the cause of your aversion to Mr. Dimple.

MARIA: No, my sweet friend, you may be assured, that though I have seen many gentlemen I could prefer to Mr. Dimple, yet I never saw one that I thought I could give my hand to, until this morning.

CHARLOTTE: This morning!

MARIA: Yes; one of the strangest accidents in the world. The odious Dimple, after disgusting me with his conversation, had just left me, when a gentleman, who, it seems, boards in the same house with him, saw him coming out of our door, and, the houses looking very much alike, he came into our house instead of his lodgings; nor did he discover his mistake until he got into the parlour, where I was; he then bowed so gracefully, made such a genteel apology, and looked so manly and noble!———

CHARLOTTE: I see some folks, though it is so great an impropriety, can praise a gentleman, when he happens to be the man of their fancy. (*Aside.*)

MARIA: I don't know how it was,—I hope he did not think me indelicate,—but I asked him, I believe, to sit down, or pointed to a chair. He sat down, and, instead of having recourse to observations upon the weather, or hackneyed criticisms upon the theatre, he entered readily into a conversation worthy a man of sense to speak, and a lady of delicacy and sentiment to hear. He was not strictly handsome, but he spoke the language of sentiment, and his eyes looked tenderness and honour.

CHARLOTTE: Oh! (*eagerly*) you sentimental, grave girls, when your hearts are once touched, beat us rattles a bar's length. And so you are quite in love with this he-angel?

MARIA: In love with him! How can you rattle so, Charlotte? am I not going to be miserable? (*Sighs.*) In love with a gentleman I never saw but one hour in my life, and don't know his name! No; I only wished that the man I shall marry may look, and talk, and act, just like him. Besides, my dear, he is a married man.

CHARLOTTE: Why, that was good-natured—he told you so, I suppose, in mere charity, to prevent you falling in love with him?

MARIA: He didn't tell me so; (*peevishly*) he looked as if he was married.

CHARLOTTE: How, my dear; did he look sheepish?

MARIA: I am sure he has a susceptible heart, and the ladies of his acquaintance must be very stupid not to———

CHARLOTTE: Hush! I hear some person coming.

(*Enter* LETITIA.)

LETITIA: My dear Maria, I am happy to see you. Lud! what a pity it is that you have purchased your wedding clothes.

MARIA: I think so. (*Sighing.*)

LETITIA: Why, my dear, there is the sweetest parcel of silks come over you ever saw! Nancy Brilliant has a full suit come; she sent over her measure, and it fits her to a hair; it is immensely dressy, and made for a court-hoop. I thought they said the large hoops were going out of fashion.

CHARLOTTE: Did you see the hat? Is it a fact that the deep laces round the border is still the fashion?

DIMPLE (*within*): Upon my honour, Sir.

MARIA: Ha! Dimple's voice! My dear, I must take leave of you. There are some things necessary to be done at our house. Can't I go through the other room?

(*Enter* DIMPLE *and* MANLY.)

DIMPLE: Ladies, your most obedient.

CHARLOTTE: Miss Van Rough, shall I present my brother Henry to you? Colonel Manly, Maria, —Miss Van Rough, brother.

MARIA: Her brother! (*Turns and sees* MANLY.)

Oh! my heart! the very gentleman I have been praising.

MANLY: The same amiable girl I saw this morning!

CHARLOTTE: Why, you look as if you were acquainted.

MANLY: I unintentionally intruded into this lady's presence this morning, for which she was so good as to promise me her forgiveness.

CHARLOTTE: Oh! ho! is that the case! Have these two penserosos been together? Were they Henry's eyes that looked so tenderly? (*Aside.*) And so you promised to pardon him? and could you be so good-natured? have you really forgiven him? I beg you would do it for my sake (*whispering loud to* MARIA.) But, my dear, as you are in such haste, it would be cruel to detain you; I can show you the way through the other room.

MARIA: Spare me, my sprightly friend.

MANLY: The lady does not, I hope, intend to deprive us of the pleasure of her company so soon.

CHARLOTTE: She has only a mantua-maker who waits for her at home. But, as I am to give my opinion of the dress, I think she cannot go yet. We were talking of the fashions when you came in, but I suppose the subject must be changed to something of more importance now. Mr. Dimple, will you favour us with an account of the public entertainments?

DIMPLE: Why, really, Miss Manly, you could not have asked me a question more *mal-apropos*. For my part, I must confess that, to a man who has travelled, there is nothing that is worthy the name of amusement to be found in this city.

CHARLOTTE: Except visiting the ladies.

DIMPLE: Pardon me, Madam; that is the avocation of a man of taste. But for amusement, I positively know of nothing that can be called so, unless you dignify with that title the hopping once a fortnight to the sound of two or three squeaking fiddles, and the clattering of the old tavern windows, or sitting to see the miserable mummers, whom you call actors, murder comedy and make a farce of tragedy.

MANLY: Do you never attend the theatre, Sir?

DIMPLE: I was tortured there once.

CHARLOTTE: Pray, Mr. Dimple, was it a tragedy or a comedy?

DIMPLE: Faith, Madam, I cannot tell; for I sat with my back to the stage all the time, admiring a much better actress than any there—a lady who played the fine woman to perfection; though, by the laugh of the horrid creatures round me, I suppose it was comedy. Yet, on second thoughts, it might be some hero in a tragedy, dying so comically as to set the whole house in an uproar. Colonel, I presume you have been in Europe?

MANLY: Indeed, Sir, I was never ten leagues from the continent.

DIMPLE: Believe me, Colonel, you have an immense pleasure to come; and when you shall have seen the brilliant exhibitions of Europe, you will learn to despise the amusements of this country as much as I do.

MANLY: Therefore I do not wish to see them; for I can never esteem that knowledge valuable which tends to give me a distaste for my native country.

DIMPLE: Well, Colonel, though you have not travelled, you have read.

MANLY: I have, a little; and by it have discovered that there is a laudable partiality which ignorant, untravelled men entertain for everything that belongs to their native country. I call it laudable; it injures no one; adds to their own happiness; and, when extended, becomes the noble principle of patriotism. Travelled gentlemen rise superior, in their own opinion, to this; but if the contempt which they contract for their country is the most valuable acquisition of their travels, I am far from thinking that their time and money are well spent.

MARIA: What noble sentiments!

CHARLOTTE: Let my brother set out where he will in the fields of conversation, he is sure to end his tour in the temple of gravity.

MANLY: Forgive me, my sister. I love my country; it has its foibles undoubtedly;—some foreigners will with pleasure remark them—but such remarks fall very ungracefully from the lips of her citizens.

DIMPLE: You are perfectly in the right, Colonel—America has her faults.

MANLY: Yes, Sir; and we, her children, should blush for them in private, and endeavour, as individuals, to reform them. But, if our country has its errors in common with other countries, I am proud to say America—I mean the United States —has displayed virtues and achievements which modern nations may admire, but of which they have seldom set us the example.

CHARLOTTE: But, brother, we must introduce you to some of our gay folks, and let you see the city, such as it is. Mr. Dimple is known to almost every family in town; he will doubtless take a pleasure in introducing you?

DIMPLE: I shall esteem every service I can render your brother an honour.

MANLY: I fear the business I am upon will take up all my time, and my family will be anxious to hear from me.

MARIA: His family! but what is it to me that he is married! (*Aside.*) Pray, how did you leave your lady, Sir?

CHARLOTTE: My brother is not married (*observing her anxiety*); it is only an odd way he has of expressing himself. Pray, brother, is this business, which you make your continual excuse, a secret?

MANLY: No, sister; I came hither to solicit the honourable Congress, that a number of my brave old soldiers may be put upon the pension-list, who were, at first, not judged to be so materially wounded as to need the public assistance. My sister says true (*to* MARIA): I call my late soldiers my family. Those who were not in the field in the late glorious contest, and those who were, have their respective merits; but, I confess, my old brother-soldiers are dearer to me than the former description. Friendships made in adversity are lasting; our countrymen may forget us, but that is no reason why we should forget one another. But I must leave you; my time of engagement approaches.

CHARLOTTE: Well, but, brother, if you will go, will you please to conduct my fair friend home? You live in the same street———I was to have gone with her myself—(*Aside.*) A lucky thought.

MARIA: I am obliged to your sister, Sir, and was just intending to go. (*Going.*)

MANLY: I shall attend her with pleasure.

(*Exit with* MARIA, *followed by* DIMPLE *and* CHARLOTTE.)

MARIA: Now, pray, don't betray me to your brother.

CHARLOTTE (*Just as she sees him make a motion to take his leave.*): One word with you, brother, if you please. (*Follows them out.*)

(*Manent,* DIMPLE *and* LETITIA.)

DIMPLE: You received the billet I sent you, I presume?

LETITIA: Hush!—Yes.

DIMPLE: When shall I pay my respects to you?

LETITIA: At eight I shall be unengaged.

(*Reenter* CHARLOTTE.)

DIMPLE: Did my lovely angel receive my billet? (*To* CHARLOTTE.)

CHARLOTTE: Yes.

DIMPLE: What hour shall I expect with impatience?

CHARLOTTE: At eight I shall be at home unengaged.

DIMPLE: Unfortunate! I have a horrid engagement of business at that hour. Can't you finish your visit earlier and let six be the happy hour?

CHARLOTTE: You know your influence over me. (*Exeunt severally.*)

SCENE 2. VAN ROUGH'S *House.*

VAN ROUGH (*alone*): It cannot possibly be true! The son of my old friend can't have acted so unadvisedly. Seventeen thousand pounds! in bills! Mr. Transfer must have been mistaken. He always appeared so prudent, and talked so well upon money matters, and even assured me that he intended to change his dress for a suit of clothes which would not cost so much, and look more substantial, as soon as he married. No, no, no! it can't be; it cannot be. But, however, I must look out sharp. I did not care what his principles or his actions were, so long as he minded the main chance. Seventeen thousand pounds! If he had lost it in trade, why the best men may have ill-luck; but to game it away, as Transfer says—why, at this rate, his whole estate may go in one night, and, what is ten times worse, mine into the bargain. No, no; Mary is right. Leave women to look out in these matters; for all they look as if they didn't know a journal from a ledger, when their interest is concerned they know what's what; they mind the main chance as well as the best of us. I wonder Mary did not tell me she knew of his spending his money so foolishly. Seventeen thousand pounds! Why, if my daughter was standing up to be married, I would forbid the banns, if I found it was to a man who did not mind the main chance.—Hush! I hear somebody coming. 'Tis Mary's voice; a man with her too! I shouldn't be surprised if this should be the other string to her bow. Aye, aye, let them alone; women understand the main chance.—Though, i' faith, I'll listen a little. (*Retires into a closet.*)

(MANLY *leading in* MARIA.)

MANLY: I hope you will excuse my speaking upon so important a subject so abruptly; but, the moment I entered your room, you struck me as the lady whom I had long loved in imagination, and never hoped to see.

MARIA: Indeed, Sir, I have been led to hear more upon this subject than I ought.

MANLY: Do you, then, disapprove my suit, Madam, or the abruptness of my introducing it? If the latter, my peculiar situation, being obliged to leave the city in a few days, will, I hope, be my excuse; if the former, I will retire, for I am sure I would not give a moment's inquietude to her whom I could devote my life to please. I am not so indelicate as to seek your immediate approbation; permit me only to be near you, and by a thousand tender assiduities to endeavour to excite a grateful return.

MARIA: I have a father, whom I would die to make happy; he will disapprove——

MANLY: Do you think me so ungenerous as to seek a place in your esteem without his consent? You must—you ever ought to consider that man as unworthy of you who seeks an interest in your heart contrary to a father's approbation. A young lady should reflect that the loss of a lover may be supplied, but nothing can compensate for the loss of a parent's affection. Yet, why do you suppose your father would disapprove? In our country, the affections are not sacrificed to riches or family aggrandizement: should you approve, my family is decent, and my rank honourable.

MARIA: You distress me, Sir.

MANLY: Then I will sincerely beg your excuse for obtruding so disagreeable a subject, and retire. (*Going.*)

MARIA: Stay, Sir! your generosity and good opinion of me deserve a return; but why must I declare what, for these few hours, I have scarce suffered myself to think?—I am——

MANLY: What?

MARIA: Engaged, Sir; and, in a few days to be married to the gentleman you saw at your sister's.

MANLY: Engaged to be married! And I have been basely invading the rights of another? Why have you permitted this? Is this the return for the partiality I declared for you?

MARIA: You distress me, Sir. What would you have me say? you are too generous to wish the truth. Ought I to say that I dared not suffer myself to think of my engagement, and that I am going to give my hand without my heart? Would you have me confess a partiality for you? If so, your triumph is compleat, and can be only more so when days of misery with the man I cannot love will make me think of him whom I could prefer.

MANLY (*after a pause*): We are both unhappy; but it is your duty to obey your parent—mine to obey my honour. Let us, therefore, both follow the path of rectitude; and of this we may be assured, that if we are not happy, we shall, at least, deserve to be so. Adieu! I dare not trust myself longer with you. (*Exeunt severally.*)

ACT V

SCENE 1. DIMPLE's *Lodgings.*

(JESSAMY *meeting* JONATHAN.)

JESSAMY: Well, Mr. Jonathan, what success with the fair?

JONATHAN: Why, such a tarnal cross tike you never saw! You would have counted she had lived upon crab-apples and vinegar for a fortnight. But what the rattle makes you look so tarnation glum?

JESSAMY: I was thinking, Mr. Jonathan, what could be the reason of her carrying herself so coolly to you.

JONATHAN: Coolly, do you call it? Why, I vow, she was fire-hot angry: may be it was because I buss'd her.

JESSAMY: No, no, Mr. Jonathan; there must be some other cause; I never yet knew a lady angry at being kissed.

JONATHAN: Well, if it is not the young woman's bashfulness, I vow I can't conceive why she shouldn't like me.

JESSAMY: May be it is because you have not the Graces, Mr. Jonathan.

JONATHAN: Grace! Why, does the young woman expect I must be converted before I court her?

JESSAMY: I mean graces of person: for instance, my lord tells us that we must cut off our nails even at top, in small segments of circles—though you won't understand that; in the next place, you must regulate your laugh.

JONATHAN: Maple-log seize it! don't I laugh natural?

JESSAMY: That's the very fault, Mr. Jonathan. Besides, you absolutely misplace it. I was told by a friend of mine that you laughed outright at the play the other night, when you ought only to have tittered.

JONATHAN: Gor! I—what does one go to see fun for if they can't laugh.

JESSAMY: You may laugh; but you must laugh by rule.

JONATHAN: Swamp it—laugh by rule! Well, I should like that tarnally.

JESSAMY: Why, you know, Mr. Jonathan, that to dance, a lady to play with her fan, or a gentle-man with his cane, and all other natural motions, are regulated by art. My master has composed an immensely pretty gamut, by which any lady or gentleman, with a few years' close application, may learn to laugh as gracefully as if they were born and bred to it.

JONATHAN: Mercy on my soul! A gamut for laughing—just like fa, la, sol?

JESSAMY: Yes. It comprises every possible display of jocularity, from an *affettuoso* smile to a *piano* titter, or full chorus *fortissimo* ha, ha, ha! My master employs his leisure hours in marking out the plays, like a cathedral chanting-book, that the ignorant may know where to laugh; and that pit, box, and gallery may keep time together, and not have a snigger in one part of the house, a broad grin in the other, and a d——d grum look in the third. How delightful to see the audience all smile together, then look on their books, then twist their mouths into an agreeable simper, then altogether shake the house with a general ha, ha, ha! loud as a full chorus of Handel's at an Abbey commemoration.

JONATHAN: Ha, ha, ha! that's dang'd cute, I swear.

JESSAMY: The gentlemen, you see, will laugh the tenor; the ladies will play the counter-tenor; the beaux will squeak the treble; and our jolly friends in the gallery a thorough base, ho, ho, ho!

JONATHAN: Well, can't you let me see that gamut?

JESSAMY: Oh! yes, Mr. Jonathan; here it is (*Takes out a book.*) Oh! no, this is only a titter with its variations. Ah, here it is. (*Takes out another.*) Now, you must know, Mr. Jonathan, this is a piece written by Ben Johnson, which I have set to my master's gamut. The places where you must smile, look grave, or laugh outright, are marked below the line. Now look over me. "There was a certain man"—now you must smile.

JONATHAN: Well, read it again; I warrant I'll mind my eye.

JESSAMY: "There was a certain man, who had a sad scolding wife,"—now you must laugh.

JONATHAN: Tarnation! That's no laughing matter though.

JESSAMY: "And she lay sick a-dying";—now you must titter.

JONATHAN: What, snigger when the good woman's a-dying! Gor, I———

JESSAMY: Yes, the notes say you must—"and she asked her husband leave to make a will," —now you must begin to look grave; "and her husband said"———

JONATHAN: Ay, what did her husband say?

Something dang'd cute, I reckon.

JESSAMY: "And her husband said, you have had your will all your life-time, and would you have it after you are dead, too?"

JONATHAN: Ho, ho, ho! There the old man was even with her; he was up to the notch—ha, ha, ha!

JESSAMY: But, Mr. Jonathan, you must not laugh so. Why you ought to have tittered *piano,* and you have laughed *fortissimo.* Look here; you see these marks, A, B, C, and so on; these are the references to the other part of the book. Let us turn to it, and you will see the directions how to manage the muscles. This (*turns over*) was note D you blundered at.—You must purse the mouth into a smile, then titter, discovering the lower part of the three front upper teeth.

JONATHAN: How? read it again.

JESSAMY: "There was a certain man"—very well!—"who had a sad scolding wife,"—why don't you laugh?

JONATHAN: Now, that scolding wife sticks in my gizzard so pluckily that I can't laugh for the blood and nowns of me. Let me look grave here, and I'll laugh your belly full, where the old creature's a-dying.

JESSAMY: "And she asked her husband"—(*Bell rings.*) My master's bell! he's returned, I fear.—Here, Mr. Jonathan, take this gamut; and I make no doubt but with a few years' close application, you may be able to smile gracefully. (*Exeunt severally.*)

SCENE 2. CHARLOTTE'S *Apartment.*

(*Enter* MANLY.)

MANLY: What, no one at home? How unfortunate to meet the only lady my heart was ever moved by, to find her engaged to another, and confessing her partiality for me! Yet engaged to a man who, by her intimation, and his libertine conversation with me, I fear, does not merit her. Aye! there's the sting; for, were I assured that Maria was happy, my heart is not so selfish but that it would dilate in knowing it, even though it were with another. But to know she is unhappy! —I must drive these thoughts from me. Charlotte has some books; and this is what I believe she calls her little library. (*Enters a closet.*)

(*Enter* DIMPLE *leading* LETITIA.)

LETITIA: And will you pretend to say now, Mr. Dimple, that you propose to break with Maria?

Are not the banns published? Are not the clothes purchased? Are not the friends invited? In short, is it not a done affair?

DIMPLE: Believe me, my dear Letitia, I would not marry her.

LETITIA: Why have you not broke with her before this, as you all along deluded me by saying you would?

DIMPLE: Because I was in hopes she would, ere this, have broke with me.

LETITIA: You could not expect it.

DIMPLE: Nay, but be calm a moment; 'twas from my regard to you that I did not discard her.

LETITIA: Regard to me!

DIMPLE: Yes; I have done everything in my power to break with her, but the foolish girl is so fond of me that nothing can accomplish it. Besides, how can I offer her my hand when my heart is indissolubly engaged to you?

LETITIA: There may be reason in this; but why so attentive to Miss Manly?

DIMPLE: Attentive to Miss Manly! For heaven's sake, if you have no better opinion of my constancy, pay not so ill a compliment to my taste.

LETITIA: Did I not see you whisper her today?

DIMPLE: Possibly I might—but something of so very trifling a nature that I have already forgot what it was.

LETITIA: I believe she has not forgot it.

DIMPLE: My dear creature, how can you for a moment suppose I should have any serious thoughts of that trifling, gay, flighty coquette, that disagreeable—

(*Enter* CHARLOTTE.)

My dear Miss Manly, I rejoice to see you; there is a charm in your conversation that always marks your entrance into company as fortunate.

LETITIA: Where have you been, my dear?

CHARLOTTE: Why, I have been about to twenty shops, turning over pretty things, and so have left twenty visits unpaid. I wish you would step into the carriage and whisk round, make my apology, and leave my cards where our friends are not at home; that, you know, will serve as a visit. Come, do go.

LETITIA: So anxious to get me out! but I'll watch you. (*Aside.*) Oh! yes, I'll go; I want a little exercise. Positively (DIMPLE *offering to accompany her*), Mr. Dimple, you shall not go; why, half my visits are cake and candle visits; it won't do, you know, for you to go. (*Exit, but returns to the door in the back scene and listens.*)

DIMPLE: This attachment of your brother to Maria is fortunate.

CHARLOTTE: How did you come to the knowledge of it?

DIMPLE: I read it in their eyes.

CHARLOTTE: And I had it from her mouth. It would have amused you to have seen her! She, that thought it so great an impropriety to praise a gentleman that she could not bring out one word in your favour, found a redundancy to praise him.

DIMPLE: I have done everything in my power to assist his passion there: your delicacy, my dearest girl, would be shocked at half the instance of neglect and misbehaviour.

CHARLOTTE: I don't know how I should bear neglect; but Mr. Dimple must misbehave himself indeed, to forfeit my good opinion.

DIMPLE: Your good opinion, my angel, is the pride and pleasure of my heart; and if the most respectful tenderness for you, and an utter indifference for all your sex besides, can make me worthy of your esteem, I shall richly merit it.

CHARLOTTE: All my sex besides, Mr. Dimple!—you forgot your tête-a-tête with Letitia.

DIMPLE: How can you, my lovely angel, cast a thought on that insipid, wry-mouthed, ugly creature!

CHARLOTTE: But her fortune may have charms.

DIMPLE: Not to a heart like mine. The man, who has been blessed with the good opinion of my Charlotte, must despise the allurements of fortune.

CHARLOTTE: I am satisfied.

DIMPLE: Let us think no more on the odious subject, but devote the present hour to happiness.

CHARLOTTE: Can I be happy, when I see the man I prefer going to be married to another?

DIMPLE: Have I not already satisfied my charming angel, that I can never think of marrying the puling Maria? But, even if it were so, could that be any bar to our happiness? for, as the poet sings,

"Love, free as air, at sight of human ties,
Spreads his light wings, and in a moment flies."

Come, then, my charming angel! why delay our bliss? The present moment is ours; the next is in the hand of fate. (*Kissing her.*)

CHARLOTTE: Begone, Sir! By your delusions you had almost lulled my honour asleep.

DIMPLE: Let me lull the demon to sleep again with kisses. (*He struggles with her; she screams.*)

(*Enter* MANLY.)

MANLY: Turn, villain! and defend yourself.
———(*Draws.*)

(VAN ROUGH *enters and beats down their swords.*)

VAN ROUGH: Is the devil in you? are you going to murder one another? (*Holding* DIMPLE.)

DIMPLE: Hold him, hold him,—I can command my passion.

(*Enter* JONATHAN.)

JONATHAN: What the rattle ails you? Is the old one in you? Let the colonel alone, can't you? I feel chock-full of fight,—do you want to kill the colonel?———

MANLY: Be still, Jonathan; the gentleman does not want to hurt me.

JONATHAN: Gor! I—I wish he did; I'd shew him Yankee boys play, pretty quick.—Don't you see you have frightened the young woman into the *hystrikes?*

VAN ROUGH: Pray, some of you explain this; what has been the occasion of all this racket?

MANLY: That gentleman can explain it to you; it will be a very diverting story for an intended father-in-law to hear.

VAN ROUGH: How was this matter, Mr. Van Dumpling?

DIMPLE: Sir,—upon my honour—all I know is, that I was talking to this young lady, and this gentleman broke in on us in a very extraordinary manner.

VAN ROUGH: Why, all this is nothing to the purpose; can you explain it, Miss? (*To* CHARLOTTE.)

(*Enter* LETITIA *through the back scene.*)

LETITIA: I can explain it to that gentleman's confusion. Though long betrothed to your daughter (*to* VAN ROUGH), yet, allured by my fortune, it seems (with shame do I speak it) he has privately paid his addresses to me. I was drawn in to listen to him by his assuring me that the match was made by his father without his consent, and that he proposed to break with Maria, whether he married me or not. But, whatever were his intentions respecting your daughter, Sir, even to me he was false; for he has repeated the same story, with some cruel reflections upon my person, to Miss Manly.

JONATHAN: What a tarnal curse!

LETITIA: Nor is this all, Miss Manly. When he was with me this very morning, he made the same ungenerous reflections upon the weakness of your mind as he has so recently done upon the defects of my person.

JONATHAN: What a tarnal curse and damn, too.

DIMPLE: Ha! since I have lost Letitia, I believe I had as good make it up with Maria. Mr. Van Rough, at present I cannot enter into particulars; but, I believe, I can explain everything to your satisfaction in private.

VAN ROUGH: There is another matter, Mr. Van Dumpling, which I would have you explain. Pray, Sir, have Messrs. Van Cash & Co. presented you those bills for acceptance?

DIMPLE: The deuce! Has he heard of those bills! Nay, then, all's up with Maria, too; but an affair of this sort can never prejudice me among the ladies; they will rather long to know what the dear creature possesses to make him so agreeable. (Aside.) Sir, you'll hear from me. (To MANLY.)

MANLY: And you from me, Sir———

DIMPLE: Sir, you wear a sword———

MANLY: Yes, Sir. This sword was presented to me by that brave Gallic hero, the Marquis De la Fayette. I have drawn it in the service of my country, and in private life, on the only occasion where a man is justified in drawing his sword, in defence of a lady's honour. I have fought too many battles in the service of my country to dread the imputation of cowardice. Death from a man of honour would be a glory you do not merit; you shall live to bear the insult of man and the contempt of that sex whose general smiles afforded you all your happiness.

DIMPLE: You won't meet me, Sir? Then I'll post you for a coward.

MANLY: I'll venture that, Sir. The reputation of my life does not depend upon the breath of a Mr. Dimple. I would have you to know, however, Sir, that I have a cane to chastise the insolence of a scoundrel, and a sword and the good laws of my country to protect me from the attempts of an assassin———

DIMPLE: Mighty well! Very fine, indeed! Ladies and gentlemen, I take my leave; and you will please to observe in the case of my deportment the contrast between a gentleman who has read Chesterfield and received the polish of Europe and an unpolished, untravelled American. (Exit.)

(Enter MARIA.)

MARIA: Is he indeed gone?———

LETITIA: I hope, never to return.

VAN ROUGH: I am glad I heard of those bills; though it's plaguy unlucky; I hoped to see Mary married before I died.

MANLY: Will you permit a gentleman, Sir, to offer himself as a suitor to your daughter? Though a stranger to you, he is not altogether so to her, or unknown in this city. You may find a son-in-law of more fortune, but you can never meet with one who is richer in love for her, or respect for you.

VAN ROUGH: Why, Mary, you have not let this gentleman make love to you without my leave?

MANLY: I did not say, Sir———

MARIA: Say, Sir!———I—the gentleman, to be sure, met me accidentally.

VAN ROUGH: Ha, ha, ha! Mark me, Mary; young folks think old folks to be fools; but old folks know young folks to be fools. Why, I knew all about this affair. This was only a cunning way I had to bring it about. Hark ye! I was in the closet when you and he were at our house. (Turns to the company.) I heard that little baggage say she loved her old father, and would die to make him happy! Oh! how I loved the little baggage! And you talked very prudently, young man. I have inquired into your character, and find you to be a man of punctuality and mind the main chance. And so, as you love Mary and Mary loves you, you shall have my consent immediately to be married. I'll settle my fortune on you, and go and live with you the remainder of my life.

MANLY: Sir, I hope———

VAN ROUGH: Come, come, no fine speeches; mind the main chance, young man, and you and I shall always agree.

LETITIA: I sincerely wish you joy (advancing to MARIA); and hope your pardon for my conduct.

MARIA: I thank you for your congratulations, and hope we shall at once forget the wretch who has given us so much disquiet, and the trouble that he has occasioned.

CHARLOTTE: And I, my dear Maria,—how shall I look to you for forgiveness? I, who, in the practice of the meanest arts, have violated the most sacred rights of friendship? I never can forgive myself, or hope charity from the world; but, I confess, I have much to hope from such a brother; and I am happy that I may soon say, such a sister.

MARIA: My dear, you distress me; you have all my love.

MANLY: And mine.

CHARLOTTE: If repentance can entitle me to forgiveness, I have already much merit; for I despise the littleness of my past conduct. I now find that the heart of any worthy man cannot be gained

by invidious attacks upon the rights and characters of others;—by countenancing the addresses of
a thousand;—or that the finest assemblage of features, the greatest taste in dress, the genteelest
address, or the most brilliant wit, cannot eventually secure a coquette from contempt and ridicule.

MANLY: And I have learned that probity, virtue, honour, though they should not have received the polish of Europe, will secure to an
honest American the good graces of his fair coun-
trywomen, and I hope, the applause of THE PUB-
LIC.

THE END

Anna Cora Mowatt: *Fashion* (1845)

Fashion was written rather quickly on the suggestion of a friend, who saw that Mowatt's talents lay in the direction of comedy for the stage. Her early years in Europe made its theme perfect for her, and she discovered herself to be a skilled social critic. Trueman, the only character she drew from life, gives us the theme of the play in Act IV when he says, "Fashion! And pray what is *fashion*, madam? An agreement between certain persons to live without using their souls! to substitute etiquette for virtue—decorum for purity—manners for morals! to affect a shame for the works of their Creator! and expend all their rapture upon the works of their tailors and dressmakers!" The play shows up the nouveau riche Americans who ape European manners, rejecting democracy in favor of a mock aristocracy. *Fashion* was an instant hit in New York and Philadelphia and made celebrities of Mowatt and her husband.

The contrast between republicans and aristocractic pretensions in the play reminds us of Royall Tyler's *The Contrast*. Almost a hundred years late, Americans were beset by similar anxieties and insecurities. A new ingredient—the presence of the black servant, Zeke—adds an interesting element to Mowatt's play. On the one hand, Zeke is referred to as a nigger and is the butt of many jokes; on the other, Trueman rejects his servant's uniform (his livery) because it indicates servitude in a free country.

Zeke's role in the play is very complex. Mowatt married a southerner after her first husband died and eventually split with him over the issue of slavery and the Civil War. She moved to Florence, then London, where she died in 1870.

Of the critics who saw the play, Edgar Allen Poe thought it "an empty shell," but after he posted his review he came to see every performance. *Fashion* is a farce, and it is formulaic; but it is also lively, witty, probing, and moving. Mrs Tiffany is a deftly drawn comic figure whose counterpart will exist in all societies. *Fashion* is itself a true American statement.

Selected Readings

Barnes, Erich. *The Lady of Fashion: Anna Cora Mowatt*. New York: Scribner's, 1954.

Mowatt, Anna Cora. *The Autobiography of an Actress*. Boston: Ticknor, Reed & Fields, 1854.

Fashion, or Life in New York

A COMEDY IN FIVE ACTS

Anna Cora Mowatt

"Howe'er it be—it seems to me
'Tis only noble to be good;
Kind hearts are more than coronets,
And simple faith than Norman blood."

TENNYSON

CHARACTERS

ADAM TRUEMAN

COUNT JOLIMAITRE, *a fashionable European Importation*

COLONEL HOWARD, *an officer in the United States Army*

MR. TIFFANY, *a New York Merchant*

T. TENNYSON TWINKLE, *a modern Poet*

AUGUSTUS FOGG, *a drawing room appendage*

SNOBSON, *a rare species of confidential clerk*

ZEKE, *a colored servant*

MRS. TIFFANY, *a lady who imagines herself fashionable*

PRUDENCE, *a maiden lady of a certain age*

MILLINETTE, *a French lady's maid*

GERTRUDE, *a governess*

SERAPHINA TIFFANY, *a belle*

ACT I

SCENE 1. (*A splendid Drawing Room in the House of* MRS. TIFFANY. *Open folding doors, discovering a Conservatory. On either side glass windows down to the ground. Doors on right and left. Mirror, couches, ottomans, a table with albums, beside it an arm chair.* MILLINETTE *dusting furniture.* ZEKE *in a dashing livery, scarlet coat.*)

ZEKE: Dere's a coat to take de eyes ob all Broadway! Ah! Missy, it am de fixin's dat make de natural *born* gemman. A libery for ever! Dere's a pair ob insuppressibles to 'stonish de colored population.

MILLINETTE: Oh, *oui,* Monsieur Zeke. (*Very politely.*) I not *comprend* one word he say! (*Aside.*)

ZEKE: I tell 'ee what, Missy, I'm 'stordinary glad to find dis a bery 'spectabul. like situation!

Now, as you've made de acquaintance ob dis here family, and dere you've had a supernumerary advantage ob me—seeing dat I only receibed my appointment dis morning. What I wants to know is your publicated opinion, privately expressed, ob de domestic circle.

MILLINETTE: You mean vat *espèce,* vat kind of personnes are Monsieur and Madame Tiffany? Ah! Monsieur is not de same ting as Madame, —not at all.

ZEKE: Well, I s'pose he ain't altogether.

MILLINETTE: Monsieur is man of business, —Madame is lady of fashion. Monsieur make de money,—Madame spend it. Monsieur nobody at all,—Madame everybody altogether. Ah! Monsieur Zeke, de money is all dat is *necessaire* in dis country to make one lady of fashion. Oh! it is quite anoder ting in *la belle France!*

ZEKE: A bery lucifer explanation. Well, now we've disposed ob de heads ob de family, who come next?

MILLINETTE: First, dere is Mademoiselle Seraphina Tiffany. Mademoiselle is not at all one proper *personne.* Mademoiselle Seraphina is one coquette. Dat is not de mode in *la belle France*; de ladies, dere, never learn *la coquetrie* until dey do get one husband.

ZEKE: I tell 'ee what, Missy, I disreprobate dat proceeding altogeder!

MILLINETTE: Vait! I have not tell you all *la famille* yet. Dere is Ma'mselle Prudence— Madame's sister, one very *bizarre* personne. Den dere is Ma'mselle Gertrude, but she not anybody at all; she only teach Mademoiselle Seraphina *la musique.*

ZEKE: Well now, Missy, what's your own special defunctions?

MILLINETTE: I not understand, Monsieur Zeke.

ZEKE: Den I'll amplify. What's de nature ob your exclusive services?

MILLINETTE: *Ah, oui! je comprend.* I am Madame's *femme de chambre*—her lady's maid, Monsieur Zeke. I teach Madame *les modes de Paris,* and Madame set de fashion for all New York. You see, Monsieur Zeke, dat it is me, *moi-même,* dat do lead de fashion for all de American *beau monde!*

ZEKE: Yah! yah! yah! I hab de idea by de heel. Well now, p'raps you can 'lustrify my officials?

MILLINETTE: Vat you will have to do? Oh! much tings, much tings. You vait on de table,—you tend de door,—you clean de boots,—you run de errands,—you drive de carriage,—you rub de horses,—you take care of de flowers,—you carry de water,—you help cook de dinner,—you wash de dishes,—and den you always remember to do everything I tell you to!

ZEKE: Wheugh, am dat *all?*

MILLINETTE: All I can tink of now. To-day is Madame's day of reception, and all her grand friends do make her one *petite* visit. You mind run fast ven de bell do ring.

ZEKE: Run? If it wasn't for dese superfluminous trimmings, I tell 'ee what, Missy, I'd run—

MRS. TIFFANY (*outside*): Millinette!

MILLINETTE: Here comes Madame! You better go, Monsieur Zeke.

ZEKE: Look ahea, Massa Zeke, does n't dis open rich! (*Aside.*) (*Exit* ZEKE.)

(*Enter* MRS. TIFFANY, *dressed in the most extravagant height of fashion.*)

MRS. TIFFANY: Is everything in order, Millinette? Ah! very elegant, very elegant, indeed! There is a *jenny-says-quoi* took about this furniture,—an air of fashion and gentility perfectly bewitching. Is there not, Millinette?

MILLINETTE: Oh, *oui,* Madame!

MRS. TIFFANY: But where is Miss Seraphina? It is twelve o'clock; our visitors will be pouring in, and she has not made her appearance. But I hear that nothing is more fashionable than to keep people waiting.—None but vulgar persons pay any attention to punctuality. Is it not so, Millinette?

MILLINETTE: Quite *comme il faut.*—Great personnes always do make little personnes wait, Madame.

MRS. TIFFANY: This mode of receiving visitors only upon one specified day of the week is a most convenient custom! It saves the trouble of keeping the house continually in order and of being always dressed. I flatter myself that *I* was the first to introduce it amongst the New York ee-light. You are quite sure that it is strictly a Parisian mode, Millinette?

MILLINETTE: Oh, *oui,* Madame; entirely *mode de Paris.*

MRS. TIFFANY: This girl is worth her weight in gold. (*Aside.*) Millinette, how do you say *arm-chair* in French?

MILLINETTE: *Fauteuil,* Madame.

MRS. TIFFANY: *Fo-tool!* That has a foreign—an out-of-the-wayish sound that is perfectly charming—and so genteel! There is something about our American words decidedly vulgar. *Fowtool!* how refined. *Fowtool! Arm-chair!* what a difference!

MILLINETTE: Madame have one charmante pronunciation. *Fowtool* (*mimicking aside*) charmante, Madame!

MRS. TIFFANY: Do you think so, Millinette? Well, I believe I have. But a woman of refinement and of fashion can always accommodate herself to everything foreign! And a week's study of that invaluable work—*"French without a Master,"* has made me quite at home in the court language of Europe! But where is the new valet? I'm rather sorry that he is black, but to obtain a white American for a domestic is almost impossible; and they call this a free country! What did you say was the name of this new servant, Millinette?

MILLINETTE: He do say his name is Monsieur Zeke.

MRS. TIFFANY: Ezekiel, I suppose. Zeke! Dear me, such a vulgar name will compromise the dignity of the whole family. Can you not suggest something more aristocratic, Millinette? Something *French!*

MILLINETTE: *Oh, oui,* Madame; *Adolph* is one very fine name.

MRS. TIFFANY: A-dolph! Charming! Ring the bell, Millinette! (MILLINETTE *rings the bell.*) I will change his name immediately, besides giving him a few directions.

(*Enter* ZEKE. MRS. TIFFANY *addresses him with great dignity.*)

Your name I hear, is *Ezekiel.*—I consider it too plebeian an appellation to be uttered in my presence. In future you are called A-dolph. Don't reply,—never interrupt me when I am speaking. A-dolph, as my guests arrive, I desire that you will inquire the name of every person, and then announce it in a loud, clear tone. That is the fashion in Paris.

(MILLINETTE *retires up the stage.*)

ZEKE: Consider de office discharged, Missus. (*Speaking very loudly.*)

MRS. TIFFANY: Silence! Your business is to obey and not to talk.

ZEKE: I'm dumb, Missus!

MRS. TIFFANY: (*pointing up stage*): A-dolph, place that *fowtool* behind me.

ZEKE: (*looking about him*): I hab n't got dat far in de dictionary yet. No matter, a genus gets his learning by nature.

(*Takes up the table and places it behind* MRS. TIFFANY, *then expresses in dumb show great satisfaction.* MRS. TIFFANY, *as she goes to sit, discovers the mistake.*)

MRS. TIFFANY: You dolt! Where have you lived not to know that *fow-tool* is the French for *arm-chair?* What ignorance! Leave the room this instant.

(MRS. TIFFANY *draws forward an arm-chair and sits.* MILLINETTE *comes forward suppressing her merriment at* ZEKE's *mistake and removes the table.*)

ZEKE: Dem's de defects ob not having a liberty education. (*Exit.*)

(PRUDENCE *peeps in.*)

PRUDENCE: I wonder if any of the fine folks have come yet. Not a soul,—I knew they had n't. There's Betsy all alone. (*Walks in.*) Sister Betsy!

MRS. TIFFANY: Prudence! how many times have I desired you to call me *Elizabeth? Betsy* is the height of vulgarity.

PRUDENCE: Oh! I forgot. Dear me, how spruce we do look here, to be sure,—everything in first rate style now, Betsy. (MRS. TIFFANY *looks at her angrily.*) *Elizabeth*, I mean. Who would have thought, when you and I were sitting behind that little mahogany-colored counter, in Canal Street, making up flashy hats and caps—

MRS. TIFFANY: Prudence, *what do* you mean? Millinette, leave the room.

MILLINETTE: *Oui,* Madame.

(MILLINETTE *pretends to arrange the books upon a side table but lingers to listen.*)

PRUDENCE: But I always predicted it,—I always told you so, Betsy,—I always said you were destined to rise above your station!

MRS. TIFFANY: Prudence! Prudence! have I not told you that—

PRUDENCE: No, Besty, it was *I* that told *you,* when we used to buy our silks and ribbons of Mr. Antony Tiffany—*"talking Tony,"* you know we used to call him, and when you always put on the finest bonnet in our shop to go to his,—and when you staid so long smiling and chattering with him, I always told you that *something* would grow out of it—and didn't it?

MRS. TIFFANY: Millinette, send Seraphina here instantly. Leave the room.

MILLINETTE: *Oui,* Madame. So dis Americaine ladi of fashion vas one *milliner?* Oh, vat a fine country for *les marchandes des modes!* I shall send for all my relation by de next packet! (*Aside.*) (*Exit* MILLINETTE.)

MRS. TIFFANY: Prudence! never let me hear you mention this subject again. Forget what we *have* been, it is enough to remember that we *are* of the *upper ten thousand!*

(PRUDENCE *goes up and sits down.*)
(*Enter* SERAPHINA, *very extravagantly dressed.*)

MRS. TIFFANY: How bewitchingly you look, my dear! Does Millinette say that that head dress is strictly Parisian?

SERAPHINA: Oh, yes, Mamma, all the rage! They call it a *lady's tarpaulin,* and it is the exact pattern of one worn by the Princess Clementina at the last court ball.

MRS. TIFFANY: Now, Seraphina, my dear, don't be too particular in your attentions to gentlemen not eligible. There is Count Joli-maitre, decidedly the most fashionable foreigner in town,—and so refined,—so much accustomed to associate with the first nobility in his own country that he can hardly tolerate the vulgarity of Americans in general. You may devote yourself to him. Mrs. Proudacre is dying to become acquainted with him. By the by, if she or her daughters should happen to drop in, be sure you don't introduce them to the Count. It is not the fashion in Paris to introduce—Millinette told me so.

(*Enter* ZEKE.)

ZEKE: (*in a very loud voice*): Mister T. Tennyson Twinkle!
MRS. TIFFANY: Show him up. (*Exit* ZEKE.)
PRUDENCE: I must be running away! (*Going.*)
MRS. TIFFANY: Mr. T. Tennyson Twinkle—a very literary young man and a sweet poet! It is all the rage to patronize poets! Quick, Seraphina, hand me that magazine.—Mr. Twinkle writes for it.

(SERAPHINA *hands the magazine,* MRS. TIFFANY *seats herself in an arm-chair and opens the book.*)

PRUDENCE (*returning*): There's Betsy trying to make out that reading without her spectacles.

(*Takes a pair of spectacles out of her pocket and hands them to* MRS. TIFFANY.)

There, Betsy, I knew you were going to ask for them. Ah! they're a blessing when one is growing old!
MRS. TIFFANY: What do you mean, Prudence? A woman of fashion *never* grows old! Age is

always out of fashion.
PRUDENCE: Oh, dear! what a delightful thing it is to be fashionable.

(*Exit* PRUDENCE. MRS. TIFFANY *resumes her seat.*)
(*Enter* TWINKLE. *He salutes* SERAPHINA.)

TWINKLE: Fair Seraphina! the sun itself grows dim,
Unless you aid his light and shine on him!
SERAPHINA: Ah! Mr. Twinkle, there is no such thing as answering you.
TWINKLE (*looks around and perceives* MRS. TIFFANY): The "New Monthly Vernal Galaxy." Reading my verses by all that's charming! Sensible woman! I won't interrupt her. (*Aside.*)
MRS. TIFFANY (*rising and coming forward*): Ah! Mr. Twinkle, is that you? I was perfectly *abimé* at the perusal of your very *distingué* verses.
TWINKLE: I am overwhelmed, Madam. Permit me. (*Taking the magazine.*) Yes, they do read tolerably. And you must take into consideration, ladies, the rapidity with which they were written. Four minutes and a half by the stop watch! The true test of a poet is the *velocity* with which he composes. Really they do look very prettily, and they read tolerably—*quite* tolerably—*very* tolerably,—especially the first verse. (*Reads.*) "To Seraphina T——."
SERAPHINA: Oh! Mr. Twinkle!
TWINKLE (*reads*): "Around my heart"—
MRS. TIFFANY: How touching! Really, Mr. Twinkle, quite tender!
TWINKLE (*recommencing*): "Around my heart"—
MRS. TIFFANY: Oh, I must tell you, Mr. Twinkle! I heard the other day that poets were the aristocrats of literature. That's one reason I like them, for I do dote on all aristocracy!
TWINKLE: Oh, Madam, how flattering! Now pray lend me your ears! (*Reads.*) "Around my heart thou weavest"—
SERAPHINA: That is such a *sweet* commencement, Mr. Twinkle!
TWINKLE (*aside*): I wish she would n't interrupt me! (*Reads.*) "Around my heart thou weavest a spell"—
MRS. TIFFANY: Beautiful! But excuse me one moment, while I say a word to Seraphina! Don't be too affable, my dear! Poets are very ornamental appendages to the drawing room, but they are always as poor as their own verses. They don't make eligible husbands! (*Aside to* SERAPHINA.)
TWINKLE: Confound their interruptions! (*Aside.*) My dear Madam, unless you pay the

utmost attention you cannot catch the ideas. Are you ready? Well, now you shall hear it to the end! (*Reads.*)

"Around my heart thou weavest a spell
"Whose"—

(*Enter* ZEKE.)

ZEKE: Mister Augustus Fogg! A bery misty lookin young gemman? (*Aside.*)

MRS. TIFFANY: Show him up, Adolph!

(*Exit* ZEKE.)

TWINKLE: This is too much!

SERAPHINA: Exquisite verses, Mr. Twinkle, —exquisite!

TWINKLE: Ah, lovely Seraphina! your smile of approval transports me to the summit of Olympus.

SERAPHINA: Then I must frown, for I would not send you so far away.

TWINKLE: Enchantress! It's all over with her. (*Aside.*) (*Retire up and converse.*)

MRS. TIFFANY: Mr. Fogg belongs to one of our oldest families,—to be sure he is the most difficult person in the world to entertain, for he never takes the trouble to talk, and never notices anything or anybody,—but then I hear that nothing is considered so vulgar as to betray any emotion, or to attempt to render oneself agreeable!

(*Enter* MR. FOGG, *fashionably attired but in very dark clothes.*)

MR. FOGG (*bowing stiffly*): Mrs. Tiffany, your most obedient. Miss Seraphina, yours. How d'ye do, Twinkle?

MRS. TIFFANY: Mr. Fogg, how do you do? Fine weather,—delightful, is n't it?

MR. FOGG: I am indifferent to weather, Madam.

MRS. TIFFANY: Been to the opera. Mr. Fogg? I hear that the *bow monde* make their *debutt* there every evening.

MR. FOGG: I consider operas a bore, Madam.

SERAPHINA (*advancing*): You must hear Mr. Twinkle's verses, Mr. Fogg!

MR. FOGG: I am indifferent to verses, Miss Seraphina.

SERAPHINA: But Mr. Twinkle's verses are addressed to me!

TWINKLE: Now pay attention, Fogg! (*Reads*)—
"Around my heart thou weavest a spell
"Whose magic I"—

(*Enter* ZEKE.)

ZEKE: Mister—No, he say he ain't no Mister—

TWINKLE: "Around my heart thou weavest a spell
"Whose magic I can never tell!"

MRS. TIFFANY: Speak in a loud, clear tone, A-dolph!

TWINKLE: This is terrible!

ZEKE: Mister Count Jolly-made-her!

MRS. TIFFANY: Count Jolimaitre! Good gracious! Zeke, Zeke—A-dolph I mean,—Dear me, what a mistake! (*Aside.*) Set that chair out of the way,—put that table back. Seraphina, my dear, are you all in order? Dear me! dear me! Your dress is so tumbled! (*Arranges her dress.*) What are you grinning at? (*To* ZEKE.) Beg the Count to *honor* us by walking up! (*Exit* ZEKE.)

Seraphina, my dear (*aside to her*), remember now what I told you about the Count. He is a man of the highest,—good gracious! I am so flurried; and nothing is so ungenteel as agitation! what will the Count think! Mr. Twinkle, pray stand out of the way! Seraphina, my dear, place yourself on my right! Mr. Fogg, the conservatory —beautiful flowers,—pray amuse yourself in the conservatory.

MR. FOGG: I am indifferent to flowers, Madam.

MRS. TIFFANY: Dear me! the man stands right in the way,—just where the Count must make his *entray*! (*Aside.*) Mr. Fogg,—pray—

(*Enter* COUNT JOLIMAITRE, *very dashingly dressed, wears a moustache.*)

MRS. TIFFANY: Oh, Count, this unexpected honor—

SERAPHINA: Count, this inexpressible pleasure—

COUNT: Beg you won't mention it, Madam! Miss Seraphina, your most devoted! (*Crosses.*)

MRS. TIFFANY: What condescension! (*Aside.*) Count, may I take the liberty to introduce —Good gracious! I forgot. (*Aside.*) Count, I was about to remark that we never introduce in America. All our fashions are foreign, Count.

(TWINKLE, *who has stepped forward to be introduced, shows great indignation.*)

COUNT: Excuse me, Madam, our fashions have grown antediluvian before you Americans discover their existence. You are lamentably behind the age—lamentably! 'Pon my honor, a foreigner of refinement finds great difficulty in existing in this provincial atmosphere.

MRS. TIFFANY: How dreadful, Count! I am very much concerned. If there is anything which I can do, Count—

SERAPHINA: Or I, Count, to render your situation less deplorable—

COUNT: Ah! I find but one redeeming charm in America—the superlative loveliness of the feminine portion of creation,—and the wealth of their obliging papas. (*Aside.*)

MRS. TIFFANY: How flattering! Ah! Count, I am afraid you will turn the head of my simple girl here. She is a perfect child of nature, Count.

COUNT: Very possibly, for though you American women are quite charming, yet, demme, there's a deal of native rust to rub off!

MRS. TIFFANY: *Rust?* Good gracious, Count! where do you find any rust? (*Looking about the room.*)

COUNT: How very unsophisticated!

MRS. TIFFANY: Count, I am so much ashamed, —pray excuse me! Although a lady of large fortune, and one, Count, who can boast of the highest connection, I blush to confess that I have never travelled—while you, Count, I presume are at home in all the courts of Europe.

COUNT: *Courts?* Eh? Oh, yes, Madam, very true. I believe I am pretty well known in some of the courts of Europe—*police courts.* (*Aside, crossing.*) In a word, Madam, I had seen enough of civilized life—wanted to refresh myself by a sight of barbarous countries and customs—had my choice between the Sandwich Islands and New York—chose New York!

MRS. TIFFANY: How complimentary to our country! And, Count, I have no doubt you speak every conceivable language? You talk English like a native.

COUNT: Eh, what? Like a native? Oh, ah, demme, yes, I am something of an Englishman. Passed one year and eight months with the Duke of Wellington, six months with Lord Brougham, two and a half with Count d'Orsay—knew them all more intimately than their best friends—no heroes to me—had n't a secret from me, I assure you,—*especially of the toilet.* (*Aside.*)

MRS. TIFFANY: Think of that, my dear! Lord Wellington and Duke Broom! (*Aside to* SERAPHINA.)

SERAPHINA: And only think of Count d'Orsay, Mamma! (*Aside to* MRS. TIFFANY.) I am so wild to see Count d'Orsay!

COUNT: Oh! a mere man milliner. Very little refinement out of Paris! Why, at the very last dinner given at Lord—Lord Knowswho, would you believe it, Madam, there was an individual present who wore a *black* cravat and took *soup twice!*

MRS. TIFFANY: How shocking! the sight of him would have spoilt my appetite! Think what a great man he must be, my dear, to despise lords and counts in that way. (*Aside to* SERAPHINA.) I must leave them together. (*Aside.*) Mr. Twinkle, your arm. I have some really very *foreign exotics* to show you.

TWINKLE: I fly at your command. I wish all her exotics were blooming in their native soil! (*Aside, and glancing at the* COUNT.)

MRS. TIFFANY: Mr. Fogg, will you accompany us? My conservatory is well worthy a visit. It cost an immense sum of money.

MR. FOGG: I am indifferent to conservatories, Madam; flowers are such a bore!

MRS. TIFFANY: I shall take no refusal. Conservatories are all the rage,—I could not exist without mine! Let me show you,—let me show you.

(*Places her arm through* MR. FOGG'S, *without his consent. Exeunt* MRS. TIFFANY, FOGG, *and* TWINKLE *into the conservatory, where they are seen walking about.*)

SERAPHINA: America, then, has no charms for you, Count?

COUNT: Excuse me,—some exceptions. I find you, for instance, particularly charming! Can't say I admire your country. Ah! if you had ever breathed the exhilarating air of Paris, ate creams at Tortoni's, dined at the Café Royale, or if you had lived in London—felt at home at St. James's, and every afternoon driven a couple of Lords and a Duchess through Hyde Park, you would find America—where you have no kings, queens, lords, nor ladies—insupportable!

SERAPHINA: Not while there was a Count in it?

(*Enter* ZEKE, *very indignant.*)

ZEKE: Where's de Missus?

(*Enter* MRS. TIFFANY, FOGG, *and* TWINKLE, *from the conservatory.*)

MRS. TIFFANY: Whom do you come to announce, A-dolph?

ZEKE: He said he would n't trust me—no, not eben wid so much as his name; so I would n't trust him up stairs, den he ups wid *his stick* and I *cuts mine.*

MRS. TIFFANY: Some of Mr. Tiffany's vulgar acquaintances. I shall die with shame. (*Aside.*) A-dolph, inform him that I am *not at home.* (*Exit

ZEKE.) My nerves are so shattered, I am ready to sink. Mr. Twinkle, that *fow tool*, if you please!

TWINKLE: What? What do you wish, Madam?

MRS. TIFFANY: The ignorance of these Americans! (*Aside.*) Count, may I trouble you? That *fow tool*, if you please!

COUNT: She's not talking English, nor French, but I suppose it's American. (*Aside.*)

TRUEMAN (*outside*): Not at home!

ZEKE: No, Sar—Missus say she's not at home.

TRUEMAN: Out of the way, you grinning nigger!

(*Enter* ADAM TRUEMAN, *dressed as a farmer, a stout cane in his hand, his boots covered with dust.* ZEKE *jumps out of his way as he enters.*) (*Exit* ZEKE.)

TRUEMAN: Where's this woman that's not *at home* in her own house? May I be shot! if I wonder at it! I should n't think she'd ever feel *at home* in such a showbox as this! (*Looking round.*)

MRS. TIFFANY: What a plebeian looking old farmer! I wonder who he is? (*Aside.*) Sir —(*advancing very agitatedly*) what do you mean, Sir, by this *ow*dacious conduct? How dare you intrude yourself into my parlor? Do you know who I am, Sir? (*With great dignity.*) You are in the presence of Mrs. Tiffany, Sir!

TRUEMAN: Antony's wife, eh? Well now, I might have guessed that—ha! ha! ha! for I see you make it a point to carry half your husband's shop upon your back! No matter; that's being a good helpmate—for he carried the whole of it once in a pack on his own shoulders—now you bear a share!

MRS. TIFFANY: How dare you, you impertinent, *ow*dacious, ignorant old man! It's all an invention. You're talking of somebody else. What will the Count think! (*Aside.*)

TRUEMAN: Why, I thought folks had better manners in the city! This is a civil welcome for your husband's old friend, and after my coming all the way from Catteraugus to see you and yours! First a grinning nigger tricked out in scarlet regimentals—

MRS. TIFFANY: Let me tell you, Sir, that liveries are all the fashion!

TRUEMAN: The fashion, are they? To make men wear the *badge of servitude* in a free land,—that's the fashion, is it? Hurrah, for republican simplicity! I will venture to say now, that you have your coat of arms too!

MRS. TIFFANY: Certainly, Sir; you can see it on the panels of my *voyture*.

TRUEMAN: Oh! no need of that. I know what your escutcheon must be! A bandbox *rampant* with a bonnet *couchant*, and a peddlar's pack *passant*! Ha, ha, ha! that shows both houses united!

MRS TIFFANY: Sir! you are most profoundly ignorant,—what do you mean by this insolence, Sir? How shall I get rid of him? (*Aside.*)

TRUEMAN (*looking at* SERAPHINA): I hope that is not Getrude! (*Aside.*)

MRS. TIFFANY: Sir, I'd have you know that —Seraphina, my child, walk with the gentlemen into the conservatory.

(*Exeunt* SERAPHINA, TWINKLE, FOGG *into conservatory.*)

Count Jolimaitre, pray make due allowances for the errors of this rustic! I do assure you, Count— (*Whispers to him.*)

TRUEMAN: Count! She calls that critter with a shoe brush over his mouth, Count! To look at him, I should have thought he was a tailor's walking advertisement! (*Aside.*)

COUNT (*addressing* TRUEMAN *whom he has been inspecting through his eyeglass*): Where did you say you belonged, my friend? Dug out of the ruins of Pompeii, eh?

TRUEMAN: I belong to a land in which I rejoice to find that you are a foreigner.

COUNT: What a barbarian! He doesn't see the honor I'm doing his country! Pray, Madam, is it one of the aboriginal inhabitants of the soil? To what tribe of Indians does he belong—the Pawnee or Choctaw? Does he carry a tomahawk?

TRUEMAN: Something quite as useful,—do you see that? (*Shaking his stick.*)

(COUNT *runs behind* MRS. TIFFANY.)

MRS. TIFFANY: Oh, dear! I shall faint! Millinette! (*Approaching.*) Millinette!

(*Enter* MILLINETTE, *without advancing into the room.*)

MILLINETTE: *Oui*, Madame.

MRS. TIFFANY: A glass of water! (*Exit* MILLINETTE.) Sir, (*crossing to* TRUEMAN) I am shocked at your plebeian conduct! This is a gentleman of the highest standing, Sir! He is a *Count*, Sir!

(*Enter* MILLINETTE, *bearing a salver with a glass of water. In advancing towards* MRS. TIFFANY, *she passes in front of the* COUNT, *starts and screams. The* COUNT, *after a start of surprise, regains his composure, plays with his eye glass, and looks perfectly unconcerned.*)

MRS. TIFFANY: What is the matter? What *is* the matter?

MILLINETTE: Noting, noting,—only— (*Looks at* COUNT *and turns away her eyes again.*) only—noting at all!

TRUEMAN: Don't be afraid, girl! Why, did you never see a live Count before? He's tame,—I dare say your mistress there leads him about by the ears.

MRS. TIFFANY: This is too much! Millinette, send for Mr. Tiffany instantly!

(*Crosses to* MILLINETTE, *who is going.*)

MILLINETTE: He just come in, Madame!

TRUEMAN: My old friend! Where is he? Take me to him,—I long to have one more hearty shake of the hand!

MRS. TIFFANY (*crosses to him*): Count, honor me by joining my daughter in the conservatory, I will return immediately.

(COUNT *bows and walks towards conservatory,* MRS. TIFFANY *following part of the way and then returning to* TRUEMAN.)

TRUEMAN: What a Jezebel! These women always play the very devil with a man, and yet I don't believe such a damaged bale of goods as *that* (*looking at* MRS. TIFFANY) has smothered the heart of little Antony!

MRS. TIFFANY: This way, Sir, sal vous plait. (*Exit with great dignity.*)

TRUEMAN: *Sal vous plait.* Ha, ha, ha! We'll see what Fashion has done for him. (*Exit.*)

ACT II

SCENE 1. (*Inner apartment of* MR. TIFFANY'S *Counting House.* MR. TIFFANY, *seated at a desk looking over papers.* MR. SNOBSON, *on a high stool at another desk, with a pen behind his ear.*)

SNOBSON (*rising, advances to the front of the stage, regards* TIFFANY *and shrugs his shoulders*): How the old boy frets and fumes over those papers, to be sure! He's working himself into a perfect fever—ex-actly,—therefore *bleeding's* the prescription! So here goes! (*Aside.*) Mr. Tiffany, a word with you, if you please, Sir?

TIFFANY (*sitting still*): Speak on, Mr. Snobson, I attend.

SNOBSON: What I have to say, Sir, is a matter of the first importance to the credit of the concern—the *credit* of the concern, Mr. Tiffany!

TIFFANY: Proceed, Mr. Snobson.

SNOBSON: Sir, you 've a handsome house —fine carriage—nigger in livery—feed on the fat of the land—everything first rate—

TIFFANY: Well, Sir?

SNOBSON: My salary, Mr. Tiffany!

TIFFANY: It has been raised three times within the last year.

SNOBSON: Stil it is insufficient for the necessities of an honest man,—mark me, an *honest* man, Mr. Tiffany.

TIFFANY (*crossing*): What a weapon he has made of that word! (*Aside.*) Enough—another hundred shall be added. Does that content you?

SNOBSON: There is one other subject, which I have before mentioned, Mr. Tiffany,—your daughter,—what's the reason you can't let the folks at home know at once that I'm to be *the man?*

TIFFANY: Villain! And must the only seal upon this scoundrel's lips be placed there by the hand of my daughter? (*Aside.*) Well, Sir, it shall be as you desire.

SNOBSON: And Mrs. Tiffany shall be informed of your resolution?

TIFFANY: Yes.

SNOBSON: Enough said! That's the ticket! The CREDIT *of the concern's safe*, Sir! (*Returns to his seat.*)

TIFFANY: How low have I bowed to this insolent rascal! To rise himself he mounts upon my shoulders, and unless I can shake him off he must crush me! (*Aside.*)

(*Enter* TRUEMAN.)

TRUEMAN: Here I am, Antony, man! I told you I'd pay you a visit in your money-making quarters. (*Looks around.*) But it looks as dismal here as a cell in the States' prison!

TIFFANY (*forcing a laugh*): Ha, ha, ha! States' prison! You are so facetious! Ha, ha, ha!

TRUEMAN: Well, for the life of me I can't see anything so amusing in that! I should think the States' prison plaguy uncomfortable lodgings. And you laugh, man, as though you fancied yourself there already.

TIFFANY: Ha, ha, ha!

TRUEMAN (*imitating him*): Ha, ha, ha! What on earth do you mean by that ill-sounding laugh, that has nothing of a laugh about it! This *fashion*-worship has made heathens and hypocrites of you all! *Deception* is your household God! A man laughs as if he were crying, and cries as if he were laughing in his sleeve. Everything is something else from what it seems to be. I have lived in your house only three days, and I've heard more lies than were ever invented during a Presidential election! First your fine lady of a wife sends me word that she's not at home—I walk up stairs, and she takes good care that *I* shall not be *at home*—wants to turn me out of doors. Then *you* come in—take your old friend by the hand—whisper, the deuce knows what, in your wife's ear, and the tables are turned in a tangent! Madam curtsies—says she's enchanted to see me—and orders her grinning nigger to show me a room.

TIFFANY: We were exceedingly happy to welcome you as our guest!

TRUEMAN: Happy? *You* happy? Ah, Antony! Antony! that hatchet face of yours, and those criss-cross furrows tell quite another story! It's many a long day since you were *happy* at anything! You look as if you'd melted down your flesh into dollars, and mortgaged your soul in the bargain! Your warm heart has grown cold over your ledger—your light spirits heavy with calculation! You have traded away your youth—your hopes—your tastes, for wealth! and now you *have* the wealth you coveted, what does it profit you? Pleasure it cannot buy; for you have lost your *capacity* for enjoyment—Ease it will not bring; for the love of gain is never satisfied! It has made your counting-house a penitentiary, and your home a fashionable *museum* where there is no niche for you! You have spent so much time *ciphering* in the one, that you find yourself at last a very *cipher* in the other! See me, man! seventy-two last August!—strong as a hickory and every whit as sound!

TIFFANY: I take the greatest pleasure in remarking your superiority, Sir.

TRUEMAN: Bah! no man takes pleasure in remarking the superiority of another! Why the deuce, can't you speak the truth, man? But it's not the *fashion* I suppose! I have not seen one frank, open face since—no, no, I can't say that either, though lying *is* catching! There's that girl, Gertrude, who is trying to teach your daughter music—but Gertrude was bred in the country!

TIFFANY: A good girl; my wife and daughter find her very useful.

TRUEMAN: Useful? Well, I must say you have queer notions of *use*!—But come, cheer up, man! I'd rather see one of your old smiles, than know you'd realized another thousand! I hear you are making money on the true, American, high pressure system—better go slow and sure—the more steam, the greater danger of the boiler's

bursting! All sound, I hope? Nothing rotten at the core?

TIFFANY: Oh, sound—quite sound!

TRUEMAN: Well, that's pleasant—though I must say you don't look very pleasant about it!

TIFFANY: My good friend, although I am solvent, I may say, perfectly solvent—yet you—the fact is, you can be of some assistance to me!

TRUEMAN: That's the *fact* is it? I'm glad we've hit upon one *fact* at last! Well—

(SNOBSON, *who during this conversation has been employed in writing, but stops occasionally to listen, now gives vent to a dry chuckling laugh.*)

TRUEMAN: Hey? What's that? Another of those deuced ill-sounding, city laughs! (*Sees* SNOBSON.) Who's that perched up on the stool of repentance—eh, Antony?

SNOBSON: The old boy has missed his text there—*that's* the stool of repentance! (*Aside and looking at* TIFFANY'S *seat.*)

TIFFANY: One of my clerks—my confidential clerk!

TRUEMAN: Confidential? Why he looks for all the world like a spy—the most inquisitorial, hang-dog face—ugh! the sight of it makes my blood run cold! Come, (*crosses*) let us talk over matters where this critter can't give us the benefit of his opinion! Antony, the next time you choose a confidential clerk, take one that carries his credentials in his face—those in his pocket are not worth much without!

(*Exeunt* TRUEMAN *and* TIFFANY.)

SNOBSON (*jumping from his stool and advancing*): The old prig has got the tin, or Tiff would never be so civil! All right—Tiff will work every shiner into the concern—all the better for me! Now I'll go and make love to Seraphina. The old woman need n't try to knock me ,down with any of her French lingo! Six months from to-day if I ain't driving my two footmen tandem, down Broadway—and as fashionable as Mrs. Tiffany herself, then I ain't the trump I thought I was! that's all. (*Looks at his watch.*) Bless me! eleven o'clock and I have n't had my julep yet! Snobson, I'm ashamed of you! (*Exit.*)

SCENE 2. (*The interior of a beautiful conservatory; walk through the centre; stands of flower pots in bloom; a couple of rustic seats.* GERTRUDE, *attired in white, with a white rose in her hair; watering the flowers.* COLONEL HOWARD *regarding her.*)

HOWARD: I am afraid you lead a sad life here, Miss Gertrude?

GERTRUDE (*turning round gaily*): What! amongst the flowers? (*Continues her occupation.*)

HOWARD: No, amongst the thistles, with which Mrs. Tiffany surrounds you; the tempests, which her temper raises!

GERTRUDE: They never harm me. Flowers and herbs are excellent tutors. I learn prudence from the reed, and bend until the storm has swept over me!

HOWARD: Admirable philosophy! But still this frigid atmosphere of fashion must be uncongenial to you? Accustomed to the pleasant companionship of your kind friends in Geneva, surely you must regret this cold exchange?

GERTRUDE: Do you . think so? Can you suppose that I could possibly prefer a ramble in the woods to a promenade in Broadway? A wreath of scented wild flowers to a bouquet of these sickly exotics? The odour of new-mown hay to the heated air of this crowded conservatory? Or can you imagine that I could enjoy the quiet conversation of my Geneva friends, more than the edifying chit-chat of a fashionable drawing room? But I see you think me totally destitute of taste?

HOWARD: You have a merry spirit to jest thus at your grievances!

GERTRUDE: I have my *mania*,—as some wise person declares that all mankind have,— and mine is a love of independence! In Geneva, my wants were supplied by two kind old maiden ladies, upon whom I know not that I have any claim. I had abilities, and desired to use them. I came here at my own request; for here I am no longer *dependent! Voila tout*, as Mrs. Tiffany would say.

HOWARD: Believe me, I appreciate the confidence you repose in me!

GERTRUDE: Confidence! Truly, Colonel Howard, the confidence is entirely on your part, in supposing that I confide that which I have no reason to conceal! I think I informed you that Mrs. Tiffany only received visitors on her reception day—she is therefore not prepared to see you. Zeke—Oh! I beg his pardon—Adolph, made some mistake in admitting you.

HOWARD: Nay, Gertrude, it was not Mrs. Tiffany, nor Miss Tiffany, whom I came to see; it—it was—

GERTRUDE: The conservatory perhaps? I will leave you to examine the flowers at leisure! (*Crosses.*)

HOWARD: Gertrude—listen to me. If I only dared to give utterance to what is hovering upon my lips! (*Aside.*) Gertrude!

GERTRUDE: Colonel Howard!

HOWARD: Gertrude, I must—must—

GERTRUDE: Yes, indeed you *must*, must leave me! I think I hear somebody coming—Mrs. Tiffany would not be well pleased to find you here—pray, pray leave me—that door will lead you into the street.

(*Hurries him out through door; takes up her watering pot, and commences watering flowers, tying up branches, & c.*)

What a strange being is man! Why should he hesitate to say—nay, why should I prevent his saying, what I would most delight to hear? Truly man *is* strange—but woman is quite as incomprehensible! (*Walks about gathering flowers.*)

(*Enter* COUNT JOLIMAITRE.)

COUNT: There she is—the bewitching little creature! Mrs. Tiffany and her daughter are out of ear-shot. I caught a glimpse of their feathers floating down Broadway, not ten minutes ago. Just the opportunity I have been looking for! Now for an engagement with this captivating little piece of prudery! 'Pon honor, I am almost afraid she will not resist a *Count* long enough to give value to the conquest. (*Approaching her.*) *Ma belle petite*, were you gathering roses for me?

GERTRUDE (*starts on first perceiving him, but instantly regains her self-possession*): The roses here, Sir, are carefully guarded with thorns—if you have the right to gather, pluck for yourself!

COUNT: Sharp as ever, little Gertrude! But now that we are alone, throw off this frigidity, and be at your ease.

GERTRUDE: Permit me to *be alone*, Sir, that I *may* be at my ease!

COUNT: Very good, *ma belle*, well said! (*Applauding her with his hands.*) Never yield too soon, even to a *title*! But as the old girl may find her way back before long, we may as well come to particulars at once. I love you; but that you know already. (*Rubbing his eye-glass unconcernedly with his handkerchief.*) Before long I shall make Mademoiselle Seraphina my wife, and, of course, you shall remain in the family!

GERTRUDE (*indignantly*): Sir—

COUNT: 'Pon my honor you shall! In France we arrange these little matters without difficulty!

GERTRUDE: But I am an *American*! Your conduct proves that you are not one! (*Going, crosses.*)

COUNT (*preventing her*): Don't run away, my immaculate *petite Americaine*! Demme, you've quite overlooked my condescension—the difference of our stations—you a species of upper servant—an orphan—no friends.

(*Enter* TRUEMAN *unperceived.*)

GERTRUDE: And therefore more entitled to the respect and protection of every *true gentleman*! Had you been one, you would not have insulted me!

COUNT: My charming little orator, patriotism and declamation become you particularly! (*Approaches her.*) I feel quite tempted to taste—

TRUEMAN (*thrusting him aside*): An American hickory-switch! (*Strikes him.*) Well, how do you like it?

COUNT: Old matter-of-fact! (*Aside.*) Sir, how dare you?

TRUEMAN: My stick has answered that question!

GERTRUDE: Oh! now I am quite safe!

TRUEMAN: Safe! not a bit safer than before! All women would be safe, if they knew how virtue became them! As for you, Mr. Count, what have you to say for yourself? Come, speak out!

COUNT: Sir,—aw—aw—you don't understand these matters!

TRUEMAN: That's a fact! Not having had *your* experience, I don't believe I *do* understand them!

COUNT: A piece of pleasantry—a mere joke—

TRUEMAN: A joke was it? I'll show you a joke worth two of that! I'll teach you the way we natives joke with a puppy who don't respect an honest woman! (*Seizing him.*)

COUNT: Oh! oh! demme—you old ruffian! let me go. What do you mean?

TRUEMAN: Oh! a piece of pleasantry—a mere joke—very pleasant is n't it?

(*Attempts to strike him again;* COUNT *struggles with him. Enter* MRS. TIFFANY *hastily, in her bonnet and shawl.*)

MRS. TIFFANY: What is the matter? I am perfectly *abimé* with terror. Mr. Trueman, what has happened?

TRUEMAN: Oh! we have been *joking*!

MRS. TIFFANY (*to* COUNT, *who is re-arranging his dress*): My dear Count, I did not expect to find you here—how kind of you!

TRUEMAN: Your *dear* Count has been showing his *kindness* in a very *foreign* manner. Too *foreign* I think, he found it to be relished by an *unfashionable native*! What do you think of a puppy, who insults an innocent girl all in the way of *kindness*? This Count of yours—this importation of—

COUNT: My dear Madam, demme, permit me to explain. It would be unbecoming—demme—particular unbecoming of you—aw—aw—to pay any attention to this ignorant person. (*Crosses to* TRUEMAN.) Anything that he says concerning a man of my standing—aw—the truth is, Madam—

TRUEMAN: Let us have the truth by all means,—if it is only for the novelty's sake!

COUNT (*turning his back to* TRUEMAN): You see, Madam, hoping to obtain a few moments' private conversation with Miss Seraphina—with *Miss Seraphina* I say and—aw—and knowing her passion for flowers, I found my way to your very tasteful and *recherché* conservatory. (*Looks about him approvingly.*) Very beautifully arranged—does you great credit, madam! Here I encountered this young person. She was inclined to be talkative; and I indulged her with—with a—aw—demme—a few *common places*! What passed between us was mere *harmless badinage* —on *my* part. You, madam, you—so conversant with our European manners—you are aware that when a man of fashion—that is, when a woman—a man is bound—amongst noblemen, you know—

MRS. TIFFANY: I comprehend you perfectly —*parfittement*, my dear Count.

COUNT: 'Pon my honor, that's very obliging of her. (*Aside.*)

MRS. TIFFANY: I am shocked at the plebeian forwardness of this conceited girl!

TRUEMAN (*walking up to* COUNT): Did you ever keep a reckoning of the lies you tell in an hour?

MRS. TIFFANY: Mr. Trueman, I blush for you! (*Crosses to* TRUEMAN.)

TRUEMAN: Don't do that—you have no blushes to spare!

MRS. TIFFANY: It is a man of rank whom you are addressing, Sir!

TRUEMAN: A rank villain, Mrs. Antony Tiffany! A *rich one* he would be, had he as much *gold* as *brass*!

MRS. TIFFANY: Pray pardon him, Count; he knows nothing of *how ton*!

COUNT: Demme, he's beneath my notice. I tell you what, old fellow—(TRUEMAN *raises his stick as* COUNT *approaches, the latter starts back*) the sight of him discomposes me—aw—I feel quite uncomfortable—aw—let us join your charming daughter? I can't do you the honor to shoot you, Sir—(*to* TRUEMAN) you are beneath me—a nobleman can't fight a commoner! Good bye, old Truepenny! I—aw—I'm insensible to your insolence!

(*Exeunt* COUNT *and* MRS. TIFFANY)

TRUEMAN: You won't be insensible to a cow hide in spite of your nobility! The next time he practises any of his foreign fashions on you, Gertrude, you'll see how I'll wake up his sensibilities!

GERTRUDE: I do not know what I should have done without you, sir.

TRUEMAN: Yes, you do—you know that you would have done well enough! Never tell a lie, girl! not even for the sake of pleasing an old man! When you open your lips let your heart speak. Never tell a lie! Let your face be the looking-glass of your soul—your heart its clock—while your tongue rings the hours! But the glass must be clear, the clock true, and then there's no fear but the tongue will do its duty in a woman's head!

GERTRUDE: You are very good, Sir!

TRUEMAN: That's as it may be!—How my heart warms towards her! (*Aside.*) Gertrude, I hear that you have no mother.

GERTRUDE: Ah! no, Sir; I wish I had.

TRUEMAN: So do I! Heaven knows, so do I! (*Aside, and with emotion.*) And you have no father, Gertrude?

GERTRUDE: No, Sir—I often wish I had!

TRUEMAN (*Hurriedly.*) Don't do that, girl! don't do that! Wish you had a mother—but never wish that you had a father again! Perhaps the one you had did not deserve such a child!

(*Enter* PRUDENCE.)

PRUDENCE: Seraphina is looking for you, Gertrude.

GERTRUDE: I will go to her. (*Crosses.*) Mr. Trueman, you will not permit me to thank you, but you cannot prevent my gratitude! (*Exit.*)

TRUEMAN (*looking after her*): If falsehood harbours there, I'll give up searching after truth!

(*Crosses, retires up the stage musingly, and commences examining the flowers.*)

PRUDENCE: What a nice old man he is to be sure! I wish he would say something! (*Aside*) (*Crosses, walks after him, turning when he turns—after a pause,*) Don't mind *me*, Mr. Trueman!

TRUEMAN: Mind you? Oh! no, don't be afraid (*Crosses.*)—I was n't minding you. Nobody seems to mind you much!

(*Continues walking and examining the flowers —*PRUDENCE *follows.*)

PRUDENCE: Very pretty flowers, ain't they? Gertrude takes care of them.

TRUEMAN: Gertrude? So I hear—(*Advancing*) I suppose you can tell me now who this Gertrude—

PRUDENCE: Who she's in love with? I *knew* you were going to say that! I'll tell you all about it! Gertrude, she's in love with—Mr. Twinkle! and he's in love with her. And Seraphina she's in love with Count Jolly—what-d' ye-call-it: but Count Jolly don't take to her at all—but Colonel Howard—he's the man—he's desperate about her!

TRUEMAN: Why you feminine newspaper! Howard in love with that quintessence of affectation! Howard—the only, frank, straightforward fellow that I've met since—I'll tell him my mind on the subject! And Gertrude hunting for happiness in a rhyming dictionary! The girl's a greater fool than I took her for! (*Crosses.*)

PRUDENCE: So she is—you see I know all about them!

TRUEMAN: I see you do! You've a wonderful knowledge—wonderful—of *other people's concerns*! It may do here, but take my word for it, in the county of Cattcraugus you'd get the name of a great *busy-body*. But perhaps you know that too?

PRUDENCE: Oh! I always know what's coming. I feel it beforehand all over me. I knew something was going to happen the day you came here—and what's more I can always tell a married man from a single—I felt right off that you were a bachelor!

TRUEMAN: Felt right off I was a bachelor did you? you were sure of it—sure? quite sure? (PRUDENCE *assents delightedly.*) Then you felt wrong!—a bachelor and a widower are not the same thing!

PRUDENCE: Oh! but it all comes to the same thing—a widower's as good as a bachelor any day! And besides I knew that you were a farmer *right off.*

TRUEMAN: On the spot, eh? I suppose you saw cabbages and green peas growing out of my hat?

PRUDENCE: No, I did n't—but I knew all about you. And I knew—(*Looking down and fidgeting with her apron.*) I knew you were for getting married soon! For last night I dream't I saw your funeral going along the streets, and the mourners all dressed in white. And a funeral is a sure sign of a wedding, you know! (*Nudging him with her elbow.*)

TRUEMAN (*imitating her voice*): Well I can't say that I *know* any such thing! you know! (*Nudging her back.*)

PRUDENCE: Oh! it does, and there's no getting over it! For my part, I like farmers—and I know all about setting hens and turkeys, and feeding chickens, and laying eggs, and all that sort of thing!

TRUEMAN: May I be shot! if mistress newspaper is not putting in an advertisement for herself! This is your city mode of courting I suppose, ha, ha, ha! (*Aside.*)

PRUDENCE: I've been west, a little; but I never was in the county of Catteraugus, myself.

TRUEMAN: Oh! you were not? And you have taken a particular fancy to go there, eh?

PRUDENCE: Perhaps I should n't object—

TRUEMAN: Oh!—ah!—so I suppose. Now pay attention to what I am going to say, for it is a matter of great importance to yourself.

PRUDENCE: Now it's coming—I know what he's going to say! (*Aside.*)

TRUEMAN: The next time you want to tie a man for life to your apron-strings, pick out one that don't come from the county of Catteraugus —for greenhorns are scarce in those parts, and modest women plenty! (*Exit.*)

PRUDENCE: Now who'd have thought he was going to say that! But I won't give him up yet—I won't give him up. (*Exit.*)

ACT III

SCENE 1. (MRS. TIFFANY'S *Parlor. Enter* MRS. TIFFANY, *followed by* MR. TIFFANY.)

TIFFANY: Your extravagance will ruin me, Mrs. Tiffany!

MRS. TIFFANY: And your stinginess will ruin me, Mr. Tiffany! It is totally and *toot a fate* impossible to convince you of the necessity of *keeping up appearances*. There is a certain display which every woman of fashion is forced to make!

TIFFANY: And pray who made *you* a woman of fashion?

MRS. TIFFANY: What a vulgar question! All women of fashion, Mr. Tiffany—

TIFFANY: In this land are *self-constituted*, like you, Madam—and *fashion* is the cloak for more sins than charity ever covered! It was for *fashion's* sake that you insisted upon my purchasing this expensive house—it was for *fashion's* sake that you ran me in debt at every exorbitant upholsterer's and extravagant furniture warehouse in the city—it was for *fashion's* sake that you built that ruinous conservatory—hired more servants than they have persons to wait upon—and dressed your footman like a harlequin!

MRS. TIFFANY: Mr. Tiffany, you are thoroughly plebeian, and insufferably *American*, in your grovelling ideas! And, pray, what was the occasion of these very *mal-ap-pro-pos* remarks? Merely because I requested a paltry fifty dollars to purchase a new style of head-dress—a *bijou* of an article just introduced in France.

TIFFANY: Time was, Mrs. Tiffany, when you manufactured your own French head-dresses —took off their first gloss at the public balls, and then sold them to your shortest-sighted customers. And all you knew about France, or French either, was what you spelt out at the bottom of your fashion plates—but now you have grown so fashionable, forsooth, that you have forgotten how to speak your mother tongue!

MRS. TIFFANY: Mr. Tiffany, Mr. Tiffany! Nothing is more positively vulgarian— more *unaristocratic* than any allusion to the past!

TIFFANY: Why I thought, my dear, that *aristocrats* lived principally upon the past—and traded in the market of fashion with the bones of their ancestors for capital?

MRS. TIFFANY: Mr. Tiffany, such vulgar remarks are only suitable to the counting house, in my drawing room you should—

TIFFANY: Vary my sentiments with my locality, as you change your *manners* with your *dress*!

MRS. TIFFANY: Mr. Tiffany, I desire that you will purchase Count d'Orsay's "Science of Etiquette," and learn how to conduct yourself —especially before you appear at the grand ball, which I shall give on Friday!

TIFFANY: Confound your balls, Madam; they make *footballs* of my money, while you dance away all that I am worth! A pretty time to give a ball when you know that I am on the very brink of bankruptcy!

MRS. TIFFANY: So much the greater reason that nobody should suspect your circumstances, or you would lose your credit at once. Just at this crisis a ball is absolutely *necessary* to save your reputation! There is Mrs. Adolphus Dashaway —she gave the most splendid fête of the season—and I hear on very good authority that her husband has not paid his baker's bill in three months. Then there was Mrs. Honeywood—

TIFFANY: Gave a ball the night before her husband shot himself—perhaps you wish to drive me to follow his example? (*Crosses.*)

MRS. TIFFANY: Good gracious! Mr. Tiffany, how you talk! I beg you won't mention anything of the kind. I consider black the most unbecoming color. I'm sure I've done all that I could to gratify you. There is that vulgar old torment, Trueman, who gives one the lie fifty times a day—have n't I been very civil to him?

TIFFANY: Civil to his *wealth*, Mrs. Tiffany! I told you that he was a rich, old farmer—the early friend of my father—my own benefactor —and that I had reason to think he might assist me in my present embarrassments. Your civility was *bought*—and like most of your *own* purchases has yet to be *paid* for. (*Crosses.*)

MRS. TIFFANY: And will be, no doubt! The condescension of a woman of fashion should command any price. Mr. Trueman is insupportably indecorous—he has insulted Count Jolimaitre in the most outrageous manner. If the Count was not so deeply interested—so *abimé* with Seraphina, I am sure he would never honor us by his visits again!

TIFFANY: So much the better—he shall never marry my daughter!—I am resolved on that. Why, Madam, I am told there is in Paris a regular matrimonial stock company, who fit out indigent dandies for this market. How do I know but this fellow is one of its creatures, and that he has come here to increase its dividends by marrying a fortune?

MRS. TIFFANY: Nonsense, Mr. Tiffany. The Count, the most fashionable young man in all New York—the intimate friend of all the dukes and lords in Europe—not marry my daughter? Not permit Seraphina to become a Countess? Mr. Tiffany, you are out of your senses!

TIFFANY: That would not be very wonderful, considering how many years I have been united to you, my dear. Modern physicians pronounce lunacy infectious!

MRS. TIFFANY: Mr. Tiffany, he is a man of fashion—

TIFFANY: Fashion makes fools, but cannot *feed* them. By the bye, I have a request,—since you are bent upon ruining me by this ball, and there is no help for it,—I desire that you will send an invitation to my confidential clerk, Mr. Snobson.

MRS. TIFFANY: Mr. Snobson! Was there ever such an *you-nick* demand! Mr. Snobson would cut a pretty figure amongst my fashionable friends! I shall do no such thing, Mr. Tiffany.

TIFFANY: Then, Madam, the ball shall not take place. Have I not told you that I am in the power of this man? That there are circumstances which it is happy for you that you do not know—which you cannot comprehend,—but which render it essential that you should be civil to Mr. Snobson? Not you merely, but Seraphina also? He is a more appropriate match for her than your foreign favorite.

MRS. TIFFANY: A match for Seraphina, indeed! (*Crosses.*) Mr. Tiffany, you are determined to make a *fow pas*.

TIFFANY: Mr. Snobson intends calling this morning. (*Crosses.*)

MRS. TIFFANY: But, Mr. Tiffany, this is not reception day—my drawing-rooms are in the most terrible disorder—

TIFFANY: Mr. Snobson is not particular—he must be admitted.

(*Enter* ZEKE.)

ZEKE: Mr. Snobson.

(*Enter* SNOBSON, *exit* ZEKE.)

SNOBSON: How dye do, Marm? (*Crosses.*) How are you? Mr. Tiffany, your most!—

MRS. TIFFANY (*formally*): *Bung jure. Comment vow portè vow, Monsur Snobson?*

SNOBSON: Oh, to be sure—very good of you—fine day.

MRS. TIFFANY (*pointing to a chair with great dignity*): *Sassoyez vow,* Monsur Snobson.

SNOBSON: I wonder what she's driving at? I ain't up to the fashionable lingo yet! (*Aside.*) Eh? what? Speak a little louder, Marm?

MRS. TIFFANY: What ignorance! (*Aside.*)

TIFFANY: I presume Mrs. Tiffany means that you are to take a seat.

SNOBSON: Ex-actly—very obliging of her so I will. (*Sits.*) No ceremony amongst friends, you know—and likely to be nearer—you understand? *O.K.*, all correct. How *is* Seraphina?

MRS. TIFFANY: Miss Tiffany is not visible this morning. (*Retires up.*)

SNOBSON: Not visible? (*Jumping up.*) I suppose that's the English for can't see her? Mr. Tiffany, Sir—(*Walking up to him*) what am I to understand by this *de-fal-ca-tion*, Sir? I expected your word to be as good as your bond—beg

pardon, Sir—I mean *better*—considerably better
—no humbug about it, Sir.

TIFFANY: Have patience, Mr. Snobson. (*Rings bell.*)

(*Enter* ZEKE.)

Zeke, desire my daughter to come here.

MRS. TIFFANY: (*Coming down.*) Adolph I say, Adolph—

(ZEKE *straightens himself and assumes foppish airs, as he turns to* MRS. TIFFANY.)

TIFFANY: Zeke.

ZEKE: Don't know any such nigga, Boss.

TIFFANY: Do as I bid you instantly, or off with your livery and quit the house!

ZEKE: Wheugh! I'se all dismission! (*Exit.*)

MRS. TIFFANY: A-dolph, A-dolph! (*Calling after him.*)

SNOBSON: I brought the old boy to his bearings, did n't I though! Pull that string, and he is sure to work right. (*Aside.*) Don't make any stranger of me, Marm—I'm quite at home. If you've got any odd jobs about the house to do up, I sha'n't miss you. I'll amuse myself with Seraphina when she comes—we'll get along very cosily by ourselves.

MRS. TIFFANY: Permit me to inform you, Mr. Snobson, that a French mother never leaves her daughter alone with a young man—she knows your sex too well for that!

SNOBSON: Very *dis*-obliging of her—but as we're none French—

MRS. TIFFANY: You have yet to learn, Mr. Snobson, that the American *ee-light*—the aristocracy—the *how-ton*—as a matter of conscience, scrupulously follow the foreign fashions.

SNOBSON: Not when they are foreign to their interests, Marm—for instance—(*enter* SERAPHINA). There you are at last, eh, Miss? How d' ye do? Ma said you were n't visible. Managed to get a peep at her, eh, Mr. Tiffany?

SERAPHINA: I heard you were here, Mr. Snobson, and came without even arranging my toilette; you will excuse my negligence?

SNOBSON: Of everything but *me*, Miss.

SERAPHINA: I shall never have to ask your pardon for *that*, Mr. Snobson.

MRS. TIFFANY: Seraphina—child—really—

(*As she is approaching* SERAPHINA, MR. TIFFANY *plants himself in front of his wife.*)

TIFFANY: Walk this way, Madam, if you please. To see that she fancies the surly fellow

takes a weight from my heart. (*Aside.*)

MRS. TIFFANY: Mr. Tiffany, it is highly improper and not at all *distingué* to leave a young girl—

(*Enter* ZEKE.)

ZEKE: Mr. Count Jolly-made-her!

MRS. TIFFANY: Good gracious! The Count—Oh, dear!—Seraphina, run and change your dress,—no there's not time! A-dolph, admit him. (*Exit* ZEKE.) Mr. Snobson, get out of the way, will you? Mr. Tiffany, what are you doing at home at this hour?

(*Enter* COUNT JOLIMAITRE, *ushered by* ZEKE.)

ZEKE: Dat's de genuine article ob a gemman. (*Aside.*) (*Exit.*)

MRS· TIFFANY: My dear Count, I am overjoyed at the very sight of you.

COUNT: Flattered myself you'd be glad to see me, Madam—knew it was not your *jour de reception*.

MRS. TIFFANY: But for you, Count, all days—

COUNT: I thought so. Ah, Miss Tiffany, on my honor, you're looking beautiful. (*Crosses.*)

SERAPHINA: Count, flattery from you—

SNOBSON: What? Eh? What's that you say?

SERAPHINA: Nothing but what etiquette requires. (*Aside to him.*)

COUNT (*regarding* MR. TIFFANY *through his eye glass*): Your worthy Papa, I believe? Sir, your most obedient.

(MR. TIFFANY *bows coldly;* COUNT *regards* SNOBSON *through his glass, shrugs his shoulders and turns away.*)

SNOBSON (*to* MRS. TIFFANY): Introduce me, will you? I never knew a Count in all my life—what a strange-looking animal!

MRS. TIFFANY: Mr. Snobson, it is not the fashion to introduce in France!

SNOBSON: But, Marm, we're in America. (MRS. TIFFANY *crosses to* COUNT.) The woman thinks she's somewhere else than where she is—she wants to make an *alibi*? (*Aside.*)

MRS. TIFFANY: I hope that we shall have the pleasure of seeing you on Friday evening, Count?

COUNT: Really, madam, my invitations—my engagements—so numerous—I can hardly answer for myself: and you Americans take offence so easily—

MRS. TIFFANY: But, Count, everybody expects you at our ball—you are the principal attraction—

SERAPHINA: Count, you *must* come!

COUNT: Since you insist—aw—aw—there's no resisting you, Miss Tiffany.

MRS. TIFFANY: I am so thankful. How can I repay your condescension! (COUNT *and* SERAPHINA *converse.*) Mr. Snobson, will you walk this way?—I have *such* a cactus in full bloom —remarkable flower! Mr. Tiffany, pray come here—I have something particular to say.

TIFFANY: Then speak out, my dear—I thought it was highly improper just now to leave a girl with a young man? (*Aside to her.*)

MRS. TIFFANY: Oh, but the Count—that is different!

TIFFANY: I suppose you mean to say there's nothing of *the man* about him?

(*Enter* MILLINETTE *with a scarf in her hand.*)

MILLINETTE: Adolph, tell me he vas here. (*Aside.*) Pardon, Madame, I bring dis scarf for Mademoiselle.

MRS. TIFFANY: Very well, Millinette; you know best what is proper for her to wear.

(MR. *and* MRS. TIFFANY *and* SNOBSON *retire up; she engages the attention of both gentlemen.*)

(MILLINETTE *crosses towards* SERAPHINA, *gives the* COUNT *a threatening look, and commences arranging the scarf over* SERAPHINA'S *shoulders.*)

MILLINETTE: Mademoiselle, *permettez-moi. Perfide*! (*Aside to* COUNT.) If Mademoiselle vil stand *tranquille* one *petit* moment. (*Turns* SERAPHINA'S *back to the* COUNT, *and pretends to arrange the scarf.*) I must speak vid you to-day, or I tell all—you find me at de foot of de stair ven you go. *Prends garde!* (*Aside to* COUNT.)

SERAPHINA: What is that you say, Millinette?

MILLINETTE: Dis scarf make you so very beautiful, Mademoiselle—*Je vous salue, mes dames.* (*Curtsies.*) (*Exit.*)

COUNT: Not a moment to lose! (*Aside.*) Miss Tiffany, I have an unpleasant—a particularly unpleasant piece of intelligence—you see, I have just received a letter from my friend—the—aw —the Earl of Airshire; the truth is, the Earl's daughter—beg you won't mention it—has distinguished me by a tender *penchant*.

SERAPHINA: I understand—and they wish you to return and marry the young lady; but surely you will not leave us, Count?

COUNT: If *you* bid me stay—I shouldn't have the conscience—I could n't *afford* to tear myself away. I'm sure that's honest. (*Aside.*)

SERAPHINA: Oh, Count!

COUNT: Say but one word—say that you should n't mind being made a Countess—and I'll break with the Earl tomorrow.

SERAPHINA: Count, this surprise—but don't think of leaving the country, Count—we could not pass the time without you! I—yes—yes, Count—I do consent!

COUNT: I thought she would! (*Aside, while he embraces her.*) Enchanted, rapture, bliss, ecstacy, and all that sort of thing—words can't express it, but you understand. But it must be kept a secret—positively it *must*! If the rumour of our engagement were whispered abroad—the Earl's daughter—the delicacy of my situation, aw —you comprehend? It is even possible that our nuptials, my charming Miss Tiffany, *our nuptials* must take place in private!

SERAPHINA: Oh, that is quite impossible!

COUNT: It's the latest fashion abroad—the very latest. Ah, I knew that would determine you. Can I depend on your secrecy?

SERAPHINA: Oh, yes! Believe me.

SNOBSON (*Coming forward in spite of* MRS. TIFFANY'S *efforts to detain him*): Why, Seraphina, have n't you a word to throw to a dog?

TIFFANY: I shouldn't think she had after wasting so many upon a puppy. (*Aside.*)

(*Enter* ZEKE, *wearing a three-cornered hat.*)

ZEKE: Missus, de bran new carriage am below.

MRS. TIFFANY: Show it up,—I mean, Very well, A-dolph. (*Exit* ZEKE.) Count, my daughter and I are about to take an airing in our new *voyture*,—will you honor us with your company?

COUNT: Madam, I—I have a most *pressing* engagement. A letter to write to the *Earl of Airshire*—who is at present residing in the *Isle of Skye*. I must bid you good morning.

MRS. TIFFANY: Good morning, Count. (*Exit* COUNT.)

SNOBSON: *I'm quite at leisure, (crosses to* MRS. TIFFANY) Marm. Books balanced—ledger closed —nothing to do all the afternoon,—I'm for you.

MRS. TIFFANY (*Without noticing him*): Come, Seraphina, come!

(*As they are going* SNOBSON *follows them.*)

SNOBSON: But, Marm—I was saying, Marm, I am quite at leisure—not a thing to do; have I, Mr. Tiffany?

MRS. TIFFANY: Seraphina, child—your red shawl—remember—Mr. Snobson, *bon swear*! (*Exit, leading* SERAPHINA.)

SNOBSON: Swear! Mr. Tiffany, Sir, am I to be

fobbed off with a *bon swear*? D——n it, I will swear!

TIFFANY: Have patience, Mr. Snobson, if you will accompany me to the counting house—

SNOBSON: Don't count too much on me, Sir. I'll make up no more accounts until these are settled! I'll run down and jump into the carriage in spite of her *bon swear*. (*Exit.*)

TIFFANY: You'll jump into a hornet's nest, if you do! Mr. Snobson, Mr. Snobson! (*Exit after him.*)

SCENE 2. *Housekeeper's room.*

(*Enter* MILLINETTE.)

MILLINETTE: I have set dat bête, Adolph, to vatch for him. He say he would come back so soon as Madame's voiture drive from de door. If he not come—but he vill—he vill—he *bien etourdi*, but he have *bon coeur*.

(*Enter* COUNT.)

COUNT: Ah! Millinette, my dear, you see what a good-natured dog I am to fly at your bidding—

MILLINETTE: Fly? Ah! *trompeur*! Vat for you fly from Paris? Vat for you leave me—and I love you so much? Ven you sick—you almost die—did I not stay by you—take care of you—and you have no else friend? Vat for you leave Paris?

COUNT: Never allude to disagreeable subjects, *mon enfant*! I was forced by uncontrollable circumstances to fly to the land of liberty—

MILLINETTE: Vat you do vid all de money I give you? The last sou I had—did I not give you?

COUNT: I dare say you did, ma petite—wish you'd been better supplied! (*Aside.*) Don't ask any questions here—can't explain now—the next time we meet—

MILLINETTE: But, ah! ven shall ve meet—ven? You not deceive me, not any more.

COUNT: Deceive you! I'd rather deceive myself—I wish I could! I'd persuade myself you were once more washing linen in the Seine! (*Aside.*)

MILLINETTE: I vil tell you ven ve shall meet—On Friday night Madame give one grand ball—you come *sans doute*—den ven de supper is served—de Americans tink of noting else ven de supper come—den you steal out of de room, and

you find me here—and you give me one grand *explanation*!

(*Enter* GERTRUDE, *unperceived.*)

COUNT: Friday night—while supper is serving—*parole d'honneur* I will be here—I will explain every thing—my sudden departure from Paris—my—demme, my countship—every thing! Now let me go—if any of the family should discover us—

GERTRUDE (*who during the last speech has gradually advanced*): They might discover more than you think it advisable for them to know!

COUNT: The devil!

MILLINETTE: *Mon Dieu!* Mademoiselle Gertrude!

COUNT (*recovering himself*): My dear miss Gertrude, let me explain—aw—aw—nothing is more natural than the situation in which you find me—

GERTRUDE: I am inclined to believe that, Sir.

COUNT: Now—'pon my honor, that's not fair. Here is Millinette will bear witness to what I am about to say—

GERTRUDE: Oh, I have not the slightest doubt of that, Sir.

COUNT: You see, Millinette happened to be lady's-maid in the family of—of—the Duchess Chateau D'Espagne—and I chanced to be a particular friend of the Duchess—*very particular* I assure you! Of course I saw Millinette, and she, demme, she saw me! Did n't you, Millinette?

MILLINETTE: Oh! *oui*—Mademoiselle, I knew him ver vell.

COUNT: Well, it is a remarkable fact that —being in correspondence with this very Duchess—at this very time—

GERTRUDE: That is sufficient, Sir—I am already so well acquainted with your extraordinary talents for improvisation, that I will not further tax your invention—

MILLINETTE: Ah! Mademoiselle Gertrude do not betray us—have pity!

COUNT (*assuming an air of dignity*): Silence Millinette! My word has been doubted—the word of a nobleman! I will inform my friend, Mrs. Tiffany, of this young person's audacity. (*Going.*)

GERTRUDE: His own weapons alone can foil this villain! (*Aside.*) Sir—Sir—Count! (*At the last word the* COUNT *turns.*) Perhaps, Sir, the least said about this matter the better!

COUNT (*delightedly*): The least said? We won't say anything at all. She's coming round

—could n't resist me. (*Aside.*) Charming Gertrude—

MILLINETTE: *Quoi?* Vat that you say?

COUNT: My sweet, adorable Millinette, hold your tongue, will you? (*Aside to her.*)

MILLINETTE (*Aloud*): No, I vill not! If you do look so from out your eyes at her again, I vill tell all!

COUNT: Oh, I never could manage two women at once,—jealousy makes the dear creatures so spiteful. The only valor is in flight! (*Aside.*) Miss Gertrude, I wish you good morning. Millinette, *mon enfant*, adieu. (*Exit.*)

MILLINETTE: But I have one word more to say. Stop, Stop! (*Exit after him.*)

GERTRUDE (*musingly*): Friday night, while supper is serving, he is to meet Millinette here and explain—what? This man is an impostor! His insulting me—his familiarity with Millinette—his whole conduct—prove it. If I tell Mrs. Tiffany this she will disbelieve me, and one word may place this so-called Count on his guard. To convince Seraphina would be equally difficult, and her rashness and infatuation may render her miserable for life. No—she shall be saved! I must devise some plan for opening their eyes. Truly, if I *cannot* invent one, I shall be the first woman who was ever at a loss for a stratagem—especially to punish a villain or to shield a friend. (*Exit.*)

ACT IV

SCENE 1. (*Ball room splendidly illuminated. A curtain hung at the further end.* MR. *and* MRS. TIFFANY, SERAPHINA, GERTRUDE, FOGG, TWINKLE, COUNT, SNOBSON, COLONEL HOWARD, *a number of guests—some seated, some standing. As the curtain rises, a cotillion is danced;* GERTRUDE *dancing with* HOWARD, SERAPHINA *with* COUNT.)

COUNT (*advancing with* SERAPHINA *to the front of the stage*): To-morrow then—to-morrow—I may salute you as my bride—demme, my Countess!

(*Enter* ZEKE, *with refreshments.*)

SERAPHINA: Yes, to-morrow.

(*As the* COUNT *is about to reply,* SNOBSON *thrusts himself in front of* SERAPHINA.)

SNOBSON: You said you'd dance with me, Miss—now take my fin, and we'll walk about and see what's going on.

(COUNT *raises his eye-glass, regards* SNOBSON, *and leads* SERAPHINA *away;* SNOBSON *follows, endeavoring to attract her attention, but encountering* ZEKE, *bearing a waiter of refreshments; stops him, helps himself, and puts some in his pockets.*)

Here's the treat! get my to-morrow's luncheon out of Tiff.

(*Enter* TRUEMAN, *yawning and rubbing his eyes.*)

TRUEMAN: What a nap I've had, to be sure! (*Looks at his watch.*) Eleven o'clock, as I'm alive! Just the time when country folks are comfortably *turned in*, and here your grand *turn-out* has hardly begun yet. (*To* TIFFANY, *who approaches.*)

GERTRUDE (*advancing*): I was just coming to look for you, Mr. Trueman. I began to fancy that you were paying a visit to dream-land.

TRUEMAN: So I was, child—so I was—and I saw a face—like yours—but brighter!—even brighter. (*To* TIFFANY.) There's a smile for you, man! It makes one feel that the world has something worth living for in it yet! Do you remember a smile like that, Antony! Ah! I see you don't—but I do—I do! (*Much moved.*)

HOWARD (*advancing*): Good evening, Mr. Trueman. (*Offers his hand.*)

TRUEMAN: That's right, man; give me your whole hand! When a man offers me the tips of his fingers, I know at once there's nothing in him worth seeking beyond his fingers ends.

(TRUEMAN *and* HOWARD, GERTRUDE *and* TIFFANY *converse.*)

MRS. TIFFANY (*advancing*): I'm in such a fidget lest that vulgar old fellow should disgrace us by some of his plebeian remarks! What it is to give a ball, when one is forced to invite vulgar people!

(MRS. TIFFANY *advances towards* TRUEMAN; SERAPHINA *stands conversing flippantly with the gentlemen who surround her; amongst them is* TWINKLE, *who having taken a magazine from his pocket, is reading to her, much to the undisguised annoyance of* SNOBSON.)

Dear me, Mr. Trueman, you are very late —quite in the fashion, I declare!

TRUEMAN: Fashion! And pray what is *fashion*, madam? An agreement between certain persons to live without using their souls! to substitute etiquette for virtue—decorum for purity— manners for morals! to affect a shame for the works of their Creator! and expend all their rapture upon the works of their tailors and dressmakers!

MRS. TIFFANY: You have the most *ow-tray* ideas, Mr. Trueman—quite rustic, and deplorably *American*! But pray walk this way.

(MRS. TIFFANY *and* TRUEMAN *go up.*)

COUNT (*advancing to* GERTRUDE, HOWARD *a short distance behind her*): Miss Gertrude—no opportunity of speaking to you before—in demand you know!

GERTRUDE: I have no choice, I must be civil to him. (*Aside.*) What were you remarking, Sir?

COUNT: Miss Gertrude—charming Ger—aw—aw—I never found it so difficult to speak to a woman before. (*Aside.*)

GERTRUDE: Yes, a very charming ball—many beautiful faces here.

COUNT: Only one!—aw—aw—one—the fact is—(*Talks to her in dumb show.*)

HOWARD: What could old Trueman have meant by saying she fancied that puppy of a Count—that paste jewel thrust upon the little finger of society.

COUNT: Miss Gertrude—aw—'pon my honor—you don't understand—really—aw—aw—will you dance the polka with me?

(GERTRUDE *bows and gives him her hand; he leads her to the set forming;* HOWARD *remains looking after them.*)

HOWARD: Going to dance with him too! A few days ago she would hardly bow to him civilly—could old Trueman have had reasons for what he said? (*Retires up.*)

(*Dance, the polka;* SERAPHINA, *after having distributed her bouquet, vinaigrette and fan amongst the gentlemen, dances with* SNOBSON.)

PRUDENCE (*peeping in as dance concludes*): I don't like dancing on Friday; something strange is always sure to happen! I'll be on the look out.

(*Remains peeping and concealing herself when any of the company approach.*)

GERTRUDE (*advancing hastily*): They are preparing the supper—now if I can only dispose of Millinette while I unmask this insolent pretender! (*Exit.*)

PRUDENCE (*peeping*): What's that she said? It's coming!

(*Re-enter* GERTRUDE, *bearing a small basket filled with bouquets; approaches* MRS. TIFFANY; *they walk to the front of the stage.*)

GERTRUDE: Excuse me, Madam—I believe this is just the hour at which you ordered supper?

MRS. TIFFANY: Well, what's that to you! So you've been dancing with the Count—how dare you dance with a nobleman—*you*?

GERTRUDE: I will answer that question half an hour hence. At present I have something to propose, which I think will gratify you and please your guests. I have heard that at the most elegant balls in Paris, it is customary—

MRS. TIFFANY: What? what?

GERTRUDE: To station a servant at the door with a basket of flowers. A bouquet is then presented to every lady as she passes in—I prepared this basket a short time ago. As the company walk in to supper, might not the flowers be distributed to advantage?

MRS. TIFFANY: How *distingué!* You are a good creature, Gertrude—there, run and hand the *bokettes* to them yourself! You shall have the whole credit of the thing.

GERTRUDE: Caught in my own net! (*Aside.*) But, Madam, I know so little of fashions—Millinette, being French herself, will do it with so much more grace. I am sure Millinette—

MRS. TIFFANY: So am I. She will do it a thousand times better than you—there go call her.

GERTRUDE (*giving basket*): But, Madam, pray order Millinette not to leave her station till supper is ended—as the company pass out of the supper room she may find that some of the ladies have been overlooked.

MRS. TIFFANY: That is true—very thoughtful of you, Gertrude. (*Exit* GERTRUDE.) What a *recherché* idea!

(*Enter* MILLINETTE.)

Here, Millinette, take this basket. Place yourself there, and distribute these *bokettes* as the company pass in to supper; but remember not to stir from the spot until supper is over. It is a French fashion you know, Millinette. I am so delighted to be the first to introduce it—it will be all the rage in the *bowmonde!*

MILLINETTE: Mon Dieu! dis vill ruin all! (*Aside.*) Madame, Madame, let me tell you, Madame, dat in France, in Paris, it is de custom to present *les* bouquets ven every body first come—long before de supper. Dis vould be *outre! barbare!* not at all la mode! Ven dey do come in—dat is de fashion in Paris!

MRS. TIFFANY: Dear me! Millinette, what is

the difference? besides I'd have you to know that Americans always improve upon French fashions! here, take the basket, and let me see that you do it in the most *you-nick* and genteel manner.

(MILLINETTE *poutingly takes the basket and retires up stage. A MARCH. Curtain hung at the further end of the room is drawn back, and discloses a room, in the centre of which stands a supper table, beautifully decorated and illuminated; the company promenade two by two into the supper room;* MILLINETTE *presents bouquets as they pass;* COUNT *leads* MRS. TIFFANY.)

TRUEMAN: (*encountering* FOGG, *who is hurrying alone to the supper room*): Mr. Fogg, never mind the supper, man! Ha, ha, ha! Of course you are indifferent to suppers!

MR. FOGG: Indifferent! suppers—oh, ah—no, Sir—suppers? no—no—I'm not indifferent to suppers! (*Hurries away towards table.*)

TRUEMAN: Ha, ha, ha! Here's a new discovery I've made in the fashionable world! Fashion don't permit the critters to have *heads* or *hearts*, but it allows them stomachs! (*To* TIFFANY, *who advances.*) So it's not fashionable to *feel*, but it's fashionable to *feed*, eh, Antony? ha, ha, ha!

(TRUEMAN *and* TIFFANY *retire towards supper room. Enter* GERTRUDE, *followed by* ZEKE.)

GERTRUDE: Zeke, go to the supper room instantly—whisper to Count Jolimatre that all is ready, and that he must keep his appointment without delay,—then watch him, and as he passes out of the room, place yourself in front of Millinette in such a manner, that the Count cannot see her nor she him. Be sure that they do not see each other—everything depends upon that. (*Crosses*)

ZEKE: Missey, consider dat business brought to a scientific conclusion.

(*Exit into supper room. Exit* GERTRUDE.)

PRUDENCE (*who has been listening*): What can she want of the Count? I always suspected that Gertrude, because she is so merry and busy! Mr. Trueman thinks so much of her too—I'll tell him this! There's something wrong—but it all comes of giving a ball on a Friday! How astonished the dear old man will be when he finds out how much I know!

(*Advances timidly towards the supper room.*)

SCENE 2. *Housekeeper's room; dark stage; table, two chairs.*

(*Enter* GERTRUDE, *with a lighted candle in her hand.*)

GERTRUDE: So far the scheme prospers! and yet this imprudence—if I fail? Fail! to lack courage in a difficulty, or ingenuity in a dilemma, are not woman's failings!

(*Enter* ZEKE, *with a napkin over his arm, and a bottle of champagne in his hand.*)

Well, Zeke—Adolph!

ZEKE: Dat's right, Missey; I feels just now as if dat was my legitimate title; dis here's de stuff to make a nigger feel like a gemman!

GERTRUDE: But he is coming?

ZEKE: He's coming! (*Sound of a champagne cork heard.*) Do you hear dat, Missey? Don't it put you all in a froth, and make you feel as light as a cork? Dere's nothing like the *union brand*, to wake up de harmonies ob de heart. (*Drinks from bottle.*)

GERTRUDE: Remember to keep watch upon the outside—do not stir from the spot; when I call you, come in quickly with a light—now, will you be gone!

ZEKE: I'm off, Missey, like a champagne cork wid de strings cut. (*Exit.*)

GERTRUDE: I think I hear the Count's step. (*Crosses, stage dark; she blows out candle.*) Now if I can but disguise my voice, and make the best of my French.

(*Enter* COUNT.)

COUNT: Millinette, where are you? How am I to see you in the dark?

GERTRUDE (*imitating* MILLINETTE'S *voice in a whisper*). Hush! *parle bas*

COUNT: Come here and give me a kiss.

GERTRUDE: Non—non—(*Retreating alarmed,* COUNT *follows.*) make haste, I must know all.

COUNT: You did not use to be so deuced particular.

ZEKE (*without*): No admission, gemman! Box office closed, tickets stopped!

TRUEMAN (*without*): Out of my way; do you want me to try if your head is as hard as my stick?

GERTRUDE: What shall I do? Ruined, ruined!

(*She stands with her hands clasped in speechless despair.*)

COUNT: Halloa! they are coming here, Millinette! Millinette, why don't you speak? Where can I hide myself? (*Running about stage, feeling for a door.*) Where are all your closets? If I could only get out—or get in somewhere; may I be smothered in a clothes' basket, if you ever catch me in such a scrape again! (*His hand accidentally touches the knob of a door opening into a closet.*) Fortune's favorite yet! I'm safe!

(*Gets into closet and closes door. Enter* PRUDENCE, TRUEMAN, MRS. TIFFANY, *and* COLONEL HOWARD, *followed by* ZEKE, *bearing a light; lights up.*)

PRUDENCE: Here they are, the Count and Gertrude! I told you so!

(*Stops in surprise on seeing only* GERTRUDE.)

TRUEMAN: And you see what a lie you told!

MRS. TIFFANY: Prudence, how dare you create this disturbance in my house? To suspect the Count too—a nobleman!

HOWARD: My sweet Gertrude, this foolish old woman would—

PRUDENCE: Oh! you needn't talk—I heard her make the appointment—I know he's here—or he's been here. I wonder if she hasn't hid him away!

(*Runs peeping about the room.*)

TRUEMAN (*following her angrily*): You're what I call a confounded—troublesome—meddling—old—prying—(*as he says the last word,* PRUDENCE *opens closet where the* COUNT *is concealed.*) Thunder and lightning!

PRUDENCE: I told you so!

(*They all stand aghast;* MRS. TIFFANY, *with her hands lifted in surprise and anger;* TRUEMAN, *clutching his stick;* HOWARD, *looking with an expression of bewildered horror from the* COUNT *to* GERTRUDE.)

MRS. TIFFANY (*Shaking her fist at* GERTRUDE): You depraved little minx! this is the meaning of your dancing with the Count!

COUNT (*stepping from the closet and advancing*): I don't know what to make of it! Millinette not here! Miss Gertrude—oh! I see—a disguise—the girl's desperate about me—the way with them all. (*Aside.*)

TRUEMAN: I'm choking—I can't speak— Gertrude—no—no—it is some horrid mistake! (*Partly aside, changes his tone suddenly.*) The villain! I'll hunt the truth out of him, if there's any in—(*crosses, approaches* COUNT *threateningly*) do you see this stick? You made its first acquaintance a few days ago; it is time you were better known to each other.

(*As* TRUEMAN *attempts to seize him,* COUNT *escapes,*

and shields himself behind MRS. TIFFANY, TRUEMAN *following.*)

COUNT: You ruffian! would you strike a woman?—Madam—my dear Madam—keep off that barbarous old man, and I will explain! Madam, with—aw—your natural *bon gout*—aw —your fashionable refinement—aw—your—aw —your knowledge of *foreign customs*—

MRS. TIFFANY: Oh! Count, I hope it ain't a *foreign custom* for the nobility to shut themselves up in the dark with young women? We think such things *dreadful* in *America*.

COUNT: Demme—aw—hear what I have to say, Madam—I'll satisfy all sides—I am perfectly innocent in this affair—'pon my honor I am! That young lady shall inform you that I am so herself!—can't help it, sorry for her. Old matter-of-fact won't be convinced any other way,—that club of his is so particularly unpleasant! (*Aside.*) Madam, I was summoned here *malgré moi*, and not knowing whom I was to meet—Miss Gertrude, favor the company by saying whether or not you directed—that—aw —aw—that colored individual to conduct me here?

GERTRUDE: Sir, you well know—

COUNT: A simple yes or no will suffice.

MRS. TIFFANY: Answer the Count's question instantly, Miss.

GERTRUDE: I did—but—

COUNT: You hear, Madam—

TRUEMAN: I won't believe it—I can't! Here, you nigger, stop rolling up your eyes, and let us know whether she told you to bring that critter here?

ZEKE: I'se refuse to gib ebidence; dat's de device ob de skilfullest counsels ob de day! Can't answer, Boss—neber git a word out ob dis child—Yah! yah! (*Exit.*)

GERTRUDE: Mrs. Tiffany,—Mr. Trueman, if you will but have patience—

TRUEMAN: Patience! Oh, Gertrude, you've taken from an old man something better and dearer than his patience—the one bright hope of nineteen years of self-denial—of nineteen years of—

(*Throws himself upon a chair, his head leaning on table.*)

MRS. TIFFANY: Get out of my house, you *ow*-dacious—you ruined—you *abimé* young woman! You will corrupt all my family. Good gracious! don't touch me,—don't come near me. Never let me see your face after to-morrow.

Pack. (*Goes up.*)

HOWARD: Gertrude, I have striven to find some excuse for you—to doubt—to disbelieve—but this is beyond all endurance! (*Exit.*)

(*Enter* MILLINETTE *in haste.*)

MILLINETTE: I could not come before—(*Stops in surprise at seeing the persons assembled.*) Mon Dieu! vat does dis mean?

COUNT: Hold your tongue, fool! You will ruin everything, I will explain tomorrow. (*Aside to her.*) Mrs. Tiffany—Madam—my dear Madam, let me conduct you back to the ball-room. (*She takes his arm.*) You see I am quite innocent in this matter; a man of my standing, you know,—aw, aw—you comprehend the whole affair.

(*Exit* COUNT *leading* MRS. TIFFANY.)

MILLINETTE: I will say to him von vord, I will! (*Exit.*)

GERTRUDE: Mr. Trueman, I beseech you—I insist upon being heard,—I claim it as a right!

TRUEMAN: Right? How dare you have the face, girl, to talk of rights? (*Comes down.*) You had more rights than you thought for, but you have forfeited them all! All right to love, respect, protection, and to not a little else that you don't dream of. Go, go! I'll start for Catteraugus to-morrow,—I've seen enough of what fashion can do! (*Exit.*)

PRUDENCE: (*wiping her eyes*): Dear old man, how he takes on! I'll go and console him! (*Exit.*)

GERTRUDE: This is too much! How heavy a penalty has my imprudence cost me! his esteem, and that of one dearer—my home—my—(*Burst of lively music from hall-room*) They are dancing, and I—I should be weeping, if pride had not sealed up my tears.

(*She sinks into a chair. Band plays the polka behind till Curtain falls.*)

ACT V

SCENE 1. MRS. TIFFANY'S *Drawing Room—same Scene as Act First.* GERTRUDE *seated at a table, with her head leaning on her hand; in the other hand she holds a pen. A sheet of paper and an ink-stand before her.*

GERTRUDE: How shall I write to them? What shall I say? Prevaricate I cannot—(*Rises and comes forward.*) and yet if I write the truth—simple souls! how can they comprehend the motives for my conduct? Nay—the truly pure see no imaginary evil in others! It is only vice, that reflecting its own image, suspects, even the innocent. I have no time to lose—I must prepare them for my return. (*Resumes her seat and writes.*) What a true pleasure there is in daring to be frank! (*After writing a few lines more pauses.*) Not so frank either,—there is one name that I cannot mention. Ah! that he should suspect—should despise me. (*Writes.*)

(*Enter* TRUEMAN.)

TRUEMAN: There she is! If this girl's soul had only been as fair as her face,—yet she dared to speak the truth,—I'll not forget that! A woman who refuses to tell a lie has one spark of heaven in her still. (*Approaches her.*) Gertrude, (GERTRUDE *starts and looks up.*) what are you writing there? Plotting more mischief, eh, girl?

GERTRUDE I was writing a few lines to some friends in Geneva.

TRUEMAN: The Wilsons, eh?

GERTRUDE (*surprised, rising*): Are you acquainted with them, Sir?

TRUEMAN: I shouldn't wonder if I was. I suppose you have taken good care not to mention the dark room—that foreign puppy in the closet—the pleasant surprise—and all that sort of thing, eh?

GERTRUDE: I have no reason for concealment, Sir! for I have done nothing of which I am ashamed!

TRUEMAN: Then I can't say much for your modesty.

GERTRUDE: I should not wish you to say more than I deserve.

TRUEMAN: There's a bold minx! (*Aside.*)

GERTRUDE: Since my affairs seem to have excited your interest—I will not say *curiosity*, perhaps you even feel a desire to inspect my correspondence? There, (*Handing the letter.*) I pride myself upon my good nature,—you may like to take advantage of it?

TRUEMAN: With what an air she carries it off! (*Aside.*) Take advantage of it? So I will. (*Reads.*) What's this? "French chambermaid—Count—impostor—infatuation—Seraphina—Millinette—disguised myself—expose him." Thunder and lightning! I see it all! Come and kiss me, girl! (GERTRUDE *evinces surprise.*) No, no—I forgot—it won't do to come to that yet! She's a rare girl! I'm out of my senses with joy! I don't know what to do with myself! Tol, de rol, de rol, de ra. (*Capers and sings.*)

GERTRUDE: What a remarkable old man! (*Aside.*) Then you do me justice, Mr. Trueman?

TRUEMAN: I say I don't! Justice? You're above all dependence upon justice! Hurrah! I've found one true woman at last? *True*? (*Pauses thoughtfully.*) Humph! I didn't think of that flaw! Plotting and manoeuvering—not much truth in that? An honest girl should be above stratagems!

GERTRUDE: But my *motive*, Sir, was good.

TRUEMAN: That's not enough—your *actions* must be *good* as well as your *motives*! Why could you not tell the silly girl that man was an imposter?

GERTRUDE: I did inform her of my suspicions —she ridiculed them; the plan I chose was an imprudent one, but I could not devise—

TRUEMAN: I hate devising! Give me a woman with the *firmness* to be *frank*! But no matter—I had no right to look for an angel out of Paradise; and I am as happy—as happy as a Lord! that is, ten times happier than any Lord ever was! Tol, de rol, de rol! Oh! you—you—I'll thrash every fellow that says a word against you!

GERTRUDE: You will have plenty of employment then, Sir, for I do not know of one just now who would speak in my favor!

TRUEMAN: Not *one*, eh? Why, where's your dear Mr. Twinkle? I know all about it—can't say that I admire your choice of a husband! But there's no accounting for a girl's taste.

GERTRUDE: Mr. Twinkle! Indeed you are quite mistaken!

TRUEMAN: No—really? Then you're not taken with him, eh?

GERTRUDE: Not even with his rhymes.

TRUEMAN: Hang that old mother meddle-much! What a fool she has made of me. And so you're quite free, and I may choose a husband for you myself? Heart-whole, eh?

GERTRUDE: I—I—I trust there is nothing *unsound* about my heart.

TRUEMAN: There it is again. Don't prevaricate, girl! I tell you an *evasion* is a *lie in contemplation*, and I hate lying! Out with the truth! Is your heart *free* or not?

GERTRUDE: Nay, Sir, since you *demand* an answer, permit *me* to demand by what right you ask the question?

(*Enter* HOWARD.)

Colonel Howard here!

TRUEMAN: I'm out again! What's the Colonel to her? (*Retires up.*)

HOWARD (*crosses to her*): I have come, Gertrude, to bid you farewell. To-morrow I resign my commission and leave this city, perhaps for ever. You, Gertrude, it is you who have exiled me! After last evening—

TRUEMAN (*coming forward to* HOWARD): What the plague have you got to say about last evening?

HOWARD: Mr. Trueman!

TRUEMAN: What have you got to say about last evening? and what have you to say to that little girl at all? It's Tiffany's precious daughter you're in love with.

HOWARD: Miss Tiffany? Never! I never had the slightest pretension—

TRUEMAN: That lying old woman! But I'm glad of it! Oh! Ah! Um! (*Looking significantly at* GERTRUDE *and then at* HOWARD.) I see how it is. So you don't choose to marry Seraphina, eh? Well now, whom do you choose to marry? (*Glancing at* GERTRUDE.)

HOWARD: I shall not marry at all!

TRUEMAN: You won't? (*Looking at them both again.*) Why you don't mean to say that you don't like—(*Points with his thumb to* GERTRUDE.)

GERTRUDE: Mr. Trueman, I may have been wrong to boast of my good nature, but do not presume too far upon it.

HOWARD: You like frankness, Mr. Trueman, therefore I will speak plainly. I have long cherished a dream from which I was last night rudely awakened.

TRUEMAN: And that's what you call speaking plainly? Well, I differ with you! But I can guess what you mean. Last night you suspected Gertrude there of—(*angrily*) of what no man shall ever suspect her again while I'm above ground! You did her injustice,—it was a mistake! There, now that matter's settled. Go, and ask her to forgive you,—she's woman enough to do it! Go, go!

HOWARD: Mr. Trueman, you have forgotten to whom you dictate.

TRUEMAN: Then you won't do it? you won't ask her pardon?

HOWARD: Most undoubtedly I will not—not at any man's bidding. I must first know—

TRUEMAN: You won't do it? Then if I don't give you a lesson in politeness—

HOWARD: It will be because you find me your *tutor* in the same science. I am not a man to brook an insult, Mr. Trueman! but we'll not quarrel in presence of the lady.

TRUEMAN: Won't we? I don't know that—

GERTRUDE: Pray, Mr. Trueman—Colonel

Howard, pray desist, Mr. Trueman, for my sake! (*Taking hold of his arm to hold him back.*) Colonel Howard, if you will read this letter it will explain everything. (*Hands letter to* HOWARD, *who reads.*)

TRUEMAN: He don't deserve an explanation! Didn't I tell him that it was a mistake? Refuse to beg your pardon! I'll teach him, I'll teach him!

HOWARD (*after reading*): Gertrude, how have I wronged you!

TRUEMAN: Oh, you'll beg her pardon now? (*Between them.*)

HOWARD: Hers, Sir, and yours! Gertrude, I fear—

TRUEMAN: You needn't,—she'll forgive you. You don't know these women as well as I do,—they're always ready to pardon; it's their nature, and they can't help it. Come along, I left Antony and his wife in the dining room; we'll go and find them. I've a story of my own to tell! As for you, Colonel, you may follow. Come along. Come along!

(*Leads out* GERTRUDE, *followed by* HOWARD.)

(*Enter* MR. *and* MRS. TIFFANY, MR. TIFFANY *with a bundle of bills in his hand.*)

MRS. TIFFANY: I beg you won't mention the subject again, Mr. Tiffany. Nothing is more plebeian than a discussion upon economy —nothing more *ungenteel* than looking over and fretting over one's bills!

TIFFANY: Then I suppose, my dear, it is quite as ungenteel to *pay* one's bills?

MRS. TIFFANY: Certainly! I hear the *ee-light* never condescend to do anything of the kind. The honor of their invaluable patronage is sufficient for the persons they employ!

TIFFANY: *Patronage* then is a newly invented food upon which the working classes fatten? What convenient appetites poor people must have! Now listen to what I am going to say. As soon as my daughter marries Mr. Snobson—

(*Enter* PRUDENCE, *a three-cornered note in her hand.*)

PRUDENCE: Oh, dear! oh, dear! what shall we do! Such a misfortune! Such a disaster! Oh, dear! oh, dear!

MRS. TIFFANY: Prudence, you are the most tiresome creature! What *is* the matter?

PRUDENCE (*passing up and down the stage*): Such a disgrace to the whole family! But I always expected it. Oh, dear! oh, dear!

MRS. TIFFANY (*following her up and down the stage*): What are you talking about, Prudence?

Will you tell me what has happened?

PRUDENCE (*still pacing*, MRS. TIFFANY *following*): Oh! I can't, I can't! You'll feel so dreadfully! How could she do such a thing! But I expected nothing else! I never did, I never did!

MRS. TIFFANY (*still following*): Good gracious! what do you mean, Prudence? Tell me, will you tell me? I shall get into such a passion! What *is* the matter?

PRUDENCE (*still pacing*): Oh, Betsy, Betsy! That your daughter should have come to that! Dear me, dear me!

TIFFANY: Seraphina? Did you say Seraphina? What has happened to her? what has she done?

(*Following* PRUDENCE *up and down the stage on the opposite side from* MRS. TIFFANY.)

MRS. TIFFANY (*still following*): What *has* she done? what *has* she done?

PRUDENCE: Oh! something dreadful— dreadful—shocking!

TIFFANY (*still following*): Speak quickly and plainly—you torture me by this delay, Prudence, be calm, and speak! What is it?

PRUDENCE (*stopping*): Zeke just told me—he carried her travelling trunk himself—she gave him a whole dollar! Oh, my!

TIFFANY: Her trunk? where? where?

PRUDENCE: Round the corner!

MRS. TIFFANY: What did she want with her trunk? You are the most vexatious creature, Prudence! There is no bearing your ridiculous conduct!

PRUDENCE: Oh, you will have worse to bear—worse! Seraphina's gone!

TIFFANY: Gone! where?

PRUDENCE: Off!—eloped—eloped with the Count! Dear me, dear me! I always told you she would!

TIFFANY: Then I am ruined!

(*Stands with his face buried in his hands.*)

MRS. TIFFANY: Oh, what a ridiculous girl! And she might have had such a splendid wedding! What could have possessed her?

TIFFANY: The devil himself possessed her, for she has ruined me past all redemption! Gone, Prudence, did you say gone? Are you *sure* they are gone?

PRUDENCE: Didn't I tell you so! Just look at this note—one might know by the very fold of it—

TIFFANY (*snatching the note*): Let me see it! (*Opens the note and reads.*) "My dear Ma,—When you receive this I shall be a *countess!* Isn't it a sweet title? The Count and I were forced to be married privately, for reasons which I will explain in my next. You must pacify Pa, and put him in a good humour before I come back, though now I'm to be a countess I suppose I shouldn't care!" Undutiful huzzy! "We are going to make a little excursion and will be back in a week.

"Your dutiful daughter—Seraphina." A man's curse is sure to spring up at his own hearth,—here is mine! The solo curb upon that villain gone, I am wholly in his power! Oh! the first downward step from honor—he who takes it cannot pause in his mad descent and is sure to be hurried on to ruin!

MRS. TIFFANY: Why, Mr. Tiffany, how you do take on! And I dare say to elope was the most fashionable way after all!

(*Enter* TRUEMAN, *leading* GERTRUDE, *and followed by* HOWARD.)

TRUEMAN: Where are all the folks? Here, Antony, you are the man I want. We've been hunting for you all over the house. Why —what's the matter? There's a face for a thriving city merchant! Ah! Antony, you never wore such a hang-dog look as that when you trotted about the country with your pack upon your back! Your shoulders are no broader now—but they've a heavier load to carry—that's plain!

MRS. TIFFANY: Mr. Trueman, such allusions are highly improper! What would my daughter, *the Countess*, say!

GERTRUDE: The Countess? Oh! Madam!

MRS. TIFFANY: Yes, the Countess!" My daughter Seraphina, the Countess *dee* Jolimaitre! What have you to say to that? No wonder you are surprised after your *recherché, abimé* conduct! I have told you already, Miss Gertrude, that you were not a proper person to enjoy the inestimable advantages of my patronage. You are dismissed —do you understand? Discharged!

TRUEMAN: Have you done? Very well, it's my turn now. Antony, perhaps what I have to say don't concern you as much as some others—but I want you to listen to me. You remember, Antony, (*his tone becomes serious*), a blue-eyed, smiling girl—

TIFFANY: Your daughter, Sir? I remember her well.

TRUEMAN: None ever saw her to forget her! Give me your hand, man. There—that will do! Now let me go on. I never coveted wealth—yet twenty years ago I found myself the richest

farmer in Catteraugus. This cursed money made my girl an object of speculation. Every idle fellow that wanted to feather his nest was sure to come courting Ruth. There was one—my heart misgave me the instant I laid eyes upon him—for he was a city chap, and not over fond of the truth. But Ruth—ah! she was too pure herself to look for guile! His fine words and his fair looks—the old story—she was taken with him—I said, "no"—but the girl liked her own way better than her old father's—girls always do! and one morning—the rascal robbed me—not of my money, he would have been welcome to that—but of the only treasure I cherished—my daughter!

TIFFANY: But you forgave her!

TRUEMAN: I did! I knew she would never forgive herself—that was punishment enough! The scoundrel thought he was marrying my gold with my daughter—he was mistaken! I took care that they should never want; but that was all. She loved him—what will not woman love? The villain broke her heart—mine was tougher, or it wouldn't have stood what it did. A year after they were married, he forsook her! She came back to her old home—her old father! It couldn't last long—she pined—and pined—and —then—she died! Don't think me an old fool—though I am one—for grieving won't bring her back. (*Bursts into tears.*)

TIFFANY: It was a heavy loss!

TRUEMAN: So heavy, that I should not have cared how soon I followed her, but for the child she left! As I pressed that child in my arms, I swore that my unlucky wealth should never curse it, as it had cursed its mother! It was all I had to love—but I sent it away—and the neighbors thought it was dead. The girl was brought up tenderly but humbly by my wife's relatives in Geneva. I had her taught true independence —she had hands—capacities—and should use them! Money should never buy her a husband! for I resolved not to claim her until she had made her choice, and found the man who was willing to take her for herself alone. She turned out a rare girl! and it's time her old grandfather claimed her. Here he is to do it! And there stands Ruth's child! Old Adam's heiress! Gertrude, Gertrude!—my child! (GERTRUDE *rushes into his arms.*)

PRUDENCE (*after a pause*): Do tell; I want to know! But I knew it! I always said Gertrude would turn out somebody, after all!

MRS. TIFFANY: Dear me! Gertrude an heiress! My dear Gertrude, I always thought you a very charming girl—quite YOU-NICK—an heiress! I must give her a ball! I'll introduce her into society myself—of course an heiress must make a sensation! (*Aside.*)

HOWARD: I am too bewildered even to wish her joy. Ah! there will be plenty to do that now—but the gulf between us is wider than ever. (*Aside.*)

TRUEMAN: Step forward, young man, and let us know what you are muttering about. I said I would never claim her until she had found the man who loved her for herself. I *have* claimed her—yet I never break my word—I think I *have* found that man! and here he is. (*Strikes* HOWARD *on the shoulder.*) Gertrude's yours! There—never say a word, man—don't bore me with your thanks—you can cancel all obligations by making that child happy! There—take her! —Well, girl, and what do you say?

GERTRUDE: That I rejoice too much at having found a parent for my first act to be one of disobedience! (*Gives her hand to* HOWARD.)

TRUEMAN: How very dutiful! and how disinterested!

(TIFFANY *retires up—and paces the stage, exhibiting great agitation.*)

PRUDENCE (*to* TRUEMAN): All the *single folks* are getting married!

TRUEMAN: No they are not. You and I are single folks, and we're not likely to get married.

MRS. TIFFANY: My dear Mr. Trueman—my sweet Gertrude, when my daughter, the Countess, returns, she will be delighted to hear of this *deenooment!* I assure you that the Countess will be quite charmed!

GERTRUDE: The Countess? Pray, Madam, where *is* Seraphina?

MRS. TIFFANY: The Countess *dee* Jolimaitre, my dear, is at this moment on her way to—to Washington! Where after visiting all the fashionable curiosities of the day—including the President—she will return to grace her native city!

GERTRUDE: I hope you are only jesting, Madam? Seraphina is not married?

MRS. TIFFANY: Excuse me, my dear, my daughter had this morning the honor of being united to the Count *dee* Jolimaitre!

GERTRUDE: Madam! He is an imposter!

MRS. TIFFANY: Good gracious! Gertrude, how can you talk in that disrespectful way of a man of rank? An heiress, my dear, should have better manners! The Count—

(*Enter* MILLINETTE, *crying.*)

MILLINETTE: Oh! Madame! I will tell everything—oh! dat monstre! He break my heart!

MRS. TIFFANY: Millinette, what is the matter?

MILLINETTE: Oh! he promise to marry me—I love him much—and now Zeke say he run away vid Mademoiselle Seraphina!

MRS. TIFFANY: What insolence! The girl is mad! Count Jolimaitre marry my *femmy de chamber*!

MILLINETTE: Oh! Madame, he is not one Count, not at all! Dat is only de title he go by in dis country. De foreigners always take de large title ven dey do come here. His name *à Paris* vas Gustave Treadmill. But he not one Frenchman at all, but he do live one long time *à Paris*. First he live vid Monsieur Vermicelle—dere he vas de head cook! Den he live vid Monsieur Tire-nez, de barber! After dat he live wid Monsieur le Comte Frippon-fin—and dere he vas le Comte's valet! Dere, now I tell everyting I feel one great deal better!

MRS. TIFFANY: Oh! good gracious! I shall faint! Not a Count! What will everybody say? It's no such thing! I say he *is* a Count! One can see the foreign *jenny says quoi* in his face! Don't you think I can tell a Count when I see one? I say he *is* a Count!

(*Enter* SNOBSON, *his hat on—his hands thrust in his pocket—evidently a little intoxicated.*)

SNOBSON: I won't stand it! I say I won't

TIFFANY (*rushing up to him*): Mr. Snobson, for heaven's sake— (*Aside.*)

SNOBSON: Keep off! I'm a hard customer to get the better of! You'll see if I don't come out strong!

TRUEMAN (*quietly knocking off* SNOBSON'S *hat with his stick*): Where are your manners, man?

SNOBSON: My business ain't with you, Catteraugus; you've waked up the wrong passenger! —Now the way I'll put it into Tiff will be a caution. I'll make him wince! That extra mint julep has put the true pluck in me. Now for it! (*Aside*) Mr. Tiffany, Sir—you need n't think to come over me, Sir—you'll have to get up a little earlier in the morning before you do *that*, Sir! I'd like to know, Sir, how you came to assist your daughter in running away with that foreign loafer? It was a downright swindle, Sir. After the conversation I and you had on that subject she wasn't your property, Sir.

TRUEMAN: What, Antony, is that the way your city clerk bullies his boss?

SNOBSON: You're drunk, Catteraugus—don't expose your-self—you're drunk! Taken a little too much toddy, my old boy! Be quiet! I'll look after you, and they won't find it out. If you want to be busy, you may take care of my *hat*—I feel so deuced weak in the chest, I don't think I *could* pick it up myself.—Now to put the screws to Tiff. (*Aside.*) Mr. Tiffany, Sir—you have broken your word, as no virtuous individual—no honorable member—of—the—com—mu—ni—ty—

TIFFANY: Have some pity, Mr. Snobson, I beseech you! I had nothing to do with my daughter's elopement! I will agree to anything you desire—your salary shall be doubled—trebled—(*Aside to him.*)

SNOBSON (*aloud*): No you don't. No bribery and corruption.

TIFFANY: I implore you to be silent. You shall become partner of the concern, if you please—only do not speak. You are not yourself at this moment. (*Aside to him.*)

SNOBSON: Ain't I, though? I feel *twice* myself. I feel like two Snobsons rolled into one, and I'm chock full of the spunk of a dozen! Now Mr. Tiffany, Sir—

TIFFANY: I shall go distracted! Mr. Snobson, if you have one spark of manly feeling—(*Aside to him.*)

TRUEMAN: Antony, why do you stand disputing with that drunken jackass? Where's your nigger? Let him kick the critter out, and be of use for once in his life.

SNOBSON: Better be quiet, Catteraugus. This ain't your hash, so keep your spoon out of the dish. Don't expose yourself, old boy.

TRUEMAN: Turn him out, Antony!

SNOBSON: He daren't do it! Ain't I up to him? Ain't he in my power? Can't I knock him into a cocked hat with a word? And now he's got my steam up—I *will* do it!

TIFFANY (*beseechingly*): Mr. Snobson—my friend—

SNOBSON: It's no go—steam's up—and I don't stand at anything!

TRUEMAN: You won't *stand* here long unless you mend your manners—you're not the first man I've *upset* because he didn't know his place.

SNOBSON: I know where Tiff's place is, and that's in the *States' Prison*! It's bespoke already. He would have it! He wouldn't take pattern of me, and behave like a gentleman! He's a *forger*, Sir! (TIFFANY *throws himself into a chair in an attitude of despair; the others stand transfixed with astonishment.*) He's been forging Dick Anderson's

endorsements of his notes these ten months. He's got a couple in the bank that will send him to the wall anyhow—if he can't make a raise. I took them there myself! Now you know what he's worth. I said I'd expose him, and I have done it!

MRS. TIFFANY: Get out of the house! You ugly, little, drunken brute, get out! It's not true. Mr. Trueman, put him out; you have got a stick—put him out!

(*Enter* SERAPHINA, *in her bonnet and shawl—a parasol in her hand.*)

SERAPHINA: I hope Zeke hasn't delivered my note.

(*Stops in surprise at seeing the persons assembled.*)

MRS. TIFFANY: Oh, here is the Countess! (*Advances to embrace her.*)

TIFFANY (*starting from his seat, and seizing* SERAPHINA *violently by the arm*): Are—you—married?

SERAPHINA: Goodness, Pa, how you frighten me! No, I'm not married, *quite.*

TIFFANY: Thank heaven.

MRS. TIFFANY (*drawing* SERAPHINA *aside*): What's the matter? Why did you come back?

SERAPHINA: The clergyman wasn't at home—I came back for my jewels—the Count said nobility couldn't get on without them.

TIFFANY: I may be saved yet! Seraphina, my child, you will not see me disgraced—ruined! I have been a kind father to you—at least I have tried to be one—although your mother's extravagance made a *madman* of me! The Count is an imposter—you seemed to like him—(*pointing to* SNOBSON). Heaven forgive me! (*Aside.*) Marry *him* and save *me.* You, Mr. Trueman, you will be my friend in this hour of extreme need—you will advance the sum which I require—I pledge myself to return it. My wife—my child—who will support them were I—the thought makes me frantic! You will aid me? You had a child yourself.

TRUEMAN: But I did not *sell* her—it was her own doings. Shame on you, Antony! Put a price on your own flesh and blood! Shame on such foul traffic!

TIFFANY: Save me—I conjure you—for my father's sake.

TRUEMAN: For your *father's* SON'S sake I will *not* aid you in becoming a greater villain than you are!

GERTRUDE: Mr. Trueman—Father, I should say—save him—do not embitter our happiness by permitting this calamity to fall upon another—

TRUEMAN: Enough—I did not need your voice, child. I am going to settle this matter my own way.

(*Goes up to* SNOBSON—*who has seated himself and fallen asleep—tilts him out of the chair.*)

SNOBSON (*waking up*): Eh? Where's the fire? Oh! it's you, Catteraugus.

TRUEMAN: If I comprehend aright, you have been for some time aware of your principal's forgeries?

(*As he says this, he beckons to* HOWARD, *who advances as witness.*)

SNOBSON: You've hit the nail, Catteraugus! Old chap saw that I was up to him six months ago; left off throwing dust into my eyes—

TRUEMAN: Oh, he did!

SNOBSON: Made no bones of forging Anderson's name at my elbow.

TRUEMAN: Forged at your elbow? You saw him do it?

SNOBSON: I did.

TRUEMAN: Repeatedly.

SNOBSON: Re—pea—ted—ly.

TRUEMAN: Then you, Rattlesnake, if he goes to the States' Prison, you'll take up your quarters there too. You are an accomplice, an *accessory*!

(TRUEMAN *walks away and seats himself,* HOWARD *rejoins* GERTRUDE. SNOBSON *stands for some time bewildered.*)

SNOBSON: The deuce, so I am! I never thought of that! I must make myself scarce. I'll be off! Tif, I say, Tif! (*Going up to him and speaking confidentially*) that drunken old rip has got us in his power. Let's give him the slip and be off. They want men of genius at the West,—we're sure to get on! You—you can set up for a writing master, and teach copying *signatures*; and I—I'll give lectures on *temperance*! You won't come, eh? Then I'm off without you. Good bye, Catteraugus! Which is the way to California? (*Steals off.*)

TRUEMAN: There's one debt your city owes me. And now let us see what other nuisances we can abate. Antony, I'm not given to preaching, therefore I shall not say much about what you have done. Your face speaks for itself,—the crime has brought its punishment along with it.

TIFFANY: Indeed it has, Sir! In *one year* I have lived a *century* of misery.

TRUEMAN: I believe you, and upon one condition I will assist you—

TIFFANY: My friend—my first, ever kind friend,—only name it!

TRUEMAN: You must sell your house and all these gew gaws, and bundle your wife and daughter off to the country. There let them learn economy, true independence, and home virtues, instead of foreign follies. As for yourself, continue your business—but let moderation, in future, be your counsellor, and let *honesty* be your confidential clerk.

TIFFANY: Mr. Trueman, you have made existence once more precious to me! My wife and daughter shall quit the city to-morrow, and—

PRUDENCE: It's all coming right! It's all coming right! We'll go to the county of Catteraugus. (*Walking up to* TRUEMAN.)

TRUEMAN: No, you won't—I make that a stipulation, Antony; keep clear of Catteraugus. None of your fashionable examples there!

(JOLIMAITRE *appears in the Conservatory and peeps into the room unperceived.*)

COUNT: What can detain Seraphina? We ought to be off!

MILLINETTE (*turns round, perceives him, runs and forces him into the room.*): Here he is! Ah, Gustave, mon cher Gustave! I have you now and we never part no more. Don't frown, Gustave, don't frown—

TRUEMAN: Come forward, Mr. Count! and for the edification of fashionable society confess that your're an imposter.

COUNT: An imposter? Why, you abominable old—

TRUEMAN: Oh, your feminine friend has told us all about it, the cook—the valet—barber and all that sort of thing. Come, confess, and something may be done for you.

COUNT: Well, then, I do confess I am no count; but really, ladies and gentlemen, I may recommend myself as the most capital cook.

MRS. TIFFANY: Oh, Seraphina!

SERAPHINA: Oh, Ma! (*They embrace and retire up.*)

TRUEMAN: Promise me to call upon the whole circle of your fashionable acquaintants with your own advertisements and in your cook's attire, and I will set you up in business to-morrow. Better turn stomachs than turn heads!

MILLINETTE: But you will marry me?

COUNT: Give us your hand, Millinette! Sir, command me for the most delicate *paté*—the daintiest *croquette à la royale*—the most transcendent *omelette soufflée* that ever issued from a French pastry-cook's oven. I hope you will pardon my conduct, but I heard that in America, where you pay homage to titles while you profess to scorn them—where *Fashion* makes the basest coin current—where you have no kings, no princes, no *nobility*—

TRUEMAN: Stop there! I object to your use of that word. When justice is found only among lawyers—health among physicians—and patriotism among politicians, *then* may you say that there is no *nobility* where there are no titles! But we *have* kings, princes, and nobles in abundance —of *Nature's stamp*, if not of *Fashion's*,—we have honest men, warm hearted and brave, and we have women—gentle, fair, and true, to whom no *title* could add *nobility*.

EPILOGUE.

PRUDENCE: I told you so! And now you hear and see.

I told you *Fashion* would the fashion be!

TRUEMAN: Then both its point and moral I distrust.

COUNT: Sir, is that liberal?

HOWARD: Or is it just?

TRUEMAN: The guilty have escaped!

TIFFANY: Is, therefore, sin. Made charming? Ah! there's punishment within!

Guilt ever carries his own scourge along.

GERTRUDE: Virtue her own reward!

TRUEMAN: You're right, I'm wrong.

MRS. TIFFANY: How we have been deceived!

PRUDENCE: I told you so.

SERAPHINA: To lose at once a title and a beau!

COUNT: A count no more, I'm no more of *account*.

TRUEMAN: But to a nobler title you may mount,

And be in time—who knows?—an honest man!

COUNT: Eh, Millinette?

MILLINETTE: Oh, *oui*—I know you can!

GERTRUDE (*to audience*): But ere we close the scene, a word with you,—

We charge you answer,—Is this picture true?
Some little mercy to our efforts show,
Then let the world your honest verdict know.
Here let it see portrayed its ruling passion,
And learn to prize at its just value—*Fashion*.

George L. Aiken: *Uncle Tom's Cabin* (1852)

Six months after its publication as a novel in March, 1852, George Aiken transformed Harriet Beecher Stowe's book onto the stage as one of the most powerful and influential pieces of drama America has ever had. Stowe never thought about protecting the dramatization rights of the book for herself because she was the wife of a minister and daughter of a writer and abolitionist and felt that the stage was wicked and unchristian. A friend had written to ask permission to dramatize the book, but Stowe refused on the grounds that even if it were good, it would lure Christians to the theater and they would get into bad habits. She was so strict in her feelings on this point that she herself had never been to see a play.

A friend, Francis H. Underwood, bought her a ticket for a performance of *Uncle Tom's Cabin* after it had been a smash success. Underwood convinced her to accompany him and describes the experience: "I asked Mrs. Stowe to go with me to see the play. She had some natural reluctance, considering the position her father had taken against the theatre, and considering the position of her husband as a preacher; but she also had some curiosity as a woman and as an author to see in flesh and blood the creations of her imagination. I think she told me she had never been in a theatre in her life. I procured the manager's box, and we entered privately, she being well muffled. She sat in the shade of the curtains of our box, and watched the play attentively. I never saw such delight upon a human face as she displayed when she first comprehended the full power of Mrs. Howard's *Topsy*. She scarcely spoke during the evening; but her expression was eloquent—smiles and tears succeeding each other through the whole."

Relatively little is known of George Aiken. He did not request permission to adapt the book for the stage, but began work on his adaptation immediately after the novel became a best seller. He had written for the stage before and seems to have

63

been something of a speculator in the manner of Cute in this play. But he had the capacity, characteristic of a number of theatrical geniuses in America, of knowing when he had a property that would appeal to a mass audience. He had written a number of dime novels that addressed such an audience, so in a way he had an apprenticeship that served him well. Aiken is probably our first playwright to have a clear sense of what the public would respond to, and he went on to make characters like Uncle Tom, Little Eva, and Simon Legree as real for most Americans as their next door neighbors. Even the London stage found the play irresistible.

The play claims a first in one other area: It is the first American play produced with no ballet or other diversion between acts. When the producer insisted that nothing was to interrupt the action, the owner of the theater was sure the play would fail miserably. He was totally wrong—the first production ran 300 nights. The owner was even able to raise the price of tickets during the run and make a higher profit.

As we look at it today, the play is rather wooden. The language, particularly of the white characters, is stiff and formal. The stereotype of white evil and black goodness was relieved in several curious ways: Little Eva's goodness seemed to live after her in the form of a holy magic expressed in locks of her hair. And the portrayal of the "good master," along with Uncle Tom's devotion to him, is meant to be taken seriously. The modern reaction against Uncle Tom hinges on the refusal to accept such "goodness" as possible for a master or proper for a slave. The preferred modern model is George Harris, who acted on the theory that if the whites could rise up against their English masters and take their freedom by force, so could the blacks rise against their white masters. George Harris does this and kills (there is pointed ambiguity on this) Tom Loker as Loker closes in on Harris and his wife and son. He is aided, however, by a Quaker abolitionist. The Harrises find freedom only in Canada, although Topsy becomes the adopted daughter of Ophelia, her former mistress, in Vermont. When given her chance for freedom, Topsy, who has been "converted" from her mischievous ways by Little Eva's lock of hair and memory, chooses to stay with Ophelia. Such circumstances promoted stereotypical attitudes among whites (the main audience for the play) that blacks, generations later, worked hard to change.

The play had over a quarter of a million performances during Harriet Beecher Stowe's lifetime. And because she did not protect the dramatization rights, she never received any royalties. There was a major revival of the play in 1924, and several important film versions—one with Lillian Gish—that communicated all the stereotypes anew. Little has ever been written on George Aiken, yet his play may be considered the first—and possibly the most important—piece of mass entertainment in the history of American drama.

Uncle Tom's Cabin, or Life among the Lowly

George L. Aiken

CHARACTERS

UNCLE TOM	SAMBO
GEORGE HARRIS	QUIMBO
GEORGE SHELBY	DOCTOR
ST. CLARE	WAITER
PHINEAS FLETCHER	HARRY, *a child*
GUMPTION CUTE	EVA
MR. WILSON	ELIZA
DEACON PERRY	CASSY
SHELBY	MARIE
HALEY	OPHELIA
LEGREE	CHLOE
TOM LOKER	TOPSY
MARKS	

ACT I

SCENE 1. *Plain chamber*

(*Enter* ELIZA, *meeting* GEORGE.)

ELIZA: Ah! George, is it you? Well, I am so glad you've come! (GEORGE *regards her mournfully*.) Why don't you smile, and ask after Harry?

GEORGE (*bitterly*): I wish he'd never been born! —I wish I'd never been born myself!

ELIZA (*sinking her head upon his breast and weeping*): Oh, George!

GEORGE: There, now, Eliza; it's too bad for me to make you feel so. Oh! how I wish you had never seen me—you might have been happy!

ELIZA: George! George! how can you talk so? What dreadful thing has happened, or is going to happen? I'm sure we've been very happy till lately.

GEORGE: So we have, dear. But oh! I wish I'd never seen you, nor you me.

ELIZA: Oh, George! how can you?

GEORGE: Yes, Eliza, it's all misery! misery!

The very life is burning out of me! I'm a poor, miserable, forlorn drudge! I shall only drag you down with me, that's all! What's the use of our trying to do anything—trying to know anything—trying to be anything? I wish I was dead!

ELIZA: Oh! now, dear George, that is really wicked. I know how you feel about losing your place in the factory, and you have a hard master; but pray be patient—

GEORGE: Patient! Haven't I been patient? Did I say a word when he came and took me away—for no earthly reason—from the place where everybody was kind to me? I'd paid him truly every cent of my earnings, and they all say I worked well.

ELIZA: Well, it *is* dreadful; but, after all, he is your master, you know.

GEORGE: My master! And who made him my master? That's what I think of! What right has he to me? I'm as much a man as he is! What right has he to make a dray-horse of me?—to take me from things I can do better than he can, and put me to work that any horse can do? He tries to do it; he says he'll bring me down and humble me, and he puts me to just the hardest, meanest and dirtiest work, on purpose.

ELIZA: Oh, George! George! you frighten me. Why, I never heard you talk so. I'm afraid you'll do something dreadful. I don't wonder at your feelings at all; but oh! do be careful—for my sake, for Harry's.

GEORGE: I have been careful, and I have been patient, but it's growing worse and worse—flesh and blood can't bear it any longer. Every chance he can get to insult and torment me he takes. He says that though I don't say anything, he sees that I've got the devil in me, and he means to bring it out; and one of these days it will come out, in a way that he won't like, or I'm mistaken.

ELIZA: Well, I always thought that I must obey my master and mistress, or I couldn't be a Christian.

GEORGE: There is some sense in it in your case. They have brought you up like a child—fed you, clothed you and taught you, so that you have a good education—that is some reason why they should claim you. But I have been kicked and cuffed and sworn at, and what do I owe? I've paid for all my keeping a hundred times over. I won't bear it!—no, I *won't!* Master will find out that I'm one whipping won't tame. My day will come yet, if he don't look out!

ELIZA: What are you going to do? Oh! George, don't do anything wicked; if you only trust in heaven and try to do right, it will deliver you.

GEORGE: Eliza, my heart's full of bitterness. I can't trust in heaven. Why does it let things be so?

ELIZA: Oh, George! we must all have faith. Mistress says that when all things go wrong to us, we must believe that heaven is doing the very best.

GEORGE: That's easy for people to say who are sitting on their sofas and riding in their carriages; but let them be where I am—I guess it would come some harder. I wish I could be good; but my heart burns and can't be reconciled. You couldn't, in my place, you can't now, if I tell you all I've got to say; you don't know the whole yet.

ELIZA: What do you mean?

GEORGE: Well, lately my master has been saying that he was a fool to let me marry off the place—that he hates Mr. Shelby and all his tribe—and he says he won't let me come here any more, and that I shall take a wife and settle down on his place.

ELIZA: But you were married to *me* by the minister, as much as if you had been a white man.

GEORGE: Don't you know I can't hold you for my wife if he chooses to part us? That is why I wish I'd never seen you—it would have been better for us both—it would have been better for our poor child if he had never been born.

ELIZA: Oh! but my master is so kind.

GEORGE: Yes, but who knows?—he may die, and then Harry may be sold to nobody knows who. What pleasure is it that he is handsome and smart and bright? I tell you, Eliza, that a sword will pierce through your soul for every good and pleasant thing your child is or has. It will make him worth too much for you to keep.

ELIZA: Heaven forbid!

GEORGE: So, Eliza, my girl, bear up now, and good-by, for I'm going.

ELIZA: Going, George! Going where?

GEORGE: To Canada; and when I'm there I'll buy you—that's all the hope that's left us. You have a kind master, that won't refuse to sell you. I'll buy you and the boy—heaven helping me, I will!

ELIZA: Oh, dreadful! If you should be taken?

GEORGE: I won't be taken, Eliza—I'll *die* first! I'll be free, or I'll die!

ELIZA: You will not kill yourself?

GEORGE: No need of that; they will kill me, fast enough. I will never go down the river alive.

ELIZA: Oh, George! for my sake, do be careful.

Don't lay hands on yourself, or anybody else. You are tempted too much, but don't. Go, if you must, but go carefully, prudently, and pray heaven to help you!

GEORGE: Well, then, Eliza, hear my plan. I'm going home quite resigned, you understand, as if all was over. I've got some preparations made, and there are those that will help me; and in the course of a few days I shall be among the missing. Well, now, good-by.

ELIZA: A moment—our boy.

GEORGE (*choked with emotion*): True, I had forgotten him; one last look, and then farewell!

ELIZA: And heaven grant it be not forever! (*Exeunt.*)

SCENE 2. (*A dining-room. Table and chairs. Dessert, wine, &c., on table.* SHELBY *and* HALEY *discovered at table.*)

SHELBY: That is the way I should arrange the matter.

HALEY: I can't make trade that way—I positively can't, Mr. Shelby. (*Drinks.*)

SHELBY: Why, the fact is, Haley, Tom is an uncommon fellow! He is certainly worth that sum anywhere—steady, honest, capable, manages my whole farm like a clock!

HALEY: You mean honest, as niggers go. (*Fills glass.*)

SHELBY: No; I mean, really, Tom is a good, steady, sensible, pious fellow. He got religion at a camp-meeting, four years ago, and I believe he really *did* get it. I've trusted him since then, with everything I have—money, house, horses, and let him come and go round the country, and I always found him true and square in everything!

HALEY: Some folks don't believe there is pious niggers, Shelby, but I *do*. I had a fellow, now, in this yer last lot I took to Orleans—'twas as good as a meetin' now, really, to hear that critter pray; and he was quite gentle and quiet like. He fetched me a good sum, too, for I bought him cheap of a man that was 'bliged to sell out, so I realized six hundred on him. Yes, I consider religion a valeyable thing in a nigger, when it's the genuine article and no mistake.

SHELBY: Well, Tom's got the real article, if ever a fellow had. Why, last fall I let him go to Cincinnati alone, to do business for me and bring home five hundred dollars. "Tom," says I to him, "I trust you, because I think you are a Christian —I know you wouldn't cheat." Tom comes back sure enough; I knew he would. Some low fellows,

they say, said to him—"Tom, why don't you make tracks for Canada?" "Ah, master trusted me, and I couldn't," was his answer. They told me all about it. I am sorry to part with Tom, I must say. You ought to let him cover the whole balance of the debt, and you would, Haley, if you had any conscience.

HALEY: Well, I've got just as much conscience as any man in business can afford to keep, just a little, you know, to swear by, as 'twere; and then I'm ready to do anything in reason to 'blige friends, but this yer, you see, is a leetle too hard on a fellow—a leetle too hard! (*Fills glass again.*)

SHELBY: Well, then, Haley, how will you trade?

HALEY: Well, haven't you a boy or a girl that you could throw in with Tom?

SHELBY: Hum! none that I could well spare; to tell the truth, it's only hard necessity makes me willing to sell at all. I don't like parting with any of my hands, that's a fact.

(HARRY *runs in.*)

Hulloa! Jim Crow! (*Throws a bunch of raisins towards him.*) Pick that up now. (HARRY *does so.*)

HALEY: Bravo, little 'un! (*Throws an orange, which* HARRY *catches. He sings and dances around the stage.*) Hurrah! Bravo! What a young 'un! That chap's a case, I'll promise. Tell you what, Shelby, fling in that chap, and I'll settle the business. Come, now, if that ain't doing the thing up about the rightest!

(ELIZA *enters. Starts on beholding* HALEY, *and gazes fearfully at* HARRY, *who runs and clings to her dress, showing the orange, &c.*)

SHELBY: Well, Eliza?

ELIZA: I was looking for Harry, please, sir.

SHELBY: Well, take him away, then.

(ELIZA *grasps the child eagerly in her arms, and casting another glance of apprehension at* HALEY, *exits hastily.*)

HALEY: By Jupiter! there's an article, now. You might make your fortune on that ar gal in Orleans any day. I've seen over a thousand in my day, paid down for gals not a bit handsomer.

SHELBY: I don't want to make my fortune on her. Another glass of wine. (*Fills the glasses.*)

HALEY (*drinks and smacks his lips*): Capital wine —first chop! Come, how will you trade about the gal? What shall I say for her? What'll you take?

SHELBY: Mr. Haley, she is not to be sold. My

wife wouldn't part with her for her weight in gold.

HALEY: Ay, ay! women always say such things, 'cause they hain't no sort of calculation. Just show 'em how many watches, feathers and trinkets one's weight in gold would buy, and that alters the case, I reckon.

SHELBY: I tell you, Haley, this must not be spoken of—I say no, and I mean no.

HALEY: Well, you'll let me have the boy tho'; you must own that I have come down pretty handsomely for him.

SHELBY: What on earth can you want with the child?

HALEY: Why, I've got a friend that's going into this yer branch of the business—wants to buy up handsome boys to raise for the market. Well, what do you say?

SHELBY: I'll think the matter over and talk with my wife.

HALEY: Oh, certainly, by all means; but I'm in a devil of a hurry, and shall want to know as soon as possible, what I may depend on. (*Rises and puts on his overcoat, which hangs on a chair. Takes hat and whip.*)

SHELBY: Well, call up this evening, between six and seven, and you shall have my answer.

HALEY: All right. Take care of yourself, old boy! (*Exit.*)

SHELBY: If anybody had ever told me that I should sell Tom to those rascally traders, I should never have believed it. Now it must come for aught I see, and Eliza's child too. So much for being in debt, heigho! The fellow sees his advantage and means to push it. (*Exit.*)

SCENE 3. (*Snowy landscape.* UNCLE TOM's *Cabin. Snow on roof. Practicable door and window. Dark Stage. Music. Enter* ELIZA *hastily, with* HARRY *in her arms.*)

ELIZA: My poor boy; they have sold you, but your mother will save you yet!

(*Goes to Cabin and taps on window.* AUNT CHLOE *appears at window with a large white night-cap on.*)

CHLOE: Good Lord! what's that? My sakes alive if it ain't Lizy! Get on your clothes, old man, quick! I'm gwine to open the door.

(*The door opens and* CHLOE *enters, followed by* UN-CLE TOM, *in his shirt sleeves, holding a tallow candle.*)

TOM (*holding the light towards* ELIZA): Lord bless you! I'm skeered to look at ye, Lizy! Are ye tuck sick, or what's come over ye?

ELIZA: I'm running away, Uncle Tom and Aunt Chloe, carrying off my child! Master sold him!

TOM and CHLOE: Sold him!

ELIZA: Yes, sold him! I crept into the closet by mistress' door to-night, and heard master tell mistress that he had sold my Harry, and you, Uncle Tom, both, to a trader, and that the man was to take possession to-morrow.

CHLOE: The good Lord have pity on us! Oh! it don't seem as if it was true. What has he done that master should sell *him?*

ELIZA: He hasn't done anything—it isn't for that. Master don't want to sell, and mistress—she's always good. I heard her plead and beg for us, but he told her 'twas no use—that he was in this man's debt, and he had got the power over him, and that if he did not pay him off clear, it would end in his having to sell the place and all the people and move off.

CHLOE: Well, old man, why don't you run away, too? Will you wait to be toted down the river, where they kill niggers with hard work and starving? I'd a heap rather die than go there, any day! There's time for ye; be off with Lizy—you've got a pass to come and go any time. Come, bustle up, and I'll get your things together.

TOM: No, no—I ain't going. Let Eliza go— it's her right. I wouldn't be the one to say no —'tain't in natur for her to stay; but you heard what she said? If I must be sold, or all the people on the place, and everything go to rack, why, let me be sold. I s'pose I can bar it as well as any one. Mas'r always found me on the spot—he always will. I never have broken trust, nor used my pass no ways contrary to my word, and I never will. It's better for me to go alone, than to break up the place and sell all. Mas'r ain't to blame, and he'll take care of you and the poor little 'uns! (*Overcome.*)

CHLOE: Now, old man, what is you gwine to cry for? Does you want to break this old woman's heart? (*Crying.*)

ELIZA: I saw my husband only this afternoon, and I little knew then what was to come. He told me he was going to run away. Do try, if you can, to get word to him. Tell him how I went and why I went, and tell him I'm going to try and find Canada. You must give my love to him, and tell him if I never see him again on earth, I trust we shall meet in heaven!

TOM: Dat is right, Lizy, trust in the Lord— He is our best friend—our only comforter.

ELIZA: You won't go with me, Uncle Tom?

TOM: No; time was when I would, but the

Lord's given me a work among these yer poor souls, and I'll stay with 'em and bear my cross with 'em till the end. It's different with you—it's more'n you could stand, and you'd better go if you can.

ELIZA: Uncle Tom, I'll try it!

. TOM: Amen! The Lord help ye! (*Exit* ELIZA *and* HARRY.)

CHLOE: What is you gwine to do, old man? What's to become of you?

TOM (*solemnly*): Him that saved Daniel in the den of lions—that saved the children in the fiery furnace—Him that walked on the sea and bade the winds be still—He's alive yet! and I've faith to believe He can deliver me!

CHLOE: You is right, old man.

TOM: The Lord is good unto all that trust Him, Chloe. (*Exeunt into Cabin.*)

SCENE 4. (*Room in Tavern by the river side. A large window, through which the river is seen, filled with floating ice. Moonlight. Table and chairs brought on. Enter* PHINEAS.)

PHINEAS: Chaw me up into tobaccy ends! how in the name of all that's onpossible am I to get across that yer pesky river? It's a reg'lar blockade of ice! I promised Ruth to meet her to-night, and she'll be into my har if I don't come. (*Goes to window.*) Thar's a conglomerated prospect for a loveyer! What in creation's to be done? That thar river looks like a permiscuous ice-cream shop come to an awful state of friz. If I war on the adjacent bank, I wouldn't care a teetotal atom. Rile up, you old varmint, and shake the ice off your back!

(*Enter* ELIZA *and* HARRY.)

ELIZA: Courage, my boy—we have reached the river. Let it but roll between us and our pursuers, and we are safe! (*Goes to window.*) Gracious powers! the river is choked with cakes of ice!

PHINEAS: Holloa, gal!—what's the matter? You look kind of streaked.

ELIZA: Is there any ferry or boat that takes people over now?

PHINEAS: Well, I guess not; the boats have stopped running.

ELIZA (*in dismay*): Stopped running?

PHINEAS: Maybe you're wanting to get over—anybody sick? Ye seem mighty anxious.

ELIZA: I—I—I've got a child that's very dangerous. I never heard of it till last night, and I've walked quite a distance to-day, in hopes to get to the ferry.

PHINEAS: Well, now, that's onlucky; I'm re'lly consarned for ye. Thar's a man, a piece down here, that's going over with some truck this evening, if he duss to; he'll be in here to supper to-night, so you'd better set down and wait. That's a smart little chap. Say, young 'un, have a chaw tobaccy? (*Takes out a large plug and a bowie-knife.*)

ELIZA: No, no! not any for him.

PHINEAS: Oh! he don't use it, eh? Hain't come to it yet? Well, I have. (*Cuts off a large piece, and returns the plug and knife to pocket.*) What's the matter with the young 'un? He looks kind of white in the gills!

ELIZA: Poor fellow! he is not used to walking, and I've hurried him on so.

PHINEAS: Tuckered, eh? Well, there's a little room there, with a fire in it. Take the babby in there, make yourself comfortable till that thar ferryman shows his countenance—I'll stand the damage.

ELIZA: How shall I thank you for such kindness to a stranger?

PHINEAS: Well, if you don't know how, why, don't try; that's the teetotal. Come, vamoose! (*Exit* ELIZA *and* HARRY.) Chaw me into sassage meat, if that ain't a perpendicular fine gal! she's a reg'lar A No. 1, sort of female! How'n thunder am I to get across this refrigerated stream of water? I can't wait for that ferryman. (*Enter* MARKS.) Halloa! what sort of a critter's this? (*Advances.*) Say, stranger, will you have something to drink?

MARKS: You are excessively kind: I don't care if I do.

PHINEAS: Ah! he's a human. Halloa, thar! bring us a jug of whisky instantaneously, or expect to be teetotally chawed up! Squat yourself, stranger, and go in for enjoyment. (*They sit at table.*) Who are you, and what's your name?

MARKS: I am a lawyer, and my name is Marks.

PHINEAS: A land shark, eh? Well, I don't think no worse on you for that. The law is a kind of necessary evil; and it breeds lawyers just as an old stump does fungus. Ah! here's the whisky.

(*Enter* WAITER, *with jug and tumblers. Places them on table.*)

Here, you—take that shin-plaster. (*Gives bill.*) I don't want any change—thar's a gal stopping in that room—the balance will pay for her—d'ye hear?—vamoose! (*Exit* WAITER.—*Fills glass.*) Take hold, neighbour Marks—don't shirk the critter. Here's hoping your path of true love may never have an ice-choked river to cross! (*They drink.*)

MARKS: Want to cross the river, eh?

PHINEAS: Well, I do, stranger. Fact is, I'm in love with the teetotalist pretty girl, over on the Ohio side, that ever wore a Quaker bonnet. Take another swig, neighbour. (*Fills glasses, and they drink.*)

MARKS: A Quaker, eh?

PHINEAS: Yes—kind of strange, ain't it? The way of it was this:—I used to own a grist of niggers—had 'em to work on my plantation, just below here. Well, stranger, do you know I fell in with that gal—of course I was considerably smashed—knocked into a pretty conglomerated heap—and I told her so. She said she wouldn't hear a word from me so long as I owned a nigger!

MARKS: You sold them, I suppose?

PHINEAS: You're teetotally wrong, neighbour. I gave them all their freedom, and told 'em to vamoose!

MARKS: Ah! yes—very noble, I dare say, but rather expensive. This act won you your lady-love, eh?

PHINEAS: You're off the track again, neighbour. She felt kind of pleased about it, and smiled, and all that; but she said she could never be mine unless I turned Quaker! Thunder and earth! what do you think of that? You're a lawyer—come, now, what's your opinion? Don't you call it a knotty point?

MARKS: Most decidedly. Of course you refused.

PHINEAS: Teetotally; but she told me to think better of it, and come to-night and give her my final conclusion. Chaw me into mincemeat, if I haven't made up my mind to do it!

MARKS: You astonish me!

PHINEAS: Well, you see, I can't get along without that gal;—she's sort of fixed my flint, and I'm sure to hang fire without her. I know I shall make a queer sort of Quaker, because you see, neighbour, I ain't precisely the kind of material to make a Quaker out of.

MARKS: No, not exactly.

PHINEAS: Well, I can't stop no longer. I must try to get across that candaverous river some way. It's getting late—take care of yourself, neighbour lawyer. I'm a teetotal victim to a pair of black eyes. Chaw me up to feed hogs if I'm not in a ruinatious state! (*Exit.*)

MARKS: Queer genius, that, very!

(*Enter* TOM LOKER.)

So you've come at last.

LOKER: Yes. (*Looks into jug.*) Empty! Waiter! more whisky!

(WAITER *enters with jug, and removes the empty one. Enter* HALEY.)

HALEY: By the land! if this yer ain't the nearest, now, to what I've heard people call Providence! Why, Loker, how are ye?

LOKER: The devil! What brought you here, Haley?

HALEY (*sitting at table*): I say, Tom, this yer's the luckiest thing in the world. I'm in a devil of a hobble, and you must help me out!

LOKER: Ugh! aw! like enough. A body may be pretty sure of that when you're glad to see 'em, or can make something off of 'em. What's the blow now?

HALEY: You've got a friend here—partner, perhaps?

LOKER: Yes, I have. Here, Marks—here's that ar fellow that I was with in Natchez.

MARKS (*grasping* HALEY's *hand*): Shall be pleased with his acquaintance. Mr. Haley, I believe?

HALEY: The same, sir. The fact is, gentlemen, this morning I bought a young 'un of Shelby up above here. His mother got wind of it, and what does she do but cut her lucky with him; and I'm afraid by this time that she has crossed the river, for I tracked her to this very place.

MARKS: So, then, ye're fairly sewed up, ain't ye? He! he! he! It's neatly done, too.

HALEY: This young 'un business makes lots of trouble in the trade.

MARKS: Now, Mr. Haley, what is it? Do you want us to undertake to catch this gal?

HALEY: The gal's no matter of mine—she's Shelby's—it's only the boy. I was a fool for buying the monkey.

LOKER: You're generally a fool!

MARKS: Come now, Loker, none of your huffs; you see, Mr. Haley's a-puttin' us in a way of a good job, I reckon; just hold still—these yer arrangements are my forte. This yer gal, Mr. Haley—how is she?—what is she? (ELIZA *appears, with* HARRY, *listening.*)

HALEY: Well, white and handsome—well brought up. I'd have given Shelby eight hundred or a thousand, and then made well on her.

MARKS: White and handsome—well brought up! Look here, now, Loker, a beautiful opening. We'll do a business here on our own account. We does the catchin'; the boy, of course, goes to Mr. Haley—we takes the gal to Orleans to speculate on. Ain't it beautiful? (*They confer together.*)

ELIZA: Powers of mercy, protect me! How shall I escape these human bloodhounds? Ah! the window—the river of ice! That dark stream lies between me and liberty! Surely the ice will bear my trifling weight. It is my only chance of escape—better sink beneath the cold waters, with my child locked in my arms, than have him torn from me and sold into bondage. He sleeps upon my breast—Heaven, I put my trust in thee! (*Gets out of window.*)

MARKS: Well, Tom Loker, what do you say?

LOKER: It'll do!

(*Strikes his hand violently on the table.* ELIZA *screams. They all start to their feet.* ELIZA *disappears.*)

HALEY: By the land, there she is now! (*They all rush to the window.*)

MARKS: She's making for the river!

LOKER: Let's after her! (*They all leap through the window. Change.*)

SCENE 5. *Snowy landscape*

(*Enter* ELIZA, *with* HARRY, *hurriedly.*)

ELIZA: They press upon my footsteps—the river is my only hope! Heaven grant me strength to reach it, ere they overtake me! Courage, my child!—we will be free—or perish! (*Rushes off.*)

(*Enter* LOKER, HALEY *and* MARKS.)

HALEY: We'll catch her yet; the river will stop her!

MARKS: No, it won't, for look! she has jumped upon the ice! She's a brave gal, anyhow!

LOKER: She'll be drowned!

HALEY: Curse that young 'un! I shall lose him, after all.

LOKER: Come on, Marks, to the ferry!

HALEY: Aye, to the ferry!—a hundred dollars for a boat! (*They rush off.*)

SCENE 6. (*The entire depth of stage, representing the Ohio River filled with Floating Ice. Bank on right hand.* ELIZA *appears, with* HARRY, *on a cake of ice, and floats slowly across.* HALEY, LOKER *and* MARKS, *on bank, right hand, observing.* PHINEAS *on opposite shore.*)

ACT II

SCENE 1. *A handsome parlour*

(MARIE *discovered reclining on a sofa.*)

MARIE (*looking at a note*): What can possibly detain St. Clare? According to this note, he should have been here a fortnight ago. (*Noise of carriage without.*) I do believe he has come at last.

(EVA *runs in.*)

EVA: Mamma! (*Throws her arms around* MARIE's *neck, and kisses her.*)

MARIE: That will do—take care, child—don't you make my head ache! (*Kisses her languidly.*)

(*Enter* ST. CLARE, OPHELIA, *and* TOM, *nicely dressed.*)

ST. CLARE: Well, my dear Marie, here we are at last. The wanderers have arrived, you see. Allow me to present my cousin, Miss Ophelia, who is about to undertake the office of our housekeeper.

MARIE (*rising to a sitting posture*): I am delighted to see you. How do you like the appearance of our city?

EVA (*running to* OPHELIA): Oh! is it not beautiful? My own darling home!—is it not beautiful?

OPHELIA: Yes, it is a pretty place, though it looks rather old and heathenish to me.

ST. CLARE: Tom, my boy, this seems to suit you?

TOM: Yes, mas'r, it looks about the right thing.

ST. CLARE: See here, Marie, I've brought you a coachman, at last, to order. I tell you, he's a regular hearse for blackness and sobriety, and will drive you like a funeral, if you wish. Open your eyes, now, and look at him. Now, don't say I never think about you when I'm gone.

MARIE: I know he'll get drunk.

ST. CLARE: Oh! no he won't. He's warranted a pious and sober article.

MARIE: Well, I hope he may turn out well; it's more than I expect, though.

ST. CLARE: Have you no curiosity to learn how and where I picked up Tom?

EVA: *Uncle* Tom, papa; that's his name.

ST. CLARE: Right, my little sunbeam!

TOM: Please, mas'r, that ain't no 'casion to say nothing 'bout me.

ST. CLARE: You are too modest, my modern Hannibal. Do you know, Marie, that our little Eva took a fancy to Uncle Tom—whom we met on board the steamboat—and persuaded me to buy him?

MARIE: Ah! she is so odd!

ST. CLARE: As we approached the landing, a sudden rush of the passengers precipitated Eva into the water—

MARIE: Gracious heavens!

ST. CLARE: A man leaped into the river, and, as she rose to the surface of the water, grasped her in his arms, and held her up until she could be drawn on the boat again. Who was that man, Eva?

EVA: Uncle Tom!

(*Runs to him.—He lifts her in his arms. She kisses him.*)

TOM: The dear soul!

OPHELIA (*astonished*): How shiftless!

ST. CLARE (*overhearing her*): What's the matter now, pray?

OPHELIA: Well, I want to be kind to everybody, and I wouldn't have anything hurt, but as to kissing—

ST. CLARE: Niggers! that you're not up to, hey?

OPHELIA: Yes, that's it—how can she?

ST. CLARE: Oh! bless you, it's nothing when you are used to it!

OPHELIA: I could never be so shiftless!

EVA: Come with me, Uncle Tom, and I will show you about the house. (*Crosses with Tom.*)

TOM: Can I go, mas'r?

ST. CLARE: Yes, Tom; she is your little mistress—your only duty will be to attend to her! (TOM *bows and exits.*)

MARIE: Eva, my dear!

EVA: Well, mamma?

MARIE: Do not exert yourself too much!

EVA: No, mamma! (*Runs out.*)

OPHELIA (*lifting up her hands*): How shiftless!

(ST. CLARE *sits next to* MARIE *on sofa.* OPHELIA *next to* ST. CLARE.)

ST. CLARE: Well, what do you think of Uncle Tom, Marie?

MARIE: He is a perfect behemoth!

ST. CLARE: Come, now, Marie, be gracious, and say something pretty to a fellow!

MARIE: You've been gone a fortnight beyond the time!

ST. CLARE: Well, you know I wrote you the reason.

MARIE: Such a short, cold letter!

ST. CLARE: Dear me! the mail was just going, and it had to be that or nothing.

MARIE: That's just the way; always something to make your journeys long and letters short!

ST. CLARE: Look at this. (*Takes an elegant velvet case from his pocket.*) Here's a present I got for you in New York—a daguerreotype of Eva and myself.

MARIE (*looks at it with a dissatisfied air*): What made you sit in such an awkward position?

ST. CLARE: Well, the position may be a matter of opinion, but what do you think of the likeness?

MARIE (*closing the case snappishly*): If you don't think anything of my opinion in one case, I suppose you wouldn't in another.

OPHELIA (*sententiously, aside*): How shiftless!

ST. CLARE: Hang the woman! Come, Marie, what do you think of the likeness? Don't be nonsensical now.

MARIE: It's very inconsiderate of you, St. Clare, to insist on my talking and looking at things. You know I've been lying all day with the sick headache, and there's been such a tumult made ever since you came, I'm half dead!

OPHELIA: You're subject to the sick headache, ma'am?

MARIE: Yes, I'm perfect martyr to it!

OPHELIA: Juniper-berry tea is good for sick headache; at least, Molly, Deacon Abraham Perry's wife, used to say so; and she was a great nurse.

ST. CLARE: I'll have the first juniper-berries that get ripe in our garden by the lake brought in for that especial purpose. Come, cousin, let us take a stroll in the garden. Will you join us, Marie?

MARIE: I wonder how you can ask such a question, when you know how fragile I am. I shall retire to my chamber, and repose till dinner time. (*Exit.*)

OPHELIA (*looking after her*): How shiftless!

ST. CLARE: Come, cousin! (*As he goes out.*) Look out for the babies! If I step upon anybody, let them mention it.

OPHELIA: Babies under foot! How shiftless! (*Exeunt.*)

SCENE 2. *A garden*

(TOM *discovered, seated on a bank, with* EVA *on his knee—his button-holes are filled with flowers, and* EVA *is hanging a wreath around his neck. Enter* ST. CLARE *and* OPHELIA, *observing.*)

EVA: Oh, Tom; you look so funny.

TOM (*sees* ST. CLARE, *and puts* EVA *down*): I begs pardon, mas'r, but the young missis would do it. Look yer, I'm like the ox, mentioned in the Good Book, dressed for the sacrifice.

ST. CLARE: I say, what do you think, Pussy? Which do you like the best—to live as they do at your uncle's, up in Vermont, or to have a house full of servants, as we do?

EVA: Oh! of course our way is the pleasantest.

ST. CLARE (*patting her head*): Why so?

EVA: Because it makes so many more round you to love, you know.

OPHELIA: Now, that's just like Eva—just one of her odd speeches.

EVA: Is it an odd speech, papa?

ST. CLARE: Rather, as this world goes, Pussy. But where has my little Eva been?

EVA: Oh! I've been up in Tom's room, hearing him sing.

ST. CLARE: Hearing Tom sing, hey?

EVA: Oh, yes! he sings such beautiful things about the new Jerusalem, and bright angels, and the land of Canaan.

ST. CLARE: I dare say; it's better than the opera, isn't it?

EVA: Yes; and he's going to teach them to me.

ST. CLARE: Singing lessons, hey? You are coming on.

EVA: Yes, he sings for me, and I read to him in my Bible, and he explains what it means. Come, Tom. (*She takes his hand and they exit.*)

ST. CLARE (*aside*): Oh, Evangeline! Rightly named; hath not heaven made thee an evangel to me?

OPHELIA: How shiftless! How can you let her?

ST. CLARE: Why not?

OPHELIA: Why, I don't know; it seems so dreadful.

ST. CLARE: You would think no harm in a child's caressing a large dog, even if he was black; but a creature that can think, reason and feel, and is immortal, you shudder at. Confess it, cousin. I know the feeling among some of you Northerners well enough. Not that there is a particle of virtue in our not having it, but custom with us does what Christianity ought to do: obliterates the feeling of personal prejudice. You loathe them as you would a snake or a toad, yet you are indignant at their wrongs. You would not have them abused, but you don't want to have anything to do with them yourselves. Isn't that it?

OPHELIA: Well, cousin, there may be some truth in this.

ST. CLARE: What would the poor and lowly do without children? Your little child is your only true democrat. Tom, now, is a hero to Eva; his stories are wonders in her eyes; his songs and Methodist hymns are better than an opera, and the traps and little bits of trash in his pockets a mine of jewels, and he the most wonderful Tom that ever wore a black skin. This is one of the roses of Eden that the Lord has dropped down expressly for the poor and lowly, who get few enough of any other kind.

OPHELIA: It's strange, cousin; one might almost think you was a *professor,* to hear you talk.

ST. CLARE: A professor?

OPHELIA: Yes, a professor of religion.

ST. CLARE: Not at all; not a professor as you town folks have it, and, what is worse, I'm afraid, not a *practicer,* either.

OPHELIA: What makes you talk so, then?

ST. CLARE: Nothing is easier than talking. My forte lies in talking, and yours, cousin, lies in doing. And speaking of that puts me in mind that I have made a purchase for your department. There's the article now. Here, Topsy! (*Whistles.*)

(TOPSY *runs on.*)

OPHELIA: Good gracious! what a heathenish, shiftless looking object! St. Clare, what in the world have you brought that thing here for?

ST. CLARE: For you to educate, to be sure, and train in the way she should go. I thought she was rather a funny specimen in the Jim Crow line. Here, Topsy, give us a song, and show us some of your dancing.

(TOPSY *sings a verse and dances a breakdown.*)

OPHELIA (*paralyzed*): Well, of all things! If I ever saw the like!

ST. CLARE (*smothering a laugh*): Topsy, this is your new mistress—I'm going to give you up to her. See now that you behave yourself.

TOPSY: Yes, mas'r.

ST. CLARE: You're going to be good, Topsy, you understand?

TOPSY: Oh, yes, mas'r.

OPHELIA: Now, St. Clare, what upon earth is this for? Your house is so full of these plagues now, that a body can't set down their foot without treading on 'em. I get up in the morning and find one asleep behind the door, and see one black head poking out from under the table—one lying on the door mat, and they are moping and mowing and grinning between all the railings, and tumbling over the kitchen floor! What on earth did you want to bring this one for?

ST. CLARE: For you to educate—didn't I tell you? You're always preaching about educating; I thought I would make you a present of a fresh caught specimen, and let you try your hand on her and bring her up in the way she should go.

OPHELIA: I don't want her, I am sure; I have more to do with 'em now than I want to.

ST. CLARE: That's you Christians, all over. You'll get up a society, and get some poor missionary to spend all his days among just such heathens; but let me see one of you that would take one into your house with you, and take the labour of their conversion upon yourselves.

OPHELIA: Well, I didn't think of it in that light. It might be a real missionary work. Well, I'll do what I can. (*Advances to* TOPSY.) She's dreadful dirty and shiftless! How old are you, Topsy?

TOPSY: Dunno, missis.

OPHELIA: How shiftless! Don't know how old you are? Didn't anybody ever tell you? Who was your mother?

TOPSY (*grinning*): Never had none.

OPHELIA: Never had any mother? What do you mean? Where was you born?

TOPSY: Never was born.

OPHELIA: You mustn't answer me in that way. I'm not playing with you. Tell me where you was born, and who your father and mother were?

TOPSY: Never was born, tell you; never had no father, nor mother, nor nothin'. I war raised by a speculator, with lots of others. Old Aunt Sue used to take care on us.

ST. CLARE: She speaks the truth, cousin. Speculators buy them up cheap, when they are little, and get them raised for the market.

OPHELIA: How long have you lived with your master and mistress?

TOPSY: Dunno, missis.

OPHELIA: How shiftless! Is it a year, or more, or less?

TOPSY: Dunno, missis.

ST. CLARE: She does not know what a year is; she don't even know her own age.

OPHELIA: Have you ever heard anything about heaven, Topsy? (TOPSY *looks bewildered and grins.*) Do you know who made you?

TOPSY: Nobody, as I knows on, he, he, he! I 'spect I growed. Don't think nobody never made me.

OPHELIA: The shiftless heathen! What can you do? What did you do for your master and mistress?

TOPSY: Fetch water—and wash dishes—and rub knives—and wait on folks—and dance breakdowns.

OPHELIA: I shall break down, I'm afraid, in trying to make anything of you, you shiftless mortal!

ST. CLARE: You find virgin soil there, cousin; put in your own ideas—you won't find many to pull up. (*Exit laughing.*)

OPHELIA (*Takes out her handkerchief. A pair of gloves falls.* TOPSY *picks them up slyly and puts them in her sleeve*): Follow me, you benighted innocent!

TOPSY: Yes, missis.

(*As* OPHELIA *turns her back to her, she seizes the end of the ribbon she wears arouund her waist, and twitches it off.*—OPHELIA *turns and sees her as she is putting it in her other sleeve.*—OPHELIA *takes ribbon from her.*)

OPHELIA: What's this? You naughty, wicked girl, you've been stealing this?

TOPSY: Laws! why, that ar's missis' ribbon, ain't it? How could it got caught in my sleeve?

OPHELIA: Topsy, you naughty girl, don't you tell me a lie—you stole that ribbon!

TOPSY: Missis, I declare for't, I didn't—never seed it till dis yer blessed minnit.

OPHELIA: Topsy, don't you know it's wicked to tell lies?

TOPSY: I never tells no lies, missis; it's just de truth I've been telling now, and nothing else.

OPHELIA: Topsy, I shall have to whip you, if you tell lies so.

TOPSY: Laws, missis, if you's to whip all day, couldn't say no other way. I never seed dat ar—it must a got caught in my sleeve. (*Blubbers.*)

OPHELIA (*seizes her by the shoulders*): Don't you tell me that again, you barefaced fibber! (*Shakes her. The gloves fall on stage.*) There you, my gloves too—you outrageous young heathen! (*Picks them up.*) Will you tell me, now, you didn't steal the ribbon?

TOPSY: No missis; stole de gloves, but didn't steal de ribbon. It was permiskus.

OPHELIA: Why, you young reprobate!

TOPSY: Yes—I's knows I's wicked!

OPHELIA: Then you know you ought to be punished. (*Boxes her ears.*) What do you think of that?

TOPSY: He, he, he! De Lord, missus; dat wouldn't kill a 'skeeter! (*Runs off laughing.* OPHELIA *follows indignantly.*)

SCENE 3. (*The Tavern by the River. Table and chairs. Jug and glasses on table. On flat is a printed placard, headed:* "Four Hundred Dollars Reward —Runaway—GEORGE HARRIS!" PHINEAS *is discovered, seated at table.*)

PHINEAS: So yer I am; and a pretty business I've undertook to do. Find the husband of the gal that crossed the river on the ice two or three days ago. Ruth said I must do it, and I'll be teetotally chawed up if I don't do it. I see they've offered a reward for him, dead or alive. How in creation am I to find the varmint? He isn't likely to go round looking natural, with a full description of his hide and figure staring him in the face.

(*Enter* MR. WILSON.)

I say, stranger, how are ye? (*Rises and comes forward.*)

WILSON: Well, I reckon.

PHINEAS: Any news? (*Takes out plug and knife.*)

WILSON: Not that I know of.

PHINEAS (*cutting a piece of tobacco and offering it*): Chaw?

WILSON: No, thank ye—it don't agree with me.

PHINEAS: Don't, eh? (*Putting it in his own mouth.*) I never felt any the worse for it.

WILSON (*sees placard*): What's that?

PHINEAS: Nigger advertised. (*Advances towards it and spits on it.*) There's my mind upon that.

WILSON: Why, now stranger, what's that for?

PHINEAS: I'd do it all the same to the writer of that ar paper, if he was here. Any man that owns a boy like that, and can't find any better way of treating him than branding him on the hand with the letter H, as that paper states, *deserves* to lose him. Such papers as this ar' a shame to old Kaintuck! that's my mind right out, if anybody wants to know.

WILSON: Well, now, that's a fact.

PHINEAS: I used to have a gang of boys, sir —that was before I fell in love—and I just told 'em:—"Boys," says I, "run now! Dig! put! jest when you want to. I never shall come to look after you!" That's the way I kept mine. Let 'em know they are free to run any time, and it jest stops their wanting to. It stands to reason it should. Treat 'em like men, and you'll have men's work.

WILSON: I think you are altogether right, friend, and this man described here is a fine fellow —no mistake about that. He worked for me some half dozen years in my bagging factory, and he was my best hand, sir. He is an ingenious fellow, too; he invented a machine for the cleaning of hemp— a really valuable affair; it's gone into use in several factories. His master holds the patent of it.

PHINEAS: I'll warrant ye; holds it, and makes money out of it, and then turns round and brands the boy in his right hand! If I had a fair chance, I'd mark him, I reckon, so that he'd carry it *one* while!

(*Enter* GEORGE HARRIS, *disguised.*)

GEORGE (*speaking as he enters*): Jim, see to the trunks. (*Sees* WILSON.) Ah! Mr. Wilson here?

WILSON: Bless my soul, can it be?

GEORGE (*advances and grasps his hand*): Mr. Wilson, I see you remember me, Mr. Butler, of Oaklands, Shelby county.

WILSON: Ye—yes—yes—sir.

PHINEAS: Halloa! there's a screw loose here somewhere. That old gentleman seems to be struck into a pretty considerable heap of astonishment. May I be teetotally chawed up! if I don't believe that's the identical man I'm arter. (*Crosses to* GEORGE.) How are ye, George Harris?

GEORGE (*starting back and thrusting his hands into his breast*): You know me?

PHINEAS: Ha, ha, ha! I rather conclude I do; but don't get riled, I ain't a bloodhound in disguise.

GEORGE: How did you discover me?

PHINEAS: By a teetotal smart guess. You're the very man I want to see. Do you know I was sent after you?

GEORGE: Ah! by my master?

PHINEAS: No; by your wife.

GEORGE: My wife! Where is she?

PHINEAS: She's stopping with a Quaker family over on the Ohio side.

GEORGE: Then she is safe?

PHINEAS: Teetotally!

GEORGE: Conduct me to her.

PHINEAS: Just wait a brace of shakes and I'll do it. I've got to go and get the boat ready. 'Twon't take me but a minute—make yourself comfortable till I get back. Chaw me up! but this is what I call doing things in short order. (*Exit.*)

WILSON: George!

GEORGE: Yes, George!

WILSON: I couldn't have thought it!

GEORGE: I am pretty well disguised, I fancy; you see I don't answer to the advertisement at all.

WILSON: George, this is a dangerous game you are playing; I could not have advised you to it.

GEORGE: I can do it on my own responsibility.

WILSON: Well, George, I suppose you're running away—leaving your lawful master, George, (I don't wonder at it), at the same time, I'm sorry, George, yes, decidedly. I think I must say that it's my duty to tell you so.

GEORGE: Why are you sorry, sir?

WILSON: Why, to see you, as it were, setting yourself in opposition to the laws of your country.

GEORGE: *My* country! What country have I, but the grave? And I would to heaven that I was laid there!

WILSON: George, you've got a hard master, in fact he is—well, he conducts himself reprehensibly—I can't pretend to defend him. I'm sorry for you, now; it's a bad case—very bad; but we must all submit to the indications of Providence, George, don't you see?

GEORGE: I wonder, Mr. Wilson, if the Indians should come and take you a prisoner away from your wife and children, and want to keep you all your life hoeing corn for them, if you'd think it your duty to abide in the condition in which you were called? I rather imagine that you'd think the first stray horse you could find an indication of Providence, shouldn't you?

WILSON: Really, George, putting the case in that somewhat peculiar light—I don't know—under those circumstances—but what I might. But it seems to me you are running an awful risk. You can't hope to carry it out. If you're taken it will be worse with you than ever; they'll only abuse you, and half kill you, and sell you down river.

GEORGE: Mr. Wilson, I know all this. I *do* run a risk, but—(*Throws open coat and shows pistols and knife in his belt.*) There! I'm ready for them. Down South I never *will* go! no, if it comes to that, I can earn myself at least six feet of free soil—the first and last I shall ever own in Kentucky!

WILSON: Why, George, this state of mind is awful—it's getting really desperate. I'm concerned. Going to break the laws of your country?

GEORGE: My country again! Sir, I haven't any country any more than I have any father. I don't want anything of *your* country, except to be left alone—to go peaceably out of it; but if any man tries to stop me, let him take care, for I am desperate. I'll fight for my liberty, to the last breath I breathe! You say your fathers did it; if it was right for them, it is right for me!

WILSON (*walking up and down, and fanning his face with a large yellow silk handkerchief*): Blast 'em all! Haven't I always said so—the infernal old cusses! Bless me! I hope I ain't swearing now! Well, go ahead, George, go ahead. But be careful, my boy; don't shoot anybody, unless—well, you'd *better* not shoot—at least I wouldn't *hit* anybody, you know.

GEORGE: Only in self-defense.

WILSON: Well, well (*Fumbling in his pocket.*) I suppose, perhaps, I ain't following my judgment—hang it, I won't follow my judgment. So here, George. (*Takes out a pocket-book and offers* GEORGE *a roll of bills.*)

GEORGE: No, my kind, good sir, you've done a great deal for me, and this might get you into trouble. I have money enough, I hope, to take me as far as I need it.

WILSON: No; but you must, George. Money is a great help everywhere; can't have too much, if you get it honestly. Take it, do take it, *now* do, my boy!

GEORGE (*taking the money*): On condition, sir, that I may repay it at some future time, I will.

WILSON: And now, George, how long are you going to travel in this way? Not long or far, I hope? It's well carried on, but too bold.

GEORGE: Mr. Wilson, it is *so bold,* and this tavern is so near, that they will never think of it; they will look for me on ahead, and you yourself wouldn't know me.

WILSON: But the mark on your hand?

GEORGE (*draws off his glove and shows scar*): That is a parting mark of Mr. Harris' regard. Looks interesting, doesn't it? (*Puts on glove again.*)

WILSON: I declare, my very blood runs cold when I think of it—your condition and your risks!

GEORGE: Mine has run cold a good many years; at present, it's about up to the boiling point.

WILSON: George, something has brought you out wonderfully. You hold up your head, and move and speak like another man.

GEORGE (*proudly*): Because I'm a *freeman!* Yes, sir; I've said "master" for the last time to any man. *I'm free!*

WILSON: Take care! You are not sure; you may be taken.

GEORGE: All men are free and equal *in the grave,* if it comes to that, Mr. Wilson.

(*Enter* PHINEAS.)

PHINEAS: Them's my sentiment, to a teetotal atom, and I don't care who knows it! Neighbour, the boat is ready, and the sooner we make tracks the better. I've seen some mysterious strangers lurking about these diggings, so we'd better put.

GEORGE: Farewell, Mr. Wilson, and heaven reward you for the many kindnesses you have shown the poor fugitive!

WILSON (*grasping his hand*): You're a brave fellow, George. I wish in my heart you were safe through, though—that's what I do.

PHINEAS: And ain't I the man of all creation to put him through, stranger? Chaw me up if I don't take him to his dear little wife, in the smallest possible quantity of time. Come, neighbour, let's vamoose.

GEORGE: Farewell, Mr. Wilson.

WILSON: My best wishes go with you, George. (*Exit.*)

PHINEAS: You're a trump, old Slow-and-Easy.

GEORGE (*looking off*): Look! look!

PHINEAS: Consarn their picters, here they come! We can't get out of the house without their seeing us. We're teetotally treed!

GEORGE: Let us fight our way through them!

PHINEAS: No, that won't do; there are too many of them for a fair fight—we should be chawed up in no time. (*Looks round and sees trap door.*) Halloa! here's a cellar door. Just you step down here a few minutes, while I parley with them. (*Lifts trap.*)

GEORGE: I am resolved to perish sooner than surrender! (*Goes down trap.*)

PHINEAS: That's your sort! (*Closes trap and stands on it.*) Here they are!

(*Enter* HALEY, MARKS, LOKER *and three* MEN.)

HALEY: Say, stranger, you haven't seen a runaway darkey about these parts, eh?

PHINEAS: What kind of a darkey?

HALEY: A mulatto chap, almost as light-complexioned as a white man.

PHINEAS: Was he a pretty good-looking chap?

HALEY: Yes.

PHINEAS: Kind of tall?

HALEY: Yes.

PHINEAS: With brown hair?

HALEY: Yes.

PHINEAS: And dark eyes?

HALEY: Yes.

PHINEAS: Pretty well dressed?

HALEY: Yes.

PHINEAS: Scar on his right hand?

HALEY: Yes, yes.

PHINEAS: Well, I ain't seen him.

HALEY: Oh, bother! Come, boys, let's search the house. (*Exeunt.*)

PHINEAS (*raises trap*): Now, then, neighbour George. (GEORGE *enters, up trap.*) Now's the time to cut your lucky.

GEORGE: Follow me, Phineas. (*Exit.*)

PHINEAS: In a brace of shakes. (*Is closing trap as* HALEY, MARKS, LOKER, *&c., re-enter.*)

HALEY: Ah! he's down in the cellar. Follow me, boys! (*Thrusts* PHINEAS *aside, and rushes down trap, followed by the others.* PHINEAS *closes trap and stands on it.*)

PHINEAS: Chaw me up! but I've got 'em all in a trap. (*Knocking below.*) Be quiet, you pesky varmints! (*Knocking.*) They're getting mighty oneasy. (*Knocking.*) Will you be quiet, you savagerous critters! (*The trap is forced open.* HALEY *and* MARKS *appear.* PHINEAS *seizes a chair and stands over trap.*) Down with you or I'll smash you into apple-fritters! (*Tableau.*)

SCENE 4. *A plain chamber*

TOPSY (*without*): You go 'long. No more nigger dan you be! (*Enters—shouts and laughter without—looks off.*) You seem to think yourself white folks. You ain't nerry one—black *nor* white. I'd like to be one or turrer. Law! you niggers, does you know you's all sinners? Well, you is—everybody is. White folks is sinners too—Miss Feely says so—but I 'spects niggers is the biggest ones. But Lor'! ye ain't any on ye up to me. I's so awful wicked there can't nobody do nothin' with me. I used to keep old missis a-swarin' at me half de time. I 'spects I's de wickedest critter in de world.

(*Song and dance introduced. Enter* EVA.)

EVA: Oh, Topsy! Tospy! you have been very wrong again.

TOPSY: Well, I 'spects I have.

EVA: What makes you do so?

TOPSY: I dunno; I 'spects it's cause I's so wicked.

EVA: Why did you spoil Jane's earrings?

TOPSY: 'Cause she's so proud. She called me a little black imp, and turned up her pretty nose at me 'cause she is whiter than I am. I was gwine by her room, and I seed her coral earrings lying on de table, so I threw dem on de floor, and put my foot on 'em, and scrunched 'em all to little bits—he! he! he! I's so wicked.

EVA: Don't you know that was very wrong?

TOPSY: I don't car' I despises dem what sets up for fine ladies, when dey ain't nothin' but cream-coloured niggers! Dere's Miss Rosa—she gives me lots of 'pertinent remarks. T'other night she was gwine to ball. She put on a beau'ful dress that missis give her—wid her har curled, all nice and pretty. She hab to go down de back stairs—dey am dark—and I puts a pail of hot water on dem, and she put her foot into it, and den she go tumblin' to de bottom of de stairs, and de water go all ober her, and spile her dress, and scald her dreadful bad! He! he! he! I's so wicked!

EVA: Oh! how could you!

TOPSY: Don't dey despise me 'cause I don't know nothin'? Don't dey laugh at me 'cause I'm brack, and dey ain't?

EVA: But you shouldn't mind them.

TOPSY: Well, I don't mind dem; but when dey are passing under my winder, I trows dirty water on 'em, and dat spiles der complexions.

EVA: What does make you so bad, Topsy? Why won't you try and be good? Don't you love anybody, Topsy?

TOPSY: Can't recommember.

EVA: But you love your father and mother?

TOPSY: Never had none; ye know, I telled ye that, Miss Eva.

EVA: Oh! I know; but hadn't you any brother, or sister, or aunt, or——

TOPSY: No, none on 'em—never had nothin' nor nobody. I's brack—no one loves me!

EVA: Oh! Topsy, I love you! (*Laying her hand on* TOPSY's *shoulder.*) I love you because you haven't had any father, or mother, or friends. I love you, and I want you to be good. I wish you would try to be good for my sake. (TOPSY *looks astonished for a moment, and then bursts into tears.*) Only think of it, Topsy—*you* can be one of those spirits bright Uncle Tom sings about!

TOPSY: Oh! dear Miss Eva—dear Miss Eva! I will try—I will try! I never did care nothin' about it before.

EVA: If you try, you will succeed. Come with me. (*Takes* TOPSY's *hand.*)

TOPSY: I will try; but den, I's so wicked!

(*Exit* EVA, *followed by* TOPSY, *crying.*)

SCENE 5. *Chamber*

(*Enter* GEORGE, ELIZA *and* HARRY.)

GEORGE: At length, Eliza, after many wanderings, we are again united.

ELIZA: Thanks to these generous Quakers, who have so kindly sheltered us.

GEORGE: Not forgetting our friend Phineas.

ELIZA: I do indeed owe him much. 'Twas he I met upon the icy river's bank, after that fearful but successful attempt, when I fled from the slave-trader with my child in my arms.

GEORGE: It seems almost incredible that you could have crossed the river on the ice.

ELIZA: Yes, I did. Heaven helping me, I crossed on the ice, for they were behind me—right behind—and there was no other way.

GEORGE: But the ice was all in broken-up blocks, swinging and heaving up and down in the water.

ELIZA: I know it was—I know it; I did not think I should get over, but I did not care—I could but die if I did not! I leaped on the ice, but how I got across I don't know; the first I remember, a man was helping me up the bank—that man was Phineas.

GEORGE: My brave girl! you deserve your freedom—you have richly earned it!

ELIZA: And when we get to Canada I can help you to work, and between us we can find something to live on.

GEORGE: Yes, Eliza, so long as we have each other, and our boy. Oh, Eliza, if these people only knew what a blessing it is for a man to feel that his wife and child belong to *him!* I've often wondered to see men that could call their wives and children *their own,* fretting and worrying about anything else. Why, I feel rich and strong, though we have nothing but our bare hands. If they will only let me alone now, I will be satisfied—thankful!

ELIZA: But we are not quite out of danger; we are not yet in Canada.

GEORGE: True; but it seems as if I smelt the free air, and it makes me strong!

(*Enter* PHINEAS, *dressed as a Quaker.*)

PHINEAS (*with a snuffle*): Verily, friends, how is it with thee?—hum!

GEORGE: Why, Phineas, what means this metamorphosis?

PHINEAS: I've become a Quaker! that's the meaning on't.

GEORGE: What—you?

PHINEAS: Teetotally! I was driven to it by a strong argument, composed of a pair of sparkling eyes, rosy cheeks, and pouting lips. Them lips would persuade a man to assassinate his grandmother! (*Assumes the Quaker tone again.*) Verily, George, I have discovered something of importance to the interests of thee and thy party, and it were well for thee to hear it.

GEORGE: Keep us not in suspense!

PHINEAS: Well, after I left you on the road, I stopped at a little, lone tavern, just below here. Well, I was tired with hard driving, and, after my supper, I stretched myself down on a pile of bags in the corner, and pulled a buffalo hide over me—and what does I do but get fast asleep.

GEORGE: With one ear open, Phineas?

PHINEAS: No, I slept ears and all for an hour or two, for I was pretty well tired; but when I came to myself a little, I found that there were some men in the room, sitting round a table, drinking and talking; and I thought, before I made much muster, I'd just see what they were up to, especially as I heard them say something about the Quakers. Then I listened with both ears and found they were talking about you. So I kept quiet, and heard them lay off all their plans. They've got a right notion of the track we are going to-night, and they'll be down after us, six or eight strong. So, now, what's to be done?

ELIZA: What *shall* we do, George?

GEORGE: I know what I shall do! (*Takes out pistols.*)

PHINEAS: Ay—ay, thou seest, Eliza, how it will work—pistols—phitz—poppers!

ELIZA: I see; but I pray it come not to that!

GEORGE: I don't want to involve any one with or for me. If you will lend me your vehicle, and direct me, I will drive alone to the next stand.

PHINEAS: Ah! well, friend, but thee'll need a driver for all that. Thee's quite welcome to do all the fighting thee knows; but I know a thing or two about the road that thee doesn't.

GEORGE: But I don't want to involve you.

PHINEAS: Involve me! Why, chaw me—that is to say—when thee does involve me, please to let me know.

ELIZA: Phineas is a wise and skillful man. You will do well, George, to abide by his judgment. And, oh! George, be not hasty with these— young blood is hot! (*Laying her hand on pistols.*)

GEORGE: I will attack no man. All I ask of this country is to be left alone, and I will go out peaceably. But I'll fight to the last breath before they shall take from me my wife and son! Can you blame me?

PHINEAS: Mortal man cannot blame thee, neighbour George! Flesh and blood could not do otherwise. Woe unto the world because of offenses, but woe unto them through whom the offense cometh! That's gospel, teetotally!

GEORGE: Would not even you, sir, do the same, in my place?

PHINEAS: I pray that I be not tried; the flesh is weak—but I think my flesh would be pretty tolerably strong in such a case; I ain't sure, friend George, that I shouldn't hold a fellow for thee, if thee had any accounts to settle with him.

ELIZA: Heaven grant we be not tempted.

PHINEAS: But if we are tempted too much, why, consarn 'em! let them look out, that's all.

GEORGE: It's quite plain you was not born for a Quaker. The old nature has its way in you pretty strong yet.

PHINEAS: Well, I reckon you are pretty teetotally right.

GEORGE: Had we not better hasten our flight?

PHINEAS: Well, I rather conclude we had; we're full two hours ahead of them, if they start at the time they planned; so let's vamoose. (*Exeunt.*)

SCENE 6. *A rocky pass in the hills. Large set rock and platform.*

PHINEAS (*without*): Out with you in a twinkling, every one, and up into these rocks with me! run *now,* if you *ever* did run!

(PHINEAS *enters, with* HARRY *in his arms.* GEORGE *supporting* ELIZA.)

Come up here; this is one of our old hunting dens. Come up. (*They ascend the rock.*) Well, here we are. Let 'em get us if they can. Whoever comes here has to walk single file between those two rocks, in fair range of your pistols—d'ye see?

GEORGE: I do see. And now, as this affair is mine, let me take all the risk, and do all the fighting.

PHINEAS: Thee's quite welcome to do the fighting, George; but I may have the fun of looking on, I suppose. But see, these fellows are kind of debating down there, and looking up, like hens when they are going to fly up onto the roost. Hadn't thee better give 'em a word of advice, before they come up, jest to tell 'em handsomely they'll be shot if they do.

(LOKER, MARKS, *and three* MEN *enter.*)

MARKS: Well, Tom, your coons are fairly treed.

LOKER: Yes, I see 'em go up right here; and here's a path—I'm for going right up. They can't jump down in a hurry, and it won't take long to feret 'em out.

MARKS: But, Tom, they might fire at us from behind the rocks. That would be ugly, you know.

LOKER: Ugh! always for saving your skin, Marks. No danger; niggers are too plaguy scared!

MARKS: I don't know why I shouldn't save my skin; it's the best I've got; and niggers do fight like the devil sometimes.

GEORGE (*rising on the rock*): Gentlemen, who are you down there, and what do you want?

LOKER: We want a party of runaway niggers. One George and Eliza Harris, and their son. We've got the officers here, and a warrant to take 'em too. D'ye hear? Ain't you George Harris, that belonged to Mr. Harris, of Shelby county, Kentucky?

GEORGE: I am George Harris. A Mr. Harris, of Kentucky, did call me his property. But now I'm a freeman, standing on Heaven's free soil! My wife and child I claim as mine. We have arms to defend ourselves, and we mean to do it. You can come up if you like, but the first one that comes within range of our bullets is a dead man.

MARKS: Oh, come—come, young man, this ain't no kind of talk at all for you. You see we're officers of justice. We've got the law on our side, and the power and so forth; so you'd better give up peaceably, you see—for you'll certainly have to give up at last.

GEORGE: I know very well that you've got the law on your side, and the power; but you haven't got us. We are standing here as free as you are, and by the great power that made us, we'll fight for our liberty till we die!

(*During this,* MARKS *draws a pistol, and when he concludes fires at him.* ELIZA *screams.*)

GEORGE: It's nothing, Eliza; I am unhurt.

PHINEAS (*drawing* GEORGE *down*): Thee'd better keep out of sight with thy speechifying; they're teetotal mean scamps.

LOKER: What did you do that for, Marks?

MARKS: You see, you get jist as much for him dead as alive in Kentucky.

GEORGE: Now, Phineas, the first man that advances I fire at; you take the second, and so on. It won't do to waste two shots on one.

PHINEAS: But what if you don't hit?

GEORGE: I'll try my best.

PHINEAS: Creation! chaw me up if there ain't stuff in you!

MARKS: I think I must have hit some on 'em. I heard a squeal.

LOKER: I'm going right up for one. I never was afraid of niggers, and I ain't a going to be now. Who goes after me?

(LOKER *dashes up the rock.* GEORGE *fires. He staggers for a moment, then springs to the top.* PHINEAS *seizes him. A struggle.*)

PHINEAS: Friend, thee is not wanted here! (*Throws* LOKER *over the rock.*)

MARKS (*retreating*): Lord help us—they're perfect devils!

(MARKS *and* PARTY *run off.* GEORGE *and* ELIZA *kneel in an attitude of thanksgiving, with the* CHILD *between them.* PHINEAS *stands over them exulting.*)

ACT III

SCENE 1. *Chamber*

(*Enter* ST. CLARE, *followed by* TOM.)

ST. CLARE (*giving money and papers to* TOM): There, Tom, are the bills, and the money to liquidate them.

TOM: Yes, mas'r.

ST. CLARE: Well, Tom, what are you waiting for? Isn't all right there?

TOM: I'm 'fraid not, mas'r.

ST. CLARE: Why, Tom, what's the matter? You look as solemn as a coffin.

TOM: I feel very bad, mas'r. I allays have thought that mas'r would be good to everybody.

ST. CLARE: Well, Tom, haven't I been? Come, now, what do you want? There's something you haven't got, I suppose, and this is the preface.

TOM: Mas'r allays been good to me. I haven't nothing to complain of on that head; but there is one that mas'r isn't good to

ST. CLARE: Why, Tom, what's got into you? Speak out—what do you mean?

TOM: Last night, between one and two, I thought so. I studied upon the matter then— mas'r isn't good to *himself.*

ST. CLARE: Ah! now I understand; you allude to the state in which I came home last night. Well, to tell the truth, I *was* slightly elevated—a little more champagne on board than I could comfortably carry. That's all, isn't it?

TOM (*deeply affected—clasping his hands and weeping*): All! Oh! my dear young mas'r, I'm 'fraid it will be *loss of all—all*, body and soul. The Good Book says, "It biteth like a serpent and stingeth like an adder," my dear mas'r.

ST. CLARE: You poor, silly fool! I'm not worth crying over.

TOM: Oh, mas'r! I implore you to think of it before it gets too late.

ST. CLARE: Well, I won't go to any more of their cursed nonsense, Tom—on my honour, I won't. I don't know why I haven't stopped long ago; I've always despised *it,* and myself for it. So now, Tom, wipe up your eyes and go about your errands.

TOM: Bless you, mas'r. I feel much better now. You have taken a load from poor Tom's heart. Bless you!

ST. CLARE: Come, come, no blessings! I'm not so wonderfully good, now. There, I'll pledge my honour to you, Tom, you don't see me so again. (*Exit* TOM.) I'll keep my faith with him, too.

OPHELIA (*without*): Come along, you shiftless mortal!

ST. CLARE: What new witchcraft has Topsy been brewing? That commotion is of her raising, I'll be bound.

(*Enter* OPHELIA, *dragging in* TOPSY.)

OPHELIA: Come here now; I will tell your master.

ST. CLARE: What's the matter now?

OPHELIA: The matter is that I cannot be plagued with this girl any longer. It's past all bearing; flesh and blood cannot endure it. Here I locked her up and gave her a hymn to study; and what does she do but spy out where I put my key, and has gone to my bureau, and got a bonnet-trimming and cut it all to pieces to make dolls' jackets! I never saw anything like it in my life!

ST. CLARE: What have you done to her?

OPHELIA: What have I done? What haven't I done? Your wife says I ought to have her whipped till she couldn't stand.

ST. CLARE: I don't doubt it. Tell me of the lovely rule of woman. I never saw above a dozen women that wouldn't half kill a horse, or a servant, either, if they had their own way with them —let alone a man.

OPHELIA: I am sure, St. Clare, I don't know what to do. I've taught and taught—I've talked till I'm tired; I've whipped her, I've punished her in every way I could think of, and still she's just what she was at first.

ST. CLARE: Come here, Tops, you monkey! (TOPSY crosses to ST. CLARE, grinning.) What makes you behave so?

TOPSY: 'Spects it's my wicked heart—Miss Feely says so.

ST. CLARE: Don't you see how much Miss Ophelia has done for you? She says she has done everything she can think of.

TOPSY: Lor', yes, mas'r! old missis used to say so, too. She whipped me a heap harder, and used to pull my ha'r, and knock my head agin the door; but it didn't do me no good. I 'spects if they's to pull every spear of ha'r out o' my head, it wouldn't do no good neither—I's so wicked! Laws! I's nothin' but a nigger, no ways! (Goes up.)

OPHELIA: Well, I shall have to give her up; I can't have that trouble any longer.

ST. CLARE: I'd like to ask you one question.

OPHELIA: What is it?

ST. CLARE: Why, if your doctrine is not strong enough to save one heathen child, that you can have at home here, all to yourself, what's the use of sending one or two poor missionaries off with it among thousands of just such? I suppose this girl is a fair sample of what thousands of your heathen are.

OPHELIA: I'm sure I don't know; I never saw such a girl as this.

ST. CLARE: What makes you so bad, Tops? Why won't you try and be good? Don't you love any one, Topsy?

TOPSY: Dunno nothing 'bout love; I loves candy and sich, that's all.

OPHELIA: But, Topsy, if you'd only try to be good, you might.

TOPSY: Couldn't never be nothing but a nigger, if I was ever so good. If I could be skinned and come white, I'd try then.

ST. CLARE: People can love you, if you are black, Topsy. Miss Ophelia would love you, if you were good. (TOPSY laughs.) Don't you think so?

TOPSY: No, she can't b'ar me, 'cause I'm a nigger—she'd's soon have a toad touch her. There can't nobody love niggers, and niggers can't do nothin'! I don't car'! (Whistles.)

ST. CLARE: Silence, you incorrigible imp, and begone!

TOPSY: He! he! he! didn't get much out of dis chile! (Exit.)

OPHELIA: I've always had a prejudice against negroes, and it's a fact—I never could bear to have that child touch me, but I didn't think she knew it.

ST. CLARE: Trust any child to find that out; there's no keeping it from them. But I believe all the trying in the world to benefit a child, and all the substantial favours you can do them, will never excite one emotion of gratitude, while that feeling of repugnance remains in the heart. It's a queer kind of fact, but so it is.

OPHELIA: I don't know how I can help it— they are disagreeable to me, this girl in particular. How can I help feeling so?

ST. CLARE: Eva does, it seems.

OPHELIA: Well, she's so loving. I wish I was like her. She might teach me a lesson.

ST. CLARE: It would not be the first time a little child had been used to instruct an old disciple, if it were so. Come, let us seek Eva, in her favourite bower by the lake.

OPHELIA: Why, the dew is falling; she mustn't be out there. She is unwell, I know.

ST. CLARE: Don't be croaking, cousin—I hate it.

OPHELIA: But she has that cough.

ST. CLARE: Oh, nonsense, of that cough—it is not anything. She has taken a little cold, perhaps.

OPHELIA: Well, that was just the way Eliza Jane was taken—and Ellen—

ST. CLARE: Oh, stop these hobgoblin, nurse legends. You old hands get so wise, that a child cannot cough or sneeze, but you see desperation and ruin at hand. Only take care of the child, keep her from the night air, and don't let her play too hard, and she'll do well enough. (Exeunt.)

SCENE 2. (*The flat represents the lake. The rays of the setting sun tinge the waters with gold. A large tree. Beneath this a grassy bank, on which* EVA *and* TOM *are seated side by side.* EVA *has a Bible open on her lap.*)

TOM: Read dat passage again, please, Miss Eva?

EVA (*reading*): "And I saw a sea of glass, mingled with fire." (*Stopping suddenly and pointing to lake.*) Tom, there it is!

TOM: What, Miss Eva?

EVA: Don't you see there? There's a "sea of glass, mingled with fire."

TOM: True enough, Miss Eva. (*Sings.*)

Oh, had I the wings of the morning,
I'd fly away to Canaan's shore;
Bright angels should convey me home,
To the New Jerusalem.

EVA: Where do you suppose New Jerusalem is, Uncle Tom?

TOM: Oh, up in the clouds, Miss Eva.

EVA: Then I think I see it. Look in those clouds; they look like great gates of pearl; and you can see beyond them—far, far off—it's all gold! Tom, sing about 'spirits bright.'

TOM (*sings*):

I see a band of spirits bright,
That taste the glories there;
They are all robed in spotless white,
And conquering palms they bear.

EVA: Uncle Tom, I've seen *them.*

TOM: To be sure you have; you are one of them yourself. You are the brightest spirit I ever saw.

EVA: They come to me sometimes in my sleep —those spirits bright—
They are all robed in spotless white,
And conquering palms they bear.
Uncle Tom, I'm going there.

TOM: Where, Miss Eva?

EVA (*pointing to the sky*): I'm going *there,* to the spirits bright, Tom; I'm going before long.

TOM: It's jest no use tryin' to keep Miss Eva here; I've allays said so. She's got the Lord's mark in her forehead. She wasn't never like a child that's to live—there was always something deep in her eyes. (*Rises and comes forward.* EVA *also comes forward, leaving Bible on bank.*)

(*Enter* ST. CLARE.)

ST. CLARE: Ah! my little pussy, you look as blooming as a rose! You are better now-a-days, are you not?

EVA: Papa, I've had things I wanted to say to you a great while. I want to say them now, before I get weaker.

ST. CLARE: Nay, this is an idle fear, Eva; you know you grow stronger every day.

EVA: It's all no use, papa, to keep it to myself any longer. The time is coming that I am going to leave you; I am going, and never to come back.

ST. CLARE: Oh, now, my dear little Eva! you've got nervous and low-spirited; you mustn't indulge such gloomy thoughts.

EVA: No, papa, don't deceive yourself, I am *not* any better; I know it perfectly well, and I am going before long. I am not nervous—I am not low-spirited. If it were not for you, papa, and my friends, I should be perfectly happy. I want to go—I long to go!

ST. CLARE: Why, dear child, what has made your poor little heart so sad? You have everything to make you happy that could be given you.

EVA: I had rather be in heaven! There are a great many things here that make me sad—that seem dreadful to me; I had rather be there; but I don't want to leave you—it almost breaks my heart!

ST. CLARE: What makes you sad, and what seems dreadful, Eva?

EVA: I feel sad for our poor people; they love me dearly, and they are all good and kind to me. I wish, papa, they were all *free!*

ST. CLARE: Why, Eva, child, don't you think they are well enough off, now?

EVA (*not heeding the question*): Papa, isn't there a way to have slaves made free? When I am dead, papa, then you will think of me, and do it for my sake?

ST. CLARE: When you are dead, Eva? Oh, child, don't talk to me so! You are all I have on earth!

EVA: Papa, these poor creatures love their children as much as you do me. Tom loves his children. Oh, do something for them!

ST. CLARE: There, there darling; only don't distress yourself, and don't talk of dying, and I will do anything you wish.

EVA: And promise me, dear father, that Tom shall have his freedom as soon as—(*hesitating*)—I am gone!

ST. CLARE: Yes, dear, I will do anything in the world—anything you could ask me to. There, Tom, take her to her chamber; this evening air is too chill for her. (*Kisses her.* TOM *takes* EVA *in his arms, and exit.*)

ST. CLARE (*gazing mournfully after* EVA): Has there ever been a child like Eva? Yes, there has been; but their names are always on grave-stones, and their sweet smiles, their heavenly eyes, their singular words and ways, are among the buried treasures of yearning hearts. It is as if heaven had an especial band of angels, whose office it is to sojourn for a season here, and endear to them the wayward human heart, that they might bear it upward with them in their homeward flight. When you see that deep, spiritual light in the eye, when the little soul reveals itself in words sweeter and wiser than the ordinary words of children, hope not to retain that child; for the seal of heaven is on it, and the light of immortality looks out from its eyes! (*Exit.*)

SCENE 3. *A corridor*

(*Enter* TOM; *he listens at door and then lies down. Enter* OPHELIA, *with candle.*)

OPHELIA: Uncle Tom, what alive have you taken to sleeping anywhere and everywhere, like a dog, for? I thought you were one of the orderly sort, that liked to lie in bed in a Christian way.

TOM (*rises; mysteriously*): I do, Miss Feely, I do, but now—

OPHELIA: Well, what now?

TOM: We mustn't speak loud; Mas'r St. Clare won't hear on't; but Miss Feely, you know there must be somebody watchin' for the bridegroom.

OPHELIA: What do you mean, Tom?

TOM: You know it says in Scripture, "At midnight there was a great cry made, behold the bridegroom cometh!" That's what I'm 'spectin' now, every night, Miss Feely, and I couldn't sleep out of hearing, noways.

OPHELIA: Why, Uncle Tom, what makes you think so?

TOM: Miss Eva, she talks to me. The Lord, he sends his messenger in the soul. I must be thar, Miss Feely; for when that ar blessed child goes into the kingdom, they'll open the door so wide, we'll all get a look in at the glory!

OPHELIA: Uncle Tom, did Miss Eva say she felt more unwell than usual to-night?

TOM: No; but she told me she was coming nearer—thar's them that tells it to the child, Miss Feely. It's the angels—it's the trumpet sound afore the break o' day!

OPHELIA: Heaven grant your fears be vain! Come in, Tom. (*Exeunt.*)

SCENE 4. EVA's *chamber*

(EVA *discovered on a couch. A table stands near the couch, with a lamp on it. The light shines upon* EVA's *face, which is very pale. Scene half dark.* UNCLE TOM *is kneeling near the foot of the couch.* OPHELIA *stands at the head.* ST. CLARE *at back. Scene opens to plaintive music. Enter* MARIE, *hastily.*)

MARIE: St. Clare! Cousin! Oh! what is the matter now?

ST. CLARE (*hoarsely*): Hush! she is dying!

MARIE (*sinking on her knees, beside* TOM): Dying!

ST. CLARE: Oh! if she would only wake and speak once more. (*Bending over* EVA.) Eva, darling!

EVA (*uncloses her eyes, smiles, raises her head and tries to speak.*)

ST. CLARE: Do you know me, Eva?

EVA (*throwing her arms feebly about his neck*): Dear papa! (*Her arms drop and she sinks back.*)

ST. CLARE: Oh, heaven! this is dreadful! Oh! Tom, my boy, it is killing me!

TOM: Look at her, mas'r. (*Points to* EVA.)

ST. CLARE: Eva! (*A pause.*) She does not hear. Oh, Eva! tell us what you see. What is it?

EVA (*feebly smiling*): Oh! love! joy! peace! (*Dies.*)

TOM: Oh! bless the Lord! it's over, dear mas'r, it's over.

ST. CLARE (*sinking on his knees*): Farewell, beloved child! the bright eternal doors have closed after thee. We shall see thy sweet face no more. Oh! wo for them who watched thy entrance into heaven, when they shall wake and find only the cold, gray sky of daily life, and thou gone forever. (*Solemn music, slow curtain.*)

ACT IV

SCENE 1. *A street in New Orleans*

(*Enter* GUMPTION CUTE, *meeting* MARKS.)

CUTE: How do ye dew?

MARKS: How are you?

CUTE: Well, now, squire, it's a fact that I am dead broke and busted up.

MARKS: You have been speculating, I suppose?

CUTE: That's just it and nothing shorter.

MARKS: You have had poor success, you say?

CUTE: Tarnation bad, now I tell you. You see I came to this part of the country to make my fortune.

MARKS: And you did not do it?

CUTE: Scarcely. The first thing I tried my hand at was keeping school. I opened an academy for the instruction of youth in the various branches of orthography, geography, and other graphies.

MARKS: Did you succeed in getting any pupils?

CUTE: Oh, lots on 'em! and a pretty set of dunces they were, too. After the first quarter, I called on the respectable parents of the juveniles, and requested them to fork over. To which they politely answered—don't you wish you may get it?

MARKS: What did you do then?

CUTE: Well, I kind of pulled up stakes and left those diggin's. Well, then I went into Spiritual Rappings for a living. That paid pretty well for a short time, till I met with an accident.

MARKS: An accident?

CUTE: Yes; a tall Yahoo called on me one day, and wanted me to summon the spirit of his mother—which, of course, I did. He asked me about a dozen questions which I answered to his satisfaction. At last he wanted to know what she died of—I said, Cholera. You never did see a critter so riled as he was. "Look yere, stranger," said he, "it's my opinion that you're a pesky humbug! for my mother was blown up in a *Steamboat!*" With that he left the premises. The next day the people furnished me with a conveyance, and I rode out of town.

MARKS: Rode out of town?

CUTE: Yes; on a rail!

MARKS: I suppose you gave up the spirits, after that?

CUTE: Well, I reckon I did; it had such an effect on my spirits.

MARKS: It's a wonder they didn't tar and feather you.

CUTE: There was some mention made of that, but when they said *feathers,* I felt as if I had wings, and flew away.

MARKS: You cut and run?

CUTE: Yes; I didn't like their company and I cut it. Well, after that I let myself out as an overseer on a cotton plantation. I made a pretty good thing of that, though it was dreadful trying to my feelings to flog the darkies; but I got used to it after a while, and then I used to lather 'em like Jehu. Well, the proprietor got the fever and ague and shook himself out of town. The place and all the fixings were sold at auction, and I found myself adrift once more.

MARKS: What are you doing at present?

CUTE: I'm in search of a rich relation of mine.

MARKS: A rich relation?

CUTE: Yes, a Miss Ophelia St. Clare. You see, a niece of hers married one of my second cousins—that's how I came to be a relation of hers. She came on here from Vermont to be housekeeper to a cousin of hers, of the same name.

MARKS: I know him well.

CUTE: The deuce you do!—well, that's lucky.

MARKS: Yes, he lives in this city.

CUTE: Say, you just point out the locality, and I'll give him a call.

MARKS: Stop a bit. Suppose you shouldn't be able to raise the wind in that quarter, what have you thought of doing?

CUTE: Well, nothing particular.

MARKS: How should you like to enter into a nice, profitable business—one that pays well?

CUTE: That's just about my measure—it would suit me to a hair. What is it?

MARKS: Nigger catching.

CUTE: Catching niggers! What on airth do you mean?

MARKS: Why, when there's a large reward offered for a runaway darkey, we goes after him, catches him, and gets the reward.

CUTE: Yes, that's all right so far—but s'pose there ain't no reward offered?

MARKS: Why, then we catches the darkey on our own account, sells him, and pockets the proceeds.

CUTE: By chowder, that ain't a bad speculation!

MARKS: What do you say? I want a partner. You see, I lost my partner last year, up in Ohio —he was a powerful fellow.

CUTE: Lost him! How did you lose him?

MARKS: Well, you see, Tom and I—his name was Tom Loker—Tom and I were after a mulatto chap, called George Harris, that run away from Kentucky. We traced him through the greater part of Ohio, and came up with him near the Pennsylvania line. He took refuge among some rocks, and showed fight.

CUTE: Oh! then runaway darkies show fight, do they?

MARKS: Sometimes. Well, Tom—like a headstrong fool as he was—rushed up the rocks, and a Quaker chap, who was helping this George Harris, threw him over the cliff.

CUTE: Was he killed?

MARKS: Well, I didn't stop to find out. Seeing that the darkies were stronger than I thought, I made tracks for a safe place.

CUTE: And what became of this George Harris?

MARKS: Oh! he and his wife and child got away safe into Canada. You see, they will get away sometimes, though it isn't very often. Now what do you say? You are just the figure for a fighting partner. Is it a bargain?

CUTE: Well, I rather calculate our teams won't hitch, no how. By chowder, I hain't no idea of setting myself up, as a target for darkies to fire at—that's a speculation that don't suit my constitution.

MARKS: You're afraid, then?

CUTE: No, I ain't; it's against my principles.

MARKS: Your principles—how so?

CUTE: Because my principles are to keep a sharp lookout for No. 1. I shouldn't feel wholesome if a darkey was to throw me over that cliff to look after Tom Loker. (*Exeunt, arm-in-arm.*)

SCENE 2. *Gothic chamber*

(ST. CLARE *discovered, seated on sofa.* TOM *to the left.*)

ST. CLARE: Oh! Tom, my boy, the whole world is as empty as an egg-shell.

TOM: I know it, mas'r, I know it. But oh! if mas'r could look up—up where our dear Miss Eva is—

ST. CLARE: Ah, Tom! I do look up; but the trouble is, I don't see anything when I do. I wish I could. It seems to be given to children and poor, honest fellows like you, to see what we cannot. How comes it?

TOM: "Thou hast hid from the wise and prudent, and revealed unto babes; even so, Father, for so it seemed good in thy sight."

ST. CLARE: Tom, I don't believe—I've got the habit of doubting—I want to believe and I cannot.

TOM: Dear mas'r, pray to the good Lord: "Lord, I believe; help thou my unbelief." ·

ST. CLARE: Who knows anything about anything? Was all that beautiful love and faith only one of the ever-shifting phases of human feeling, having nothing real to rest on, passing away with the little breath? And is there no more Eva—nothing?

TOM: Oh! dear mas'r, there is. I know it; I'm sure of it. Do, do, dear mas'r, believe it!

ST. CLARE: How do you know there is, Tom? You never saw the Lord.

TOM: Felt Him in my soul, mas'r—feel Him now! Oh, mas'r, when I was sold away from my old woman and the children, I was jest a'most broken up—I felt as if there warn't nothing left —and then the Lord stood by me, and He says, "Fear not, Tom," and He brings light and joy into a poor fellow's soul—makes all peace; and I's so happy, and loves everybody, and feels willin' to be jest where the Lord wants to put me. I know it couldn't come from me, 'cause I's a poor, complaining creature—it comes from above, and I know He's willin' to do for mas'r.

ST. CLARE (*grasping* TOM's *hand*): Tom, you love me!

TOM: I's willin' to lay down my life this blessed day for you.

ST. CLARE (*sadly*): Poor, foolish fellow! I'm not worth the love of one good, honest heart like yours.

TOM: Oh, mas'r! there's more than me loves you—the blessed Saviour loves you.

ST. CLARE: How do you know that, Tom?

TOM: The love of the Saviour passeth knowledge.

ST. CLARE (*turns away*): Singular! that the story of a man who lived and died eighteen hundred years ago, can affect people so yet. But He was no man. (*Rises.*) No man ever had such long and living power. Oh! that I could believe what my mother taught me, and pray as I did when I was a boy! But, Tom, all this time I have forgotten why I sent for you. I'm going to make a freeman of you; so have your trunk packed, and get ready to set out for Kentuck.

TOM (*joyfully*): Bless the Lord!

ST. CLARE (*dryly*): You haven't had such very bad times here, that you need be in such a rapture, Tom.

TOM: No, no, mas'r, 'tain't that, it's being a *freeman*—that's what I'm joyin' for.

ST. CLARE: Why, Tom, don't you think, for your own part, you've been better off than to be free?

TOM: No, *indeed*, Mas'r St. Clare—no, indeed!

ST. CLARE: Why, Tom, you couldn't possibly have earned, by your work, such clothes and such living as I have given you.

TOM: I know all that, Mas'r St. Clare— mas'r's been too good; but I'd rather have poor clothes, poor house, poor everything, and have 'em *mine*, than have the best, if they belonged to somebody else. I had *so*, mas'r; I think it's natur', mas'r.

ST. CLARE: I suppose so, Tom; and you'll be going off and leaving me in a month or so— though why you shouldn't no mortal knows.

TOM: Not while mas'r is in trouble. I'll stay with mas'r as long as he wants me, so as I can be any use.

ST. CLARE (sadly): Not while I'm in trouble, Tom? And when will my trouble be over?

TOM: When you are a believer.

ST. CLARE: And you really mean to stay by me till that day comes? (Smiling and laying his hand on TOM's shoulder.) Ah, Tom! I won't keep you till that day. Go home to your wife and children, and give my love to all.

TOM: I's faith to think that day will come —the Lord has a work for mas'r.

ST. CLARE: A work, hey? Well, now, Tom, give me your views on what sort of a work it is—let's hear.

TOM: Why, even a poor fellow like me has a work; and Mas'r St. Clare, that has larnin', and riches, and friends, how much he might do for the Lord.

ST CLARE: Tom, you seem to think the Lord needs a great deal done for him.

TOM: We does for him when we does for his creatures.

ST. CLARE: Good theology, Tom. Thank you, my boy; I like to hear you talk. But go now, Tom, and leave me alone. (Exit TOM.) That faithful fellow's words have excited a train of thoughts that almost bear me, on the strong tide of faith and feeling to the gates of that heaven I so vividly conceive. They seem to bring me nearer to Eva.

OPHELIA (outside): What are you doing there, you limb of Satan? You've been stealing something. I'll be bound.

(OPHELIA drags in TOPSY.)

TOPSY: You go 'long, Miss Feely, 'tain't none o' your business.

ST. CLARE: Heyday! what is all this commotion?

OPHELIA: She's been stealing.

TOPSY (sobbing): I hain't neither.

OPHELIA: What have you got in your bosom?

TOPSY: I've got my hand dar.

OPHELIA: But what have you got in your hand?

TOPSY: Nuffin'.

OPHELIA: That's a fib, Topsy.

TOPSY: Well, I 'spects it is.

OPHELIA: Give it to me, whatever it is.

TOPSY: It's mine—I hope I may die this bressed minute, if it don't b'long to me.

OPHELIA: Topsy, I order you to give me that article; don't let me have to ask you again. (TOP-

SY reluctantly takes the foot of an old stocking from her bosom and hands it to OPHELIA.) Sakes alive! what is all this? (Takes from it a lock of hair, and a small book, with a bit of crape twisted around it.)

TOPSY: Dat's a lock of ha'r dat Miss Eva give me—she cut it from her own beau'ful head herself.

ST. CLARE (takes book): Why did you wrap this (pointing to crape) around the book?

TOPSY: 'Cause—'cause—'cause 'twas Miss Eva's. Oh! don't take 'em away, please! (Sits down on stage, and, putting her apron over her head, begins to sob vehemently.)

OPHELIA: Come, come, don't cry; you shall have them.

TOPSY (jumps up joyfully and takes them): I wants to keep 'em, 'cause dey makes me good; I ain't half so wicked as I used to was. (Runs off.)

ST. CLARE: I really think you can make something of that girl. Any mind that is capable of a real sorrow is capable of good. You must try and do something with her.

OPHELIA: The child has improved very much; I have great hopes of her.

ST. CLARE: I believe I'll go down the street, a few moments, and hear the news.

OPHELIA: Shall I call Tom to attend you?

ST. CLARE: No, I shall be back in an hour. (Exit.)

OPHELIA: He's got an excellent heart, but then he's so dreadful shiftless! (Exit.)

[In a prompt copy of this play, owned by the New York Public Library, the following scene is inserted in manuscript:]

SCENE. (A bar-room. Tables and chairs. Newspapers on table. MARKS and CUTE discovered.)

CUTE: Any news, Squire?

MARKS: . . . 'scaped to death!

CUTE: Squire, it's lucky that the staves of that barrel wasn't made of yellow pine.

MARKS: Why so, Cute?

CUTE: Because she might have got a pine-knot hole in both her eyes, and been blind for life.

MARKS: . . . from him immediately.

CUTE: Don't want to enter into any such speculation. Hello, Squire, who is this feller coming up street?

MARKS: Can't say, Cute, never having seen the individual before.

CUTE: Rather an odd-looking fish, ain't he, Judge?

MARKS: . . . Mr. Simon Legree.

CUTE: Do you think him and I will agree?

MARKS: . . . pretty rough.

CUTE: Trot him out, Squire, I'm tough!

(LEGREE *enters.*)

LEGREE: How are you, Marks? What are you doing down here?

MARKS: . . . Cute, Legree; Legree, Cute. (LEGREE *squeezes* CUTE'*s hand.*)

CUTE: I'll trouble for that when you get through with it. Darn his picture! My hand's like a duck's foot. (ST. CLARE *enters, and seats himself at table.*)

CUTE: I cal'ate you're some on your muscle, Squire?

LEGREE: Just so, stranger.

CUTE: Say, I cal'ate you'd handle a fellar pretty rough.

LEGREE: Just so, stranger.

CUTE: Well, say, do you want to hire an overseer to boss your darkies?

LEGREE: Why so?

CUTE: 'Cause I'd like to hire myself out for a few months to oversee.

LEGREE: I can oversee my own niggers, I reckon.

CUTE: You look as if you could, by thunder!

LEGREE: 'Umph! Do you see that 'ere right hand? There's a fist that's grown hard a smacking down niggers! Just feel the weight on't, stranger!

CUTE: Land of hope and blessed promise! Now, I shouldn't wonder if your heart was just about as hard as your hand.

LEGREE: Just so, stranger.

CUTE: Nevertheless, you've one soft spot about you.

LEGREE: 'Umph, indeed, whereabouts?

CUTE: Your head, you darned cuss!

LEGREE: What! (*Rushes at him with bowie-knife.* ST. CLARE *attempts to separate them. Business and scene closes.*)

SCENE 3. *Front chamber*

(*Enter* TOPSY.)

TOPSY: Dar's somethin' de matter wid me—I isn't a bit like myself. I haven't done anything wrong since poor Miss Eva went up in de skies and left us. When I's gwine to do anything wicked, I tinks of her, and somehow I can't do it. I's getting to be good, dat's a fact. I 'spects when I's dead I shall be turned into a little brack angel.

(*Enter* OPHELIA.)

OPHELIA: Topsy, I've been looking for you; I've got something very particular to say to you.

TOPSY: Does you want me to say the catechism?

OPHELIA: No, not now.

TOPSY (*aside*): Golly! dat's one comfort.

OPHELIA: Now, Topsy, I want you to try and understand what I am going to say to you.

TOPSY: Yes, missis, I'll open my ears drefful wide.

OPHELIA: Mr. St. Clare has given you to me, Topsy.

TOPSY: Den I b'longs to you, don't I? Golly! I thought I always belonged to you.

OPHELIA: Not till to-day have I received any authority to call you my property.

TOPSY: I's your property, am I? Well, if you say so, I 'spects I am.

OPHELIA: Topsy, I can give you your liberty.

TOPSY: My liberty?

OPHELIA: Yes, Topsy.

TOPSY: Has you got 'um with you?

OPHELIA: I have, Topsy.

TOPSY: Is it clothes or wittles?

OPHELIA: How shiftless! Don't you know what your liberty is, Topsy?

TOPSY: How should I know when I never seed 'um?

OPHELIA: Topsy, I am going to leave this place; I am going many miles away—to my own home in Vermont.

TOPSY: Den what's to become of dis chile?

OPHELIA: If you wish to go, I will take you with me.

TOPSY: Miss Feely, I doesn't want to leave you no how, I loves you, I does.

OPHELIA: Then you shall share my home for the rest of your days. Come, Topsy.

TOPSY: Stop, Miss Feely; does dey hab any oberseers in Varmount?

OPHELIA: No, Topsy.

TOPSY: Nor cotton plantations, nor sugar factories, nor darkies, nor whipping, nor nothing?

OPHELIA: No, Topsy.

TOPSY: By golly! de quicker you is gwine de better den.

(*Enter* TOM, *hastily.*)

TOM: Oh, Miss Feely! Miss Feely!

OPHELIA: Gracious me, Tom! what's the matter?

TOM: Oh, Mas'r St. Clare! Mas'r St. Clare!

OPHELIA: Well, Tom, well?

TOM: They've just brought him home and I do believe he's killed.

OPHELIA: Killed?

TOPSY: Oh, dear! what's to become of de poor darkies now?

TOM: He's dreadful weak. It's just as much as he can do to speak. He wanted me to call you.

OPHELIA: My poor cousin! Who would have thought of it? Don't say a word to his wife, Tom; the danger may not be so great as you think; it would only distress her. Come with me; you may be able to afford some assistance. (*Exeunt.*)

SCENE 4. *Handsome chamber*

(ST. CLARE *discovered seated on sofa.* OPHELIA, TOM *and* TOPSY *are clustered around him.* DOCTOR *back of sofa, feeling his pulse.*)

ST. CLARE (*raising himself feebly*): Tom—poor fellow!

TOM: Well, mas'r?

ST. CLARE: I have received my death wound.

TOM: Oh, no, no, mas'r!

ST. CLARE: I feel that I am dying—Tom, pray!

TOM (*sinking on his knees*): I do pray, mas'r! I do pray!

ST. CLARE (*after a pause*): Tom, one thing preys upon my mind.—I have forgotten to sign your freedom papers. What will become of you when I am gone?

TOM: Don't think of that, mas'r.

ST. CLARE: I was wrong, Tom, very wrong, to neglect it. I may be the cause of much suffering to you hereafter. Marie, my wife—she—oh!—

OPHELIA: His mind is wandering.

ST. CLARE (*energetically*): No! it is coming *home* at last! (*Sinks back.*) at last! at last! Eva, I come! (*Dies.*)

ACT V

SCENE 1. *An auction mart*

(UNCLE TOM *and* EMMELINE *at back.* ADOLF, SKEGGS, MARKS, MANN, *and various spectators discovered.* MARKS *and* MANN *come forward.*)

MARKS: Hulloa, Alf! what brings you here?

MANN: Well, I was wanting a valet, and I heard that St. Clare's lot was going; I thought I'd just look at them.

MARKS: Catch me ever buying any of St. Clare's people. Spoilt niggers, every one —impudent as the devil.

MANN: Never fear that; if I get 'em, I'll soon have their airs out of them—they'll soon find that they've another kind of master to deal with than St. Clare. 'Pon my word, I'll buy that fellow—I like the shape of him. (*Pointing to* ADOLF.)

MARKS: You'll find it'll take all you've got to keep him— he's deucedly extravagant.

MANN: Yes, but my lord will find that he *can't* be extravagant with *me.* Just let him be sent to the calaboose a few times, and thoroughly dressed down, I'll tell you if it don't bring him to a sense of his ways. Oh! I'll reform him, up hill and down, you'll see. I'll buy him, that's flat.

(*Enter* LEGREE; *he goes up and looks at* ADOLF, *whose boots are nicely blacked.*)

LEGREE: A nigger with his boots blacked —bah! (*Spits on them.*) Holloa, you! (*To* TOM.) Let's see your teeth. (*Seizes* TOM *by the jaw and opens his mouth.*) Strip up your sleeve and show your muscle. (TOM *does so.*) Where was you raised?

TOM: In Kentuck, mas'r.

LEGREE: What have you done?

TOM: Had care of mas'r's farm.

LEGREE: That's a likely story. (*Turns to* EMMELINE.) You're a nice looking girl enough. How old are you? (*Grasps her arm.*)

EMMELINE (*shrieking*): Ah! you hurt me.

SKEGGS: Stop that, you minx! No whimpering here. The sale is going to begin. (*Mounts the rostrum.*) Gentlemen, the next article I shall offer you to-day is Adolf, late valet to Mr. St. Clare. How much am I offered? (*Various bids are made.* ADOLF *is knocked down to* MANN *for eight hundred dollars.*) Gentlemen, I now offer a prime article—the quadroon girl, Emmeline, only fifteen years of age, warranted in every respect. (*Business as before.* EMMELINE *is sold to* LEGREE *for one thousand dollars.*) Now, I shall close to-day's sale by offering you the valuable article known as Uncle Tom, the most useful nigger ever raised. Gentlemen in want of an overseer, now is the time to bid.

(*Business as before.* TOM *is sold to* LEGREE *for twelve hundred dollars.*)

LEGREE: Now look here, you two belong to me. (TOM *and* EMMELINE *sink on their knees.*)

TOM: Heaven help us, then!

(*Music.* LEGREE *stands over them exulting. Picture.*)

SCENE 2. *The garden of* MISS OPHELIA's *house in Vermont*

(*Enter* OPHELIA *and* DEACON PERRY.)

DEACON: Miss Ophelia, allow me to offer you my congratulations upon your safe arrival in your native place. I hope it is your intention to pass the remainder of your days with us?

OPHELIA: Well, Deacon, I have come here with that express purpose.

DEACON: I presume you were not over pleased with the South?

OPHELIA: Well, to tell the truth, Deacon, I wasn't; I liked the country very well, but the people there are so dreadful shiftless.

DEACON: The result, I presume, of living in a warm climate.

OPHELIA: Well, Deacon, what is the news among you all here?

DEACON: Well, we live on in the same even jog-trot pace. Nothing of any consequence has happened.—Oh! I forgot. (*Takes out his handkerchief.*) I've lost my wife; my Molly has left me. (*Wipes his eyes.*)

OPHELIA: Poor soul! I pity you, Deacon.

DEACON: Thank you. You perceive I bear my loss with resignation.

OPHELIA: How you must miss her tongue!

DEACON: Molly certainly was fond of talking. She always would have the last word—heigho!

OPHELIA: What was her complaint, Deacon?

DEACON: A very mild and soothing one, Miss Ophelia; she had a severe attack of the lockjaw.

OPHELIA: Dreadful!

DEACON: Wasn't it? When she found she couldn't use her tongue, she took it so much to heart that it struck to her stomach and killed her. Poor dear! Excuse my handkerchief; she's been dead only eighteen months.

OPHELIA: Why, Deacon, by this time you ought to be setting your cap for another wife.

DEACON: Do you think so, Miss Ophelia?

OPHELIA: I don't see why you shouldn't—you are still a good-looking man, Deacon.

DEACON: Ah! well, I think I do wear well—in fact, I may say remarkably well. It has been observed to me before.

OPHELIA: And you are not much over fifty?

DEACON: Just turned of forty, I assure you.

OPHELIA: Hale and hearty?

DEACON: Health excellent—look at my eye! Strong as a lion—look at my arm! A No. 1 constitution—look at my leg!!!

OPHELIA: Have you no thoughts of choosing another partner?

DEACON: Well, to tell you the truth, I have.

OPHELIA: Who is she?

DEACON: She is not far distant. (*Looks at* OPHELIA *in a languishing manner.*) I have her in my eye at this present moment.

OPHELIA (*aside*): Really, I believe he's going to pop. Why, surely, Deacon, you don't mean to—

DEACON: Yes, Miss Ophelia, I do mean; and believe me, when I say—(*Looking off.*) The Lord be good to us, but I believe there is the devil coming!

(TOPSY *runs on with bouquet. She is now dressed very neatly.*)

TOPSY: Miss Feely, here is some flowers dat I hab been gathering for you. (*Gives bouquet.*)

OPHELIA: That's a good child.

DEACON: Miss Ophelia, who is this young person?

OPHELIA: She is my daughter.

DEACON (*aside*): Her daughter! Then she must have married a colored man off South. I was not aware that you had been married, Miss Ophelia?

OPHELIA: Married? Sakes alive! what made you think I had been married?

DEACON: Good gracious! I'm getting confused. Didn't I understand you to say that this somewhat tanned young lady was your daughter?

OPHELIA: Only by adoption. She is my adopted daughter.

DEACON: O—oh! (*Aside.*) I breathe again.

TOPSY (*aside*): By golly! dat old man's eyes stick out of 'um head dre'ful. Guess he never seed anything like me afore.

OPHELIA: Deacon, won't you step into the house and refresh yourself after your walk?

DEACON: I accept your polite invitation (*Offers his arm.*) Allow me.

OPHELIA: As gallant as ever, Deacon. I declare, you grow younger every day.

DEACON: You can never grow old, madam.

OPHELIA: Ah, you flatterer! (*Exeunt.*)

TOPSY: Dar dey go, like an old goose and gander. Guess dat ole gemblemun feels kind of confectionary—rather sweet on my old missis. By golly! she's been dre'ful kind to me ever since I come away from de South; and I loves her, I does, 'cause she takes such car' on me and gives me dese fine clothes. I tries to be good, too, and I's getting 'long 'mazin' fast. I'se not so wicked as I used to was. (*Looks out.*) Hulloa! dar's some one comin' here. I wonder what he wants now. (*Retires, observing.*)

(*Enter* GUMPTION CUTE, *very shabby—a small bundle, on a stick, over his shoulder.*)

CUTE: By chowder, here I am again. Phew! it's a pretty considerable tall piece of walking between here and New Orleans, not to mention the wear of shoe-leather. I guess I'm about done up. If this streak of bad luck lasts much longer, I'll borrow sixpence to buy a rope, and hang myself right straight up! When I went to call on Miss Ophelia, I swow if I didn't find out that she had left for Vermont; so I kind of concluded to make tracks in that direction myself, and as I didn't have any money left, why I had to foot it, and here I am in Old Varmount once more. They told me Miss Ophelia lived up here. I wonder if she will remember the relationship. (*Sees* TOPSY.) By chowder, there's a darkey. Look here, Charcoal!

TOPSY (*comes forward*): My name isn't Charcoal —it's Topsy.

CUTE: Oh! your name is Topsy, is it, you juvenile specimen of Day & Martin?

TOPSY: Tell you I don't know nothin' 'bout Day & Martin. I's Topsy and I belong to Miss Feely St. Clare.

CUTE: I'm much obleeged to you, you small extract of Japan, for your information. So Miss Ophelia lives up there in the white house, does she?

TOPSY: Well, she don't do nothin' else.

CUTE: Well, then, just locomote your pins.

TOPSY: What—what's dat?

CUTE: Walk your chalks!

TOPSY: By golly! dere ain't no chalk 'bout me.

CUTE: Move your trotters.

TOPSY: How you does spoke! What you mean by trotters?

CUTE: Why, your feet, Stove Polish.

TOPSY: What does you want me to move my feet for?

CUTE: To tell your mistress, you ebony angel, that a gentleman wishes to see her.

TOPSY: Does you call yourself a gentleman? By golly! you look more like a scar'-crow.

CUTE: Now look here, you Charcoal, don't you be sassy. I'm a gentleman in distress; a done-up speculator; one that has seen better days—long time ago—and better clothes too, by chowder! My creditors are like my boots —they've no soles. I'm a victim to circumstances. I've been through much and survived it. I've taken walking exercise for the benefit of my health; but as I was trying to live on air at the same time, it was a losing speculation, 'cause it gave me such a dreadful appetite.

TOPSY: Golly! you look as if you could eat an ox, horns and all.

CUTE: Well, I calculate I could, if he was roasted—it's a speculation I should like to engage in. I have returned like the fellow that run away in Scripture; and if anybody's got a fatted calf they want to kill, all they got to do is to fetch him along. Do you know, Charcoal, that your mistress is a relation of mine?

TOPSY: Is she your uncle?

CUTE: No, no, not quite so near as that. My second cousin married her niece.

TOPSY: And does you want to see Miss Feely?

CUTE: I do. I have come to seek a home beneath her roof, and take care of all the spare change she don't want to use.

TOPSY: Den just yo' follow me, mas'r.

CUTE: Stop! By chowder, I've got a great idee. Say, you Day & Martin, how should you like to enter into a speculation?

TOPSY: Golly! I doesn't know what a spec —spec—cu—what-do-you-call-'um am.

CUTE: Well, now, I calculate I've hit upon about the right thing. Why should I degrade the manly dignity of the Cutes by becoming a beggar—expose myself to the chance of receiving the cold shoulder as a poor relation? By chowder, my blood biles as I think of it! Topsy, you can make my fortune, and your own, too. I've an idee in my head that is worth a million of dollars.

TOPSY: Golly! is your head worth dat? Guess you wouldn't bring dat out South for de whole of you.

CUTE: Don't you be too severe, now, Charcoal; I'm a man of genius. Did you ever hear of Barnum?

TOPSY: Barnum! Barnum! Does he live out South?

CUTE: No, he lives in New York. Do you know how he made his fortin?

TOPSY: What is him fortin, hey? Is it something he wears?

CUTE: Chowder, how green you are!

TOPSY (*indignantly*): Sar, I hab you to know I's not green; I's brack.

CUTE: To be sure you are, Day & Martin. I calculate, when a person says another has a fortune, he means he's got plenty of money, Charcoal.

TOPSY: And did he make the money?

CUTE: Sartin sure, and no mistake.

TOPSY: Golly! now I thought money always growed.

CUTE: Oh, git out! You are too cute—you are cuter than I am; and I'm Cute by name and cute by nature. Well, as I was saying, Barnum made his money by exhibiting a *woolly* horse; now wouldn't it be an all-fired speculation to show you as the woolly gal?

TOPSY: You want to make a sight of me?

CUTE: I'll give you half the receipts, by chowder!

TOSPY: Should I have to leave Miss Feely?

CUTE: To be sure you would.

TOPSY: Den you hab to get a woolly gal somewhere else, Mas'r Cute. (*Runs off.*)

CUTE: There's another speculation gone to smash, by chowder! (*Exit.*)

SCENE 3. *A rude chamber*

(TOM *is discovered, in old clothes, seated on a stool; he holds in his hand a paper containing a curl of* EVA's *hair. The scene opens to the symphony of "Old Folks at Home."*)

TOM: I have come to de dark places; I's going through de vale of shadows. My heart sinks at times and feels just like a big lump of lead. Den it gits up in my throat and chokes me till de tears roll out of my eyes; den I take out dis curl of little Miss Eva's hair, and the sight of it brings calm to my mind and I feels strong again. (*Kisses the curl and puts it in his breast—takes out a silver dollar, which is suspended around his neck by a string.*) Dere's de bright silver dollar dat Mas'r George Shelby gave me the day I was sold away from Old Kentuck, and I've kept it ever since. Mas'r George must have grown to be a man by this time. I wonder if I shall ever see him again.

SONG. *"Old Folks at Home."*

(*Enter* LEGREE, EMMELINE, SAMBO *and* QUIMBO.)

LEGREE: Shut up, you black cuss! Did you think I wanted any of your infernal howling? (*Turns to* EMMELINE.) We've home. (EMMELINE *shrinks from him. He takes hold of her ear.*) You didn't ever wear earrings?

EMMELINE (*trembling*): No, master.

LEGREE: Well, I'll give you a pair, if you're a good girl. You needn't be so frightened; I don't mean to make you work very hard. You'll have fine times with me and live like a lady; only be a good girl.

EMMELINE: My soul sickens as his eyes gaze upon me. His touch makes my very flesh creep.

LEGREE (*turns to* TOM, *and points to* SAMBO *and* QUIMBO): Ye see what ye'd get if ye'd try to run off. These yer boys have been raised to track niggers, and they'd just as soon chaw one on ye up as eat their suppers; so mind yourself. (*To* EMMELINE.) Come, mistress, you go in here with me. (*Taking* EMMELINE's *hand, and leading her away.*)

EMMELINE (*withdrawing her hand, and shrinking back*): No, no! let me work in the fields; I don't want to be a lady.

LEGREE: Oh! you're going to be contrary, are you? I'll soon take all that out of you.

EMMELINE: Kill me, if you will.

LEGREE: Oh! you want to be killed, do you? Now, come here, you Tom—you see I told you I didn't buy you jest for the common work; I mean to promote you and make a driver of you, and to-night ye may jest as well begin to get yer hand in. Now, ye jest take this yer gal, and flog her; ye've seen enough on't to know how.

TOM: I beg mas'r's pardon—hopes mas'r won't set me at that. It's what I ain't used to—never did, and can't do—no way possible.

LEGREE: Ye'll larn a pretty smart chance of things ye never did know before I've done with ye. (*Strikes* TOM *with whip, three blows. Music chord each blow.*) There! now will ye tell me ye can't do it?

TOM: Yes, mas'r! I'm willing to work night and day, and work while there's life and breath in me; but this yer thing I can't feel it right to do, and, mas'r, I *never* shall do it, *never!*

LEGREE: What! ye black beast! tell *me* ye don't think it right to do what I tell ye! What have any of you cussed cattle to do with thinking what's right? I'll put a stop to it. Why, what do ye think ye are? Maybe ye think yer a gentleman, master Tom, to be telling your master what's right and what ain't! So you pretend it's wrong to flog the gal?

TOM: I think so, mas'r; 'twould be downright cruel, and it's what I never will do, mas'r. If you mean to kill me, kill me; but as to raising my hand agin any one here, I never shall—I'll die first!

LEGREE: Well, here's a pious dog at last, let down among us sinners—powerful holy critter he must be. Here, you rascal! you make believe to be so pious, didn't you never read out of your Bible, "Servants, obey your masters?" Ain't I your master? Didn't I pay twelve hundred dollars, cash, for all there is inside your cussed old black shell? Ain't you mine, body and soul?

TOM: No, no! My soul ain't yours, mas'r; you haven't bought it—ye can't buy it; it's been bought and paid for by one that is able to keep it, and you can't harm it!

LEGREE: I can't? we'll see, we'll see! Here, Sambo! Quimbo! give this dog such a breaking in as he won't get over this month!

EMMELINE: Oh, no! you will not be so cruel—have some mercy! (*Clings to* TOM.)

LEGREE: Mercy? you won't find any in this shop! Away with the black cuss! Flog him within an inch of his life!

(SAMBO *and* QUIMBO *seize* TOM *and drag him up stage.* LEGREE *seizes* EMMELINE, *and throws her. She falls on her knees, with her hands lifted in supplication.* LEGREE *raises his whip, as if to strike* TOM. *Picture.*)

SCENE 4. *Plain chamber*

(*Enter* OPHELIA, *followed by* TOPSY.)

OPHELIA: A person inquiring for me, did you say, Topsy?

TOPSY: Yes, missis.

OPHELIA: What kind of a looking man is he?

TOPSY: By golly! he's very queer looking man, anyway; and den he talks so dre'ful funny. What does you think?—yah! yah! he wanted to 'xibite me as de woolly gal! yah! yah!

OPHELIA: Oh! I understand. Some cute Yankee, who wants to purchase you, to make a show of—the heartless wretch!

TOPSY: Dat's just him, missis; dat's just his name. He tole me dat it was Cute—Mr. Cute Speculashum—dat's him.

OPHELIA: What did you say to him, Topsy?

TOPSY: Well, I didn't say much; it was brief and to the point—I tole him I wouldn't leave you, Miss Feely, no how.

OPHELIA: That's right, Topsy; you know you are very comfortable here—you wouldn't fare quite so well if you went away among strangers.

TOPSY: By golly! I know dat; you takes care on me, and makes me good. I don't steal any now, and I don't swar, and I don't dance breakdowns. Oh! I isn't so wicked as I used to was.

OPHELIA: That's right, Topsy; now show the gentleman, or whatever he is, up.

TOPSY: By golly! I guess he won't make much out of Miss Feely. (*Exit.*)

OPHELIA: I wonder who this person can be? Perhaps it is some old acquaintance, who has heard of my arrival, and who comes on a social visit.

(*Enter* CUTE.)

CUTE: Aunt, how do ye do? Well, I swan, the sight of you is good for weak eyes. (*Offers his hand.*)

OPHELIA (*coldly drawing back*): Really, sir, I can't say that I ever had the pleasure of seeing you before.

CUTE: Well, it's a fact that you never did. You see I never happened to be in your neighborhood afore now. Of course you've heard of me? I'm one of the Cutes—Gumption Cute, the first and only son of Josiah and Maria Cute, of Oniontown, on the Onion river, in the north part of this ere State of Varmount.

OPHELIA: Can't say I ever heard the name before.

CUTE: Well then, I calculate your memory must be a little ricketty. I'm a relation of yours.

OPHELIA: A relation of mine! Why, I never heard of any Cutes in our family.

CUTE: Well, I shouldn't wonder if you never did. Don't you remember your niece, Mary?

OPHELIA: Of course I do. What a shiftless question!

CUTE: Well, you see, my second cousin, Abijah Blake, married her; so you see that makes me a relation of yours.

OPHELIA: Rather a distant one, I should say.

CUTE: By chowder! I'm *near* enough, just at present.

OPHELIA: Well, you certainly are a sort of connection of mine.

CUTE: Yes, kind of sort of.

OPHELIA: And of course you are welcome to my house, as long as you choose to make it your home.

CUTE: By chowder! I'm booked for the next six months—this isn't a bad speculation.

OPHELIA: I hope you left all your folks well at home?

CUTE: Well, yes, they're pretty comfortably disposed of. Father and mother's dead, and Uncle Josh has gone to California. I am the only representative of the Cutes left.

OPHELIA: There doesn't seem to be a great deal of *you* left. I declare, you are positively in rags.

CUTE: Well, you see, the fact is, I've been speculating—trying to get bank-notes—specie-rags, as they say—but I calculate I've turned out rags of another sort.

OPHELIA: I'm sorry for your ill luck, but I am afraid you have been shiftless.

CUTE: By chowder! I've done all that a fellow could do. You see, somehow, everything I take hold of kind of bursts up.

OPHELIA: Well, well, perhaps you'll do better for the future; make yourself at home. I have got to see to some household matters, so excuse me for a short time. (*Aside.*) Impudent and shiftless! (*Exit.*)

CUTE: By chowder! I rather guess that this speculation will hitch. She's a good-natured old critter; I reckon I'll be a son to her while she lives, and take care of her valuables arter she's a defunct departed. I wonder if they keep the vittles in this ere room? Guess not. I've got extensive accommodations for all sorts of eatables. I'm a regular vacuum, throughout —pockets and all. I'm chuck full of emptiness. (*Looks out.*) Halloa! who's this elderly individual coming upstairs? He looks like a compound essence of starch and dignity. I wonder if he isn't another relation of mine. I should like a rich old fellow now for an uncle.

(*Enter* DEACON PERRY.)

DEACON: Ha! a stranger here!

CUTE: How d'ye do?

DEACON: You are a friend to Miss Ophelia, I presume?

CUTE: Well, I rather calculate that I am a leetle more than a friend.

DEACON (*aside*): Bless me! what can he mean by those mysterious words? Can he be her—no, I don't think he can. She said she wasn't—well, at all events, it's very suspicious.

CUTE: The old fellow seems kind of stuck up.

DEACON: You are a particular friend to Miss Ophelia, you say?

CUTE: Well, I calculate I am.

DEACON: Bound to her by any tender tie?

CUTE: It's something more than a tie—it's a regular double-twisted knot.

DEACON: Ah! just as I suspected. (*Aside.*) Might I inquire the nature of that tie?

CUTE: Well, it's the natural tie of relationship.

DEACON: A relation—what relation!

CUTE: Why, you see, my second cousin, Abijah Blake, married her niece, Mary.

DEACON: Oh! is that all?

CUTE: By chowder, ain't that enough?

DEACON: Then you are not her husband?

CUTE: To be sure I ain't. What put that 'ere idee into your cranium?

DEACON (*shaking him vigorously by the hand*): My dear sir, I'm delighted to see you.

CUTE: Holloa! you ain't going slightly insane, are you?

DEACON: No, no fear of that; I'm only happy, that's all.

CUTE: I wonder if he's been taking a nipper?

DEACON: As you are a relation of Miss Ophelia's, I think it proper that I should make you my confidant; in fact, let you into a little scheme that I have lately conceived.

CUTE: Is it a speculation?

DEACON: Well, it is, just at present; but I trust before many hours to make it a surety.

CUTE: By chowder! I hope it won't serve you the way my speculations have served me. But fire away, old boy, and give us the prospectus.

DEACON: Well, then, my young friend, I have been thinking, ever since Miss Ophelia returned to Vermont, that she was just the person to fill the place of my lamented Molly.

CUTE: Say, you couldn't tell us who your lamented Molly was, could you?

DEACON: Why, the late Mrs. Perry, to be sure.

CUTE: Oh! then the lamented Polly was your wife?

DEACON: She was.

CUTE: And now you wish to marry Miss Ophelia?

DEACON: Exactly.

CUTE (*aside*): Consarn this old porpoise! if I let him do that he'll Jew me out of my living. By chowder! I'll put a spoke in his wheel.

DEACON: Well, what do you say? will you intercede for me with your aunt?

CUTE: No! bust me up if I do!

DEACON: No?

CUTE: No, I tell you. I forbid the bans. Now, ain't you a purty individual, to talk about getting married, you old superannuated Methuselah specimen of humanity! Why, you've got one foot in eternity already, and t'other ain't fit to stand on. Go home and go to bed! have your head shaved, and send for a lawyer to make your will; leave your property to your heirs—if you hain't got any, why leave it to me—I'll take care of it, and charge nothing for the trouble.

DEACON: Really, sir, this language, to one of my standing, is highly indecorous—it's more, sir, than I feel willing to endure, sir. I shall expect an explanation, sir.

CUTE: Now, you see, old gouty toes, you're losing your temper.

DEACON: Sir, I'm a deacon; I never lost my temper in all my life, sir.

CUTE: Now, you see, you're getting excited; you had better go; we can't have a disturbance here!

DEACON: No, sir! I shall not go, sir! I shall not go until I have seen Miss Ophelia. I wish to know if she will countenance this insult.

CUTE: Now keep cool, old stick-in-the-mud! Draw it mild, old timber-toes!

DEACON: Damn it all, sir, what—

CUTE: Oh! only think, now, what would people say to hear a deacon swearing like a trooper?

DEACON: Sir—I—you—this is too much, sir.

CUTE: Well, now, I calculate that's just about my opinion, so we'll have no more of it. Get out of this! start your boots, or by chowder! I'll pitch you from one end of the stairs to the other.

(Enter OPHELIA.)

OPHELIA: Hoity toity! What's the meaning of all these loud words.

CUTE: } (together) { Well, you see, Aunt—
DEACON: } { Miss Ophelia, I beg—

CUTE: Now, look here, you just hush your yap! How can I fix up matters if you keep jabbering?

OPHELIA: Silence! for shame, Mr. Cute. Is that the way you speak to the deacon?

CUTE: Darn the deacon!

OPHELIA: Deacon Perry, what is all this?

DEACON: Madam, a few words will explain everything. Hearing from this person that he was your nephew, I ventured to tell him that I cherished hopes of making you my wife, whereupon he flew into a violent passion, and ordered me out of the house.

OPHELIA: Does this house belong to you or me, Mr. Cute?

CUTE: Well, to you, I reckon.

OPHELIA: Then how dare you give orders in it?

CUTE: Well, I calculated you wouldn't care about marrying old half-a-century there.

OPHELIA: That's enough; I will marry him; and as for you, (points to the right) get out.

CUTE: Get out?

OPHELIA: Yes; the sooner the better.

CUTE: Darned if I don't serve him our first though.

(CUTE makes a dash at DEACON, who gets behind OPHELIA. TOPSY enters with a broom and beats CUTE around stage. OPHELIA faints in DEACON's arms. CUTE falls, and TOPSY butts him, keeling over him. Quick drop.)

ACT VI

SCENE 1. Dark landscape. An old, roofless shed.

(TOM is discovered in shed, lying on some old cotton bagging. CASSY kneels by his side, holding a cup to his lips.)

CASSY: Drink all ye want. I knew how it would be. It isn't the first time I've been out in the night, carrying water to such as you.

TOM (returning cup): Thank you, missis.

CASSY: Don't call me missis. I'm a miserable slave like yourself—a lower one than you can ever be! It's no use, my poor fellow, this you've been trying to do. You were a brave fellow. You had the right on your side; but it's all in vain for you to struggle. You are in the Devil's hands: he is the strongest, and you must give up.

TOM: Oh! how can I give up?

CASSY: You see you don't know anything about it; I do. Here you are, on a lone plantation, ten miles from any other, in the swamps; not a white person here who could testify, if you were burned alive. There's no law here that can do you, or any of us, the least good; and this man! there's no earthly thing that he is not bad enough to do. I could make one's hair rise, and their teeth chatter, if I should only tell what I've seen and been knowing to here; and it's no use resisting! Did I want to live with him? Wasn't I a woman delicately bred? and he! —Father in Heaven! what was he and is he? And yet I've lived with him these five years, and cursed every moment of my life, night and day.

TOM: Oh, heaven! have you quite forgot us poor critters?

CASSY: And what are these miserable low dogs you work with, that you should suffer on their account? Every one of them would turn against you the first time they get a chance. They are all of them as low and cruel to each other as they can be; there's no use in your suffering to keep from hurting them!

TOM: What made 'em cruel? If I give out, I shall get used to it and grow, little by little, just like 'em. No, no, missis, I've lost everything, wife, and children, and home, and a kind master, and he would have set me free if he'd only lived a day longer—I've lost everything in *this* world, and now I can't lose heaven, too; no, I can't get to be wicked besides all.

CASSY: But it can't be that He will lay sin to our account; he won't charge it to us when we are forced to it; he'll charge it to them that drove us to it. Can I do anything more for you? Shall I give you some more water?

TOM: Oh missis! I wish you'd go to Him who can give you living waters!

CASSY: Go to Him! Where is He? Who is He?

TOM: Our Heavenly Father!

CASSY: I used to see the picture of Him, over the altar, when I was a girl; but *he isn't here!* there's nothing here but sin, and long, long despair! There, there, don't talk any more, my poor fellow. Try to sleep, if you can. I must hasten back, lest my absence be noted. Think of me when I am gone, Uncle Tom, and pray, pray for me. (*Exit* CASSY. TOM *sinks back to sleep.*)

SCENE 2. *Street in New Orleans*

(*Enter* GEORGE SHELBY.)

GEORGE: At length my mission of mercy is nearly finished; I have reached my journey's end. I have now but to find the house of Mr. St. Clare, re-purchase old Uncle Tom, and convey him back to his wife and children, in old Kentucky. Some one approaches; he may, perhaps, be able to give me the information I require. I will accost him.

(*Enter* MARKS.)

Pray, sir, can you tell me where Mr. St. Clare dwells?

MARKS: Where I don't think you'll be in a hurry to seek him.

GEORGE: And where is that?

MARKS: In the grave!

GEORGE: Stay, sir! you may be able to give me some information concerning Mr. St. Clare.

MARKS: I beg pardon, sir, I am a lawyer; I can't afford to *give* anything.

GEORGE: But you would have no objections to selling it?

MARKS: Not the slightest.

GEORGE: What do you value it at?

MARK: Well, say five dollars, that's reasonable.

GEORGE: There they are. (*Gives money.*) Now answer me to the best of your ability. Has the death of St. Clare caused his slaves to be sold?

MARKS: It has.

GEORGE: How were they sold?

MARKS: At auction—they went dirt cheap.

GEORGE: How were they bought—all in one lot?

MARKS: No, they went to different bidders.

GEORGE: Was you present at the sale?

MARKS: I was.

GEORGE: Do you remember seeing a negro among them called Tom.

MARKS: What, Uncle Tom?

GEORGE: The same—who bought him?

MARKS: A Mr. Legree.

GEORGE: Where is his plantation?

MARKS: Up in Louisiana, on the Red River; but a man never could find it unless he had been there before.

GEORGE: Who could I get to direct me there?

MARKS: Well, stranger, I don't know of any one just at present, 'cept myself, could find it for you; it's such an out-of-the-way sort of hole; and if you are a mind to come down handsomely, why, I'll do it.

GEORGE: The reward shall be ample.

MARKS: Enough said, stranger; let's take the steamboat at once. (*Exeunt.*)

SCENE 3. *A rough chamber*

(*Enter* LEGREE. *Sits.*)

LEGREE: Plague on that Sambo, to kick up this yer row between me and the new hands.

(CASSY *steals on, and stands behind him.*)

The fellow won't be fit to work for a week now, right in the press of the season.

CASSY: Yes, just like you.

LEGREE: Hah! you she-devil! you've come back, have you? (*Rises.*)

CASSY: Yes, I have; come to have my own way, too.

LEGREE: You lie, you jade! I'll be up to my word. Either behave yourself, or stay down in the quarters and fare and work with the rest.

CASSY: I'd rather, ten thousand times, live in the dirtiest hole in the quarters, than be under your hoof!

LEGREE: But you are under my hoof, for all that, that's one comfort; so sit down here and listen to reason. (*Grasps her wrist.*)

CASSY: Simon Legree, take care! (LEGREE *lets go his hold.*) You're afraid of me, Simon, and you've reason to be; for I've got the Devil in me!

LEGREE: I believe to my soul you have. After all, Cassy, why can't you be friends with me, as you used to?

CASSY (*bitterly*): Used to!

LEGREE: I wish, Cassy, you'd behave yourself decently.

CASSY: *You* talk about behaving decently! and what have you been doing? You haven't even sense enough to keep from spoiling one of your best hands, right in the most pressing season, just for your devilish temper.

LEGREE: I was a fool, it's a fact, to let any such brangle come up; but when Tom set up his will he had to be broke in.

CASSY: You'll never break *him* in.

LEGREE: Won't I? I'd like to know if I won't! He'll be the first nigger that ever come it round me! I'll break every bone in his body but he shall give up.

(*Enter* SAMBO, *with a paper in his hand; he stands bowing.*)

LEGREE: What's that, you dog?

SAMBO: It's a witch thing, mas'r.

LEGREE: A what?

SAMBO: Something that niggers gits from witches. Keep 'em from feeling when they's flogged. He had it tied round his neck with a black string.

(LEGREE *takes the paper and opens it. A silver dollar drops on the stage, and a long curl of light hair twines around his finger.*)

LEGREE: Damnation. (*Stamping and writhing, as if the hair burned him.*) Where did this come from? Take if off! burn it up! burn it up! (*Throws the curl away.*) What did you bring it to me for?

SAMBO (*trembling*): I beg pardon, mas'r; I thought you would like to see 'um.

LEGREE: Don't you bring me any more of your devilish things. (*Shakes his fist at* SAMBO *who runs off.* LEGREE *kicks the dollar after him.*) Blast it! where did he get that? If it didn't look just like—whoo! I thought I'd forgot that. Curse me if I think there's any such thing as forgetting anything, any how.

CASSY: What is the matter with you, Legree? What is there in a simple curl of fair hair to appal a man like you—you who are familiar with every form of cruelty.

LEGREE: Cassy, to-night the past has been recalled to me—the past that I have so long and vainly striven to forget.

CASSY: Hast aught on this earth power to move a soul like thine?

LEGREE: Yes, for hard and reprobate as I now seem, there has been a time when I have been rocked on the bosom of a mother, cradled with prayers and pious hymns, my now seared brow bedewed with the waters of holy baptism.

CASSIE (*aside*): What sweet memories of childhood can thus soften down that heart of iron?

LEGREE: In early childhood a fair-haired woman has led me, at the sound of Sabbath bells, to worship and to pray. Born of a hard-tempered sire, on whom that gentle woman had wasted a world of unvalued love, I followed in the steps of my father. Boisterous, unruly and tyrannical, I despised all her counsel, and would have none of her reproof, and, at an early age, broke from her to seek my fortunes on the sea. I never came home but once after that; and then my mother, with the yearning of a heart that must love something, and had nothing else to love, clung to me, and sought with passionate prayers and entreaties to win me from a life of sin.

CASSY: That was your day of grace, Legree; then good angels called you, and mercy held you by the hand.

LEGREE: My heart inly relented; there was a conflict, but sin got the victory, and I set all the force of my rough nature against the conviction of my conscience. I drank and swore, was wilder and more brutal than ever. And one night, when my mother, in the last agony of her despair, knelt at my feet, I spurned her from me, threw her senseless on the floor, and with brutal curses fled to my ship.

CASSY: Then the fiend took thee for his own.

LEGREE: The next I heard of my mother was one night while I was carousing among drunken companions. A letter was put in my hands. I opened it, and a lock of long, curling hair fell from it, and twined about my fingers, even as that lock twined but now. The letter told me that my mother was dead, and that dying she blest and forgave me! (*Buries his face in his hands.*)

CASSY: Why did you not even then renounce your evil ways?

LEGREE: There is a dread, unhallowed necromancy of evil, that turns things sweetest and holiest to phantoms of horror and affright. That pale, loving mother,—her dying prayers, her forgiving love,—wrought in my demoniac heart of sin only as a damning sentence, bringing with it a fearful looking for of judgment and fiery indignation.

CASSY: And yet you would not strive to avert the doom that threatened you.

LEGREE: I burned the lock of hair and I burned the letter; and when I saw them hissing and crackling in the flame, inly shuddered as I thought of everlasting fires! I tried to drink and revel, and swear away the memory; but often in the deep night, whose solemn stillness arraigns the soul in forced communion with itself, I have seen that pale mother rising by my bed-side, and felt the soft twining of that hair around my fingers, 'till the cold sweat would roll down my face, and I would spring from my bed in horror—horror! (*Falls in chair. After a pause.*) What the devil ails me? Large drops of sweat stand on my forehead, and my heart beats heavy and thick with fear. I thought I saw something white rising and glimmering in the gloom before me, and it seemed to bear my mother's face! I know one thing; I'll let that fellow Tom alone, after this. What did I want with his cussed paper? I believe I am bewitched sure enough! I've been shivering and sweating ever since! Where did he get that hair? It couldn't have been that! I *burn'd* that up, I know I did! It would be a joke if hair could rise from the dead! I'll have Sambo and Quimbo up here to sing and dance one of their dances, and keep off these horrid notions. Here, Sambo! Quimbo! (*Exit.*)

CASSY: Yes, Legree, that golden tress was charmed; each hair had in it a spell of terror and remorse for thee, and was used by a mightier power to bind thy cruel hands from inflicting uttermost evil on the helpless! (*Exit.*)

SCENE 4. *Street*

(*Enter* MARKS, *meeting* CUTE, *who enters, dressed in an old faded uniform.*)

MARKS: By the land, stranger, but it strikes me that I've seen you somewhere before.

CUTE: By chowder! do you know now, that's just what I was going to say?

MARKS: Isn't your name Cute?

CUTE: You're right, I calculate. Yours is Marks, I reckon.

MARKS: Just so.

CUTE: Well, I swow, I'm glad to see you. (*They shake hands.*) How's your wholesome?

MARKS: Hearty as ever. Well, who would have thought of ever seeing you again. Why, I thought you was in Vermont?

CUTE: Well, so I was. You see I went there after that rich relation of mine—but the speculation didn't turn out well.

MARKS: How so?

CUTE: Why, you see, she took a shine to an old fellow—Deacon Abraham Perry—and married him.

MARKS: Oh, that rather put your nose out of joint in that quarter.

CUTE: Busted me right up, I tell you. The deacon did the handsome thing though; he said if I would leave the neighbourhood and go out South again, he'd stand the damage. I calculate I didn't give him much time to change his mind, and so, you see, here I am again.

MARKS: What are you doing in that soldier rig?

CUTE: Oh, this is my sign.

MARKS: Your sign?

CUTE: Yes; you see, I'm engaged just at present in an all-fired good speculation; I'm a Fillibusterow.

MARKS: A what?

CUTE: A Fillibusterow! Don't you know what that is? It's Spanish for Cuban Volunteer; and means a chap that goes the whole porker for glory and all that ere sort of thing.

MARKS: Oh! you've joined the order of the Lone Star!

CUTE: You've hit it. You see I bought this uniform at a second-hand clothing store; I puts it on and goes to a benevolent individual and I says to him,—appealing to his feelings,—I'm one of the fellows that went to Cuba and got massacred by the bloody Spaniards. I'm in a destitute condition—give me a trifle to pay my passage back, so I can whop the tyrannical cusses and avenge my brave fellow soger what got slewed there.

MARKS: How pathetic!

CUTE: I tell you it works up the feelings of benevolent individuals dreadfully. It draws tears from their eyes and money from their pockets. By chowder! one old chap gave me a hundred dollars to help on the cause.

MARKS: I admire a genius like yours.

CUTE: But I say, what are you up to?

MARKS: I am the travelling companion of a young gentleman by the name of Shelby, who is going to the plantation of a Mr. Legree, on the Red River, to buy an old darky who used to belong to his father.

CUTE: Legree—Legree? Well, now, I calculate I've heard that ere name afore.

MARKS: Do you remember that man who drew a bowie knife on you in New Orleans?

CUTE: By chowder! I remember the circumstance just as well as if it was yesterday; but I can't say that I recollect much about the man, for you see I was in something of a hurry about that time and didn't stop to take a good look at him.

MARKS: Well, that man was this same Mr. Legree.

CUTE: Do you know, now, I should like to pay that critter off?

MARKS: Then I'll give you an opportunity.

CUTE: Chowder! how will you do that?

MARKS: Do you remember the gentleman that interfered between you and Legree?

CUTE: Yes—well?

MARKS: He received the blow that was intended for you, and died from the effects of it. So, you see, Legree is a murderer, and we are the only witnesses of the deed. His life is in our hands.

CUTE: Let's have him right up and make him dance on nothing to the tune of Yankee Doodle!

MARKS: Stop a bit. Don't you see a chance for a profitable speculation?

CUTE: A speculation! Fire away, don't be bashful; I'm the man for a speculation.

MARKS: I have made a deposition to the Governor of the State of all the particulars of that affair at Orleans.

CUTE: What did you do that for?

MARKS: To get a warrant for his arrest.

CUTE: Oh! and have you got it?

MARKS: Yes; here it is. (*Takes out paper.*)

CUTE: Well, now, I don't see how you are going to make anything by that bit of paper?

MARKS: But I do. I shall say to Legree, I have got a warrant against you for murder; my friend, Mr. Cute, and myself are the only witnesses who can appear against you. Give us a thousand dollars, and we will tear up the warrant and be silent.

CUTE: Then Mr. Legree forks over a thousand dollars, and your friend Cute pockets five hundred of it. Is that the calculation?

MARKS: If you will join me in the undertaking.

CUTE: I'll do it, by chowder!

MARKS: Your hand to bind the bargain.

CUTE: I'll stick by you thro' thick and thin.

MARKS: Enough said.

CUTE: Then shake. (*They shake hands.*)

MARKS: But I say, Cute, he may be contrary and show fight.

CUTE: Never mind, we've got the law on our side, and we're bound to stir him up. If he don't come down handsomely, we'll present him with a neck-tie made of hemp!

MARKS: I declare you're getting spunky.

CUTE: Well, I reckon I am. Let's go and have something to drink. Tell you what, Marks, if we don't get *him,* we'll have his hide, by chowder! (*Exeunt, arm in arm.*)

SCENE 5. *Rough chamber*

(*Enter* LEGREE, *followed by* SAMBO.)

LEGREE: Go and send Cassy to me.

SAMBO: Yes, mas'r. (*Exit.*)

LEGREE: Curse the woman! she's got a temper worse than the devil! I shall do her an injury one of these days if she isn't careful.

(*Re-enter* SAMBO, *frightened.*)

What's the matter with you, you black scoundrel?

SAMBO: S'help me, mas'r, she isn't dere.

LEGREE: I suppose she's about the house somewhere?

SAMBO: No, she isn't, mas'r; I's been all over de house and I can't find nothing of her nor Emmeline.

LEGREE: Bolted, by the Lord! Call out the dogs! saddle my horse! Stop! are you sure they really have gone?

SAMBO: Yes, mas'r; I's been in every room 'cept the haunted garret, and dey wouldn't go dere.

LEGREE: I have it! Now, Sambo, you jest go and walk that Tom up here, right away! (*Exit* SAMBO.) The old cuss is at the bottom of this yer whole matter; and I'll have it out of his infernal black hide, or I'll know the reason why! I *hate* him—I *hate* him! And isn't he *mine?* Can't I do what I like with him? Who's to hinder, I wonder?

(TOM *is dragged on by* SAMBO *and* QUIMBO.)

LEGREE (*grimly confronting* TOM): Well, Tom, do you know I've made up my mind to *kill* you?

TOM: It's very likely, Mas'r.

LEGREE: I—*have—done—just—that—thing,* Tom, unless you tell me what do you know about these yer gals? (TOM *is silent.*) D'ye hear? Speak!

TOM: I hain't got anything to tell, mas'r.

LEGREE: Do you dare to tell me, you old black rascal, you don't know? Speak! Do you know anything?

TOM: I know, mas'r; but I can't tell anything. I *can die!*

LEGREE: Hark ye, Tom! ye think, 'cause I have let you off before, I don't mean what I say; but, this time, I have made *up my mind,* and counted the cost. You've always stood it out agin me; now, I'll *conquer ye or kill ye!* one or t'other. I'll count every drop of blood there is in you, and take 'em one by one, 'till ye give up!

TOM: Mas'r, if you was sick, or in trouble, or dying, and I could save, I'd *give* you my heart's blood; and, if taking every drop of blood in this poor old body would save your precious soul, I'd give 'em freely. Do the worst you can, my troubles will be over soon; but if you don't repent, yours won't never end.

(LEGREE *strikes* TOM *down with the butt of his whip.*)

LEGREE: How do you like that?

SAMBO: He's most gone, mas'r!

TOM (*rises feebly on his hands*): There ain't no more you can do! I forgive you with all my soul. (*Sinks back, and is carried off by* SAMBO *and* QUIMBO.)

LEGREE: I believe he's done for finally. Well, his mouth is shut up at last—that's one comfort.

(*Enter* GEORGE SHELBY, MARKS *and* CUTE.)

Strangers! Well, what do you want?

GEORGE: I understand that you bought in New Orleans a negro named Tom?

LEGREE: Yes, I did buy such a fellow, and a devil of a bargain I had of it, too! I believe he's trying to die, but I don't know as he'll make it out.

GEORGE: Where is he? Let me see him!

SAMBO: Dere he is! (*Points to* TOM.)

LEGREE: How dare you speak? (*Drives* SAMBO *and* QUIMBO *off.* GEORGE *exits.*)

CUTE: Now's the time to nab him.

MARKS: How are you, Mr. Legree?

LEGREE: What the devil brought you here?

MARKS: This little bit of paper. I arrest you for the murder of Mr. St. Clare. What do you say to that?

LEGREE: This is my answer! (*Makes a blow at* MARKS, *who dodges, and* CUTE *receives the blow. He cries out and runs off.* MARKS *fires at* LEGREE, *and follows* CUTE.) I am hit!—the game's up! (*Falls dead.* QUIMBO *and* SAMBO *return and carry him off laughing.*)

(GEORGE SHELBY *enters, supporting* TOM. *Music. They advance and* TOM *falls, centre.*)

GEORGE: Oh! dear Uncle Tom! do wake—do speak once more! look up! Here's Master George—your own little Master George. Don't you know me?

TOM (*opening his eyes and speaking in a feeble tone*): Mas'r George! Bless de Lord! it's all I wanted! They hav'n't forgot me! It warms my soul; it does my old heart good! Now I shall die content!

GEORGE: You sha'n't die! you mustn't die, nor think of it. I have come to buy you, and take you home.

TOM: Oh, Mas'r George, you're too late. The Lord has bought me, and is going to take me home.

GEORGE: Oh! don't die. It will kill me—it will break my heart to think what you have suffered, poor, poor fellow!

TOM: Don't call me poor fellow. I *have* been poor fellow; but that's all past and gone now. I'm right in the door, going into glory! Oh, Mas'r George! *Heaven has come!* I've got the victory! the Lord has given it to me! Glory be to His name! (*Dies.*)

(*Solemn music.* GEORGE *covers* UNCLE TOM *with his cloak, and kneels over him. Clouds work on and conceal them, and then work off.*)

SCENE 7. (*Gorgeous clouds, tinted with sunlight.* EVA, *robed in white, is discovered on the back of a milk-white dove, with expanded wings, as if just soaring upward. Her hands are extended in benediction over* ST. CLARE *and* UNCLE TOM, *who are kneeling and gazing up to her. Impressive music. Slow curtain.*)

THE END

Dion Boucicault: *The Octoroon* (1859)

Although he was born in Dublin and achieved his first great stage successes in London, Boucicault played an important part in the American theater. He was lured across the ocean by an actress, Agnes Robertson, whom he married in 1853. He not only wrote for her, but he also acted with her in many dramas. Like most theatrical people of the time, Boucicault was an all-round talent in the theater rather than a specialist. He did write 400 dramas, including many adaptations of novels and translations of French plays, but he never lost his interest in acting.

His great successes began in his early twenties with *London Assurance*, which was revived by the Royal Shakespeare Company in 1978. *The Colleen Bawn* (1860), *Arrah-na-Pogue* (1864), *The Shaughraun* (1874) and *The Octoroon* are his best-known plays. His output was so immense that he must be considered one of the two or three most productive playwrights of all time. Boucicault is credited with having developed the nineteenth-century sentimental, melodramatic play of immense popular appeal and equally immense commercial success.

The Octoroon ranks among his most successful plays. Its theme was clearly controversial when it played in 1859 because a lengthy debate had been going on in America over the issue of slavery. The original material for the drama came from the novel, *The Quadroon,* by Mayne Reid (1856), but Boucicault's adaptation was quite liberal, particularly in terms of the depth he added to the characters. Boucicault played Wahnotee and his wife played Zoe, the Octoroon.

The play was popular in most regions of America, which may well be a strike against it in a sense. The northerners saw the play as anti-slavery, while the southerners loved the sympathetic portrait of the difficulties of life on the plantations. Southerners thrilled to the thought that the arch-villain of the drama, M'Closky, was a transplanted Connecticut Yankee. Yankees in general are sadly portrayed in the play, including the well-meaning Scudder; this helped the southerners respond warmly to the play. But the fact that North and South enjoyed the play equally indicates that *The Octoroon* really takes no explicit stand against the enslavement of blacks in America, and that Boucicault was adept at making his play offend no one.

On the other hand, it is fair to say that Boucicault uses the play to explore some of the implications of slavery in general. Zoe's transformation from a free woman to a slave, while not developed as fully as it might be, is touching and intense. Moreover, Zoe is a victim of laws that prevent marriage across racial lines, and in 1859 it was quite an achievement for Boucicault to convince anyone, North or South, that such a law might not be good. When Zoe is about to die, she says she is heading for a world in which color is not a bar between people, and in which there is not law, but justice. In a rather telling change, the play ended happily with Zoe able to marry George—but only on the London stage. In America, because of the laws and the sentimental requirements of the time, Zoe had to die. Indeed, the play is much stronger in its American version, since the serious nature of the dramatic complications is thereby felt.

Stage effects were among Boucicault's fortes. The burning ship, the men swimming through the dark water, even the rather novel apparatus of the camera all marked the drama as Boucicault's. He did not originate the concept of the camera as witness to a murder, but it is an interesting touch, carefully prepared for in the portrayal of Scudder as a feckless inventor always tinkering with apparatus of some kind.

The Octoroon is still a strong play. Despite its stereotypical melodramatic plot of the plantation about to be sold to the evil mortgage-holder, and despite its last-minute reprieve from the worst of fates, its straightforwardness and simplicity of language make it possible for us to respond to it positively. Its portrait of blacks is perhaps more complex than we might expect for the time, just as its portrayal of George and Dora is perhaps less complex than might be desired.

Boucicault died in 1890 at the age of 70, with his successes behind him. He had spent his money, run off from his wife, returned to America, and was teaching for $50 a week—a sad ending for the first all-round genius of the American stage.

Selected Readings

Boucicault, Dion. *Forbidden Fruit and Other Plays,* ed. Allardyce Nicoll and F. Theodore Cloak. Princeton: Princeton University Press, 1940.

Enkvist, Nils E. *"The Octoroon* and English Opinions of Slavery." *American Quarterly,* 8 (1956), pp. 166–170.

Faulkner, Seldon. "The Octoroon War." *Educational Theatre Journal*, 15 (1963), pp. 33–38.

Gambone, Kenneth. "Boucicault's Contributions to Theatre." *Ball State Teachers College Forum*, 4 (1963), pp. 73–78.

Hogan, Robert Goode. *Dion Boucicault*. New York: Twayne, 1969.

Walsh, Townsend. *The Career of Dion Boucicault*. New York: Benjamin Blom, 1967.

The Octoroon, or Life in Louisiana

Dion Boucicault

CHARACTERS

GEORGE PEYTON	JACKSON
SALEM SCUDDER	OLD PETE
MR. SUNNYSIDE	PAUL, *a boy slave*
JACOB M'CLOSKY	SOLON
WAHNOTEE	MRS. PEYTON
LAFOUCHE	ZOE
CAPTAIN RATTS	DORA SUNNYSIDE
COLONEL POINTDEXTER	GRACE
JULES THIBODEAUX	MINNIE
JUDGE CAILLOU	DIDO

ACT 1

(*The scene opens on a view of the Plantation Terrebonne, in Louisiana. A branch of the Mississippi is seen winding through the Estate. A low built, but extensive Planter's Dwelling, surrounded with a veranda, and raised a few feet from the ground, occupies the left side. On the right stand a table and chairs.* GRACE *is discovered sitting at breakfast-table with the negro children.*)

(SOLON *enters, from the house.*)

SOLON: Yah! you bomn'ble fry—git out—a gen'leman can't pass for you.

GRACE (*seizing a fly whisk*): Hee!—ha git out!

(*She drives the children away: in escaping they tumble against* SOLON, *who falls with the tray; the children steal the bananas and rolls that fall about.*)

(*Enter* PETE, *who is lame; he carries a mop and pail.*)

PETE: Hey! laws a massey! why, clar out! drop dat banana! I'll murder this yer crowd.

(*He chases children about; they leap over railing at back.*) (*Exit* SOLON.)

Dem little niggers is a judgment upon dis generation.

(*Enter* GEORGE, *from the house.*)

GEORGE: What's the matter, Pete?

PETE: It's dem black trash, Mas'r George; dis ere property wants claring; dem's getting too numerous round: when I gets time I'll kill some on 'em, sure!

GEORGE: They don't seem to be scared by the threat.

PETE: Stop, you varmin! Stop till I get enough of you in one place!

GEORGE: Were they all born on this estate?

PETE: Guess they nebber was born—dem tings! what, dem?—get away! Born here—dem darkies? What, on Terrebonne! Don't b'lieve it, Mas'r George; dem black tings never was born at all; dey swarmed one mornin' on a sassafras tree in the swamp; I cotched 'em; dey ain't no 'count. Don't believe dey'll turn out niggers when dey're growed; dey'll come out sunthin' else.

GRACE: Yes, Mas'r George, dey was born here; and old Pete is fonder on 'em dan he is of his fiddle on a Sunday.

PETE: What? dem tings—dem?—get away. (*Makes blow at the children.*) Born here! dem darkies! What, on Terrebonne? Don't b'lieve it, Mas'r George,—no. One morning dey swarmed on a sassafras tree in de swamp, and I cotched 'em all in a sieve,—dat's how dey come on top of dis yearth—git out, you,—ya, ya! (*Laughs.*) (*Exit* GRACE.)

(*Enter* MRS. PEYTON, *from the house.*)

MRS. PEYTON: So, Pete, you are spoiling those children as usual!

PETE: Dat's right, missus! gib it to ole Pete! he's allers in for it. Git away dere! Ya! if dey ain't all lighted, like coons, on dat snake fence, just out of shot. Look dar! Ya, ya! Dem debils. Ya!

MRS. PEYTON: Pete, do you hear?

PETE: Git down dar! I'm arter you! (*Hobbles off.*)

MRS. PEYTON: You are out early this morning, George.

GEORGE: I was up before daylight. We got the horses saddled, and galloped down the shell road over the Piney Patch; then coasting the Bayou Lake, we crossed the long swamps, by Paul's Path, and so came home again.

MRS. PEYTON (*laughing*): You seem already familiar with the names of every spot on the estate.

(*Enter* PETE, *who arranges breakfast.*)

GEORGE: Just one month ago I quitted Paris. I left that siren city as I would have left a beloved woman.

MRS. PEYTON: No wonder! I dare say you left at least a dozen beloved women there, at the same time.

GEORGE: I feel that I departed amid universal and sincere regret. I left my loves and my creditors equally inconsolable.

MRS. PEYTON: George, you are incorrigible. Ah! you remind me so much of your uncle, the judge.

GEORGE: Bless his dear old handwriting, it's all I ever saw of him. For ten years his letters came every quarter-day, with a remittance and a word of advice in his formal cavalier style; and then a joke in the postcript, that upset the dignity of the foregoing. Aunt, when he died, two years ago, I read over those letters of his, and if I didn't cry like a baby—

MRS. PEYTON: No, George; say you wept like a man. And so you really kept those foolish letters?

GEORGE: Yes; I kept the letters, and squandered the money.

MRS. PEYTON (*embracing him*): Ah! why were you not my son—you are so like my dear husband.

(*Enter* SALEM SCUDDER.)

SCUDDER: Ain't he! Yes—when I saw him and Miss Zoe galloping through the green sugar crop, and doing ten dollars' worth of damage at every stride, says I, how like his old uncle he do make the dirt fly.

GEORGE: O, aunt! what a bright, gay creature she is!

SCUDDER: What, Zoe! Guess that you did n't leave anything female in Europe that can lift an eyelash beside that gal. When she goes along, she just leaves a streak of love behind her. It's a good drink to see her come into the cotton fields —the niggers get fresh on the sight of her. If she ain't worth her weight in sunshine you may take one of my fingers off, and choose which you like.

MRS. PEYTON: She need not keep us waiting breakfast, though. Pete, tell Miss Zoe that we are waiting.

PETE: Yes, missus. Why, Minnie, why don't you run when you hear, you lazy crittur? (*Minnie runs off.*) Dat's de laziest nigger on dis yere property. (*Sitting down.*) Don't do nuffin.

MRS. PEYTON: My dear George, you are left in your uncle's will heir to this estate.

GEORGE: Subject to your life interest and an annuity to Zoe, is it not so?

MRS. PEYTON: I fear that the property is so involved that the strictest economy will scarcely recover it. My dear husband never kept any accounts, and we scarcely know in what condition the estate really is.

SCUDDER: Yes, we do, ma'am; it's in a darned bad condition. Ten years ago the judge took as overseer a bit of Connecticut hardware called M'Closky. The judge did n't understand accounts —the overseer did. For a year or two all went fine. The judge drew money like Bourbon whisky from a barrel, and never turned off the tap. But out it flew, free for everybody or anybody to beg, borrow, or steal. So it went, till one day the judge found the tap would n't run. He looked in to see what stopped it, and pulled out a big mortgage. "Sign that," says the overseer; "it's only a formality." "All right," says the judge, and away went a thousand acres; so at the end of eight years, Jacob M'Closky, Esquire, finds himself proprietor of the richest half of Terrebonne—

GEORGE: But the other half is free.

SCUDDER: No, it ain't; because, just then, what does the judge do, but hire another overseer—a Yankee—a Yankee named Salem Scudder.

MRS. PEYTON: O, no, it was—

SCUDDER: Hold on, now! I'm going to straighten this account clear out. What was this here Scudder? Well, he lived in New York by sittin' with his heels up in front of French's Hotel, and inventin'—

GEORGE: Inventing what?

SCUDDER: Improvements—anything, from a stay-lace to a fire-engine. Well, he cut that for the photographing line. He and his apparatus arrived here, took the judge's likeness and his fancy, who made him overseer right off. Well, sir, what does this Scudder do but introduces his inventions and improvements on this estate. His new cotton gins broke down, the steam sugar-mills burst up, until he finished off with his folly what Mr. M'Closky with his knavery began.

MRS. PEYTON: O, Salem! how can you say so? Have n't you worked like a horse?

SCUDDER: No, ma'am, I worked like an ass —an honest one, and that's all. Now, Mr. George, between the two overseers, you and that good old lady have come to the ground; that is the state of things, just as near as I can fix it. (ZOE *sings without.*)

GEORGE: 'T is Zoe.

SCUDDER: O, I have not spoiled that anyhow. I can't introduce any darned improvement there. Ain't that a cure for old age; it kinder lifts the heart up, don't it?

MRS. PEYTON: Poor child! what will become of her when I am gone? If you have n't spoiled her, I fear I have. She has had the education of a lady.

GEORGE: I have remarked that she is treated by the neighbors with a kind of familiar condescension that annoyed me.

SCUDDER: Don't you know that she is the natural daughter of the judge, your uncle, and that old lady thar just adored anything her husband cared for; and this girl, that another woman would 'a' hated, she loves as if she'd been her own child.

GEORGE: Aunt, I am prouder and happier to be your nephew and heir to the ruins of Terrebonne, than I would have been to have had half Louisiana without you.

(*Enter* ZOE, *from the house.*)

ZOE: Am I late? Ah! Mr. Scudder, good morning.

SCUDDER: Thank'ye. I'm from fair to middlin', like a bamboo cane, much the same all the year round.

ZOE: No; like a sugar cane; so dry outside, one would never think there was so much sweetness within.

SCUDDER: Look here: I can't stand that gal! if I stop here, I shall hug her right off. (*He sees* PETE, *who has set his pail down up stage, and goes to sleep on it.*) If that old nigger ain't asleep, I'm blamed. Hillo! (*He kicks pail from under* PETE, *and lets him down. Exit.*)

PETE: Hi! Debbel's in de pail! Whar's breakfass?

(*Enter* SOLON *and* DIDO *with coffee-pot and dishes.*)

DIDO: Bless'ee, Missey Zoe, here it be. Dere's a dish of penpans—jess taste, Mas'r George— and here's fried bananas; smell 'em do, sa glosh.

PETE: Hole yer tongue, Dido. Whar's de coffee? (*He pours it out.*) If it don't stain de cup, your wicked ole life's in danger, sure! dat right! black as nigger; clar as ice. You may drink dat, Mas'r George. (*Looks off.*) Yah! here's Mas'r Sunnyside, and Missey Dora, jist drove up. Some of you niggers run and hole de hosses; and take dis, Dido. (*He gives her coffee-pot to hold, and hobbles off, followed by* SOLON *and* DIDO.)

(*Enter* SUNNYSIDE *and* DORA.)

SUNNYSIDE: Good day, ma'am. (*He shakes hands with George.*) I see we are just in time for breakfast. (*He sits.*)

DORA: O, none for me; I never eat. (*She sits.*)

GEORGE (*aside*): They do not notice Zoe—(*Aloud.*) You don't see Zoe, Mr. Sunnyside.

SUNNYSIDE: Ah! Zoe, girl; are you there?

DORA: Take my shawl, Zoe. (ZOE *helps her.*) What a good creature she is.

SUNNYSIDE: I dare say, now, that in Europe you have never met any lady more beautiful in person, or more polished in manners, than that girl.

GEORGE: You are right, sir; though I shrank from expressing that opinion in her presence, so bluntly.

SUNNYSIDE: Why so?

GEORGE: It may be considered offensive.

SUNNYSIDE (*astonished*): What? I say, Zoe, do you hear that?

DORA: Mr. Peyton is joking.

MRS. PEYTON: My nephew is not acquainted with our customs in Louisiana, but he will soon understand.

GEORGE: Never, aunt! I shall never understand how to wound the feelings of any lady; and, if that is the custom here, I shall never acquire it.

DORA: Zoe, my dear, what does he mean?

ZOE: I don't know.

GEORGE: Excuse me, I'll light a cigar. (*He goes up.*)

DORA (*aside to* ZOE): Is n't he sweet! O, dear, Zoe, is he in love with anybody?

ZOE: How can I tell?

DORA: Ask him, I want to know; don't say I told you to inquire, but find out. Minnie, fan me, it is so nice—and his clothes are French, ain't they?

ZOE: I think so; shall I ask him that too?

DORA: No, dear. I wish he would make love to me. When he speaks to one he does it so easy, so gentle; it is n't bar-room style; love lined with drinks, sighs tinged with tobacco—and they say all the women in Paris were in love with him, which I feel *I* shall be. Stop fanning me; what nice boots he wears.

SUNNYSIDE (*to* MRS. PEYTON): Yes, ma'am, I hold a mortgage over Terrebonne; mine's a ninth, and pretty near covers all the property,

except the slaves. I believe Mr. M'Closky has a bill of sale on them. O, here he is.

(*Enter* M'CLOSKY.)

SUNNYSIDE: Good morning, Mr. M'Closky.

M'CLOSKY: Good morning, Mr. Sunnyside; Miss Dora, your servant.

DORA (*seated*): Fan me, Minnie.—(*Aside.*) I don't like that man.

M'CLOSKY (*aside*): Insolent as usual—(*Aloud.*) You begged me to call this morning. I hope I'm not intruding.

MRS. PEYTON: My nephew, Mr. Peyton.

M'CLOSKY: O, how d' ye do sir? (*He offers his hand,* GEORGE *bows coldly.*) (*Aside.*) A puppy—if he brings any of his European airs here we'll fix him.—(*Aloud.*) Zoe, tell Pete to give my mare a feed, will ye?

GEORGE (*angrily*): Sir!

M'CLOSKY: Hillo! did I tread on ye?

MRS. PEYTON: What is the matter with George?

ZOE (*she takes fan from* MINNIE): Go, Minnie, tell Pete; run! (*Exit* MINNIE.)

MRS. PEYTON: Grace, attend to Mr. M'Closky.

M'CLOSKY: A julep, gal, that's my breakfast, and a bit of cheese.

GEORGE (*aside to* MRS. PEYTON): How can you ask that vulgar ruffian to your table!

MRS. PEYTON: Hospitality in Europe is a courtesy; here, it is an obligation. We tender food to a stranger, not because he is a gentleman, but because he is hungry.

GEORGE: Aunt, I will take my rifle down to the Atchafalaya. Paul has promised me a bear and a deer or two. I see my little Nimrod yonder, with his Indian companion. Excuse me, ladies. Ho! Paul! (*He enters house.*)

PAUL (*outside*): I'ss, Mas'r George.

(*Enter* PAUL *with the Indian.*)

SUNNYSIDE: It's a shame to allow that young cub to run over the swamps and woods, hunting and fishing his life away instead of hoeing cane.

MRS. PEYTON: The child was a favorite of the judge, who encouraged his gambols. I could n't bear to see him put to work.

GEORGE (*returning with rifle*): Come, Paul, are you ready?

PAUL: I'ss, Mas'r George. O, golly! ain't that a pooty gun.

M'CLOSKY: See here, you imp; if I catch you, and your redskin yonder, gunning in my swamps, I'll give you rats, mind. Them vagabonds, when the game's about, shoot my pigs. (*Exit* GEORGE *into house*.)

PAUL: You gib me rattan, Mas'r Clostry, but I guess you take a berry long stick to Wahnotee. Ugh, he make bacon of you.

M'CLOSKY: Make bacon of me, you young whelp! Do you mean that I'm a pig? Hold on a bit. (*He seizes whip, and holds* PAUL.)

ZOE: O, sir! don't, pray, don't.

M'CLOSKY (*slowly lowering his whip*): Darn you, redskin, I'll pay you off some day, both of ye. (*He returns to table and drinks*.)

SUNNYSIDE: That Indian is a nuisance. Why don't he return to his nation out West?

M'CLOSKY: He's too fond of thieving and whiskey.

ZOE: No; Wahnotee is a gentle, honest creature, and remains here because he loves that boy with the tenderness of a woman. When Paul was taken down with the swamp fever the Indian sat outside the hut, and neither ate, slept, nor spoke for five days, till the child could recognize and call him to his bedside. He who can love so well is honest—don't speak ill of poor Wahnotee.

MRS. PEYTON: Wahnotee, will you go back to your people?

WAHNOTEE: Sleugh.

PAUL: He don't understand; he speaks a mash-up of Indian and Mexican. Wahnotee Patira na sepau assa wigiran?

WAHNOTEE: Weal Omenee.

PAUL: Says he'll go if I'll go with him. He calls me Omenee, the Pigeon, and Miss Zoe is Ninemoosha, the Sweetheart.

WAHNOTEE (*pointing to* ZOE): Ninemoosha.

ZOE: No, Wahnotee, we can't spare Paul.

PAUL: If Omenee remain, Wahnotee will die in Terrebonne.

(*During the dialogue,* WAHNOTEE *has taken* GEORGE'S *gun*.)

(*Enter* GEORGE.)

GEORGE: Now I'm ready.

(GEORGE *tries to regain his gun;* WAHNOTEE *refuses to give it up;* PAUL *quietly takes it from him and remonstrates with him*.)

DORA: Zoe, he's going; I want him to stay and make love to me; that's what I came for to-day.

MRS. PEYTON: George, I can't spare Paul for an hour or two; he must run over to the landing; the steamer from New Orleans passed up the river last night, and if there's a mail they have thrown it ashore.

SUNNYSIDE: I saw the mail-bags lying in the shed this morning.

MRS. PEYTON: I expect an important letter from Liverpool; away with you, Paul; bring the mail-bags here.

PAUL: I'm 'most afraid to take Wahnotee to the shed, there's rum there.

WAHNOTEE: Rum!

PAUL: Come, then, but if I catch you drinkin', O, laws a mussey, you'll get snakes! I'll gib it you! now mind. (*Exit with Indian*.)

GEORGE: Come, Miss Dora, let me offer you my arm.

DORA: Mr. George, I am afraid, if all we hear is true, you have led a dreadful life in Europe.

GEORGE: That's a challenge to begin a description of my feminine adventures.

DORA: You have been in love, then?

GEORGE: Two hundred and forty-nine times! Let me relate you the worst cases.

DORA: No! no!

GEORGE: I'll put the naughty parts in French.

DORA: I won't hear a word! O, you horrible man! go on. (*Exit* GEORGE *and* DORA *to the house*.)

M'CLOSKY: Now, ma'am I'd like a little business, if agreeable. I bring you news; your banker, old Lafouche, of New Orleans, is dead; the executors are winding up his affairs, and have foreclosed on all overdue mortgages, so Terrebonne is for sale. Here's the *Picayune* (*Producing paper*.) with the advertisement.

ZOE: Terrebonne for sale!

MRS. PEYTON: Terrebonne for sale, and you, sir, will doubtless become its purchaser.

M'CLOSKY: Well, ma'am, I s'pose there's no law agin my bidding for it. The more bidders, the better for you. You'll take care, I guess, it don't go too cheap.

MRS. PEYTON: O, sir, I don't value the place for its price, but for the many happy days I've spent here; that landscape, flat and uninteresting though it may be, is full of charm for me; those poor people, born around me, growing up about my heart, have bounded my view of life; and now to lose that homely scene, lose their black, ungainly faces! O, sir, perhaps you should be as old as I am, to feel as I do, when my past life is torn away from me.

M'CLOSKY: I'd be darned glad if somebody would tear my past life away from *me*. Sorry I can't help you, but the fact is, you're in such an all-fired mess that you could n't be pulled out without a derrick.

MRS. PEYTON: Yes, there is a hope left yet, and I cling to it. The house of Mason Brothers, of

Liverpool, failed some twenty years ago in my husband's debt.

M'CLOSKY: They owed him over fifty thousand dollars.

MRS. PEYTON: I cannot find the entry in my husband's accounts; but you, Mr. M'Closky, can doubtless detect it. Zoe, bring here the judge's old desk; it is in the library. (*Exit* ZOE *to the house*.)

M'CLOSKY: You don't expect to recover any of this old debt, do you?

MRS. PEYTON: Yes; the firm has recovered itself, and I received a notice two months ago that some settlement might be anticipated.

SUNNYSIDE: Why, with principal and interest this debt has been more than doubled in twenty years.

MRS. PEYTON: But it may be years yet before it will be paid off, if ever.

SUNNYSIDE: If there's a chance of it, there's not a planter round here who would n't lend you the whole cash, to keep your name and blood amongst us. Come, cheer up, old friend.

MRS. PEYTON: Ah! Sunnyside, how good you are; so like my poor Peyton. (*Exit* MRS. PEYTON *and* SUNNYSIDE *to the house*.)

M'CLOSKY: Curse their old families—they cut me—a bilious, conceited, thin lot of dried up aristocracy. I hate 'em. Just because my grandfather was n't some broken-down Virginia transplant, or a stingy old Creole, I ain't fit to sit down to the same meat with them. It makes my blood so hot I feel my heart hiss. I'll sweep these Peytons from this section of the country. Their presence keeps alive the reproach against me that I ruined them. Yet, if this money should come! Bah! There's no chance of it. Then, if they go, they'll take Zoe—she'll follow them. Darn that girl; she makes me quiver when I think of her; she's took me for all I'm worth. (*Enter* ZOE *from house, with the desk*.) O, here, do you know what the annuity the old judge left you is worth to-day? Not a picayune.

ZOE: It's surely worth the love that dictated it; here are the papers and accounts. (*Putting the desk on the table*.)

M'CLOSKY: Stop, Zoe; come here! How would you like to rule the house of the richest planter on Atchafalaya—eh? or say the word, and I'll buy this old barrack, and you shall be mistress of Terrebonne.

ZOE: O, sir, do not speak so to me!

M'CLOSKY: Why not! look here, these Peytons are bust; cut 'em; I am rich, jine me; I'll set you up grand, and we'll give these first families here our dust, until you'll see their white skins shrivel up with hate and rage; what d' ye say?

ZOE: Let me pass! O, pray, let me go!

M'CLOSKY: What, you won't, won't ye? If young George Peyton was to make you the same offer, you'd jump at it pretty darned quick, I guess. Come, Zoe, don't be a fool; I'd marry you if I could, but you know I can't; so just say what you want. Here, then, I'll put back these Peytons in Terrebonne, and they shall know you done it; yes, they'll have you to thank for saving them from ruin.

ZOE: Do you think they would live here on such terms?

M'CLOSKY: Why not? We'll hire out our slaves, and live on their wages.

ZOE: But I'm not a slave.

M'CLOSKY: No; if you were I'd buy you, if you cost all I'm worth.

ZOE: Let me pass!

M'CLOSKY: Stop.

(*Enter* SCUDDER.)

SCUDDER: Let her pass.

M'CLOSKY: Eh?

SCUDDER: Let her pass! (*He takes out his knife. Exit* ZOE *to house*.)

M'CLOSKY: Is that you, Mr. Overseer? (*He examines paper*.)

SCUDDER: Yes, I'm here, somewhere, interferin'.

M'CLOSKY (*sitting*): A pretty mess you've got this estate in—

SCUDDER: Yes—me and Co.—we done it; but, as you were senior partner in the concern, I reckon you got the big lick.

M'CLOSKY: What d' ye mean?

SCUDDER: Let me proceed by illustration. (*Sits*.) Look thar! (*Points with his knife off*.) D' ye see that tree?—it's called a live oak, and is a native here; beside it grows a creeper; year after year that creeper twines its long arms round and round the tree—sucking the earth dry all about its roots —living on its life—overrunning its branches, until at last the live oak withers and dies out. Do you know what the niggers round here call that sight? they call it the Yankee hugging the Creole.

M'CLOSKY: Mr. Scudder, I've listened to a great many of your insinuations, and now I'd like to come to an understanding what they mean. If you want a quarrel—

SCUDDER: No, I'm the skurriest crittur at a fight you ever see; my legs have been too well brought up to stand and see my body abused; I take good care of myself, I can tell you.

M'CLOSKY: Because I heard that you had traduced my character.

SCUDDER: Traduced! Whoever said so lied. I always said you were the darndest thief that ever escaped a white jail to misrepresent the North to the South.

M'CLOSKY (*he raises hand to back of his neck*): What!

SCUDDER: Take your hand down—take it down. (M'CLOSKY *lowers his hand.*) Whenever I gets into company like yours, I always start with the advantage on my side.

M'CLOSKY: What d' ye mean?

SCUDDER: I mean that before you could draw that bowie-knife, you wear down your back, I'd cut you into shingles. Keep quiet, and let's talk sense. You wanted to come to an understanding, and I'm coming thar as quick as I can. Now, Jacob M'Closky, you despise me because you think I'm a fool; I despise you because I know you to be a knave. Between us we've ruined these Peytons; you fired the judge, and I finished off the widow. Now, I feel bad about my share in the business. I'd give half the balance of my life to wipe out my part of the work. Many a night I've laid awake and thought how to pull them through, till I've cried like a child over the sum I could n't do; and you know how darned hard 't is to make a Yankee cry.

M'CLOSKY: Well, what's that to me?

SCUDDER: Hold on, Jacob, I'm coming to that —I tell ye, I'm such a fool—I can't bear the feeling, it keeps at me like a skin complaint, and if this family is sold up—

M'CLOSKY: What then?

SCUDDER (*rising*): I'd cut my throat—or yours —yours I'd prefer.

M'CLOSKY: Would you now? why don't you do it?

SCUDDER: 'Cos I's skeered to try! I never killed a man in my life—and civilization is so strong in me I guess I could n't do it—I'd like to, though!

M'CLOSKY: And all for the sake of that old woman and that young puppy—eh? No other cause to hate—to envy me—to be jealous of me —eh?

SCUDDER: Jealous? what for?

M'CLOSKY: Ask the color in your face: d' ye think I can't read you, like a book? With your New England hypocrisy, you would persuade yourself that it was this family alone you cared for; it ain't—you know it ain't—'t is the "Octoroon"; and you love her as I do; and you hate me because I'm your rival—that's where the tears come from, Salem Scudder, if you ever shed any—that's

where the shoe pinches.

SCHUDDER: Wal, I do like the gal; she's a—

M'CLOSKY: She's in love with young Peyton; it made me curse whar it made you cry, as it does now; I see the tears on your cheeks now.

SCUDDER: Look at 'em, Jacob, for they are honest water from the well of truth. I ain't ashamed of it—I do love the gal; but I ain't jealous of you, because I believe the only sincere feeling about you is your love for Zoe, and it does your heart good to have her image thar; but I believe you put it thar to spile. By fair means I don't think you can get her, and don't you try foul with her, 'cause if you do, Jacob, civilization be darned, I'm on you like a painter, and when I'm drawed out I'm pizin. (*Exit* SCUDDER *to house.*)

M'CLOSKY: Fair or foul, I'll have her—take that home with you! (*He opens desk.*) What's here —judgments? yes, plenty of 'em; bill of costs, account with Citizens' Bank—what's this? "Judgment, $40,000, Thibodeaux against Peyton,'"—surely, that is the judgment under which this estate is now advertised for sale—(*He takes up paper and examines it.*) yes, "Thibodeaux against Peyton, 1838." Hold on! whew! this is worth taking to—in this desk the judge used to keep one paper I want—this should be it. (*Reads.*) "The free papers of my daughter Zoe, registered February 4th, 1841." Why, judge, was n't you lawyer enough to know that while a judgment stood against you it was a lien on your slaves? Zoe is your child by a quadroon slave, and you did n't free her; blood! if this is so, she's mine! this old Liverpool debt—that may cross me—if it only arrive too late—if it don't come by this mail—Hold on! this letter the old lady expects—that's it; let me only head off that letter, and Terrebonne will be sold before they can recover it. That boy and the Indian have gone down to the landing for the post-bags; they'll idle on the way as usual; my mate will take me across the swamp, and before they can reach the shed, I'll have purified them bags—ne'er a letter shall show this mail. Ha, ha!—(*Calls.*) Pete, you old turkey-buzzard, saddle my mare. Then, if I sink every dollar I'm worth in her purchase, I'll own that Octoroon.

ACT II

(*The Wharf with goods, boxes, and bales scattered about—a camera on a stand;* DORA *being photographed by* SCUDDER, *who is arranging photographic apparatus,* GEORGE *and* PAUL *looking on at back.*)

SCUDDER: Just turn your face a leetle this way—fix your—let's see—look here.

DORA: So?

SCUDDER: That's right. (*Putting his head under the darkening apron.*) It's such a long time since I did this sort of thing, and this old machine has got so dirty and stiff, I'm afraid it won't operate. That's about right. Now don't stir.

PAUL: Ugh! she looks as though she war gwine to have a tooth drawed!

SCUDDER: I've got four plates ready, in case we miss the first shot. One of them is prepared with a self-developing liquid that I've invented. I hope it will turn out better than most of my notions. Now fix yourself. Are you ready?

DORA: Ready!

SCUDDER: Fire!—one, two, three. (SCUDDER *takes out watch.*)

PAUL: Now it's cooking; laws mussey! I feel it all inside, as if I was at a lottery.

SCUDDER: So! (*Throws down apron.*) That's enough. (*Withdrawing slide, turns and sees* PAUL.) What! what are you doing there, you young varmint! Ain't you took them bags to the house yet?

PAUL: Now, it ain't no use trying to get mad, Mas'r Scudder. I'm gwine! I only come back to find Wahnotee; whar is dat ign' ant Ingiun?

SCUDDER: You'll find him scenting round the rum store, hitched up by the nose. (*Exit into the room.*)

PAUL (*calling at the door*): Say, Mas'r Scudder, take me in dat telescope?

SCUDDER (*inside the room*): Get out, you cub! clar out!

PAUL: You got four of dem dishes ready. Gosh, would n't I like to hab myself took! What's de charge, Mas'r Scudder? (*He runs off.*)

(*Enter* SCUDDER, *from the room.*)

SCUDDER: Job had none of them critters on his plantation, else he'd never ha' stood through so many chapters. Well, that has come out clear, ain't it? (*Showing the plate.*)

DORA: O, beautiful! Look, Mr. Peyton.

GEORGE (*looking*): Yes, very fine!

SCUDDER: The apparatus can't mistake. When I travelled round with this machine, the homely folks used to sing out, "Hillo, mister, this ain't like me!" "Ma'am," says I, "the apparatus can't mistake." "But, mister, that ain't my nose." "Ma'am, your nose drawed it. The machine can't err—you may mistake your phiz but the apparatus don't." "But, sir, it ain't agreeable." "No, ma'am, the truth seldom is."

(*Enter* PETE, *puffing.*)

PETE: Mas'r Scudder! Mas'r Scudder!

SCUDDER: Hillo! what are you blowing about like a steamboat with one wheel for?

PETE: *You* blow, Mas'r Scudder, when I tole you: dere's a man from Noo Aleens just arriv'd at de house, and he's stuck up two papers on de gates: "For sale—dis yer property," and a heap of oder tings—an he seen missus, and arter he shown some papers she burst out crying—I yelled; den de corious of little niggers dey set up, den de hull plantation children—de live stock reared up and created a purpiration of lamentation as did de ole heart good to har.

DORA: What's the matter?

SCUDDER: He's come.

PETE: Dass it—I saw 'm!

SCUDDER: The sheriff from New Orleans has taken possession—Terrebonne is in the hands of the law.

(*Enter* ZOE.)

ZOE: O, Mr. Scudder! Dora! Mr. Peyton! come home—there are strangers in the house.

DORA: Stay, Mr. Peyton: Zoe, a word! (*She leads her forward—aside.*) Zoe, the more I see of George Peyton the better I like him; but he is too modest—that is a very impertinent virtue in a man.

ZOE: I'm no judge, dear.

DORA: Of course not, you little fool; no one ever made love to you, and you can't understand; I mean, that George knows I am an heiress; my fortune would release this estate from debt.

ZOE: O, I see!

DORA: If he would only propose to marry me I would accept him, but he don't know that, and he will go on fooling, in his slow European way, until it is too late.

ZOE: What's to be done?

DORA: You tell him.

ZOE: What? that he is n't to go on fooling in his slow—

DORA: No, you goose! twit him on his silence and abstraction—I'm sure it's plain enough, for he has not spoken two words to me all the day; then joke round the subject, and at last speak out.

SCUDDER: Pete, as you came here, did you pass Paul and the Indian with the letter-bags?

PETE: No, sar; but dem vagabonds neber take

the 'specable straight road, dey goes by de swamp. (*Exit up the path.*)

SCUDDER: Come, sir!

DORA (*to* ZOE.): Now's your time.—(*Aloud.*) Mr. Scudder, take us with you—Mr. Peyton is so slow, there's no getting him on. (*Exit* DORA *and* SCUDDER.)

ZOE: They are gone!—(*Glancing at* GEORGE.) Poor fellow, he has lost all.

GEORGE: Poor child! how sad she looks now she has no resource.

ZOE: How shall I ask him to stay?

GEORGE: Zoe, will you remain here? I wish to speak to you.

ZOE (*aside*): Well, that saves trouble.

GEORGE: By our ruin you lose all.

ZOE: O, I'm nothing; think of yourself.

GEORGE: I can think of nothing but the image that remains face to face with me; so beautiful, so simple, so confiding, that I dare not express the feelings that have grown up so rapidly in my heart.

ZOE (*aside*): He means Dora.

GEORGE: If I dared to speak!

ZOE: That's just what you must do, and do it at once, or it will be too late.

GEORGE: Has my love been divined?

ZOE: It has been more than suspected.

GEORGE: Zoe, listen to me, then. I shall see this estate pass from me without a sigh, for it possesses no charm for me; the wealth I covet is the love of those around me—eyes that are rich in fond looks, lips that breathe endearing words; the only estate I value is the heart of one true woman, and the slaves I'd have are her thoughts.

ZOE: George, George, your words take away my breath!

GEORGE: The world, Zoe, the free struggle of minds and hands is before me; the education bestowed on me by my dear uncle is a noble heritage which no sheriff can seize; with that I can build up a fortune, spread a roof over the heads I love, and place before them the food I have earned; I will work—

ZOE: Work! I thought none but colored people worked.

GEORGE: Work, Zoe, is the salt that gives savor to life.

ZOE: Dora said you were slow; if she could hear you now—

GEORGE: Zoe, you are young; your mirror must have told you that you are beautiful. Is your heart free?

ZOE: Free? of course it is!

GEORGE: We have known each other but a few days, but to me those days have been worth all the rest of my life. Zoe, you have suspected the feeling that now commands an utterance—you have seen that I love you.

ZOE: Me! you love *me?*

GEORGE: As my wife,—the sharer of my hopes, my ambitions, and my sorrows; under the shelter of your love I could watch the storms of fortune pass unheeded by.

ZOE: *My* love! *My* love? George, you know not what you say! *I* the sharer of your sorrows—your wife! Do you know what I am?

GEORGE: Your birth—I know it. Has not my dear aunt forgotten it—she who had the most right to remember it? You are illegitimate, but love knows no prejudice.

ZOE (*aside*): Alas! he does not know, he does not know! and will despise me, spurn me, loathe me, when he learns who, what, he has so loved.—(*Aloud.*) George, O, forgive me! Yes, I love you—I did not know it until your words showed me what has been in my heart; each of them awoke a new sense, and now I know how unhappy—how very unhappy I am.

GEORGE: Zoe, what have I said to wound you?

ZOE: Nothing; but you must learn what I thought you already knew. George, you cannot marry me; the laws forbid it!

GEORGE: Forbid it?

ZOE: There is a gulf between us, as wide as your love, as deep as my despair; but, O, tell me, say you will pity me! that you will not throw me from you like a poisoned thing!

GEORGE: Zoe, explain yourself—your language fills me with shapeless fears.

ZOE: And what shall I say? I—my mother was—no, no—not her! Why should I refer the blame to her? George, do you see that hand you hold? look at these fingers; do you see the nails are of a bluish tinge?

GEORGE: Yes, near the quick there is a faint blue mark.

ZOE: Look in my eyes; is not the same color in the white?

GEORGE: It is their beauty.

ZOE: Could you see the roots of my hair you would see the same dark, fatal mark. Do you know what that is?

GEORGE: No.

ZOE: That is the ineffaceable curse of Cain. Of the blood that feeds my heart, one drop in eight is black—bright red as the rest may be, that one drop poisons all the flood; those seven bright drops give me love like yours—hope like yours—ambition like yours—life hung with passions like dew-drops on the morning flowers; but the one black drop gives me despair, for I'm an unclean thing—forbidden by the laws—I'm an Octoroon!

GEORGE: Zoe, I love you none the less; this knowledge brings no revolt to my heart, and I can overcome the obstacle.

ZOE: But *I* cannot.

GEORGE: We can leave this country, and go far away where none can know.

ZOE: And our mother, she who from infancy treated me with such fondness, she who, as you said, has most reason to spurn me, can she forget what I am? Will she gladly see you wedded to the child of her husband's slave? No! she would revolt from it, as all but you would; and if I consented to hear the cries of my heart, if I did not crush out my infant love, what would she say to the poor girl on whom she had bestowed so much? No, no!

GEORGE: Zoe, must we immolate our lives on her prejudice?

ZOE: Yes, for I'd rather be black than ungrateful! Ah, George, our race has at least one virtue—it knows how to suffer!

GEORGE: Each word you utter makes my love sink deeper into my heart.

ZOE: And I remained here to induce you to offer that heart to Dora!

GEORGE: If you bid me do so I will obey you—

ZOE: No, no! if you cannot be mine, O, let me not blush when I think of you.

GEORGE: Dearest Zoe! (*Exit* GEORGE *and* ZOE.)

(*As they exit,* M'CLOSKY *rises from behind a rock and looks after them.*)

M'CLOSKY: She loves him! I felt it—and how she can love! (*Advances.*) That one black drop of blood burns in her veins and lights up her heart like a foggy sun. O, how I lapped up her words, like a thirsty bloodhound! I'll have her, if it costs me my life! Yonder the boy still lurks with those mailbags; the devil still keeps him here to tempt me, darn his yellow skin! I arrived just too late, he had grabbed the prize as I came up. Hillo! he's coming this way, fighting with his Injiun. (*Conceals himself.*)

(*Enter* PAUL, *wrestling with* WAHNOTEE.)

PAUL: It ain't no use now: you got to gib it up!

WAHNOTEE: Ugh!

PAUL: It won't do! You got dat bottle of rum hid under your blanket—gib it up now, you—. Yar! (*Wrenching it from him.*) You nasty, lying Injiun! It's no use you putting on airs; I ain't gwine to sit up wid you all night and you drunk. Hillo! war's de crowd gone? And dar's de 'paratus—O, gosh, if I could take a likeness ob dis child! Uh—uh, let's have a peep. (*Looking through camera.*) O, golly! yar, you Wahnotee! you stan' dar, I see you. Ta demine usti.

(*He looks at* WAHNOTEE *through the camera;* WAHNOTEE *springs back with an expression of alarm.*)

WAHNOTEE: No tue Wahnotee.

PAUL: Ha, ha! he tinks it's a gun. You ign'ant Injiun, it can't hurt you! Stop, here's dem dishes—plates—dat's what he call 'em, all fix: I see Mas'r Scudder do it often—tink I can take likeness—stay dere, Wahnotee.

WAHNOTEE: No, carabine tue.

PAUL: I must operate and take my own likeness too—how debbel I do dat? Can't be ober dar an' here too—I ain't twins. Ugh! ach! 'Top; you look, you Wahnotee; you see dis rag, eh? Well when I say go, den lift dis rag like dis, see! den run to dat pine tree up dar (*Points.*) and back ag'in, and den pull down de rag so, d'ye see?

WAHNOTEE: Hugh!

PAUL: Den you hab glass ob rum.

WAHNOTEE: Rum!

PAUL: Dat wakes him up. Coute, Wahnotee in omenee dit go Wahnotee, poina la fa, comb a pine tree, la revieut sala, la fa.

WAHNOTEE: Fire-water!

PAUL: Yes, den a glass ob fire-water; now den. (*Throwing mail-bags down and sitting on them.*) Pret, now den go.

(WAHNOTEE *raises the apron and runs off.* PAUL *sits for his picture—*M'CLOSKY *appears.*)

M'CLOSKY: Where are they? Ah, yonder goes the Indian!

PAUL: De time he gone just 'bout enough to cook dat dish plate.

M'CLOSKY: Yonder is the boy—now is my time! What's he doing; is he asleep? (*Advancing.*) He is sitting on my prize! darn his carcass! I'll clear him off there—he'll never know what stunned him. (*He takes Indian's tomahawk and steals to* PAUL.)

PAUL: Dam dat Injiun! is dat him creeping dar? I dare n't move fear to spile myself.

(M'CLOSKY *strikes him on the head—he falls dead.*)

M'CLOSKY: Hooraw; the bags are mine—now for it!—(*Opening the mail-bags.*) What's here? Sunnyside, Pointdexter, Jackson, Peyton; here it is—the Liverpool postmark, sure enough!—(*Opening letter—reads.*) "Madam, we are instructed by the firm of Mason and Co., to inform you that a dividend of forty per cent. is payable on the 1st proximo, this amount in consideration of position, they send herewith, and you will find enclosed by draft to your order, on the Bank of Louisiana, which please acknowledge—the balance will be paid in full, with interest, in three, six, and nine months—your drafts on Mason Brothers at those dates will be accepted by La Palisse and Compagnie, N. O., so that you may command immediate use of the whole amount at once, if required. Yours, etc., James Brown." What a find! this infernal letter would have saved all. (*During the reading of letter he remains nearly motionless under the focus of the camera.*) But now I guess it will arrive too late—these darned U. S. mails are to blame. The Injiun! he must not see me. (*Exit rapidly.*)

(WAHNOTEE *runs on, and pulls down the apron. He sees* PAUL, *lying on the ground and speaks to him, thinking that he is shamming sleep. He gesticulates and jabbers to him and moves him with his feet, then kneels down to rouse him. To his horror he finds him dead. Expressing great grief he raises his eyes and they fall upon the camera. Rising with a savage growl, he seizes the tomahawk and smashes the camera to pieces. Going to* PAUL *he expresses in pantomime grief, sorrow, and fondness, and takes him in his arms to carry him away.*)

ACT III

(*A Room in* MRS. PEYTON's *house showing the entrance on which an auction bill is pasted.* SOLON *and* GRACE *are there.*)

PETE (*outside*): Dis way—dis way.

(*Enter* PETE, POINTDEXTER, JACKSON, LAFOUCHE *and* CAILLOU.)

PETE: Dis way, gen'l'men; now, Solon—Grace—dey's hot and tirsty—sangaree, brandy, rum.

JACKSON: Well, what d'ye say, Lafouche—d'ye smile?

(*Enter* THIBODEAUX *and* SUNNYSIDE.)

THIBODEAUX: I hope we don't intrude on the family.

PETE: You see dat hole in dar, sar? I was raised on dis yar plantation—nebber see no door in it—always open, sar, for stranger to walk in.

SUNNYSIDE: And for substance to walk out.

(*Enter* RATTS.)

RATTS: Fine southern style that, eh!

LAFOUCHE (*reading the bill*): "A fine, well-built old family mansion, replete with every comfort."

RATTS: There's one name on the list of slaves scratched, I see.

LAFOUCHE: Yes; No. 49, Paul, a quadroon boy, aged thirteen.

SUNNYSIDE: He's missing.

POINTDEXTER: Run away, I suppose.

PETE (*indignantly*): No, sar; nigger nebber cut stick on Terrebonne; dat boy's dead, sure.

RATTS: What, Picayune Paul, as we called him, that used to come aboard my boat?—poor little darkey, I hope not; many a picayune he picked up for his dance and nigger songs, and he supplied our table with fish and game from the Bayous.

PETE: Nebber supply no more, sar—nebber dance again. Mas'r Ratts, you hard him sing about de place where de good niggers go, de last time.

RATTS: Well!

PETE: Well, he gone dar hisself; why I tink so—'cause we missed Paul for some days, but nebber tout nothin' till one night dat Injiun Wahnotte suddenly stood right dar 'mongst us—was in his war paint, and mightly cold and grave—he sit down by de fire. "Whar's Paul?" I say—he smoke and smoke, but nebber look out of de fire; well knowing dem critters, I wait a long time—den he say, "Wahnotee great chief;" den I say nothing—smoke anoder time—last, rising to go, he turn round at door, and say berry low—O, like a woman's voice he say, "Omenee Pangeuk,"—dat is, Paul is dead—nebber see him since.

RATTS: That red-skin killed him.

SUNNYSIDE: So we believe; and so mad are the folks around, if they catch the red-skin they'll lynch him sure.

RATTS: Lynch him! Darn his copper carcass, I've got a set of Irish deckhands aboard that just loved that child; and after I tell them this, let them get a sight of the red-skin, I believe they would eat him, tomahawk and all. Poor little Paul!

THIBODEAUX: What was he worth?

RATTS: Well, near on five hundred dollars.

PETE (*scandalized*): What, sar! You p'tend to be sorry for Paul, and prize him like dat! Five hundred dollars! (*To* THIBODEAUX.)Tousand dollars, Massa Thibodeau.

(*Enter* SCUDDER.)

SCUDDER: Gentlemen, the sale takes place at three. Good morning, Colonel. It's near that now, and there's still the sugar-houses to be inspected. Good day, Mr. Thibodeaux—shall we drive down that way? Mr. Lafouche, why, how do you do, sir? you're looking well.

LAFOUCHE: Sorry I can't return the compliment.

RATTS: Salem's looking a kinder hollowed out.

SCUDDER: What, Mr. Ratts, are you going to invest in swamps?

RATTS: No; I want a nigger.

SCUDDER: Hush.

PETE: Eh! wass dat?

SCUDDER: Mr. Sunnyside, I can't do this job of showin' round the folks; my stomach goes agin it. I want Pete here a minute.

SUNNYSIDE: I'll accompany them certainly.

SCUDDER (*eagerly*): Will ye? Thank ye; thank ye.

SUNNYSIDE: We must excuse Scudder, friends. I'll see you round the estate.

(*Enter* GEORGE *and* MRS. PEYTON.)

LAFOUCHE: Good morning, Mrs. Peyton. (*All salute.*)

SUNNYSIDE: This way, gentlemen.

RATTS (*aside to* SUNNYSIDE): I say, I'd like to say summit soft to the old woman; perhaps it would n't go well, would it?

THIBODEAUX: No; leave it alone.

RATTS: Darn it, when I see a woman in trouble, I feel like selling the skin off my back.

(*Exit* THIBODEAUX, SUNNYSIDE, RATTS, POINTDEXTER, GRACE, JACKSON, LAFOUCHE, CAILLOU, SOLON.)

SCUDDER (*aside to* PETE): Go outside there; listen to what you hear, then go down to the quarters and tell the boys, for I can't do it. O, get out.

PETE: He said "I want a nigger." Laws, mussey! What am goin' to cum ob us!

(*Exit slowly, as if trying to conceal himself.*)

GEORGE: My dear aunt, why do you not move from this painful scene? Go with Dora to Sunnyside.

MRS. PEYTON: No, George; your uncle said to me with his dying breath, "Nellie, never leave Terrebonne," and I never *will* leave it, till the law compels me.

SCUDDER: Mr. George, I'm going to say somethin' that has been chokin' me for some time. I know you'll excuse it. Thar's Miss Dora—that girl's in love with you; yes, sir, her eyes are startin' out of her head with it: now her fortune would redeem a good part of this estate.

MRS. PEYTON: Why, George, I never suspected this!

GEORGE: I did, aunt, I confess, but—

MRS. PEYTON: And you hesitated from motives of delicacy?

SCUDDER: No, ma'am, here's the plan of it. Mr. George is in love with Zoe.

GEORGE: Scudder!

MRS. PEYTON: George!

SCUDDER: Hold on, now! things have got so jammed in on top of us, we ain't got time to put kid gloves on to handle them. He loves Zoe, and has found out that she loves him. (*Sighing.*) Well, that's all right; but as he can't marry her, and as Miss Dora would jump at him—

MRS. PEYTON: Why did n't you mention this before?

SCUDDER: Why, because *I* love Zoe, too, and I could n't take that young feller from her; and she's jist living on the sight of him, as I saw her do; and they so happy in spite of this yer misery around them, and they reproachin' themselves with not feeling as they ought. I've seen it, I tell you; and darn it, ma'am, can't you see that's what's been a hollowing me out so—I beg your pardon.

MRS. PEYTON: O, George,—my son, let me call you,—I do not speak for my own sake, nor for the loss of the estate, but for the poor people here: they will be sold, divided, and taken away—they have been born here. Heaven has denied me children; so all the strings of my heart have grown around and amongst them, like the fibres and roots of an old tree in its native earth. O, let all go, but save them! With them around us, if we have not wealth, we shall at least have the home that they alone can make—

GEORGE: My dear mother—Mr. Scudder—you teach me what I ought to do; if Miss Sunnyside will accept me as I am, Terrebonne shall be saved; I will sell myself, but the slaves shall be protected.

MRS. PEYTON: *Sell* yourself, George! Is not Dora worth any man's—

SCUDDER: Don't say that, ma'am; don't say that to a man that loves another gal. He's going to do an heroic act; don't spile it.

MRS. PEYTON: But Zoe is only an Octoroon.

SCUDDER: She's won this race agin the white, anyhow; it's too late now to start her pedigree. (*As* DORA *enters.*) Come. Mrs. Peyton, take my arm. Hush! here's the other one: she's a little too thoroughbred—too much of the greyhound; but that heart's there, I believe. (*Exeunt* SCUDDER *and* MRS. PEYTON.)

DORA: Poor Mrs. Peyton.

GEORGE: Miss Sunnyside, permit me a word: a feeling of delicacy has suspended upon my lips an avowal, which—

DORA (*aside*): O, dear, has he suddenly come to his senses?

(*Enter* ZOE, *stopping at back.*)

GEORGE: In a word, I have seen and admired you!

DORA (*aside*): He has a strange way of showing it. European, I suppose.

GEORGE: If you would pardon the abruptness of the question, I would ask you, Do you think the sincere devotion of my life to make yours happy would succeed?

DORA (*aside*): Well, he has the oddest way of making love.

GEORGE: You are silent?

DORA: Mr. Peyton, I presume you have hesitated to make this avowal because you feared, in the present condition of affairs here, your object might be misconstrued, and that your attention was rather to my fortune than myself. (*A pause.*) Why don't he speak?—I mean, you feared I might not give you credit for sincere and pure feelings. Well, you wrong me. I don't think you capable of anything else but—

GEORGE: No, I hesitated because an attachment I had formed before I had the pleasure of seeing you had not altogether died out.

DORA (*smiling*): Some of those sirens of Paris, I presume. (*Pausing.*) I shall endeavor not to be jealous of the past; perhaps I have no right to be. (*Pausing.*) But now that vagrant love is—eh, faded—is it not? Why don't you speak, sir?

GEORGE: Because, Miss Sunnyside, I have not learned to lie.

DORA: Good gracious—who wants you to?

GEORGE: I do, but I can't do it. No, the love I speak of is not such as you suppose,—it is a passion that has grown up here since I arrived; but it is a hopeless, mad, wild feeling, that must perish.

DORA: Here! since you arrived! Impossible: you have seen no one; whom can you mean?

ZOE (*advancing*): Me.

GEORGE: Zoe!

DORA: You!

ZOE: Forgive him, Dora; for he knew no better until I told him. Dora, you are right. He is incapable of any but sincere and pure feelings —so are you. He loves me—what of that? You know you can't be jealous of a poor creature like me. If he caught the fever, were stung by a snake, or possessed of any other poisonous or unclean thing, you could pity, tend, love him through it, and for your gentle care he would love you in return. Well, is he not thus afflicted now? I am his love—he loves an Octoroon.

GEORGE: O, Zoe, you break my heart!

DORA: At college they said I was a fool—I must be. At New Orleans, they said, "She's pretty, very pretty, but no brains." I'm afraid they must be right; I can't understand a word of all this.

ZOE: Dear Dora, try to understand it with your heart. You love George; you love him dearly; I know it; and you deserve to be loved by him. He will love you—he must. His love for me will pass away—it shall. You heard him say it was hopeless. O, forgive him and me!

DORA (*weeping*): O, why did he speak to me at all then? You've made me cry, then, and I hate you both! (*Exit through room.*)

(*Enter* MRS. PEYTON *and* SCUDDER, M'CLOSKY *and* POINTDEXTER.)

M'CLOSKY: I'm sorry to intrude, but the business I came upon will excuse me.

MRS. PEYTON: Here is my nephew, sir.

ZOE: Perhaps I had better go.

M'CLOSKY: Wal, as it consarns you, perhaps you better had.

SCUDDER: Consarns Zoe?

M'CLOSKY: I don't know; she may as well hear the hull of it. Go on, Colonel—Colonel Pointdexter, ma'am—the mortgagee, auctioneer, and general agent.

POINTDEXTER: Pardon me, madam, but do you know these papers?

(*He hands the papers to* MRS. PEYTON.)

MRS. PEYTON (*taking them*): Yes, sir; they were the free papers of the girl Zoe; but they were in my husband's secretary. How came they in your possession?

M'CLOSKY: I—I found them.

GEORGE: And you purloined them?

M'CLOSKY: Hold on, you'll see. Go on, Colonel.

POINTDEXTER: The list of your slaves is incomplete—it wants one.

SCUDDER: The boy Paul—we know it.

POINTDEXTER: No, sir, you have omitted the Octoroon girl, Zoe.

MRS. PEYTON: Zoe

ZOE: Me!

POINTDEXTER: At the time the judge executed those free papers to his infant slave, a judgment stood recorded against him; while that was on record he had no right to make away with his property. That judgment still exists: under it and others this estate is sold to-day. Those free papers ain't worth the sand that's on 'em.

MRS. PEYTON: Zoe a slave! It is impossible!

POINTDEXTER: It is certain, madam: the judge was negligent, and doubtless forgot this small formality.

SCUDDER: But the creditors will not claim the gal?

M'CLOSKY: Excuse me; one of the principal mortgages has made the demand. (*Exeunt* M'CLOSKY *and* POINTDEXTER.)

SCUDDER: Hold on yere, George Peyton; you sit down there. You're trembling so, you'll fall down directly. This blow has staggered me some.

MRS. PEYTON: O, Zoe, my child! don't think too hard of your poor father.

ZOE: I shall do so if you weep. See, I'm calm.

SCUDDER: Calm as a tombstone, and with about out as much life. I see it in your face.

GEORGE: It cannot be! It shall not be!

SCUDDER: Hold your tongue—it must. Be calm—darn the things; the proceeds of this sale won't cover the debts of the estate. Consarn those Liverpool English fellers, why couldn't they send something by the last mail? Even a letter, promising something—such is the feeling round amongst the planters. Darn me, if I could n't raise thirty thousand on the envelope alone, and ten thousand more on the postmark.

GEORGE: Zoe, they shall not take you from us while I live.

SCUDDER: Don't be a fool; they'd kill you, and then take her, just as soon as—stop; old Sunnyside, he'll buy her; that'll save her.

ZOE: No, it won't; we have confessed to Dora that we love each other. How can she then ask her father to free me?

SCUDDER: What in thunder made you do that?

ZOE: Because it was the truth, and I had rather be a slave with a free soul, than remain free with a slavish, deceitful heart. My father gives me freedom—at least he thought so. May Heaven bless him for the thought, bless him for the happiness he spread around my life. You say the proceeds of the sale will not cover his debts. Let me be sold then, that I may free his name. I give him back the liberty he bestowed upon me; for I can never repay him the love he bore his poor Octoroon child, on whose breast his last sigh was drawn, into whose eyes he looked with the last gaze of affection.

MRS. PEYTON: O, my husband! I thank Heaven you have not lived to see this day.

ZOE: George, leave me! I would be alone a little while.

GEORGE: Zoe! (*Turning away overpowered.*)

ZOE: Do not weep, George. Dear George, you now see what a miserable thing I am.

GEORGE: Zoe!

SCUDDER: I wish they could sell *me!* I brought half this ruin on this family, with my all-fired improvements. I deserve to be a nigger this day—I feel like one, inside. (*Exit* SCUDDER.)

ZOE: Go now, George—leave me—take her with you. (*Exit* MRS. PEYTON *and* GEORGE.) A slave! a slave! Is this a dream—for my brain reels with the blow? He said so. What! then I shall be sold!—sold! and my master—O! (*She falls on her knees, with her face in her hands.*) No—no master but one. George—George—hush—they come! save me! No, (*Looks off.*) 't is Pete and the servants—they come this way. (*Enters the inner room.*)

(*Enter* PETE, GRACE, MINNIE, SOLON, DIDO, *and all Niggers.*)

PETE: Cum yer now—stand round, 'cause I've got to talk to you darkies—keep dem chil'n quiet—don't make no noise, de missus up dar har us.

SOLON: Go on, Pete.

PETE: Gen'l'men, my colored frens and ladies, dar's mighty bad news gone round. Dis yer prop'ty to be sold—old Terrebonne—whar we all been raised, is gwine—dey's gwine to take it away—can't stop here nohow.

OMNES: O-o! O-o!

PETE: Hold quiet, you trash o' niggers! tink

anybody wants you to cry? Who's you to set up screeching?—be quiet! But dis ain't all. Now, my cullud brethren, gird up your lines, and listen—hold on yer bref—it's a comin'. We tought dat de niggers would belong to de ole missus, and if she lost Terrebonne, we must live dere allers, and we would hire out, and bring our wages to ole Missus Peyton.

OMNES: Ya! ya! Well—

PETE: Hush! I tell ye, 't ain't so—we can't do it—we've got to be sold—

OMNES: Sold!

PETE: Will you hush? she will har you. Yes! I listen dar jess now—dar was ole lady cryin'—Mas'r George—ah! you seen dem big tears in his eyes. O, Mas'r Scudder, he did n't cry zackly; both ob his eyes and cheek look like de bad Bayou in low season—so dry dat I cry for him. (Raising his voice.) Den say de missus, "'T ain't for de land I keer, but for dem poor niggers—dey'll be sold—dat wot stagger me." "No," say Mas'r George, "I'd rather sell myself fuss; but dey shan't suffer, nohow,—I see 'em dam fuss."

OMNES: O, bless 'um! Bless Mas'r George.

PETE: Hole yer tongues. Yes, for you, for me, for dem little ones, dem folks cried. Now, den, if Grace dere wid her chil'n were all sold, she'll begin screechin' like a cat. She did n't mind how kind old judge was to her; and Solon, too, he'll holler, and break de ole lady's heart.

GRACE: No, Pete; no, I won't. I'll bear it.

PETE: I don't think you will any more, but dis here will; 'cause de family spile Dido, dey has. She nebber was worth much a' dat nigger.

DIDO: How dar you say dat, you black nigger, you? I fetch as much as any odder cook in Louisiana.

PETE: What's the use of your rakin' it kind, and comfortin' de missus' heart, if Minnie dere, and Louise, and Marie, and Julie is to spile it?

MINNIE: We won't, Pete; we won't.

PETE (to the men): Dar, do ye hear dat, ye mis-'able darkies; dem gals is worth a boat load of kinder men dem is. Cum, for de pride of de family, let every darky look his best for the judge's sake—dat ole man so good to us, and dat ole woman—so dem strangers from New Orleans shall say, Dem's happy darkies, dem's a fine set of niggers; every one say when he's sold, "Lor' bless dis yer family I'm gwine out of, and send me as good a home."

OMNES: We'll do it, Pete; we'll do it.

PETE: Hush! hark! I tell ye dar's somebody in dar. Who is it?

GRACE: It's Missy Zoe. See! see!

PETE: Come along; she har what we say, and she's cryin' for us. None o' ye ign'rant niggers could cry for yerselves like dat. Come here quite: now quite.

(Exeunt PETE and all the Negroes, slowly.)

(Enter ZOE who is supposed to have overheard the last scene.)

ZOE: O! must I learn from these poor wretches how much I owe, and how I ought to pay the debt? Have I slept upon the benefits I received, and never saw, never felt, never knew that I was forgetful and ungrateful? O, my father! my dear, dear father! forgive your poor child. You made her life too happy, and now these tears will flow. Let me hide them till I teach my heart. O, my —my heart! (Exit, with a low, wailing, suffocating cry.)

(Enter M'CLOSKY, LAFOUCHE, JACKSON, SUNNYSIDE and POINTDEXTER.)

POINTDEXTER (looking at his watch): Come, the hour is past. I think we may begin business. Where is Mr. Scudder?

JACKSON: I want to get to Ophelensis tonight.

(Enter DORA.)

DORA: Father, come here.

SUNNYSIDE: Why, Dora, what's the matter? Your eyes are red.

DORA: Are they? thank you. I don't care, they were blue this morning, but it don't signify now.

SUNNYSIDE: My darling! who has been teasing you?

DORA: Never mind. I want you to buy Terrebonne.

SUNNYSIDE: Buy Terrebonne! What for?

DORA: No matter—buy it!

SUNNYSIDE: It will cost me all I'm worth. This is folly, Dora.

DORA: Is my plantation at Comptableau worth this?

SUNNYSIDE: Nearly—perhaps.

DORA: Sell it, then, and buy this.

SUNNYSIDE: Are you mad, my love?

DORA: Do you want me to stop here and bid for it?

SUNNYSIDE: Good gracious, no!

DORA: Then I'll do it if you don't.

SUNNYSIDE: I will! I will! But for Heaven's sake go—here comes the crowd. (Exit DORA.)

What on earth does that child mean or want?

(*Enter* SCUDDER, GEORGE, RATTS, CAILLOU, PETE, GRACE, MINNIE, *and all the Negroes. A large table is in the center of the background.* POINTDEXTER *mounts the table with his hammer, his clerk sitting at his feet. The Negro mounts the table from behind. The rest sit down.*)

POINTDEXTER: Now, gentlemen, we shall proceed to business. It ain't necessary for me to dilate, describe or enumerate; Terrebonne is known to you as one of the richest bits of sile in Louisiana, and its condition reflects credit on them as had to keep it. I'll trouble you for that piece of baccy, Judge—thank you—so, gentlemen, as life is short, we'll start right off. The first lot on here is the estate in block, with its sugar-houses, stock, machines, implements, good dwelling-houses and furniture. If there is no bid for the estate and stuff, we'll sell it in smaller lots. Come, Mr. Thibodeaux, a man has a chance once in his life—here's yours.

THIBODEAUX: Go on. What's the reserve bid?

POINTDEXTER: The first mortgagee bids forty thousand dollars.

THIBODEAUX: Forty-five thousand.

SUNNYSIDE: Fifty thousand.

POINTDEXTER: When you have done joking, gentlemen, you'll say one hundred and twenty thousand. It carried that easy on mortgage.

LAFOUCHE: Then why don't you buy it yourself, Colonel?

POINTDEXTER: I'm waiting on your fifty thousand bid.

CAILLOU: Eighty thousand.

POINTDEXTER: Don't be afraid: it ain't going for that, Judge.

SUNNYSIDE: Ninety thousand.

POINTDEXTER: We're getting on.

THIBODEAUX: One hundred—

POINTDEXTER: One hundred thousand bid for this mag—

CAILLOU: One hundred and ten thousand—

POINTDEXTER: Good again—one hundred and—

SUNNYSIDE: Twenty.

POINTDEXTER: And twenty thousand bid. Squire Sunnyside is going to sell this at fifty thousand advance to-morrow. (*Looking round.*) Where's that man from Mobile that wanted to give one hundred and eight thousand?

THIBODEAUX: I guess he ain't left home yet, Colonel.

POINTDEXTER: I shall knock it down to the Squire—going—gone—for one hundred and

twenty thousand dollars. (*Raising hammer.*) Judge, you can raise the hull on mortgage—going for half its value. (*Knocking on the table.*) Squire Sunnyside, you've got a pretty bit o' land, Squire. Hillo, darkey, hand me a smash dar.

SUNNYSIDE: I got more than I can work now.

POINTDEXTER: Then buy the hands along with the property. Now, gentlemen, I'm proud to submit to you the finest lot of field hands and house servants that was ever offered for competition: they speak for themselves, and do credit to their owners. (*Reading.*) "No. 1, Solon, a guest boy, and a good waiter."

PETE: That's my son—buy him, Mas'r Ratts; he's sure to sarve you well.

POINTDEXTER: Hold your tongue!

RATTS: Let the old darkey alone—eight hundred for that boy.

CAILLOU: Nine.

RATTS: A thousand.

SOLON: Thank you, Mas'r Ratts: I die for you, sar; hold up for me, sar.

RATTS: Look here, the boy knows and likes me, Judge; let him come my way?

CAILLOU: Go on—I'm dumb.

POINTDEXTER: One thousand bid. He's yours, Captain Ratts, Magnolia steamer. (SOLON *goes and stands behind* RATTS.) "No. 2, the yellow girl, Grace, with two children—Saul, aged four, and Victoria, five." (*They got on table.*)

SCUDDER: That's Solon's wife and children Judge.

GRACE (*to* RATTS): Buy me, Mas'r Ratts, do buy me, sar?

RATTS: What in thunder should I do with you and those devils on board my boat?

GRACE: Wash, sar—cook, sar—anything.

RATTS: Eight hundred agin, then—I'll go it.

JACKSON: Nine.

RATTS: I'm broke, Solon—I can't stop the Judge.

THIBODEAUX: What's the matter, Ratts? I'll lend you all you want. Go it, if you're a mind to.

RATTS: Eleven.

JACKSON: Twelve.

SUNNYSIDE: O, O!

SCUDDER (*to* JACKSON): Judge, my friend. The Judge is a little deaf. Hello! (*Speaking in his ear-trumpet.*) This gal and them children belong to that boy Solon there. You're bidding to separate them, Judge.

JACKSON: The devil I am! (*Rising.*) I'll take back my bid, Colonel.

POINTDEXTER: All right, Judge; I thought there was a mistake. I must keep you, Captain, to the eleven hundred.

RATTS: Go it.

POINTDEXTER: Eleven hundred—going—going—sold! "No. 3, Pete, a house servant."

PETE: Dat's me—yer, I'm comin'—stand around dar. (*Tumbles upon the table.*)

POINTDEXTER: Aged seventy-two.

PETE: What's dat? A mistake, sar—forty-six.

POINTDEXTER: Lame.

PETE: But don't mount to nuffin—kin work cannel. Come, Judge, pick up. Now's your time, sar.

JACKSON: One hundred dollars.

PETE: What, sar? me! for me—look ye here! (*He dances.*)

GEORGE: Five hundred.

PETE: Mas'r George—ah, no, sar—don't buy me—keep your money for some uder dat is to be sold. I ain't no 'count, sar.

POINTDEXTER: Five hundred bid—it's a good price. He's yours, Mr. George Peyton. (*Pete goes down.*) "No. 4, the Octoroon girl, Zoe."

(*Enter* ZOE, *very pale, and stands on table.* M'CLOSKY *who hitherto has taken no interest in the sale, now turns his chair.*)

SUNNYSIDE (*rising*): Gentlemen, we are all acquainted with the circumstances of this girl's position, and I feel sure that no one here will oppose the family who desires to redeem the child of our esteemed and noble friend, the late Judge Peyton.

OMNES: Hear! bravo! hear!

POINTDEXTER: While the proceeds of this sale promises to realize less than the debts upon it, it is my duty to prevent any collusion for the depreciation of the property.

RATTS: Darn ye! You're a man as well as an auctioneer, ain't ye?

POINTDEXTER: What is offered for this slave?

SUNNYSIDE: One thousand dollars.

M'CLOSKY: Two thousand.

SUNNYSIDE: Three thousand.

M'CLOSKY: Five thousand.

GEORGE: Demon!

SUNNYSIDE: I bid seven thousand, which is the last dollar this family possesses.

M'CLOSKY: Eight.

THIBODEAUX: Nine.

OMNES: Bravo!

M'CLOSKY: Ten. It's no use, Squire.

SCUDDER: Jacob M'Closky, you shan't have that girl. Now, take care what you do. Twelve thousand.

M'CLOSKY: Shan't I! Fifteen thousand. Beat that any of ye.

POINTDEXTER: Fifteen thousand bid for the Octoroon.

(*Enter* DORA.)

DORA: Twenty thousand.

OMNES: Bravo!

M'CLOSKY: Twenty-five thousand.

OMNES (*groan*): O! O!

GEORGE: Yelping hound—take that. (*He rushes on* M'CLOSKY. M'CLOSKY *draws his knife.*)

SCUDDER (*darting between them*): Hold on, George Peyton—stand back. This is your own house; we are under your uncle's roof; recollect yourself. And, strangers, ain't we forgetting there's a lady present? (*The knives disappear.*) If we can't behave like Christians, let's try and act like gentlemen. Go on, Colonel.

LAFOUCHE: He didn't ought to bid against a lady.

M'CLOSKY: O, that's it, is it? Then I'd like to hire a lady to go to auction and buy my hands.

POINTDEXTER: Gentlemen, I believe none of us have two feelings about the conduct of that man; but he has the law on his side—we may regret, but we must respect it. Mr. M'Closky has bid twenty-five thousand dollars for the Octoroon. Is there any other bid? For the first time, twenty-five thousand—last time! (*Brings hammer down.*) To Jacob M'Closky, the Octoroon girl, Zoe, twenty-five thousand dollars.

ACT IV

SCENE. *The Wharf. The Steamer "Magnolia," alongside, a bluff rock.* RATTS *discovered, superintending the loading of ship.*

(*Enter* LAFOUCHE *and* JACKSON.)

JACKSON: How long before we start, captain?

RATTS: Just as soon as we put this cotton on board.

(*Enter* PETE, *with a lantern, and* SCUDDER, *with note book.*)

SCUDDER: One hundred and forty-nine bales. Can you take any more?

RATTS: Not a bale. I've got engaged eight

hundred bales at the next landing, and one hundred hogsheads of sugar at Patten's Slide—that'll take my guards under—hurry up thar.

VOICE (outside): Wood's aboard.

RATTS: All aboard then.

(Enter M'CLOSKY.)

SCUDDER: Sign that receipt, captain, and save me going up to the clerk.

M'CLOSKY: See here—there's a small freight of turpentine in the fore hold there, and one of the barrels leaks; a spark from your engines might set the ship on fire, and you'll go with it.

RATTS: You be darned! Go and try it, if you've a mind to.

LAFOUCHE: Captain, you've loaded up here until the boat is sunk so deep in the mud she won't float.

RATTS (calling off): Wood up thar, you Pollo —hang on to the safety valve—guess she'll crawl off on her paddles. (Shouts heard.)

JACKSON: What's the matter?

(Enter SOLON.)

SOLON: We got him!

SCUDDER: Who?

SOLON: The Injiun!

SCUDDER: Wahnotee? Where is he? D'ye call running away from a fellow catching him?

RATTS: Here he comes.

OMNES: Where? Where?

(Enter WAHNOTEE. They are all about to rush on him.)

SCUDDER: Hold on! stan' round thar! no violence—the critter don't know what we mean.

JACKSON: Let him answer for the boy then.

M'CLOSKY: Down with him—lynch him.

OMNES: Lynch him! (Exit LAFOUCHE.)

SCUDDER: Stan' back, I say! I'll nip the first that lays a finger on him. Pete, speak to the red-skin.

PETE: Whar's Paul, Wahnotee? What's come ob de child?

WAHNOTEE: Paul wunce—Paul pangeuk.

PETE: Pangeuk—dead!

WAHNOTEE: Mort!

M'CLOSKY: And you killed him? (They approach him.)

SCUDDER: Hold on!

PETE: Um, Paul reste?

WAHNOTEE: Hugh vieu. (Goes.) Paul reste ci!

SCUDDER: Here, stay! (Examining the ground.) The earth has been stirred here lately.

WAHNOTEE: Weenee Paul. (He points down, and shows by pantomime how he buried PAUL.)

SCUDDER: The Injun means that he buried him there! Stop! here's a bit of leather (Drawing out the mail-bags.) The mail-bags that were lost! (Sees the tomahawk in WAHNOTEE's belt—draws it out and examines it.) Look! here are marks of blood—look thar, red-skin, what's that?

WAHNOTEE: Paul! (Makes a sign that PAUL was killed by a blow on the head.)

M'CLOSKY: He confesses it; the Indian got drunk, quarrelled with him, and killed him.

(Re-enter LAFOUCHE, with smashed apparatus.)

LAFOUCHE: Here are evidences of the crime; this rum-bottle half emptied—this photographic apparatus smashed—and there are marks of blood and foot-steps around the shed.

M'CLOSKY: What more d'ye want—ain't that proof enough? Lynch him!

OMNES: Lynch him! Lynch him!

SCUDDER: Stan' back, boys! He's an Injiun—fair play.

JACKSON: Try him, then—try him on the spot of his crime.

OMNES: Try him! Try him!

LAFOUCHE: Don't let him escape!

RATTS: I'll see to that. (Drawing revolver.) If he stirs, I'll put a bullet through his skull, mighty quick.

M'CLOSKY: Come, form a court then, choose a jury—we'll fix this varmin.

(Enter THIBODEAUX and CAILLOU.)

THIBODEAUX: What's the matter?

LAPOUCHE: We've caught this murderer Injiun, and are going to try him. (WAHNOTEE sits, rolled in blanket.)

PETE: Poor little Paul—poor little nigger!

SCUDDER: This business goes agin me, Ratts —'t ain't right.

LAFOUCHE: We're ready; the jury's impanelled —go ahead—who'll be accuser?

RATTS: M'Closky.

M'CLOSKY: Me?

RATTS: Yes; you was the first to hail Judge Lynch.

M'CLOSKY: Well, what's the use of argument whar guilt sticks out so plain; the boy and Injiun were alone when last seen.

SCUDDER: Who says that?

M'CLOSKY: Everybody—that is, I heard so.

SCUDDER: Say what you know—not what you heard.

M'CLOSKY: I know then that the boy was killed with that tomahawk—the redskin owns it—the signs of violence are all round the shed—this apparatus smashed—ain't it plain that in a drunken fit he slew the boy, and when sober concealed the body yonder?

OMNES: That's it—that's it.

RATTS: Who defends the Injiun?

SCUDDER: I will; for it is agin my natur' to b'lieve him guilty; and if he be, this ain't the place, nor you the authority to try him. How are we sure the boy is dead at all? There are no witnesses but a rum bottle and an old machine. Is it on such evidence you'd hang a human being?

RATTS: His own confession.

SCUDDER: I appeal against your usurped authority. This lynch law is a wild and lawless proceeding. Here's a pictur' for a civilized community to afford; yonder, a poor, ignorant savage, and round him a circle of hearts, white with revenge and hate, thirsting for his blood: you call yourselves judges—you ain't—you're a jury of executioners. It is such scenes as these that bring disgrace upon our Western life.

M'CLOSKY: Evidence! Evidence! Give us evidence. We've had talk enough; now for proof.

OMNES: Yes, yes! Proof, proof!

SCUDDER: Where am I to get it? The proof is here, in my heart.

PETE (who has been looking about the camera): 'Top, sar! 'Top a bit! O, laws-a-mussey, see dis! here's a pictur' I found stickin' in that yar telescope machine, sar! look, sar!

SCUDDER: A photographic plate. (PETE holds his lantern up.) What's this, eh? two forms! The child—'t is he! dead—and above him—Ah! ah! Jacob M'Closky, 't was you murdered that boy!

M'CLOSKY: Me?

SCUDDER: You! You slew him with that tomahawk; and as you stood over his body with the letter in your hand, you thought that no witness saw the deed, that no eye was on you—but there was, Jacob M'Closky, there was. The eye of the Eternal was on you—the blessed sun in heaven, that, looking down, struck upon this plate the image of the deed. Here you are, in the very attitude of your crime!

M'CLOSKY: 'T is false!

SCUDDER: 'T is true! the apparatus can't lie. Look there, jurymen. (Showing plate to jury.) Look there. O, you wanted evidence—you called for proof—Heaven has answered and convicted you.

M'CLOSKY: What court of law would receive such evidence? (Going.)

RATTS: Stop! this would! you called it yourself; you wanted to make us murder that Injiun; and since we've got our hands in for justice, we'll try it on you. What say ye? shall we have one law for the red-skin and another for the white?

OMNES: Try him! Try him!

RATTS: Who'll be accuser?

SCUDDER: I will! Fellow-citizens, you are convened and assembled here under a higher power than the law. What's the law? When the ship's abroad on the ocean, when the army is before the enemy, where in thunder's the law? It is in the hearts of brave men, who can tell right from wrong, and from whom justice can't be bought. So it is here, in the wilds of the West, where our hatred of crime is measured by the speed of our executions—where necessity is law! I say, then, air you honest men? air you true? Put your hands on your naked breasts, and let every man as don't feel a real American heart there, bustin' up with freedom, truth, and right, let that man step out—that's the oath I put to ye—and then say, Darn ye, go it!

OMNES: Go on! Go on!

SCUDDER: No! I won't go on; that man's down. I won't strike him, even with words. Jacob, your accuser is that picter of the crime—let that speak—defend yourself.

M'CLOSKY (drawing knife): I will, quicker than lightning.

RATTS: Seize him, then! (They rush on M'CLOSKY, and disarm him.) He can fight though he's a painter: claws all over.

SCUDDER: Stop! Search him, we may find more evidence.

M'CLOSKY: Would you rob me first, and murder me afterwards?

RATTS (searching him): That's his programme—here's a pocket-book.

SCUDDER (opening it): What's here? Letters! Hello! To "Mrs. Peyton, Terrebonne, Louisiana, United States." Liverpool postmark. Ho! I've got hold of the tail of a rat—come out. (Reading.) What's this? A draft for eighty-five thousand dollars, and credit on Palisse and Co., of New Orleans, for the balance. Hi! the rat's out. You killed the boy to steal this letter from the mail-bags—you stole this letter, that the money should not arrive in time to save the Octoroon; had it done so, the lien on the estate would have ceased, and Zoe be free.

OMNES: Lynch him! Lynch him! Down with him!

SCUDDER: Silence in the court: stand back, let

the gentlemen of the jury retire, consult, and return their verdict.

RATTS: I'm responsible for the crittur—go on.

PETE (*to* WAHNOTEE): See, Injiun; look dar, (*Showing him the plate.*) see dat innocent; look, dar's de murderer of poor Paul.

WAHNOTEE: Ugh! (*Examining the plate.*)

PETE: Ya! as he? Closky tue Paul—kill de child with your tomahawk dar: 't was n't you, no—ole Pete allus say so. Poor Injiun lub our little Paul.

(WAHNOTEE *rises and looks at* M'CLOSKY—*he is in his war paint and fully armed.*)

SCUDDER: What say ye, gentlemen? Is the prisoner guilty, or is he not guilty?

OMNES: Guilty!

SCUDDER: And what is to be his punishment?

OMNES: Death! (*All advance.*)

WAHNOTEE (*crosses to* M'CLOSKY): Ugh!

SCUDDER: No, Injiun; we deal out justice here, not revenge. 'T ain't you he has injured, 't is the white man, whose laws he has offended.

RATTS: Away with him—put him down the aft hatch, till we rig his funeral.

M'CLOSKY: Fifty against one! O! if I had you one by one alone in the swamp, I'd rip ye all. (*He is borne off in boat struggling.*)

SCUDDER: Now, then, to business.

PETE (*re-enters from boat*): O, law, sir, dat debil Closky, he tore hisself from de gen'lam, knock me down, take my light, and trows it on de turpentine barrels, and de shed's all afire! (*Fire seen.*)

JACKSON (*re-entering*): We are catching fire forward: quick, cut free from the shore.

RATTS: All hands aboard there—cut the starn ropes—give her headway!

ALL: Ay, ay!

(*Cry of "Fire" heard—Engine bells heard—steam whistle noise.*)

RATTS: Cut all away, for'ard—overboard with every bale afire.

(*The Steamer moves off with the fire still blazing.*)
(M'CLOSKY *re-enters, swimming.*)

M'CLOSKY: Ha! have I fixed ye? Burn! burn! that's right. You thought you had cornered me, did ye? As I swam down, I thought I heard something in the water, as if pursuing me—one of them darned alligators, I suppose—they swarm hereabout—may they crunch every limb of ye. (*Exit.*)

(WAHNOTEE *is seen swimming. He finds trail and follows* M'CLOSKY. *The Steamer floats on at back, burning.*)

ACT V

SCENE 1. *Negroes' Quarters.*

(*Enter* ZOE.)

ZOE: It wants an hour yet to daylight—here is Pete's hut—(*Knocks.*) He sleeps—no; I see a light.

DIDO (*enters from hut*): Who dat?

ZOE: Hush, aunty! 'T is I—Zoe.

DIDO: Missey Zoe? Why you out in de swamp dis time ob night; you catch de fever sure—you is all wet.

ZOE: Where's Pete?

DIDO: He gone down to de landing last night wid Mas'r Scudder; not come back since—kint make it out.

ZOE: Aunty, there is sickness up at the house; I have been up all night beside one who suffers, and I remembered that when I had the fever you gave me a drink, a bitter drink, that made me sleep—do you remember it?

DIDO: Did n't I? Dem doctors ain't no 'count; dey don't know nuffin.

ZOE: No; but you, aunty, you are wise—you know every plant, don't you, and what it is good for?

DIDO: Dat you drink is fust rate for red fever. Is de folks' head bad?

ZOE: Very bad, aunty; and the heart aches worse, so they can get no rest.

DIDO: Hold on a bit, I get you de bottle. (*Exit.*)

ZOE: In a few hours that man, my master, will come for me: he has paid my price, and he only consented to let me remain here this one night, because Mrs. Peyton promised to give me up to him to-day.

DIDO (*re-enters with phial*): Here 't is —now you give one timble-full—dat's nuff.

ZOE: All there is there would kill one, would n't it?

DIDO: Guess it kill a dozen—nebber try.

ZOE: It's not a painful death, aunty, is it? You told me it produced a long, long sleep.

DIDO: Why you tremble so? Why you speak so wild? What you's gwine to do, missey?

ZOE: Give me the drink.

DIDO: No. Who dat sick at de house?

ZOE: Give it to me.

DIDO: No. You want to hurt yourself. O, Miss Zoe, why you ask old Dido for dis pizen?

ZOE: Listen to me. I love one who is here, and he loves me—George. I sat outside his door all night—I heard his sighs—his agony—torn from him by my coming fate; and he said, "I'd rather see her dead than this!"

DIDO: Dead!

ZOE: He said so—then I rose up, and stole from the house, and ran down to the bayou; but its cold, black, silent stream terrified me—drowning must be so horrible a death. I could not do it. Then, as I knelt there, weeping for courage, a snake rattled beside me. I shrunk from it and fled. Death was there beside me, and I dared not take it. O! I'm afraid to die; yet I am more afraid to live.

DIDO: Die!

ZOE: So I came here to you; to you, my own dear nurse; to you, who so often hushed me to sleep when I was a child; who dried my eyes and put your little Zoe to rest. Ah! give me the rest that no master but One can disturb—the sleep from which I shall awake free! You can protect me from that man—do let me die without pain.

DIDO: No, no—life is good for young ting like you.

ZOE: O! good, good nurse: you will, you will.

DIDO: No—g' way.

ZOE: Then I shall never leave Terrebonne—the drink, nurse; the drink; that I may never leave my home—my dear, dear home. You will not give me to that man? Your own Zoe, that loves you, aunty, so much, so much. (*She gets the phial.*) Ah! I have it.

DIDO: No missey. O! no—don't.

ZOE: Hush! (*Runs off.*)

DIDO: Here, Solon, Minnie, Grace.

(*They enter.*)

ALL: Was de matter?

DIDO: Miss Zoe got de pizen. (*Exit.*)

ALL: O! O! (*Exeunt.*)

SCENE 2. *In a Cane-brake Bayou, on a bank, with a canoe near by,* M'CLOSKY *is seen asleep.*

M'CLOSKY: Burn, burn! blaze away! How the flames crack. I'm not guilty; would ye murder me? Cut, cut the rope—I choke—choke!—Ah! (*Waking.*) Hello! where am I? Why, I was dreaming—curse it! I can never sleep now without dreaming. Hush! I thought I heard the sound of a paddle in the water. All night, as I fled through the cane-brake, I heard footsteps behind me. I lost them in the cedar swamp—again they haunted my path down the bayou, moving as I moved, resting when I rested—hush! there again!—no; it was only the wind over the canes. The sun is rising. I must launch my dug-out, and put for the bay, and in a few hours I shall be safe from pursuit on board of one of the coasting schooners that run from Galveston to Matagorda. In a little time this darned business will blow over, and I can show again. Hark! there's that noise again! If it was the ghost of that murdered boy haunting me! Well—I did n't mean to kill him, did I? Well, then, what has my all-cowardly heart got to skeer me so for?

(*He gets in canoe and rows off.* WAHNOTEE *appears in another canoe. He gets out and finds trail and paddles off after* M'CLOSKY.)

SCENE 3. *A cedar Swamp.*

(*Enter* SCUDDER *and* PETE.)

SCUDDER: Come on, Pete, we shan't reach the house before midday.

PETE: Nebber mind, sa, we bring good news—it won't spile for de keeping.

SCUDDER: Ten miles we've had to walk, because some blamed varmin onhitched our dug-out. I left it last night all safe.

PETE: P'r'aps it floated away itself.

SCUDDER: No; the hitching line was cut with a knife.

PETE: Say, Mas'r Scudder, s'pose we go in round by de quarters and raise de darkies, den dey cum long wid us, and we 'proach dat ole house like Gin'ral Jackson when he took London out dar.

SCUDDER: Hello, Pete, I never heard of that affair.

PETE: I tell you, sa—hush!

SCUDDER: What?

PETE: Was dat?—a cry out dar in the swamp—dar again!

SCUDDER: So it is. Something forcing its way through the undergrowth—it comes this way—it's either a bear or a runaway nigger.

(*He draws a pistol.* M'CLOSKY *rushes on, and falls at* SCUDDER'S *feet.*)

SCUDDER: Stand off—what are ye?

PETE: Mas'r Clusky.

M'CLOSKY: Save me—save me! I can go no farther. I heard voices.

SCUDDER: Who's after you?

M'CLOSKY: I don't know, but I feel it's death! In some form, human, or wild beast, or ghost, it has tracked me through the night. I fled; it followed. Hark! there it comes—it comes—don't you hear a footstep on the dry leaves!

SCUDDER: Your crime has driven you mad.

M'CLOSKY: D'ye hear it—nearer—nearer—ah!

(WAHNOTEE *rushes on, and attacks* M'CLOSKY.)

SCUDDER: The Injiun! by thunder.

PETE: You'se a dead man, Mas'r Clusky—you got to b'lieve dat.

M'CLOSKY: No—no. If I must die, give me up to the law; but save me from the tomahawk. You are a white man; you'll not leave one of your own blood to be butchered by the red-skin?

SCUDDER: Hold on now, Jacob; we've got to figure on that—let us look straight at the thing. Here we are on the selvage of civilization. It ain't our side, I believe, rightly; but Nature has said that where the white man sets his foot, the red man and the black man shall up sticks and stand around. But what do we pay for that possession? In cash? No—in kind—that is, in protection, forbearance, gentleness, in all them goods that show the critters the difference between the Christian and the savage. Now, what have you done to show them the distinction? for, darn me, if I can find out.

M'CLOSKY: For what I have done, let me be tried.

SCUDDER: You have been tried—honestly tried and convicted. Providence has chosen your executioner. I shan't interfere.

PETE: O, no; Mas'r Scudder, don't leave Mas'r Closky like dat—don't, sa—'t ain't what good Christian should do.

SCUDDER: D'ye hear that, Jacob? This old nigger, the grandfather of the boy you murdered, speaks for you—don't that go through you? D' ye feel it? Go on, Pete, you've waked up the Christian here, and the old hoss responds. (*He throws bowie-knife to* M'CLOSKY.) Take that, and defend yourself.

(*Exeunt* SCUDDER *and* PETE. WAHNOTEE *faces him. They fight.* M'CLOSKY *runs off,* WAHNOTEE *follows him.—Screams outside.*)

SCENE 4. *Parlor at Terrebonne.*

(*Enter* ZOE.)

ZOE: My home, my home! I must see you no more. Those little flowers can live, but I cannot. To-morrow they'll bloom the same—all will be here as now, and I shall be cold. O! my life, my happy life; why has it been so bright?

(*Enter* MRS. PEYTON *and* DORA.)

DORA: Zoe, where have you been?

MRS. PEYTON: We felt quite uneasy about you.

ZOE: I've been to the negro quarters. I suppose I shall go before long, and I wished to visit all the places, once again, to see the poor people.

MRS. PEYTON: Zoe, dear, I'm glad to see you more calm this morning.

DORA: But how pale she looks, and she trembles so.

ZOE: Do I? (*Enters* GEORGE.) Ah! he is here.

DORA: George, here she is.

ZOE: I have come to say good-by, sir; two hard words—so hard, they might break many a heart; might n't they?

GEORGE: O, Zoe! can you smile at this moment?

ZOE: You see how easily I have become reconciled to my fate—so it will be with you. You will not forget poor Zoe! but her image will pass away like a little cloud that obscured your happiness a while—you will love each other; you are both too good not to join your hearts. Brightness will return amongst you. Dora, I once made you weep; those were the only tears I caused anybody. Will you forgive me?

DORA: Forgive you—(*Kisses her.*)

ZOE: I feel you do, George.

GEORGE: Zoe, you are pale. Zoe!—she faints!

ZOE: No; a weakness, that's all—a little water. (DORA *gets some water.*) I have a restorative here—will you pour it in the glass? (DORA *attempts to take it.*) No; not you—George. (GEORGE *pours the contents of the phial into glass.*) Now, give it to me. George, dear George, do you love me?

GEORGE: Do you doubt it, Zoe?

ZOE: No! (*She drinks.*)

DORA: Zoe, if all I possess would buy your freedom, I would gladly give it.

ZOE: I am free! I had but one Master on earth, and he has given me my freedom!

DORA: Alas! but the deed that freed you was not lawful.

ZOE: Not lawful—no—but I am going to where there is no law—where there is only justice.

GEORGE: Zoe, you are suffering—your lips are white—your cheeks are flushed.

ZOE: I must be going—it is late. Farewell, Dora. (*Retiring.*)

PETE (*outside*): Whar's Missus—whar's Mas'r George?

GEORGE: They come.

(*Enter* SCUDDER)

SCUDDER: Stand around and let me pass—room thar! I feel so big with joy, creation ain't wide enough to hold me. Mrs. Peyton, George Peyton, Terrebonne is yours. It was that rascal M'Closky—but he got rats, I swow—he killed the boy, Paul, to rob this letter from the mailbags—the letter from Liverpool you know—he sot fire to the shed—that was how the steamboat got burned up.

MRS. PEYTON: What d' ye mean?

SCUDDER: Read—read that. (*He gives letter to them.*)

GEORGE: Explain yourself.

(*Enter* SUNNYSIDE.)

SUNNYSIDE: Is it true?

SCUDDER: Every word of it, Squire. Here, you tell it, since you know it. If I was to try, I'd bust.

MRS. PEYTON: Read, George. Terrebonne is yours.

(*Enter* PETE, DIDO, SOLON, MINNIE, *and* GRACE.)

PETE: Whar is she—whar is Miss Zoe?

SCUDDER: What's the matter?

PETE: Don't ax me. Whar's de gal? I say.

SCUDDER: Here she is—Zoe!—water—she faints.

PETE: No—no. 'T ain't no faint—she's a dying, sa: she got pizon from old Dido here, this mornin'.

GEORGE: Zoe!

SCUDDER: Zoe! is this true?—no, it ain't—darn it, say it ain't. Look here, you're free, you know; nary a master to hurt you now: you will stop here as long as you're a mind to, only don't look so.

DORA: Her eyes have changed color.

PETE: Dat's what her soul 's gwine to do. It's going up dar, whar dere's no line atween folks.

GEORGE: She revives.

ZOE (*on the sofa*): George—where—where—

GEORGE: O, Zoe! what have you done?

ZOE: Last night I overheard you weeping in your room, and you said, "I'd rather see her dead than so!"

GEORGE: Have I then prompted you to this?

ZOE: No; but I loved you so, I could not bear my fate; and then I stood between your heart and hers. When I am dead she will not be jealous of your love for me, no laws will stand between us. Lift me; so—(GEORGE *raises her head*)—let me look at you, that your face may be the last I see of this world. O! George, you may, without a blush, confess your love for the Octoroon.

(*She dies.* GEORGE *lowers her head gently and kneels beside her.*)

Bronson Howard: *Shenandoah* (1888)

The Civil War had been the subject of drama before Bronson Howard's work, but few writers saw the potential for melodrama as clearly as he did. William Gillette, who became famous in the title role of his own play, *Sherlock Holmes,* had written two plays on the subject of the war. One, *Secret Service,* was perhaps even more successful than Howard's. But few playwrights of any time seem to have known their audience and its taste as well as Howard did.

Bronson Howard was born in Detroit, Michigan, in 1842. His family had means; and one of his forebears had fought in the French and Indian War and had later been killed in the Revolutionary War in the battle of Monmouth. Howard's early plans were to school himself for Yale, so he studied in New Haven for some time in preparation. Eye trouble seems to have kept him from attending Yale, and he returned to Detroit to work for the Detroit *Free Press.* His first play, *Fantine,* was an adaptation of a segment of Victor Hugo's *Les Misérables,* and its success encouraged him to head for New York at the age of twenty-two. He began to make his living as a journalist, but soon he was lionized with the success of his play, *Saratoga,* a farce and social commentary about a man engaged to four women. Its run, one hundred one nights, enabled him to turn to playwriting as a career.

Howard was a good student of social mores, and most of his plays reflect the ways of his audiences. When he made them laugh at themselves, he was cautious enough not to indict them or to treat them with rough satire. Indeed, in his revelation of their nature he ended by praising their warmth, their humor, their courage. Yet, by modern standards we could hardly consider his analysis of society either deep or truly realistic. For these very reasons his plays were generally well received. He established—or, more properly, contributed to—the tradition of rewarding his audiences with humor and wit, but was careful not to abuse them or jolt them out of their own sense of security. One pictures the audiences in the large cities of 1888 as somewhat complacent, very secure, and thoroughly certain of their values. Nothing Bronson Howard did on stage would have challenged their sense of themselves.

To a large extent, Howard's qualities as a dramatist can be seen fully in *Shenandoah,* possibly his most popular play. Its focus is on Civil War, yet there is very little about war itself in the play. The question of slavery is omitted altogether. Perhaps it is just as well that Howard avoided making the play a propaganda piece defending one side or the other. The result, however, is that the most representative play of the Civil War theme is almost devoid of any insight into the Civil War. Ironically, this may be what made the play as successful as it was —there was little to irritate adherents of either side.

The focus is on personal matters. And, as in most comedies, the emphasis is especially on romance and marriage. The opening of the play is authentic in portraying the anticipation of Charleston concerning the bombing of Fort Sumter. The citizens did regard it as a social event, a virtual fireworks. The romance of Colonel Kerchival West, the northerner, and his southern sweetheart, Gertrude Ellingham, is the principal focus of the play. Their falling-out over the question of war dominates the first act, with a wonderful bit of coquettishness on the part of Gertrude at the end of the act, when Kerchival asks whether she loves him. They part as enemies, just as the men who had been fellow officers under the United States flag and who must now obey the flag of their respective "countries."

The theme of brother against brother, of sweetheart against sweetheart, interests Howard more than any of the deeper issues that have engaged subsequent historians. Even the social issues of Harriet Beecher Stowe and George L. Aiken receive no attention from Howard, since the failings of any of the characters, as well as the complications all of them suffer, stem usually from personal problems of character. Apart from the necessary evils of occupation and separation—themes that actually "arise" between Acts I and II—the forces of personal pride, of scoundrelism (on the part of Thornton), and of gallantry dominate the drama. The suspicion of infidelity on the part of the Haverills is balanced by the extraordinary fidelity of Kerchival and Gertrude, even while enemies; and the reunion of all four in the last act can be seen as a symbol of the uncertainties the future of the republic faced in 1865, and the will the nation exerted in trying to mend the damage done by separation.

Serious students of the period will realize that the metaphor of an older married couple and a young pair of newlyweds may not be totally suitable for exploring the theme of a nation united after having been rent apart. The pain of the period of reconstruction is now only hinted at in the play, and returning to normalcy seems unlikely to offer real difficulties for these people.

Yet, for all its shortcomings, *Shenandoah* reveals people as they were, shows them as they themselves probably wished to be seen, and offers us a view of America as it really appeared to be to a great number of theatergoers. Were we to wish for something quite different, we would be demanding what the contemporary late twentieth-century stage has taught us to demand. Bronson Howard would have been a terrible failure had he in any way attempted to answer this demand; that was reserved for a much later generation, the one that was writing at the time Howard died in 1908.

Selected Readings

Bronson Howard, *Autobiography of a Play* (New York: Dramatic Museum of Columbia University, 1915).

————. *The Banker's Daughter and Other Plays*, ed. Allan G. Halline. Princeton: Princeton University Press, 1941.

Shenandoah

Bronson Howard

CHARACTERS

GENERAL HAVERILL
COLONEL KERCHIVAL WEST
CAPTAIN HEARTSEASE
LIEUTENANT FRANK BEDLOE
MAJOR-GENERAL FRANCIS BUCKTHORN,
    Commander of the 19th Army Corps
SERGEANT BARKET
COLONEL ROBERT ELLINGHAM, *10th Virginia*
CAPTAIN THORNTON, *Secret Service, C.S.A.*
MRS. CONSTANCE HAVERILL
GERTRUDE ELLINGHAM
MADELINE WEST

JENNY BUCKTHORN
MRS. EDITH HAVERILL
HARDWICK, *Surgeon*
CAPTAIN LOCKWOOD, *U. S. Signal Corps*
LIEUTENANT OF SIGNAL CORPS
LIEUTENANT OF INFANTRY
CORPORAL DUNN
BENSON
OLD MARGERY
JANNETTE
WILKINS

ACT I

Charleston Harbor in 1861. "After the Ball."

(*The Interior of a Southern Residence on the shore of Charleston Harbor. Large double doors at the rear of the stage are open. A large, wide window, with low sill, extends down the right side of the stage. A veranda is seen through the doors and the window. There is a wide opening on the left with a corridor beyond. The furniture and appointments are quaint and old-fashioned, but lighted candles nearly burned down, light the general tone of the walls and upholstery is that of the old Colonial period in its more ornamental and decorative phase, as shown in the early days of Charleston. Old candlesticks and candelabra, with lighted candles nearly burned down, light the room, and in addition the moon-light streams in. Beyond the central doors and the window there is a lawn, with Southern foliage, extending down to the shores of the harbor; a part of the bay lies in the distance, with low-lying land beyond. The lights of Charleston are seen over the water along the shore. The gray twilight of early morning gradually steals over the scene as the Act progresses. As the curtain rises,* KERCHIVAL WEST *is sitting in a chair, his feet extended and his head thrown back, a handkerchief over his face.* ROBERT ELLINGHAM *strolls in on the veranda,* beyond the window, smoking. He looks to the right, starts and moves to the window; leans against the upper side of the window and looks across.*)

ELLINGHAM: Kerchival!

KERCHIVAL (*under the handkerchief*): Eh? H'm!

ELLINGHAM: Can you sleep at a time like this? My own nerves are on fire.

KERCHIVAL: Fire? Oh—yes—I remember. Any more fire-works, Bob?

ELLINGHAM: A signal rocket from one of the batteries, now and then. (*He goes up beyond the window.* KERCHIVAL *arouses himself, taking the handkerchief from his eyes.*)

KERCHIVAL: What a preposterous hour to be up. The ball was over an hour ago, all the guests are gone, and it's nearly four o'clock. (*Looking at his watch.*) Exactly ten minutes of four. (*He takes out a cigar.*) Our Southern friends assure us that General Beauregard is to open fire on Fort Sumter this morning. I don't believe it. (*Lighting the cigar and rising, he looks out through the window.*) There lies the old fort—solemn and grim as ever, and the flag-staff stands above it, like a warning finger. If they do fire upon it (*shutting his teeth for a moment and looking down at the cigar in his hand*) the echo of that first shot will be heard above their graves, and Heaven knows how many of our own, also; but the flag will still float!—over the graves of both sides.

(ELLINGHAM *enters from the central door and approaches him.*)

Are you Southerners all mad, Robert?

ELLINGHAM: Are you Northerners all blind? (KERCHIVAL *sits down.*) We Virginians would prevent a war if we could. But your people in the North do not believe that one is coming. You do not understand the determined frenzy of my fellow Southerners. Look! (*Pointing toward the rear of the stage.*) Do you see the lights of the city, over the water? The inhabitants of Charleston are gathering, even now, in the gray, morning twilight, to witness the long-promised bombardment of Fort Sumter. It is to be a gala day for them. They have talked and dreamed of nothing else for weeks. The preparations have become a part of their social life—of their amusement—their gayeties. This very night at the ball—here—in the house of my own relatives—what was their talk? What were the jests they laughed at? Sumter! War! Ladies were betting bonbons that the United States would not dare to fire a shot in return, and pinning ribbons on the breasts of their "heroes." There was a signal rocket from one of the forts, and the young men who were dancing here left their partners standing on the floor to return to the batteries—as if it were the night before another Waterloo. The ladies themselves hurried away to watch the "spectacle" from their own verandas. You won't see the truth! I tell you, Kerchival, a war between the North and South is inevitable!

KERCHIVAL: And if it does come, you Virginians will join the rest.

ELLINGHAM: Our State will be the battle ground I fear. But every loyal son of Virginia will follow her flag. It is our religion!

KERCHIVAL: My State is New York. If New York should go against the old flag, New York might go to the devil. That is my religion.

ELLINGHAM: So differently have we been taught what the word "patriotism" means!

KERCHIVAL: You and I are officers of the same regiment of the United States Regular Army, Robert; we were classmates at West Point, and we have fought side by side on the plains. You saved my scalp once; I'd have to wear a wig, now, if you had n't. I say, old boy, are we to be enemies?

ELLINGHAM (*laying his hand over his shoulder*): My dear old comrade, whatever else comes, our friendship shall be unbroken!

KERCHIVAL: Bob! (*looking up at him*) I only hope that we shall never meet in battle!

ELLINGHAM: In battle? The idea is horrible!

KERCHIVAL (*rising and crossing to him*): My dear old comrade, one of us will be wrong in this great fight, but we shall both be honest in it. (*He gives his hand;* ELLINGHAM *grasps it warmly, then turns away.*)

ELLINGHAM: Colonel Haverill is watching the forts, also; he has been as sad to-night as we have. Next to leaving you, my greatest regret is that I must resign from his regiment.

KERCHIVAL: You are his favorite officer.

ELLINGHAM: Naturally, perhaps; he was my guardian.

(*Enter* HAVERILL *from the rear. He walks down, stopping in the center of the stage.*)

HAVERILL: Kerchival! I secured the necessary passports to the North yesterday afternoon; this one is yours; I brought it down for you early in the evening. (KERCHIVAL *takes the paper and goes to the window.*) I am ordered direct to Washington at once, and shall start with Mrs. Haverill this forenoon. You will report to Captain Lyon, of the 2d Regiment, in St. Louis. Robert! I have hoped for peace to the last, but it is hoping against hope. I feel certain, now, that the fatal blow will be struck this morning. Our old regiment is already broken up, and you, also, will now resign, I suppose, like nearly all your fellow Southerners in the Service.

ELLINGHAM: You know how sorry I am to leave your command, Colonel!

HAVERILL: I served under your father in Mexico; he left me, at his death, the guardian of you and your sister, Gertrude. Even since you became of age, I have felt that I stood in his place. But you must be your sister's only guardian now. Your father fell in battle, fighting for our common country, but you—

ELLINGHAM: He would have done as I shall do, had he lived. He was a Virginian!

HAVERILL: I am glad, Robert, that he was never called upon to decide between two flags. He never knew but one, and we fought under it together. (*Exit.*)

ELLINGHAM: Kerchival! Something occurred in this house to-night which—which I should n't mention under ordinary circumstances, but I—I feel that it may require my further attention, and you, perhaps, can be of service to me. Mrs. Haverill, the wife of the Colonel—

KERCHIVAL: Fainted away in her room.

ELLINGHAM: You know?

KERCHIVAL: I was one of the actors in the little drama.

ELLINGHAM: Indeed!

KERCHIVAL: About half-past nine this evening, while the ladies were dressing for the ball, I was going upstairs; I heard a quick, sharp cry, sprang forward, found myself at an open door. Mrs. Haverill lay on the floor inside, as if she had just reached the door to cry for help, when she fell. After doing all the unnecessary and useless things I could think of, I rushed out of the room to tell your sister, Gertrude, and my own sister, Madeline, to go and take care of the lady. Within less than twenty minutes afterwards, I saw Mrs. Haverill sail into the drawing-room, a thing of beauty, and with the glow of perfect health on her cheek. It was an immense relief to me when I saw her. Up to that time I had a vague idea that I had committed a murder.

ELLINGHAM: Murder!

KERCHIVAL: M—m. A guilty conscience. Every man, of course, does exactly the wrong thing when a woman faints. When I rushed out of Mrs. Haverills's room, I left my handkerchief soaked with water upon her face. I must ask her for it, it's a silk one. Luckily, the girls got there in time to take if off; she would n't have come to if they had n't. It never occurred to me that she'd need to breathe in my absence. That's all I know about the matter. What troubles you? I suppose every woman has a right to faint whenever she chooses. The scream that I heard was so sharp, quick and intense that—

ELLINGHAM: That the cause must have been a serious one.

KERCHIVAL: Yes! So I thought. It must have been a mouse.

ELLINGHAM: Mr. Edward Thornton has occupied the next room to that of Mrs. Haverill to-night.

KERCHIVAL (quickly): What do you mean?

ELLINGHAM: During the past month or more he has been pressing, not to say insolent, in his attentions to Mrs. Haverill.

KERCHIVAL: I've noticed that myself.

ELLINGHAM: And he is an utterly unscrupulous man; it is no fault of mine that he was asked to be a guest at this house to-night. He came to Charleston, some years ago, from the North, but if there are any vices and passions peculiarly strong in the South, he has carried them all to the extreme. In one of the many scandals connected with Edward Thornton's name, it was more than whispered that he entered a lady's room unexpectedly at night. But, as he killed the lady's husband in a duel a few days afterwards, the scandal dropped.

KERCHIVAL: Of course; the gentleman received ample satisfaction as an outraged husband, and Mr. Thornton apologized, I suppose, to his widow.

ELLINGHAM: He has repeated the adventure.

KERCHIVAL: Do—you—think—that?

ELLINGHAM: I was smoking on the lawn, and glanced up at the window; my eyes may have deceived me, and I must move cautiously in the matter; but it could n't have been imagination; the shadow of Edward Thornton's face and head appeared upon the curtain.

KERCHIVAL: Whew! The devil!

ELLINGHAM: Just at that moment, I too, heard the stifled scream.

(*Enter* EDWARD THORNTON.)

THORNTON: Gentlemen!

ELLINGHAM: Your name was just on my tongue, Mr. Thornton.

THORNTON: I thought I heard it, but you are welcome to it. Miss Gertrude has asked me to ride over to Mrs. Pinckney's with her, to learn if there is further news from the batteries. I am very glad the time to attack Fort Sumter has come at last!

ELLINGHAM: I do not share your pleasure.

THORNTON: You are a Southern gentleman.

ELLINGHAM: And you are a Northern "gentleman."

THORNTON: A Southerner by choice; I shall join the cause.

ELLINGHAM: We native Southerners will defend our own rights, sir; you may leave them in our keeping. It is my wish, Mr. Thornton, that you do not accompany my sister.

THORNTON: Indeed!

ELLINGHAM: Her groom, alone, will be sufficient.

THORNTON: As you please, sir. Kindly offer my excuses to Miss Gertrude. You and I can chat over the subject later in the day, when we are alone. (*Moving up the stage.*)

ELLINGHAM: By all means, and another subject, also, perhaps.

THORNTON: I shall be entirely at your service. (*Exit to the veranda.*)

ELLINGHAM: Kerchival, I shall learn the whole truth, if possible, to-day. If it is what I suspect—what I almost know—I will settle with him myself. He has insulted our Colonel's wife and outraged the hospitality of my friends. (*Walking to the right.*)

KERCHIVAL (*walking to the left*): I think it ought to be my quarrel. I'm sure I'm mixed up in it enough.

MADELINE (*without, calling*): Kerchival!

ELLINGHAM: Madeline. (*Aside, starting,* KERCHIVAL *looks across at him sharply.*)

KERCHIVAL (*aside*): I distinctly saw Bob give a start when he heard Madeline. Now, what can there be about my sister's voice to make a man jump like that?

GERTRUDE (*without*): Brother Robert!

KERCHIVAL: Gertrude! (*Aside, starting,* ELLINGHAM *looks at him sharply.*) How the tones of a woman's voice thrill through a man's soul!

(*Enter* MADELINE.)

MADELINE: Oh, Kerchival—here you are.

(*Enter* GERTRUDE, *from the apartment, in a riding habit, with a whip.*)

GERTRUDE: Robert, dear! (*Coming down to* ROBERT; *they converse in dumb show.*)

MADELINE: Where are your field glasses? I've been rummaging all through your clothes, and swords, and sashes, and things. I've turned everything in your room upside down.

KERCHIVAL: Have you?

MADELINE: I can't find your glasses anywhere. I want to look at the forts. Another rocket went up just now. (*Runs up the stage and stands on the piazza looking off.*)

KERCHIVAL: A sister has all the privileges of a wife to upset a man's things, without her legal obligation to put them straight again. (*Glances at* GERTRUDE.) I wish Bob's sister had the same privileges in my room that my own has.

GERTRUDE: Mr. Thornton isn't going with me, you say?

ELLINGHAM: He requested me to offer you his apologies.

KERCHIVAL: May *I* accompany you? (ELLINGHAM *turns to the window on the right.*)

GERTRUDE: My groom, old Pete, will be with me, of course; there's no particular need of anyone else. But you may go along, if you like. I've got my hands full of sugar plums for Jack. Dear old Jack—he always has his share when we have company. I'm going over to Mrs. Pinckney's to see if she's had any more news from General Beauregard; her son is on the General's staff.

MADELINE (*looking off to the right*): There's another rocket from Fort Johnson, and it is answered from Fort Moultrie. Ah! (*Angrily.*) General Beauregard is a bad, wicked man! (*Coming down.*)

GERTRUDE: Oh! Madeline! You are a bad, wicked Northern girl to say such a thing.

MADELINE: I *am* a Northern girl.

GERTRUDE: And I am a Southern girl. (*They face each other.*)

KERCHIVAL (*dropping into a chair*): The war has begun.

(ELLINGHAM *has turned from the window; he strolls across the stage, watching the girls.*)

GERTRUDE: General Beauregard is a patriot.

MADELINE: He is a Rebel.

GERTRUDE: So am I.

MADELINE: Gertrude!—You—you—

GERTRUDE: Madeline! You

MADELINE: I—I—

GERTRUDE: I—

BOTH: O—O-h! (*Bursting into tears and rushing into each other's arms, sobbing, then suddenly kissing each other vigorously.*)

KERCHIVAL: I say, Bob, if the North and South do fight, that will be the end of it.

GERTRUDE: I've got something to say to you, Madeline, dear. (*Confidentially and turning with her arms about her waist. The girls sit down talking earnestly.*)

ELLINGHAM: Kerchival, old boy! There's—there's something I'd like to say to you before we part to-day.

KERCHIVAL: I'd like a word with you, also!

MADELINE: You don't really mean that, Gertrude—with me?

ELLINGHAM: I'm in love with your sister, Madeline.

KERCHIVAL: The devil you are!

ELLINGHAM: I never suspected such a thing until last night.

GERTRUDE: Robert was in love with you six weeks ago. (MADELINE *kisses her.*)

KERCHIVAL: *I've* made a discovery, too, Bob.

MADELINE: *I've* got something to say to *you,* Gertrude.

KERCHIVAL: I'm in love with *your* sister.

ELLINGHAM (*astonished*): You are?

MADELINE: Kerchival has been in love with you for the last three months. (GERTRUDE *offers her lips—they kiss.*)

KERCHIVAL: I fell in love with her the day before yesterday. (*The two gentlemen grasp each other's hands warmly.*)

ELLINGHAM: We understand each other, Kerchival. (*He turns up the stage and stops at the door.*) Miss Madeline, you said just now that you wished to watch the forts. Would you like to walk down to the shore?

MADELINE: Yes! (*Rising and going up to him. He takes one of her hands in his own and looks at her earnestly.*)

ELLINGHAM: This will be the last day that we shall be together, for the present. But we shall meet again—sometime—if we both live.

MADELINE: If we both live! You mean—if *you* live. You must go into this dreadful war, if it comes.

ELLINGHAM: Yes, Madeline, I must. Come let us watch for our fate. (*Exeunt to the veranda.*)

KERCHIVAL (*aside*): I must leave Charleston to-day. ((*He sighs.*) Does she love me?

GERTRUDE: I am ready to start, Mr. West, when you are.

KERCHIVAL: Oh! Of course, I forgot. (*Rising.*) I shall be delighted to ride at your side.

GERTRUDE: At my side! (*Rising.*) There is n't a horse in America that can keep by the side of my Jack, when I give him his head, and I'm sure to do it. You may follow us. But you can hardly ride in that costume; while you are changing it, I'll give Jack his bonbons. (*Turning to the window.*) There he is, bless him! Pawing the ground, and impatient for me to be on his back. Let him come, Pete. (*Holding up bonbons at window.*) I love you.

KERCHIVAL: Eh? (*Turning suddenly.*)

GERTRUDE (*looking at him*): What?

KERCHIVAL: You were saying—

GERTRUDE: Jack! (*Looking out. The head of a large black horse appears through the window.*) You dear old fellow. (*She feeds him with bonbons.*) Jack has been my boy ever since he was a little colt. I brought you up, did n't I, Jack? He's the truest, and kindest, and best of friends; I would n't be parted from him for the world, and I'm the only woman he'll allow to be near him.

KERCHIVAL (*earnestly*): You are the only woman, Miss Gertrude, that I—

GERTRUDE: Dear Jack!

KERCHIVAL (*aside*): Jack embarrasses me. He's a third party.

GERTRUDE: There! That will do for the present, Jack. Now go along with Pete! If you are a very good boy, and don't let Lieutenant Kerchival West come within a quarter of a mile of me, after the first three minutes, you shall have some more sugar plums when we get to Mrs. Pinckney's. (*An old negro leads the horse away.* GERTRUDE *looks around at* KERCHIVAL.) You

have n't gone to dress, yet; we shall be late. Mrs. Pinckney asked a party of friends to witness the bombardment this morning, and breakfast together on the piazza while they are looking at it. We can remain and join them, if you like.

KERCHIVAL: I hope they won't wait for breakfast until the bombardment begins.

GERTRUDE: I'll bet you an embroidered cigar-case, Lieutenant, against a box of gloves that it will begin in less than an hour.

KERCHIVAL: Done! You will lose the bet. But you shall have the gloves; and one of the hands that go inside them shall be—(*Taking one of her hands; she withdraws it.*)

GERTRUDE: My own—until some one wins it. You don't believe that General Beauregard will open fire on Fort Sumter this morning?

KERCHIVAL: No; I don't.

GERTRUDE: Everything is ready.

KERCHIVAL: It's so much easier to get everything ready to do a thing than it is to do it. I have been ready a dozen times, this very night, to say to you, Miss Gertrude, that I—that I—(*Pauses.*)

GERTRUDE (*looking down and tapping her skirt with her whip*): Well?

KERCHIVAL: But I did n't.

GERTRUDE (*glancing up at him suddenly*): I dare say, General Beauregard has more nerve than you have.

KERCHIVAL: It is easy enough to set the batteries around Charleston Harbor, but the man who fires the first shot at a woman—

GERTRUDE: Woman!

KERCHIVAL: At the American flag—must have nerves of steel.

GERTRUDE: You Northern men are so slow, to—

KERCHIVAL: I have been slow; but I assure you, Miss Gertrude, that my heart—

GERTRUDE: What subject are we on now?

KERCHIVAL: You were complaining because I was too slow.

GERTRUDE: I was doing nothing of the kind, sir!—let me finish, please. You Northern men are so slow, to believe that our Southern heroes—Northern *men* and Southern *heroes*—you recognize the distinction I make—you won't believe that they will keep their promises. They have sworn to attack Fort Sumter this morning, and—they—will do it. This "American Flag" you talk of is no longer our flag: it is foreign to us!—It is the flag of an enemy!

KERCHIVAL (*tenderly and earnestly*): Am I your enemy?

GERTRUDE: You have told me that you will

return to the North, and take the field.

KERCHIVAL: Yes, I will. (*Decisively.*)

GERTRUDE: You will be fighting against my friends, against my own brother, against me. We *shall* be enemies.

KERCHIVAL (*firmly*): Even that, Gertrude— (*She looks around at him, he looks squarely into her eyes as he proceeds*)—if you will have it so. If my country needs my services, I shall not refuse them, though it makes us enemies! (*She wavers a moment, under strong emotion, and turns away; sinks upon the seat, her elbow on the back of it, and her lightly-clenched fist against her cheek, looking away from him.*)

GERTRUDE: I will have it so! I am a Southern woman!

KERCHIVAL: We have more at stake between us, this morning, than a cigar-case and a box of gloves. (*Turning up the stage.*)

(*Enter* MRS. HAVERILL *from apartment.*)

MRS. HAVERILL: Mr. West! I've been looking for you. I have a favor to ask.

KERCHIVAL: Of me?—with pleasure.

MRS. HAVERILL: But I am sorry to have interrupted you and Gertrude. (*As she passes down* KERCHIVAL *moves up the stage.* GERTRUDE *rises.*) (*Apart.*) There are tears in your eyes, Gertrude, dear!

GERTRUDE (*apart*): They have no right there.

MRS. HAVERILL (*apart*): I'm afraid I know what has happened. A quarrel! and you are to part with each other so soon. Do not let a girl's coquetry trifle with her heart until it is too late. You remember the confession you made to me last night?

GERTRUDE (*apart*): Constance! (*Starting.*) That is my secret; more a secret now than ever.

MRS. HAVERILL (*apart*): Yes, dear; but you do love him. (GERTRUDE *moves up the stage.*)

GERTRUDE: You need not ride over with me, Mr. West.

KERCHIVAL: I can be ready in one moment.

GERTRUDE: I choose to go alone! Old Pete will be with me; and Jack, himself, is a charming companion.

KERCHIVAL: If you prefer Jack's company to mine—

GERTRUDE: I do. (*Exit on the veranda.*)

KERCHIVAL: Damn Jack! But you will let me assist you to mount. (*Exit after her.*)

MRS. HAVERILL: We leave for the North before noon, but every hour seems a month. If my husband should learn what happened in my room to-night, he would kill that man. What

encouragement could I have given him? Innocence is never on its guard—but, (*drawing up*) the last I remember before I fell unconscious, he was crouching before me like a whipped cur! (*She starts as she looks out of the window.*) There is Mr. Thornton, now—Ah! (*Angrily.*) No—I must control my own indignation. I must keep him and Colonel Haverill from meeting before we leave Charleston. Edward Thornton would shoot my husband down without remorse. But poor Frank! I must not forget him, in my own trouble. I have but little time left to care for his welfare.

(*Re-enter* KERCHIVAL.)

KERCHIVAL: You said I could do you a favor, Mrs. Haverill?

MRS. HAVERILL: Yes, I wanted to speak with you about General Haverill's son, Frank. I should like you to carry a message to Charleston for me as soon as it is light. It is a sad errand. You know too well the great misfortune that has fallen upon my husband in New York.

KERCHIVAL: His only son has brought disgrace upon his family name, and tarnished the reputation of a proud soldier. Colonel Haverill's fellow officers sympathize with him most deeply.

MRS. HAVERILL: And poor young Frank! I could hardly have loved the boy more if he had been my own son. If he had not himself confessed the crime against the bank, I could not have believed him guilty. He has escaped from arrest. He is in the City of Charleston. I am the only one in all the world he could turn to. He was only a lad of fourteen when his father and I were married, six years ago; and the boy has loved me from the first. His father is stern and bitter now in his humiliation. This note from Frank was handed to me while the company were here last evening. I want you to find him and arrange for me to meet him, if you can do it with safety. I shall give you a letter for him.

KERCHIVAL: I'll get ready at once; and I will do all I can for the boy.

MRS. HAVERILL: And—Mr. West! Gertrude and Madeline have told me that—that—I was under obligations to you last evening.

KERCHIVAL: Don't mention it. I merely ran for them, and I—I'm very glad you did n't choke—before they reached you. I trust you are quite well now?

MRS. HAVERILL: I am entirely recovered, thank you. And I will ask another favor of you, for we are old friends. I desire very much that General Haverill should not know that—that any accident occurred to me to-night—or that my health has not been perfect.

KERCHIVAL: Certainly, madam!

MRS. HAVERILL: It would render him anxious without cause.

KERCHIVAL (aside): It looks as if Robert was right; she does n't want the two men to meet.

(Enter HAVERILL, a white silk handkerchief in his hand.)

HAVERILL: Constance, my dear, I've been all over the place looking for you. I thought you were in your room. But—by the way, Kerchival, this is your handkerchief; your initials are on it.

(KERCHIVAL turns and stares at him a second. MRS. HAVERILL starts slightly and turns front. HAVERILL glances quickly from one to the other, then extends his hands toward KERCHIVAL, with the handkerchief. KERCHIVAL moves to him and takes it. MRS. HAVERILL drops into the chair.)

KERCHIVAL: Thank you. (He walks up and exits with a quick glance back. HAVERILL looks at MRS. HAVERILL, who sits nervously, looking away. He then glances up after KERCHIVAL. A cloud comes over his face and he stands a second in thought. Then, with a movement as if brushing away a passing suspicion, he smiles pleasantly and approaches MRS. HAVERILL; leaning over her.)

HAVERILL: My fair Desdemona! (Smiling.) I found Cassio's handkerchief in your room. Have you a kiss for me? (She looks up, he raises her chin with a finger and kisses her.) That's the way I shall smother you.

MRS. HAVERILL (rising and dropping her head upon his breast): Husband!

HAVERILL: But what is this they have been telling me?

MRS. HAVERILL: What have they said to you?

HAVERILL: There was something wrong with you in the early part of the evening; you are trembling and excited, my girl!

MRS. HAVERILL: It was nothing, John; I—I —was ill, for a few moments, but I am well now.

HAVERILL: You said nothing about it to me.

MRS. HAVERILL: Do not give it another thought.

HAVERILL: Was there anything besides your health involved in the affair? There was. (Aside.) How came this handkerchief in her room?

MRS. HAVERILL: My husband! I do not want to say anything more—at—at present—about what happened to-night. There has never been a shadow between us—will you not trust me?

HAVERILL: Shadow! You stand in a bright light of your own, my wife; it shines upon my whole life—there can be no shadow there. Tell me as much or as little as you like, and in your own time. I am sure you will conceal nothing from me that I ought to know. I trust my honor and my happiness to you, absolutely.

MRS. HAVERILL: They will both be safe, John, in my keeping. But there is something else that I wish to speak with you about; something very near to your heart—your son!

HAVERILL: My son!

MRS. HAVERILL: He is in Charleston.

HAVERILL: And not—in prison? To me he is nowhere. I am childless.

MRS. HAVERILL: I hope to see him to-day; may I not take him some kind word from you?

HAVERILL: My lawyers in New York had instructions to provide him with whatever he needed.

MRS. HAVERILL: They have done so, and he wants for nothing; he asks for nothing, except that I will seek out the poor young wife—only a girl herself—whom he is obliged to desert, in New York.

HAVERILL: His marriage was a piece of reckless folly, but I forgave him that.

MRS. HAVERILL: I am sure that it was only after another was dependent on him that the debts of a mere spendthrift were changed to fraud—and crime.

HAVERILL: You may tell him that I will provide for her.

MRS. HAVERILL: And may I take him no warmer message from his father?

HAVERILL: I am an officer of the United States Army. The name which my son bears came to me from men who had borne it with honor, and I transmitted it to him without a blot. He has disgraced it, by his own confession.

MRS. HAVERILL: I cannot forget the poor mother who died when he was born; her whose place I have tried to fill, to both Frank and to you. I never saw her, and she is sleeping in the old graveyard at home. But I am doing what she would do today, if she were living. No pride—no disgrace—could have turned her face from him. The care and the love of her son has been to me the most sacred duty which one woman can assume for another.

HAVERILL: You have fulfilled that duty, Constance. Go to my son! I would go with you, but he is a man now; he could not look into my eyes, and I could not trust myself. But I will send him something which a man will understand. Frank loves you as if you were his own mother; and I—I would like him to—to think tenderly of me, also. He will do it when he looks at this picture. (*Taking a miniature from his pocket.*)

MRS. HAVERILL: Of me!

HAVERILL: I have never been without it one hour, before, since we were married. He will recognize it as the one that I have carried through every campaign, in every scene of danger on the Plains; the one that has always been with me. He is a fugitive from justice. At times, when despair might overcome him, this may give him nerve to meet his future life manfully. It has often nerved me, when I might have failed without it. Give it to him, and tell him that I send it. (*Giving her the miniature.*) I could not send a kinder message, and he will understand it. (*Turning, he stands a moment in thought.* THORNTON *appears at the window looking at them quietly, over his shoulder, a cigar in his hand.* MRS. HAVERILL *sees him, and starts with a suppressed breath, then looks at* HAVERILL, *who moves away. He speaks aside.*) My son! My son! We shall never meet again! (*Exit.*)

(MRS. HAVERILL *looks after him earnestly, then turns and looks at* THORNTON, *drawing up to her full height.* THORNTON *moves up the stage, beyond the window.*)

MRS. HAVERILL: Will he dare to speak to me again?

(*Enter* THORNTON; *he comes down the stage quietly. He has thrown away the cigar.*)

THORNTON: Mrs. Haverill! I wish to offer you an apology.

MRS. HAVERILL: I have not asked for one, sir!

THORNTON: Do you mean by that, that you will not accept one?

MRS. HAVERILL (*aside*): What can I say? (*Aloud.*) Oh, Mr. Thornton!—for my husband's sake, I—

THORNTON: Ah! You are afraid that your husband may become involved in an unpleasant affair. Your solicitude for his safety, madame, makes me feel that my offense to-night was indeed unpardonable. No gentleman can excuse himself for making such a mistake as I have made. I had supposed that it was Lieutenant Kerchival West, who—

MRS. HAVERILL: What do you mean, sir?

THORNTON: But if it is your husband that stands between us—

MRS. HAVERILL: Let me say this, sir: whatever I may fear for my husband, he fears nothing for himself.

THORNTON: He knows? (*Looking at her, keenly.*)

(*Enter* KERCHIVAL WEST, *now in riding suit.*)
(*He stops, looking at them.*)

You are silent. Your husband does know what occurred to-night; that relieves my conscience. (*Lightly.*) Colonel Haverill and I can now settle it between us.

MRS. HAVERILL: No, Mr. Thornton! My husband knows nothing, and, I beg of you, do not let this horrible affair go further. (*Sees* KERCHIVAL.)

KERCHIVAL: Pardon me. (*Stepping forward.*) I hope I am not interrupting you. (*Aside.*) It *was* Thornton. (*Aloud.*) You said you would have a letter for me to carry, Mrs. Haverill.

MRS. HAVERILL: Yes, I—I will go up and write it at once. (*As she leaves she stops and looks back. Aside.*) I wonder how much he overheard.

KERCHIVAL (*quietly*): I suppose eight o'clock will be time enough for me to go?

MRS. HAVERILL: Oh, yes! (*glancing at him a moment*)—quite. (*Exit.*)

KERCHIVAL (*quietly*): Mr. Thornton! you are a scoundrel! Do I make myself plain?

THORNTON: You make the fact that you desire to pick a quarrel with me quite plain, sir; but I choose my own quarrels and my own enemies.

KERCHIVAL: Colonel Haverill is my commander, and he is beloved by every officer in the regiment.

THORNTON: On what authority, may I ask, do you—

KERCHIVAL: The honor of Colonel Haverill's wife is under our protection.

THORNTON: Under your protection? You have a better claim than that, perhaps, to act as her champion. Lieutenant Kerchival West is Mrs. Haverill's favourite officer in the regiment.

KERCHIVAL (*approaching him*): You dare to suggest that I—

THORNTON: If I accept your challenge, I shall do so not because you are her protector, but my rival.

KERCHIVAL: Bah! (*Striking him sharply on the cheek with his glove. The two men stand facing each other a moment.*) Is it my quarrel now?

THORNTON: I think you are entitled to my attention, sir.

KERCHIVAL: My time here is limited.

THORNTON: We need not delay. The Bayou

La Forge is convenient to this place.

KERCHIVAL: I'll meet you there, with a friend, at once.

THORNTON: It will be light enough to see the sights of our weapons in about one hour. (*They bow to each other, and* THORNTON *goest out.*)

KERCHIVAL: I've got ahead of Bob.

GERTRUDE (*without*): Whoa! Jack! Old boy! Steady, now—that's a good fellow.

KERCHIVAL: She has returned. I *must* know whether Gertrude Ellingham loves me—before Thornton and I meet. He is a good shot.

GERTRUDE (*without, calling*): O—h! Pete! You may take Jack to the stable. Ha—ha—ha! (*She appears at window; to* KERCHIVAL.) Old Pete, on the bay horse, has been doing his best to keep up with us; but Jack and I have led him such a race! Ha—ha—ha—ha! (*Disappearing beyond the window.*)

KERCHIVAL: Does she love me?

GERTRUDE (*entering at the rear and coming down.*): I have the very latest news from the headquarters of the Confederate Army in South Carolina. At twenty minutes after three this morning General Beauregard sent this message to Major Anderson in Fort Sumter: "I shall open fire in one hour!" The time is up!—and he will keep his word! (*Turning and looking out of the window.* KERCHIVAL *moves across to her.*)

KERCHIVAL: Gertrude! I must speak to you; we may never meet again; but I must know the truth. I love you. (*Seizing her hand.*) Do you love me? (*She looks around at him as if about to speak; hesitates.*) Answer me! (*She looks down with a coquettish smile, tapping her skirt with her riding whip.*) Well? (*A distant report of a cannon, and low rumbling reverberations over the harbor.* GERTRUDE *turns suddenly, looking out.* KERCHIVAL *draws up, also looking off.*)

GERTRUDE: A low—bright—line of fire—in the sky! It is a shell. (*A second's pause; she starts slightly*). It has burst upon the fort. (*Looks over her shoulder at* KERCHIVAL, *drawing up to her full height.*) Now!—do you believe that we Southerners are in deadly earnest?

KERCHIVAL: We Northerners are in deadly earnest, too. I have received my answer. (*He crosses quickly and then turns.*) We are—enemies! (*They look at each other for a moment.*)

(*Exit* KERCHIVAL.)

GERTRUDE: Kerchival! (*Moving quickly half across stage, looking after him eagerly, then stops.*) Enemies! (*She drops into the chair sobbing bitterly.*)

Another distant report, and low, long reverberations as the curtain descends.)

ACT II

(*The scene is the exterior of the Ellingham Homestead in the Shenandoah Valley. Three-Top Mountain is seen in the distance. A corner of the house, with the projecting end of the veranda is seen on the left. A low wall extends from the veranda across the stage to the center, then with a turn to the right it is continued off the stage. There is a wide opening in the wall at the center, with a low, heavy stone post, with flat top, on each side. Beyond the wall and the opening, a road runs across the stage. At the back of this road there is an elevation of rock and turf. This slopes up to the rear, is level on the top about twelve feet, then slopes down to the road, and also out behind the wood, which is seen at the right. The level part in the centre rises to about four feet above the stage. Beyond this elevation in the distance is a broad valley, with Three Top Mountain rising on the right. The foliage is appropriate to Northern Virginia. Rustic seats and table are on the right. There is a low rock near the stone post. When curtain rises it is sunset. As the act proceeds this fades into twilight and then brightens into moonlight. At the rise of the curtain a trumpet signal is heard, very distant.* GERTRUDE *and* MADELINE *are standing on the elevation.* GERTRUDE *is shading her eyes with her hand and looking off to the left.* MADELINE *stands a little below her, on the incline, resting her arm about* GERTRUDE's *waist, also looking off.*)

GERTRUDE: It is a regiment of Union Cavalry. The Federal troops now have their lines three miles beyond us, and only a month ago the Confederate Army was north of Winchester. One army or the other has been marching up and down the Shenandoah Valley for three years. I wonder what the next change will be. We in Virginia have had more than our share of the war. (*Looking off.*)

MADELINE: You have, indeed, Gertrude. (*Walking down to a seat.*) And we at home in Washington have pitied you so much. But everybody says that there will be peace in the valley after this. (*Dropping into the seat.*)

GERTRUDE: Peace! (*Coming down.*) That word means something very different to us poor Southerners from what it means to you.

MADELINE: I know, dear; and we in the North

know how you have suffered, too. We were very glad when General Buckthorn was appointed to the command of the Nineteenth Army Corps, so that Jenny could get permission for herself and me to come and visit you.

GERTRUDE: The old General will do anything for Jenny, I suppose.

MADELINE: Yes. (*Laughing.*) We say in Washington that Jenny is in command of the Nineteenth Army Corps herself.

GERTRUDE: I was never more astonished or delighted in my life than when you and Jenny Buckthorn rode up, this morning, with a guard from Winchester; and Madeline, dear, I—I only wish that my brother Robert could be here, too. Do you remember in Charleston, darling—that morning—when I told you that—that Robert loved you?

MADELINE: He—(*looking down*)—he told me so himself only a little while afterwards, and while we were standing there, on the shore of the bay—the—the shot was fired which compelled him to enter this awful war—and me to return to my home in the North.

GERTRUDE: I was watching for that shot, too. (*Turning.*)

MADELINE: Yes—(*rising*)—you and brother Kerchival—

GERTRUDE: We won't talk about that, my dear. We were speaking of Robert. As I told you this morning, I have not heard from him since the battle of Winchester, a month ago. Oh, Madeline! the many, many long weeks, like these, we have suffered, after some terrible battle in which he has been engaged. I do not know, now, whether he is living or dead.

MADELINE: The whole war has been one long suspense to me. (*Dropping her face into her hands.*)

GERTRUDE: My dear sister! (*Placing her arm about her waist and moving to the left.*) You are a Northern girl, and I am a Rebel—but we are sisters. (*They mount the veranda and pass out. An old countryman comes in. He stops and glances back, raises a broken portion of the capstone of the post, and places a letter under it.* GERTRUDE *has stepped back on the veranda and is watching him. He raises his head sharply, looking at her and bringing his finger to his lips. He drops his head again, as with age, and goes out.* GERTRUDE *moves down to the stage and up to the road, looks to the right and left, raises the broken stone, glancing back as she does so, then takes the letter and moves down.*) Robert is alive! It is his handwriting! (*She tears open the wrapper.*) Only a line from him! and this—a dispatch—and also a

letter to me! Why, it is from Mrs. Haverill—from Washington—with a United States postmark. (*She reads from a scrap of paper.*) "The enclosed dispatch must be in the hands of Captain Edward Thornton before eight o'clock tonight. We have signaled to him from Three Top Mountain, and he is waiting for it at the bend in Oak Run. Our trusty scout at the Old Forge will carry it if you will put it in his hands." The scout is not there, now; I will carry it to Captain Thornton myself. I—I have n't my own dear horse to depend on now; Jack knew every foot of the way through the woods about here; he could have carried a dispatch himself. I can't bear to think of Jack; it's two years since he was captured by the enemy—and if he is still living—I—I suppose he is carrying one of their officers No! Jack would n't fight on that side. He was a Rebel—as I am. He was one of the Black Horse Cavalry—his eyes always flashed towards the North. Poor Jack! my pet. (*Brushing her eyes.*) But this is no time for tears. I must do the best I can with the gray horse. Captain Thornton shall have the dispatch. (*She reads from note.*) "I also inclose a letter for you. I found it in a United States mail-bag which we captured from the enemy." Oh—that's the way Mrs. Haverill's letter came—Ha—ha—ha—by way of the Rebel army! (*Opens it; reads.*) "My Darling Gertrude: When Colonel Kerchival West was in Washington last week, on his way from Chattanooga, to serve under Sheridan in the Shenandoah Valley, he called upon me. It was the first time I had seen him since the opening of the war. I am certain that he still loves you, dear." (*She kisses the letter eagerly, then draws up.*) It is quite immaterial to me whether Kerchival West still loves me or not. (*Reads.*) "I have kept your secret, my darling."—Ah! My secret! —"but I was sorely tempted to betray the confidence you reposed in me at Charleston. If Kerchival West had heard you say, as I did, when your face was hidden in my bosom, that night, that you loved him with your whole heart—"—Oh! I could bite my tongue out now for making that confession—(*She looks down at letter with a smile.*) "I am certain that he still loves you." (*A Trumpet Signal. She kisses the letter repeatedly. The Signal is repeated louder than at first. She starts, listening.*)

(JENNY BUCKTHORN *runs in, on the veranda.*)

JENNY: Do you hear, Gertrude, they are going to pass this very house. (*A Military band is playing "John Brown" in the distance. A chorus of soldiers is heard.*) I've been watching them through my glass; it is Colonel Kerchival West's regiment.

GERTRUDE (*eagerly, then coldly*): Colonel West's! It is perfectly indifferent to me whose regiment it is.

JENNY: Oh! Of course. (*coming down.*) It is equally indifferent to me; Captain Heartsease is in command of the first troop. (*Trumpet Signal sounds.*) Column right! (*She runs up to the road. Looking off to the left.*) They are coming up the hill.

GERTRUDE: At my very door! And Kerchival West in command! I will not stand here and see them pass. The dispatch for Captain Thornton! I will carry it to him as soon as they are gone. (*Exit up the veranda, the band and chorus increasing in volume.*)

JENNY: Cavalry! That's the branch of the service I was born in; I was in a fort at the time—on the Plains. Sergeant Barket always said that my first baby squall was a command to the garrison; if any officer or soldier, from my father down, failed to obey my orders, I court-martialed him on the spot. I'll make 'em pass in review. (*Jumping up on the rustic seat.*) Yes! (*Looking off to the left.*) There's Captain Heartsease himself, at the head of the first troop. Draw sabre! (*With parasol.*) Present! (*Imitating the action. The band and chorus are now full and loud; she swings the parasol in time. A trumpet Signal. Band and chorus suddenly cease.*) Halt! Why, they are stopping here. (*Trumpet Signal sounds.*) Dismount! I—I wonder if they are going to—I do believe—(*Looking eagerly. Trumpet Signal.*) Assembly of Guard Details! As sure as fate, they are going into camp here. We girls will have a jolly time. (*Jumping down.*) Ha—ha—ha—ha! Let me see. How shall I receive Captain Heartsease? He deserves a court-martial, for he stole my lace handkerchief—at Mrs. Grayson's reception—in Washington. He was called away by orders to the West that very night, and we have n't met since. (*Sighs.*) He's been in lots of battles since then; I suppose he's forgotten all about the handkerchief. We girls, at home, don't forget such things. We are n't in battles. All we do is to—to scrape lint and flirt with other officers.

(*Enter* CAPTAIN HEARTSEASE. *followed by* COLONEL ROBERT ELLINGHAM, *then stops at the gate.*)

HEARTSEASE: This way, Colonel Ellingham. (*They enter. As they come down* HEARTSEASE *stops*

suddenly, looking at JENNY, *and puts up his glasses.*) Miss Buckthorn!

JENNY: Captain Heartsease!

HEARTSEASE (*very quietly and with perfect composure.*): I am thunderstruck. The unexpected sight of you has thrown me into a fever of excitement.

JENNY: Has it? (*Aside.*) If he gets so excited as that in battle it must be awful. (*Aloud.*) Colonel Ellingham!

ELLINGHAM: Miss Buckthorn! You are visiting my sister? I am what may be called a visitor—by force—myself.

JENNY: Oh! You're a prisoner!

ELLINGHAM: I ventured too far within the Union lines to-night, and they have picked me up. But Major Wilson has kindly accepted my parole, and I shall make the best of it.

JENNY: Is Major Wilson in command of the regiment?

HEARTSEASE: Yes. Colonel West is to join us at this point, during the evening.

ELLINGHAM: I am very glad you are here, Miss Buckthorn, with Gertrude.

JENNY: Somebody here will be delighted to see you, Colonel.

ELLINGHAM: My sister can hardly be pleased to see me as a prisoner.

JENNY: Not your sister. (*Passing him and crossing to the veranda. She turns and beckons to him. She motions with her thumb, over her shoulder. He goes up the steps of the veranda and turns.*)

ELLINGHAM: What do you mean?

JENNY: I mean this—(*Reaching up her face, he leans down, placing his ear near her lips*)—somebody else's sister! When she first sees you, be near enough to catch her.

ELLINGHAM: I understand you! Madeline! (*Exit on veranda.* JENNY *runs up steps after him, then stops and looks back at* HEARTSEASE *over the railing.* HEARTSEASE *takes a lace handkerchief from his pocket.*)

JENNY: I do believe that's my handkerchief.

(*A guard of Sentries marches in and across the stage in the road. The Corporal in command orders halt and a sentry to post, then marches the guard out. The sentry stands with his back to the audience, afterwards moving out and in, appearing and disappearing during the Act.*)

HEARTSEASE: Miss Buckthorn! I owe you an apology. After I left your side, the last time we met, I found your handkerchief in my possession. I assure you, it was an accident.

JENNY (*aside, pouting*): I thought he *intended*

to steal it. (*Aloud.*) That was more than a year ago. (*Then brightly.*) Do you always carry it with you?

HEARTSEASE: Always; there. (*Indicating his left breast pocket.*)

JENNY: Next to his heart!

HEARTSEASE: Shall I return it to you?

JENNY: Oh, if a lace handkerchief can be of any use to you, Captain, during the hardships of a campaign—you—you may keep that one. You soldiers have so few comforts—and it's real lace.

HEARTSEASE: Thank you. (*Returning the handkerchief to his pocket.*) Miss Buckthorn, your father is in command of the Nineteenth Army Corps. He does n't like me.

JENNY: I know it.

HEARTSEASE: But you are in command of him.

JENNY: Yes; I always have been.

HEARTSEASE: If ever you decide to assume command of any other man, I—I trust you will give *me* your orders.

JENNY (*aside, starting back.*): If that was intended for a proposal, it's the queerest-shaped one I ever heard of. (*Aloud.*) Do you mean, Captain, that—that you—I must command myself now. (*Shouldering her parasol.*) 'Bout —face! March! (*Turning squarely around, marching up and out, on the veranda.*)

HEARTSEASE: I have been placed on waiting orders. (*Stepping up the stage and looking after her; then very quietly and without emotion.*) I am in an agony of suspense. The sight of that girl always arouses the strongest emotions of my nature.

(*Enter* COLONEL KERCHIVAL WEST, *looking at the paper in his hand. The sentinel, in the road, comes to a salute.*)

Colonel West!

KERCHIVAL: Captain!

HEARTSEASE: You have rejoined the regiment sooner than we expected.

KERCHIVAL (*looking at the paper*): Yes; General Haverill is to meet me here at seven o'clock. Major Wilson tells me that some of your company captured Colonel Robert Ellingham, of the Tenth Virginia.

HEARTSEASE: He is here under parole.

KERCHIVAL: And this is the old Ellingham homestead. (*Aside.*) Gertrude herself is here, I suppose; almost a prisoner to me, like her brother; and my troops surround their home. She must, indeed, feel that I am her enemy now. Ah, well, war is war. (*Aloud.*) By the bye, Heartsease, a young Lieutenant, Frank Bedloe, has joined our troop?

HEARTSEASE: Yes; an excellent young officer.

KERCHIVAL: I sent for him as I came through the camp. Lieutenant Frank "Bedloe" is the son of General Haverill.

HEARTSEASE: Indeed! Under an assumed name!

KERCHIVAL: He was supposed to have been killed in New Orleans more than a year ago; but he was taken prisoner instead.

HEARTSEASE: He is here.

KERCHIVAL: I should never have known him; with his full beard and bronzed face. His face was as smooth as a boy's when I last met him in Charleston.

(*Enter* LIEUTENANT FRANK BEDLOE; *he stops, saluting.*)

FRANK: You wished me to report to you, Colonel?

KERCHIVAL: You have been assigned to the regiment during my absence.

FRANK: Yes, sir.

(KERCHIVAL *moves to him and grasps his hand; looks into his eyes a moment before speaking.*)

KERCHIVAL: Frank Haverill.

FRANK: You—you know me, sir?

KERCHIVAL: I saw Mrs. Haverill while I was passing through Washington on Saturday. She told me that you had escaped from prison in Richmond, and had re-entered the service. She did not know then that you had been assigned to my regiment. I received a letter from her, in Winchester, this morning, informing me of the fact, and asking for my good offices in your behalf. But here is the letter. (*Taking a letter from wallet and giving it to him.*) It is for you rather than for me. I shall do everything I can for you, my dear fellow.

FRANK: Thank you, sir. (*He opens the letter, dropping the envelope upon the table.*) Kind, thoughtful and gentle to my faults, as ever —(*Looking at the letter*)—and always thinking of my welfare. My poor little wife, too, is under her protection. Gentlemen, I beg of you not to reveal my secret to my father.

KERCHIVAL: General Haverill shall know nothing from us, my boy, you have my word for that.

HEARTSEASE: Nothing.

KERCHIVAL: And he cannot possibly recognize you. What with your full beard, and thinking as he does, that you are—

FRANK: That I am dead. I am dead to him. It would have been better if I had died. Nothing but my death—not even that—can wipe out the disgrace which I brought upon his name.

HEARTSEASE: General Haverill has arrived.

(*Enter* GENERAL HAVERILL, *with a Staff Officer.*)

FRANK (*moving down*): My father!

HAVERILL (*after exchanging salutes with the three officers, he turns to the Staff Officer, giving him a paper and brief instructions in dumb show. The Officer goes out over the incline. Another Staff Officer enters, salutes and hands him a paper, than stands up.*): Ah! The men are ready. (*Looking at the paper, then to* KERCHIVAL.) Colonel! I have a very important matter to arrange with you; there is not a moment to be lost. I will ask Captain Heartsease to remain. (FRANK *salutes and starts up the stage;* HAVERILL *looks at him, starting slightly; raises his hand to detain him.*) One moment; your name!

HEARTSEASE: Lieutenant Bedloe, General, of my own troop, and one of our best officers.

(HAVERILL *steps to* FRANK, *looking into his face a moment.*)

HAVERILL: Pardon me! (*He steps down the stage.* FRANK *moves away from him, then stops and looks back at him.* HAVERILL *stands up a moment in thought, covers his face with one hand, then draws up.*) Colonel West! We have a most dangerous piece of work for a young officer—(FRANK *starts joyfully*)—to lead a party of men, whom I have already selected. I cannot *order* an officer to undertake anything so nearly hopeless; he must be a volunteer.

FRANK: Oh, sir, General! Let me be their leader.

HAVERILL: I thought you had passed on.

FRANK: Do not refuse me, sir. (HAVERILL *looks at him a moment.* HEARTSEASE *and* KERCHIVAL *exchange glances.*)

HAVERILL: You are the man we need, my young friend. You shall go. Listen! We wish to secure a key to the cipher dispatches, which the enemy are now sending from their signal station on Three Top Mountain. There is another Confederate Signal Station in the valley, just beyond Buckton's Ford. (*Pointing to the left.*) Your duty will be this: First, to get inside the enemy's line; then to follow a path through the woods, with one of our scouts as your guide; attack the Station suddenly, and secure their code, if possible. I have this moment received word that the scout and the men are at the fort, now, awaiting their leader. Major McCandless,

of my staff, will take you to the place. (*Indicating the Staff Officer.* FRANK *exchanges salutes with him.*) My young friend! I do not conceal from you the dangerous nature of the work on which I am sending you. If—if you do not return, I—I will write, myself, to your friends. (*Taking out a note book.*) Have you a father living?

FRANK: My—father—is—is—he is—

HAVERILL: I understand you. A mother? Or—

KERCHIVAL: I have the address of Lieutenant Bedloe's friends, General.

HAVERILL: I will ask you to give it to me, if necessary. (*He extends his hand.*) Good-bye, my lad. (FRANK *moves to him.* HAVERILL *grasps his hand, warmly.*) Keep a brave heart and come back to us.

(FRANK *moves up the stage. Exit Staff Officer.*)

FRANK: He is my father still. (*Exit.*)

HAVERILL: My dead boy's face! (*Dropping his face into both hands.*)

HEARTSEASE (*apart to* KERCHIVAL): He shall not go alone. (*Aloud.*) General! Will you kindly give me leave of absence from the command?

HAVERILL: Leave of absence! To an officer in active service—and in the presence of the enemy?

KERCHIVAL (*taking his hand. Apart*): God bless you, old fellow! Look after the boy.

HAVERILL: A—h—(*With a sudden thought, turns.*) I think I understand you, Captain Heartsease. Yes; you may have leave of absence.

HEARTSEASE: Thank you. (*He salutes.* HAVERILL *and* KERCHIVAL *salute. Exit* HEARTSEASE.)

KERCHIVAL: Have you any further orders for me, General?

HAVERILL: I wish you to understand the great importance of the duty to which I have just assigned this young officer. General Sheridan started for Washingtom this noon, by way of Front Royal. Since his departure, we have had reason· to believe that the enemy are about to move, and we must be able to read their signal dispatches, if possible. (*Sitting down.*) I have ordered Captain Lockwood, of our own Signal Corps to report to you here, with officers and men. (*He takes up the empty envelope on table, unconsciously, as he speaks, tapping it on the table.*) If Lieutenant Bedloe succeeds in getting the key to the enemy's cipher, we can signal from this point—(*pointing to the elevation*)—to our station at Front Royal. Men and horses are waiting there now, to carry forward a message, if necessary, to General Sheridan himself. (*He starts suddenly, looking at the envelope in his hand; reads address.*

Aside.) "Colonel Kerchival West"—in my wife's handwriting!

KERCHIVAL: I'll attend to your orders.

HAVERILL: Postmarked at Washington, yesterday. (*Reads.*) "Private and confidential." (*Aloud.*) Colonel West! I found a paragraph, to-day, in a paper published in Richmond, taken from a prisoner. I will read it to you. (*He takes a newspaper slip from his wallet and reads.*) "From the *Charleston Mercury.* Captain Edward Thornton, of the Confederate Secret Service, has been assigned to duty in the Shenandoah Valley. Our gallant Captain still bears upon his face the mark of his meeting, in 1861, with Lieutenant, now Colonel Kerchival West, who is also to serve in the valley, with Sheridan's Army. Another meeting between these two men would be one of the strange coincidences of the war, as they were at one time, if not indeed at present, interested in the same beautiful woman." (*Rises.*) I will ask you to read the last few lines, yourself. (*Crossing, he hands* KERCHIVAL *the slip.*)

KERCHIVAL (*reading*): "The scandal connected with the lovely wife of a Northern officer, at the opening of the war, was over-shadowed, of course, by the attack on Fort Sumter; but many Charlestonians will remember it. The lady in defense of whose good name Captain Thornton fought the duel"—he defended her good name!—"is the wife of General Haverill, who will be Colonel West's immediate commander." (*He pauses a moment, then hands back the slip.*) General! I struck Mr. Thornton, after a personal quarrel.

HAVERILL: And the cause of the blow? There is much more in this than I have ever known of. I need hardly say that I do not accept the statement of this scandalous paragraph as correct. I will ask you to tell me the whole story, frankly, as man to man.

KERCHIVAL (*after a moment's thought*): I will tell you—all—frankly, General.

(*Enter* SERGEANT BARKET.)

BARKET: Colonel Wist? Adjutant Rollins wishes to report—a prisoner—just captured.

HAVERILL: We will meet again later, to-night when the camp is at rest. We are both soldiers, and have duties before us, at once. For the present, Colonel, be on the alert; we must watch the enemy. (*He moves up the stage.* BARKET *salutes.* HAVERILL *stops and looks at envelope in his hands, reading.*) "Private and confidence." (*Exit.*)

KERCHIVAL: Sergeant Barket! Lieutenant Bedloe has crossed the enemy's line, at Buckton's

Ford, with a party of men. I wish you to ride to the ford yourself, and remain there with your horse in readiness and fresh. As soon as any survivor of the party returns, ride back with the first news at full speed.

BARKET: Yes, sir. (*Starting.*)

KERCHIVAL: You say a prisoner has been captured? Is it a spy?

BARKET: Worse—a petticoat.

KERCHIVAL: A female prisoner! (*Dropping into the seat.*)

BARKET: I towld the byes your honor would n't thank us fer the catchin' of her. The worst of it is she's a lady; and what's worse still, it's a purty one.

KERCHIVAL: Tell Major Wilson, for me, to let her take the oath, and everything else she wants. The Government of the United States will send her an apology and a new bonnet.

BARKET: The young lady is to take the oath, is it? She says she'll see us damned first.

KERCHIVAL: A lady, Barket?

BARKET: Well! she did n't use thim exact words. That's the way I understand her emphasis. Ivery time she looks at me, I feel like getting under a boom-proof. She was dashing through the woods on a gray horse, sur; and we had the divil's own chase. But we came up wid her, at last, down by the bend in Oak Run. Just at that moment we saw the figure of a Confederate officer, disappearing among the trays on the ither side.

KERCHIVAL: A—h!

BARKET: Two of us rayturned wid the girl; and the rist wint after the officer. Nothing has been heard of thim yet.

KERCHIVAL: Have you found any dispatches on the prisoner?

BARKET: Well!—yer honor, I'm a bachelor, meself; and I'm not familiar with the taypography of the sex. We byes are in mortal terror for fear somebody might order us to go on an exploring expedition.

KERCHIVAL: Tell them to send the prisoner here, Barket, and hurry to Buckton's Ford yourself, at once.

BARKET: As fast as me horse can carry me, sir, and it's a good one. (*Exit.*)

KERCHIVAL: I'd rather deal with half the Confederate army than with one woman, but I must question her. They captured her down by the Bend in Oak Run. (*Taking out the map, and looking at it.*) I see. She had just met, or was about to meet, a Confederate officer at that point. It is evident that she was either taking him a dispatch or was there to receive one. Oak Run. (CORPORAL DUNN *and two soldiers enter, with* GERTRUDE *as a prisoner. They stop,* KERCHIVAL *sits, studying the map.* GERTRUDE *glances at him and marches down with her head erect; she stops, with her back to him.*)

DUNN: The prisoner, Colonel West!

KERCHIVAL: Ah! Very well, Corporal; you can go. (*Rising; he motions the guard to retire.* CORPORAL DUNN *gives the necessary orders and exit with guard.*) Be seated, madam. (GERTRUDE *draws up, folding her arms and planting her foot, spitefully.* KERCHIVAL *shrugs his shoulders. Aside.*) I wish they'd capture a tigress for me, or some other female animal that I know how to manage better than I do a woman. (*Aloud.*) I am very sorry, madam; but, of course, my duty as a military officer is paramount to all other considerations. You have been captured within the lines of this army, and under circumstances which lead me to think that you have important dispatches upon your person. I trust that you will give me whatever you have, at once. I shall be exceedingly sorry if you compel me to adopt the extreme—and the very disagreeable course—for both of us—of having—you—I—I hesitate even to use the word, madame—but military law is absolute —having you—

GERTRUDE: Searched! If you dare, Colonel West! (*Turning to him suddenly and drawing up to her full height.*)

KERCHIVAL: Gertrude Ellingham! (*Springs across to her, with his arms extended.*) My dear Gertrude!

GERTRUDE (*turning her back upon him*): Not "dear Gertrude" to you, sir!

KERCHIVAL: Not?—Oh! I forgot.

GERTRUDE (*coldly*): I am your prisoner.

KERCHIVAL: Yes. (*Drawing up firmly, with a change of manner.*) We will return to the painful realities of war. I am very sorry that you have placed yourself in a position like this, and, believe me, Gertrude—(*With growing tenderness.*) —I am still more sorry to be in such a position myself. (*Resting one hand on her arm, and his other arm about waist.*)

GERTRUDE (*after looking down at his hands*): You don't like the position? (*He starts back, drawing up with dignity.*) Is that the paramount duty of a military officer?

KERCHIVAL: You will please hand me whatever dispatches or other papers may be in your possession.

GERTRUDE (*looking away*): You will *force* me, I suppose. I am a woman; you have the power.

Order in the guard! A Corporal and two men—you'd better make it a dozen—I am dangerous! Call the whole regiment to arms! Beat the long roll! I won't give up, if all the armies of the United States surround me.

(*Enter* GENERAL BUCKTHORN.)

KERCHIVAL: General Buckthorn! (*Saluting.*)

BUCKTHORN: Colonel West.

GERTRUDE (*aside*): Jenny's father! (BUCKTHORN *glances at* GERTRUDE, *who still stands looking away. He moves down to* KERCHIVAL.)

BUCKTHORN (*apart, gruffly*): I was passing with my staff, and I was informed that you had captured a woman bearing dispatches to the enemy. Is this the one?

KERCHIVAL: Yes, General.

BUCKTHORN: Ah! (*Turning, he looks at her.*)

GERTRUDE: I wonder if he will recognize me. He hasn't seen since I was a little girl. (*She turns toward him.*)

BUCKTHORN (*turning to* KERCHIVAL *and punching him in the ribs.*): Fine young woman!—(*He turns and bows to her very gallantly, removing his hat. She bows deeply in return*) A-h-e-m! (*Suddenly pulling himself up to a stern, military air; then gruffly to* KERCHIVAL, *extending his hand.*) Let me see the dispatches.

KERCHIVAL: She declines positively to give them up.

BUCKTHORN: Oh! Does she? (*Walks up the stage thoughtfully, and turns.*) My dear young lady! I trust you will give us no further trouble. Kindly let us have those dispatches.

GERTRUDE (*looking away*): I have no dispatches, and I would not give them to you if I had.

BUCKTHORN: What! You defy my authority? Colonel West, I command you! Search the prisoner!

(GERTRUDE *turns suddenly towards* KERCHIVAL, *facing him defiantly. He looks across at her, aghast. A moment's pause.*)

KERCHIVAL: General Buckthorn—I decline to obey that order.

BUCKTHORN: You—you decline to obey my order! (*Moves down to him fiercely.*)

KERCHIVAL (*apart*): General! It is the woman I love.

BUCKTHORN (*apart*): Is it? Damn you, sir! I would n't have an officer in my army corps who *would* obey me, under such circumstances. I'll have to look for those dispatches myself.

KERCHIVAL (*facing him, angrily*): If you dare, General Buckthorn!

BUCKTHORN (*apart*):   Blast your eyes! I'd kick you out of the army if you'd *let* me search her; but it's my military duty to swear at you. (*To* GERTRUDE.) Colonel West has sacrificed his life to protect you.

GERTRUDE: His life!

BUCKTHORN: I shall have him shot for insubordination to his commander, immediately. (*Gives* KERCHIVAL *a huge wink, and turns up stage.*)

GERTRUDE: Oh, sir! General! I have told you the truth. I have no dispatches. Believe me, sir, I have n't so much as a piece of paper about me, except—

BUCKTHORN: Except? (*Turning sharply.*)

GERTRUDE: Only a letter. Here it is. (*Taking letter from the bosom of her dress.*) Upon my soul, it is all I have. Truly, it is.

BUCKTHORN (*taking the letter*): Colonel West, you're reprieved. (*Winks at* KERCHIVAL, *who turns away, laughing.* BUCKTHORN *reads letter.*) "Washington"—Ho—ho! From within our own lines—"Colonel Kerchival West"—

KERCHIVAL: Eh?

GERTRUDE: Please, General!—Don't read it aloud.

BUCKTHORN: Very well! I won't.

KERCHIVAL (*aside*): I wonder what it has to do with me.

BUCKTHORN (*reading; aside*): "If Kerchival West had heard you say, as I did—m—m— that you loved him with your whole heart—" (*He glances up at* GERTRUDE *who drops her head, coyly.*) This is a very important military document. (*Turns to the last page.*) "Signed, Constance Haverill." (*Turns to front page.*) "My dear Gertrude!" Is this Miss Gertrude Ellingham?

GERTRUDE: Yes, General.

BUCKTHORN: I sent my daughter, Jenny, to your house, with an escort, this morning.

GERTRUDE: She is here.

BUCKTHORN (*tapping her under the chin*): You're an arrant little Rebel, my dear; but I like you immensely. (*Draws up suddenly, with an Ahem!, then turns to* KERCHIVAL.) Colonel West, I leave this dangerous young woman in your charge. (KERCHIVAL *approaches.*) If she disobeys you in any way, or attempts to escape—read that letter! (*Giving him the letter.*)

GERTRUUDE: Oh! General!

BUCKTHORN: But not till then.

KERCHIVAL (*tenderly, taking her hand*): My —prisoner!

GERTRUDE (*aside*): I could scratch my own eyes out—or his, either—rather than have him read that letter.

(*Enter* CORPORAL DUNN, *with a guard of four soldiers and* CAPTAIN EDWARD THORNTON *as a prisoner.*)

KERCHIVAL: Edward Thornton!

GERTRUDE: They have taken him, also! He has the dispatch!

DUNN: The Confederate Officer, Colonel, who was pursued by our troops at Oak Run, after they captured the young lady.

BUCKTHORN: The little witch has been communicating with the enemy!

KERCHIVAL (*to* GERTRUDE): You will give me your parole of honor until we next meet?

GERTRUDE: Yes. (*Aside.*) That letter! I *am* his prisoner. (*She walks up the steps, looking back at* CAPTAIN THORNTON, *and then leaves the stage.*)

KERCHIVAL: We will probably find the dispatches we have been looking for now, General.

BUCKTHORN: Prisoner! You will hand us what papers you may have.

THORNTON: I will hand you nothing.

BUCKTHORN: Colonel!

(KERCHIVAL *motions to* THORNTON, *who looks at him sullenly.*)

KERCHIVAL: Corporal   Dunn!—search   the prisoner. (DUNN *steps to* THORNTON, *taking him by the shoulder and turning him rather roughly so that* THORNTON's *back is to the audience.* DUNN *throws open his coat, takes the paper from his breast, hands it to* KERCHIVAL, *who gives it to* BUCKTHORN.) Proceed with the search.

(DUNN *continues the search.* BUCKTHORN *drops upon the seat, lights a match and looks at the paper.*)

BUCKTHORN (*reading*): "General Rosser will rejoin General Early with all the cavalry in his command, at—" This is important.

(*Continues to read with matches. The* CORPORAL *hands a packet to* KERCHIVAL. *He removes the covering.*)

KERCHIVAL (*starting*): A portrait of Mrs. Haverill! (*He touches* CORPORAL DUNN *on the shoulder quickly and motions him to retire.* DUNN *falls back to the guard.* KERCHIVAL *speaks apart to* THORNTON, *who has turned front.*) How did this portrait come into your possession?

THORNTON: That is my affair, not yours!

BUCKTHORN: Anything else, Colonel?

KERCHIVAL (*placing the miniature in his pocket*): Nothing!

THORNTON (*apart, over* KERCHIVAL's *shoulder*): A time will come, perhaps, when I can avenge the insult of this search, and also this scar. (*Pointing to a scar on his face.*) Your aim was better than mine in Charleston, but we shall meet again; give me back that picture.

KERCHIVAL: Corporal! Take your prisoner!

THRONTON: Ah!

(*He springs viciously at* KERCHIVAL; CORPORAL DUNN *springs forward, seizes* THORNTON *and throws him back to the Guard.* KERCHIVAL *walks to the right,* DUNN *stands with his carbine levelled at* THORNTON, *looks at* KERCHIVAL, *who quietly motions him out.* CORPORAL DUNN *gives the orders to the men and marches out, with* THORNTON.)

BUCKTHORN: Ah! (*Still reading with matches.*) Colonel! (*Rising.*) The enemy has a new movement on foot, and General Sheridan has left the army! Listen! (*reads from dispatches with matches.*) "Watch for a signal from Three Top Mountain to-night."

KERCHIVAL: We hope to be able to read that signal ourselves.

BUCKTHORN: Yes, I know. Be on your guard. I will speak with General Haverill, and then ride over to General Wright's headquarters. Keep us informed.

KERCHIVAL: I will, General. (*Saluting.* BUCKTHORN *salutes and exit.*)

KERCHIVAL: "Watch for a signal from Three Top Mountain to-night." (*Looking up at Mountain.*) We shall be helpless to read it unless Lieutenant Bedloe is successful. I only hope the poor boy is not lying dead, already in those dark woods beyond the ford. (*He turns down, taking the miniature from his pocket.*) How came Edward Thornton to have this portrait of Mrs. Haverill in his possession?

(GERTRUDE *runs in on the veranda.*)

GERTRUDE: Oh, Colonel West! He's here! (*Looks back.*) They are coming this way with him.

KERCHIVAL: Him! Who?

GERTRUDE: Jack.

KERCHIVAL: Jack!

GERTRUDE: My own horse!

KERCHIVAL: Ah, I remember! He and I were acquainted in Charleston.

GERTRUDE: Two troopers are passing through the camp with him.

KERCHIVAL: He is not in your possession?

GERTRUDE: He was captured at the battle of Fair Oaks, but I recognized him the moment I saw him; and I am sure he knew me, too, when I went up to him. He whinnied and looked so happy. You are in command here—(*Running*

down.)—you will compel them to give him up to me?

KERCHIVAL: If he is in my command, your pet shall be returned to you. I'll give one of my own horses to the Government as a substitute, if necessary.

GERTRUDE: Oh, thank you, my dear Kerchival! (*Going to him; he takes her hand, looking into her eyes.*) I—I could almost—

KERCHIVAL: Can you almost confess, at last, Gertrude, that you—love me? (*Tenderly; she draws back, hanging her head, but leaving her hand in his.*) Have I been wrong? I felt that that confession was hovering on your tongue when we were separated in Charleston. Have I seen that confession in your eyes since we met again to-day—even among the angry flashes which they have shot out at me? During all this terrible war—in the camp and the trench—in the battle—I have dreamed of a meeting like this. You are still silent?

(*Her hand is still in his. She is looking down. A smile steals over her face, and she raises her eyes to his, taking his hand in both her own.*)

GERTRUDE: Kerchival! I— (*Enter* BENSON. *She looks around over her shoulder.* KERCHIVAL *looks up. A trooper leading a large black horse, now caparisoned in military saddle, bridle, follows* BENSON *across; another trooper follows.*) Jack!

(*She runs up the stage, meeting the horse.* KERCHIVAL *turns.*)

KERCHIVAL: Confound Jack! That infernal horse was always in my way!

GERTRUDE (*with her arm about her horse's neck*): My darling old fellow! Is he not beautiful, Kerchival? They have taken good care of him. How soft his coat is!

KERCHIVAL: Benson, explain this!

BENSON: I was instructed to show this horse and his leader through the lines, sir.

KERCHIVAL: What are your orders, my man?

(*Moving up, the trooper hands him a paper. He moves down a few steps, reading it.*)

GERTRUDE: You are to be mine again, Jack, mine! (*Resting her cheek against the horse's head and patting it.*) The Colonel has promised it to me.

KERCHIVAL: Ah! (*With a start, as he reads the paper.* GERTRUDE *raises her head and looks at him.*) This is General Sheridan's horse, on his way to Winchester, for the use of the General when he returns from Washington.

GETRUDE: General Sheridan's horse? He is mine!

KERCHIVAL: I have no authority to detain him. He must go on.

GERTRUDE: I have hold of Jack's bridle, and you may order your men to take out their sabres and cut my hand off.

KERCHIVAL (*he approaches her and gently takes her hand as it holds the bridle.*): I would rather have my own hand cut off, Gertrude, than bring tears to your eyes, but there is no alternative! (GERTRUDE *releases the bridle and turns front, brushing her eyes, her hand still held in his, his back to the audience. He returns the order and motions troopers out; they move out, with the horse.* KERCHIVAL *turns to move.* GERTRUDE *starts after the horse; he turns quickly to check her.*) You forget—that—you are my prisoner.

GERTRUDE: I *will* go!

KERCHIVAL: General Buckthorn left me special instructions—(*taking out the wallet and letter*)—in case you declined to obey my orders—

GERTRUDE: Oh, Colonel! Please don't read that letter. (*She stands near him, dropping her head. He glances up at her from the letter. She glances up at him and drops her eyes again.*) I will obey you.

KERCHIVAL (*aside*): What the deuce can there be in that letter?

GERTRUDE: Colonel West! Your men made me a prisoner this afternoon; to-night you have robbed me, by your own orders, of—of—Jack is only a pet, but I love him; and my brother is also a captive in your hands. When we separated in Charleston you said that we were enemies. What is there lacking to make those words true to-day? You *are* my enemy! A few moments ago you asked me to make a confession to you. You can judge for yourself whether it is likely to be a confession of—love—or of hatred!

KERCHIVAL: Hatred!

GERTRUDE (*facing him*): Listen to my confession, sir! From the bottom of my heart—

KERCHIVAL: Stop!

GERTRUDE: I will not stop!

KERCHIVAL: I command you.

GERTRUDE: Indeed! (*He throws open the wallet in his hand and raises the letter.*) Ah! (*She turns away; turns again, as if to speak. He half opens the letter. She stamps her foot and walks up steps of the veranda. Here she turns again.*) I tell you, I—(*He opens the letter. She turns, and exits with a spiteful step.*)

KERCHIVAL: I wonder if that document orders me to cut her head off! (*Returning it to wallet and pocket.*) Was ever lover in such a position? I am obliged to cross the woman I love at every step.

(*Enter* CORPORAL DUNN, *very hurriedly.*)

DUNN: A message from Adjutant Rollins, sir! The prisoner, Captain Thornton, dashed away from the special guard which was placed over him, and he has escaped. He had a knife concealed, and two of the Guard are badly wounded. Adjutant Rollins thinks the prisoner is still within the lines of the camp—in one of the houses or the stables.

KERCHIVAL: Tell Major Wilson to place the remainder of the Guard under arrest, and to take every possible means to recapture the prisoner. (CORPORAL DUNN *salutes, and exit.*) So! Thornton has jumped his guard, and he is armed. I wonder if he is trying to get away, or to find me. From what I know of the man, he does n't much care which he succeeds in doing. That scar which I gave him in Charleston is deeper in his heart than it is in his face. (*A signal light suddenly appears on Three Top Mountain. The "Call."*) Ah!—the enemy's signal!

(*Enter* CAPTAIN LOCKWOOD, *followed by the* LIEUTENANT OF SIGNAL CORPS.)

Captain Lockwood! You are here! Are your signalmen with you?

LOCKWOOD: Yes, Colonel; and one of my Lieutenants.

(*The* LIEUTENANT *is looking up at the signal with his glass.* CAPTAIN LOCKWOOD *does the same.*)
(HAVERILL *enters, followed by two staff officers.*)

HAVERILL (*as he enters*): Can you make anything of it, Captain?

LOCKWOOD: Nothing, General! Our services are quite useless unless Lieutenant Bedloe returns with the key to their signals.

HAVERILL: A—h! We shall fail. It is time he had returned, if successful.

SENTINEL (*without*): Halt! Who goes there? (KERCHIVAL *runs up the stage and half way up the incline, looking off.*) Halt! (*A shot is heard without.*)

BARKET (*without*): Och!—Ye murtherin spalpeen!

KERCHIVAL: Sentinel! Let him pass; it is Sergeant Barket.

SENTINEL (*without*): Pass on.

KERCHIVAL: He did n't give the countersign. News from Lieutenant Bedloe, General!

BARKET (*hurrying in, up the slope*): Colonel Wist, our brave byes wiped out the enemy, and here's the papers.

KERCHIVAL: Ah! (*Taking the papers.—Then to* LOCKWOOD.) Is that the key?

LOCKWOOD: Yes, Lieutenant!

(LIEUTENANT *hurries up to the elevation, looking through his glass.* LOCKWOOD *opens the book.*)

HAVERILL: What of Lieutenant Bedloe, Sergeant?

BARKET: Sayreously wounded, and in the hands of the inimy!

HAVERILL (*sighing*): A—h.

BARKET (*coming down the stone steps*): It is reported that Captain Heartsease was shot dead at his side.

KERCHIVAL: Heartsease dead!

LIEUTENANT OF SIGNAL CORPS (*reading Signals*): Twelve—Twenty-two—Eleven.

BARKET: Begorra! I forgot the Sintinil entirely, but he did n't forget me. (*Holding his left arm.*)

HAVERILL: Colonel West! We must make every possible sacrifice for the immediate exchange of Lieutenant Bedloe, if he is still living. It is due to him. Colonel Robert Ellingham is a prisoner in this camp; offer him his own exchange for young Bedloe.

KERCHIVAL: He will accept, of course. I will ride to the front with him myself, General, and show him through the lines.

HAVERILL: At once! (KERCHIVAL *crosses front and exit on the veranda.*) Can you follow the dispatch, Captain?

LOCKWOOD: Perfectly; everything is here.

HAVERILL: Well!

LIEUTENANT OF SIGNAL CORPS.: Eleven—Twenty-two—One—Twelve.

LOCKWOOD (*from the book*): "General Longstreet is coming with—"

HAVERILL: Longstreet!

LIEUTENANT OF SIGNAL CORPS.: One—Twenty-one.

LOCKWOOD: "With eighteen thousand men."

HAVERILL: Longstreet and his corps!

LIEUTENANT OF SIGNAL CORPS.: Two—Eleven—Twenty-two.

LOCKWOOD: "Sheridan is away!"

HAVERILL: They have discovered his absence!

LIEUTENANT OF SIGNAL CORPS.: Two—Twenty-two—Eleven—One—Twelve—One.

LOCKWOOD: "We will crush the Union Army before he can return."

HAVERILL: Signal that dispatch from here to our Station at Front Royal. Tell them to send it after General Sheridan—and ride for their lives. (LOCKWOOD *hurries out.*) Major Burton! We will ride to General Wright's headquarters at once—our horses!

(*The noise of a struggle is heard without.*)

BARKET: What the devil is the row out there? (*Exit, also one of the Staff Officers.*)

HAVERILL (*looking off to the left*): What is this! Colonel West wounded!

(*Enter* KERCHIVAL WEST, *his coat thrown open; with* ELLINGHAM, BARKET *assisting.*)

ELLINGHAM: Steady, Kerchival, old boy! You should have let us carry you.

KERCHIVAL: Nonsense, old fellow! It's a mere touch with the point of the knife. I—I'm faint—with the loss of a little blood—that's all. Bob!—I—

(*He reels suddenly and is caught by* ELLINGHAM *as he sinks to the ground, insensible.*)

ELLINGHAM: Kerchival. (*Kneeling at his side.*)

HAVERILL: Go for the Surgeon! (*To the Staff Officer, who goes out quickly on veranda.*) How did this happen?

(*Enter* CORPORAL DUNN *and Guard, with* THORNTON. *He is in his shirt sleeves and disheveled, his arms folded. They march down.*)

Captain Thornton!

ELLINGHAM: We were leaving the house together; a hunted animal sprang suddenly across our path, like a panther. (*Looking over his shoulder.*) There it stands. Kerchival!—my brother!

DUNN: We had just brought this prisoner to bay, but I'm afraid we were too late.

HAVERILL: This is assassination, sir, not war. If you have killed him—

THORNTON: Do what you like with me; we need waste no words. I had an old account to settle, and I have paid my debt.

ELLINGHAM: General Haverill! I took these from his breast when he first fell.

(*Handing up wallet and miniature to* HAVERILL. HAVERILL *starts as he looks at the miniature.* THORNTON *watches him.*)

HAVERILL (*aside*): My wife's portrait!

THORNTON: If I have killed him—your honor will be buried in the same grave.

HAVERILL: Her picture on his breast! She gave it to him—not to my son!

(*Dropping into the seat.* CAPTAIN LOCKWOOD *enters with a Signalman, who has a burning torch on a long pole; he hurries up the elevation.* CAPTAIN LOCKWOOD *stands below, facing him. Almost simultaneously with the entrance of the Signalman,* GERTRUDE *runs in on veranda.)*

GERTRUDE: They are calling for a surgeon! Who is it? Brother!—you are safe. Ah! (*Uttering a scream, as she sees* KERCHIVAL, *and falling on her knees at his side.*) Kerchival! Forget those last bitter words I said to you. Can't you hear my confession? I do love you. Can't you hear me? I love you!

(*The Signalman is swinging the torch as the curtain descends,* LOCKWOOD *looking out to the right.*)

ACT III

(*The scene is the same as in Act II. It is now bright daylight, with sunshine flecking the foreground and bathing the distant valley and mountains. As the curtain rises* JENNY BUCKTHORN *is sitting on the low stone post, in the center of the stage, looking toward the left. She imitates a Trumpet Signal on her closed fists.*)

JENNY: What a magnificent line! Guides posts! Every man and every horse is eager for the next command. There comes the flag! (*As the scene progresses, trumpet signals are heard without and she follows their various meanings in her speech.*) To the standard! The regiment is going to the front. Oh! I do wish I could go with it. I always do, the moment I hear the trumpets. Boots and Saddles! Mount! I wish I was in command of the regiment. It was born in me. Fours right! There they go! Look at those horses' ears! Forward. (*A military band is heard without, playing "The Battle Cry of Freedom."* JENNY *takes the attitude of holding a bridle and trotting.*) Bappity—plap—plap —plap, etc. (*She imitates the motions of a soldier on horseback, stepping down to the rock at side of post; thence to the ground and about the stage, with the various curvellings of a spirited horse. A chorus of soldiers is heard without, with the band. The music becomes more and more distant.* JENNY *gradually stops as the music is dying away, and stands, listening. As it dies entirely away, she suddenly starts to an enthusiastic attitude.*) Ah! If I were only a man! The enemy! On Third Battalion, left, front, into line, march! Draw sabres! Charge! (*Imitates a trumpet signal. As she finishes, she rises to her full height, with both arms raised, and trembling with enthusiasm.*) Ah! (*She suddenly drops her arms and changes to an attitude and expression of disappoint-*

ment—pouting.) And the first time Old Margery took me to Father, in her arms, she had to tell him I was a girl. Father was as much disgusted as I was. But he'd never admit it; he says I'm as good a soldier as any of 'em—just as I am.

(*Enter* BARKET, *on the veranda, his arm in a sling.*)

BARKET: Miss Jenny!
JENNY: Barket! The regiment has marched away to the front, and we girls are left here, with just you and a corporal's guard to look after us.
BARKET: I've been watching the byes mesilf. (*Coming down.*) If a little military sugar-plum like you, Miss Jenny, objects to not goin' wid 'em, what do you think of an ould piece of hard tack like me? I can't join the regiment till I've taken you and Miss Madeline back to Winchester, by your father's orders. But it is n't the first time I've escorted you, Miss Jenny. Many a time, when you was a baby, on the Plains, I commanded a special guard to accompany ye's from one fort to anither, and we gave the command in a whisper, so as not to wake ye's up.
JENNY: I told you to tell Father that I'd let him know when Madeline and I were ready to go.
BARKET: I tould him that I'd as soon move a train of army mules.
JENNY: I suppose we must start for home again to-day?
BARKET: Yes, Miss Jenny, in charge of an ould Sargeant wid his arm in a sling and a couple of convalescent throopers. This department of the United States Army will move to the rear in half an hour.
JENNY: Madeline and I only came yesterday morning.
BARKET: Whin your father got ye's a pass to the front, we all thought the fightin' in the Shenandocy Valley was over. It looks now as if it was just beginning. This is no place for women, now. Miss Gertrude Ellingham ought to go wid us, but she won't.
JENNY: Barket! Captain Heartsease left the regiment yesterday, and he has n't rejoined it; he is n't with them, now, at the head of his company. Where is he?
BARKET: I can't say where he is, Miss Jenny. (*Aside.*) Lyin' unburied in the woods, where he was shot, I'm afraid.
JENNY: When Captain Heartsease does rejoin the regiment, Barket, please say to him for me, that—that I—I may have some orders for him,

when we next meet. (*Exit, on veranda.*)

BARKET: Whin they nixt mate. They tell us there is no such thing as marriage in Hiven. If Miss Jenny and Captain Heartsease mate there, they'll invint somethin' that's mighty like it. While I was lyin' wounded in General Buckthorn's house at Washington, last summer, and ould Margery was taking care of me, Margery tould me, confidentially, that they was in love wid aitch ither; and I think she was about right. I've often seen Captain Heartsease take a sly look at a little lace handkerchief, just before we wint into battle. (*Looking off the stage.*) Here's General Buckthorn himself. He and I must make it as aisy as we can for Miss Jenny's poor heart.

(*Enter* GENERAL BUCKTHORN.)

BUCKTHORN: Sergeant Barket! You have n't started with those girls yet?

BARKET: They're to go in half an hour, sir.

BUCKTHORN: Be sure they do go. Is General Haverill here?

BARKET: Yes, sur; in the house with some of his staff, and the Surgeon.

BUCKTHORN: Ah! The Surgeon. How is Colonel West, this morning, after the wound he received last night?

BARKET: He says, himself, that he's as well as iver he was; but the Colonel and Surgeon don't agray on that subject. The dochter says he must n't lave his room for a month. The knife wint dape; and there's something wrong inside of him. But the Colonel bein' on the outside himsilf, can't see it. He's as cross as a bear, baycause they would n't let him go to the front this morning, at the head of his regiment. I happened to raymark that the Chaplain was prayin' for his raycovery. The Colonel said he'd courtmartial him if he did n't stop that—quick; there's more important things for the Chaplain to pray for in his official capacity. Just at that moment the trumpets sounded, "Boots and Saddles." I had to dodge one of his boots, and the Surgeon had a narrow escape from the ither one. It was lucky for us both his saddle was n't in the room.

BUCKTHORN: That looks encouraging. I think Kerchival will get on.

BARKET: Might I say a word to you, sur, about Miss Jenny?

BUCKTHORN: Certainly, Barket. You and old Margery and myself have been a sort of triangular mother, so to speak, to the little girl since her own poor mother left her to our care, when she was only a baby, in the old fort on the

Plains. (*He unconsciously rests his arm over* BARKET'S *shoulder, familiarly, and then suddenly draws up.*) Ahem! (*Gruffly.*) What is it? Proceed.

BARKET: Her mother's bosom would have been the softest place for her poor little head to rest upon, now, sur.

BUCKTHORN (*touching his eyes*): Well!

BARKET: Ould Margery tould me in Washington that Miss Jenny and Captain Heartsease were in love wid aitch ither.

BUCKTHORN (*starting*): In love!

BARKET: I approved of the match.

BUCKTHORN: What the devil!

(BARKET *salutes quickly and starts up stage and out.* BUCKTHORN *moves up after him, and stops at the post.* BARKET *stops in the road.*)

BARKET: So did ould Margery.

BUCKTHORN (*angrily*): March! (BARKET *salutes suddenly and marches off.*) Heartsease! That young jackanapes! A mere fop; he'll never make a soldier. My girl in love with—bah! I don't believe it; she's too good a soldier, herself.

(*Enter* HAVERILL, *on the veranda.*)

Ah, Haverill!

HAVERILL: General Buckthorn! Have you heard anything of General Sheridan since I sent that dispatch to him last evening?

BUCKTHORN: He received it at midnight and sent back word that he considers it a ruse of the enemy. General Wright agrees with him. The reconnoissance yesterday showed no hostile force, on our right, and Crook reports that Early is retreating up the valley. But General Sheridan may, perhaps, give up his journey to Washington, and he has ordered some changes in our line, to be executed this afternoon at four o'clock. I rode over to give you your instructions in person. You may order General McCuen to go into camp on the right of Meadow Brook, with the second division.

(HAVERILL *is writing in his note-book.*)
(*Enter* JENNY, *on the veranda.*)

JENNY: Oh, Father! I'm so glad you've come. I've got something to say to you.

(*Running down and jumping into his arms, kissing him. He turns with her, and sets her down, squarely on her feet and straight before him.*)

BUCKTHORN: And I've got something to say to you—about Captain Heartsease.

JENNY: Oh! That's just what I wanted to talk about.

BUCKTHORN: Fall in! Front face! (*She jumps into military position, turning towards him.*) What's this I hear from Sergeant Barket? He says you've been falling in love.

JENNY: I have (*Saluting.*)

BUCKTHORN: Young woman! Listen to my orders. Fall out! (*Turns sharply and marches to* HAVERILL.) Order the Third Brigade of Cavalry, under Colonel Lowell, to occupy the left of the pike.

JENNY: Father! (*Running to him and seizing the tail of his coat.*) Father, dear!

BUCKTHORN: Close in Colonel Powell on the extreme left—(*slapping his coat-tails out of* JENNY'S *hands, without looking around*)—and hold Custer on the second line, at Old Forge Road. That is all at present. (*Turning to* JENNY.) Goodbye, my darling! (*Kisses her.*) Remember your orders! You little pet! (*Chuckling, as he taps her chin; draws up suddenly and turns to* HAVERILL.) General! I bid you good-day.

HAVERILL: Good-day, General Buckthorn.

(*They salute with great dignity.* BUCKTHORN *starts up stage;* JENNY *springs after him, seizing his coat-tails.*)

JENNY: But I want to talk with you, Father; I can't fall out. I—I—have n't finished yet.

(*Clinging to his coat, as* BUCKTHORN *marches out rapidly, in the road, holding back with all her might.*)

HAVERILL: It may have been a ruse of the enemy, but I hope that General Sheridan has turned back from Washington. (*Looking at his note-book.*) We are to make changes in our line at four o'clock this afternoon. (*Returning the book to his pocket, he stands in thought.*) The Surgeon tells me that Kerchival West will get on well enough if he remains quiet; otherwise not. He shall not die by the hand of a common assassin; he has no right to die like that. My wife gave my own picture of herself to him—not to my son—and she looked so like an angel when she took it from my hand! They were both false to me, and they have been true to each other. I will save his life for myself.

(*Enter* GERTRUDE, *on the veranda.*)

GERTRUDE: General Haverill! (*Anxiously, coming down.*) Colonel West persists in disobeying the injunctions of the Surgeon. He is preparing to join his regiment at the front. Give him your orders to remain here. Compel him to be prudent!

HAVERILL (*quickly*): The honor of death at the front is not in reserve for him.

GERTRUDE: Eh? What did you say, General?

HAVERILL: Gertrude! I wish to speak to you, as your father's old friend; and I was once your guardian. Your father was my senior officer in the Mexican War. Without his care I should have been left dead in a foreign land. He, himself, afterwards fell fighting for the old flag.

GERTRUDE: The old flag. (*Aside.*) My father died for it, and he—(*looking toward the left*)—is suffering for it—the old flag!

HAVERILL: I can now return the kindness your father did to me, by protecting his daughter from something that may be worse than death.

GERTRUDE: What do you mean?

HAVERILL: Last night I saw you kneeling at the side of Kerchival West; you spoke to him with all the tender passion of a Southern woman. You said you loved him. But you spoke into ears that could not hear you. Has he ever heard those words from your lips? Have you ever confessed your love to him before?

GERTRUDE: Never. Why do you ask?

HAVERILL: Do not repeat those words. Keep your heart to yourself, my girl.

GERTRUDE: General! Why do you say this to me? And at such a moment—when his life—

HAVERILL: His life! (*Turning sharply.*) It belongs to me!

GERTRUDE: Oh!

KERCHIVAL: Sergeant! (*Without. He steps into the road, looking back.* HAVERILL *comes down.*) See that my horse is ready at once. General! (*Saluting.*) Are there any orders for my regiment beyond those given to Major Wilson, in my absence, this morning? I am about to ride on after the troops and reassume my command.

HAVERILL (*quietly*): It is my wish, Colonel, that you remain here under the care of the Surgeon.

KERCHIVAL: My wound is a mere trifle. This may be a critical moment in the campaign, and I cannot rest here. I must be with my own men.

HAVERILL (*quietly*): I beg to repeat the wish I have already expressed.

(KERCHIVAL *walks to him, and speaks apart, almost under his breath, but very earnest in tone.*)

KERCHIVAL: I have had no opportunity, yet, to explain certain matters, as you requested me to do yesterday; but whatever there may be between us, you are now interfering with my duty and my privilege as a soldier; and it is my right to be at the head of my regiment.

HAVERILL (*quietly*): It is my positive order that you do not reassume your command.

KERCHIVAL: General Haverill, I protest against this—

HAVERILL (*quietly*): You are under arrest, sir.

KERCHIVAL: Arrest!

GERTRUDE: Ah!

(KERCHIVAL *unclasps his belt and offers his sword to* HAVERILL.)

HAVERILL (*quietly*): Keep your sword; I have no desire to humiliate you; but hold yourself subject to further orders from me.

KERCHIVAL: My regiment at the front!—and I under arrest! (*Exit.*)

HAVERILL: Gertrude! If your heart refuses to be silent—if you feel that you must confess your love to that man—first tell him what I have said to you, and refer him to me for an explanation. (*Exit.*)

GERTRUDE: What can he mean? He would save me from something worse than death, he said. "His life—It belongs to me!" What can he mean? Kerchival told me that he loved me—it seems many years since that morning in Charleston—and when we met again, yesterday, he said that he had never ceased to love me. I will not believe that he has told me a falsehood. I have given him my love, my whole soul and my faith. (*Drawing up to her full height.*) My perfect faith!

(JENNY *runs in, to the road, and up the slope. She looks down the hill, then toward the left and enters.*)

JENNY: A flag of truce, Gertrude. And a party of Confederate soldiers, with an escort, coming up the hill. They are carrying someone; he is wounded.

(*Enter, up the slope, a Lieutenant of Infantry with an escort of Union Soldiers, their arms at right shoulder, and a party of Confederate Soldiers bearing a rustic stretcher.* LIEUTENANT FRANK BEDLOE *lies on the stretcher.* MAJOR HARDWICK, *a Confederate Surgeon, walks at his side.* MADELINE *appears at the veranda, watching them.* GERTRUDE *stands with her back to the audience. The Lieutenant gives orders in a low tone, and the front escort moves toward the right, in the road. The Confederate bearers and the Surgeon pass through the gate. The rear escort moves on in the road, under the Lieutenant's orders. The bearers halt in the front of the stage; on a sign from the Surgeon, they leave the stretcher on the ground, stepping back.*)

MAJOR HARDWICK: Is General Haverill here?

GERTRUDE: Yes; what can we do, sir?

MADELINE: The General is just about mount-ing with his staff, to ride away. Shall I go for him, sir?

MAJOR HARDWICK: Say to him, please, that Colonel Robert Ellingham, of the Tenth Virginia, sends his respects and sympathy. He instructed me to bring this young officer to this point, in exchange for himself, as agreed upon between them last evening.

(*Exit* MADELINE.)

JENNY: Is he unconscious or sleeping, sir?

MAJOR HARDWICK: Hovering between life and death. I thought he would bear the removal better. He is waking. Here, my lad! (*Placing his canteen to the lips of* FRANK, *who moves, reviving.*) We have reached the end of our journey.

FRANK: My father!

MAJOR HARDWICK: He is thinking of his home.

(FRANK *rises on one arm, assisted by the Surgeon.*)

FRANK: I have obeyed General Haverill's orders, and I have a report to make.

GERTRUDE: We have already sent for him. (*Stepping to him.*) He will be here in a moment.

FRANK (*looking into her face, brightly*): Is not this—Miss—Gertrude Ellingham?

GERTRUDE: You know me? You have seen me before?

FRANK: Long ago! Long ago! You know the wife of General Haverill?

GERTRUDE: I have no dearer friend in the world.

FRANK: She will give a message for me to the dearest friend *I* have in the world. My little wife! I must not waste even the moment we are waiting. Doctor! My note-book! (*Trying to get it from his coat. The Surgeon takes it out. A torn and blood stained lace handkerchief also falls out.* GERTRUDE *kneels at his side.*) Ah! I—I—have a message from another—(*holding up the handkerchief*)—from Captain Heartsease. (JENNY *makes a quick start towards him.*) He lay at my side in the hospital, when they brought me away; he had only strength enough to put this in my hand, and he spoke a woman's name; but I—I—forget what it is. The red spots upon it are the only message he sent.

(GERTRUDE *takes the handkerchief and looks back at* JENNY, *extending her hand.* JENNY *moves to her, takes the handkerchief and turns back, looking down on it. She drops her face into her hands and goes out sobbing, on the veranda.*)

(*Enter* MADELINE *on the veranda.*)

MADELINE: General Haverill is coming. I was just in time. He was already on his horse.

FRANK: Ah! He is coming. (*Then suddenly.*) Write! Write! (GERTRUDE *writes in the note-book as he dictates.*) "To—my wife—Edith:—Tell our little son, when he is old enough to know—how his father died; not how he lived. And tell her who filled my own mother's place so lovingly —she is your mother, too—that my father's portrait of her, which she gave to me in Charleston, helped me to be a better man!" And—Oh! I must not forget this—"It was taken away from me while I was a prisoner in Richmond, and it is in the possession of Captain Edward Thornton, of the Confederate Secret Service. But her face is still beside your own in my heart. My best—warmest, last—love—to you, darling." I will sign it.

(GERTRUDE *holds the book, and he signs it, then sinks back very quietly, supported by the Surgeon.* GERTRUDE *rises and walks away.*)

MADELINE: General Haverill is here.

(*The Surgeon lays the fold of the blanket over* FRANK's *face and rises.*)

GERTRUDE: Doctor!

MAJOR HARDWICK: He is dead.

(MADELINE, *on the veranda, turns and looks away. The Lieutenant orders the guard, "Present Arms."*)

(*Enter* HAVERILL, *on the veranda. He salutes the guard as he passes. The Lieutenant orders, "Carry Arms."* HAVERILL *comes down.*)

HAVERILL: I am too late?

MAJOR HARDWICK: I'm sorry, General. His one eager thought as we came was to reach here in time to see you.

(HAVERILL *moves to the bier, looks down at it, then folds back the blanket from the face. He starts slightly as he first sees it.*)

HAVERILL: Brave boy! I hoped once to have a son like you. I shall be in your father's place to-day, at your grave. (*He replaces the blanket and steps back.*) We will carry him to his comrades in the front. He shall have a soldier's burial, in sight of the mountain-top beneath which he sacrificed his young life; that shall be his monument.

MAJOR HARDWICK: Pardon me, General. We Virginians are your enemies, but you cannot honor this young soldier more than we do. Will you allow my men the privilege of carrying him to his grave?

(HAVERILL *inclines his head. The Surgeon motions to the Confederate Soldiers, who step to the bier and raise it gently.*)

HAVERILL: Lieutenant!

(*The Lieutenant orders the guard "Left Face." The Confederate bearers move through the gate, preceded by* LIEUTENANT HARDWICK. HAVERILL *draws his sword, reverses it, and moves up behind the bier with bowed head. The Lieutenant orders "Forward March," and the cortège disappears. While the girls are still watching it, the heavy sound of distant artillery is heard, with booming reverberations among the hills and in the valley.*)

MADELINE: What is that sound, Gertrude?
GERTRUDE: Listen!

(*Another and more prolonged distant sound, with long reverberations.*)

MADELINE: Again! Gertrude!

(GERTRUDE *raises her hand to command silence; listens. Distant cannon again.*)

GERTRUDE: It is the opening of a battle.
MADELINE: Ah! (*Running down stage. The sounds are heard again, prolonged.*)
GERTRUDE: How often have I heard that sound! (*Coming down.*) This is war, Madeline! You are face to face with it now.
MADELINE: And Robert is there! He may be in the thickest of the danger—at this very moment.
GERTRUDE: Yes. Let our prayers go up for him; mine do, with all a sister's heart.

(KERCHIVAL *enters on veranda, without coat or vest, his sash about his waist, looking back as he comes in.*)

Kerchival!
KERCHIVAL: Go on! Go on! Keep the battle to yourselves. I'm out of it. (*The distant cannon and reverberations are rising in volume.*)
MADELINE: I pray for Robert Ellingham—and for the *cause* in which he risks his life! (KERCHIVAL *looks at her, suddenly; also* GERTRUDE.) Heaven forgive me if I am wrong, but I am praying for the enemies of my country. His people are my people, his enemies are my enemies. Heaven defend him and his, in this awful hour.
KERCHIVAL: Madeline! My sister!
MADELINE: Oh, Kerchival! (*Turning and dropping her face on his breast.*) I cannot help it—I cannot help it!
KERCHIVAL: My poor girl! Every woman's

heart, the world over, belongs not to any country or any flag, but to her husband—and her lover. Pray for the man you love, sister—it would be treason not to. (*Passes her before him to the left of the stage. Looks across to* GERTRUDE.) Am I right? (GERTRUDE *drops her head.* MADELINE *moves up veranda and out.*) Is what I have said to Madeline true?

GERTRUDE: Yes! (*Looks up.*) Kerchival!

KERCHIVAL: Gertrude! (*Hurries across to her, clasps her in his arms. He suddenly staggers and brings his hand to his breast.*)

GERTRUDE: Your wound!

(*Supporting him as he reels and sinks into seat.*)

KERCHIVAL: Wound! I have no wound! You do love me! (*Seizing her hand.*)

GERTRUDE: Let me call the Surgeon, Kerchival.

KERCHIVAL: You can be of more service to me than he can. (*Detaining her. Very heavy sounds of the battle; she starts, listening.*) Never mind that! It's only a battle. You love me!

GERTRUDE: Be quiet, Kerchival, dear. I do love you. I told you so, when you lay bleeding here, last night. But you could not hear me. (*At his side, resting her arm about him, stroking his head.*) I said that same thing to—to—another, more than three years ago. It is in that letter that General Buckthorn gave you. (KERCHIVAL *starts.*) No—no—you must be very quiet, or I will not say another word. If you obey me, I will repeat that part of the letter, every word; I know it by heart, for I read it a dozen times. The letter is from Mrs. Haverill.

KERCHIVAL (*quietly*): Go on.

GERTRUDE: "I have kept your secret, my darling, but I was sorely tempted to betray the confidence you reposed in me at Charleston. If Kerchival West—(*she retires backward from him as she proceeds*)—had heard you say, as I did, when your face was hidden in my bosom, that night, that you loved him with your whole heart—"

KERCHIVAL: Ah!

(*Starting to his feet. He sinks back. She springs to support him.*)

GERTRUDE: I will go for help.

KERCHIVAL: Do not leave me at such a moment as this. You have brought me a new life. (*Bringing her to her knees before him and looking down at her.*) Heaven is just opening before me. (*His hands drop suddenly and his head falls back.*)

GERTRUDE: Ah! Kerchival! You are dying!

(*Musketry. A sudden sharp burst of musketry,* mingled with the roar of artillery near by. KERCHIVAL *starts, seizing* GERTRUDE's *arm and holding her away, still on her knees. He looks eagerly toward the left.*)

KERCHIVAL: The enemy is close upon us!

(BARKET *runs in, up the slope.*)

BARKET: Colonel Wist! The devils have sprung out of the ground. They're pouring over our lift flank like Noah's own flood. The Union Army has started back for Winchester, on its way to the North Pole; our own regiment, Colonel, is coming over the hill in full retrate.

KERCHIVAL: My own regiment! (*Starting up.*) Get my horse, Barket. (*Turns.*) Gertrude, my life! (*Embraces* GERTRUDE.)

BARKET: Your horse is it? I'm wid ye! There's a row at Finnegan's ball, and we're in it. (*Springs to the road, and runs out.*)

KERCHIVAL (*turns away; stops*): I am under arrest.

(*The retreat begins. Fugitives begin to straggle across the stage from the left.*)

GERTRUDE: You must not go, Kerchival; it will kill you.

KERCHIVAL: Arrest be damned! (*Starts up toward the center, raising his arms above his head with clenched fist, and rising to full height.*) Stand out of my way, you cowards!

(*They cower away from him as he rushes out among them. The stream of fugitives passing across the stage swells in volume.* GERTRUDE *runs throught them and up to the elevation, turning.*)

GERTRUDE: Men! Are you soldiers? Turn back! There is a leader for you! Turn back! Fight for your flag—and mine!—the flag my father died for! Turn back! (*She looks out toward the left and then turns toward the front.*) He has been marked for death already, and I—I can only pray. (*Dropping to her knees.*)

(*The stream of fugitives continues, now over the elevation also. Rough and torn uniforms, bandaged arms and legs; some limping and supported by others, some dragging their muskets after them, others without muskets, others using them as crutches. There is a variety of uniforms, both cavalry and infantry; flags are dragged on the ground, the rattle of near musketry and roar of cannon continue; two or three wounded fugitives drop down beside the hedge.* BENSON *staggers in and drops upon a rock near the post. Artillerists, rough, torn and wounded, drag and force a field-piece across.* CORPORAL DUNN, *wounded, staggers to the top of elevation. There is a lull in the sounds of the battle. Distant cheers are heard without.*)

DUNN: Listen, fellows! Stop! Listen! Sheridan! General Sheridan is coming! (*Cheers from those on stage.* GERTRUDE *rises quickly. The wounded soldiers rise, looking over the hedge. All on stage stop, looking eagerly toward the left. The cheers without come nearer, with shouts of "Sheridan! Sheridan!"*) The horse is down; he is worn out.

GERTRUDE: No! He is up again! He is on my Jack! Now, for your life, Jack, and for me! You've never failed me yet. (*The cheers without now swell to full volume and are taken up by those on the stage. The horse sweeps by with General Sheridan.*) Jack! Jack!! Jack!!!

(*Waving her arms as he passes. She throws up her arms and falls backward, caught by* DUNN. *The stream of men is reversed and surges across the stage to the left, in the road and on the elevation, with shouts, and throwing up of hats. The field-piece is forced up the slope with a few bold, rough movements; the artillerists are loading it, and the stream of returning fugitives is still surging by in the road as the curtain falls.*)

ACT IV

(*A living room in the residence of* GENERAL BUCKTHORN *in Washington. There is a fireplace slanting upward from the left toward the center of the stage. On the right toward the center there is a small alcove. On the left there is an opening to the hall with a stair case beyond. There is a door on the right and a wide opening with portières leads on the left toward another room. There is an upright piano toward the front of the stage on the right and an armchair and low stool stand before the fireplace. A small table is set for tea. It is afternoon;* MRS. HAVERILL, *in an armchair, is resting her face upon her hand, and looking into the fire.* EDITH *is on a low stool at her side, sewing a child's garment.*)

EDITH: It seems hardly possible that the war is over, and that General Lee has really surrendered. There is music in the streets nearly all the time, now, and everybody looks so cheerful and bright. (*Distant fife and drums are heard playing "Johnnie Comes Marching Home."* EDITH *springs up and runs up to window, looking out.*) More troops returning! The old tattered battle-flag is waving in the wind, and people are running after them

so merrily. Every day, now, seems like a holiday. The war is over. All the women ought to feel very happy, whose—whose husbands are—coming back to them.

MRS. HAVERILL: Yes, Edith; those women whose—husbands are coming back to them. (*Still looking into the fire.*)

EDITH: Oh! (*Dropping upon the stool, her head upon the arm of the chair.*)

MRS. HAVERILL (*resting her arm over her*): My poor, little darling! *Your* husband will not come back.

EDITH: Frank's last message has never reached me.

MRS. HAVERILL: No; but you have one sweet thought always with you. Madeline West heard part of it, as Gertrude wrote it down. His last thought was a loving one, of you.

EDITH: Madeline says that he was thinking of you, too. He knew that you were taking such loving care of his little one, and of me. You have always done that, since you first came back from Charleston, and found me alone in New York.

MRS. HAVERILL: I found a dear, sweet little daughter. (*Stroking her head.*) Heaven sent you, darling! You have been a blessing to me. I hardly know how I should have got through the past few months at all without you at my side.

EDITH: What is your own trouble, dear? I have found you in tears so often; and since last October, after the battle of Cedar Creek, you—you have never shown me a letter from—from my—Frank's father. General Haverill arrived in Washington yesterday, but has not been here yet. Is it because I am here? He has never seen me, and I fear that he has never forgiven Frank for marrying me.

MRS. HAVERILL: Nonsense, my child; he did think the marriage was imprudent, but he told me to do everything I could for you. If General Haverill has not been to see either of us, since his arrival in Washington, it is nothing that you need to worry your dear little head about. How are you getting on with your son's wardrobe?

EDITH: Oh! Splendidly! Frankie isn't a baby any longer; he's a man, now, and he has to wear a man's clothes. (*Holding up a little pair of trousers, with maternal pride.*) He's rather young to be dressed like a man, but I want Frank to grow up as soon as possible. I long to have him old enough to understand me when I repeat to him the words in which General Haverill told the whole world how his father died! (*Rising.*) And yet, even in his official report to the Government, he only honored him as Lieutenant Bedloe. He has never forgiven his son for the disgrace he brought upon his name.

MRS. HAVERILL: I know him so well—(*rising*) —the unyielding pride, that conquers even the deep tenderness of his nature. He can be silent, though his own heart is breaking. (*Aside.*) He can be silent, too, though *my* heart is breaking. (*Dropping her face in her hand.*)

EDITH: *Mother!* (*Putting her arm about her.*)

(*Enter* JANNETTE.)

JANNETTE: A letter for you, Madam.

MRS. HAVERILL (*taking note; aside*): He has answered me. (*She opens and reads the letter, and inclines her head to* JANNETTE, *who goes out to the hall. Aloud.*) General Haverill will be here this afternoon, Edith. (*Exit.*)

EDITH: There is something that she cannot confide to me, or to anyone. General Haverill returned to Washington yesterday, and he has not been here yet. He will be here to-day. I always tremble when I think of meeting him.

(GENERAL BUCKTHORN *appears in the hall.*)

BUCKTHORN: Come right in; this way, Barket. Ah, Edith!

BARKET (*entering*): As I was saying, sur—just after the battle of Sayder Creek began—

BUCKTHORN (*to* EDITH): More good news! The war is, indeed, over now!

BARKET: Whin Colonel Wist rode to the front to mate his raytrating rigiment—

BUCKTHORN: General Johnston has surrendered his army, also; and that, of course, does end the war.

EDITH: I'm very glad that all the fighting is over.

BUCKTHORN: So am I; but my occupation, and old Barket's too, is gone. Always at work on new clothes for our little soldier?

EDITH: He's growing so, I can hardly make them fast enough for him. But this is the time for his afternoon nap. I must go now, to see if he is sleeping soundly.

BUCKTHORN: Our dear little mother! (*Tapping her chin.*) I always claim the privilege of my white hair, you know. (*She puts up her lips; he kisses her. She goes out.*) The sweetest young widow I ever saw! (BARKET *coughs.* BUCKTHORN *turns sharply;* BARKET *salutes.*) Well! What the devil are you thinking about now?

BARKET: The ould time, sur. Yer honor used to claim the same privilege for brown hair.

BUCKTHORN: You old rascal! What a memory you have! You were telling me for the hundredth time about the battle of Cedar Creek; go on. I can never hear it often enough. Kerchival West was a favorite of mine, poor fellow!

BARKET: Just afther the battle of Sayder Creek began, when the Colonel rode to the front to mate his raytrating rigiment—

BUCKTHORN: I'll tell Old Margery to bring in tea for both of us, Barket.

BARKET: For both of us, sur?

BUCKTHORN: Yes; and later in the evening we'll have something else, together. This is a great day for all of us. I'm not your commander to-day, but your old comrade in arms—(*Laying his arm over* BARKET's *shoulder*)—and I'm glad I don't have to pull myself up now every time I forget my dignity. Ah! you and I will be laid away before long, but we'll be together again in the next world. won't we, Barket?

BARKET: Wid yer honor's permission. (*Saluting.*)

BUCKTHORN: Ha—ha—ha! (*Laughing.*) If we do meet there, I'm certain you'll salute me as your superior officer. There's old Margery, now. (*Looking toward the door and calling.*) Margery! Tea for two!

MARGERY (*without*): The tay be waiting for ye, sur; and it be boilin' over wid impatience.

BUCKTHORN: Bring up a chair, Barket. (*Sitting down in the arm-chair.*)

BARKET (*having placed table and drawing up a chair*): Do you know, Gineral. I don't fale quite aisy in my moind. I'm not quite sure that Margery will let us take our tay together. (*Sits down, doubtfully.*)

BUCKTHORN: I had n't thought of that. I— (*Glancing to the right.*)—I hope she will, Barket. But, of course, if she won't—she's been commander-in-chief of my household ever since Jenny was a baby.

BARKET: At Fort Duncan, in Texas.

BUCKTHORN: You and Old Margery never got along very well in those days; but I thought you had made it all up; she nursed you through your wound, last summer, and after the battle of Cedar Creek, also.

BARKET: Yis, sur, bliss her kind heart, she's been like a wife to me; and that's the trouble. A man's wife is such an angel when he's ill that he dreads to get well; good health is a misfortune to him. Auld Margery and I have had anither misunderstanding.

BUCKTHORN: I'll do the best I can for both of us, Barket. You were telling me about the battle of—

BARKET: Just afther the battle of Sayder Creek began, whin Colonel Wist rode to the front to mate his raytrating rigiment—

(*Enter* OLD MARGERY, *with a tea-tray. She stops abruptly, looking at* BARKET. *He squirms in his chair.* BUCKTHORN *rises and stands with his back to the mantel.* OLD MARGERY *moves to the table, arranges things on it, glances at* BARKET, *then at* BUCKTHORN, *who looks up at the ceiling, rubbing his chin.* OLD MARGERY *takes up one of the cups, with saucer.*)

OLD MARGERY: I misunderstood yer order, sur. I see there's no one here but yerself. (*Going.*)

BUCKTHORN: Ah, Margery! (*She stops.*) Barket tells me that there has been a slight misunderstanding between you and him.

OLD MARGERY: Day before yisterday, the ould Hibernian dhrone had the kitchen upside down, to show anither old milithary vagabone loike himself how the battle of Sayder Creek was fought. He knocked the crame pitcher into the basket of clane clothes, and overturned some raspberry jam and the flat-irons into a pan of fresh eggs. There *has* been a misunderstanding betwane us.

BUCKTHORN: I see there has. I suppose Barket was showing his friend how Colonel Kerchival West rode forward to meet his regiment, when he was already wounded dangerously.

OLD MARGERY: Bliss the poor, dear young man! He and I was always good frinds, though he was something of a devil in the kitchen himself, whin he got there. (*Wiping her eye with one corner of her apron.*) And bliss the young Southern lady that was in love wid him, too. (*Changing the cup and wiping the other eye with the corner of her apron.*) Nothing was iver heard of ayther of thim afther that battle was over, to this very day.

BUCKTHORN: Barket was at Kerchival's side when he rode to the front. (OLD MARGERY *hesitates a moment, then moves to the table; sets down the cup and marches out.* BUCKTHORN *sits in the arm-chair again, pouring tea.*) I could always find some way to get Old Margery to do what I wanted her to do.

BARKET: You're a great man, Giniral; we'd niver have conquered the South widout such men.

BUCKTHORN: Now go on, Barket; you were interrupted.

BARKET: Just afther the battle of Sayder Creek began, whin—

(*Enter* JANNETTE, *with a card, which she hands to* BUCKTHORN.)

BUCKTHORN (*reading card*): Robert Ellingham! (*Rises.*) I will go to him. (*To* JANNETTE.) Go upstairs and tell Miss Madeline to come down.

JANNETTE: Yes, sir. (*Going.*)

BUCKTHORN: And, Jannette, simply say there is a caller; don't tell her who is here. (*Exit* JANNETTE. BUCKTHORN *follows her out to the hall.*) Ellingham! My dear fellow!

(*Extending his hand and disappearing.*)

BARKET: Colonel Ellingham and Miss Madeline—lovers! That's the kind o' volunteers the country nades now!

(*Enter* BUCKTHORN *and* ELLINGHAM.)

BUCKTHORN (*as he enters*): We've been fighting four years to keep you out of Washington, Colonel, but we are delighted to see you within the lines, now.

ELLINGHAM: I am glad, indeed, General, to have so warm a welcome. But can you tell me anything about my sister, Gertrude?

BUCKTHORN: About your sister? Why, can't you tell us? And have you heard nothing of Kerchival West on your side of the line?

ELLINGHAM: All I can tell you is this: As soon as possible after our surrender at Appomattox, I made my way to the Shenandoah Valley. Our home there is utterly deserted. I have hurried down to Washington in the hopes that I might learn something of you. There is no human being about the old homestead; it is like a haunted house—empty, and dark, and solitary. You do not even know where Gertrude is?

BUCKTHORN: We only know that Kerchival was not found among the dead of his own regiment at Cedar Creek, though he fell among them during the fight. The three girls searched the field for him, but he was not there. As darkness came on, and they were returning to the house, Gertrude suddenly seized the bridle of a stray horse, sprang upon its back and rode away to the South, into the woods at the foot of Three Top Mountain. The other two girls watched for her in vain. She did not return, and we have heard nothing from her since.

ELLINGHAM: Poor girl! I understand what was in her thoughts, and she was right. We captured fourteen hundred prisoners that day, although we were defeated, and Kerchival must have been among them. Gertrude rode away, alone, in the darkness, to find him. I shall return to the South at once and learn where she now is.

(JANNETTE *has re-entered, down the stairs.*)

JANNETTE: Miss Madeline will be down in a moment. (*Exit in hall.*)

BARKET (*aside*): That name wint through his chist like a rifle ball.

BUCKTHORN: Will you step into the drawing-room, Colonel? I will see Madeline myself, first. She does not even know that you are living.

ELLINGHAM: I hardly dared ask for her. Is she well?

BUCKTHORN: Yes; and happy—or soon will be.

ELLINGHAM: Peace, at last!

(*Exit to the apartment.* BUCKTHORN *closes the portières.*)

BUCKTHORN: I ought to prepare Madeline a little, Barket; you must help me.

BARKET: Yis, sur, I will.

(*Enter* MADELINE, *down the stairs.*)

MADELINE: Uncle! Jannette said you wished to see me; there is a visitor here. Who is it?

BARKET: Colonel Robert Ellingham.

MADELINE: Ah! (*Staggering.*)

BUCKKTHORN (*supporting her*): You infernal idiot! I'll put you in the guard-house!

BARKET: You wanted me to help ye, Gineral.

MADELINE: Robert is alive—and here?

(*Rising from his arms, she moves to the portières, holds them aside, peeping in; gives a joyful start, tosses aside the portières and runs through.*)

BUCKTHORN: Barket! There's nothing but that curtain between us and Heaven.

BARKET: I don't like stayin' out o' Hiven, myself, sur. Gineral! I'll kiss Ould Margery—if I die for it! (*Exit.*)

BUCKTHORN: Kiss Old Margery! I'll give him a soldier's funeral.

(*Enter* JENNY *from hall, demurely.*)

Ah! Jenny, my dear! I have news for you. Colonel Robert Ellingham is in the drawing-room.

JENNY: Oh! I am delighted. (*Starting.*)

BUCKTHORN: A-h-e-m!

JENNY: Oh!—exactly. I see. I have some news for *you,* papa. Captain Heartsease has arrived in Washington.

BUCKTHORN: Oh! My dear! I have often confessed to you how utterly mistaken I was about that young man. He is a soldier—as good a soldier as you are. I'll ask him to the house.

JENNY (*demurely*): He is here now.

BUCKTHORN: Now?

JENNY: He's been here an hour; in the library.

BUCKTHORN: Why! Barket and I were in the library fifteen minutes ago.

JENNY: Yes, sir. We were in the bay-window; the curtains were closed.

BUCKTHORN: Oh! exactly; I see. You may tell him he has my full consent.

JENNY: He has n't asked for it.

BUCKTHORN: Has n't he? And you've been in the bay-window an hour? Well, my darling—I was considered one of the best Indian fighters in the old army, but it took me four years to propose to your mother. I'll go and see the Captain. (*Exit.*)

JENNY: I wonder if it will take Captain Heartsease four years to propose to me. Before he left Washington, nearly two years ago, he told everybody in the circle of my acquaintance, except me, that he was in love with me. I'll be an old lady in caps before our engagement commences. Poor, dear mother! The idea of a girl's waiting four years for a chance to say, "Yes." It's been on the tip of my tongue so often, I'm afraid it'll pop out, at last, before he pops the question.

(*Enter* BUCKTHORN *and* HEARTSEASE *from the hall.*)

BUCKTHORN: Walk right in, Captain; this is the family room. You must make yourself quite at home here.

HEARTSEASE: Thank you. (*Walking down toward the right.*)

BUCKTHORN: My dear! (*Apart to* JENNY.) The very first thing he said to me, after our greeting, was that he loved my daughter.

JENNY: Now he's told my father!

BUCKTHORN: He's on fire!

JENNY: Is he? (*Looking at* HEARTSEASE, *who stands quietly stroking his mustache.*) Why does n't he tell *me?*

BUCKTHORN: You may have to help him a little; your mother assisted me. When you and Jenny finish your chat, Captain—(*Lighting a cigar at the mantel*)—you must join me in the smoking room.

HEARTSEASE: I shall be delighted. By the way, General—I have been in such a fever of excitement since I arrived at this house—

JENNY (*aside*): Fever? Chills!

HEARTSEASE: That I forgot it entirely. I have omitted a very important and a very sad commission. I have brought with me the note-book of Lieutenant Frank Bedloe—otherwise Haverill—

in which Miss Gertrude Ellingham wrote down his last message to his young wife.

JENNY: Have you seen Gertrude?

BUCKTHORN (*taking the book*): How did this note-book come into your possession?

HEARTSEASE: Miss Ellingham visited the prison in North Carolina where I was detained. She was going from hospital to hospital, from prison to prison, and from burial-place to burial-place, to find Colonel Kerchival West, if living—or some record of his death.

BUCKTHORN: Another Evangeline! Searching for her lover through the wilderness of this great war!

HEARTSEASE: I was about to be exchanged at the time, and she requested me to bring this to her friends in Washington. She had not intended to carry it away with her. I was not exchanged, as we then expected, but I afterwards escaped from prison to General Sherman's Army.

BUCKTHORN: I will carry this long-delayed message to the widowed young mother. (*Exit.*)

JENNY: I remember so well, when poor Lieutenant Haverill took out the note-book and asked Gertrude to write for him. He he brought me a message at the same time.

(*Their eyes meet. He puts up his glasses. She turns away, touching her eyes.*)

HEARTSEASE: I—I remember the circumstances you probably allude too; that is—when he left my side—I—I gave him my—I mean your—lace handkerchief.

JENNY: It is sacred to me!

HEARTSEASE: Y-e-s—I would say—is it?

JENNY (*wiping her eyes*): It was stained with the life-blood of a hero!

HEARTSEASE: I must apologize to you for its condition. I had n't any chance to have it washed and ironed.

JENNY (*looking around at him, suddenly; then, aside*): What could any girl do with a lover like that? (*Turning up the stage.*)

HEARTSEASE (*aside*): She seems to remember that incident so tenderly! My blood boils!

JENNY: Did n't you long to see your—your friends at home—when you were in prison, Captain?

HEARTSEASE: Yes—especially—I longed especially, Miss Buckthorn, to see—

JENNY: Yes!—to see—

HEARTSEASE: But there were lots of jolly fellows in the prison. (JENNY *turns away.*)

HEARTSEASE: We had a dramatic society, and

a glee club, and an orchestra. I was one of the orchestra. I had a banjo, with one string; I played one tune on it, that I used to play on the piano, with one finger. But, Miss Buckthorn, I am a prisoner again, to-night—your prisoner.

JENNY (*aside*): At last!

HEARTSEASE: I'll show you how that tune went. (*Turns to the piano and sits.*)

JENNY (*aside*): Father said I'd have to help him, but I don't see an opening.

(HEARTSEASE *plays part of an air with one finger and strikes two or three wrong notes.*)

HEARTSEASE: There are two notes down there, somewhere, that I never could get right. The fellows in prison used to dance while I played—(*Playing*)—that is, the lame ones did; those that were n't lame could n't keep the time.

JENNY: You must have been in great danger, Captain, when you escaped from prison.

HEARTSEASE: Y-e-s. I was badly frightened several times. One night I came face to face, on the road, with a Confederate Officer. It was Captain Thornton.

JENNY: Oh! What did you do?

HEARTSEASE: I killed him. (*Very quietly, and trying the tune again at once. Enter* JANNETTE, *from the hall; she glances into the room and goes up the stairs.*) I used to skip those two notes on the banjo. It's very nice for a soldier to come home from the war, and meet those—I mean the one particular person that he—you see, when a soldier loves a woman, as—as—

JENNY (*aside*): As he loves me. (*Approaches him.*)

HEARTSEASE: As soldiers often do—(*Plays; she turns away, petulantly; he plays the tune through correctly.*) That's it!

JENNY (*aside*): I'm not going to be made love to by piece-meal, like this, any longer. (*Aloud.*) Captain Heartsease! Have you anything in particular to say to me? (*He looks up.*)

HEARTSEASE: Y-e-s. (*Rising.*)

JENNY: Say it! You told my father, and all my friends, that you were in love with me. Whom are you going to tell next?

HEARTSEASE: I *am* in love with you.

JENNY: It was my turn.

HEARTSEASE ((*going near to her*): Do you love me?

JENNY (*laying her head quietly on his breast*): I must take time to consider.

HEARTSEASE (*quietly*): I assume that this means "Yes."

JENNY: It isn't the way a girl says "No."

HEARTSEASE: My darling!

JENNY: Why! His heart is beating as fast as mine is!

HEARTSEASE (*quietly*): I am frantic with joy. (*He kisses her. She hides her face on his breast. Enter* MRS. HAVERILL, *down-stairs, followed by* JANNETTE. MRS. HAVERILL *stops suddenly.* JANNETTE *stands in the doorway.* HEARTSEASE *inclines his head to her, quietly looking at her over* JENNY.) I am delighted to see you, after so long an absence; I trust that we shall meet more frequently hereafter.

JENNY (*looking at him*): Eh?

HEARTSEASE (*looking down at her*): I think, perhaps, it might be as well for us to repair to another apartment, and continue our interview, there!

JENNY (*dropping her head on his breast again*): This room is very comfortable.

MRS. HAVERILL: Jenny dear!

(JENNY *starts up; looks from* MRS. HAVERILL *to* HEARTSEASE.)

JENNY: Constance! I—'Bout face! March! (*She turns and goes out.*)

MRS. HAVERILL: I am glad to see you again, Captain, and happy as well as safe.

HEARTSEASE: Thank you, Madam. I am happy. If you will excuse me, I will join—my father —in the smoking-room.

(MRS. HAVERILL *inclines her head, and* HEARTSEASE *walks out.*)

MRS. HAVERILL: Jannette! You may ask General Haverill to come into this room. (*Exit* JANNETTE. MRS. HAVERILL *walks down the stage, reading a note.*) "I have hesitated to come to you personally, as I have hesitated to write to you. If I have been silent, it is because I could not bring my hand to write what was in my mind and in my heart. I do not know that I can trust my tongue to speak it, but I will come."

(*Enter* HAVERILL, *from the hall; he stops.*)

HAVERILL: Constance!

MRS. HAVERILL: My husband! May I call you husband? After all these months of separation, with your life in almost daily peril, and my life —what? Only a weary longing for one loving word—and you are silent.

HAVERILL: May I call you wife? I do not wish to speak that word except with reverence. You have asked me to come to you. I am here. I will be plain, direct and brief. Where is the portrait of yourself, which I gave you, in Charleston, for my son?

MRS. HAVERILL: Your son is dead, sir; and my portrait lies upon his breast, in the grave. (HAVERILL *takes the miniature from his pocket and holds it towards her in his extended hand. She starts back.*) He gave it to you? And you ask me where it is?

HAVERILL: It might have lain in the grave of Kerchival West!

MRS. HAVERILL: Ah!

HAVERILL: Not in my son's. I found it upon *his* breast. (*She turns front dazed.*) Well! I am listening! It was not I that sought this interview, madam; and if you prefer to remain silent, I will go. You know, now, why I have been silent so long.

MRS. HAVERILL: My only witnesses to the truth are both dead. I shall remain silent. (*Turning towards him.*) We stand before each other, living, but not so happy as they. We are parted, forever. Even if you should accept my unsupported word —if I could so far forget my pride as to give it to you—suspicion would still hang between us. I remain silent.

(HAVERILL *looks at her, earnestly, for a moment, then approaches her.*)

HAVERILL: I cannot look into your eyes and not see truth and loyalty there. Constance!

MRS. HAVERILL: No, John! (*Checking him.*) I will not accept your blind faith! (*Moving.*)

HAVERILL (*looking down at the picture in his hand*): My faith is blind; blind as my love! I do not wish to see!

(*Enter* EDITH. *She stops and looks at* HAVERILL. *He raises his head and looks at her.*)

EDITH: This is General Haverill? (*Dropping her eyes.*) I am Edith, sir.

HAVERILL (*gently*): My son's wife. (*Kisses her forehead.*) You shall take the place he once filled in my heart. His crime and his disgrace are buried in a distant grave.

EDITH: And you have not forgiven him, even yet?

MRS. HAVERILL: Is there no atonement for poor Frank's sin—not even his death? Can you only bury the wrong and forget the good?

HAVERILL: The good?

MRS. HAVERILL: Your own words to the Government, as his commander!

HAVERILL: What do you mean?

MRS. HAVERILL: "The victory of Cedar Creek

would have been impossible without the sacrifice of this young officer."

HAVERILL: My own words, yes—but—

EDITH: "His name must take its place forever, in the roll of names which his countrymen honor."

HAVERILL: Lieutenant Bedloe!

MRS. HAVERILL: Haverill! You did not know?

HAVERILL: My—son.

EDITH: You did not receive mother's letter? —after his death?

HAVERILL: My son! (*Sinking upon a chair.*) I left him alone in his grave, unknown; but my tears fell for him then, as they do now. He died before I reached him.

EDITH: Father! (*Laying her hand gently on his shoulder.*) You shall see Frank's face again. His little son is lying asleep upstairs; and when he wakes up, Frank's own eyes will look into yours. I have just received his last message. I will read it to you. (*She opens the note-book and reads.*) "Tell our little son how his father died, not how he lived. And tell her who filled my own mother's place so lovingly." (*She looks at* MRS. HAVERILL, *moves to her and hides her face in her bosom.*) My mother!

MRS. HAVERILL: Edith—my child! Frank loved us both.

EDITH (*reading*): "Father's portrait of her, which she gave to me in Charleston—(HAVERILL *starts*)—helped me to be a better man."

HAVERILL (*rising to his feet*): Constance!

EDITH (*reading*): "It was taken from me in Richmond, and it is in the possession of Captain Edward Thornton."

HAVERILL: One moment! Stop! Let me think! (EDITH *looks at him.*) Thornton was a prisoner— and to Kerchival West. A dispatch had been found upon him—he was searched! (*He moves to her and takes both her hands in his own, bowing his head over them.*) My head is bowed in shame.

MRS. HAVERILL: Speak to me, John, as you used to speak! Tell me you still love me!

HAVERILL: The—the words will come—but they are—choking me—now. (*He presses her hand to his lips.*)

MRS. HAVERILL: We will think no more of the past, except of what was bright in it. Frank's memory, and our own love, will be with us always.

(*Enter* BUCKTHORN, *followed by* HEARTSEASE.)

BUCKTHORN: Haverill! You are back from the war, too. It begins to look like peace in earnest.

HAVERILL: Yes. Peace and home.

(*Shaking hands with him.* MRS. HAVERILL *joins* EDITH.)

(*Enter* BARKET.)

BARKET: Gineral! (BUCKTHORN *moves to him.* HAVERILL *joins* MRS. HAVERILL *and* EDITH. BARKET *speaks apart, twisting one side of his face.*) I kissed her!

BUCKTHORN: Have you sent for a surgeon?

BARKET: I felt as if the inimy had surprised us agin, and Sheridan was sixty miles away.

HAVERILL: This is old Sergeant Barket. (BARKET *salutes.*) You were the last man of us all that saw Colonel West.

BARKET: Just afther the battle of Sayder Creek began—whin Colonel Wist rode to the front to mate his retrayting rigiment—the byes formed in line, at sight of him, to raysist the victorious inimy. It was just at the brow of a hill—about there, sur—(*pointing with his cane*) and—here! (*He takes the tray from the table and sets it on the carpet, then lays the slices of bread in a row.*) That be the rigiment. (*All are interested.* MADELINE *and* ELLINGHAM *enter, and look on.* BARKET *arranges the two cups and saucers in a row.*) That be the inimy's batthery, sur.

(*Enter* MARGERY. *She goes to the table, then looks around, sharply at* BARKET.)

OLD MARGERY: Ye ould Hibernian dhrone! What are yez doin' wid the china on the floor? You'll break it all!

BUCKTHORN: Ah—Margery! Barket is telling us where he last saw Colonel Kerchival West.

OLD MARGERY: The young Colonel! The taycups and saucers be's the inimy's batthery? Yez may smash 'em, if ye loike!

BUCKTHORN: Go on, Barket.

(JENNY *and* HEARTSEASE *have entered, as* BARKET *proceeds, the whole party lean forward, intensely interested.* GERTRUDE *enters in the hall, looks in, beckons as if to some one without, and* KERCHIVAL *follows. They move to the center of the stage, back of the rest and listen unseen.*)

BARKET: Just as the rigiment was ray-formed in line, and Colonel Wist was out in front— widout any coat or hat, and wid only a shtick in his hand—we heard cheers in the rear. Gineral Sheridan was coming! One word to the men— and we swept over the batthery like a whirlwind! (*Slashing his cane through the cups and saucers.*)

OLD MARGERY: Hoo-roo!

BARKET: The attack on the lift flank was checked. But when we shtopped to take breath, Colonel Wist was n't wid us. (GERTRUDE *turns lovingly to* KERCHIVAL. *He places his arm about her.*) Heaven knows where he is now. Afther the battle was over, pooor Miss Gertrude wint off by hersilf into the wilderness to find him.

KERCHIVAL: My wife! You saved my life, at last. (*Embracing her.*)

BARKET: They'll niver come together in this world. I saw Miss Gertrude, myself, ride away into the woods and disappear behind a schoolhouse on the battle-field, over there.

GERTRUDE: No, Barket—(*All start and look*) —it was the little church; we were married there this morning!

Susan Glaspell: *Suppressed Desires* (1914)

Susan Glaspell was born in Davenport, Iowa, in 1882. She once said she could not remember a time when she did not want to be a writer, and she began her publishing career while a student at Drake University in Des Moines. After college, she worked for a newspaper and met her husband-to-be, George Cram Cook, in 1908. At that time there was no chance that he, a Harvard-educated teacher at Iowa University, would be drawn to a woman of simple, middle-class background such as Susan Glaspell, so their paths separated. She decided to go to Paris to write, while he married a woman of his own social class. In five years' time, he was divorced, and Glaspell was ready to live in America again and write. In 1913, when they met once more and married, they had the feeling that fate had intended them for one another all the time. Friends had attracted them to Provincetown, where they made their home.

They made history in Provincetown. The Provincetown players, which began modestly in a living room with a reading of *Suppressed Desires,* eventually produced the first plays of Eugene O'Neill and became a focal point for serious theater in America. Although it was on a vastly smaller scale, it matched in seriousness, and perhaps in talent, the great European theater movements, such as the growing Abbey Theater in Ireland. It was a theater designed to show the work of serious writers. Unlike the work of Bronson Howard, who was, like Dion Boucicault, gifted in knowing how to please an audience, the work of Susan Glaspell and the other Provincetown playwrights was meant to be challenging, demanding, and something far beyond entertainment.

Suppressed Desires, however, is an entertaining play. It is still performed and hardly ever stopped being given during her lifetime. It began as a kind of joke, with Susan Glaspell and her husband Jig Cook making fun of the faddishness associated with Freudian psychology. The intellectuals in New York's Greenwich Village were caught up in the interpretation of dreams, which were seen to reveal our subconscious desires and wishes. The couple were tossing off casual quips about the Oedipus complex, the unconscious desire we are all supposed to possess to kill off our same-sex parent and marry our opposite-sex one. The very sense of outrage this provokes in commonsensical people made the intellectuals delight in it all the more. As Susan Glaspell and her husband bandied the idea around, they found themselves supplying lines of dialogue and a comic situation. They worked out the circumstances of the play and Susan finished it. The play is usually considered a collaborative effort, but it is clear from her subsequent work that Susan Glaspell was the playwright in the family. Jig Cook was extremely supportive of his wife's work in the theater, but his interests lay mainly in writing novels.

The tension in the play is drawn from the conflict of theory and practice. Henrietta is anxious to convince everyone that psychoanalysis is important enough that her friends should be "psyched," as Steve puts it. She is writing learned papers on the subject, reading Freud, "the new Messiah," and "Jung, the new St. Paul." Her efforts to convince all around her come to grief when she discovers that her own Dr. Russell advises her husband that he has a suppressed desire to leave their marriage and advises Mabel that she has a suppressed desire to marry Henrietta's husband. The comical way all this is revealed, through the interpretation of symbols in dreams—including two conflicting interpretations—is a satirical barb at the early adherents of psychoanalysis and their methods.

The treatment of psychoanalysis is light and deft. Glaspell actually had a serious interest in the subject, so there was no effort on her part to demolish Freud or Jung. Instead, she saw the opportunity to deal amusingly with the hypocrisy of a "practitioner" who suddenly saw the practice turning against her.

The play was produced in Provincetown because no one who read it in New York, including the celebrated Washington Square Playhouse, would give it a production. The New York theater felt it was too specialized in its interest in psychoanalysis, presumably fearing the general audiences would be too ignorant of the field to make sense of the play. After its first reading, word got around Provincetown, and people who hadn't seen the first version demanded a second performance. Eventually, it became a hit of the first "season" of the Provincetown Players.

Glaspell went on to write several books, among them a memoir of her husband, who died in Delphi, Greece, where he had adopted the ways of the Greek peasants living on Mount Parnassus near the temple of Apollo. Even though she continued writing after her husband's death, her output of plays was very small, and it is more reasonable to think of her as a critical influence in the drama of the early twentieth century than as a major playwright. She died in 1948, having broken in 1925 with the revised Provincetown Playhouse, which had taken a very new direction under the influence of Eugene O'Neill, while she and Jig Cook were in Greece. O'Neill had tried to placate her bad feelings about using the name she and her husband had invented, and while she put up a good front, she never worked with the Provincetown Playhouse again.

Suggested Readings

Bach, Gerhard. "Susan Glaspell (1876–1948): A Bibliography of Dramatic Criticism." *Great Lakes Review: A Journal of Midwest Culture, 3*, pp. 1–34.

Glaspell, Susan. *The Road to the Temple, the Life of George Cram Cook.* New York: Stokes, 1927.

———. *Alison's House: A Play in Three Acts.* New York: Samuel French, 1930.

Noc, Marcia. "Susan Glaspell's Analysis of the Midwestern Character." *Books at Iowa*, 27, pp. 3–14.

Waterman, Arthur E. *Susan Glaspell.* New York: Twayne, 1966.

Suppressed Desires

A COMEDY

Susan Glaspell

In collaboration with
George Cram Cook

CHARACTERS

HENRIETTA BREWSTER
STEPHEN BREWSTER
MABEL

SCENE 1

(A *studio apartment in an upper story, Washington Square South. Through an immense north window in the back wall appear tree tops and the upper part of the Washington Arch. Beyond it you look up Fifth Avenue. Near the window is a big table, loaded at one end with serious-looking books and austere scientific periodicals. At the other end are architect's drawings, blue prints, dividing compasses, square, ruler, etc. At the left is a door leading to the rest of the apartment; at the right the outer door. A breakfast table is set for three, but only two are seated at it*—HENRIETTA *and* STEPHEN BREWSTER. As the curtains withdraw STEVE *pushes back his coffee cup and sits dejected.*)

HENRIETTA: It isn't the coffee, Steve dear. There's nothing the matter with the coffee. There's something the matter with *you*.

STEVE (*doggedly*): There may be something the matter with my stomach.

HENRIETTA (*scornfully*): Your stomach! The trouble is not with your stomach but in your subconscious mind.

STEVE: Subconscious piffle! (*Takes morning paper and tries to read.*)

HENRIETTA: Steve, you never used to be so disagreeable. You certainly have got some sort of a complex. You're all inhibited. You're no long-er open to new ideas. You won't listen to a word about psychoanalysis.

STEVE: A word! I've listened to volumes!

HENRIETTA: You've ceased to be creative in architecture—your work isn't going well. You're not sleeping well———

STEVE: How can I sleep, Henrietta, when you're always waking me up to find out what I'm dreaming?

HENRIETTA: But dreams are so important, Steve. If you'd tell yours to Dr. Russell he'd find out exactly what's wrong with you.

STEVE: There's nothing wrong with me.

HENRIETTA: You don't even talk as well as you used to.

STEVE: Talk? I can't say a thing without you looking at me in that dark fashion you have when you're on the trail of a complex.

HENRIETTA: This very irritability indicates that you're suffering from some suppressed desire.

STEVE: I'm suffering from a suppressed desire for a little peace.

HENRIETTA: Dr. Russell is doing simply wonderful things with nervous cases. Won't you go to him, Steve?

STEVE (*slamming down his newspaper*): No, Henrietta, I won't!

HENRIETTA: But Stephen———!

STEVE: Tst! I hear Mabel coming. Let's not be

166

at each other's throats the first day of her visit.

(*He takes out cigarettes.* MABEL *comes in from door left, the side opposite* STEVE, *so that he is facing her. She is wearing a rather fussy negligee in contrast to* HENRIETTA, *who wears "radical" clothes.* MABEL *is what is called plump.*)

MABEL: Good morning.

HENRIETTA: Oh, here you are, little sister.

STEVE: Good morning, Mabel.

(MABEL *nods to him and turns, her face lighting up, to* HENRIETTA.)

HENRIETTA (*giving* MABEL *a hug as she leans against her*): It's so good to have you here. I was going to let you sleep, thinking you'd be tired after the long trip. Sit down. There'll be fresh toast in a minute and (*rising*) will you have————

MABEL: Oh, I ought to have told you, Henrietta. Don't get anything for me. I'm not eating breakfast.

HENRIETTA (*at first in mere surprise*): Not eating breakfast? (*She sits down, then leans toward* MABEL *who is seated now, and scrutinizes her.*)

STEVE (*half to himself*): The psychoanalytical look!

HENRIETTA: Mabel, why are you not eating breakfast?

MABEL (*a little startled*): Why, no particular reason. I just don't care much for breakfast, and they say it keeps down————(*a hand on her hip —the gesture of one who is reducing*) that is, it's a good thing to go without it.

HENRIETTA: Don't you sleep well? Did you sleep well last night?

MABEL: Oh, yes, I slept all right. Yes, I slept fine last night, only (*laughing*) I did have the funniest dream!

STEVE: S-h! S-t!

HENRIETTA (*moving closer*): And what did you dream, Mabel?

STEVE: Look-a-here, Mabel, I feel it's my duty to put you on. Don't tell Henrietta your dreams. If you do she'll find out that you have an underground desire to kill your father and marry your mother————

HENRIETTA: Don't be absurd, Stephen Brewster. (*Sweetly to* MABEL.) What was your dream, dear?

MABEL (*laughing*): Well, I dreamed I was a hen.

HENRIETTA: A hen?

MABEL: Yes; and I was pushing along through a crowd as fast as I could, but being a hen I couldn't walk very fast—it was like having a tight skirt, you know; and there was some sort of creature in a blue cap—you know how mixed up dreams are—and it kept shouting after me, "Step, Hen! Step, Hen!" until I got all excited and just couldn't move at all.

HENRIETTA (*resting chin in palm and peering*): You say you became much excited?

MABEL (*laughing*): Oh, yes; I was in a terrible state.

HENRIETTA (*leaning back, murmurs*) This is significant.

STEVE: She dreams she's a hen. She is told to step lively. She becomes violently agitated. What can it mean?

HENRIETTA (*turning impatiently from him*): Mabel, do you know anything about psychoanalysis?

MABEL (*feebly*): Oh—not much. No—I————(*Brightening.*) It's something about the war, isn't it?

STEVE: Not that kind of war.

MABEL (*abashed*): I thought it might be the name of a new explosive.

STEVE: It *is*.

MABEL (*apologetically to* HENRIETTA, *who is frowning*): You see, Henrietta, I—we do not live in touch with intellectual things, as you do. Bob being a dentist—somehow our friends————

STEVE (*softly*): Oh, to be a dentist! (*Goes to window and stands looking out.*)

HENRIETTA: Don't you see anything more of that editorial writer—what was his name?

MABEL: Lyman Eggleston?

HENRIETTA: Yes, Eggleston. He was in touch with things. Don't you see him?

MABEL: Yes, I see him once in a while. Bob doesn't like him very well.

HENRIETTA: Your husband does not like Lyman Eggleston? (*Mysteriously.*) Mabel, are you perfectly happy with your husband?

STEVE (*sharply*): Oh, come now, Henrietta— that's going a little strong!

HENRIETTA: Are you perfectly happy with him, Mabel?

(STEVE *goes to work-table.*)

MABEL: Why—yes—I guess so. Why———— of course I am!

HENRIETTA: Are you happy? Or do you only think you are? Or do you only think you *ought* to be?

MABEL: Why, Henrietta, I don't know what you mean!

STEVE (*seizes stack of books and magazines and dumps them on the breakfast table*): This is what she means, Mable. Psychoanalysis. My work-table groans with it. Books by Freud, the new Messiah; books by Jung, the new St. Paul; the Psychoanalytical Review—back numbers two-fifty per.

MABEL: But what's it all about?

STEVE: All about your sub-un-non-conscious mind and desires you know not of. They may be doing you a great deal of harm. You may go crazy with them. Oh, yes! People are doing it right and left. Your dreaming you're a hen ———(*Shakes his head darkly.*)

HENRIETTA: Any fool can ridicule anything.

MABEL (*hastily, to avert a quarrel*): But what do you say it is, Henrietta?

STEVE (*looking at his watch*): Oh, if Henrietta's going to start that! (*During* HENRIETTA'S *next speech settles himself at work-table and sharpens a lead pencil.*)

HENRIETTA: It's like this, Mable. You want something. You think you can't have it. You think it's wrong. So you try to think you don't want it. Your mind protects you—avoids pain —by refusing to think the forbidden thing. But it's there just the same. It stays there shut up in your unconscious mind, and it festers.

STEVE: Sort of an ingrowing mental toenail.

HENRIETTA: Precisely. The forbidden impulse is there full of energy which has simply got to do something. It breaks into your consciousness in disguise, masks itself in dreams, makes all sorts of trouble. In extreme cases it drives you insane.

MABEL (*with a gesture of horror*): Oh!

HENRIETTA (*reassuring*): But psychoanalysis has found out how to save us from that. It brings into consciousness the suppressed desire that was making all the trouble. Psychoanalysis is simply the latest scientific method of preventing and curing insanity.

STEVE (*from his table*): It is also the latest scientific method of separating families.

HENRIETTA (*mildly*): Families that ought to be separated.

STEVE: The Dwights, for instance. You must have met them, Mabel, when you were here before. Helen was living, apparently, in peace and happiness with good old Joe. Well—she went to this psychoanalyzer—she was "psyched," and biff!—bang!—home she comes with an unsuppressed desire ·to leave her husband. (*He starts work, drawing lines on a drawing board with a T-square.*)

MABEL: How terrible! Yes, I remember Helen

Dwight. But—but did she have such a desire?

STEVE: First she'd known of it.

MABEL: And she *left* him?

HENRIETTA (*coolly*): Yes, she did.

MABEL: Wasn't he good to her?

HENRIETTA: Why, yes, good enough.

MABEL: Wasn't he kind to her?

HENRIETTA: Oh, yes———kind to her.

MABEL: And she left her good, kind husband———!

HENRIETTA: Oh, Mabel! "Left her good, kind husband!" How naïve———forgive me, dear, but how bourgeois you are! She came to know herself. And she had the courage!

MABEL: I may be very naïve and—bourgeois —but I don't see the good of a new science that breaks up homes.

(STEVE *applauds.*)

STEVE: In enlightening Mabel, we mustn't neglect to mention the case of Art Holden's private secretary, Mary Snow, who has just been informed of her suppressed desire for her employer.

MABEL: Why, I think it is terrible, Henrietta! It would be better if we didn't know such things about ourselves.

HENRIETTA: No, Mabel, that is the old way.

MABEL: But—but her employer? Is he married?

STEVE (*grunts*): Wife and four children.

MABEL: Well, then, what good does it do the girl to be told she has a desire for him? There's nothing can be done about it.

HENRIETTA: Old institutions will have to be reshaped so that something can be done in such cases. It happens, Mabel, that this suppressed desire was on the point of landing Mary Snow in the insane asylum. Are you so tight-minded that you'd rather have her in the insane asylum than break the conventions?

MABEL: But—but have people always had these awful suppressed desires?

HENRIETTA: Always.

STEVE: But they've just been discovered.

HENRIETTA: The harm they do has just been discovered. And free, sane people must face the fact that they have to be dealt with.

MABEL (*stoutly*): I don't believe they have them in Chicago.

HENRIETTA (*business of giving* MABEL *up*): People "have them" wherever the living Libido—the center of the soul's energy—is in conflict with petrified moral codes. That means everywhere in civilization. Psychoanalysis———

STEVE: Good God! I've got the roof in the cellar!

HENRIETTA: The roof in the cellar!

STEVE (*holding plan at arm's length*): That's what psychoanalysis does!

HENRIETTA: That's what psychoanalysis could *un*-do. It is any wonder I'm concerned about Steve? He dreamed the other night that the walls of his room melted away and he found himself alone in a forest. Don't you see how significant it is for an architect to have *walls* slip away from him? It symbolizes his loss of grip in his work. There's some suppressed desire——

STEVE (*hurling his ruined plan viciously to the floor*): Suppressed hell!

HENRIETTA: You speak more truly than you know. It is through suppressions that hells are formed in us.

MABEL (*looking at* STEVE, *who is tearing his hair*): Don't you think it would be a good thing, Henrietta, if we went somewhere else?

(*They rise and begin to pick up the dishes.* MABEL *drops a plate which breaks.* HENRIETTA *draws up short and looks at her—the psychoanalytic look.*)

I'm sorry, Henrietta. One of the Spode plates, too. (*Surprised and resentful as* HENRIETTA *continues to peer at her.*) Don't take it so to heart, Henrietta.

HENRIETTA: I can't help taking it to heart.

MABEL: I'll get you another. (*Pause. More sharply as* HENRIETTA *does not answer.*) I said I'll get you another plate, Henrietta.

HENRIETTA: It's not the plate.

MABEL: For heaven's sake, what is it then?

HENRIETTA: It's the significant little false movement that made you drop it

MABEL: Well, I suppose everyone makes a false movement once in a while.

HENRIETTA: Yes, Mabel, but these false movements all mean something.

MABEL (*about to cry*): I don't think that's very nice! It was just because I happened to think of that Mabel Snow you were talking about——

HENRIETTA: *Mabel* Snow!

MABEL: Snow—Snow—well, what was her name, then?

HENRIETTA: Her name is Mary. You substituted *your own* name for hers.

MABEL: Well, *Mary* Snow, then; *Mary* Snow. I never heard her name but once. I don't see anything to make such a fuss about.

HENRIETTA (*gently*): Mabel dear—mistakes like that in names——

MABEL (*desperately*): They don't mean some-thing, too, do they?

HENRIETTA (*gently*): I am sorry, dear, but they do.

MABEL: But I'm always doing that!

HENRIETTA (*after a start of horror*): My poor little sister, tell me about it.

MABEL: About what?

HENRIETTA: About your not being happy. About your longing for another sort of life.

MABEL: But I *don't*.

HENRIETTA: Ah, I understand these things, dear. You feel Bob is limiting you to a life in which you do not feel free——

MABEL: Henrietta! When did I ever say such a thing?

HENRIETTA: You said you are not in touch with things intellectual. You showed your feeling that it is Bob's profession—that has engendered a resentment which has colored your whole life with him.

MABEL: Why—Henrietta!

HENRIETTA: Don't be afraid of me, little sister. There's nothing can shock me or turn me from you. I am not like that. I wanted you to come for this visit because I had a feeling that you needed more from life than you were getting. No one of these things I have seen would excite my suspicion. It's the combination. You don't eat breakfast. (*Enumerating on her fingers.*) You make false moves; you substitute your own name for the name of another *whose love is misdirected.* You're nervous; you *look* queer; in your eyes there's a frightened look that is most unlike you. And this dream. A *hen.* Come with me this afternoon to Dr. Russell! Your whole life may be at stake, Mabel.

MABEL (*gasping*): Henrietta, I—you—you always were the smartest in the family, and all that, but—this is terrible! I don't think we *ought* to think such things. (*Brightening.*) Why, I'll tell you why I dreamed I was a hen. It was because last night, telling about that time in Chicago, you said I was as mad as a wet hen.

HENRIETTA (*superior*): Did you dream you were a *wet* hen?

MABEL (*forced to admit it*): No.

HENRIETTA: No. You dreamed you were a *dry* hen. And why, being a hen, were you urged to step?

MABEL: Maybe it's because when I am getting on a street car it always irritates me to have them call "Step lively."

HENRIETTA: No, Mabel, that is only a child's view of it—if you will forgive me. You see merely the elements used in the dream. You do not see into the dream; you do not see its meaning. This dream of the hen————

STEVE: Hen—hen—wet hen—dry hen—mad hen! (*Jumps up in a rage.*) Let me out of this!

HENRIETTA (*hastily picking up dishes, speaks soothingly*): Just a minute, dear, and we'll have things so you can work in quiet. Mabel and I are going to sit in my room. (*She goes out left, carrying dishes.*)

STEVE (*seizing hat and coat from an alcove near the outside door*): I'm going to be psychoanalyzed. I'm going now! I'm going straight to that infallible doctor of hers—that priest of this new religion. If he's got honesty enough to tell Henrietta there's nothing the matter with my unconscious mind, perhaps I can be let alone about it, and then I *will* be all right. (*From the door in a loud voice.*) Don't tell Henrietta I'm going. It might take weeks, and I couldn't stand all the talk. (*He hurries out.*)

HENRIETTA (*returning*): Where's Steve? Gone? (*With a hopeless gesture.*) You see how impatient he is—how unlike himself! I tell you, Mabel, I'm nearly distracted about Steve.

MABEL: I think he's a little distracted, too.

HENRIETTA: Well, if he's gone—you might as well stay here. I have a committee meeting at the bookshop, and will have to leave you to yourself for an hour or two. (*As she puts her hat on, taking it from the alcove where STEVE found his, her eye, lighting up almost carnivorously, falls on an enormous volume on the floor beside the work-table. The book has been half hidden by the wastebasket. She picks it up and carries it around the table toward MABEL.*) Here, dear, is one of the simplest statements of psychoanalysis. You just read this and then we can talk more intelligently.

(MABEL *takes volume and staggers back under its weight to chair rear center,* HENRIETTA *goes to outer door, stops and asks abruptly.*)

How old is Lyman Eggleston?

MABEL (*promptly*): He isn't forty yet. Why, what made you ask that, Henrietta? (*As she turns her head to look at* HENRIETTA *her hands move toward the upper corners of the book balanced on her knees.*)

HENRIETTA: Oh, nothing. Au revoir.

(*She goes out.* MABEL *stares at the ceiling. The book slides to the floor. She starts; looks at the book, then at the broken plate on the table.*)

MABEL: The plate! The book! (*She lifts her eyes, leans forward, elbow on knee, chin on knuckles and plaintively queries.*)

Am I unhappy?

SCENE 2

(*Two weeks later. The stage is as in Scene 1, except that the breakfast table has been removed. During the first few minutes the dusk of a winter afternoon deepens. Out of the darkness spring rows of double street-lights almost meeting in the distance.* HENRIETTA *is at the psychoanalytical end of* STEVE's *work-table, surrounded by open books and periodicals, writing.* STEVE *enters briskly.*)

STEVE: What are you doing, my dear?

HENRIETTA: My paper for the Liberal Club.

STEVE: Your paper on————?

HENRIETTA: On a subject which does not have your sympathy.

STEVE: Oh, I'm not sure I'm wholly out of sympathy with psychoanalysis, Henrietta. You worked it so hard. I couldn't even take a bath without its meaning something.

HENRIETTA (*loftily*): I talked it because I knew you needed it.

STEVE: You haven't said much about it these last two weeks. Uh—your faith in it hasn't weakened any?

HENRIETTA: Weakened? It's grown stronger with each new thing I've come to know. And Mabel. She is with Dr. Russell now. Dr. Russell is wonderful! From what Mabel tells me I believe his analysis is going to prove that I was right. Today I discovered a remarkable confirmation of my theory in the hen-dream.

STEVE: What is your theory?

HENRIETTA: Well, you know about Lyman Eggleston. I've wondered about him. I've never seen him, but I know he's less bourgeois than Mabel's other friends—more intellectual—and (*Significantly.*) she doesn't see much of him because Bob doesn't like him.

STEVE: But what's the confirmation?

HENRIETTA: Today I noticed the first syllable of his name.

STEVE: Ly?

HENRIETTA: No—egg.

STEVE: Egg?

HENRIETTA (*patiently*): Mabel dreamed she was a hen. (STEVE *laughs.*) You wouldn't laugh if you knew how important names are in interpreting dreams. Freud is full of just such cases in which a whole hidden complex is revealed by a single significant syllable—like this egg.

STEVE: Doesn't the traditional relation of hen and egg suggest rather a maternal feeling?

HENRIETTA: There is something maternal in Mabel's love, of course, but that's only one element.

STEVE: Well, suppose Mabel hasn't a suppressed desire to be this gentleman's mother, but his beloved. What's to be done about it? What about Bob? Don't you think it's going to be a little rough on him?

HENRIETTA: That can't be helped. Bob, like everyone else, must face the facts of life. If Dr. Russell should arrive independently at this same interpretation I shall not hesitate to advise Mabel to leave her present husband.

STEVE: Um—hum! (*The lights go up on Fifth Avenue.* STEVE *goes to the window and looks out.*) How long is it we've lived here, Henrietta?

HENRIETTA: Why, this is the third year, Steve.

STEVE: I—we—one would miss this view if one went away, wouldn't one?

HENRIETTA: How strangely you speak! Oh, Stephen, I *wish* you'd go to Dr. Russell. Don't think my fears have abated because I've been able to restrain myself. I had to on account of Mabel. But now, dear—won't you go?

STEVE: I—(*He breaks off, turns on the light, then comes and sits beside* HENRIETTA.) How long have we been married, Henrietta?

HENRIETTA: Stephen, I don't understand you! You *must* go to Dr. Russell.

STEVE: I have gone.

HENRIETTA: You—what?

STEVE (*jauntily*): Yes, Henrietta, I've been psyched.

HENRIETTA: You went to Dr. Russell?

STEVE: The same.

HENRIETTA: And what did he say?

STEVE: He said—I—I was a little surprised by what he said, Henrietta.

HENRIETTA (*breathlessly*): Of course—one can so seldom anticipate. But tell me—your dream, Stephen? It means———?

STEVE: It means—I was considerably surprised by what it means.

HENRIETTA: *Don't* be so exasperating!

STEVE: It means—you really want to know, Henrietta?

HENRIETTA: Stephen, you'll drive me mad!

STEVE: He said—of course he may be wrong in what he said.

HENRIETTA: He *isn't* wrong. *Tell* me!

STEVE: He said my dream of the walls receding and leaving me alone in a forest indicates a suppressed desire———

HENRIETTA: Yes—yes!

STEVE: To be freed from———

HENRIETTA: Yes—freed from———?

STEVE: Marriage.

HENRIETTA (*crumples; stares*): Marriage!

STEVE: He—he may be mistaken, you know.

HENRIETTA: *May* be mistaken?

STEVE: I—well, of course, I hadn't taken any stock in it myself. It was only your great confidence———

HENRIETTA: Stephen, are you telling me that Dr. Russell—Dr. A.E. Russell—told you this?

(STEVE *nods.*)

Told you you have a suppressed desire to separate from *me?*

STEVE: That's what he said.

HENRIETTA: Did he know who you were?

STEVE: Yes.

HENRIETTA: That you were married to me?

STEVE: Yes, he knew that.

HENRIETTA: And he told you to leave me?

STEVE: It seems he must be wrong, Henrietta.

HENRIETTA (*rising*): And I've sent him more patients———! (*Catches herself and resumes coldly.*) What reason did he give for this analysis?

STEVE: He says the confining walls are a symbol of my feeling about marriage and that their fading away is a wish-fulfillment.

HENRIETTA (*gulping*): Well, is it? Do you want our marriage to end?

STEVE: It was a great surprise to me that I did. You see I hadn't known what was in my unconscious mind.

HENRIETTA (*flaming*): What did you tell Dr. Russell about me to make him think you weren't happy?

STEVE: I never told him a thing, Henrietta. He got it all from his confounded clever inferences. I—I tried to refute them, but he said that was only part of my self-protective lying.

HENRIETTA: And that's why you were so —happy—when you came in just now!

STEVE: Why, Henrietta, how can you say such a thing? I was *sad*. Didn't I speak sadly of—of the view? Didn't I ask how long we had been married?

HENRIETTA (*rising*): Stephen Brewster, have you no sense of the seriousness of this? Dr. Russell doesn't know what our marriage has been. You do. You should have laughed him down! Confined—in life with me? Did you tell him that I *believe* in freedom?

STEVE: I very emphatically told him that his results were a great surprise to me.

HENRIETTA: But you accepted them.

STEVE: Oh, not at all. I merely couldn't refute his arguments. I'm not a psychologist. I came home to talk it over with you. You being a disciple of psychoanalysis————

HENRIETTA: If you are going, I wish you would go tonight!

STEVE: Oh, my dear! I—surely I couldn't do that! Think of my feelings. And my laundry hasn't come home.

HENRIETTA: I ask you to go tonight. Some women would falter at this, Steve, but I am not such a woman. I leave you free. I do not repudiate psychoanalysis; I say again that it has done great things. It has also made mistakes, of course. But since you accept this analysis—(*She sits down and pretends to begin work.*) I have to finish this paper. I wish you would leave me.

STEVE (*scratches his head, goes to the inner door*): I'm sorry, Henrietta, about my unconscious mind.

(*Alone,* HENRIETTA'S *face betrays her outraged state of mind—disconcerted, resentful, trying to pull herself together. She attains an air of bravely bearing an outrageous thing. The outer door opens and* MABEL *enters in great excitement.*)

MABEL (*breathless*): Henrietta, I'm so glad you're here. And alone? (*Looks toward the inner door.*) Are you alone, Henrietta?

HENRIETTA (*with reproving dignity*): Very much so.

MABEL (*rushing to her*): Henrietta, he's found it!

HENRIETTA (*aloof*): Who has found what?

MABEL: Who has found what? Dr. Russell has found my suppressed desire!

HENRIETTA: That is interesting.

MABEL: He finished with me today—he got hold of my complex—in the most amazing way! But, oh, Henrietta—it is so terrible!

HENRIETTA: Do calm yourself, Mabel. Surely there's no occasion for all this agitation.

MABEL: But there is! And when you think of the lives that are affected—the readjustments that must be made in order to bring the suppressed hell out of me and save me from the insane asylum————!

HENRIETTA: The insane asylum!

MABEL: You said that's where these complexes brought people!

HENRIETTA: What did the doctor tell you, Mabel?

MABEL: Oh, I don't know how I can tell you—it is so awful—so unbelievable.

HENRIETTA: I rather have my hand in at hearing the unbelievable.

MABEL: Henrietta, who would ever have thought it? How can it be true? But the doctor is perfectly certain that I have a suppressed desire for————(*Looks at* HENRIETTA, *is unable to continue.*)

HENRIETTA: Oh, go on, Mable. I'm not unprepared for what you have to say.

MABEL: Not unprepared? You mean you have suspected it?

HENRIETTA: From the first. It's been my theory all along.

MABEL: But, Henrietta, I didn't know myself that I had this secret desire for Stephen.

HENRIETTA (*jumps up*): Stephen!

MABEL: My brother-in-law! My own sister's husband!

HENRIETTA: *You* have a suppressed desire for *Stephen!*

MABEL: Oh, Henrietta, aren't these unconscious selves terrible? They seem so unlike *us!*

HENRIETTA: What insane thing are you driving at?

MABEL (*blubbering*): Henrietta, don't you use that word to me. I don't *want* to go to the insane asylum.

HENRIETTA: What did Dr. Russell say?

MABEL: Well, you see—oh, it's the strangest thing! But you know the voice in my dream that called "Step, Hen!" Dr. Russell found out today that when I was a little girl I had a story-book in words of one syllable and I read the name Stephen wrong. I used to read it S-t-e-p, step, h-e-n, hen. (*Dramatically.*) Step Hen is Stephen.

(*Enter* STEPHEN, *his head bent over a time-table.*)

Stephen is Step Hen!

STEVE: I? Step Hen?

MABEL (*triumphantly*): S-t-e-p, step, H-e-n, hen, Stephen!

HENRIETTA (*exploding*): Well, what if Stephen is Step Hen? (*Scornfully.*) Step Hen! Step Hen! For that ridiculous coincidence————

MABEL: Coincidence! But it's childish to look at the mere elements of a dream. You have to look *into* it—you have to see what it *means!*

HENRIETTA: On account of that trivial, meaningless play on syllables—on that flimsy basis—you are ready————(*Wails.*) O-h!

STEVE: What on earth's the matter? What has happened? Suppose I *am* Step Hen? What about it? What does it mean?

MABEL (*crying*): It means—that I—have a suppressed desire for *you!*

STEVE: For me! The deuce you have! (*Feebly.*) What —er—makes you think so?

MABEL: Dr. Russell has worked it out scientifically.

HENRIETTA: Yes. Through the amazing discovery that Step Hen equals Stephen!

MABEL (*tearfully*): Oh, that isn't all—that isn't near all. Henrietta won't give me a chance to tell it. She'd rather I'd go to the insane asylum than be unconventional.

HENRIETTA: We'll all go there if you can't control yourself. We are still waiting for some rational report.

MABEL (*drying her eyes*): Oh, there's such a lot about names. (*With some pride.*) I don't see how I ever did it. It all works in together. I dreamed I was a hen because that's the first syllable of *Hen*rietta's name, and when I dreamed I was a hen, I was putting myself in Henrietta's place.

HENRIETTA: With Stephen?

MABEL: With Stephen.

HENRIETTA (*outraged*): Oh!

(*Turns in rage upon* STEPHEN, *who is fanning himself with the time-table.*)

What are you doing with that time-table?

STEVE: Why—I thought—you were so keen to have me go tonight—I thought I'd just take a run up to Canada, and join Billy—a little shooting—but———

MABEL: But there's more about the names.

HENRIETTA: Mabel, have you thought of Bob—dear old Bob—your good, kind husband?

MABEL: Oh, Henrietta, "my good, kind husband!"

HENRIETTA: Think of him, Mabel, out there alone in Chicago, working his head off, fixing people's teeth—for you!

MABEL: Yes, but think of the living Libido—in conflict with petrified moral codes! And think of the perfectly wonderful way the names all prove it. Dr. Russell said he's never seen anything more convincing. Just look at Stephen's last name—Brewster. I dream I'm a hen, and the name Brewster—you have to say its first letter by itself—and then the hen, that's me, she says to him: "Stephen, Be Rooster!"

(HENRIETTA *and* STEPHEN *collapse into the nearest chairs.*)

MABEL: I think it's perfectly wonderful! Why, if it wasn't for psychoanalysis you'd never find out how wonderful your own mind is!

STEVE (*begins to chuckle*): Be Rooster! Stephen, Be Rooster!

HENRIETTA: You think it's funny, do you?

STEVE: Well, what's to be done about it.

Does Mabel have to go away with me?

HENRIETTA: Do you want Mabel to go away with you?

STEVE: Well, but Mabel herself—her complex, her suppressed desire———!

HENRIETTA (*going to her*): Mabel, are you going to insist on going away with Stephen?

MABEL: I'd rather go with Stephen than go to the insane asylum!

HENRIETTA: For heaven's sake, Mabel, drop that insane asylum! If you *did* have a suppressed desire for Stephen hidden away in you—God knows it isn't hidden now. Dr. Russell has brought it into your consciousness—with a vengeance. That's all that's necessary to break up a complex. Psychoanalysis doesn't say you have to *gratify* every suppressed desire.

STEVE (*softly*): Unless it's for Lyman Eggleston.

HENRIETTA (*turning on him*): Well, if it comes to that, Stephen Brewster, I'd like to know why that interpretation of mine isn't as good as this one? Step, Hen!

STEVE: But Be Rooster! (*He pauses, chuckling to himself.*) Step-Hen Be rooster. And *Hen*rietta. Pshaw, my dear, Doc Russell's got you beat a mile! (*He turns away and chuckles.*) Be rooster!

MABEL: What has Lyman Eggleston got to do with it?

STEVE: According to Henrietta, you, the hen, have a suppressed desire for *Egg*leston, the egg.

MABEL: Henrietta, I think that's indecent of you! He is bald as an egg and little and fat—the idea of you thinking such a thing of me!

HENRIETTA: Well, Bob isn't little and bald and fat! Why don't you stick to your own husband? (*To* STEPHEN.) What if Dr. Russell's interpretation has got mine "beat a mile"? (*Resentful look at him.*) It would only mean that Mabel doesn't want Eggleston and does want you. Does that mean she has to have you?

MABEL: But you said Mabel Snow———

HENRIETTA: *Mary* Snow! You're not as much like her as you think—substituting your name for hers! The cases are entirely different. Oh, I wouldn't have *believed* this of you, Mabel. (*Beginning to cry.*) I brought you here for a pleasant visit—thought you needed brightening *up*—wanted to be *nice* to you—and now you—my husband—you insist———(*In fumbling her way to her chair she brushes to the floor some sheets from the psychoanalytical table.*)

STEVE (*with solicitude*): Careful dear. Your paper on psychoanalysis! (*Gathers up sheets and offers them to her.*)

HENRIETTA: I don't want my paper on psychoanalysis! I'm sick of psychoanalysis!

STEVE (*eagerly*): Do you mean that, Henrietta?

HENRIETTA: Why shouldn't I mean it? Look at all I've done for psychoanalysis—and— (*Raising a tear-stained face.*) What has psychoanalysis done for me?

STEVE: Do you mean, Henrietta, that you're going to stop *talking* psychoanalysis?

HENRIETTA: Why shouldn't I stop talking it? Haven't I seen what it does to people? Mabel has gone crazy about psychoanalysis!

(*At the word "crazy" with a moan* MABEL *sinks to chair and buries her face in her hands.*)

STEVE (*solemnly*): Do you swear never to wake me up in the night to find out what I'm dreaming?

HENRIETTA: Dream what you please—I don't care what you're dreaming.

STEVE: Will you clear off my work-table so the Journal of Morbid Psychology doesn't stare me in the face when I'm trying to plan a house?

HENRIETTA (*pushing a stack of periodicals off the table*): I'll *burn* the Journal of Morbid Psychology!

STEVE: My dear Henrietta, if you're going to separate from psychoanalysis, there's no reason why I should separate from *you*.

(*They embrace ardently.* MABEL *lifts her head and looks at them woefully.*)

MABEL (*jumping up and going toward them*): But what about me? What am I to do with my suppressed desire?

STEVE (*with one arm still around* HENRIETTA, *gives* MABEL *a brotherly hug*): Mabel, you just keep right on suppressing it!

Eugene O'Neill: *The Emperor Jones* (1920)

If there is a single figure who dominated the American stage in the first half of the twentieth century, it is Eugene O'Neill. He was born in 1888, the son of an actor, James O'Neill, who toured with his own small company giving performances of *The Count of Monte Cristo*, in which, for a brief time, Eugene took a small part before he began to influence the theater through his own work.

O'Neill is virtually the stereotype of the vagrant writer of the early part of this century. He had a year at Princeton, got wanderlust, and sailed off to South America, where he worked in Buenos Aires at a variety of jobs. He spent time totally unemployed in Argentina, returned to America, and studied briefly with the greatest drama teacher in his time: George Pierce Baker of Harvard (later of Yale). Eventually he found his way to Provincetown, where he wrote a number of plays based on his adventures as a seaman. There he met Susan Glaspell and the first stirrings of the Provincetown Players.

Most of his early plays were given their first performances through the Provincetown Players. Once he began writing, he began to attract enormous attention and won numerous prizes. The Pulitzer Prize was his several times, for plays such as *Beyond the Horizon* (1920), *Anna Christie* (1922), and *Strange Interlude* (1928). Ultimately, he was awarded the Nobel Prize in 1936, but he was already quite sick with the neurological disease that ultimately killed him in 1953.

O'Neill's plays are usually marked by an unyielding realism, sometimes extremely brutal for its time, as in the dismal surroundings of *Anna Christie* and the brutal ways of *The Hairy Ape*, which were both strong and shocking plays in their time. Like others in the Provincetown Players group, O'Neill was hardly interested in babying his audiences. He did not want them to have a candy-coated view of the world, but instead wanted to share some of his own deep feelings about the world he had known. It was not the world of the average middle-class, well-off theatergoer. And there were many times when the roughness of his vision failed to please his audiences.

His output was enormous, including a number of plays he wished to have forgotten, published in 1950 as *The Lost Plays of Eugene O'Neill*. The last period of his life was spent working on a massive project of at least eleven plays that would record the Irish struggle in America. Before he died, he destroyed the bulk of these plays in the belief that they were unsuccessful. We have, of the proposed opus, *A Tale of the Possessed Dispossessed*, only two pieces: *A Touch of the Poet* and *Hughie*, the first of which is a most impressive play. He also worked on a series of plays dealing with more personal themes, somewhat more auto-biographical material. *The Iceman Cometh* (1939), *A Moon for the Misbegotten* (1941), and *Long Day's Journey Into Night* (1942) are all striking, original, and remarkable plays. They have been performed frequently since O'Neill's death, and to considerable critical acclaim.

Some of the other truly memorable plays he wrote are *All God's Chillun Got Wings* (1924), *Desire Under the Elms* (1925), *The Great God Brown* (1926), *Marco Millions* (1927), *Mourning Becomes Electra* (1931), and *Ah, Wilderness* (1933). The extraor-dinary intensity of the realism of the earliest plays gave way to a kind of symbolic drama, sometimes resorting to the Greek de-vice of masks, and other unusual techniques. Some critics speculated that O'Neill developed a brand of mysticism that expressed itself through a symbolic language. They also felt, some of them, that this language was unintelligible to the ordinary viewer. Not all his critics have been kind. Some have felt him to be a minor writer whose huge energies make him seem larger than he is. Others, however, recognize in him a creative vision totally unmatched by the other playwrights of his generation.

The Emperor Jones is presented in scenes, rather than in acts. The scenes shift rapidly, almost like dream sequences, and some are fantasy moments, meant to parallel the feverish anxiety of Brutus Jones as he tries to flee from his rebellious people through the jungle. The setting, in a West Indian island before organized government comes (in the form of the white marines), has been interpreted symbolically in a variety of ways. Perhaps it owes something to O'Neill's reading of Joseph Conrad, whose *Lord Jim* and *Heart of Darkness* treat locales in a similarly symbol-ic way. The play is a study of power and politics, just as much as it is a study in racial awareness.

To a certain extent, the play moves in a throbbing fashion, establishing a rhythm of action that parallels the intensity and the anguish of Jones' fears. The sense that these scenes are rhythmically related may have influenced the great dancer, Jose Limon, to base his famous ballet on this play. There already is something dancelike in the drama, with its shifts, its rapid movement on stage, the motion and power of physical movement alone. The play has been read as an allegory, with an apparent commentary on the relative merits of empires and democracies, but such readings will vary as the politics of the commentators vary. *The Emperor Jones* is an interpretation of deep, and perhaps dark, motives that lie within all humanity. It is a story of pride and power, of egoism and independence, of free will and fate.

Selected Readings

Alexander, Doris M. *The Tempering of Eugene O'Neill*. New York: Harcourt, Brace & World, 1962.

Atkinson, Jennifer M. *Eugene O'Neill: A Descriptive Bibliography*. Pittsburgh: Pittsburgh University Press, 1974.

Bogard, Travis. *Contour in Time: The Plays of Eugene O'Neill*. New York: Oxford University Press, 1972.

Cargill, Oscar, N. Bryllion Fagin, and William J. Fisher, eds., *O'Neill and His Plays: Four Decades of Criticism*. New York: New York University Press, 1961.

Carpenter, Frederic I. *Eugene O'Neill*. New York: Twayne, 1964.

Chabrowe, Ernest G. *Eugene O'Neill: A Collection of Criticism*. New York: McGraw-Hill, 1976.

Cronin, Harry. *Eugene O'Neill, Irish and American: A Study in Cultural Context*. New York: Arno: 1978.

Falk, Doris V. *Eugene O'Neill and the Tragic Tension*. New Brunswick: Rutgers University Press, 1958.

Gassner, John. *Eugene O'Neill*. Minneapolis: University of Minnesota Press, 1965.

――――. *O'Neill: A Collection of Critical Essays*. Englewood Cliffs: Prentice-Hall, 1964.

Gelb, Arthur, and Barbara Gelb. *O'Neill*. New York: Harper, 1975.

Griffin, Ernest G. *Eugene O'Neill: A Collection of Criticism*. New York: McGraw-Hill, 1976.

Raleigh, John H. *The Plays of Eugene O'Neill*. Carbondale: Southern Illinois University Press, 1965.

Sanborn, Ralph, and Barret H. Clark. *A Bibliography of the Works of Eugene O'Neill*. New York: Random House, 1971.

The Emperor Jones

Eugene O'Neill

CHARACTERS

BRUTUS JONES, *Emperor*
HENRY SMITHERS, *A Cockney Trader*
AN OLD NATIVE WOMAN
LEM, *A Native Chief*
SOLDIERS, *Adherents of Lem*
The Little Formless Fears; Jeff; The Negro Convicts; The Prison Guard; The Planters; The Auctioneer; The Slaves; The Congo Witch-Doctor; The Crocodile God.

The action of the play takes place on an island in the West Indies as yet not self-determined by White Marines. The form of native government is, for the time being, an Empire.

SCENES

SCENE 1: In the palace of the Emperor Jones. Afternoon.
SCENE 2: The edge of the Great Forest. Dusk.
SCENE 3: In the Forest. Night.
SCENE 4: In the Forest. Night.
SCENE 5: In the Forest. Night.
SCENE 6: In the Forest. Night.
SCENE 7: In the Forest. Night.
SCENE 8: Same as Scene Two—the edge of the Great Forest. Dawn.

SCENE 1

(*The audience chamber in the palace of the Emperor—a spacious, high-ceilinged room with bare, white-washed walls. The floor is of white tiles. In the rear, to the left of center, a wide archway giving out on a portico with white pillars. The palace is evidently situated on high ground for beyond the portico nothing can be seen but a vista of distant hills, their summits crowned with thick groves of palm trees. In the right wall, center, a smaller arched doorway leading to the living quarters of the palace. The room is bare of furniture with the exception of one huge chair made of uncut wood which stands at center, its back to rear. This is very apparently the Emperor's throne. It is* painted a dazzling, eye-smiting scarlet. There is a brilliant orange cushion on the seat and another smaller one is placed on the floor to serve as a footstool. Strips of matting, dyed scarlet, lead from the foot of the throne to the two entrances.

It is late afternoon but the sunlight still blazes yellowly beyond the portico and there is an oppressive burden of exhausting heat in the air.

As the curtain rises, a native negro woman sneaks in cautiously from the entrance on the right. She is very old, dressed in cheap calico, bare-footed, a red bandana handkerchief covering all but a few stray wisps of white hair. A bundle bound in colored cloth is carried over her shoulder on the end of a stick. She hesitates beside the doorway, peering back as if in extreme dread of being discovered. Then she begins to glide noiselessly, a step at a time, toward the doorway in the rear. At this moment, SMITHERS *appears beneath the portico.*

SMITHERS *is a tall, stoop-shouldered man about forty. His bald head, perched on a long neck with an enormous Adam's apple, looks like an egg. The tropics have tanned his naturally pasty face with its small, sharp features to a sickly yellow, and native rum has painted his pointed nose to a startling red. His little, washy-blue eyes are red-rimmed and dart about him like a ferret's. His expression is one of unscrupulous meanness, cowardly and dangerous. He is dressed in a worn riding suit of dirty white drill, puttees, spurs, and wears a white cork helmet. A cartridge belt with an automatic revolver is around his waist. He carries a riding whip in his hand. He sees the woman and stops to watch her suspiciously. Then, making up his mind, he steps quickly on tiptoe into the room. The woman, looking back over her shoulder continually, does not see him until it is too late. When she does* SMITHERS *springs forward and grabs her firmly by the shoulder. She struggles to get away, fiercely but silently.)*

SMITHERS (*tightening his grasp—roughly*): Easy! None o' that, me birdie. You can't wiggle out, now I got me 'ooks on yer.

WOMAN (*seeing the uselessness of struggling, gives way to frantic terror, and sinks to the ground, embracing his knees supplicatingly*): No tell him! No tell him, Mister!

SMITHERS (*with great curiosity*): Tell 'im? (*Then scornfully.*) Oh, you mean 'is bloomin' Majesty. What's the gaime, any'ow? What are you sneakin' away for? Been stealin' a bit, I s'pose. (*He taps her bundle with his riding whip significantly.*)

WOMAN (*shaking her head vehemently*): No, me no steal.

SMITHERS: Bloody liar! But tell me what's up. There's somethin' funny goin' on. I smelled it in the air first thing I got up this mornin'. You blacks are up to some devilment. This palace of 'is is like a bleedin' tomb. Where's all the 'ands? (*The* WOMAN *keeps sullenly silent.* SMITHERS *raises his whip threateningly.*) Ow, yer won't, won't yer? I'll show yer what's what.

WOMAN (*coweringly*): I tell, Mister. You no hit. They go—all go. (*She makes a sweeping gesture toward the hills in the distance.*)

SMITHERS: Run away—to the 'ills?

WOMAN: Yes, Mister. Him Emperor—Great Father (*She touches her forehead to the floor with a quick mechanical jerk.*) Him sleep after eat. Then they go—all go. Me old woman. Me left only. Now me go too.

SMITHERS (*his astonishment giving way to an immense, mean satisfaction*): Ow! So that's the ticket! Well, I know bloody well wot's in the air—when they runs orf to the 'ills. The tom-tom 'll be thumping out there bloomin' soon. (*With extreme vindictiveness.*) And I'm bloody glad of it, for one! Serve 'im right! Puttin' on airs, the stinkin' nigger! 'Is Majesty! Gawd blimey! I only 'opes I'm there when they takes 'im out to shoot 'im. (*Suddenly.*) 'E's still 'ere all right, ain't 'e?

WOMAN: Him sleep.

SMITHERS: 'E's bound to find out soon as 'e wakes up. 'E's cunnin' enough to know when 'is time's come. (*He goes to the doorway on right and whistles shrilly with his fingers in his mouth. The old woman springs to her feet and runs out of the doorway, rear.* SMITHERS *goes after her, reaching for his revolver.*) Stop or I'll shoot! (*Then stopping—indifferently.*) Pop orf then, if yer like, yer black cow. (*He stands in the doorway, looking after her.*)

(JONES *enters from the right. He is a tall, powerfully-built, full-blooded negro of middle age. His features are typically negroid, yet there is something decidedly distinctive about his face—an underlying strength of will, a hardy, self-reliant confidence in himself that inspires respect. His eyes are alive with a keen, cunning intelligence. In manner he is shrewd, suspicious, evasive. He wears a light blue uniform coat, sprayed with brass buttons, heavy gold chevrons on his shoulders, gold braid on the collar, cuffs, etc. His pants are bright red with a light blue stripe down the side. Patent leather laced boots with brass spurs, and a belt with a long-barreled, pearl-handled revolver in a holster complete his make up. Yet there is something not altogether ridiculous about his grandeur. He has a way of carrying it off.)*

JONES (*not seeing anyone—greatly irritated and blinking sleepily—shouts*): Who dare whistle dat way in my palace? Who dare wake up de Emperor? I'll git de hide frayled off some o' you niggers sho'!

SMITHERS (*showing himself—in a manner half-afraid and half-defiant*): It was me whistled to yer. (*As* JONES *frowns angrily.*) I got news for yer.

JONES (*putting on his suavest manner, which fails to cover up his contempt for the white man*): Oh, it's you, Mister Smithers. (*He sits down on his throne with easy dignity.*) What news you got to tell me?

SMITHERS (*coming close to enjoy his discomfiture*): Don't yer notice nothin' funny today?

JONES (*coldly*): Funny? No. I ain't perceived nothin' of de kind!

SMITHERS: Then yer ain't so foxy as I thought yer was. Where's all your court? (*Sarcastically.*) The Generals and the Cabinet Ministers and all?

JONES (*imperturbably*): Where dey mostly runs to minute I closes my eyes—drinkin' rum and talkin' big down in de town. (*Sarcastically.*) How come you don't know dat? Ain't you sousin' with 'em most every day?

SMITHERS (*stung but pretending indifference—with a wink*): That's part of the day's work. I got ter—ain't I—in my business?

JONES (*contemptuously*): Yo' business!

SMITHERS (*imprudently enraged*): Gawd blimey, you was glad enough for me ter take yer in on it when you landed here first. You didn' 'ave no 'igh and mighty airs in them days!

JONES (*his hand going to his revolver like a flash—menacingly*): Talk polite, white man! Talk polite, you heah me! I'm boss heah now, is you fergettin'? (*The Cockney seems about to challenge this last statement with the facts but something in the other's eyes holds and cows him.*)

SMITHERS (*in a cowardly whine*): No 'arm meant, old top.

JONES (*condescendingly*): I accepts yo' apology. (*Lets his hand fall from his revolver.*) No use'n you rakin' up ole times. What I was den is one thing. What I is now's another. You didn't let me in on yo' crooked work out o' no kind feelin's dat time. I done de dirty work fo' you—and most o' de brain work, too, fo' dat matter—and I was wu'th money to you, dat's de reason.

SMITHERS: Well, blimey, I give yer a start, didn't I?—when no one else would. I wasn't afraid to 'ire you like the rest was—'count of the story about your breakin' jail back in the States.

JONES: No, you didn't have no s'cuse to look down on me fo' dat. You been in jail you'self more'n once.

SMITHERS (*furiously*): It's a lie! (*Then trying to pass it off by an attempt at scorn.*) Garn! Who told yer that fairy tale?

JONES: Dey's some tings I ain't got to be tole. I kin see 'em in folk's eyes. (*Then after a pause—meditatively.*) Yes, you sho' give me a start. And it didn't take long from dat time to git dese fool, woods' niggers right where I wanted dem. (*With pride.*) From stowaway to Emperor in two years! Dat's goin' some!

SMITHERS (*with curiosity*): And I bet you got yer pile o' money 'id safe some place.

JONES (*with satisfaction*): I sho' has! And it's in a foreign bank where no pusson don't ever git it out but me no matter what come. You didn't

s'pose I was holdin' down dis Emperor job for de glory in it, did you? Sho'! De fuss and glory part of it, dat's only to turn de heads o' de low-flung, bush niggers dat's here. Dey wants de big circus show for deir money. I gives it to 'em an' I gits de money. (*With a grin.*) De long green, dat's me every time! (*Then rebukingly.*) But you ain't got no kick agin me, Smithers. I'se paid you back all you done for me many times. Ain't I pertected you and winked at all de crooked tradin' you been doin' right out in de broad day? Sho' I has—and me makin' laws to stop it at de same time! (*He chuckles.*)

SMITHERS (*grinning*): But, meanin' no 'arm, you been grabbin' right and left yourself, ain't yer? Look at the taxes you've put on 'em! Blimey! You've squeezed 'em dry!

JONES (*chuckling*): No, dey ain't *all* dry yet. I'se still heah, ain't I?

SMITHERS (*smiling at his secret thought*): They're dry right now, you'll find out. (*Changing the subject abruptly.*) And as for me breakin' laws, you've broke 'em all yerself just as fast as yer made 'em.

JONES: Ain't I de Emperor? De laws don't go for him. (*Judicially.*) You heah what I tells you, Smithers. Dere's little stealin' like you does, and dere's big stealin' like I does. For de little stealin' dey gits you in jail soon or late. For de big stealin' dey makes you Emperor and puts you in de Hall o' Fame when you croaks. (*Reminiscently.*) If dey's one thing I learns in ten years on de Pullman ca's listenin' to de white quality talk, it's dat same fact. And when I gits a chance to use it I winds up Emperor in two years.

SMITHERS (*unable to repress the genuine admiration of the small fry for the large*): Yes, yer turned the bleedin' trick, all right. Blimey, I never seen a bloke 'as 'ad the bloomin' luck you 'as.

JONES (*severely*): Luck? What you mean—luck?

SMITHERS: I suppose you'll say as that swank about the silver bullet ain't luck—and that was what first got the fool blacks on yer side the time of the revolution, wasn't it?

JONES (*with a laugh*): Oh, dat silver bullet! Sho' was luck. But I makes dat luck, you heah? I loads de dice! Yessuh! When dat murderin' nigger ole Lem hired to kill me takes aim ten feet away and his gun misses fire and I shoots him dead, what you heah me say?

SMITHERS: You said yer'd got a charm so's no lead bullet'd kill yer. You was so strong only a silver bullet could kill yer, you told 'em. Blimey, wasn't that swank for yer—and plain, fat-'eaded luck?

JONES (*proudly*): I got brains and I uses 'em quick. Dat ain't luck.

SMITHERS: Yer know they wasn't 'ardly liable to get no silver bullets. And it was luck 'e didn't 'it you that time.

JONES (*laughing*): And dere all dem fool bush niggers was kneelin' down and bumpin' deir heads on de ground like I was a miracle out o' de Bible. Oh, Lawd, from dat time on I has dem all eatin' out of my hand. I cracks de whip and dey jumps through.

SMITHERS (*with a sniff*): Yankee bluff done it.

JONES: Ain't a man's talkin' big what makes him big—long as he makes folks believe it? Sho', I talks large when I ain't got nothin' to back it up, but I ain't talkin' wild just de same. I knows I kin fool 'em—I *knows* it—and dat's backin' enough fo' my game. And ain't I got to learn deir lingo and teach some of dem English befo' I kin talk to 'em? Ain't dat wuk? You ain't never learned ary word er it, Smithers, in de ten years you been heah, dough you knows it's money in yo' pocket tradin' wid 'em if you does. But you'se too shiftless to take de trouble.

SMITHERS (*flushing*): Never mind about me. What's this I've 'eard about yer really 'avin' a silver bullet moulded for yourself?

JONES: It's playin' out my bluff. I has de silver bullet moulded and I tells 'em when de time comes I kills myself wid it. I tells 'em dat's 'cause I'm de on'y man in de world big enuff to git me. No use'n deir tryin'. And dey falls down and bumps deir heads. (*He laughs.*) I does dat so's I kin take a walk in peace widout no jealous nigger gunnin' at me from behind de trees.

SMITHERS (*astonished*): Then you 'ad it made—'onest?

JONES: Sho' did. Heah she be. (*He takes out his revolver, breaks it, and takes the silver bullet out of one chamber.*) Five lead an' dis silver baby at de last. Don't she shine pretty? (*He holds it in his hand, looking at it admiringly, as if strangely fascinated.*)

SMITHERS: Let me see. (*Reaches out his hand for it.*)

JONES (*harshly*): Keep yo' hands whar dey b'long, white man. (*He replaces it in the chamber and puts the revolver back on his hip.*)

SMITHERS (*snarling*): Gawd blimey! Think I'm a bleedin' thief, you would.

JONES: No, 'tain't dat. I knows you'se scared to steal from me. On'y I ain't 'lowin' nary body to touch dis baby. She's my rabbit's foot.

SMITHERS (*sneering*): A bloomin' charm, wot? (*Venomously.*) Well, you'll need all the bloody charms you 'as before long, s' 'elp me!

JONES (*judicially*): Oh, I'se good for six months yit 'fore dey gits sick o' my game. Den, when I sees trouble comin', I makes my getaway.

SMITHERS: Ho! You got it all planned, ain't yer?

JONES: I ain't no fool. I knows dis Emperor's time is sho't. Dat why I make hay when de sun shine. Was you thinkin' I'se aimin' to hold down dis job for life? No, suh! What good is gittin' money if you stays back in dis raggedy country? I wants action when I spends. And when I sees dese niggers gittin' up deir nerve to tu'n me out, and I'se got all de money in sight, I resigns on de spot and beats it quick.

SMITHERS: Where to?

JONES: None o' yo' business.

SMITHERS: Not back to the bloody States, I'll lay my oath.

JONES (*suspiciously*): Why don't I? (*Then with an easy laugh.*) You mean 'count of dat story 'bout me breakin' from jail back dere? Dat's all talk.

SMITHERS (*skeptically*): Ho, yes!

JONES (*sharply*): You ain't 'sinuatin' I'se a liar, is you?

SMITHERS (*hastily*): No, Gawd strike me! I was only thinkin' o' the bloody lies you told the blacks 'ere about killin' white men in the States.

JONES (*angered*): How come dey're lies?

SMITHERS: You'd 'ave been in jail if you 'ad, wouldn't yer then? (*With venom.*) And from what I've 'card, it ain't 'ealthy for a black to kill a white man in the States. They burns 'em in oil, don't they?

JONES (*with cool deadliness*): You mean lynchin' 'd scare me? Well, I tells you, Smithers, maybe I does kill one white man back dere. Maybe I does. And maybe I kills another right heah 'fore long if he don't look out.

SMITHERS (*trying to force a laugh*): I was on'y spoofin' yer. Can't yer take a joke? And you was just sayin' you'd never been in jail.

JONES (*in the same tone—slightly boastful*): Maybe I goes to jail dere for gettin' in an argument wid razors ovah a crap game. Maybe I gits twenty years when dat colored man die. Maybe I gits in 'nother argument wid de prison guard was overseer ovah us when we're wukin' de road. Maybe he hits me wid a whip and I splits his head wid a shovel and runs away and files de chain off my leg and gits away safe. Maybe I does all dat an' maybe I don't. It's a story I tells you so's you knows I'se de kind of man dat if you evah repeats one word of it, I ends yo' stealin' on dis yearth mighty damn quick!

SMITHERS (*terrified*): Think I'd peach on yer? Not me! Ain't I always been yer friend?

JONES (*suddenly relaxing*): Sho' you has—and you better be.

SMITHERS (*recovering his composure—and with it his malice*): And just to show yer I'm yer friend, I'll tell yer that bit o' news I was goin' to.

JONES: Go ahead! Shoot de piece. Must be bad news from de happy way you look.

SMITHERS (*warningly*): Maybe it's gettin' time for you to resign—with that bloomin' silver bullet, wot? (*He finishes with a mocking grin.*)

JONES (*puzzled*): What's dat you say? Talk plain.

SMITHERS: Ain't noticed any of the guards or servants about the place today, I 'aven't.

JONES (*carelessly*): Dey're all out in de garden sleepin' under de trees. When I sleeps, dey sneaks a sleep, too, and I pretends I never suspicions it. All I got to do is to ring de bell and dey come flyin', makin' a bluff dey was wukin' all de time.

SMITHERS (*in the same mocking tone*): Ring the bell now an' you'll bloody well see what I means.

JONES (*startled to alertness, but preserving the same careless tone*): Sho' I rings. (*He reaches below the throne and pulls out a big, common dinner bell which is painted the same vivid scarlet as the throne. He rings this vigorously—then stops to listen. Then he goes to both doors, rings again, and looks out.*)

SMITHERS (*watching him with malicious satisfaction, after a pause—mockingly*): The bloody ship is sinkin' an' the bleedin' rats 'as slung their 'ooks.

JONES (*in a sudden fit of anger flings the bell clattering into a corner*): Low-flung, woods' niggers! (*Then catching* SMITHERS' *eye on him, he controls himself and suddenly bursts into a low chuckling laugh.*) Reckon I overplays my hand dis once! A man can't take de pot on a bob-tailed flush all de time. Was I sayin' I'd sit in six months mo'? Well, I'se changed my mind den. I cashes in and resigns de job of Emperor right dis minute.

SMITHERS (*with real admiration*): Blimey, but you're a cool bird, and no mistake.

JONES: No use'n fussin'. When I knows de game's up I kisses it good-by widout no long waits. Dey've all run off to de hills, ain't dey?

SMITHERS: Yes—every bleedin' man jack of 'em.

JONES: Den de revolution is at de post. And de Emperor better git his feet smokin' up de trail. (*He starts for the door in rear.*)

SMITHERS: Goin' out to look for your 'orse? Yer won't find any. They steals the 'orses first thing. Mine was gone when I went for 'im this mornin'. That's wot first give me a suspicion of wot was up.

JONES (*alarmed for a second, scratches his head, then philosophically*): Well, den I hoofs it. Feet, do yo' duty! (*He pulls out a gold watch and looks at it.*) Three-thuty. Sundown's at six-thuty or dereabouts. (*Puts his watch back—with cool confidence.*) I got plenty o' time to make it easy.

SMITHERS: Don't be so bloomin' sure of it. They'll be after you 'ot and 'eavy. Ole Lem is at the bottom o' this business an' 'e 'ates you like 'ell. 'E'd rather do for you than eat 'is dinner, 'e would!

JONES (*scornfully*): Dat fool no-count nigger! Does you think I'se scared o' him? I stands him on his thick head more'n once befo' dis, and I does it again if he comes in my way—(*Fiercely.*) And dis time I leave him a dead nigger fo' sho'!

SMITHERS: You'll 'ave to cut through the big forest—an' these blacks 'ere can sniff and follow a trail in the dark like 'ounds. You'd 'ave to 'ustle to get through that forest in twelve hours even if you knew all the bloomin' trails like a native.

JONES (*with indignant scorn*): Look-a-heah, white man! Does you think I'se a natural bo'n fool? Give me credit fo' havin' some sense, fo' Lawd's sake! Don't you s'pose I'se looked ahead and made sho' of all de chances? I'se gone out in dat big forest, pretendin' to hunt, so many times dat I knows it high an' low like a book. I could go through on dem trails wid my eyes shut. (*With great contempt.*) Think dese ign'rent bush niggers dat ain't got brains enuff to know deir own names even can catch Brutus Jones? Huh, I s'pects not! Not on yo' life! Why, man, de white men went after me wid blood-hounds where I come from an' I jes' laughs at 'em. It's a shame to fool dese black trash around heah, dey're so easy. You watch me, man. I'll make dem look sick, I will. I'll be 'cross de plain to de edge of de forest by time dark comes. Once in de woods in de night dey got a swell chance o' findin' dis baby! Dawn tomorrow I'll be out at de oder side and on de coast whar dat French gunboat is stayin'. She picks me up, takes me to Martinique when she go dar, and dere I is safe wid a mighty big bankroll in my jeans. It's easy as rollin' off a log.

SMITHERS (*maliciously*): But s'posin' somethin' 'appens wrong an' they do nab yer?

JONES (*decisively*): Dey don't—dat's de answer.

SMITHERS: But, just for argyment's sake —what'd you do?

JONES (*frowning*): I'se got five lead bullets in dis gun good enuff fo' common bush niggers —and after dat I got de silver bullet left to cheat 'em out o' gittin' me.

SMITHERS (*jeeringly*): Ho, I was fergettin' that silver bullet. You'll bump yourself orf in style, won't yer? Blimey!

JONES (*gloomily*): You kin bet yo' whole roll on one thing, white man. Dis baby plays out his string to de end and when he quits, he quits wid a bang de way he ought. Silver bullet ain't none too good for him when he go, dat's a fac'! (*Then shaking off his nervousness—with a confident laugh.*) Sho'! What is I talkin' about? Ain't come to dat yit and I never will—not wid trash niggers like dese yere. (*Boastfully.*) Silver bullet bring me luck anyway. I kin outguess, outrun, outfight, an' outplay de whole lot o' dem all ovah de board any time o' de day er night! You watch me! (*From the distant hills comes the faint, steady thump of a tom-tom, low and vibrating. It starts at a rate exactly corresponding to normal pulse beat—72 to the minute—and continues at a gradually accelerating rate from this point uninterruptedly to the very end of the play.*)

(*JONES starts at the sound. A strange look of apprehension creeps into his face for a moment as he listens. Then he asks, with an attempt to regain his most casual manner.*) What's dat drum beatin' fo'?

SMITHERS (*with a mean grin*): For you. That means the bleedin' ceremony 'as started. I've 'eard it before and I knows.

JONES: Cer'mony? What cer'mony?

SMITHERS: The blacks is 'oldin' a bloody meetin', 'avin' a war dance, gettin' their courage worked up b'fore they starts after you.

JONES: Let dem! Dey'll sho' need it!

SMITHERS: And they're there 'oldin' their 'eathen religious service—makin' no end of devil spells and charms to 'elp 'em against your silver bullet. (*He guffaws loudly.*) Blimey, but they're balmy as 'ell!

JONES (*a tiny bit awed and shaken in spite of himself*): Huh! Takes more'n dat to scare dis chicken!

SMITHERS (*scenting the other's feeling— maliciously*): Ternight when it's pitch black in the forest, they'll 'ave their pet devils and ghosts 'oundin' after you. You'll find yer bloody 'air 'll be standin' on end before termorrow mornin'. (*Seriously.*) It's a bleedin' queer place, that stinkin' forest, even in daylight. Yer don't know what might 'appen in there, it's that rotten still. Always sends the cold shivers down my back minute I gets in it.

JONES (*with a contemptuous sniff*): I ain't no chicken-liver like you is. Trees an' me, we'se friends, and dar's a full moon comin' bring me light. And let dem po' niggers make all de fool spells dey'se a min' to. Does yo' s'pect I'se silly enuff to b'lieve in ghosts an' ha'nts an' all dat ole woman's talk? G'long, white man! You ain't talkin' to me. (*With a chuckle.*) Doesn't you know dey's got to do wid a man was member in good standin' o' de Baptist Church? Sho' I was dat when I was porter on de Pullmans, befo' I gits into my little trouble. Let dem try deir heathen tricks. De Baptist Church done pertect me and land dem all in hell. (*Then with more confident satisfaction.*) And I'se got little silver bullet o' my own, don't forgit!

SMITHERS: Ho! You 'aven't give much 'eed to your Baptist Church since you been down 'ere. I've 'eard myself you 'ad turned yer coat an' was takin' up with their blarsted witch-doctors, or whatever the 'ell yer calls the swine.

JONES (*vehemently*): I pretends to! Sho' I pretends! Dat's part o' my game from de fust. If I finds out dem niggers believes dat black is white, den I yells it out louder 'n deir loudest. It don't git me nothin' to do missionary work for de Baptist Church. I'se after de coin, an' I lays my Jesus on de shelf for de time bein'. (*Stops abruptly to look at his watch—alertly.*) But I ain't got de time to waste on no more fool talk wid you. I'se gwine away from heah dis secon'. (*He reaches in under the throne and pulls out an expensive Panama hat with a bright multi-colored band and sets it jauntily on his head.*) So long, white man! (*With a grin.*) See you in jail sometime, maybe!

SMITHERS: Not me, you won't. Well, I wouldn't be in yer bloody boots for no bloomin' money, but 'ere's wishin' yer luck just the same.

JONES (*contemptuously*): You're de frightenedest man evah I see! I tells you I'se safe's 'f I was in New York City. It takes dem niggers from now to dark to git up de nerve to start somethin'. By dat time, I'se got a head start dey never kotch up wid.

SMITHERS (*maliciously*): Give my regards to any ghosts yer meets up with.

JONES (*grinning*): If dat ghost got money, I'll

tell him never ha'nt you less'n he wants to lose it.

SMITHERS (*flattered*): Garn! (*Then curiously.*) Ain't yer takin' no luggage with yer?

JONES: I travels light when I wants to move fast. And I got tinned grub buried on de edge o' de forest. (*Boastfully.*) Now say dat I don't look ahead an' use my brains! (*With a wide, liberal gesture.*) I will all dat's left in de palace to you—and you better grab all you kin sneak away wid befo' dey gits here.

SMITHERS (*gratefully*): Righto—and thanks ter yer. (*As* JONES *walks toward the door in rear —cautioningly.*) Say! Look 'ere, you ain't goin' out chat way, are yer?

JONES: Does you think I'd slink out de back door like a common nigger? I'se Emperor yit, ain't I? And de Emperor Jones leaves de way he comes, and dat black trash don't dare stop him—not yit, leastways (*He stops for a moment in the doorway, listening to the far-off but insistent beat of the tom-tom.*) Listen to dat roll-call, will you? Must be mighty big drum carry dat far. (*Then with a laugh.*) Well, if dey ain't no whole brass band to see me off, I sho' got de drum part of it. So long, white man. (*He puts his hands in his pockets and with studied carelessness, whistling a tune, he saunters out of the doorway and off to the left.*)

SMITHERS (*looks after him with a puzzled admiration*): 'E's got 'is bloomin' nerve with 'im, s'elp me! (*Then angrily.*) Ho—the bleedin' nigger—puttin' on 'is bloody airs! I 'opes they nabs 'im an' gives 'im what's what!

SCENE 2

(*The end of the plain where the Great Forest begins. The foreground is sandy, level ground dotted by a few stones and clumps of stunted bushes cowering close against the earth to escape the buffeting of the trade wind. In the rear the forest is a wall of darkness dividing the world. Only when the eye becomes accustomed to the gloom can the outlines of separate trunks of the nearest trees be made out, enormous pillars of deeper blackness. A somber monotone of wind lost in the leaves moans in the air. Yet this sound serves but to intensify the impression of the forest's relentless immobility, to form a background throwing into relief its brooding, implacable silence.*)

JONES *enters from the left, walking rapidly. He stops as he nears the edge of the forest, looks around him quickly, peering into the dark as if searching for some familiar landmark. Then, apparently satisfied that he is where he ought to be, he throws himself on the ground, dog-tired*).

Well, heah I is. In de nick o' time, too! Little mo' an' it'd be blacker'n de ace of spades heahabouts. (*He pulls a bandana handkerchief from his hip pocket and mops off his perspiring face.*) Sho'! Gimme air! I'se tuckered out sho' 'nuff. Dat soft Emperor job ain't no trainin' fo' a long hike ovah dat plain in de brilin' sun. (*Then with a chuckle.*) Cheer up, nigger, de worst is yet to come. (*He lifts his head and stares at the forest. His chuckle peters out abruptly. In a tone of awe.*) My goodness, look at dem woods, will you? Dat no-count Smithers said dey'd be black an' he sho' called de turn. (*Turning away from them quickly and looking down at his feet, he snatches at a chance to change the subject—solicitously.*) Feet, you is holdin' up yo' end fine an' I sutinly hopes you ain't blisterin' none. It's time you git a rest. (*He takes off his shoes, his eyes studiously avoiding the forest. He feels of the soles of his feet gingerly.*) You is still in de pink—on'y a little mite feverish. Cool yo'selfs. Remember you done got a long journey yit befo' you. (*He sits in a weary attitude, listening to the rhythmic beating of the tom-tom. He grumbles in a loud tone to cover up a growing uneasiness.*) Bush niggers! Wonder dey wouldn't git sick o' beatin' dat drum. Sound louder, seem like. I wonder if dey's startin' after me? (*He scrambles to his feet, looking back across the plain.*) Couldn't see dem now, nohow, if dey was hundred feet away. (*Then shaking himself like a wet dog to get rid of these depressing thoughts.*) Sho', dey's miles an' miles behind. What you gittin' fidgety about? (*But he sits down and begins to lace up his shoes in great haste, all the time muttering reassuringly.*) You know what? Yo' belly is empty, dat's what's de matter wid you. Come time to eat! Wid nothin' but wind on yo' stumach, o' course you feels jiggedy. Well, we eats right heah an' now soon's I gits dese pesky shoes laced up. (*He finishes lacing up his shoes.*) Dere! Now le's see! (*Gets on his hands and knees and searches the ground around him with his eyes.*) White stone, white stone, where is you? (*He sees the first white stone and crawls to it—with satisfaction.*) Heah you is! I knowed dis was de right place. Box of grub, come to me. (*He turns over the stone and feels in under it—in a tone of dismay.*) Ain't heah! Gorry, is I in de right place or isn't I? Dere's 'nother stone. Guess dat's it. (*He scrambles to the next stone and turns it over.*) Ain't heah, neither! Grub, whar is you? Ain't heah. Gorry, has I got to go hungry into dem woods— all de night? (*While he is talking he scrambles from one stone to another, turning them over in frantic haste. Finally, he jumps to his feet excitedly.*) Is I lost de place? Must have! But how dat happen when I was followin' de trail across de plain in broad daylight? (*Almost plaintively.*) I'se hungry, I is! I gotta git my feed. Whar's my strength gonna come from if I doesn't? Gorry, I gotta find dat grub high an' low somehow! Why it come dark so quick like dat? Can't see nothin'. (*He scratches a match on his trousers and peers about him. The rate of the beat of the far-off tom-tom increases perceptibly as he does so. He mutters in a bewildered voice.*) How come all dese white stones come heah when I only remembers one? (*Suddenly, with a frightened gasp, he flings the match on the ground and stamps on it.*) Nigger, is you gone crazy mad? Is you lightin' matches to show dem whar you is? Fo' Lawd's sake, use yo' haid. Gorry, I'se got to be careful! (*He stares at the plain behind him apprehensively, his hand on his revolver.*) But how come all dese white stones? And whar's dat tin box o' grub I hid all wrapped up in oilcloth?

(*While his back is turned, the* LITTLE FORMLESS FEARS *creep out from the deeper blackness of the forest. They are black, shapeless, only their glittering little eyes can be seen. If they have any describable form at all it is that of a grubworm about the size of a creeping child. They move noiselessly, but with deliberate, painful effort, striving to raise themselves on end, failing and sinking prone again.* JONES *turns about to face the forest. He stares up at the tops of the trees, seeking vainly to discover his whereabouts by their conformation.*)

Can't tell nothin' from dem trees! Gorry, nothin' 'round heah looks like I evah seed it befo'. I'se done lost de place sho' 'nuff! (*With mournful foreboding.*) It's mighty queer! It's mighty queer! (*With sudden forced defiance—in an angry tone.*) Woods, is you tryin' to put somethin' ovah on me?

(*From the formless creatures on the ground in front of him comes a tiny gale of low mocking laughter like a rustling of leaves. They squirm upward toward him in twisted attitudes.* JONES *looks down, leaps backward with a yell of terror, yanking out his revolver as he does so—in a quavering voice.*) What's dat? Who's dar? What is you? Git away from me befo' I shoots you up! You don't?—

(*He fires. There is a flash, a loud report, then silence broken only by the far-off, quickened throb of the tom-tom. The formless creatures have scurried back into the forest.* JONES *remains fixed in his position, listening intently. The sound of the shot, the reassuring feel of the revolver in his hand, have somewhat restored his shaken nerve. He addresses himself with renewed confidence.*)

Dey're gone. Dat shot fix 'em. Dey was only little animals—little wild pigs, I reckon. Dey've maybe rooted out yo' grub an' eat it. Sho', you fool nigger, what you think dey is—ha'nts? (*Excitedly.*) Gorry, you give de game away when you fire dat shot. Dem niggers heah dat fo' su'tin! Time you beat it in de woods widout no long waits. (*He starts for the forest—hesitates before the plunge—then urging himself in with manful resolution.*) Git in, nigger! What you skeered at? Ain't nothin' dere but de trees! Git in! (*He plunges boldly into the forest.*)

SCENE 3

(*In the forest. The moon has just risen. Its beams, drifting through the canopy of leaves, make a barely perceptible, suffused, eerie glow. A dense low wall of underbrush and creepers is in the nearer foreground, fencing in a small triangular clearing. Beyond this is the massed blackness of the forest like an encompassing barrier. A path is dimly discerned leading down to the clearing from left, rear, and winding away from it again toward the right. As the scene opens nothing can be distinctly made out. Except for the beating of the tom-tom, which is a trifle louder and quicker than at the close of the previous scene, there is silence, broken every few seconds by a queer, clicking sound. Then gradually the figure of the negro,* JEFF, *can be discerned crouching on his haunches at the rear of the triangle. He is middle-aged, thin, brown in color, is dressed in a Pullman porter's uniform and cap. He is throwing a pair of dice on the ground before him, picking them up, shaking them, casting them out with the regular, rigid, mechanical movements of an automaton. The heavy, plodding footsteps of someone approaching along the trail from the left are heard and* JONES' *voice, pitched on a slightly higher key and strained in a cheery effort to overcome its own tremors.*)

De moon's rizen. Does you heah dat, nigger? You gits more light from dis out. No mo' buttin' yo' fool head agin' de trunks an' scratchin' de hide off yo' legs in de bushes. Now you sees whar yo'se gwine. So cheer up! From now on you has a snap. (*He steps just to the rear of the triangular clearing and mops off his face on his sleeve. He has lost his Panama hat. His face is scratched, his brilliant uniform shows several large rents.*) What time's it gittin' to be, I wonder? I dassent light no match to find out. Phoo'. It's wa'm an' dat's a fac'! (*Wearily.*) How long I been makin' tracks in dese woods? Must be hours an' hours. Seems like fo'evah! Yit can't be, when de moon's jes' riz. Dis am a long night fo' yo', yo' Majesty! (*With a mournful chuckle.*) Majesty! Der ain't much majesty 'bout dis baby now. (*With attempted cheerfulness.*) Never min'. It's all part o' de game. Dis night come to an end like everything else. And when you gits dar safe and has dat bankroll in yo' hands you laughs at all dis. (*He starts to whistle but checks himself abruptly.*) What yo' whistlin' for, you po' dope! Want all de worl' to heah you? (*He stops talking to listen.*) Heah dat ole drum! Sho' gits nearer from de sound. Dey's packin' it along wid 'em. Time fo' me to move. (*He takes a step forward, then stops—worriedly.*) What's dat odder queer clickety sound I heah? Dere it is! Sound close! Sound like—sound like—Fo' God sake, sound like some nigger was shootin' crap! (*Frightenedly.*) I better beat it quick when I gits dem notions. (*He walks quickly into the clear space—then stands transfixed as he sees* JEFF—*in a terrified gasp.*) Who dar? Who dat? Is dat you, Jeff? (*Starting toward the other, forgetful for a moment of his surroundings and really believing it is a living man that he sees—in a tone of happy relief.*) Jeff! I'se sho' mighty glad to see you! Dey tol' me you done died from dat razor cut I gives you. (*Stopping suddenly, bewilderedly.*) But how you come to be heah, nigger? (*He stares fascinatedly at the other who continues his mechanical play with the dice.* JONES' *eyes begin to roll wildly. He stutters.*) Ain't you gwine—look up—can't you speak to me? Is you—is you—a ha'nt? (*He jerks out his revolver in a frenzy of terrified rage.*) Nigger, I kills you dead once. Has I got to kill you ag'in? You take it den. (*He fires. When the smoke clears away* JEFF *has disappeared.* JONES *stands trembling—then with a certain reassurance.*) He's gone, anyway. Ha'nt or not ha'nt, dat shot fix him. (*The beat of the far-off tom-tom is perceptibly louder and more rapid.* JONES *becomes conscious of it—with a start, looking back over his shoulder.*) Dey's gittin' near! Dey's comin' fast! And heah I is shootin' shots to let 'em know jes' whar I is! Oh, Gorry, I'se got to run. (*Forgetting the path he plunges wildly into the underbrush in the rear and disappears in the shadow.*)

SCENE 4

(*In the forest. A wide dirt road runs diagonally from right, front, to left, rear. Rising sheer on both sides the forest walls it in. The moon is now up. Under its light the road glimmers ghastly and unreal. It is as if the forest had stood aside momentarily to let the road pass through and accomplish its veiled purpose. This done, the forest will fold in upon itself again and the road will be no more.* JONES *stumbles in from the forest on the right. His uniform is ragged and torn. He looks about him with numbed surprise when he sees the road, his eyes blinking in the bright moonlight. He flops down exhaustedly and pants heavily for a while. Then with sudden anger.*)

I'm meltin' wid heat! Runnin' an' runnin' an' runnin'! Damn dis heah coat! Like a straitjacket! (*He tears off his coat and flings it away from him, revealing himself stripped to the waist.*) Dere! Dat's better! Now I kin breathe! (*Looking down at his feet, the spurs catch his eye.*) And to hell wid dese high-fangled spurs. Dey're what's been a-trippin' me up an' breakin' my neck. (*He unstraps them and flings them away disgustedly.*) Dere! I gits rid o' dem frippety Emperor trappin's an' I travels lighter. Lawd! I'se tired! (*After a pause, listening to the insistent beat of the tom-tom in the distance.*) I must 'a' put some distance between myself an' dem—runnin' like dat—an' yit—dat damn drum sounds jes' de same—nearer, even. Well, I guess I a'most holds my lead anyhow. Dey won't never catch up. (*With a sigh.*) If on'y my fool legs stands up. Oh, I'se sorry I evah went in for dis. Dat Emperor job is sho' hard to shake. (*He looks around him suspiciously.*) How'd dis road evah git heah? Good level road, too. I never remembers seein' it befo'. (*Shaking his head apprehensively.*) Dese woods is sho' full o' de queerest things at night. (*With a sudden terror.*) Lawd God, don't let me see no more o' dem ha'nts! Dey gits my goat! (*Then trying to talk himself into confidence.*) Ha'nts! You fool nigger, dey ain't no such things! Don't de Baptist parson tell you dat many time? Is you civilized, or is you like dese ign'rent black niggers heah? Sho'! Dat was all in yo' own head. Wasn't nothin' dere. Wasn't no Jeff! Know what? You jus' get seein' dem things 'cause yo' belly's empty and you's sick wid hunger inside. Hunger 'fects yo' head and yo' eyes. Any fool know dat. (*Then pleading fervently.*) But bless God, I don't come across no more o' dem, whatever dey is! (*Then cautiously.*) Rest! Don't talk! Rest! You needs it. Den you gits on yo' way again. (*Looking at the moon.*) Night's half gone a'most. You hits de coast in de mawning! Den you's all safe.

(*From the right forward a small gang of negroes enter. They are dressed in striped convict suits, their heads are shaven, one leg drags limpingly, shackled to a heavy ball and chain. Some carry picks, the others shovels. They are followed by a white man dressed in the uniform of a prison guard. A Winchester rifle is slung across his shoulders and he carries a heavy whip. At a signal from the* GUARD *they stop on the road opposite where* JONES *is sitting.* JONES, *who has been staring up at the sky, unmindful of their noiseless approach, suddenly looks down and sees them. His eyes pop out, he tries to get to his feet and fly, but sinks back, too numbed by fright to move. His voice catches in a choking prayer.*)

Lawd Jesus!

(*The* PRISON GUARD *cracks his whip—noiselessly —and at that signal all the convicts start to work on the road. They swing their picks, they shovel, but not a sound comes from their labor. Their movements, like those of* JEFF *in the preceding scene, are those of automatons,—rigid, slow, and mechanical. The* PRISON GUARD *points sternly at* JONES *with his whip, motions him to take his place among the other shovelers.* JONES *gets to his feet in a hypnotized stupor. He mumbles subserviently.*)

Yes, suh! Yes, suh! I'se comin'.

(*As he shuffles, dragging one foot, over to his place, he curses under his breath with rage and hatred.*)

God damn yo' soul, I gits even wid you yit, sometime.

(*As if there were a shovel in his hands he goes through weary, mechanical gestures of digging up dirt, and throwing it to the road-side. Suddenly the* GUARD *approaches him angrily, threateningly. He raises his whip and lashes* JONES *viciously across the shoulders with it.* JONES *winces with pain and cowers abjectly. The* GUARD *turns his back on him and walks away contemptuously. Instantly* JONES *straightens up. With arms upraised as if his shovel were a club in his hands he springs murderously at the unsuspecting* GUARD. *In the act of crashing down his shovel on the white man's skull,* JONES *suddenly becomes aware that his hands are empty. He cries despairingly.*)

Whar's my shovel! Gimme my shovel 'til I splits his damn head! (*Appealing to his fellow convicts.*) Gimme a shovel, one o' you, fo' God's sake!

(*They stand fixed in motionless attitudes, their eyes on the ground. The* GUARD *seems to wait expectantly, his back turned to the attacker.* JONES *bellows with baffled, terrified rage, tugging frantically at his revolver.*)

I kills you, you white debil, if it's de last thing I evah does! Ghost or debil, I kill you agin!

(*He frees the revolver and fires point blank at the* GUARD's *back. Instantly the walls of the forest close in from both sides, the road and the figures of the convict gang are blotted out in an ensbrouding darkness. The only sounds are a crashing in the underbrush as* JONES *leaps away in mad flight and the throbbing of the tom-tom, still far distant, but increased in volume of sound and rapidity of beat.*)

SCENE 5

(*A large circular clearing, enclosed by the serried ranks of gigantic trunks of tall trees whose tops are lost to view. In the center is a big dead stump worn by time into a curious resemblance to an auction block. The moon floods the clearing with a clear light.* JONES *forces his way in through the forest on the left. He looks wildly about the clearing with hunted, fearful glances. His pants are in tatters, his shoes cut and misshapen, flapping about his feet. He slinks cautiously to the stump in the center and sits down in a tense position, ready for instant flight. Then he holds his head in his hands and rocks back and forth, moaning to himself miserably.*)

Oh, Lawd, Lawd! Oh, Lawd, Lawd!.(*Suddenly he throws himself on his knees and raises his clasped hands to the sky—in a voice of agonized pleading.*) Lawd Jesus, heah my prayer! I'se a po' sinner, a po' sinner! I knows I done wrong, I knows it! When I cotches Jeff cheatin' wid loaded dice my anger overcomes me and I kills him dead! Lawd, I done wrong! When dat guard hits me wid de whip, my anger overcomes me, and I kills him dead! Lawd, I done wrong! And down heah whar dese fool bush niggers raises me up to the seat o' de mighty, I steals all I could grab. Lawd, I done wrong! I knows it! I'se sorry! Forgive me, Lawd! Forgive dis po' sinner! (*Then beseeching terrifiedly.*) And keep dem away, Lawd! Keep dem away from me! And stop dat drum soundin' in my ears! Dat begin to sound ha'nted, too. (*He gets to his feet, evidently slightly reassured by his prayer—with attempted confidence.*) De Lawd'll preserve me from dem ha'nts after dis. (*Sits down on the stump again.*) I ain't skeered o' real men. Let dem come. But dem odders—(*He shudders —then looks down at his feet, working his toes inside the shoes—with a groan.*) Oh, my po' feet! Dem shoes ain't no use no more 'ceptin' to hurt. I'se better off widout dem. (*He unlaces them and pulls them off—holds the wrecks of the shoes in his hands and regards them mournfully.*) You was real, A-one patin' leather, too. Look at you now. Emperor, you'se gittin' mighty low!

(*He sighs dejectedly and remains with bowed shoulders, staring down at the shoes in his hands as if reluctant to throw them away. While his attention is thus occupied, a crowd of figures silently enter the clearing from all sides. All are dressed in Southern costumes of the period of the fifties of the last century. There are middle-aged men who are evidently well-to-do planters. There is one spruce, authoritative individual—the* AUCTIONEER. *There is a crowd of curious spectators, chiefly young belles and dandies who have come to the slave-market for diversion. All exchange courtly greetings in dumb show and chat silently together. There is something stiff, rigid, unreal, marionettish about their movements. They group themselves about the stump. Finally a batch of slaves is led in from the left by an attendant—three men of different ages, two women, one with a baby in her arms, nursing. They are placed to the left of the stump, beside* JONES.*

The white planters look them over appraisingly as if they were cattle, and exchange judgments on each. The dandies point with their fingers and make witty remarks. The belles titter bewitchingly. All this in silence save for the ominous throb of the tom-tom. The* AUCTIONEER *holds up his hand, taking his place at the stump. The groups strain forward attentively. He touches* JONES *on the shoulder peremptorily, motioning for him to stand on the stump—the auction block.*

JONES *looks up, sees the figures on all sides, looks wildly for some opening to escape, sees none, screams and leaps madly to the top of the stump to get as far away from them as possible. He stands there, cowering, paralyzed with horror. The* AUCTIONEER *begins his silent spiel. He points to* JONES, *appeals to the planters to see for themselves. Here is a good field hand, sound in wind and limb as they can see. Very strong still in spite of his being middle-aged. Look at that back. Look at those shoulders. Look at the muscles in his arms and his sturdy legs. Capable of any amount of hard labor. Moreover, of a good disposition, intelligent and tractable. Will any gentleman start the bidding? The* PLANTERS *raise their fingers, make their bids. They are apparently all eager to possess* JONES.)

The bidding is lively, the crowd interested. While this has been going on, JONES *has been seized by the courage of desperation. He dares to look down and around him. Over his face abject terror gives way to mystification, to gradual realization—stutteringly.*)

What you all doin', white folks? What's all dis? What you all lookin' at me fo'? What you doin' wid me, anyhow? (*Suddenly convulsed with raging hatred and fear.*) Is dis a auction? Is you sellin' me like dey uster befo' de war? (*Jerking out his revolver just as the* AUCTIONEER *knocks him down to one of the planters—glaring from him to the purchaser.*) And *you* sells me? And *you* buys me? I shows you I'se a free nigger, damn yo' souls! (*He fires at the* AUCTIONEER *and at the* PLANTER *with such rapidity that the two shots are almost simultaneous. As if this were a signal the walls of the forest fold in. Only blackness remains and silence broken by* JONES *as he rushes off, crying with fear—and by the quickened, ever louder beat of the tom-tom.*)

SCENE 6

(*A cleared space in the forest. The limbs of the trees meet over it forming a low ceiling about five feet from the ground. The interlocked ropes of creepers reaching upward to entwine the tree trunks give an arched appearance to the sides. The space thus enclosed is like the dark, noisome hold of some ancient vessel. The moonlight is almost completely shut out and only a vague wan light filters through. There is the noise of someone approaching from the left, stumbling and crawling through the undergrowth.* JONES' *voice is heard between chattering moans.*)

Oh, Lawd, what I gwine do now? Ain't got no bullet left on'y de silver one. If mo' o' dem ha'nts come after me, how I gwine skeer dem away? Oh, Lawd, on'y de silver one left—an' I gotta save dat fo' luck. If I shoots dat one I'm a goner sho'! Lawd, it's black heah! Whar's de moon? Oh, Lawd, don't dis night evah come to an end? (*By the sounds, he is feeling his way cautiously forward.*) Dere! Dis feels like a clear space. I gotta lie down an' rest. I don't care if dem niggers does cotch me. I gotta rest.

(*He is well forward now where his figure can be dimly made out. His pants have been so torn away that what is left of them is no better than a breech cloth. He flings himself full length, face downward on the ground, panting with exhaustion. Gradually it seems to grow lighter in the enclosed space and two rows* of seated figures can be seen behind JONES. They are sitting in crumpled, despairing attitudes, hunched, facing one another with their backs touching the forest walls as if they were shackled to them. All are negroes, naked save for loin cloths. At first they are silent and motionless. Then they begin to sway slowly forward toward each and back again in unison, as if they were laxly letting themselves follow the long roll of a ship at sea. At the same time, a low, melancholy murmur rises among them, increasing gradually by rhythmic degrees which seem to be directed and controlled by the throb of the tom-tom in the distance, to a long, tremulous wail of despair that reaches a certain pitch, unbearably acute, then falls by slow gradations of tone into silence and is taken up again. JONES starts, looks up, sees the figures, and throws himself down again to shut out the sight. A shudder of terror shakes his whole body as the wail rises up about him again. But the next time, his voice, as if under some uncanny compulsion, starts with the others. As their chorus lifts he rises to a sitting posture similar to the others, swaying back and forth. His voice reaches the highest pitch of sorrow, of desolation. The light fades out, the other voices cease, and only darkness is left. JONES can be heard scrambling to his feet and running off, his voice sinking down the scale and receding as he moves farther and farther away in the forest. The tom-tom beats louder, quicker, with a more insistent, triumphant pulsation.)

SCENE 7

(The foot of a gigantic tree by the edge of a great river. A rough structure of boulders, like an altar, is by the tree. The raised river bank is in the nearer background. Beyond this the surface of the river spreads out, brilliant and unruffled in the moonlight, blotted out and merged into a veil of bluish mist in the distance. JONES' voice is heard from the left rising and falling in the long, despairing wail of the chained slaves, to the rhythmic beat of the tom-tom. As his voice sinks into silence, he enters the open space. The expression of his face is fixed and stony, his eyes have an obsessed glare, he moves with a strange deliberation like a sleep-walker or one in a trance. He looks around at the tree, the rough stone altar, the moonlit surface of the river beyond, and passes his hand over his head with a vague gesture of puzzled bewilderment. Then, as if in obedience to some obscure impulse, he sinks into a kneeling, devotional posture before the altar. Then he seems to come to himself partly, to have an uncertain realization of what he is doing, for he straightens up

and stares about him horrifiedly—in an incoherent mumble.)

What—what is I doin'? What is—dis place? Seems like I know dat tree—an' dem stones —an' de river. I remember—seems like I been heah befo'. (Tremblingly.) Oh, Gorry, I'se skeered in dis place! I'se skeered. Oh, Lawd, pertect dis sinner!

(Crawling away from the altar, he cowers close to the ground, his face hidden, his shoulders heaving with sobs of hysterical fright. From behind the trunk of the tree, as if he had sprung out of it, the figure of the CONGO WITCH-DOCTOR appears. He is wizened and old, naked except for the fur of some small animal tied about his waist, its bushy tail hanging down in front. His body is stained all over a bright red. Antelope horns are on each side of his head, branching upward. In one hand he carries a bone rattle, in the other a charm stick with a bunch of white cockatoo feathers tied to the end. A great number of glass beads and bone ornaments are about his neck, ears, wrists, and ankles. He struts noiselessly with a queer prancing step to a position in the clear ground between JONES and the altar. Then with a preliminary, summoning stamp of his foot on the earth, he begins to dance and to chant. As if in response to his summons the beating of the tom-tom grows to a fierce, exultant boom whose throbs seem to fill the air with vibrating rhythm. JONES looks up, starts to spring to his feet, reaches a half-kneeling, half-squatting position and remains rigidly fixed there, paralyzed with awed fascination by this new apparition. The WITCH-DOCTOR sways, stamping with his foot, his bone rattle clicking the time. His voice rises and falls in a weird, monotonous croon, without articulate word divisions. Gradually his dance becomes clearly one of a narrative in pantomime, his croon is an incantation, a charm to allay the fierceness of some implacable deity demanding sacrifice. He flees, he is pursued by devils, he hides, he flees again. Ever wilder and wilder becomes his flight, nearer and nearer draws the pursuing evil, more and more the spirit of terror gains possession of him. His croon, rising to intensity, is punctuated by shrill cries. JONES has become completely hypnotized. His voice joins in the incantation, in the cries, he beats time with his hands and sways his body to and fro from the waist. The whole spirit and meaning of the dance has entered into him, has become his spirit. Finally the theme of the pantomime halts on a howl of despair, and is taken up again in a note of savage hope. There is a salvation. The forces of evil demand sacrifice. They must be appeased. The WITCH-DOCTOR points with his wand to the sacred tree, to the river beyond, to the altar, and *finally to* JONES *with a ferocious command.* JONES *seems to sense the meaning of this. It is he who must offer himself for sacrifice. He beats his forehead abjectly to the ground, moaning hysterically.*)

Mercy, Oh, Lawd! Mercy! Mercy on dis po' sinner.

(*The* WITCH-DOCTOR *springs to the river bank. He stretches out his arms and calls to some God within its depths. Then he starts backward slowly, his arms remaining out. A huge head of a crocodile appears over the bank and its eyes, glittering greenly, fasten upon* JONES. *He stares into them fascinatedly. The* WITCH-DOCTOR *prances up to him, touches him with his wand, motions with hideous command toward the waiting monster.* JONES *squirms on his belly nearer and nearer, moaning continually.*)

Mercy, Lawd! Mercy!

(*The crocodile heaves more of his enormous hulk onto the land.* JONES *squirms toward him. The* WITCH-DOCTOR's *voice shrills out in furious exultation, the tom-tom beats madly.* JONES *cries out in a fierce, exhausted spasm of anguished pleading.*)

Lawd, save me! Lawd Jesus, heah my prayer!

(*Immediately, in answer to his prayer, comes the thought of the one bullet left him. He snatches at his hip, shouting defiantly.*)

De silver bullet! You don't git me yit!

(*He fires at the green eyes in front of him. The head of the crocodile sinks back behind the river bank, the* WITCH-DOCTOR *springs behind the sacred tree and disappears.* JONES *lies with his face to the ground, his arms outstretched, whimpering with fear as the throb of the tom-tom fills the silence about him with a somber pulsation, a baffled but revengeful power.*)

SCENE 8

(*Dawn. Same as Scene Two, the dividing line of forest and plain. The nearest tree trunks are dimly revealed but the forest behind them is still a mass of glooming shadow. The tom-tom seems on the very spot, so loud and continuously vibrating are its beats.* LEM *enters from the left, followed by a small squad of his soldiers, and by the Cockney trader,* SMITHERS. LEM *is a heavy-set, ape-faced old savage of the extreme African type, dressed only in a loin cloth. A revolver and cartridge belt are about his waist. His soldiers are in different degrees of rag-concealed nakedness. All wear broad palm-leaf hats. Each one carries a rifle.* SMITHERS *is the same as in Scene One. One of the soldiers, evidently a tracker, is peering about keenly on the ground. He points to the spot where* JONES *entered the forest.* LEM *and* SMITHERS *come to look.*)

SMITHERS (*after a glance, turns away in disgust*): That's where 'e went in right enough. Much good it'll do yer. 'E's miles orf by this an' safe to the Coast, damn 's 'ide! I tole yer yer'd lose im, didn't I?—wastin' the 'ole bloomin' night beatin' yer bloody drum and castin' yer silly spells! Gawd blimey, wot a pack!

LEM (*gutturally*): We cotch him. (*He makes a motion to his soldiers who squat down on their haunches in a semi-circle.*)

SMITHERS (*exasperatedly*): Well, ain't yer goin' in an' 'unt 'im in the woods? What the 'ell's the good of waitin'?

LEM (*imperturbably—squatting down himself*): We cotch him.

SMITHERS (*turning away from him contemptuously*): Aw! Garn! 'E's a better man than the lot o' you put together. I 'ates the sight o' 'im but I'll say that for 'im. (*A sound comes from the forest. The soldiers jump to their feet, cocking their rifles alertly.* LEM *remains sitting with an imperturbable expression, but listening intently. He makes a quick signal with his hand. His followers creep quickly into the forest, scattering so that each enters at a different spot.*)

SMITHERS: You ain't thinkin' that would be 'im, I 'ope?

LEM (*calmly*): We cotch him.

SMITHERS: Blarsted fat 'eads! (*Then after a second's thought—wonderingly.*) Still an' all, it might 'appen. If 'e lost 'is bloody way in these stinkin' woods 'e'd likely turn in a circle without 'is knowin' it.

LEM (*peremptorily*): Sssh! (*The reports of several rifles sound from the forest, followed a second later by savage, exultant yells. The beating of the tom-tom abruptly ceases.* LEM *looks up at the white man with a grin of satisfaction.*) We cotch him. Him dead.

SMITHERS (*with a snarl*): 'Ow d'yer know it's 'im an' 'ow d'yer know 'e's dead?

LEM: My mens dey got um silver bullets. Lead bullet no kill him. He got um strong charm. I cook um money, make um silver bullet, make um strong charm, too.

SMITHERS (*astonished*): So that's wot you was up to all night, wot? You was scared to put after 'im till you'd moulded silver bullets, eh?

LEM (*simply stating a fact*): Yes. Him got strong charm. Lead no good.

SMITHERS (*slapping his thigh and guffawing*): Haw-haw! If yer don't beat all 'ell! (*Then recovering himself—scornfully.*) I'll bet yer it ain't 'im they shot at all, yer bleedin' looney!

LEM (*calmly*): Dey come bring him now. (*The soldiers come out of the forest, carrying* JONES' *limp body. He is dead. They carry him to* LEM, *who examines his body with great satisfaction.* SMITHERS *leans over his shoulder—in a tone of frightened awe.*) Well, they did for yer right enough, Jonesey, me lad! Dead as a 'erring! (*Mockingly.*) Where's yer 'igh an' mighty airs now, yer bloomin' Majesty? (*Then with a grin.*) Silver bullets! Gawd blimey, but yer died in the 'eighth o' style, any'ow!

CURTAIN

Elmer Rice: *The Adding Machine* (1923)

When compared with the beginnings of most American playwrights, Elmer Rice's start in the theater seems ridiculously simple. When he was twenty, he graduated from law school, but instead of opening a law practice, he calmly told his family that he intended to be a playwright. He knew nothing of the usual means by which someone got the attention of the stage. It is said that he simply wrote a play, put it in an envelope, and sent it to a producer, who remarkably enough, accepted it immediately. The play *On Trial* (1914) reflects Rice's experience with the law. One of the reasons for its success was its dependence upon some of the technical innovations of the films, an industry that had thoroughly captured the modern imagination by that time.

Elmer Rice was born Elmer Reizenstein in New York in 1892, changing his name to something much simpler and more memorable. Most of his early years in theater were spent on amateur productions of intense seriousness. So in a sense, Rice's apprenticeship in the theater came after his commercial success rather than before it. In these years, in New York City, Rice developed a considerable social conscience. Perhaps because of this background, or possibly just because of his residing in a huge metropolis, where he could observe people in many conditions, he found himself committed to an examination of the human condition in America. Some of his convictions were expressed rather directly in his dramas.

The Adding Machine was produced by the Theatre Guild in 1922. It was advanced for its time, and yet it was successful. Even now it seems contemporary. It is organized into scenes rather than acts, and there is little effort at keeping the play realistic in style. It is usually described as an expressionistic play, which is a way of suggesting that its style includes elements of the fantastic and surreal. The American theater was not burgeoning with such plays, but there were several examples in English literature of surrealism and "expressionistic" techniques.

For our time, Rice's themes seem extraordinarily *a propos*. Mr. Zero is putting in his time on a job that has reduced him to being an adding machine for the last twenty-five years. Even the little dignity that is left him is stripped away when he finds that in the interests of efficiency and business, he is being replaced by a machine that never tires, is never late, and never makes a mistake. The ordinarily passive Mr. Zero strikes back, but to no avail.

It may not be that Rice was simply looking ahead, since there are a number of other interesting themes in the play that attract him equally. He does not examine the question of whether it is better to keep people employed at meaningless tasks machines could do better or to simply replace them entirely. That seems a more modern theme. Rice's answer—or Mr. Zero's answer—is to demand one's dignity as a worker. Twenty-five years of service mean something to him, as he reveals late in the play when he translates that time into months, weeks, and days.

But the question of employment is only one theme in the play. The further questions of social relations, marriage and sexuality, and even evolution and reincarnation enter into the drama. One of the most remarkable moments in the play is in Scene 2, when Daisy and Mr. Zero are tabulating columns of figures. Their principal communication concerns the tabulation of dollars and cents, but beneath that they give utterance to a "subtext" in which their anxieties and deeper feelings are expressed. Neither is aware that the other is speaking deep feelings: they speak at cross purposes. Mr. Zero thinks about a woman, Judy, whose exhibitionism got her arrested, and he believes that "Women are all alike." Daisy, meanwhile, wonders why he won't notice her, and thinks, "I wish I was dead."

The satiric portrait of a social gathering at the Zeros is brilliantly revealed in Scene 3. The couples separate upon arriving and begin talking among themselves, men in one circle, women in another. The weather is the first topic of the conversation. Then the women talk disparagingly about the men, while the men talk disparagingly about the women. The talk then turns to women's suffrage, the gloomy economic outlook, and foreigners and minority groups. Ironically, the topics of conversation for many Americans have hardly altered in sixty years.

The play ends with the prospect of Mr. Zero's reincarnation and beginning again as a baby. He is told that his progress through the eons of time is downward, that his next incarnation will be worse than his last. He is hardly brightened by the prospect.

Selected Readings

Durham, Frank. *Elmer Rice*. New York: Twayne, 1970.
Hogan, Robert. *The Independence of Elmer Rice*. Carbondale: Southern Illinois
    University Press, 1965.
Rice, Elmer. *The Living Theatre*. New York: Harper, 1959.
————. *Seven Plays*. New York: Viking; 1959.

The Adding Machine

A PLAY IN EIGHT SCENES

Elmer Rice

CHARACTERS

MR. ZERO	MRS. FIVE
MRS. ZERO	MR. SIX
DAISY DIANA	MRS. SIX
DOROTHEA DEVORE	POLICEMAN
THE BOSS	GUIDE
MR. ONE	THE FIXER
MRS. ONE	A GUARD
MR. TWO	JUDY O'GRADY
MRS. TWO	YOUNG MAN
MR. THREE	SHRDLU
MRS. THREE	A HEAD
MR. FOUR	LIEUTENANT CHARLES
MRS. FOUR	JOE
MR. FIVE	SIGHTSEERS

SCENE 1

(*A small bedroom containing an "installment plan" bed, dresser, and chairs. An ugly electric-light fixture over the bed with a single glaring, naked lamp. One small window with the shade drawn. The walls are papered with sheets of foolscap covered with columns of figures.*

MR. ZERO *is lying on the bed, facing the audience, his head and shoulders visible. He is thin, sallow, undersized, and partially bald.* MRS. ZERO *is standing before the dresser arranging her hair for the night. She is forty-five, sharp-featured, gray streaks in her hair. She is shapeless in her long-sleeved cotton nightgown. She is wearing her shoes, over which sag her ungartered stockings.*)

MRS. ZERO (*as she takes down her hair*): I'm gettin' sick o' them. Westerns. All them cowboys ridin' around an' foolin' with them ropes. I don't care nothin' about that. I'm sick of 'em. I don't see why they don't have more of them stories like *For Love's Sweet Sake*. I like them sweet little love stories. They're nice an' wholesome. Mrs. Twelve was sayin' to me only yesterday, "Mrs. Zero," says she, "what I like is one of them wholesome stories, with just a sweet, simple love story." "You're right, Mrs. Twelve," I says. "That's what I like too." They're showin' too many Westerns at the Rosebud. I'm gettin' sick of them. I think we'll start goin' to the Peter Stuyvesant. They got a good bill there Wednesday night. There's a Chubby Delano comedy called *Sea-Sick*. Mrs. Twelve was tellin' me about it. She says it's a scream. They're havin' a picnic in the country and they sit Chubby next to an old maid with a great big mouth. So he gets sore an' when she ain't lookin' he goes and catches a frog and drops it in her clam chowder. An' when she goes to eat the chowder the frog jumps out of it an' right into her mouth. Talk about laugh! Mrs. Twelve was tellin' me she laughed so she nearly passed out. He sure can pull some funny ones. An' they got that big Grace Darling feature, *A Mother's Tears*. She's sweet. But I don't like her clothes. There's no style to them. Mrs. Nine was tellin' me she read in *Pictureland* that she ain't livin' with her husband. He's her second too. I don't know whether they're divorced or just separated. You wouldn't think it to see her on the screen. She looks so sweet and innocent. Maybe it ain't true. You can't believe all you read. They say some Pittsburgh millionaire is crazy about her and that's why she ain't livin' with her husband. Mrs. Seven was tellin' me her brother-in-law has a friend that used to go to school with Grace Darling. He says her name ain't Grace Darling at all. Her right name is Elizabeth Dugan, he says, an' all them stories about her gettin' five thousand a week is the bunk, he says. She's sweet though. Mrs. Eight was tellin' me that *A Mother's Tears* is the best picture she ever made. "Don't miss it, Mrs. Zero," she says. "It's sweet," she says. "Just sweet and wholesome. Cry!" she says, "I nearly cried my eyes out." There's one part in it where this big bum of an Englishman—he's a married man too—an' she's this little simple country girl. An' she nearly falls for him too. But she's sittin' out in the garden, one day, and she looks up and there's her mother lookin' at her, right out of the clouds. So that night she locks the door of her room. An' sure enough, when everybody's in bed, along comes this big bum of an Englishman an' when she won't let him in what does he do but go an' kick open the door. "Don't

miss it, Mrs. Zero," Mrs. Eight was tellin' me. It's at the Peter Stuyvesant Wednesday night, so don't be tellin' me you want to go to the Rosebud. The Eights seen it downtown at the Strand. They go downtown all the time. Just like us—nit! I guess by the time it gets to the Peter Stuyvesant all that part about kickin' in the door will be cut out. Just like they cut out that big cabaret scene in *The Price of Virtue*. They sure are pullin' some rough stuff in the pictures nowadays. "It's no place for a young girl," I was tellin' Mrs. Eleven, only the other day. An' by the time they get uptown half of it is cut out. But you wouldn't go downtown—not if wild horses was to drag you. You can wait till they come uptown! Well, I don't want to wait, see? I want to see 'em when everybody else is seein' 'em an' not a month later. Now don't go tellin' me you ain't got the price. You could dig up the price all right, all right, if you wanted to. I notice you always got the price to go to the ball game. But when it comes to me havin' a good time, then it's always: "I ain't got the price. I gotta start savin'." A fat lot you'll ever save! I got all I can do now makin' both ends meet, an' you talkin' about savin'. (*She seats herself on a chair and begins removing her shoes and stockings.*) An' don't go pullin' that stuff about bein' tired. "I been workin' hard all day. Twice a day in the subway's enough for me." Tired! Where do you get that tired stuff, anyhow? What about me? Where do I come in? Scrubbin' floors an' cookin' your meals an' washin' your dirty clothes. An' you sittin' on a chair all day, just addin' figgers an' waitin' for five-thirty. There's no five-thirty for me. I don't wait for no whistle. I don't get no vacations neither. And what's more I don't get no pay envelope every Saturday night neither. I'd like to know where you'd be without me. An' what have I got to show for it?—slavin' my life away to give you a home. What's in it for me, I'd like to know? But it's my own fault, I guess. I was a fool for marryin' you. If I'd 'a' had any sense, I'd 'a' known what you were from the start. I wish I had it to do over again, I hope to tell you. You was goin' to do wonders, you was! You wasn't goin' to be a bookkeeper long—oh, no, not you. Wait till you got started—you was goin' to show 'em. There wasn't no job in the store that was too big for you. Well, I've been waitin'—waitin' for you to get started—see? It's been a good long wait too. Twenty-five years! An' I ain't seen nothin' happen. Twenty-five years in the same job. Twenty-five years tomorrow! You're proud of it, ain't you? Twenty-five years in the same job an' never missed a day! That's somethin' to be proud of, ain't it? Sittin' for twenty-five years on the same chair, addin' up figgers. What about bein' store manager? I guess you forgot about that, didn't you? An' me at home here lookin' at the same four walls an' workin' my fingers to the bone to make both ends meet. Seven years since you got a raise! An' if you don't get one tomorrow, I'll bet a nickel you won't have the guts to go an' ask for one. I didn't pick much when I picked you, I'll tell the world. You ain't much to be proud of. (*She rises, goes to the window, and raises the shade. A few lighted windows are visible on the other side of the closed court. Looking out for a moment.*) She ain't walkin' around tonight, you can bet your sweet life on that. An' she won't be walkin' around any more nights neither. Not in this house, anyhow. (*She turns away from the window.*) The dirty bum! The idea of her comin' to live in a house with respectable people. They should 'a' gave her six years, not six months. If I was the judge I'd of gave her life. A bum like that. (*She approaches the bed and stands there a moment.*) I guess you're sorry she's gone. I guess you'd like to sit home every night an' watch her goin's-on. You're somethin' to be proud of, you are! (*She stands on the bed and turns out the light. A thin stream of moonlight filters in from the court. The two figures are dimly visible. MRS. ZERO gets into bed.*) You'd better not start nothin' with women, if you know what's good for you. I've put up with a lot, but I won't put up with that. I've been slavin' away for twenty-five years, makin' a home for you an' nothin' to show for it. If you was any kind of a man you'd have a decent job by now an' I'd be gettin' some comfort out of life—instead of bein' just a slave, washin' pots an' standin' over the hot stove. I've stood it for twenty-five years an' I guess I'll have to stand it twenty-five more. But don't you go startin' nothin' with women———

(*She goes on talking as the curtain falls.*)

SCENE 2

(*An office in a department store. Wood and glass partitions. In the middle of the room two tall desks back to back. At one desk on a high stool is ZERO. Opposite him at the other desk, also on a high stool, is DAISY DIANA DOROTHEA DEVORE, a plain, middle-aged woman. Both wear green eyeshades and paper sleeve-protectors. A pendent electric lamp throws light upon both desks. DAISY reads aloud figures from a pile of slips which lie before her. As she reads the figures ZERO enters them upon a large square sheet of ruled paper which lies before him.*)

DAISY (*reading aloud*): Three ninety-eight. Forty-two cents. A dollar fifty. A dollar fifty. A dollar twenty-five. Two dollars. Thirty-nine cents. Twenty-seven fifty.

ZERO (*petulantly*): Speed it up a little, cancha?

DAISY: What's the rush? Tomorrer's another day.

ZERO: Aw, you make me sick.

DAISY: An' you make me sicker.

ZERO: Go on. Go on. We're losin' time.

DAISY: Then quit bein' so bossy. (*She reads.*) Three dollars. Two sixty-nine. Eighty-one fifty. Forty dollars. Eight seventy-five. Who do you think you are, anyhow?

ZERO: Never mind who I think I am. You tend to your work.

DAISY: Aw, don't be givin' me so many orders. Sixty cents. Twenty-four cents. Seventy-five cents. A dollar fifty. Two fifty. One fifty. One fifty. Two fifty. I don't have to take it from you and what's more I won't.

ZERO: Aw, quit talkin'.

DAISY: I'll talk all I want. Three dollars. Fifty cents. Fifty cents. Seven dollars. Fifty cents. Two fifty. Three fifty. Fifty cents. One fifty. Fifty cents.

(*She goes on, bending over the slips and transferring them from one pile to another. ZERO bends over his desk, busily entering the figures.*)

ZERO (*without looking up*): You make me sick. Always shootin' off your face about somethin'. Talk, talk, talk. Just like all the other women. Women make me sick.

DAISY (*busily fingering the slips*): Who do you think you are, anyhow? Bossin' me around. I don't have to take it from you, and what's more I won't.

(*They both attend closely to their work, neither looking up. Throughout, each intones figures during the other's speeches.*)

ZERO: Women make me sick. They're all alike. The judge gave her six months. I wonder what they do in the workhouse. Peel potatoes. I'll bet she's sore at me. Maybe she'll try to kill me when she gets out. I better be careful. Hello Girl Slays Betrayer. Jealous Wife Slays Rival. You can't tell what a woman's liable to do. I better be careful.

DAISY: I'm gettin' sick of it. Always pickin'

on me about somethin'. Never a decent word out of you. Not even the time o' day.

ZERO: I guess she wouldn't have the nerve at that. Maybe she don't even know it's me. They didn't even put my name in the paper, the big bums. Maybe she's been in the workhouse before. A bum like that. She didn't have nothin' on that one time—nothin' but a shirt. (*He glances up quickly, then bends over again.*) You make me sick. I'm sick of lookin' at your face.

DAISY: Gee, ain't that whistle ever goin' to blow? You didn't used to be like that. Not even good mornin' or good evenin'. I ain't done nothin' to you. It's the young girls. Goin' around without corsets.

ZERO: Your face is gettin' all yeller. Why don't you put some paint on it? She was puttin' on paint that time. On her cheeks and on her lips. And that blue stuff on her eyes. Just sittin' there in a shimmy puttin' on the paint. An' walkin' around the room with her legs all bare.

DAISY: I wish I was dead.

ZERO: I was a goddam fool to let the wife get on to me. She oughta get six months at that. The dirty bum. Livin' in a house with respectable people. She'd be livin' there yet if the wife hadn't o' got on to me. Damn her!

DAISY: I wish I was dead.

ZERO: Maybe another one'll move in. Gee, that would be great. But the wife's got her eye on me now.

DAISY: I'm scared to do it though.

ZERO: You oughta move into that room. It's cheaper than where you're livin' now. I better tell you about it. I don't mean to be always pickin' on you.

DAISY: Gas. The smell of it makes me sick. (ZERO *looks up and clears his throat.* DAISY *looks up, startled.*) Whadja say?

ZERO: I didn't say nothin'.

DAISY: I thought you did.

ZERO: You thought wrong.

(*They bend over their work again.*)

DAISY: A dollar sixty. A dollar fifty. Two ninety. One sixty-two.

ZERO: Why the hell should I tell you? Fat chance of you forgettin' to pull down the shade!

DAISY: If I asked for carbolic they might get on to me.

ZERO: Your hair's gettin' gray. You don't wear them shirtwaists any more with the low collars. When you'd bend down to pick somethin' up———

DAISY: I wish I knew what to ask for. Girl Takes Mercury After All-Night Party. Woman In Ten-Story Death Leap.

ZERO: I wonder where'll she go when she gets out. Gee, I'd like to make a date with her. Why didn't I go over there the night my wife went to Brooklyn? She never woulda found out.

DAISY: I seen Pauline Frederick do it once. Where could I get a pistol though?

ZERO: I guess I didn't have the nerve.

DAISY: I'll bet you'd be sorry then that you been so mean to me. How do I know though? Maybe you wouldn't.

ZERO: Nerve! I got as much nerve as anybody. I'm on the level, that's all. I'm a married man and I'm on the level.

DAISY: Anyhow, why ain't I got a right to live? I'm as good as anybody else. I'm too refined, I guess. That's the whole trouble.

ZERO: The time the wife had pneumonia I thought she was goin' to pass out. But she didn't. The doctor's bill was eighty-seven dollars. (*Looking up.*) Hey, wait a minute! Didn't you say eighty-seven dollars?

DAISY (*looking up*): What?

ZERO: Was the last you said eighty-seven dollars?

DAISY (*consulting the slip*): Forty-two fifty.

ZERO: Well, I made a mistake. Wait a minute. (*He busies himself with an eraser.*) All right. Shoot.

DAISY: Six dollars. Three fifteen. Two twenty-five. Sixty-five cents. A dollar twenty. You talk to me as if I was dirt.

ZERO: I wonder if I could kill the wife without anybody findin' out. In bed some night. With a pillow.

DAISY: I used to think you was stuck on me.

ZERO: I'd get found out though. They always have ways.

DAISY: We used to be so nice and friendly together when I first came here. You used to talk to me then.

ZERO: Maybe she'll die soon. I noticed she was coughin' this mornin'.

DAISY: You used to tell me all kinds o' things. You were goin' to show them all. Just the same, you're still sittin' here.

ZERO: Then I could do what I damn please. Oh, boy!

DAISY: Maybe it ain't all your fault neither. Maybe if you'd had the right kind o' wife—somebody with a lot of common sense, somebody refined—me!

ZERO: At that, I guess I'd get tired of bummin' around. A feller wants some place to hang his hat.

DAISY: I wish she would die.

ZERO: And when you start goin' with women you're liable to get into trouble. And lose your job maybe.

DAISY: Maybe you'd marry me.

ZERO: Gee, I wish I'd gone over there that night.

DAISY: Then I could quit workin'.

ZERO: Lots o' women would be glad to get me.

DAISY: You could look a long time before you'd find a sensible, refined girl like me.

ZERO: Yes, sir, they could look a long time before they'd find a steady meal ticket like me.

DAISY: I guess I'd be too old to have any kids. They say it ain't safe after thirty-five.

ZERO: Maybe I'd marry you. You might be all right, at that.

DAISY: I wonder—if you don't want kids—whether—if there's any way———

ZERO (looking up): Hey! Hey! Can't you slow up? What do you think I am—a machine?

DAISY (looking up): Say, what do you want, anyhow? First it's too slow an' then it's too fast. I guess you don't know what you want.

ZERO: Well, never mind about that. Just slow up.

DAISY: I'm gettin' sick o' this. I'm goin' to ask to be transferred.

ZERO: Go ahead. You can't make me mad.

DAISY: Aw, keep quiet. (She reads.) Two forty-five. A dollar twenty. A dollar fifty. Ninety cents. Sixty-three cents.

ZERO: Marry you! I guess not! You'd be as bad as the one I got.

DAISY: You wouldn't care if I did ask. I got a good mind to ask.

ZERO: I was a fool to get married.

DAISY: Then I'd never see you at all.

ZERO: What chance has a guy got with a woman tied around his neck?

DAISY: That time at the store picnic—the year your wife couldn't come—you were nice to me then.

ZERO: Twenty-five years holdin' down the same job!

DAISY: We were together all day—just sittin' around under the trees.

ZERO: I wonder if the boss remembers about it bein' twenty-five years.

DAISY: And comin' home that night—you sat next to me in the big delivery wagon.

ZERO: I got a hunch there's a big raise comin' to me.

DAISY: I wonder what it feels like to be really kissed. Men—dirty pigs! They want the bold ones.

ZERO: If he don't come across I'm goin' right up to the front office and tell him where he gets off.

DAISY: I wish I was dead.

ZERO: "Boss," I'll say, "I want to have a talk with you." "Sure," he'll say, "sit down. Have a Corona Corona." "No," I'll say, "I don't smoke." "How's that?" he'll say. "Well, boss," I'll say, "it's this way. Every time I feel like smokin' I just take a nickel and put it in the old sock. A penny saved is a penny earned, that's the way I look at it." "Damn sensible," he'll say. "You got a wise head on you, Zero."

DAISY: I can't stand the smell of gas. It makes me sick. You coulda kissed me if you wanted to.

ZERO: "Boss," I'll say, "I ain't quite satisfied. I been on the job twenty-five years now and if I'm gonna stay I gotta see a future ahead of me." "Zero," he'll say, "I'm glad you came in. I've had my eye on you, Zero. Nothin' gets by me." "Oh, I know that, boss," I'll say. That'll hand him a good laugh, that will. "You're a valuable man, Zero," he'll say, "and I want you right up here with me in the front office. You're done addin' figgers. Monday mornin' you move up here."

DAISY: Them kisses in the movies—them long ones—right on the mouth—

ZERO: I'll keep a-goin' right on up after that. I'll show some of them birds where they get off.

DAISY: That one the other night—*The Devil's Alibi*—he put his arms around her—and her head fell back—and her eyes closed—like she was in a daze.

ZERO: Just give me about two years and I'll show them birds where they get off.

DAISY: I guess that's what it's like—a kinda daze—when I see them like that, I just seem to forget everything.

ZERO: Then me for a place in Jersey. And maybe a little Buick. No tin Lizzie for mine. Wait till I get started—I'll show 'em.

DAISY: I can see it now when I kinda half close my eyes. The way her head fell back. And his mouth pressed right up against hers. Oh, Gawd! it must be grand!

(There is a sudden shrill blast from a steam whistle.)

DAISY *and* ZERO *(together):* The whistle! *(With great agility they get off their stools, remove their eyeshades and sleeve-protectors and put them on the desks. Then each produces from behind the desk a hat—* ZERO, *a dusty derby,* DAISY, *a frowsy straw.* DAISY *puts on her hat and turns toward* ZERO *as though she were about to speak to him. But he is busy cleaning his pen and pays no attention to her. She sighs and goes toward the door at the left.)*

ZERO *(looking up):* G'night, Miss Devore.

(But she does not hear him and exits. ZERO *takes up his hat and goes left. The door at the right opens and the* BOSS *enters—middle-aged, stoutish, bald, well dressed.)*

THE BOSS *(calling):* Oh—er—Mister—er——

*(*ZERO *turns in surprise, sees who it is, and trembles nervously.)*

ZERO *(obsequiously):* Yes, sir. Do you want me, sir?

BOSS: Yes. Just come here a moment, will you?

ZERO: Yes, sir. Right away, sir. *(He fumbles his hat, picks it up, stumbles, recovers himself, and approaches the* BOSS, *every fiber quivering.)*

BOSS: Mister—er—er——

ZERO: Zero.

BOSS: Yes, Mr. Zero. I wanted to have a little talk with you.

ZERO *(with a nervous grin.):* Yes, sir, I been kinda expectin' it.

BOSS *(staring at him):* Oh, have you?

ZERO: Yes, sir.

BOSS: How long have you been with us, Mister—er—Mister——

ZERO: Zero.

BOSS: Yes, Mr. Zero.

ZERO: Twenty-five years today.

BOSS: Twenty-five years! That's a long time.

ZERO: Never missed a day.

BOSS: And you've been doing the same work all the time?

ZERO: Yes, sir. Right here at this desk.

BOSS: Then, in that case, a change probably won't be unwelcome to you.

ZERO: No sir, it won't. And that's the truth.

BOSS: We've been planning a change in this department for some time.

ZERO: I kinda thought you had your eye on me.

BOSS: You were right. The fact is that my efficiency experts have recommended the installation of adding machines.

ZERO *(staring at him):* Addin' machines?

BOSS: Yes, you've probably seen them. A mechanical device that adds automatically.

ZERO: Sure, I've seen them. Keys—and a handle that you pull. *(He goes through the motions in the air.)*

BOSS: That's it. They do the work in half the time and a high-school girl can operate them. Now, of course, I'm sorry to lose an old and faithful employee——

ZERO: Excuse me, but would you mind sayin' that again?

BOSS: I say I'm sorry to lose an employee who's been with me for so many years—— *(Soft music is heard—the sound of the mechanical player of a distant merry-go-round. The part of the floor upon which the desk and stools are standing begins to revolve very slowly.)* But, of course, in an organization like this, efficiency must be the first consideration——*(The music becomes gradually louder and the revolutions more rapid.)* You will draw your salary for the full month. And I'll direct my secretary to give you a letter of recommendation——

ZERO: Wait a minute, boss. Let me get this right. You mean I'm canned?

BOSS *(barely making himself heard above the increasing volume of sound):* I'm sorry—no other alternative—greatly regret—old employee— efficiency—economy—business—business— BUSINESS——

(His voice is drowned by the music. The platform is revolving rapidly now. ZERO *and the* BOSS *face each other. They are entirely motionless save for the* BOSS's *jaws, which open and close incessantly. But the words are inaudible. The music swells and swells. To it is added every off-stage effect of the theater: the wind, the waves, the galloping horses, the locomotive whistle, the sleigh bells, the automobile siren, the glass-crash. New Year's Eve, Election Night, Armistice Day, and Mardi Gras. The noise is deafening, maddening, unendurable. Suddenly it culminates in a terrific peal of thunder. For an instant there is a flash of red and then everything is plunged into blackness.)*

SCENE 3

(The ZERO *dining room. Entrance door at right. Doors to kitchen and bedroom at left. The walls, as in the first scene, are papered with foolscap sheets covered*

with columns of figures. *In the middle of the room, upstage, a table set for two. Along each side wall seven chairs are ranged in symmetrical rows.*

At the rise of the curtain MRS. ZERO *is seen seated at the table looking alternately at the entrance door and a clock on the wall. She wears a bungalow apron over her best dress.*

After a few moments the entrance door opens and ZERO *enters. He hangs his hat on a rack behind the door and, coming over to the table, seats himself at the vacant place. His movements throughout are quiet and abstracted.*)

MRS. ZERO (*breaking the silence*): Well, it was nice of you to come home. You're only an hour late and that ain't very much. The supper don't get very cold in an hour. An' of course the part about our havin' a lot of company tonight don't matter. (*They begin to eat.*)

Ain't you even got sense enough to come home on time? Didn't I tell you we're goin' to have a lot o' company tonight? Didn't you know the Ones are comin'? An' the Twos? An' the Threes? An' the Fours? An' the Fives? And the Sixes? Didn't I tell you to be home on time? I might as well talk to a stone wall. (*They eat for a few moments in silence.*)

I guess you musta had some important business to attend to. Like watchin' the scoreboard. Or was two kids havin' a fight an' you was the referee? You sure do have a lot of business to attend to. It's a wonder you have time to come home at all. You gotta tough life, you have. Walk in, hang up your hat, an' put on the nosebag. An' me in the hot kitchen all day, cookin' your supper an' waitin' for you to get good an' ready to come home! (*Again they eat in silence.*)

Maybe the boss kept you late tonight. Tellin' you what a big noise you are and how the store couldn't 'a' got along if you hadn't been pushin' a pen for twenty-five years. Where's the gold medal he pinned on you? Did some blind old lady take it away from you or did you leave it on the seat of the boss's limousine when he brought you home? (*Again a few moments of silence.*)

I'll bet he gave you a big raise, didn't he? Promoted you from the third floor to the fourth, maybe. Raise? A fat chance you got o' gettin' a raise. All they gotta do is put an ad in the paper. There's ten thousand like you layin' around the streets. You'll be holdin' down the same job at the end of another twenty-five years—if you ain't forgot how to add by that time.

(*A noise is heard offstage, a sharp clicking such as is made by the operation of the keys and levers of an adding machine.* ZERO *raises his head for a moment but lowers it almost instantly.*)

MRS. ZERO: There's the doorbell. The company's here already. And we ain't hardly finished supper. (*She rises.*) But I'm goin' to clear off the table whether you're finished or not. If you want your supper, you got a right to be home on time. Not standin' around lookin' at scoreboards. (*As she piles up the dishes* ZERO *rises and goes toward the entrance door.*) Wait a minute! Don't open the door yet. Do you want the company to see all the mess? An' go an' put on a clean collar. You got red ink all over it. (ZERO *goes toward bedroom door.*) I should think after pushin' a pen for twenty-five years, you'd learn how to do it without gettin' ink on your collar. (ZERO *exits to bedroom.* MRS. ZERO *takes dishes to kitchen, talking as she goes.*)

I guess I can stay up all night now washin' dishes. You should worry! That's what a man's got a wife for, ain't it? Don't he buy her her clothes an' let her eat with him at the same table? An' all she's gotta do is cook the meals an' do the washin' an' scrub the floor, an' wash the dishes when the company goes. But, believe me, you're goin' to sling a mean dish towel when the company goes tonight!

(*While she is talking* ZERO *enters from bedroom. He wears a clean collar and is cramming the soiled one furtively into his pocket.* MRS. ZERO *enters from kitchen. She has removed her apron and carries a table cover which she spreads hastily over the table. The clicking noise is heard again.*)

MRS. ZERO: There's the bell again. Open the door, cancha?

(ZERO *goes to the entrance door and opens it. Six men and six women file into the room in a double column. The men are all shapes and sizes, but their dress is identical with that of* ZERO *in every detail. Each, however, wears a wig of a different color. The women are all dressed alike too, except that the dress of each is of a different color.*)

MRS. ZERO (*taking the first woman's hand*): How de do, Mrs. One.

MRS. ONE: How de do, Mrs. Zero.

(MRS. ZERO *repeats this formula with each woman in turn.* ZERO *does the same with the men except that he is silent throughout. The files now separate, each man taking a chair from the right wall and each woman one from the left wall. Each sex forms a circle with the chairs very close together. The men—all except* ZERO—*smoke cigars. The women munch chocolates.*)

SIX: Some rain we're havin'.

FIVE: Never saw the like of it.

FOUR: Worst in fourteen years, paper says.

THREE: Y' can't always go by the papers.

TWO: No, that's right too.

ONE: We're liable to forget from year to year.

SIX: Yeh, come t' think, last year was pretty bad too.

FIVE: An' how about two years ago?

FOUR: Still, this year's pretty bad.

THREE: Yeh, no gettin' away from that.

TWO: Might be a whole lot worse.

ONE: Yeh, it's all the way you look at it. Some rain though.

MRS. SIX: I like them little organdic dresses.

MRS. FIVE: Yeh, with a little lace trimmin' on the sleeves.

MRS. FOUR: Well, I like 'em plain myself.

MRS. THREE: Yeh, what I always say is the plainer the more refined.

MRS. TWO: Well, I don't think a little lace does any harm.

MRS. ONE: No, it kinda dresses it up.

MRS. ZERO: Well, I always say it's all a matter of taste.

MRS. SIX: I saw you at the Rosebud Movie Thursday night, Mr. One.

ONE: Pretty punk show, I'll say.

TWO: They're gettin' worse all the time.

MRS. SIX: But who was the charming lady, Mr. One?

ONE: Now don't you go makin' trouble for me. That was my sister.

MRS. FIVE: Oho! That's what they all say.

MRS. FOUR: Never mind! I'll bet Mrs. One knows what's what, all right.

MRS. ONE: Oh, well, he can do what he likes —'slong as he behaves himself.

THREE: You're in luck at that, One. Fat chance I got of gettin' away from the frau even with my sister.

MRS. THREE: You oughta be glad you got a good wife to look after you.

THE OTHER WOMEN (in unison): That's right, Mrs. Three.

FIVE: I guess I know who wears the pants in your house, Three.

MRS. ZERO: Never mind. I saw them holdin' hands at the movie the other night.

THREE: She musta been tryin' to get some money away from me.

MRS. THREE: Swell chance anybody'd have of gettin' any money away from you.

(General laughter.)

FOUR: They sure are a loving couple.

MRS. TWO: Well, I think we oughta change the subject.

MRS. ONE: Yes, let's change the subject.

SIX (sotto voce): Did you hear the one about the travelin' salesman?

FIVE: It seems this guy was in a sleeper.

FOUR: Goin' from Albany to San Diego.

THREE: And in the next berth was an old maid.

TWO: With a wooden leg.

ONE: Well, along about midnight————

(They all put their heads together and whisper.)

MRS. SIX (sotto voce): Did you hear about the Sevens?

MRS. FIVE: They're gettin' a divorce.

MRS. FOUR: It's the second time for him.

MRS. THREE: They're two of a kind, if you ask me.

MRS. TWO: One's as bad as the other.

MRS. ONE: Worse.

MRS. ZERO: They say that she————

(They all put their heads together and whisper.)

SIX: I think this woman suffrage is the bunk.

FIVE: It sure is! Politics is a man's business.

FOUR: Woman's place is in the home.

THREE: That's it! Lookin' after the kids, 'stead of hangin' around the streets.

TWO: You hit the nail on the head that time.

ONE: The trouble is they don't know what they want.

MRS. SIX: Men sure get me tired.

MRS. FIVE: They sure are a lazy lot.

MRS. FOUR: And dirty.

MRS. THREE: Always grumblin' about somethin'.

MRS. TWO: When they're not lyin'!

MRS. ONE: Or messin' up the house.

MRS. ZERO: Well, believe me, I tell mine where he gets off.

SIX: Business conditions are sure bad.

FIVE: Never been worse.

FOUR: I don't know what we're comin' to.

THREE: I look for a big smash-up in about three months.

TWO: Wouldn't surprise me a bit.

ONE: We're sure headin' for trouble.

MRS. SIX: My aunt has gallstones.

MRS. FIVE: My husband has bunions.

MRS. FOUR: My sister expects next month.

MRS. THREE: My cousin's husband has erysipelas.

MRS. TWO: My niece has St. Vitus's dance.

MRS. ONE: My boy has fits.

MRS. ZERO: I never felt better in my life. Knock wood!

SIX: Too damn much agitation, that's at the bottom of it.

FIVE: That's it! Too damn many strikes.

FOUR: Foreign agitators, that's what it is.

THREE: They oughta be run outa the country.

TWO: What the hell do they want anyhow?

ONE: They don't know what they want, if you ask me.

SIX: America for the Americans is what I say!

ALL (*in unisons*): That's it! Damn foreigners! Damn dagoes! Damn Catholics! Damn sheenies! Damn niggers! Jail 'em! Shoot 'em! Hang 'em! Lynch 'em! Burn 'em! (*They all rise. Sing in unison.*)

My country 'tis of thee,
Sweet land of liberty!

MRS. FOUR: Why so pensive, Mr. Zero?

ZERO (*speaking for the first time*): I'm thinkin'.

MRS. FOUR: Well, be careful not to sprain your mind. (*Laughter.*)

MRS. ZERO: Look at the poor men all by themselves. We ain't very sociable.

ONE: Looks like we're neglectin' the ladies.

(*The women cross the room and join the men, all chattering loudly. The doorbell rings.*)

MRS. ZERO: Sh! The doorbell!

(*The volume of sound slowly diminishes. Again the doorbell.*)

ZERO (*quietly*): I'll go. It's for me.

(*They watch curiously as ZERO goes to the door and opens it, admitting a POLICEMAN. There is a murmur of surprise and excitement.*)

POLICEMAN: I'm lookin' for Mr. Zero.

(*They all point to ZERO.*)

ZERO: I've been expectin' you.

POLICEMAN: Come along!

ZERO: Just a minute. (*He puts his hand in his pocket.*)

POLICEMAN: What's he tryin' to pull? (*He draws a revolver.*) I got you covered.

ZERO: Sure, that's all right. I just want to give you somethin'. (*He takes the collar from his pocket and gives it to the POLICEMAN.*)

POLICEMAN (*suspiciously*): What's that?

ZERO: The collar I wore.

POLICEMAN: What do I want it for?

ZERO: It's got bloodstains on it.

POLICEMAN (*pocketing it*): All right, come along!

ZERO (*turning to MRS. ZERO*): I gotta go with him. You'll have to dry the dishes yourself.

MRS. ZERO (*rushing forward*): What are they takin' you for?

ZERO (*calmly*): I killed the boss this afternoon. (*The POLICEMAN takes him off.*)

SCENE 4

(*A court of justice. Three bare white walls without doors or windows except for a single door in the right wall. At the right is a jury box in which are seated MESSRS. ONE, TWO, THREE, FOUR, FIVE, and SIX and their respective wives. On either side of the jury box stands a uniformed officer. Opposite the jury box is a long, bare oak table piled high with law books. Behind the books ZERO is seated, his face buried in his hands. There is no other furniture in the room. A moment after the rise of the curtain one of the officers rises and, going around the table, taps ZERO on the shoulder. ZERO rises and accompanies the officer. The officer escorts him to the great empty space in the middle of the courtroom, facing the jury. He motions to ZERO to stop, then points to the jury and resumes his place beside the jury box. ZERO stands there looking at the jury, bewildered and half afraid. The jurors give no sign of having seen him. Throughout they sit with folded arms, staring stolidly before them.*)

ZERO (*beginning to speak, haltingly*): Sure I killed him. I ain't sayin' I didn't, am I? Sure I killed him. Them lawyers! They give me a good stiff pain, that's what they give me. Half the time I don't know what the hell they're talkin' about. Objection sustained. Objection overruled. What's the big idea anyhow? You ain't heard me do any objectin', have you? Sure not! What's the idea of objectin'? You got a right to know. What I say is, if one bird kills another bird, why you got a right to call him for it. That's what I say. I know all about that. I been on the jury too. Them lawyers! Don't let 'em fill you full of bunk. All that bull about it bein' red ink on the bill file. Red ink nothin'! It was blood, see? I want you to get that right—all of you. One, two, three, four, five, six, seven, eight, nine, ten, eleven, twelve. Twelve of you. Six and six. That makes twelve. I figgered it up often enough. Six and six makes twelve. And five is seventeen. And eight is twenty-five. And three is twenty-eight. Eight and carry two. Aw, cut it out! Them damn figgers! I can't forget 'em. Twenty-five years, see? Eight hours a day, exceptin' Sundays. And July and August half-day Saturday. One week's vacation with pay. And another week without pay if you want it. Who the hell wants it? Layin' around the house listenin' to the wife tellin' you where you get off. Nix! An' legal holidays. I nearly forgot them. New Year's, Washington's Birthday, Decoration Day, Fourth o' July, Labor Day, Election Day, Thanksgivin', Christmas. Good Friday if you want it. An' if you're a Jew, Young Kipper an' the other one—I forget what they call it. The dirty sheenies—always gettin' two to the other bird's one. An' when a holiday comes on Sunday, you get Monday off. So that's fair enough. But when the Fourth o' July comes on Saturday, why you're out o' luck on account of Saturday bein' a half-day anyhow. Get me? Twenty-five years— I'll tell you somethin' funny. Decoration Day an' the Fourth o' July are always on the same day o' the week. Twenty-five years. Never missed a day, and never more'n five minutes late. Look at my time card if you don't believe me. Eight twenty-seven, eight thirty, eight twenty-nine, eight twenty-seven, eight thirty-two. Eight an' thirty-two's forty an'—Goddam them figgers! I can't forget 'em. They're funny things, them figgers. They look like people sometimes. The eights, see? Two dots for the eyes and a dot for the nose. An' a line. That's the mouth, see? An' there's others remind you of other things—but I can't talk about them on account of there bein' ladies here. Sure I killed him. Why didn't he shut up? If he'd only shut up! Instead o' talkin' an' talkin' about how sorry he was an' what a good guy I was an' this an' that. I felt like sayin' to him: "For Christ's sake shut up!" But I didn't have the nerve, see? I didn't have the nerve to say that to the boss. An' he went on talkin', sayin' how sorry he was, see? He was standin' right close to me. An' his coat only had two buttons on it. Two an' two makes four an'—aw, can it. An' there was the bill file on the desk. Right where I could touch it. It ain't right to kill a guy. I know that. When I read all about him in the paper an' about his three kids I felt like a cheapskate, I tell you. They had the kids' pictures in the paper, right next to mine. An' his wife too. Gee, it must be swell to have a wife like that. Some guys sure is lucky An' he left fifty thousand dollars just for a rest room for the girls in the store. He was a good guy at that.

Fifty thousand. That's more'n twice as much as I'd have if I saved every nickel I ever made. Let's see. Twenty-five an' twenty-five an' twenty-five an'—aw, cut it out! An' the ads had a big, black border around 'em; an' all it said was that the store would be closed for three days on account of the boss bein' dead. That nearly handed me a laugh, that did. All them floorwalkers an' buyers an' high-muck-a-mucks havin' me to thank for gettin' three days off. I hadn't oughta killed him. I ain't sayin' nothin' about that. But I thought he was goin' to give me a raise, see? On account of bein' there twenty-five years. He never talked to me before, see? Except one mornin' we happened to come in the store together and I held the door open for him and he said "Thanks." Just like that, see? "Thanks!" That was the only time he ever talked to me. An' when I seen him comin' up to my desk, I didn't know where I got off. A big guy like that comin' up to my desk. I felt like I was chokin' like and all of a sudden I got a kind o' bad taste in my mouth like when you get up in the mornin'. I didn't have no right to kill him. The district attorney is right about that. He read the law to you, right out o' the book. Killin' a bird—that's wrong. But there was that girl, see? Six months they gave her. It was a dirty trick tellin' the cops on her like that. I shouldn't 'a' done that. But what was I gonna do? The wife wouldn't let up on me. I hadda do it. She used to walk around the room, just in her undershirt, see? Nothin' else on. Just her undershirt. An' they gave her six months. That's the last I'll ever see of her. Them birds—how do they get away with it? Just grabbin' women, the way you see 'em do in the pictures. I've seen lots I'd like to grab like that, but I ain't got the nerve—in the subway an' on the street an' in the store buyin' things. Pretty soft for them shoe salesmen, I'll say, lookin' at women's legs all day. Them lawyers! They give me a pain, I tell you—a pain! Sayin' the same thing over an' over again. I never said I didn't kill him. But that ain't the same as bein' a regular murderer. What good did it do me to kill him? I didn't make nothin' out of it. Answer yes or no! Yes or no, me elbow! There's some things you can't answer yes or no. Give me the once-over, you guys. Do I look like a murderer? Do I? I never did no harm to nobody. Ask the wife. She'll tell you. Ask anybody. I never got into trouble. You wouldn't count that one time at the Polo Grounds. That was just fun like. Everybody was yellin', "Kill the empire! Kill the empire!" An' before I knew what I was doin' I fired the pop bottle. It was on account of everybody yellin' like that. Just in fun like, see? The yeller dog! Callin' that one a strike—a mile away from the plate. Anyhow, the bottle didn't hit him. An' when I seen the cop comin' up the aisle, I beat it. That didn't hurt nobody. It was just in fun like, see? An' that time in the subway. I was readin' about a lynchin', see? Down in Georgia. They took the nigger an' they tied him to a tree. An' they poured kerosene on him and lit a big fire under him. The dirty nigger! Boy, I'd of liked to been there, with a gat in each hand, pumpin' him full of lead. I was readin' about it in the subway, see? Right at Times Square where the big crowd gets on. An' all of a sudden this big nigger steps right on my foot. It was lucky for him I didn't have a gun on me. I'd of killed him sure, I guess. I guess he couldn't help it all right on account of the crowd, but a nigger's got no right to step on a white man's foot. I told him where he got off all right. The dirty nigger. But that didn't hurt nobody either. I'm a pretty steady guy, you gotta admit that. Twenty-five years in one job an' I never missed a day. Fifty-two weeks in a year. Fifty-two an' fifty-two an' fifty-two an'—They didn't have t' look for me, did they? I didn't try to run away, did I? Where was I goin' to run to! I wasn't thinkin' about it at all, see? I'll tell you what I was thinkin' about—how I was goin' to break it to the wife about bein' canned. He canned me after twenty-five years, see? Did the lawyers tell you about that? I forget. All that talk gives me a headache. Objection sustained. Objection overruled. Answer yes or no. It gives me a headache. And I can't get the figgers outta my head neither. But that's what I was thinkin' about—how I was goin' t' break it to the wife about bein' canned. An' what Miss Devore would think when she heard about me killin' him. I bet she never thought I had the nerve to do it. I'd of married her if the wife had passed out. I'd be holdin' down my job yet if he hadn't o' canned me. But he kept talkin' an' talkin'. An' there was the bill file right where I could reach it. Do you get me? I'm just a regular guy like anybody else. Like you birds, now. (For the first time the jurors relax, looking indignantly at each other and whispering.)

Suppose you was me, now. Maybe you'd 'a' done the same thing. That's the way you oughta look at it, see? Suppose you was me——

JURORS (rising as one and shouting in unison): GUILTY!

(ZERO falls back, stunned for a moment by their vociferousness. The JURORS right-face in their places and file quickly out of the jury box and toward the door in a double column.)

ZERO (recovering speech as the JURORS pass out at the door): Wait a minute. Jest a minute. You don't get me right. Jest give me a chance an' I'll tell you how it was. I'm all mixed up, see? On account of them lawyers. And the figgers in my head. But I'm goin' to tell you how it was. I was there twenty-five years, see? An' they gave her six months, see?

(He goes on haranguing the empty jury box as the curtain falls.)

SCENE 5*

(In the middle of the stage is a large cage with bars on all four sides. The bars are very far apart and the interior of the cage is clearly visible. The floor of the cage is about six feet above the level of the stage. A flight of wooden steps lead up to it on the side facing the audience. ZERO is discovered in the middle of the cage seated at a table above which is suspended a single naked electric light. Before him is an enormous platter of ham and eggs which he eats voraciously with a large wooden spoon. He wears a uniform of very broad black and white horizontal stripes. A few moments after the rise of the curtain a man enters at left, wearing the blue uniform and peaked cap of a GUIDE. He is followed by a miscellaneous crowd of Men, Women, and Children—about a dozen in all.)

GUIDE (stopping in front of the cage): Now ladies and gentlemen, if you'll kindly step right this way! (The crowd straggles up and forms a loose semi-circle around him.) Step right up, please. A little closer so's everybody can hear. (They move up closer. ZERO pays no attention whatever to them.) This, ladies and gentlemen, is a very inter-est-in' specimen; the North American murderer, Genus homo sapiens, Habitat North America. (A titter of excitement. They all crowd up around the cage.) Don't push. There's room enough for everybody.

TALL LADY: Oh, how interesting!

---

* Note: This scene was part of the original script. It was omitted, however, when the play was produced, and was performed for the first time (in its present revised form) when the play was revived at the Phoenix Theatre in New York in February, 1956.—ELMER RICE

STOUT LADY (*excitedly*): Look, Charley, he's eating!

CHARLEY (*bored*): Yeh, I see him.

GUIDE (*repeating by rote*): This specimen, ladies and gentlemen, exhibits the characteristics which are typical of his kind———

SMALL BOY (*in a Little Lord Fauntleroy suit, whiningly*): Mama!

MOTHER: Be quiet, Eustace, or I'll take you right home.

GUIDE: He has the opposable thumbs, the large cranial capacity, and the highly developed prefrontal areas which distinguish him from all other species.

YOUTH (*who has been taking notes*): What areas did you say?

GUIDE (*grumpily*): Pre-front-al areas. He learns by imitation and has a language which is said by some eminent philiologists to bear many striking resemblances to English.

BOY OF FOURTEEN: Pop, what's a philiologist?

FATHER: Keep quiet, can't you, and listen to what he's sayin'.

GUIDE: He thrives and breeds freely in captivity. This specimen was taken alive in his native haunts shortly after murdering his boss. (*Murmurs of great interest.*)

TALL LADY: Oh, how charming!

YOUTH (*again taking notes*): What was that last? I didn't get it.

SEVERAL (*helpfully*): Murdering his boss.

YOUTH: Oh—thanks.

GUIDE: He was tried, convicted and sentenced in one hour, thirteen minutes and twenty-four seconds, which sets a new record for the territory east of the Rockies and north of the Mason and Dixon line.

LITTLE LORD FAUNTLEROY (*whiningly*): Ma-ma!

MOTHER: Be quiet, Eustace, or Mama won't let you ride in the choo-choo.

GUIDE: Now take a good look at him, ladies and gents. It's his last day here. He's goin' to be executed at noon. (*Murmurs of interest.*)

TALL LADY: Oh, how lovely!

MAN: What's he eating?

GUIDE: Ham and eggs.

STOUT LADY: He's quite a big eater, ain't he?

GUIDE: Oh, he don't always eat that much. You see we always try to make 'em feel good on their last day. So about a week in advance we let them order what they want to eat on their last day. They can have eight courses and they can order anything they want—don't make no difference what it costs or how hard it is to get. Well, he couldn't make up his mind till last night and then he ordered eight courses of ham and eggs. (*They all push and stare.*)

BOY OF FOURTEEN: Look, Pop! He's eatin' with a spoon. Don't he know how to use a knife and fork?

GUIDE (*overhearing him*): We don't dare trust him with a knife and fork, sonny. He might try to kill himself.

TALL LADY: Oh, how fascinating!

GUIDE (*resuming his official tone*): And now, friends, if you'll kindly give me your kind attention for just a moment. (*He takes a bundle of folders from his pocket.*) I have a little souvenir folder, which I'm sure you'll all want to have. It contains twelve beautiful colored views relating to the North American Murderer you have just been looking at. These include a picture of the murderer, a picture of the murderer's wife, the blood-stained weapon, the murderer at the age of six, the spot where the body was found, the little red schoolhouse where he went to school, and his vine-covered boyhood home in southern Illinois, with his sweet-faced, white-haired old mother plainly visible in the foreground. And many other interesting views. I'm now going to distribute these little folders for your examination. (*Sotto voce.*) Just pass them back, will you. (*In louder tones.*) Don't be afraid to look at them. You don't have to buy them if you don't want to. It don't cost anything to look at them. (*To the* YOUTH, *who is fumbling with a camera.*) Hey, there, young feller, no snapshots allowed. All right now, friends, if you'll just step this way. Keep close together and follow me. A lady lost her little boy here one time and by the time we found him, he was smoking cigarettes and hollering for a razor.

(*Much laughter as they all follow him off left.* ZERO *finishes eating and pushes away his plate. As the crowd goes at left,* MRS. ZERO *enters at right. She is dressed in mourning garments. She carries a large parcel. She goes up the steps to the cage, opens the door, and enters.* ZERO *looks up and sees her.*)

MRS. ZERO: Hello.

ZERO: Hello, I didn't think you were comin' again.

MRS. ZERO: Well, I thought I'd come again. Are you glad to see me?

ZERO: Sure, Sit down. (*She complies.*) You're all dolled up, ain't you?

MRS. ZERO: Yeh, don't you like it? (*She gets up and turns about like a mannequin.*)

ZERO: Gee. Some class.

MRS. ZERO: I always look good in black.

There's some weight to this veil though; I'll tell the world. I got a fierce headache.

ZERO: How much did all that set you back?

MRS. ZERO: Sixty-four dollars and twenty cents. And I gotta get a pin yet and some writin' paper—you know, with black around the edges.

ZERO: You'll be scrubbin' floors in about a year, if you go blowin' your coin like that.

MRS. ZERO: Well, I gotta do it right. It don't happen every day. (*She rises and takes up the parcel.*) I brought you somethin'.

ZERO (*interested*): Yeh, what?

MRS. ZERO (*opening the parcel*): You gotta guess.

ZERO: Er—er—gee, search me.

MRS. ZERO: Somethin' you like. (*She takes out a covered plate.*)

ZERO (*with increasing interest*): Looks like somethin' to eat.

MRS. ZERO (*nodding*): Yeh. (*She takes off the top plate.*) Ham an' eggs!

ZERO (*joyfully*): Oh, boy! Just what I feel like eatin'. (*He takes up the wooden spoon and begins to eat avidly.*)

MRS. ZERO (*pleased*): Are they good?

ZERO (*his mouth full*): Swell.

MRS. ZERO (*a little sadly*): They're the last ones I'll ever make for you.

ZERO (*busily eating*): Uh-huh.

MRS. ZERO: I'll tell you somethin'—shall I?

ZERO: Sure.

MRS. ZERO (*hesitantly*): Well, all the while they were cookin' I was cryin'.

ZERO: Yeh? (*He leans over and pats her hand.*)

MRS. ZERO: I jest couldn't help it. The thought of it jest made me cry.

ZERO: Well—no use cryin' about it.

MRS. ZERO: I jest couldn't help it.

ZERO: Maybe this time next year you'll be fryin' eggs for some other bird.

MRS. ZERO: Not on your life.

ZERO: You never can tell.

MRS. ZERO: Not me. Once is enough for me.

ZERO: I guess you're right at that. Still, I dunno. You might jest happen to meet some guy———

MRS. ZERO: Well, if I do, there'll be time enough to think about it. No use borrowin' trouble.

ZERO: How do you like bein' alone in the house?

MRS. ZERO: Oh, it's all right.

ZERO: You got plenty room in the bed now, ain't you?

MRS. ZERO: Oh yeh. (*A brief pause.*) It's kinda lonesome though—you know, wakin' up in the mornin' and nobody around to talk to.

ZERO: Yeh, I know. It's the same with me.

MRS. ZERO: Not that we ever did much talkin'.

ZERO: Well, that ain't it. It's just the idea of havin' somebody there in case you want to talk.

MRS. ZERO: Yeh, that's it. (*Another brief pause.*) I guess maybe I use t'bawl you out quite a lot, didn't I?

ZERO: Oh well—no use talkin' about it now.

MRS. ZERO: We were always at it, weren't we?

ZERO: No more than any other married folks, I guess.

MRS. ZERO (*dubiously*): I dunno———

ZERO: I guess I gave you cause, all right.

MRS. ZERO: Well, I got my faults too.

ZERO: None of us are perfect.

MRS. ZERO: We got along all right, at that, didn't we?

ZERO: Sure! Better'n most.

MRS. ZERO: Remember them Sundays at the beach, in the old days?

ZERO: You bet. (*With a laugh.*) Remember that time I ducked you? Gee, you was mad!

MRS. ZERO (*with a laugh*): I didn't talk to you for a whole week.

ZERO (*chuckling*): Yeh, I remember.

MRS. ZERO: And the time I had pneumonia and you brought me them roses. Remember?

ZERO: Yeh, I remember. And when the doctor told me maybe you'd pass out, I nearly sat down and cried.

MRS. ZERO: Did you?

ZERO: I sure did.

MRS. ZERO: We had some pretty good times at that, didn't we?

ZERO: I'll say we did!

MRS. ZERO (*with a sudden soberness*): It's all over now.

ZERO: All over is right. I ain't got much longer.

MRS. ZERO (*rising and going over to him*): Maybe—maybe—If we had to do it over again, it would be different.

ZERO (*taking her hand*): Yeh. We live and learn.

MRS. ZERO (*crying*): If we only had another chance.

ZERO: It's too late now.

MRS. ZERO: It don't seem right, does it?

ZERO: It ain't right. But what can you do about it?

MRS. ZERO: Ain't there somethin'—somethin' I can do for you—before———

ZERO: No. Nothin'. Not a thing.

MRS. ZERO: Nothin' at all?

ZERO: No. I can't think of anything. (*Suddenly.*) You're takin' good care of that scrapbook, ain't you? With all the clippings in it?

MRS. ZERO: Oh, sure. I got it right on the parlor table. Right where everybody can see it.

ZERO (*pleased*): It must be pretty near full, ain't it?

MRS. ZERO: All but about three pages.

ZERO: Well, there'll be more tomorrow. Enough to fill it, maybe. Be sure to get them all, will you?

MRS. ZERO: I will. I ordered the papers already.

ZERO: Gee, I never thought I'd have a whole book full of clippings all about myself. (*Suddenly.*) Say, that's somethin' I'd like to ask you.

MRS. ZERO: What?

ZERO: Suppose you should get sick or be run over or somethin', what would happen to the book?

MRS. ZERO: Well, I kinda thought I'd leave it to little Beatrice Elizabeth.

ZERO: Who? Your sister's kid?

MRS. ZERO: Yeh.

ZERO: What would she want with it?

MRS. ZERO: Well, it's nice to have, ain't it? And I wouldn't know who else to give it to.

ZERO: Well, I don't want her to have it. That fresh little kid puttin' her dirty fingers all over it.

MRS. ZERO: She ain't fresh and she ain't dirty. She's a sweet little thing.

ZERO: I don't want her to have it.

MRS. ZERO: Who do you want to have it then?

ZERO: Well, I kinda thought I'd like Miss Devore to have it.

MRS. ZERO: Miss Devore?

ZERO: Yeh. You know. Down at the store.

MRS. ZERO: Why should she have it?

ZERO: She'd take good care of it. And anyhow, I'd like her to have it.

MRS. ZERO: Oh you would, would you?

ZERO: Yes.

MRS. ZERO: Well, she ain't goin' to have it. Miss Devore! Where does she come in, I'd like to know, when I got two sisters and a niece.

ZERO: I don't care nothin' about your sisters and your niece.

MRS. ZERO: Well, I do! And Miss Devore ain't goin' to get it. Now put that in your pipe and smoke it.

ZERO: What have you got to say about it? It's my book, ain't it?

MRS. ZERO: No, it ain't. It's mine now—or it will be tomorrow. And I'm goin' to do what I like with it.

ZERO: I should of given it to her in the first place, that's what I should of done.

MRS. ZERO: Oh, should you? And what about me? Am I your wife or ain't I?

ZERO: Why remind me of my troubles?

MRS. ZERO: So it's Miss Devore all of a sudden, is it? What's been goin' on, I'd like to know, between you and Miss Devore?

ZERO: Aw, tie a can to that!

MRS. ZERO: Why didn't you marry Miss Devore, if you think so much of her?

ZERO: I would have if I'd of met her first.

MRS. ZERO (*shrieking*): Ooh! A fine way to talk to me. After all I've done for you. You bum! You dirty bum! I won't stand for it! I won't stand for it!

(*In a great rage* MRS. ZERO *takes up the dishes and smashes them on the floor. Then crying hysterically she opens the cage door, bangs it behind her, comes down the steps, and goes off toward left.* ZERO *stands gazing the ruefully after her for a moment and then with a shrug and a sigh begins picking up the pieces of broken crockery.*

As MRS. ZERO *exits at left a door in the back of the cage opens and a* MAN *enters. He is dressed in a sky-blue padded silk dressing gown which is fitted with innumerable pockets. Under this he wears a pink silk union suit. His bare feet are in sandals. He wears a jaunty Panama hat with a red feather stuck in the brim. Wings are fastened to his sandals and to the shoulders of his dressing gown.* ZERO, *who is busy picking up the broken crockery, does not notice him at first. The* MAN *takes a gold toothpick and begins carefully picking his teeth, waiting for* ZERO *to notice him.* ZERO *happens to look up and suddenly sees the* MAN. *He utters a cry of terror and shrinks into a corner of the cage, trembling with fear.*)

ZERO (*hoarsely*): Who are you?

MAN (*calmly, as he pockets his toothpick*): I'm the Fixer—from the Claim Department.

ZERO: Whaddya want?

THE FIXER: It's no use, Zero. There are no miracles.

ZERO: I don't know what you're talkin' about.

THE FIXER: Don't lie, Zero. (*Holding up his hand.*) And now that your course is run—now that the end is already in sight, you still believe that some thunderbolt, some fiery bush, some celestial apparition will intervene between you and extinction. But it's no use, Zero. You're done for.

ZERO (*vehemently*): It ain't right! It ain't fair! I ain't gettin' a square deal!

THE FIXER (*wearily*): They all say that, Zero. (*Mildly.*) Now just tell me why you're not getting a square deal.

ZERO: Well, that addin' machine. Was that a square deal—after twenty-five years?

THE FIXER: Certainly—from any point of view, except a sentimental one. (*Looking at his wrist watch.*) The machine is quicker, it never makes a mistake, it's always on time. It presents no problems of housing, traffic congestion, water supply, sanitation.

ZERO: It costs somethin' to buy them machines, I'll tell you that!

THE FIXER: Yes, you're right there. In one respect you have the advantage over the machine —the cost of manufacture. But we've learned from many years' experience, Zero, that the original cost is an inconsequential item compared to upkeep. Take the dinosaurs, for example. They literally ate themselves out of existence. I held out for them to the last. They were damned picturesque—but when it came to a question of the nitrate supply, I simply had to yield. (*He begins to empty and clean his pipe.*) And so with you, Zero. It costs a lot to keep up all that delicate mechanism of eye and ear and hand and brain which you've never put to any use. We can't afford to maintain it in idleness—and so you've got to go. (*He puts the pipe in one of his pockets.*)

ZERO (*falling to his knees, supplicatingly*): Gimme a chance, gimme another chance!

THE FIXER: What would you do if I gave you another chance?

ZERO: Well—first thing I'd go out and look for a job.

THE FIXER: Adding figures?

ZERO: Well, I ain't young enough to take up somethin' new.

(THE FIXER *takes out a police whistle and blows shrilly. Instantly two guards enter.*)

THE FIXER: Put the skids under him, boys, and make it snappy. (*He strolls away to the other side of the cage, and taking a nail clipper from a pocket, begins to clip his nails as the* GUARDS *seize* ZERO.)

ZERO (*struggling and shrieking*): No! No! Don't take me away! Don't kill me! Gimme a chance! Gimme another chance!

GUARD (*soothingly*): Ah, come on! Be a good fellow! It'll all be over in a minute!

ZERO: I don't want to die! I don't want to die! I want to live!

(THE GUARDS *look at each other dubiously. Then one of them walks rather timidly over to* THE FIXER, *who is busy with his nails.*)

GUARD (*clearing his throat*): H'm!

THE FIXER (*looking up*): Well?

GUARD (*timidly*): He says he wants to live.

THE FIXER: No. He's no good.

GUARD (*touching his cap, deferentially*): Yes sir! (*He goes back to his companion and the two of them drag* ZERO *out at the back of the cage, still struggling and screaming.*)

(THE FIXER *puts away his nail clippers, yawns, then goes to the table and sits on the edge of it. From a pocket he takes an enormous pair of horn-rimmed spectacles. Then from another pocket he takes a folded newspaper, which he unfolds carefully. It is a colored comic supplement. He holds it up in front of him and becomes absorbed in it.*

A moment later the door at the back of the cage opens and a tall, brawny, bearded MAN *enters. He wears a red flannel undershirt and carries a huge blood-stained axe.* THE FIXER, *absorbed in the comic supplement, does not look up.*)

MAN (*hoarsely*): O.K.

THE FIXER (*looking up*): What?

MAN: O.K.

THE FIXER (*nodding*): Oh, all right. (*The* MAN *bows deferentially and goes out at the back.* THE FIXER *puts away his spectacles and folds the comic supplement carefully. As he folds the paper.*) That makes a total of 2,137 black eyes for Jeff.

(*He puts away the paper, turns out the electric light over his head, and leaves the cage by the front door. Then he takes a padlock from a pocket, attaches it to the door, and saunters off.*)

SCENE 6

(*A graveyard in full moonlight. It is a second-rate graveyard—no elaborate tombstones or monuments, just simple headstones and here and there a cross. At the back is an iron fence with a gate in the middle. At first no one is visible, but there are occasional sounds throughout: the hooting of an owl, the whistle of a distant whippoorwill, the croaking of a bullfrog, and the yowling of a serenading cat. After a few moments two figures appear outside the gate—a man and a woman. She pushes the gate and it opens with a rusty creak. The couple enter. They are now fully visible in the moonlight—*JUDY O'GRADY *and a* YOUNG MAN.)

JUDY (*advancing*): Come on, this is the place.

YOUNG MAN (*hanging back*): This! Why this here is a cemetery.

JUDY: Aw, quit yer kiddin'!

YOUNG MAN: You don't mean to say——

JUDY: What's the matter with this place?

YOUNG MAN: A cemetery!

JUDY: Sure. What of it?

YOUNG MAN: You must be crazy.

JUDY: This place is all right, I tell you. I been here lots o' times.

YOUNG MAN: Nix on this place for me!

JUDY: Ain't this place as good as another? Whaddya afraid of? They're all dead ones here! They don't bother you. (*With sudden interest.*) Oh, look, here's a new one.

YOUNG MAN: Come on out of here.

JUDY: Wait a minute. Let's see what it says. (*She kneels on a grave in the foreground and putting her face close to the headstone spells out the inscription.*) Z-E-R-O. Z-e-r-o. Zero! Say, that's the guy——

YOUNG MAN: Zero? He's the guy killed his boss, ain't he?

JUDY: Yeh, that's him, all right. But what I'm thinkin' of is that I went to the hoosegow on account of him.

YOUNG MAN: What for?

JUDY: You know, same old stuff. Tenement House Law. (*Mincingly.*) Section blaa-blaa of the Penal Code. Third offense. Six months.

YOUNG MAN: And this bird——

JUDY (*contemptuously*): Him? He was mama's white-haired boy. We lived in the same house. Across the airshaft, see? I used to see him lookin' in my window. I guess his wife musta seen him too. Anyhow, they went and turned the bulls on me. And now I'm out and he's in. (*Suddenly.*) Say—say——(*She bursts into a peal of laughter.*)

YOUNG MAN (*nervously*): What's so funny?

JUDY (*rocking with laughter*): Say, wouldn't it be funny—if—if——(*She explodes again.*) That would be a good joke on him, all right. He can't do nothin' about it now, can he?

YOUNG MAN: Come on out of here. I don't like this place.

JUDY: Aw, you're a bum sport. What do you want to spoil my joke for?

(*A cat yammers mellifluously.*)

YOUNG MAN (*half hysterically*): What's that?

JUDY: It's only the cats. They seem to like it here all right. But come on if you're afraid. (*They go toward the gate. As they go out.*) You nervous men sure are the limit.

(*They go out through the gate. As they disappear* ZERO'S *grave opens suddenly and his head appears.*)

ZERO (*looking about*): That's funny! I thought I heard her talkin' and laughin'. But I don't see nobody. Anyhow, what would she be doin' here? I guess I must 'a' been dreamin'. But how could I be dreamin' when I ain't been asleep? (*He looks about again.*) Well, no use goin' back. I can't sleep anyhow. I might as well walk around a little. (*He rises out of the ground, very rigidly. He wears a full-dress suit of very antiquated cut and his hands are folded stiffly across his breast. Walking woodenly.*) Gee! I'm stiff! (*He slowly walks a few steps, then stops.*) Gee, it's lonesome here! (*He shivers and walks on aimlessly.*) I should 'a' stayed where I was. But I thought I heard her laughin'. (*A loud sneeze is heard.* ZERO *stands motionless, quaking with terror. The sneeze is repeated.* ZERO *says hoarsely.*) What's that?

A MILD VOICE: It's all right. Nothing to be afraid of.

(*From behind a headstone* SHRDLU *appears. He is dressed in a shabby and ill-fitting cutaway. He wears silver-rimmed spectacles and is smoking a cigarette.*)

SHRDLU: I hope I didn't frighten you.

ZERO (*still badly shaken*): No-o. It's all right. You see, I wasn't expectin' to see anybody.

SHRDLU: You're a newcomer, aren't you?

ZERO: Yeh, this is my first night. I couldn't seem to get to sleep.

SHRDLU: I can't sleep either. Suppose we keep each other company, shall we?

ZERO (*eagerly*): Yeh, that would be great. I been feelin' awful lonesome.

SHRDLU (*nodding*): I know. Let's make ourselves comfortable.

(*He seats himself easily on a grave.* ZERO *tries to follow his example but he is stiff in every joint and groans with pain.*)

ZERO: I'm kinda stiff.

SHRDLU: You mustn't mind the stiffness. It wears off in a few days. (*He produces a package of cigarettes.*) Will you have a Camel?

ZERO: No, I don't smoke.

SHRDLU: I find it helps keep the mosquitoes away. (*He lights a cigarette. Suddenly taking the cigarette out of his mouth.*) Do you mind if I smoke, Mr.—Mr.—?

ZERO: No, go right ahead.

SHRDLU (*replacing the cigarette*): Thank you. I didn't catch your name. (ZERO *does not reply,*

Mildly.) I say I didn't catch your name.

ZERO: I heard you the first time. (*Hesitantly.*) I'm scared if I tell you who I am and what I done, you'll be off me.

SHRDLU (*sadly*): No matter what your sins may be, they are as snow compared to mine.

ZERO: You got another guess comin'. (*He pauses dramatically.*) My names's Zero. I'm a murderer.

SHRDLU (*nodding calmly*): Oh, yes, I remember reading about you, Mr. Zero.

ZERO (*a little piqued*): And you still think you're worse than me?

SHRDLU (*throwing away his cigarette*): Oh, a thousand times worse, Mr. Zero—a million times worse.

ZERO: What did you do?

SHRDLU: I, too, am a murderer.

ZERO (*looking at him in amazement*): Go on! You're kiddin' me!

SHRDLU: Every word I speak is the truth, Mr. Zero. I am the foulest, the most sinful of murderers! You only murdered your employer, Mr. Zero. But I—I murdered my mother. (*He covers his face with his hands and sobs.*)

ZERO (*horrified*): The hell yer say!

SHRDLU (*sobbing*): Yes, my mother! My beloved mother!

ZERO (*suddenly*): Say, you don't mean to say you're Mr.———

SHRDLU (*nodding*): Yes. (*He wipes his eyes, still quivering with emotion.*)

ZERO: I remember readin' about you in the papers.

SHRDLU: Yes, my guilt has been proclaimed to all the world. But that would be a trifle if only I could wash the stain of sin from my soul.

ZERO: I never heard of a guy killin' his mother before. What did you do it for?

SHRDLU: Because I have a sinful heart—there is no other reason.

ZERO: Did she always treat you square and all like that?

SHRDLU: She was a saint—a saint, I tell you. She cared for me and watched over me as only a mother can.

ZERO: You mean to say you didn't have a scrap or nothin'?

SHRDLU: Never a harsh or an unkind word. Nothing except loving care and good advice. From my infancy she devoted herself to guiding me on the right path. She taught me to be thrifty, to be devout, to be unselfish, to shun evil companions, and to shut my ears to all the temptations of the flesh—in short, to become a virtuous, respectable, and God-fearing man. (*He groans.*) But it was a hopeless task. At fourteen I began to show evidence of my sinful nature.

ZERO (*breathlessly*): You didn't kill anybody else, did you?

SHRDLU: No, thank God, there is only one murder on my soul. But I ran away from home.

ZERO: You did!

SHRDLU: Yes, A companion lent me a profane book—the only profane book I have ever read, I'm thankful to say. It was called *Treasure Island.* Have you ever read it?

ZERO: No, I never was much on readin' books.

SHRDLU: It is a wicked book—a lurid tale of adventure. But it kindled in my sinful heart a desire to go to sea. And so I ran away from home.

ZERO: What did you do—get a job as a sailor?

SHRDLU: I never saw the sea—not to the day of my death. Luckily my mother's loving intuition warned her of my intention and I was sent back home. She welcomed me with open arms. Not an angry word, not a look of reproach. But I could read the mute suffering in her eyes as we prayed together all through the night.

ZERO (*sympathetically*): Gee, that must 'a' been tough. Gee, the mosquitoes are bad, ain't they? (*He tries awkwardly to slap at them with his stiff hands.*)

SHRDLU (*absorbed in his narrative*): I thought that experience had cured me of evil and I began to think about a career. I wanted to go in foreign missions at first, but we couldn't bear the thought of the separation. So we finally decided that I should become a proofreader.

ZERO: Say, slip me one o' them Camels, will you? I'm gettin' all bit up.

SHRDLU: Certainly. (*He hands* ZERO *cigarettes and matches.*)

ZERO (*lighting up*): Go ahead. I'm listenin'.

SHRDLU: By the time I was twenty I had a good job reading proof for a firm that printed catalogues. After a year they promoted me and let me specialize in shoe catalogues.

ZERO: Yeh? That must 'a' been a good job.

SHRDLU: It was a very good job. I was on the shoe catalogues for thirteen years. I'd been on them yet, if I hadn't———(*He chokes back a sob.*)

ZERO: They oughta put a shot o' citronella in that embalmin' fluid.

SHRDLU (*sighs*): We were so happy together. I

had my steady job. And Sundays we would go to morning, afternoon, and evening service. It was an honest and moral mode of life.

ZERO: It sure was.

SHRDLU: Then came that fatal Sunday. Dr. Amaranth, our minister, was having dinner with us—one of the few pure spirits on earth. When he had finished saying grace, we had our soup. Everything was going along as usual—we were eating our soup and discussing the sermon, just like every other Sunday I could remember. Then came the leg of lamb————(*He breaks off, then resumes in a choking voice.*) I see the whole scene before me so plainly—it never leaves me—Dr. Amaranth at my right, my mother at my left, the leg of lamb on the table in front of me, and the cuckoo clock on the little shelf between the windows. (*He stops and wipes his eyes.*)

ZERO: Yeh, but what happened?

SHRDLU: Well, as I started to carve the lamb ————Did you ever carve a leg of lamb?

ZERO: No, corned beef was our speed.

SHRDLU: It's very difficult on account of the bone. And when there's gravy in the dish there's danger of spilling it. So Mother always used to hold the dish for me. She leaned forward, just as she always did, and I could see the gold locket around her neck. It had my picture in it and one of my baby curls. Well, I raised my knife to carve the leg of lamb—and instead I cut my mother's throat! (*He sobs.*)

ZERO: You must 'a' been crazy!

SHRDLU (*raising his head, vehemently*): No! Don't try to justify me. I wasn't crazy. They tried to prove at the trial that I was crazy. But Dr. Amaranth saw the truth! He saw it from the first! He knew that it was my sinful nature—and he told me what was in store for me.

ZERO (*trying to be comforting*): Well, your troubles are over now.

SHRDLU (*his voice rising*): Over! Do you think this is the end?

ZERO: Sure. What more can they do to us?

SHRDLU (*his tones growing shriller and shriller*): Do you think there can ever be any peace for such as we are—murderers, sinners? Don't you know what awaits us—flames, eternal flames!

ZERO (*nervously*): Keep your shirt on, buddy —they wouldn't do that to us.

SHRDLU: There's no escape—no escape for us, I tell you. We're doomed! We're doomed to suffer unspeakable torments through all eternity. (*His voice rises higher and higher.*)

(*A grave opens suddenly and a head appears.*)

THE HEAD: Hey, you birds! Can't you shut up and let a guy sleep?

(ZERO *scrambles painfully to his feet.*)

ZERO (*to* SHRDLU): Hey, put on the soft pedal.

SHRDLU (*too wrought up to attend*): It won't be long now! We'll receive our summons soon.

THE HEAD: Are you goin' to beat it or not? (*He calls into the grave.*) Hey, Bill, lend me your head a minute. (*A moment later his arm appears holding a skull.*)

ZERO (*warningly*): Look out! (*He seizes* SHRDLU *and drags him away just as* THE HEAD *throws the skull.*)

THE HEAD (*disgustedly*): Missed 'em. Damn old tabby cats! I'll get 'em next time. (*A prodigious yawn.*) Ho-hum! Me for the worms!

(THE HEAD *disappears as the curtain falls.*)

SCENE 7

(*A pleasant place. A scene of pastoral loveliness. A meadow dotted with fine old trees and carpeted with rich grass and field flowers. In the background are seen a number of tents fashioned of gay-striped silks, and beyond gleams a meandering river. Clear air and a fleckless sky. Sweet distant music throughout.*

At the rise of the curtain SHRDLU *is seen seated under a tree in the foreground in an attitude of deep dejection. His knees are drawn up and his head is buried in his arms. He is dressed as in the preceding scene.*

A few minutes later ZERO *enters at right. He walks slowly and looks about him with an air of half-suspicious curiosity. He too is dressed as in the preceding scene. Suddenly he sees* SHRDLU *seated under the tree. He stands still and looks at him half fearfully. Then, seeing something familiar in him, goes closer.* SHRDLU *is unaware of his presence. At last* ZERO *recognizes him and grins in pleased surprise.*)

ZERO: Well, if it ain't————! (*He claps* SHRDLU *on the shoulder.*) Hello, buddy!

(SHRDLU *looks up slowly, then, recognizing* ZERO, *he rises gravely and extends his hand courteously.*)

SHRDLU: How do you do, Mr. Zero? I'm very glad to see you again.

ZERO: Same here. I wasn't expectin' to see you either. (*Looking about.*) This is a kinda nice place. I wouldn't mind restin' here a while.

SHRDLU: You may if you wish.

ZERO: I'm kinda tired. I ain't used to bein' outdoors. I ain't walked so much in years.

SHRDLU: Sit down here, under the tree.

ZERO: Do they let you sit on the grass?

SHRDLU: Oh, yes.

ZERO (seating himself): Boy, this feels good. I'll tell the world my feet are sore. I ain't used to so much walkin'. Say, I wonder would it be all right if I took my shoes off; my feet are tired.

SHRDLU: Yes. Some of the people here go barefoot.

ZERO: Ych? They sure must be nuts. But I'm goin' t' leave 'em off for a while. So long as it's all right. The grass feels nice and cool. (He stretches out comfortably.) Say, this is the life of Riley all right, all right. This sure is a nice place. What do they call this place, anyhow?

SHRDLU: The Elysian Fields.

ZERO: The which?

SHRDLU: The Elysian Fields.

ZERO (dubiously): Oh! Well, it's a nice place all right.

SHRDLU: They say that this is the most desirable of all places. Only the most favored remain here.

ZERO: Yeh? Well, that lets me out, I guess. (Suddenly.) But what are you doin' here? I thought you'd be burned by now.

SHRDLU (sadly): Mr. Zero, I am the most unhappy of men.

ZERO (in mild astonishment): Why, because you ain't bein' roasted alive?

SHRDLU (nodding): Nothing is turning out as I expected. I saw everything so clearly—the flames, the tortures, an eternity of suffering as the just punishment for my unspeakable crime. And it has all turned out so differently.

ZERO: Well, that's pretty soft for you, ain't it?

SHRDLU (wailingly): No, no, no! It's right and just that I should be punished. I could have endured it stoically. All through those endless ages of indescribable torment I should have exulted in the magnificence of divine justice. But this— this is maddening! What becomes of justice? What becomes of morality? What becomes of right and wrong? It's maddening—simply maddening! Oh, if Dr. Amaranth were only here to advise me! (He buries his face and groans.)

ZERO (trying to puzzle it out): You mean to say they ain't called you for cuttin' your mother's throat?

SHRDLU: No! It's terrible—terrible! I was prepared for anything—anything but this.

ZERO: Well, what did they say to you?

SHRDLU (looking up): Only that I was to come here and remain until I understood.

ZERO: I don't get it. What do they want you to understand?

SHRDLU (despairingly): I don't know—I don't know! If I only had an inkling of what they meant————(Interrupting himself.) Just listen quietly for a moment: do you hear anything? (They are both silent, straining their ears.)

ZERO (at last): Nope.

SHRDLU: You don't hear any music? Do you?

ZERO: Music? No, I don't hear nothin'.

SHRDLU: The people here say that the music never stops.

ZERO: They're kiddin' you.

SHRDLU: Do you think so?

ZERO: Sure thing. There ain't a sound.

SHRDLU: Perhaps. They're capable of anything. But I haven't told you of the bitterest of my disappointments.

ZERO: Well, spill it. I'm gettin' used to hearin' bad news.

SHRDLU: When I came to this place my first thought was to find my dear mother. I wanted to ask her forgiveness. And I wanted her to help me to understand.

ZERO: An' she couldn't do it?

SHRDLU (with a deep groan): She's not here, Mr. Zero! Here where only the most favored dwell, that wisest and purest of spirits is nowhere to be found. I don't understand it.

A WOMAN'S VOICE (in the distance): Mr. Zero! Oh, Mr. Zero! (ZERO raises his head and listens attentively.)

SHRDLU (going on, unheedingly): If you were to see some of the people here—the things they do————

ZERO (interrupting): Wait a minute, will you? I think somebody's callin' me.

VOICE (somewhat nearer): Mr. Ze-ro! Oh! Mr. Ze-ro!

ZERO: Who the hell's that now? I wonder if the wife's on my trail already. That would be swell, wouldn't it? An' I figgered on her bein' good for another twenty years anyhow.

VOICE (nearer): Mr. Ze-ro! Yoo-hoo!

ZERO: No. That ain't her voice. (Calling savagely.) Yoo-hoo. (To SHRDLU.) Ain't that always the way? Just when a guy is takin' life easy an' havin' a good time! (He rises and looks off left.) Here she comes, whoever she is. (In sudden amaze-

ment.) Well, I'll be—! Well, what do you know about that!

(*He stands looking in wonderment as* DAISY DIANA DOROTHEA DEVORE *enters. She wears a much-beruffled white muslin dress which is a size too small and fifteen years too youthful for her. She is red-faced and breathless.*)

DAISY (*panting*): Oh! I thought I'd never catch up to you. I've been followin' you for days—callin' an' callin'. Didn't you hear me?

ZERO: Not till just now. You look kinda winded.

DAISY: I sure am. I can't hardly catch my breath.

ZERO: Well, sit down an' take a load off your feet. (*He leads her to the tree.*)

(DAISY *sees* SHRDLU *for the first time and shrinks back a little.*)

ZERO: It's all right, he's a friend of mine. (*To* SHRDLU.) Buddy, I want you to meet my friend, Miss Devore.

SHRDLU (*rising and extending his hand courteously*): How do you do, Miss Devore?

DAISY (*self-consciously*): How do!

ZERO (*to* DAISY): He's a friend of mine. (*To* SHRDLU.) I guess you don't mind if she sits here a while an' cools off, do you?

SHRDLU: No, no, certainly not.

(*They all seat themselves under the tree.* ZERO *and* DAISY *are a little self-conscious.* SHRDLU *gradually becomes absorbed in his own thoughts.*)

ZERO: I was just takin' a rest myself. I took my shoes off on account of my feet bein' so sore.

DAISY: Yeh, I'm kinda tired too. (*Looking about.*) Say, ain't it pretty here though?

ZERO: Yeh, it is at that.

DAISY: What do they call this place?

ZERO: Why—er—let's see. He was tellin' me just a minute ago. The—er—I don't know. Some kind o' fields. I forget now. (*To* SHRDLU.) Say, buddy, what do they call this place again? (SHRDLU, *absorbed in his thoughts, does not hear him. To* DAISY.) He don't hear me. He's thinkin' again.

DAISY (*sotto voce*): What's the matter with him?

ZERO: Why, he's the guy that murdered his mother—remember?

DAISY (*interested*): Oh, yeh! Is that him?

ZERO: Yeh. An' he had it all figgered out how they was goin' t' roast him or somethin'.

And now they ain't goin' to do nothin' to him an' it's kinda got his goat.

DAISY (*sympathetically*): Poor feller!

ZERO: Yeh. He takes it kinda hard.

DAISY: He looks like a nice young feller.

ZERO: Well, you sure are good for sore eyes. I never expected to see you here.

DAISY: I thought maybe you'd be kinda surprised.

ZERO: Surprised is right. I thought you was alive an' kickin'. When did you pass out?

DAISY: Oh, right after you did—a coupla days.

ZERO (*interested*): Yeh? What happened? Get hit by a truck or somethin'?

DAISY: No. (*Hesitantly.*) You see—it's this way. I blew out the gas.

ZERO (*astonished*): Go on! What was the big idea?

DAISY (*falteringly*): Oh, I don't know. You see, I lost my job.

ZERO: I'll bet you're sorry you did it now, ain't you?

DAISY (*with conviction*): No, I ain't sorry. Not a bit. (*Then hesitantly.*) Say, Mr. Zero, I been thinkin'———(*She stops.*)

ZERO: What?

DAISY (*plucking up courage*): I been thinkin' it would be kinda nice—if you an' me—if we could kinda talk things over.

ZERO: Yeh. Sure. What do you want to talk about?

DAISY: Well—I don't know—but you and me—we ain't really ever talked things over, have we?

ZERO: No, that's right, we ain't. Well, let's go to it.

DAISY: I was thinkin' if we could be alone —just the two of us, see?

ZERO: Oh, yeh! Yeh, I get you. (*He turns to* SHRDLU *and coughs loudly.* SHRDLU *does not stir.*)

ZERO (*to* DAISY): He's dead to the world. (*He turns to* SHRDLU.) Say, buddy. (*No answer.*) Say, buddy!

SHRDLU (*looking up with a start*): Were you speaking to me?

ZERO: Yeh. How'd you guess it? I was thinkin' that maybe you'd like to walk around a little and look for your mother.

SHRDLU (*shaking his head*): It's no use. I've looked everywhere. (*He relapses into thought again.*)

ZERO: Maybe over there they might know.

SHRDLU: No, no! I've searched everywhere. She's not here.

(ZERO *and* DAISY *look at each other in despair.*)

ZERO: Listen, old shirt, my friend here and me—see?—we used to work in the same store. An' we got some things to talk over—business, see?—kinda confidential. So if it ain't askin' too much————

SHRDLU (*springing to his feet*): Why, certainly! Excuse me! (*He bows politely to* DAISY *and walks off.* DAISY *and* ZERO *watch him until he has disappeared.*)

ZERO (*with a forced laugh*): He's a good guy at that.

(*Now that they are alone, both are very self-conscious, and for a time they sit in silence.*)

DAISY (*breaking the silence*): It sure is pretty here, ain't it?

ZERO: Sure is.

DAISY: Look at the flowers! Ain't they just perfect! Why, you'd think they was artificial, wouldn't you?

ZERO: Yeh, you would.

DAISY: And the smell of them. Like perfume.

ZERO: Yeh.

DAISY: I'm crazy about the country, ain't you?

ZERO: Yeh. It's nice for a change.

DAISY: Them store picnics—remember?

ZERO: You bet. They sure was fun.

DAISY: One time—I guess you don't remember—the two of us—me and you—we sat down on the grass together under a tree—just like we're doin' now.

ZERO: Sure I remember.

DAISY: Go on! I'll bet you don't.

ZERO: I'll bet I do. It was the year the wife didn't go.

DAISY (*her face brightening*): That's right! I didn't think you'd remember.

ZERO: An' comin' home we sat together in the truck.

DAISY (*eagerly, rather shamefacedly*): Yeh! There's somethin' I've always wanted to ask you.

ZERO: Well, why didn't you?

DAISY: I don't know. It didn't seem refined. But I'm goin' to ask you now anyhow.

ZERO: Go ahead. Shoot.

DAISY (*falteringly*): Well—while we was comin' home—you put your arm up on the bench behind me—and I could feel your knee kinda pressin' against mine. (*She stops.*)

ZERO (*becoming more and more interested*): Yeh—well, what about it?

DAISY: What I wanted to ask you was—was it just kinda accidental?

ZERO (*with a laugh*): Sure it was accidental. Accidental on purpose.

DAISY (*eagerly*): Do you mean it?

ZERO: Sure I mean it. You mean to say you didn't know it?

DAISY: No. I've been wantin' to ask you————

ZERO: Then why did you get sore at me?

DAISY: Sore? I wasn't sore! When was I sore?

ZERO: That night. Sure you was sore. If you wasn't sore why did you move away?

DAISY: Just to see if you meant it. I thought if you meant it you'd move up closer. An' then when you took your arm away I was sure you didn't mean it.

ZERO: An' I thought all the time you was sore. That's why I took my arm away. I thought if I moved up you'd holler and then I'd be in a jam, like you read in the paper all the time about guys gettin' pulled in for annoyin' women.

DAISY: An' I was wishin' you'd put your arm around me—just sittin' there wishin' all the way home.

ZERO: What do you know about that? That sure is hard luck, that is. If I'd 'a' only knew! You know what I felt like doin'—only I didn't have the nerve?

DAISY: What?

ZERO: I felt like kissin' you.

DAISY (*fervently*): I wanted you to.

ZERO (*astonished*): You would 'a' let me?

DAISY: I wanted you to! I wanted you to! Oh, why didn't you—why didn't you?

ZERO: I didn't have the nerve. I sure was a dumbbell.

DAISY: I would 'a' let you all you wanted to. I wouldn't 'a' cared. I know it would 'a' been wrong but I wouldn't 'a' cared. I wasn't thinkin' about right an' wrong at all. I didn't care—see? I just wanted you to kiss me.

ZERO (*feelingly*): If I'd only knew. I wanted to do it, I swear I did. But I didn't think you cared nothin' about me.

DAISY (*passionately*): I never cared nothin' about nobody else.

ZERO: Do you mean it—on the level? You ain't kiddin' me, are you?

DAISY: No, I ain't kiddin'. I mean it. I'm tellin' you the truth. I ain't never had the nerve to tell you before—but now I don't care. It don't make no difference now. I mean it—every word of it.

ZERO (*dejectedly*): If I'd only knew it.

DAISY: Listen to me. There's somethin' else I want to tell you. I may as well tell you everything now. It don't make no difference now.

About my blowin' out the gas—see? Do you know why I done it?

ZERO: Yeh, you told me—on account o' bein' canned.

DAISY: I just told you that. That ain't the real reason. The real reason is on account o' you.

ZERO: You mean to say on account o' me passin' out?

DAISY: Yeh. That's it. I didn't want to go on livin'. What for? What did I want to go on livin' for? I didn't have nothin' to live for with you gone. I often thought of doin' it before. But I never had the nerve. An' anyhow I didn't want to leave you.

ZERO: An' me bawlin' you out, about readin' too fast an' readin' too slow.

DAISY (reproachfully): Why did you do it?

ZERO: I don't know, I swear I don't. I was always stuck on you. An' while I'd be addin' them figgers, I'd be thinkin' how if the wife died, you an' me could get married.

DAISY: I used to think o' that too.

ZERO: An' then before I knew it I was bawlin' you out.

DAISY: Them was the times I'd think o' blowin' out the gas. But I never did till you was gone. There wasn't nothin' to live for then. But it wasn't so easy to do anyhow. I never could stand the smell o' gas. An' all the while I was gettin' ready, you know, stuffin' up all the cracks, the way you read about in the paper—I was thinkin' of you and hopin' that maybe I'd meet you again. An' I made up my mind if I ever did see you, I'd tell you.

ZERO (taking her hand): I'm sure glad you did. I'm sure glad. (Ruefully.) But it don't do much good now, does it?

DAISY: No, I guess it don't. (Summoning courage.) But there's one thing I'm goin' to ask you.

ZERO: What's that?

DAISY (in a low voice): I want you to kiss me.

ZERO: You bet I will! (He leans over and kisses her cheek.)

DAISY: Not like that. I don't mean like that. I mean really kiss me. On the mouth. I ain't never been kissed like that.

(ZERO puts his arms about her and presses his lips to hers. A long embrace. At last they separate and sit side by side in silence.)

DAISY (putting her hands to her cheeks): So that's what it's like. I didn't know it could be like that. I didn't know anythin' could be like that.

ZERO (fondling her hand): Your cheeks are red. They're all red. And your eyes are shinin'. I never seen your eyes shinin' like that before.

DAISY (holding up her hand): Listen—do you hear it? Do you hear the music?

ZERO: No, I don't hear nothin'!

DAISY: Yeh—music. Listen an' you'll hear it. (They are both silent for a moment.)

ZERO (excitedly): Yeh! I hear it! He said there was music, but I didn't hear it till just now.

DAISY: Ain't it grand?

ZERO: Swell! Say, do you know what?

DAISY: What?

ZERO: It makes me feel like dancin'.

DAISY: Yeh? Me too.

ZERO (springing to his feet): Come on! Let's dance! (He seizes her hands and tries to pull her up.)

DAISY (resisting laughingly): I can't dance. I ain't danced in twenty years.

ZERO: That's nothin'. I ain't neither. Come on! I feel just like a kid! (He pulls her to her feet and seizes her about the waist.)

DAISY: Wait a minute! Wait till I fix my skirt. (She turns back her skirts and pins them above the ankles.)

(ZERO seizes her about the waist. They dance clumsily but with gay abandon. DAISY's hair becomes loosened and tumbles over her shoulders. She lends herself more and more to the spirit of the dance. But ZERO soon begins to tire and dances with less and less zest.)

ZERO (stopping at last, panting for breath): Wait a minute! I'm all winded. (He releases DAISY, but before he can turn away, she throws her arms about him and presses her lips to his. Freeing himself.) Wait a minute! Let me get my wind! (He limps to the tree and seats himself under it, gasping for breath. DAISY looks after him, her spirits rather dampened.) Whew! I sure am winded! I ain't used to dancin'. (He takes off his collar and tie and opens the neckband of his shirt. DAISY sits under the tree near him, looking at him longingly. But he is busy catching his breath.) Gee, my heart's goin' a mile a minute.

DAISY: Why don't you lay down an' rest? You could put your head on my lap.

ZERO: That ain't a bad idea. (He stretches out, his head in DAISY's lap.)

DAISY (fondling his hair): It was swell, wasn't it?

ZERO: Yeh. But you gotta be used to it.

DAISY: Just imagine if we could stay here all the time—you an' me together—wouldn't it be swell?

ZERO: Yeh. But there ain't a chance.

DAISY: Won't they let us stay?

ZERO: No. This place is only for the good ones.

DAISY: Well, we ain't so bad, are we?

ZERO: Go on! Me a murderer an' you committin' suicide. Anyway, they wouldn't stand for this—the way we been goin' on.

DAISY: I don't see why.

ZERO: You don't! You know it ain't right. Ain't I got a wife?

DAISY: Not any more you ain't. When you're dead that ends it. Don't they always say "until death do us part"?

ZERO: Well, maybe you're right about that but they wouldn't stand for us here.

DAISY: It would be swell—the two of us together—we could make up for all them years.

ZERO: Yeh, I wish we could.

DAISY: We sure were fools. But I don't care. I've got you now. (*She kisses his forehead and cheeks and mouth.*)

ZERO: I'm sure crazy about you. I never saw you lookin' so pretty before, with your cheeks all red. An' your hair hangin' down. You got swell hair. (*He fondles and kisses her hair.*)

DAISY (*ecstatically*): We got each other now, ain't we?

ZERO: Yeh. I'm crazy about you. Daisy! That's a pretty name. It's a flower, ain't it? Well —that's what you are—just like a flower.

DAISY (*happily*): We can always be together now, can't we?

ZERO: As long as they'll let us. I sure am crazy about you. (*Suddenly he sits upright.*) Watch your step!

DAISY (*alarmed*): What's the matter?

ZERO (*nervously*): He's comin' back.

DAISY: Oh, is that all? Well, what about it?

ZERO: You don't want him to see us layin' around like this, do you?

DAISY: I don't care if he does.

ZERO: Well, you oughta care. You don't want him to think you ain't a refined girl, do you? He's an awful moral bird, he is.

DAISY: I don't care nothin' about him. I don't care nothin' about anybody but you.

ZERO: Sure, I know. But we don't want people talkin' about us. You better fix your hair an' pull down your skirts. (DAISY *complies rather sadly. They are both silent as* SHRDLU *enters. With feigned nonchalance.*) Well, you got back all right, didn't you?

SHRDLU: I hope I haven't returned too soon.

ZERO: No, that's all right. We were just havin' a little talk. You know—about business an' things.

DAISY (*boldly*): We were wishin' we could stay here all the time.

SHRDLU: You may if you like.

ZERO *and* DAISY (*in astonishment*): What!

SHRDLU: Yes, Anyone who likes may remain———

ZERO: But I thought you were tellin' me———

SHRDLU: Just as I told you, only the most favored do remain. But anyone may.

ZERO: I don't get it. There's a catch in it somewheres.

DAISY: It don't matter as long as we can stay.

ZERO (*to* SHRDLU): We were thinkin' about gettin' married, see?

SHRDLU: You may or may not, just as you like.

ZERO: You don't mean to say we could stay if we didn't, do you?

SHRDLU: Yes. They don't care.

ZERO: An' there's some here that ain't married?

SHRDLU: Yes.

ZERO (*to* DAISY): I don't know about this place, at that. They must be kind of a mixed crowd.

DAISY: It don't matter, so long as we got each other.

ZERO: Yeh, I know, but you don't want to mix with people that ain't respectable.

DAISY (*to* SHRDLU): Can we get married right away? I guess there must be a lot of ministers here, ain't there?

SHRDLU: Not as many as I had hoped to find. The two who seem most beloved are Dean Swift and the Abbé Rabelais. They are both much admired for some indecent tales which they have written.

ZERO (*shocked*): What! Ministers writin' smutty stories! Say, what kind of a dump is this anyway?

SHRDLU (*despairingly*): I don't know, Mr. Zero. All these people here are so strange, so unlike the good people I've known. They seem to think of nothing but enjoyment or of wasting their time in profitless occupations. Some paint pictures from morning until night, or carve blocks of stone. Others write songs or put words together, day in and day out. Still others do nothing but lie under the trees and look at the sky. There are men who spend all their time reading books and women who think only of adorning themselves. And forever they are telling stories and laughing and singing and drinking and dancing. There are drunkards, thieves, vagabonds, blasphemers, adulterers. There is one

———

ZERO: That's enough. I heard enough. (*He seats himself and begins putting on his shoes.*)

DAISY (*anxiously*): What are you goin' to do?

ZERO: I'm goin' to beat it, that's what I'm goin' to do.

DAISY: You said you liked it here.

ZERO (*looking at her in amazement*): Liked it! Say, you don't mean to say you want to stay here, do you, with a lot of rummies an' loafers an' bums?

DAISY: We don't have to bother with them. We can just sit here together an' look at the flowers an' listen to the music.

SHRDLU (*eagerly*): Music! Did you hear music?

DAISY: Sure, Don't you hear it?

SHRDLU: No, they say it never stops. But I've never heard it.

ZERO (*listening*): I thought I heard it before but I don't hear nothin' now. I guess I must 'a' been dreamin'. (*Looking about.*) What's the quickest way out of this place?

DAISY (*pleadingly*): Won't you stay just a little longer?

ZERO: Didn't yer hear me say I'm goin'? Good-by, Miss Devore. I'm goin' to beat it. (*He limps off at right.* DAISY *follows him slowly.*)

DAISY (*to* SHRDLU): I won't ever see him again.

SHRDLU: Are you goin' to stay here?

DAISY: It don't make no difference now. Without him I might as well be alive.

(*She goes off right.* SHRDLU *watches her a moment, then sighs and seating himself under the tree, buries his head on his arm.*)

SCENE 8

(*Before the curtain rises the clicking of an adding machine is heard. The curtain rises upon an office similar in appearance to that of Scene 2 except that there is a door in the back wall through which can be seen a glimpse of the corridor outside. In the middle of the room* ZERO *is seated completely absorbed in the operation of an adding machine. He presses the keys and pulls the lever with mechanical precision. He still wears his full-dress suit but he has added to it sleeve-protectors and a green eyeshade. A strip of white paper-tape flows steadily from the machine as* ZERO *operates. The room is filled with this tape—streamers, festoons. billows of it everywhere. It covers the floor and the furniture, it climbs the walls and chokes the doorways. A few moments later* LIEUTENANT CHARLES *and* JOE *enter at the left.* LIEUTENANT CHARLES *is middle-aged and inclined to corpulence. He has an air of world-weariness. He is barefooted, wears a Panama hat, and is dressed in bright red tights which are a very bad fit—too tight in some places, badly wrinkled in others.* JOE *is a youth with a smutty face dressed in dirty blue overalls.*)

CHARLES (*after contemplating* ZERO *for a few moments*): All right, Zero, cease firing.

ZERO (*looking up, surprised*): Whaddja say?

CHARLES: I say stop punching that machine.

ZERO (*bewildered*): Stop? (*He goes on working mechanically.*)

CHARLES (*impatiently*): Yes. Can't you stop? Here, Joe, give me a hand. He can't stop.

(JOE *and* CHARLES *each take one of* ZERO's *arms and with enormous effort detach him from the machine. He resists passively—mere inertia. Finally they succeed and swing him around on his stool.* CHARLES *and* JOE *mop their foreheads.*)

ZERO (*querulously*): What's the idea? Can't you lemme alone?

CHARLES (*ignoring the question*): How long have you been here?

ZERO: Jes' twenty-five years. Three hundred months, ninety-one hundred and thirty-one days, one hundred thirty-six thousand—

CHARLES (*impatiently*): That'll do! That'll do!

ZERO (*proudly*): I ain't missed a day, not an hour, not a minute. Look at all I got done. (*He points to the maze of paper.*)

CHARLES: It's time to quit.

ZERO: Quit? Whaddya mean quit. I ain't goin' to quit!

CHARLES: You've got to.

ZERO: What for? What do I have to quit for?

CHARLES: It's time for you to go back.

ZERO: Go back where? Whaddya talkin' about?

CHARLES: Back to earth, you dub. Where do you think?

ZERO: Aw, go on, Cap, who are you kiddin'?

CHARLES: I'm not kidding anybody. And don't call me Cap. I'm a lieutenant.

ZERO: All right, Lieutenant, all right. But what's this you're tryin' to tell me about goin' back?

CHARLES: Your time's up, I'm telling you. You must be pretty thick. How many times do you want to be told a thing?

ZERO: This is the first time I heard about goin' back. Nobody ever said nothin' to me about it before.

CHARLES: You didn't think you were going to stay here forever, did you?

ZERO: Sure. Why not? I did my bit, didn't I? Forty-five years of it. Twenty-five years in the store. Then the boss canned me and I knocked him cold. I guess you ain't heard about that——

CHARLES (*interrupting*): I know all about that. But what's that got to do with it?

ZERO: Well, I done my bit, didn't I? That oughta let me out.

CHARLES (*jeeringly*): So you think you're all through, do you?

ZERO: Sure, I do. I did the best I could while I was there and then I passed out. And now I'm sittin' pretty here.

CHARLES: You've got a fine idea of the way they run things, you have. Do you think they're going to all of the trouble of making a soul just to use it once?

ZERO: Once is often enough, it seems to me.

CHARLES: It seems to you, does it? Well, who are you? And what do you know about it? Why, man, they use a soul over and over again—over and over until it's worn out.

ZERO: Nobody ever told me.

CHARLES: So you thought you were all through, did you? Well, that's a hot one, that is.

ZERO (*sullenly*): How was I to know?

CHARLES: Use your brains! Where would we put them all! We're crowded enough as it is. Why, this place is nothing but a kind of repair and service station—a sort of cosmic laundry, you might say. We get the souls in here by the bushelful. Then we get busy and clean them up. And you ought to see some of them. The muck and the slime. Phoo! And as full of holes as a flour sifter. But we fix them up. We disinfect them and give them a kerosene rub and mend the holes and back they go—practically as good as new.

ZERO: You mean to say I've been here before—before the last time, I mean?

CHARLES: Been here before! Why, you poor boob—you've been here thousands of times—fifty thousand at least.

ZERO (*suspiciously*): How is it I don't remember nothin' about it?

CHARLES: Well—that's partly because you're stupid. But it's mostly because that's the way they fix it. (*Musingly.*) They're funny that way—every now and then they'll do something white like that—when you'd least expect it. I guess economy's at the bottom of it though. They figure that the souls would get worn out

quicker if they remembered.

ZERO: And don't any of 'em remember?

CHARLES: Oh, some do. You see there's different types: there's the type that gets a little better each time it goes back—we just give them a wash and send them right through. Then there's another type—the type that gets a little worse each time. That's where you belong!

ZERO (*offended*): Me? You mean to say I'm gettin' worse all the time?

CHARLES (*nodding*): Yes, A little worse each time.

ZERO: Well—what was I when I started? Somethin' big? A king or somethin'?

CHARLES (*laughing derisively*): A king! That's a good one! I'll tell you what you were the first time—if you want to know so much—a monkey.

ZERO (*shocked and offended*): A monkey!

CHARLES (*nodding*): Yes, sir—just a hairy, chattering, long-tailed monkey.

ZERO: That musta been a long time ago.

CHARLES: Oh, not so long. A million years or so. Seems like yesterday to me.

ZERO: Then look here, whaddya mean by sayin' I'm gettin' worse all the time?

CHARLES: Just what I said. You weren't so bad as a monkey. Of course, you did just what all the other monkeys did, but still it kept you out in the open air. And you weren't woman-shy—there was one little red-headed monkey—Well, never mind. Yes, sir, you weren't so bad then. But even in those days there must have been some bigger and brainer monkey that you kowtowed to. The mark of the slave was on you from the start.

ZERO (*sullenly*): You ain't very particular about what you call people, are you?

CHARLES: You wanted the truth, didn't you? If there ever was a soul in the world that was labeled slave it's yours. Why, all the bosses and kings that there ever were have left their trademarks on your backside.

ZERO: It ain't fair, if you ask me.

CHARLES (*shrugging his shoulders*): Don't tell me about it. I don't make the rules. All I know is, you've been getting worse—worse each time. Why, even six thousand years ago you weren't so bad. That was the time you were hauling stones for one of those big pyramids in a place they call Africa. Ever hear of the pyramids?

ZERO: Them big pointy things?

CHARLES (*nodding*): That's it.

ZERO: I seen a picture of them in the movies.

CHARLES: Well, you helped build them. It

was a long step down from the happy days in the jungle, but it was a good job—even though you didn't know what you were doing and your back was striped by the foreman's whip. But you've been going down, down. Two thousand years ago you were a Roman galley slave. You were on one of the triremes that knocked the Carthaginian fleet for a goal. Again the whip. But you had muscles then—chest muscles, back muscles, biceps. (*He feels* ZERO's *arm gingerly and turns away in disgust.*) Phoo! A bunch of mush! (*He notices that* JOE *has fallen asleep. Walking over, he kicks him in the shin.*) Wake up, you mutt! Where do you think you are! (*He turns to* ZERO *again.*) And then another thousand years and you were a serf—a lump of clay digging up other lumps of clay. You wore an iron collar then—white ones hadn't been invented yet. Another long step down. But where you dug, potatoes grew, and that helped fatten the pigs. Which was something. And now —well, I don't want to rub it in———

ZERO: Rub it in is right! Seems to me I got a pretty healthy kick comin'. I ain't had a square deal! Hard work! That's all I've ever had!

CHARLES (*callously*): What else were you ever good for?

ZERO: Well, that ain't the point. The point is I'm through! I had enough! Let 'em find somebody else to do the dirty work. I'm sick of bein' the goat! I quit right here and now! (*He glares about defiantly. There is a thunderclap and a bright flash of lightning. Screaming.*) Ooh! What's that? (*He clings to* CHARLES.)

CHARLES: It's all right. Nobody's going to hurt you. It's just their way of telling you that they don't like you to talk that way. Pull yourself together and calm down. You can't change the rules—nobody can—they've got it all fixed. It's a rotten system—but what are you going to do about it?

ZERO: Why can't they stop pickin' on me? I'm satisfied here—doin' my day's work. I don't want to go back.

CHARLES: You've got to, I tell you. There's no way out of it.

ZERO: What chance have I got—at my age? Who'll give me a job?

CHARLES: You big boob, you don't think you're going back the way you are, do you?

ZERO: Sure, how then?

CHARLES: Why, you've got to start all over.

ZERO: All over?

CHARLES (*nodding*): You'll be a baby again—a bald, red-faced little animal, and then you'll go through it all again. There'll be millions of others like you—all with their mouths open, squalling for food. And then when you get a little older you'll begin to learn things—and you'll learn all the wrong things and learn them all in the wrong way. You'll eat the wrong food and wear the wrong clothes, and you'll live in swarming dens where there's no light and no air! You'll learn to be a liar and a bully and a braggart and a coward and a sneak. You'll learn to fear the sunlight and to hate beauty. By that time you'll be ready for school. There they'll tell you the truth about a great many things that you don't give a damn about, and they'll tell you lies about all the things you ought to know— and about all the things you want to know they'll tell you nothing at all. When you get through you'll be equipped for your life work. You'll be ready to take a job.

ZERO (*eagerly*): What'll my job be? Another adding machine?

CHARLES: Yes. But not one of these antiquated adding machines. It will be a superb, super-hyper-adding machine, as far from this old piece of junk as you are from God. It will be something to make you sit up and take notice, that adding machine. It will be an adding machine which will be installed in a coal mine and which will record the individual output of each miner. As each miner down in the lower galleries takes up a shovelful of coal, the impact of his shovel will automatically set in motion a graphite pencil in your gallery. The pencil will make a mark in white upon a blackened, sensitized drum. Then your work comes in. With the great toe of your right foot you release a lever which focuses a violet ray on the drum. The ray, playing upon and through the white mark, falls upon a selenium cell which in turn sets the keys of the adding apparatus in motion. In this way the individual output of each miner is recorded without any human effort except the slight pressure of the great toe of your right foot.

ZERO (*in breathless, round-eyed wonder*): Say, that'll be some machine, won't it?

CHARLES: Some machine is right. It will be the culmination of human effort—the final triumph of the evolutionary process. For millions of years the nebulous gases swirled in space. For more millions of years the gases cooled and then through inconceivable ages they hardened into rocks. And then came life. Floating green things on the waters that covered the earth. More millions of years and a step upward—an animate organism in the ancient slime. And so on—step by step, down through the ages—a gain here, a gain there—the mollusk, the fish, the reptile, then mammal, man! And all so that you might sit in the gallery of a coal mine and operate the super-hyper-adding machine with the great toe of your right foot!

ZERO: Well, then—I ain't so bad after all.

CHARLES: You're a failure, Zero, a failure. A waste product. A slave to a contraption of steel and iron. The animal's instinct, but not his strength and skill. The animal's appetites, but not his unashamed indulgence of them. True, you move and eat and digest and excrete and reproduce. But any microscopic organism can do as much. Well—time's up! Back you go—back to your sunless groove—the raw material of slums and wars—the ready prey of the first jingo or demagogue or political adventurer who takes the trouble to play upon your ignorance and credulity and provincialism. You poor, spineless, brainless boob—I'm sorry for you!

ZERO (falling to his knees): Then keep me here! Don't send me back! Let me stay!

CHARLES: Get up. Didn't I tell you I can't do anything for you? Come on, time's up!

ZERO: I can't! I can't! I'm afraid to go through it all again.

CHARLES: You've got to, I tell you. Come on, now!

ZERO: What did you tell me so much for? Couldn't you just let me go, thinkin' everythin' was goin' to be all right?

CHARLES: You wanted to know, didn't you?

ZERO: How did I know what you were goin' to tell me? Now I can't stop thinkin' about it! I can't stop thinkin'! I'll be thinkin' about it all the time.

CHARLES: All right! I'll do the best I can for you. I'll send a girl with you to keep you company.

ZERO: A girl? What for? What good will a girl do me?

CHARLES: She'll help make you forget.

ZERO (eagerly): She will? Where is she?

CHARLES: Wait a minute, I'll call her. (He calls in a loud voice.) Oh! Hope! Yoo-hoo! (He turns his head aside and speaks in the manner of a ventriloquist imitating a distant feminine voice.) Ye-es. (Then in his own voice.) Come here, will you? There's a fellow who wants you to take him back. (Ventriloquously again.) All right. I'll be

right over, Charlie dear. (He turns to ZERO.) Kind of familiar, isn't she? Charlie dear!

ZERO: What did you say her name is?

CHARLES: Hope. H-o-p-e.

ZERO: Is she good-lookin'?

CHARLES: Is she good-looking! Oh, boy, wait until you see her! She's a blonde with big blue eyes and red lips and little white teeth and—

ZERO: Say, that listens good to me. Will she be long?

CHARLES: She'll be here right away. There she is now! Do you see her?

ZERO: No. Where?

CHARLES: Out in the corridor. No, not there. Over farther. To the right. Don't you see her blue dress? And the sunlight on her hair?

ZERO: Oh, sure! Now I see her! What's the matter with me anyhow? Say, she's some jane! Oh, you baby vamp!

CHARLES: She'll make you forget your troubles.

ZERO: What troubles are you talkin' about?

CHARLES: Nothing. Go on. Don't keep her waiting.

ZERO: You bet I won't! Oh, Hope! Wait for me! I'll be right with you! I'm on my way! (He stumbles out eagerly. JOE bursts into uproarious laughter.)

CHARLES (eying him in surprise and anger): What in hell's the matter with you?

JOE (shaking with laughter): Did you get that? He thinks he saw somebody and he's following her! (He rocks with laughter.)

CHARLES (punching him in the jaw): Shut your face!

JOE (nursing his jaw): What's the idea? Can't I even laugh when I see something funny?

CHARLES: Funny! You keep your mouth shut or I'll show you something funny. Go on, hustle out of here and get something to clean up this mess with. There's another fellow moving in. Hurry now. (He makes a threatening gesture. JOE exits hastily. CHARLES goes to chair and seats himself. He looks weary and dispirited. Shaking his head.) Hell, I'll tell the world this is a lousy job! (He takes a flask from his pocket, uncorks it, and slowly drains it.)

CURTAIN.

Marc Connelly: *The Green Pastures* (1930)

Born in McKeesport, Pennsylvania, in 1890, Marc Connelly began a career as a journalist in Pittsburgh, where he eventually became well known for a humor column in a local paper. His interest in theater was stimulated when he went to New York to see a musical for which he had written the song lyrics. After that success, he decided to stay and see what he could do on his own. He spent five years there with relatively little to show for them and then met George Kaufman, one of the great collaborators of American drama. They agreed to work jointly and Connelly's first hit play, *Dulcy* (1921), was the result. By modern standards, it is a somewhat difficult play, since it is based on a character whose appeal is supposed to be through haplessness, and on the general ineptitude of women. Today we would regard it as being abjectly sexist, but then it was a stunning success and signaled the beginning of a number of hits of a light, frothy, popular sort.

Connelly might have continued writing such plays with George Kaufman (who kept on collaborating with others), but he broke away to write plays of a somewhat different nature. His comic touch was sure enough that he did not want to leave humor entirely, but his vision was not the same as that of his former collaborator. His success did not come immediately, however. Not until his 1929 play, *The Green Pastures*, was Connelly able to write the play that would establish him on the American stage. That success made up for any number of other failures since it is the kind of play that establishes a reputation once and for all.

The play, with an all-black cast, won the Pulitzer Prize and was made into a popular film. The idea for *The Green Pastures* was suggested to him when he read Roark Bradford's *Ol' Man Adam and His Chillun*, a retelling of black folktales from the South. He was struck by the warmth, the humor, and the very human way in which the black versions of Bible stories were retold. Connelly's own version of the stories is, in essence, a retelling of the Pentateuch, the first five books of the Bible, the books of Moses. He includes a reference to the New Testament Jesus in the last pages of the play, but the rest of the play is notable for the absence of such references. *The Green Pastures* is an emphatically Old-Testament drama.

The play's success was huge. To some extent modern audiences might regard Connelly's vision as tainted by a desire to view all blacks as the "happy Negroes" of the first-scene fish-fry, but that may not be a totally fair criticism. Connelly seems to have regarded the language of black southerners as particularly supple and responsive to spiritual matters. The play is a tolerant, concerned view of the nature of humanity as interpreted through Bible stories. Its appeal was almost guaranteed by the nature of its theme and its basic material, yet its success was assured by the rich characterization of its principal players. In particular, the role of God was notable, drawn with subtlety and an extraordinary good humor without being "sappy."

In a sense, the play is a kind of "progress report," a review of the state of things by God. He wanders over the earth looking for good people, but he mainly runs into sinners of various stripes. Our first view of Adam as a thirty-year-old bewildered man is rather comical, as is the talk God has with the flowers, who he reveals are much better behaved than the men and women he's seen. Such touches are as unexpected as they are humorous, and they tend to warm us to the theme of such a searching divinity. Naturally, we meet the principal actors in the Pentateuch: Adam, Eve, but not the serpent, who like Satan is totally absent from the drama. In this sense, Connelly's version of the story, unlike John Milton's, is quite optimistic in its emphasis on goodness. Milton is no less optimistic, but Connelly, by emphasizing the positive so strongly because he focuses our attention almost wholly on God, seems less negative and more uplifting. Some of the other actors in the Old Testament that take part in *The Green Pastures* are Cain, Noah, and the Pharaoh, all striking figures in the vivid black folktale retellings of the Bible. They are no less vivid in Connelly's version.

The theology of *The Green Pastures* is not to be examined closely. It does not conform to any sect or religion, although it has rarely been condemned or attacked for heterodoxy. Most viewers simply took it to be what it is—a very loose, folksy retelling of stories that are powerful in themselves, with little or no regard for the niceties of religious truth. One curious moment that might have aroused the ire of some comes close to the middle of the drama when God says in his worrying about what to do about all the sinfulness on earth: "Man is a kind of pet of mine and it ain't right fo' me to give up tryin' to do somethin' wid him. Doggone, mankin' *mus'* be all right at de core or else why did I ever bother wid him in de first place?" This is a basically optimistic view, and it permeates the play, making it a rather joyful comedy despite its emphasis on human foibles and the bafflement of God in his efforts to set the world straight. God's final observation concerning the need for suffering comes as an insight about God himself, and its meaning is left us to unravel.

None of Marc Connelly's subsequent plays achieved the success of this one, yet he continued to write and produce plays into the 1940s. Some of his short stories have attracted attention and won prizes, but they were only adjuncts to his theatrical work.

Selected Readings

Connelly, Marc. *Voices Offstage*. New York: Holt, Rinehart, & Winston, 1968.
————. *Dulcy*. New York: Holt, Rinehart, & Winston, 1921.
Nolan, Paul T. *Marc Connelly*. New York: Twayne, 1968.

The Green Pastures
Marc Connelly

CHARACTERS

MR. DESHEE, *the Preacher*
MYRTLE
FIRST BOY
SECOND BOY
FIRST COOK
A VOICE
SECOND COOK
FIRST MAN ANGEL
FIRST MAMMY ANGEL
A STOUT ANGEL
A SLENDER ANGEL
ARCHANGEL
GABRIEL
GOD
CHOIR LEADER
CUSTARD MAKER
ADAM
EVE
CAIN
CAIN'S GIRL
ZEBA
CAIN THE SIXTH
BOY GAMBLER
FIRST GAMBLER
SECOND GAMBLER
VOICE IN SHANTY
NOAH
NOAH'S WIFE
SHEM
FIRST WOMAN

SECOND WOMAN
THIRD WOMAN
FIRST MAN
FLATFOOT
HAM
JAPHETH
FIRST CLEANER
SECOND CLEANER
ABRAHAM
ISAAC
JACOB
MOSES
ZIPPORAH
AARON
A CANDIDATE MAGICIAN
GENERAL
HEAD MAGICIAN
FIRST WIZARD
SECOND WIZARD
JOSHUA
FIRST SCOUT
MASTER OF CEREMONIES
PHARAOH
KING OF BABYLON
PROPHET
HIGH PRIEST
CORPORAL
HEZDREL
SECOND OFFICER

SCENES

Part I

1. The Sunday School
2. A Fish Fry
3. A Garden
4. Outside the Garden
5. A Roadside
6. A Private Office
7. Another Roadside and a House
8. A House
9. A Hillside
10. A Mountain Top

PART I

SCENE 1

(*A corner in a Negro church. Ten children and an elderly preacher. The costumes are those that might be seen in any lower Louisiana town at Sunday-School time. As the curtain rises,* MR. DESHEE, *the preacher, is reading from a Bible. The* CHILDREN *are listening with varied degrees of interest. Three or four are wide-eyed in their attention. Two or three are obviously puzzled, but interested, and the smallest ones are engaged in more physical concerns. One is playing with a little doll, and another runs his finger on all the angles of his chair.*)

DESHEE: "An' Adam lived a hundred and thirty years, an' begat a son in his own likeness, after his image; an' called his name Seth. An' de days of Adam, after he had begotten Seth, were eight hundred years; an' he begat sons an' daughters; an' all de days dat Adam lived were nine hundred an' thirty years; an' he died. An' Seth lived a hundred an' five years an' begat Enos; an' Seth lived after he begat Enos eight hundred an' seven years and begat sons and daughters. An' all de days of Seth were nine hundred and twelve years; an' he died." An' it go on like dat till we come to Enoch an' de book say: "An' Enoch lived sixty an' five years and begat Methuselah." Den it say: "An' all de days of Methuselah were nine hund'ed an' sixty an' nine years an' he died." An' dat was de oldest man dat ever was. Dat's why we call ol' Mr. Gurney's mammy ol' Mrs. Methuselah, caize she's so ol'. Den a little later it tell about another member of de fam'ly. His name was Noah. Maybe some of you know about him already. I'm gonter tell you all about him next Sunday. Anyway dat's de meat an' substance of de first five chapters of Genesis. Now, how you think you gonter like de Bible?

MYRTLE: I think it's jest wonderful, Mr. Deshee. I cain't understand any of it.

FIRST BOY: Why did dey live so long, Mr. Deshee?

DESHEE: Why? Caize dat was de way God felt.

SECOND BOY: Dat made Adam a way back.

DESHEE: Yes, he certainly 'way back by de time Noah come along. Want to ask me any mo' questions?

SECOND BOY: What de worl' look like when de Lawd begin, Mr. Deshee?

DESHEE: How yo' mean what it look like?

MYRTLE: Carlisle mean who was in N'Orleans den.

DESHEE: Dey wasn't nobody in N'Orleans on 'count dey wasn't any N'Orleans. Dat's de whole idea I tol' you at de end of de first Chapter. Yo' got to git yo' minds fixed. Dey wasn't any Rampart Street. Dey wasn't any Canal Street. Dey wasn't any Louisiana. Dey wasn't nothin' on de earth at all caize fo' de reason dey wasn't any earth.

MYRTLE: Yes, but what Carlisle wanter know is—

DESHEE (*interrupting and addressing little boy who has been playing with his chair and paying no attention*): Now Randolph, if you don't listen, how yo' gonter grow up and be a good man? Yo' wanter grow up an' be a transgressor?

LITTLE BOY (*frightened*): No.

DESHEE: You tell yo' mammy yo' sister got to come wid you next time. She kin git de things done in time to bring you to de school. You content yo'self. (*The little boy straightens up in his chair.*) Now, what do Carlisle want to know?

CARLISLE: How he decide he want de worl' to be right yere and how he git de idea he wanted it?

MYRTLE: Caize de Book say, don't it, Mr. Deshee?

DESHEE: De Book say, but at de same time dat's a good question. I remember when I was a little boy de same thing recurred to me. An' ol' Mr. Dubois, he was a wonderful preacher at New Hope Chapel over in East Gretna, he said: "De answer is dat de Book ain't got time to go into all de details." And he was right. You know sometimes I think de Lawd expects us to figure out a few things for ourselves. We know that at one time dey wasn't anything except Heaven, we don't know jest where it was but we know it was dere. Maybe it was everywhere. Den one day de

Lawd got the idea he'd like to make some places. He made de sun and de moon, de stars. An' he made de earth.

MYRTLE: Who was aroun' den, nothin' but angels?

DESHEE: I suppose so.

FIRST BOY: What was de angels doin' up dere?

DESHEE: I suppose dey jest flew aroun' and had a good time. Dey wasn't no sin, so dey musta had a good time.

FIRST BOY: Did dey have picnics?

DESHEE: Sho, dey had the nicest kind of picnics. Dey probably had fish frys, wid b'iled custard and ten cent seegars for de adults. God gives us humans lotsa ideas about havin' good times. Maybe dey were things he'd seen de angels do. Yes, sir, I bet dey had a fish fry every week.

MYRTLE: Did dey have Sunday School, too?

DESHEE: Yes, dey musta had Sunday School for de cherubs.

MYRTLE: What did God look like, Mr. Deshee?

DESHEE: Well, nobody knows exactly what God looked like. But when I was a little boy I used to imagine dat he looked like de Reverend Dubois. He was de finest looking ol' man I ever knew. Yes, I used to bet de Lawd looked exactly like Mr. Dubois in de days when he walked de earth in de shape of a natchel man.

MYRTLE: When was dat, Mr. Deshee?

DESHEE: Why, when he was gettin' things started down heah. When He talked to Adam and Eve and Noah and Moses and all dem. He made mighty men in dem days. But aldo they was awful mighty dey always knew dat He was beyond dem all. Pretty near one o'clock, time fo' you chillun to go home to dinner, but before I let you go I wan' you to go over wid me de main facts of de first lesson. What's de name of de book?

CHILDREN: Genesis.

DESHEE: Dat's right. And what's de other name?

CHILDREN: First Book of Moses.

DESHEE: Dat's right. And dis yere's Chapter One. (*The lights begin to dim.*) "In de beginnin' God created de heaven an' de earth. An' de earth was widout form an' void. An' de darkness was upon de face of de deep."

SCENE 2

(*In the darkness many voices are heard singing "Rise, Shine, Give God The Glory." They sing it gayly and rapidly. The lights go up as the second verse ends. The chorus is being sung diminuendo by a mixed company of angels. That is they are angels in that they wear brightly colored robes and have wings protruding from their backs. Otherwise they look and act like a company of happy negroes at a fish fry. The scene itself is a pre-Creation Heaven with compromises. In the distance is an unbroken stretch of blue sky. Companionable varicolored clouds billow down to the floor of the stage and roll overhead to the branches of a live oak tree which is up left. The tree is leafy and dripping with Spanish moss, and with the clouds makes a frame for the scene. In the cool shade of the tree are the usual appurtenances of a fish fry; a large kettle of hot fat set on two small parallel logs, with a fire going underneath, and a large rustic table formed by driving four stakes into the ground and placing planks on top of the small connecting boards. On the table are piles of biscuits and corn bread and the cooked fish in dish pans. There are one or two fairly large cedar or crock "churns" containing boiled custard, which looks like milk. There is a gourd dipper beside the churns and several glasses and cups of various sizes and shapes from which the custard is drunk.*

The principal singers are marching two by two in a small area at the R. of the stage. Two MAMMY ANGELS are attending to the frying beside the kettle. Behind the table a MAN ANGEL is skinning fish and passing them to the cooks. Another is ladling out the custard. A MAMMY ANGEL is putting fish on bread for a brood of cherubs, and during the first scene they seat themselves on a grassy bank upstage. Another MAMMY ANGEL is clapping her hands disapprovingly and beckoning a laughing BOY CHERUB down from a cloud a little out of her reach. Another MAMMY ANGEL is solicitously slapping the back of a girl cherub who has a large fish sandwich in her hand and a bone in her throat. There is much movement about the table, and during the first few minutes several individuals go up to the table to help themselves to the food and drink. Many of the women angels wear hats and a few of the men are smoking cigars. A large boxful is on the table. There is much laughter and chatter as the music softens, but continues, during the early part of the action. The following short scenes are played almost simultaneously.)

FIRST COOK (*at kettle, calling off*): Hurry up, Cajey. Dis yere fat's cryin' fo' mo' feesh.

A VOICE (*offstage*): We comin', fas' we kin. Dey got to be ketched, ain't dey? We cain't say. "C'm'on little fish. C'm'on an' git fried," kin we?

SECOND COOK (*at table*): De trouble is de mens is all worm fishin'.

FIRST MAN ANGEL (*at table*): Whut dif'runce do it make? Yo' all de time got to make out like somebody's doin' somethin' de wrong way.

SECOND COOK (*near table*): I s'pose you got de per'fec' way fo' makin' bait.

FIRST MAN ANGEL: I ain't sayin' dat. I is sayin' whut's wrong wid worm fishin'.

SECOND COOK: Whut's wrong wid worm fishin'? Ever'thing, dat's all. Dey's only one good way fo' catfishin', an' dat's minny fishin'. Anybody know dat.

FIRST MAN ANGEL: Well, it jest so happen dat minny fishin' is de doggondest fool way of fishin' dey is. You kin try minny fishin' to de cows come home an' all you catch'll be de backache. De trouble wid you, sister, is you jest got minny fishin' on de brain.

SECOND COOK: Go right on, loud mouf. You tell me de news. My, my! You jest de wisest person in de worl'. First you, den de Lawd God.

FIRST MAN ANGEL (*to the custard ladler*): You cain't tell dem nothin'. (*Walks away to the custard churn.*) Does you try to 'splain some simple fac' dey git man-deaf.

FIRST MAMMY ANGEL (*to* CHERUB *on the cloud*): Now, you heerd me. (*The* CHERUB *assumes several mocking poses, as she speaks.*) You fly down yere. You wanter be put down in de sin book? (*She goes to the table, gets a drink for herself and points out the* CHERUB *to one of the men behind the table.*) Dat baby must got imp blood in him he so vexin'. (*She returns to her position under the cloud.*) You want me to fly up dere an' slap you down? Now, I tol' you. (*The* CHERUB *starts to come down.*)

STOUT ANGEL (*to the* CHERUB *with a bone in her throat*): I tol' you you was too little fo' cat fish. What you wanter git a bone in yo' troat to'? (*She slaps the* CHERUB'S *back.*)

SLENDER ANGEL (*leisurely eating a sandwich as she watches the backslapping*): What de trouble wid Leonetta?

STOUT ANGEL: She got a catfish bone down her froat. (*To the* CHERUB·) Doggone, I tol' you to eat grinnel instead.

SLENDER ANGEL: Ef'n she do git all dat et, she gonter have de bellyache.

STOUT ANGEL: Ain't I tol' her dat? (*To* CHERUB.) Come on now; let go dat bone. (*She slaps* CHERUB'S *back again. The bone is dislodged and the* CHERUB *grins her relief.*) Dat's good.

SLENDER ANGEL (*comfortingly*): Now she all right.

STOUT ANGEL: Go on an' play wid yo' cousins. (*The* CHERUB *joins the Cherubs sitting on the embank-*

ment. The concurrency of scenes ends here.) I ain't see you lately, Lily. How you been?

SLENDER ANGEL: Me, I'm fine. I been visitin' my mammy. She waitin' on de welcome table over by de throne of grace.

STOUT ANGEL: She always was pretty holy.

SLENDER ANGEL: Yes, ma'am. She like it dere. I guess de Lawd's took quite a fancy to her.

STOUT ANGEL: Well, dat's natural. I declare yo' mammy one of de finest lady angels I know.

SLENDER ANGEL: She claim you de best one she know.

STOUT ANGEL: Well, when you come right down to it, I suppose we is all pretty near per-fec'.

SLENDER ANGEL: Yes, ma'am. Why is dat, Mis' Jenny?

STOUT ANGEL: I s'pose it's caize de Lawd he don' 'low us 'sociatin' wid de devil any mo' so dat dey cain' be no mo' sinnin'.

SLENDER ANGEL: Po' ol' Satan. Whutevah become of him?

STOUT ANGEL: De Lawd put him some place I s'pose.

SLENDER ANGEL: But dey ain't any place but Heaven, is dey?

STOUT ANGEL: De Lawd could make a place, couldn't he?

SLENDER ANGEL: Dat's de truth. Dey's one thing confuses me though.

STOUT ANGEL: What's dat?

SLENDER ANGEL: I do a great deal of travelin' an' I ain't never come across any place but Heaven anywhere. So if de Lawd kick Satan out of Heaven jest whereat did he go? Dat's my question.

STOUT ANGEL: You bettah let de Lawd keep his own secrets, Lily. De way things is goin' now dey ain't been no sinnin' since dey give dat scamp a kick in de pants. Nowadays Heaven's free of sin an' if a lady wants a little constitutional she kin fly 'til she wing-weary widout gittin' insulted.

SLENDER ANGEL: I was jest a baby when Satan lef'. I don't even 'member what he look like.

STOUT ANGEL: He was jest right fo' a devil. (*An* ARCHANGEL *enters. He is older than the others and wears a white beard. His clothing is much darker than that of the others and his wings a trifle more imposing.*) Good mo'nin', Archangel.

(*Others say good morning.*)

ARCHANGEL: Good mo'nin', folks. I wonder kin I interrup' de fish fry an' give out de Sunday school cyards? (*Cries of Suttingly! "Mah goodness,* yes"—etc. The marching CHOIR stops.) You kin keep singin' if you want to. Why don' you sing "When de Saints Come Marchin' In?" Seem to me I ain' heard dat lately. (The CHOIR begins "When the Saints Come Marching In," rather softly, but does not resume marching. The ARCHANGEL looks off left.) All right, bring 'em yere. (A prim looking WOMAN TEACHER-ANGEL enters, shepherding ten BOY and GIRL CHERUBS. The TEACHER carries ten beribboned diplomas, which she gives to the ARCHANGEL. The cherubs are dressed in stiffly starched white suits and dresses, the little girls having enormous ribbons at the backs of their dresses and smaller ones in their hair and on the tips of their wings. They line up in front of the ARCHANGEL and receive the attention of the rest of the company. The CHOIR sings through the ceremony.) Now den cherubs, why is you yere?

CHILDREN: Because we so good.

ARCHANGEL: Dat's right. Now who de big boss?

CHILDREN: Our dear Lawd.

ARCHANGEL: Dat's right. When you all grow up what you gonter be?

CHILDREN: Holy angels at de throne of grace.

ARCHANGEL: Dat's right. Now, you passed yo' 'xaminations and it gives me great pleasure to hand out de cyards for de whole class. Gineeva Chaproe. (The FIRST GIRL CHERUB goes to him and gets her diploma. The CHOIR sings loudly and resumes marching, as the ARCHANGEL calls out another name —and presents diplomas.) Corey Moulter. (SECOND GIRL CHERUB gets her diploma.) Nootzie Winebush. (THIRD GIRL CHERUB.) Harriet Prancy. (FOURTH GIRL CHERUB.) I guess you is Brozain Stew't. (He gives the FIFTH GIRL CHERUB the paper. Each of the presentations has been accompanied by hand-clapping from the bystanders.) Now you boys know yo' own names. Suppose you come yere and help me git dese 'sorted right?

(BOY CHERUBS gather about him and receive their diplomas. The little GIRLS have scattered about the stage, joining groups of the adult angels. The angel GABRIEL enters. He is bigger and more elaborately winged than even the ARCHANGEL, but he is also much younger and beardless. His costume is less conventional than that of the other men, resembling more the Gabriel of the Doré drawings. His appearance causes a flutter among the others. They stop their chattering with the children. The CHOIR stops as three or four audible whispers of "Gabriel!" are heard. In a moment the heavenly company is all attention.)

GABRIEL (lifting his hand): Gangway! Gangway for de Lawd God Jehovah!

(There is a reverent hush and GOD enters. He is the tallest and biggest of them all. He wears a white shirt with a white bow tie, a long Prince Albert coat of black alpaca, black trousers and congress gaiters. He looks at the assemblage. There is a pause. He speaks in a rich, bass voice.)

GOD: Is you been baptized?

OTHERS (chanting): Certainly, Lawd.

GOD: Is you been baptized?

OTHERS: Certainly, Lawd.

GOD (with the beginning of musical notation): Is you been baptized?

OTHERS (now half-singing): Certainly, Lawd. Certainly, certainly, certainly, Lawd.

(They sing the last two verses with equivalent part division.)

Is you been redeemed?
 Certainly, Lawd.
Is you been redeemed?
 Certainly, Lawd.
Is you been redeemed?
 Certainly, Lawd. Certainly, certainly,
  certainly, Lawd.
Do you bow mighty low?
 Certainly, Lawd.
Do you bow mighty low?
 Certainly, Lawd.
Do you bow mighty low?
 Certainly, Lawd. Certainly, certainly,
  certainly, Lawd.

(As the last response ends all heads are bowed. God looks at them for a moment; then lifts His hand.)

GOD: Let de fish fry proceed.

(EVERYONE rises. The ANGELS relax and resume their inaudible conversations. The activity behind the table and about the cauldron is resumed. Some of the choir members cross to the table and get sandwiches and cups of the boiled custard. Three or four of the children in the Sunday School class and the little girl who had the bone in her throat affectionately group themselves about GOD as he speaks with the ARCHANGEL. He pats their heads, they hang to his coat-tails, etc.)

ARCHANGEL: Good mo'nin', Lawd.

GOD: Good mo'nin', Deacon. You lookin' pretty spry.

ARCHANGEL: I cain' complain. We just been givin' our cyards to de chillun.

GOD: Dat's good.

(A small CHERUB, his feet braced against one of GOD's shoes is using GOD's coat-tail as a trapeze. One *of the* COOKS *offers a fish sandwich which* GOD *politely declines.*)

FIRST MAMMY ANGEL: Now, you leave go de Lawd's coat, Herman. You heah me?

GOD: Dat's all right, sister. He jest playin'.

FIRST MAMMY ANGEL: He playin' too rough.

(GOD *picks up the* CHERUB *and spanks him goodnaturedly. The* CHERUB *squeals with delight and runs to his mother.* GABRIEL *advances to* GOD *with a glass of the custard.*)

GABRIEL: Little b'iled custud, Lawd?

GOD: Thank you very kindly. Dis looks nice.

CUSTARD MAKER (*offering a box*): Ten cent seegar, Lawd?

GOD (*taking it*): Thank you, thank you. How de fish fry goin'? (*Ad lib. cries of* "O.K. Lawd," "Fine an' dandy, Lawd," "De best one yit, Lawd," *etc. To the choir.*) How you shouters gittin' on?

CHOIR LEADER: We been marchin' and singin' de whole mo'nin'.

GOD: I heerd you. You gittin' better all de time. You gittin' as good as de one at de throne. Why don' you give us one dem ol' time jump ups?

CHOIR LEADER: Anythin' you say, Lawd. (*To the others.*) "So High!"

(*The* CHOIR *begins to sing* "So High You Can't Get Over It." *They sing softly, but do not march. An* ANGEL *offers his cigar to* GOD *from which He can light His own.*)

GOD: No, thanks. I'm gonter save dis a bit.

(*He puts the cigar in his pocket and listens to the singers a moment. Then he sips his custard. After the second sip, a look of displeasure comes on his face.*)

GABRIEL: What's de matter, Lawd?

GOD (*sipping again*): I ain't jest sure, yit. Dey's something 'bout dis custahd. (*Takes another sip.*)

CUSTARD MAKER: Ain't it all right, Lawd?

GOD: It don't seem seasoned jest right. You make it?

CUSTARD MAKER: Yes, Lawd. I put everythin' in it like I allus do. It's supposed to be perfec'.

GOD: Yeah. I kin taste de eggs and de cream and de sugar. (*Suddenly.*) I know what it is. It needs jest a little bit mo' firmament.

CUSTARD MAKER: Dey's firmament in it, Lawd.

GOD: Maybe, but it ain' enough.

CUSTARD MAKER: It's all we had, Lawd. Dey ain't a drap in de jug.

GOD: Dat's all right. I'll jest r'ar back an' pass a miracle. (CHOIR *stops singing.*) Let it be some firmament! An' when I say let it be some firmament, I don't want jest a little bitty dab o' firmament caize I'm sick an' tired of runnin' out of it when we need it. Let it be a whole mess of firmament! (*The stage has become misty until* GOD *and the heavenly company are obscured. As he finishes the speech there is a burst of thunder. As the stage grows darker.*) Dat's de way I like it.

(*Murmurs from the others;* "Dat's a lot of firmament." "My, dat is firmament!" "Look to me like he's created rain," *etc.*)

FIRST MAMMY ANGEL (*when the stage is dark*): Now, look Lawd, dat's too much firmament. De Cherubs is gettin' all wet.

SECOND MAMMY ANGEL: Look at my Carlotta, Lawd. She's soaked to de skin. Dat's *plenty* too much firmament.

GOD: Well, 'co'se we don't want de chillun to ketch cold. Can't you dreen it off?

GABRIEL: Dey's no place to dreen it, Lawd.

FIRST MAMMY ANGEL: Why don't we jest take de babies home, Lawd?

GOD: No, I don' wanta bust up de fish fry. You angels keep quiet an' I'll pass another miracle. Dat's always de trouble wid miracles. When you pass one you always gotta r'ar back an' pass another. (*There is a hush.*) Let dere be a place to dreen off dis firmament. Let dere be mountains and valleys an' let dere be oceans an' lakes. An' let dere be rivers and bayous to dreen it off in, too. As a matter of fac' let dere be de earth. An' when dat's done let dere be de sun, an' let it come out and dry my Cherubs' wings.

(*The lights go up until the stage is bathed in sunlight. On the embankment upstage there is now a waist-high wrought iron railing such as one sees on the galleries of houses in the French quarter of New Orleans. The* CHERUBS *are being examined by their parents and there is an ad lib. murmur of,* "You all right, honey?" "You feel better now, Albert?" "Now you all dry, Vangy?" *until the* ARCHANGEL, *who has been gazing in awe at the railing, drowns them out.*)

ARCHANGEL: Look yere!

(*There is a rush to the embankment accompanied by exclamations,* "My goodness!" "What's dis?" "I declah!" *etc.* GABRIEL *towers above the group on the middle of the embankment.* GOD *is wrapped in thought, facing the audience. The* CHOIR *resumes singing* "So High You Can't Get Over It" *softly. The babbling at the balustrade dies away as the people lean over the railing.* GABRIEL *turns and faces* GOD *indicating the earth below the railing with his left hand.*)

GABRIEL: Do you see it, Lawd?

GOD (*quietly, without turning his head upstage*): Yes, Gabriel.

GABRIEL: Looks mighty nice, Lawd.

GOD: Yes.

(GABRIEL *turns and looks over the railing.*)

GABRIEL (*gazing down*): Yes, suh. Dat'd make mighty nice farming country. Jest look at dat South forty over dere. You ain't going to let dat go to waste is you, Lawd? Dat would be a pity an' a shame.

GOD (*not turning*): It's a good earth. (GOD *turns, room is made for him beside* GABRIEL *on the embankment.*) Yes. I ought to have somebody to enjoy it. (*He turns, facing the audience. The others, save for the* CHOIR *who are lined up in two rows of six on an angle up right, continue to look over the embankment.*) Gabriel! (GOD *steps down from the embankment two paces.*)

GABRIEL (*joining him*): Yes, Lawd.

GOD: Gabriel, I'm goin' down dere.

GABRIEL: Yes, Lawd.

GOD: I want you to be my working boss yere while I'm gone.

GABRIEL: Yes, Lawd.

GOD: You know dat matter of dem two stars?

GABRIEL: Yes, Lawd.

GOD: Git dat fixed up! You know dat sparrow dat fell a little while ago? 'Tend to dat, too.

GABRIEL: Yes, Lawd.

GOD: I guess dat's about all. I'll be back Saddy. (*To the* CHOIR.) Quiet, angels. (*The* CHOIR *stops singing. Those on the embankment circle down stage.* GOD *goes to embankment. Turns and faces the company.*) I'm gonter pass one more miracle. You all gonter help me an' not make a soun' caize it's one of de most impo'tant miracles of all. (*Nobody moves.* GOD *turns, facing the sky and raises his arms above his head.*) Let there be man.

(*There is growing roll of thunder as stage grows dark. The* CHOIR *bursts into "Hallelujah," and continues until the lights go up on the next scene.*)

SCENE 3

(*Enclosing the stage is a heterogeneous cluster of cottonwood, camphor, live oak and sycamore trees, youpon and turkey berry bushes, with their purple and red*

berries, sprays of fern-like indigo fiera and splashes of various Louisiana flowers. In the middle of the stage, disclosed when the mistiness at rise grows into warm sunlight, stands ADAM. *He is a puzzled man of 30, of medium height, dressed in the clothing of the average field hand. He is bare-headed. In the distance can be heard the choir continuing. "Bright Mansions Above." A bird begins to sing.* ADAM *smiles and turns to look at the source of this novel sound. He senses his strength and raises his forearms, his fists clenched. With his left hand he carefully touches the muscles of his upper right arm. He smiles again, realizing his power. He looks at his feet which are stretched wide apart. He stamps once or twice and now almost laughs in his enjoyment. Other birds begin trilling and* ADAM *glances up joyfully toward the foliage.* GOD *enters.*)

GOD: Good mo'nin', Son.

ADAM (*with a little awe*): Good mo'nin', Lawd.

GOD: What's yo' name, Son?

ADAM: Adam.

GOD: Adam which?

ADAM (*frankly, after a moment's puzzled groping*): Jest Adam, Lawd.

GOD: Well, Adam, how dey treatin' you? How things goin'?

ADAM: Well, Lawd, you know it's kind of a new line of wukk.

GOD: You'll soon get de hang of it. You know yo' kind of a new style with me.

ADAM: Oh, I guess I'm gonter make out all right soon as I learn de ropes.

GOD: Yes, I guess you will. Yo' a nice job.

ADAM: Yes, Lawd.

GOD: Dey's jest one little thing de matter with you. Did you notice it?

ADAM: Well, now you mentioned it, Lawd, I kind of thought dey was somethin' wrong.

GOD: Yes suh, you ain't quite right. Adam, you need a family. De reason for dat is in yo' heart you is a family man. (*Flicking the ash off his cigar.*) I'd say dat was de main trouble at de moment.

ADAM (*smiling*): Yes sir. (*His smile fades and he is puzzled again.*) At de same time—dey's one thing puzzlin' me, Lawd. Could I ask you a question?

GOD: Why, certainly, Adam.

ADAM: Lawd, jest what *is* a family?

GOD: I'm gonter show you. (*Indicates a spot.*) Jest lie down dere, Adam. Make out like you was goin' to slumber.

ADAM (*gently*): Yes, Lawd.

(*He lies down.* GOD *stands beside him and as he*

raises his arms above his head the lights go down. In the darkness GOD speaks.)

GOD: Eve (Lights go up. EVE is standing beside ADAM. She is about twenty-six, and quite pretty. She is dressed like a country girl. Her gingham dress is quite new and clean. GOD is now at the other side of the stage, looking at them critically. EVE looks at ADAM in timid wonder and slowly turns her head until she meets the glance of GOD. ADAM stands beside EVE. They gaze at each other for a moment. GOD smiles.) Now you all right, Eve. (ADAM and EVE face him.) Now I'll tell you what I'm gonter do. I'm gonter put you in charge here. I'm gonter give you de run of dis whole garden. Eve, you take care of dis man an' Adam you take care of dis woman. You belong to each other. I don' want you to try to do too much caize yo' both kind of experiment wid me an' I ain't sho' whether you could make it. You two jest enjoy yo'self. Drink de water from de little brooks an' de wine from de grapes an' de berries, an' eat de food dat's hangin' for you in de trees. (He pauses, startled by a painful thought.) Dat is, in all but one tree. (He pauses. Then, not looking at them.) You know what I mean, my children?

ADAM and EVE: Yes, Lawd. (They slowly turn their heads left, toward the branches of an offstage tree. Then they look back at GOD.)

ADAM: Thank you, Lawd.

EVE: Thank you, Lawd.

GOD: I gotter be gittin' along now. I got a hund'ed thousan' things to do 'fo' you take yo' nex' breath. Enjoy yo'selves—

(GOD exits.)

(ADAM and EVE stand looking after Him for a moment, then each looks down and watches their hands meet and clasp.)

(After a moment they lift their heads slowly until they are again gazing at the tree.)

EVE: Adam.

ADAM (looking at the tree, almost in terror): What?

EVE (softly as she too continues to look at the tree.): Adam.

(The CHOIR begins singing "Turn You Round" and as the lights go down the CHOIR continues until there is blackness. The CHOIR suddenly stops. The following scene is played in the darkness.)

MR. DESHEE'S VOICE: Now, I s'pose you chillun know what happened after God made Adam 'n' Eve. Do you?

FIRST GIRL'S VOICE: I know, Mr. Deshee.

MR. DESHEE'S VOICE: Jest a minute, Randolph. Didn't I tell you you gotta tell yo' mammy let yo' sister bring you. Carlisle, take way dat truck he's eatin'. You sit by him, see kin you keep him quiet. Now, den, Myrtle what happened?

FIRST GIRL'S VOICE: Why, den dey ate de fo'bidden fruit and den dey got driv' out de garden.

MR. DESHEE'S VOICE: An' den what happened?

FIRST GIRL'S VOICE: Den dey felt ver bad.

MR. DESHEE'S VOICE: I don' mean how dey feel, I mean how dey do. Do dey have any children or anything like dat?

FIRST GIRL'S VOICE: Oh, yes, suh, dey have Cain 'n' Abel.

MR. DESHEE'S VOICE: Dat's right, dey have Cain an' Abel.

BOY'S VOICE: Dat was a long time after dey got married, wasn't it, Mr. Deshee? My mammy say it was a hund'ed years.

MR. DESHEE'S VOICE: Well, nobody kin be so sure. As I tol' you befo' dey was jest beginnin' to be able to tell de time an' nobody was any too sure 'bout anythin' even den. So de bes' thing to do is jest realize dat de thing happened an' don't bother 'bout how many years it was. Jest remember what I told you about it gittin' dark when you go to sleep an' it bein' light when you wake up. Dat's de way time went by in dem days. One thing we do know an' dat was dis boy Cain was a mean rascal.

(The lights go up on the next scene.)

SCENE 4

(A roadside.

CAIN, a husky young Negro, stands over the body of the dead ABEL. Both are dressed as laborers. CAIN is looking at the body in awe, a rock in his right hand. GOD enters.)

GOD: Cain, look what you done to Abel

CAIN: Lawd, I was min'in' my own business and he come monkeyin' aroun' wit' me. I was wukkin' in de fiel' an' he was sittin' in de shade of de tree. He say "Me, I'd be skeered to git out in dis hot sun. I be 'fraid my brains git cooked. Co'se you ain't got no brains so you ain't in no danger." An' so I up and flang de rock. If it miss 'im all right, an' if it hit 'im, all right. Dat's de way I feel.

GOD: All right, but I'm yere to tell you dat's called a crime. When de new Judge is done talkin' to you you'll be draggin' a ball and chain de rest of yo' life.

CAIN: Well, what'd he want to come monkeyin' aroun' me fo' den? I was jest plowin', min'in' my own business, and not payin' him no min', and yere he come makin' me de fool. I'd bust anybody what make me de fool.

GOD: Well, I ain' sayin' you right an' I ain' sayin' you wrong. But I do say was I you I'd jest git myself down de road 'til I was clean out of de county. An' you better take an' git married an' settle down an' raise some chillun. Dey ain' nothin' to make a man fo'git his troubles like raisin' a family. Now, you better git.

CAIN: Yessuh.

(CAIN *walks off.*)

(GOD *watches him from the forestage and as the lights begin to dim looks off. The* CHOIR *begins 'Run, Sinner, Run.''*)

GOD: Adam an' Eve you better try again. You better have Seth an' a lot mo' chillun.

(*There is darkness. The* CHOIR *continues until the lights go up on the next scene.*)

SCENE 5

(CAIN *is discovered walking on an unseen treadmill. A middle distance of trees, hillsides and shrubbery passes him on an upper treadmill. Behind is the blue sky. He stops under the branches of a tree to look at a sign on a fence railing. Only half the tree is visible on the stage. The sign reads,* "NOD PARISH. COUNTY LINE.")

CAIN (*sitting down with a sigh of relief under the tree*): At las'! Phew! (*Wipes his forehead with a handkerchief.*) Feels like I been walkin' fo'ty years. (*He looks back.*) Well, dey cain' git me now. Now I kin raise a fam'ly. (*An idea occurs to him, and suddenly he begins looking right and left.*) Well, I'll be hit by a mule! Knock me down for a trustin' baby! Where I gonter git dat fam'ly? Dat preacher fooled me. (*He is quite dejected.*) Doggone!

CAIN'S GIRL (*off stage*): Hello, Country Boy!

(CAIN *glances up to the offstage branches of the tree.*)

CAIN: Hey-ho, Good lookin'! Which way is it to town?

CAIN'S GIRL (*offstage*): What you tryin' to do? You tryin' to mash me? I be doggone if it ain't gittin' so a gal cain't hardly leave de house 'out some of dese fast men ain' passin' remarks at her.

CAIN: I ain' passin' remarks.

CAIN'S GIRL (*offstage*): If I thought you was tryin' to mash me, I'd call de police an' git you tooken to de first precinct.

CAIN: Look yere, gal, I ast you a question, an' if you don' answer me I'm gonter bend you 'cross my pants an' burn you up.

CAIN'S GIRL (*offstage*): I'm comin' down.

(CAIN *takes his eyes from the tree.*)

CAIN: Yes, an' you better hurry.

(CAIN'S GIRL *enters. She is as large as* CAIN, *wickedly pretty, and somewhat flashily dressed. She smiles at* CAIN.)

CAIN'S GIRL: I bet you kin handle a gal mean wid dem big stout arms of your'n. I sho' would hate to git you mad at me, Country Boy.

CAIN (*smiling*): Come yere. (*She goes a little closer to him.*) Don't be 'fraid, I ain' so mean.

CAIN'S GIRL: You got two bad lookin' eyes. I bet yo' hot coffee 'mong de women folks.

CAIN: I ain' never find out. What was you doin' in dat tree?

CAIN'S GIRL: Jest coolin' myself in de element.

CAIN: Is you a Nod Parish gal?

CAIN'S GIRL: Bo'n an' bred.

CAIN: You know yo' kinda pretty.

CAIN'S GIRL: Who tol' you dat?

CAIN: Dese yere two bad eyes of mine.

CAIN'S GIRL: I bet you say dat to everybody all de way down de road.

CAIN: Comin' down dat road I didn't talk to nobody.

CAIN'S GIRL: Where you boun' for, Beautiful?

CAIN: I'm jest seein' de country. I thought I might settle down yere fo' a spell. You live wit' yo' people?

CAIN'S GIRL: Co'se I does.

CAIN: 'Spose dey'd like to take in a boarder?

CAIN'S GIRL: Be nice if dey would, wouldn't it?

CAIN: I think so. You got a beau?

CAIN'S GIRL: Huh-uh!

CAIN (*smiling*): You has *now*.

CAIN'S GIRL: I guess—I guess if you wanted to kiss me an' I tried to stop you, you could pretty nearly crush me wit' dem stout arms.

CAIN: You wouldn't try too much, would you?

CAIN'S GIRL: Maybe for a little while.

CAIN: An' den what?

CAIN'S GIRL: Why don' we wait an' see?

CAIN: When would dat be?

CAIN'S GIRL: Tonight. After supper. Think you kin walk a little further now, City Boy?

CAIN: Yeh, I ain't so weary now.

(*She takes his hand.*)

CAIN'S GIRL: What yo' name? (*Takes his arm.*)

CAIN: Cain.

CAIN'S GIRL: Then I'm Cain's Gal. Come on, honey, an' meet de folks.

(*They exit.*)

(*The choir is heard singing "You Better Mind," as* GOD *enters.* GOD *watches the vanished* CAIN *and his girl.*)

GOD (*after shaking his head*): Bad business. I don' like de way things is goin' atall.

(*The stage is darkened.*)

(*The* CHOIR *continues singing until the lights go up on the next scene.*)

SCENE 6

(GOD's *private office in Heaven. It is a small room, framed by tableau curtains. A large window up center looks out on the sky. There is a battered roll-top desk. On the wall next to the window is a framed religious oleograph with a calendar attached to it underneath. A door is at the left. A hat rack is on the wall above the door. There are two or three cheap pine chairs beside the window, and beyond the door. In front of the desk is an old swivel armchair which creaks every time* GOD *leans back in it. The desk is open and various papers are stuck in the pigeonholes. Writing implements, etc. are on the desk. On a shelf above the desk is a row of law books. A cuspidor is near the desk, and a waste basket by it. The general atmosphere is that of the office of a Negro lawyer in a Louisiana town. As the lights go up* GOD *takes a fresh cigar from a box on the desk and begins puffing it without bothering to light it. There is no comment on this minor miracle from* GABRIEL *who is sitting in one of the chairs with a pencil and several papers in his hand. The singing becomes pianissimo.*)

GABRIEL (*looking at the papers*): Well, I guess dat's about all de impo'tant business this mornin', Lawd.

GOD: How 'bout dat Cherub over to Archangel Montgomery's house?

GABRIEL: Where do dey live, Lawd?

(*The singing stops.*)

GOD: Dat little two story gold house, over by de pearly gates.

GABRIEL: Oh, *dat* Montgomery. I thought you was referrin' to de ol' gentleman. Oh, yeh. (*He sorts through the papers and finds one he is looking for.*) Yere it 'tis. (*Reads.*) "Cherub Christina Montgomery; wings is moltin' out of season an' nobody knows what to do."

GOD: Well, now, take keer of dat. You gotter be more careful, Gabe.

GABRIEL: Yes, Lawd.

(*Folds the papers and puts them in a pocket.* GOD *turns to his desk, takes another puff or two of the cigar, and with a pencil, begins checking off items on a sheet of paper before him. His back is turned toward* GABRIEL. GABRIEL *takes his trumpet from the hat rack and burnishes it with his robe. He then wets his lips and puts the mouthpiece to his mouth.*)

GOD (*without turning around*): Now, watch yo'self, Gabriel.

GABRIEL: I wasn't goin' to blow, Lawd. I jest do dat every now an' den so I can keep de feel of it.

(*He leans trumpet against the wall.* GOD *picks up the papers and swings his chair around toward* GABRIEL.)

GOD: What's dis yere about de moon?

GABRIEL (*suddenly remembering*): Oh! De moon people say it's beginnin' to melt a little, on 'count caize de sun's so hot.

GOD: It's goin' 'roun' 'cordin' to schedule, ain't it?

GABRIEL: Yes, Lawd.

GOD: Well, tell 'em to stop groanin'. Dere's nothin' de matter wid dat moon. Trouble is so many angels is flyin' over dere on Saddy night. Dey git to beatin' dere wings when dey dancin' an' dat makes de heat. Tell dem dat from now on dancin' 'roun' de moon is sinnin'. Dey got to stop it. Dat'll cool off de moon. (*He swings back and puts the paper on the desk. He leans back in the chair comfortably, his hands clasped behind his head.*) Is dere anythin' else you ought to remin' me of?

GABRIEL: De prayers, Lawd.

GOD (*puzzled, slowly swinging chair around again*): De prayers?

GABRIEL: From mankind. You know, down on de earth.

GOD: Oh, yeh, de poor little earth. Bless my soul, I almos' forgot about dat. Mus' be three or four hund'ed years since I been down dere. I wasn't any too pleased wid dat job.

GABRIEL (*laughing*): You know you don' make mistakes, Lawd.

GOD (*soberly, with introspective detachment*): So dey tell me. (*He looks at* GABRIEL, *then through the window again.*) So dey tell me. I fin' I kin be displeased though, an' I was displeased wid de mankind I las' seen. Maybe I ought to go down dere agin—I need a little holiday.

GABRIEL: Might do you good, Lawd.

GOD: I think I will. I'll go down an' walk de earth agin an' see how dem poor humans is makin' out. What time is it, by de sun an' de stars?

GABRIEL (*glancing out of the window*): Jest exactly half-past, Lawd.

(GOD *is taking his hat and stick from the hat rack.*)

GOD (*opening the door*): Well, take keer o' yo'self. I'll be back Saddy. (*He exists.*)

(*The stage is darkened. The* CHOIR *begins "Dere's no Hidin' Place," and continues until the lights go up on the next scene.*)

SCENE 7

(GOD *is walking along a country road. He stops to listen. Church bells are heard in the distance.*)

GOD: Dat's nice. Nice an' quiet. Dat's de way I like Sunday to be. (*The sound is broken by a shrill voice of a girl. It is* ZEBA *singing a "blues."*) Now, dat ain't so good. (GOD *resumes his walk and the upper treadmill brings on a tree stump on which* ZEBA *is sitting. She is accompanying her song with a ukulele.* GOD *and the treadmills stop. When the stump reaches the center of the stage, it is seen that* ZEBA *is a rouged and extremely flashily dressed chippy of about eighteen.*) Stop dat!

ZEBA: What's de matter wid you, Country Boy? Pull up yo' pants. (*She resumes singing.*)

GOD: Stop dat!

ZEBA (*stops again*): Say, listen to me, Banjo Eyes. What right you got to stop a lady enjoyin' herself?

GOD: Don't you know dis is de Sabbath? Da's no kin' o' song to sing on de Lawd's day.

ZEBA: Who care 'bout de Lawd's day, anymo'? People jest use Sunday now to git over Saddy.

GOD: You a awful sassy little girl.

ZEBA: I come fum sassy people! We even speak mean of de dead.

GOD: What's yo' name?

ZEBA (*flirtatiously*): "What's my name?" Ain't you de ol'-time gal hunter! Fust, "What's my name?" den I s'pose, what would it be like if you tried to kiss me? You preachers' is de debbils.

GOD: I ain't aimin' to touch you daughter. (*A sudden sternness frightens* ZEBA. *She looks at him sharply.*) What is yo' name?

ZEBA: Zeba.

GOD: Who's yo' fam'ly?

ZEBA: I'm de great-great gran' daughter of Seth.

GOD: Of Seth? But Seth was a good man.

ZEBA: Yeh, he too good, he die of holiness.

GOD: An' yere's his little gran' daughter reekin' wid cologne. Ain't nobody even tol' you yo' on de road to Hell?

ZEBA (*smiling*): Sho' dat's what de preacher say. Exceptin' of course, I happens to know dat I'm on de road to de picnic groun's, an' at de present time I'm waitin' to keep a engagement wid my sweet papa. He don't like people talkin' to me.

(CAIN THE SIXTH *enters. He is a young buck, wearing a "box" coat and the other flashy garments of a Rampart Street swell.*)

CAIN THE SIXTH: Hello, sugah! (*He crosses in front of* GOD *and faces* ZEBA.) Hello, mamma! Sorry I'm late baby, but de gals in de barrelhouse jest wouldn't let me go. Doggone, one little wirehead swore she'd tear me down.

(ZEBA *smiles and takes his hand.*)

GOD: What's yo' name, son?

CAIN THE SIXTH (*contemptuously; without turning*): Soap 'n water, Country Boy.

GOD (*sternly*): What's yo' name, son?

(CAIN *slowly turns and for a moment his manner is civil.*)

CAIN THE SIXTH: Cain the Sixth.

GOD: I was afraid so.

CAIN THE SIXTH (*his impudence returning*): You a new preacher?

GOD: Where you live?

CAIN THE SIXTH: Me, I live mos' any place.

GOD: Yes, an' you gonter see dem all. Is de udder young men all like you?

CAIN THE SIXTH (*smiling*): De gals don' think so.

(*He turns towards* ZEBA *again, picks her up and sits on the stump with the laughing* ZEBA *on his lap.*)

ZEBA: Dey ain't nobody in de worl' like my honey-cake.

(CAIN *kisses her and she resumes her song.*)

(GOD *watches them.* ZEBA *finishes a verse of the song and begins another softly.* CAIN THE SIXTH's *eyes have been closed during the singing.*)

CAIN THE SIXTH (*his eyes closed*): Is de preacher gone?

(ZEBA *looks quickly at* GOD *without seeing him, and then looks off. She stops the song.*)

ZEBA: Yeh, I guess he walks fast.

(CAIN *pushes her off his lap and rises.*)

CAIN THE SIXTH (*with acid sweetness*): Dey tell me las' night you was talkin' to a creeper man, baby.

ZEBA: Why, you know dey ain't nobody in de world fo' me but you.

CAIN THE SIXTH (*smiling*): I know dey ain't. I even got dat guaranteed. (*Takes a revolver from his pocket.*) See dat, baby?

ZEBA: Sho' I see it, honey

CAIN THE SIXTH: Dat jest makes me positive. (*Puts the gun back.*)

ZEBA (*pushing him back on the stump*): You don' wanter believe dem stories, papa.

CAIN THE SIXTH (*with sinister lightness*): No, I didn't believe dem, baby. Co'se dat big gorilla, Flatfoot, from de other side of de river *is* in town ag'in.

ZEBA: Dat don' mean nothin'. Flatfoot ain't nothin' to me.

CAIN THE SIXTH (*sitting again*): Co'se he ain't. Go 'head, sing some mo', baby.

(ZEBA *resumes singing.*)

GOD: Bad business. (*The treadmills start turning.* GOD *resumes his walk.* ZEBA, *still singing, and* CAIN THE SIXTH *recede with the landscape.* GOD *is again alone on the country road. There is a twitter of birds.* GOD *looks up and smiles.*) De birds is goin' 'bout dere business, all right. (*A patch of flowers goes by, black-eyed Susans, conspicuously.*) How you flowers makin' out? (*Children's voices answer, "We O.K., Lawd."*) Yes, an' you looks very pretty. (*Childrens' voices: "Thank you, Lawd." The flowers pass out of sight.*) It's only de human bein's makes me downhearted. Yere's as nice a Sunday as dey is turnin' out anywhere, an' nobody makin' de right use of it. (*Something ahead of him attracts his attention. His face brightens.*) Well, now dis is mo' like it. Now dat's nice to see people prayin'. It's

a wonder dey don' do it in de church. But I fin' I don' min' it if dey do it outdoors.

(*A group of five adult Negroes and a boy on their knees in a semicircle, appears. The treadmills stop. The* BOY, *his head bent, swings his hands rhythmically up to his head three or four times. There is a hush.*)

GAMBLER: Oh, Lawd, de smoke-house is empty. Oh, Lawd, lemme git dem groceries. Oh, Lawd, lemme see dat little *six.* (*He casts the dice.*) Wham! Dere she is, frien's.

(*Exclamations from the others: "Well damn my eyes!" "Doggone, dat's de eighth pass he made." "For God's sake, can't you ever crap?" etc. The* BOY *is picking up the money.*)

GOD: Gamblin'! (*Looks over the group's shoulders.*) An' wid frozen dice!

BOY GAMBLER: Dey's a dolla' 'n' a half talkin' fo' me. How much you want of it, Riney?

FIRST GAMBLER: I take fo' bits. Wait a minute. Mebbe I take a little mo'. (*He counts some money in his hand.*)

SECOND GAMBLER (*glancing up at* GOD): Hello, Liver Lips. (*To the others.*) Looka ol' Liver Lips.

(*The others look up and laugh good-naturedly, repeating "Liver Lips."*)

FIRST GAMBLER: Ain't his pockets high from de groun'? Ol' High-Pockets.

(*The others keep saying "Ole Liver Lips." "Ol' Liver Lips don't like to see people dicin'." "Dats a good name, 'High Pockets'."*)

BOY GAMBLER (*to others*): Come on, you gonter fade me or not?

(GOD *seizes the boy's ears and drags him to his feet. The others do not move, but watch, amused.*)

GOD: Come yere, son. Why, yo' jest a little boy. Gamblin' an' sinnin'. (GOD *looks at the boy's face.*) You been chewin' tobacco, too, like you was yo' daddy. (GOD *sniffs.*) An' you been drinkin' sonny-kick-mammy-wine. You oughta be 'shamed. (*To the others.*) An' you gamblers oughta be 'shamed, leadin' dis boy to sin.

FIRST GAMBLER: He de bes' crap shooter in town, mister.

GOD: I'm gonter tell his mammy. I bet she don' know 'bout dis.

FIRST GAMBLER: No, she don' know. (*The others laugh.*) She don' know anythin'.

SECOND GAMBLER: Das de God's truth.

FIRST GAMBLER: See kin you beat 'im, High Pockets. Dey's a dolla' open yere.

GOD: I ain't gonter beat 'im. I'm gonter teach 'im. I may have to teach you all.

(*He starts walking from them. The* BOY *sticks out his tongue the moment* GOD'*s back is turned.*)

BOY GAMBLER: If you fin' my mammy you do mo'n I kin. Come on, gamblers, see kin you gimme a little action. Who wants any part of dat dollar?

(*The treadmill carries them off. The* FIRST GAMBLER *is heard saying: "I'll take anoder two bits," and the others, "Gimme a dime's wo'th," "I ain't only got fifteen cents left," etc. as they disappear.*)

GOD (*walking*): Where's dat little boy's home? (*The front of a shanty appears and* GOD *stops in front of the door.*) Yere's de place. It ain't any too clean, either.

(*Knocks on the door with his cane.*)

VOICE IN SHANTY: Who dar?

GOD: Never you min' who's yere. Open de door.

VOICE IN SHANTY: You gotta search warrant?

GOD: I don' need one.

VOICE IN SHANTY: Who you wanter see?

GOD: I wanter see de mammy of de little gamblin' boy.

VOICE IN SHANTY: You mean little Johnny Rucker?

GOD: Dat may be his name.

VOICE IN SHANTY: Well, Mrs. Rucker ain't home.

GOD: Where's she at?

VOICE IN SHANTY: Who, Mrs. Rucker?

GOD: You heerd me.

VOICE IN SHANTY: Oh, she run away las' night wid a railroad man. She's eloped.

GOD: Where's Rucker?

VOICE IN SHANTY: He's flat under de table. He so drunk he cain't move.

GOD: Who are you?

VOICE IN SHANTY: I'se jest a fren' an' neighbor. I come in las' night to de party, an' everybody in yere's dead drunk but me. De only reason I kin talk is I drank some new white mule I made myself, an' it burn my throat so I cain't drink no mo'. You got any mo' questions?

GOD: Not for you.

(*The shanty begins to move off as* GOD *starts walking again.*)

VOICE IN SHANTY: Good riddance, I say.

(*Shanty disappears.*)

GOD: Dis ain't gittin' me nowheres. All I gotta say dis yere mankind I been peoplin' my earth wid sho' ain't much. (*He stops and looks back.*) I got good min' to wipe 'em all off an' people de earth wid angels. No. Angels is all right, singin' an' playin' an' flyin' around, but dey ain't much on workin' de crops and buildin' de levees. No, suh, mankind's jest right for my earth, if he wasn't so doggone sinful. I'd rather have my earth peopled wit' a bunch of channel catfish, dan I would mankin' an' his sin. I jest cain't stan' sin.

(*He is about to resume his walk when* NOAH *enters.* NOAH *is dressed like a country preacher. His coat is of the "hammer-tail" variety. He carries a prayer book under his arm.*)

NOAH: Mo'nin', brother.

GOD: Mo'nin', brother. I declare you look like a good man.

NOAH: I try to be, brother. I'm de preacher yere. I don't think I seen you to de meetin'.

(*They resume walking.*)

GOD: I jest come to town a little while ago an' I been pretty busy.

NOAH: Yeh, mos' everybody say dey's pretty busy dese days. Dey so busy dey cain't come to meetin'. It seem like de mo' I preaches de mo' people ain't got time to come to church. I ain't hardly got enough members to fill up de choir. I gotta do de preachin' an' de bassin' too.

GOD: Is dat a fac'?

NOAH: Yes, suh, brother. Everybody is mighty busy, gamblin', good-timin', an' goin' on. You jest wait, though. When Gabriel blow de horn you gonter fin' dey got plenty of time to punch chunks down in Hell. Yes, suh.

GOD: Seems a pity. Dey all perfec'ly healthy?

NOAH: Oh, dey healthy, all right. Dey jest all lazy, and mean, and full of sin. You look like a preacher, too, brother.

GOD: Well, I am, in a way.

NOAH: You jest passin' through de neighborhood?

GOD: Yes. I wanted to see how things was goin' in yo' part of de country, an' I been feelin' jest 'bout de way you do. It's enough to discourage you.

NOAH: Yes, but I gotta keep wres'lin' wid 'em. Where you boun' for right now, brother?

GOD: I was jest walkin' along. I thought I might stroll on to de nex' town.

NOAH: Well, dat's a pretty good distance. I

live right yere. (*He stops walking.*) Why don' you stop an' give us de pleasure of yo' comp'ny for dinner? I believe my ol' woman has kilt a chicken.

GOD: Why, dat's mighty nice of you, brother. I don' believe I caught yo' name.

NOAH: Noah, jest brother Noah. Dis is my home, brother. Come right in.

(GOD *and* NOAH *start walking towards Noah's house which is just coming into view on the treadmill.*)

(*The stage darkens, the* CHOIR *sings "Feastin' Table," and when the lights go up again, the next scene is disclosed.*)

SCENE 8

(*Interior of Noah's house. The ensemble suggests the combination living-dining room in a fairly prosperous Negro's cabin. Clean white curtains hang at the window. A table and chairs are in the center of the room. There is a cheerful checked tablecloth on the table, and on the wall, a framed, highly colored picture reading "God Bless Our Home."*)

(NOAH'S WIFE, *an elderly Negress, simply and neatly dressed,* GOD *and* NOAH *are discovered grouped about the table.*)

NOAH: Company, darlin'. (*Noah's wife takes Noah's and God's hats.*) Dis gemman's a preacher, too. He's jest passin' through de country.

GOD: Good mo'nin', sister.

NOAH'S WIFE: Good mo'nin'. You jest ketch me when I'm gittin' dinner ready. You gonter stay with us?

GOD: If I ain't intrudin'. Brother Noah suggested—

NOAH'S WIFE: You set right down yere. I got a chicken in de pot an' it'll be ready in 'bout five minutes. I'll go out de back an' call Shem, Ham 'n' Japheth. (*To* GOD.) Dey's our sons. Dey live right acrost de way but always have Sunday dinner wid us. You mens make yo'selves comf'table.

GOD: Thank you, thank you very kindly.

NOAH: You run along, we all right.

(GOD *and* NOAH *seat themselves.* NOAH'S WIFE *exits.*)

GOD: You got a fine wife, Brother Noah.

NOAH: She pretty good woman.

GOD: Yes, suh, an' you got a nice little home. Have a ten cent seegar? (GOD *offers him one.*)

NOAH: Thank you, much obliged.

(*Both men lean back restfully in their chairs.*)

GOD: Jest what seems to be de main trouble 'mong mankind, Noah?

NOAH: Well, it seems to me de main trouble is dat de whol' distric' is wide open. Now you know dat makes fo' loose livin'. Men folks spen's all dere time fightin', loafin' an' gamblin', an' makin' bad likker.

GOD: What about de women?

NOAH: De women is worse dan de men. If dey ain't makin' love powder dey out beg, borrow an' stealin' money for policy tickets. Doggone, I come in de church Sunday 'fo' las' 'bout an' hour befo' de meetin' was to start, and dere was a woman stealin' de altar cloth. She was goin' to hock it. Dey ain't got no moral sense. Now you take dat case las' month, over in East Putney. Case of dat young Willy Roback.

GOD: What about him?

NOAH: Dere is a boy sebenteen years old. Doggone, if he didn't elope with his aunt. Now, you know, dat kin' of goin' on is bad fo' a neighborhood.

GOD: Terrible, terrible.

NOAH: Yes, suh. Dis use' to be a nice, decent community. I been doin' my best to preach de Word, but seems like every time I preach de place jest goes a little mo' to de dogs. De good Lawd only knows what's gonter happen.

GOD: Dat is de truth.

(*There is a pause. Each puffs his cigar.*)

(*Suddenly* NOAH *grasps his knee, as if it were paining him, and twists his foot.*)

NOAH: Huh!

GOD: What's de matter?

NOAH: I jest got a twitch. My buck-aguer I guess. Every now and den I gets a twitch in de knee. Might be a sign of rain.

GOD: That's just what it is. Noah, what's de mos' rain you ever had 'round dese parts?

NOAH: Well, de water come down fo' six days steady last April an' de ribber got so swole it bust down de levee up 'bove Freeport. Raise cain all de way down to de delta.

GOD: What would you say was it to rain for forty days and forty nights?

NOAH: I'd say dat was a *complete* rain!

GOD: Noah, you don't know who I is, do you?

NOAH (*puzzled*): Yo' face looks easy, but I don't think I recall de name.

(GOD *rises slowly, and as he reaches his full height there is a crash of lightning, a moment's darkness, and a roll of thunder. It grows light again.* NOAH *is on his knees in front of* GOD.)

I should have known you. I should have seen de glory.

GOD: Dat's all right, Noah. You didn't know who I was.

NOAH: I'm jes' ol' preacher Noah, Lawd, an' I'm yo' servant. I ain' very much, but I'se all I got.

GOD: Sit down, Noah. Don' let me hear you shamin' yo'se'f, caize yo' a good man. (*Timidly* NOAH *waits until* GOD *is seated, and then sits, himself.*) I jest wanted to fin' out if you was good, Noah. Dat's why I'm walkin' de earth in de shape of a natchel man. I wish dey was mo' people like you. But, far as I kin see you and yo' fam'ly is de only respectable people in de worl'.

NOAH: Dey jest all poor sinners, Lawd.

GOD: I know. I am your Lawd. I am a god of wrath and vengeance an' dat's why I'm gonter destroy dis worl'.

NOAH (*almost in a whisper, drawing back*): Jest as you say, Lawd.

GOD: I ain't gonter destroy you, Noah. You and yo' fam'ly, yo' sheep an' cattle, an' all de udder things dat ain't human I'm gonter preserve. But de rest is gotta go. (*Takes a pencil and a sheet of paper from his pocket.*) Look yere, Noah. (NOAH *comes over and looks over his shoulder.*) I want you to build me a boat. I want you to call it de "Ark," and I want it to look like dis. (*He is drawing on the paper. Continues to write as he speaks.*) I want you to take two of every kind of animal and bird dat's in de country. I want you to take seeds an' sprouts an' everythin' like dat an' put dem on dat Ark, because dere is gonter be all dat rain. Dey's gonter to be a deluge, Noah, an' dey's goin' to be a flood. De levees is gonter bust an' everything dat's fastened down is comin' loose, but it ain't gonter float long, caize I'm gonter make a storm dat'll sink everythin' from a hencoop to a barn. Dey ain't a ship on de sea dat'll be able to fight dat tempest. Dey all got to go. Everythin'. Everythin' in dis pretty worl' I made, except one thing, Noah. You an' yo' fam'ly an' de things I said are going to ride dat storm in de Ark. Yere's de way it's to be. (*He hands* NOAH *the paper.* NOAH *takes it and reads.*)

NOAH (*pause; looks at paper again*): Yes, suh, dis seems to be complete. Now 'bout the animals, Lawd, you say you want everythin'?

GOD: Two of everythin'.

NOAH: Dat would include jayraffes an' hippopotamusses?

GOD: Everythin' dat is.

NOAH: Dey was a circus in town las' week. I guess I kin fin' dem. Co'se I kin git all de rabbits an' possums an' wil' turkeys easy. I'll sen' de boys out. Hum, I'm jest wonderin'—

GOD: 'Bout what?

NOAH: 'Bout snakes? Think you'd like snakes, too?

GOD: Certainly, I want snakes.

NOAH: Oh, I kin git snakes, lots of 'em. Co'se, some of 'em's a little dangerous. Maybe I better take a kag of likker, too?

GOD: You kin have a kag of likker.

NOAH (*musingly*): Yes, suh, dey's a awful lot of differ'nt kin's of snakes, come to think about it. Dey's water moccasins, cotton-moufs, rattlers —mus' be a hund'ed kin's of other snakes down in de swamps. Maybe I better take two kags of likker.

GOD (*mildly*): I think de one kag's enough.

NOAH: No, I better take two kags. Besides I kin put one on each side of de boat, an' balance de ship wid dem as well as havin' dem fo' medicinal use.

GOD: You kin put one kag in de middle of de ship.

NOAH (*buoyantly*): Jest as easy to take de two kags, Lawd.

GOD: I think one kag's enough.

NOAH: Yes, Lawd, but you see forty days an' forty nights—

(*There is a distant roll of thunder.*)

GOD (*firmly*): One kag, Noah.

NOAH: Yes, Lawd. One kag.

(*The door in the back opens and* NOAH'S WIFE *enters with a tray of dishes and food.*)

NOAH'S WIFE: Now, den, gen'lemen , if you'll jest draw up cheers.

(*The stage is darkened. The* CHOIR *is heard singing "I Want to Be Ready." They continue in the darkness until the lights go up on the next scene.*)

SCENE 9

(*In the middle of the stage is the ark. On the hillside, below the Ark, a dozen or more men and women, townspeople, are watching* NOAH, SHEM, HAM *and* JAPHETH *on the deck of the Ark. The three sons are busily nailing boards on the cabin.* NOAH *is smoking a pipe. He wears a silk hat, captain's uniform and a "slicker."*)

NOAH (*to* SHEM): You, Shem, tote up some ol' rough lumber, don' bring up any planed up lumber, caize dat ain't fo' de main deck.

SHEM: Pretty near supper time, daddy.

NOAH: Maybe 'tis, but I got de feelin' we ought to keep goin'.

FIRST WOMAN: You gonter work all night, Noah, maybe, huh?

NOAH (*without looking at her*): If de sperrit move me.

SECOND WOMAN: Look yere, Noah, whyn't you give up all dis damn foolishness? Don' you know people sayin' yo' crazy? What you think you doin' anyway?

NOAH: I'se buildin' a Ark. (*Other men and women join those in the foreground.*) Ham, you better stop for a while 'n see whether dey bringin' de animals up all right. (*He looks at his watch.*) Dey ought to be pretty near de foot o' de hill by dis time; if dey ain't you wait fo' dem and bring 'em yo'se'f.

(HAM *goes down a ladder at the side of the ship and exits during the following scene. The newcomers in group have been speaking to some of the early arrivals.*)

SECOND WOMAN (*to* THIRD WOMAN, *one of the newcomers*): No, you don't mean it!

THIRD WOMAN: I do so. Dat's what de talk is in de town.

FIRST MAN: You hear dat, Noah? Dey say yo' ol' lady is tellin' everybody it's gonter rain fo' fo'ty days and fo'ty nights. You know people soon gonter git de idea you *all* crazy.

NOAH: Lot I keer what you think. (*To* JAPHETH.) Straighten up dem boards down dere, Japheth. (*Indicates floor of deck.*)

FIRST MAN (*to* THIRD WOMAN): Was I you, I wouldn't go 'round with Mrs. Noah anymore, lady. Fust thing you know you'll be gittin' a hard name, too.

THIRD WOMAN: Don' I know?

SECOND WOMAN: A lady cain't be too partic'lar dese days.

(ZEBA *and* FLATFOOT, *a tall, black, wicked-looking buck, enter, their arms around each other's waist.*)

ZEBA: Dere it is baby. Was I lyin'?

FLATFOOT: Well, I'll be split in two!

FIRST MAN: What you think of it, Flatfoot?

FLATFOOT: I must say! Look like a house wit' a warpin' cellar.

NOAH: Dis yere vessel is a boat.

FLATFOOT: When I was a little boy dey used to build boats down near de ribber, where de water was.

(*The others laugh.*)

NOAH: Dis time it's been arranged to have de water come up to de boat. (JAPHETH *looks belligerently over the rail of the Ark at* FLATFOOT. *To* JAPHETH.) Keep yo' shirt on, son.

SECOND WOMAN (*to* THIRD WOMAN): Now, you see de whole fam'ly's crazy.

THIRD WOMAN: Listen, dey ain't gonter 'taminate me. It was me dat started resolvin' dem both out o' de buryin' society.

ZEBA: When all dis water due up yere, Noah?

NOAH: You won't know when it gits yere, daughter.

ZEBA: Is she goin' to be a side-wheeler, like de Bessy-Belle?

FLATFOOT: No! if she was a side-wheeler she'd get her wheels all clogged wid sharks. She gonter have jus' one great big stern wheel, like de Commodore. Den if dey ain't 'nuf water why de big wheel kin stir some up.

(*General laughter. Two or three of the* GAMBLERS *enter and join the group, followed by* CAIN THE SIXTH.)

CAIN THE SIXTH: Dere's de fool an' his monument, jest like I said!

(*The* GAMBLERS *and* CAIN THE SIXTH *roar with laughter, slap their legs, etc., the members of the main group talk sotto voce to each other as* CAIN THE SIXTH *catches* ZEBA' *eye.* FLATFOOT *is on her right and is not aware of* CAIN *the* SIXTH'S *presence.*)

NOAH: See how dey makin' out inside, son. (*Stops hammering.*)

(JAPHETH *exits into Ark.*)
(NOAH *turns and gazes towards the east.*)

CAIN THE SIXTH: Hello, honey.

ZEBA (*frightened but smiling*): Hello, Sugah.

CAIN THE SIXTH (*pleasantly*): Ain't dat my ol' frien' Flatfoot wid you?

ZEBA: Why, so 'tis! (FLATFOOT *is now listening.*) (*To* FLATFOOT.) He's got a gun.

CAIN THE SIXTH: No, I ain't.

(*He lifts his hands over his head.* ZEBA *quickly advances and runs her hands lightly over his pockets.*)

ZEBA (*relieved*): I guess he ain't.

CAIN THE SIXTH: No, I ain't got no gun for my ol' friend, Flatfoot.

(*He walks up to him.*)

FLATFOOT (*smiling*): Hi, Cain. How's de boy?

(CAIN *quickly presses his chest against* FLATFOOT's, *his downstage arm sweeps around* FLATFOOT's *body and his hand goes up to the small of* FLATFOOT's *back.*)

CAIN THE SIXTH (*quietly, but triumphantly*): I got a little *knife* fo' *him*.

(FLATFOOT *falls dead.*)

(*The laughter of the others stops and they look at the scene.* ZEBA *for a moment is terrified, her clenched hand pressed to her mouth. She looks at* CAIN THE SIXTH, *who is smiling at her. He tosses the knife on the ground and holds his hands out to her. She goes to him, smiling.*)

ZEBA: You sho' take keer of me, honey.

CAIN THE SIXTH: Dat's caize I think yo' wo'th takin' keer of. (*To the others.*) It's all right, folks. I jest had to do a little cleanin' up.

FIRST WOMAN (*smiling*): You is de quickes' scoundrel.

FIRST GAMBLER: It was a nice quick killin'. Who was he?

SECOND WOMAN (*casually*): Dey called him Flatfoot. From over de river. He wa'nt any good. He owed me for washin' for over a year.

THIRD WOMAN: Used to peddle muggles. Said it had a kick like reg'lar snow. Wasn't no good.

SECOND GAMBLER: Think we ought to bury him?

FIRST MAN: No, just leave him dere. Nobody comes up yere, 'cept ol' Manatee.

(*Indicates* NOAH. *Cries of "Ol' Manatee! Ol' Manatee, dat's good!"*)

NOAH (*still looking off*): You bettah pray, you po' chillun.

(*They all laugh.*)

FIRST WOMAN: We bettah pray? You bettah pray, Ol' Manatee?

ZEBA: You bettah pray for rain. (*Laughter again.*)

NOAH: Dat's what I ain't doin', sinners. Shem! Japheth! (*To others, as he points off. Patter of rain.*) Listen!

CAIN THE SIXTH (*casually*): Doggone, I believe it *is* gonter shower a little.

FIRST GAMBLER: It do looks like rain.

FIRST WOMAN: I think I'll git on home. I got a new dress on.

ZEBA: Me, too. I wants to keep lookin' nice fo' my sweet papa.

(*She pats* CAIN THE SIXTH's *cheek.* CAIN THE SIXTH *hugs her.*)

NOAH (*almost frantically*): Ham! Is de animals dere?

HAM (*offstage*): Yes, sir, dere yere. We're comin'.

NOAH: Den bring 'em on.

(SHEM *and* JAPHETH *come on deck with their hammers. The stage begins to darken.*)

THIRD WOMAN: I guess we all might go home 'til de shower's over. Come on, papa.

SECOND GAMBLER: See you after supper, Noah. (*Crowd starts moving off* R.)

NOAH: God's gittin' ready to start, my sons. Let's git dis plankin' done.

ZEBA: Put a bix Texas on it, Noah, an' we'll use it fo' excursions.

(*There is a distant roll of thunder, there are cries of "Good night, Admiral." "See you later." "So long, Manatee," as the crowd goes off. The thunder rumbles again. There is the sound of increasing rain. The hammers of* SHEM *and* JAPHETH *sound louder and are joined by the sounds of other hammerers. There is a flash of lightning. The* CHOIR *begins "Dey Ol' Ark's a-Movering," the sounds on the Ark become faster and louder. The rush of rain grows heavier.*)

NOAH: Hurry! Hurry! Where are you, Ham?

HAM (*just off stage*): Yere, I am, father, wid de animals.

NOAH: God's give us his sign. Send 'em up de gangplank.

(*An inclined plane is thrown against the Ark from the side of the stage by* HAM, *who cracks a whip.*)

HAM: Get on, dere.

(*The heads of two elephants are seen.*)

NOAH: Bring 'em on board! De Lawd is strikin' down de worl'!

(*The singing and the noises reach fortissimo as* HAM *cracks his whip again, and the rain falls on the stage.*)

(*The stage is darkened. The* CHOIR *continues singing in the darkness.*)

SCENE 10

(*When the lights go up on scene, the Ark is at sea. Stationary waves run in front of it. The hillside has disappeared. The Ark is in the only lighted area.*)

SHEM *is smoking a pipe on the deck, leaning on the rail. A steamboat whistle blows three short and one long blast.* SHEM *is surprised. In a moment* HAM *appears, also with a pipe, and joins* SHEM *at the rail.*)

SHEM: Who'd you think you was signallin'?
HAM: Dat wasn't me, dat was daddy.
SHEM: He think he gonter git a reply?
HAM: I don' know. He's been gittin' a heap of comfort out of dat likker.
SHEM: De kag's nearly empty, ain't it?
HAM: Pretty nearly almos'. (*They look over the rail. A pause.*) Seen anythin'?
SHEM: Dis mornin' I seen somethin' over dere migh'a' been a fish.
HAM: Dat's de big news of de week.
SHEM: How long you think dis trip's gonter las'?
HAM: I don' know! Rain fo'ty days 'n' fo'ty nights an' when dat stop' I thought sho' we'd come up ag'inst a san' bar o' somethin'. Looks now like all dat rain was jest a little incident of de trip. (*The whistle blows again.*) Doggone! I wish he wouldn't do dat. Fust thing we know he'll wake up dem animals ag'in.

(JAPHETH *appears.*)

SHEM: What de matter wit' de ol' man, Jape?
JAPHETH: Doggone, he say he had a dream dat we're nearly dere. Dat's why he pullin de whistle cord. See kin he git a' answer. (*He looks over the rail.*) Look to me like de same ol' territory.

(MRS. NOAH *appears on deck.*)

NOAH'S WIFE: You boys go stop yo' paw pullin' dat cord. He so full of likker he think he's in a race.
JAPHETH: He claim he know what he's doin'.
NOAH'S WIFE: I claim he gittin' to be a perfec' nuisance. Me an' yo' wives cain't hardly heah ou'sel'es think. (NOAH *appears, his hat rakishly tilted on his head. He goes to the railing and looks out.*) You 'spectin' company?
NOAH: Leave me be, woman. De watah don' look so rough today. De ol' boat's ridin' easier.
NOAH'S WIFE: Ridin' like a ol' mule!
NOAH: Yes, suh, de air don't feel so wet. Shem! 'Spose you sen' out 'nother dove. (SHEM *goes into the Ark.*) Ham, go git de soundin' line. Jape, keep yo' eye on de East.

(JAPHETH *goes to the end of the boat.*)

NOAH'S WIFE: As fo' you, I s'pose you'll help things along by takin' a little drink.

NOAH: Look yere, who's de pilot of dis vessel?
NOAH'S WIFE: Ol' Mister Dumb Luck.
NOAH: Well, see dat's where you don' know anythin'.
NOAH'S WIFE: I s'pose you ain't drunk as a fool?
NOAH (*cordially*): I feel congenial.
NOAH'S WIFE: An' you look it. You look jest wonderful. I wonder if you'd feel so congenial if de Lawd was to show up?
NOAH: De Lawd knows what I'm doin', don' you worry 'bout dat.
NOAH'S WIFE: I wouldn't say anythin' ag'inst de Lawd. He suttinly let us know dey'd be a change in de weather. But I bet even de Lawd wonders sometimes why he ever put you in charge.
NOAH: Well, you let de Lawd worry' bout dat.

(SHEM *appears with the dove.*)

SHEM: Will I leave her go, Paw?
NOAH: Leave 'er go.

(*There is a chorus of "Good Luck, Dove," from the group as the dove flies off stage.* HAM *appears with the sounding line.*)

Throw 'er over, Boy.

(HAM *proceeds to do so.*)

NOAH'S WIFE: An' another thing————
HAM: Hey!
NOAH (*rushing to his side*): What is it?
HAM: Only 'bout a inch! Look! (*They lean over.*)
JAPHETH: It's gettin' light in de East.

(*As* HAM *works the cord up and down,* NOAH *and* NOAH'S WIFE *turn toward* JAPHETH. *The* CHOIR *begins "My Soul Is a Witness for the Lord."*)

NOAH: Praise de Lawd, so it is.
NOAH'S WIFE: Oh, dat's pretty.
NOAH (*to* HAM): An' de boat's stopped. We've landed. Shem, go down n' drag de fires an' dreen de boiler. Yo go help 'im, Ham.
JAPHETH: Look, Paw.

(*The dove wings back to the Ark with an olive branch in its mouth.*)

NOAH: 'N' yere's de little dove wid greenery in its mouth! Take 'er down, Jape, so she kin tell de animals. (JAPHETH *exits after* SHEM *and* HAM *carrying the dove. To* MRS. NOAH.) Now, maybe you feel little different.

NOAH'S WIFE (*contritely*): It was jes' gittin' to be so tiresome. I'm sorry, Noah.

NOAH: Dat's all right, ol' woman. (NOAH'S WIFE *exits.* NOAH *looks about him. The lights have changed and the water piece is gone and the ark is again on the hillside. Two mountains can be seen in the distance and a rainbow slowly appears over the Ark. The singing has grown louder.*) Thank you, Lawd, thank you very much indeed. Amen.

(*The singing stops with the "Amen."* GOD *appears on the deck.*)

GOD: Yo' welcome, Noah.

(NOAH *turns and sees him.*)

NOAH: O, Lawd, it's wonderful.

GOD (*looking about him*): I sort of like it. I like de way you handled de ship, too, Noah.

NOAH: Was you watchin', Lawd?

GOD: Every minute. (*He smiles.*) Didn't de ol' lady light into you?

NOAH (*apologetically*): She was kinda restless.

GOD: That's all right. I ain't blamin' nobody. I don' even min' you' cussin' an drinkin'. I figure a steamboat cap'n on a long trip like you had has a right to a little redeye, jest so he don't go crazy.

NOAH: Thank you, Lawd. What's de orders now?

GOD: All de animals safe?

NOAH: Dey all fin'n' dandy, Lawd.

GOD: Den I want you to open dat starboard door, an' leave 'em all out. Let 'em go down de hill. Den you an' de family take all de seeds 'n de sprouts an' begin plantin' ag'in. I'm startin' all over, Noah.

(NOAH *exits.* GOD *looks around.*)

GOD: Well, now we'll see what happens. (GOD *listens with a smile, as noises accompanying the debarking of the animals are heard. There are the cracks of whips, the voices of the men on the Ark, shouting: "Git along dere." "Whoa, take it easy." "Duck yo' head." "Keep in line dere," etc. Over the Ark there is a burst of centrifugal shadows, and the sound of a myriad of wings.* GOD *smiles at the shadows.*) Dat's right, birds, fin' yo' new homes. (*Bird twitters are heard again.* GOD *listens a moment and rests an arm on the railing. He speaks softly.*) Gabriel, kin you spare a minute?"

(GABRIEL *appears.*)

GABRIEL: Yes, Lawd?

(*The sounds from the other side of the Ark are by* now almost hushed. The LORD *indicates the new world with a wave of the hand.*)

GOD: Well, it's did.

GABRIEL (*respectfully, but with no enthusiasm*): So I take notice.

GOD: Yes, suh, startin' all over again.

GABRIEL: So I see.

GOD (*looking at him suddenly*): Don' seem to set you up much.

GABRIEL: Well, Lawd, you see—(*He hesitates.*) 'Tain't none of my business.

GOD: What?

GABRIEL: I say, I don' know very much about it.

GOD: I know you don'. I jest wanted you to see it. (*A thought strikes him.*) Co'se, it ain' yo' business, Gabe. It's my business. 'Twas my idea. De whole thing was my idea. An' every bit of it's my business 'n nobody else's. De whole thing rests on my shoulders. I declare, I guess *dat's* why I feel so solemn an' serious, at dis particklar time. You know *dis* thing's turned into quite a proposition.

GABRIEL (*tenderly*): But, it's all right, Lawd, as you say, it's did.

GOD: Yes, suh, it's did. (*Sighs deeply. Looks slowly to the right and the left. Then softly.*) I only hope it's goin' to work out all right.

PART II

SCENE 1

(*God's Office again.*

Somewhere the CHOIR *is singing: "A City Called Heaven." In the office are* TWO WOMEN CLEANERS. *One is scrubbing the floor, the other dusting the furniture. The one dusting stops and looks out the window. There is a whirr and a distant faint Boom. The* CHOIR *stops.*)

FIRST CLEANER: Dat was a long way off.

SECOND CLEANER (*at window*): Yes, ma'am. An' dat must a' been a big one. Doggone, de Lawd mus' be mad fo' sho', dis mo'nin'. Dat's de fo'ty-six' thunde'-bolt since breakfast.

FIRST CLEANER: I wonder where at He's pitchin' dem.

SECOND CLEANER: My goodness, don' you know?

FIRST CLEANER (*a little hurt*): Did I know I wouldn't ask de question.

SECOND CLEANER: Every one of dem's bound fo' de earth.

FIRST CLEANER: De earth? You mean dat little ol' dreenin' place?

SECOND CLEANER: Dat's de planet. (*Another faint whirr and boom.*) Dere goes another.

FIRST CLEANER: Well, bless me. I didn't know dey was thunde'bolts.

SECOND CLEANER: Wha'd you think dey was?

FIRST CLEANER (*above desk*): I wasn't sho', but I thought maybe He might be whittlin' a new star o' two, an' de noise was jest de chips fallin'.

SECOND CLEANER: Carrie, where you been? Don' you know de earth is de new scandal? Ever'body's talkin' 'bout it.

FIRST CLEANER: Dey kep' it from me.

SECOND CLEANER: Ain't you noticed de Lawd's been unhappy lately?

FIRST CLEANER (*thoughtfully*): Yeah, He ain't been his old self.

SECOND CLEANER: What did you think was de matteh? Lumbago?

FIRST CLEANER (*petulantly*): I didn't know. I didn't think it was fo' me t'inquieh.

SECOND CLEANER: Well, it jest so happens dat de Lawd is riled as kin be by dat measly little earth. Or I should say de scum dat's on it.

FIRST CLEANER: Dat's mankind down dere.

SECOND CLEANER: Dey mus' be scum, too, to git de Lawd so wukked up.

FIRST CLEANER: I s'pose so. (*Another whirr and boom.*) Looks like He's lettin' dem feel de wrath. Ain' dat a shame to plague de Lawd dat way?

SECOND CLEANER: From what I hear dey been beggin' fo' what dey're gittin'. My brother flew down to bring up a saint de other day and he say from what he see mos' of de population down dere has made de debbil king an' dey wukkin' in three shifts fo' him.

FIRST CLEANER: You cain't blame de Lawd.

SECOND CLEANER: Co'se you cain't. Dem human bein's 'd make anybody bile oveh. Ev'ry-time de Lawd try to do sompin' fo' dem, dog-gone if dey don't staht some new ruckus.

FIRST CLEANER: I take notice He's been wuk-kin' in yere mo' dan usual.

SECOND CLEANER: I wish He'd let us ladies fix it up. Wouldn't take a minute to make dis desk gold-plated.

FIRST CLEANER: I 'spose He likes it dis way. De Lawd's kind o' ol' fashioned in some ways. I s'pose He keeps dis office plain an' simple on purpose.

SECOND CLEANER (*finishing her work*): I don' see why.

FIRST CLEANER (*looking off*): Well, it's kind of a nice place to come to when He's studyin' some-thin' impo'tant. 'Most evahthin' else in heaven's so fin' 'n' gran', maybe ev'ry now an den He jest gits sick an' tired of de glory. (*She is also collecting her utensils.*)

SECOND CLEANER: Maybe so. Jest de same I'd like to have a free hand wid dis place for a while, so's I could gold it up.

(GOD *appears in the doorway.*)

GOD: Good mo'nin', daughters.

FIRST AND SECOND CLEANERS: Good mo'nin', Lawd. We was jest finishin'.

GOD: Go ahead den, daughters. (*Goes to the window.*)

FIRST AND SECOND CLEANERS: Yes, Lawd. (*They exeunt. Off stage.*) Good mo'nin', Gabriel.

(*Off stage* GABRIEL *says, "Good mo'nin', sisters," and enters immediately. He stands in the doorway for a moment watching* GOD—*a notebook and pencil in his hand.*)

GOD: What's de total?

GABRIEL (*consulting the book*): Eighteen thou-sand nine hund'ed an' sixty for de mo'nin'. Dat's includin' de village wid de fo'tune tellers. Dey certainly kin breed fast.

GOD (*solemnly*): Dey displease me. Dey dis-please me greatly.

GABRIEL: Want some more bolts, Lawd?

GOD (*looking through window*): Look at 'em dere. Squirmin' an' fightin' an' bearin' false wit-ness. Listen to dat liar, dere. He don' intend to marry dat little gal. He don' even love her. What did you say?

GABRIEL: Should I git mo' bolts?

GOD: Wait a minute. (*He carefully points his finger down through the window.*) I'm goin' to git dat wicked man myself. (*From a great distance comes an agonized cry: "Oh, Lawd!"* GOD *turns from the window.*) No use gittin' mo' thunde'bolts. Dey don' do de trick. (*He goes to the swivel chair and sits.*) It's got to be somethin' else.

GABRIEL: How would it be if you was to doom 'em all ag'in, like dat time you sent down de flood? I bet dat would make dem mind.

GOD: You see how much good de flood did. Dere dey is, jest as bad as ever.

GABRIEL: How about cleanin' up de whole mess of 'em and sta'tin' all over ag'in wid some new kind of animal?

GOD: An' admit I'm licked?

GABRIEL (*ashamedly*): No, of co'se not, Lawd.

GOD: No, suh. No, suh. Man is a kind of pet

of mine and it ain't right fo' me to give up tryin' to do somethin' wid him. Doggone, mankin' *mus'* be all right at de core or else why did I ever bother wid him in de first place? (*Sits at desk.*)

GABRIEL: It's jest dat I hates to see you worryin' about it, Lawd.

GOD: Gabe, dere ain't anythin' worth while anywheres dat didn't 'cause somebody some worryin'. I ain't never tol' you de trouble I had gittin' things started up yere. Dat's a story in itself. No, suh, de more I keep on bein' de Lawd de more I know I got to keep improvin' things. An' dat takes time and worry. De main trouble wid mankin' is he takes up so much of my time. He ought to be able to help hisself a little. (*He stops suddenly and cogitates.*) Hey, dere! I think I got it!

GABRIEL (*eagerly*): What's de news?

GOD (*still cogitating*): Yes, suh, dat seems like an awful good idea.

GABRIEL: Tell me, Lawd.

GOD: Gabriel, have you noticed dat every now an' den, mankin' turns out some pretty good specimens?

GABRIEL: Dat's de truth.

GOD: Yes, suh. Dey's ol' Abraham and Isaac an' Jacob an' all dat family.

GABRIEL: Dat's so, Lawd.

GOD: An' everyone of dem boys was a hard wukker an' a good citizen. We got to admit dat.

GABRIEL: Dey wouldn't be up yere flyin' wid us if dey hadn't been.

GOD: No, suh. An' I don' know but what de answer to de whole trouble is right dere.

GABRIEL: How you mean, Lawd?

GOD: Why, doggone it, de good man is de man dat keeps busy. I mean I been goin' along on de principle dat he was something like you angels—dat you ought to be able to give him somethin' an' den jest let him sit back an' enjoy it. Dat ain't so. Now dat I recollec' I put de first one down dere to take keer o' dat garden an' den I let him go ahead an' do nothin' but git into mischief. (*He rises.*) Sure, *dat's* it. He ain't *built* jest to fool 'roun' an' not do nothin'. Gabe, I'm gonter try a new scheme.

GABRIEL (*eagerly*): What's de scheme, Lawd?

GOD: I'll tell you later. Send in Abraham, Isaac an' Jacob. (*A voice outside calls: "Right away, Lawd."*) You go tell dem to put dem bolts back in de boxes. I ain't gonter use dem ag'in a while.

GABRIEL: O.K., Lawd.

GOD: Was you goin' anywhere near de Big Pit?

GABRIEL: I could go.

GOD: Lean over de brink and tell Satan he's jest a plain fool if he thinks he kin beat anybody as big as me.

GABRIEL: Yes, suh, Lawd. Den I'll spit right in his eye. (GABRIEL *exits.*)

(GOD *looks down through the window again to the earth below.*)

GOD: Dat new polish on de sun makes it powerful hot. (*He "r'ar back."*) Let it be jest a little bit cooler. (*He feels the air.*) Dat's nice. (*Goes to His desk. A knock on the door.*) Come in.

(ABRAHAM, ISAAC and JACOB *enter. All are very old men, but the beard of* ABRAHAM *is the longest and whitest, and they suggest their three generations. They have wings that are not quite so big as those of the native angels.*)

ISAAC: Sorry we so long comin', Lawd. But Pappy and me had to take de boy (*Pointing to* JACOB) over to git him a can of wing ointment.

GOD: What was de matter, son?

JACOB: Dey was chafin' me a little. Dey fine now, thank you, Lawd.

GOD: Dat's good. Sit down an' make yo'selves comf'table. (*The three sit.* MEN: *"Thank you, Lawd."*) Men, I'm goin' to talk about a little scheme I got. It's one dat's goin' to affec' yo' fam'lies an' dat's why I 'cided I'd talk it over wid you, 'fo' it goes into ee-fect. I don' know whether you boys know it or not, but you is about de three best men of one fam'ly dat's come up yere since I made little apples. Now I tell you what I'm gonter do. Seein' dat you human bein's cain't 'preciate anythin' lessen you fust wukk to git it and den keep strugglin' to hold it, why I'm gonter turn over a very valuable piece of property to yo' fam'ly, and den see what kin dey do with it. De rest of de worl' kin go jump in de river fo' all I keer. I'm gonter be lookin' out fo' yo' descendents only. Now den, seein' dat you boys know de country pretty tho'ly, where at does you think is de choice piece of property in de whole worl'? Think it over for a minute. I'm gonter let you make de s'lection.

ABRAHAM: If you was to ask me, Lawd, I don't think dey come any better dan de Land of Canaan.

GOD (*to* ISAAC *and* JACOB): What's yo' feelin' in de matter?

JACOB (*after a nod from* ISAAC): Pappy an' me think do we get a pick, dat would be it.

GOD (*goes to window again; looks out*): De Land of Canaan. Yes, I guess dat's a likely neighborhood. It's all run over wid Philistines and things right now, but we kin clean dat up. (*He turns from the window and resumes his seat.*) All right. Now who do you boys think is de best of yo' men to put in charge down dere? You see I ain't been payin' much attention to anybody in partic'lar lately.

ISAAC: Does you want de brainiest or de holiest, Lawd? (MEN *look up.*)

GOD: I want de holiest. I'll make him brainy. (MEN *appreciate the miracle.*)

ISAAC (*as* ABRAHAM *and* ISAAC *nod to him*): Well, if you want A Number One, goodness, Lawd, I don't know where you'll git more satisfaction dan in a great-great-great-great grandson of mine.

GOD: Where's he at?

ISAAC: At de moment I b'lieve he's in de sheep business over in Midian County. He got in a little trouble down in Egypt, but t'wan't his doin'. He killed a man dat was abusin' one of our boys in de brick works. Of co'se you know old King Pharaoh's got all our people in bondage.

GOD: I heard of it. (*With some ire.*) Who did you think put them dere? (*The visitors lower their heads.*) It's all right, boys. (*All rise.*) I'm gonter take dem out of it. An' I'm gonter turn over de whole Land of Canaan to dem. An' do you know whose gonter lead dem dere? Yo' great, great, great, great grandson. Moses, ain't it?

ISAAC: Yes, Lawd.

GOD (*smiling*): Yes. I been noticin' *him.*

ABRAHAM: It's quite a favor fo' de fam'ly, Lawd.

GOD: Dat's why I tol' you. You see, it so happens I love yo' fam'ly, an' I delight to honor it. Dat's all, gen'lemen. (*The three others rise and cross to the door, murmuring, "Yes, Lawd," "Thank you, Lawd," "Much obliged, Lawd." etc. The* CHOIR *begins, "My Lord's A-Writin' All De Time" pianis- simo.* GOD *stands watching the men leave.*) Enjoy yo' selves. (*He goes to the window. The singing grows softer. He speaks through the window to the earth.*) I'm comin' down to see you, Moses, an' dis time my scheme's *got* to wukk.

(*The stage is darkened. The singing grows louder and continues until the lights go up on the next scene.*)

SCENE 2

(*The tableau curtains frame the opening of a cave, which is dimly lighted. A large turkey-berry bush is somewhere near the foreground.* MOSES *is seated on the grass eating his lunch from a basket in his lap.* ZIP- PORAH, *his wife, stands watching him. He is about*

forty, ZIPPORAH *somewhat younger. They are dressed inconspicuously. Moses stutters slightly when he speaks. He looks up to see* ZIPPORAH *smiling.*)

MOSES: What you smilin' at, Zipporah?

ZIPPORAH: Caize you enjoyin' yo'self.

MOSES: You is a good wife, Zipporah.

ZIPPORAH: You is a good husband, Moses. (MOSES *wipes his mouth with a handkerchief and begins putting into the basket the various implements of the meal which had been on the ground about him.*) Why you suppose it's so dark yere today? Dey's no rain in de air.

MOSES: Seems like it's jest aroun' dis cave. Yo' father's house is got de sun on it. (*He looks in another direction.*) Looks all clear down toward Egypt.

ZIPPORAH: Co'se it *would* be fine weather in Egypt. De sky looks all right. Maybe it's gonter rain jest right yere. Why don't you move de sheep over to de other pasture?

MOSES (*a bit puzzled*): I don' know. It got dark like dis befo' you come along wid de dinner an' I was gonter stop you on de top of de hill. Den somethin' kep' me yere.

ZIPPORAH: S'pose it could be de Lawd warnin' you dat dey's 'Gyptians hangin' 'roun'?

MOSES: Dey may have fo'gotten all about dat killin' by now. Dey got a new Pharaoh down dere.

ZIPPORAH: An' I hear he's jest as mean to yo' people as his pappy was. I wouldn't put it pas' him to send soljahs all the way up yere fo' you.

MOSES: Dat's all right. De Lawd's looked after me so far, I don't 'spect him to fall down on me now. You better be gittin' home.

ZIPPORAH (*taking the basket*): I'll be worryin' about you.

MOSES (*kissing her and then smiling*): 'Parently de Lawd ain't. He knows I'm safe as kin be. Lemme see you feel dat way.

ZIPPORAH: You is a good man, Moses.

MOSES: I's a lucky man. (ZIPPORAH *exits with the basket.* MOSES *looks up at the sky.*) Dat's funny. De sun seems to be shinin' everyplace but right yere. It's shinin' on de sheep. Why ain't dey no cloud dere?

GOD (*offstage*): Caize I want it to be like dat, Moses.

MOSES (*looking about him*): Who's dat?

GOD (*offstage again*): I'm de Lawd, Moses.

MOSES (*smiling*): Dat's what you say. Dis yere shadow may be de Lawd's wukk, but dat voice soun' pretty much to me like my ol' brother Aaron.

GOD (*offstage*): Den keep yo' eyes open, son. (*The turkey-berry bush begins to glow and then turns completely red.* MOSES *looks at it fascinated.*) Maybe you notice de bush ain't burnin' up.

MOSES: Dat's de truth.

(MOSES *is full of awe but not frightened.*)

GOD (*offstage*): Now you believe me?

MOSES: Co'se I does. It's wonderful.

(*The light in the bush dies and* GOD *appears from behind it.*)

GOD: No, it ain't, Moses. It was jest a trick.

MOSES: 'Scuse me doubtin' you, Lawd. I always had de feelin' you wuz takin' keer of me, but I never 'spected you'd fin' de time to talk wid me pussunly. (*He laughs.*) Dat was a good trick, Lawd. I'se seen some good ones, but dat was de beatenest.

GOD: Yo' gonter see lots bigger tricks dan dat, Moses. In fac', yo' gonter perfo'm dem.

MOSES (*incredulously*): Me? I'm gonter be a tricker?

GOD: Yes, suh.

MOSES: An' do magic? Lawd, my mouth ain't got de quick talk to go wid it.

GOD: It'll come to you now.

MOSES (*now cured of stuttering*): Is I goin' wid a circus?

GOD (*slowly and solemnly*): Yo' is goin' down into Egypt, Moses, and lead my people out of bondage. To do dat I'm gonter make you de bes' tricker in de worl'.

MOSES (*a little frightened*): Egypt! You know I killed a man dere, Lawd. Won't dey kill me?

GOD: Not when dey see yo' tricks. You ain't skeered, is you?

MOSES (*simply and bravely*): No, suh, Lawd.

GOD: Den yere's what I'm gonter do. Yo' people is my chillun, Moses. I'm sick and tired o' de way ol' King Pharaoh is treatin' dem, so I'se gonter take dem away, and yo' gonter lead dem. You gonter lead 'em out of Egypt an' across de river Jordan. It's gonter take a long time, and you ain't goin' on no excursion train. Yo' gonter wukk awful hard for somethin' yo' goin' to fin' when de trip's over.

MOSES: What's dat, Lawd?

GOD: It's de Land of Canaan. It's de bes' land I got. I've promised it to yo' people, an' I'm gonter give it to dem.

MOSES: Co'se, ol' King Pharaoh will do everything he kin to stop it.

GOD: Yes, an' dat's where de tricks come in.

Dey tell me he's awful fond of tricks.

MOSES: I hear dat's *all* he's fon' of. Dey say if you can't take a rabbit out of a hat you cain't even git in to see him.

GOD: Wait'll you see de tricks you an' me's goin' to show him.

MOSES (*delightedly*): Doggone! Huh, Lawd?

GOD: Yes, suh. Now de first trick—

(GOD *is lifting a stick which he carries.*)

MOSES: Jest a minute, Lawd. (GOD *halts the demonstration.*) I'm gonter learn de tricks and do just like you tell me, but I *know* it's gonter take me a little time to learn all dat quick talkin'. Cain't I have my brother Aaron go wid me? He's a good man.

GOD: I was gonter have him help you wid de Exodus. I guess he can watch, too.

MOSES: I'll call 'im. (*He turns as if to shout.*)

GOD: Wait. (MOSES *turns and looks at* GOD.) I'll bring him. (*Softly.*) Aaron!

(AARON *appears between* GOD *and* MOSES *in the mouth of the cave. He is a little taller than* MOSES *and slightly older. He, too, is dressed like a field hand.*)

AARON (*blankly*): Hey!

(MOSES *goes to him, takes his hand and leads him, bewildered, down to where* MOSES *had been standing alone.* AARON *then sees* GOD.)

MOSES (*almost in a whisper*): It's all right.

GOD: Don't worry, son, I'm jest showin' some tricks. Bringin' you yere was one of dem. (AARON *stares at* GOD *as if hypnotized.*) Now den, you see dis yere rod? Looks like a ordinary walking stick, don' it?

MOSES: Yes, Lawd.

GOD: Well, it ain't no ordinary walkin' stick, caize look. (MOSES *leans forward.*) When I lays it down on de groun'—

(*The stage is darkened. The* CHOIR *begins, "Go Down, Moses," and continues until the lights go up on the next scene.*)

SCENE 3

(*The throne room of* PHARAOH. *It suggests a Negro lodge room. The plain board walls are colored by several large parade banners of varying sizes, colors and materials, bordered with gold fringe and tassels on them. Some of the inscriptions on them read:*)

SUBLIME ORDER OF PRINCES OF THE HOUSE OF PHARAOH
HOME CHAPTER

MYSTIC BROTHERS OF THE EGYPTIAN HOME GUARD
LADIES AUXILIARY, NO. I

SUPREME MAGICIANS AND WIZARDS OF THE UNIVERSE

PRIVATE FLAG OF HIS HONOR OLD KING PHARAOH

ROYAL YOUNG PEOPLE'S PLEASURE CLUB

ENCHANTED AND INVISIBLE CADETS OF EGYPT BOYS'
BRIGADE

There is one door up right and a window. The throne, an ordinary armchair with a drapery over its back, is on a dais. PHARAOH *is seated on the throne. His crown and garments might be those worn by a high officer in a Negro lodge during a ritual. About the throne itself are high officials, several of them with plumed hats, clothing that suggests military uniforms, and rather elaborate sword belts, swords and scabbards. A few soldiers carrying spears are also in his neighborhood and one or two bearded ancients in brightly colored robes with the word "Wizard" on their conical hats. In the general group of men and women scattered elsewhere in the room Sunday finery is noticeable everywhere. Most of the civilians have bright "parade" ribbons and wear medals. In a cleared space immediately before the throne a* CANDIDATE MAGICIAN *is performing a sleight-of-hand trick with cards.* PHARAOH *watches him apathetically. He is receiving earnest attention from a few of the others, but the majority of the men and women are talking quietly among themselves. Beside the* CANDIDATE MAGICIAN *are several paraphernalia of previously demonstrated tricks.*)

CANDIDATE MAGICIAN (*holding up some cards*): Now den, ol' King Pharaoh, watch dis. (*He completes a trick. There is a murmur of "Not Bad," "Pretty Good," etc. from a few of the watchers.* PHARAOH *makes no comment.*) Now, I believe de cyard I ast you to keep sittin' on was de trey of diamonds, wasn't it?

PHARAOH: Yeah.

CANDIDATE MAGICIAN: Den kin I trouble you to take a look at it now? (PHARAOH *half rises to pick up a card he has been sitting on, and looks at it.*) I believe you'll now notice dat it's de King of Clubs? (PHARAOH *nods and shows the card to those nearest him. The* CANDIDATE MAGICIAN *waits for an audible approval and gets practically none.*) An' dat, ol' King Pharaoh, completes de puffohmance.

(*An elderly man in a uniform steps forward.*)

GENERAL: On behalf of my nephew I beg Yo' Honor to let him jine de ranks of de royal trickers and magicians.

PHARAOH (*to the two* WIZARDS): What do de committee think? (*The* WIZARDS *shake their heads.*) Dat's what I thought. He ain't good enough. I'd like to help you out, General, but you know a man's got to be a awful good tricker to git in de royal society dese days. You better go back an' steddy some mo', son. (*He lifts his voice and directs two soldiers guarding the door.*) Is de head magician reached de royal waitin' room yit? (*One of the soldiers opens the door to look out.*) If he is, send him in.

(*The soldier beckons to some one off stage, throws the door open, and announces to the court.*)

SOLDIER: De Head Magician of de land of Egypt.

(*A very old and villainous man enters. His costume is covered with cabalistic and zodiacal signs. He advances to the King, the other magician and his uncle making way for him. He bows curtly to* PHARAOH.)

HEAD MAGICIAN: Good mo'nin', ol' King Pharaoh.

PHARAOH: Mo'nin', Professor. What's de news?

HEAD MAGICIAN: Evahthing's bein' carried out like you said.

PHARAOH: How's de killin' of de babies 'mongst de Hebrews comin' 'long?

HEAD MAGICIAN: Jes' like you ordered.

PHARAOH (*genially*): Dey killed all of 'em, huh?

HEAD MAGICIAN: Do dey see one, dey kill 'im. You teachin' 'em a great lesson. Dey don' like it a-tall.

PHARAOH (*smiling*): What do dey say?

HEAD MAGICIAN (*pawing the air inarticulately*): I hates to tell in front of de ladies.

PHARAOH: Dey feels pretty bad, huh?

HEAD MAGICIAN: Dat's jest de beginnin' of it. Betwixt de poleece and de soljahs we killed about a thousan' of 'em las' night. Dat's purty good.

PHARAOH (*thoughtfully*): Yeh, it's fair. I guess you boys is doin' all you kin. But I fin' I ain't satisfied, though.

HEAD MAGICIAN: How you mean, Yo' Honor?

PHARAOH: I mean I'd like to make dose Hebrew chillun realize dat I kin be even mo' of a pest. I mean I hates dem chillun. An' I'm gonter think of a way of makin' 'em even mo' mizzable.

HEAD MAGICIAN: But dey *ain't* anythin' mean-er dan killin' de babies, King.

PHARAOH: Dey must be sump'n. Doggone, you is my head tricker, you put yo' brains on it. (*To the others.*) Quiet, whilst de Head Magician go into de silence.

HEAD MAGICIAN (*after turning completely around twice, and a moment's cogitation*): I tell you what I kin do. All de Hebrews dat ain't out to de bury-in' grounds or in de hospitals is laborin' in de brick wukks.

PHARAOH: Yeh?

HEAD MAGICIAN (*after a cackling laugh*): How would it be to take de straw away from 'em and tell 'em dey's got to turn out jest as many bricks as usual? Ain't dat nasty?

PHARAOH: Purty triflin', but I s'pose it'll have to do for de time bein'. Where's de extreme inner guard? (*One of the military attendants comes forward.*) Go on out an' tell de sup'intendent to put dat into ee-ffect. (*The attendant bows and starts for the door. He stops as* PHARAOH *calls to him.*) Wait a minute! Tell 'im to chop off de hands of anybody dat say he cain't make de bricks dat way. (*The attendant salutes and exits, the door being opened and closed by one of the soldiers.*) Now what's de news in de magic line?

HEAD MAGICIAN: I ain't got very many novel-ties today, King, I bin wukkin' too hard on de killin's. I'm so tired I don' believe I could lift a wand.

(*There are murmurs of protest from the assemblage.*)

PHARAOH: Doggone, you was to 'a been de chief feature o' de meetin' dis mawnin'. Look at de turn-out you got account of me tellin' 'em you was comin'.

HEAD MAGICIAN: Well, dat's de way it is, King. Why don' you git de wizards to do some spell castin'?

PHARAOH: Dey say it's in dec yards dat dey cain't wukk till high noon. (*He glances at the* WIZARDS.) Think mebbe you kin cheat a little?

FIRST WIZARD: Oh dat cain't be done, King.

PHARAOH: Well, we might as well adjourn, den. Looks to me like de whole program's shot to pieces. (*He starts to rise, when there is a furious banging on the door.*) What's de idea, dere? See who dat is. (*The soldiers open the door.* MOSES *and* AARON *enter, pushing the two soldiers aside and coming down in front of* PHARAOH. *The soldiers are bewildered and* PHARAOH *is angry.*) Say, who tol' you two baboons you could come in yere?

MOSES: Is you ol' King Pharaoh?

PHARAOH: Dat's me. Did you heah what I asked you?

MOSES: My name is Moses, and dis is my brother Aaron. (*Murmur of "Hebrews" spreads through the room.*)

PHARAOH (*in a rage*): Is you Hebrews?

MOSES: Yes, suh.

PHARAOH (*almost screaming*): Put 'em to de sword!

(*As the courtiers approach,* AARON *suddenly discloses the rod, which he swings once over his head. The courtiers draw back as if their hands had been stung. Cries of "Hey!" "Lookout," etc.*)

MOSES: Keep outside dat circle.

(*The courtiers nearest* MOSES *and* AARON *look at each other, exclaiming ad lib., "Did you feel dat?" "What is dat?" "What's goin' on, heah?" "My hands is stingin'!" etc.*)

PHARAOH (*puzzled but threatening*): What's de idea yere?

MOSES: We is magicians, ol' King Pharaoh.

PHARAOH (*to the* HEAD MAGICIAN): Put a spell on 'em. (*The* HEAD MAGICIAN *stands looking at them bewildered. To* MOSES.) I got some magicians, too. We'll see who's got de bes' magic. (MOSES *and* AARON *laugh. Most of the courtiers are cowering. To the* HEAD MAGICIAN.) Go ahead, give 'em gri-gri.

MOSES: Sure, go ahead.

PHARAOH: Hurry up, dey's laughin' at you. What's de matter?

HEAD MAGICIAN: I cain't think of de right spell.

PHARAOH (*now frightened himself*): You mean dey got even *you* whupped?

HEAD MAGICIAN: Dey's got a new kind of magic.

PHARAOH (*gazes at* HEAD MAGICIAN *a moment, bewildered; to the* WIZARDS): I s'pose if de Professor cain't, you cain't.

FIRST WIZARD: Dat's a new trick, King.

HEAD MAGICIAN (*rubbing his fingers along his palms*): It's got 'lectricity in it!

PHARAOH: Hm, well dat may make it a little diff'rent. So you boys is magicians, too?

MOSES: Yes, suh.

PHARAOH: Well, we's always glad to see some new trickers in de co't, dat is if dey good. (*He glances about him.*) You look like you is O.K.

MOSES: Dat's what we claims, ol' King Pha-raoh. We think we's de best in de worl'.

PHARAOH: You certainly kin talk big. Jest

what is it you boys would like?

MOSES: We came to show you some tricks. Den we's goin' to ask you to do somethin' for us.

PHARAOH: Well, I s'pose you know I'm a fool for conjurin'. If a man kin show me some tricks I ain't seen, I goes out of my way to do him a favor.

MOSES: Dat's good. Want to see de first trick?

PHARAOH: It ain't goin' to hurt nobody?

MOSES: Dis one won't.

PHARAOH: Go ahead.

MOSES: Dis yere rod my brother has looks jes' like a walkin' stick, don' it?

(*The courtiers now join the King in interest.*)

PHARAOH: Uh huh. Le's see.

(AARON *hands him the rod, which* PHARAOH *inspects and returns.*)

MOSES: Well, look what happens when he lays it on de groun'.

(AARON *places the rod on the second step of the throne. It turns into a lifelike snake. There are exclamations from the assemblage.*)

PHARAOH: Dat's a good trick! Now turn it back into a walkin' stick again. (AARON *picks it up and it is again a rod. Exclamations of "Purty good!" "Dat's all right!" "What do you think of that!" etc*) Say, you is good trickers!

MOSES: You ain't never seen de beat of us. Now I'm goin' to ask de favor.

PHARAOH: Sure, what is it?

MOSES (*solemnly*): Let de Hebrew chillun go!

PHARAOH (*rises and stares at them. There is a murmur of "Listen to 'im!" "He's got nerve!" "I never in my life!" "My goodness!" etc.*): What did you say?

MOSES: Let de Hebrew chillun go.

(PHARAOH *seats himself again.*)

PHARAOH (*slowly*): Don' you know de Hebrews is my slaves?

MOSES: Yes, suh.

PHARAOH: Yes, suh, my slaves. (*There is a distant groaning.*) Listen, and you kin hear 'em bein' treated like slaves. (*He calls toward the window.*) What was dey doin' den?

MAN NEAR THE WINDOW: Dey's jest gettin' de news down in de brick-yard.

PHARAOH: I won't let them go. (*He snorts contemptuously.*) Let's see another trick.

MOSES: Yes, suh, yere's a better one. (*He lowers his head.*) Let's have a plague of de flies.

(AARON *raises the rod. The room grows dark and a great buzzing of flies is heard. The courtiers break out in cries of "Get away fum me!" "Take 'em away!" "De place is filled with flies!" "Dis is terrible!" "Do sump'n, Pharaoh!"*)

PHARAOH (*topping the others*): All right—stop de trick!

MOSES: Will you let de Hebrews go?

PHARAOH: Sho' I will. Go ahead stop it!

MOSES (*also above the others*): Begone!

(*The buzzing stops and the room is filled with light again, as* AARON *lowers the rod. All except* MOSES *and* AARON *are brushing the flies from their persons.*)

PHARAOH (*laughing*): Doggone, dat was a good trick! (*The others, seeing they are uninjured, join in the laughter, with exclamations of "Doggone!" "You all right?" "Sho' I'm all right." "Didn' hurt me," etc.*) You is good trickers.

MOSES: Will you let de Hebrew chillun go?

PHARAOH (*sitting down again*): Well, I'll tell you, boys, I'll tell you sump'n you didn' know. You take me, *I'm* a pretty good tricker, an' I jest outtricked you. So, bein' de bes' tricker, I don' think I will let 'em go. You got any mo' tricks yo'self.

MOSES: Yes, suh. Dis is a little harder one. (AARON *lifts the rod.*) Gnats in de mill pon', gnats in de clover, gnats in de tater patch, stingin' all over.

(*The stage grows dark again. There is the humming of gnats and the slapping of hands against faces and arms, and the same protests as were heard with the flies, but with more feeling, "I'm gittin' stung to death!" "I'm all stung!" "Dey're like hornets!" "Dey's on my face!" etc.*)

PHARAOH: Take 'em away, Moses!

MOSES (*his voice drowning the others*): If I do, will you let 'em go?

PHARAOH: Sho' I will, dis time.

MOSES: Do you mean it?

PHARAOH: Co'se I mean it! Doggone, one just stang me on de nose.

MOSES: Begone! (*Lights come up as* AARON *lowers the rod. There is a moment of general recovery again.* PHARAOH *rubs his nose, looks at his hands, etc., as do the others.*) Now, how about it?

PHARAOH (*smiling*): Well, I'll tell you, Moses. Now dat de trick's over—

(MOSES *takes a step toward* PHARAOH.)

MOSES: Listen, Pharaoh. You been lyin' to

me, and I'm gittin' tired of it.

PHARAOH: I ain't lyin', I'm trickin', too. You been trickin' me and I been trickin' you.

MOSES: I see. Well, I got one mo' trick up my sleeve which I didn't aim to wukk unless I had to. Caize when I does it, I cain't undo it.

PHARAOH: Wukk it an' I'll trick you right back. I don' say you ain't a good tricker, Moses. You is one of de best I ever seen. But I kin out-trick you. Dat's all.

MOSES: It ain't only me dat's goin' to wukk dis trick. It's me an' de Lawd.

PHARAOH: Who?

MOSES: De Lawd God of Israel.

PHARAOH: I kin outtrick you an' de Lawd too!

MOSES (angrily): Now you done it, ol' King Pharaoh. You been mean to de Lawd's people, and de Lawd's been easy on you caize you didn' know no better. You been givin' me a lot of say-so-and no do-so, and I didn' min' dat. But now you've got to braggin' dat you's better dan de Lawd, and dat's too many.

PHARAOH: You talk like a preacher, an' I never like to hear preachers talk.

MOSES: You ain't goin' to like it any better, when I strikes down de oldes' boy in every one of yo' people's houses.

PHARAOH: Now you've given up trickin' and is jest lyin'. (He rises.) Listen, I'm Pharaoh. I do de strikin' down yere. I strike down my enemies, and dere's no one in all Egypt kin kill who he wants to, 'ceptin' me.

MOSES: I'm sorry, Pharaoh. Will you let de Hebrews go?

PHARAOH: You heard my word. (AARON is lifting his rod again at a signal from MOSES.) Now, no more tricks or I'll—

MOSES: Oh, Lawd, you'll have to do it, I guess. Aaron, lift de rod.

(There is a thunderclap, darkness and screams. The lights go up. Several of the younger men on the stage have fallen to the ground or are being held in the arms of the horrified elders.)

PHARAOH: What have you done yere? Where's my boy?

(Through the door come four men bearing a young man's body.)

FIRST OF THE FOUR MEN: King Pharaoh.

(PHARAOH drops into his chair, stunned, as the dead boy is brought to the throne.)

PHARAOH (grief-stricken): Oh, my son, my fine son.

(The courtiers look at him with mute appeal.)

MOSES: I'm sorry, Pharaoh, but you cain't fight de Lawd. Will you let his people go?

PHARAOH: Let them go.

(The lights go out. The CHOIR begins, "Mary Don't You Weep," and continues until it is broken by the strains of "I'm Noways Weary and I'm Noways Tired." The latter is sung by many more voices than the former, and the cacophony ends as the latter grows in volume and the lights go up on the next scene.)

SCENE 4

(The CHILDREN OF ISRAEL are marching on the treadmill and now singing fortissimo. They are of all ages and most of them are ragged. The men have packs on their shoulders, one or two have hand carts. The line stretches across the stage. It is nearing twilight, and the faces of the assemblage are illumined by the rays of the late afternoon sun. The upper treadmill carries a gradually rising and falling middle distance past the marchers. The foot of a mountain appears; a trumpet call is heard as the foot of the mountain reaches stage center. The marchers halt. The picture now shows the mountain running up out of sight off right. The singing stops. A babel of "What's de matter?" "Why do we stop?" "Tain't sundown yet!" "What's happened?" "What's goin' on?" "What are they blowin' for?" etc. Those looking ahead begin to murmur. "It's Moses," "Moses." "What's happened to him?" The others take up the repetition of "Moses," and MOSES enters, on the arm of AARON. He is now an old man, as is his brother, and he totters toward the center of the stage. Cries of "What's de matter, Moses?" "You ain't hurt, is you?" "Ain't that too bad?" etc. He slowly seats himself on the rock at the foot of the mountain.)

AARON: How you feelin' now, brother?

MOSES: I'm so weary, Aaron. Seems like I was took all of a sudden.

AARON: Do we camp yere?

MOSES (pathetically): No, you got to keep goin'.

AARON: But you cain't go no further tonight, brother.

MOSES: Dis never happened to me befo'.

A YOUNG WOMAN: But you's a ol' man, now, Father Moses. You cain't expect to go as fas' as we kin.

MOSES: But de Lawd said I'd do it. He said I was to show you de Promised Land. Fo'ty years, I bin leadin' you. I led you out o' Egypt. I led you past Sinai, and through de wilderness. Oh, I cain't fall down on you now!

AARON: Le's res' yere fo' de night. Den we'll see how you feel in de mo'nin'.

MOSES: We tol' de scouts we'd meet 'em three miles furder on. I hate fo' 'em to come back all dis way to report. 'Tis gettin' a little dark, ain't it?

AARON: It ain't dark, Brother.

MOSES: No, it's my eyes.

AARON: Maybe it's de dust.

MOSES: No, I jest cain't seem to see. Oh, Lawd, dey cain't have a blind man leadin' 'em! Where is you, Aaron?

AARON: I'se right yere, Moses.

MOSES: Do you think—(Pause.) Oh! Do you think it's de time He said?

AARON: How you mean, Moses?

(*Crowd look from one to another in wonder.*)

MOSES: He said I could lead 'em to de Jordan, dat I'd *see* de Promised Land, and dat's all de further I could go, on account I broke de laws. Little while back I thought I *did* see a river ahead, and a pretty land on de other side. (*Distant shouts "Hooray!" "Yere dey are!" "Dey travelled quick." etc.*) Where's de young leader of de troops? Where's Joshua?

(*The call "Joshua" is taken up by those on the right of the stage, followed almost immediately by "Yere he is!" "Moses wants you!" etc.*)

(JOSHUA *enters. He is a fine looking Negro of about thirty.*)

JOSHUA (*going to* MOSES' *side*): Yes, suh.

MOSES: What's de shoutin' 'bout, Joshua?

JOSHUA: De scouts is back wid de news. De Jordan is right ahead of us, and Jericho is jest on de other side. Moses, we're dere! (*There are cries of "Hallelujah!" "De Lawd be praised!" "Hooray!" "De Kingdom's comin'!" etc. With a considerable stir among the marchers, several new arrivals crowd in from right, shouting "Moses, we're dere!"* JOSHUA *seeing the newcomers.*) Yere's de scouts!

(*Three very ragged and dusty young men advance to* MOSES.)

MOSES (*as the shouting dies*): So it's de River Jordan?

FIRST SCOUT: Yes, suh.

MOSES: All we got to take is de city of Jericho.

FIRST SCOUT: Yes, suh.

MOSES: Joshua, you got to take charge of de fightin' men, an' Aaron's gotta stay by de priests.

JOSHUA: What about you?

MOSES: You are leavin' me behind. Joshua, you gonter get de fightin' men together and take dat city befo' sundown.

JOSHUA: It's a big city, Moses, wid walls all 'round it. We ain't got enough men.

MOSES: You'll take it, Joshua.

JOSHUA: Yes, suh, but how?

MOSES: Move up to de walls wid our people. Tell de priests to go wid you with de rams' horns. You start marchin' 'roun' dem walls, and den—

JOSHUA: Yes, suh.

MOSES: De Lawd'll take charge, jest as he's took charge ev'y time I've led you against a city. He ain't never failed, has he?

SEVERAL VOICES: No, Moses. (*All raise their heads.*)

MOSES: And he ain't goin' to fail us now. (*He prays. All bow.*) Oh, Lawd, I'm turnin' over our brave young men to you, caize I know you don' want me to lead 'em any further. (*Rises.*) Jest like you said, I've got to de Jordan but I cain't git over it. An' yere dey goin' now to take de city of Jericho. In a little while dey'll be marchin' 'roun' it. An' would you please be so good as to tell 'em what to do? Amen. (*To* JOSHUA.) Go ahead. Ev'ybody follows Joshua now. Give de signal to move on wid e'vything. (*A trumpet is heard.*) You camp fo' de night in de City of Jericho. (MOSES *seats himself on the rock.*)

JOSHUA: Cain't we help you, Moses?

MOSES: You go ahead. De Lawd's got his plans fo' me. Soun' de signal to march. (*Another trumpet call is heard. The company starts marching off.* AARON *lingers a moment.*) Take care of de Ark of de Covenant, Aaron.

AARON: Yes, Brother. Good-bye.

MOSES: Good-bye, Aaron. (*The singing is resumed softly and dies away. The last of the marchers has disappeared.*) Yere I is, Lawd. De chillun is goin' into de Promised Land. (GOD *enters from behind the hill. He walks to* MOSES, *puts his hands on his shoulders.*) You's with me, ain't you, Lawd?

GOD: Co'se I is.

MOSES: Guess I'm through, Lawd. Jest like you said I'd be, when I broke de tablets of de law. De ol' machine's broke down.

GOD: Jest what was it I said to you, Moses? Do you remember?

MOSES: You said I couldn't go into de Promised Land.

GOD: Dat's so. But dat ain't all dey was to it.

MOSES: How you mean, Lawd?

GOD: Moses, you been a good man. You been a good leader of my people. You got me angry once, dat's true. And when you anger me I'm a God of Wrath. But I never meant you wasn't gonter have what was comin' to you. An' I ain't goin' to do you out of it, Moses. It's jest de country acrost de River dat you ain't gonter enter. You gonter have a Promised Land. I been gettin' it ready fo' you, fo' a long time. Kin you stand up?

MOSES (*rising, with* GOD's *help*): Yes, suh, Lawd.

GOD: Come on, I'm goin' to show it to you. We goin' up dis hill to see it. Moses, it's a million times nicer dan de Land of Canaan. (*They start up the hill.*)

MOSES: I cain't hardly see.

GOD: Don't worry. Dat's jest caize you so old.

(*They take a step or two up the hill, when* MOSES *stops suddenly.*)

MOSES: Oh!

GOD: What's de matter?

MOSES: We cain't be doin' dis!

GOD: Co'se we kin!

MOSES: But I fo'got! I fo'got about Joshua and de fightin' men!

GOD: How about 'em?

MOSES: Dey're marchin' on Jericho. I tol' 'em to march aroun' de walls and den de Lawd would be dere to tell 'em what to do.

GOD: Dat's all right. He's dere.

MOSES: Den who's dis helpin' me up de hill?

GOD: Yo' faith, yo' God.

MOSES: And is you over dere helpin' them too, Lawd? Is you goin' to tell dem poor chillun what to do?

GOD: Co'se I is. Listen, Moses. I'll show you how I'm helpin' dem.

(*From the distance comes the blast of the rams' horns, the sound of crumbling walls, a roar, and a moment's silence. The* CHOIR *begins "Joshua Fit De Battle of Jericho" and continues through the rest of the scene.*)

MOSES: You did it, Lawd! You've tooken it! Listen to de chillun'—dey's in de Land of Ca-naan at last! You's de only God dey ever was, ain't you, Lawd?

GOD (*quietly*): Come on, ol' man. (*They continue up the hill.*)

(*The stage is darkened.*)

MR. DESHEE (*in the dark*): But even dat scheme didn' work. Caize after dey got into the Land of Canaan dey went to de dogs again. And dey went into bondage again. Only dis time it was in de City of Babylon.

(*The* CHOIR, *which has been singing "Cain't Stay Away," stops as the next scene begins.*)

SCENE 5

(*Under a low ceiling is a room vaguely resembling a Negro night club in New Orleans. Two or three long tables run across the room, and on the left is a table on a dais with a gaudy canopy above it. The table bears a card marked "Reserved for King and guests."*

Flashy young men and women are seated at the tables. About a dozen couples are dancing in the foreground to the tune of a jazz orchestra. The costumes are what would be worn at a Negro masquerade to represent the debauchees of Babylon.)

FIRST MAN: When did yuh git to Babylon?

SECOND MAN: I jes' got in yesterday.

THIRD MAN (*dancing*): How do you like dis baby, Joe?

FOURTH MAN: Hot damn! She could be de King's pet!

A WOMAN: Anybody seen my papa?

THIRD MAN: Don' fo'git de dance at de High Priest's house tomorrow.

(*The dance stops as a bugle call is heard. Enter* MASTER OF CEREMONIES.)

MASTER OF CEREMONIES: Stop! Tonight's guest of honor, de King of Babylon an' party of five.

(*Enter the* KING *and five girls. The* KING *has on an imitation ermine cloak over his conventional evening clothes and wears a diamond tiara. All rise as the* KING *enters, and sing, "Hail, de King of Bab—Bab—Babylon."*)

KING: Wait till you see de swell table I got. (*He crosses the stage to his table. The girls are jabbering.*) Remind me to send you a peck of rubies in de mo'nin'.

MASTER OF CEREMONIES: Ev'nin', King!

KING: Good ev'nin'. How's de party goin'?

MASTER OF CEREMONIES: Bes' one we ever had in Babylon, King.

KING: Any Jew boys yere?

MASTER OF CEREMONIES (indicating some of the others): Lot o' dem yere. I kin go git mo' if you want 'em.

KING: I was really referrin' to de High Priest. He's a 'ticlar frien' o' mine an' he might drop in. You know what he look like?

MASTER OF CEREMONIES: No, suh, but I'll be on de look-out fo' him.

KING: O.K. Now let's have a li'l good time.

MASTER OF CEREMONIES: Yes, suh. (To the orchestra.) Let 'er go, boys.

(The music begins, waiters appear with food and great urns painted gold and silver, from which they pour out wine for the guests. The MASTER OF CEREMONIES exits. The KING's dancing-girls go to the middle of the floor, and start to dance. The KING puts his arms about the waists of two girls, and draws them to him.)

KING: Hot damn! Da's de way! Let de Jew boys see our gals kin dance better'n dere's. (There is an ad lib. babel of "Da's de truth, King!" "I don' know—we got some good gals, too!" etc.) Dey ain' nobody in de worl' like de Babylon gals.

(The dancing grows faster, the watchers keep time with hand-claps. The door at the left opens suddenly, and the PROPHET, a patriarchal, ragged figure enters. He looks belligerently about the room, and is followed almost immediately by the MASTER OF CEREMONIES.)

PROPHET: Stop! (The music and the dancers halt.)

KING: What's the idea, bustin' up my party?

MASTER OF CEREMONIES: He said he was expected, King. I thought mebbe he was de—

KING: Did you think he was de High Priest of de Hebrews? Why, he's jest an ol' bum! De High Priest is a fashion plate. T'row dis ole bum out o' yere!

PROPHET: Stop!

(Those who have been advancing to seize him stop, somewhat amused.)

KING: Wait a minute. Don't throw him out. Let's see what he has to say.

PROPHET: Listen to me, King of Babylon! I've been sent yere by de Lawd God Jehovah. Don't you dare lay a hand on de Prophet!

KING: Oh, you're a prophet, is yuh? Well, you know we don' keer much fo' prophets in dis part of de country.

PROPHET: Listen to me, sons and daughters of Babylon! Listen, you children of Israel dat's given yo'selves over to de evil ways of yo' oppressors! You're all wallowin' like hogs in sin, an' de wrath of Gawd ain' goin' to be held back much longer! I'm tellin' you, repent befo' it's too late. Repent befo' Jehovah casts down de same fire dat burned up Sodom and Gomorrah. Repent befo' de—(During this scene yells increase as the PROPHET continues.)

(The HIGH PRIEST enters Left. He is a fat voluptuary, elaborately clothed in brightly colored robes. He walks in hand in hand with a gaudily dressed "chippy.")

HIGH PRIEST (noise stops): Whoa, dere! What you botherin' the King fo'?

PROPHET (wheeling): And you, de High Priest of all Israel, walkin' de town wid a dirty li'l tramp.

KING: Seems to be a frien' o' yours, Jake.

HIGH PRIEST (crossing to the KING with his girl): Aw, he's one of dem wild men, like Jeremiah and Isaiah. Don' let him bother you none. (Pushes PROPHET aside and goes to KING's table.)

PROPHET: You consort with harlots, an' yo' pollution in the sight of de Lawd. De Lawd God's goin' to smite you down, jest as he's goin' to smite down all dis wicked world! (Grabs HIGH PRIEST and turns him around.)

KING (angrily against the last part of the preceding speech): Wait a minute. I'm getting tired of this. Don' throw him out. Jest kill him! (There is the sound of a shot. The PROPHET falls.)

PROPHET: Smite 'em down, Lawd, like you said. Dey ain't a decent person left in de whole world.

(He dies. MASTER OF CEREMONIES, revolver in hand, looks down at the PROPHET.)

MASTER OF CEREMONIES: He's dead, King.

KING: Some of you boys take him out.

(A couple of young men come from the background and walk off with the body.)

HIGH PRIEST: Don' know whether you should'a done that, King.

KING: Why not?

HIGH PRIEST: I don' know whether de Lawd would like it.

KING: Now, listen, Jake. You know yo' Lawd ain't payin' much attention to dis man's town. Except fo' you boys, it's tho'ly protected by de Gods o' Babylon.

HIGH PRIEST: I know, but jest de same—

KING: Look yere, s'pose I give you a couple hund'ed pieces of silver. Don' you s'pose you kin arrange to persuade yo' Gawd to keep his hands off?

HIGH PRIEST (*oilily*): Well of co'se we could try. I dunno how well it would work.

(*As the* HIGH PRIEST *speaks, The* KING *claps his hands.* MASTER OF CEREMONIES *enters with bag of money.*)

KING: Yere it is.

HIGH PRIEST (*smiling*): I guess we kin square things up. (*He prays—whiningly.*) Oh Lawd, please forgive my po' frien' de King o' Babylon. He didn't know what he was doin' an'—

(*There is a clap of thunder, darkness for a second. The lights go up and* GOD *is standing in the center of the room.*)

GOD (*in a voice of doom*): Dat's about enough. (*The guests are horrified.*) I's stood all I kin from you. I tried to make dis a good earth. I helped Adam, I helped Noah, I helped Moses, an' I helped David. What's de grain dat grew out of de seed? Sin! Nothin' but sin throughout de whole world. I've given you ev'y chance. I sent you warriors and prophets. I've given you laws and commandments, an' you betrayed my trust. Ev'ything I've given you, you've defiled. Ev'y time I've fo'given you, you've mocked me. An' now de High Priest of Israel tries to trifle wid my name. Listen, you chillun of darkness, yo' Lawd is tried. I'm tired of de struggle to make you worthy of de breath I gave you. I put you in bondage ag'in to cure you an' yo' worse dan you was amongst de flesh pots of Egypt. So I renounce you. Listen to the words of yo' lawd God Jehovah, for dey is de last words yo' ever hear from me. I repent of dese people dat I have made and I will deliver dem no more.

(*There is darkness and cries of* "Mercy!" "Have pity, Lawd!" "We didn' mean it, Lawd!" "Forgive us, Lawd!" *etc. The* CHOIR *sings* "Death's Gwinter Lay His Cold Icy Hands On Me" *until the lights go up on the next scene.*)

SCENE 6

(GOD *is writing at his desk. Outside, past the door, goes* HOSEA, *a dignified old man, with wings like*

JACOB'S. GOD, *sensing his presence, looks up from the paper he is examining, and follows him out of the corner of his eye. Angrily he resumes his work as soon as* HOSEA *is out of sight. There is a knock on the door.*)

GOD: Who is it?

(GABRIEL *enters.*)

GABRIEL: It's de delegation, Lawd.
GOD (*wearily*): Tell 'em to come in.

(ABRAHAM, ISAAC, JACOB, *and* MOSES *enter.*)

Good mo'nin', gen'lemen.
THE VISITORS: Good mo'nin', Lawd.
GOD: What kin I do for you?
MOSES: You know, Lawd. Go back to our people.

GOD (*shaking his head*): Ev'ry day fo' hund'ed's of years you boys have come in to ask dat same thing. De answer is still de same. I repented of de people I made. I said I would deliver dem no more. Good mo'nin', gen'lemen. (*The four visitors rise and exeunt.* GABRIEL *remains.*) Gabe, why do dey do it?

GABRIEL: I 'spect dey think you gonter change yo' mind.

GOD (*sadly*): Dey don' know me. (HOSEA *again passes the door. His shadow shows on wall.* GABRIEL *is perplexed, as he watches.* GOD *again looks surreptitiously over His shoulder at the passing figure.*) I don' like dat, either.

GABRIEL: What, Lawd?
GOD: Dat man.
GABRIEL: He's jest a prophet, Lawd. Dat's jest old Hosea. He jest come up the other day.

GOD: I know. He's one of de few dat's come up yere since I was on de earth last time.

GABRIEL: Ain' been annoyin' you, has he?
GOD: I don' like him walkin' past de door.
GABRIEL: All you got to do is tell him to stop, Lawd.

GOD: Yes, I know. I don' want to tell him. He's got a right up yere or he wouldn't be yere.

GABRIEL: You needn' be bothered by him hangin' aroun' de office all de time. I'll tell 'im. Who's he think he—

GOD: No, Gabe. I find it ain't in me to stop him. I sometimes jest wonder why he don' come in and say hello.

GABRIEL: You want him to do dat?

(*He moves as if to go to the door.*)

GOD: He never has spoke to me, and if he don' wanta come in, I ain't gonter make him.

But dat ain't de worst of it, Gabriel.

GABRIEL: What is, Lawd?

GOD: Ev'y time he goes past de door I hears a voice.

GABRIEL: One of de angels?

GOD (shaking his head): It's from de earth. It's a man.

GABRIEL: You mean he's prayin'?

GOD: No, he ain't exactly prayin'. He's jest talkin' in such a way dat I got to lissen. His name is Hezdrel.

GABRIEL: Is he on de books?

GOD: No, not yet. But ev'y time dat Hosea goes past I hear dat voice.

GABRIEL: Den tell it to stop.

GOD: I find I don' want to do that, either. Dey's gettin' ready to take Jerusalem down dere. Dat was my big fine city. Dis Hezdrel, he's jest one of de defenders. (Suddenly and passionately, almost wildly.) I ain't comin' down. You hear me? I ain't comin' down. (He looks at GABRIEL.) Go ahead, Gabriel. 'Tend to yo' chores. I'm gonter keep wukkin' yere.

GABRIEL: I hates to see you feelin' like dis, Lawd.

GOD: Dat's all right. Even bein' Gawd ain't a bed of roses. (GABRIEL exits. HOSEA's shadow is on the wall. For a second HOSEA hesitates. GOD looks at the wall. Goes to window.) I hear you. I know yo' fightin' bravely, but I ain't comin' down. Oh, why don' you leave me alone? You know you ain't talkin' to me. Is you talkin' to me? I cain't stand yo' talkin' dat way. I kin only hear part of what you' sayin', and it puzzles me. Don' you know you cain't puzzle God? (A pause. Then, tenderly.) Do you want me to come down dere ve'y much? You know I said I wouldn't come down? (Fiercely.) Why don' he answer me a little? (With clenched fists, looks down through the window.) Listen! I'll tell you what I'll do. I ain't goin' to promise you anythin', and I ain't goin' to do nothin' to help you. I'm jest feelin' a little low, an' I'm only comin' down to make myself feel a little better, dat's all.

(The stage is darkened. CHOIR begins "A Blind Man Stood In De Middle of De Road," and continues until the lights go up on the next scene.)

SCENE 7

(It is a shadowed corner beside the walls of the temple in Jerusalem. The light of camp fires flickers on the figure of HEZDREL, who was ADAM in Part I. He stands in the same position ADAM held when first discovered but in his right hand is a sword, and his left is in a sling. Around him are several prostrate bodies. Pistol and cannon shots, then a trumpet call. Six young men enter from left in command of a CORPORAL. They are all armed.)

CORPORAL: De fightin's stopped fo' de night, Hezdrel.

HEZDREL: Yes?

CORPORAL: Dey're goin' to begin ag'in at cockcrow. (Man enters, crosses the stage and exits.) Herod say he's goin' to take de temple tomorrow, burn de books and de Ark of de Covenant, and put us all to de sword.

HEZDREL: Yo' ready, ain't you?

EVERYBODY: Yes, Hezdrel.

HEZDREL: Did de food get in through de hole in de city wall?

(Two soldiers enter, cross the stage and exit.)

CORPORAL: Yessuh, we's goin' back to pass it out now.

HEZDREL: Good. Any mo' of our people escape today?

CORPORAL: Ol' Herod's got de ol' hole covered up now, but fifteen of our people got out a new one we made.

(Other soldiers enter, cross the stage and exit.)

HEZDREL: Good. Take dese yere wounded men back and git 'em took care of.

CORPORAL: Yes, suh.

(They pick up the bodies on the ground and carry them offstage as HEZDREL speaks.)

HEZDREL: So dey gonter take de temple in de mo'nin'? We'll be waitin' for 'em. Jest remember, boys, when dey kill us we leap out of our skins, right into de lap of God.

(The men disappear with the wounded; from the deep shadow upstage comes GOD.)

GOD: Hello, Hezdrel—Adam.

HEZDREL (rubbing his forehead): Who is you?

GOD: Me? I'm jest an ol' preacher, from back in de hills.

HEZDREL: What you doin' yere?

GOD: I heard you boys was fightin'. I jest wanted to see how it was goin'.

HEZDREL: Well, it ain't goin' so well.

GOD: Dey got you skeered, huh?

HEZDREL: Look yere, who is you, a spy in my brain?

GOD: Cain't you see I's one of yo' people?

HEZDREL: Listen, Preacher, we ain't skeered. We's gonter be killed, but we ain't skeered.

GOD: I's glad to hear dat. Kin I ask you a question, Hezdrel?

HEZDREL: What is it?

GOD: How is it you is so brave?

HEZDREL: Caize we got faith, dat's why!

GOD: Faith! In who?

HEZDREL: In our dear Lawd God.

GOD: But God say he abandoned ev' one down yere.

HEZDREL: Who say dat? Who dare say dat of de Lawd God of Hosea?

GOD: De God of Hosea?

HEZDREL: You heard me. Look yere, you *is* a spy in my brain!

GOD: No, I ain't, Hezdrel. I'm jest puzzled. You ought to know dat.

HEZDREL: How come you so puzzled 'bout de God of Hosea?

GOD: I don' know. Maybe I jest don' hear things. You see, I live 'way back in de hills.

HEZDREL: What you wanter find out?

GOD: Ain't de God of Hosea de same Jehovah dat was de God of Moses?

HEZDREL (*contemptuously*): No. Dat ol' God of wrath and vengeance? We have de God dat Hosea preached to us. He's de one God.

GOD: Who's he?

HEZDREL (*reverently*): De God of mercy.

GOD: Hezdrel, don' you think dey must be de same God?

HEZDREL: I don' know. I ain't bothered to think much about it. Maybe dey is. Maybe our God is de same ol' God. I guess we jest got tired of his appearance dat ol' way.

GOD: What you mean, Hezdrel?

HEZDREL: Oh, dat ol' God dat walked de earth in de shape of a man. I guess he lived wid man so much dat all he seen was de sins in man. Dat's what made him de God of wrath and vengeance. Co'se he made Hosea. An' Hosea never would a found what mercy was unless dere was a little of it in God, too. Anyway, he ain't a fearsome God no mo'. Hosea showed us dat.

GOD: How you s'pose Hosea found dat mercy?

HEZDREL: De only way he could find it. De only way I found it. De only way anyone kin find it.

GOD: How's dat?

HEZDREL: Through sufferin'.

GOD (*after a pause*): What if dey kill you in de mo'nin', Hezdrel.

HEZDREL: If dey do, dey do. Dat's all.

GOD: Herod say he's goin' to burn de temple—

HEZDREL: So he say.

GOD: And burn de Ark an' de books. Den dat's de end of de books, ain't it?

HEZDREL (*buoyantly*): What you mean? If he burns dem things in dere? Naw. Dem's jest copies.

GOD: Where is de others?

HEZDREL (*tapping his head*): Dey's a set in yere. Fifteen got out through de hole in the city wall today. A hundred and fifty got out durin' de week. Each of 'em is a set of de books. Dey's scattered safe all over de countryside now, jest waitin' to git pen and paper fo' to put 'em down agin.

GOD (*proudly*): Dey cain't lick you, kin dey Hezdrel?

HEZDREL (*smiling*): I know dey cain't. (*Trumpet.*) You better get out o' yere, Preacher, if you wanter carry de news to yo' people. It'll soon be daylight.

GOD: I'm goin'. (*He takes a step upstage and stops.*) Want me to take any message?

HEZDREL: Tell de people in de hills dey ain't nobody like de Lawd God of Hosea.

GOD: I will. If dey kill you tomorrow I'll bet dat God of Hosea'll be waitin' for you.

HEZDREL: I *know* he will.

GOD (*quietly*): Thank you, Hezdrel.

HEZDREL: Fo' what?

GOD: Fo' tellin' me so much. You see I been so far away, I guess I was jest way behin' de times.

(*He exits. Pause, then trumpet sounds.*) (HEZDREL *paces back and forth once or twice. Another young soldier appears. Other men enter and stand grouped about* HEZDREL.)

SECOND OFFICER (*excitedly*): De cock's jest crowed, Hezdrel. Dey started de fightin' ag'in.

HEZDREL: We's ready for 'em. Come on, boys. (*From the darkness upstage comes another group of soldiers.*) Dis is de day dey say dey'll git us. Le's fight till de last man goes. What d'you say?

CORPORAL: Le's go. Hezdrel!

HEZDREL (*calling left*): Give 'em ev'ything, boys!

(*There is a movement toward the left, a bugle call and the sound of distant battle. The lights go out. The* CHOIR *is heard singing, "March On," triumphantly. They continue to sing after the lights go up on the next scene.*)

SCENE 8

(*It is the same setting as the Fish Fry Scene in Part I. The same angels are present but the* CHOIR, *instead of marching, is standing in a double row on an angle upstage right.* GOD *is seated in an armchair near center. He faces the audience. As the* CHOIR *continues to sing,* GABRIEL *enters, unnoticed by the chattering angels. He looks at* GOD *who is staring thoughtfully toward the audience.*)

GABRIEL: You look a little pensive, Lawd. (GOD *nods his head.*) Have a seegar, Lawd?

GOD: No thanks, Gabriel.

(GABRIEL *goes to the table, accepts a cup of custard; chats with the angel behind the table for a moment as he sips, puts the cup down and returns to the side of* GOD.)

GABRIEL: You look awful pensive, Lawd. You been sittin' yere, lookin' dis way, an awful long time. Is it somethin' serious, Lawd?

GOD: Very serious, Gabriel.

GABRIEL (*awed by His tone*): Lawd, is de time come for me to blow?

GOD: Not yet, Gabriel. I'm just thinkin'.

GABRIEL: What about, Lawd? (*Puts up hand. Singing stops.*)

GOD: 'Bout somethin' de boy tol' me. Somethin' 'bout Hosea, and himself. How dey foun' somethin'.

GABRIEL: What, Lawd?

GOD: Mercy. (*A pause.*) Through *sufferin'*, he said.

GABRIEL: Yes, Lawd.

GOD: I'm tryin' to find it, too. It's awful impo'tant. It's awful impo'tant to all de people on my earth. Did he mean dat even God must suffer?

(GOD *continues to look out over the audience for a moment and then a look of surprise comes into his face. He sighs. In the distance a voice cries.*)

THE VOICE: Oh, look at him! Oh, look, dey goin' to make him carry it up dat high hill! Dey goin' to nail him to it! Oh, dat's a terrible burden for one man to carry!

(GOD *rises and murmurs "Yes!" as if in recognition. The heavenly beings have been watching him closely, and now, seeing him smile gently, draw back, relieved. All the angels burst into "Hallelujah, King Jesus."* GOD *continues to smile as the lights fade away. The singing becomes fortissimo.*)

CURTAIN

Clifford Odets: *Waiting for Lefty* (1935)

Born in Philadelphia, but raised in New York City, Odets maintained an urban outlook in all his work. He is sensitive to the political and economic strains of city life as only a person who came of age during the Great Depression would be. His views of the free and open economic policies of *laissez faire* and rugged individualism are colored by memories of his own neighborhoods and his own parents, who were hard-working, apparently comfortable, but never well off. Clifford Odets left high school early to become a radio announcer. He soon found his way into the theater, joining such notables as Harold Clurman and Lee Strasberg, with whom he formed the Group Theatre in 1930. He acted small parts in a number of plays while also writing his first play, eventually titled *Awake and Sing*. The Group reluctantly decided not to produce it because they feared it would not run long enough to recover costs. It was a strong play, with a pronounced social theme—like all of Odets' major work—centering on a poor family in the Bronx (obviously modeled on his own) whose difficulties in the early years of the Depression were its main focus.

Waiting for Lefty was written in three days, while Odets locked himself (so the story goes) in a Boston hotel room. He wrote it expressly for a one-act play contest and it easily won the first prize. When it was produced, it was a sensation. Some critics feel it is his most stimulating play and perhaps his best. Others prefer *Golden Boy* (1937), the story of a city youth who was forced to choose between his talent as a violinist and his remarkable abilities as a prize fighter. Even *Awake and Sing*, which was finally produced in 1935 in response to the success of *Waiting for Lefty*, has its following, and some critics have maintained that it is his finest work. However, few critics cite any of his later plays as being as distinctive and effective as these three; yet Clifford Odets remained thoroughly committed and active in the theater throughout his life.

Soon after his early success, Odets found it necessary to supplement the income of the Group Theater by going to Hollywood to become a screenwriter. He apparently sent much of the money he made back to the Group to support important productions of minor plays. His work as a screenwriter was by no means all pleasant, even though he had some success. Eventually, he wrote a play about some of his experiences and about the entire phenomenon of Hollywood and the marketing of a writer's talent. Its title, *The Big Knife* (1949), says it all.

From the first production of *Waiting for Lefty*, Clifford Odets became something of a darling to the political left. Many people associated him with the 1930s enthusiasm for Communism, although Odets maintained that he was committed to a "vague socialism." The theme of Communism, extremely timely in the early 1930s, is apparent in *Waiting for Lefty*, although it is also clear that the taxi drivers who are the central characters of the drama are much more interested in fair wages and more personal economic independence than in any specific economic ideologies. The play was based on the actual 1934 strike of New York taxi drivers. The portrait of management is certainly not favorable. In a flashback scene interrupting the ongoing union meeting, Joe's wife Edna puts things rather forcefully when she accuses him of not being manly, of not sticking up for her and her children, and of not measuring up to her expectations. Joe's willingness to put up with low wages and bad working conditions translates directly into her threatening to leave him for another more manly man. Even the union is indicted for being controlled by mobsters and gunmen and not having the workers' best interests at heart. They constantly advise against a strike and want everyone to wait for Lefty, who will tell them the truth.

The technique of flashback is used effectively in the play, bringing it in some ways close in style to such expressionistic plays as *The Adding Machine* and even *The Emperor Jones*. Flashback was common in the films of the period, so it was familiar to most audiences. Played against the impending union strike vote, it was a particularly effective device, using switches in locale and time and giving the feeling that the play was full-length rather than a one-acter.

The 1950s were not kind to Clifford Odets. He might have been the dean of American playwrights, but instead he found himself under a cloud of suspicion during the infamous period of Hollywood blacklisting and the purges of the House Committee on Un-American Activities Anti-Communist groups. fed on the tensions of the cold war years and brought terrible pressure on those whose views were in any way left-leaning and liberal. Yet he survived and has established himself as one of the strongest voices of the 1930s in America. He is our Depression playwright, celebrating the struggles of the common citizen.

Suggested reading

Cantor, Harold. *Clifford Odets, Playwright-Poet.* Metuchen: Scarecrow Press, 1973

Mendelsohn, Michael J. *Clifford Odets, Humane Dramatist.* Deland: Everett/Edwards, 1969

Murray, Edward. *Clifford Odets: The Thirties and After.* New York: Ungar, 1968.

Odets, Clifford. *Night Music.* New York: Random House, 1949.

———. *Six Plays.* New York: Random House, 1939.

———. *The Big Knife.* New York: Random House, 1949.

Waiting for Lefty

Clifford Odets

CHARACTERS

FATT	CLAYTON
JOE	AGATE KELLER
EDNA	HENCHMAN
MILLER	REILLY
FAYETTE	DR. BARNES
IRV	DR. BENJAMIN
FLORRIE	A MAN
SID	

(As the curtain goes up we see a bare stage. On it are sitting six or seven men in a semi-circle. Lolling against the proscenium down left is a young man chewing a toothpick: a gunman. A fat man of porcine appearance is talking directly to the audience. In other words he is the head of a union and the men ranged behind him are a committee of workers. They are now seated in interesting different attitudes and present a wide diversity of type, as we shall soon see. The fat man is hot and heavy under the collar, near the end of a long talk, but not too hot: he is well fed and confident. His name is HARRY FATT.*)*

FATT: You're so wrong I ain't laughing. Any guy with eyes to read knows it. Look at the textile strike—out like lions and in like lambs. Take the San Francisco tie-up—starvation and broken heads. The steel boys wanted to walk out too, but they changed their minds. It's the trend of the times, that's what it is. All we workers got a good man behind us now. He's top man of the country—looking out for our interests—the man in the White House is the one I'm referrin' to. That's why the times ain't ripe for a strike. He's working day and night—

VOICE (*from the audience*): For who? (*The* GUNMAN *stirs himself.*)

FATT: For you! The records prove it. If this was the Hoover régime, would I say don't go out, boys? Not on your tin-type! But things is different now. You read the papers as well as me. You know it. And that's why I'm against the strike. Because we gotta stand behind the man who's standin' behind us! The whole country

――――

ANOTHER VOICE: Is on the blink! (*The* GUNMAN *looks grave.*)

FATT: Stand up and show yourself, you damn red! Be a man, let's see what you look like! (*Waits in vain.*) Yellow from the word go! Red and yellow makes a dirty color, boys. I got my eyes on four or five of them in the union here. What the hell'll they do for you? Pull you out and run away when trouble starts. Give those birds a chance and they'll have your sisters and wives in the whore houses, like they done in Russia. They'll tear Christ off his bleeding cross. They'll wreck your homes and throw your babies in the river. You think that's bunk? Read the papers! Now listen, we can't stay here all night. I gave you the facts in the case. You boys got hot suppers to go to and――――

ANOTHER VOICE: Says you!

GUNMAN: Sit down, Punk!

ANOTHER VOICE: Where's Lefty? (*Now this question is taken up by the others in unison.* FATT *pounds with gavel.*)

FATT: That's what I wanna know. Where's your pal, Lefty? You elected him chairman —where the hell did he disappear?

VOICES: We want Lefty! Lefty! Lefty!

FATT (*pounding*): What the hell is this—a circus? You got the committee here. This bunch of cowboys you elected. (*Pointing to man on extreme right end.*)

MAN: Benjamin.

FATT: Yeah, Doc Benjamin. (*Pointing to other men in circle in seated order.*) Benjamin, Miller, Stein, Mitchell, Phillips, Keller. It ain't my fault Lefty took a run-out powder. If you guys—

A GOOD VOICE: What's the committee say?

OTHERS: The committee! Let's hear from the committee! (FATT *tries to quiet the crowd, but one of the seated men suddenly comes to the front. The* GUNMAN *moves over to center stage, but* FATT *says:*)

FATT: Sure, let him talk. Let's hear what the red boys gotta say! (*Various shouts are coming from the audience.* FATT *insolently goes back to his seat in the middle of the circle. He sits on his raised platform and relights his cigar. The* GUNMAN *goes back to his post.* JOE, *the new speaker, raises his hand for quiet. Gets it quickly. He is sore.*)

JOE: You boys know me. I ain't a red boy one bit! Here I'm carryin' a shrapnel that big I picked up in the war. And maybe I don't know it when it rains! Don't tell me red! You know what we are? The black and blue boys! We been kicked around so long we're black and blue from head to toes. But I guess anyone who says straight out he don't like it, he's a red boy to the leaders of the union. What's this crap about goin' home to hot suppers? I'm asking to your faces how many's got hot suppers to go home to? Anyone who's sure of his next meal, raise your hand! A certain gent sitting behind me can raise them both. But not in front here! And that's why we're talking strike—to get a living wage!

VOICE: Where's Lefty?

JOE: I honest to God don't know, but he didn't take no run-out powder. That Wop's got more guts than a slaughter house. Maybe a traffic jam got him, but he'll be here. But don't let this red stuff scare you. Unless fighting for a living scares you. We gotta make up our minds. My wife made up my mind last week, if you want the truth. It's plain as the nose on Sol Feinberg's face we need a strike. There's us comin' home every night—eight, ten hours on the cab. "God," the wife says, "eighty cents ain't money—don't buy beans almost. You're workin' for the company," she says to me, "Joe! you ain't workin' for me or the family no more!" She says to me, "If you don't start . . ."

ACT 1

JOE AND EDNA

(*The lights fade out and a white spot picks out the playing space within the space of seated men. The seated men are very dimly visible in the outer dark, but more prominent is* FATT *smoking his cigar and often blowing the smoke in the lighted circle.*

A tired but attractive woman of thirty comes into the room, drying her hands on an apron. She stands there sullenly as JOE *comes in from the other side, home from work. For a moment they stand and look at each other in silence.*)

JOE: Where's all the furniture, honey?

EDNA: They took it away. No installments paid.

JOE: When?

EDNA: Three o'clock.

JOE: They can't do that.

EDNA: Can't? They did it.

JOE: Why, the palookas, we paid three-quarters.

EDNA: The man said read the contract.

JOE: We must have signed a phoney. . . .

EDNA: It's a regular contract and you signed it.

JOE: Don't be so sour, Edna. . . .(*Tries to embrace her.*)

EDNA: Do it in the movies, Joe—they pay Clark Gable big money for it.

JOE: This is a helluva house to come home to. Take my word!

EDNA: Take MY word! Whose fault is it?

JOE: Must you start that stuff again?

EDNA: Maybe you'd like to talk about books?

JOE: I'd like to slap you in the mouth!

EDNA: No you won't.

JOE (*sheepishly*): Jeez, Edna, you get me sore some time. . . .

EDNA: But just look at me—I'm laughing all over!

JOE: Don't insult me. Can I help it if times are bad? What the hell do you want me to do, jump off a bridge or something?

EDNA: Don't yell. I just put the kids to bed so they won't know they missed a meal. If I don't have Emmy's shoes soled tomorrow, she can't go to school. In the meantime let her sleep.

JOE: Honey, I rode the wheels off the chariot today. I cruised around five hours without a call. It's conditions.

EDNA: Tell it to the A & P!

JOE: I booked two-twenty on the clock. A lady with a dog was lit . . . she gave me a quarter tip by mistake. If you'd only listen to me—we're rolling in wealth.

EDNA: Yeah? How much?

JOE: I had "coffee and—" in a beanery. (*Hands her silver coins.*) A buck four.

EDNA: The second month's rent is due tomorrow.

JOE: Don't look at me that way, Edna.

EDNA: I'm looking through you, not at you. . . . Everything was gonna be so ducky! A cottage by the waterfall, roses in Picardy. You're a four-star-bust! If you think I'm standing for it much longer, you're crazy as a bedbug.

JOE: I'd get another job if I could. There's no work—you know it.

EDNA: I only know we're at the bottom of the ocean.

JOE: What can I do?

EDNA: Who's the man in the family, you or me?

JOE: That's no answer. Get down to brass tacks. Christ, gimme a break, too! A coffee and java all day. I'm hungry, too, Babe. I'd work my fingers to the bone if—

EDNA: I'll open a can of salmon.

JOE: Not now. Tell me what to do!

EDNA: I'm not God!

JOE: Jeez, I wish I was a kid again and didn't have to think about the next minute.

EDNA: But you're not a kid and you do have to think about the next minute. You got two blondie kids sleeping in the next room. They need food and clothes. I'm not mentioning anything else—But we're stalled like a flivver in the snow. For five years I laid awake at night listening to my heart pound. For God's sake, do something, Joe, get wise. Maybe get your buddies together, maybe go on strike for better money. Poppa did it during the war and they won out. I'm turning into a sour old nag.

JOE (*defending himself*): Strikes don't work!

EDNA: Who told you?

JOE: Besides that means not a nickel a week while we're out. Then when it's over they don't take you back.

EDNA: Suppose they don't! What's to lose?

JOE: Well, we're averaging six-seven dollars a week now.

EDNA: That just pays for the rent.

JOE: That is something, Edna.

EDNA: It isn't. They'll push you down to three and four a week before you know it. Then you'll say, "That's somethin'," too!

JOE: There's too many cabs on the street, that's the whole damn trouble.

EDNA: Let the company worry about that, you big fool! If their cabs didn't make a profit, they'd take them off the streets. Or maybe you think they're in business just to pay Joe Mitchell's rent!

JOE: You don't know a-b-c, Edna.

EDNA: I know this—your boss is making suckers outa you boys every minute. Yes, and suckers out of all the wives and the poor innocent kids who'll grow up with crooked spines and sick bones. Sure, I see it in the papers, how good orange juice is for kids. But damnit our kids get colds one on top of the other. They look like little ghosts. Betty never saw a grapefruit. I took her to the store last week and she pointed to a stack of grapefruits. "What's that!" she said. My God, Joe—the world is supposed to be for all of us.

JOE: You'll wake them up.

EDNA: I don't care, as long as I can maybe wake you up.

JOE: Don't insult me. One man can't make a strike.

EDNA: Who says one? You got hundreds in your rotten union!

JOE: The union ain't rotten.

EDNA: No? Then what are they doing? Collecting dues and patting your back?

JOE: They're making plans.

EDNA: What kind?

JOE: They don't tell us.

EDNA: It's too damn bad about you. They don't tell little Joey what's happening in his bitsie witsie union. What do you think it is—a ping pong game?

JOE: You know they're racketeers. The guys at the top would shoot you for a nickel.

EDNA: Why do you stand for that stuff?

JOE: Don't you wanna see me alive?

EDNA (after a deep pause): No . . . I don't think I do, Joe. Not if you can lift a finger to do something about it, and don't. No, I don't care.

JOE: Honey, you don't understand what—

EDNA: Take your hand away! Only they don't . . . let them all be ground to hamburger!

JOE: It's one thing to—

EDNA: Take you hand away! Only they don't grind me to little pieces! I got different plans. (Starts to take off her apron.)

JOE: Where are you going?

EDNA: None of your business.

JOE: What's up your sleeve?

EDNA: My arm'd be up my sleeve, darling if I had a sleeve to wear. (Puts neatly folded apron on back of chair.)

JOE: Tell me!

EDNA: Tell you what?

JOE: Where are you going?

EDNA: Don't you remember my old boy friend?

JOE: Who?

EDNA: Bud Haas. He still has my picture in his watch. He earns a living.

JOE: What the hell are you talking about?

EDNA: I heard worse than I'm talking about.

JOE: Have you seen Bud since we got married?

EDNA: Maybe.

JOE: If I thought . . . (He stands looking at her.)

EDNA: See much? Listen, boy friend, if you think I won't do this it just means you can't see straight.

JOE: Stop talking bull!

EDNA: This isn't five years ago, Joe.

JOE: You mean you'd leave me and the kids?

EDNA: I'd leave you like a shot!

JOE: No. . . .

EDNA: Yes! (JOE turns away, sitting in a chair with his back to her. Outside the lighted circle of the playing stage we hear the other seated members of the strike committee. "She will . . . she will . . . it happens that way," etc. This group should be used throughout for various comments. political. emotional and as general chorus. Whispering. . . . The fat boss now blows a heavy cloud of smoke into the scene.)

JOE (finally): Well, I guess I ain't got a leg to stand on.

EDNA: No?

JOE (suddenly mad): No, you lousy tart, no! Get the hell out of here. Go pick up that bull-thrower on the corner and stop at some cushy hotel downtown. He's probably been coming here every morning and laying you while I hacked my guts out!

EDNA: You're crawling like a worm!

JOE: You'll be crawling in a minute.

EDNA: You don't scare me that much! (Indicates a half inch on her finger.)

JOE: This is what I slaved for!

EDNA: Tell it to your boss!

JOE: He don't give a damn for you or me!

EDNA: That's what I say.

JOE: Don't change the subject!

EDNA: This is the subject, the exact subject! Your boss makes this subject. I never saw him in my life, but he's putting ideas in my head a mile a minute. He's giving your kids that fancy disease called the rickets. He's making a jelly-fish outa you and putting wrinkles in my face. This is the subject every inch of the way! He's throwing me into Bud Haas' lap. When in hell will you get wise—

JOE: I'm not so dumb as you think! But you are talking like a red.

EDNA: I don't know what that means. But when a man knocks you down you get up and kiss his fist! You gutless piece of boloney.

JOE: One man can't—

EDNA (with great joy): I don't say one man! I say a hundred, a thousand, a whole million, I say. But start in your own union. Get those hack boys together! Sweep out those racketeers like a pile of dirt! Stand up like men and fight for the crying kids and wives. Goddamnit! I'm tired of slavery and sleepless nights.

JOE (*with her*): Sure, sure! . . .

EDNA: Yes. Get brass toes on your shoes and know where to kick!

JOE (*suddenly jumping up and kissing his wife full on the mouth*): Listen, Edna, I'm goin' down to 174th Street to look up Lefty Costello. Lefty was saying the other day . . . (*He suddenly stops.*) How about this Haas guy?

EDNA: Get out of here!

JOE: I'll be back! (*Runs out. For a moment* EDNA *stands triumphant. There is a blackout and when the regular lights come up,* JOE MITCHELL *is concluding what he has been saying*):

JOE: You guys know this stuff better than me. We gotta walk out! (*Abruptly he turns and goes back to his seat.*)

ACT II

LAB ASSISTANT EPISODE

(*Discovered:* MILLER, *a lab assistant, looking around; and* FAYETTE, *an industrialist.*)

FAYETTE: Like it?

MILLER: Very much. I've never seen an office like this outside the movies.

FAYETTE: Yes, I often wonder if interior decorators and bathroom fixture people don't get all their ideas from Hollywood. Our country's extraordinary that way. Soap, cosmetics, electric refrigerators just let Mrs. Consumer know they're used by the Crawfords and Garbos —more volume of sale than one plant can handle!

MILLER: I'm afraid it isn't that easy, Mr. Fayette.

FAYETTE: No, you're right—gross exaggeration on my part. Competition is cutthroat today. Market's up flush against a stone wall. The astronomers had better hurry—open Mars to trade expansion.

MILLER: Or it will be just too bad!

FAYETTE: Cigar?

MILLER: Thank you, don't smoke.

FAYETTE: Drink?

MILLER: Ditto, Mr. Fayette.

FAYETTE: I like sobriety in my workers . . . the trained ones, I mean. The pollacks and niggers, they're better drunk—keeps them out of mischief. Wondering why I had you come over?

MILLER: If you don't mind my saying—very much.

FAYETTE (*patting him on the knee*): I like your work.

MILLER: Thanks.

FAYETTE: No reason why a talented young man like yourself shouldn't string along with us—a growing concern. Loyalty is well repaid in our organization. Did you see Siegfried this morning?

MILLER: He hasn't been in the laboratory all day.

FAYETTE: I told him yesterday to raise you twenty dollars a month. Starts this week.

MILLER: You don't know how happy my wife'll be.

FAYETTE: Oh, I can appreciate it. (*He laughs.*)

MILLER: Was that all, Mr. Fayette?

FAYETTE: Yes, except that we're switching you to laboratory A tomorrow. Siegfried knows about it. That's why I had you in. The new work is very important. Siegfried recommended you very highly as a man to trust. You'll work directly under Dr. Brenner. Make you happy?

MILLER: Very. He's an important chemist!

FAYETTE (*leaning over seriously*): We think so, Miller. We think so to the extent of asking you to stay within the building throughout the time you work with him.

MILLER: You mean sleep and eat in?

FAYETTE: Yes. . . .

MILLER: It can be arranged.

FAYETTE: Fine. You'll go far, Miller.

MILLER: May I ask the nature of the new work?

FAYETTE (*looking around first*): Poison gas. . . .

MILLER: Poison!

FAYETTE: Orders from above. I don't have to tell you from where. New type poison gas for modern warfare.

MILLER: I see.

FAYETTE: You didn't know a new war was that close, did you?

MILLER: I guess I didn't.

FAYETTE: I don't have to stress the importance of absolute secrecy.

MILLER: I understand!

FAYETTE: The world is an armed camp today. One match sets the whole world blazing in forty-eight hours. Uncle Sam won't be caught napping!

MILLER (*addressing his pencil*): They say 12 million men were killed in that last one and 20 million more wounded or missing.

FAYETTE: That's not our worry. If big business went sentimental over human life there wouldn't be big business of any sort!

MILLER: My brother and two cousins went in the last one.

FAYETTE: They died in a good cause.

MILLER: My mother says "no!"

FAYETTE: She won't worry about you this time. You're too valuable behind the front.

MILLER: That's right.

FAYETTE: All right, Miller. See Siegfried for further orders.

MILLER: You should have seen my brother —he could ride a bike without hands. . . .

FAYETTE: You'd better move some clothes and shaving tools in tomorrow. Remember what I said—you're with a growing organization.

MILLER: He could run the hundred yards in 9:8 flat. . . .

FAYETTE: Who?

MILLER: My brother. He's in the Meuse-Argonne Cemetery. Mama went there in 1926. . . .

FAYETTE: Yes, those things stick. How's your handwriting, Miller, fairly legible?

MILLER: Fairly so.

FAYETTE: Once a week I'd like a little report from you.

MILLER: What sort of report?

FAYETTE: Just a few hundred words once a week on Dr. Brenner's progress.

MILLER: Don't you think it might be better coming from the Doctor?

FAYETTE: I didn't ask you that.

MILLER: Sorry.

FAYETTE: I want to know what progress he's making, the reports to be purely confidential —between you and me.

MILLER: You mean I'm to watch him?

FAYETTE: Yes!

MILLER: I guess I can't do that. . . .

FAYETTE: Thirty a month raise. . . .

MILLER: You said twenty. . . .

FAYETTE: Thirty!

MILLER: Guess I'm not built that way.

FAYETTE: Forty. . . .

MILLER: Spying's not in my line, Mr. Fayette!

FAYETTE: You use ugly words, Mr. Miller!

MILLER: For ugly activity? Yes!

FAYETTE: Think about it, Miller. Your chances are excellent. . . .

MILLER: No.

FAYETTE: You're doing something for your country. Assuring the United States that when those gaddamn Japs start a ruckus we'll have offensive weapons to back us up! Don't you read your newspapers, Miller?

MILLER: Nothing but Andy Gump.

FAYETTE: If you were on the inside you'd know I'm talking cold sober truth! Now, I'm not asking you to make up your mind on the spot. Think about it over your lunch period.

MILLER: No.

FAYETTE: Made up your mind already?

MILLER: Afraid so.

FAYETTE: You understand the consequences?

MILLER: I lose my raise——

Simultaneously: {
MILLER: And my job!
FAYETTE: And your job!
MILLER: You misunderstand——
}

MILLER: Rather dig ditches first!

FAYETTE: That's a big job for foreigners.

MILLER: But sneaking—and making poison gas—that's for Americans?

FAYETTE: It's up to you.

MILLER: My mind's made up.

FAYETTE: No hard feelings?

MILLER: Sure hard feelings! I'm not the civilized type, Mr. Fayette. Nothing suave or sophisticated about me. Plenty of hard feelings! Enough to want to bust you and all your kind square in the mouth! (*Does exactly that.*)

ACT III

THE YOUNG HACK AND HIS GIRL

(*Opens with girl and brother.* FLORENCE *waiting for* SID *to take her to a dance.*)

FLORRIE: I gotta right to have something out of life. I don't smoke, I don't drink. So if Sid wants to take me to a dance, I'll go. Maybe if you was in love you wouldn't talk so hard.

IRV: I'm saying it for your good.

FLORRIE: Don't be so good to me.

IRV: Mom's sick in bed and you'll be worryin' her to the grave. She don't want that boy hanging around the house and she don't want you meeting him in Crotona Park.

FLORRIE: I'll meet him anytime I like!

IRV: If you do, yours truly'll take care of it in his own way. With just one hand, too!

FLORRIE: Why are you all so set against him?

IRV: Mom told you ten times—it ain't him. It's that he ain't got nothing. Sure, we know he's serious, that he's stuck on you. But that don't cut no ice.

FLORRIE: Taxi drivers used to make good money.

IRV: Today they're makin' five and six dollars a week. Maybe you wanta raise a family on that.

Then you'll be back here living with us again and I'll be supporting two families in one. Well . . . over my dead body.

FLORRIE: Irv, I don't care—I love him!

IRV: You're a little kid with half-baked ideas!

FLORRIE: I stand there behind the counter the whole day. I think about him—

IRV: If you thought more about Mom it would be better.

FLORRIE: Don't I take care of her every night when I come home? Don't I cook supper and iron your shirts and . . . you give me a pain in the neck, too. Don't try to shut me up! I bring a few dollars in the house, too. Don't you see I want something else out of life. Sure, I want romance, love, babies. I want everything in life I can get.

IRV: You take care of Mom and watch your step!

FLORRIE: And if I don't?

IRV: Yours truly'll watch it for you!

FLORRIE: You can talk that way to a girl. . . .

IRV: I'll talk that way to your boy friend too, and it won't be with words! Florrie, if you had a pair of eyes you'd see it's for your own good we're talking. This ain't no time to get married. Maybe later—

FLORRIE: "Maybe Later" never comes for me, though. Why don't we send Mom to a hospital? She can die in peace there instead of looking at the clock on the mantelpiece all day.

IRV: That needs money. Which we don't have!

FLORRIE: Money, Money, Money!

IRV: Don't change the subject.

FLORRIE: This is the subject!

IRV: You gonna stop seeing him? (She turns away.) Jesus, kiddie, I remember when you were a baby with curls down your back. Now I gotta stand here yellin' at you like this.

FLORRIE: I'll talk to him, Irv.

IRV: When?

FLORRIE: I asked him to come here tonight. We'll talk it over.

IRV: Don't get soft with him. Nowadays is no time to be soft. You gotta be hard as a rock or go under.

FLORRIE: I found that out. There's the bell. Take the egg off the stove I boiled for Mom. Leave us alone Irv. (SID comes in—the two men look at each other for a second. IRV exits.)

SID (enters): Hello, Florrie.

FLORRIE: Hello, Honey. You're looking tired.

SID: Naw, I just need a shave.

FLORRIE: Well, draw your chair up to the fire and I'll ring for brandy and soda . . . like in the movies.

SID: If this was the movies I'd bring a big bunch of roses.

FLORRIE: How big?

SID: Fifty or sixty dozen—the kind with long, long stems—big as that. . . .

FLORRIE: You dope. . . .

SID: Your Paris gown is beautiful.

FLORRIE (acting grandly): Yes, Percy, velvet panels are coming back again. Madame La Farge told me today that Queen Marie herself designed it.

SID: Gee . . .!

FLORRIE: Every princess in the Balkans is wearing one like this. (Poses grandly.)

SID: Hold it. (Does a nose camera—thumbing nose and imitating grinding of camera with other hand. Suddenly she falls out of the posture and swiftly goes to him, to embrace him, to kiss him with love. Finally):

SID: You look tired, Florrie.

FLORRIE: Naw, I just need a shave. (She laughs tremulously.)

SID: You worried about your mother?

FLORRIE: No.

SID: What's on your mind?

FLORRIE: The French and Indian War.

SID: What's on your mind?

FLORRIE: I got us on my mind, Sid. Night and day, Sid!

SID: I smacked a beer truck today. Did I get hell! I was driving along thinking of US, too. You don't have to say it—I know what's on your mind. I'm rat poison around here.

FLORRIE: Not to me. . . .

SID: I know to who . . . and I know why. I don't blame them. We're engaged now for three years . . .

FLORRIE: That's a long time. . . .

SID: My brother Sam joined the navy this morning—get a break that way. They'll send him down to Cuba with the hootchy-kootchy girls. He don't know from nothing, that dumb basket ball player!

FLORRIE: Don't you do that.

SID: Don't you worry, I'm not the kind who runs away. But I'm so tired of being a dog, Baby, I could choke. I don't even have to ask what's going on in your mind. I know from the word go, 'cause I'm thinking the same things, too.

FLORRIE: It's yes or no—nothing in between.

SID: The answer is no—a big electric sign looking down on Broadway!

FLORRIE: We wanted to have kids. . . .

SID: But that sort of life ain't for the dogs which is us. Christ, Baby! I get like thunder in my chest when we're together. If we went off together I could maybe look the world straight in the face, spit in its eye lika a man should do. Goddamnit, it's trying to be a man on the earth. Two in life together.

FLORRIE: But something wants us to be lonely like that—crawling alone in the dark. Or they want us trapped.

SID: Sure, the big shot money men want us like that.

FLORRIE: Highly insulting us——

SID: Keeping us in the dark about what is wrong with us in the money sense. They got the power and mean to be damn sure they keep it. They know if they give in just an inch, all the dogs like us will be down on them together—an ocean knocking them to hell and back and each singing cuckoo with stars coming from their nose and ears. I'm not raving, Florrie——

FLORRIE: I know you're not, I know.

SID: I don't have the words to tell you what I feel. I never finished school. . . .

FLORRIE: I know. . . .

SID: But it's relative, like the professors say. We worked like hell to send him to college—my kid brother Sam, I mean—and look what he done—joined the navy! The damn fool don't see the cards is stacked for all of us. The money man dealing himself a hot royal flush. Then giving you and me a phony hand like a pair of tens or something. Then keep on losing the pots 'cause the cards is stacked against you. Then he says, what's the matter you can't win—no stuff on the ball, he says to you. And kids like my brother believe it 'cause they don't know better. For all their education, they don't know from nothing. But wait a minute! Don't he come around and say to you—this millionaire with a jazz band—listen Sam or Sid or what's-your-name, you're no good, but here's a chance. The whole world'll know who you are. Yes sir, he says, get up on that ship and fight those bastards who's making the world a lousy place to live in. The Japs, the Turks, the Greeks. Take this gun—kill the slobs like a real hero, he says, a real American. Be a hero! And the guy you're poking at? A real louse, just like you, 'cause they don't let him catch more than a pair of tens, too. On that foreign soil he's a guy like me and Sam, a guy who wants his baby like you and hot sun on

his face! They'll teach Sam to point the guns the wrong way, that dumb basket ball player!

FLORRIE: I got a lump in my throat, Honey.

SID: You and me—we never even had a room to sit in somewhere.

FLORRIE: The park was nice . . .

SID: In winter? The hallways . . . I'm glad we never got together. This way we don't know what we missed.

FLORRIE (in a burst): Sid, I'll go with you—we'll get a room somewhere.

SID: Naw . . . they're right. If we can't climb higher than this together—we better stay apart.

FLORRIE: I swear to God I wouldn't care.

SID: You would, you would—in a year, two years, you'd curse the day. I seen it happen.

FLORRIE: Oh, Sid. . . .

SID: Sure, I know. We got the blues, Babe—the 1935 blues. I'm talkin' this way 'cause I love you. If I didn't, I wouldn't care. . . .

FLORRIE: We'll work together, we'll—

SID: How about the backwash? Your family needs your nine bucks. My family—

FLORRIE: I don't care for them!

SID: You're making it up, Florrie. Little Florrie Canary in a cage.

FLORRIE: Don't make fun of me.

SID: I'm not, Baby.

FLORRIE: Yes, you're laughing at me.

SID: I'm not. (They stand looking at each other, unable to speak. Finally, he turns to a small portable phonograph and plays a cheap, sad, dance tune. He makes a motion with his hand; she comes to him. They begin to dance slowly. They hold each other tightly, almost as though they would merge into each other. The music stops, but the scratching record continues to the end of the scene. They stop dancing. He finally looses her clutch and seats her on the couch, where she sits, tense and expectant.)

SID: Hello, Babe.

FLORRIE: Hello. (For a brief time they stand as though in a dream.)

SID (finally): Good-bye, Babe. (He waits for an answer, but she is silent. They look at each other.)

SID: Did you ever see my Pat Rooney imitation? (He whistles Rosy O'Grady and soft-shoes to it. Stops. He asks):

SID: Don't you like it?

FLORRIE (finally): No. (Buries her face in her hands. Suddenly he falls on his knees and buries his face in her lap.)

ACT IV

LABOR SPY EPISODE

FATT: You don't know how we work for you. Shooting off your mouth won't help. Hell, don't you guys ever look at the records like me? Look in your own industry. See what happened when the hacks walked out in Philly three months ago! Where's Philly? A thousand miles away? An hour's ride on the train.

VOICE: Two hours!!

FATT: Two hours ... what the hell's the difference. Let's hear from someone who's got the practical experience to back him up. Fellers, there's a man here who's seen the whole parade in Philly, walked out with his pals, got knocked down like the rest—and blacklisted after they went back. That's why he's here. He's got a mighty interestin' word to say. (*Announces*): *Tom Clayton!* (*As* CLAYTON *starts up from the audience,* FATT *gives him a hand which is sparsely followed in the audience.* CLAYTON *comes forward.*)

Fellers, this is a man with practical strike experience—Tom Clayton from little ole Philly.

CLAYTON *a thin, modest individual*: Fellers, I don't mind your booing. If I thought it would help us hacks get better living conditions, I'd let you walk all over me, cut me up to little pieces. I'm one of you myself. But what I wanna say is that Harry Fatt's right. I only been working here in the big town five weeks, but I know conditions just like the rest of you. You know how it is—don't take long to feel the sore spots, no matter where you park.

CLEAR VOICE (*from audience*): Sit down!

CLAYTON: But Fatt's right. Our officers is right. The time ain't ripe. Like a fruit don't fall off the tree until it's ripe.

CLEAR VOICE: Sit down, you fruit!

FATT (*on his feet*): Take care of him, boys.

VOICE (*in audience, struggling*): No one takes care of me. (*Struggle in house and finally the owner of the voice runs up on stage, says to speaker*):

SAME VOICE: Where the hell did you pick up that name! Clayton! This rat's name is Clancy, from the old Clancys, way back! Fruit! I almost wet myself listening to that one!

FATT (*gunman with him*): This ain't a barn! What the hell do you think you're doing here!

SAME VOICE: Exposing a rat!

FATT: You can't get away with this. Throw him the hell outa here.

VOICE (*preparing to stand his ground*): Try it yourself. . . . When this bozo throws that slop around. You know who he is? That's a company spy.

FATT: Who the hell are you to make—

VOICE: I paid dues in this union for four years, that's who's me! I gotta right and this pussy-footed rat ain't coming in here with ideas like that. You know his record. Lemme say it out——

FATT: You'll prove all this or I'll bust you in every hack outfit in town!

VOICE: I gotta right. I gotta right. Looka *him*, he don't say boo!

CLAYTON: You're a liar and I never seen you before in my life!

VOICE: Boys, he spent two years in the coal fields breaking up any organization he touched. Fifty guys he put in jail. He's ranged up and down the east coast—shipping, textiles, steel —he's been in everything you can name. Right now——

CLAYTON: That's a lie!

VOICE: Right now he's working for that Bergman outfit on Columbus Circle who furnishes rats for any outfit in the country, before, during, and after strikes. (*The man who is the hero of the next episode goes down to his side with other committee men.*)

CLAYTON: He's trying to break up the meeting, fellers!

VOICE: We won't search you for credentials. . . .

CLAYTON: I got nothing to hide. Your own secretary knows I'm straight.

VOICE: Sure. Boys, you know who this sonovabitch is?

CLAYTON: I never seen you before in my life!

VOICE: Boys, I slept with him in the same bed sixteen years. HE'S MY OWN LOUSY BROTHER!!

FATT (*after pause*): Is this true? (*No answer from* CLAYTON.)

VOICE (*to* CLAYTON): Scram, before I break your neck! (CLAYTON *scrams down center aisle.* VOICE *says, watching him*): Remember his map—he can't change that—Clancy! (*Standing in his place says*): Too bad you didn't know about this, Fatt! (*After a pause.*) The Clancy family tree is bearing nuts! (*Standing isolated clear on the stage is the hero of the next espisode.*)

ACT V

INTERNE EPISODE

Dr. Barnes, an elderly distinguished man, is speaking on the telephone. He wears a white coat.

DR. BARNES: No, I gave you my opinion twice. You outvoted me. You did this to Dr. Benjamin yourself. That is why you can tell him yourself. (*Hangs up phone, angrily. As he is about to pour himself a drink from a bottle on the table, a knock is heard.*)

BARNES: Who is it?

BENJAMIN (*without*): Can I see you a minute, please?

BARNES (*hiding the bottle*): Come in, Dr. Benjamin, come in.

BENJAMIN: It's important—excuse me—they've got Leeds up there in my place—He's operating on Mrs. Lewis—the historectomy —it's my job. I washed up, prepared . . . they told me at the last minute. I don't mind being replaced, Doctor, but Leeds is a damn fool! He shouldn't be permitted————

BARNES (*dryily*): Leeds is the nephew of Senator Leeds.

BENJAMIN: He's incompetent as hell.

BARNES (*obviously changing subject, picks up lab. jar*): They're doing splendid work in brain surgery these days. This is a very fine specimen. . . .

BENJAMIN: I'm sorry, I thought you might be interested.

BARNES (*still examining jar*): Well, I am, young man, I am! Only remember it's a charity case!

BENJAMIN: Of course. They wouldn't allow it for a second, otherwise.

BARNES: Her life is in danger?

BENJAMIN: Of course! You know how serious the case is!

BARNES: Turn your gimlet eyes elsewhere, Doctor. Jigging around like a cricket on a hot grill won't help. Doctors don't run these hospitals. He's the Senator's nephew and there he stays.

BENJAMIN: It's too bad.

BARNES: I'm not calling you down either. (*Plopping down jar suddenly.*) Goddamnit, do you think it's my fault?

BENJAMIN (*about to leave*): I know . . . I'm sorry.

BARNES: Just a minute. Sit down.

BENJAMIN: Sorry, I can't sit.

BARNES: Stand then!

BENJAMIN (*sits*): Understand, Dr. Barnes, I don't mind being replaced at the last minute this way, but . . . well, this flagrant bit of class distinction—because she's poor————

BARNES: Be careful of words like that—"class distinction." Don't belong here. Lots of energy, you brilliant young men, but idiots. Discretion! Ever hear that word?

BENJAMIN: Too radical?

BARNES: Precisely. And some day like in Germany, it might cost you your head.

BENJAMIN: Not to mention my job.

BARNES: So they told you?

BENJAMIN: Told me what?

BARNES: They're closing Ward C next month. I don't have to tell you the hospital isn't self-supporting. Until last year that board of trustees met deficits. . . . You can guess the rest. At a board meeting Tuesday, our fine feathered friends discovered they couldn't meet the last quarter's deficit—a neat little sum well over $100,000. If the hospital is to continue at all, its damn————

BENJAMIN: Necessary to close another charity ward!

BARNES: So they say. . . . (*A wait.*)

BENJAMIN: But that's not all?

BARNES (*ashamed*): Have to cut down on staff too. . . .

BENJAMIN: That's too bad. Does it touch me?

BARNES: Afraid it does.

BENJAMIN: But after all I'm top man here. I don't mean I'm better than others, but I've worked harder.

BARNES: And shown more promise. . . .

BENJAMIN: I always supposed they'd cut from the bottom first.

BARNES: Usually.

BENJAMIN: But in this case?

BARNES: Complications.

BENJAMIN: For instance? (BARNES *hesitant.*)

BARNES: I like you, Benjamin. It's one ripping shame.

BENJAMIN: I'm no sensitive plant—what's the answer?

BARNES: An old disease, malignant, tumescent. We need an anti-toxin for it.

BENJAMIN: I see.

BARNES: What?

BENJAMIN: I met that disease before—at Harvard first.

BARNES: You have seniority here, Benjamin.

BENJAMIN: But I'm a Jew! (BARNES *nods his head in agreement.* BENJAMIN *stands there a moment and blows his nose.*)

BARNES (*blows his nose*): Microbes!

BENJAMIN: Pressure from above?

BARNES: Don't think Kennedy and I didn't fight for you!

BENJAMIN: Such discrimination, with all those wealthy brother Jews on the board?

BARNES: I've remarked before—doesn't seem to be much difference between wealthy Jews and rich Gentiles. Cut from the same piece!

BENJAMIN: For myself I don't feel sorry. My parents gave up an awful lot to get me this far. They ran a little dry goods shop in the Bronx until their pitiful savings went in the crash last year. Poppa's peddling neckties. . . . Saul Ezra Benjamin—a man who's read Spinoza all his life.

BARNES: Doctors don't run medicine in this country. The men who know their jobs don't run anything here, except the motormen on trolley cars. I've seen medicine change—plenty—anesthesia, sterilization—but not because of rich men—in *spite* of them! In a rich man's country your true self's buried deep. Microbes! Less. . . . Vermin! See this ankle, this delicate sensitive hand? Four hundred years to breed that. Out of a revolutionary background! Spirit of '76! Ancestors froze at Valley Forge! What's it all mean! Slops! The honest workers were sold out then, in '76. The Constitution's for rich men then and now. Slops! (*The phone rings.*)

BARNES (*angrily*): Dr. Barnes. (*Listens a moment, looks at* BENJAMIN.) I see. (*Hangs up, turns slowly to the younger Doctor.*) They lost your patient. (BENJAMIN *stands solid with the shock of this news but finally hurls his operation gloves to the floor.*)

BARNES: That's right . . . that's right. Young, hot, go and do it! I'm very ancient, fossil, but life's ahead of you. Dr. Benjamin, and when you fire the first shot say, "This one's for old Doc Barnes!" Too much dignity—bullets. Don't shoot vermin! Step on them! If I didn't have an invalid daughter——(BARNES *goes back to his seat, blows his nose in silence.*) I have said my piece, Benjamin.

BENJAMIN: Lots of things I wasn't certain of. Many things these radicals say . . . you don't believe theories until they happen to you.

BARNES: You lost a lot today, but you won a great point.

BENJAMIN: Yes, to know I'm right? To really begin believing in something? Not to say, "What a world!", but to say, "Change the world!" I wanted to go to Russia. Last week I was thinking about it—the wonderful opportunity to do good work in their socialized medicine——

BARNES: Beautiful, beautiful!

BENJAMIN: To be able to work——

BARNES: Why don't you go? I might be able——

BENJAMIN: Nothing's nearer what I'd like to do!

BARNES: Do it!

BENJAMIN: No! Our work's here—America! I'm scared. . . . What future's ahead, I don't know. Get some job to keep alive—maybe drive a cab—and study and work and learn my place——

BARNES: And step down hard!

BENJAMIN: Fight! Maybe get killed, but goddamn! We'll go ahead! (BENJAMIN *stands with clenched fist raised high.*)

Blackout

AGATE: *Ladies and Gentlemen,* and don't let anyone tell you we ain't got some ladies in this sea of upturned faces! Only they're wearin' pants. Well, maybe I don't know a thing; maybe I fell outa the cradle when I was a kid and ain't been right since—you can't tell!

VOICE: Sit down, cockeye!

AGATE: Who's paying you for those remarks, Buddy?—Moscow Gold? Maybe I got a glass eye, but it come from working in a factory at the age of eleven. They hooked it out because they didn't have a shield on the works. But I wear it like a medal 'cause it tells the world where I belong—deep down in the working class! We had delegates in the union there—all kinds of secretaries and treasurers . . . walkin' delegates, but not with blisters on their feet! Oh no! On their fat little ass from sitting on cushions and raking in mazuma. (SECRETARY *and* GUNMAN *remonstrate in words and actions here.*) Sit down, boys. I'm just sayin' that about unions in general. I know it ain't true here! Why no, our officers is all aces. Why, I seen our own secretary Fatt walk outa his way not to step on a cockroach. No boys, don't think—

FATT (*breaking in*): You're out of order!

AGATE (*to audience*): Am I outa order?

ALL: No, no. Speak. Go on, etc.

AGATE: Yes, our officers is all aces. But I'm a member here—and no experience in Philly either! Today I couldn't wear my union button. The damnest thing happened. When I take the old coat off the wall, I see she's smoking. I'm a sonovagun if the old union button isn't on fire! Yep, the old celluloid was makin' the most god-awful stink: the landlady come up and give me hell! You know what happened? That old union button just blushed itself to death! Ashamed! Can you beat it?

FATT: Sit down, Keller! Nobody's interested!

AGATE: Yes they are!

GUNMAN: Sit down like he tells you!

AGATE (*continuing to audience*): And when I finish——(*His speech is broken by* FATT *and* GUNMAN *who physically handle him. He breaks away and gets to other side of stage. The two are about to make for him when some of the committee men come forward and get in between the struggling parties.* AGATE's *shirt has been torn.*)

AGATE (*to audience*): What's the answer, boys? The answer is, if we're reds because we wanna strike, then we take over their salute too! Know how they do it? (*Makes Communist salute.*) What is it? An uppercut! The good old uppercut to the chin! Hell, some of us boys ain't even got a shirt to our backs. What's the boss class tryin' to do—make a nudist colony outa us?

(*The audience laughs and suddenly* AGATE *comes to the middle of the stage so that the other cabmen back him up in a strong clump.*)

AGATE: Don't laugh! Nothing's funny! This is your life and mine! It's skull and bones every incha the road! Christ, we're dyin' by inches! For what? For the debutant-ees to have their sweet comin' out parties in the Ritz! Poppa's got a daughter she's gotta get her picture in the papers. Christ, they make 'em with our blood. Joe said it. Slow death or fight. It's war!

(*Throughout this whole speech* AGATE *is backed up by the other six workers, so that from their activity it is plain that the whole group of them are saying these things. Several of them may take alternate lines out of this long last speech.*)

You Edna, God love your mouth! Sid and Florrie, the other boys, old Doc Barnes—fight with us for right! It's war! Working class, unite and fight! Tear down the slaughter house of our old lives! Let freedom really ring.

These slick slobs stand here telling us about bogeymen. That's a new one for the kids—the reds is bogeymen! But the man who got me food in 1932, he called me Comrade! The one who picked me up where I bled—he called me Comrade too! What are we waiting for. . . . Don't wait for Lefty! He might never come. Every minute——(*This is broken into by a man who has dashed up the center aisle from the back of the house. He runs up on stage, says*):

MAN: Boys, they just found Lefty!

OTHERS: What? What? What?

SOME: Shhh. . . . Shhh. . . .

MAN: They found Lefty. . . .

AGATE: Where?

MAN: Behind the car barns with a bullet in his head!

AGATE (*crying*): Hear it, boys, hear it? Hell, listen to me! Coast to coast! HELLO AMERICA! HELLO. WE'RE STORMBIRDS OF THE WORKING-CLASS. WORKERS OF THE WORLD. . . . OUR BONES AND BLOOD! And when we die they'll know what we did to make a new world! Christ, cut us up to little pieces. We'll die for what is right! put fruit trees where our ashes are! (*To audience*): Well, what's the answer?

ALL: STRIKE!

AGATE: LOUDER!

ALL: STRIKE!

AGATE and OTHERS on Stage: AGAIN!

ALL: STRIKE, STRIKE, STRIKE!!!

CURTAIN

Lillian Hellman: *The Little Foxes* (1939)

Although she was born in New Orleans and returned there often, Lillian Hellman was raised, from the age of 5, in New York City, where her father was a businessman. She did, however, until she was sixteen, spend half the year in New Orleans and the other half in New York, so her knowledge of the South was tempered by some objectivity. Her college education was mainly at New York University, and her first job after graduation was as a reader of manuscripts for the then legendary literary publisher Horace Liveright. She was trying at the time to write stories, most of which were rejected; eventually she began reviewing books for the *Herald Tribune*. She met Arthur Kober, a struggling writer working for the Schubert Theater organization, and found herself on the fringes of the theater world. When they married, they headed for the Paris of 1925, where so many great American writers were in bohemian residence. Kober worked for a Paris magazine that published a few of Lillian Hellman's stories, but in 1930 the couple returned to America and looked to Hollywood for work as writers. Kober stayed on as a successful writer, but Hellman grew disaffected and, having met Dashiell Hammett, decided to leave Kober and return to New York. "Dash" and Lillian lived in rather impoverished circumstances at the Sutton Hotel, where the noted comic novelist, Nathaniel West, was the manager—a job given him by a kindly uncle. A great many well-known writers, among them William Faulkner, lived in the Sutton, and the place became famous as a "seminary" for young authors.

By this time Lillian Hellman had been reading plays for Hollywood producers as well as for New York producers and their level of quality was so low that she decided to try writing her own. Hammett got a book of legal trials, suggested she read it, and urged her to write about something that really happened. Out of that suggestion and that book came her first play, *The Children's Hour* (1934). It was about a neurotic child in a girl's school who accused her two teachers of being lesbians The portrait of evil in that girl, Mary Tilford, was extraordinarily powerful, and the play itself was such an instant hit that Lillian Hellman was transformed into a celebrity almost overnight. The play ran almost 700 performances and made her independent enough to devote all her time to writing.

The Little Foxes was written after Lillian Hellman had traveled extensively in Europe, particularly in Russia and Spain. She was, like many writers and intellectuals of the period, somewhat dissatisfied with the American economic system —which gave evidence, in the face of the Great Depression, of being unfair and in need of great change. Her interest in Communism was strong, and her experience in Spain, watching the horrors of the Franco war against the Republicans, convinced her she could not side with the Nazis and that the Communists offered a more workable alternative.

Her writing of the play was a difficult ordeal. She had such great success with *The Children's Hour* that people expected too much of her. Her next play, *Days to Come* (1936), about a strike, was a total failure and left her deeply depressed. She began *The Little Foxes* slowly, showing various drafts of it to Hammett for criticism. He was a tough, difficult, and unyielding critic. She wrote six drafts of the play, then left the final draft by his door with a note: "I hope *this* satisfies you." His response the next morning was hardly satisfying, and she went back and rewrote it again.

It is not a play about the South, although there is much insight into Southern ways. There is a clear effort to cut across regional bounds in the portrait of Marshall, who has come down from Massachusetts looking for cheap labor and stable conditions. He, like the inbred Hubbards, is anxious to make a fortune and is not above obtaining it at the expense of poor whites and poor blacks. Their zeal in oppressing the poor is hardly concealed, just as their zest for outdoing one another is perfectly apparent. One of the play's most powerful aspects is the internecine struggle of the Hubbards: Regina, Oscar, and Ben. Beneath that surface is the proposed marriage of Alexandra and her cousin Leo, a man whose brutality and unscrupulousness is revealed again and again in the early part of the drama. Clearly, the future for Alexandra, should she do what her mother wants her to do, would be as bleak and painful as her mother's.

Alexandra is not as central to the play as she might be. The original production starred Talullah Bankhead as Regina (Bette Davis played the part in the film version), and her performance was so striking that it concealed the strength that lay within

Alexandra. One cannot escape thinking that something of the fiber of Lillian Hellman resides in the character Alexandra, if only in her resolve to leave and to do something to fight against such people who plot against the poor and behave like those in the biblical phrase that gave the play its title. "Beware the little foxes that steal the grapes."

Lillian Hellman has had many successes on Broadway since 1939, and her Hollywood screenwriting credits were also substantial until the 1950s McCarthy purge of the Screenwriter's Guild. Dashiell Hammett was questioned and refused testimony; he was sentenced to six months in jail even though he was a very sick man. Lillian Hellman was also subpoenaed and she too refused to testify, but, convinced that her own background and commitments were artistic and nonpolitical, the committee did not hold her in contempt. Hollywood would not offer her work except under conditions she could not accept.

Her memoir, *Pentimento* (1973), was in part the basis of a popular film of the 1970s called *Julia*, in which Jane Fonda played the title role. Its success brought Lillian Hellman back into the public eye; she enjoys, as she should, the role of an honored elder in the world of American theater.

Selected Readings

Falk, Doris. *Lillian Hellman*. New York: Ungar, 1978
Hellman, Lillian. *Six Plays*. New York: Random House, 1969.
———. *Collected Plays*. Boston: Little, Brown, 1972.
———. *An Unfinished Woman*. Boston: Little, Brown, 1969.
———. *Pentimento*. Boston: Little, Brown, 1973.
———. *Scoundrel Time*. Boston: Little, Brown, 1976.
Moody, Richard. *Lillian Hellman, Playwright*. New York: Pegasus, 1972.

The Little Foxes

Lillian Hellman

CHARACTERS

ADDIE	REGINA GIDDENS
CAL	WILLIAM MARSHALL
BIRDIE HUBBARD	BENJAMIN HUBBARD
OSCAR HUBBARD	ALEXANDRA GIDDENS
LEO HUBBARD	HORACE GIDDENS

The scene of the play is the living room of the Giddens house, in a small town in the South.

ACT I: The Spring of 1900, evening.
ACT II: A week later, early morning.
ACT III: Two weeks later, late afternoon.

There has been no attempt to write Southern dialect. It is to be understood that the accents are Southern.

ACT I

(SCENE: *The living room of the Giddens house, in a small town in the deep South, the Spring of 1900. Upstage is a staircase leading to the second story. Upstage, right, are double doors to the dining room. When these doors are open we see a section of the dining room and the furniture. Upstage, left, is an entrance hall with a coat-rack and umbrella stand. There are large lace-curtained windows on the left wall. The room is lit by a center gas chandelier and painted china oil lamps on the tables. Against the wall is a large piano. Downstage, right, are a high couch, a large table, several chairs. Against the left back wall are a table and several chairs. Near the window there are a smaller couch and tables. The room is good-looking, the furniture expensive; but it reflects no particular taste. Everything is of the best and that is all.*

AT RISE: ADDIE, *a tall, nice-looking Negro woman of about fifty-five, is closing the windows. From behind the closed dining-room doors there is the sound of voices. After a second,* CAL, *a middle-aged Negro, comes in from the entrance hall carrying a tray with glasses and a bottle of port.* ADDIE *crosses, takes the tray from him, puts it on table, begins to arrange it.*)

ADDIE (*pointing to the bottle*): You gone stark out of your head?

CAL: No, smart lady, I ain't. Miss Regina told me to get out that bottle. (*Points to bottle.*) That very bottle for the mighty honored guest. When Miss Regina changes orders like that you can bet your dime she got her reason.

ADDIE (*points to dining room*): Go on. You'll be needed.

CAL: Miss Zan she had two helpings frozen fruit cream and she tell that honored guest, she tell him that you make the best frozen fruit cream in all the South.

ADDIE (*smiles, pleased*): Did she? Well, see that Belle saves a little for her. She like it right before she go to bed. Save a few little cakes, too, she like—

(*The dining-room doors are opened and quickly closed again by* BIRDIE HUBBARD. BIRDIE *is a woman of about forty, with a pretty, well-bred, faded face.*

278

Her movements are usually nervous and timid, but now, as she comes running into the room, she is gay and excited. CAL *turns to* BIRDIE.)

BIRDIE: Oh, Cal. (*Closes door.*) I want you to get one of the kitchen boys to run home for me. He's to look in my desk drawer and—(*To* ADDIE.) My, Addie. What a good supper! Just as good as good can be.

ADDIE: You look pretty this evening, Miss Birdie, and young.

BIRDIE (*laughing*): Me, young? (*Turns back to* CAL.) Maybe you better find Simon and tell him to do it himself. He's to look in my desk, the left drawer, and bring my music album right away. Mr. Marshall is very anxious to see it because of his father and the opera in Chicago. (*To* ADDIE.) Mr. Marshall is such a polite man with his manners and very educated and cultured and I've told him all about how my mama and papa used to go to Europe for the music—(*Laughs. To* ADDIE.) Imagine going all the way to Europe just to listen to music. Wouldn't that be nice, Addie? Just to sit there and listen and—(*Turns and steps to* CAL.) *Left* drawer, Cal. Tell him that twice because he forgets. And tell him not to let any of the things drop out of the album and to bring it right in here when he comes back.

(*The dining-room doors are opened and quickly closed by* OSCAR HUBBARD. *He is a man in his late forties.*)

CAL: Yes'm. But Simon he won't get it right. But I'll tell him.

BIRDIE: Left drawer, Cal, and tell him to bring the blue book and—

OSCAR (*sharply*): Birdie.

BIRDIE (*turning nervously*): Oh, Oscar. I was just sending Simon for my music album.

OSCAR (*to* CAL): Never mind about the album. Miss Birdie has changed her mind.

BIRDIE: But, really, Oscar. Really I promised Mr. Marshall. I—(CAL *looks at them, exits.*)

OSCAR: Why do you leave the dinner table and go running about like a child?

BIRDIE (*trying to be gay*): But, Oscar, Mr. Marshall said most specially he *wanted* to see my album. I told him about the time Mama met Wagner, and Mrs. Wagner gave her the signed program and the big picture. Mr. Marshall wants to see that. Very, very much. We had such a nice talk and—

OSCAR (*taking a step to her*): You have been chattering to him like a magpie. You haven't let him be for a second. I can't think he came South

to be bored with you.

BIRDIE (*quickly, hurt*): He wasn't bored. I don't believe he was bored. He's a very educated, cultured gentleman. (*Her voice rises.*) I just don't believe it. You always talk like that when I'm having a nice time.

OSCAR (*turning to her, sharply*): You have had too much wine. Get yourself in hand now.

BIRDIE (*drawing back, about to cry shrilly*): What am I doing? I am not doing anything. What am I doing?

OSCAR (*taking a step to her, tensely*): I said get yourself in hand. Stop acting like a fool.

BIRDIE (*turns to him, quietly*): I don't believe he was bored. I just don't believe it. Some people like music and like to talk about it. That's all I was doing.

(LEO HUBBARD *comes hurrying through the dining-room door. He is a young man of twenty, with a weak kind of good looks.*)

LEO: Mama! Papa! They are coming in now.

OSCAR (*softly*): Sit down, Birdie. Sit down now. (BIRDIE *sits down, bows her head as if to hide her face.*)

(*The dining-room doors are opened by* CAL. *We see people beginning to rise from the table.* REGINA GIDDENS *comes in with* WILLIAM MARSHALL. REGINA *is a handsome woman of forty.* MARSHALL *is forty-five, pleasant-looking, self-possessed. Behind them comes* ALEXANDRA GIDDENS, *a very pretty, rather delicate-looking girl of seventeen. She is followed by* BENJAMIN HUBBARD, *fifty-five, with a large jovial face and the light graceful movements that one often finds in large men.*)

REGINA: Mr. Marshall, I think you're trying to console me. Chicago may be the noisiest, dirtiest city in the world but I should still prefer it to the sound of our horses and the smell of our azaleas. I should like crowds of people, and theatres, and lovely women—*Very* lovely women, Mr. Marshall?

MARSHALL (*crossing to sofa*): In Chicago? Oh, I suppose so. But I can tell you this: I've never dined there with three *such* lovely ladies.

(ADDIE *begins to pass the port.*)

BEN: Our Southern women are well favored.

LEO (*laughs*): But one must go to Mobile for the ladies, sir. Very elegant worldly ladies, too.

BEN (*looks at him very deliberately*): Worldly, eh? *Worldly*, did you say?

OSCAR (*hastily, to* LEO): Your uncle Ben means

that worldliness is not a mark of beauty in any woman.

LEO (*quickly*): Of course, Uncle Ben. I didn't mean.

MARSHALL: Your port is excellent, Mrs. Giddens.

REGINA: Thank you, Mr. Marshall. We had been saving that bottle, hoping we could open it just for you.

ALEXANDRA (*as* ADDIE *comes to her with the tray*): Oh. May I *really*, Addie?

ADDIE: Better ask Mama.

ALEXANDRA: May I, Mama?

REGINA (*nods, smiles*): In Mr. Marshall's honor.

ALEXANDRA (*smiles*): Mr. Marshall, this will be the first taste of port I've ever had.

(ADDIE *serves* LEO.)

MARSHALL: No one ever had their first taste of a better port. (*He lifts his glass in a toast; she lifts hers; they both drink.*) Well, I suppose it is all true, Mrs. Giddens.

REGINA: What is true?

MARSHALL: That you Southerners occupy a unique position in America. You live better than the rest of us, you eat better, you drink better. I wonder you find time, or want to find time, to do business.

BEN: A great many Southerners don't.

MARSHALL: Do all of you live here together?

REGINA: Here with me? (*Laughs.*) Oh, no. My brother Ben lives next door. My brother Oscar and his family live in the next square.

BEN: But we are a very close family. We've always *wanted* it that way.

MARSHALL: That is very pleasant. Keeping your family together to share each other's lives. My family moves around too much. My children seem never to come home. Away at school in the winter; in the summer, Europe with their mother—

REGINA (*eagerly*): Oh yes. Even down here we read about Mrs. Marshall in the society pages.

MARSHALL: I dare say. She moves about a great deal. And all of you are part of the same business? Hubbard Sons?

BEN (*motions to* OSCAR): Oscar and me. (*Motions to* REGINA.) My sister's good husband is a banker.

MARSHALL (*looks at* REGINA, *surprised*): Oh.

REGINA: I am so sorry that my husband isn't here to meet you. He's been very ill. He is at Johns Hopkins. But he will be home soon. We think he is getting better now.

LEO: I work for Uncle Horace. (REGINA *looks*

at him.) I mean I work for Uncle Horace at his bank. I keep an eye on things while he's away.

REGINA (*smiles*): Really, Leo?

BEN (*looks at* LEO, *then to* MARSHALL): Modesty in the young is as excellent as it is rare. (*Looks at* LEO *again.*)

OSCAR (*to* LEO): Your uncle means that a young man should speak more modestly.

LEO (*hastily, taking a step to* BEN): Oh, I didn't mean, sir—

MARSHALL: Oh, Mrs. Hubbard. Where's that Wagner autograph you promised to let me see? My train will be leaving soon and—

BIRDIE: The autograph? Oh. Well. Really, Mr. Marshall, I didn't mean to chatter so about it. Really I—(*Nervously, looking at* OSCAR.) You must excuse me. I didn't get it because, well, because I had—I—I had a little headache and—

OSCAR: My wife is a miserable victim of headaches.

REGINA (*quickly*): Mr. Marshall said at supper that he would like you to play for him, Alexandra.

ALEXANDRA (*who has been looking at* BIRDIE): It's not I who play well, sir. It's my aunt. She plays just wonderfully. She's my teacher. (*Rises. Eagerly.*) May we play a duet? May we, Mama?

BIRDIE (*taking* ALEXANDRA's *hand*): Thank you, dear. But I have my headache now. I—

OSCAR (*sharply*): Don't be stubborn, Birdie. Mr. Marshall wants you to play.

MARSHALL: Indeed I do. If your headache isn't—

BIRDIE (*hesitates, then gets up, pleased*): But I'd like to, sir. Very much. (*She and* ALEXANDRA *go to the piano.*)

MARSHALL: It's very remarkable how you Southern aristocrats have kept together. Kept together and kept what belonged to you.

BEN: You misunderstand, sir. Southern aristocrats have *not* kept together and have *not* kept what belonged to them.

MARSHALL (*laughs, indicates room*): You don't call this keeping what belongs to you?

BEN: But we are not aristocrats. (*Points to* BIRDIE *at the piano.*) Our brother's wife is the only one of us who belongs to the Southern aristocracy.

(BIRDIE *looks towards* BEN.)

MARSHALL (*smiles*): My information is that you people have been here, and solidly here, for a long time.

OSCAR: And so we have. Since our great-grandfather.

BEN (*smiles*): Who was *not* an aristocrat, like Birdie's.

MARSHALL (*a little sharply*): You make great distinctions.

BEN: Oh, they have been made for us. And maybe they are important distinctions. (*Leans forward, intimately.*) Now you take Birdie's family. When my great-grandfather came here they were the highest-tone plantation owners in this state.

LEO (*steps to* MARSHALL, *proudly*): My mother's grandfather was *governor* of the state before the war.

OSCAR: They owned the plantation, Lionnet. You may have heard of it, sir?

MARSHALL (*laughs*): No, I've never heard of anything but brick houses on a lake, and cotton mills.

BEN: Lionnet in its day was the best cotton land in the South. It still brings us in a fair crop. (*Sits back.*) Ah, they were great days for those people—even when I can remember. They had the best of everything. (BIRDIE *turns to them.*) Cloth from Paris, trips to Europe, horses you can't raise any more, niggers to lift their fingers—

BIRDIE (*suddenly*): We were good to our people. Everybody knew that. We were better to them than—

(MARSHALL *looks up at* BIRDIE.)

REGINA: Why, Birdie. You aren't playing.

BEN: But when the war comes these fine gentlemen ride off and leave the cotton, *and* the women, to rot.

BIRDIE: My father was killed in the war. He was a fine soldier, Mr. Marshall. A fine man.

REGINA: Oh, certainly, Birdie. A famous soldier.

BEN (*to* BIRDIE): But that isn't the tale I am telling Mr. Marshall. (*To* MARSHALL.) Well, sir the war ends. (BIRDIE *goes back to piano.*) Lionnet is almost ruined, and the sons finish ruining it. And there were thousands like them. Why? (*Leans forward.*) Because the Southern aristocrat can adapt himself to nothing. Too high-tone to try.

MARSHALL: Sometimes it is difficult to learn new ways. (BIRDIE *and* ALEXANDRA *begin to play.* MARSHALL *leans forward, listening.*)

BEN: Perhaps, perhaps. (*He sees that* MARSHALL *is listening to the music. Irritated, he turns to* BIRDIE *and* ALEXANDRA *at the piano, then back to* MARSHALL.*) You're right, Mr. Marshall. It is difficult to learn new ways. But maybe that's why it's profitable. *Our* grandfather and *our* father learned the new ways and learned how to make them pay. They work. (*Smiles nastily.*) *They* are in trade. Hubbard Sons, Merchandise. Others, Birdie's family, for example, look down on them. (*Settles back in chair.*) To make a long story short, Lionnet now belongs to *us*. (BIRDIE *stops playing.*) Twenty years ago we took over their land, their cotton, and their daughter. (BIRDIE *rises and stands stiffly by the piano.* MARSHALL, *who has been watching her, rises.*)

MARSHALL: May I bring you a glass of port, Mrs. Hubbard?

BIRDIE (*softly*): No, thank you, sir. You are most polite.

REGINA (*sharply, to* BEN): You are boring Mr. Marshall with these ancient family tales.

BEN: I hope not. I hope not. I am trying to make an important point—(*bows to* MARSHALL) for our future business partner.

OSCAR (*to* MARSHALL): My brother always says that it's folks like us who have struggled and fought to bring to our land some of the prosperity of your land.

BEN: Some people call that patriotism.

REGINA (*laughs gaily*): I hope you don't find my brothers too obvious, Mr. Marshall. I'm afraid they mean that this is the time for the ladies to leave the gentlemen to talk business.

MARSHALL (*hastily*): Not at all. We settled everything this afternoon. (MARSHALL *looks at his watch.*) I have only a few minutes before I must leave for the train. (*Smiles at her.*) And I insist they be spent with you.

REGINA: *And* with another glass of port.

MARSHALL: Thank you.

BEN (*to* REGINA): My sister is right. (*To* MARSHALL.) I am a plain man and I am trying to say a plain thing. A man ain't only in business for what he can get out of it. It's got to give him something here. (*Puts hand to his breast.*) That's every bit as true for the nigger picking cotton for a silver quarter, as it is for you and me. (REGINA *gives* MARSHALL *a glass of port.*) If it don't give him something here, then he don't pick the cotton right. Money isn't all. Not by three shots.

MARSHALL: Really? Well, I always thought it was a great deal.

REGINA: And so did I, Mr. Marshall.

MARSHALL (*leans forward; pleasantly, but with meaning*): Now you don't have to convince me that you are the right people for the deal. I wouldn't be here if you hadn't convinced me six months ago. You want the mill here, and I want it here. It isn't my business to find out *why* you want it.

BEN: To bring the machine to the cotton, and not the cotton to the machine.

MARSHALL (*amused*): You have a turn for neat phrases, Hubbard. Well, however grand your reasons are, mine are simple: I want to make money and I believe I'll make it on you. (*As* BEN *starts to speak, he smiles.*) Mind you, I have no objections to more high-minded reasons. They are mighty valuable in business. It's fine to have partners who so closely follow the teachings of Christ. (*Gets up.*) And now I must leave for my train.

REGINA: I'm sorry you won't stay over with us, Mr. Marshall, but you'll come again. Any time you like.

BEN (*motions to* LEO, *indicating the bottle*): Fill them up, boy, fill them up. (LEO *moves around filling the glasses as* BEN *speaks.*) Down here, sir, we have a strange custom. We drink the *last* drink for a toast. That's to prove that the Southerner is always still on his feet for the last drink. (*Picks up his glass.*) It was Henry Frick, your Mr. Henry Frick, who said, "Railroads are the Rembrandts of investments." Well, *I* say, "Southern cotton mills *will be* the Rembrandts of investment." So I give you the firm of Hubbard Sons and Marshall, Cotton Mills, and to it a long and prosperous life.

(*They all pick up their glasses.* MARSHALL *looks at them, amused. Then he, too, lifts his glass, smiles.*)

OSCAR: The children will drive you to the depot. Leo! Alexandra! You will drive Mr. Marshall down.

LEO (*eagerly, looks at* BEN *who nods*): Yes, sir. (*To* MARSHALL.) Not often Uncle Ben lets *me* drive the horses. And a beautiful pair they are. (*Starts for hall.*) Come on, Zan.

ALEXANDRA: May I drive tonight, Uncle Ben, please? I'd like to and—

BEN (*shakes his head, laughs*): In your evening clothes? Oh, no, my dear.

ALEXANDRA: But Leo always—(*Stops, exits quickly.*)

REGINA: I don't like to say good-bye to you, Mr. Marshall.

MARSHALL: Then we won't say good-bye. You have promised that you would come and let me show you Chicago. Do I have to make you promise again?

REGINA (*looks at him as he presses her hand*): I promise again.

MARSHALL (*touches her hand again, then moves to* BIRDIE): Good-bye, Mrs. Hubbard.

BIRDIE (*shyly, with sweetness and dignity*): Good-bye, sir.

MARSHALL (*as he passes* REGINA): Remember.

REGINA: I will.

OSCAR: We'll see you to the carriage.

(MARSHALL *exits, followed by* BEN *and* OSCAR. *For a second* REGINA *and* BIRDIE *stand looking after them. Then* REGINA *throws up her arms, laughs happily.*)

REGINA: And there, Birdie, goes the man who has opened the door to our future.

BIRDIE (*surprised at the unaccustomed friendliness*): What?

REGINA (*turning to her*): Our future. Yours and mine, Ben's and Oscar's, the children—(*Looks at* BIRDIE's *puzzled face, laughs.*) Our future! (*Gaily.*) You were charming at supper, Birdie. Mr. Marshall certainly thought so.

BIRDIE (*pleased*): Why, Regina! Do you think he did?

REGINA: Can't you tell when you're being admired?

BIRDIE: Oscar said I bored Mr. Marshall. (*Then quietly.*) But he admired *you*. He told me so.

REGINA: What did he say?

BIRDIE: He said to me, "I hope your sister-in-law will come to Chicago. Chicago will be at her feet." He said the ladies would bow to your manners and the gentlemen to your looks.

REGINA: Did he? He seems a lonely man. Imagine being lonely with all that money. I don't think he likes his wife.

BIRDIE: Not like his wife? What a thing to say.

REGINA: She's away a great deal. He said that several times. And once he made fun of her being so social and high-tone. But that fits in all right. (*Sits back, arms on back of sofa, stretches.*) Her being social, I mean. She can introduce me. It won't take long with an introduction from her.

BIRDIE (*bewildered*): Introduce you? In Chicago? You mean you really might go? Oh, Regina, you can't leave here. What about Horace?

REGINA: Don't look so scared about everything, Birdie. I'm going to live in Chicago. I've always wanted to. And now there'll be plenty of money to go with.

BIRDIE: But Horace won't be able to move around. You know what the doctor wrote.

REGINA: There'll be millions, Birdie, millions. You know what I've always said when people told me we were rich? I said I think you should either be a nigger or a millionaire. In between, like us, what for? (*Laughs. Looks at* BIRDIE.) But I'm not going away tomorrow, Birdie. There's plenty of time to worry about Horace when he comes home. If he ever decides to come home.

BIRDIE: Will we be going to Chicago? I mean, Oscar and Leo and me?

REGINA: You? I shouldn't think so. (*Laughs.*) Well, we must remember tonight. It's a very important night and we mustn't forget it. We shall plan all the things we'd like to have and then we'll really have them. Make a wish, Birdie, any wish. It's bound to come true now.

(BEN *and* OSCAR *enter.*)

BIRDIE (*laughs*): Well. Well, I don't know. Maybe. (REGINA *turns to look at* BEN.) Well, I guess I'd know right off what I wanted.

(OSCAR *stands by the upper window, waves to the departing carriage.*)

REGINA (*looks up at* BEN, *smiles; he smiles back at her*): Well, you did it.

BEN: Looks like it might be we did.

REGINA (*springs up, laughs*): Looks like it! Don't pretend. You're like a cat who's been licking the cream. (*Crosses to wine bottle.*) Now we must all have a drink to celebrate.

OSCAR: The children, Alexandra and Leo, make a very handsome couple, Regina. Marshall remarked himself what fine young folks they were. How well they looked together!

REGINA (*sharply*): Yes. You said that before, Oscar.

BEN: Yes, sir. It's beginning to look as if the deal's all set. I may not be a subtle man—but—(*Turns to them. After a second.*) Now somebody ask me how I know the deal is set.

OSCAR: What do you mean, Ben?

BEN: You remember I told him that down here we drink the *last* drink for a toast?

OSCAR (*thoughtfully*): Yes. I never heard that before.

BEN: Nobody's ever heard it before. God forgives those who invent what they need. I already had his signature. But we've all done business with men whose word over a glass is better than a bond. Anyway it don't hurt to have both.

OSCAR (*turns to* REGINA): You understand what Ben means?

REGINA (*smiles*): Yes, Oscar. I understand. I understood immediately.

BEN (*looks at her admiringly*): Did you, Regina? Well, when he lifted his glass to drink, I closed my eyes and saw the bricks going into place.

REGINA: And *I* saw a lot more than that.

BEN: Slowly, slowly. As yet we have only our hopes.

REGINA: Birdie and I have just been planning what we want. I know what I want. What will you want, Ben?

BEN: Caution. Don't count the chickens. (*Leans back, laughs.*) Well, God would allow us a little daydreaming. Good for the soul when you've worked hard enough to deserve it. (*Pauses.*) I think I'll have a stable. For a long time I've had my good eyes on Carter's in Savannah. A rich man's pleasure, the sport of kings, why not the sport of Hubbards? Why not?

REGINA (*smiles*): Why not? What will you have, Oscar?

OSCAR: I don't know. (*Thoughtfully.*) The pleasure of seeing the bricks grow will be enough for me.

BEN: Oh, of course. Our *greatest* pleasure will be to see the bricks grow. But we are all entitled to a little side indulgence.

OSCAR: Yes, I suppose so. Well, then, I think we might take a few trips here and there, eh, Birdie?

BIRDIE (*surprised at being consulted*): Yes, Oscar. I'd like that.

OSCAR: We might even make a regular trip to Jekyll Island. I've heard the Cornelly place is for sale. We might think about buying it. Make a nice change. Do you good, Birdie, a change of climate. Fine shooting on Jekyll, the best.

BIRDIE: I'd like —

OSCAR (*indulgently*): What would you like?

BIRDIE: *Two* things. Two things I'd like most.

REGINA: Two! I should like a thousand. You are modest, Birdie.

BIRDIE (*warmly, delighted with the unexpected interest*): I should like to have Lionnet back. I know you own it now, but I'd like to see it fixed up again, the way Mama and Papa had it. Every year it used to get a nice coat of paint—Papa was very particular about the paint—and the lawn was so smooth all the way down to the river, with the trims of zinnias and red-feather plush. And the figs and blue little plums and the scuppernongs—(*Smiles. Turns to* REGINA.) The organ is still there and it wouldn't cost much to fix. We could have parties for Zan, the way Mama used to have for me.

BEN: That's a pretty picture, Birdie. Might be a most pleasant way to live. (*Dismissing* BIR-

DIE.) What do you want, Regina?

BIRDIE (*very happily, not noticing that they are no longer listening to her*): I could have a cutting garden. Just where Mama's used to be. Oh, I do think we could be happier there. Papa used to say that *nobody* had ever lost their temper at Lionnet, and *nobody* ever would. Papa would never let anybody be nasty-spoken or mean. No, sir. He just didn't like it.

BEN: What do you want, Regina?

REGINA: I'm going to Chicago. And when I'm settled there and know the right people and the right things to buy—because I certainly don't now—I shall go to Paris and buy them. (*Laughs.*) I'm going to leave you and Oscar to count the bricks.

BIRDIE: Oscar. Please let me have Lionnet back.

OSCAR (*to* REGINA): You are serious about moving to Chicago?

BEN: She is going to see the great world and leave us in the little one. Well, we'll come and visit you and meet all the great and be proud to think you are our sister.

REGINA (*gaily*): Certainly. And you won't even have to learn to be subtle, Ben. Stay as you are. You will be rich and the rich don't have to be subtle.

OSCAR: But what about Alexandra? She's seventeen. Old enough to be thinking about marrying.

BIRDIE: And, Oscar, I have one more wish. Just one more wish.

OSCAR (*turns*): What is it, Birdie? What are you saying?

BIRDIE: I want you to stop shooting. I mean, so much. I don't like to see animals and birds killed just for the killing. You only throw them away—

BEN (*to* REGINA): It'll take a great deal of money to live as you're planning, Regina.

REGINA: Certainly. But there'll be plenty of money. You have estimated the profits very high.

BEN: I have—

BIRDIE (OSCAR *is looking at her furiously*): And you never let anybody else shoot, and the niggers need it so much to keep from starving. It's wicked to shoot food just because you like to shoot, when poor people need it so—

BEN (*laughs*): I have estimated the profits very high—for myself.

REGINA: What did you say?

BIRDIE: I've always wanted to speak about it, Oscar.

OSCAR (*slowly, carefully*): What are you chattering about?

BIRDIE (*nervously*): I was talking about Lionnet and—and about your shooting—

OSCAR: You are exciting yourself.

REGINA (*to* BEN): I didn't hear you. There was so much talking.

OSCAR (*to* BIRDIE): You have been acting very childish, very excited, all evening.

BIRDIE: Regina asked me what I'd like.

REGINA: What did you say, Ben?

BIRDIE: Now that we'll be so rich everybody was saying what they would like, so *I* said what *I* would like, too.

BEN: I said—(*He is interrupted by* OSCAR.)

OSCAR (*to* BIRDIE): Very well. We've all heard you. That's enough now.

BEN: I am waiting. (*They stop.*) I am waiting for you to finish. You and Birdie. Four conversations are three too many. (BIRDIE *slowly sits down.* BEN *smiles, to* REGINA.) I said that I had, and I do, estimate the profits very high—for myself, and Oscar, of course.

REGINA (*slowly*): And what does that mean?

(BEN *shrugs, looks towards* OSCAR.)

OSCAR (*looks at* BEN, *clears throat*): Well, Regina, it's like this. For forty-nine per cent Marshall will put up four hundred thousand dollars. For fifty-one per cent—(*smiles archly*) a controlling interest, mind you, we will put up two hundred and twenty-five thousand dollars besides offering him certain benefits that our (*looks at* BEN) local position allows us to manage. Ben means that two hundred and twenty-five thousand dollars is a lot of money.

REGINA: I know the terms and I know it's a lot of money.

BEN (*nodding*): It is.

OSCAR: Ben means that we are ready with our two-thirds of the money. Your third, Horace's I mean, doesn't seem to be ready. (*Raises his hand as* REGINA *starts to speak.*) Ben has written to Horace, I have written, and you have written. He answers. But he never mentions this business. Yet we have explained it to him in great detail, and told him the urgency. Still he never mentions it. Ben has been very patient, Regina. Naturally, you are our sister and we want you to benefit from anything we do.

REGINA: And in addition to your concern for me, you do not want control to go out of the family. (*To* BEN.) That right, Ben?

BEN: That's cynical. (*Smiles.*) Cynicism is an unpleasant way of saying the truth.

OSCAR: No need to be cynical. We'd have no trouble raising the third share, the share that you want to take.

REGINA: I am sure you could get the third share, the share you were saving for me. But that would give you a strange partner. And strange partners sometimes want a great deal. (*Smiles unpleasantly.*) But perhaps it would be wise for you to find him.

OSCAR: Now, now. Nobody says we *want* to do that. We would like to have you in and you would like to come in.

REGINA: Yes. I certainly would.

BEN (*laughs, puts up his hand*): But we haven't heard from Horace.

REGINA: I've given my word that Horace will put up the money. That should be enough.

BEN: Oh, it was enough. I took your word. But I've got to have more than your word now. The contracts will be signed this week, and Marshall will want to see our money soon after. Regina, Horace has been in Baltimore for five months. I know that you've written him to come home, and that he hasn't come.

OSCAR: It's beginning to look as if he doesn't want to come home.

REGINA: Of course he wants to come home. You can't move around with heart trouble at any moment you choose. You know what doctors are like once they get their hands on a case like this—

OSCAR: They can't very well keep him from answering letters, can they? (REGINA *turns to* BEN.) They couldn't keep him from arranging for the money if he wanted to —

REGINA: Has it occurred to you that Horace is also a good business man?

BEN: Certainly. He is a shrewd trader. Always has been. The bank is proof of that.

REGINA: Then, possibly, he may be keeping silent because he doesn't think he is getting enough for his money. (*Looks at* OSCAR.) Seventy-five thousand he has to put up. That's a lot of money, too.

OSCAR: Nonsense. He knows a good thing when he hears it. He knows that we can make *twice* the profit on cotton goods manufactured *here* than can be made in the North.

BEN: That isn't what Regina means. (*Smiles.*) May I interpret you, Regina? (*To* OSCAR.) Regina is saying that Horace wants *more* than a third of our share.

OSCAR: But he's only putting up a third of the money. You put up a third and you get a third. What else *could* he expect?

REGINA: Well, *I* don't know. I don't know about these things. It would seem that if you put up a third you should only get a third. But then again, there's no law about it, is there? I should think that if you knew your money was very badly needed, well, you just might say, I want more, I want a bigger share. You boys have done that. I've heard you say so.

BEN (*after a pause, laughs*): So you believe he has deliberately held out? For a larger share? (*Leaning forward.*) Well, I *don't* believe it. But I *do* believe that's what *you* want. Am I right, Regina?

REGINA: Oh, I shouldn't like to be too definite. But I *could* say that I wouldn't like to persuade Horace unless he did get a larger share. I must look after his interests. It seems only natural—

OSCAR: And where would the larger share come from?

REGINA: I don't know. That's not my business. (*Giggles.*) But perhaps it could come off your share, Oscar.

(REGINA *and* BEN *laugh.*)

OSCAR (*rises and wheels furiously on both of them as they laugh*): What kind of talk is this?

BEN: I haven't said a thing.

OSCAR (*to* REGINA): *You* are talking very big tonight.

REGINA (*stops laughing*): Am I? Well, you should know me well enough to know that I wouldn't be asking for things I didn't think I could get.

OSCAR: Listen. I don't believe you can even get Horace to come home, much less get money from him or talk quite so big about what you want.

REGINA: Oh, I can get him home.

OSCAR: Then why haven't you?

REGINA: I thought I should fight his battles for him, before he came home. Horace is a very sick man. And even if *you* don't care how sick he is, I do.

BEN: Stop this foolish squabbling. How can you get him home?

REGINA: I will send Alexandra to Baltimore. She will ask him to come home. She will say that she *wants* him to come home, and that *I* want him to come home.

BIRDIE (*suddenly*): Well, of course she wants him here, but he's sick and maybe he's happy where he is.

REGINA (*ignores* BIRDIE, *to* BEN): You agree that he will come home if she asks him to, if she says that I miss him and want him—

BEN (*looks at her, smiles*): I admire you, Regina. And I agree. That's settled now and—(*Starts to rise.*)

REGINA (*quickly*): But before she brings him home, I want to know what he's going to get.

BEN: What do you want?

REGINA: Twice what you offered.

BEN: Well, you won't get it.

OSCAR (*to* REGINA): I think you've gone crazy.

REGINA: I don't want to fight, Ben—

BEN: I don't either. You won't get it. There isn't any chance of that. (*Roguishly.*) You're holding us up, and that's not pretty, Regina, not pretty. (*Holds up his hand as he sees she is about to speak.*) But we need you, and I don't want to fight. Here's what I'll do: I'll give Horace forty per cent, instead of the thirty-three and a third he really should get. I'll do that, provided he is home and his money is up within two weeks. How's that?

REGINA: All right.

OSCAR: I've asked before: where is this extra share coming from?

BEN (*pleasantly*): From you. From your share.

OSCAR (*furiously*): From me, is it? That's just fine and dandy. That's my reward. For thirty-five years I've worked my hands to the bone for you. For thirty-five years I've done all the things you didn't want to do. And this is what I—

BEN (*turns slowly to look at* OSCAR. OSCAR *breaks off*): My, my. I am being attacked tonight on all sides. First by my sister, then by my brother. And I ain't a man who likes being attacked. I can't believe that God wants the strong to parade their strength, but I don't mind doing it if it's got to be done. (*Leans back in his chair.*) You ought to take these things better, Oscar. I've made you money in the past. I'm going to make you more money now. You'll be a very rich man. What's the difference to any of us if a little more goes here, a little less goes there—it's all in the family. And it will stay in the family. I'll never marry. (ADDIE *enters, begins to gather the glasses from the table.* OSCAR *turns to* BEN.) So my money will go to Alexandra and Leo. They may even marry some day and—(ADDIE *looks at* BEN.)

BIRDIE (*rising*): Marry—Zan and Leo—

OSCAR (*carefully*): That would make a great difference in my feelings. If they married.

BEN: Yes, that's what I mean. Of course it would make a difference.

OSCAR (*carefully*): Is that what *you* mean, Regina?

REGINA: Oh, it's too far away. We'll talk about it in a few years.

OSCAR: I want to talk about it now.

BEN (*nods*): Naturally.

REGINA: There's a lot of things to consider. They are first cousins, and—

OSCAR: That isn't unusual. Our grandmother and grandfather were first cousins.

REGINA (*giggles*): And look at us.

(BEN *giggles.*)

OSCAR (*angrily*): You're both being very gay with my money.

BEN (*sighs*): These quarrels. I dislike them so. (*Leans forward to* REGINA.) A marriage might be a very wise arrangement, for several reasons. And then, Oscar has given up something for you. You should try to manage something for him.

REGINA: I haven't said I was opposed to it. But Leo is a wild boy. There were those times when he took a little money from the bank and—

OSCAR: That's all past history—

REGINA: Oh, I know. And I know all young men are wild. I'm only mentioning it to show you that there are considerations—

BEN (*irritated because she does not understand that he is trying to keep* OSCAR *quiet*): All right, so there are. But please assure Oscar that you will think about it very seriously.

REGINA (*smiles, nods*): Very well. I assure Oscar that I will think about it seriously.

OSCAR (*sharply*): That is not an answer.

REGINA (*rises*): My, you're in a bad humor and you shall put me in one. I have said all that I am willing to say now. After all, Horace has to give his consent, too.

OSCAR: Horace will do what you tell him to.

REGINA: Yes, I think he will.

OSCAR: And I have your word that you will try to—

REGINA (*patiently*): Yes, Oscar. You have my word that I will think about it. Now do leave me alone.

(*There is the sound of the front door being closed.*)

BIRDIE: I—Alexandra is only seventeen. She—

REGINA (*calling*): Alexandra? Are you back?

ALEXANDRA: Yes, Mama.

LEO (*comes into the room*): Mr. Marshall got off safe and sound. Weren't those fine clothes he had? You can always spot clothes made in a good place. Looks like maybe they were done in England. Lots of men in the North send all the way to England for their stuff.

BEN (*to* LEO): Were you careful driving the horses?

LEO: Oh, yes, sir. I was.

(ALEXANDRA *has come in on* BEN's *question, hears the answer, looks angrily at* LEO.)

ALEXANDRA: It's a lovely night. You should have come, Aunt Birdie.

REGINA: Were you gracious to Mr. Marshall?

ALEXANDRA: I think so, Mama. I liked him.

REGINA: Good. And now I have great news for you. You are going to Baltimore in the morning to bring your father home.

ALEXANDRA (*gasps, then delighted*): Me? Papa said I should come? That must mean—(*Turns to* ADDIE.) Addie, he must be well. Think of it, he'll be back home again. We'll bring him home.

REGINA: You are going alone, Alexandra.

ADDIE (ALEXANDRA *has turned in surprise*): Going alone? Going by herself? A child that age! Mr. Horace ain't going to like Zan traipsing up there by herself.

REGINA (*sharply*): Go upstairs and lay out Alexandra's things.

ADDIE: He'd expect me to be along—

REGINA: I'll be up in a few minutes to tell you what to pack. (ADDIE *slowly begins to climb the steps. To* ALEXANDRA.) I should think you'd like going alone. At your age it certainly would have delighted me. You're a strange girl, Alexandra. Addie has babied you so much.

ALEXANDRA: I only thought it would be more fun if Addie and I went together.

BIRDIE (*timidly*): Maybe I could go with her, Regina. I'd really like to.

REGINA: She is going alone. She is getting old enough to take some responsibilities.

OSCAR: She'd better learn now. She's almost old enough to get married. (*Jovially, to* LEO, *slapping him on shoulder.*) Eh, son?

LEO: Huh?

OSCAR (*annoyed with* LEO *for not understanding*): Old enough to get married, you're thinking, eh?

LEO: Oh, yes, sir. (*Feebly.*) Lots of girls get married at Zan's age. Look at Mary Prester and Johanna and—

REGINA: Well, she's not getting married tomorrow. But she is going to Baltimore tomorrow, so let's talk about that. (*To* ALEXANDRA.)

You'll be glad to have Papa home again.

ALEXANDRA: I wanted to go before, Mama. You remember that. But you said *you* couldn't go, and that *I* couldn't go alone.

REGINA: I've changed my mind. (*Too casually.*) You're to tell Papa how much you missed him, and that he must come home now—for your sake. Tell him that you *need* him home.

ALEXANDRA: Need him home? I don't understand.

REGINA: There is nothing for you to understand. You are simply to say what I have told you.

BIRDIE (*rises*): He may be too sick. She couldn't do that—

ALEXANDRA: Yes. He may be too sick to travel. I couldn't make him think he had to come home for me, if he is too sick to—

REGINA (*looks at her, sharply, challengingly*): You *couldn't* do what I tell you to do, Alexandra?

ALEXANDRA (*quietly*): No. I couldn't. If I thought it would hurt him.

REGINA (*after a second's silence, smiles pleasantly*): But you are doing this for Papa's own good. (*Takes* ALEXANDRA's *hand.*) You must let me be the judge of his condition. It's the best possible cure for him to come home and be taken care of here. He mustn't stay there any longer and listen to those alarmist doctors. You are doing this entirely for his sake. Tell your papa that I want him to come home, that I miss him very much.

ALEXANDRA (*slowly*): Yes, Mama.

REGINA (*to the others; rises*): I must go and start getting Alexandra ready now. Why don't you all go home?

BEN (*rises*): I'll attend to the railroad ticket. One of the boys will bring it over. Good night, everybody. Have a nice trip, Alexandra. The food on the train is very good. The celery is so crisp. Have a good time and act like a little lady. (*Exits.*)

REGINA: Good night, Ben. Good night, Oscar—(*Playfully.*) Don't be so glum, Oscar. It makes you look as if you had chronic indigestion.

BIRDIE: Good night, Regina.

REGINA: Good night, Birdie. (*Exits upstairs.*)

OSCAR (*starts for hall*): Come along.

LEO (*to* ALEXANDRA): Imagine your not wanting to go! What a little fool you are. Wish it were me. What I could do in a place like Baltimore!

ALEXANDRA (*angrily, looking away from him*): Mind your business. I can guess the kind of things *you* could do.

LEO (*laughs*): Oh, no, you couldn't. (*He exits.*)

REGINA (*calling from the top of the stairs*): Come on, Alexandra.

BIRDIE (*quickly, softly*): Zan.

ALEXANDRA: I don't understand about my going, Aunt Birdie. (*Shrugs.*) But anyway, Papa will be home again. (*Pats* BIRDIE's *arm.*) Don't worry about me. I can take care of myself. Really I can.

BIRDIE (*shakes her head, softly*): That's not what I'm worried about. Zan—

ALEXANDRA (*comes close to her*): What's the matter?

BIRDIE: It's about Leo—

ALEXANDRA (*whispering*): He beat the horses. That's why we were late getting back. We had to wait until they cooled off. He always beats the horses as if—

BIRDIE (*whispering frantically, holding* ALEXANDRA's *hands*): He's my son. My own son. But you are more to me—more to me than my own child. I love you more than anybody else—

ALEXANDRA: Don't worry about the horses. I'm sorry I told you.

BIRDIE (*her voice rising*): *I am not worrying about the horses.* I am worrying about *you*. You are *not* going to marry Leo. I am not going to let them do that to you—

ALEXANDRA: Marry? To Leo? (*Laughs.*) I wouldn't marry, Aunt Birdie. I've never even thought about it—

BIRDIE: But they have thought about it. (*Wildly.*) Zan, I couldn't stand to think about such a thing. You and—

(OSCAR *has come into the doorway on* ALEXANDRA's *speech. He is standing quietly, listening.*)

ALEXANDRA (*laughs*): But I'm not going to marry. And I'm certainly not going to marry Leo.

BIRDIE: Don't you understand? They'll make you. They'll make you—

ALEXANDRA (*takes* BIRDIE's *hands, quietly, firmly*): That's foolish, Aunt Birdie. I'm grown now. Nobody can make me do anything.

BIRDIE: I just couldn't stand—

OSCAR (*sharply*): Birdie. (BIRDIE *looks up, draws quickly away from* ALEXANDRA. *She stands rigid, frightened. Quietly.*) Birdie, get your hat and coat.

ADDIE (*calls from upstairs*): Come on, baby. Your mama's waiting for you, and she ain't nobody to keep waiting.

ALEXANDRA: All right. (*Then softly, embracing* BIRDIE.) Good night, Aunt Birdie. (*As she passes* OSCAR.) Good night, Uncle Oscar. (BIRDIE *begins to move slowly towards the door as* ALEXANDRA *climbs the stairs.* ALEXANDRA *is almost out of view when* BIRDIE *reaches* OSCAR *in the doorway. As* BIRDIE *quickly attempts to pass him, he slaps her hard, across the face.* BIRDIE *cries out, puts her hand to her face. On the cry,* ALEXANDRA *turns, begins to run down the stairs.*) Aunt Birdie! What happened? What happened? I—

BIRDIE (*softly, without turning*): Nothing, darling. Nothing happened. (*Quickly, as if anxious to keep* ALEXANDRA *from coming close.*) Now go to bed. (OSCAR *exits.*) Nothing happened. (*Turns to* ALEXANDRA *who is holding her hand.*) I only—I only twisted my ankle. (*She goes out.* ALEXANDRA *stands on the stairs looking after her as if she were puzzled and frightened.*)

ACT II

(SCENE: *Same as Act I. A week later, morning.*

AT RISE: *The light comes from the open shutter of the right window; the other shutters are tightly closed.* ADDIE *is standing at the window, looking out. Near the dining-room doors are brooms, mops, rags, etc. After a second,* OSCAR *comes into the entrance hall, looks in the room, shivers, decides not to take his hat and coat off, comes into the room. At the sound of the door,* ADDIE *turns to see who has come in.*)

ADDIE (*without interest*): Oh, it's you, Mr. Oscar.

OSCAR: What is this? It's not night. What's the matter here? (*Shivers.*) Fine thing at this time of the morning. Blinds all closed. (ADDIE *begins to open shutters.*) Where's Miss Regina? It's cold in here.

ADDIE: Miss Regina ain't down yet.

OSCAR: She had any word?

ADDIE (*wearily*): No, sir.

OSCAR: Wouldn't you think a girl that age could get on a train at one place and have sense enough to get off at another?

ADDIE: Something must have happened. If Zan say she was coming last night, she's coming last night. Unless something happened. Sure fire disgrace to let a baby like that go all that way alone to bring home a sick man without—

OSCAR: You do a lot of judging around here, Addie, eh? Judging of your white folks, I mean.

ADDIE (*looks at him, sighs*): I'm tired. I been

up all night watching for them.

REGINA (*speaking from the upstairs hall*): Who's downstairs, Addie? (*She appears in a dressing gown, peers down from the landing.* ADDIE *picks up broom, dustpan and brush and exits.*) Oh, it's you, Oscar. What are you doing here so early? I haven't been down yet. I'm not finished dressing.

OSCAR (*speaking up to her*): You had any word from them?

REGINA: No.

OSCAR: Then something certainly has happened. People don't just say they are arriving on Thursday night, and they haven't come by Friday morning.

REGINA: Oh, nothing has happened. Alexandra just hasn't got sense enough to send a message.

OSCAR: If nothing's happened, then why aren't they here?

REGINA: You asked me that ten times last night. My, you do fret so, Oscar. Anything might have happened. They may have missed connections in Atlanta, the train may have been delayed—oh, a hundred things could have kept them.

OSCAR: Where's Ben?

REGINA (*as she disappears upstairs*): Where should he be? At home, probably. Really, Oscar I don't tuck him in his bed and I don't take him out of it. Have some coffee and don't worry so much.

OSCAR: Have some coffee? There isn't any coffee. (*Looks at his watch, shakes his head. After a second* CAL *enters with a large silver tray, coffee urn, small cups, newspaper.*) Oh, there you are. Is everything in this fancy house always late?

CAL (*looks at him surprised*): You ain't out shooting this morning, Mr. Oscar?

OSCAR: First day I missed since I had my head cold. First day I missed in eight years.

CAL: Yes, sir. I bet you. Simon he say you had a mighty good day yesterday morning. That's what Simon say. (*Brings* OSCAR *coffee and newspaper.*)

OSCAR: Pretty good, pretty good.

CAL (*laughs, slyly*): Bet you got enough bobwhite and squirrel to give every nigger in town a Jesus-party. Most of 'em ain't had no meat since the cotton picking was over. Bet they'd give anything for a little piece of that meat—

OSCAR (*turns his head to look at* CAL): Cal, if I catch a nigger in this town going shooting, you know what's going to happen.

(LEO *enters.*)

CAL (*hastily*): Yes, sir, Mr. Oscar. I didn't say nothing about nothing. It was Simon who told me and—Morning, Mr. Leo. You gentlemen having your breakfast with us here?

LEO: The boys in the bank don't know a thing. They haven't had any message.

(CAL *waits for an answer, gets none, shrugs, moves to door, exits.*)

OSCAR (*peers at* LEO): What you doing here, son?

LEO: You told me to find out if the boys at the bank had any message from Uncle Horace or Zan—

OSCAR: I told you if they had a message to bring it here. I told you that if they didn't have a message to stay at the bank and do your work.

LEO: Oh, I guess I misunderstood.

OSCAR: You didn't misunderstand. You just were looking for any excuse to take an hour off. (LEO *pours a cup of coffee.*) You got to stop that kind of thing. You got to start settling down. You going to be a married man one of these days.

LEO: Yes, sir.

OSCAR: You also got to stop with that woman in Mobile. (*As* LEO *is about to speak.*) You're young and I haven't got no objections to outside women. That is, I haven't got no objections so long as they don't interfere with serious things. Outside women are all right in their place, but *now* isn't their place. You got to realize that.

LEO (*nods*): Yes, sir. I'll tell her. She'll act all right about it.

OSCAR: Also, you got to start working harder at the bank. You got to convince your Uncle Horace you going to make a fit husband for Alexandra.

LEO: What do you think has happened to them? Supposed to be here last night—(*Laughs.*) Bet you Uncle Ben's mighty worried. Seventy-five thousand dollars worried.

OSCAR (*smiles happily*): Ought to be worried. Damn well ought to be. First he don't answer the letters, then he don't come home—(*Giggles.*)

LEO: What will happen if Uncle Horace don't come home or don't—

OSCAR: Or don't put up the money? Oh, we'll get it from outside. Easy enough.

LEO (*surprised*): But *you* don't want outsiders.

OSCAR: What do I care who gets my share? I been shaved already. Serve Ben right if he had to give away some of his.

LEO: Damn shame what they did to you.

OSCAR (*looking up the stairs*): Don't talk so

loud. Don't you worry. When I die, you'll have as much as the rest. You might have yours *and* Alexandra's. I'm not so easily licked.

LEO: I wasn't thinking of myself, Papa—

OSCAR: Well, you should be, you should be. It's every man's duty to think of himself.

LEO: You think Uncle Horace don't want to go in on this?

OSCAR (*giggles*): That's my hunch. He hasn't showed any signs of loving it yet.

LEO (*laughs*): But he hasn't listened to Aunt Regina yet, either. Oh, he'll go along. It's too good a thing. Why wouldn't he want to? He's got plenty and plenty to invest with. He don't even have to sell anything. Eighty-eight thousand worth of Union Pacific bonds sitting right in his safe deposit box. All he's got to do is open the box.

OSCAR (*after a pause; looks at his watch*): Mighty late breakfast in this fancy house. Yes, he's had those bonds for fifteen years. Bought them when they were low and just locked them up.

LEO: Yeah. Just has to open the box and take them out. That's all. Easy as easy can be. (*Laughs.*) The things in that box! There's all those bonds, looking mighty fine. (OSCAR *slowly puts down his newspaper and turns to* LEO.) Then right next to them is a baby shoe of Zan's and a cheap old cameo on a string, and, and—nobody'd believe this—a piece of an old violin. Not even a whole violin. Just a piece of an old thing, a piece of a violin.

OSCAR (*very softly, as if he were trying to control his voice*): A piece of a violin! What do you think of that!

LEO: Yes, sirree. A lot of other crazy things, too. A poem, I guess it is, signed with his mother's name, and two old schoolbooks with notes and—(LEO *catches* OSCAR's *look. His voice trails off. He turns his head away.*)

OSCAR (*very softly*): How do you know what's in the box, son?

LEO (*stops, draws back, frightened, realizing what he has said*): Oh, well. Well, er. Well, one of the boys, sir. It was one of the boys at the bank. He took old Manders' keys. It was Joe Horns. He just up and took Manders' keys and, and—well, took the box out. (*Quickly.*) Then they all asked me if I wanted to see, too. So I looked a little, I guess, but then I made them close up the box quick and I told them never—

OSCAR (*looks at him*): Joe Horns, you say? He opened it?

LEO: Yes, sir, yes, he did. My word of honor.

(*Very nervously looking away.*) I suppose that don't excuse *me* for looking—(*looking at* OSCAR) but I did make him close it up and put the keys back in Manders' drawer—

OSCAR (*leans forward, very softly*): Tell me the truth, Leo. I am not going to be angry with you. Did you open the box yourself?

LEO: *No, sir, I didn't.* I told you I didn't. No, I—

OSCAR (*irritated, patient*): I am *not* going to be angry with you. (*Watching* LEO *carefully.*) Sometimes a young fellow deserves credit for looking round him to see what's going on. Sometimes that's a good sign in a fellow your age. (OSCAR *rises.*) Many great men have made their fortune with their eyes. Did you open the box?

LEO (*very puzzled*): No. I—

OSCAR (*moves to* LEO): Did you open the box? It may have been—well, it may have been a good thing if you had.

LEO (*after a long pause*): I opened it.

OSCAR (*quickly*): Is that the truth? (LEO *nods.*) Does anybody else know that you opened it? Come, Leo, don't be afraid of speaking the truth to me.

LEO: No. Nobody knew. Nobody was in the bank when I did it. But—

OSCAR: Did your Uncle Horace ever know you opened it?

LEO (*shakes his head*): He only looks in it once every six months when he cuts the coupons, and sometimes Manders even does that for him. Uncle Horace don't even have the keys. Manders keeps them for him. Imagine not looking at all that. You can bet if I had the bonds, I'd watch 'em like—

OSCAR: If you had them. (LEO *watches him.*) If you had them. Then you could have a share in the mill, you and me. A fine, big share, too. (*Pauses, shrugs.*) Well, a man can't be shot for wanting to see his son get on in the world, can he, boy?

LEO (*looks up, begins to understand*): No, he can't. Natural enough. (*Laughs.*) But I haven't got the bonds and Uncle Horace has. And now he can just sit back and wait to be a millionaire.

OSCAR (*innocently*): You think your Uncle Horace likes you well enough to lend you the bonds if he decides not to use them himself?

LEO: Papa, it must be that you haven't had your breakfast! (*Laughs loudly.*) Lend me the bonds! My God—

OSCAR (*disappointed*): No, I suppose not. Just a fancy of mine. A loan for three months, maybe four, easy enough for us to pay it back then.

Anyway, this is only April—(*Slowly counting the months on his fingers.*) And if he doesn't look at them until Fall, he wouldn't even miss them out of the box.

LEO: That's it. He wouldn't even miss them. Ah, well—

OSCAR: No, sir. Wouldn't even miss them. How could he miss them if he never looks at them? (*Sighs as* LEO *stares at him.*) Well, here we are sitting around waiting for him to come home and invest his money in something he hasn't lifted his hand to get. But I can't help thinking he's acting strange. You laugh when I say he could lend you the bonds if he's not going to use them himself. But would it hurt him?

LEO (*slowly looking at* OSCAR): No. No, it wouldn't.

OSCAR: People ought to help other people. But that's not always the way it happens. (BEN *enters, hangs his coat and hat in hall. Very carefully.*) And so sometimes you got to think of yourself. (*As* LEO *stares at him,* BEN *appears in the doorway.*) Morning, Ben.

BEN (*coming in, carrying his newspaper*): Fine sunny morning. Any news from the runaways?

REGINA (*on the staircase*): There's no news or you would have heard it. Quite a convention so early in the morning, aren't you all? (*Goes to coffee urn.*)

OSCAR: You rising mighty late these days. Is that the way they do things in Chicago society?

BEN (*looking at his paper*): Old Carter died up in Senateville. Eighty-one is a good time for us all, eh? What do you think has really happened to Horace, Regina?

REGINA: Nothing.

BEN (*too casually*): You don't think maybe he never started from Baltimore and never intends to start?

REGINA (*irritated*): Of course they've started. Didn't I have a letter from Alexandra? What is so strange about people arriving late? He has that cousin in Savannah he's so fond of. He may have stopped to see him. They'll be along today some time, very flattered that you and Oscar are so worried about them.

BEN: I'm a natural worrier. Especially when I am getting ready to close a business deal and one of my partners remains silent *and* invisible.

REGINA (*laughs*): Oh, is that it? I thought you were worried about Horace's health.

OSCAR: Oh, that too. Who could help but worry? I'm worried. This is the first day I haven't shot since my head cold.

REGINA (*starts towards dining room*): Then you haven't had your breakfast. Come along. (OSCAR *and* LEO *follow her.*)

BEN: Regina. (*She turns at dining-room door.*) That cousin of Horace's has been dead for years and, in any case, the train does not go through Savannah.

REGINA (*laughs, continues into dining room, seats herself*): Did he die? You're always remembering about people dying. (BEN *rises.*) Now I intend to eat my breakfast in peace, and read my newspaper.

BEN (*goes towards dining room as he talks*): This is second breakfast for me. My first was bad. Celia ain't the cook she used to be. Too old to have taste any more. If she hadn't belonged to Mama, I'd send her off to the country.

(OSCAR *and* LEO *start to eat.* BEN *seats himself.*)

LEO: Uncle Horace will have some tales to tell, I bet. Baltimore is a lively town.

REGINA (*to* CAL): The grits isn't hot enough. Take it back.

CAL: Oh, yes'm. (*Calling into kitchen as he exits.*) Grits didn't hold the heat. Grits didn't hold the heat.

LEO: When I was at school three of the boys and myself took a train once and went over to Baltimore. It was so big we thought we were in Europe. I was just a kid then—

REGINA: I find it very pleasant (ADDIE *enters.*) to have breakfast alone. I hate chattering before I've had something hot. (CAL *closes the dining-room doors.*) Do be still, Leo.

(ADDIE *comes into the room, begins gathering up the cups, carries them to the large tray. Outside there are the sounds of voices. Quickly* ADDIE *runs into the hall. A few seconds later she appears again in the doorway, her arm around the shoulders of* HORACE GIDDENS, *supporting him.* HORACE *is a tall man of about forty-five. He has been good looking, but now his face is tired and ill. He walks stiffly, as if it were an enormous effort, and carefully, as if he were unsure of his balance.* ADDIE *takes off his overcoat and hangs it on the hall tree. She then helps him to a chair.*)

HORACE: How are you, Addie? How have you been?

ADDIE: I'm all right, Mr. Horace. I've just been worried about you.

(ALEXANDRA *enters. She is flushed and excited, her hat awry, her face dirty. Her arms are full of packages, but she comes quickly to* ADDIE.)

ALEXANDRA: Now don't tell me how worried you were. We couldn't help it and there was no way to send a message.

ADDIE (*begins to take packages from* ALEXANDRA): Yes, sir, I was mighty worried.

ALEXANDRA: We had to stop in Mobile over night. Papa—(*Looks at him.*) Papa didn't feel well. The trip was too much for him, and I made him stop and rest—(*As* ADDIE *takes the last package.*) No, don't take that. That's father's medicine. I'll hold it. It mustn't break. Now, about the stuff outside. Papa must have his wheel chair. I'll get that and the valises—

ADDIE (*very happy, holding* ALEXANDRA's *arms*): Since when you got to carry your own valises? Since when I ain't old enough to hold a bottle of medicine?. (HORACE *coughs.*) You feel all right, Mr. Horace?

HORACE (*nods*): Glad to be sitting down.

ALEXANDRA (*opening package of medicine*): He doesn't feel all right. (ADDIE *looks at her, then at* HORACE.) He just says that. The trip was very hard on him, and now he must go right to bed.

ADDIE (*looking at him carefully*): Them fancy doctors, they give you help?

HORACE: They did their best.

ALEXANDRA (*has become conscious of the voices in the dining room*): I bet Mama was worried. I better tell her we're here now. (*She starts for door.*)

HORACE: Zan. (*She stops.*) Not for a minute, dear.

ALEXANDRA: Oh, Papa, you feel bad again. I knew you did. Do you want your medicine?

HORACE: No, I don't feel that way. I'm just tired, darling. Let me rest a little.

ALEXANDRA: Yes, but Mama will be mad if I don't tell her we're here.

ADDIE: They're all in there eating breakfast.

ALEXANDRA: Oh, are they all here? Why do they *always* have to be here? I was hoping Papa wouldn't have to see anybody, that it would be nice for him and quiet.

ADDIE: Then let your papa rest for a minute.

HORACE: Addie, I bet your coffee's as good as ever. They don't have such good coffee up North. (*Looks at the urn.*) Is it as good, Addie? (ADDIE *starts for coffee urn.*)

ALEXANDRA: No. Dr. Reeves said not much coffee. Just now and then. I'm the nurse now, Addie.

ADDIE: You'd be a better one if you didn't look so dirty. Now go and take a bath, Miss Grown-up. Change your linens, get out a fresh dress and give your hair a good brushing—go on—

ALEXANDRA: Will you be all right, Papa?

ADDIE: Go on.

ALEXANDRA (*on stairs, talks as she goes up*): The pills Papa must take once every four hours. And the bottle only when—only if he feels very bad. Now don't move until I come back and don't talk much and remember about his medicine, Addie—

ADDIE: Ring for Belle and have her help you and then I'll make you a fresh breakfast.

ALEXANDRA (*as she disappears*): How's Aunt Birdie? Is she here?

ADDIE: It ain't right for you to have coffee? It will hurt you?

HORACE (*slowly*): Nothing can make much difference now. Get me a cup, Addie. (*She looks at him, crosses to urn, pours a cup.*) Funny. They can't make coffee up North. (ADDIE *brings him a cup.*) They don't like red pepper, either. (*He takes the cup and gulps it greedily.*) God, that's good. You remember how I used to drink it? Ten, twelve cups a day. So strong it had to stain the cup. (*Then slowly.*) Addie, before I see anybody else, I want to know why Zan came to fetch me home. She's tried to tell me, but she doesn't seem to know herself.

ADDIE (*turns away*): I don't know. All I know is big things are going on. Everybody going to be high-tone rich. Big rich. You too. All because smoke's going to start out of a building that ain't even up yet.

HORACE: I've heard about it.

ADDIE: And, er—(*Hesitates—steps to him.*) And—well, Zan, she going to marry Mr. Leo in a little while.

HORACE (*looks at her, then very slowly*): What are you talking about?

ADDIE: That's right. That's the talk, God help us.

HORACE (*angrily*): What's the talk?

ADDIE: I'm telling you. There's going to be a wedding—(*Angrily turns away.*) Over my dead body there is.

HORACE (*after a second, quietly*): Go and tell them I'm home.

ADDIE (*hesitates*): Now you ain't to get excited. You're to be in your bed—

HORACE: Go on, Addie. Go and say I'm back. (ADDIE *opens dining-room doors. He rises with difficulty, stands stiff, as if he were in pain, facing the dining room.*)

ADDIE: Miss Regina. They're home. They got here—

REGINA: Horace! (REGINA *quickly rises. runs into the room. Warmly.*) Horace! You've finally arrived. (*As she kisses him, the others come forward, all talking together.*)

BEN (*in doorway, carrying a napkin*): Well, sir, you had us all mighty worried. (*He steps forward. They shake hands.* ADDIE *exits.*)

OSCAR: You're a sight for sore eyes.

HORACE: Hello, Ben.

(LEO *enters, eating a biscuit.*)

OSCAR: And how you feel? Tip-top, I bet, because that's the way you're looking.

HORACE (*coldly, irritated with* OSCAR's *lie*): Hello, Oscar. Hello, Leo, how are you?

LEO (*shaking hands*): I'm fine, sir. But a lot better now that you're back.

REGINA: Now sit down. What did happen to you and where's Alexandra? I am so excited about seeing you that I almost forgot about her.

HORACE: I didn't feel good, a little weak, I guess, and we stopped over night to rest. Zan's upstairs washing off the train dirt.

REGINA: Oh, I am so sorry the trip was hard on you. I didn't think that—

HORACE: Well, it's just as if I had never been away. All of you here—

BEN: Waiting to welcome you home.

(BIRDIE *bursts in. She is wearing a flannel kimono and her face is flushed and excited.*)

BIRDIE (*runs to him, kisses him*): Horace!

HORACE (*warmly pressing her arm*): I was just wondering where you were, Birdie.

BIRDIE (*excited*): Oh, I would have been here. I didn't know you were back until Simon said he saw the buggy. (*She draws back to look at him. Her face sobers.*) Oh, you don't look well, Horace. No, you don't.

REGINA (*laughs*): Birdie, what a thing to say—

HORACE (*looking at* OSCAR): Oscar thinks I look very well.

OSCAR (*annoyed; turns on* LEO): Don't stand there holding that biscuit in your hand.

LEO: Oh, well. I'll just finish my breakfast, Uncle Horace, and then I'll give you all the news about the bank—(*He exits into the dining room.*)

OSCAR: And what is that costume you have on?

BIRDIE (*looking at* HORACE): Now that you're home, you'll feel better. Plenty of good rest and we'll take such fine care of you. · (*Stops.*) But where is Zan? I missed her so much.

OSCAR: I asked you what is that strange costume you're parading around in?

BIRDIE (*nervously, backing towards stairs*): Me?

Oh! It's my wrapper. I was so excited about Horace I just rushed out of the house—

OSCAR: Did you come across the square dressed that way? My dear Birdie, I—

HORACE (*to* REGINA, *wearily*): Yes, it's just like old times.

REGINA (*quickly to* OSCAR): Now, no fights. This is a holiday.

BIRDIE (*runs quickly up the stairs*): Zan! Zannie!

OSCAR: Birdie! (*She stops.*)

BIRDIE: Oh. Tell Zan I'll be back in a little while. (*Whispers.*) Sorry, Oscar. (*Exits.*)

REGINA (*to* OSCAR *and* BEN): Why don't you go finish your breakfast and let Horace rest for a minute?

BEN (*crossing to dining room with* OSCAR): Never leave a meal unfinished. There are too many poor people who need the food. Mighty glad to see you home, Horace. Fine to have you back. Fine to have you back.

OSCAR (*to* LEO *as* BEN *closes dining-room doors*): Your mother has gone crazy. Running around the streets like a woman—

(*The moment* REGINA *and* HORACE *are alone, they become awkward and self-conscious.*)

REGINA (*laughs awkwardly*): Well. Here we are. It's been a long time. (HORACE *smiles.*) Five months. You know, Horace, I wanted to come and be with you in the hospital, but I didn't know where my duty was. Here, or with you. But you know how much I *wanted* to come.

HORACE: That's kind of you, Regina. There was no need to come.

REGINA: Oh, but there was. Five months lying there all by yourself, no kinfolks, no friends. Don't try to tell me you didn't have a bad time of it.

HORACE: I didn't have a bad time. (*As she shakes her head, he becomes insistent.*) No, I didn't, Regina. Oh, at first when I—when I heard the news about myself—but after I got used to that, I liked it there.

REGINA: You *liked* it? (*Coldly.*) Isn't that strange. You liked it so well you didn't want to come home?

HORACE: That's not the way to put it. (*Then, kindly, as he sees her turn her head away.*) But there I was and I got kind of used to it, kind of to like lying there and thinking. (*Smiles.*) I never had much time to think before. And time's become valuable to me.

REGINA: It sounds almost like a holiday.

HORACE (*laughs*): It was, sort of. The first holiday I've had since I was a little kid.

REGINA: And here I was thinking you were in pain and—

HORACE (*quietly*): I was in pain.

REGINA: And instead you were having a holiday! A holiday of thinking. Couldn't you have done that here?

HORACE: I wanted to do it before I came here. I was thinking about us.

REGINA: About us? About you and me? Thinking about you and me after all these years. (*Unpleasantly.*) You shall tell me everything you thought—some day.

HORACE (*there is silence for a minute*): Regina. (*She turns to him.*) Why did you send Zan to Baltimore?

REGINA: Why? Because I wanted you home. You can't make anything suspicious out of that, can you?

HORACE: I didn't mean to make anything suspicious about it. (*Hesitantly, taking her hand.*) Zan said you wanted me to come home. I was so pleased at that and touched, it made me feel good.

REGINA (*taking away her hand, turns*): Touched that I should want you home?

HORACE (*sighs*): I'm saying all the wrong things as usual. Let's try to get along better. There isn't so much more time. Regina, what's all this crazy talk I've been hearing about Zan and Leo? Zan and Leo marrying?

REGINA (*turning to him, sharply*): Who gossips so much around here?

HORACE (*shocked*): Regina!

REGINA (*annoyed, anxious to quiet him*): It's some foolishness that Oscar thought up. I'll explain later. I have no intention of allowing any such arrangement. It was simply a way of keeping Oscar quiet in all this business I've been writing you about—

HORACE (*carefully*): What has Zan to do with any business of Oscar's? Whatever it is, you had better put it out of Oscar's head immediately. You know what I think of Leo.

REGINA: But there's no need to talk about it now.

HORACE: There is no need to talk about it ever. Not as long as I live. (HORACE *stops, slowly turns to look at her.*) As long as I live. I've been in a hospital for five months. Yet since I've been here you have not once asked me about—about my health. (*Then gently.*) Well, I suppose they've written you. I can't live very long.

REGINA (*coldly*): I've never understood why people have to talk about this kind of thing.

HORACE (*there is a silence. Then he looks up at her, his face cold*): You misunderstand. I don't intend to gossip about my sickness. I thought it was only fair to tell you. I was not asking for your sympathy.

REGINA (*sharply, turns to him*): What do the doctors think caused your bad heart?

HORACE: What do you mean?

REGINA: They didn't think it possible, did they, that your fancy women may have—

HORACE (*smiles unpleasantly*): Caused my heart to be bad? I don't think that's the best scientific theory. You don't catch heart trouble in bed.

REGINA (*angrily*): I didn't think you did. I only thought you might catch a bad conscience—in bed, as you say.

HORACE: I didn't tell them about my bad conscience. Or about my fancy women. Nor did I tell them that my wife has not wanted me in bed with her for—(*Sharply.*) How long is it, Regina? (REGINA *turns to him.*) Ten years? Did you bring me home for this, to make me feel guilty again? That means you want something. But you'll not make me feel guilty any more. My "thinking" has made a difference.

REGINA: I see that it has. (*She looks towards dining-room door. Then comes to him, her manner warm and friendly.*) It's foolish for us to fight this way. I didn't mean to be unpleasant. I was stupid.

HORACE (*wearily*): God knows I didn't either. I came home wanting so much not to fight, and then all of a sudden there we were. I got hurt and—

REGINA (*hastily*): It's all my fault. I didn't ask about—about your illness because I didn't want to remind you of it. Anyway I never believe doctors when they talk about—(*brightly*) when they talk like that.

HORACE (*not looking at her*): Well, we'll try our best with each other. (*He rises.*)

REGINA (*quickly*): I'll try. Honestly, I will. Horace, Horace, I know you're tired but, but—couldn't you stay down here a few minutes longer? I want Ben to tell you something.

HORACE: Tomorrow.

REGINA: I'd like to now. It's very important to me. It's very important to all of us. (*Gaily, as she moves toward dining room.*) Important to your beloved daughter. She'll be a very great heiress——

HORACE: Will she? That's nice.

REGINA (*opens doors*): Ben, are you finished breakfast?

HORACE: Is this the mill business I've had so many letters about?

REGINA (*to* BEN): Horace would like to talk to you now.

HORACE: Horace would not like to talk to .you now. I am very tired, Regina—

REGINA (*comes to him*): Please. You've said we'll try our best with each other. I'll try. Really, I will. Please do this for me now. You will see what I've done while you've been away. How I watched your interests. (*Laughs gaily.*) And I've done very well too. But things can't be delayed any longer. Everything must be settled this week —(HORACE *sits down.* BEN *enters.* OSCAR *has stayed in the dining room, his head turned to watch them.* LEO *is pretending to read the newspaper.*) Now you must tell Horace all about it. Only be quick because he is very tired and must go to bed. (HORACE *is looking up at her. His face hardens as she speaks.*) But I think your news will be better for him than all the medicine in the world.

BEN (*looking at* HORACE): It could wait. Horace may not feel like talking today.

REGINA: What an old faker you are! You know it can't wait. You know it must be finished this week. You've been just as anxious for Horace to get here as I've been.

BEN (*very jovial*): I suppose I have been. And why not? Horace has done Hubbard Sons many a good turn. Why shouldn't I be anxious to help him now?

REGINA (*laughs*): Help him! Help him when you need him, that's what you mean.

BEN: What a woman you married, Horace. (*Laughs awkwardly when* HORACE *does not answer.*) Well, then I'll make it quick. You know what I've been telling you for years. How I've always said that every one of us little Southern business men had great things—(*extends his arm*)—right beyond our finger tips. It's been my dream: my dream to make those fingers grow longer. I'm a lucky man, Horace, a lucky man. To dream and to live to get what you've dreamed of. That's *my* idea of a lucky man. (*Looks at his fingers as his arm drops slowly.*) For thirty years I've cried bring the cotton mills to the cotton. (HORACE *opens medicine bottle.*) Well, finally I got up nerve to go to Marshall Company in Chicago.

HORACE: I know all this. (*He takes the medicine.* REGINA *rises, steps to him.*)

BEN: Can I get you something?

HORACE: Some water, please.

REGINA (*turns quickly*): Oh, I'm sorry. Let me. (*Brings him a glass of water. He drinks as they wait in silence.*) You feel all right now?

HORACE: Yes. You wrote me. I know all that.

(OSCAR *enters from dining room.*)

REGINA (*triumphantly*): But you don't know that in the last few days Ben has agreed to give us—you, I mean—a much larger share.

HORACE: Really? That's very generous of him.

BEN (*laughs*): It wasn't so generous of me. It was smart of Regina.

REGINA (*as if she were signaling* HORACE): I explained to Ben that perhaps you hadn't answered his letters because you didn't think he was offering you enough, and that the time was getting short and you could guess how much he needed you—

HORACE (*smiles at her, nods*): And I could guess that he wants to keep control in the family?

REGINA (*to* BEN, *triumphantly*): Exactly. (*To* HORACE.) So I did a little bargaining for you and convinced my brothers they weren't the only Hubbards who had a business sense.

HORACE: Did you have to convince them of that? How little people know about each other! (*Laughs.*) But you'll know better about Regina next time, eh, Ben? (BEN, REGINA, HORACE *laugh together.* OSCAR's *face is angry.*) Now let's see. We're getting a bigger share. (*Looking at* OSCAR.) Who's getting less?

BEN: Oscar.

HORACE: Well, Oscar, you've grown very unselfish. What's happened to you?

(LEO *enters from dining room.*)

BEN (*quickly, before* OSCAR *can answer*): Oscar doesn't mind. Not worth fighting about now, eh, Oscar?

OSCAR (*angrily*): I'll get mine in the end. You can be sure of that. I've got my son's future to think about.

HORACE (*sharply*): Leo? Oh, I see. (*Puts his head back, laughs.* REGINA *looks at him nervously.*) I am beginning to see. Everybody will get theirs.

BEN: I knew you'd see it. Seventy-five thousand, and that seventy-five thousand will make you a million.

REGINA (*steps to table, leaning forward*): It will, Horace, it will.

HORACE: I believe you. (*After a second.*) Now I can understand Oscar's self-sacrifice, but what did you have to promise Marshall Company besides the money you're putting up?

BEN: They wouldn't take promises. They wanted guarantees.

HORACE: Of what?

BEN (*nods*): Water power. Free and plenty of it.

HORACE: You got them that, of course.

BEN: Cheap. You'd think the Governor of a great state would make his price a little higher. From pride, you know. (HORACE *smiles.* BEN *smiles.*) Cheap wages. "What do you mean by cheap wages?" I say to Marshall. "Less than Massachusetts," he says to me, "and that averages eight a week." "Eight a week! By God," I tell him, "*I'd* work for eight a week myself." Why, there ain't a mountain white or a town nigger but wouldn't give his right arm for three silver dollars every week, eh, Horace?

HORACE: Sure. And they'll take less than that when you get around to playing them off against each other. You can save a little money that way, Ben. (*Angrily.*) And make them hate each other just a little more than they do now.

REGINA: What's all this about?

BEN (*laughs*): There'll be no trouble from anybody, white or black. Marshall said that to me. "What about strikes? That's all we've had in Massachusetts for the last three years." I say to him, "What's a strike? I never heard of one. Come South, Marshall. We got good folks and we don't stand for any fancy fooling."

HORACE: You're right. (*Slowly.*) Well, it looks like you made a good deal for yourselves, and for Marshall, too. (*To* BEN.) Your father used to say he made the thousands and you boys would make the millions. I think he was right. (*Rises.*)

REGINA (*they are all looking at* HORACE; *she laughs nervously*): Millions for *us,* too.

HORACE: Us? You and me? I don't think so. We've got enough money, Regina. We'll just sit by and watch the boys grow rich. (*They watch* HORACE *tensely as he begins to move towards the staircase. He passes* LEO, *looks at him for a second.*) How's everything at the bank, Leo?

LEO: Fine, sir. Everything is fine.

HORACE: How are all the ladies in Mobile? (HORACE *turns to* REGINA, *sharply.*) Whatever made you think I'd let Zan marry—

REGINA: Do you mean that you are turning this down? Is it possible that's what you mean?

BEN: No, that's not what he means. Turning down a fortune. Horace is tired. He'd rather talk about it tomorrow—

REGINA: We can't keep putting it off this way. Oscar must be in Chicago by the end of the week with the money and contracts.

OSCAR (*giggles, pleased*): Yes, sir. Got to be there end of the week. No sense going without the money.

REGINA (*tensely*): I've waited long enough for your answer. I'm not going to wait any longer.

HORACE (*very deliberately*): I'm very tired now, Regina.

BEN (*hastily*): Now, Horace probably has his reasons. Things he'd like explained. Tomorrow will do. I can—

REGINA (*turns to* BEN, *sharply*): I want to know his reasons now! (*Turns back to* HORACE.)

HORACE (*as he climbs the steps*): I don't know them all myself. Let's leave it at that.

REGINA: We shall not leave it at that! We have waited for you here like children. Waited for you to come home.

HORACE: So that you could invest my money. So this is why you wanted me home? Well, I had hoped—(*Quietly.*) If you are disappointed, Regina, I'm sorry. But I must do what I think best. We'll talk about it another day.

REGINA: We'll talk about it now. Just you and me.

HORACE (*looks down at her; his voice is tense*): Please, Regina. It's been a hard trip. I don't feel well. Please leave me alone now.

REGINA (*quietly*): I want to talk to you, Horace. I'm coming up. (*He looks at her for a minute, then moves on again out of sight. She begins to climb the stairs.*)

BEN (*softly;* REGINA *turns to him as he speaks*): Sometimes it is better to wait for the sun to rise again. (*She does not answer.*) And sometimes, as our mother used to tell you, (REGINA *starts up stairs*) it's unwise for a good-looking woman to frown. (BEN *rises, moves towards stairs.*) Softness and a smile do more to the heart of men —(*She disappears.* BEN *stands looking up the stairs. There is a long silence. Then, suddenly,* OSCAR *giggles.*)

OSCAR: Let us hope she'll change his mind. Let us hope. (*After a second* BEN *crosses to table, picks up his newspaper.* OSCAR *looks at* BEN. *The silence makes* LEO *uncomfortable.*)

LEO: The paper says twenty-seven cases of yellow fever in New Orleans. Guess the floodwaters caused it. (*Nobody pays attention.*) Thought they were building the levees high enough. Like the niggers always say: a man born of woman can't build nothing high enough for the Mississippi. (*Gets no answer. Gives an embarrassed laugh.*)

(*Upstairs there is the sound of voices. The voices are not loud, but* BEN, OSCAR, LEO *become conscious of them.* LEO *crosses to landing, looks up, listens.*)

OSCAR (*pointing up*): Now just suppose she

don't change his mind? Just suppose he keeps on refusing?

BEN (*without conviction*): He's tired. It was a mistake to talk to him today. He's a sick man, but he isn't a crazy one.

OSCAR (*giggles*): But just suppose he is crazy. What then?

BEN (*puts down his paper, peers at* OSCAR): Then we'll go outside for the money. There's plenty who would give it.

OSCAR: And plenty who will want a lot for what they give. The ones who are rich enough to give will be smart enough to want. That means we'd be working for them, don't it, Ben?

BEN: You don't have to tell me the things I told you six months ago.

OSCAR: Oh, you're right not to worry. She'll change his mind. She always has. (*There is a silence. Suddenly* REGINA's *voice becomes louder and sharper. All of them begin to listen now. Slowly* BEN *rises, goes to listen by the staircase.* OSCAR, *watching him, smiles. As they listen* REGINA's *voice becomes very loud.* HORACE's *voice is no longer heard.*) Maybe. But I don't believe it. I never did believe he was going in with us.

BEN (*turning to him*): What the hell do you expect me to do?

OSCAR (*mildly*): Nothing. You done your almighty best. Nobody could blame you if the whole thing just dripped away right through our fingers. You can't do a thing. But there may be something I could do for us. (OSCAR *rises.*) Or, I might better say, Leo could do for us. (BEN *stops, turns, looks at* OSCAR. LEO *is staring at* OSCAR.) Ain't that true, son? Ain't it true you might be able to help your own kinfolks?

LEO (*nervously taking a step to him*): Papa, I—

BEN (*slowly*): How would he help us, Oscar?

OSCAR: Leo's got a friend. Leo's friend owns eighty-eight thousand dollars in Union Pacific bonds. (BEN *turns to look at* LEO.) Leo's friend don't look at the bonds much—not for five or six months at a time.

BEN (*after a pause*): Union Pacific. Uh, huh. Let me understand. Leo's friend would—would lend him these bonds and he—

OSCAR (*nods*): Would be kind enough to lend them to us.

BEN: Leo.

LEO (*excited, comes to him*): Yes, sir?

BEN: When would your friend be wanting the bonds back?

LEO (*very nervous*): I don't know. I—well, I—

OSCAR (*sharply; steps to him*): You told me he won't look at them until Fall—

LEO: Oh, that's right. But I—not till Fall. Uncle Horace never—

BEN (*sharply*): Be still.

OSCAR (*smiles at* LEO): Your uncle doesn't wish to know your friend's name.

LEO (*starts to laugh*): That's a good one. Not know his name—

OSCAR: Shut up, Leo! (LEO *turns away slowly, moves to table.* BEN *turns to* OSCAR.) He won't look at them again until September. That gives us five months. Leo will return the bonds in three months. And we'll have no trouble raising the money once the mills are going up. Will Marshall accept bonds?

(BEN *stops to listen to sudden sharp voices from above. The voices are now very angry and very loud.*)

BEN (*smiling*): Why not? Why not? (*Laughs.*) Good. We are lucky. We'll take the loan from Leo's friend—I think he will make a safer partner than our sister. (*Nods towards stairs. Turns to* LEO.) How soon can you get them?

LEO: Today. Right now. They're in the safe-deposit box and—

BEN (*sharply*): I don't want to know where they are.

OSCAR (*laughs*): We will keep it secret from you. (*Pats* BEN's *arm.*)

BEN (*smiles*): Good. Draw a check for our part. You can take the night train for Chicago. Well, Oscar (*holds out his hand*), good luck to us.

OSCAR: Leo will be taken care of?

LEO: I'm entitled to Uncle Horace's share. I'd enjoy being a partner—

BEN (*turns to stare at him*): You would? You can go to hell, you little—(*Starts towards* LEO.)

OSCAR (*nervously*): Now, now. He didn't mean that. I only want to be sure he'll get something out of all this.

BEN: Of course. We'll take care of him. We won't have any trouble about that. I'll see you at the store.

OSCAR (*nods*): That's settled then. Come on, son. (*Starts for door.*)

LEO (*puts out his hand*): I didn't mean just that. I was only going to say what a great day this was for me and—(BEN *ignores his hand.*)

BEN: Go on.

(LEO *looks at him, turns, follows* OSCAR *out.* BEN *stands where he is, thinking. Again the voices upstairs can be heard.* REGINA's *voice is high and furious.* BEN *looks up, smiles, winces at the noise.*)

ALEXANDRA (*upstairs*): Mama—Mama—don't ... (*The noise of running footsteps is heard and* ALEX-

ANDRA *comes running down the steps, speaking as she comes.*) Uncle Ben! Uncle Ben! Please go up. Please make Mama stop. Uncle Ben, he's sick, he's so sick. How can Mama talk to him like that—please, make her stop. She'll—

BEN: Alexandra, you have a tender heart.

ALEXANDRA (*crying*): Go on up, Uncle Ben, please—

(*Suddenly the voices stop. A second later there is the sound of a door being slammed.*)

BEN: Now you see. Everything is over. Don't worry. (*He starts for the door.*) Alexandra, I want you to tell your mother how sorry I am that I had to leave. And don't worry so, my dear. Married folk frequently raise their voices, unfortunately. (*He starts to put on his hat and coat as RE-GINA appears on the stairs.*)

ALEXANDRA (*furiously*): How can you treat Papa like this? He's sick. He's very sick. Don't you know that? I won't let you.

REGINA: Mind your business, Alexandra. (*To BEN. Her voice is cold and calm.*) How much longer can you wait for the money?

BEN (*putting on his coat*): He has refused? My, that's too bad.

REGINA: He will change his mind. I'll find a way to make him. What's the longest you can wait now?

BEN: I could wait until next week. But I can't wait until next week. (*He giggles, pleased at the joke.*) I could but I can't. Could and can't. Well, I must go now. I'm very late—

REGINA (*coming downstairs towards him*): You're not going. I want to talk to you.

BEN: I was about to give Alexandra a message for you. I wanted to tell you that Oscar is going to Chicago tonight, so we can't be here for our usual Friday supper.

REGINA (*tensely*): Oscar is going to Chi— (*Softly.*) What do you mean?

BEN: Just that. Everything is settled. He's going on to deliver to Marshall—

REGINA (*taking a step to him*): I demand to know what—You are lying. You are trying to scare me. *You haven't got the money.* How could you have it? You can't have—(BEN *laughs.*) You will wait until I—

(HORACE *comes into view on the landing.*)

BEN: You are getting out of hand. Since when do I take orders from you?

REGINA: Wait, you—(BEN *stops.*) How *can* he go to Chicago? Did a ghost arrive with the money? (BEN *starts for the hall.*) I don't believe

you. Come back here. (REGINA *starts after him.*) Come back here, you—(*The door slams. She stops in the doorway, staring, her fists clenched. After a pause she turns slowly.*)

HORACE (*very quietly*): It's a great day when you and Ben cross swords. I've been waiting for it for years.

ALEXANDRA: Papa, Papa, please go back! You will—

HORACE: And so they don't need you, and so you will not have your millions, after all.

REGINA (*turns slowly*): You hate to see anybody live now, don't you? You hate to think that I'm going to be alive and have what I want.

HORACE: I should have known you'd think that was the reason.

REGINA: Because you're going to die and you know you're going to die.

ALEXANDRA (*shrilly*): Mama! Don't—Don't listen, Papa. Just don't listen. Go away—

HORACE: Not to keep you from getting what you want. Not even partly that. (*Holding to the rail.*) I'm sick of you, sick of this house, sick of my life here. I'm sick of your brothers and their dirty tricks to make a dime. There must be better ways of getting rich than cheating niggers on a pound of bacon. Why should I give you the money? (*Very angrily.*) To pound the bones of this town to make dividends for you to spend? You wreck the town, you and your brothers, *you* wreck the town and live on it. Not me. Maybe it's easy for the dying to be honest. But it's not my fault I'm dying. (ADDIE *enters, stands at door quietly.*) I'll do no more harm now. I've done enough. I'll die my own way. And I'll do it without making the world any worse. I leave that to you.

REGINA (*looks up at him slowly, calmly*): I hope you die. I hope you die soon. (*Smiles.*) I'll be waiting for you to die.

ALEXANDRA (*shrieking*): Papa! Don't—Don't listen—Don't—

ADDIE: Come here, Zan. Come out of this room.

(ALEXANDRA *runs quickly to* ADDIE, *who holds her.* HORACE *turns slowly and starts upstairs.*)

ACT III

(SCENE: *Same as Act I. Two weeks later. It is late afternoon and it is raining.*

AT RISE: HORACE *is sitting near the window in a wheel chair. On the table next to him is a safe-*

deposit box, and a small bottle of medicine. BIRDIE *and* ALEXANDRA *are playing the piano. On a chair is a large sewing basket.*)

BIRDIE (*counting for* ALEXANDRA): One and two and three and four. One and two and three and four. (*Nods—turns to* HORACE.) We once played together, Horace. Remember?

HORACE (*has been looking out of the window*): What, Birdie?

BIRDIE: We played together. You and me.

ALEXANDRA: *Papa* used to play?

BIRDIE: Indeed he did. (ADDIE *appears at the door in a large kitchen apron. She is wiping her hands on a towel.*) He played the fiddle and very well, too.

ALEXANDRA (*turns to smile at* HORACE): I never knew—

ADDIE: Where's your mama?

ALEXANDRA: Gone to Miss Safronia's to fit her dresses.

(ADDIE *nods, starts to exit.*)

HORACE: Addie.

ADDIE: Yes, Mr. Horace.

HORACE (*speaks as if he had made a sudden decision*): Tell Cal to get on his things. I want him to go an errand.

(ADDIE *nods, exits.* HORACE *moves nervously in his chair, looks out of the window.*)

ALEXANDRA (*who has been watching him*): It's too bad it's been raining all day, Papa. But you can go out in the yard tomorrow. Don't be restless.

HORACE: I'm not restless, darling.

BIRDIE: I remember so well the time we played together, your papa and me. It was the first time Oscar brought me here to supper. I had never seen all the Hubbards together before, and you know what a ninny I am and how shy. (*Turns to look at* HORACE.) You said you could play the fiddle and you'd be much obliged if I'd play with you. *I* was obliged to *you,* all right, all right. (*Laughs when he does not answer her.*) Horace, you haven't heard a word I've said.

HORACE: Birdie, when did Oscar get back from Chicago?

BIRDIE: Yesterday. Hasn't he been here yet?

ALEXANDRA (*stops playing*): No. Neither has Uncle Ben since—since that day.

BIRDIE: Oh, I didn't know it was *that* bad. Oscar never tells me anything—

HORACE (*smiles, nods*): The Hubbards have had their great quarrel. I knew it would come some day. (*Laughs.*) It came.

ALEXANDRA: It came. It certainly came all right.

BIRDIE (*amazed*): But Oscar was in such a good humor when he got home, I didn't—

HORACE: Yes, I can understand that.

(ADDIE *enters carrying a large tray with glasses, a carafe of elderberry wine and a plate of cookies, which she puts on the table.*)

ALEXANDRA: Addie! A party! What for?

ADDIE: Nothing for. I had the fresh butter, so I made the cakes, and a little elderberry does the stomach good in the rain.

BIRDIE: Isn't this nice! A party just for us. Let's play party music, Zan.

(ALEXANDRA *begins to play a gay piece.*)

ADDIE (*to* HORACE, *wheeling his chair to center*): Come over here, Mr. Horace, and don't be thinking so much. A glass of elderberry will do more good.

(ALEXANDRA *reaches for a cake.* BIRDIE *pours herself a glass of wine.*)

ALEXANDRA: Good cakes, Addie. It's nice here. Just us. Be nice if it could always be this way.

BIRDIE (*nods happily*): Quiet and restful.

ADDIE: Well, it won't be that way long. Little while now, even sitting here, you'll hear the red bricks going into place. The next day the smoke'll be pushing out the chimneys and by church time that Sunday every human born of woman will be living on chicken. That's how Mr. Ben's been telling the story.

HORACE (*looks at her*): They believe it that way?

ADDIE: Believe it? They use to believing what Mr. Ben orders. There ain't been so much talk around here since Sherman's army didn't come near.

HORACE (*softly*): They are fools.

ADDIE (*nods, sits down with the sewing basket*): You ain't born in the South unless you're a fool.

BIRDIE (*has drunk another glass of wine*): But we didn't play together after that night. Oscar said he didn't like me to play on the piano. (*Turns to* ALEXANDRA.) You know what he said that night?

ALEXANDRA: Who?

BIRDIE: Oscar. He said that music made him nervous. He said he just sat and waited for the next note. (ALEXANDRA *laughs.*) He wasn't poking fun. He meant it. Ah, well—(*She finishes her glass, shakes her head.* HORACE *looks at her, smiles.*)

Your papa don't like to admit it, but he's been mighty kind to me all these years. (*Running the back of her hand along his sleeve.*) Often he'd step in when somebody said something and once— (*She stops, turns away, her face still.*) Once he stopped Oscar from—(*She stops, turns. Quickly.*) I'm sorry I said that. Why, here I am so happy and yet I think about bad things. (*Laughs nervously.*) That's not right, now, is it? (*She pours a drink.* CAL *appears in the door. He has on an old coat and is carrying a torn umbrella.*)

ALEXANDRA: Have a cake, Cal.

CAL (*comes in, takes a cake*): Yes'm. You want me, Mr. Horace?

HORACE: What time is it, Cal?

CAL: 'Bout ten minutes before it's five.

HORACE: All right. Now you walk yourself down to the bank.

CAL: It'll be closed. Nobody'll be there but Mr. Manders, Mr. Joe Horns, Mr. Leo—

HORACE: Go in the back way. They'll be at the table, going over the day's business. (*Points to the deposit box.*) See that box?

CAL (*nods*): Yes, sir.

HORACE: You tell Mr. Manders that Mr. Horace says he's much obliged to him for bringing the box, it arrived all right.

CAL (*bewildered*): He know you got the box He bring it himself Wednesday. I opened the door to him and he say, "Hello, Cal, coming on to summer weather."

HORACE: You say just what I tell you. Understand?

(BIRDIE *pours another drink, stands at table.*)

CAL: No, sir. I ain't going to say I understand. I'm going down and tell a man he give you something he already know he give you, and you say "understand."

HORACE: Now, Cal.

CAL: Yes, sir. I just going to say you obliged for the box coming all right. I ain't going to understand it, but I'm going to say it.

HORACE: And tell him I want him to come over here after supper, and to bring Mr. Sol Fowler with him.

CAL (*nods*): He's to come after supper and bring Mr. Sol Fowler, your attorney-*at*-law, with him.

HORACE (*smiles*): That's right. Just walk right in the back room and say your piece. (*Slowly.*) In front of everybody.

CAL: Yes, sir. (*Mumbles to himself as he exits.*)

ALEXANDRA (*who has been watching* HORACE): Is anything the matter, Papa?

HORACE: Oh, no. Nothing.

ADDIE: Miss Birdie, that elderberry going to give you a headache spell.

BIRDIE (*beginning to be drunk; gaily*): Oh, I don't think so. I don't think it will.

ALEXANDRA (*as* HORACE *puts his hand to his throat*): Do you want your medicine, Papa?

HORACE: No, no. I'm all right, darling.

BIRDIE: Mama used to give me elderberry wine when I was a little girl. For hiccoughs. (*Laughs.*) You know, I don't think people get hiccoughs any more. Isn't that funny? (BIRDIE *laughs.* HORACE *and* ALEXANDRA *laugh.*) I used to get hiccoughs just when I shouldn't have.

ADDIE (*nods*): And nobody gets growing pains no more. That is funny. Just as if there was some style in what you get. One year an ailment's stylish and the next year it ain't.

BIRDIE (*turns*): I remember. It was my first big party, at Lionnet I mean, and I was so excited, and there I was with hiccoughs and Mama laughing. (*Softly. Looking at carafe.*) Mama always laughed. (*Picks up carafe.*) A big party, a lovely dress from Mr. Worth in Paris, France, and hiccoughs. (*Pours drink.*) My brother pounding me on the back and Mama with the elderberry bottle, laughing at me. Everybody was on their way to come, and I was such a ninny, hiccoughing away. (*Drinks.*) You know, that was the first day I ever saw Oscar Hubbard. The Ballongs were selling their horses and he was going there to buy. He passed and lifted his hat—we could see him from the window—and my brother, to tease Mama, said maybe we should have invited the Hubbards to the party. He said Mama didn't like them because they kept a store, and he said that was old-fashioned of her. (*Her face lights up.*) And then, and *then,* I saw Mama angry for the first time in my life. She said that wasn't the reason. She said she was old-fashioned, but not that way. She said she was old-fashioned enough not to like people who killed animals they couldn't use, and who made their money charging awful interest to poor, ignorant niggers and cheating them on what they bought. She was very angry, Mama was. I had never seen her face like that. And then suddenly she laughed and said, "Look, I've frightened Birdie out of the hiccoughs." (*Her head drops. Then softly.*) And so she had. They were all gone. (*Moves to sofa, sits.*)

ADDIE: Yeah, they got mighty well off cheating niggers. Well, there are people who eat the earth and eat all the people on it like in the Bible with the locusts. Then there are people who stand around and watch them eat it. (*Softly.*)

Sometimes I think it ain't right to stand and watch them do it.

BIRDIE (*thoughtfully*): Like I say, if we could only go back to Lionnet. Everybody'd be better there. They'd be good and kind. I like people to be kind. (*Pours drink.*) Don't you, Horace; don't you like people to be kind?

HORACE: Yes, Birdie.

BIRDIE (*very drunk now*): Yes, that was the first day I ever saw Oscar. Who would have thought —(*Quickly.*) You all want to know something? Well, I don't like Leo. My very own son, and I don't like him. (*Laughs, gaily.*) My, I guess I even like Oscar more.

ALEXANDRA: Why did you marry Uncle Oscar?

ADDIE (*sharply*): That's no question for you to be asking.

HORACE (*sharply*): Why not? She's heard enough around here to ask anything.

ALEXANDRA: Aunt Birdie, why did you marry Uncle Oscar?

BIRDIE: I don't know. I thought I liked him. He was kind to me and I thought it was because he liked me too. But that wasn't the reason— (*Wheels on* ALEXANDRA.) Ask why *he* married *me*. I can tell you that: He's told it to me often enough.

ADDIE (*leaning forward*): Miss Birdie, don't—

BIRDIE (*speaking very rapidly, tensely*): My family was good and the cotton on Lionnet's fields was better. Ben Hubbard wanted the cotton and (*rises*) Oscar Hubbard married it for him. He was kind to me, then. He used to smile at me. He hasn't smiled at me since. Everybody knew that's what he married me for. (ADDIE *rises.*) Everybody but me. Stupid, stupid me.

ALEXANDRA (*to* HORACE, *holding his hand, softly*): I see. (*Hesitates.*) Papa, I mean—when you feel better couldn't we go away? I mean, by ourselves. Couldn't we find a way to go—

HORACE: Yes, I know what you mean. We'll try to find a way. I promise you, darling.

ADDIE (*moves to* BIRDIE): Rest a bit, Miss Birdie. You get talking like this you'll get a headache and—

BIRDIE (*sharply, turning to her*): I've never had a headache in my life. (*Begins to cry hysterically.*) You know it as well as I do. (*Turns to* ALEXANDRA.) I never had a headache, Zan. That's a lie they tell for me. I drink. All by myself, in my own room, by myself, I drink. Then, when they want to hide it, they say, "Birdie's got a headache again"—

ALEXANDRA (*comes to her quickly*): Aunt Birdie.

BIRDIE (*turning away*): Even you won't like me now. You won't like me any more.

ALEXANDRA: I love you. I'll always love you.

BIRDIE (*furiously*): Well, don't. Don't love me. Because in twenty years you'll just be like me. They'll do all the same things to you. (*Begins to laugh hysterically.*) You know what? In twenty-two years I haven't had a whole day of happiness. Oh, a little, like today with you all. But never a single, whole day. I say to myself, if only I had one more *whole* day, then—(*The laugh stops.*) And that's the way you'll be. And you'll trail after them, just like me, hoping they won't be so mean that day or say something to make you feel so bad—only you'll be worse off because you haven't got my Mama to remember—(*Turns away, her head drops. She stands quietly, swaying a little, holding onto the sofa.* ALEXANDRA *leans down, puts her cheek on* BIRDIE's *arm.*)

ALEXANDRA (*to* BIRDIE): I guess we were all trying to make a happy day. You know, we sit around and try to pretend nothing's happened. We try to pretend we are not here. We make believe we are just by ourselves, some place else, and it doesn't seem to work. (*Kisses* BIRDIE's *hand.*) Come now, Aunt Birdie, I'll walk you home. You and me. (*She takes* BIRDIE's *arm. They move slowly out.*)

BIRDIE (*softly as they exit*): You and me.

ADDIE (*after a minute*): Well. First time I ever heard Miss Birdie say a word. (HORACE *looks at her.*) Maybe it's good for her. I'm just sorry Zan had to hear it. (HORACE *moves his head as if he were uncomfortable.*) You feel bad, don't you? (*He shrugs.*)

HORACE: So you didn't want Zan to hear? It would be nice to let her stay innocent, like Birdie at her age. Let her listen now. Let her see everything. How else is she going to know that she's got to get away? I'm trying to show her that. I'm trying, but I've only got a little time left. She can even hate me when I'm dead, if she'll only learn to hate and fear this.

ADDIE: Mr. Horace—

HORACE: Pretty soon there'll be nobody to help her but you.

ADDIE (*crossing to him*): What can I do?

HORACE: Take her away.

ADDIE: How can I do that? Do you think they'd let me just go away with her?

HORACE: I'll fix it so they can't stop you when you're ready to go. You'll go, Addie?

ADDIE (*after a second, softly*): Yes, sir. I promise. (*He touches her arm, nods.*)

HORACE (*quietly*): I'm going to have Sol Fowler make me a new will. They'll make trouble, but you make Zan stand firm and Fowler'll do the rest. Addie, I'd like to leave you something for yourself. I always wanted to.

ADDIE (*laughs*): Don't you do that, Mr. Horace. A nigger woman in a white man's will! I'd never get it nohow.

HORACE: I know. But upstairs in the armoire drawer there's seventeen hundred dollar bills. It's money left from my trip. It's in an envelope with your name. It's for you.

ADDIE: Seventeen hundred dollar bills! My God, Mr. Horace, I won't know how to count up that high. (*Shyly.*) It's mighty kind and good of you. I don't know what to say for thanks—

CAL (*appears in doorway*): I'm back. (*No answer.*) I'm back.

ADDIE: So we see.

HORACE: Well?

CAL: Nothing. I just went down and spoke my piece. Just like you told me. I say, "Mr. Horace he thank you mightily for the safe box arriving in good shape and he say you come right after supper to his house and bring Mr. Attorney-at-law Sol Fowler with you." Then I wipe my hands on my coat. Every time I ever told a lie in my whole life, I wipe my hands right after. Can't help doing it. Well, while I'm wiping my hands, Mr. Leo jump up and say to me, "What box? What you talking about?"

HORACE (*smiles*): Did he?

CAL: And Mr. Leo say he got to leave a little early cause he got something to do. And then Mr. Manders say Mr. Leo should sit right down and finish up his work and stop acting like somebody made him Mr. President. So he sit down. Now, just like I told you, Mr. Manders was mighty surprised with the message because he knows right well he brought the box—(*Points to box, sighs.*) But he took it all right. Some men take everything easy and some do not.

HORACE (*puts his head back, laughs*): Mr. Leo was telling the truth; he *has* got something to do. I hope Manders don't keep him too long. (*Outside there is the sound of voices.* CAL *exits.* ADDIE *crosses quickly to* HORACE, *puts basket on table, begins to wheel his chair towards the stairs. Sharply.*) No. Leave me where I am.

ADDIE: But that's Miss Regina coming back.

HORACE (*nods, looking at door*): Go away, Addie.

ADDIE (*hesitates*): Mr. Horace. Don't talk no more today. You don't feel well and it won't do no good—

HORACE (*as he hears footsteps in the hall*): Go

on. (*She looks at him for a second, then picks up her sewing from table and exits as* REGINA *comes in from hall.* HORACE's *chair is now so placed that he is in front of the table with the medicine.* REGINA *stands in the hall, shakes umbrella, stands it in the corner, takes off her cloak and throws it over the banister. She stares at* HORACE.)

REGINA (*as she takes off her gloves*): We had agreed that you were to stay in your part of this house and I in mine. This room is *my* part of the house. Please don't come down here again.

HORACE: I won't.

REGINA (*crosses towards bell-cord*): I'll get Cal to take you upstairs.

HORACE (*smiles*): Before you do I want to tell you that after all, we have invested our money in Hubbard Sons and Marshall, Cotton Manufacturers.

REGINA (*stops, turns, stares at him*): What are you talking about? You haven't seen Ben— When did you change your mind?

HORACE: I didn't change my mind. *I* didn't invest the money. (*Smiles.*) It was invested for me.

REGINA (*angrily*): What—?

HORACE: I had eighty-eight thousand dollars' worth of Union Pacific bonds in that safe-deposit box. They are not there now. Go and look. (*As she stares at him, he points to the box.*) Go and look, Regina. (*She crosses quickly to the box, opens it.*) Those bonds are as negotiable as money.

REGINA (*turns back to him*): What kind of joke are you playing now? Is this for my benefit?

HORACE: I don't look in that box very often, but three days ago, on Wednesday it was, because I had made a decision—

REGINA: I want to know what you are talking about.

HORACE (*sharply*): Don't interrupt me again. Because I had made a decision, I sent for the box. The bonds were gone. Eighty-eight thousand dollars gone. (*He smiles at her.*)

REGINA (*after a moment's silence, quietly*): Do you think I'm crazy enough to believe what you're saying?

HORACE (*shrugs*): Believe anything you like.

REGINA (*stares at him, slowly*): Where did they go to?

HORACE: They are in Chicago. With Mr. Marshall, I should guess.

REGINA: What did they do? Walk to Chicago? Have you really gone crazy?

HORACE: Leo took the bonds.

REGINA (*turns sharply then speaks softly, without conviction*): I don't believe it.

HORACE (*leans forward*): I wasn't there but I can guess what happened. This fine gentleman, to whom you were willing to marry your daughter, took the keys and opened the box. You remember that the day of the fight Oscar went to Chicago? Well, he went with my bonds that his son Leo had stolen for him. (*Pleasantly.*) And for Ben, of course, too.

REGINA (*slowly, nods*): When did you find out the bonds were gone?

HORACE: Wednesday night.

REGINA: I thought that's what you said. Why have you waited three days to do anything? (*Suddenly laughs.*) This *will* make a fine story.

HORACE (*nods*): Couldn't it?

REGINA (*still laughing*): A fine story to hold over their heads. How could they be such fools? (*Turns to him.*)

HORACE: But I'm not going to hold it over their heads.

REGINA (*the laugh stops*): What?

HORACE (*turns his chair to face her*): I'm going to let them keep the bonds—as a loan from you. An eighty-eight-thousand-dollar loan; they should be grateful to you. They will be, I think.

REGINA (*slowly, smiles*): I see. You are punishing me. But I won't let you punish me. If you won't do anything, I will. Now. (*She starts for door.*)

HORACE: You won't do anything. Because you can't. (REGINA *stops.*) It won't do you any good to make trouble because I shall simply say that I lent them the bonds.

REGINA (*slowly*): You would do that?

HORACE: Yes. For once in your life I am tying your hands. There is nothing for you to do. (*There is silence. Then she sits down.*)

REGINA: I see. You are going to lend them the bonds and let them keep all the profit they make on them, 'and there is nothing I can do about it. Is that right?

HORACE: Yes.

REGINA (*softly*): Why did you say that I was making this gift?

HORACE: I was coming to that. I am going to make a new will, Regina, leaving you eighty-eight thousand dollars in Union Pacific bonds. The rest will go to Zan. It's true that your brothers have borrowed your share for a little while. After my death I advise you to talk to Ben and Oscar. They won't admit anything and Ben, I think, will be smart enough to see that he's safe. Because I knew about the theft and said nothing. Nor will I say anything as long as I live. Is that clear to you?

REGINA (*nods, softly, without looking at him*): You will not say anything as long as you live.

HORACE: That's right. And by that time they will probably have replaced your bonds, and then they'll belong to you and nobody but us will ever know what happened. (*Stops, smiles.*) They'll be around any minute to see what I am going to do. I took good care to see that word reached Leo. They'll be mighty relieved to know I'm going to do nothing and Ben will think it all a capital joke on you. And that will be the end of that. There's nothing you can do to them, nothing you can do to me.

REGINA: You hate me very much.

HORACE: No.

REGINA: Oh, I think you do. (*Puts her head back, sighs.*) Well, we haven't been very good together. Anyway, I don't hate you either. I have only contempt for you. I've always had.

HORACE: From the very first?

REGINA: I think so.

HORACE: I was in love with *you*. But why did *you* marry *me*?

REGINA: I was lonely when I was young.

HORACE: *You* were lonely?

REGINA: Not the way people usually mean. Lonely for all the things I wasn't going to get. Everybody in this house was so busy and there was so little place for what I wanted. I wanted the world. Then, and then—(*Smiles.*) Papa died and left the money to Ben and Oscar.

HORACE: And you married me?

REGINA: Yes, I thought—But I was wrong You were a small-town clerk then. You haven't changed.

HORACE (*nods, smiles*): And that wasn't what you wanted.

REGINA: No. No, it wasn't what I wanted. (*Pauses, leans back, pleasantly.*) It took me a little while to find out I had made a mistake. As for you—I don't know. It was almost as if I couldn't stand the kind of man you were—(*Smiles, softly.*) I used to lie there at night, praying you wouldn't come near—

HORACE: Really? It was as bad as that?

REGINA (*nods*): Remember when I went to Doctor Sloan and I told you he said there was something the matter with me and that you shouldn't touch me any more?

HORACE: I remember.

REGINA: But you believed it. I couldn't understand that. I couldn't understand that anybody could be such a soft fool. That was when I began to despise you.

HORACE (*puts his hand to his throat, looks at the

bottle of medicine on table): Why didn't you leave me?

REGINA: I told you I married you for something. It turned out it was only for this. (*Carefully.*) This wasn't what I wanted, but it was something. I never thought about it much but if I had (HORACE *puts his hand to his throat*) I'd have known that you would die before I would. But I couldn't have known that you would get heart trouble so early and so bad. I'm lucky, Horace. I've always been lucky. (HORACE *turns slowly to the medicine.*) I'll be lucky again. (HORACE *looks at her. Then he puts his hand to his throat. Because he cannot reach the bottle he moves the chair closer. He reaches for the medicine, takes out the cork, picks up the spoon. The bottle slips and smashes on the table. He draws in his breath, gasps.*)

HORACE: Please. Tell Addie—The other bottle is upstairs. (REGINA *has not moved. She does not move now. He stares at her. Then, suddenly as if he understood, he raises his voice. It is a panic-stricken whisper, too small to be heard outside the room*) Addie! Addie! Come—(*Stops as he hears the softness of his voice. He makes a sudden, furious spring from the chair to the stairs, taking the first few steps as if he were a desperate runner. On the fourth step he slips, gasps, grasps the rail, makes a great effort to reach the landing. When he reaches the landing, he is on his knees. His knees give way, he falls on the landing, out of view.* REGINA *has not turned during his climb up the stairs. Now she waits a second. Then she goes below the landing, speaks up.*)

REGINA: Horace. Horace. (*When there is no answer, she turns, calls*) Addie! Cal! Come in here. (*She starts up the steps.* ADDIE *and* CAL *appear. Both run towards the stairs.*) He's had an attack. Come up here. (*They run up the steps quickly.*)

CAL: My God. Mr. Horace—(*They cannot be seen now.*)

REGINA (*her voice comes from the head of the stairs*): Be still, Cal. Bring him in here.

(*Before the footsteps and the voices have completely died away,* ALEXANDRA *appears in the hall door, in her raincloak and hood. She comes into the room, begins to unfasten the cloak, suddenly looks around, sees the empty wheel chair, stares, begins to move swiftly as if to look in the dining room. At the same moment* ADDIE *runs down the stairs.* ALEXANDRA *turns and stares up at* ADDIE.)

ALEXANDRA: Addie! What?

ADDIE (*takes* ALEXANDRA *by the shoulders*): I'm going for the doctor. Go upstairs. (ALEXANDRA *looks at her, then quickly breaks away and runs up the steps.* ADDIE *exits. The stage is empty for a minute.*

Then the front door bell begins to ring. When there is no answer, it rings again. A second later LEO *appears in the hall, talking as he comes in.*)

LEO (*very nervous*): Hello. (*Irritably.*) Never saw any use ringing a bell when a door was open. If you are going to ring a bell, then somebody should answer it. (*Gets in the room, looks around, puzzled, listens, hears no sound.*) Aunt Regina. (*He moves around restlessly.*) Addie. (*Waits.*) Where the hell—(*Crosses to the bell cord, rings it impatiently, waits, gets no answer, calls.*) Cal! Cal! (CAL *appears on the stair landing.*)

CAL (*his voice is soft, shaken*): Mr. Leo. Miss Regina says you stop that screaming noise.

LEO (*angrily*): Where is everybody?

CAL: Mr. Horace he got an attack. He's bad. Miss Regina says you stop that noise.

LEO: Uncle Horace—What—What happened? (CAL *starts down the stairs, shakes his head, begins to move swiftly off.* LEO *looks around wildly.*) But when—You seen Mr. Oscar or Mr. Ben? (CAL *shakes his head. Moves on.* LEO *grabs him by the arm.*) Answer me, will you?

CAL: No, I ain't seem 'em. I ain't got time to answer you. I got to get things. (CAL *runs off.*)

LEO: But what's the matter with him? When did this happen—(*Calling after* CAL.) You'd think Papa'd be some place where you could find him. I been chasing him all afternoon.

(OSCAR *and* BEN *come into the room, talking excitedly.*)

OSCAR: I hope it's not a bad attack.

BEN: It's the first one he's had since he came home.

LEO: Papa, I've been looking all over town for you and Uncle Ben—

BEN: Where is he?

OSCAR: Addie said it was sudden.

BEN (*to* LEO): Where is he? When did it happen?

LEO: Upstairs. Will you listen to me, please? I been looking for you for—

OSCAR (*to* BEN): You think we should go up? (BEN, *looking up the steps, shakes his head.*)

BEN: I don't know. I don't know.

OSCAR (*shakes his head*): But he was all right—

LEO (*yelling*): *Will you listen to me?*

OSCAR (*sharply*): What is the matter with you?

LEO: I been trying to tell you. I been trying to find you for an hour—

OSCAR: Tell me what?

LEO: Uncle Horace knows about the bonds.

He knows about them. He's had the box since Wednesday—

BEN (*sharply*): Stop shouting! What the hell are you talking about?

LEO (*furiously*): I'm telling you he knows about the bonds. Ain't that clear enough—

OSCAR (*grabbing* LEO's *arm*): You God-damn fool! Stop screaming!

BEN: Now what happened? Talk quietly.

LEO: You heard me. Uncle Horace knows about the bonds. He's known since Wednesday.

BEN (*after a second*): How do you know that?

LEO: Because Cal comes down to Manders and says the box came O.K. and—

OSCAR (*trembling*): That might not mean a thing—

LEO (*angrily*): No? It might not, huh? Then he says Manders should come here tonight and bring Sol Fowler with him. I guess that don't mean a thing either.

OSCAR (*to* BEN): Ben—What—Do you think he's seen the—

BEN (*motions to the box*): There's the box. (*Both* OSCAR *and* LEO *turn sharply.* LEO *makes a leap to the box.*) You ass. Put it down. What are you going to do with it, eat it?

LEO: I'm going to—(*Starts.*)

BEN (*furiously*): Put it down. Don't touch it again. Now sit down and shut up for a minute.

OSCAR: Since Wednesday. (*To* LEO.) You said he had it since Wednesday. Why didn't he say something—(*To* BEN.) I don't understand—

LEO (*taking a step*): I can put it back. I can put it back before anybody knows.

BEN (*who is standing at the table, softly*): He's had it since Wednesday. Yet he hasn't said a word to us.

OSCAR: Why? Why?

LEO: What's the difference why? He was getting ready to say plenty. He was going to say it to Fowler tonight—

OSCAR (*angrily*): Be still. (*Turns to* BEN, *looks at him, waits.*)

BEN (*after a minute*): I don't believe that.

LEO (*wildly*): *You* don't believe it? What do I care what *you* believe? I do the dirty work and then—

BEN (*turning his head sharply to* LEO): I'm remembering that. I'm remembering that, Leo.

OSCAR: What do you mean?

LEO: You—

BEN (*to* OSCAR): If you don't shut that little fool up, I'll show you what I mean. For some reason he knows, but he don't say a word.

OSCAR: Maybe he didn't know that *we*—

BEN (*quickly*): That *Leo*—He's no fool. Does Manders know the bonds are missing?

LEO: How could I tell? I was half crazy. I don't think so. Because Manders seemed kind of puzzled and—

OSCAR: But we got to find out—(*He breaks off as* CAL *comes into the room carrying a kettle of hot water.*)

BEN: How is he, Cal?

CAL: I don't know, Mr. Ben. He was bad. (*Going towards stairs.*)

OSCAR: But when did it happen?

CAL (*shrugs*): He wasn't feeling bad early. (ADDIE *comes in quickly from the hall.*) Then there he is next thing on the landing, fallen over, his eyes tight—

ADDIE (*to* CAL): Dr. Sloan's over at the Ballongs. Hitch the buggy and go get him. (*She takes the kettle and cloths from him, pushes him, runs up the stairs.*) Go on. (*She disappears.* CAL *exits.*)

BEN: Never seen Sloan anywhere when you need him.

OSCAR (*softly*): Sounds bad.

LEO: He would have told *her* about it. Aunt Regina. He would have told his own wife—

BEN (*turning to* LEO): Yes, he might have told her. But they weren't on such pretty terms and maybe he didn't. Maybe he didn't. (*Goes quickly to* LEO.) Now, listen to me. If she doesn't know, it may work out all right. If she does know, you're to say he lent you the bonds.

LEO: Lent them to me! Who's going to believe that?

BEN: Nobody.

OSCAR (*to* LEO): Don't you understand? It can't do no harm to say it—

LEO: Why should I say he lent them to me? Why not to you? (*Carefully.*) Why not to Uncle Ben?

BEN (*smiles*): Just because he didn't lend them to me. Remember that.

LEO: But all he has to do is say he didn't lend them to me—

BEN (*furiously*): But for some reason, he doesn't seem to be talking, does he?

(*There are footsteps above. They all stand looking at the stairs.* REGINA *begins to come slowly down.*)

BEN: What happened?

REGINA: He's had a bad attack.

OSCAR: Too bad. I'm so sorry we weren't here when—when Horace needed us.

BEN: When *you* needed us.

REGINA (*looks at him*): Yes.

BEN: How is he? Can we—can we go up?

REGINA (*shakes her head*): He's not conscious.

OSCAR (*pacing around*): It's that—it's that bad? Wouldn't you think Sloan could be found quickly, just once, just once?

REGINA: I don't think there is much for him to do.

BEN: Oh, don't talk like that. He's come through attacks before. He will now.

(REGINA *sits down. After a second she speaks softly.*)

REGINA: Well. We haven't seen each other since the day of our fight.

BEN (*tenderly*): That was nothing. Why, you and Oscar and I used to fight when we were kids.

OSCAR (*hurriedly*): Don't you think we should go up? Is there anything we can do for Horace—

BEN: You don't feel well. Ah—

REGINA (*without looking at them*): No, I don't. (*Slight pause.*) Horace told me about the bonds this afternoon. (*There is an immediate shocked silence.*)

LEO: The bonds. What do you mean? What bonds? What—

BEN (*looks at him furiously. Then to* REGINA): The Union Pacific bonds? *Horace's* Union Pacific bonds?

REGINA: Yes.

OSCAR (*steps to her, very nervously*): Well. Well what—what about them? What—what could he say?

REGINA: He said that Leo had stolen the bonds and given them to you.

OSCAR (*aghast, very loudly*): That's ridiculous, Regina, absolutely—

LEO: I don't know what you're talking about. What would I—Why—

REGINA (*wearily to* BEN): Isn't it enough that he stole them from me? Do I have to listen to this in the bargain?

OSCAR: You are talking—

LEO: I didn't steal anything. I don't know why—

REGINA (*to* BEN): Would you ask them to stop that, please? (*There is silence for a minute.* BEN *glowers at* OSCAR *and* LEO.)

BEN: Aren't we starting at the wrong end, Regina? What did Horace tell you?

REGINA (*smiles at him*): He told me that Leo had stolen the bonds.

LEO: I didn't steal—

REGINA: Please. Let me finish. Then he told me that he was going to pretend that he had lent them to you (LEO *turns sharply to* REGINA, *then*

looks at OSCAR, *then looks back at* REGINA.) as a present from me—to my brothers. He said there was nothing I could do about it. He said the rest of his money would go to Alexandra. That is all. (*There is a silence.* OSCAR *coughs,* LEO *smiles slyly.*)

LEO (*taking a step to her*): I told you he had lent them—I could have told you—

REGINA (*ignores him, smiles sadly at* BEN): So I'm very badly off, you see. (*Carefully.*) But Horace said there was nothing I could do about it as long as he was alive to say he had lent you the bonds.

BEN: You shouldn't feel that way. It can all be explained, all be adjusted. It isn't as bad—

REGINA: So you, at least, are willing to admit that the bonds were stolen?

BEN (OSCAR *laughs nervously*): I admit no such thing. It's possible that Horace made up that part of the story to tease you—(*Looks at her.*) Or perhaps to punish you. Punish you.

REGINA (*sadly*): It's not a pleasant story. I feel bad, Ben, naturally. I hadn't thought—

BEN: Now you shall have the bonds safely back. That was the understanding, wasn't it, Oscar?

OSCAR: Yes.

REGINA: I'm glad to know that. (*Smiles.*) Ah, I had greater hopes—

BEN: Don't talk that way. That's foolish. (*Looks at his watch.*) I think we ought to drive out for Sloan ourselves. If we can't find him we'll go over to Senateville for Doctor Morris. And don't think I'm dismissing this other business. I'm not. We'll have it all out on a more appropriate day.

REGINA (*looks up, quietly*): I don't think you had better go yet. I think you had better stay and sit down.

BEN: We'll be back with Sloan.

REGINA: Cal has gone for him. I don't want you to go.

BEN: Now don't worry and—

REGINA: You will come back in this room and sit down. I have something more to say.

BEN (*turns, comes towards her*): Since when do I take orders from you?

REGINA (*smiles*): You don't—yet. (*Sharply.*) Come back, Oscar. You too, Leo.

OSCAR (*sure of himself, laughs*): My dear Regina—

BEN (*softly, pats her hand*): Horace has already clipped your wings and very wittily. Do I have to clip them, too? (*Smiles at her.*) You'd get farther with a smile, Regina. I'm a soft man for a woman's smile.

REGINA: I'm smiling, Ben. I'm smiling because you are quite safe while Horace lives. But I don't think Horace will live. And if he doesn't live I shall want seventy-five per cent in exchange for the bonds.

BEN (*steps back, whistles, laughs*): Greedy! What a greedy girl you are! You want so much of everything.

REGINA: Yes. And if I don't get what I want I am going to put all three of you in jail.

OSCAR (*furiously*): You're mighty crazy. Having just admitted—

BEN: And on what evidence would you put Oscar and Leo in jail?

REGINA (*laughs, gaily*): Oscar, listen to him. He's getting ready to swear that it was you and Leo! What do you say to that? (OSCAR *turns furiously towards* BEN.) Oh, don't be angry, Oscar. I'm going to see that he goes in with you.

BEN: Try anything you like, Regina. (*Sharply.*) And now we can stop all this and say goodbye to you. (ALEXANDRA *comes slowly down the steps.*) It's his money and he's obviously willing to let us borrow it. (*More pleasantly.*) Learn to make threats when you can carry them through. For how many years have I told you a good-looking woman gets more by being soft and appealing? Mama used to tell you that. (*Looks at his watch.*) Where the hell is Sloan? (*To* OSCAR.) Take the buggy and—(*As* BEN *turns to* OSCAR, *he sees* ALEXANDRA. *She walks stiffly. She goes slowly to the lower window, her head bent. They all turn to look at her.*)

OSCAR (*after a second, moving towards her*): What? Alexandra—(*She does not answer. After a second* ADDIE *comes slowly down the stairs, moving as if she were very tired. At foot of steps, she looks at* ALEXANDRA, *then turns and slowly crosses to door and exits.* REGINA *rises.* BEN *looks nervously at* ALEXANDRA, *at* REGINA.)

OSCAR (*as* ADDIE *passes him, irritably to* ALEXANDRA): Well, what is—(*Turns into room—sees* ADDIE *at foot of steps*)—what's? (BEN *puts up a hand, shakes his head.*) My God, I didn't know—who *could* have known—I didn't know he was that sick. Well, well—I—(REGINA *stands quietly, her back to them.*)

BEN (*softly, sincerely*): Seems like yesterday when he first came here.

OSCAR (*sincerely, nervously*): Yes, that's true. (*Turns to* BEN) The whole town loved him and respected him.

ALEXANDRA (*turns*): Did you love him, Uncle Oscar?

OSCAR: Certainly, I—What a strange thing to ask! I—

ALEXANDRA: Did you love him, Uncle Ben?

BEN (*simply*): He had—

ALEXANDRA (*suddenly starts to laugh very loudly*): And you, Mama, did you love him, too?

REGINA: I know what you feel, Alexandra, but please try to control yourself.

ALEXANDRA (*still laughing*): I'm trying, Mama. I'm trying very hard.

BEN: Grief makes some people laugh and some people cry. It's better to cry, Alexandra.

ALEXANDRA (*the laugh has stopped; tensely moves toward* REGINA): What was Papa doing on the staircase?

(BEN *turns to look at* ALEXANDRA.)

REGINA: Please go and lie down, my dear. We all need time to get over shocks like this. (ALEXANDRA *does not move.* REGINA's *voice becomes softer, more insistent.*) Please go, Alexandra.

ALEXANDRA: No, Mama. I'll wait. I've got to talk to you.

REGINA: Later. Go and rest now.

ALEXANDRA (*quietly*): I'll wait, Mama. I've plenty of time.

REGINA (*hesitates, stares, makes a half shrug, turns back to* BEN): As I was saying. Tomorrow morning I am going up to Judge Simmes. I shall tell him about Leo.

BEN (*motioning toward* ALEXANDRA): Not in front of the child, Regina. I—

REGINA (*turns to him; sharply*): I didn't ask her to stay. Tomorrow morning I go to Judge Simmes—

OSCAR: And what proof? What proof of all this—

REGINA (*turns sharply*): None. I won't need any. The bonds are missing and they are with Marshall. That will be enough. If it isn't, I'll add what's necessary.

BEN: I'm sure of that.

REGINA (*turns to* BEN): You can be quite sure.

OSCAR: We'll deny—

REGINA: Deny your heads off. You couldn't find a jury that wouldn't weep for a woman whose brothers steal from her. And you couldn't find twelve men in this state you haven't cheated and hate you for it.

OSCAR: What kind of talk is this? You couldn't do anything like that! We're your own brothers. (*Points upstairs.*) How can you talk that way when upstairs not five minutes ago—

REGINA (*slowly*): There are people who can never go back, who must finish what they start.

I am one of those people, Oscar. (*After a slight pause.*) Where was I? (*Smiles at* BEN.) Well, they'll convict you. But I won't care much if they don't. (*Leans forward, pleasantly.*) Because by that time you'll be ruined. I shall also tell my story to Mr. Marshall, who likes me, I think, and who will not want to be involved in your scandal. A respectable firm like Marshall and Company. The deal would be off in an hour. (*Turns to them angrily.*) And you know it. Now I don't want to hear any more from any of you. *You'll do no more bargaining in this house.* I'll take my seventy-five per cent and we'll forget the story forever. That's one way of doing it, and the way I prefer. You know me well enough to know that I don't mind taking the other way.

BEN (*after a second, slowly*): None of us have ever known you well enough, Regina.

REGINA: You're getting old, Ben. Your tricks aren't as smart as they used to be. (*There is no answer. She waits, then smiles.*) All right. I take it that's settled and I get what I asked for.

OSCAR (*furiously to* BEN): Are you going to let her do this—

BEN (*turns to look at him, slowly*): You have a suggestion?

REGINA (*puts her arms above her head, stretches, laughs*): No, he hasn't. All right. Now, Leo, I have forgotten that you ever saw the bonds. (*Archly, to* BEN *and* OSCAR.) And as long as you boys both behave yourselves, I've forgotten that we ever talked about them. You can draw up the necessary papers tomorrow. (BEN *laughs.* LEO *stares at him, starts for door. Exits.* OSCAR *moves towards door angrily.* REGINA *looks at* BEN, *nods, laughs with him. For a second,* OSCAR *stands in the door, looking back at them. Then he exits.*)

REGINA: You're a good loser, Ben. I like that.

BEN (*he picks up his coat, then turns to her*): Well, I say to myself, what's the good? You and I aren't like Oscar. We're not sour people. I think that comes from a good digestion. Then, too, one loses today and wins tomorrow. I say to myself, years of planning and I get what I want. Then I don't get it. But I'm not discouraged. The century's turning, the world is open. Open for people like you and me. Ready for us, waiting for us. After all this is just the beginning. There are hundreds of Hubbards sitting in rooms like this throughout the country. All their names aren't Hubbard, but they are all Hubbards and they will own this country some day. We'll get along.

REGINA (*smiles*): I think so.

BEN: Then, too, I say to myself, things may change. (*Looks at* ALEXANDRA.) I agree with Alexandra. What is a man in a wheel chair doing on a staircase? I ask myself that.

REGINA (*looks up at him*): And what do you answer?

BEN: I have no answer. But maybe some day I will. Maybe never, but maybe some day. (*Smiles. Pats her arm.*) When I do, I'll let you know. (*Goes towards hall.*)

REGINA: When you do, write me. I will be in Chicago. (*Gaily*) Ah, Ben, if Papa had only left me his money.

BEN: I'll see you tomorrow.

REGINA: Oh, yes. Certainly. You'll be sort of working for me now.

BEN (*as he passes* ALEXANDRA, *smiles*): Alexandra, you're turning out to be a right interesting girl. (*Looks at* REGINA.) Well, good night all. (*He exits.*)

REGINA (*sits quietly for a second, stretches, turns to look at* ALEXANDRA): What do you want to talk to me about, Alexandra?

ALEXANDRA (*slowly*): I've changed my mind. I don't want to talk. There's nothing to talk about now.

REGINA: You're acting very strange. Not like yourself. You've had a bad shock today. I know that. And you loved Papa, but you must have expected this to come some day. You knew how sick he was.

ALEXANDRA: I knew. We all knew.

REGINA: It will be good for you to get away from here. Good for me, too. Time heals most wounds, Alexandra. You're young, you shall have all the things I wanted. I'll make the world for you the way I wanted it to be for me. (*Uncomfortably.*) Don't sit there staring. You've been around Birdie so much you're getting just like her.

ALEXANDRA (*nods*): Funny. That's what Aunt Birdie said today.

REGINA (*nods*): Be good for you to get away from all this.

(ADDIE *enters.*)

ADDIE: Cal is back, Miss Regina. He says Dr. Sloan will be coming in a few minutes.

REGINA: We'll go in a few weeks. A few weeks! That means two or three Saturdays, two or three Sundays. (*Sighs.*) Well, I'm very tired. I shall go to bed. I don't want any supper. Put the lights out and lock up. (ADDIE *moves to the piano lamp, turns it out.*) You go to your room, Alexandra. Addie will bring you something hot. You look very tired. (*Rises. To* ADDIE.) Call me when Dr. Sloan gets here. I don't want to see anybody else. I don't want any condolence calls tonight. The whole town will be over.

ALEXANDRA: Mama, I'm not coming with you. I'm not going to Chicago.

REGINA (*turns to her*): You're very upset, Alexandra.

ALEXANDRA (*quietly*): I mean what I say. With all my heart.

REGINA: We'll talk about it tomorrow. The morning will make a difference.

ALEXANDRA: It won't make any difference. And there isn't anything to talk about. I am going away from you. Because I want to. Because I know Papa would want me to.

REGINA (*puzzled, careful, polite*): You *know* your papa wanted you to go away from me?

ALEXANDRA: Yes.

REGINA (*softly*): And if I say no?

ALEXANDRA (*looks at her*): Say it, Mama, say it. And see what happens.

REGINA (*softly, after a pause*): And if I make you stay?

ALEXANDRA: That would be foolish. It wouldn't work in the end.

REGINA: You're very serious about it, aren't you? (*Crosses to stairs.*) Well, you'll change your mind in a few days.

ALEXANDRA: You only change your mind when you want to. And I won't want to.

REGINA (*going up the steps*): Alexandra, I've come to the end of my rope. Somewhere there

has to be what I want, too. Life goes too fast. Do what you want; think what you want; go where you want. I'd like to keep you with me, but I won't make you stay. Too many people used to make me do too many things. No, I won't make you stay.

ALEXANDRA: You couldn't, Mama, because I want to leave here. As I've never wanted anything in my life before. Because now I understand what Papa was trying to tell me. (*Pause.*) All in one day: Addie said there were people who ate the earth and other people who stood around and watched them do it. And just now Uncle Ben said the same thing. Really, he said the same thing. (*Tensely.*) Well, tell him for me, Mama, I'm not going to stand around and watch you do it. Tell him I'll be fighting as hard as he'll be fighting (*rises*) some place where people don't just stand around and watch.

REGINA: Well, you have spirit, after all. I used to think you were all sugar water. We don't have to be bad friends. I don't want us to be bad friends, Alexandra. (*Starts, stops, turns to* ALEXANDRA.) Would you like to come and talk to me, Alexandra? Would you—would you like to sleep in my room tonight?

ALEXANDRA (*takes a step towards her*): Are you afraid, Mama? (REGINA *does not answer. She moves slowly out of sight.* ADDIE *comes to* ALEXANDRA, *presses her arm.*)

THE CURTAIN FALLS

Thornton Wilder: *The Skin of Our Teeth* (1942)

Most critics have treated Wilder as the most learned, the most "literary" of our major playwrights. He was a friend of Sigmund Freud, James Joyce, and Gertrude Stein—the most important traceable influence in his work. He was born in Madison, Wisconsin, in 1897, and began his schooling in Hong Kong when his father, a newspaperman, became an ambassador there. His mother soon removed him to Berkeley, California, for five years of American schools. When his father was transferred to Shanghai, the family was reunited, and Wilder attended The American School. He saw very little of China, although he learned some Chinese. After graduating from Berkeley High in 1915, he first went to Oberlin College, then Yale when his father was moved to New Haven. His first play was published in the *Yale Literary Magazine* when he was a senior.

Wilder's college career was interrupted by a brief tour of military duty with the Coast Guard Artillery. It was the first of two tours; the second came during World War II, when, because of his fluency in Italian, French, and German, he was assigned to the Intelligence Corps. Between the wars, he spent a year in Italy at the American Academy in Rome, then taught French at Lawrenceville School in New Jersey for seven years, with two years off for an M.A. in French Literature at Princeton. During this time he wrote a novel and a play, but neither was notably successful. His second novel, *The Bridge of San Luis Rey* (1927), was a sudden and complete success, however, bringing with it not only financial independence, but the Pulitzer Prize, the first of many. After that, he left Lawrenceville and devoted himself more fully to writing.

He did not, however, completely abandon academic life. Wilder founded the MacDowell Colony, a retreat for artists, in Peterborough, New Hampshire, and from 1930 to 1936 spent half the year there and the other half lecturing at the University of Chicago, which at that time was one of the most intense and exciting intellectual environments in American education, led by its new president, Robert Hutchins, a classmate of Wilder's at Yale. Wilder also taught at the University of Hawaii and at Harvard, and critics have said that he was always more comfortable in an academic atmosphere than in the more rough and tumble world of the theater.

Wilder had been writing a number of short plays, some of which were eventually published. One variety, called "three-minute plays," interested him greatly, but few opportunities existed for him to produce them. Some of his one-act plays, *The Long Christmas Dinner and Other Plays* (1931), have been performed by school and college groups. But his first real success came with the production of *Our Town* (1938), one of the few genuine classics of modern American theater. The play was an outgrowth of his summers in Peterborough, New Hampshire, where he had taken long walks through the countryside and had grown sensitive to the ways of New England and its people. Grover's Corners is Peterborough, and the Peterborough Players used to give an annual performance of the play in their own honor, often with Thornton Wilder playing the part of the Stage Manager. The freshness of the setting—which used nothing but a bare stage—and the directness of the examination of the details of everyday life combined well with a deep, humanistic optimism that was clearly not a bluff, nor the easy sentiment of melodrama. The understanding that only a person with Wilder's background could bring out of a thorough classical education—a training in thought and literature—revealed itself quietly but firmly. The play enjoyed a long run and won the Pulitzer Prize.

Wilder's second Pulitzer Prize play, *The Skin of Our Teeth,* was also a commercial success. It was written on the eve of World War II, and it clearly portrays the fears the entire world felt as it stood on the brink of self-destruction. The play is about humanity's struggle for survival, beginning with the ice age, proceeding to the era of the Great Flood, and continuing to the age of wholesale war. The characters are archetypal; they are working within huge mythic structures centering on the idea of the fall of man, the concept of sin—with Cain playing a prominent part—and on the final "promise" that humanity seems to have; the promise to begin again, to refuse to let any superficial defeat stymie the hopefulness that we will somehow survive and struggle onward to something better.

The play was mystifying to early audiences, since it was rather experimental. It used multiple time-sequences, unusual staging, and some unsettling techniques, such as breaking the action to remind the audience that this was just a play, but one in which they had a serious stake. The influence of James Joyce's highly experimental novel, *Finnegans Wake,* is clear throughout, as is the work of many other writers. Wilder saw the play produced after World War II in the bombed-out buildings of Germany—one of the first pieces of theater post-war Germans experienced—and found himself deeply moved, particularly in the final scene when Hester asks, "How will a man choose the ruler that shall rule over him? Will he not choose a man who has first established order in himself?"

Before Thornton Wilder died in 1976, he had a number of other successes as a writer and playwright. One play, *The Matchmaker,* was eventually turned into a musical, *Hello, Dolly!* Its success alone would have guaranteed Wilder a niche in the American theater, but it would not have been a representative one. His two greatest works, *Our Town* and *The Skin of Our Teeth,* serve as the best examples of his faith in humanity—the central theme of his work.

Suggested Readings

Burbank, Rex. *Thornton Wilder,* 2d ed. Boston: Twayne, 1978.

Edelstein, J.M. *A Bibliographical Checklist of the Writings of Thornton Wilder.* New Haven: Yale University Press, 1959.

Goldstein, Malcolm. *The Art of Thornton Wilder.* Lincoln: University of Nebraska Press, 1965.

Grebanier, Bernard. *Thornton Wilder.* University of Minnesota Pamphlets, No. 34. Minneapolis: University of Minnesota Press, 1964.

Haberman, Donald. *The Plays of Thornton Wilder: A Critical Study.* Middletown: Wesleyan University Press, 1967.

Kuner, Mildred Cristophe. *Thornton Wilder: The Bright and the Dark.* New York: Crowell, 1972.

Stresau, Hermann. *Thornton Wilder,* tr. Frieda Schutze. New York: Ungar, 1971.

Wilder, Thornton. *The Angel That Troubled the Waters and Other Plays.* New York: Coward McCann, 1928.

———. *The Long Christmas Dinner and Other Plays in One Act.* New York: Coward McCann, 1931.

———. *Three Plays.* New York: Harper, 1957.

The Skin of Our Teeth

Thornton Wilder

CHARACTERS

ANNOUNCER	MISS E. MUSE
SABINA	MISS T. MUSE
MR. FITZPATRICK	MISS M. MUSE
MRS. ANTROBUS	TWO USHERS
DINOSAUR	TWO DRUM MAJORETTES
MAMMOTH	FORTUNE TELLER
TELEGRAPH BOY	TWO CHAIR PUSHERS
GLADYS	SIX CONVEENERS
HENRY	BROADCAST OFFICIAL
MR. ANTROBUS	DEFEATED CANDIDATE
DOCTOR	MR. TREMAYNE
PROFESSOR	HESTER
JUDGE	IVY
HOMER	FRED BAILEY

ACT I: Home, Excelsior, New Jersey.
ACT II: Atlantic City Boardwalk.
ACT III: Home, Excelsior, New Jersey.

ACT I

(A projection screen in the middle of the curtain. The first lantern side: the name of the theatre, and the words: NEWS EVENTS OF THE WORLD. *An* ANNOUNCER's *voice is heard.)*

ANNOUNCER: The management takes pleasure in bringing to you—The News Events of the World. *(Slide of the sun appearing above the horizon.)*

Freeport, Long Island:

The sun rose this morning at 6:32 a.m. This gratifying event was first reported by Mrs. Dorothy Stetson of Freeport, Long Island, who promptly telephoned the Mayor.

The Society for Affirming the End of the World at once went into a special session and postponed the arrival of that event for TWEN-TY-FOUR HOURS.

All honor to Mrs. Stetson for her public spirit.

New York City. *(Slide of the front doors of the theatre in which this play is playing; three cleaning* WOMEN *with mops and pails.)*

The X Theatre. During the daily cleaning of this theatre a number of lost objects were collected as usual by Mesdames Simpson, Pateslewski, and Moriarty.

Among these objects found today was a wedding ring, inscribed: To Eva from Adam. Genesis II:18

The ring will be restored to the owner or owners, if their credentials are satisfactory.

Tippehatchee, Vermont. *(Slide representing a glacier.)*

The unprecedented cold weather of this summer has produced a condition that has not yet been satisfactorily explained. There is a report that a wall of ice is moving southward across these counties. The disruption of communications by the cold wave now crossing the country has rendered exact information difficult, but little credence is given to the rumor that the ice had pushed the Cathedral of Montreal as far as St. Albans, Vermont.

For further information see your daily papers. Excelsior, New Jersey. (*Slide of a modest suburban home.*)

The home of Mr. George Antrobus, the inventor of the wheel. The discovery of the wheel, following so closely on the discovery of the lever, has centered the attention of the country on Mr. Antrobus of this attractive suburban residence district. This is his home, a commodious seven-room house, conveniently situated near a public school, a Methodist church, and a firehouse; it is right handy to an A. and P. (*Slide of* MR. ANTROBUS *on his front steps, smiling and lifting his straw hat. He holds a wheel.*)

Mr. Antrobus, himself. He comes of very old stock and has made his way up from next to nothing.

It is reported that he was once a gardener, but left that situation under circumstances · that have been variously reported.

Mr. Antrobus is a veteran of foreign wars, and bears a number of scars, front and back. (*Slide of* MRS. ANTROBUS, *holding some roses.*)

This is Mrs. Antrobus, the charming and gracious president of the Excelsior Mothers' Club.

Mrs. Antrobus is an excellent needlewoman; it is she who invented the apron on which so many interesting changes have been rung since. (*Slide of the* FAMILY *and* SABINA.)

Here we see the Antrobuses with their two children, Henry and Gladys, and friend. The friend in the rear, is Lily Sabina, the maid.

I know we all want to congratulate this typical American family on its enterprise. We all wish Mr. Antrobus a successful future. Now the management takes you to the interior of this home for a brief visit. (*Curtain rises. Living room of a commuter's home.* SABINA—*straw-blonde, over-rouged—is standing by the window back center, a feather duster under her elbow.*)

SABINA: Oh, oh, oh! Six o'clock and the master not home yet.

Pray God nothing serious has happened to him crossing the Hudson River. If anything happened to him, we would certainly be inconsolable and have to move into a less desirable residence district.

The fact is I don't know what'll become of us. Here it is the middle of August and the coldest day of the year. It's simply freezing; the dogs are sticking to the sidewalks; can anybody explain that? No.

But I'm not surprised. The whole world's at sixes and sevens, and why the house hasn't fallen down about our ears long ago is a miracle to me. (*A fragment of the right wall leans precariously over the stage.* SABINA *looks at it nervously and it slowly rights itself.*)

Every night this same anxiety as to whether the master will get home safely: whether he'll bring home anything to eat. In the midst of life we are in the midst of death, a truer word was never said. (*The fragment of scenery flies up into the lofts.* SABINA *is struck dumb with surprise, shrugs her shoulders and starts dusting* MR. ANTROBUS' *chair, including the under side.*)

Of course, Mr. Antrobus is a very fine man, an excellent husband and father, a pillar of the church, and has all the best interests of the community at heart. Of course, every muscle goes tight every time he passes a policeman; but what I think is that there are certain charges that ought not to be made, and I think I may add, ought not to be allowed to be made; we're all human; who isn't? (*She dusts* MRS. ANTROBUS' *rocking chair.*)

Mrs. Antrobus is as fine a woman as you could hope to see. She lives only for her children; and if it would be any benefit to her children she'd see the rest of us stretched out dead at her feet without turning a hair,—that's the truth. If you want to know anything more about Mrs. Antrobus, just go and look at a tigress, and look hard.

As to the children—

Well, Henry Antrobus is a real, clean cut American boy. He'll graduate from High School one of these days, if they make the alphabet any easier.—Henry, when he has a stone in his hand, has a perfect aim; he can hit anything from a bird to an older brother—Oh! I didn't mean to say that!—but it certainly was an unfortunate accident, and it was very hard getting the police out of the house.

Mr. and Mrs. Antrobus' daughter is named Gladys. She'll make some good man a good wife some day, if he'll just come down off the movie screen and ask her.

So here we are!

We've managed to survive for some time now, catch as catch can, the fat and the lean, and if the dinosaurs don't trample us to death, and if the grasshoppers don't eat up our garden, we'll all live to see better days, knock on wood.

Each new child that's born to the Antrobuses seems to them to be sufficient reason for the whole universe's being set in motion; and each new child that dies seems to them to have been spared a whole world of sorrow, and what the end of it will be is still very much an open question.

We've rattled along, hot and cold, for some time now—(*A portion of the wall above the door, right, flies up into the air and disappears.*) and my advice to you is not to inquire into why or whither, but just enjoy your ice cream while it's on your plate,—that's my philosophy.

Don't forget that a few years ago we came through the depression by the skin of our teeth! One more tight squeeze like that and where will we be? (*This is a cue line,* SABINA *looks angrily at the kitchen door and repeats.*) . . . we came through the depression by the skin of our teeth; one more tight squeeze like that and where will we be? (*Flustered, she looks through the opening in the right wall; then goes to the window and reopens the Act.*)

Oh, oh, oh! Six o'clock and the master not home yet. Pray God nothing has happened to him crossing the Hudson. Here it is the middle of August and the coldest day of the year. It's simply freezing; the dogs are sticking. One more tight squeeze like that and where will we be?

VOICE (*off stage*): Make up something! Invent something!

SABINA: Well . . . uh . . . this certainly is a fine American home . . . and—uh . . . everybody's very happy . . . and—uh . . . (*Suddenly flings pretense to the winds and coming downstage says with indignation.*) I can't invent any words for this play, and I'm glad I can't. I hate this play and every word in it.

As for me, I don't understand a single word of it, anyway—all about the troubles the human race has gone through, there's a subject for you.

Besides, the author hasn't made up his silly mind as to whether we're all living back in caves or in New Jersey today, and that's the way it is all the way through.

Oh—why can't we have plays like we used to have—*Peg o' My Heart,* and *Smilin' Thru,* and *The Bat*—good entertainment with a message you can take home with you?

I took this hateful job because I had to. For two years I've sat up in my room living on a sandwich and a cup of tea a day, waiting for better times in the theatre. And look at me now: I—I who've played *Rain* and *The Barretts of Wimpole Street* and *First Lady*—God in Heaven!

(*The* STAGE MANAGER *puts his head out from the hole in the scenery.*)

MR. FITZPATRICK: Miss Somerset! Miss Somerset!

SABINA: Oh! Anyway!—nothing matters! It'll all be the same in a hundred years. (*Loudly.*) We came through the depression by the skin of our teeth,—that's true!—one more tight squeeze like that and where will we be? (*Enter* MRS. ANTROBUS, *a mother.*)

MRS. ANTROBUS: Sabina, you've let the fire go out.

SABINA (*in a lather*): One-thing-and-another; don't-know-whether-my-wits-are-upside-or-down; might-as-well-be-dead-as-alive-in-a-house-all-sixes-and-sevens. . . .

MRS. ANTROBUS: You've let the fire go out. Here it is the coldest day of the year right in the middle of August, and you've let the fire go out.

SABINA: Mrs. Antrobus, I'd like to give my two weeks' notice, Mrs. Antrobus. A girl like I can get a situation in a home where they're rich enough to have a fire in every room, Mrs. Antrobus, and a girl don't have to carry the responsibility of the whole house on her two shoulders. And a home without children, Mrs. Antrobus, because children are a thing only a parent can stand, and a truer word was never said; and a home, Mrs. Antrobus, where the master of the house don't pinch decent, self-respecting girls when he meets them in a dark corridor. I mention no names and make no charges. So you have my notice, Mrs. Antrobus. I hope that's perfectly clear.

MRS. ANTROBUS: You've let the fire go out!—Have you milked the mammoth?

SABINA: I don't understand a word of this play.—Yes, I've milked the mammoth.

MRS. ANTROBUS: Until Mr. Antrobus comes home we have no food and we have no fire. You'd better go over to the neighbors and borrow some fire.

SABINA: Mrs. Antrobus! I can't! I'd die on the way, you know I would. It's worse than January. The dogs are sticking to the sidewalks. I'd die.

MRS. ANTROBUS: Very well, I'll go.

SABINA (*even more distraught, coming forward and sinking on her knees*): You'd never come back alive; we'd all perish; if you weren't here, we'd just perish. How do we know Mr. Antrobus'll be back? We don't know. If you go out, I'll just kill myself.

MRS. ANTROBUS: Get up, Sabina.

SABINA: Every night it's the same thing. Will

he come back safe, or won't he? Will we starve to death, or freeze to death, or boil to death or will we be killed by burglars? I don't know why we go on living. I don't know why we go on living at all. It's easier being dead. (*She flings her arms on the table and buries her head in them. In each of the succeeding speeches she flings her head up—and sometimes her hands—then quickly buries her head again.*)

MRS. ANTROBUS: The same thing! Always throwing up the sponge, Sabina. Always announcing your own death. But give you a new hat—or a plate of ice-cream—or a ticket to the movies, and you want to live forever.

SABINA: You don't care whether we live or die; all you care about is those children. If it would be any benefit to them you'd be glad to see us all stretched out dead.

MRS. ANTROBUS: Well, maybe I would.

SABINA: And what do they care about? Themselves—that's all they care about. (*Shrilly.*) They make fun of you behind your back. Don't tell me: they're ashamed of you. Half the time, they pretend they're someone else's children. Little thanks you get from them.

MRS. ANTROBUS: I'm not asking for any thanks.

SABINA: And Mr. Antrobus—you don't understand *him*. All that work he does—trying to discover the alphabet and the multiplication table. Whenever he tries to learn anything you fight against it.

MRS. ANTROBUS: Oh, Sabina, I know you.

When Mr. Antrobus raped you home from your Sabine hills, he did it to insult me.

He did it for your pretty face, and to insult me.

You were the new wife, weren't you?

For a year or two you lay on your bed all day and polished the nails on your hands and feet:

You made puff-balls of the combings of your hair and you blew them up to the ceiling.

And I washed your underclothes and I made you chicken broths.

I bore children and between my very groans I stirred the cream that you'd put on your face.

But I knew you wouldn't last.

You didn't last.

SABINA: But it was I who encouraged Mr. Antrobus to make the alphabet. I'm sorry to say it, Mrs. Antrobus, but you're not a beautiful woman, and you can never know what a man could do if he tried. It's girls like I who inspire the multiplication table.

I'm sorry to say it, but you're not a beautiful woman, Mrs. Antrobus, and that's the God's truth.

MRS. ANTROBUS: And you didn't last— you sank to the kitchen. And what do you do there? You let the fire go out!

No wonder to you it seems easier being dead.

Reading and writing and counting on your fingers is all very well in their way,—but I keep the home going.

MRS. ANTROBUS: —There's that dinosaur on the front lawn again.—Shoo! Go away. Go away. (*The baby* DINOSAUR *puts his head in the window.*)

DINOSAUR: It's cold.

MRS. ANTROBUS: You go around to the back of the house where you belong.

DINOSAUR: It's cold. (*The* DINOSAUR *disappears.* MRS. ANTROBUS *goes calmly out.* SABINA *slowly raises her head and speaks to the audience. The central portion of the center wall rises, pauses, and disappears into the loft.*)

SABINA: Now that you audience are listening to this too, I understand it a little better.

I wish eleven o'clock were here; I don't want to be dragged through this whole play again. (*The* TELEGRAPH BOY *is seen entering the back wall of the stage from the right. She catches sight of him and calls.*) Mrs. Antrobus! Mrs. Antrobus! Help! There's a strange man coming to the house. He's coming up the walk, help! (*Enter* MRS. ANTROBUS *in alarm, but efficient.*)

MRS. ANTROBUS: Help me quick! (*They barricade the door by piling the furniture against it.*) Who is it? What do you want?

TELEGRAPH BOY: A telegram for Mrs. Antrobus from Mr. Antrobus in the city.

SABINA: Are you sure, are you sure? Maybe it's just a trap!

MRS. ANTROBUS: I know his voice, Sabina. We can open the door. (*Enter the* TELEGRAPH BOY, *12 years old, in uniform. The* DINOSAUR *and* MAMMOTH *slip by him into the room and settle down front right.*) I'm sorry we kept you waiting. We have to be careful, you know. (*To the* ANIMALS.) Hm! . . . Will you be quiet? (*They nod.*) Have you had your supper? (*They nod.*) Are you ready to come in? (*They nod.*) Young man, have you any fire with you? Then light the grate, will you? (*He nods, produces something like a briquet; and kneels by the imagined fireplace, footlights center. Pause.*) What are people saying about this cold weather? (*He makes a doubtful shrug with his shoulders.*) Sabina, take this stick and go and light the stove.

SABINA: Like I told you, Mrs. Antrobus; two weeks. That's the law. I hope that's perfectly clear. (*Exit.*)

MRS. ANTROBUS: What about this cold weather?

TELEGRAPH BOY (*lowered eyes*): Of course, I don't know anything . . . but they say there's a wall of ice moving down from the North, that's what they say. We can't get Boston by telegraph, and they're burning pianos in Hartford. . . . It moves everything in front of it, churches and post offices and city halls.

I live in Brooklyn myself.

MRS. ANTROBUS: What are people doing about it?

TELEGRAPH BOY: Well . . . uh . . . Talking, mostly.

Or just what you'd do a day in February.

There are some that are trying to go South and the roads are crowded; but you can't take old people and children very far in a cold like this.

MRS. ANTROBUS: —What's this telegram you have for me?

TELEGRAPH BOY (*fingertips to his forehead*): If you wait just a minute; I've got to remember it. (*The* ANIMALS *have left their corner and are nosing him. Presently they take places on either side of him, leaning aginst his hips, like heraldic beasts.*)

This telegram was flashed from Murray Hill to University Heights! And then by puffs of smoke from University Heights to Staten Island.

And then by lantern from Staten Island to Plainfield, New Jersey. What hath God wrought! (*He clears his throat.*)

To Mrs. Antrobus, Excelsior, New Jersey:

My dear wife, will be an hour late. Busy day at the office.

Don't worry the children about the cold just keep them warm burn everything except Shakespeare. (*Pause.*)

MRS. ANTROBUS: Men!—He knows I'd burn ten Shakespeares to prevent a child of mine from having one cold in the head. What does it say next? (*Enter* SABINA.)

TELEGRAPH BOY: 'Have made great discoveries today have separated em from en.'

SABINA: I know what that is, that's the alphabet, yes it is. Mr. Antrobus is just the cleverest man. Why, when the alphabet's finished, we'll be able to tell the future and everything.

TELEGRAPH BOY: Then listen to this: 'Ten tens make a hundred semi-colon consequences far-reaching.' (*Watches for effect.*)

MRS. ANTROBUS: The earth's turning to ice,

and all he can do is to make up new numbers.

TELEGRAPH BOY: Well, Mrs. Antrobus, like the head man at our office said: a few more discoveries like that and we'll be worth freezing.

MRS. ANTROBUS: What does he say next?

TELEGRAPH BOY: I . . . I can't do this last part very well. (*He clears his throat and sings.*) 'Happy w'dding ann'vers'ry to you, Happy ann'vers'ry to you—' (*The* ANIMALS *begin to howl soulfully;* SABINA *screams with pleasure.*)

MRS. ANTROBUS: Dolly! Frederick! Be quiet.

TELEGRAPH BOY (*above the din*): 'Happy w'dding ann'vers'ry, dear Eva; happy w'dding ann'vers'ry to you.'

MRS. ANTROBUS: Is that in the telegram? Are they singing telegrams now? (*He nods.*) The earth's getting so silly no wonder the sun turns cold.

SABINA: Mrs. Antrobus, I want to take back the notice I gave you. Mrs. Antrobus, I don't want to leave a house that gets such interesting telegrams and I'm sorry for anything I said. I really am.

MRS. ANTROBUS: Young man, I'd like to give you something for all this trouble; Mr. Antrobus isn't home yet and I have no money and no food in the house—

TELEGRAPH BOY: Mrs. Antrobus . . . I don't like to . . . appear to . . . ask for anything, but . . .

MRS. ANTROBUS: What is it you'd like?

TELEGRAPH BOY: Do you happen to have an old needle you could spare? My wife just sits home all day thinking about needles.

SABINA (*shrilly*): We only got two in the house. Mrs. Antrobus, you know we only got two in the house.

MRS. ANTROBUS (*after a look at* SABINA *taking a needle from her collar*): Why yes, I can spare this.

TELEGRAPH BOY (*lowered eyes*): Thank you, Mrs. Antrobus. Mrs. Antrobus, can I ask you something else? I have two sons of my own; if the cold gets worse, what should I do?

SABINA: I think we'll all perish, that's what I think. Cold like this in August is just the end of the whole world. (*Silence.*)

MRS. ANTROBUS: I don't know. After all, what does one do about anything? Just keep as warm as you can. And don't let your wife and children see that you're worried.

TELEGRAPH BOY: Yes . . . Thank you, Mrs. Antrobus. Well, I'd better be going.—Oh, I forgot! There's one more sentence in the telegram. 'Three cheers have invented the wheel.'

MRS. ANTROBUS: A wheel? What's a wheel?

TELEGRAPH BOY: I don't know. That's what it said. The sign for it is like this. Well, goodbye. (*The* WOMEN *see him to the door, with goodbyes and injunctions to keep warm.*)

SABINA (*apron to her eyes, wailing*): Mrs. Antrobus, it looks to me like all the nice men in the world are already married; I don't know why that is. (*Exit.*)

MRS. ANTROBUS (*thoughtful; to the* ANIMALS): Do you ever remember hearing tell of any cold like this in August? (*The* ANIMALS *shake their heads.*) From your grandmothers or anyone? (*They shake their heads.*) Have you any suggestions? (*They shake their heads. She pulls her shawl around, goes to the front door and opening it an inch calls.*) HENRY. GLADYS. CHILDREN. Come right in and get warm. No, no, when mama says a thing she means it.

Henry! HENRY. Put down that stone. You know what happened last time. (*Shriek.*) HENRY! Put down that stone!

Gladys! Put down your dress!! Try and be a lady. (*The* CHILDREN *bound in and dash to the fire. They take off their winter things and leave them in heaps on the floor.*)

GLADYS: Mama, I'm hungry. Mama, why is it so cold?

HENRY (*at the same time*): Mama, why doesn't it snow? Mama, when's supper ready? Maybe, it'll snow and we can make snowballs.

GLADYS: Mama, it's so cold that in one more minute I just couldn't of stood it.

MRS. ANTROBUS: Settle down, both of you, I want to talk to you. (*She draws up a hassock and sits front center over the orchestra pit before the imaginary fire. The* CHILDREN *stretch out on the floor, leaning against her lap. Tableau by Raphael. The* ANIMALS *edge up and complete the triangle.*)

It's just a cold spell of some kind. Now listen to what I'm saying:

When your father comes home I want you to be extra quiet. He's had a hard day at the office and I don't know but what he may have one of his moods.

I just got a telegram from him very happy and excited, and you know what that means. Your father's temper's uneven; I guess you know that. (*Shriek.*)

Henry! Henry!

Why—why can't you remember to keep your hair down over your forehead? You must keep that scar covered up. Don't you know that when your father sees it he loses all control over himself? He goes crazy. He wants to die. (*After a moment's despair she collects herself decisively, wets the*

hem of her apron in her mouth and starts polishing his forehead vigorously.*)

Lift your head up. Stop squirming. Blessed me, sometimes I think that it's going away— and then there it is; just as red as ever.

HENRY: Mama, today at school two teachers forgot and called me by my old name. They forgot, Mama. You'd better write another letter to the principal, so that he'll tell them I've changed my name. Right out in class they called me: Cain.

MRS. ANTROBUS (*putting her hand on his mouth, too late; hoarsely*): Don't say it. (*Polishing feverishly.*) If you're good they'll forget it. Henry, you didn't hit anyone . . . today, did you?

HENRY: Oh . . . no-o-o!

MRS. ANTROBUS (*still working, not looking at Gladys*): And, Gladys, I want you to be especially nice to your father tonight. You know what he calls you when you're good—his little angel, his little star. Keep your dress down like a little lady. And keep your voice nice and low. Gladys Antrobus!! What's that red stuff you have on your face? (*Slaps her.*) You're a filthy detestable child! (*Rises in real, though temporary, repudiation and despair.*) Get away from me, both of you! I wish I'd never seen sight or sound of you. Let the cold come! I can't stand it. I don't want to go on. (*She walks away.*)

GLADYS (*weeping*): All the girls at school do, Mama.

MRS. ANTROBUS (*shrieking*): I'm through with you, that's all!—Sabina! Sabina!—Don't you know your father'd go crazy if he saw that paint on your face? Don't you know your father thinks you're perfect? Don't you know he couldn't live if he didn't think you were perfect?—Sabina! (*Enter* SABINA.)

SABINA: Yes, Mrs. Antrobus!

MRS. ANTROBUS: Take this girl out into the kitchen and wash her face with the scrubbing brush.

MR. ANTROBUS (*outside, roaring*): 'I've been working on the railroad, all the livelong day . . . etc.' (*The* ANIMALS *start running around in circles, bellowing.* SABINA *rushes to the window.*)

MRS. ANTROBUS: Sabina, what's that noise outside?

SABINA: Oh, it's a drunken tramp. It's a giant, Mrs. Antrobus. We'll all be killed in our beds, I know it!

MRS. ANTROBUS: Help me quick. Quick. Everybody. (*Again they stack all the furniture against the door.* MR. ANTROBUS *pounds and bellows.*) Who is it? What do you want?—Sabina, have you any boiling water ready?—Who is it?

MR. ANTROBUS: Broken-down camel of a pig's snout, open this door.

MRS. ANTROBUS: God be praised! It's your father.—Just a minute, George!—Sabina, clear the door, quick. Gladys, come here while I clean your nasty face!

MR. ANTROBUS: She-bitch of a goat's gizzard, I'll break every bone in your body. Let me in or I'll tear the whole house down.

MRS. ANTROBUS: Just a minute, George, something's the matter with the lock.

MR. ANTROBUS: Open the door or I'll tear your livers out. I'll smash your brains on the ceiling, and Devil take the hindmost.

MRS. ANTROBUS: Now you can open the door, Sabina. I'm ready. (*The door is flung open. Silence. MR. ANTROBUS—face of a Keystone Comedy Cop— stands there in fur cap and blanket. His arms are full of parcels, including a large stone wheel with a center in it. One hand carries a railroad man's lantern. Suddenly he bursts into joyous roar.*)

MR. ANTROBUS: Well, how's the whole crooked family? (*Relief. Laughter. Tears. Jumping up and down. ANIMALS cavorting. ANTROBUS throws the parcels on the ground. Hurls his cap and blanket after them. Heroic embraces. Melee of HUMANS and ANIMALS, SABINA included.*) I'll be scalded and tarred if a man can't get a little welcome when he comes home. Well, Maggie, you old gunny-sack, how's the broken down old weather hen? —Sabina, old fishbait, old skunkpot.—And the children,—how've the little smellers been?

GLADYS: Papa, Papa, Papa, Papa, Papa.

MR. ANTROBUS: How've they been, Maggie?

MRS. ANTROBUS: Well, I must say, they've been as good as gold. I haven't had to raise my voice once. I don't know what's the matter with them.

ANTROBUS (*kneeling before GLADYS*): Papa's little weasel, eh?—Sabina, there's some food for you. —Papa's little gopher?

GLADYS (*her arm around his neck*): Papa, you're always teasing me.

ANTROBUS: And Henry? Nothing rash today, I hope. Nothing rash?

HENRY: No, Papa.

ANTROBUS (*roaring*): Well that's good, that's good—I'll bet Sabina let the fire go out.

SABINA: Mr. Antrobus, I've given my notice. I'm leaving two weeks from today. I'm sorry, but I'm leaving.

ANTROBUS (*roar*): Well, if you leave now you'll freeze to death, so go and cook the dinner.

SABINA: Two weeks, that's the law. (*Exit.*)

ANTROBUS: Did you get my telegram?

MRS. ANTROBUS: Yes.—What's a wheel? (*He indicates the wheel with a glance. HENRY is rolling it around the floor. Rapid, hoarse interchange.*) MRS. ANTROBUS: What does this cold weather mean? It's below freezing. ANTROBUS: Not before the children! MRS. ANTROBUS: Shouldn't we do something about it?—start off, move? ANTROBUS: Not before the children!!! (*He gives HENRY a sharp slap.*)

HENRY: Papa, you hit me!

ANTROBUS: Well, remember it. That's to make you remember today. Today. The day the alphabet's finished; and the day that we *saw* the hundred—the hundred, the hundred, the hundred, the hundred, the hundred—there's no end to 'em.

I've had a day at the office!

Take a look at that wheel, Maggie—when I've got that to rights: you'll see a sight.

There's a reward there for all the walking you've done.

MRS. ANTROBUS: How do you mean?

ANTROBUS (*on the hassock looking into the fire; with awe*): Maggie, we've reached the top of the wave. There's not much more to be done. We're there!

MRS. ANTROBUS (*cutting across his mood sharply*): And the ice?

ANTROBUS: The ice!

HENRY (*playing with the wheel*): Papa, you could put a chair on this.

ANTROBUS (*broodingly*): Ye-e-s, any booby can fool with it now,—but I thought of it first.

MRS. ANTROBUS: Children, go out in the kitchen. I want to talk to your father alone. (*The CHILDREN go out. ANTROBUS has moved to his chair up left. He takes the goldfish bowl on his lap; pulls the canary cage down to the level of his face. Both the ANIMALS put their paws up on the arm of his chair. MRS. ANTROBUS faces him across the room, like a judge.*)

MRS. ANTROBUS: Well?

ANTROBUS (*shortly*): It's cold.—How things been, eh? Keck, keck, keck.—And you, Millicent?

MRS. ANTROBUS: I know it's cold.

ANTROBUS (*to the canary*): No spilling of sunflower seed, eh? No singing after lights-out, y'know what I mean?

MRS. ANTROBUS: You can try and prevent us freezing to death, can't you? You can do something? We can start moving. Or we can go on the animals' backs?

ANTROBUS: The best thing about animals is that they don't talk much.

MAMMOTH: It's cold.

ANTROBUS: Eh, eh, eh! Watch that!—
—By midnight we'd turn to ice. The roads are full of people now who can scarcely lift a foot from the ground. The grass out in front is like iron,—which reminds me, I have another needle for you.—The people up north—where are they?
Frozen . . . crushed . . .

MRS. ANTROBUS: Is that what's going to happen to us?—Will you answer me?

ANTROBUS: I don't know. I don't know anything. Some say that the ice is going slower. Some say that it's stopped. The sun's growing cold. What can I do about that? Nothing we can do but burn everything in the house, and the fenceposts and the barn. Keep the fire going. When we have no more fire, we die.

MRS. ANTROBUS: Well, why didn't you say so in the first place? (MRS. ANTROBUS *is about to march off when she catches sight of two* REFUGEES, *men, who have appeared against the back wall of the theatre and who are soon joined by others.*)

REFUGEES: Mr. Antrobus! Mr. Antrobus! Mr. An-nn-tro-bus!

MRS. ANTROBUS: Who's that? Who's that calling you?

ANTROBUS (*clearing his throat guiltily*): Hm— let me see. (*Two* REFUGEES *come up to the window.*)

REFUGEE: Could we warm our hands for a moment, Mr. Antrobus. It's very cold, Mr. Antrobus.

ANOTHER REFUGEE: Mr. Antrobus, I wonder if you have a piece of bread or something that you could spare. (*Silence. They wait humbly.* MRS. ANTROBUS *stands rooted to the spot. Suddenly a knock at the door, then another hand knocking in short rapid blows.*)

MRS. ANTROBUS: Who are these people? Why, they're all over the front yard. What have they come *here* for? (*Enter* SABINA.)

SABINA: Mrs. Antrobus! There are some tramps knocking at the back door.

MRS. ANTROBUS: George, tell these people to go away. Tell them to move right along. I'll go and send them away from the back door. Sabina, come with me. (*She goes out energetically.*)

ANTROBUS: Sabina! Stay here! I have something to say to you. (*He goes to the door and opens it a crack and talks through it.*) Ladies and gentlemen! I'll have to ask you to wait a few minutes longer. It'll be all right . . . while you're waiting you might each one pull up a stake of the fence. We'll need them all for the fireplace. There'll be coffee and sandwiches in a moment. (SABINA *looks out door over his shoulder and suddenly extends her arm pointing, with a scream.*)

SABINA: Mr. Antrobus, what's that??—that big white thing? Mr. Antrobus, it's ICE. It's ICE!!

ANTROBUS: Sabina, I want you to go in the kitchen and make a lot of coffee. Make a whole pail full.

SABINA: Pail full!!

ANTROBUS (*with gesture*): And sandwiches . . . piles of them . . . like this.

SABINA: Mr. An . . . !! (*Suddenly she drops the play, and says in her own person as* MISS SOMERSET, *with surprise.*) Oh, I see what this part of the play means now! This means refugees. (*She starts to cross to the proscenium.*) Oh, I don't like it. I don't like it. (*She leans against the proscenium and bursts into tears.*)

ANTROBUS: Miss Somerset!

VOICE OF THE STAGE MANAGER: Miss Somerset!

SABINA (*energetically, to the audience*): Ladies and gentlemen! Don't take this play serious. The world's not coming to an end. You know it's not. People exaggerate! Most people really have enough to eat and a roof over their heads. Nobody actually starves—you can always eat grass or something. That ice-business—why, it was a long, long time ago. Besides they were only savages. Savages don't love their families—not like we do.

ANTROBUS *and* STAGE MANAGER: Miss Somerset!! (*There is renewed knocking at the door.*)

SABINA: All right. I'll say the lines, but I won't think about the play. (*Enter* MRS. ANTROBUS.)

SABINA (*parting thrust at the audience*): And I advise you not to think about the play, either. (*Exit* SABINA.)

MRS. ANTROBUS: George, these tramps say that you asked them to come to the house. What does this mean? (*Knocking at the door.*)

ANTROBUS: Just . . . uh . . . There are a few friends, Maggie, I met on the road. Real nice, real useful people. . . .

MRS. ANTROBUS (*back to the door*): Now, don't you ask them in!
George Antrobus, not another soul comes in here over my dead body.

ANTROBUS: Maggie, there's a doctor there. Never hurts to have a good doctor in the house. We've lost a peck of children, one way and another. You can never tell when a child's throat will get stopped up. What you and I have seen—!!! (*He puts his fingers on his throat, and imitates diphtheria.*)

MRS. ANTROBUS: Well, just one person then,

the Doctor. The others can go right along the road.

ANTROBUS: Maggie, there's an old man, particular friend of mine—

MRS. ANTROBUS: I won't listen to you.

ANTROBUS: It was he that really started off the A.B.C.'s.

MRS. ANTROBUS: I don't care if he perishes. We can do without reading or writing. We can't do without food.

ANTROBUS: Then let the ice come!! Drink your coffee!! I don't want any coffee if I can't drink it with some good people.

MRS. ANTROBUS: Stop shouting. Who else is there trying to push us off the cliff?

ANTROBUS: Well, there's the man ... who makes all the laws. Judge Moses!

MRS. ANTROBUS: Judges can't help us now.

ANTROBUS: And if the ice melts? ... and if we pull through? Have you and I been able to bring up Henry? What have we done?

MRS. ANTROBUS: Who are those old women?

ANTROBUS (coughs): Up in town there are nine sisters. There are three or four of them here. They're sort of music teachers ... and one of them recites and one of them—

MRS. ANTROBUS: That's the end. A singing troupe! Well, take your choice, live or die. Starve your own children before your face.

ANTROBUS (gently): These people don't take much. They're used to starving. They'll sleep on the floor.

Besides, Maggie, listen: no, listen:

Who've we got in the house, but Sabina? Sabina's always afraid the worst will happen. Whose spirits can she keep up? Maggie, these people never give up. They think they'll live and work forever.

MRS. ANTROBUS (walks slowly to the middle of the room): All right, let them in. Let them in. You're master here. (Softly.) —But these animals must go. Enough's enough. They'll soon be big enough to push the walls down, anyway. Take them away.

ANTROBUS (sadly): All right. The dinosaur amd mammoth—! Come on, baby, come on Frederick. Come for a walk. That's a good little fellow.

DINOSAUR: It's cold.

ANTROBUS: Yes, nice cold fresh air. Bracing. (He holds the door open and the ANIMALS go out. He beckons to his friends. The REFUGEES are typical elderly out-of-works from the streets of New York today. JUDGE MOSES wears a skull cap. HOMER is a blind beggar with a guitar. The seedy crown shuffles in and waits humbly and expectantly. ANTROBUS introduces them to his wife who bows to each with a stately bend of her head.) Make yourself at home, Maggie, this the doctor ... m ... Coffee'll be here in a minute. ... Professor, this is my wife. ... And: ... Judge ... Maggie, you know the Judge. (An old blind man with a guitar.) Maggie, you know ... you know Homer?—Come right in, Judge. —Miss Muse—are some of your sisters here? Come right in ... Miss E. Muse; Miss T. Muse, Miss M. Muse.

MRS. ANTROBUS: Pleased to meet you. Just ... make yourself comfortable. Supper'll be ready in a minute. (She goes out, abruptly.)

ANTROBUS: Make yourselves at home, friends. I'll be right back. (He goes out. The REFUGEES stare about them in awe. Presently several voices start whispering "Homer! Homer!" All take it up. HOMER strikes a chord or two on his guitar, then starts to speak:)

HOMER:

Μῆνιν ἄειδε, θεὰ, Πηληϊάδεω ᾿Αχιλῆος, οὐλομένην, ἣ μυρί᾿ ᾿Αχαιοῖς ἄλγε᾿ ἔθηκεν, πολλὰς δ᾿ ἰφθίμους ψυχὰς—

(HOMER's face shows he is lost in thought and memory and the words die away on his lips. The REFUGEES likewise nod in dreamy recollection. Soon the whisper "Moses, Moses!" goes around. An aged Jew parts his beard and recites dramatically.)

MOSES:

בְּרֵאשִׁית בָּרָא אֱלֹהִים אֵת הַשָּׁמַיִם וְאֵת הָאָרֶץ: וְהָאָרֶץ הָיְתָה תֹהוּ וָבֹהוּ וְחֹשֶׁךְ עַל־פְּנֵי תְהוֹם וְרוּחַ אֱלֹהִים מְרַחֶפֶת עַל־פְּנֵי הַמָּיִם:

(The same dying away of the words takes place, and on the part of the REFUGEES the same retreat into recollection. Some of them murmur, "Yes, yes." The mood is broken by the abrupt entrance of MR. and MRS. ANTROBUS and SABINA bearing platters of sandwiches and a pail of coffee. SABINA stops and stares at the guests.)

MR. ANTROBUS: Sabina, pass the sandwiches.

SABINA: I thought I was working in a respectable house that had respectable guests. I'm giving my notice, Mr. Antrobus: two weeks, that's the law.

MR. ANTROBUS: Sabina! Pass the sandwiches.

SABINA: Two weeks, that's the law.

MR. ANTROBUS: There's the law. That's Moses.

SABINA (stares): The Ten Commandments —FAUGH!!—(To Audience.) That's the worst line I've ever had to say on any stage.

ANTROBUS: I think the best thing to do is just not to stand on ceremony, but pass the sandwiches around from left to right.—Judge, help yourself to one of these.

MRS. ANTROBUS: The roads are crowded, I hear?

THE GUESTS (*all talking at once*): Oh, ma'am, you can't imagine. . . . You can hardly put one foot before you . . . people are trampling one another. (*Sudden silence.*)

MRS. ANTROBUS: Well, you know what I think it is,—I think it's sun-spots!

THE GUESTS (*discreet hubbub*): Oh, you're right, Mrs. Antrobus . . . that's what it is . . . That's what I was saying the other day. (*Sudden silence.*)

ANTROBUS: Well, I don't believe the whole world's going to turn to ice. (*All eyes are fixed on him, waiting.*) I can't believe it. Judge! Have we worked for nothing? Professor! Have we just failed in the whole thing?

MRS. ANTROBUS: It is certainly very strange— well fortunately on both sides of the family we come of very hearty stock.—Doctor, I want you to meet my children. They're eating their supper now. And of course I want them to meet you.

MISS M. MUSE: How many children have you, Mrs. Antrobus?

MRS. ANTROBUS: I have two,—a boy and a girl.

MOSES (*softly*): I understand you had two sons, Mrs. Antrobus. (MRS. ANTROBUS *in blind suffering; she walks toward the footlights.*)

MRS. ANTROBUS (*in a low voice*): Abel, Abel, my son, my son, Abel, my son, Abel, Abel, my son. (*The* REFUGEES *move with few steps toward her as though in comfort murmuring words in Greek, Hebrew, German, et cetera. A piercing shriek from the kitchen,—* SABINA's *voice. All heads turn.*)

ANTROBUS: What's that? (SABINA *enters, bursting with indignation, pulling on her gloves.*)

SABINA: Mr. Antrobus—that son of yours, that boy Henry Antrobus—I don't stay in this house another moment!—He's not fit to live among respectable folks and that's a fact.

MRS. ANTROBUS: Don't say another word, Sabina. I'll be right back. (*Without waiting for an answer she goes past her into the kitchen.*)

SABINA: Mr. Antrobus, Henry has thrown a stone again and if he hasn't killed the boy that lives next door, I'm very much mistaken. He finished his supper and went out to play; and I heard such a fight; and then I saw it. I saw it with my own eyes. And it looked to me like stark murder. (MRS. ANTROBUS *appears at the kitchen door, shielding* HENRY *who follows her. When she steps aside, we see on* HENRY's *forehead a large ochre and scarlet scar in the shape of a C.* MR. ANTROBUS

starts toward him. A pause. HENRY *is heard saying under his breath.*)

HENRY: He was going to take the wheel away from me. He started to throw a stone at me first.

MRS. ANTROBUS: George, it was just a boyish impulse. Remember how young he is. (*Louder, in an urgent wail.*) George, he's only four thousand years old.

SABINA: And everything was going along so nicely! (*Silence.* ANTROBUS *goes back to the fireplace.*)

ANTROBUS: Put out the fire! Put out all the fires. (*Violently.*) No wonder the sun grows cold. (*He starts stamping on the fireplace.*)

MRS. ANTROBUS: Doctor! Judge! Help me!— George, have you lost your mind?

ANTROBUS: There is no mind. We'll not try to live. (*To the guests.*) Give it up. Give up trying. (MRS. ANTROBUS *seizes him.*)

SABINA: Mr. Antrobus! I'm downright ashamed of you.

MRS. ANTROBUS: George, have some more coffee.—Gladys! Where's Gladys gone? (GLADYS *steps in, frightened.*)

GLADYS: Here I am, Mama.

MRS. ANTROBUS: Go upstairs and bring your father's slippers. How could you forget a thing like that, when you know how tired he is? (ANTROBUS *sits in his chair. He covers his face with his hands.* MRS. ANTROBUS *turns to the* REFUGEES.) Can't some of you sing? It's your business in life to sing, isn't it? Sabina! (*Several of the women clear their throats tentatively, and with frightened faces gather around* HOMER's *guitar. He establishes a few chords. Almost inaudibly they start singing, led by* SABINA: *"Jingle Bells,"* MRS. ANTROBUS *continues to* ANTROBUS *in a low voice, while taking off his shoes.*) George, remember all the other times. When the volcanoes came right up in the front yard.

And the time the grasshoppers ate every single leaf and blade of grass, and all the grain and spinach you'd grown with your own hands. And the summer there were earthquakes every night.

ANTROBUS: Henry! Henry! (*Puts his hand on his forehead.*) Myself. All of us, we're covered with blood.

MRS. ANTROBUS: Then remember all the times you were pleased with him and when you were proud of yourself.—Henry! Henry! Come here and recite to your father the multiplication table that you do so nicely. (HENRY *kneels on one knee beside his father and starts whispering the multiplication table.*)

HENRY (*finally*): Two times six is twelve; three times six is eighteen—I don't think I know the sixes. (*Enter* GLADYS *with the slippers.*

MRS. ANTROBUS *makes stern gestures to her.*) Go in there and do your best. (*The* GUESTS *are now singing "Tenting Tonight."*)

GLADYS (*putting slippers on his feet*): Papa . . . papa . . . I was very good in school today. Miss Conover said right out in class that if all the girls had as good manners as Gladys Antrobus, that the world would be a very different place to live in.

MRS. ANTROBUS: You recited a piece at assembly, didn't you? Recite it to your father.

GLADYS: Papa, do you want to hear what I recited in class? (*Fierce directorial glance from her mother.*) 'THE STAR' by Henry Wadsworth LONGFELLOW.

MRS. ANTROBUS: Wait!!! The fire's going out. There isn't enough wood! Henry, go upstairs and bring down the chairs and start breaking up the beds. (*Exit* HENRY. *The singers return to "Jingle Bells," still very softly.*)

GLADYS: Look, Papa, here's my report card. Lookit. Conduct A! Look, Papa. Papa, do you want to hear the Star, by Henry Wadsworth Longfellow? Papa, you're not mad at me, are you?—I know it'll get warmer. Soon it'll be just like spring, and we can go to a picnic at the Hibernian Picnic Grounds like you always like to do, don't you remember? Papa, just look at me once. (*Enter* HENRY *with some chairs.*)

ANTROBUS: You recited in assembly, did you? (*She nods eagerly.*) You didn't forget it?

GLADYS: No!!! I was perfect. (*Pause. Then* ANTROBUS *rises, goes to the front door and opens it. The* REFUGEES *draw back timidly; the song stops; he peers out of the door, then closes it.*)

ANTROBUS (*with decision, suddenly*): Build up the fire. It's cold. Build up the fire. We'll do what we can. Sabina, get some more wood. Come around the fire, everybody. At least the young ones may pull through. Henry, have you eaten something?

HENRY: Yes, papa.

ANTROBUS: Gladys, have you had some supper?

GLADYS: I ate in the kitchen, papa.

ANTROBUS: If you do come through this— what'll you be able to do? What do you know? Henry, did you take a good look at that wheel?

HENRY: Yes, papa.

ANTROBUS (*sitting down in his chair.*): Six times two are—

HENRY: —twelve; six times three are eighteen; six times four are—Papa, it's hot and cold. It makes my head all funny. It makes me sleepy.

ANTROBUS (*gives him a cuff*): Wake up. I don't care if your head is sleepy. Six times four are twenty-four. Six times five are—

HENRY: Thirty. Papa!

ANTROBUS: Maggie, put something into Gladys' head on the chance she can use it.

MRS. ANTROBUS: What do you mean, George?

ANTROBUS: Six times six are thirty-six.

Teach her the beginnings of the Bible.

GLADYS: But, Mama, it's so cold and close. (HENRY *has all but drowsed off. His father slaps him sharply and the lesson goes on.*)

MRS. ANTROBUS: 'In the beginning God created the heavens and the earth; and the earth was waste and void; and the darkness was upon the face of the deep—' (*The singing starts up again louder.* SABINA *has returned with wood.*)

SABINA (*after placing wood on the fireplace comes down to the footlights and addresses the audience*): Will you please start handing up your chairs? We'll need everything for this fire. Save the human race.—Ushers, will you pass the chairs up here? Thank you.

HENRY: Six times nine are fifty-four; six times ten are sixty. (*In the back of the auditorium the sound of chairs being ripped up can be heard.* USHERS *rush down the aisles with chairs and hand them over.*)

GLADYS: 'And God called the light Day and the darkness he called Night.'

SABINA: Pass up your chairs, everybody. Save the human race.

ACT II

(*Toward the end of the intermission, though with the house-lights still up, lantern slide projections begin to appear on the curtain. Timetables for trains leaving Pennsylvania Station for Atlantic City. Advertisements of Atlantic City hotels, drugstores, churches, rug merchants; fortune tellers, Bingo parlors.*

When the house-lights go down, the voice of an ANNOUNCER *is heard.*)

ANNOUNCER: The Management now brings you the News Events of the World. Atlantic City, New Jersey. (*Projection of a chrome postcard of the waterfront, trimmed in mica with the legend:* FUN AT THE BEACH).

This great convention city is playing host this week to the anniversary convocation of that great fraternal order,—the Ancient and Honorable Order of Mammals, Subdivision Humans. This great fraternal, militant and burial society is celebrating on the Boardwalk, ladies and gentlemen, its six hundred thousandth Annual Convention.

It has just elected its president for the ensuing term,—(*Projection of* MR. *and* MRS. ANTROBUS *posed as they will be shown a few moments later.*)

Mr. George Antrobus of Excelsior, New Jersey. We show you President Antrobus and his gracious and charming wife, every inch a mammal. Mr. Antrobus has had a long and chequered career. Credit has been paid to him for many useful enterprises including the introduction of the lever, of the wheel and the brewing of beer. Credit has also been extended to President Antrobus's gracious and charming wife for many practical suggestions, including the hem, the gore, and the gusset; and the novelty of the year,—frying in oil. Before we show you Mr. Antrobus accepting the nomination, we have an important announcement to make. As many of you know, this great celebration of the Order of the Mammals has received delegations from the other rival Orders,—or shall we say: esteemed concurrent Orders: the WINGS, the FINS, the SHELLS, and so on. These Orders are holding their conventions also, in various parts of the world, and have sent representatives to our own, two of a kind.

Later in the day we will show you President Antrobus broadcasting his words of greeting and congratulation to the collected assemblies of the whole natural world.

Ladies and Gentlemen! We give you President Antrobus! (*The screen becomes a Transparency.* MR. ANTROBUS *stands beside a pedestal;* MRS. ANTROBUS *is seated wearing a corsage of orchids.* ANTROBUS *wears an untidy Prince Albert; spats; from a red rosette in his buttonhole hangs a fine long purple ribbon of honor. He wears a gay lodge hat,—something between a fez and a legionnaire's cap.*)

ANTROBUS: Fellow-mammals, fellow vertebrates, fellow-humans, I thank you. Little did my dear parents think,—when they told me to stand on my own two feet,—that I'd arrive at this place.

My friends, we have come a long way.

During this week of happy celebration it is perhaps not fitting that we dwell on some of the difficult times we have been through. The dinosaur is extinct—(*Applause.*)—the ice has retreated; and the common cold is being pursued by every means within our power. (MRS. ANTROBUS *sneezes, laughs prettily, and murmurs:* "I beg your pardon.")

In our memorial service yesterday we did honor to all our friends and relatives who are no longer with us, by reason of cold, earthquakes, plagues and . . . and . . . (*Coughs.*) differences of opinion.

As our Bishop so ably said . . . uh . . . so ably said. . . .

MRS. ANTROBUS (*closed lips*): Gone, but not forgotten.

ANTROBUS: 'They are gone, but not forgotten.'

I think I can say, I think I can prophesy with complete . . . uh . . . with complete. . . .

MRS. ANTROBUS: Confidence.

ANTROBUS: Thank you, my dear,—With complete lack of confidence, that a new day of security is about to dawn.

The watchword of the closing year was: Work. I give you the watchword for the future: Enjoy Yourselves.

MRS. ANTROBUS: George, sit down!

ANTROBUS: Before I close, however, I wish to answer one of those unjust and malicious accusations that were brought against me during this last electoral campaign.

Ladies and gentlemen, the charge was made that at various points in my career I leaned toward joining some of the rival orders,—that's a lie.

As I told reporters of the *Atlantic City Herald*, I do not deny that a few months before my birth I hesitated between . . . uh . . . between pinfeathers and gill-breathing,—and so did many of us here,—but for the last million years I have been viviparous, hairy and diaphragmatic. (*Applause. Cries of 'Good old Antrobus,' 'The Prince chap!' 'Georgie,' etc.*)

ANNOUNCER: Thank you. Thank you very much, Mr. Antrobus.

Now I know that our visitors will wish to hear a word from that gracious and charming mammal, Mrs. Antrobus, wife and mother,—Mrs. Antrobus! (MRS. ANTROBUS *rises, lays her program on her chair, bows and says:*)

MRS. ANTROBUS: Dear friends, I don't really think I should say anything. After all, it was my husband who was elected and not I.

Perhaps, as president of the Women's Auxiliary Bed and Board Society,—I had some notes here, oh, yes, here they are:—I should give a short report from some of our committees that have been meeting in this beautiful city.

Perhaps it may interest you to know that it has at last been decided that the tomato is edible. Can you all hear me? The tomato *is* edible.

A delegate from across the sea reports that the

thread woven by the silkworm gives a cloth . . . I have a sample of it here . . . can you see it? smooth, elastic. I should say that it's rather attractive,—though personally I prefer less shiny surfaces. Should the windows of a sleeping apartment be open or shut? I know all mothers will follow our debates on this matter with close interest. I am sorry to say that the most expert authorities have not yet decided. It does seem to me that the night air would be bound to be unhealthy for our children, but there are many distinguished authorities on both sides. Well, I could go on talking forever,—as Shakespeare says: a woman's work is seldom done; but I think I'd better join my husband in saying thank you, and sit down. Thank you. (*She sits down.*)

ANNOUNCER: Oh, Mrs. Antrobus!

MRS. ANTROBUS: Yes?

ANNOUNCER: We understand that you are about to celebrate a wedding anniversary. I know our listeners would like to extend their felicitations and hear a few words from you on that subject.

MRS. ANTROBUS: I have been asked by this kind gentleman . . . yes, my friends, this Spring Mr. Antrobus and I will be celebrating our five thousandth wedding anniversary. .

I don't know if I speak for my husband, but I can say that, as for me, I regret every moment of it. (*Laughter of confusion.*) I beg your pardon. What I *mean* to say is that I do not regret one moment of it. I hope none of you catch my cold. We have two children. We've always had two children, though it hasn't always been the same two. But as I say, we have two fine children, and we're very grateful for that. Yes, Mr. Antrobus and I have been married five thousand years. Each wedding anniversary reminds me of the times when there were no weddings. We had to crusade for marriage. Perhaps there are some women within the sound of my voice who remember that crusade and those struggles; we fought for it, didn't we? We chained ourselves to lampposts and we made disturbances in the Senate,—anyway, at last we women got the ring.

A few men helped us, but I must say that most men blocked our way at every step: they said we were unfeminine.

I only bring up these unpleasant memories, because I see some signs of backsliding from that great victory.

Oh, my fellow mammals, keep hold of that.

My husband says that the watchword for the year is Enjoy Yourselves. I think that's very open to misunderstanding. My watchword for the year is: Save the Family. It's held together for over five thousand years: Save it! Thank you.

ANNOUNCER: Thank you, Mrs. Antrobus. (*The transparency disappears.*) We had hoped to show you the Beauty Contest that took place here today.

President Antrobus, an experienced judge of pretty girls, gave the title of Miss Atlantic City 1942, to Miss Lily-Sabina Fairweather, charming hostess of our Boardwalk Bingo Parlor.

Unfortunately, however, our time is up, and I must take you to some views of the Convention City and conveeners,—enjoying themselves.

(*A burst of music; the curtain rises.*
The Boardwalk. The audience is sitting in the ocean. A hand rail of scarlet cord stretches across the front of the stage. A ramp—also with scarlet hand rail—descends to the right corner of the orchestra pit where a great scarlet beach umbrella or a cabana stands. Front and right stage left are benches facing the sea; attached to each bench is a street-lamp.

The only scenery is two cardboard cut-outs six feet high, representing shops at the back of the stage. Reading from left to right they are: SALT WATER TAFFY: FORTUNE TELLER; *then the blank space;* BINGO PARLOR; TURKISH BATH. *They have practical doors, that of the Fortune Teller's being hung with bright gypsy curtains.*

By the left proscenium and rising from the orchestra pit is the weather signal; it is like the mast of a ship with cross bars. From time to time black discs are hung on it to indicate the storm and hurricane warnings. Three roller chairs, pushed by melancholy NEGROES *file by empty. Throughout the act they traverse the stage in both directions.*

From time to time, CONVEENERS, *dressed like* MR. ANTROBUS, *cross the stage. Some walk sedately by; others engage in inane horseplay. The old gypsy* FORTUNE TELLER *is seated at the door of her shop, smoking a corncob pipe.*

From the Bingo Parlor comes the voice of the CALLER.)

BINGO CALLER: A-Nine; A-Nine. C-Twenty-six; C-Twenty-six. A-Four; A-Four. B-Twelve.

CHORUS (*back-stage*): Bingo!!! (*The front of the Bingo Parlor shudders, rises a few feet in the air and returns to the ground trembling.*)

FORTUNE TELLER (*mechanically, to the unconscious back of a passerby, pointing with her pipe*): Bright's disease! Your partner's deceiving you in that Kansas City deal. You'll have six grandchildren. Avoid high places. (*She rises and shouts after another.*) Cirrhosis of the liver! (SABINA *appears at the door of the Bingo Parlor. She hugs about her a blue raincoat that almost conceals her red bathing suit. She tries to catch the* FORTUNE TELLER'S *attention.*)

SABINA: Sssst! Esmeralda! Sssst!

FORTUNE TELLER: Keck!

SABINA: Has President Antrobus come along yet?

FORTUNE TELLER: No, no, no. Get back there. Hide yourself.

SABINA: I'm afraid I'll miss him. Oh, Esmeralda, if I fail in this, I'll die; I know I'll die. President Antrobus!!! And I'll be his wife! If it's the last thing I'll do, I'll be Mrs. George Antrobus.—Esmeralda, tell me my future.

FORTUNE TELLER: Keck!

SABINA: All right, I'll tell *you* my future. (*Laughing dreamily and tracing it out with one finger on the palm of her hand.*) I've won the Beauty Contest in Atlantic City,—well, I'll win the Beauty Contest of the whole world. I'll take President Antrobus away from that wife of his. Then I'll take every man away from his wife. I'll turn the whole earth upside down.

FORTUNE TELLER: Keck!

SABINA: When all those husbands just think about me they'll get dizzy. They'll faint in the streets. They'll have to lean against lampposts.—Esmeralda, who was Helen of Troy?

FORTUNE TELLER (*furiously*): Shut your foolish mouth. When Mr. Antrobus comes along you can see what you can do. Until then,—go away. (SABINA *laughs. As she returns to the door of her Bingo Parlor a group of* CONVEENERS *rush over and smother her with attention.*) Oh, Miss Lily, you know me. You've known me for years.

SABINA: Go away, boys, go away. I'm after bigger fry than you are —Why, Mr. Simpson!! How *dare* you!! I expect that even you nobodies must have girls to amuse you; but where you find them and what you do with them, is of absolutely no interest to me. (*Exit. The* CONVEENERS *squeal with pleasure and stumble in after her. The* FORTUNE TELLER *rises, puts her pipe down on the stool, unfurls her voluminous skirts, gives a sharp wrench to her bodice and strolls towards the audience, swinging her hips like a young woman.*)

FORTUNE TELLER: I tell the future. Keck. Nothing easier. Everybody's future is in their face. Nothing easier.

But who can tell your past,—eh? Nobody!

Your youth,—where did it go? It slipped away while you weren't looking. While you were asleep. While you were drunk? Puh! You're like our friend, Mr. and Mrs. Antrobus; you lie awake nights trying to know your past. What did it mean? What was it trying to say to you?

Think! Think! Split your heads. I can't tell the past and neither can you. If anybody tries to tell you the past, take my word for it, they're charlatans! Charlatans! But I can tell you the future. (*She suddenly barks at a passing chair-pusher.*) Apoplexy! (*She returns to the audience.*) Nobody listens.—Keck! I see a face among you now—I won't embarrass him by pointing him out, but, listen, it may be you: Next year the watchsprings inside you will crumple up. Death by regret,—Type Y. It's in the corners of your mouth. You'll decide that you should have lived for pleasure, but that you missed it. Death by regret,—Type Y. . . . Avoid mirrors. You'll try to be angry,—but no!—no anger. (*Far forward, confidentially.*) And now what's the immediate future of our friends, the Antrobuses? Oh, you've seen it as well as I have, keck,—that dizziness of the head; that Great Man dizziness? The inventor of beer and gunpowder? The sudden fits of temper and then the long stretches of inertia? 'I'm a sultan; let my slave-girls fan me?'

You know as well as I do what's coming. Rain. Rain. Rain in floods. The deluge. But first you'll see shameful things—shameful things. Some of you will be saying: 'Let him drown. He's not worth saving. Give the whole thing up.' I can see it in your faces. But you're wrong. Keep your doubts and despairs to yourselves.

Again there'll be the narrow escape. The survival of a handful. From destruction,—(*She points sweeping with her hand to the stage.*) Even of the animals, a few will be saved: two of a kind, male and female, two of a kind. (*The heads of* CONVEENERS *appear about the stage and in the orchestra pit, jeering at her.*)

CONVEENERS: Charlatan! Madam Kill-joy! Mrs. Jeremiah! Charlatan!

FORTUNE TELLER: And *you!* Mark my words before it's too late. Where'll *you* be?

CONVEENERS: The croaking raven. Old dust and ashes. Rags, bottles, sacks.

FORTUNE TELLER: Yes, stick out your tongues. You can't stick your tongues out far enough to lick the death-sweat from your foreheads. It's too late to work now—bail out the flood with your soup spoons. You've had your chance and you've lost.

CONVEENERS: Enjoy yourselves!!! (*They disappear. The* FORTUNE TELLER *looks off left and puts her finger on her lip.*)

FORTUNE TELLER: They're coming—the Antrobuses. Keck. Your hope. Your despair. Your selves. (*Enter from the left,* MR. *and* MRS. ANTROBUS *and* GLADYS.)

MRS. ANTROBUS: Gladys Antrobus, stick your stummick in.

GLADYS: But it's easier this way.

MRS. ANTROBUS: Well, it's too bad the new president has such a clumsy daughter, that's all I can say. Try and be a lady.

FORTUNE TELLER: Aijah! That's been said a hundred billion times.

MRS. ANTROBUS: Goodness! Where's Henry? He was here just a minute ago. Henry! (*Sudden violent stir. A roller-chair appears from the left. About it are dancing in great excitement* HENRY *and a* NEGRO CHAIR-PUSHER.)

HENRY (*slingshot in hand*): I'll put your eye out. I'll make you yell, like you never yelled before.

NEGRO (*at the same time*): Now, I warns you. I warns you. If you make me mad, you'll get hurt.

ANTROBUS: Henry! What is this? Put down that slingshot.

MRS. ANTROBUS (*at the same time*): Henry! HENRY! Behave yourself.

FORTUNE TELLER: That's right, young man. There are too many people in the world as it is. Everybody's in the way, except one's self.

HENRY: All I wanted to do was—have some fun.

NEGRO: Nobody can't touch my chair, nobody, without I allow 'em to. You get clean away from me and you get away fast. (*He pushes his chair off, muttering.*)

ANTROBUS: What were you doing, Henry?

HENRY: Everybody's always getting mad. Everybody's always trying to push you around. I'll make him sorry for this; I'll make him sorry.

ANTROBUS: Give me that slingshot.

HENRY: I won't. I'm sorry I came to this place. I wish I weren't here. I wish I weren't anywhere.

MRS. ANTROBUS: Now, Henry, don't get so excited about nothing. I declare I don't know what we're going to do with you. Put your slingshot in your pocket, and don't try to take hold of things that don't belong to you.

ANTROBUS: After this you can stay home. I wash my hands of you.

MRS. ANTROBUS: Come now, let's forget all about it. Everybody take a good breath of that sea air and calm down. (*A passing* CONVEENER *bows to* ANTROBUS *who nods to him.*) Who was that you spoke to, George?

ANTROBUS: Nobody, Maggie. Just the candidate who ran against me in the election.

MRS. ANTROBUS: The man who ran against you in the election!! (*She turns and waves her umbrella after the disappearing* CONVEENER.) My husband didn't speak to you and he never will speak to you.

ANTROBUS: Now, Maggie.

MRS. ANTROBUS: After those lies you told about him in your speeches! Lies, that's what they were.

GLADYS *and* HENRY: Mama, everybody's looking at you. Everybody's laughing at you.

MRS. ANTROBUS: If you must know, my husband's a SAINT, a downright SAINT, and you're not fit to speak to him on the street.

ANTROBUS: Now, Maggie, now, Maggie, that's enough of that.

MRS. ANTROBUS: George Antrobus, you're a perfect worm. If you won't stand up for yourself, I will.

GLADYS: Mama, you just act awful in public.

MRS. ANTROBUS (*laughing*): Well, I must say I enjoyed it. I feel better. Wish his wife had been there to hear it. Children, what do you want to do?

GLADYS: Papa, can we ride in one of those chairs? Mama, I want to ride in one of those chairs.

MRS. ANTROBUS: No, sir. If you're tired you just sit where you are. We have no money to spend on foolishness.

ANTROBUS: I guess we have enough for a thing like that. It's one of the things you do at Atlantic City.

MRS. ANTROBUS: Oh, we have? I tell you it's a miracle my children have shoes to stand up in. I didn't think I'd ever live to see them pushed around in chairs.

ANTROBUS: We're on a vacation, aren't we? We have a right to some treats, I guess. Maggie, some day you're going to drive me crazy.

MRS. ANTROBUS: All right, go. I'll just sit here and laugh at you. And you can give me my dollar right in my hand. Mark my words, a rainy day is coming. There's a rainy day ahead of us. I feel it in my bones. Go on, throw your money around. I can starve. I've starved before. I know how. (*A* CONVEENER *puts his head through Turkish Bath window, and says with raised eyebrows.*)

CONVEENER: Hello, George. How are ya? I see where you brought the WHOLE family along.

MRS. ANTROBUS: And what do you mean by that? (CONVEENER *withdraws head and closes window.*)

ANTROBUS: Maggie, I tell you there's a limit to what I can stand. God's Heaven, haven't I worked *enough?* Don't I get *any* vacation? Can't I even give my children so much as a ride in a roller-chair?

MRS. ANTROBUS (*putting her hand out for rain-drops*): Anyway, it's going to rain very soon and you have your broadcast to make.

ANTROBUS: Now, Maggie, I warn you. A man can stand a family only just so long. I'm warning you. (*Enter* SABINA *from the Bingo-Parlor. She wears a flounced red silk bathing suit, 1905. Red stockings, shoes, parasol. She bows demurely to* ANTROBUS *and starts down the ramp.* ANTROBUS *and the* CHILDREN *stare at her.* ANTROBUS *bows gallantly.*)

MRS. ANTROBUS: Why, George Antrobus, how can you say such a thing! You have the best family in the world.

ANTROBUS: Good morning, Miss Fairweather. (SABINA *finally disappears behind the beach umbrella or in a cabana in the orchestra pit.*)

MRS. ANTROBUS: Who on earth was that you spoke to, George?

ANTROBUS (*complacent; mock-modest*): Hm . . . m . . . just a . . . solambaka keray.

MRS. ANTROBUS: What? I can't understand you.

GLADYS: Mama, wasn't she beautiful?

HENRY: Papa, introduce her to me.

MRS. ANTROBUS: Children, will you be quiet while I ask your father a simple question?—Who did you say it was, George?

ANTROBUS: Why-uh . . . a friend of mine. Very nice refined girl.

MRS. ANTROBUS: I'm waiting.

ANTROBUS: Maggie, that's the girl I gave the prize to in the beauty contest,—that's Miss Atlantic City 1942.

MRS. ANTROBUS: Hm! She looked like Sabina to me.

HENRY (*at the railing*): Mama, the life-guard knows her, too. Mama, he knows her well.

ANTROBUS: Henry, come here.—She's a very nice girl in every way and the sole support of her aged mother.

MRS. ANTROBUS: So was Sabina, so was Sabina; and it took a wall of ice to open your eyes about Sabina.—Henry, come over and sit down on this bench.

ANTROBUS: She's a very different matter from Sabina. Miss Fairweather is a college graduate, Phi Beta Kappa.

MRS. ANTROBUS: Henry, you sit here by mama. Gladys—

ANTROBUS (*sitting*): Reduced circumstances have required her taking a position as hostess in a Bingo Parlor; but there isn't a girl with higher principles in the country.

MRS. ANTROBUS: Well, let's not talk about it.—Henry, I haven't seen a whale yet.

ANTROBUS: She speaks seven languages and has more culture in her little finger than you've acquired in a lifetime.

MRS. ANTROBUS (*assuming amiability*): All right, all right, George. I'm glad to know there are such superior girls in the Bingo Parlors.—Henry, what's that? (*Pointing at the storm signal, which has one black disk.*)

HENRY: What is it, Papa?

ANTROBUS: What? Oh, that's the storm signal. One of those black disks means bad weather; two means storms; three means hurricane; and four means the end of the world. (*As they watch it a second black disk rolls into place.*)

MRS. ANTROBUS: Goodness! I'm going this very minute to buy you all some raincoats.

GLADYS (*putting her cheek against her father's shoulder*): Mama, don't go yet. I like sitting this way. And the ocean coming in and coming in. Papa, don't you like it?

MRS. ANTROBUS: Well, there's only one thing I lack to make me a perfectly happy woman: I'd like to see a whale.

HENRY: Mama, we saw two. Right out there. They're delegates to the convention. I'll find you one.

GLADYS: Papa, ask me something. Ask me a question.

ANTROBUS: Well . . . how big's the ocean?

GLADYS: Papa, you're teasing me. It's — three-hundred and sixty million square-miles — and — its — covers — three-fourths — of — the — earth's — surface — and — its — deepest-place — is — five — and — a — half — miles — deep — and — its — average — depth — is — twelve-thousand — feet. No, Papa, ask me something hard, real hard.

MRS. ANTROBUS (*rising*): Now I'm going off to buy those raincoats. I think that bad weather's going to get worse and worse. I hope it doesn't come before your broadcast. I should think we have about an hour or so.

HENRY: I hope it comes zzzzzz everything before it. I hope it—

MRS. ANTROBUS: Henry!—George, I think . . . maybe, it's one of those storms that are just as bad on land as on the sea. When you're just as safe and safer in a good stout boat.

HENRY: There's a boat out at the end of the pier.

MRS. ANTROBUS: Well, keep your eye on it. George, you shut your eyes and get a good rest before the broadcast.

ANTROBUS: Thundering Judas, do I have to be told when to open and shut my eyes? Go and buy your raincoats.

MRS. ANTROBUS: Now, children, you have ten minutes to walk around. Ten minutes. And, Henry: control yourself. Gladys, stick by your brother and don't get lost. (*They run off.*)

MRS. ANTROBUS: Will you be all right. George? (CONVEENERS *suddenly stick their heads out of the Bingo Parlor and Salt Water Taffy store, and voices rise from the orchestra pit.*)

CONVEENERS: George, Geo-r-r-rge! George! Leave the old hen-coop at home, George. Do-mes-ticated Georgie!

MRS. ANTROBUS (*shaking her umbrella*): Low common oafs! That's what they are. Guess a man has a right to bring his wife to a convention, if he wants to. (*She starts off.*) What's the matter with a family, I'd like to know. What else have they got to offer? (*Exit.* ANTROBUS *has closed his eyes. The* FORTUNE TELLER *comes out of her shop and goes over to the left proscenium. She leans against it watching* SABINA *quizzically.*)

FORTUNE TELLER: Heh! Here she comes!

SABINA (*loud whisper*): What's he doing?

FORTUNE TELLER: Oh, he's ready for you. Bite your lips, dear, take a long breath and come on up.

SABINA: I'm nervous. My whole future depends on this. I'm nervous.

FORTUNE TELLER: Don't be a fool. What more could you want? He's forty-five. His head's a little dizzy. He's just been elected president. He's never known any other woman than his wife. Whenever he looks at her he realizes that she knows every foolish thing he's ever done.

SABINA (*still whispering*): I don't know why it is, but every time I start one of these I'm nervous. (*The* FORTUNE TELLER *stands in the center of the stage watching the following.*)

FORTUNE TELLER: You make me tired.

SABINA: First tell me my fortune. (*The* FORTUNE TELLER *laughs drily and makes the gesture of brushing away a nonsensical question.* SABINA *coughs and says.*) Oh, Mr. Antrobus,—dare I speak to you for a moment?

ANTROBUS: What?—Oh, certainly, certainly, Miss Fairweather.

SABINA: Mr. Antrobus . . . I've been so unhappy. I've wanted . . . I've wanted to make sure that you don't think that I'm the kind of girl who goes out for beauty contests.

FORTUNE TELLER: That's the way!

ANTROBUS: Oh, I understand. I understand perfectly.

FORTUNE TELLER: Give it a little more. Lean on it.

SABINA: I knew you would. My mother said to me this morning: Lily, she said, that fine Mr. Antrobus gave you the prize because he saw at once that you weren't the kind of girl who'd go in for a thing like that. But, honestly, Mr. Antrobus, in this world, honestly, a good girl doesn't know where to turn.

FORTUNE TELLER: Now you've gone too far.

ANTROBUS: My dear Miss Fairweather!

SABINA: You wouldn't know how hard it is. With that lovely wife and daughter you have. Oh, I think Mrs. Antrobus is the finest woman I ever saw. I wish I were like her.

ANTROBUS: There, there. There's . . . uh . . . room for all kinds of people in the world, Miss Fairweather.

SABINA: How wonderful of you to say that. How generous!—Mr. Antrobus, have you a moment free? . . . I'm afraid I may be a little conspicuous here . . . could you come down, for just a moment, to my beach cabana . . . ?

ANTROBUS: Why-uh . . . yes, certainly . . . for a moment . . . just for a moment.

SABINA: There's a deck chair there. Because: you know you *do* look tired. Just this morning my mother said to me: Lily, she said, I hope Mr. Antrobus is getting a good rest. His fine strong face has deep deep lines in it. Now isn't it true, Mr. Antrobus: you work too hard?

FORTUNE TELLER: Bingo! (*She goes into her shop.*)

SABINA: Now you will just stretch out. No, I shan't say a word, not a word. I shall just sit there,—privileged. That's what I am.

ANTROBUS (*taking her hand*): Miss Fairweather . . . you'll . . . spoil me.

SABINA: Just a moment. I have something I wish to say to the audience.—Ladies and gentlemen. I'm not going to play this particular scene tonight. It's just a short scene and we're going to skip it. But I'll tell you what takes place and then we can continue the play from there on. Now in this scene—

ANTROBUS (*between his teeth*): But, Miss Somerset!

SABINA: I'm sorry. I'm sorry. But I have to skip it. In this scene, I talk to Mr. Antrobus, and at the end of it he decides to leave his wife, get a divorce at Reno and marry me. That's all.

ANTROBUS: Fitz!—Fitz!

SABINA: So that now I've told you we can jump to the end of it,—where you say: (*Enter in fury* MR. FITZPATRICK, *the stage manager.*)

MR. FITZPATRICK: Miss Somerset, we insist on

your playing this scene.

SABINA: I'm sorry, Mr. Fitzpatrick, but I can't and I won't. I've told the audience all they need to know and now we can go on. (Other ACTORS begin to appear on the stage, listening.)

MR. FITZPATRICK: And why can't you play it?

SABINA: Because there are some lines in that scene that would hurt some people's feelings and I don't think the theatre is a place where people's feelings ought to be hurt.

MR. FITZPATRICK: Miss Somerset, you can pack up your things and go home. I shall call the understudy and I shall report you to Equity.

SABINA: I sent the understudy up to the corner for a cup of coffee and if Equity tries to penalize me I'll drag the case right up to the Supreme Court. Now listen, everybody, there's no need to get excited.

MR. FITZPATRICK and ANTROBUS: Why can't you play it . . . what's the matter with the scene?

SABINA: Well, if you must know, I have a personal guest in the audience tonight. Her life hasn't been exactly a happy one. I wouldn't have my friend hear some of these lines for the whole world. I don't suppose it occurred to the author that some other women might have gone through the experience of losing their husbands like this. Wild horses wouldn't drag from me the details of my friend's life . . . well, they'd been married twenty years, and before he got rich, why, she'd done the washing and everything.

MR. FITZPATRICK: Miss Somerset, your friend will forgive you. We must play this scene.

SABINA: Nothing, nothing will make me say some of those lines . . . about 'a man outgrows a wife every seven years' and . . . and that one about 'the Mohammedans being the only people who looked the subject square in the face.' Nothing.

MR. FITZPATRICK: Miss Somerset! Go to your dressing room. I'll read your lines.

SABINA: Now everybody's nerves are on edge.

MR. ANTROBUS: Skip the scene. (MR. FITZPATRICK and the other ACTORS go off.)

SABINA: Thank you. I knew you'd understand. We'll do just what I said. So Mr. Antrobus is going to divorce his wife and marry me. Mr. Antrobus, you say: 'It won't be easy to lay all this before my wife.' (The ACTORS withdraw. ANTROBUS walks about, his hand to his forehead, muttering.)

ANTROBUS: Wait a minute. I can't get back into it as easily as all that. 'My wife is a very obstinate woman.' Hm . . . then you say . . . hm

. . . Miss Fairweather, I mean Lily, it won't be easy to lay all this before my wife. It'll hurt her feelings a little.

SABINA: Listen, George: other people haven't got feelings. Not in the same way that we have, —we who are presidents like you and prizewinners like me. Listen, other people haven't got feelings; they just imagine they have. Within two weeks they go back to playing bridge and going to the movies.

Listen, dear: everybody in the world except a few people like you and me are just people of straw. Most people have no insides at all. Now that you're president you'll see that. Listen, darling, there's a kind of secret society at the top of the world,—like you and me,—that know this. The world was made for us. What's life anyway? Except for two things, pleasure and power, what is life? Boredom! Foolishness. You know it is. Except for those two things, life's nau-se-at-ing. So,—come here! (she moves close. They kiss.) So.

Now when your wife comes, it's really very simple; just tell her.

ANTROBUS: Lily, Lily, you're a wonderful woman.

SABINA: Of course I am. (They enter the cabana and it hides them from view. Distant roll of thunder. A third black disk appears on the weather signal. Distant thunder is heard. MRS. ANTROBUS appears carrying parcels. She looks about, seats herself on the bench left, and fans herself with her handkerchief. Enter GLADYS right, followed by two CONVEENERS. She is wearing red stockings.)

MRS. ANTROBUS: Gladys!

GLADYS: Mama, here I am.

MRS. ANTROBUS: Gladys Antrobus!!! Where did you get those dreadful things?

GLADYS: Wh-a-t? Papa liked the color.

MRS. ANTROBUS: You go back to the hotel this minute!

GLADYS: I won't. I won't. Papa liked the color.

MRS. ANTROBUS: All right. All right. You stay here. I've a good mind to let your father see you that way. You stay right here.

GLADYS: I . . . I don't want to stay . . . if you don't think he'd like it.

MRS. ANTROBUS: Oh . . . it's all one to me. I don't care what happens. I don't care if the biggest storm in the whole world comes. Let it come. (She folds her hands.) Where's your brother?

GLADYS (in a small voice.): He'll be here.

MRS. ANTROBUS: Will he? Well, let him get into trouble. I don't care. I don't know where your father is, I'm sure. (*Laughter from the cabana.*)

GLADYS (*leaning over the rail*): I think he's . . . Mama, he's talking to the lady in the red dress.

MRS. ANTROBUS: Is that so? (*Pause.*) We'll wait till he's through. Sit down here beside me and stop fidgeting . . . what are you crying about? (*Distant thunder. She covers* GLADY's *stockings with a raincoat.*)

GLADYS: You don't like my stockings. (*Two* CONVEENERS *rush in with a microphone on a standard and various paraphernalia. The* FORTUNE TELLER *appears at the door of her shop. Other characters gradually gather.*)

BROADCAST OFFICIAL: Mrs. Antrobus! Thank God we've found you at last. Where's Mr. Antrobus? We've been hunting everywhere for him. It's about time for the broadcast to the conventions of the world.

MRS. ANTROBUS (*calm*): I expect he'll be here in a minute.

BROADCAST OFFICIAL: Mrs. Antrobus, if he doesn't show up in time, I hope you will consent to broadcast in his place. It's the most important broadcast of the year. (SABINA *enters from the cabana followed by* ANTROBUS.)

MRS. ANTROBUS: No, I shan't. I haven't one single thing to say.

BROADCAST OFFICIAL: Then won't you help us find him, Mrs. Antrobus? A storm's coming up. A hurricane. A deluge!

SECOND CONVEENER (*who has sighted* ANTROBUS *over the rail*): Joe! Joe! Here he is.

BROADCAST OFFICIAL: In the name of God, Mr. Antrobus, you're on the air in five minutes. Will you kindly please come and test the instrument? That's all we ask. If you just please begin the alphabet slowly. (ANTROBUS, *with set face, comes ponderously up the ramp. He stops at the point where his waist is level with the stage and speaks authoritatively to the* OFFICIALS.)

ANTROBUS: I'll be ready when the time comes. Until then, move away. Go away. I have something I wish to say to my wife.

BROADCAST OFFICIAL (*whimpering*): Mr. Antrobus! This is the most important broadcast of the year. (*The* OFFICIALS *withdraw to the edge of the stage.* SABINA *glides up the ramp behind* ANTROBUS.)

SABINA (*whispering*): Don't let her argue. Remember arguments have nothing to do with it.

ANTROBUS: Maggie, I'm moving out of the hotel. In fact, I'm moving out of everything. For good. I'm going to marry Miss Fairweather. I shall provide generously for you and the children. In a few years you'll be able to see that it's all for the best. That's all I have to say.

BROADCAST OFFICIAL: Mr. Antrobus! I hope you'll be ready. This is the most important broadcast of the year.

GLADYS: What did Papa say, Mama? I didn't hear what Papa said.

BROADCAST OFFICIAL: Mr. Antrobus. All we want to do is test your voice with the alphabet.

ANTROBUS: Go away. Clear out.

MRS. ANTROBUS (*composedly with lowered eyes*): George, I can't talk to you until you wipe those silly red marks off your face.

ANTROBUS: I think there's nothing to talk about. I've said what I have to say.

SABINA: Splendid!!

ANTROBUS: You're a fine woman, Maggie, but . . . but a man has his own life to lead in the world.

MRS. ANTROBUS: Well, after living with you for five thousand years I guess I have a right to a word or two, haven't I?

ANTROBUS (*to* SABINA): What can I answer to that?

SABINA: Tell her that conversation would only hurt her feelings. It's-kinder-in-the-long-run-to-do-it-short-and-quick.

ANTROBUS: I want to spare your feelings in every way I can, Maggie.

BROADCAST OFFICIAL: Mr. Antrobus, the hurricane signal's gone up. We could begin right now.

MRS. ANTROBUS (*calmly, almost dreamily*): I didn't marry you because you were perfect. I didn't even marry you because I loved you. I married you because you gave me a promise. (*She takes off her ring and looks at it.*) That promise made up for your faults. And the promise I gave you made up for mine. Two imperfect people got married and it was the promise that made the marriage.

ANTROBUS: Maggie, . . . I was only nineteen.

MRS. ANTROBUS (*she puts her ring back on her finger*): And when our children were growing up, it wasn't a house that protected them; and it wasn't our love, that protected them—it was that promise.

And when that promise is broken—this can

BINGO ANNOUNCER: A—nine; A—nine. D—forty-two; D—forty-two. C—thirty; C—thirty. B—seventeen; B—seventeen. C—forty; C—forty.

CHORUS: Bingo!!

happen! (*With a sweep of the hand she removes the raincoat from* GLADYS' *stockings.*)

ANTROBUS (*stretches out his arm, apoplectic*): Gladys!! Have you gone crazy? Has everyone gone crazy? (*Turning on* SABINA.) You did this. You gave them to her.

SABINA: I never said a word to her.

ANTROBUS (*to* GLADYS): You go back to the hotel and take those horrible things off.

GLADYS (*pert*): Before I go, I've got something to tell you,—it's about Henry.

MRS. ANTROBUS (*claps her hands peremptorily*): Stop your noise,—I'm taking her back to the hotel. George. Before I go I have a letter. . . . I have a message to throw into the ocean. (*Fumbling in her handbag.*) Where is the plagued thing? Here it is. (*She flings something—invisible to us—far over the heads of the audience to the back of the auditorium.*) It's a bottle. And in the bottle's a letter. And in the letter is written all the things that a woman knows.

It's never been told to any man and it's never been told to any woman, and if it finds its destination, a new time will come. We're not what books and plays say we are. We're not what advertisements say we are. We're not in the movies and we're not on the radio.

We're not what you're all told and what you think we are: We're ourselves. And if any man can find one of us he'll learn why the whole universe was set in motion. And if any man harm any one of us, his soul—the only soul he's got—had better be at the bottom of that ocean,—and that's the only way to put it. Gladys, come here. We're going back to the hotel. (*She drags* GLADYS *firmly off by the hand, but* GLADYS *breaks away and comes down to speak to her father.*)

SABINA: Such goings-on. Don't give it a minute's thought.

GLADYS: Anyway, I think you ought to know that Henry hit a man with a stone. He hit one of those colored men that push the chairs and the man's very sick. Henry ran away and hid and some policemen are looking for him very hard. And I don't care a bit if you don't want to have anything to do with mama and me, because I'll never like you again and I hope nobody ever likes you again,—so there! (*She runs off.* ANTROBUS *starts after her.*)

ANTROBUS: I . . . I have to go and see what I can do about this.

SABINA: You stay right here. Don't go now while you're excited. Gracious sakes, all these things will be forgotten in a hundred years. Come, now, you're on the air. Just say anything,

—it doesn't matter what. Just a lot of birds and fishes and things.

BROADCAST OFFICIAL: Thank you, Miss Fairweather. Thank you very much. Ready, Mr. Antrobus.

ANTROBUS (*touching the microphone*): What is it, what is it? Who am I talking to?

BROADCAST OFFICIAL: Why, Mr. Antrobus! To our order and to all the other orders.

ANTROBUS (*raising his head*): What are all those birds doing?

BROADCAST OFFICIAL: Those are just a few of the birds. Those are the delegates to our convention,—two of a kind.

ANTROBUS (*pointing into the audience*): Look at the water. Look at them all. Those fishes jumping. The children should see this!—There's Maggie's whales!! Here are your whales, Maggie!!

BROADCAST OFFICIAL: I hope you're ready, Mr. Antrobus.

ANTROBUS: And look on the beach! You didn't tell me these would be here!

SABINA: Yes, George. Those are the animals.

BROADCAST OFFICIAL (*busy with the apparatus*): Yes, Mr. Antrobus, those are the vertebrates. We hope the lion will have a word to say when you're through. Step right up, Mr. Antrobus, we're ready. We'll just have time before the storm. (*Pause. In a hoarse whisper.*) They're wait-ing. (*It has grown dark. Soon after he speaks a high whistling noise begins. Strange veering lights start whirling about the stage. The other characters disappear from the stage.*)

ANTROBUS: Friends. Cousins. Four score and ten billion years ago our forefather brought forth upon this planet the spark of life,—(*He is drowned out by thunder. When the thunder stops the* FORTUNE TELLER *is seen standing beside him.*)

FORTUNE TELLER: Antrobus, there's not a minute to be lost. Don't you see the four disks on the weather signal? Take your family into that boat at the end of the pier.

ANTROBUS: My family? I have no family. Maggie! Maggie! They won't come.

FORTUNE TELLER: They'll come.—Antrobus! Take these animals into that boat with you. All of them,—two of each kind.

SABINA: George, what's the matter with you? This is just a storm like any other storm.

ANTROBUS: Maggie!

SABINA: Stay with me, we'll go . . . (*Losing conviction.*) This is just another thunderstorm,—isn't it? Isn't it?

ANTROBUS: Maggie!!! (MRS. ANTROBUS *appears*

beside him with GLADYS.)

MRS. ANTROBUS (*matter-of-fact*): Here I am and here's Gladys.

ANTROBUS: Where've you been? Where have you been? Quick, we're going into that boat out there.

MRS. ANTROBUS: I know we are. But I haven't found Henry. (*She wanders off into the darkness calling "Henry!"*)

SABINA (*low urgent babbling, only occasionally raising her voice*): I don't believe it. I don't believe it's anything at all. I've seen hundreds of storms like this.

FORTUNE TELLER: There's no time to lose. Go. Push the animals along before you. Start a new world. Begin again.

SABINA: Esmeralda! George! Tell me,—is it really serious?

ANTROBUS (*suddenly very busy*): Elephants first. Gently, gently.—Look where you're going.

GLADYS (*leaning over the ramp and striking an animal on the back*): Stop it or you'll be left behind!

ANTROBUS: Is the Kangaroo there? *There* you are! Take those turtles in your pouch, will you? (*To some other animals, pointing to his shoulder.*) Here! You jump up here. You'll be trampled on.)

GLADYS (*to her father, pointing below*): Papa, look,—the snakes!

MRS. ANTROBUS: I can't find Henry. Hen-ry!

ANTROBUS: Go along. Go along. Climb on their backs.—Wolves! Jackals,—whatever you are,—tend to your own business!

GLADYS (*pointing, tenderly*): Papa,—look.

SABINA: Mr. Antrobus—take me with you. Don't leave me here. I'll work. I'll help. I'll do anything. (THREE CONVEENERS *cross the stage, marching with a banner.*)

CONVEENERS: George! What are you scared of?—George! Fellas, it looks like rain.— 'Maggie, where's my umbrella?'—George, setting up for Barnum and Bailey.

ANTROBUS (*again catching his wife's hand*): Come on now, Maggie—the pier's going to break any minute.

MRS. ANTROBUS: I'm not going a step without Henry. Henry!

GLADYS (*on the ramp*): Mama! Papa! Hurry. The pier's cracking, Mama. It's going to break.

MRS. ANTROBUS: Henry! Cain! CAIN! (HENRY *dashes into the stage and joins his mother.*)

HENRY: Here I am, Mama.

MRS. ANTROBUS: Thank God!—now come quick.

HENRY: I didn't think you wanted me.

MRS. ANTROBUS: Quick! (*She pushes him down before her into the aisle.*)

SABINA (*all the* ANTROBUSES *are now in the theatre aisle.* SABINA *stands at the top of the ramp*): Mrs. Antrobus, take me. Don't you remember me? I'll work. I'll help. Don't leave me here!'

MRS. ANTROBUS (*impatiently, but as though it were of no importance*): Yes, yes. There's a lot of work to be done. Only hurry.

FORTUNE TELLER (*now dominating the stage. To* SABINA *with a grim smile*): Yes, go—back to the kitchen with you.

SABINA (*half-down the ramp. To* FORTUNE TELLER): I don't know why my life's always being interrupted—just when everything's going fine!! (*She dashes up the aisle. Now the* CONVEENERS *emerge doing a serpentine dance on the stage. They jeer at the* FORTUNE TELLER.)

CONVEENERS: Get a canoe—there's not a minute to be lost! Tell me my future. Mrs. Croaker.

FORTUNE TELLER: Paddle in the water, boys— enjoy yourselves.

VOICE *from the* BINGO PARLOR: A-nine; A-nine. C-Twenty-four. C-Twenty-four.

CONVEENERS: Rags, bottles, and sacks.

FORTUNE TELLER: Go back and climb on your roofs. Put rags in the cracks under your doors. —Nothing will keep out the flood. You've had your chance. You've had your day. You've failed. You've lost.

VOICE *from the* BINGO PARLOR: B-fifteen. B-Fifteen.

FORTUNE TELLER (*shading her eyes and looking out to sea*): They're safe. George Antrobus! Think it over! A new world to make.—think it over!

ACT III

(*Just before the curtain rises, two sounds are heard from the stage: a cracked bugle call.*

The curtain rises on almost total darkness. Almost all the flats composing the walls of MR. ANTROBUS's *house, as of Act I, are up, but they lean helter-skelter against one another, leaving irregular gaps. Among the flats missing are two in the back wall, leaving the frames of the window and door crazily out of line. Off stage, back right, some red Roman fire is burning. The bugle call is repeated. Enter* SABINA *through the tilted door. She is dressed as a Napoleonic camp follower, "la fille du regiment," in begrimed reds and blues.*)

SABINA: Mrs. Antrobus! Gladys! Where are you?

The war's over. The war's over. You can come out. The peace treaty's been signed.

Where are they?—Hmpf! Are they dead, too? Mrs. Annnn-trobus! Glaaaadus! Mr. Antrobus'll be here this afternoon. I just saw him downtown. Huuuurry and put things in order. He says that now that the war's over we'll all have to settle down and be perfect. (*Enter* MR. FITZPATRICK, *the stage manager, followed by the whole company, who stand waiting at the edges of the stage.* MR. FITZPATRICK *tries to interrupt* SABINA.)

MR. FITZPATRICK: Miss Somerset, we have to stop a moment.

SABINA: They may be hiding out in the back—

MR. FITZPATRICK: Miss Somerset! We have to stop a moment.

SABINA: What's the matter?

MR. FITZPATRICK: There's an explanation we have to make to the audience.—Lights, please. (*To the actor who plays* MR. ANTROBUS,) Will you explain the matter to the audience? (*The lights go up. We now see that a balcony or elevated runway has been erected at the back of the stage, back of the wall of the Antrobus house. From its extreme right and left ends ladder-like steps descend to the floor of the stage.*)

ANTROBUS: Ladies and gentlemen, an unfortunate accident has taken place back stage. Perhaps I should say *another* unfortunate accident.

SABINA: I'm sorry. I'm sorry.

ANTROBUS: The management feels, in fact, we all feel that you are due an apology. And now we have to ask your indulgence for the most serious mishap of all. Seven of our actors have . . . have been taken ill. Apparently, it was something they ate. I'm not exactly clear what happened. (*All the* ACTORS *start to talk at once.* ANTROBUS *raises his hand.*) Now, now—not all at once. Fitz, do you know what it was?

MR. FITZPATRICK: Why, it's perfectly clear. These seven actors had dinner together, and they ate something that disagreed with them.

SABINA: Disagreed with them!!! They have ptomaine poisoning. They're in Bellevue Hospital this very minute in agony. They're having their stomachs pumped out this very minute, in perfect agony.

ANTROBUS: Fortunately, we've just heard they'll all recover.

SABINA: It'll be a miracle if they do, a downright miracle. It was the lemon meringue pie.

ACTORS: It was the fish . . . it was the canned tomatoes . . . it was the fish.

SABINA: It was the lemon meringue pie. I saw it with my own eyes; it had blue mould all over the bottom of it.

ANTROBUS: Whatever it was, they're in no condition to take part in this performance. Naturally, we haven't enough understudies to fill all those roles; but we do have a number of splendid volunteers who have kindly consented to help us out. These friends have watched our rehearsals, and they assure me that they know the lines and the business very well. Let me introduce them to you—my dresser, Mr. Tremayne,—himself a distinguished Shakespearean actor for many years; our wardrobe mistress, Hester; Miss Somerset's maid, Ivy; and Fred Bailey, captain of the ushers in this theatre. (*These persons bow modestly.* IVY *and* HESTER *are colored girls.*) Now this scene takes place near the end of the act. And I'm sorry to say we'll need a short rehearsal, just a short run-through. And as some of it takes place in the auditorium, we'll have to keep the curtain up. Those of you who wish can go out in the lobby and smoke some more. The rest of you can listen to us, or . . . or just talk quietly among yourselves, as you choose. Thank you. Now will you take it over, Mr. Fitzpatrick?

MR. FITZPATRICK: Thank you.—Now for those of you who are listening perhaps I should explain that at the end of this act, the men have come back from the War and the family's settled down in the house. And the author wants to show the hours of the night passing by over their heads, and the planets crossing the sky . . . uh . . . over their heads. And he says—this is hard to explain —that each of the hours of the night is a philosopher, or a great thinker. Eleven o'clock, for instance, is Aristotle. And nine o'clock is Spinoza. Like that. I don't suppose it means anything. It's just a kind of poetic effect.

SABINA: Not mean anything! Why, it certainly does. Twelve o'clock goes by saying those wonderful things. I think it means that when people are asleep they have all those lovely thoughts, much better than when they're awake.

IVY: Excuse me, I think it means,—excuse me, Mr. Fitzpatrick—

SABINA: What were you going to say, Ivy?

IVY: Mr. Fitzpatrick, you let my father come to a rehearsal; and my father's a Baptist minister, and he said that the author meant that—just like the hours and stars go by over our heads at night, in the same way the ideas and thoughts of the great men are in the air around us all the time and they're working on us, even when we don't know it.

MR. FITZPATRICK: Well, well, maybe that's it. Thank you, Ivy. Anyway,—the hours of the night are philosophers. My friends, are you ready? Ivy, can you be eleven o'clock? 'This good estate of the mind possessing its object in energy we call divine.' Aristotle.

IVY: Yes, sir. I know that and I know twelve o'clock and I know nine o'clock.

MR. FITZPATRICK: Twelve o'clock? Mr. Tremayne, the Bible.

TREMAYNE: Yes.

MR. FITZPATRICK: Ten o'clock? Hester — Plato? (she nods eagerly.) Nine o'clock, Spinoza, —Fred?

BAILEY: Yes, sir. (FRED BAILEY picks up a great gilded cardboard numeral IX and starts up the steps to the platform. MR. FITZPATRICK strikes his forehead.)

MR. FITZPATRICK: The planets!! We forgot all about the planets.

SABINA: O my God! The planets! Are they sick too? (ACTORS nod.)

MR. FITZPATRICK: Ladies and gentlemen, the planets are singers. Of course, we can't replace them, so you'll have to imagine them singing in this scene. Saturn sings from the orchestra pit down here. The Moon is way up there. And Mars with a red lantern in his hand, stands in the aisle over there—Tz-tz-tz. It's too bad; it all makes a very fine effect. However! Ready—nine o'clock: Spinoza.

BAILEY (walking slowly across the balcony, left to right): 'After experience had taught me that the common occurrences of daily life are vain and futile—'

FITZPATRICK: Louder, Fred. 'And I saw that all the objects of my desire and fear—'

BAILEY: 'And I saw that all the objects of my desire and fear were in themselves nothing good nor bad save insofar as the mind was affeccted by them—'

FITZPATRICK: Do you know the rest? All right. Ten o'clock. Hester. Plato.

HESTER: 'Then tell me, O Critias, how will a man choose the ruler that shall rule over him? Will he not—'

FITZPATRICK: Thank you. Skip to the end, Hester.

HESTER: '. . . can be multiplied a thousand fold in its effects among the citizens.'

FITZPATRICK: Thank you.—Aristotle, Ivy?

IVY: This good estate of the mind possessing its objects in energy we call divine. This we mortals have occasionally and it is this energy which is pleasantest and best. But God has it always. It is wonderful in us; but in Him how much more wonderful.'

FITZPATRICK: Midnight. Midnight, Mr. Tremayne. That's right,—you've done it before.— All right, everybody. You know what you have to do.—Lower the curtain. House lights up. Act Three of THE SKIN OF OUR TEETH. (As the curtain descends he is heard saying.) You volunteers, just wear what you have on. Don't try to put on the costumes today. (House lights go down. The Act begins again. The Bugle call. Curtain rises. Enter SABINA.)

SABINA: Mrs. Antrobus! Gladys! Where are you? The war's over.—You've heard all this— (She gabbles the main points.) Where—are—they? Are—they—dead, too, et cetera. I—just—saw —Mr.—Antrobus—down town, et cetera. (Slowing up.) He says that now that the war's over we'll all have to settle down and be perfect. They may be hiding out in the back somewhere. Mrs. An-tro-bus. (She wanders off. It has grown lighter. A trapdoor is cautiously raised and MRS. ANTROBUS emerges waist-high and listens. She is disheveled and worn; she wears a tattered dress and a shawl half covers her head. She talks down through the trapdoor.)

MRS. ANTROBUS: It's getting light. There's still something burning over there—Newark, or Jersey City. What? Yes, I could swear I heard someone moving about up here. But I can't see anybody. I say: I can't see anybody. (She starts to move about the stage. GLADYS' head appears at the trapdoor. She is holding a BABY.)

GLADYS: Oh, Mama. Be careful.

MRS. ANTROBUS: Now, Gladys, you stay out of sight.

GLADYS: Well, let me stay here just a minute. I want the baby to get some of this fresh air.

MRS. ANTROBUS: All right, but keep your eyes open. I'll see what I can find. I'll have a good hot plate of soup for you before you can say Jack Robinson. Gladys Antrobus! Do you know what I think I see? There's old Mr. Hawkins sweeping the sidewalk in front of his A. and P. store. Sweeping it with a broom. Why, he must have gone crazy, like the others! I see some other people moving about, too.

GLADYS: Mama, come back, come back. (MRS. ANTROBUS returns to the trapdoor and listens.)

MRS. ANTROBUS: Gladys, there's something in the air. Everybody's movement's sort of different. I see some women walking right out in the middle of the street.

SABINA'S VOICE: Mrs. An-tro-bus!

MRS. ANTROBUS and GLADYS: What's that?!!

SABINA'S VOICE: Glaaaadys! Mrs. An-tro-bus! (Enter SABINA.)

MRS. ANTROBUS: Gladys, that's Sabina's voice as sure as I live.—Sabina! Sabina!—Are you a-live?!!

SABINA: Of course, I'm alive. How've you girls been?—Don't try and kiss me. I never want to kiss another human being as long as I live. Sh'sh, there's nothing to get emotional about. Pull yourself together, the war's over. Take a deep breath,—the war's over.

MRS. ANTROBUS: The war's over!! I don't believe you. I don't believe you. I can't believe you.

GLADYS: Mama!

SABINA: Who's that?

MRS. ANTROBUS: That's Gladys and her baby. I don't believe you. Gladys, Sabina says the war's over. Oh, Sabina.

SABINA (leaning over the BABY): Goodness! Are there any babies left in the world! Can it see? And can it cry and everything?

GLADYS: Yes, he can. He notices everything very well.

SABINA: Where on earth did you get it? Oh, I won't ask.—Lord, I've lived all these seven years around camp and I've forgotten how to behave. — Now we've got to think about the men coming home.—Mrs. Antrobus, go and wash your face, I'm ashamed of you. Put your best clothes on. Mr. Antrobus'll be here this afternoon. I just saw him downtown.

MRS. ANTROBUS and GLADYS: He's alive!! He'll be here!! Sabina, you're not joking?

MRS. ANTROBUS: And Henry?

SABINA (dryly): Yes, Henry's alive, too, that's what they say. Now don't stop to talk. Get yourselves fixed up. Gladys, you look terrible. Have you any decent clothes? (SABINA has pushed them toward the trapdoor.)

MRS. ANTROBUS (half down): Yes, I've something to wear just for this very day. But, Sabina, — who won the war?

SABINA: Don't stop now,—just wash your face. (A whistle sounds in the distance.) Oh, my God, what's that silly little noise?

MRS. ANTROBUS: Why, it sounds like . . . it sounds like what used to be the noon whistle at the shoe-polish factory. (Exit.)

SABINA: That's what it is. Seems to me like peacetime's coming along pretty fast—shoe polish!

GLADYS (half down): Sabina, how soon after peacetime begins does the milkman start coming to the door?

SABINA: As soon as he catches a cow. Give him time to catch a cow, dear. (Exit GLADYS. SABINA walks about a moment, thinking.) Shoe polish! My, I'd forgotten what peacetime was like. (She shakes her head, then sits down by the trapdoor and starts talking down the hole.) Mrs. Antrobus, guess what I saw Mr. Antrobus doing this morning at dawn. He was tacking up a piece of paper on the door of the Town Hall. You'll die when you hear: it was a recipe for grass soup, for a grass soup that doesn't give you the diarrhea. Mr. Antrobus is still thinking up new things.—He told me to give you his love. He's got all sorts of ideas for peacetime, he says. No more laziness and idiocy, he says. And oh, yes! Where are his books? What? Well, pass them up. The first thing he wants to see are his books. He says if you've burnt those books, or if the rats have eaten them, he says it isn't worthwhile starting over again. Everybody's going to be beautiful, he says, and diligent, and very intelligent. (A hand reaches up with two volumes.) What language is that? Pu-u-gh,—mold! And he's got such plans for you, Mrs. Antrobus. You're going to study history and algebra—and so are Gladys and I— and philosophy. You should hear him talk. (Taking two more volumes.) Well, these are in English, anyway.—To hear him talk, seems like he expects you to be a combination, Mrs. Antrobus, of a saint and a college professor, and a dancehall hostess, if you know what I mean. (Two more volumes.) Ugh. German! (She is lying on the floor; one elbow bent, her cheek on her hand, meditatively.) Yes, peace will be here before we know it. In a week or two we'll be asking the Perkinses in for a quiet evening of bridge. We'll turn on the radio and hear how to be big successes with a new toothpaste. We'll trot down to the movies and see how girls with wax faces live—all that will begin again. Oh, Mrs. Antrobus, God forgive me but I enjoyed the war. Everybody's at their best in wartime. I'm sorry it's over. And, oh, I forgot! Mr. Antrobus sent you another message—can you hear me?—(Enter HENRY, blackened and sullen. He is wearing torn overalls, but has one gaudy admiral's epaulette hanging by a thread from his right shoulder, and there are vestiges of gold and scarlet braid running down his left trouser leg. He stands listening.) Listen! Henry's never to put foot in this house again, he says. He'll kill Henry on sight, if he sees him.

You don't know about Henry??? Well, where have you been? What? Well, Henry rose right to the top. Top of *what?* Listen, I'm telling you. Henry rose from corporal to captain, to major, to general.—I don't know how to say it, but the enemy is *Henry; Henry is* the enemy. Everybody knows that.

HENRY: He'll kill me, will he?

SABINA: Who are *you?* I'm not afraid of you. The war's over.

HENRY: I'll kill him so fast. I've spent seven years trying to find him; the others I killed were just substitutes.

SABINA: Goodness! It's Henry!—(*He makes an angry gesture.*) Oh, I'm not afraid of you. The war's over, Henry Antrobus, and you're not any more important than any other unemployed. You go away and hide yourself, until we calm your father down.

HENRY: The first thing to do is to burn up those old books; it's the ideas he gets out of those old books that . . . that makes the whole world so you can't live in it. (*He reels forward and starts kicking the books about, but suddenly falls down in a sitting position.*)

SABINA: You leave those books alone!! Mr. Antrobus is looking forward to them a-special. —Gracious sakes, Henry, you're so tired you can't stand up. Your mother and sister'll be here in a minute and we'll think what to do about you.

HENRY: What did they ever care about me?

SABINA: There's that old whine again. All you people think you're not loved enough, no-body loves you. Well, you start being lovable and we'll love you.

HENRY (*outraged*): I don't want anybody to love me.

SABINA: Then stop talking about it all the time.

HENRY: I *never* talk about it. The last thing I want is anybody to pay any attention to me.

SABINA: I can hear it behind every word you say.

HENRY: I want everybody to hate me.

SABINA: Yes, you've decided that's second best, but it's still the same thing.—Mrs. Antrobus! Henry's here. He's so tired he can't stand up (MRS. ANTROBUS *and* GLADYS, *with her* BABY, *emerge. They are dressed as in Act I.* MRS. ANTROBUS *carries some objects in her apron, and* GLADYS *has a blanket over her shoulder.*)

MRS. ANTROBUS *and* GLADYS: Henry! Henry! Henry!

HENRY (*glaring at them*): Have you anything to eat?

MRS. ANTROBUS: Yes, I have, Henry. I've been saving it for this very day,—two good baked potatoes. no! Henry! one of them's for your father. Henry!! Give me that other potato back this minute. (SABINA *sidles up behind him and snatches the other potato away.*)

SABINA: He's so dog-tired he doesn't know what he's doing.

MRS. ANTROBUS: Now you just rest there, Henry, until I can get your room ready. Eat that potato good and slow, so you can get all the nourishment out of it.

HENRY: You all might as well know right now that I haven't come back here to live.

MRS. ANTROBUS: Sh. . . . I'll put this coat over you. Your room's hardly damaged at all. Your football trophies are a little tarnished, but Sabina and I will polish them up tomorrow.

HENRY: Did you hear me? I don't live here. I don't belong to anybody.

MRS. ANTROBUS: Why, how can you say a thing like that! You certainly do belong right here. Where else would you want to go? Your forehead's feverish, Henry, seems to me. You'd better give me that gun, Henry. You won't need that any more.

GLADYS (*whispering*): Look, he's fallen asleep already, with his potato half-chewed.

SABINA: Puh! The terror of the world.

MRS. ANTROBUS: Sabina, you mind your own business, and start putting the room to rights. (HENRY *has turned his face to the back of the sofa.* MRS. ANTROBUS *gingerly puts the revolver in her apron pocket, then helps* SABINA. SABINA *has found a rope hanging from the ceiling. Grunting, she hangs all her weight on it, and as she pulls the walls begin to move into their right places.* MRS. ANTROBUS *brings the over-turned tables, chairs and hassock into the positions of Act I.*)

SABINA: That's all we do—always beginning again! Over and over again. Always beginning again. (*She pulls on the rope and a part of the wall moves into place. She stops. Meditatively.*) How do we know that it'll be any better than before? Why do we go on pretending? Some day the whole earth's going to have to turn cold anyway, and until that time all these other things'll be happening again: it will be more wars and more walls of ice and floods and earthquakes.

MRS. ANTROBUS: Sabina!! Stop arguing and go on with your work.

SABINA: All right. I'll go on just out of *habit,* but I won't believe in it.

MRS. ANTROBUS (*aroused*): Now, Sabina. I've let you talk long enough. I don't want to hear any more of it. Do I have to explain to you what everybody knows,—everybody who keeps a home going? Do I have to say to you what nobody should ever *have* to say, because they can read it in each other's eyes?

Now listen to me: (MRS. ANTROBUS *takes hold of the rope.*)

I could live for seventy years in a cellar and make soup out of grass and bark, without ever doubting that this world has a work to do and will do it.

Do you hear me?

SABINA (*frightened*): Yes, Mrs. Antrobus.

MRS. ANTROBUS: Sabina, do you see this house,—216 Cedar Street,—do you see it?

SABINA: Yes, Mrs. Antrobus.

MRS. ANTROBUS: Well, just to have known this house is to have seen the idea of what we can do someday if we keep our wits about us. Too many people have suffered and died for my children for us to start reneging now. So we'll start putting this house to rights. Now, Sabina, go and see what you can do in the kitchen.

SABINA: Kitchen! Why is it that however far I go away, I always find myself back in the kitchen? (*Exit.*)

MRS. ANTROBUS (*still thinking over her last speech, relaxes and says with a reminiscent smile*): Goodness gracious, wouldn't you know that my father was a parson? It was just like I heard his own voice speaking and he's been dead five thousand years. There! I've gone and almost waked Henry up.

HENRY (*talking in his sleep, indistinctly*): Fellows . . . what have they done for us? . . . Blocked our way at every step. Kept everything in their own hands. And you've stood it. When are you going to wake up?

MRS. ANTROBUS: Sh, Henry. Go to sleep. Go to sleep.—Well, that looks better. Now let's go and help Sabina.

GLADYS: Mama, I'm going out into the backyard and hold the baby right up in the air. And show him that we don't have to be afraid any more. (*Exit GLADYS to the kitchen. MRS. ANTROBUS glances at HENRY, exits into kitchen. HENRY thrashes about in his sleep. Enter ANTROBUS, his arms full of bundles, chewing the end of a carrot. He has a slight limp. Over the suit of Act I he is wearing an overcoat too long for him, its skirts trailing on the ground. He lets his bundles fall and stands looking about. Presently his attention is fixed on HENRY, whose words grow clearer.*)

HENRY: All right! What have you got to lose? What have they done for us? That's right—nothing. Tear everything down. I don't care what you smash. We'll begin again and we'll

show 'em. (ANTROBUS *takes out his revolver and holds it pointing downwards. With his back towards the audience he moves toward the footlights.* HENRY's *voice grows louder and he wakes with a start. They stare at one another. Then* HENRY *sits up quickly. Throughout the following scene* HENRY *is played, not as a misunderstood or misguided young man, but as a representation of strong unreconciled evil.*) All right! Do something. (*Pause.*) Don't think I'm afraid of you, either. All right, do what you were going to do. Do it. (*Furiously.*) Shoot me, I tell you. You don't have to think I'm any relation of yours. I haven't got any father or any mother, or brothers or sisters. And I don't want any. And what's more I haven't got anybody over me; and I never will have. I'm alone, and that's all I want to be: alone. So you can shoot me.

ANTROBUS: You're the last person I wanted to see. The sight of you dries up all my plans and hopes. I wish I were back at war still, because it's easier to fight you than to live with you. War's a pleasure—do you hear me?—War's a pleasure compared to what faces us now: trying to build up a peacetime with you in the middle of it. (ANTROBUS *walks up to the window.*)

HENRY: I'm not going to be a part of any peacetime of yours. I'm going a long way from here and make my own world that's fit for a man to live in. Where a man can be free, and have a chance, and do what he wants to do in his own way.

ANTROBUS (*his attention arrested; thoughtfully. He throws the gun out of the window and turns with hope*): . . . Henry, let's try again.

HENRY: Try what? Living here?—Speaking polite downtown to all the old men like you? Standing like a sheep at the street corner until the red light turns to green? Being a good boy and a good sheep, like all the stinking ideas you get out of your books? Oh, no. I'll make a world, and I'll show you.

ANTROBUS (*hard*): How can you make a world for people to live in, unless you've first put order in yourself? Mark my words: I shall continue fighting you until my last breath as long as you mix up your idea of liberty with your idea of hogging everything for yourself. I shall have no pity on you. I shall pursue you to the far corners of the earth. You and I want the same thing; but until you think of it as something that everyone has a right to, you are my deadly enemy and I will destroy you.—I hear your mother's voice in the kitchen. Have you seen her?

HENRY: I have no mother. Get it into your head. I don't belong here. I have nothing to do here. I have no home.

ANTROBUS: Then why did you come here? With the whole world to choose from, why did you come to this one place: 216 Cedar Street, Excelsior, New Jersey. . . . Well?

HENRY: What if I did? What if I wanted to look at it once more, to see if—

ANTROBUS: Oh, you're related, all right— When your mother comes in you must behave yourself. Do you hear me?

HENRY (*wildly*): What is this?———*must behave* yourself. Don't you say *must* to me.

ANTROBUS: Quiet! (*Enter* MRS. ANTROBUS *and* SABINA.)

HENRY: Nobody can say *must* to me. All my life everybody's been crossing me,—everybody, everything, all of you. I'm going to be free, even if I have to kill half the world for it. Right now, too. Let me get my hands on his throat. I'll show him. (*He advances toward* ANTROBUS. *Suddenly,* SABINA *jumps between them and calls out in her own person.*)

SABINA: Stop! Stop! Don't play this scene. You know what happened last night. Stop the play. (*The men fall back, panting.* HENRY *covers his face with his hands.*) Last night you almost strangled him. You became a regular savage. Stop it!

HENRY: It's true. I'm sorry. I don't know what comes over me. I have nothing against him personally. I respect him very much . . . I . . . I admire him. But something comes over me. It's like I become fifteen years old again. I . . . I . . . listen: my own father used to whip me and lock me up every Saturday night. I never had enough to eat. He never let me have enough money to buy decent clothes. I was ashamed to go downtown. I never could go to the dances. My father and my uncle put rules in the way of everything I wanted to do. They tried to prevent my living at all.—I'm sorry. I'm sorry.

MRS. ANTROBUS (*quickly*): No, go on. Finish what you were saying. Say it all.

HENRY: In this scene it's as though I were back in High School again. It's like I had some big emptiness inside me,—the emptiness of being hated and blocked at every turn. And the emptiness fills up with the one thought that you have to strike and fight and kill. Listen, it's as though you have to kill somebody else so as not to end up killing yourself.

SABINA: That's not true. I knew your father and your uncle and your mother. You imagined all that. Why, they did everything they could for you. How can you say things like that? They didn't lock you up.

HENRY: They did. They did. They wished I hadn't been born.

SABINA: That's not true.

ANTROBUS (*in his own person, with self-condemnation, but cold and proud*): Wait a minute. I have something to say, too. It's not wholly his fault that he wants to strangle me in this scene. It's my fault, too. He wouldn't feel that way unless there were something in me that reminded him of all that. He talks about an emptiness. Well, there's an emptiness in me, too. Yes.— work, work, work,—that's all I do. I've ceased to *live*. No wonder he feels that anger coming over him.

MRS. ANTROBUS: There! At least you've said it.

SABINA: We're all just as wicked as we can be, and that's the God's truth.

MRS. ANTROBUS (*nods a moment, then comes forward; quietly*): Come. Come and put your head under some cold water.

SABINA (*in a whisper*): I'll go with him. I've known him a long while. You have to go on with the play. Come with me. (HENRY *starts out with* SABINA, *but turns at the exit and says to* ANTROBUS.)

HENRY: Thanks. Thanks for what you said. I'll be all right tomorrow. I won't lose control in that place. I promise. (*Exeunt* HENRY *and* SABINA. ANTROBUS *starts toward the front door, fastens it.* MRS. ANTROBUS *goes up stage and places the chair close to table.*)

MRS. ANTROBUS: George, do I see you limping?

ANTROBUS: Yes, a little. My old wound from the other war started smarting again. I can manage.

MRS. ANTROBUS (*looking out of the window*): Some lights are coming on,—the first in seven years. People are walking up and down looking at them. Over in Hawkins' open lot they've built a bonfire to celebrate the peace. They're dancing around it like scarecrows.

ANTROBUS: A bonfire! As though they hadn't seen enough things burning.—Maggie,—the dog died?

MRS. ANTROBUS: Oh, yes. Long ago. There are no dogs left in Excelsior.—You're back again! All these years. I gave up counting on letters. The few that arrived were anywhere from six months to a year late.

ANTROBUS: Yes, the ocean's full of letters, along with the other things.

MRS. ANTROBUS: George, sit down, you're tired.

ANTROBUS: No, you sit down. I'm tired but

I'm restless. (*Suddenly, as she comes forward.*) Maggie! I've lost it. I've lost it.

MRS. ANTROBUS: What, George? What have you lost?

ANTROBUS: The most important thing of all: the desire to begin again, to start building.

MRS. ANTROBUS (*sitting in the chair right of the table*): Well, it will come back.

ANTROBUS (*at the window*): I've lost it. This minute I feel like all those people dancing around the bonfire—just relief. Just the desire to settle down; to slip into the old grooves and keep the neighbors from walking over my lawn.— Hm. But during the war,—in the middle of all that blood and dirt and hot and cold—every day and night, I'd have moments, Maggie, when I *saw* the things that we could do when it was over. When you're at war you think about a better life; when you're at peace you think about a more comfortable one. I've lost it. I feel sick and tired.

MRS. ANTROBUS: Listen! The baby's crying.

I hear Gladys talking. Probably she's quieting Henry again. George, while Gladys and I were living here—like moles, like rats, and when we were at out wits' end to save the baby's life—the only thought we clung to was that you were going to bring something good out of this suffering. In the night, in the dark, we'd whisper about it, starving and sick.—Oh, George, you'll have to get it back again. Think! What else kept us alive all these years? Even now, it's not comfort we want. We can suffer whatever's necessary; only give us back that promise. (*Enter* SABINA *with a lighted lamp. She is dressed as in Act I.*)

SABINA: Mrs. Antrobus . . .

MRS. ANTROBUS: Yes, Sabina?

SABINA: Will you need me?

MRS. ANTROBUS: No, Sabina, you can go to bed.

SABINA: Mrs. Antrobus, if it's all right with you, I'd like to go to the bonfire and celebrate seeing the war's over. And, Mrs. Antrobus, they've opened the Gem Movie Theatre and they're giving away a hand-painted soup tureen to every lady, and I thought one of us ought to go.

ANTROBUS: Well, Sabina, I haven't any money. I haven't seen any money for quite a while.

SABINA: Oh, you don't need money. They're taking anything you can give them. And I have some . . . some . . . Mrs. Antrobus, promise you won't tell anyone. It's a little against the law. But I'll give you some, too.

ANTROBUS: What is it?

SABINA: I'll give you some, too. Yesterday I picked up a lot of . . . of beef-cubes! (MRS. ANTROBUS *turns and says calmly.*)

MRS. ANTROBUS: But, Sabina, you know you ought to give that in to the Center downtown. They know who needs them most.

SABINA (*outburst*): Mrs. Antrobus, I didn't make this war. I didn't ask for it. And, in my opinion, after anybody's gone through what we've gone through, they have a right to grab what they can find. You're a very nice man, Mr. Antrobus, but you'd have got on better in the world if you'd realized that dog-eat-dog was the rule in the beginning and always will be. And most of all now. (*In tears.*) Oh, the world's an awful place, and you know it is. I used to think something could be done about it; but I know better now. I hate it. I hate it. (*She comes forward slowly and brings six cubes from the bag.*) All right. All right. You can have them.

ANTROBUS: Thank you, Sabina.

SABINA: Can I have . . . can I have one to go to the movies? (ANTROBUS *in silence gives her one.*) Thank you.

ANTROBUS: Good night, Sabina.

SABINA: Mr. Antrobus, don't mind what I say. I'm just an ordinary girl, you know what I mean, I'm just an ordinary girl. But you're a bright man, you're a very bright man, and of course you invented the alphabet and the wheel, and, my God, a lot of things . . . and if you've got any other plans, my God, don't let me upset them. Only every now and then I've got to go to the movies. I mean my nerves can't stand it. But if you have any ideas about improving the crazy old world, I'm really with you. I really am. Because it's . . . it's . . . Good night. (*She goes out.* ANTROBUS *starts laughing softly with exhilaration.*)

ANTROBUS: Now I remember what three things always went together when I was able to see things most clearly: three things. Three things. (*He points to where* SABINA *has gone out.*) The voice of the people in their confusion and their need. And the thought of you and the children and this house . . . And . . . Maggie! I didn't dare ask you: my books! They haven't been lost, have they?

MRS. ANTROBUS: No. There are some of them right here. Kind of tattered.

ANTROBUS: Yes.—Remember, Maggie, we almost lost them once before? And when we finally did collect a few torn copies out of old cellars they ran in everyone's head like a fever. They as good as rebuilt the world. (*Pauses, book in hand, and looks up.*) Oh, I've never forgotten for long at a time that living is struggle. I know that every good and excellent thing in the world stands moment by moment on the razor-edge of danger and must be fought for—whether it's a field, or a home, or a country. All I ask is the chance to build new worlds and God has always given us that. And has given us (*opening the book*) voices to guide us; and the memory of our mistakes to warn us. Maggie, you and I will remember in peacetime all the resolves that were so clear to us in the days of war. We've come a long ways. We've learned. We're learning. And the steps of our journey are marked for us here. (*He stands by the table turning the leaves of a book.*) Sometimes out there in the war,—standing all night on a hill—I'd try and remember some of the words in these books. Parts of them and phrases would come back to me. And after a while I used to give names to the hours of the night. (*He sits, hunting for a passage in the book.*) Nine o'clock I used to call Spinoza. Where is it: 'After experience had taught me—' (*The back wall has disappeared, revealing the platform.* FRED BAILEY *carrying his numeral has started from left to right.* MRS. ANTROBUS *sits by the table sewing.*)

BAILEY: 'After experience had taught me that the common occurrences of daily life are vain and futile; and I saw that all the objects of my desire and fear were in themselves nothing good nor bad save insofar as the mind was affected by them; I at length determined to search out whether there was something truly good and communicable to man.' (*Almost without break* HESTER, *carrying a large Roman numeral ten, starts crossing the platform.* GLADYS *appears at the kitchen door and moves towards her mother's chair.*)

HESTER: Then tell me, O Critias, how will a man choose the ruler that shall rule over him?

Will he not choose a man who has first established order in himself, knowing that any decision that has its spring from anger or pride or vanity can be multiplied a thousand fold in its effects upon the citizens?' (HESTER *disappears and* IVY, *as eleven o'clock starts speaking.*)

IVY: 'This good estate of the mind possessing its object in energy we call divine. This we mortals have occasionally and it is this energy which is pleasantest and best. But God has it always. It is wonderful in us; but in Him how much more wonderful.' (*As* MR. TREMAYNE *starts to speak,* HENRY *appears at the edge of the scene, brooding and unreconciled, but present.*)

TREMAYNE: 'In the beginning, God created the Heavens and the Earth; and the Earth was waste and void; And the darkness was upon the face of the deep. And the Lord said let there be light and there was light.' (*Sudden black-out and silence, except for the last strokes of the midnight bell. Then just as suddenly the lights go up, and* SABINA *is standing at the window, as at the opening of the play.*)

SABINA: Oh, oh, oh. Six o'clock and the master not home yet. Pray God nothing serious has happened to him crossing the Hudson River. But I wouldn't be surprised. The whole world's at sixes and sevens, and why the house hasn't fallen down about our ears long ago is a miracle to me. (*She comes down to the footlights.*) This is where you came in. We have to go on for ages and ages yet.

You go home.

The end of this play isn't written yet.

Mr. and Mrs. Antrobus! Their heads are full of plans and they're as confident as the first day they began,—and they told me to tell you: good night.

William Inge: *Come Back, Little Sheba* (1950)

Inge is virtually the only playwright to have four hit plays in his first four tries: *Come Back, Little Sheba* (1950), *Picnic* (1953), *Bus Stop* (1955), and *The Dark at the Top of the Stairs* (1957). His plays, and the films made of them, rank Inge as one of the most powerful forces in American drama in the 1950s.

Born in Independence, Kansas, in 1913, Inge spent most of his youth on the fringes of the theater, studying and acting. His mother was descended from the great actor Edwin Booth, so she was able to encourage him. He taught at Culver Military Academy for a year, after a stint as a touring actor, then went to Peabody Teachers College in Nashville, Tennessee, where he prepared for a career as a high school drama teacher. He finally gave up teaching after he moved to Stephens College for Women in Missouri. By 1943 he had become a drama critic for a St. Louis paper.

His newspaper work led him fortuitously to interview Tennessee Williams who returned briefly to St. Louis in 1944 to avoid publicity after the success of *The Glass Menagerie*. When Inge told him that he too wanted to be a successful playwright, Williams was encouraging. He said he'd read any play Inge wrote and, if he liked it, would send it to his agent. Three years later, Inge's first play, *Farther Off from Heaven* (1947), was produced in Dallas. Ten years later it would reappear on Broadway with the title *The Dark at the Top of the Stairs*.

Picnic won almost all the theater awards in 1953, including the Pulitzer Prize. *Come Back, Little Sheba* also won several awards, including the George Jean Nathan Award, and many critics have considered it his best work. Its appeal is based on its simplicity and its clarity in presenting the pain of two people whose dreams have been reduced to a humdrum reality. Lola and Doc were once young and filled with promise until pregnancy forced them to marry and give up their individual ambitions. And—perhaps the greatest cruelty—their unwanted child died, leaving Lola unable to have more children. She depends on Little Sheba, her lost dog, for the expression of her maternal feelings.

Marie and Turk and Bruce are examples of a new generation of indifferent youth. Marie is a boarder with Lola and Doc, but she is also something of a substitute child, the girl they never had; Marie has helped them stabilize their own lives. Doc has sworn off alcohol and Lola even cleans house when Marie's "intended" is coming to visit. Not until Marie's virtue is revealed as imperfect does Doc, in reaction, start drinking again. In a sense, the conflict is based on a generation gap, particularly in reference to sexual behavior. Lola and Doc have been faithful to one another, but Marie actually sleeps with Bruce the night before her fiancée arrives. There is no way Lola and Doc can understand Marie's behavior.

Because Inge spent some time in psychotherapy, he is able to introduce details drawn from modern psychology. He is even said to have shown the play to some psychologists for their examination of relevant facts and details. The ending of the play focuses on the recitation of dreams that have a clear and weighty psychological message. For Lola, Doc merges in her dream with her father, giving us the sense that Lola has problems to work out, just as Doc does.

Despite complaints of pessimism, Inge felt the ending of the drama was optimistic. Lola and Doc Delaney must start again, and they must begin in relation only to one another. Lola forgoes Little Sheba and Doc renounces alcohol and his dreams of Marie. Their world may be drab, but they resolve to live in it together out of a genuine need for one another.

William Inge died in 1973 without duplicating his earlier triumphs. Yet his influence in drama is still significant; many younger playwrights have developed themes he began to explore.

Selected Readings

Brustein, Robert. "The Men-Taming Women of William Inge." *Harper's,*
    217 (1958), pp. 52–57.
Inge, William. *Four Plays.* New York: Random House, 1958.
Suhman, R. Baird. *William Inge.* New York: Twayne, 1965.

Come Back, Little Sheba

William Inge

CHARACTERS

DOC	MILKMAN
MARIE	MESSENGER
LOLA	BRUCE
TURK	ED ANDERSON
POSTMAN	ELMO HUSTON
MRS. COFFMAN	

SCENE

An old house in a run-down neighborhood of a Midwestern city.

ACT I
SCENE 1: Morning in late spring.
SCENE 2: The same evening, after supper.

ACT II
SCENE 1: The following morning.
SCENE 2: Late afternoon the same day.
SCENE 3: 5:30 the next morning.
SCENE 4: Morning, a week later.

ACT I

SCENE 1

(The stage is empty.

It is the downstairs of an old house in one of those semi-respectable neighborhoods in a Midwestern city. The stage is divided into two rooms, the living room at right and the kitchen at left, with a stairway and a door between. At the foot of the stairway is a small table with a telephone on it. The time is about 8:00 A.M., a morning in the late spring.

At rise of curtain the sun hasn't come out in full force and outside the atmosphere is a little gray. The house is extremely cluttered and even dirty. The living room somehow manages to convey the atmosphere of the twenties, decorated with cheap pretense at niceness and respectability. The general effect is one of fussy awkwardness. The furniture is all heavy and rounded-looking, the chairs and davenport being covered with a shiny mohair. The davenport is littered and there are lace antimacassars on all the chairs. In such areas, houses are so close together, they hide each other from the sunlight. What sun could come through the window, at right, is dimmed by the smoky glass curtains. In the kitchen there is a table, center. On it are piled dirty dishes from supper the night before. Woodwork in the kitchen is dark and grimy. No industry whatsoever has been spent in making it one of those white, cheerful rooms that we commonly think kitchens should be. There is no action on stage for several seconds.

DOC comes downstairs to kitchen. His coat is on back of chair, center. He straightens chair, takes roll from bag on drainboard, folds bag and tucks it behind sink. He lights stove and goes to table, fills dishpan there and takes it to sink. Turns on water, tucks towel in vest for apron. He goes to chair and says prayer.

345

Then he crosses to stove, takes frying pan to sink and turns on water.

MARIE, *a young girl of eighteen or nineteen who rooms in the house, comes out of her bedroom [next to the living room], skipping airily into the kitchen. Her hair is piled in curls on top of her head and she wears a sheer dainty negligee and smart, feathery mules on her feet. She has the cheerfulness only youth can feel in the morning.)*

MARIE (*goes to chair, opens pocketbook there*): Hi!

DOC: Well, well, how is our star boarder this morning?

MARIE: Fine.

DOC: Want your breakfast now?

MARIE: Just my fruit juice. I'll drink it while I dress and have my breakfast later.

DOC (*places two glasses on table*): Up a little early, aren't you?

MARIE: I have to get to the library and check out some books before anyone else gets them.

DOC: Yes, you want to study hard, Marie, learn to be a fine artist some day. Paint lots of beautiful pictures. I remember a picture my mother had over the mantelpiece at home, a picture of a cathedral in a sunset, one of those big cathedrals in Europe somewhere. Made you feel religious just to look at it.

MARIE: These books aren't for art, they're for biology. I have an exam.

DOC: Biology? Why do they make you take biology?

MARIE (*laughs*): It's required. Didn't you have to take biology when you were in college?

DOC: Well . . . yes, but I was preparing to study medicine, so of course I *had* to take biology and things like that. You see—I was going to be a real doctor then—only I left college my third year.

MARIE: What's the matter? Didn't you like the pre-med course?

DOC: Yes, of course . . . I had to give it up.

MARIE: Why?

DOC (*goes to stove with roll on plate—evasive*): I'll put your sweet roll in now, Marie, so it will be nice and warm for you when you want it.

MARIE: Dr. Delaney, you're so nice to your wife, and you're so nice to me, as a matter of fact, you're so nice to everyone. I hope my husband is as nice as you are. Most husbands would never think of getting their own breakfast.

DOC (*very pleased with this*): . . . uh . . . you might as well sit down now and . . . yes, sit here and I'll serve you your breakfast now, Marie, and we can eat it together, the two of us.

MARIE (*a light little laugh as she starts dancing away from him*): No, I like to bathe first and feel that I'm fresh and clean to start the day. I'm going to hop into the tub now. See you later. (*She goes upstairs.*)

DOC (*the words appeal to him*): Yes, fresh and clean—(DOC *shows disappointment but goes on in businesslike way setting his breakfast on the table.*)

MARIE (*offstage*): Mrs. Delaney.

LOLA (*offstage*): 'Mornin', honey.

(*Then LOLA comes downstairs. She is a contrast to DOC's neat cleanliness, and MARIE's. Over a nightdress she wears a lumpy kimono. Her eyes are dim with a morning expression of disillusionment, as though she had had a beautiful dream during the night and found on waking none of it was true. On her feet are worn dirty comfies.*)

LOLA (*with some self-pity*): I can't sleep late like I used to. It used to be I could sleep till noon if I wanted to, but I can't any more. I don't know why.

DOC: Habits change. Here's your fruit juice.

LOLA (*taking it*): I oughta be gettin' your breakfast, Doc, instead of you gettin' mine.

DOC: I have to get up anyway, Baby.

LOLA (*sadly*): I had another dream last night.

DOC (*pours coffee*): About Little Sheba?

LOLA (*with sudden animation*): It was just as real. I dreamt I put her on a leash and we walked downtown—to do some shopping. All the people on the street turned around to admire her, and I felt so proud. Then we started to walk, and the blocks started going by so fast that Little Sheba couldn't keep up with me. Suddenly, I looked around and Little Sheba was gone. Isn't that funny? I looked everywhere for her but I couldn't find her. And I stood there feeling sort of afraid. (*Pause.*) Do you suppose that means anything?

DOC: Dreams are funny.

LOLA: Do you suppose it means Little Sheba is going to come back?

DOC: I don't know, Baby.

LOLA (*petulant*): I miss her so, Doc. She was such a cute little puppy. Wasn't she cute?

DOC (*smiles with the reminiscence*): Yes, she was cute.

LOLA: Remember how white and fluffy she used to be after I gave her a bath? And how her little hind-end wagged from side to side when she walked?

DOC (*an appealing memory*): I remember.

LOLA: She was such a cute little puppy. I hated to see her grow old, didn't you, Doc?

DOC: Yah. Little Sheba should have stayed young forever. Some things should never grow old. That's what it amounts to, I guess.

LOLA: She's been gone for such a long time. What do you suppose ever happened to her?

DOC: You can't ever tell.

LOLA (with anxiety): Do you suppose she got run over by a car? Or do you think that old Mrs. Coffman next door poisoned her? I wouldn't be a bit surprised.

DOC: No, Baby. She just disappeared. That's all we know.

LOLA (redundantly): Just vanished one day . . . vanished into thin air. (As though in a dream.)

DOC: I told you I'd find you another one, Baby.

LOLA (pessimistically): You couldn't ever find another puppy as cute as Little Sheba.

DOC (back to reality): Want an egg?

LOLA: No. Just this coffee. (He pours coffee and sits down to breakfast. LOLA, suddenly.) Have you said your prayer, Doc?

DOC: Yes, Baby.

LOLA: And did you ask God to be with you —all through the day, and keep you strong?

DOC: Yes, Baby.

LOLA: Then God will be with you, Docky. He's been with you almost a year now and I'm so proud of you.

DOC (preening a little): Sometimes I feel sorta proud of myself.

LOLA: Say your prayer, Doc. I like to hear it.

DOC (matter-of-factly): God grant me the serenity to accept the things I cannot change, courage to change the things I can, and wisdom always to tell the difference.

LOLA: That's nice. That's so pretty. When I think of the way you used to drink, always getting into fights, we had so much trouble. I was so scared! I never knew what was going to happen.

DOC: That was a long time ago, Baby.

LOLA: I know it, Daddy. I know how you're going to be when you come home now. (She kisses him lightly.)

DOC: I don't know what I would have done without you.

LOLA: And now you've been sober almost a year.

DOC: Yep. A year next month. (He rises and goes to the sink with coffee cup and two glasses, rinsing them.)

LOLA: Do you have to go to the meeting tonight?

DOC: No. I can skip the meetings now for a while.

LOLA: Oh, good! Then you can take me to a movie.

DOC: Sorry, Baby. I'm going out on some Twelfth Step work with Ed Anderson.

LOLA: What's that?

DOC (drying the glasses): I showed you that list of twelve steps the Alcoholics Anonymous have to follow. This is the final one. After you learn to stay dry yourself, then you go out and help other guys that need it.

LOLA: Oh!

DOC (goes to sink): When we help others, we help ourselves.

LOLA: I know what you mean. Whenever I help Marie in some way, it makes me feel good.

DOC: Yah. (LOLA takes her cup to DOC and he washes it.) Yes, but this is a lot different, Baby. When I go out to help some poor drunk, I have to give him courage—to stay sober like I've stayed sober. Most alcoholics are disappointed men . . . They need courage . . .

LOLA: You weren't ever disappointed, were you, Daddy?

DOC (after another evasive pause): The important thing is to forget the past and live for the present. And stay sober doing it.

LOLA: Who do you have to help tonight?

DOC: Some guy they picked up on Skid Row last night. (Gets his coat from back of chair.) They got him at the City Hospital. I kinda dread it.

LOLA: I thought you said it helped you.

DOC (puts on coat): It does, if you can stand it. I did some Twelfth Step work down there once before. They put alcoholics right in with the crazy people. It's horrible—these men all twisted and shaking—eyes all foggy and full of pain. Some guy there with his fists clamped together, so he couldn't kill anyone. There was a young man, just a young man, had scratched his eyes out.

LOLA (cringing): Don't, Daddy. Seems a shame to take a man there just 'cause he got drunk.

DOC: Well, they'll sober a man up. That's the important thing. Let's not talk about it any more.

LOLA (with relief): Rita Hayworth's on tonight, out at the Plaza. Don't you want to see it?

DOC: Maybe Marie will go with you.

LOLA: Oh, no. She's probably going out with Turk tonight.

DOC: She's too nice a girl to be going out with a guy like Turk.

LOLA: I don't know why, Daddy. Turk's nice. (*Cuts coffee cake.*)

DOC: A guy like that doesn't have any respect for *nice* young girls. You can tell that by looking at him.

LOLA: I never saw Marie object to any of the love-making.

DOC: A big, brawny bozo like Turk, he probably forces her to kiss him.

LOLA: Daddy, that's not so at all. I came in the back way once when they were in the living room, and she was kissing him like he was Rudolph Valentino.

DOC (*an angry denial*): Marie is a nice girl.

LOLA: I know she's nice. I just said she and Turk were doing some tall spooning. It wouldn't surprise me any if . . .

DOC: Honey, I don't want to hear any more about it.

LOLA: You try to make out like every young girl is Jennifer Jones in the *Song of Bernadette*.

DOC: I do not. I just like to believe that young people like her are clean and decent . . .

(MARIE *comes downstairs*.)

MARIE: Hi! (*Gets cup and saucer from drainboard*.)

LOLA (*at stove*): There's an extra sweet roll for you this morning, honey. I didn't want mine.

MARIE: One's plenty, thank you.

DOC: How soon do you leave this morning?

(LOLA *brings coffee*.)

MARIE (*eating*): As soon as I finish my breakfast.

DOC: Well, I'll wait and we can walk to the corner together.

MARIE: Oh, I'm sorry, Doc. Turk's coming by. He has to go to the library, too.

DOC: Oh, well, I'm not going to be competition with a football player. (*To* LOLA.) It's a nice spring morning. Wanta walk to the office with me?

LOLA: I look too terrible, Daddy. I ain't even dressed.

DOC: Kiss Daddy good-bye.

LOLA (*gets up and kisses him softly*): Bye, bye, Daddy. If you get hungry, come home and I'll have something for you.

MARIE (*joking*): Aren't you going to kiss *me*, Dr. Delaney?

(LOLA *eggs* DOC *to go ahead*.)

DOC (*startled, hesitates, forces himself to realize she is only joking and manages to answer*): Can't

spend my time kissing all the girls.

(MARIE *laughs*. DOC *goes into living room while* LOLA *and* MARIE *continue talking*. MARIE'S *scarf is tossed over his hat on chair, so he picks it up, then looks at it fondly, holding it in the air inspecting its delicate gracefulness. He drops it back on chair and goes out*.)

MARIE: I think Dr. Delaney is so nice.

LOLA (*She is by the closet now, where she keeps a few personal articles. She is getting into a more becoming smock*): When did you say Turk was coming by?

MARIE: Said he'd be here about 9:30. (DOC *exits, hearing the line about* TURK.) That's a pretty smock.

LOLA (*goes to table, sits in chair and changes shoes*): It'll be better to work around the house in.

MARIE (*not sounding exactly cheerful*): Mrs. Delaney, I'm expecting a telegram this morning. Would you leave it on my dresser for me when it comes?

LOLA: Sure, honey. No bad news, I hope.

MARIE: Oh, no! It's from Bruce.

LOLA (MARIE'S *boy friends are one of her liveliest interests*): Oh, your boy friend in Cincinnati. Is he coming to see you?

MARIE: I guess so.

LOLA: I'm just dying to meet him.

MARIE (*changing the subject*): Really, Mrs. Delaney, you and Doc have been so nice to me. I just want you to know I appreciate it.

LOLA: Thanks, honey.

MARIE: You've been like a father and mother to me. I appreciate it.

LOLA: Thanks, honey.

MARIE: Turk was saying just the other night what good sports you both are.

LOLA (*brushing hair*): That so?

MARIE: Honest. He said it was just as much fun being with you as with kids our own age.

LOLA (*couldn't be more flattered*): Oh, I like that Turk. He reminds me of a boy I used to know in high school, Dutch McCoy. Where did you ever meet him?

MARIE: In art class.

LOLA: Turk take art?

MARIE (*laughs*): No. It was in a life class. He was modeling. Lots of the athletes do that. It pays them a dollar an hour.

LOLA: That's nice.

MARIE: Mrs. Delaney? I've got some corrections to make in some of my drawings. Is it all right if I bring Turk home this morning to pose for me? It'll just take a few minutes.

LOLA: Sure, honey.

MARIE: There's a contest on now. They're giving a prize for the best drawing to use for advertising the Spring Relays.

LOLA: And you're going to do a picture of Turk? That's nice. (*A sudden thought.*) Doc's gonna be gone tonight. You and Turk can have the living room if you want to. (*A little secretively.*)

MARIE (*this is a temptation*): O.K. Thanks. (*Exit to bedroom.*)

LOLA: Tell me more about Bruce. (*Follows her to bedroom door.*)

MARIE (*offstage in bedroom; remembering her affinity*): Well, he comes from one of the best families in Cincinnati. And they have a great big house. And they have a maid, too. And he's got a wonderful personality. He makes $300 a month.

LOLA: That so?

MARIE: And he stays at the best hotels. His company insists on it. (*Enters.*)

LOLA: Do you like him as well as Turk? (*Buttoning up back of* MARIE's *blouse.*)

MARIE (*evasive*): Bruce is so dependable, and . . . he's a gentleman, too.

LOLA: Are you goin' to marry him, honey?

MARIE: Maybe, after I graduate from college and he feels he can support a wife and children. I'm going to have lots and lots of children.

LOLA: I wanted children, too. When I lost my baby and found out I couldn't have any more, I didn't know what to do with myself. I wanted to get a job, but Doc wouldn't hear of it.

MARIE: Bruce is going to come into a lot of money some day. His uncle made a fortune in men's garters. (*Exits into her room.*)

LOLA (*leaning on door frame*): Doc was a rich boy when I married him. His mother left him $25,000 when she died. (*Disillusioned.*) It took him a lot to get his office started and everything . . . then, he got sick. (*She makes a futile gesture, then on the bright side.*) But Doc's always good to me . . . now.

MARIE (*re-enters*): Oh, Doc's a peach.

LOLA: I used to be pretty, something like you. (*She gets her picture from table.*) I was Beauty Queen of the senior class in high school. My dad was awful strict, though. Once he caught me holding hands with that good-looking Dutch McCoy. Dad sent Dutch home, and wouldn't let me go out after supper for a whole month. Daddy would never let me go out with boys much. Just because I was pretty. He was afraid all the boys would get the wrong idea—*you* know. I never

had any fun at all until I met Doc.

MARIE: Sometimes I'm glad I didn't know my father. Mom always let me do pretty much as I please.

LOLA: Doc was the first boy my dad ever let me go out with. We got married that spring. (*Replaces picture.* MARIE *sits on couch, puts on shoes and socks.*)

MARIE: What did your father think of that?

LOLA: We came right to the city then. And, well, Doc gave up his pre-med course and went to Chiropractor School instead.

MARIE: You must have been married awful young.

LOLA: Oh, yes. Eighteen.

MARIE: That must have made your father really mad.

LOLA: Yes, it did. I never went home after that, but my mother comes down here from Green Valley to visit me sometimes.

TURK (*Bursts into the front room from outside. He is a young, big, husky, good-looking boy, nineteen or twenty. He has the openness, the generosity, vigor and health of youth. He's had a little time in the service, but he is not what one would call disciplined. He wears faded dungarees and T-shirt. He always enters unannounced. He hollers for* MARIE): Hey, Marie! Ready?

MARIE (*calling; runs and exits into bedroom, closing door*): Just a minute, Turk.

LOLA (*confidentially*): I'll entertain him until you're ready. (*She is by nature coy and kittenish with any attractive man. Picks up papers—stuffs them under table.*) The house is such a mess, Turk! I bet you think I'm an awful housekeeper. Some day I'll surprise you. But you're like one of the family now. (*Pause.*) My, you're an early caller.

TURK: Gotta get to the library. Haven't cracked a book for a biology exam and Marie's gotta help me.

LOLA (*unconsciously admiring his stature and physique and looking him over*): My, I'd think you'd be chilly running around in just that thin little shirt.

TURK: Me? I go like this in the middle of winter.

LOLA: Well, you're a big husky man.

TURK (*laughs*): Oh, I'm a brute, *I* am.

LOLA: You should be out in Hollywood making those Tarzan movies.

TURK: I had enough of that place when I was in the Navy.

LOLA: That so?

TURK (*calling*): Hey, Marie, hurry up.

MARIE: Oh, be patient, Turk.

TURK (*to* LOLA): She doesn't realize how busy I am. I'll only have a half hour to study at most. I gotta report to the coach at 10:30.

LOLA: What are you in training for now?

TURK: Spring track. They got me throwing the javelin.

LOLA: The javelin? What's that?

TURK (*laughs at her ignorance*): It's a big, long lance. (*Assumes the magnificent position.*) You hold it like this, erect—then you let go and it goes singing through the air, and lands yards away, if you're any good at it, and sticks in the ground, quivering like an arrow. I won the State championship last year.

LOLA (*She has watched as though fascinated*): My!

TURK (*very generous*): Get Marie to take you to the track field some afternoon, and you can watch me.

LOLA: That would be thrilling.

MARIE (*comes dancing in*): Hi, Turk.

TURK: Hi, juicy.

LOLA (*as the young couple move to the doorway*): Remember, Marie, you and Turk can have the front room tonight. All to yourselves. You can play the radio and dance and make a plate of fudge, or anything you want.

MARIE (*to* TURK): O.K.?

TURK (*with eagerness*): Sure.

MARIE: Let's go. (*Exits.*)

LOLA: 'Bye, kids.

TURK: 'Bye, Mrs. Delaney. (*Gives her a chuck under the chin.*) You're a swell skirt.

(LOLA *couldn't be more flattered. For a moment she is breathless. They speed out the door and* LOLA *stands, sadly watching them depart. Then a sad, vacant look comes over her face. Her arms drop in a gesture of futility. Slowly she walks out on the front porch and calls.*)

LOLA: Little Sheba! Come, Little She-ba. Come back . . . come back, Little Sheba! (*She waits for a few moments, then comes wearily back into the house, closing the door behind her. Now the morning has caught up with her. She goes to the kitchen, kicks off her pumps and gets back into comfies. The sight of the dishes on the drainboard depresses her. Clearly she is bored to death. Then the telephone rings with the promise of relieving her. She answers it.*) Hello—Oh, no, you've got the wrong number— Oh, that's all right. (*Again it looks hopeless. She hears the* POSTMAN. *Now her spirits are lifted. She runs to the door, opens it and awaits him. When he's within distance, she lets loose a barrage of welcome.*) 'Morning, Mr. Postman.

POSTMAN: 'Morning, ma'am.

LOLA: You better have something for me today. Sometimes I think you don't even know I live here. You haven't left me anything for two whole weeks. If you can't do better than that, I'll just have to get a new postman.

POSTMAN (*on the porch*): You'll have to get someone to write you some letters, lady. Nope, nothing for you.

LOLA: Well, I was only joking. You knew I was joking, didn't you? I bet you're thirsty. You come right in here and I'll bring you a glass of cold water. Come in and sit down for a few minutes and rest your feet awhile.

POSTMAN: I'll take you up on that, lady. I've worked up quite a thirst. (*Coming in.*)

LOLA: You sit down. I'll be back in just a minute. (*Goes to kitchen, gets pitcher out of refrigerator and brings it back.*)

POSTMAN: Spring is turnin' into summer awful soon.

LOLA: You feel free to stop here and ask me for a drink of water any time you want to. (*Pouring drink.*) That's what we're all here for, isn't it? To make each other comfortable?

POSTMAN: Thank you, ma'am.

LOLA (*clinging, not wanting to be left alone so soon; she hurries her conversation to hold him*): You haven't been our postman very long, have you?

POSTMAN (*she pours him a glass of water, stands holding pitcher as he drinks*): No.

LOLA: You postmen have things pretty nice, don't you? I hear you get nice pensions after you been working for the government twenty years. I think that's dandy. It's a *good* job, too. (*Pours him a second glass.*) You may get tired but I think it's good for a man to be outside and get a lot of exercise. Keeps him strong and healthy. My husband, he's a doctor, a *chiro*practor; he has to stay inside his office all day long. The only exercise he gets is rubbin' people's backbones. (*They laugh.* LOLA *goes to table, leaves pitcher.*) It makes his hands strong. He's got the strongest hands you ever did see. But he's got a poor digestion. I keep tellin' him he oughta get some fresh air once in a while and some exercise. (POSTMAN *rises as if to go, and this hurries her into a more absorbing monologue.*) You know what? My husband is an Alcoholics Anonymous. He doesn't care if I tell you that 'cause he's proud of it. He hasn't touched a drop in almost a year. All that time we've had a quart of whiskey in the pantry for company and he hasn't even gone near it. Doesn't even want to. You know, alcoholics can't drink like ordinary people; they're *allergic* to it. It affects them different. They get started drinking and can't stop. Liquor transforms them. Sometimes they get mean and violent and wanta fight, but if they let liquor alone, they're perfectly all right, just like you and me. (POSTMAN *tries to leave.*) You should have seen Doc before he gave it up. He lost all his patients, wouldn't even go to the office; just wanted to stay drunk all day long and he'd come home at night and . . . You just wouldn't believe it if you saw him now. He's got his patients all back, and he's just doing fine.

POSTMAN: Sure, I know Dr. Delaney. I deliver his office mail. He's a fine man.

LOLA: Oh, thanks. You don't ever drink, do you?

POSTMAN: Oh, a few beers once in a while. (*He is ready to go.*)

LOLA: Well, I guess that stuff doesn't do any of us any good.

POSTMAN: No. (*Crosses down for mail on floor center.*) Well, good day, ma'am.

LOLA: Say, you got any kids?

POSTMAN: Three grandchildren.

LOLA (*getting it from console table*): We don't have any kids, and we got this toy in a box of breakfast food. Why don't you take it home to them?

POSTMAN: Why, that's very kind of you, ma'am. (*He takes it, and goes.*)

LOLA: Good-bye, Mr. Postman.

POSTMAN (*on porch*): I'll see that you get a letter, if I have to write it myself.

LOLA: Thanks. Good-bye. (*Left alone, she turns on radio. Then she goes to kitchen to start dishes, showing her boredom in the half-hearted way she washes them. Takes water back to icebox. Then she spies* MRS. COFFMAN *hanging baby clothes on lines just outside kitchen door. Goes to door.*) My, you're a busy woman this morning, Mrs. Coffman.

MRS. COFFMAN (*German accent. She is outside, but sticks her head in for some of the following*): Being busy is being happy.

LOLA: I guess so.

MRS. COFFMAN: I don't have it as easy as you. When you got seven kids to look after, you got no time to sit around the house, Mrs. Delaney.

LOLA: I s'pose not.

MRS. COFFMAN: But you don't hear me complain.

LOLA: Oh, no. You never complain. (*Pause.*) I guess my little doggie's gone for good, Mrs. Coffman. I sure miss her.

MRS. COFFMAN: The only way to keep from missing one dog is to get another.

LOLA (*goes to sink, turns off water*): Oh, I never could find another doggie as cute as Little Sheba.

MRS. COFFMAN: Did you put an ad in the paper?

LOLA: For two whole weeks. No one answered it. It's just like she vanished—into thin air. (*She likes this metaphor.*) Every day, though, I go out on the porch and call her. You can't tell; she might be around. Don't you think?

MRS. COFFMAN: You should get busy and forget her. You should get busy, Mrs. Delaney.

LOLA: Yes, I'm going to. I'm going to start my spring house-cleaning one of these days real soon. Why don't you come in and have a cup of coffee with me, Mrs. Coffman, and we can chat awhile?

MRS. COFFMAN: I got work to do, Mrs. Delaney. I got work. (*Exit.*)

(LOLA *turns from the window, annoyed at her rejection. Is about to start in on the dishes when the* MILKMAN *arrives. She opens the back door and detains him.*)

MILKMAN: 'Morning, Mrs. Coffman.

MRS. COFFMAN: 'Morning.

LOLA: Hello there, Mr. Milkman. How are you today?

MILKMAN: 'Morning, Lady.

LOLA: I think I'm going to want a few specials today. Can you come in a minute? (*Goes to icebox.*)

MILKMAN (*coming in*): What'll it be? (*He probably is used to her. He is not a handsome man but husky and attractive in his uniform.*)

LOLA (*at refrigerator*): Well, now, let's see. You got any cottage cheese?

MILKMAN: We always got cottage cheese, Lady. (*Showing her card.*) All you gotta do is check the items on the card and we leave 'em. Now I gotta go back to the truck.

LOLA: Now, don't scold me. I always mean to do that but you're always here before I think of it. Now, I guess I'll need some coffee cream, too —half a pint.

MILKMAN: Coffee cream. O.K.

LOLA: Now let me see . . . Oh, yes, I want a quart of buttermilk. My husband has liked buttermilk ever since he stopped drinking. My husband's an alcoholic. Had to give it up. Did I ever tell you? (*Starts out. Stops at sink.*)

MILKMAN: Yes, Lady. (*Starts to go. She follows.*)

LOLA: Now he can't get enough to eat. Eats six times a day. He comes home in the middle of the morning, and I fix him a snack. In the middle of the afternoon he has a malted milk with an egg in it. And then another snack before he goes to bed.

MILKMAN: What'd ya know?

LOLA: Keeps his energy up.

MILKMAN: I'll bet. Anything else. Lady?

LOLA: No, I guess not.

MILKMAN (*going out*): Be back in a jiffy. (*Gives her slip.*)

LOLA: I'm just so sorry I put you to so much extra work. (*He goes. Returns shortly with dairy products.*) After this I'm going to do my best to remember to check the card. I don't think it's right to put people to extra work. (*Goes to icebox, puts things away.*)

MILKMAN (*smiles, is willing to forget*): That's all right, Lady.

LOLA: Maybe you'd like a piece of cake or a sandwich. Got some awfully good cold cuts in the icebox.

MILKMAN: No, thanks, Lady.

LOLA: Or maybe you'd like a cup of coffee.

MILKMAN: No, thanks. (*He's checking the items, putting them on the bill.*)

LOLA: You're just a young man. You oughta be going to college. I think everyone should have an education. Do you like your job?

MILKMAN: It's O.K. (*Looks at LOLA.*)

LOLA: You're a husky young man. You oughta be out in Hollywood making those Tarzan movies.

MILKMAN (*steps back; feels a little flattered*): When I first began on this job I didn't get enough exercise, so I started working out on the bar-bell.

LOLA: Bar-bells?

MILKMAN: Keeps you in trim.

LOLA (*fascinated*): Yes, I imagine.

MILKMAN: I sent my picture in to *Strength and Health* last month. (*Proudly.*) It's a physique study! If they print it, I'll bring you a copy.

LOLA: Oh, will you? I think we should all take better care of ourselves, don't you?

MILKMAN: If you ask me, Lady, that's what's wrong with the world today. We're not taking care of ourselves.

LOLA: I wouldn't be surprised.

MILKMAN: Every morning, I do forty push-ups before I eat my breakfast.

LOLA: Push-ups?

MILKMAN: Like this. (*He spreads himself on the floor and demonstrates, doing three rapid push-ups. LOLA couldn't be more fascinated. Then he springs to his feet.*) That's good for shoulder development. Wanta feel my shoulders?

LOLA: Why . . . why, yes. (*He makes one arm tense and puts her hand on his shoulder.*) Why, it's just like a rock.

MILKMAN: I can do seventy-nine without stopping.

LOLA: Seventy-nine!

MILKMAN: Now feel my arm.

LOLA (*does so*): Goodness!

MILKMAN: You wouldn't believe what a puny kid I was. Sickly, no appetite.

LOLA: Is that a fact? And, my! Look at you now.

MILKMAN (*very proud*): Shucks, any man could do the same . . . if he just takes care of himself.

LOLA: Oh, sure, sure.

(*A horn is heard offstage.*)

MILKMAN: There's my buddy. I gotta beat it. (*Picks up his things, shakes hands, leave hurriedly.*) See you tomorrow, Lady.

LOLA: 'Bye.

(*She watches him from kitchen window until he gets out of sight. There is a look of some wonder on her face, an emptiness, as though she were unable to understand anything that ever happened to her. She looks at clock, runs into living room, turns on radio. A pulsating tomtom is heard as a theme introduction. Then the* ANNOUNCER.)

ANNOUNCER (*in dramatic voice*): TA-BOOoooo! (*Now in a very soft, highly personalized voice.* LOLA *sits on couch, eats candy.*) It's Ta-boo, radio listeners, your fifteen minutes of temptation. (*An alluring voice.*) Won't you join me? (LOLA *swings feet up.*) Won't you leave behind your routine, the dull cares that make up your day-to-day existence, the little worries, the uncertainties, the confusions of the work-a-day world and follow me where pagan spirits hold sway, where lithe natives dance on a moon-enchanted isle, where palm trees sway with the restless ocean tide, restless surging on the white shore? Won't you come along?

(*More tom-tom*)
(*Now in an oily voice*)

But remember, it's TA-BOOOOOooooo-OOO!

(*Now the tom-tom again, going into a sensual, primitive rhythm melody.* LOLA *has been transfixed from the beginning of the program. She lies down on the davenport, listening, then slowly, growing more and more comfortable.*)

WESTERN UNION BOY (*at door*): Telegram for Miss Marie Buckholder.

LOLA: She's not here.

WESTERN UNION BOY: Sign here.

(LOLA *does, then she closes the door and brings the envelope into the house, looking at it wonderingly. This is a major temptation for her. She puts the envelope on the table but can't resist looking at it. Finally she gives in and takes it to the kitchen to steam it open. Then* MARIE *and* TURK *burst into the room.* LOLA, *confused, wonders what to do with the telegram, then decides, just in the nick of time, to jam it in her apron pocket.*)

MARIE: Mrs. Delaney! (*Turns off radio. At the sound of* MARIE's *voice,* LOLA *embarrassedly slips the message into her pocket and runs in to greet them*) Mind if we turn your parlor into an art studio?

LOLA: Sure, go right ahead. Hi, Turk.

(TURK *gives a wave of his arm.*)

MARIE (*to* TURK, *indicating her bedroom*): You can change in there, Turk. (*Exit to bedroom.*)

LOLA (*puzzled*): Change?

MARIE: He's gotta take off his clothes.

LOLA: Huh? (*Closes door.*)

MARIE: These drawings are for my life class.

LOLA (*consoled but still mystified*): Oh.

MARIE (*sits on couch*): Turk's the best male model we've had all year. Lotsa athletes pose for us 'cause they've all got muscles. They're easier to draw.

LOLA: You mean . . . he's gonna pose *naked?*

MARIE (*laughs*): No. The women do, but the men are always more proper. Turk's going to pose in his track suit.

LOLA: Oh. (*Almost to herself.*) The women pose naked but the men don't. (*This strikes her as a startling inconsistency.*) If it's all right for a woman, it oughta be for a man.

MARIE (*businesslike*): The man always keeps covered. (*Calling to* TURK.) Hurry up, Turk.

TURK (*With all his muscles in place, he comes out. He is not at all self-conscious about his semi-nudity. His body is something he takes very much for granted.* LOLA *is a little dazed by the spectacle of flesh*). How do you want this lovely body? Same pose I took in Art Class?

MARIE: Yah. Over there where I can get more light on you.

TURK (*opens door; starts pose*): Anything in the house I can use for a javelin?

MARIE: Is there, Mrs. Delaney?

LOLA: How about the broom?

TURK: O.K.

(LOLA *runs out to get it.* TURK *goes to her in kitchen, takes it, returns to living room and resumes pose.*)

MARIE (*from her sofa, studying* TURK *in relation to her sketch-pad, moves his leg*): Your left foot a little more this way. (*Studying it.*) O.K., hold it. (*Starts sketching rapidly and industriously.* LOLA *looks on, lingeringly.*)

LOLA (*starts unwillingly into kitchen, changes her mind and returns to the scene of action.* MARIE *and* TURK *are too busy to comment.* LOLA *looks at sketch, inspecting it.*): Well . . . that's real pretty, Marie. (MARIE *is intent.* LOLA *moves closer to look at the drawing.*) It . . . it's real artistic. (*Pause.*) I wish *I* was artistic.

TURK: Baby, I can't hold this pose very long at a time.

MARIE: Rest whenever you feel like it.

TURK: O.K.

MARIE (*to* LOLA): If I make a good drawing, they'll use it for the posters for the Spring Relays.

LOLA: Ya. You told me.

MARIE (*to* TURK): After I'm finished with these sketches I won't have to bother you any more.

TURK: No bother. (*Rubs his shoulder—he poses.*) Hard pose, though. Gets me in the shoulder.

(MARIE *pays no attention.* LOLA *peers at him so closely, he becomes a little self-conscious and breaks pose. This also breaks* LOLA's *concentration.*)

LOLA: I'll heat you up some coffee. (*Goes to kitchen.*)

TURK (*softly to* MARIE): Hey, can't you keep her out of here? She makes me feel naked.

MARIE (*laughs*): I can't keep her out of her own house, can I?

TURK: Didn't she ever see a man before?

MARIE: Not a big, beautiful man like you, Turky. (TURK *smiles, is flattered by any recognition of his physical worth, takes it as an immediate invitation to lovemaking. Pulling her up, he kisses her as* DOC *comes up on porch.* MARIE *pushes* TURK *away.*)

Turk, get back in your corner.

(DOC *comes in from outside.*)

DOC (*cheerily*): Hi, everyone.

MARIE: Hi.

TURK: Hi, Doc. (DOC *then sees* TURK, *feels immediate resentment. Goes into kitchen to* LOLA.) What's goin' on here?

LOLA (*getting cups*): Oh, hello, Daddy. Marie's doin' a drawin'.

DOC (*trying to size up the situation.* MARIE *and* TURK *are too busy to speak.*): Oh.

LOLA: I've just heated up the coffee, want some?

DOC: Yeah. What happened to Turk's clothes?

LOLA: Marie's doing some drawings for her *life* class, Doc.

DOC: Can't she draw him with his clothes on?

LOLA (*with coffee; very professional now*): No, Doc, it's not the same. See, it's a *life* class. They draw bodies. They all do it, right in the classroom.

DOC: Why, Marie's just a young girl; she shouldn't be drawing things like that. I don't care if they do teach it at college. It's not right.

LOLA (*disclaiming responsibility*): I don't know, Doc.

TURK (*turns*): I'm tired.

MARIE (*squats at his feet*): Just let me finish the foot.

DOC: Why doesn't she draw something else, a bowl of flowers or a cathedral . . . or a sunset?

LOLA: All she told me, Doc, was if she made a good drawing of Turk, they'd use it for the posters for the Spring Relay. (*Pause.*) So I guess they don't want sunsets.

DOC: What if someone walked into the house now? What would they think?

LOLA: Daddy, Marie just asked me if it was all right if Turk came and posed for her. Now that's all she said, and I said O.K. But if you think it's wrong I won't let them do it again.

DOC: I just don't like it.

MARIE: Hold it a minute more.

TURK: O.K.

LOLA: Well, then you speak to Marie about it if . . .

DOC (*he'd never mention anything disapprovingly to* MARIE): No, Baby. I couldn't do that.

LOLA: Well, then . . .

DOC: Besides, it's not her fault. If those college people make her do drawings like that, I suppose she has to do them. I just don't think it's right she should have to, that's all.

LOLA: Well, if you think it's wrong . . .

DOC (*ready to dismiss it*): Never mind.

LOLA: I don't see any harm in it, Daddy.

DOC: Forget it.

LOLA (*goes to icebox*): Would you like some buttermilk?

DOC: Thanks.

(MARIE *finishes sketch.*)

MARIE: O.K. That's all I can do for today.

TURK: Is there anything I can do for *you?*

MARIE: Yes—get your clothes on.

TURK: O.K., coach.

(TURK *exits.*)

LOLA: You know what Marie said, Doc? She said that the women pose naked, but the men don't.

DOC: Why, of course, honey.

LOLA: Why is that?

DOC (*stumped*): Well . . .

LOLA: If it's all right for a woman it oughta be for a man. But the man always keeps covered. That's what she said.

DOC: Well, that's the way it should be, honey. A man, after all, is a man, and he . . . well, he has to protect himself.

LOLA: And a woman doesn't?

DOC: It's different, honey.

LOLA: Is it? I've got a secret, Doc. Bruce is comin'.

DOC: Is that so?

LOLA (*after a glum silence*): You know Marie's boy friend from Cincinnati. I promised Marie a long time ago, when her fiancé came to town, dinner was on me. So I'm getting out the best china and cooking the best meal you ever sat down to.

DOC: When did she get the news?

LOLA: The telegram came this morning.

DOC: That's fine. That Bruce sounds to me like just the fellow for her. I think I'll go in and congratulate her.

LOLA (*nervous*): Not now, Doc.

DOC: Why not?

LOLA: Well, Turk's there. It might make him feel embarrassed.

DOC: Well, why doesn't Turk clear out now that Bruce is coming? What's he hanging around for? She's engaged to marry Bruce, isn't she?

(TURK *enters from bedroom and goes to* MARIE, *starting to make advances.*)

LOLA: Marie's just doing a picture of him, Doc.

DOC: You always stick up for him. You encourage him.

LOLA: Shhh, Daddy. Don't get upset.

DOC (*very angrily*): All right, but if anything happens to the girl I'll never forgive you.

(DOC *goes upstairs.* TURK *then grabs* MARIE, *kisses her passionately.*)

SCENE 2

(*The same evening, after supper. Outside it is dark. There has been an almost miraculous transformation of the entire house.* LOLA, *apparently, has been working hard and fast all day. The rooms are spotlessly clean and there are such additions as new lampshades, fresh curtains, etc. In the kitchen all the enamel surfaces glisten, and piles of junk that have lain around for months have been disposed of.* LOLA *and* DOC *are in the kitchen, he washing up the dishes and she puttering around putting the finishing touches on her housecleaning.*)

LOLA (*at stove*): There's still some beans left. Do you want them, Doc?

DOC: I had enough.

LOLA: I hope you got enough to eat tonight, Daddy. I been so busy cleaning I didn't have time to fix you much.

DOC: I wasn't very hungry.

LOLA (*at table, cleaning up*): You know what? Mrs. Coffman said I could come over and pick all the lilacs I wanted for my centerpiece tomorrow. Isn't that nice? I don't think she poisoned Little Sheba, do you?

DOC: I never did think so, Baby. Where'd you get the new curtains?

LOLA: I went out and bought them this afternoon. Aren't they pretty? Be careful of the woodwork, it's been varnished.

DOC: How come, honey?

LOLA (*gets broom and dustpan from closet*): Bruce is comin'. I figured I had to do my spring housecleaning some time.

DOC: You got all this done in one day? The house hasn't looked like this in years.

LOLA: I can be a good housekeeper when I want to be, can't I, Doc?

DOC (*holding dustpan for* LOLA): I never had any complaints. Where's Marie now.

LOLA: I don't know, Doc. I haven't seen her since she left here this morning with Turk.

DOC (*with a look of disapproval*): Marie's too nice to be wasting her time with him.

LOLA: Daddy, Marie can take care of herself. Don't worry. (*Returns broom to closet.*)

DOC (*goes into living room*): 'Bout time for Fibber McGee and Molly.

LOLA (*untying apron; goes to closet and then back door*): Daddy, I'm gonna run over to Mrs. Coffman's and see if she's got any silver polish. I'll be right back.

(DOC *goes to radio.* LOLA *exits*)

(*At the radio* DOC *starts twisting the dial. He rejects one noisy program after another, then very unexpectedly he comes across a rendition of Shubert's famous "Ave Maria," sung in a high soprano voice. Probably he has encountered the piece before somewhere, but it is now making its first impression on him. Gradually he is transported into a world of ethereal beauty which he never knew existed. He listens intently. The music has expressed some ideal of beauty he never fully realized and he is even a little mystified. Then* LOLA *comes in the back door, letting it slam, breaking the spell, and announcing in a loud, energetic voice:*)

Isn't it funny? I'm not a bit tired tonight. You'd think after working so hard all day I'd be pooped.

DOC (*in the living room; he cringes*): Baby, don't use that word.

LOLA (*to* DOC *on couch. Sets silver polish down and joins* DOC): I'm sorry, Doc. I hear Marie and Turk say it all the time, and I thought it was kinda cute.

DOC: It . . . it sounds vulgar.

LOLA (*kisses* DOC): I won't say it again, Daddy. Where's Fibber McGee?

DOC: Not quite time yet.

LOLA: Let's get some peppy music.

DOC (*tuning in a sentimental dance band*): That what you want?

LOLA: That's O.K. (DOC *takes a pack of cards off radio and starts shuffling them, very deftly.*) I love to watch you shuffle cards, Daddy. You use your hands so gracefully. (*She watches closely.*) Do me one of your card tricks.

DOC: Baby, you've seen them all.

LOLA: But I never get tired of them.

DOC: O.K. Take a card. (LOLA *does.*) Keep it now. Don't tell me what it is.

LOLA: I won't.

DOC (*shuffling cards again*): Now put it back in the deck. I won't look. (*He closes his eyes.*)

LOLA (*with childish delight*): All right.

DOC: Put it back.

LOLA: Uh-huh.

DOC: O.K. (*Shuffles cards again, cutting them, taking top half off, exposing* LOLA'S *card, to her astonishment.*) That your card?

LOLA (*unbelievingly*): Daddy, how did you do it?

DOC: Baby, I've pulled that trick on you dozens of times.

LOLA: But I never understand how you do it.

DOC: Very simple.

LOLA: Docky, show me how you do that.

DOC (*you can forgive him a harmless feeling of superiority*): Try it for yourself.

LOLA: Doc, you're clever. I never could do it.

DOC: Nothing to it.

LOLA: There is *too*. Show me how you do it. Doc.

DOC: And give away all my secrets? It's a gift, honey. A magic gift.

LOLA: Can't you give it to me?

DOC (*picks up newspaper*): A man has to keep some things to himself.

LOLA: It's not a gift at all, it's just some trick you *learned*.

DOC: O.K., Baby, any way you want to look at it.

LOLA: Let's have some music. How soon do you have to meet Ed Anderson?

(DOC *turns on radio.*)

DOC: I still got a little time. (*Pleased.*)

LOLA: Marie's going to be awfully happy when she sees the house all fixed up. She can entertain Bruce here when he comes, and maybe we could have a little party here and you can do your card tricks.

DOC: O.K.

LOLA: I think a young girl should be able to bring her friends home.

DOC: Sure.

LOLA: We never liked to sit around the house 'cause the folks always stayed there with us. (*Rises—starts dancing alone.*) Remember the dances we used to go to, Daddy?

DOC: Sure.

LOLA: We had awful good times—for a while, didn't we?

DOC: Yes, Baby.

LOLA: Remember the homecoming dance, when Charlie Kettlekamp and I won the Charleston contest?

DOC: Please, honey. I'm trying to read.

LOLA: And you got mad at him 'cause he thought he should take me home afterwards.

DOC: I did not.

LOLA: Yes, you did—Charlie was all right, Doc, really he was. You were just jealous.

DOC: I *wasn't jealous.*

LOLA (*She has become very coy and flirtatious now, an old dog playing old tricks*): You got jealous every time we went out any place and I even looked at another boy. There was never anything between Charlie and me; there never was.

DOC: That was a long time ago . . .

LOLA: Lots of other boys called me up for dates . . . Sammy Knight . . . Hand Biderman . . . Dutch McCoy.

DOC: Sure, Baby. You were the "it" girl.

LOLA (*pleading for his attention now*): But I saved all my dates for *you,* didn't I, Doc?

DOC (*trying to joke*): As far as *I* know, Baby.

LOLA (*hurt*): Daddy, I did. You *got* to believe that. I never took a date with any other boy but you.

DOC (*a little weary and impatient*): That's all forgotten now. (*Turns off radio.*)

LOLA: How can you talk that way, Doc? That was the happiest time of our lives. I'll never forget it.

DOC (*disapprovingly*): Honey!

LOLA (*at the window*): That was a nice spring. The trees were so heavy and green and the air smelled so sweet. Remember the walks we used to take, down to the old chapel, where it was so quiet and still? (*Sits on couch.*)

DOC: In the spring a young man's fancy turns . . . pretty fancy.

LOLA (*in the same tone of reverie*): I was pretty then, wasn't I, Doc? Remember the first time you kissed me? You were scared as a young girl, I believe, Doc; you trembled so. (*She is being very soft and delicate. Caught in the reverie, he chokes a little and cannot answer.*) We'd been going together all year and you were always so shy. Then for the first time you grabbed me and kissed me. Tears came to your eyes, Doc, and you said you'd love me forever and ever. Remember? You said . . . if I didn't marry you, you wanted to die . . . I remember 'cause it scared me for anyone to say a thing like that.

DOC (*in a repressed tone*): Yes, Baby.

LOLA: And when the evening came on, we stretched out on the cool grass and you kissed me all night long.

DOC (*opens doors*): Baby, you've got to forget those things. That was twenty years ago.

LOLA: I'll soon be forty. Those years have just vanished—vanished into thin air.

DOC: Yes.

LOLA: Just disappeared—like Little Sheba. (*Pause.*) Maybe you're sorry you married me now. You didn't know I was going to get old and fat and sloppy . . .

DOC: Oh, Baby!

LOLA: It's the truth. That's what I am. But I didn't know it, either. Are you sorry you married me, Doc?

DOC: Of course not.

LOLA: I mean, are you sorry you *had* to marry me?

DOC (*goes to porch*): We were never going to talk about that, Baby.

LOLA (*following* DOC *out*): You *were* the first one, Daddy, the *only* one. I'd just die if you didn't believe that.

DOC (*tenderly*): I know, Baby.

LOLA: You were so nice and so proper. Doc;

I thought nothing we could do together could ever be wrong—or make us unhappy. Do you think we did wrong, Doc?

DOC (*consoling*): No, Baby, of course I don't.

LOLA: I don't think anyone knows about it except my folks, do you?

DOC: Of course not, Baby.

LOLA (*follows him in*): I wish the baby had lived, Doc. I don't think that woman knew her business, do you, Doc?

DOC: I guess not.

LOLA: If we'd gone to a doctor, she would have lived, don't you think?

DOC: Perhaps.

LOLA: A doctor wouldn't have known we'd just got married, would he? Why were we so afraid?

DOC (*sits on couch*): We were just kids. Kids don't know how to look after things.

LOLA (*sits on couch*): If we'd had the baby she'd be a young girl now; then maybe you'd have *saved* your money, Doc, and she could be going to college—like Marie.

DOC: Baby, what's done is done.

LOLA: It must make you feel bad at times to think you had to give up being a doctor and to think you don't have any money like you used to.

DOC: No . . . no, Baby. We should never feel bad about what's past. What's in the past can't be helped. You . . . you've got to forget it and live for the present. If you can't forget the past, you stay in it and never get out. I might be a big M.D. today, instead of a chiropractor; we might have had a family to raise and be with us now; I might still have a lot of money if I'd used my head and invested it carefully, instead of gettin' drunk every night. We might have a nice house, and comforts, and friends. But we don't have any of those things. So what! We gotta keep on living, don't we? I can't stop just 'cause I made a few mistakes. I gotta keep goin' . . . somehow.

LOLA: Sure, Daddy.

DOC (*sighs and wipes brow*): I . . . I wish you wouldn't ask me questions like that, Baby. Let's not talk about it any more. I gotta keep goin', and not let things upset me, or . . . or . . . I saw enough at the City Hospital to keep me sober for a long time.

LOLA: I'm sorry, Doc. I didn't mean to upset you.

DOC: I'm not upset.

LOLA: What time'll you be home tonight?

DOC: 'Bout eleven o'clock.

LOLA: I wish you didn't have to go tonight. I feel kinda lonesome.

DOC: Ya, so am I, Baby, but some time soon, we'll go *out* together. I kinda hate to go to those night clubs and places since I stopped drinking, but some night I'll take you out to dinner.

LOLA: Oh, will you, Daddy?

DOC: We'll get dressed up and go to the Windermere and have a fine dinner and dance between courses.

LOLA (*eagerly*): Let's do, Daddy. I got a little money saved up. I got about forty dollars out in the kitchen. We can take that if you need it.

DOC: I'll have plenty of money the first of the month.

LOLA (*she has made a quick response to the change of mood, seeing a future evening of carefree fun.*): What are we sitting round here so serious for? (*Turns to radio.*) Let's have some music. (LOLA *gets a lively foxtrot on the radio, dances with* DOC. *They begin dancing vigorously as though to dispense with the sadness of the preceding dialogue, but slowly it winds them and leaves* LOLA *panting.*) We oughta go dancing . . . all the time, Docky . . . It'd be good for us. Maybe if I danced more often, I'd lose . . . some of . . . this fat. I remember . . . I used to be able to dance like this . . . all night . . . and not even notice . . . it. (LOLA *breaks into a Charleston routine as of yore.*) Remember the Charleston, Daddy?

(DOC *is clapping his hands in rhythm. Then* MARIE *bursts in through the front door, the personification of the youth that* LOLA *is trying to recapture.*)

DOC: Hi, Marie.

MARIE: What are you trying to do, a jig, Mrs. Delaney? (MARIE *doesn't intend her remark to be cruel, but it wounds* LOLA. LOLA *stops abruptly in her dancing, losing all the fun she has been able to create for herself. She feels she might cry; so to hide her feelings she hurries quietly out to kitchen, but* DOC *and* MARIE *do not notice.* MARIE *notices the change in atmosphere.*) Hey, what's been happening around here?

DOC: Lola got to feeling industrious. You oughta see the kitchen.

MARIE (*running to kitchen, where she is too observant of the changes to notice* LOLA *weeping in corner.* LOLA, *of course, straightens up as soon as* MARIE *enters*): What got into you, Mrs. Delaney? You've done wonders with the house. It looks marvelous.

LOLA (*quietly*): Thanks, Marie.

MARIE (*darting back into living room*): I can

hardly believe I'm in the same place.

DOC: Think your boy friend'll like it? (*Meaning* BRUCE.)

MARIE (*thinking of* TURK): You know how men are. Turk never notices things like that.

(*Starts into her room blowing a kiss to* DOC *on her way.* LOLA *comes back in, dabbing at her eyes.*)

DOC: Turk? (MARIE *is gone; he turns to* LOLA.) What's the matter, honey?

LOLA: I don't know.

DOC: Feel bad about something?

LOLA: I didn't want her to see me dancing that way. Makes me feel sorta silly.

DOC: Why, you're a fine dancer.

LOLA: I feel kinda silly.

MARIE (*jumps back into the room with her telegram*): My telegram's here. When did it come?

LOLA: It came about an hour ago, honey.

(LOLA *looks nervously at* DOC. DOC *looks puzzled and a little sore.*)

MARIE: Bruce is coming! "Arriving tomorrow 5:00 P.M. CST, Flight 22, Love, Bruce." When did the telegram come?

DOC (*looking hopelessly at* LOLA): So it came an hour ago.

LOLA (*nervously*): Isn't it nice I got the house all cleaned? Marie, you bring Bruce to dinner with us tomorrow night. It'll be a sort of wedding present.

MARIE: That would be wonderful, Mrs. Delaney, but I don't want you to go to any trouble.

LOLA: No trouble at all. Now I insist. (*Front doorbell rings.*) That must be Turk.

MARIE (*whisper*): Don't tell *him.* (*Goes to door.* LOLA *scampers to kitchen.*) Hi, Turk. Come on in.

TURK (*entering; stalks her*): Hi. (*Looks around to see if anyone is present, then takes her in his arms and starts to kiss her.*)

LOLA: I'm sorry, Doc. I'm sorry about the telegram.

DOC: Baby, people don't do things like that. Don't you understand? *Nice* people don't.

MARIE: Stop it!

TURK: What's the matter?

MARIE: They're in the kitchen.

(TURKS *sits with book.*)

DOC: Why didn't you give it to her when it came?

LOLA: Turk was posing for Marie this morning and I couldn't give it to her while he was here.

(TURK *listens at door.*)

DOC: Well, it just isn't nice to open other people's mail.

(TURK *goes to* MARIE'S *door.*)

LOLA: I guess I'm not nice then. That what you mean?

MARIE: Turk, will you get away from that door?

DOC: No, Baby, but . . .

LOLA: I don't see any harm in it, Doc. I steamed it open and sealed it back. (TURK *at switch in living room.*) She'll never know the difference. I don't see any harm in that, Doc.

DOC (*gives up*): O.K., Baby, if you don't see any harm in it, I guess I can't explain it. (*Starts getting ready to go.*)

LOLA: I'm sorry, Doc. Honest, I'll never do it again. Will you forgive me?

DOC (*giving her a peck of a kiss*): I forgive you.

MARIE (*comes back with book*): Let's look like we're studying.

TURK: Biology? Hot dog!

LOLA (*after* MARIE *leaves her room.*): Now I feel better. Do you have to go now?

(TURK *sits by* MARIE *on the couch.*)

DOC: Yah.

LOLA: Before you go, why don't you show your tricks to Marie?

DOC (*reluctantly*): Not now.

LOLA: Oh, please do. They'd be crazy about them.

DOC (*with pride*): O.K. (*Preens himself a little.*) If you think they'd enjoy them . . .

(LOLA, *starting to living room, stops suddenly upon seeing* MARIE *and* TURK *spooning behind a book. A broad, pleased smile breaks on her face and she stands silently watching.* DOC *is at sink.*)

Well . . . what's the matter, Baby?

LOLA (*in a soft voice*): Oh . . . nothing . . . nothing . . . Doc.

DOC: Well, do you want me to show 'em my tricks or don't you?

LOLA (*coming back to center kitchen; in a secretive voice with a little giggle*): I guess they wouldn't be interested now.

DOC (*with injured pride; a little sore*): Oh, very well.

LOLA: Come and look, Daddy.

DOC (*shocked and angry*): No!

LOLA: Just one little look. They're just kids, Daddy. It's sweet. (*Drags him by arm.*)

DOC (*jerking loose*): Stop it, Baby. I won't do it. It's not decent to snoop around spying on people like that. It's cheap and mischievous and mean.

LOLA (*this had never occurred to her*): Is it?

DOC: Of course it is.

LOLA: I don't spy on Marie and Turk to be mischievous and mean.

DOC: Then why *do* you do it?

LOLA: You watch young people make love in the movies, don't you, Doc? There's nothing wrong with that. And I *know* Marie and I like her, and Turk's nice, too. They're both so young and pretty. Why shouldn't I watch them?

DOC: I give up.

LOLA: Well, why shouldn't I?

DOC: I don't know, Baby, but it's not nice.

(TURK *kisses* MARIE'S *ear*.)

LOLA (*plaintive*): I think it's one of the nicest things I know.

MARIE: Let's go out on the porch.

(*They steal out.*)

DOC: It's not right for Marie to do that, particularly since Bruce is coming. We shouldn't allow it.

LOLA: Oh, they don't do any harm, Doc. I think it's all right.

(TURK *and* MARIE *go to porch.*)

DOC: It's not all right. I don't know why you encourage that sort of thing.

LOLA: I don't encourage it.

DOC: You do, too. You like that fellow Turk. You said so. And I say he's no good. Marie's sweet and innocent; she doesn't understand guys like him. I think I oughta run him outa the house.

LOLA: Daddy, you wouldn't do that.

DOC (*very heated*): Then you talk to her and tell her how we feel.

LOLA: Hush, Daddy. They'll hear you.

DOC: I don't care if they do hear me.

LOLA (*to* DOC *at stove*): Don't get upset, Daddy. Bruce is coming and Turk won't be around any longer. I promise you.

DOC: All right. I better go.

LOLA: I'll go with you, Doc. Just let me run up and get a sweater. Now wait for me.

DOC: Hurry, Baby.

(LOLA *goes upstairs.* DOC *is at platform when he hears* TURK *laugh on the porch.* DOC *sees whisky bottle. Reaches for it and hears* MARIE *giggle. Turns away as* TURK *laughs again. Turns back to the bottle and hears* LOLA's *voice from upstairs.*)

LOLA: I'll be there in a minute, Doc. (*Enters downstairs.*) I'm all ready. (DOC *turns out kitchen lights and they go into living room.*) I'm walking Doc down to the bus. (DOC *sees* TURK *with* LOLA's *picture. Takes it out of his hand, puts it on shelf as* LOLA *leads him out.* DOC *is offstage.*) Then I'll go for a long walk in the moonlight. Have a good time. (*She exits.*)

MARIE: 'Bye, Mrs. Delaney. (*Exits.*)

TURK: He hates my guts. (*Goes to front door.*)

MARIE: Oh, he does not. (*Follows* TURK, *blocks his exit in door.*)

TURK: Yes, he does. If you ask me, he's jealous.

MARIE: Jealous?

TURK: I've always thought he had a crush on you.

MARIE: Now, Turk, don't be silly. Doc is nice to me. It's just in a few little things he does, like fixing my breakfast, but he's nice to everyone.

TURK: He ever make a pass?

MARIE: No. He'd never get fresh.

TURK: He better not.

MARIE: Turk, don't be ridiculous. Doc's such a nice, quiet man; if he gets any fun out of being nice to me, why not?

TURK: He's got a wife of his own, hasn't he? Why doesn't he make a few passes at her?

MARIE: Thing like that are none of our business.

TURK: O.K. How about a snuggle, lovely?

MARIE (*a little prim and businesslike*): No more for tonight, Turk.

TURK: Why's tonight different from any other night?

MARIE: I think we should make it a rule, every once in a while, just to sit and talk. (*Starts to sit on couch, but goes to chair.*)

TURK (*restless, sits on couch*): O.K. What'll we talk about?

MARIE: Well . . . there's lotsa things.

TURK: O.K. Start in.

MARIE: A person doesn't start a conversation that way.

TURK: Start it any way you want to.

MARIE: Two people should have something to talk about, like politics or psychology or religion.

TURK: How 'bout sex?

MARIE: Turk!

TURK (*chases her around couch*): Have you read

the Kinsey Report, Miss Buckholder?

MARIE: I should say not.

TURK: How old were you when you had your first affair, Miss Buckholder? And did you ever have relations with your grandfather?

MARIE: Turk, stop it.

TURK: You wanted to talk about something; I was only trying to please. Let's have a kiss.

MARIE: Not tonight.

TURK: Who you savin' it up for?

MARIE: Don't talk that way.

TURK (*gets up, yawns*): Well, thanks, Miss Buckholder, for a nice evening. It's been a most enjoyable talk.

MARIE (*anxious*): Turk, where are you going?

TURK: I guess I'm a man of action, Baby.

MARIE: Turk, don't go.

TURK: Why not? I'm not doin' any good here.

MARIE: Don't go.

TURK (*returns and she touches him; they sit on couch*): Now why didn't you think of this before? C'mon, let's get to work.

MARIE: Oh, Turk, this is all we ever do.

TURK: Are you complaining?

MARIE (*weakly*): No.

TURK: Then what do you want to put on such a front for?

MARIE: It's not a front.

TURK: What else is it? (*Mimicking.*) Oh, no, Turk. Not tonight, Turk. I want to talk about philosophy, Turk. (*Himself again.*) When all the time you know that if I went outa here without givin' you a good lovin' up you'd be sore as hell . . . Wouldn't you?

MARIE (*she has to admit to herself it's true; she chuckles*): Oh . . . Turk . . .

TURK: It's true, isn't it?

MARIE: Maybe.

TURK: How about tonight, lovely; going to be lonesome?

MARIE: Turk, you're in training.

TURK: What of it? I can throw that old javelin any old time, *any* old time. C'mon, Baby, we've got by with it before, haven't we?

MARIE: I'm not so sure.

TURK: What do you mean?

MARIE: Sometimes I think Mrs. Delaney knows.

TURK: Well, bring her along. I'll take care of her, too, if it'll keep her quiet.

MARIE (*a pretense of being shocked*): Turk!

TURK: What makes you think so?

MARIE: Women just sense those things. She asks so many questions.

TURK: She ever *say* anything?

MARIE: No.

TURK: Now *you're* imagining things.

MARIE: Maybe.

TURK: Well, stop it.

MARIE: O.K.

TURK (*follows* MARIE): Honey, I know I talk awful rough around you at times; I never was a very gentlemanly bastard, but you really don't mind it . . . do you? (*She only smiles mischievously.*) Anyway, you know I'm nuts about you.

MARIE (*smug*): Are you?

(*Now they engage in a little rough-house, he cuffing her like an affectionate bear, she responding with "Stop it," "Turk, that hurt," etc. And she slaps him playfully. Then they laugh together at their own pretense. Now* LOLA *enters the back way very quietly, tiptoeing through the dark kitchen, standing by the doorway where she can peek at them. There is a quiet, satisfied smile on her face. She watches every move they make, alertly.*)

TURK: Now, Miss Buckholder, what is your opinion of the psychodynamic pressure of living in the atomic age?

MARIE (*playfully*): Turk, don't make fun of me.

TURK: Tonight?

MARIE (*her eyes dance as she puts him off just a little longer*): Well.

TURK: Tonight will never come again. (*This is true. She smiles.*) O.K.?

MARIE: Tonight will never come again . . . (*They embrace and start to dance.*) Let's go out somewhere first and have a few beers. We can't come back till they're asleep.

TURK: O.K.

(*They dance slowly out the door. Then* LOLA *moves quietly into the living room and out onto the porch. There she can be heard calling plaintively in a lost voice.*)

LOLA: Little Sheba . . . Come back . . . Come back, Little Sheba. Come back.

ACT II

SCENE 1

(*The next morning.* LOLA *and* DOC *are at breakfast again.* LOLA *is rambling on while* DOC *sits meditatively, his head down, his face in his hands.*)

LOLA (*in a light, humorous way, as though the faults of youth were as blameless as the uncontrollable actions of a puppy; chuckles*): Then they danced for a while and went out together, arm in arm . . .

DOC (*sitting at table, very nervous and tense*): I don't wanta hear any more about it, Baby.

LOLA: What's the matter, Docky?

DOC: Nothing.

LOLA: You look like you didn't feel very good.

DOC: I didn't sleep well last night.

LOLA: You didn't take any of those sleeping pills, did you?

DOC: No.

LOLA: Well, don't. The doctors say they're terrible for you.

DOC: I'll feel better after a while.

LOLA: Of course you will.

DOC: What time did Marie come in last night?

LOLA: I don't know, Doc. I went to bed early and went right to sleep. Why?

DOC: Oh . . . nothing.

LOLA: You musta slept if you didn't hear her.

DOC: I heard her; it was after midnight.

LOLA: Then what did you ask me for?

DOC: I wasn't sure it was her.

LOLA: What do you mean?

DOC: I thought I heard a man's voice.

LOLA: Turk probably brought her inside the door.

DOC (*troubled*): I thought I heard someone laughing. A man's laugh . . . I guess I was just hearing things.

LOLA: Say your prayer?

DOC (*gets up*): Yes.

LOLA: Kiss me 'bye. (*He leans over and kisses her, then puts on his coat and starts to leave.*) Do you think you could get home a little early? I want you to help me entertain Bruce. Marie said he'd be here about 5:30. I'm going to have a lovely dinner: stuffed pork chops, twice-baked potatoes, and asparagus, and for dessert a big chocolate cake and maybe ice cream . . .

DOC: Sounds fine.

LOLA: So you get home and help me.

DOC: O.K.

(DOC *leaves kitchen and goes into living room. Again on the chair is* MARIE's *scarf. He picks it up as before and fondles it. Then there is the sound of* TURK's *laughter, soft and barely audible. It sounds like the laugh of a sated Bacchus.* DOC's *body stiffens. It is a sickening fact he must face and it has been revealed to him in its ugliest light. The lyrical grace,*

the spiritual ideal of Ave Maria is shattered. He has been fighting the truth, maybe suspecting all along that he was deceiving himself. Now he looks as though he might vomit. All his blind confusion is inside him. With an immobile expression of blankness on his face, he stumbles into the table above the sofa.)

LOLA (*still in kitchen*): Haven't you gone yet, Docky?

DOC (*dazed*): No . . . no, Baby.

LOLA (*in doorway*): Anything the matter?

DOC: No . . . no. I'm all right now. (*Drops scarf, takes hat, exits. He has managed to sound perfectly natural. He braces himself and goes out.* LOLA *stands a moment, looking after him with a little curiosity. Then* MRS. COFFMAN *enters, sticks her head in back door.*)

MRS. COFFMAN: Anybody home?

LOLA (*on platform*): 'Morning, Mrs. Coffman.

MRS. COFFMAN (*inspecting the kitchen's new look*): So this is what you've been up to, Mrs. Delaney.

LOLA (*proud*): Yes, I been busy.

(MARIE's *door opens and closes.* MARIE *sticks her head out of her bedroom door to see if the coast is clear, then sticks her head back in again to whisper to* TURK *that he can leave without being observed.*)

MRS. COFFMAN: Busy? Good Lord, I never seen such activity. What got into you, Lady?

LOLA: Company tonight. I thought I'd fix things up a little.

MRS. COFFMAN: You mean you done all this in one day?

LOLA (*with simple pride*): I said I been busy.

MRS. COFFMAN: Dear God, you done your spring house cleaning all in one day.

(TURK *appears in living room.*)

LOLA (*appreciating this*): I fixed up the living room a little, too.

MRS. COFFMAN: I must see it. (*Goes into living room.* TURK *overhears her and ducks back into* MARIE's *room, shutting the door behind himself and* MARIE.) I declare! Overnight you turn the place into something really swanky.

LOLA: Yes, and I bought a few new things, too.

MRS. COFFMAN: Neat as a pin, and so warm and cozy. I take my hat off to you, Mrs. Delaney. I didn't know you had it in you. All these years, now, I been sayin' to myself, "That Mrs. Delaney is a good for nothing, sits around the house all day, and never so much as shakes a dust mop." I guess it just shows, we never really know what people are like.

LOLA: I still got some coffee.

MRS. COFFMAN: Not now, Mrs. Delaney. Seeing your house so clean makes me feel ashamed. I gotta get home and get to work. (*Goes to kitchen.*)

LOLA (*follows*): I hafta get busy, too. I got to get out all the silver and china. I like to set the table early, so I can spend the rest of the day looking at it.

(*Both laugh.*)

MRS. COFFMAN: Good day, Mrs. Delaney. (*Exits.*)

(*Hearing the screen door slam,* MARIE *guards the kitchen door and* TURK *slips out the front. But neither has counted on* DOC's *reappearance. After seeing that* TURK *is safe,* MARIE *blows a good-bye kiss to him and joins* LOLA *in the kitchen. But* DOC *is coming in the front door just as* TURK *starts to go out. There is a moment of blind embarrassment, during which* DOC *only looks stupefied and* TURK, *after mumbling an unintelligible apology, runs out. First* DOC *is mystified, trying to figure it all out. His face looks more and more troubled. Meanwhile,* MARIE *and* LOLA *are talking in the kitchen.*)

MARIE: Boo! (*Sneaking up behind* LOLA *at back porch.*)

LOLA (*jumping around*): Heavens! You scared me, Marie. You up already?

MARIE: Yah.

LOLA: This is Saturday. You could sleep as late as you wanted.

MARIE (*pouring a cup of coffee*): I thought I'd get up early and help you.

LOLA: Honey, I'd sure appreciate it. You can put up the table in the living room, after you've had your breakfast. That's where we'll eat. Then you can help me set it.

(DOC *closes door.*)

MARIE: O.K.

LOLA: Want a sweet roll?

MARIE: I don't think so. Turk and I had so much beer last night. He got kinda tight.

LOLA: He shouldn't do that, Marie.

MARIE (*starts for living room*): Just keep the coffee hot for me. I'll want another cup in a minute. (*Stops on seeing* DOC.) Why, Dr. Delaney! I thought you'd gone.

DOC (*trying to sustain his usual manner*): Good morning, Marie. (*But not looking at her.*)

MARIE (*she immediately wonders*): Why . . . why . . . how long have you been here, Doc?

DOC: Just got here, just this minute.

LOLA (*comes in*): That you, Daddy?

DOC: It's me.

LOLA: What are you doing back?

DOC: I . . . I just thought maybe I'd feel better . . . if I took a glass of soda water . . .

LOLA: I'm afraid you're not well, Daddy.

DOC: I'm all right. (*Starts for kitchen.*)

LOLA (*helping* MARIE *with table*): The soda's on the drainboard.

(DOC *goes to kitchen, fixes some soda, and stands a moment, just thinking. Then he sits sipping the soda, as though he were trying to make up his mind about something.*)

Marie, would you help me move the table? It'd be nice now if we had a dining room, wouldn't it? But if we had a dining room, I guess we wouldn't have you, Marie. It was my idea to turn the dining room into a bedroom and rent it. I thought of lots of things to do for extra money . . . a few years ago . . . when Doc was so . . . so sick.

(*They set up table—*LOLA *gets cloth from cabinet.*)

MARIE: This is a lovely tablecloth.

LOLA: Irish linen. Doc's mother gave it to us when we got married. She gave us all our silver and china, too. The china's Havelin. I'm so proud of it. It's the most valuable possession we own. I just washed it . . . Will you help me bring it in? (*Getting china from kitchen.*) Doc was sortuva Mama's boy. He was an only child and his mother thought the sun rose and set in him. Didn't she, Docky? She brought Doc up like a real gentleman.

MARIE: Where are the napkins?

LOLA: Oh, I forgot them. They're so nice I keep them in my bureau drawer with my handkerchiefs. Come upstairs and we'll get them.

(LOLA *and* MARIE *go upstairs. Then* DOC *listens to be sure* LOLA *and* MARIE *are upstairs, looks cautiously at the whiskey bottle on pantry shelf but manages to resist several times. Finally he gives in to temptation, grabs bottle off shelf, then starts wondering how to get past* LOLA *with it. Finally, it occurs to him to wrap it inside his trench coat which he gets from pantry and carries over his arm.* LOLA *and* MARIE *are heard upstairs. They return to the living room and continue setting table as* DOC *enters from kitchen on his way out.*)

LOLA (*coming downstairs*): Did you ever notice how nice he keeps his fingernails? Not many men think of things like that. And he used to take his mother to church every Sunday.

MARIE (*at table*): Oh, Doc's a real gentleman.

LOLA: Treats women like they were all beautiful angels. We went together a whole year before he even kissed me. (DOC *comes through the living room with coat and bottle, going to front door.*) On your way back to the office now, Docky?

DOC (*his back to them*): Yes.

LOLA: Aren't you going to kiss me good-bye before you go, Daddy? (*She goes to him and kisses him.* MARIE *catches* DOC'*s eye and smiles. Then she exits to her room, leaving door open.*) Get home early as you can. I'll need you. We gotta give Bruce a royal welcome.

DOC: Yes, Baby.

LOLA: Feeling all right?

DOC: Yes.

LOLA (*in doorway,* DOC *is on porch*): Take care of yourself.

DOC (*in a toneless voice*): Good-bye. (*He goes.*)

LOLA (*coming back to table with pleased expression, which changes to a puzzled look, calls to* MARIE): Now that's funny. Why did Doc take his raincoat? It's a beautiful day. There isn't a cloud in sight.

SCENE 2

(*It is now 5:30. The scene is the same as the preceding except that more finishing touches have been added and the two women, still primping the table, lighting the tapers, are dressed in their best.* LOLA *is arranging the centerpiece.*)

LOLA (*above table, fixing flowers*): I just love lilacs, don't you, Marie? (*Takes one and studies it.*) Mrs. Coffman was nice; she let me have all I wanted. (*Looks at it very closely.*) Aren't they pretty? And they smell so sweet. I think they're the nicest flower there is.

MARIE: They don't last long.

LOLA (*respectfully*): No. Just a few days. Mrs. Coffman's started blooming just day before yesterday.

MARIE: By the first of the week they'll all be gone.

LOLA: Vanish . . . they'll vanish into thin air. (*Gayer now.*) Here, honey, we have them to spare now. Put this in your hair. There. (MARIE *does.*) Mrs. Coffman's been so nice lately. I didn't use to like her. Now where could Doc be? He promised he'd get here early. He didn't even come home for lunch.

MARIE (*gets two chairs from bedroom*): Mrs. De-

laney, you're a peach to go to all this trouble.

LOLA (*gets salt and pepper*): Shoot, I'm gettin' more fun out of it than you are. Do you think Bruce is going to like us?

MARIE: If he doesn't, I'll never speak to him again.

LOLA (*eagerly*): I'm just dying to meet him. But I feel sorta bad I never got to do anything nice for Turk.

MARIE (*carefully prying*): Did . . . Doc ever say anything to you about Turk . . . and me?

LOLA: About Turk and you? No, honey. Why?

MARIE: I just wondered.

LOLA: What if Bruce finds out that you've been going with someone else?

MARIE: Bruce and I had a very businesslike understanding before I left for school that we weren't going to sit around lonely just because we were separated.

LOLA: Aren't you being kind of mean to Turk?

MARIE: I don't think so.

LOLA: How's he going to feel when Bruce comes?

MARIE: He may be sore for a little while, but he'll get over it.

LOLA: Won't he feel bad?

MARIE: He's had his eye on a pretty little Spanish girl in his history class for a long time. I like Turk, but he's not the marrying kind.

LOLA: No! Really?

(LOLA, *with a look of sad wonder on her face, sits on arm of couch. It's been a serious disillusionment.*)

MARIE: What's the matter?

LOLA: I . . . I just felt kinda tired.

(*Sharp buzzing of doorbell.* MARIE *runs to answer it.*)

MARIE: That must be Bruce. (*She skips to the mirror again, then to door.*) Bruce!

BRUCE: How are you, sweetheart?

MARIE: Wonderful.

BRUCE: Did you get my wire?

MARIE: Sure.

BRUCE: You're looking swell.

MARIE: Thanks. What took you so long to get here?

BRUCE: Well, honey, I had to go to my hotel and take a bath.

MARIE: Bruce, this is Mrs. Delaney.

BRUCE (*now he gets the cozy quality out of his voice*): How do you do, ma'am?

LOLA: How d'ya do?

BRUCE: Marie has said some very nice things about you in her letters.

MARIE: Mrs. Delaney has fixed the grandest dinner for us.

BRUCE: Now that was to be my treat. I have a big expense account now, honey. I thought we could all go down to the hotel and have dinner there, and celebrate first with a few cocktails.

LOLA: Oh, we can have cocktails, too. Excuse me, just a minute.

(*She hurries to the kitchen and starts looking for the whiskey.* BRUCE *kisses* MARIE.)

MARIE (*whispers*): Now, Bruce, she's been working on this dinner all day. She even cleaned the house for you.

BRUCE (*with a surveying look*): Did she?

MARIE: And Doc's joining us. You'll like Doc.

BRUCE: Honey, are we going to have to stay here the whole evening?

MARIE: We just can't eat and run. We'll get away as soon as we can.

BRUCE: I hope so. I got the raise, sweetheart. They're giving me new territory.

(LOLA *is frantic in the kitchen, having found the bottle missing. She hurries back into the living room.*)

LOLA: You kids are going to have to entertain yourselves awhile 'cause I'm going to be busy in the kitchen. Why don't you turn on the radio, Marie? Get some dance music. I'll shut the door so . . . so I won't disturb you.

(LOLA *does so, then goes to the telephone.*)

MARIE: Come and see my room, Bruce. I've fixed it up just darling. And I've got your picture in the prettiest frame right on my dresser.

(*They exit and their voices are heard from the bedroom while* LOLA *is phoning.*)

LOLA (*at the phone*): This is Mrs. Delaney. Is . . . Doc there? Well, then, is Ed Anderson there? Well, would you give me Ed Anderson's telephone number? You see, he sponsored Doc into the club and helped him . . . you know . . . and . . . and I was a little worried tonight . . . Oh, thanks. Yes, I've got it. (*She writes down number.*) Could you have Ed Anderson call me if he comes in? Thank you. (*She hangs up. On her face is a dismal expression of fear, anxiety and doubt. She searches flour bin, icebox, closet. Then she goes into the living room, calling to* MARIE *and* BRUCE *as she comes.*) I . . . I guess we'll go ahead without Doc, Marie.

MARIE (*enters from her room*): What's the matter with Doc, Mrs. Delaney?

LOLA: Well . . . he got held up at the office . . . just one of those things, you know. It's too bad. It would have to happen when I needed him most.

MARIE: Sure you don't need any help?

LOLA: Huh? Oh, no. I'll make out. Everything's ready. I tell you what I'm going to do. Three's a crowd, so I'm going to be the butler and serve the dinner to you two young lovebirds . . . (*The telephone rings.*) Pardon me . . . pardon me just a minute. (*She rushes to phone, closing the door behind her.*) Hello? Ed? Have you seen Doc? He went out this morning and hasn't come back. We're having company for dinner and he was supposed to be home early. . . . That's not all. This time we've had a quart of whiskey in the kitchen and Doc's never gone near it. I went to get it tonight. I was going to serve some cocktails. It was *gone*. Yes, I saw it there yesterday. No, I don't think so. . . . He said this morning he had an upset stomach but . . . Oh, would you? . . . Thank you, Mr. Anderson. Thank you a million times. And you let me know when you find out anything. Yes, I'll be here . . . yes. (*Hangs up and crosses back to living room.*) Well, I guess we're all ready.

BRUCE: Aren't you going to look at your present?

MARIE: Oh, sure, let's get some scissors.

(*Their voices continue in bedroom.*)

MARIE (*enters with* BRUCE): Mrs. Delaney, we think you should eat with us.

LOLA: Oh, no, honey, I'm not very hungry. Besides, this is the first time you've been together in months and I think you should be alone. Marie, why don't you light the candles? Then we'll have just the right atmosphere.

(*She goes into kitchen, gets tomato-juice glasses from icebox while* BRUCE *lights the candles.*)

BRUCE: Do we have to eat by candlelight? I won't be able to see.

(LOLA *returns.*)

LOLA: Now, Bruce, you sit here. (*He and* MARIE *sit.*) Isn't that going to be cozy? Dinner for two. Sorry we won't have time for cocktails. Let's have a little music. (*She turns on the radio and a Viennese waltz swells up as the curtain falls with* LOLA *looking at the young people eating.*)

SCENE 3

(*Funereal atmosphere. It is about 5:30 the next morning. The sky is just beginning to get light outside, while inside the room the shadows still cling heavily to the corners. The remains of last night's dinner clutter the table in the living room. The candles have guttered down to stubs amid the dirty dinner plates, and the lilacs in the centerpiece have wilted.* LOLA *is sprawled on the davenport, sleeping. Slowly she awakens and regards the morning light. She gets up and looks about strangely, beginning to show despair for the situation she is in. She wears the same spiffy dress she had on the night before but it is wrinkled now, and her marcelled coiffure is awry. One silk stocking has twisted loose and falls around her ankle. When she is sufficiently awake to realize her situation, she rushes to the telephone and dials a number.*)

LOLA (*at telephone; she sounds frantic*): Mr. Anderson? Mr. Anderson, this is Mrs. Delaney again. I'm sorry to call you so early, but I just *had* to . . . Did you find Doc? . . . No, he's not home yet. I don't suppose he'll come home till he's drunk all he can hold and wants to sleep. . . . I don't know what else to think, Mr. Andersons. I'm scared, Mr. Anderson. I'm awful scared. Will you come right over? . . . . Thanks, Mr. Anderson. (*She hangs up and goes to kitchen to make coffee. She finds some left from the night before, so turns on the fire to warm it up. She wanders around vaguely, trying to get her thoughts in order, jumping at every sound. Pours herself a cup of coffee, then takes it to living room, sits and sips it. Very quietly* DOC *enters through the back way into the kitchen. He carries a big bottle of whiskey which he carefully places back in the pantry, not making a sound, hangs up overcoat, then puts suitcoat on back of chair. Starts to go upstairs. But* LOLA *speaks.*) Doc? That you, Doc? (*Then* DOC *quietly walks in from kitchen. He is staggering drunk, but he is managing for a few minutes to appear as though he were perfectly sober and nothing had happened. His steps, however, are not too sure and his eyes are like blurred ink pots.* LOLA *is too frightened to talk. Her mouth is gaping and she is breathless with fear.*)

DOC: Good morning, honey.

LOLA: Doc! You all right?

DOC: The morning paper here? I wanta see the morning paper.

LOLA: Doc, we don't get a morning paper. *You* know that.

DOC: Oh, then I suppose I'm drunk or something. That what you're trying to say?

LOLA: No, Doc . . .

DOC: Then give me the morning paper.

LOLA (*scampering to get last night's paper from console table*): Sure, Doc. Here it is. Now you just sit there and be quiet.

DOC (*resistance rising*): Why shouldn't I be quiet?

LOLA: Nothin', Doc . . .

DOC (*Has trouble unfolding paper. He places it before his face in order not to be seen. But he is too blind even to see*): Nothing, Doc. (*Mockingly.*)

LOLA (*cautiously, after a few minutes' silence*): Doc, are you all right?

DOC: Of course, I'm all right. Why shouldn't I be all right?

LOLA: Where you been?

DOC: What's it your business where I been? I been to London to see the Queen. What do you think of that? (*Apparently she doesn't know what to think of it.*) Just let me alone. That's all I ask. I'm all right.

LOLA (*whimpering*): Doc, what made you do it? You said you'd be home last night . . . 'cause we were having company. Bruce was here and I had a big dinner fixed . . . and you never came. What was the matter, Doc?

DOC (*mockingly*): We had a big dinner for *Bruce.*

LOLA: Doc, it was for you, too.

DOC: Well . . . I don't want it.

LOLA: Don't get mad, Doc.

DOC (*threateningly*): Where's Marie?

LOLA: I don't know, Doc. She didn't come in last night. She was out with Bruce.

DOC (*back to audience*): I suppose you tucked them in bed together and peeked through the keyhole and applauded.

LOLA (*sickened*): Doc, don't talk that way. Bruce is a nice boy. They're gonna get married.

DOC: He probably *has* to marry her, the poor bastard. Just 'cause she's pretty and he got amorous one day . . . Just like I had to marry *you.*

LOLA: Oh, Doc!

DOC: You and Marie are both a couple of sluts.

LOLA: Doc, please don't talk like that.

DOC: What are you good for? You can't even get up in the morning and cook my breakfast.

LOLA (*mumbling*): I will, Doc. I will after this.

DOC: You won't even sweep the floors, till some bozo comes along to make love to Marie, and then you fix things up like Buckingham Palace or a Chinese whorehouse with perfume on the lampbulbs, and flowers, and the gold-trimmed china *my mother* gave us. We're not going to use these any more. My mother didn't buy those dishes for whores to eat off of.

(*He jerks the cloth off the table, sending the dishes rattling to the floor.*)

LOLA: Doc! Look what you done.

DOC: Look what I *did,* not *done.* I'm going to get me a drink. (*Goes to kitchen.*)

LOLA (*follows to platform*): Oh, no, Doc! You know what it does to you!

DOC: You're damn right I know what it does to me. It makes me willing to come home here and look at you, you two-ton old heifer. (*Takes a long swallow.*) There! And pretty soon I'm going to have another, then another.

LOLA (*with dread*): Oh, Doc! (LOLA *takes phone.* DOC *sees this, rushes for the butcher-knife from kitchen-cabinet drawer. Not finding it, he gets a hatchet from the back porch.*) Mr. Anderson? Come quick, Mr. Anderson. He's back. He's *back!* He's got a hatchet!

DOC: God damn you! Get away from that telephone. (*He chases her into living room where she gets the couch between them.*) That's right, phone! Tell the world I'm drunk. Tell the whole damn world. Scream your head off, you fat slut. Holler till all the neighbors think I'm beatin' hell outuv you. Where's Bruce now—under Marie's bed? You got all fresh and pretty for him, didn't you? Combed your hair for once—you even washed the back of your neck and put on a girdle. You were willing to harness all that fat into one bundle.

LOLA (*about to faint under the weight of the crushing accusations*): Doc, don't say any more ... I'd rather you hit me with an axe, Doc ... Honest I would. But I can't stand to hear you talk like that.

DOC: I oughta hack off all that fat, and then wait for Marie and chop off those pretty ankles she's always dancing around on ... then start lookin' for Turk and fix him too.

LOLA: Daddy, you're talking crazy!

DOC: I'm making sense for the first time in my life. You didn't know I knew about it, did you? But I saw him coming outa there, I saw him. You knew about it all the time and thought you were hidin' something ...

LOLA: Daddy, I didn't know anything about it at all. Honest, Daddy.

DOC: Then *you're* the one that's crazy, if you think I didn't know. You were running a regular house, weren't you? It's probably been going on for years, ever since we were married.

(*He lunges for her. She breaks for kitchen. They struggle in front of sink.*)

LOLA: Doc, it's not so; it's not so. You gotta believe me, Doc.

DOC: You're lyin'. But none a that's gonna happen any more. I'm gonna fix you now, once and for all. . . .

LOLA: Doc ... don't do that to me. (LOLA, *in a frenzy of fear, clutches him around the neck holding arm with axe by his side.*) Remember, Doc. It's *me,* Lola! You said I was the prettiest girl you ever saw. Remember, Doc! It's me! Lola!

DOC (*the memory has overpowered him; he collapses, slowly mumbling*): Lola ... my pretty Lola.

(*He passes out on the floor.* LOLA *stands now, as though in a trance. Quietly* MRS. COFFMAN *comes creeping in through the back way.*)

MRS. COFFMAN (*calling softly*): Mrs. Delaney! (LOLA *doesn't even hear.* MRS. COFFMAN *comes in.*) Mrs. Delaney! Here you are, Lady. I heard screaming and I was frightened for you.

LOLA: I ... I'll be all right ... some men are comin' pretty soon; everything'll be all right.

MRS. COFFMAN: I'll stay until they get here.

LOLA (*feeling a sudden need*): Would you ... would you *please,* Mrs. Coffman? (*Breaks into sobs.*)

MRS. COFFMAN: Of course, Lady. (*Regarding* DOC.) The doctor got "sick" again?

LOLA (*mumbling*): Some men ... 'll be here pretty soon ...

MRS. COFFMAN: I'll try to straighten things up before they get here. . . .

(*She rights chair, hangs up telephone and picks up the axe, which she is holding when* ED ANDERSON *and* ELMO HUSTON *enter unannounced. They are experienced AA's. Neatly dressed businessmen approaching middle-age.*)

ED: Pardon us for walking right in, Mrs. Delaney, but I didn't want to waste a second. (*Kneels by* DOC.)

LOLA (*weakly*): It's all right. . . .

(*Both men observe* DOC *on the floor, and their expressions hold understanding mixed with a feeling of irony. There is even a slight smile of irony on* ED's *face. They have developed the surgeon's objectivity.*)

ED: Where is the hatchet? (*To* ELMO *as though appraising* DOC's *condition.*) What do you think, Elmo?

ELMO: We can't leave him here if he's gonna play around with hatchets.

ED: Give me a hand, Elmo. We'll get him to sit up and then try to talk some sense into him. (*They struggle with the lumpy body,* DOC *grunting his resistance.*) Come on, Doc, old boy. It's Ed and Elmo. We're going to take care of you. (*They seat him at table.*)

DOC (*through a thick fog*): Lemme alone.

ED: Wake up. We're taking you away from here.

DOC: Lemme 'lone, God damn it. (*Falls forward, head on table.*)

ELMO (*To* MRS. COFFMAN): Is there any coffee?

MRS. COFFMAN: I think so, I'll see. (*Goes to stove with cup from drainboard. Lights fire under coffee and waits for it to get heated.*)

ED: He's way beyond coffee.

ELMO: It'll help some. Get something hot into his stomach.

ED: If we could get him to eat. How 'bout some hot food, Doc?

(DOC *gestures and they don't push the matter.*)

ELMO: City Hospital, Ed?

ED: I guess that's what it will have to be.

LOLA: Where you going to take him?

(ELMO *goes to phone; speaks quietly to City Hospital.*)

ED: Don't know. Wanta talk to him first.

MRS. COFFMAN (*coming in with the coffee*): Here's the coffee.

ED (*taking cup*): Hold him, Elmo, while I make him swallow this.

ELMO: Come on, Doc, drink your coffee.

(DOC *only blubbers.*)

DOC (*after the coffee is down*): Uh . . . what . . . what's goin' on here?

ED: It's me, Doc. Your old friend Ed. I got Elmo with me.

DOC (*twisting his face painfully*): Get out, both of you. Lemme 'lone.

ED (*with certainty*): We're takin' you with us, Doc.

DOC: Hell you are. I'm all right. I just had a little slip. We all have slips. . . .

ED: Sometimes, Doc, but we gotta get over 'em.

DOC: I'll be O.K. Just gimme a day to sober up. I'll be as good as new.

ED: Remember the last time, Doc? You said you'd be all right in the morning and we found you with a broken collar bone. Come on.

DOC: Boys, I'll be all right. Now lemme alone.

ED: How much has he had, Mrs. Delaney?

LOLA: I don't know. He had a quart when he left here yesterday and he didn't get home till now.

ED: He's probably been through a *couple* of quarts. He's been dry for a long time. It's going to hit him pretty hard. Yah, he'll be a pretty sick man for a few days. (*Louder to* DOC, *as though he were talking to a deaf man.*) Wanta go to the City Hospital, Doc?

DOC (*this has a sobering effect on him; he looks about him furtively for possible escape*): No . . . no, boys. Don't take me there. That's a torture chamber. No, Ed. You wouldn't do that to me.

ED: They'll sober you up.

DOC: Ed, I been there; I've seen the place. That's where they take the crazy people. You can't do that to me, Ed.

ED: Well, *you're* crazy, aren't you? Goin' after your wife with a hatchet.

(*They lift* DOC *to his feet.* DOC *looks with dismal pleading in his eyes at* LOLA, *who has her face in her hands.*)

DOC (*so plaintive, a sob in his voice*): Honey! Honey!

(LOLA *can't look at him. Now* DOC *tries to make a getaway, bolting blindly into the living room before the two men catch him and hold him in front of living-room table*)

Honey, don't let 'em take me there. They'll believe *you.* Tell 'em you won't *let* me take a drink.

LOLA: Isn't there any place else you could take him?

ED: Private sanitariums cost a lotta dough.

LOLA: I got forty dollars in the kitchen.

ED: That won't be near enough.

DOC: I'll be at the meeting tomorrow night sober as you are now.

ED (*to* LOLA): All the king's horses couldn't keep him from takin' another drink now, Mrs. Delaney. He got himself into this; he's gotta sweat it out.

DOC: I won't go to the City Hospital. That's where they take the crazy people. (*Stumbles into chair.*)

ED (*using all his patience now*): Look, Doc. Elmo and I are your friends. You know that. Now if you don't come along peacefully, we're going to call the cops and you'll have to wear off this jag in the cooler. How'd you like that? (DOC *is as though stunned.*) The important thing is for you to get sober.

DOC: I don't wanta go.

ED: The City Hospital or the City Jail. Take your choice. We're not going to leave you here. Come on, Elmo.

(*They grab hold of him.*)

DOC (*has collected himself and now given in*): O.K., boys. Gimme another drink and I'll go.

LOLA: Oh, no, Doc.

ED: Might as well humor him, ma'am. Another few drinks couldn't make much difference now.

(MRS. COFFMAN *runs for bottle and glass in pantry and comes right back with them. She hands them to* LOLA.)

O.K., Doc, we're goin' to give you a drink. Take a good one; it's gonna be your last for a long, long time to come.

(ED *takes the bottle, removes the cork and gives* DOC *a glass of whiskey.* DOC *takes his fill, straight, coming up once or twice for air. Then* ED *takes the bottle from him and hands it to* LOLA. *To* LOLA.)

They'll keep him three or four days, Mrs. Delaney; then he'll be home again, good as new. (*Modestly.*) I . . . I don't want to pry into personal affairs, ma'am . . . but he'll need you then, pretty bad . . . Come on, Doc. Let's go.

(ED *has a hold of* DOC's *coat sleeve trying to maneuver him. A faraway look is in* DOC's *eyes, a dazed look containing panic and fear. He gets to his feet.*)

DOC (*struggling to sound reasonable*): Just a minute, boys . . .

ED: What's the matter?

DOC: I . . . I wanta glass of water.

ED: You'll get a glass of water later. Come on.

DOC (*beginning to twist a little in* ED's *grasp*): . . . a glass of water . . . that's all . . . (*One furious, quick twist of his body and he eludes* ED.)

ED: Quick, Elmo.

(ELMO *acts fast and they get* DOC *before he gets away. Then* DOC *struggles with all his might, kicking and screaming like a pampered child,* ED *and* ELMO *holding him tightly to usher him out.*)

DOC (*as he is led out*): Don't let 'em take me there. Don't take me there. Stop them, somebody. Stop them. That's where they take the crazy people. Oh, God, stop them, somebody. Stop them.

(LOLA *looks on blankly while* ED *and* ELMO *depart with* DOC. *Now there are several moments of deep silence.*)

MRS. COFFMAN (*clears up; very softly*): Is there anything more I can do for you now, Mrs. Delaney?

LOLA: I guess not.

MRS. COFFMAN (*puts a hand on* LOLA's *shoulder*): Get busy, Lady. Get busy and forget it.

LOLA: Yes . . . I'll get busy right away. Thanks, Mrs. Coffman.

MRS. COFFMAN: I better go. I've got to make breakfast for the children. If you want me for anything, let me know.

LOLA: Yes . . . yes . . . good-bye, Mrs. Coffman.

(MRS. COFFMAN *exits.* LOLA *is too exhausted to move from the big chair. At first she can't even cry; then the tears come slowly, softly. In a few moments* BRUCE *and* MARIE *enter, bright and merry.* LOLA *turns her head slightly to regard them as creatures from another planet.*)

MARIE (*springing into room;* BRUCE *follows*): Congratulate me, Mrs. Delaney.

LOLA: Huh?

MARIE: We're going to be married.

LOLA: Married? (*It barely registers.*)

MARIE (*showing ring*): Here it is. My engagement ring.

(MARIE *and* BRUCE *are too engrossed in their own happiness to notice* LOLA's *stupor.*)

LOLA: That's lovely . . . lovely.

MARIE: We've had the most wonderful time. We danced all night and then drove out to the lake and saw the sun rise.

LOLA: That's nice.

MARIE: We've made all our plans. I'm quitting school and flying back to Cincinnati with Bruce this afternoon. His mother has invited me to visit them before I go home. Isn't that wonderful?

LOLA: Yes . . . yes, indeed.

MARIE: Going to miss me?

LOLA: Yes, of course, Marie. We'll miss you very much .... uh . . . congratulations.

MARIE: Thanks, Mrs Delaney. (*Goes to bedroom door.*) Come on, Bruce, help me get my stuff. (*To* LOLA.) Mrs. Delaney, would you throw everything into a big box and send it to me at home? We haven't had breakfast yet. We're going down to the hotel and celebrate.

BRUCE: I'm sorry we're in such a hurry, but we've got a taxi waiting.

(*They go into room.*)

LOLA (*goes to telephone, dials*): Long-distance? I want to talk to Green Valley 223. Yes. This is Delmar 1887.

(*She hangs up.* MARIE *comes from bedroom, followed by* BRUCE, *who carries suitcase.*)

MARIE: Mrs. Delaney, I sure hate to say good-bye to you. You've been so wonderful to me. But Bruce says I can come and visit you once in a while, didn't you, Bruce?

BRUCE: Sure thing.

LOLA: You're going?

MARIE: We're going downtown and have our breakfast, then do a little shopping and catch our plane. And thanks for everything, Mrs. Delaney.

BRUCE: It was very nice of you to have us to dinner.

LOLA: Dinner? Oh, don't mention it.

MARIE (*to* LOLA): There isn't much time for good-bye now, but I just want you to know Bruce and I wish you the best of everything. You and Doc both. Tell Doc good-bye for me, will you, and remember I think you're both a coupla peaches.

BRUCE: Hurry, honey.

MARIE: 'Bye, Mrs. Delaney! (*She goes out.*)

BRUCE: 'Bye, Mrs. Delaney. Thanks for being nice to my girl.

(*He goes out and off porch with* MARIE.)

LOLA (*Waves. The phone rings. She goes to it quickly*): Hello. Hello, Mom. It's Lola, Mom. How are you? Mom, Doc's sick again. Do you think Dad would let me come home for a while? I'm awfully unhappy, Mom. Do you think . . . just till I made up my mind? . . . All right. No, I guess it wouldn't do any good for you to come here . . . I . . . I'll let you know what I decide to do. That's all, Mom. Thanks. Tell Daddy hello.

(*She hangs up.*)

SCENE 4

(*It is morning, a week later. The house is neat again.* LOLA *is dusting in the living room as* MRS. COFFMAN *enters.*)

MRS. COFFMAN: Mrs. Delaney! Good morning, Mrs. Delaney.

LOLA: Come in, Mrs. Coffman.

MRS. COFFMAN (*coming in*): It's a fine day for the games. I've got a box lunch ready, and I'm taking all the kids to the Stadium. My boy's got a ticket for you, too. You better get dressed and come with us.

LOLA: Thanks, Mrs. Coffman, but I've got work to do.

MRS. COFFMAN: But it's a big day. The Spring Relays . . . All the athletes from the colleges are supposed to be there.

LOLA: Oh, yes. You know that boy, Turk, who used to come here to see Marie—he's one of the big stars.

MRS. COFFMAN: Is that so? Come on . . . do. We've got a ticket for you. . . .

LOLA: Oh, no, I have to stay here and clean up the house. Doc may be coming home today. I talked to him on the phone. He wasn't sure what time they'd let him out, but I wanta have the place all nice for him.

MRS. COFFMAN: Well, I'll tell you all about it when I come home. Everybody and his brother will be there.

LOLA: Have a good time.

MRS. COFFMAN: 'Bye, Mrs. Delaney.

LOLA: 'Bye.

(MRS. COFFMAN *leaves, and* LOLA *goes into kitchen. The* MAILMAN *comes onto porch and leaves a letter, but* LOLA *doesn't even know he's there. Then the* MILKMAN *knocks on the kitchen door.*)

LOLA: Come in.

MILKMAN (*entering with armful of bottles, etc.*): I see you checked the list, lady. You've got a lot of extras.

LOLA: Ya—I think my husband's coming home.

MILKMAN (*he puts the supplies on table, then pulls out magazine*): Remember, I told you my picture was going to appear in *Strength and Health*. (*Showing her magazine.*) Well, see that pile of muscles? That's me.

LOLA: My goodness. You got your picture in a magazine.

MILKMAN: Yes, ma'am. See what it says about my chest development? For the greatest self-improvement in a three months' period.

LOLA: Goodness sakes. You'll be famous, won't you?

MILKMAN: If I keep busy on these bar-bells. I'm working now for "muscular separation."

LOLA: That's nice.

MILKMAN (*cheerily*): Well, good day, ma'am.

LOLA: You forgot your magazine.

MILKMAN: That's for you.

(*Exits.* LOLA *puts away the supplies in the icebox. Then* DOC *comes in the front door, carrying the little suitcase she previously packed for him. His quiet manner and his serious demeanor are the same as before.* LOLA *is shocked by his sudden appearance. She jumps and can't help showing her fright.*)

LOLA: Docky! (*Without thinking she assumes an attitude of fear.* DOC *observes this and it obviously pains him.*)

DOC: Good morning, honey. (*Pause.*)

LOLA (*on platform*): Are . . . are you all right, Doc?

DOC: Yes, I'm all right. (*An awkward pause. Then* DOC *tries to reassure her.*) Honest, I'm all right, honey. Please don't stand there like that . . . like I was gonna . . . gonna . . .

LOLA (*tries to relax*): I'm sorry, Doc.

DOC: How you been?

LOLA: Oh, I been all right, Doc. Fine.

DOC: Any news?

LOLA: I told you about Marie—over the phone.

DOC: Yah.

LOLA: He was a very nice boy, Doc. Very nice.

DOC: That's good. I hope they'll be happy.

LOLA (*trying to sound bright*): She said . . . maybe she'd come back and visit us some time. That's what she *said.*

DOC (*pause*): It . . . it's good to be home.

LOLA: Is it, Daddy?

DOC: Yah. (*Beginning to choke up, just a little.*)

LOLA: Did everything go all right . . . I mean . . . did they treat you well and . . .

DOC (*now loses control of his feelings. Tears in his eyes, he all but lunges at her, gripping her arms, drilling his head into her bosom*): Honey, don't ever leave me. *Please* don't ever leave me. If you do, they'd have to keep me down at that place all the time. I don't know what I said to you or what I did, I can't remember hardly anything. But please forgive me . . . please . . . please . . . And I'll try to make everything up.

LOLA (*there is surprise on her face and new contentment. She becomes almost angelic in demeanor. Tenderly she places a soft hand on his head*): Daddy! Why, of course I'll never leave you. (*A smile of satisfaction.*) You're all I've got. You're all I ever had. (*Very tenderly he kisses her.*)

DOC (*collecting himself now;* LOLA *sits beside* DOC): I . . . I feel better . . . already.

LOLA (*almost gay*): So do I. Have you had your breakfast?

DOC: No. The food there was terrible. When they told me I could go this morning, I decided to wait and fix myself breakfast here.

LOLA (*happily*): Come on out in the kitchen and I'll get you a nice, big breakfast. I'll scramble some eggs and . . . You see I've got the place all cleaned up just the way you like it. (DOC *goes to kitchen.*) Now you sit down here and I'll get your fruit juice. (*He sits and she gets fruit juice from refrigerator.*) I've got bacon this morning, too. My, it's expensive now. And I'll light the oven and make you some toast, and here's some orange marmalade, and . . .

DOC (*with a new feeling of control*): Fruit juice. I'll need lots of fruit juice for a while. The doctor said it would restore the vitamins. You see, that damn whiskey kills all the vitamins in your system, eats up all the sugar in your kidneys. They came around every morning and shot vitamins in my arm. Oh, it didn't hurt. And the doctor told me to drink a quart of fruit juice every day. And you better get some candy bars for me at the grocery this morning. Doctor said to eat lots of candy, try to replace the sugar.

LOLA: I'll do that, Doc. Here's another glass of this pineapple juice now. I'll get some candy bars first thing.

DOC: The doctor said I should have a hobby. Said I should go out more. That's all that's wrong with me. I thought maybe I'd go hunting once in a while.

LOLA: Yes, Doc. And bring home lots of good things to eat.

DOC: I'll get a big bird dog, too. Would you like a sad-looking old bird dog around the house?

LOLA: Of course, I would. (*All her life and energy have been restored.*) You know what, Doc? I had another dream last night.

DOC: About Little Sheba?

LOLA: Oh, it was about everyone and everything. (*In a raptured tone. She gets bacon from icebox and starts to cook it.*) Marie and I were going to the Olympics back in our high school stadium. There were thousands of people there. There was Turk out in the center of the field throwing the javelin. Every time he threw it, the crowd would roar . . . and you know who the man in charge was? It was my father. Isn't that funny? . . . But Turk kept changing into someone else all the time. And then my father disqualified him. So he had to sit on the sidelines . . . and guess who took his place, Daddy? You! You came trotting out there on the field just as big as you please . . .

DOC (*smilingly*): How did I do, Baby?

LOLA: Fine. You picked the javelin up real careful, like it was awful heavy. But you threw it, Daddy, clear, *clear* up into the sky. And it never came down again. (DOC *looks very pleased with himself.* LOLA *goes on.*) Then it started to rain. And I couldn't find Little Sheba. I almost went crazy looking for her and there were so many people, I didn't even know where to look. And you were waiting to take me home. And we walked and walked through the slush and mud, and people were hurrying all around us and . . . and . . . (*Leaves stove and sits. Sentimental tears come to her eyes.*) But this part is sad, Daddy. All of a sudden I saw Little Sheba . . . she was lying in the middle of the field . . . dead. . . . It made me cry, Doc. No one paid any attention . . . I cried and cried. It made me feel so bad, Doc. That sweet little puppy . . . her curly white fur all smeared with mud, and no one to stop and take care of her . . .

DOC: Why couldn't *you?*

LOLA: I wanted to, but you wouldn't let me. You kept saying, "We can't stay here, honey; we gotta go on. We gotta go on." (*Pause.*) Now, isn't that strange?

DOC: Dreams are funny.

LOLA: I don't think Little Sheba's ever coming back, Doc. I'm not going to call her any more.

DOC: Not much point in it, Baby. I guess she's gone for good.

LOLA: I'll fix your eggs.

(*She gets up, embraces* DOC, *and goes to stove.* DOC *remains at the table sipping his fruit juice. The curtain comes slowly down.*)

CURTAIN

Tennessee Williams: *Camino Real* (1953)

Tennessee Williams' childhood sounds almost like a case history in psychology. His father, a travelling shoe salesman, hardly appeared at home during his earliest years and Williams lived with his mother's parents in Mississippi. He became profoundly close with his grandfather, a preacher, and deeply attached to his mother and his older sister, Rose. But when his father finally came in off the road and took a manager's job in St. Louis, the family had to move and live together there. Neither Rose nor Tennessee liked St. Louis—it was large, noisy, and gloomy. A third child was born shortly after they moved, and the house they bought—quickly, and without much thought to its beauty—turned out to be dark and dreary. Family arguments started soon after. Tennessee became so seriously ill that he was partially paralyzed and, when he recovered and began school, his weakness (principally in his legs) made him the butt of bullies and taunts from more robust and threatening boys. His father also taunted him; he wanted his son to grow up to be a rugged athlete, but things were not working out that way. Nothing Williams did seemed to satisfy his father, and much the same could be said about Rose. She took refuge from the torment by closeting herself in her room with her large collection of glass-spun animals. Her eventual mental breakdown came after the death of a suitor, and it grew to be more and more serious. She underwent a lobotomy to relieve the mental strain and restore her to some peace, but the operation was not a success.

Tennessee Williams was writing throughout much of his youth. His mother had given him a typewriter when he was eleven, and he used it to construct more interesting worlds than the one around him. He wrote constantly, and achieved some early success with short stories that earned him small sums of money. He eventually went to the University of Missouri, but when he flunked ROTC—largely because his physical weakness discouraged him—his father was infuriated and refused to pay his tuition. It was the depths of the Depression and the next thirty months were spent as "my time in hell" with Tennessee working in a shoe factory at $65 a month, a good salary for 1931. He wrote as much as possible and often worked late into the night; this was his touch with the real world. The experience ended with a nervous collapse, a period of recuperation with his grandparents now in Memphis (from which he got his nickname), and a return to college, at Washington University in St. Louis, where he wrote and produced several plays. His bachelor's degree finally came from the State University of Iowa, where he studied playwriting.

The following years were spent in struggling toward recognition. He lived in many places—Chicago, St. Louis, New Orleans, and even Mexico—and seems to have developed a feeling for the kind of characters he portrays in *Camino Real*: lonely, struggling, uncertain. His early plays were recognized as good by some people, but they went unproduced. He obtained a Rockefeller award in 1940, but it only helped in supporting him; he had to maintain several small jobs to keep from starving. In 1943, he found a job as a scriptwriter for MGM but no one liked his scripts, so he was let go. That year he wrote his first truly successful play, *The Glass Menagerie*, which has been described as an atonement for his sister's insanity. MGM turned it down, but when the play opened in New York in 1945 it was an instant hit with 561 performances. Williams won the Pulitzer Prize in 1947 for his even greater success, *A Streecar Named Desire*, which introduced Marlon Brando. It ran 855 performances and inspired a number of imitations and adaptations. By 1947, at the age of 36, Williams was regarded as the most promising and significant young playwright in the country.

Camino Real was by no means as successful as his first two hits. It ran only 60 performances, but it was a play Williams believed was tremendously important and profoundly significant. He invested it with feeling, as he later indicated, instead of the kind of systematic thought the critics seemed to want. Yet, the play is filled with thought as well as feeling. It builds on Williams' experiences as a down-and-outer, experiences he shares with many other great writers, such as Jack London, Eugene O'Neill, and George Orwell. The figure of Gutman seems influenced by Thornton Wilder's Stage Manager in *Our Town*, guiding the motion of the drama block by block. The main characters are all romantics: Kilroy, the wandering American, former prize fighter, former lover, still with hope in his huge heart; Don Quixote, who opens and ends the play, the symbol of striving in the face of defeat; Lord Byron, the living embodiment of romanticism; and many others drawn from romantic literature from Dumas to Proust.

As a *tour de force,* the play has a number of scenes and set speeches designed to rock an audience. When Kilroy runs out into the aisles, Williams is invading the audience's space in a threatening way. As Quixote says, it is a crime to be alone when so many are lonely; Williams must involve the audience in the action.

Some have regarded the play as pessimistic, almost as if it were part of the theatre of cruelty, but perhaps our current perspective has restored some of the hopefulness Williams tried to express. The incurable romantic Kilroy, who dies and is resurrected in a scene that recalls Michelangelo's *Pieta,* survives at the end of the play. His heart, his capacity for feeling and hope, is still intact. When Don Quixote points out that violets in the mountains have broken the rocks, he reminds us that nature has a way of surmounting what often seem impossible difficulties—if flowers can split rocks, then the human spirit can attain equally impossible goals.

William's later dramatic successes have included *The Rose Tattoo* (1951); *Cat on a Hot Tin Roof* (1955); *Orpheus Descending* (1957); *Sweet Bird of Youth* (1959); *The Night of the Iguana* (1961); and *Small Craft Warnings* (1972). Williams is still actively writing, although some of his most recent work has closed on Broadway after only a few performances. He must still be considered one of America's two or three most significant living playwrights.

Selected Readings

Donahue, Francis. *The Dramatic World of Tennessee Williams.* New York: Ungar, 1964.

Falk, Signi Lenea. "Tennessee Williams: A Selected Bibliography," *Modern Drama,* 1 (1958), pp. 220–223.

———. *Tennessee Williams,* 2d. ed., New York: Twayne, 1978.

Fedder, Norman J. *The Influence of D.H. Lawrence on Tennessee Williams.* The Hague: Mouton, 1966.

Freeman, Lucy. *Remember Me to Tom.* New York: Putnam, 1963.

Hirsch, Foster. *A Portrait of the Artist: The Plays of Tennessee Williams.* Port Washington, N.Y.: Kennikat Press, 1979.

Jackson, Esther M. *The Broken World of Tennessee Williams.* Madison: University of Wisconsin Press, 1965.

Leavitt, Richard Freeman, ed. *The World of Tennessee Williams.* New York: Putnam, 1977.

Maxwell, Gilbert. *Tennessee Williams and Friends.* Cleveland: World, 1965.

Stanton, Stephens, ed. *Tennessee Williams: A Collection of Critical Essays.* Englewood Cliffs, N.J.: Prentice-Hall, 1978.

Steen, Mike. *A Look at Tennessee Williams.* New York: Hawthorn, 1969.

Tischler, Nancy M. *Tennessee Williams: Rebellious Puritan.* New York: Citadel, 1961.

Weales, Gerald. *Tennessee Williams.* Univ. of Minnesota Pamphlets, No. 53. Minneapolis: University of Minnesota Press, 1965.

Williams, Tennessee. *American Blues: Five Short Plays by Tennessee Williams*. New York: Dramatists Play Service, 1943.

———. *Three Plays*. New York: New Directions, 1948.

———. *27 Wagon Loads of Cotton and Other One-Act Plays*. New York: New Directions, 1945.

———. *Memoirs*. Garden City, N.Y.: Doubleday, 1975.

Camino Real

Tennessee Williams

CHARACTERS

GUTMAN	WAITER
SURVIVOR	LORD BYRON
ROSITA	NAVIGATOR OF THE
FIRST OFFICER	FUGITIVO
JACQUES CASANOVA	PILOT OF THE FUGITIVO
LA MADRECITA DE LOS	MARKET WOMAN
PERDIDOS	SECOND MARKET WOMAN
HER SON	STREET VENDOR
KILROY	LORD MULLIGAN
FIRST STREET CLEANER	THE GYPSY
SECOND STREET CLEANER	HER DAUGHTER, ESMERALDA
ABDULLAH	NURSIE
A BUM IN A WINDOW	EVA
A. RATT	THE INSTRUCTOR
THE LOAN SHARK	ASSISTANT INSTRUCTOR
BARON DE CHARLUS	MEDICAL STUDENT
LOBO	DON QUIXOTE
SECOND OFFICER	SANCHO PANZA
A GROTESQUE MUMMER	PRUDENCE DUVERNOY
MARGUERITE GAUTIER	OLYMPE
LADY MULLIGAN	

PROLOGUE

(*As the curtain rises, on an almost lightless stage, there is a loud singing of wind, accompanied by distant, measured reverberations like pounding surf or distant shellfire. Above the ancient wall that backs the set and the perimeter of mountains visible above the wall, are flickers of a white radiance as though daybreak were a white bird caught in a net and struggling to rise.*

The plaza is seen fitfully by this light. It belongs to a tropical seaport that bears a confusing, but somehow harmonious, resemblance to such widely scattered ports as Tangiers, Havana, Vera Cruz, Casablanca, Shanghai, New Orleans.

On stage left is the luxury side of the street, containing the façade of the Siete Mares hotel and its low terrace on which are a number of glass-topped white iron tables and chairs. In the downstairs there is a great bay window in which are seen a pair of elegant "dummies," one seated, one standing behind, looking out into the plaza with painted smiles. Upstairs is a small balcony and behind it a large window exposing a wall on which is hung a phoenix painted on silk: this should be softly lighted now and then in the play, since resurrections are so much a part of its meaning.

Opposite the hotel is Skid Row which contains the GYPSY's *gaudy stall,* THE LOAN SHARK's *establishments with a window containing a variety of pawned articles, and the "Ritz Men Only" which is a flea-bag hotel or flophouse and which has a practical window above its downstairs entrance, in which a bum will appear from time to time to deliver appropriate or contrapuntal song titles.*

Upstage is a great flight of stairs that mount the ancient wall to a sort of archway that leads out into "Terra Incognita," as it is called in the play, a wasteland between the walled town and the distant perimeter of snow-topped mountains.

Downstage right and left are a pair of arches which give entrance to dead-end streets.

Immediately after the curtain rises a shaft of blue light is thrown down a central aisle of the theatre, and in this light, advancing from the back of the house, appears DON QUIXOTE DE LA MANCHA, *dressed like an old "desert rat." As he enters the aisle he shouts, "Hola!", in a cracked old voice which is still full of energy and is answered by another voice which is impatient and tired, that of his squire,* SANCHO PANZA. *Stumbling with a fatigue which is only physical, the old knight comes down the aisle, and* SANCHO *follows a couple of yards behind him, loaded down with equipment that ranges from a medieval shield to a military canteen or Thermos bottle. Shouts are exchanged between them.*)

QUIXOTE (*ranting above the wind in a voice which is nearly as old*): Blue is the color of distance!

SANCHO (*wearily behind him*): Yes, distance is blue.

QUIXOTE: Blue is also the color of nobility.

SANCHO: Yes, nobility's blue.

QUIXOTE: Blue is the color of distance and nobility, and that's why an old knight should always have somewhere about him a bit of blue ribbon . . .

(*He jostles the elbow of an aisle-sitter as he staggers with fatigue; he mumbles an apology.*)

SANCHO: Yes, a bit of blue ribbon.

QUIXOTE: A bit of faded blue ribbon, tucked away in whatever remains of his armor, or borne on the tip of his lance, his—unconquerable lance! It serves to remind an old knight of distance that he has gone and distance he has yet to go . . .

(SANCHO *mutters the Spanish word for excrement as several pieces of rusty armor fall into the aisle.*)

(QUIXOTE *has now arrived at the foot of the steps onto the forestage. He pauses there as if wandering out of or into a dream.* SANCHO *draws up clanking behind him.*)

(MR. GUTMAN, *a lordly fat man wearing a linen suit and a pith helmet, appears dimly on the balcony of the Siete Mares, a white cockatoo on his wrist. The bird cries out harshly.*)

GUTMAN: Hush, Aurora.

QUIXOTE: It also reminds an old knight of that green country he lived in which was the youth of his heart, before such singing words as *Truth!*

SANCHO (*panting*): —Truth.

QUIXOTE: *Valor!*

SANCHO: —Valor.

QUIXOTE (*elevating his lance*). *Devoir!*

SANCHO: —Devoir . . .

QUIXOTE: —turned into the meaningless mumble of some old monk hunched over cold mutton at supper!

(GUTMAN *alters a pair of* GUARDS *in the plaza, who cross with red lanterns to either side of the proscenium where they lower black and white striped barrier gates as if the proscenium marked a frontier. One of them, with a hand on his holster, advances toward the pair on the steps.*)

GUARD: Vien aquí.

(SANCHO *hangs back but* QUIXOTE *stalks up to the barrier gate. The* GUARD *turns a flashlight on his long and exceedingly grave red face, "frisks" him casually for concealed weapons, examines a rusty old knife and tosses it contemptuously away.*)

Sus papeles! Sus documentos!

(QUIXOTE *fumblingly produces some tattered old papers from the lining of his hat.*)

GUTMAN (*impatiently*): Who is it?

GUARD: An old desert rat named Quixote.

GUTMAN: Oh!—Expected!—Let him in.

(*The* GUARDS *raise the barrier gate and one sits down to smoke on the terrace.* SANCHO *hangs back still. A dispute takes place on the forestage and steps into the aisle.*)

QUIXOTE: Forward!

SANCHO: Aw, naw. I know this place. (*He produces a crumpled parchment.*) Here it is on the chart. Look, it says here: "Continue until you come to the square of a walled town which is the end of the Camino Real and the beginning of the Camino Real. Halt there," it says, "and turn back, Traveler, for the spring of humanity has gone dry in this place and—"

QUIXOTE (*he snatches the chart from him and reads the rest of the inscription*): "—there are no birds in the country except wild birds that are tamed and kept in—" (*He holds the chart close to his nose.*) —Cages!

SANCHO (*urgently*): Let's go back to La Mancha!

QUIXOTE: Forward!

SANCHO:: The time has come for retreat!

QUIXOTE: The time for retreat never comes!

SANCHO: *I'm going back to La Mancha!*

(*He dumps the knightly equipment into the orchestra pit.*)

QUIXOTE: *Without me?*

SANCHO (*bustling up the aisle*): With you or without you, old tireless and tiresome master!

QUIXOTE (*imploringly*): *Saaaaaan-chooooooooo!*

SANCHO (*near the top of the aisle*): I'm going back to La *Maaaaaaaaan-chaaaaaaa* . . .

(*He disappears as the blue light in the aisle dims out. The* GUARD *puts out his cigarette and wanders out of the plaza. The wind moans and* GUTMAN *laughs softly as the* ANCIENT KNIGHT *enters the plaza with such a desolate air.*)

QUIXOTE (*looking about the plaza*): —Lonely . . .

(*To his surprise the word is echoed softly by almost unseen figures huddled below the stairs and against the wall of the town.* QUIXOTE *leans upon his lance and observes with a wry smile—*)

—When so many are lonely as seem to be lonely, it would be inexcusably selfish to be lonely alone.

(*He shakes out a dusty blanket. Shadowy arms extend toward him and voices murmur.*)

VOICE: Sleep. Sleep. Sleep.

QUIXOTE (*arranging his blanket*): Yes, I'll sleep for a while, I'll sleep and dream for a while against the wall of this town . . .

(*A mandolin or guitar plays "The Nightingale of France."*)

—And my dream will be a pageant, a masque in which old meanings will be remembered and possibly new ones discovered, and when I wake from this sleep and this disturbing pageant of a dream, I'll choose one among its shadows to take along with me in the place of Sancho . . .

(*He blows his nose between his fingers and wipes them on his shirttail.*)

—For new companions are not as familiar as old ones but all the same—they're old ones with only slight differences of face and figure, which may or may not be improvements, and it would be selfish of me to be lonely alone . . .

(*He stumbles down the incline into the Pit below the stairs where most of the Street People huddle beneath awnings of open stalls.*

The white cockatoo squawks.)

GUTMAN: Hush, Aurora.

QUIXOTE: And tomorrow at this same hour, which we call madrugada, the loveliest of all words, except the word alba, and that word also means daybreak—

—Yes, at daybreak tomorrow I will go on from here with a new companion and this old bit of blue ribbon to keep me in mind of distance that I have gone and distance I have yet to go, and also to keep me in mind of—

(*The cockatoo cries wildly.*

QUIXOTE *nods as if in agreement with the outcry and folds himself into his blanket below the great stairs.*)

GUTMAN (*stroking the cockatoo's crest*): Be still, Aurora. I know it's morning, Aurora.

(*Daylight turns the plaza silver and slowly gold.* VENDORS *rise beneath white awnings of stalls. The* GYPSY's *stall opens. A tall, courtly figure, in his late middle years* (JACQUES CASANOVA) *crosses from the Siete Mares to the* LOAN SHARK's, *removing a silver snuff box from his pocket as* GUTMAN *speaks. His costume, like that of all the legendary characters in the play* (*except perhaps* QUIXOTE) *is generally "modern" but with vestigial touches of the period to which he was actually related. The cane and the snuff box and perhaps a brocaded vest may be sufficient to give this historical suggestion in* CASANOVA's *case. He bears his hawklike head with a sort of anxious pride on most occasions, a pride maintained under a steadily mounting pressure.*)

—It's morning and after morning. It's afternoon, ha ha! And now I must go downstairs to announce the beginning of that old wanderer's dream . . .

(*He withdraws from the balcony as old* PRUDENCE DUVERNOY *stumbles out of the hotel, as if not yet quite awake from an afternoon siesta. Chattering with beads and bracelets, she wanders vaguely down into the plaza, raising a faded green silk parasol, damp henna-streaked hair slipping under a monstrous hat of faded silk roses; she is searching for a lost poodle.*)

PRUDENCE: Trique? Trique?

(JACQUES *comes out of the* LOAN SHARK's *replacing his case angrily in his pocket.*)

JACQUES: Why, I'd rather give it to a street beggar! This case is a Boucheron, I won it at faro at the summer palace, at Tsarkoe Selo in the winter of—

(*The* LOAN SHARK *slams the door.* JACQUES *glares, then shrugs and starts across the plaza.* OLD PRUDENCE *is crouched over the filthy gray bundle of a dying mongrel by the fountain.*)

PRUDENCE: Trique, oh, Trique!

(*The* GYPSY's *son,* ABDULLAH, *watches, giggling.*)

JACQUES (*reproving*): It is a terrible thing for an old woman to outlive her dogs.

(*He crosses to* PRUDENCE *and gently disengages the animal from her grasp.*)

Madam, this is not Trique.

PRUDENCE: —When I woke up she wasn't in her basket . . .

JACQUES: Sometimes we sleep too long in the afternoon and when we wake we find things changed, Signora.

PRUDENCE: Oh, you're Italian!

JACQUES: I am from Venice, Signora.

PRUDENCE: Ah, Venice, city of pearls! I saw you last night on the terrace dining with—Oh, I'm so worried about her! I'm an old friend of hers, perhaps she's mentioned me to you. Prudence Duvernoy? I was her best friend in the old days in Paris, but now she's forgotten so much . . .

I hope you have influence with her!

(*A waltz of* CAMILLE's *time in Paris is heard.*)

I want you to give her a message from a certain wealthy old gentleman that she met at one of those watering places she used to go to for her

health. She resembled his daughter who died of consumption and so he adored Camille, lavished everything on her! What did she do? Took a young lover who hadn't a couple of pennies to rub together, disinherited by his father because of *her!* Oh, you can't do that, not now, not any more, you've got to be realistic on the Camino Real!

(GUTMAN *has come out on the terrace: he announces quietly.*)

GUTMAN: Block One on the Camino Real.

BLOCK ONE

PRUDENCE (*continuing*): Yes, you've got to be practical on it! Well, give her this message, please, Sir. He wants her back on any terms whatsoever! (*Her speech gathers furious momentum.*) Her evenings will be free. He wants only her mornings, mornings are hard on old men because their hearts beat slowly, and he wants only her mornings! Well, that's how it should be! A sensible arrangement! Elderly gentlemen have to content themselves with a lady's spare time before supper! Isn't that so? Of course so! And so I told him! I told him, Camille isn't well! She requires delicate care! Has many debts, creditors storm her door! "How much does she owe?" he asked me, and, oh, did I do some lightning mathematics! Jewels in pawn, I told him, pearls, rings, necklaces, bracelets, diamond ear-drops are in pawn! Horses put up for sale at a public auction!

JACQUES (*appalled by this torrent*): Signora, Signora, all of these things are—

PRUDENCE:—What?

JACQUES: *Dreams!*

(GUTMAN *laughs. A woman sings at a distance.*)

PRUDENCE (*continuing with less assurance*): —You're not so young as I thought when I saw you last night on the terrace by candlelight on the—Oh, but—Ho ho!—I bet there is *one* old fountain in this plaza that hasn't gone dry!

(*She pokes him obscenely. He recoils.* GUTMAN *laughs.* JACQUES *starts away but she seizes his arm again, and the torrent of speech continues.*)

PRUDENCE: Wait, wait, listen! Her candle is burning low. But how can you tell? She might have a lingering end, and charity hospitals?

Why, you might as well take a flying leap into the Streetcleaners' barrel. Oh, I've told her and told her not to live in a dream! A dream is nothing to live in, why, it's gone like a—

Don't let her elegance fool you! That girl has done the Camino in carriages but she has also done it on foot! She knows every stone the Camino is paved with! So tell her this. You tell her, she won't listen to me!—Times and conditions have undergone certain changes since we were friends in Paris, and now we dismiss young lovers with skins of silk and eyes like a child's first prayer, we put them away as lightly as we put away white gloves meant only for summer, and pick up a pair of black ones, suitable for winter . . .

(*The singing voice rises: then subsides.*)

JACQUES: Excuse me, Madam.

(*He tears himself from her grasp and rushes into the Siete Mares.*)

PRUDENCE (*dazed, to* GUTMAN): —What block is this?

GUTMAN: Block one.

PRUDENCE: I didn't hear the announcement . . .

GUTMAN (*coldly*): Well, now you do.

(OLYMPE *comes out of the lobby with a pale orange silk parasol like a floating moon.*)

OLYMPE: Oh, there you are, I've looked for you high and low!—mostly low . . .

(*They float vaguely out into the dazzling plaza as though a capricious wind took them, finally drifting through the Moorish arch downstage right.*
The song dies out.)

GUTMAN (*lighting a thin cigar*): Block Two on the Camino Real.

BLOCK TWO

(*After* GUTMAN'S *announcement, a hoarse cry is heard. A figure in rags, skin blackened by the sun, tumbles crazily down the steep alley to the plaza. He turns about blindly, murmuring: "A donde la fuente?" He stumbles against the hideous old prostitute* ROSITA *who grins horribly and whispers something to him, hitching up her ragged, filthy skirt. Then she gives him a jocular push toward the fountain. He falls upon his belly and thrusts his hands into the dried-up basin. Then he staggers to his feet with a despairing cry.*)

THE SURVIVOR: La fuente está seca!

(ROSITA *laughs madly but the other* STREET PEOPLE *moan. A dry gourd rattles.*)

ROSITA: The fountain is dry, but there's plenty to drink in the Siete Mares!

(*She shoves him toward the hotel. The proprietor,* GUTMAN, *steps out, smoking a thin cigar, fanning himself with a palm leaf. As the* SURVIVOR *advances,* GUTMAN *whistles. A man in military dress comes out upon the low terrace.*)

OFFICER: Go back!

(*The* SURVIVOR *stumbles forward. The* OFFICER *fires at him. He lowers his hands to his stomach, turns slowly about with a lost expression, looking up at the sky, and stumbles toward the fountain. During the scene that follows, until the entrance of* LA MADRECITA *and her* SON, *the* SURVIVOR *drags himself slowly about the concrete rim of the fountain, almost entirely ignored, as a dying pariah dog in a starving country.* JACQUES CASANOVA *comes out upon the terrace of the Siete Mares. Now he passes the hotel proprietor's impassive figure, descending a step beneath and a little in advance of him, and without looking at him.*)

JACQUES (*with infinite weariness and disgust*): What has happened?

GUTMAN (*serenely*): We have entered the second in a progress of sixteen blocks on the Camino Real. It's five o'clock. That angry old lion, the Sun, looked back once and growled and then went switching his tail toward the cool shade of the Sierras. Our guests have taken their afternoon siestas . . .

(*The* SURVIVOR *has come out upon the forestage, now, not like a dying man but like a shy speaker who has forgotten the opening line of his speech. He is only a little crouched over with a hand obscuring the red stain over his belly. Two or three* STREET PEOPLE *wander about calling their wares: "Tacos, tacos, fritos . . ."* —"Lotería, lotería"—ROSITA *shuffles around, calling "Love? Love?"—pulling down the filthy décolletage of her blouse to show more of her sagging bosom. The* SURVIVOR *arrives at the top of the stairs descending into the orchestra of the theatre, and hangs onto it, looking out reflectively as a man over the rail of a boat coming into a somewhat disturbingly strange harbor.*)

GUTMAN (*continuing*): —They suffer from extreme fatigue, our guests at the Siete Mares, all of them have a degree or two of fever. Questions are passed amongst them like something illicit and shameful, like counterfeit money or drugs or indecent postcards—

(*He leans forward and whispers.*)

—"What is this place? Where are we? What is the meaning of—*Shhhh!*"—Ha ha . . .

THE SURVIVOR (*very softly to the audience*): I once had a pony named Peeto. He caught in his nostrils the scent of thunderstorms coming even before the clouds had crossed the Sierra . . .

VENDOR: Tacos, tacos, fritos . . .

ROSITA: Love? Love?

LADY MULLIGAN (*to waiter on terrace*): Are you sure no one called me? I was expecting a call . . .

GUTMAN (*smiling*): My guests are confused and exhausted but at this hour they pull themselves together, and drift downstairs on the wings of gin and the lift, they drift into the public rooms and exchange notes again on fashionable couturiers and custom tailors, restaurants, vintages of wine, hair-dressers, plastic surgeons, girls and young men susceptible to offers . . .

(*There is a hum of light conversation and laughter within.*)

—Hear them? They're exchanging notes . . .

JACQUES (*striking the terrace with his cane*): I asked you what has happened in the plaza!

GUTMAN: Oh, in the plaza, ha ha!—Happenings in the plaza don't concern us . . .

JACQUES: I heard shots fired.

GUTMAN: Shots were fired to remind you of your good fortune in staying here. The public fountains have gone dry, you know, but the Siete Mares was erected over the only perpetual never-dried-up spring in Tierra Caliente, and of course that advantage has to be—protected—sometimes by—martial law . . .

(*The guitar resumes.*)

THE SURVIVOR: When Peeto, my pony, was born—he stood on his four legs at once, and accepted the world!—He was wiser than I . . .

VENDOR: Fritos, fritos, tacos!

ROSITA: Love!

THE SURVIVOR: —When Peeto was one year old he was wiser than God!

(*A wind sings across the plaza; a dry gourd rattles.*)

"Peeto, Peeto!" the Indian boys call after him, trying to stop him—trying to stop the wind!

(*The SURVIVOR's head sags forward. He sits down as slowly as an old man on a park bench. JACQUES*

strikes the terrace again with his cane and starts toward the SURVIVOR. *The* GUARD *seizes his elbow.*)

JACQUES: Don't put your hand on *me!*

GUARD: *Stay here.*

GUTMAN: Remain on the terrace, please, Signor Casanova.

JACQUES (*fiercely*): —*Cognac!*

(*The* WAITER *whispers to* GUTMAN. GUTMAN *chuckles.*)

GUTMAN: The Maître 'D' tells me that your credit has been discontinued in the restaurant and bar, he says that he has enough of your tabs to pave the terrace with!

JACQUES: What a piece of impertinence! I told the man that the letter that I'm expecting has been delayed in the mail. The postal service in this country is fantastically disorganized, and you know it! You also know that Mlle. Gautier will guarantee my tabs!

GUTMAN: Then let her pick them up at dinner tonight if you're hungry!

JACQUES: I'm not accustomed to this kind of treatment on the Camino Real!

GUTMAN: Oh, you'll be, you'll be, after a single night at the "Ritz Men Only." That's where you'll have to transfer your patronage if the letter containing the remittance check doesn't arrive tonight.

JACQUES: I assure you that I shall do nothing of the sort!—Tonight or ever!

GUTMAN: Watch out, old hawk, the wind is ruffling your feathers!

(JACQUES *sinks trembling into a chair.*)

—Give him a thimble of brandy before he collapses . . . Fury is a luxury of the young, their veins are resilient, but his are brittle. . . .

JACQUES: Here I sit, submitting to insult for a thimble of brandy—while directly in front of me—

(*The singer,* LA MADRECITA, *enters the plaza. She is a blind woman led by a ragged* YOUNG MAN. *The* WAITER *brings* JACQUES *a brandy.*)

—a man in the plaza dies like a pariah dog! —I take the brandy! I sip it!—My heart is too tired to break, my heart is too tired to—break . . .

(LA MADRECITA *chants softly. She slowly raises her arm to point at the* SURVIVOR *crouched on the steps from the plaza.*)

GUTMAN (*suddenly*): Give me the phone! Connect me with the Palace. Get me the Generalissimo, quick, quick, quick!

(*The* SURVIVOR *rises feebly and shuffles very slowly toward the extended arms of "The Little Blind One."*)

Generalissimo? Gutman speaking! Hello, sweetheart. There has been a little incident in the plaza. You know that party of young explorers that attempted to cross the desert on foot? Well, one of them's come back. He was very thirsty. He found the fountain dry. He started toward the hotel. He was politely advised to advance no further. But he disregarded this advice. Action had to be taken. And now, and now—that old blind woman they call "La Madrecita"? —She's come into the plaza with the man called "The Dreamer" . . .

SURVIVOR: Donde?

THE DREAMER: Aquí!

GUTMAN (*continuing*): You remember those two! I once mentioned them to you. You said "They're harmless dreamers and they're loved by the people."—"What," I asked you, "is harmless about a dreamer, and what," I asked you, "is harmless about the love of the people?— Revolution only needs good dreamers who remember their dreams, and the love of the people belongs safely only to you—their Generalissimo!"—Yes, now the blind woman has recovered her sight and is extending her arms to the wounded Survivor, and the man with the guitar is leading him to her . . .

(*The described action is being enacted.*)

Wait one moment! There's a possibility that the forbidden word may be spoken! Yes! The forbidden word is about to be spoken!

(*The* DREAMER *places an arm about the blinded* SURVIVOR, *and cries out.*)

THE DREAMER: *Hermano!*

(*The cry is repeated like springing fire and a loud murmur sweeps the crowd. They push forward with cupped hands extended and the gasping cries of starving people at the sight of bread. Two* MILITARY GUARDS *herd them back under the colonnades with clubs and drawn revolvers.* LA MADRECITA *chants softly with her blind eyes lifted. A* GUARD *starts toward her. The* PEOPLE *shout* "NO!")

LA MADRECITA (*chanting*): "Rojo está el sol! Rojo está el sol de sangre! Blanca está la luna! Blanca está la luna de miedo!"

(*The crowd makes a turning motion.*)

GUTMAN (*to the waiter*): *Put up the ropes!*

(*Velvet ropes are strung very quickly about the terrace of the Siete Mares. They are like the ropes on decks of steamers in rough waters.* GUTMAN *shouts into the phone again.*)

The word was spoken. The crowd is agitated. Hang on!

(*He lays down instrument.*)

JACQUES (*hoarsely, shaken*): He said "Hermano." That's the word for brother.

GUTMAN (*calmly*): Yes, the most dangerous word in any human tongue is the word for brother. It's inflammatory.—I don't suppose it can be struck out of the language altogether but it must be reserved for strictly private usage in back of soundproof walls. Otherwise it disturbs the population . . .

JACQUES: The people need the word. They're thirsty for it!

GUTMAN: What are these creatures? Mendicants. Prostitutes. Thieves and petty vendors in a bazaar where the human heart is a part of the bargain.

JACQUES: Because they need the word and the word is forbidden!

GUTMAN: The word is said in pulpits and at tables of council where its volatile essence can be contained. But on the lips of these creatures, what is it? A wanton incitement to riot, without understanding. For what is a brother to them but someone to get ahead of, to cheat, to lie to, to undersell in the market. Brother, you say to a man whose wife you sleep with!—But now, you see, the word has disturbed the people and made it necessary to invoke martial law!

(*Meanwhile the* DREAMER *has brought the* SURVIVOR *to* LA MADRECITA, *who is seated on the cement rim of the fountain. She has cradled the dying man in her arms in the attitude of a Pietà. The* DREAMER *is crouched beside them, softly playing a guitar. Now he springs up with a harsh cry.*)

THE DREAMER: *Muerto!*

(*The* STREETCLEANERS' *piping commences at a distance.* GUTMAN *seizes the phone again.*)

GUTMAN (*into phone*): Generalissimo, the Survivor is no longer surviving. I think we'd better have some public diversion right away. Put the Gypsy on! Have her announce the Fiesta!

LOUDSPEAKER (*responding instantly*): Damas y Caballeros! The next voice you hear will be the voice of—the Gypsy!

GYPSY (*over loudspeaker*): Hoy! Noche de Fiesta! Tonight the moon will restore the virginity of my daughter!

GUTMAN: Bring on the Gypsy's daughter, Esmeralda. Show the virgin-to-be!

(ESMERALDA *is led from the* GYPSY's *stall by a severe duenna, "Nursie," out upon the forestage. She is manacled by the wrist to the duenna. Her costume is vaguely Levantine.*
Guards are herding the crowd back again.)

GUTMAN: Ha ha! Ho ho ho! Music!

(*There is gay music.* ROSITA *dances.*)

Abdullah! You're on!

(ABDULLAH *skips into the plaza, shouting histrionically.*)

ABDULLAH: Tonight the moon will restore the virginity of my sister, Esmeralda!

GUTMAN: *Dance, boy!*

(ESMERALDA *is led back into the stall. Throwing off his burnoose,* ABDULLAH *dances with* ROSITA. *Behind their dance, armed* GUARDS *force* LA MADRECITA *and the* DREAMER *to retreat from the fountain, leaving the lifeless body of the survivor. All at once there is discordant blast of brass instruments.*)

KILROY *comes into the plaza. He is a young American vagrant, about twenty-seven. He wears dungarees and a skivvy shirt, the pants faded nearly white from long wear and much washing, fitting him as closely as the clothes of sculpture. He has a pair of golden boxing gloves slung about his neck and he carries a small duffle bag. His belt is ruby-and-emerald-studded with the word CHAMP in bold letters. He stops before a chalked inscription on a wall downstage which says: "Kilroy Is Coming!" He scratches out "Coming" and over it prints "Here!"*)

GUTMAN: Ho ho!—a clown! The Eternal Punchinella! That's exactly what's needed in a time of crisis!
Block Three on the Camino Real.

BLOCK THREE

KILROY (*genially, to all present*): Ha ha!

(*Then he walks up to the* OFFICER *by the terrace of the Siete Mares.*)

Buenas dias, señor.

(*He gets no response—barely even a glance.*)

Habla Inglesia? Usted?

OFFICER: What is it you want?

KILROY: Where is Western Union or Wells-Fargo? I got to send a wire to some friends in the States.

OFFICER: No hay Western Union, no hay Wells-Fargo.

KILROY: That is very peculiar. I never struck a town yet that didn't have one or the other. I just got off a boat. Lousiest frigging tub I ever shipped on, one continual hell it was, all the way up from Rio. And me sick, too. I picked up one of those tropical fevers. No sick-bay on that tub, no doctor, no medicine or nothing, not even one quinine pill, and I was burning up with Christ knows how much fever. I couldn't make them understand I was sick. I got a bad heart, too. I had to retire from the prize ring because of my heart. I was the light heavyweight champion of the West Coast, won these gloves!—before my ticker went bad.—Feel my chest! Go on, feel it! Feel it. I've got a heart in my chest as big as the head of a baby. Ha ha! They stood me in front of a screen that makes you transparent and that's what they seen inside me, a heart in my chest as big as the head of a baby! With something like that you don't need the Gypsy to tell you, "Time is short, Baby—get ready to hitch on wings!" The medics wouldn't okay me for no more fights. They said to give up liquor smoking and sex!—To give up sex!—I used to believe a man couldn't live without sex—but he can—if he wants to! My real true woman, my wife, she would of stuck with me, but it was all spoiled with her being scared and me, too, that a real hard kiss would kill me!—So one night while she was sleeping I wrote her good-bye . . .

(*He notices a lack of attention in the* OFFICER: *he grins.*)

No comprendo the lingo?

OFFICER: What is it you want?

KILROY: Excuse my ignorance, but what place is this? What is this country and what is the name of this town? I know is seems funny to me to ask such a question. Loco! But I was so glad to get off that rotten tub that I didn't ask nothing of no one except my pay—and I got short-changed on that. I have trouble counting these pesos or Whatzit-you-call-'em.

(*He jerks out his wallet.*)

All-a-this-here. In the States that pile of lettuce would make you a plutocrat!—But I bet you this stuff don't add up to fifty dollars American coin. Ha ha!

OFFICER: Ha ha.

KILROY: Ha ha!

OFFICER (*making a sound like a death-rattle*): Ha-ha-ha-ha-ha.

(*He turns and starts into the cantina.* KILROY *grabs his arm.*)

KILROY: Hey!

OFFICER: What is it you want?

KILROY: What is the name of this country and this town?

(*The* OFFICER *thrusts his elbow in* KILROY's *stomach and twists his arm loose with a Spanish curse. He kicks the swinging doors open and enters the cantina.*)

Brass hats are the same everywhere.

(*As soon as the* OFFICER *goes, the* STREET PEOPLE *come forward and crowd about* KILROY *with their wheedling cries.*)

STREET PEOPLE: Dulces, dulces! Lotería! Lotería! Pasteles, café con leche!

KILROY: No caree, no caree!

(*The* PROSTITUTE *creeps up to him and grins.*)

ROSITA: Love? Love?

KILROY: What did you say?

ROSITA: *Love?*

KILROY: Sorry—I don't feature that. (*To audience.*) I have ideals.

(*The* GYPSY *appears on the roof of her establishment with* ESMERALDA *whom she secures by handcuffs to the iron railing.*)

GYPSY: Stay there while I give the pitch!

(*She then advances with a portable microphone.*)

Testing! One, two, three, four!

NURSIE (*from offstage*): You're on the air!

GYPSY'S LOUDSPEAKER: Are you perplexed by something? Are you tired out and confused? Do you have a fever?

(KILROY *looks around for the source of the voice.*)

Do you feel yourself to be spiritually unprepared for the age of exploding atoms? Do you distrust the newspapers? Are you suspicious of governments? Have you arrived at a point on the Camino Real where the walls converge not in the distance but right in front of your nose? Does further progress appear impossible to you? Are

you afraid of anything at all? Afraid of your heartbeat? Or the eyes of strangers! Afraid of breathing? Afraid of not breathing? Do you wish that things could be straight and simple again as they were in your childhood? Would you like to go back to Kindy Garten?

(ROSITA *has crept up to* KILROY *while he listens. She reaches out to him. At the same time a* PICKPOCKET *lifts his wallet.*)

KILROY (*catching the whore's wrist*): Keep y'r hands off me, y' dirty ole bag! No caree putas! No loteria, no dulces, nada—so get away! Vamoose! All of you! Quit picking at me!

(*He reaches in his pocket and jerks out a handful of small copper and silver coins which he flings disgustedly down the street. The grotesque people scramble after it with their inhuman cries.* KILROY *goes on a few steps—then stops short—feeling the back pocket of his dungarees. Then he lets out a startled cry.*)

Robbed! My God, I've been robbed!

(*The* STREET PEOPLE *scatter to the walls.*)

Which of you got my wallet? *Which* of you dirty—? Shh—Uh!

(*They mumble with gestures of incomprehension. He marches back to the entrance to the hotel.*)

Hey! Officer! Official!—General!

(*The* OFFICER *finally lounges out of the hotel entrance and glances at* KILROY.)

Tiende? One of them's got my wallet! Picked it out of my pocket while that old whore there was groping me! Don't you comprendo?

OFFICER: Nobody rob you. You don't have no pesos.

KILROY: Huh?

OFFICER: You just dreaming that you have money. You don't ever have money. Nunca! Nada!

(*He spits between his teeth.*)

Loco . . .

(*The* OFFICER *crosses to the fountain.* KILROY *stares at him, then bawls out.*)

KILROY (*to the* STREET PEOPLE): We'll see what the American Embassy has to say about this! I'll go to the American Consul. Whichever of you rotten spivs lifted my wallet is going to jail—calaboose! I hope I have made myself plain. If not, I will make myself plainer!

(There are scattered laughs among the crowd. He crosses to the fountain. He notices the body of the no longer SURVIVOR, *kneels beside it, shakes it, turns it over, springs up and shouts.)*

Hey! This guy is dead!

(There is the sound of the STREETCLEANERS' *piping. They trundle their white barrel into the plaza from one of the downstage arches. The appearance of these men undergoes a progressive alteration through the play. When they first appear they are almost like any such public servants in a tropical country; their white jackets are dirtier than the musicians' and some of the stains are red. They have on white caps with black visors. They are continually exchanging sly jokes and giggling unpleasantly together.* LORD MULLIGAN *has come out upon the terrace and as they pass him, they pause for a moment, point at him, snicker. He is extremely discomfited by this impertinence, touches his chest as if he felt a palpitation and turns back inside.* KILROY *yells to the advancing* STREETCLEANERS.)

There's a dead man layin' here!

(They giggle again. Briskly they lift the body and stuff it into the barrel; then trundle it off, looking back at KILROY, *giggling, whispering. They return under the downstage arch through which they entered.* KILROY, *in a low, shocked voice.)*

What *is* this place? What kind of a hassle have I got myself into?

LOUDSPEAKER: If anyone on the Camino is bewildered, come to the Gypsy. A poco dinero will tickle the Gypsy's palm and give her visions!

ABDULLAH *(giving* KILROY *a card)*: If you got a question, ask my mama, the Gypsy!

KILROY: Man, whenever you see those three brass balls on a street, you don't have to look a long ways for a Gypsy. Now le' me think. I am faced with three problems. One: I'm hungry. Two: I'm lonely. Three: I'm in a place where I don't know what it is or how I got there! First action that's indicated is to—cash in on something—Well ... let's see ...

(Honky-tonk music fades in at this point and the Skid Row façade begins to light up for the evening. There is the GYPSY's *stall with its cabalistic devices, its sectional cranium and palm, three luminous brass balls overhanging the entrance to the* LOAN SHARK *and his window filled with a vast assortment of hocked articles for sale: trumpets, banjos, fur coats, tuxedos, a gown of scarlet sequins, loops of pearls and rhinestones. Dimly behind this display is a neon sign in three pastel colors, pink, green, and blue. It fades softly in and*

out and it says: "Magic Tricks Jokes." There is also the advertisement of a flea-bag hotel or flophouse called "Ritz Men Only." This sign is also pale neon or luminous paint, and only the entrance is on the street floor, the rooms are above the* LOAN SHARK *and* GYPSY's *stall. One of the windows of this upper story is practical. Figures appear in it sometimes, leaning out as if suffocating or to hawk and spit into the street below. This side of the street should have all the color and animation that are permitted by the resources of the production. There may be moments of dancelike action* [*a fight, a seduction, sale of narcotics, arrest, etc.*].)

KILROY *(to the audience from the apron)*: What've I got to cash in on? My golden gloves? Never! I'll say that once more, never! The silver-framed photo of my One True Woman? Never! Repeat that! Never! What else have I got of a detachable and a negotiable nature? Oh! My ruby-and-emerald-studded belt with the word CHAMP on it.

(He whips if off his pants.)

This is not necessary to hold on my pants, but this is a precious reminder of the sweet used-to-be. Oh, well. Sometimes a man has got to hock his sweet used-to-be in order to finance his present situation ...

(He enters the LOAN SHARK's. *A* DRUNKEN BUM *leans out the practical window of the "Ritz Men Only" and shouts.)*

BUM: O Jack o' Diamonds, you robbed my pockets, you robbed my pockets of silver and gold!

(He jerks the window shade down.)

GUTMAN *(on the terrace)*: Block Four on the Camino Real!

BLOCK FOUR

(There is a phrase of light music as the BARON DE CHARLUS, *an elderly foppish sybarite in a light silk suit, a carnation in his lapel, crosses from the Siete Mares to the honky-tonk side of the street. On his trail is a wild-looking young man of startling beauty called* LOBO. CHARLUS *is aware of the follower and, during his conversation with* A. RATT, *he takes out a pocket mirror to inspect him while pretending to comb his hair and point his moustache. As* CHARLUS *approaches, the* MANAGER *of the flea-bag puts up a vacancy sign and calls out.)*

A. RATT: Vacancy here! A bed at the "Ritz Men Only"! A little white ship to sail the dangerous night in . . .

THE BARON: Ah, bon soir, Mr. Ratt.

A. RATT: Cruising?

THE BARON: No, just—walking!

A. RATT: That's all you need to do.

THE BARON: I sometimes find it suffices. You have a vacancy, do you?

A. RATT: For you?

THE BARON: And a possible guest. You know the requirements. An iron bed with no mattress and a considerable length of stout knotted rope. No! Chains this evening, metal chains. I've been very bad, I have a lot to atone for . . .

A. RATT: Why don't you take these joy-rides at the Siete Mares?

THE BARON (with the mirror focused on LOBO): They don't have Ingreso Libero at the Siete Mares. Oh, I don't like places in the haute saison, the alta staggione, and yet if you go between the fashionable seasons, it's too hot or too damp or appallingly overrun by all the wrong sort of people who rap on the wall if canaries sing in your bed-springs after midnight. I don't know why such people don't stay at home. Surely a Kodak, a Brownie, or even a Leica works just as well in Milwaukee or Sioux City as it does in these places they do on their whirlwind summer tours, and don't look now, but I think I am being followed!

A. RATT: Yep, you've made a pickup!

THE BARON: Attractive?

A. RATT: That depends on who's driving the bicycle, Dad.

THE BARON: Ciao, Caro! Expect me at ten.

(He crosses elegantly to the fountain.)

A. RATT: Vacancy here! A little white ship to sail the dangerous night in!

(The music changes. KILROY backs out of the LOAN SHARK's, belt unsold, engaged in a violent dispute. The LOAN SHARK is haggling for his golden gloves. CHARLUS lingers, intrigued by the scene.)

LOAN SHARK: I don't want no belt! I want the gloves! Eight-fifty!

KILROY: No dice.

LOAN SHARK: Nine, nine-fifty!

KILROY: Nah, nah, nah!

LOAN SHARK: Yah, yah, yah.

KILROY: I say nah.

LOAN SHARK: I say yah.

KILROY: The nahs have it.

LOAN SHARK: Don't be a fool. What can you do with a pair of golden gloves?

KILROY: I can remember the battles I fought to win them! I can remember that I used to be —CHAMP!

(Fade in Band Music: "March of the Galdiators" —ghostly cheers, etc.)

LOAN SHARK: You can remember that you used to be—Champ?

KILROY: Yes! I used to be—CHAMP!

THE BARON: Used to be is the past tense, meaning useless.

KILROY: Not to me, Mister. These are my gloves, these gloves are gold, and I fought a lot of hard fights to win 'em! I broke clean from the clinches. I never hit a low blow, the referee never told me to mix it up! And the fixers never got to me!

LOAN SHARK: In other words, a sucker!

KILROY: Yep, I'm a sucker that won the golden gloves!

LOAN SHARK: Congratulations. My final offer is a piece of green paper with Alexander Hamilton's picture on it. Take it or leave it.

KILROY: I leave it for you to *stuff* it! I'd hustle my heart on this street, I'd peddle my heart's true blood before I'd leave my golden gloves hung up in a loan shark's window between a rusted trombone and some poor lush's long ago mildewed tuxedo!

LOAN SHARK: So you say but I will see you later.

THE BARON: The name of the Camino is not unreal!

(The BUM sticks his head out the window and shouts.)

BUM: Pa dam, Pa dam, Pa dam!

THE BARON (continuing the BUM's song): Echoes the beat of my heart!

Pa dam, Pa dam—hello!

(He has crossed to KILROY as he sings and extends his hand to him.)

KILROY (uncertainly): Hey, mate. It's wonderful to see you.

THE BARON: Thanks, but why?

KILROY: A normal American. In a clean white suit.

THE BARON: My suit is pale yellow. My nationality is French, and my normality has been often subject to question.

KILROY: I still say your suit is clean.

THE BARON: Thanks. That's more than I can say for your apparel.

KILROY: Don't judge a book by the covers. I'd take a shower if I could locate the "Y".

THE BARON: What's the "Y"?

KILROY: Sort of a Protestant church with a swimmin' pool in it. Sometimes it also has an employment bureau. It does good in the community.

THE BARON: Nothing in this community does much good.

KILROY: I'm getting the same impression. This place is confusing to me. I think it must be the aftereffects of fever. Nothing seems real. Could you give me the scoop?

THE BARON: Serious questions are referred to the Gypsy. Once upon a time. Oh, once upon a time. I used to wonder. Now I simply wander. I stroll about the fountain and hope to be followed. Some people call it corruption. I call it —simplification . . .

BUM (*very softly at the window*): I wonder what's become of Sally, that old gal of mine?

(*He lowers the blind.*)

KILROY: Well, anyhow . . .

THE BARON: Well, anyhow?

KILROY: How about the hot-spots in this town?

THE BARON: Oh, the hot-spots, ho ho! There's the Pink Flamingo, the Yellow Pelican, the Blue Heron, and the Prothonotary Warbler! They call it the Bird Circuit. But I don't care for such places. They stand three-deep at the bar and look at themselves in the mirror and what they see is depressing. One sailor comes in—they faint! My own choice of resorts is the Bucket of Blood downstairs from the "Ritz Men Only."— How about a match?

KILROY: Where's your cigarette?

THE BARON (*gently and sweetly*): Oh, I don't smoke. I just wanted to see your eyes more clearly . . .

KILROY: Why?

THE BARON: The eyes are the windows of the soul, and yours are too gentle for someone who has as much as I have to atone for.

(*He starts off.*)

Au revoir . . .

KILROY: —A very unusual type character . . .

(CASANOVA *is on the steps leading to the arch, looking out at the desert beyond. Now he turns and descends a few steps, laughing with a note of tired incredulity.* KILROY *crosses to him.*)

Gee, it's wonderful to see you, a normal American in a—

(*There is a strangulated outcry from the arch under which the* BARON *has disappeared.*)

Excuse me a minute!

(*He rushes toward the source of the outcry.* JACQUES *crosses to the bench before the fountain. Rhubarb is heard through the arch.* JACQUES *shrugs wearily as if it were just a noisy radio.* KILROY *comes plummeting out backwards, all the way to* JACQUES.)

I tried to interfere, but what's th' use?!

JACQUES: No use at all!

(*The* STREETCLEANERS *come through the arch with the* BARON *doubled up in their barrel. They pause and exchange sibilant whispers, pointing and snickering at* KILROY.)

KILROY: Who are they pointing at? At me, Kilroy?

(*The* BUM *laughs from the window.* A. RATT *laughs from his shadowy doorway. The* LOAN SHARK *laughs from his.*)

Kilroy is here and he's not about to be there!—If he can help it . . .

(*He snatches up a rock and throws it at the* STREETCLEANERS. *Everybody laughs louder and the laughter seems to reverberate from the mountains. The light changes, dims a little in the plaza.*)

Sons a whatever you're sons of! Don't look at me, I'm not about to take no ride in the barrel!

(*The* BARON, *his elegant white shoes protruding from the barrel, is wheeled up the Alleyway Out. Figures in the square resume their dazed attitudes and one or two* GUESTS *return to the terrace of the Siete Mares as—*)

GUTMAN: Block Five on the Camino Real!

(*He strolls off.*)

BLOCK FIVE

KILROY (*to* JACQUES): Gee, the blocks go fast on this street!

JACQUES: Yes. The blocks go fast.

KILROY: My name's Kilroy. I'm here.

JACQUES: Mine is Casanova. I'm here, too.

KILROY: But you been here longer than me and maybe could brief me on it. For instance, what do they do with a stiff picked up in this town?

(*The* GUARD *stares at them suspiciously from the terrace.*

JACQUES *whistles "La Golondrina" and crosses downstage. Kilroy follows.*)

Did I say something untactful?

JACQUES (*smiling into a sunset glow*): The exchange of serious questions and ideas, especially between persons from opposite sides of the plaza, is regarded unfavorably here. You'll notice I'm talking as if I had acute laryngitis. I'm gazing into the sunset. If I should start to whistle "La Golondrina" it means we're being overheard by the Guards on the terrace. Now you want to know what is done to a body from which the soul has departed on the Camino Real!—Its disposition depends on what the Streetcleaners happen to find in its pockets. If its pockets are empty as the unfortunate Baron's turned out to be, and as mine are at this moment—the "stiff" is wheeled straight off to the Laboratory. And there the individual becomes an undistinguished member of a collectivist state. His chemical components are separated and poured into vats containing the corresponding elements of countless others. If any of his vital organs or parts are at all unique in size or structure, they're placed on exhibition in bottles containing a very foul-smelling solution called formaldehyde. There is a charge of admission to this museum. The proceeds go to the maintenance of the military police.

(*He whistles "La Golondrina" till the* GUARD *turns his back again. He moves toward the front of the stage.*)

KILROY (*following*): —I guess that's—sensible . . .

JACQUES: Yes, but not romantic. And romance is important. Don't you think?

KILROY: Nobody thinks romance is more important than me!

JACQUES: Except possibly me!

KILROY: Maybe that's why fate has brung us together! We're buddies under the skin!

JACQUES: Travelers born?

KILROY: Always looking for something!

JACQUES: Satisfied by nothing!

KILROY: Hopeful?

JACQUES: Always!

OFFICER: Keep moving!

(*They move apart till the* OFFICER *exits.*)

KILROY: And when a joker on the Camino gets fed up with one continual hassle—how does he get *off* it?

JACQUES: You see the narrow and very steep stairway that passes under what is described in the travel brochures as a "Magnificent Arch of Triumph"?—Well, that's the Way Out!

KILROY: That's the way out?

(KILROY *without hesitation plunges right up to almost the top step; then pauses with a sound of squealing brakes. There is a sudden loud wind.*)

JACQUES (*shouting with hand cupped to mouth*): Well, how does the prospect please you, Traveler born?

KILROY (*shouting back in a tone of awe*): It's too unknown for my blood. Man, I seen nothing like it except through a telescope once on the pier on Coney Island. "Ten cents to see the craters and plains of the moon!"—And here's the same view in three dimensions for nothing!

(*The desert wind sings loudly:* KILROY *mocks it.*)

JACQUES: Are you—ready to cross it?

KILROY: Maybe sometime with someone but not right now and alone! How about you?

JACQUES: I'm not alone.

KILROY: You're with a party?

JACQUES: No, but I'm sweetly encumbered with a—lady . . .

KILROY: It wouldn't do with a lady. I don't see nothing but nothing—and then more nothing. And then I see some mountains. But the mountains are covered with snow.

JACQUES: Snowshoes would be useful!

(*He observes* GUTMAN *approaching through the passage at upper left. He whistles "La Golondrina" for* KILROY'S *attention and points with his cane as he exits.*)

KILROY (*descending steps disconsolately*): Mush, mush.

(*The* BUM *comes to his window.* A. RATT *enters his doorway.* GUTMAN *enters below* KILROY.)

BUM: It's sleepy time down South!

GUTMAN (*warningly as* KILROY *passes him*): Block Six in a progress of sixteen blocks on the Camino Real.

BLOCK SIX

KILROY (*from the stairs*): Man, I could use a bed now.—I'd like to make a cool pad on this camino now and lie down and sleep and dream of being with someone—friendly . . .

(*He crosses to the "Ritz Men Only."*)

A. RATT (*softly and sleepily*): Vacancy here! I got a single bed at the "Ritz Men Only," a little white ship to sail the dangerous night in.

(KILROY *crosses down to his doorway.*)

KILROY: —You got a vacancy here?

A. RATT: I got a vacancy here if you got the one-fifty there.

KILROY: Ha ha! I been in countries where money was not legal tender. I mean it was legal but it wasn't tender.

(*There is a loud groan from offstage above.*)

—Somebody dying on you or just drunk?

A. RATT: Who knows or cares in this pad, Dad?

KILROY: I heard once that a man can't die while he's drunk. Is that a fact or fiction?

A RATT: Strictly a fiction.

VOICE ABOVE: *Stiff in number seven! Call the Streetcleaners!*

A. RATT (*with absolutely no change in face or voice*): Number seven is vacant.

(STREETCLEANERS' *piping is heard. The* BUM *leaves the window.*)

KILROY: Thanks, but tonight I'm going to sleep under the stars.

(A. RATT *gestures "Have it your way" and exits.* KILROY, *left alone, starts downstage. He notices that* LA MADRECITA *is crouched near the fountain, holding something up, inconspicuously, in her hand. Coming to her he sees that it's a piece of food. He takes it, puts it in his mouth, tries to thank her but her head is down, muffled in her rebozo and there is no way for him to acknowledge the gift. He starts to cross.* STREET PEOPLE *raise up their heads in their Pit and motion him invitingly to come in with them. They call softly, "Sleep, sleep . . ."*)

GUTMAN (*from his chair on the terrace*): Hey, Joe.

(*The* STREET PEOPLE *duck immediately.*)

KILROY: Who? Me?

GUTMAN: Yes, you, Candy Man. Are you disocupado?

KILROY: —That means unemployed, don't it?

(*He sees* OFFICERS *converging from right.*)

GUTMAN: Jobless. On the bum. Carrying the banner!

KILROY: —Aw, no, aw, no, don't try to hang no vagrancy rap on me! I was robbed on this square and I got plenty of witnesses to prove it.

GUTMAN (*with ironic courtesy*): Oh?

(*He makes a gesture asking "Where?"*)

KILROY (*coming down to apron left and crossing to the right*): Witnesses! Witness! Witnesses!

(*He comes to* LA MADRECITA.)

You were a witness!

(*A gesture indicates that he realizes her blindness. Opposite the* GYPSY'S *balcony he pauses for a second.*)

Hey, Gypsy's daughter!

(*The balcony is dark. He continues up to the Pit. The* STREET PEOPLE *duck as he calls down.*)

You were witnesses!

(*An* OFFICER *enters with a Patsy outfit. He hands it to* GUTMAN.)

GUTMAN: Here, Boy! Take these.

(GUTMAN *displays and then tosses on the ground at* KILROY'S *feet the Patsy outfit—the red fright wig, the big crimson nose that lights up and has horn rimmed glasses attached, a pair of clown pants that have a huge footprint on the seat.*)

KILROY: What is this outfit?

GUTMAN: The uniform of a Patsy.

KILROY: I know what a Patsy is—he's a clown in the circus who takes prat-falls but *I'm no Patsy!*

GUTMAN: Pick it up.

KILROY: Don't give me orders. Kilroy is a free agent—

GUTMAN (*smoothly*): But a Patsy isn't. Pick it up and put it on, Candy Man. You are now the Patsy.

KILROY: So you say but you are completely mistaken.

(*Four* OFFICERS *press in on him.*)

And don't crowd me with your torpedoes! I'm a stranger here but I got a clean record in all the places I been, I'm not in the books for nothin' but vagrancy and once when I was hungry I walked by a truck-load of pineapples without picking one, because I was brought up good—

(*Then, with a pathetic attempt at making friends with the* OFFICER *to his right.*)

and there was a cop on the corner!

OFFICER: Ponga selo!

KILROY: What'd you say? (*Desperately to audience he asks.*) What did he say?

OFFICER: Ponga selo!

KILROY: What'd you say?

(*The* OFFICER *shoves him down roughly to the Patsy outfit.* KILROY *picks up the pants, shakes them out carefully as if about to step into them and says very politely.*)

Why, surely. I'd be delighted. My fondest dreams have come true.

(*Suddenly he tosses the Patsy dress into* GUTMAN's *face and leaps into the aisle of the theatre.*)

GUTMAN: Stop him! Arrest that vagrant! Don't let him get away!

LOUDSPEAKER: Be on the lookout for a fugitive Patsy. The Patsy has escaped. Stop him, stop that Patsy!

(*A wild chase commences. The two* GUARDS *rush madly down either side to intercept him at the back of the house.* KILROY *wheels about at the top of the center aisle, and runs back down it, panting, gasping out questions and entreaties to various persons occupying aisle seats, such as.*)

KILROY: How do I git out? Which way do I go, which way do I get out? Where's the Greyhound depot? Hey, do you know where the Greyhound bus depot is? What's the best way out, if there is any way out? I got to find one. I had enough of this place. I had too much of this place. I'm free. I'm a free man with equal rights in this world! You better believe it because that's news for you and you had better believe it! Kilroy's a free man with equal rights in this world! All right, now, help me, somebody, help me find a way out, I got to find one, I don't like this place! It's not for me and I am not buying any! Oh! Over there! I see a sign that says EXIT. That's a sweet word to me, man, that's a lovely word, EXIT! That's the entrance to paradise for Kilroy! Exit, I'm coming, Exit, I'm coming!

(*The* STREET PEOPLE *have gathered along the forestage to watch the chase.* ESMERALDA, *barefooted, wearing only a slip, bursts out of the* GYPSY's *establishment like an animal broken out of a cage, darts among the* STREET PEOPLE *to the front of the* CROWD *which is shouting like the spectators at the climax of a corrida. Behind her,* NURSIE *appears, a male actor, wigged and dressed austerely as a duenna, crying out in both languages.*)

NURSIE: Esmeralda! Esmeralda!

GYPSY: Police!

NURSIE: Come back here, Esmeralda!

GYPSY: Catch her, idiot!

NURSIE: Where is my lady bird, where is my precious treasure?

GYPSY: Idiot! I told you to keep her door locked!

NURSIE: She jimmied the lock, Esmeralda!

(*These shouts are mostly lost in the general rhubarb of the chase and the shouting* STREET PEOPLE. ESMERALDA *crouches on the forestage, screaming encouragement in Spanish to the fugitive.* ABDULLAH *catches sight of her, seizes her wrist, shouting.*)

ABDULLAH: Here she is! I got her!

(ESMERALDA *fights savagely. She nearly breaks loose, but* NURSIE *and the* GYPSY *close upon her, too, and she is overwhelmed and dragged back, fighting all the way, toward the door from which she escaped. Meanwhile—timed with the above action—shots are fired in the air by* KILROY's *pursuers. He dashes, panting, into the boxes of the theatre, darting from one box to another, shouting incoherently, now, sobbing for breath, crying out.*)

KILROY: *Mary, help a Christian! Help a Christian, Mary!*

ESMERALDA: *Yankee! Yankee, jump!*

(*The* OFFICERS *close upon him in the box nearest the stage. A dazzling spot of light is thrown on him. He lifts a little gilded chair to defend himself. The chair is torn from his grasp. He leaps upon the ledge of the box.*)

Jump! Jump, Yankee!

(*The* GYPSY *is dragging the girl back by her hair.*)

KILROY: *Watch out down there! Geronimo!*

(*He leaps onto the stage and crumples up with a twisted ankle.* ESMERALDA *screams demoniacally, breaks from her mother's grasp and rushes to him, fighting off his pursuers who have leapt after him from the box.* ABDULLAH, NURSIE *and the* GYPSY *seize her again, just as* KILROY *is seized by his pursuers. The* OFFICERS *beat him to his knees. Each time he is struck,* ESMERALDA *screams as if she received the blow herself. As his cries subside into sobbing, so do hers, and at the end, when he is quite helpless, she is also overcome by her captors and as they drag her back to the* GYPSY's *she cries to him.*)

ESMERALDA: *They've got you! They've got me!*

(*Her mother slaps her fiercely.*)

Caught! Caught! We're caught!

(*She is dragged inside. The door is slammed shut on her continuing outcries. For a moment nothing is heard but* KILROY's *hoarse panting and sobbing.* GUTMAN *takes command of the situation, thrusting his way through the crowd to face* KILROY *who is pinioned by two* GUARDS.)

GUTMAN (*smiling serenely*): Well, well, how do you do! I understand that you're seeking employment here. We need a Patsy and the job is yours for the asking!

KILROY: I don't. Accept. This job. I been. Shanghied!

(KILROY *dons Patsy outfit.*)

GUTMAN: Hush! The Patsy doesn't talk. He lights his nose, that's all!

GUARD: Press the little button at the end of the cord.

GUTMAN: That's right. Just press the little button at the end of the cord!

(KILROY *lights his nose. Everybody laughs.*)

GUTMAN: Again, ha ha! Again, ha ha! Again!

(*The nose goes off and on like a firefly as the stage dims out. The curtain falls. There is a short intermission.*)

BLOCK SEVEN

(*The* DREAMER *is singing with mandolin, "Noche de Ronde." The* GUESTS *murmur, "cool-cool . . ."* GUTMAN *stands on the podiumlike elevation downstage right, smoking a long thin cigar, signing an occasional tab from the bar or café. He is standing in an amber spot. The rest of the stage is filled with blue dusk. At the signal the song fades to a whisper and* GUTMAN *speaks.*)

GUTMAN: Block Seven on the Camino Real— I like this hour.

(*He gives the audience a tender gold-toothed smile.*)

The fire's gone out of the day but the light of it lingers . . . In Rome the continual fountains are bathing stone heroes with silver, in Copenhagen the Tivoli gardens are lighted, they're selling the lottery on San Juan de Latrene . . .

(*The* DREAMER *advances a little, playing the mandolin softly.*)

LA MADRECITA (*holding up glass beads and shell necklaces*): Recuerdos, recuerdos?

GUTMAN: And these are the moments when we look into ourselves and ask with a wonder which never is lost altogether: "Can this be all? Is there nothing more? Is this what the glittering wheels of the heavens turn for?"

(*He leans forward as if conveying a secret.*)

—Ask the Gypsy! Un poco dinero will tickle the Gypsy's palm and give her visions!

(ABDULLAH *emerges with a silver tray, calling.*)

ABDULLAH: Letter for Signor Casanova, letter for Signor Casanova!

(JACQUES *springs up but stands rigid.*)

GUTMAN: Casanova, you have received a letter. Perhaps it's the letter with the remittance check in it!

JACQUES (*in a hoarse, exalted voice*): Yes! It is! The letter! With the remittance check in it!

GUTMAN: Then why don't you take it so you can maintain your residence at the Siete Mares and so avoid the more somber attractions of the "Ritz Men Only"?

JACQUES: My hand is—

GUTMAN: Your hand is paralyzed? . . . By what? *Anxiety? Apprehension?* . . . Put the letter in Signor Casanova's pocket so he can open it when he recovers the use of his digital extremities. Then give him a shot of brandy on the house before he falls on his face!

(JACQUES *has stepped down into the plaza. He looks down at* KILROY *crouched to the right of him and wildly blinking his nose.*)

JACQUES: Yes. I know the Morse code.

(KILROY's *nose again blinks on and off.*)

Thank you, brother.

(*This is said as if acknowledging a message.*)

I knew without asking the Gypsy that something of this sort would happen to you. You have a spark of anarchy in your spirit and that's not to be tolerated. Nothing wild or honest is tolerated here! It has to be extinguished or used only to light up your nose for Mr. Gutman's amusement . . .

(JACQUES *saunters around* KILROY *whistling "La Golondrina." Then satisfied that no one is suspicious of this encounter . . .*)

Before the final block we'll find some way out of here! Meanwhile, patience and courage, little brother!

(JACQUES *feeling he's been there too long starts away giving* KILROY *a reassuring pat on the shoulder and saying.*)

Patience! . . . Courage!

LADY MULLIGAN (*from the* MULLIGAN's *table*): Mr. Gutman!

GUTMAN: Lady Mulligan! And how are you this evening, Lord Mulligan?

LADY MULLIGAN (*interrupting* LORD MULLIGAN's *rumblings*): He's not at all well. This . . . climate is so enervating!

LORD MULLIGAN: I was so weak this morning . . . I couldn't screw the lid on my tooth paste!

LADY MULLIGAN: Raymond, tell Mr. Gutman about those two impertinent workmen in the square! . . . These two idiots pushing a white barrel! Pop up every time we step outside the hotel!

LORD MULLIGAN: —point and giggle at me!

LADY MULLIGAN: Can't they be discharged?

GUTMAN: They can't be discharged, disciplined nor bribed! All you can do is pretend to ignore them.

, LADY MULLIGAN: I can't eat . . . Raymond, stop stuffing!

LORD MULLIGAN: *Shut up!*

GUTMAN (*to the audience*): When the big wheels crack on this street it's like the fall of a capital city, the destruction of Carthage, the sack of Rome by the white-eyed giants from the North! I've seen them fall! I've seen the destruction of them! Adventurers suddenly frightened of a dark room! Gamblers unable to choose between odd and even! Con men and pitchmen and plume-hatted cavaliers turned baby-soft at one note of the Streetcleaners' pipes! When I observe this change, I say to myself: "Could it happen to ME?"—The answer is "YES!" And that's what curdles my blood like milk on the doorstep of someone gone for the summer!

(*A* HUNCHBACK MUMMER *somersaults through his hoop of silver bells, springs up and shakes it excitedly toward a downstage arch which begins to flicker with a diamond-blue radiance; this marks the advent of each legendary character in the play. The music follows: a waltz from the time of* CAMILLE *in Paris.*)

GUTMAN (*downstage to the audience*): Ah, there's the music of another legend, one that everyone knows, the legend of the sentimental whore, the courtesan who made the mistake of love. But now you see her coming into this plaza not as she was when she burned with fever that cast a thin light over Paris, but changed, yes, faded as lanterns and legends fade when they burn into day!

(*He turns and shouts.*)

Rosita, sell her a flower!

(MARGUERITE *has entered the plaza. A beautiful woman of indefinite age. The* STREET PEOPLE *cluster about her with wheedling cries, holding up glass beads, shell necklaces and so forth. She seems confused, lost, half-awake.* JACQUES *has sprung up at her entrance but has difficulty making his way through the cluster of vendors.* ROSITA *has snatched up a tray of flowers and cries out.*)

ROSITA: Camellias, camellias! Pink or white, whichever a lady finds suitable to the moon!

GUTMAN: That's the ticket!

MARGUERITE: Yes, I would like a camellia.

ROSITA (*in a bad French accent*): Rouge ou blanc ce soir?

MARGUERITE: It's always a white one, now . . . but there used to be five evenings out of the month when a pink camellia, instead of the usual white one, let my admirers know that the moon those nights was unfavorable to pleasure, and so they called me—Camille . . .

JACQUES: Mia cara!

(*Imperiously, very proud to be with her, he pushes the* STREET PEOPLE *aside with his cane.*)

Out of the way, make way, let us through, please!

MARGUERITE: Don't push them with your cane.

JACQUES: If they get close enough they'll snatch your purse.

(MARGUERITE *utters a low, shocked cry.*)

What is it?

MARGUERITE: *My purse is gone! It's lost! My papers were in it!*

JACQUES: Your passport was in it?

MARGUERITE: My passport and my permiso de residencia!

(*She leans faint against the arch during the following scene.* ABDULLAH *turns to run.* JACQUES *catches him.*)

JACQUES (*seizing* ABDULLAH's *wrist*): Where did you take her?

ABDULLAH: Oww!—P'tit Zoco.

JACQUES: The Souks?

ABDULLAH: The Souks!

JACQUES: Which cafés did she go to?

ABDULLAH: Ahmed's, she went to—

JACQUES: Did she smoke at Ahmed's?

ABDULLAH: Two kif pipes!

JACQUES: Who was it took her purse? Was it *you?* We'll see!

(*He strips off the boy's burnoose. He crouches whimpering, shivering in a ragged slip.*)

MARGUERITE: Jacques, let the boy go, he didn't take it!

JACQUES: He doesn't have it on him but knows who does!

ABDULLAH: No, no, I don't know!

JACQUES: You little son of a Gypsy! Senta! . . . You know who I am? I am Jacques Casanova! I belong to the Secret Order of the Rose-colored Cross! . . . Run back to Ahmed's. Contact the spiv that took the lady's purse. Tell him to keep it but give her back her papers! There'll be a large reward.

(*He thumps his cane on the ground to release* ABDULLAH *from the spell. The boy dashes off.* JACQUES *laughs and turns triumphantly to* MARGUERITE.)

LADY MULLIGAN: Waiter! The adventurer and his mistress must not be seated next to Lord Mulligan's table!

JACQUES (*loudly enough for* LADY MULLIGAN *to hear*): This hotel has become a mecca for black marketeers and their expensively kept women!

LADY MULLIGAN: Mr. Gutman!

MARGUERITE: Let's have dinner upstairs!

WAITER (*directing them to terrace table*): This way, M'sieur.

JACQUES: We'll take our usual table.

(*He indicates one.*)

MARGUERITE: Please!

WAITER (*overlapping* MARGUERITE's *"please!"*): This table is reserved for Lord Byron!

JACQUES (*masterfully*): This table is always our table.

MARGUERITE: I'm not hungry.

JACQUES: Hold out the lady's chair, cretino!

GUTMAN (*darting over to* MARGUERITE's *chair*): Permit me!

(JACQUES *bows with mock gallantry to* LADY MULLI-GAN *as he turns to his chair during seating of* MAR-GUERITE.)

LADY MULLIGAN: We'll move to *that* table!

JACQUES: —You must learn how to carry the banner of Bohemia into the enemy camp.

(*A screen is put up around them.*)

MARGUERITE: Bohemia has no banner. It survives by discretion.

JACQUES: I'm glad that you value discretion. *Wine list!* Was it discretion that led you through the bazaars this afternoon wearing your cabochon sapphire and diamond ear-drops? You were fortunate that you lost only your purse and papers!

MARGUERITE: Take the wine list.

JACQUES: Still or sparkling?

MARGUERITE: Sparkling.

GUTMAN: May I make a suggestion, Signor Casanova?

JACQUES: Please do.

GUTMAN: It's a very cold and dry wine from only ten metres below the snowline in the mountains. The name of the wine is Quando!—meaning when! Such as "When are remittances going to be received?" "When are accounts to be settled?" Ha ha ha! Bring Signor Casanova a bottle of Quando with the compliments of the house!

JACQUES: I'm sorry this had to happen in—your presence . . .

MARGUERITE: That doesn't matter, my dear. But why don't you *tell* me when you are short of money?

JACQUES: I thought the fact was apparent. It is to everyone else.

MARGUERITE: The letter you were expecting, it still hasn't come?

JACQUES (*removing it from his pocket*): It came this afternoon—Here it is!

MARGUERITE: You haven't opened the letter!

JACQUES: I haven't had the nerve to! I've had so many unpleasant surprises that I've lost faith in my luck.

MARGUERITE: Give the letter to me. Let me open it for you.

JACQUES: Later, a little bit later, after the—wine . . .

MARGUERITE: Old hawk, anxious old hawk!

(*She clasps his hand on the table: he leans toward her: she kisses her fingertips and places them on his lips.*)

JACQUES: Do you call that a kiss?

MARGUERITE: I call it the ghost of a kiss. It will have to do for now. (*She leans back, her blue-tinted eyelids closed.*)

JACQUES: Are you tired? Are you tired, Marguerite? You know you should have rested this afternoon.

MARGUERITE: I looked at silver and rested.

JACQUES: You looked at silver at Ahmed's?

MARGUERITE: No, I rested at Ahmed's, and had mint-tea.

(*The* DREAMER *accompanies their speech with his guitar. The duologue should have the style of an antiphonal poem, the cues picked up so that there is scarcely a separation between the speeches, and the tempo quick and the voices edged.*)

JACQUES: You had mint-tea downstairs?

MARGUERITE: No, upstairs.

JACQUES: Upstairs where they burn the poppy?

MARGUERITE: Upstairs where it's cool and there's music and the haggling of the bazaar is soft as the murmur of pigeons.

JACQUES: That sounds restful. Reclining among silk pillows on a divan, in a curtained and perfumed alcove above the bazaar?

MARGUERITE: Forgetting for a while where I am, or that I don't know where I am . . .

JACQUES: Forgetting alone or forgetting with some young companion who plays the lute or the flute or who had silver to show you? Yes. That sounds very restful. And yet you do seem tired.

MARGUERITE: If I seem tired, it's your insulting solicitude that I'm tired of!

JACQUES: Is it insulting to feel concern for your safety in this place?

MARGUERITE: Yes, it is. The implication is.

JACQUES: What is the implication?

MARGUERITE: You know what it is: that I am one of those *aging*—*voluptuaries*—who used to be paid for pleasure but now have to pay!—Jacques, I won't be followed, I've gone too far to be followed!—*What is it?*

(*The* WAITER *has presented an envelope on a salver.*)

WAITER: A letter for the lady.

MARGUERITE: How strange to receive a letter in a place where nobody knows I'm staying! Will you open it for me?

(*The* WAITER *withdraws.* JACQUES *takes the letter and opens it.*)

Well! What is it?

JACQUES: Nothing important. An illustrated brochure from some resort in the mountains.

MARGUERITE: What is it called?

JACQUES: Bide-a-While.

(*A chafing dish bursts into startling blue flame at the* MULLIGANS' *table.* LADY MULLIGAN *clasps her hands and exclaims with affected delight, the* WAITER *and* MR. GUTMAN *laugh agreeably.* MARGUERITE *springs up and moves out upon the forestage.* JACQUES *goes to her.*)

Do you know this resort in the mountains?

MARGUERITE: Yes. I stayed there once. It's one of those places with open sleeping verandahs, surrounded by snowy pine woods. It has rows and rows of narrow white iron beds as regular as tombstones. The invalids smile at each other when axes flash across valleys, ring, flash, ring again! Young voices shout across valleys Hola! And mail is delivered. The friend that used to write you ten-page letters contents himself now with a postcard bluebird that tells you to "Get well Quick!"

(JACQUES *throws the brochure away.*)

—And when the last bleeding comes, not much later nor earlier than expected, you're wheeled discreetly into a little tent of white gauze, and the last thing you know of this world, of which you've known so little and yet so much, is the smell of an empty ice box.

(*The blue flame expires in the chafing dish.* GUTMAN *picks up the brochure and hands it to the* WAITER, *whispering something.*)

JACQUES: You won't go back to that place.

(*The* WAITER *places the brochure on the salver again and approaches behind them.*)

MARGUERITE: I wasn't released. I left without permission. They sent me this to remind me.

WAITER (*presenting the salver*): You dropped this.

JACQUES: We threw it away!

WAITER: Excuse me.

JACQUES: Now, from now on, Marguerite, you must take better care of yourself. Do you hear me?

MARGUERITE: I hear you. No more distractions for me? No more entertainers in curtained and perfumed alcoves above the bazaar, no more young men that a pinch of white powder or a puff of gray smoke can almost turn to someone devoutly remembered?

JACQUES: No, from now on—

MARGUERITE: What "from now on," old hawk?

JACQUES: Rest. Peace.

MARGUERITE: Rest in peace is that final bit of advice they carve on grave-stones, and I'm not ready for it! Are you? Are *you* ready for it?

(*She returns to the table. He follows her.*)

Oh, Jacques, when are we going to leave here, how are we going to leave here, you've got to tell me!

JACQUES: I've told you all I know.

MARGUERITE: Nothing, you've given up hope!

JACQUES: I haven't, that's not true.

(GUTMAN *has brought out the white cockatoo which he shows to* LADY MULLIGAN *at her table.*)

GUTMAN (*his voice rising above the murmurs*): Her name is Aurora.

LADY MULLIGAN: Why do you call her Aurora?

GUTMAN: She cries at daybreak.

LADY MULLIGAN: Only at daybreak?

GUTMAN: Yes, at daybreak only?

(*Their voices and laughter fade under.*)

MARGUERITE: How long is it since you've been to the travel agencies?

JACQUES: This morning I made the usual round of Cook's, American Express, Wagon-lits Universal, and it was the same story. There are no flights out of here till further orders from someone higher up.

MARGUERITE: Nothing, nothing at all?

JACQUES: Oh, there's a rumor of something called the Fugitivo, but—

MARGUERITE: The What!!!?

JACQUES: The Fugitivo. It's one of those non-scheduled things that—

MARGUERITE: When, when, when?

JACQUES: I told you it was non-scheduled Non-scheduled means it comes and goes at no predictable—

MARGUERITE: Don't give me the dictionary! I want to know how does one get on it? Did you bribe them? Did you offer them money? No. Of course you didn't! And I know why! You really don't want to leave here. You *think* you don't want to go because you're brave as an old hawk. But the truth of the matter—the real not the royal truth—is that you're terrified of the Terra Incognita outside that wall.

JACQUES: You've hit upon the truth. I'm terrified of the unknown country inside or outside this wall or any place on earth without you with me! The only country, known or unknown that I can breathe in, or care to, is the country in which we breathe together, as we are now at this table. And later, a little while later, even closer than this, the sole inhabitants of a tiny world whose limits are those of the light from a rose-colored lamp—beside the sweetly, completely known country of your cool bed!

MARGUERITE: The little comfort of love?

JACQUES: Is that comfort so little?

MARGUERITE: Caged birds accept each other but flight is what they long for.

JACQUES: I want to stay here with you and love you and guard you until the time or way comes that we both can leave with honor.

MARGUERITE: "Leave with honor"? Your vocabulary is almost as out-of-date as your cape and your cane. How could anyone quit this field with honor, this place where there's nothing but the gradual wasting away of everything decent in us . . . the sort of desperation that comes after even desperation has been worn out through long wear! . . . Why have they put these screens around the table?

(*She springs up and knocks one of them over.*)

LADY MULLIGAN: There! You see? I don't understand why you let such people stay here.

GUTMAN: They pay the price of admission the same as you.

LADY MULLIGAN: What price is that?

GUTMAN: Desperation!—With cash here!

(*He indicates the Siete Mares.*)

Without cash there!

(*He indicates Skid Row.*)

Block Eight on the Camino Real!

BLOCK EIGHT

(*There is the sound of loud desert wind and a flamenco cry followed by a dramatic phrase of music.*

A flickering diamond blue radiance floods the hotel entrance. The crouching, grimacing HUNCHBACK *shakes his hoop of bells which is the convention for the appearance of each legendary figure.*

LORD BYRON *appears in the doorway readied for departure.* GUTMAN *raises his hand for silence.*)

GUTMAN: You're leaving us, Lord Byron?

BYRON: Yes, I'm leaving you, Mr. Gutman.

GUTMAN: What a pity! But this is a port of entry and departure. There are no permanent guests. Possibly you are getting a little restless?

BYRON: The luxuries of this place have made me soft. The metal point's gone from my pen, there's nothing left but the feather.

GUTMAN: That may be true. But what can you do about it?

BYRON: Make a departure!

GUTMAN: From yourself?

BYRON: From my present self to myself as I used to be!

GUTMAN: *That's* the *furthest* departure a man could make! I guess you're sailing to Athens? There's another war there and like all wars since the beginning of time it can be interpreted as a—struggle for *what?*

BYRON: —For *freedom!* You may laugh at it, but it still means something to *me!*

GUTMAN: Of course it does! I'm not laughing a bit, I'm beaming with admiration.

BYRON: I've allowed myself many distractions.

GUTMAN: Yes, indeed!

BYRON: But I've never altogether forgotten my old devotion to the—

GUTMAN: —To the *what,* Lord Byron?

(BYRON *passes nervous fingers through his hair.*)

You can't remember the object of your one-time devotion?

(*There is a pause.* BYRON *limps away from the terrace and goes toward the fountain.*)

BYRON: When Shelley's corpse was recovered from the sea . . .

(GUTMAN *beckons the* DREAMER *who approaches and accompanies* BYRON's *speech.*)

—It was burned on the beach of Viareggio. —I watched the spectacle from my carriage because the stench was revolting . . . Then it— fascinated me! I got out of my carriage. Went nearer, holding a handkerchief to my nostrils!— I saw that the front of the skull had broken away in the flames, and there—

(*He advances out upon the stage apron, followed by* ABDULLAH *with the pine torch or lantern.*)

And there was the brain of Shelley, indistinguishable from a cooking stew!—*boiling, bubbling, hissing!*—in the *blackening*—*cracked*—*pot*—of his skull!

(MARGUERITE *rises abruptly.* JACQUES *supports her.*)

—Trelawney, his friend, Trelawney, threw salt and oil and frankincense in the flames and finally the almost intolerable stench—

(ABDULLAH *giggles.* GUTMAN *slaps him.*)

—was *gone* and the burning was *pure!*—as a man's burning should be . . .

A man's burning *ought* to be pure!—*not* like mine—(a crepe suzette—burned in brandy . . .) *Shelley's* burning was finally very *pure!*

But the body, the corpse, split open like a grilled pig!

(ABDULLAH *giggles irrepressibly again.* GUTMAN *grips the back of his neck and he stands up stiff and assumes an expression of exaggerated solemnity.*)

—And then Trelawney—as the ribs of the corpse unlocked—reached into them as a baker reaches quickly into an oven!

(ABDULLAH *almost goes into another convulsion.*)

—And snatched out—as a baker would a biscuit!—the *heart* of Shelley! Snatched the heart of Shelley out of the blistering corpse!—Out of the purifying—blue-flame . . .

(MARGUERITE *resumes her seat;* JACQUES *his.*)

—And it was *over!*—I thought—

(*He turns slightly from the audience and crosses upstage from the apron. He faces* JACQUES *and* MARGUERITE.)

—I thought it was a disgusting thing to do, to snatch a man's heart from his body! What can one man do with another man's heart?

(JACQUES *rises and strikes the stage with his cane.*)

JACQUES (*passionately*): He can do this with it!

(*He seizes a loaf of bread on his table, and descends from the terrace.*)

He can twist it like this!

(*He twists the loaf.*)

He can tear it like this!

(*He tears the loaf in two.*)

He can crush it under his foot!

(*He drops the bread and stamps on it.*)

—And kick it away—like this!

(*He kicks the bread off the terrace.* LORD BYRON *turns away from him and limps again out upon the stage apron and speaks to the audience.*)

BYRON: That's very true, Señor. But a poet's vocation, which used to be my vocation, is to influence the heart in a gentler fashion than you have made your mark on that loaf of bread. He ought to purify it and lift it above its ordinary level. For what is the heart but a sort of—

(He makes a high, groping gesture in the air.)

—A sort of—*instrument!*—that translates *noise* into *music,* chaos into—*order* . . .

(ABDULLAH ducks almost to the earth in an effort to stifle his mirth. GUTMAN *coughs to cover his own amusement.)*

—a mysterious order!

(He raises his voice till it fills the plaza.)

—That was my vocation once upon a time, before it was obscured by vulgar plaudits!—Little by little it was lost among gondolas and palazzos!—masked balls, glittering salons, huge shadowy courts and torch-lit entrances!—Baroque façades, canopies and carpets, candelabra and gold plate among snowy damask, ladies with throats as slender as flower-stems, bending and breathing toward me their fragrant breath——

—Exposing their breasts to me!

Whispering, half-smiling!—And everywhere marble, the visible grandeur of marble, pink and gray marble, veined and tinted as flayed corrupting flesh,—all these provided agreeable distractions from the rather frightening solitude of a poet. Oh, I wrote many cantos in Venice and Constantinople and in Ravenna and Rome, on all of those Latin and Levantine excursions that my twisted foot led me into—but I wonder about them a little. They seem to improve as the wine in the bottle—dwindles . . . *There is a passion for declivity in this world!*

And lately I've found myself listening to hired musicians behind a row of artificial palm trees—instead of the single—pure-stringed instrument of my heart . . .

Well, then, it's time to leave here!

(He turns back to the stage.)

—There is a time for departure even when there's no certain place to go!

I'm going to look for one, now. I'm sailing to Athens. At least I can look up at the Acropolis, I can stand at the foot of it and look up at broken columns on the crest of a hill—if not purity, at least its recollection . . .

I can sit quietly looking for a long, long time in absolute silence, and possibly, yes, *still* possibly—

The old pure music will come to me again. Of course on the other hand I may hear only the little noise of insects in the grass . . .

But I am sailing to Athens! *Make voyages!—Attempt them!*—there's nothing else . . .

MARGUERITE *(excitedly)*: *Watch where he goes!*

(LORD BYRON limps across the plaza with his head bowed, making slight, apologetic gestures to the wheedling BEGGARS who shuffle about him. There is music. He crosses toward the steep Alleyway Out. The following is played with a quiet intensity so it will be in a lower key than the later Fugitivo Scene.)

Watch him, watch him, see which way he goes. Maybe he knows of a way that we haven't found out.

JACQUES: Yes, I'm watching him, Cara.

(LORD and LADY MULLIGAN half rise, staring anxiously through monocle and lorgnon.)

MARGUERITE: Oh, my God, I believe he's going up that alley.

JACQUES: Yes, he is. He has.

LORD and LADY MULLIGAN: Oh, the fool, the idiot, he's going under the arch!

MARGUERITE: Jacques, run after him, warn him, tell him about the desert he has to cross.

JACQUES: I think he knows what he's doing.

MARGUERITE: I can't look!

(She turns to the audience, throwing back her head and closing her eyes. The desert wind sings loudly as BYRON climbs to the top of the steps.)

BYRON *(to several porters carrying luggage—which is mainly caged birds)*: THIS WAY!

(He exits. KILROY *starts to follow. He stops at the steps, cringing and looking at GUTMAN. GUTMAN motions him to go ahead.* KILROY *rushes up the stairs. He looks out, loses his nerve and sits—blinking his nose.* GUTMAN *laughs as he announces—)*

GUTMAN: Block Nine on the Camino Real!

(He goes into the hotel.)

BLOCK NINE

(ABDULLAH runs back to the hotel with the billowing flambeau. A faint and far away humming sound becomes audible . . . MARGUERITE *opens her eyes with a startled look. She searches the sky for something. A very low percussion begins with the humming sound, as if excited hearts are beating.)*

MARGUERITE: Jacques! I hear something in the sky!

JACQUES: I think what you hear is—

MARGUERITE *(with rising excitement)*: —No, it's

a plane, a great one, I see the lights of it, now!
JACQUES: Some kind of fireworks, Cara.
MARGUERITE: Hush! LISTEN!

(*She blows out the candle to see better above it. She rises, peering into the sky.*)

I see it! I see it! There! It's circling over us!
LADY MULLIGAN: Raymond, Raymond, sit down, your face is flushed!
HOTEL GUESTS (*overlapping*): What is it?
The FUGITIVO!
THE FUGITIVO! THE FUGITIVO!
Quick, get my jewelry from the hotel safe!
Cash a check!
Throw some things in a bag! I'll wait here!
Never mind luggage, we have our money and papers!
Where is it now?
There, there!
It's turning to land!
To go like this?
Yes, go anyhow, just go anyhow, just go!
Raymond! Please!
Oh, it's rising again!
Oh, it's—*SHH! MR. GUTMAN!*

(GUTMAN *appears in the doorway. He raises a hand in a commanding gesture.*)

GUTMAN: Signs in the sky should not be mistaken for wonders!

(*The* VOICES *modulate quickly.*)

Ladies, gentlemen, please resume your seats!

(*Places are resumed at tables, and silver is shakily lifted. Glasses are raised to lips, but the noise of concerted panting of excitement fills the stage and a low percussion echoes frantic heart beats.* GUTMAN *descends to the plaza, shouting furiously to the* OFFICER.)

Why wasn't I told the Fugitivo was coming?

(*Everyone, almost as a man, rushes into the hotel and reappears almost at once with hastily collected possessions.* MARGUERITE *rises but appears stunned.*

There is a great whistling and screeching sound as the aerial transport halts somewhere close by, accompanied by rainbow splashes of light and cries like children's on a roller-coaster. Some incoming PASSENGERS *approach the stage down an aisle of the theatre, preceded by* REDCAPS *with luggage.*)

PASSENGERS: What a heavenly trip!
The scenery was thrilling!
It's so quick!
The only way to travel! Etc., etc.

(*A uniformed man, the* PILOT, *enters the plaza with a megaphone.*)

PILOT (*through the megaphone*): Fugitivo now loading for departure! Fugitivo loading immediately for departure! Northwest corner of the plaza!
MARGUERITE: Jacques, it's the Fugitivo, it's the non-scheduled thing you heard of this afternoon!
PILOT: All out-going passengers on the Fugitivo are requested to present their tickets and papers immediately at this station.
MARGUERITE: He said "out-going passengers"!
PILOT: Out-going passengers on the Fugitivo report immediately at this station for custom inspection.
MARGUERITE (*with a forced smile*): Why are you just standing there?
JACQUES (*with an Italian gesture*): Che cosa possa fare!
MARGUERITE: Move, move, do something!
JACQUES: *What!*
MARGUERITE: Go to them, ask, find out!
JACQUES: I have no idea what the damned thing is!
MARGUERITE: I do, I'll tell you! It's a way to escape from this abominable place!
JACQUES: Forse, forse, non so!
MARGUERITE: It's a way *out* and *I'm* not going to miss it!
PILOT: Ici la Douáne! Customs inspection here!
MARGUERITE: Customs. That means luggage. Run to my room! Here! Key! Throw a few things in a bag, my jewels, my furs, but hurry! Vite, vite, vite! I don't believe there's much time! No, everybody is—

(*Outgoing* PASSENGERS *storm the desk and table.*)

—Clamoring for tickets! There must be limited space! Why don't you do what I tell you?

(*She rushes to a man with a rubber stamp and a roll of tickets.*)

Monsieur! Señor! Pardonnez-moi! I'm going, I'm going out! I want my ticket!
PILOT (*coldly*): Name, please.
MARGUERITE: Mademoiselle—Gautier—but I—
PILOT: Gautier? Gautier? We have no Gautier listed.
MARGUERITE: I'm—*not* listed! I mean I'm—traveling under another name.

TRAVEL AGENT: What name are you traveling under?

(PRUDENCE *and* OLYMPE *rush out of the hotel half dressed, dragging their furs. Meanwhile* KILROY *is trying to make a fast buck or two as a* REDCAP. *The scene gathers wild momentum, is punctuated by crashes of percussion. Grotesque mummers act as demon custom inspectors and immigration authorities, etc. Baggage is tossed about, ripped open, smuggled goods seized, arrests made, all amid the wildest importunities, protests, threats, bribes, entreaties; it is a scene for improvisation.*)

PRUDENCE: Thank God I woke up!

OLYMPE: Thank God I wasn't asleep!

PRUDENCE: I knew it was non-scheduled but I *did* think they'd give you time to get in your girdle.

OLYMPE: Look who's trying to crash it! I know damned well *she* don't have a reservation!

PILOT (*to* MARGUERITE): What name did you say, Mademoiselle? Please! People are waiting, you're holding up the line!

MARGUERITE: I'm so confused! Jacques! What name did you make my reservation under?

OLYMPE: She has no reservation!

PRUDENCE: *I have, I got mine!*

OLYMPE: *I got mine!*

PRUDENCE: *I'm* next!

OLYMPE: Don't push *me*, you old bag!

MARGUERITE: I was here first! I was here before anybody! Jacques, quick! Get my money from the hotel safe!

(JACQUES *exits.*)

AGENT: *Stay in line!*

(*There is a loud warning whistle.*)

PILOT: Five minutes. The Fugitivo leaves in five minutes. Five, five minutes only!

(*At this announcement the scene becomes riotous.*)

TRAVEL AGENT: *Four minutes! The Fugitivo leaves in four minutes!*

(PRUDENCE *and* OLYMPE *are shrieking at him in French. The warning whistle blasts again.*)

Three minutes, the Fugitivo leaves in three minutes!

MARGUERITE (*topping the turmoil*): Monsieur! Please! I was here first, I was here before anybody! Look!

(JACQUES *returns with her money.*)

I have thousands of francs! Take whatever you want! Take all of it, it's yours!

PILOT: Payment is only accepted in pounds sterling or dollars. Next, please.

MARGUERITE: You don't accept francs? They do at the hotel! They accept my francs at the Siete Mares!

PILOT: Lady, don't argue with me, I don't make the rules!

MARGUERITE (*beating her forehead with her fist*): Oh, God, Jacques! Take these back to the cashier!

(*She thrusts the bills at him.*)

Get them changed to dollars or—*Hurry! Tout de suite!* I'm—going to faint . . .

JACQUES: But Marguerite—

MARGUERITE: *Go! Go! Please!*

PILOT: Closing, we're closing now! The Fugitivo leaves in two minutes!

(LORD *and* LADY MULLIGAN *rush forward.*)

LADY MULLIGAN: Let Lord Mulligan through.

PILOT (*to* MARGUERITE): You're standing in the way.

(OLYMPE *screams as the* CUSTOMS INSPECTOR *dumps her jewels on the ground. She and* PRUDENCE *butt heads as they dive for the gems. the fight is renewed.*)

MARGUERITE (*detaining the* PILOT): Oh, look, Monsieur! Regardez ça! My diamond, a solitaire —two carats! Take that as security!

PILOT: Let me go. The Loan Shark's across the plaza!

(*There is another warning blast.* PRUDENCE *and* OLYMPE *seize hat boxes and rush toward the whistle.*)

MARGUERITE (*clinging desperately in the* PILOT): You don't understand! Señor Casanova has gone to change money! He'll be here in a second. And I'll pay five, ten, twenty times the price of— *JACQUES! JACQUES! WHERE ARE YOU?*

VOICE (*back of auditorium*): We're closing the gate!

MARGUERITE: You can't close the gate!

PILOT: Move, Madame!

MARGUERITE: I won't move!

LADY MULLIGAN: I tell you, Lord Mulligan is the Iron & Steel man from Cobh! Raymond! They're closing the gate!

LORD MULLIGAN: I can't seem to get through!

GUTMAN: Hold the gate for Lord Mulligan!

PILOT (*to* MARGUERITE): Madame, stand back or I will have to use force!

MARGUERITE: Jacques! Jacques!

LADY MULLIGAN: Let us through! We're clear!

PILOT: Madame! Stand back and let these passengers through!

MARGUERITE: No, No! I'm first! I'm next!

LORD MULLIGAN: Get her out of our way! That woman's a whore!

LADY MULLIGAN: How dare you stand in our way?

PILOT: Officer, take this woman!

LADY MULLIGAN: Come on, Raymond!

MARGUERITE (as the OFFICER pulls her away): Jacques! Jacques! Jacques!

(JACQUES returns with changed money.)

Here! Here is the money!

PILOT: All right, give me your papers.

MARGUERITE: —My papers? Did you say my papers?

PILOT: Hurry, hurry, your passport!

MARGUERITE: —Jacques! He wants my papers! Give him my papers, Jacques!

JACQUES: —The lady's papers are lost!

MARGUERITE (wildly): No, no, no, THAT IS NOT TRUE! HE WANTS TO KEEP ME HERE! HE'S LYING ABOUT IT!

JACQUES: Have you forgotten that your papers were stolen?

MARGUERITE: I gave you my papers, I gave you my papers to keep, you've got my papers.

(Screaming, LADY MULLIGAN breaks past her and descends the stairs.)

LADY MULLIGAN: Raymond! Hurry!

LORD MULLIGAN (staggering on the top step): I'm sick! I'm sick!

(The STREETCLEANERS disguised as expensive morticians in swallowtail coats come rapidly up the aisle of the theatre and wait at the foot of the stairway for the tottering tycoon.)

LADY MULLIGAN: You cannot be sick till we get on the Fugitivo!

LORD MULLIGAN: Forward all cables to Guaranty Trust in Paris.

LADY MULLIGAN: Place de la Concorde.

LORD MULLIGAN: Thank you! All purchases C.O.D. to Mulligan Iron & Steel Works in Cobh—Thank you!

LADY MULLIGAN: Raymond! Raymond! Who are these men?

LORD MULLIGAN: I know these men! I recognize their faces!

LADY MULLIGAN: Raymond! They're the Streetcleaners!

(She screams and runs up the aisle screaming repeatedly, stopping half-way to look back. The TWO STREETCLEANERS seize LORD MULLIGAN by either arm as he crumples.)

Pack Lord Mulligan's body in dry ice! Ship Air Express to Cobh care of Mulligan Iron & Steel Works, in Cobh!

(She runs sobbing out of the back of the auditorium as the whistle blows repeatedly and a VOICE shouts.)

I'm coming! I'm coming!

MARGUERITE: Jacques! Jacques! Oh, God!

PILOT: The Fugitivo is leaving, all aboard!

(He starts toward the steps. MARGUERITE clutches his arm.)

Let go of me!

MARGUERITE: You can't go without me!

PILOT: Officer, hold this woman!

JACQUES: Marguerite, let him go!

(She releases the PILOT's arms and turns savagely on JACQUES. She tears his coat open, seizes a large envelope of papers and rushes after the PILOT who has started down the steps over the orchestra pit and into a center aisle of the house. Timpani build up as she starts down the steps, screaming—)

MARGUERITE: Here! I have them here! Wait! I have my papers now, I have my papers!

(The PILOT runs cursing up the center aisle as the Fugitivo whistle gives repeated short, shrill blasts; timpani and dissonant brass are heard. Outgoing PASSENGERS burst into hysterical song, laughter, shouts of farewell. These can come over a loudspeaker at the back of the house.)

VOICE IN DISTANCE: Going! Going! Going!

MARGUERITE (attempting as if half-paralyzed to descend the steps): NOT WITHOUT ME, NO, NO, NOT WITHOUT ME!

(Her figure is caught in the dazzling glacial light of the follow-spot. It blinds her. She makes violent, crazed gestures, clinging to the railing of the steps; her breath is loud and hoarse as a dying person's, she holds a blood-stained handkerchief to her lips.

There is a prolonged, gradually fading, rocketlike roar as the Fugitivo takes off. Shrill cries of joy from departing passengers; something radiant passes above the stage and streams of confetti and tinsel fall into the plaza. Then there is a great calm, the ship's receding roar diminished to the hum of an insect.)

GUTMAN (somewhat compassionately): Block Ten on the Camino Real.

BLOCK TEN

(There is something about the desolation of the plaza that suggests a city devastated by bombardment. Reddish lights flicker here and there as if ruins were smoldering and wisps of smoke rise from them.)

LA MADRECITA *(almost inaudibly)*: Donde?

THE DREAMER: Aqui. Aqui, Madrecita.

MARGUERITE: Lost! Lost! Lost! Lost!

(She is still clinging brokenly to the railing of the steps. JACQUES *descends to her and helps her back up the steps.)*

JACQUES: Lean against me, Cara. Breathe quietly, now.

MARGUERITE: Lost!

JACQUES: Breathe quietly, quietly, and look up at the sky.

MARGUERITE: Lost . . .

JACQUES: These tropical nights are so clear. There's the Southern Cross. Do you see the Southern Cross, Marguerite?

(He points through the proscenium. They are now on the bench before the fountain; she is resting in his arms.)

And there, over there, is Orion, like a fat, golden fish swimming North in the deep clear water, and we are together, breathing quietly together, leaning together, quietly, quietly together, completely, sweetly together, not frightened, now, not alone, but completely quietly together . . .

*(*LA MADRECITA, *led into the center of the plaza by her son, has begun to sing very softly; the reddish flares dim out and the smoke disappears.)*

All of us have a desperate bird in our hearts, a memory of—some distant mother with—wings . . .

MARGUERITE: I would have—left—without you . . .

JACQUES: I know, I know!

MARGUERITE: Then how can you—still—?

JACQUES: Hold you?

*(*MARGUERITE *nods slightly.)*

Because you've taught me that part of love which is tender. I never knew it before. Oh, I had—mistresses that circled me like moons! I scrambled from one bed-chamber to another bed-chamber with shirttails always aflame, from girl to girl, like buckets of coal-oil poured on a con-flagration! But never loved until now with the part of love that's tender . . .

MARGUERITE: —We're used to each other. That's what you think is love . . . You'd better leave me now, you'd better go and let me go because there's a cold wind blowing out of the mountains and over the desert and into my heart, and if you stay with me now, I'll say cruel things, I'll wound your vanity, I'll taunt you with the decline of your male vigor!

JACQUES: Why does disappointment make people unkind to each other?

MARGUERITE: Each of us is very much alone.

JACQUES: Only if we distrust each other.

MARGUERITE: We have to distrust each other. It is our only defense against betrayal.

JACQUES: I think our defense is love.

MARGUERITE: Oh, Jacques, we're used to each other, we're a pair of captive hawks caught in the same cage, and so we've grown used to each other. That's what passes for love at this dim, shadowy end of the Camino Real . . .

What are we sure of? Not even of our existence, dear comforting friend! And whom can we ask the questions that torment us? "What is this place?" "Where are we?"—a fat old man who gives sly hints that only bewilder us more, a fake of a Gypsy squinting at cards and tea-leaves. What else are we offered? The never-broken procession of little events that assure us that we and strangers about us are still going on! Where? Why? and the perch that we hold is unstable! We're threatened with eviction, for this is a port of entry and departure, there are no permanent guests! And where else have we to go when we leave here? Bide-a-While? "Ritz Men Only"? Or under that ominous arch into Terra Incognita? We're lonely. We're frightened. We hear the Streetcleaners' piping not far away. So now and then, although we've wounded each other time and again—we stretch out hands to each other in the dark that we can't escape from—we huddle together for some dim-communal comfort—and that's what passes for love on this terminal stretch of the road that used to be royal. What is it, this feeling between us? When you feel my exhausted weight against your shoulder—when I clasp your anxious old hawk's head to my breast, what is it we feel in whatever is left of our hearts? Something, yes, something—delicate, unreal, bloodless! The sort of violets that could grow on the moon, or in the crevices of those far away mountains, fertilized by the droppings of carrion birds. Those birds are familiar to us. Their shadows inhabit the plaza. I've heard them flapping their wings like old charwomen beating worn-out carpets with gray brooms . . .

But tenderness, the violets in the mountains —can't break the rocks!

JACQUES: The violets in the mountains can break the rocks if you believe in them and allow them to grow!

(*The plaza has resumed its usual aspect.* ABDULLAH *enters through one of the downstage arches.*)

ABDULLAH: Get your carnival hats and noise-makers here! Tonight the moon will restore the virginity of my sister!

MARGUERITE (*almost tenderly touching his face*): Don't you know that tonight I am going to betray you?

JACQUES: —Why would you do that?

MARGUERITE: Because I've out-lived the tenderness of my heart. Abdullah, come here! I have an errand for you! Go to Ahmed's and deliver a message!

ABDULLAH: I'm working for Mama, making the Yankee dollar! Get your carnival hats and—

MARGUERITE: *Here, boy!*

(*She snatches a ring off her finger and offers it to him.*)

JACQUES: —Your cabochon sapphire?

MARGUERITE: Yes, my cabochon sapphire!

JACQUES: Are you mad?

MARGUERITE: Yes, I'm mad, or nearly! The specter of lunacy's at my heels tonight!

(JACQUES *drives* ABDULLAH *back with his cane.*)

Catch, boy! The other side of the fountain! Quick!

(*The guitar is heard molto vivace. She tosses the ring across the fountain.* JACQUES *attempts to hold the boy back with his cane.* ABDULLAH *dodges in and out like a little terrier, laughing.* MARGUERITE *shouts encouragement in French. When the boy is driven back from the ring, she snatches it up and tosses it to him again, shouting.*)

Catch, boy! Run to Ahmed's! Tell the charming young man that the French lady's bored with her company tonight! Say that the French lady missed the Fugitivo and wants to forget she missed it! Oh, and reserve a room with a balcony so I can watch your sister appear on the roof when the moonrise makes her a virgin!

(ABDULLAH *skips shouting out of the plaza.* JACQUES *strikes the stage with his cane. She says, without looking at him.*)

Time betrays us and we betray each other.

JACQUES: Wait, Marguerite.

MARGUERITE: No! I can't! The wind from the desert is sweeping me away!

(*A loud singing wind sweeps her toward the terrace, away from him. She looks back once or twice as if for some gesture of leave-taking but he only stares at her fiercely, striking the stage at intervals with his cane, like a death-march.* GUTMAN *watches, smiling, from the terrace, bows to* MARGUERITE *as she passes into the hotel. The drum of* JACQUES' *cane is taken up by other percussive instruments, and almost unnoticeably at first, weird-looking celebrants or carnival murmurs creep into the plaza, silently as spiders descending a wall.*

A sheet of scarlet and yellow rice paper bearing some cryptic device is lowered from the center of the plaza. The percussive effects become gradually louder. JACQUES *is oblivious to the scene behind him, standing in front of the plaza, his eyes closed.*)

GUTMAN: Block Eleven on the Camino Real.

BLOCK ELEVEN

GUTMAN: The Fiesta has started. The first event is the coronation of the King of Cuckolds.

(*Blinding shafts of light are suddenly cast upon* CASANOVA *on the forestage. He shields his face, startled, as the crowd closes about him. The blinding shafts of light seem to strike him like savage blows and he falls to his knees as—*

The HUNCHBACK *scuttles out of the* GYPSY's *stall with a crown of gilded antlers on a velvet pillow. He places it on* JACQUES' *head. The celebrants form a circle about him chanting.*)

JACQUES: What is this?—a crown—

GUTMAN: A crown of horns!

CROWD: Cornudo! Cornudo! Cornudo! Cornudo! Cornudo!

GUTMAN: Hail, all hail, the King of Cuckolds on the Camino Real!

(JACQUES *springs up, first striking out at them with his cane. Then all at once he abandons self-defense, throws off his cape, casts away his cane, and fills the plaza with a roar of defiance and self-derision.*)

JACQUES: Si, si, sono cornudo! Cornudo! Cornudo! Casanova is the King of Cuckolds on the Camino Real! Show me crowned to the world! Announce the honor! Tell the world of the honor bestowed on Casanova, Chevalier de Seingalt! Knight of the Golden Spur by the Grace of His Holiness the Pope . . . Famous adventurer! Con man Extraordinary! Gambler! Pitch-man par excellence! Shill! Pimp! Spiv! *And—great—lover . . .*

(*The* CROWD *howls with applause and laughter but his voice rises above them with sobbing intensity.*)

Yes, I said GREAT LOVER! The greatest lover wears the longest horns on the Camino! GREAT! LOVER!

GUTMAN: Attention! Silence! The moon is rising! The restoration is about to occur!

(*A white radiance is appearing over the ancient wall of the town. The mountains become luminous. There is music. Everyone, with breathless attention, faces the light.*

KILROY *crosses to* JACQUES *and beckons him out behind the crowd. There he snatches off the antlers and returns him his fedora.* JACQUES *reciprocates by removing* KILROY's *fright wig and electric nose. They embrace as brothers. In a Chaplinesque dumb-play,* KILROY *points to the wildly flickering three brass balls of the* LOAN SHARK *and to his golden gloves: then with a terrible grimace he removes the gloves from about his neck, smiles at* JACQUES *and indicates that the two of them together will take flight over the wall.* JACQUES *shakes his head sadly, pointing to his heart and then to the Siete Mares.* KILROY *nods with regretful understanding of a human and manly folly. A* GUARD *has been silently approaching them in a soft shoe dance.* JACQUES *whistles "La Golondrina."* KILROY *assumes a very nonchalant pose. The* GUARD *picks up curiously the discarded fright wig and electric nose. Then glancing suspiciously at the pair, he advances.* KILROY *makes a run for it. He does a baseball slide into the* LOAN SHARK's *welcoming doorway. The door slams. The* COP *is about to crash it when a gong sounds and* GUTMAN *shouts.*)

GUTMAN: SILENCE! ATTENTION! THE GYPSY!

GYPSY (*appearing on the roof with a gong*): The moon has restored the virginity of my daughter Esmeralda!

(*The gong sounds.*)

STREET PEOPLE: Ahh!

GYPSY: The moon in its plenitude has made her a virgin!

(*The gong sounds.*)

STREET PEOPLE: Ahh!

GYPSY: Praise her, celebrate her, give her suitable homage!

(*The gong sounds.*)

STREET PEOPLE: Ahh!

GYPSY: Summon her to the roof!

(*She shouts.*)

ESMERALDA!

(DANCERS *shout the name in rhythm.*)

RISE WITH THE MOON, MY DAUGHTER! CHOOSE THE HERO!

(ESMERALDA *appears on the roof in dazzling light. She seems to be dressed in jewels. She raises her jeweled arms with a harsh flamenco cry.*)

ESMERALDA: OLE!
DANCERS: OLE!

(*The details of the Carnival are a problem for director and choreographer but it has already been indicated in the script that the Fiesta is a sort of serio-comic, grotesque-lyric "Rites of Fertility" with roots in various pagan cultures.*

It should not be over-elaborated or allowed to occupy much time. It should not be more than three minutes from the appearance of ESMERALDA *on the* GYPSY's *roof till the return of* KILROY *from the* LOAN SHARK's.

KILROY *emerges from the Pawn Shop in grotesque disguise, a turban, dark glasses, a burnoose and an umbrella or sunshade.*)

KILROY (*to* JACQUES): So long pal, I wish you could come with me.

(JACQUES *clasps his cross in* KILROY's *hands.*)

ESMERALDA: Yankee!
KILROY (*to the audience*): So long, everybody. Good luck to you all on the Camino! I hocked my golden gloves to finance this expedition. I'm going. Hasta luega. I'm going. I'm gone!

ESMERALDA: Yankee!

(*He has no sooner entered the plaza than the riotous women strip off everything but the dungarees and skivvy which he first appeared in.*)

KILROY (*to the women*): Let me go. Let go of me! Watch out for my equipment!

ESMERALDA: Yankee! Yankee!

(*He breaks away from them and plunges up the stairs of the ancient wall. He is half-way up them when* GUTMAN *shouts out.*)

GUTMAN: Follow-spot on that gringo, light the stairs!

(*The light catches* KILROY. *At the same instant* ESMERALDA *cries out to him.*)

ESMERALDA: *Yankee! Yankee!*
GYPSY: What's goin' on down there?

(*She rushes into the plaza.*)

KILROY: Oh, no, I'm on my way out!
ESMERALDA: Espere un momento!

(*The* GYPSY *calls the police, but is ignored in the crowd.*)

KILROY: Don't tempt me, baby! I hocked my golden gloves to finance this expedition!
ESMERALDA: Querido!
KILROY: Querido means sweetheart, a word which is hard to resist but I must resist it.
ESMERALDA: Champ!
KILROY: I used to be Champ but why remind me of it?
ESMERALDA: Be champ again! Contend in the contest! Compete in the competition!
GYPSY (*shouting*): *Naw, naw, not eligible!*
ESMERALDA: *Pl-eeeeeeze!*
GYPSY: Slap her, Nursie, she's flippin'.

(ESMERALDA *slaps* NURSIE *instead.*)

ESMERALDA: Hero! Champ!
KILROY: I'm not in condition!
ESMERALDA: You're still the Champ, the undefeated Champ of the golden gloves!
KILROY: Nobody's called me that in a long, long time!
ESMERALDA: Champ!
KILROY: My resistance is crumbling!
ESMERALDA: Champ!
KILROY: It's crumbled!
ESMERALDA: Hero!
KILROY: GERONIMO!

(*He takes a flying leap from the stairs into the center of the plaza. He turns toward* ESMERALDA *and cries.*)

DOLL!!

(KILROY *surrounded by cheering* STREET PEOPLE *goes into a triumphant eccentric dance which reviews his history as fighter, traveler and lover.*
At finish of the dance, the music is cut off, as KILROY *lunges, arm uplifted towards* ESMERALDA, *and cries.*)

KILROY: *Kilroy the Champ!*
ESMERALDA: *KILROY the Champ!*

(*She snatches a bunch of red roses from the stunned* Nursie *and tosses them to* KILROY.)

CROWD (*sharply*): OLE!

(*The* GYPSY, *at the same instant, hurls her gong down, creating a resounding noise.*
KILROY *turns and comes down towards the audience, saying to them.*)

KILROY: *Y'see?*

(*Cheering* STREET PEOPLE *surge towards him and lift him in the air. The lights fade as the curtain descends.*)

CROWD (*in a sustained yell*): OLE!

(*The curtain falls. There is a short intermission.*)

BLOCK TWELVE

(*The stage is in darkness except for a spot of light which picks out* ESMERALDA *on the* GYPSY's *roof.*)

ESMERALDA: Mama, what happened?—Mama, the lights went out!—Mama, where are you? It's so dark I'm scared!—MAMA!

(*The lights are turned on displaying a deserted plaza. The* GYPSY *is seated at a small table before her stall.*)

GYPSY: Come on downstairs, Doll. The mischief is done. You've chosen your hero!
GUTMAN (*from the balcony of the Siete Mares*): Block Twelve on the Camino Real.
NURSIE (*at the fountain*): Gypsy, the fountain is still dry!
GYPSY: What d'yuh expect? There's nobody left to uphold the old traditions! You raise a girl. She watches television. Plays be-bop. Reads *Screen Secrets.* Comes the Big Fiesta. The moonrise makes her a virgin—which is the neatest trick of the week! And what does she do? Chooses a Fugitive Patsy for the Chosen Hero! Well, show him in! Admit the joker and get the virgin ready!
NURSIE: You're going through with it?
GYPSY: Look, Nursie! I'm operating a legitimate joint! This joker'll get the same treatment he'd get if he breezed down the Camino in a blizzard of G-notes! Trot, girl! Lubricate your means of locomotion!

(NURSIE *goes into the* GYPSY's *stall. The* GYPSY *rubs her hands together and blows on the crystal ball, spits on it and gives it the old one-two with a "shammy" rag . . . She mutters "Crystal ball, tell me all . . . crystal ball tell me all" . . . as* KILROY *bounds into the plaza from her stall . . . a rose between his teeth.*)

GYPSY: Siente se, por favor.

KILROY: No comprendo the lingo.

GYPSY: Put it down!

NURSIE (offstage): Hey, Gypsy!

GYPSY: Address me as Madam!

NURSIE (entering): Madam! Winchell has scooped you!

GYPSY: In a pig's eye!

NURSIE: The Fugitivo has "fftt . . ."!

GYPSY: In Elizabeth, New Jersey . . . ten fifty seven P.M. . . . Eastern Standard Time—while you were putting them kiss-me-quicks in your hair-do! Furthermore, my second exclusive is that the solar system is drifting towards the constellation of Hercules: Skiddoo!

(NURSIE exits. Stamping is heard offstage.)

Quiet, back there! God damn it!

NURSIE (offstage): She's out of control!

GYPSY: Give her a double-bromide!

(To KILROY.)

Well, how does it feel to be the Chosen Hero?

KILROY: I better explain something to you.

GYPSY: Save your breath. You'll need it.

KILROY: I want to level with you. Can I level with you?

GYPSY (rapidly stamping some papers): How could you help but level with the Gypsy?

KILROY: I don't know what the hero is chosen for.

(ESMERALDA and NURSIE shriek offstage.)

GYPSY: Time will brief you . . . Aw, I hate paper work! . . . NURSEHH!

(NURSIE comes out and stands by the table.)

This filing system is screwed up six ways from Next Sunday . . . File this crap under crap!—

(To KILROY.)

The smoking lamp is lit. Have a stick on me!

(She offers him a cigarette.)

KILROY: No thanks.

GYPSY: Come on, indulge yourself. You got nothing to lose that won't be lost.

KILROY: If that's a professional opinion, I don't respect it.

GYPSY: Resume your seat and give me your full name.

KILROY: Kilroy.

GYPSY (writing all this down): Date of birth and place of that disaster?

KILROY: Both unknown.

GYPSY: Address?

KILROY: Traveler.

GYPSY: Parents?

KILROY: Anonymous.

GYPSY: Who brought you up?

KILROY: I was brought up and down by an eccentric old aunt in Dallas.

GYPSY: Raise both hands simultaneously and swear that you have not come here for the purpose of committing an immoral act.

ESMERALDA (from offstage): Hey, Chico!

GYPSY: QUIET! Childhood diseases?

KILROY: Whooping cough, measles and mumps.

GYPSY: Likes and dislikes?

KILROY: I like situations I can get out of. I don't like cops and—

GYPSY: Immaterial! Here! Signature on this! (She hands him a blank.)

KILROY: What is it?

GYPSY: You always sign something, don't you?

KILROY: Not till I know what it is.

GYPSY: It's just a little formality to give a tone to the establishment and make an impression on our out-of-town trade. Roll up your sleeve.

KILROY: What for?

GYPSY: A shot of some kind.

KILROY: What kind?

GYPSY: Any kind. Don't they always give you some kind of a shot?

KILROY: "They"?

GYPSY: Brass-hats, Americanos!

(She injects a hypo.)

KILROY: I am no guinea pig!

GYPSY: Don't kid yourself. We're all of us guinea pigs in the laboratory of God. Humanity is just a work in progress.

KILROY: I don't make it out.

GYPSY: Who does? The Camino Real is a funny paper read backwards!

(There is weird piping outside. KILROY shifts on his seat. The GYPSY grins.)

Tired? The altitude makes you sleepy?

KILROY: It makes me nervous.

GYPSY: I'll show you how to take a slug of tequila! It dilates the capillaries. First you sprinkle salt on the back of your hand. Then lick it off with your tongue. Now then you toss the shot down!

(*She demonstrates.*)

—And then you bite into the lemon. That way it goes down easy, but what a bang!—You're next.

KILROY: No, thanks, I'm on the wagon.

GYPSY: There's an old Chinese proverb that says, "When your goose is cooked you might as well have it cooked with plenty of gravy."

(*She laughs.*)

Get up, baby. Let's have a look at yuh!—You're not a bad-looking boy. Sometimes working for the Yankee dollar isn't a painful profession. Have you ever been attracted by older women?

KILROY: Frankly, no, ma'am.

GYPSY: Well, there's a first time for everything.

KILROY: That is a subject I cannot agree with you on.

GYPSY: You think I'm an old bag?

(KILROY *laughs awkwardly. The* GYPSY *slaps his face.*)

Will you take the cards or the crystal?

KILROY: It's immaterial.

GYPSY: All right, we'll begin with the cards.

(*She shuffles and deals.*)

Ask me a question.

KILROY: Has my luck run out?

GYPSY: Baby, your luck ran out the day you were born. Another question.

KILROY: Ought I to leave this town?

GYPSY: It don't look to me like you've got much choice in the matter . . . Take a card.

(KILROY *takes one.*)

GYPSY: Ace?

KILROY: Yes, ma'am.

GYPSY: What color?

KILROY: Black.

GYPSY: Oh, oh—That does it. How big is your heart?

KILROY: As big as the head of a baby.

GYPSY: It's going to break.

KILROY: That's what I was afraid of.

GYPSY: The Streetcleaners are waiting for you outside the door.

KILROY: Which door, the front one? I'll slip out the back!

GYPSY: Leave us face it frankly, your number is up! You must've known a long time that the name of Kilroy was on the Streetcleaners' list.

KILROY: Sure. But not on top of it!

GYPSY: It's always a bit of a shock. Wait a minute! Here's good news. The Queen of Hearts has turned up in proper position.

KILROY: What's that mean?

GYPSY: Love, Baby!

KILROY: Love?

GYPSY: The Booby Prize!—Esmeralda!

(*She rises and hits a gong. A divan is carried out. The* GYPSY'S DAUGHTER *is seated in a reclining position, like an odalisque, on this low divan. A spangled veil covers her face. From this veil to the girdle below her navel, that supports her diaphanous bifurcated skirt, she is nude except for a pair of glittering emerald snakes coiled over her breasts.* KILROY'S *head moves in a dizzy circle and a canary warbles inside it.*)

KILROY: WHAT'S—WHAT'S *HER* SPE-CIALTY?—Tea-leaves?

(*The* GYPSY *wags a finger.*)

GYPSY: You know what curiosity did to the tom cat!—Nursie, give me my glamour wig and my forty-five. I'm hitting the street! I gotta go down to Walgreen's for change.

KILROY: What change?

GYPSY: The change from that ten-spot you're about to give me.

NURSIE: Don't argue with her. She has a will of iron.

KILROY: I'm not arguing!

(*He reluctantly produces the money.*)

But let's be *fair* about this! I hocked my golden gloves for this saw-buck!

NURSIE: All of them Yankee bastids want something for nothing!

KILROY: I want a receipt for this bill.

NURSIE: No one is gypped at the Gypsy's!

KILROY: That's wonderful! How do I know it?

GYPSY: It's in the cards, it's in the crystal ball, it's in the tea-leaves! Absolutely no one is gypped at the Gypsy's!

(*She snatches the bill. The wind howls.*)

Such changeable weather! I'll slip on my summer furs! Nursie, break out my summer furs!

NURSIE (*leering grotesquely*): *Mink or sable?*

GYPSY: *Ha ha, that's a doll!* Here! Clock him!

(NURSIE *tosses her a greasy blanket, and the* GYPSY *tosses* NURSIE *an alarm clock. The* GYPSY *rushes through the beaded string curtains.*)

Adios! Ha ha!!

(She is hardly offstage when two shots ring out. KILROY *starts.)*

ESMERALDA *(plaintively)*: Mother has such an awful time on the street.

KILROY: You mean that she is insulted on the street?

ESMERALDA: By strangers.

KILROY *(to the audience)*: I shouldn't think acquaintances would do it.

(She curls up on the low divan. KILROY *licks his lips.)*

—You seem very different from—this afternoon . . .

ESMERALDA: This afternoon?

KILROY: Yes, in the plaza when I was being roughed up by them gorillas and you was being dragged in the house by your Mama!

*(*ESMERALDA *stares at him blankly.)*

You don't remember?

ESMERALDA: I never remember what happened before the moonrise makes me a virgin.

KILROY: —That—comes as a shock to you, huh?

ESMERALDA: Yes. It comes as a shock.

KILROY *(smiling)*: You have a little temporary amnesia they call it!

ESMERALDA: Yankee . . .

KILROY: Huh?

ESMERALDA: I'm glad I chose you. I'm glad that you were chosen. *(Her voice trails off.)* I'm glad. I'm very glad . . .

NURSIE: Doll!

ESMERALDA: —What is it, Nursie?

NURSIE: How are things progressing?

ESMERALDA: Slowly, Nursie—

*(*NURSIE *comes lumbering in.)*

NURSIE: I want some light reading matter.

ESMERALDA: He's sitting on *Screen Secrets.*

KILROY *(jumping up)*: Aw. Here. *(He hands her the fan magazine. She lumbers back out, coyly.)*—I—I feel——self-conscious . . .

(He suddenly jerks out a silver-framed photo.)

—D'you—like pictures?

ESMERALDA: Moving pictures?

KILROY: No, a—motionless—snapshot!

ESMERALDA: Of you?

KILROY: Of my—real—true woman . . . She was a platinum blonde the same as Jean Harlow. Do you remember Jean Harlow? No, you wouldn't remember Jean Harlow. It shows you are getting old when you remember Jean Harlow.

(He puts the snapshot away.)

. . . They say that Jean Harlow's ashes are kept in a little private cathedral in Forest Lawn . . . Wouldn't it be wonderful if you could sprinkle them ashes over the ground like seeds, and out of each one would spring another Jean Harlow? And when spring comes you could just walk out and pick them off the bush! . . . You don't talk much.

ESMERALDA: You want me to *talk?*

KILROY: Well, that's the way we do things in the States. A little vino, some records on the victrola, some quiet conversation—and then if both parties are in a mood for romance . . . Romance—

ESMERALDA: Music!

(She rises and pours some wine from a slender crystal decanter as music is heard.)

They say that the monetary system has got to be stabilized all over the world.

KILROY *(taking the glass)*: Repeat that, please. My radar was not wide open.

ESMERALDA: I said that *they* said that—uh, skip it! But we couldn't care less as long as we keep on getting the Yankee dollar . . . plus federal tax!

KILROY: That's for surely!

ESMERALDA: How do you feel about the class struggle? Do you take sides in that?

KILROY: Not that I—

ESMERALDA: Neither do we because of the dialectics.

KILROY: Who! Which?

ESMERALDA: Languages with accents, I suppose. But Mama don't care as long as they don't bring the Pope over here and put him in the White House.

KILROY: Who would do that?

ESMERALDA: Oh, the Bolsheviskies, those nasty old things with whiskers! *Whiskers scratch!* But little moustaches tickle . . .

(She giggles.)

KILROY: I always got a smooth shave . . .

ESMERALDA: And how do you feel about the Mumbo Jumbo? Do you think they've got the Old Man in the bag yet?

KILROY: The Old Man?

ESMERALDA: God. We don't think so. We think there has been so much of the Mumbo Jumbo it's put Him to sleep!

(KILROY *jumps up impatiently.*)

KILROY: This is not what I mean by a quiet conversation. I mean this is no where! *No where!*

ESMERALDA: What sort of talk do you want?

KILROY: Something more—intimate sort of! You know, like—

ESMERALDA: —Where did you get those eyes?

KILROY: *PERSONAL!* Yeah . . .

ESMERALDA: Well,—where did you get those eyes?

KILROY: Out of a dead cod-fish!

NURSIE (*shouting offstage*): DOLL!

(KILROY *springs up, pounding his left palm with his right fist.*)

ESMERALDA: What?

NURSIE: Fifteen minutes!

KILROY: I'm no hot-rod mechanic.

(*To the audience.*)

I bet she's out there holding a stop watch to see that I don't over-stay my time in this place!

ESMERALDA (*calling through the string curtains*): Nursie, go to bed, Nursie!

KILROY (*in a fierce whisper*): That's right, go to bed, Nursie!!

(*There is a loud crash offstage.*)

ESMERALDA: —Nursie has gone to bed . . .

(*She drops the string curtains and returns to the alcove.*)

KILROY (*with vast relief*): —Ahhhhhhhhhh . . .

ESMERALDA: What've you got your eyes on?

KILROY: Those green snakes on you—what do you wear them for?

ESMERALDA: Supposedly for protection, but really for fun.

(*He crosses to the divan.*)

What are you going to do?

KILROY: I'm about to establish a beach-head on that sofa.

(*He sits down.*)

How about—lifting your veil?

ESMERALDA: I can't lift it.

KILROY: Why not?

ESMERALDA: I promised Mother I wouldn't.

KILROY: I thought your mother was the broadminded type.

ESMERALDA: Oh, she is, but you know how mothers are. You can lift it for me, if you say pretty please.

KILROY: Aww—

ESMERALDA: Go on, say it! Say pretty please!

KILROY: No!!

ESMERALDA: Why not?

KILROY: It's silly.

ESMERALDA: Then you can't lift my veil!

KILROY: Oh, all right. Pretty please.

ESMERALDA: Say it again!

KILROY: Pretty please.

ESMERALDA: Now say it once more like you meant it.

(*He jumps up. She grabs his hand.*)

Don't go away.

KILROY: You're making a fool out of me.

ESMERALDA: I was just teasing a little. Because you're so cute. Sit down again, please— *pretty* please!

(*He falls on the couch.*)

KILROY: What is that wonderful perfume you've got on?

ESMERALDA: Guess!

KILROY: Chanel Number Five?

ESMERALDA: No.

KILROY: Tabu?

ESMERALDA: No.

KILROY: I give up.

ESMERALDA: It's *Noche en Acapulco!* I'm just dying to go to Acapulco. I wish that you would take me to Acapulco.

(*He sits up.*)

What's the matter?

KILROY: You gypsies' daughters are invariably reminded of something without which you cannot do—just when it looks like everything has been fixed.

ESMERALDA: That isn't nice at all. I'm not the gold-digger type. Some girls see themselves in silver foxes. I only see myself in Acapulco!

KILROY: At Todd's Place?

ESMERALDA: Oh, no, at the Mirador! Watching those pretty boys dive off the Quebrada!

KILROY: Look again, Baby. Maybe you'll see yourself in Paramount Pictures or having a Singapore Sling at a Statler bar!

ESMERALDA: You're being sarcastic?

KILROY: Nope. Just realistic. All of you gypsies' daughters have hearts of stone, and I'm not whistling "Dixie"! But just the same, the night before a man dies, he says, "Pretty please—will you let me lift your veil?"—while the Street-cleaners wait for him right outside the door!—Because to be warm for a little longer is life.

And love?—that's a four-letter word which is sometimes no better than one you see printed on fences by kids playing hooky from school!—Oh, well—what's the use of complaining? You gypsies' daughters have ears that only catch sounds like the snap of a gold cigarette case! Or, pretty please, Baby,—we're going to Acapulco!

ESMERALDA: *Are* we?

KILROY: See what I mean?

(*To the audience.*)

Didn't I tell you?!

(*To* ESMERALDA.)

Yes! In the morning!

ESMERALDA: Ohhhh! I'm dizzy with joy! My little heart is going pitty-pat!

KILROY: My big heart is going boom-boom! Can I lift your veil now?

ESMERALDA: If you will be gentle.

KILROY: I would not hurt a fly unless it had on leather mittens.

(*He touches a corner of her spangled veil.*)

ESMERALDA: Ohhh . . .

KILROY: What?

ESMERALDA: Ohhhhhh!!

KILROY: Why! What's the matter?

ESMERALDA: You are not being gentle!

KILROY: I *am* being gentle.

ESMERALDA: You are *not* being gentle.

KILROY: What was I being, then?

ESMERALDA: Rough!

KILROY: I am *not* being rough.

ESMERALDA: Yes, you *are* being rough. You have to be gentle with me because you're the first.

KILROY: Are you kidding?

ESMERALDA: No.

KILROY: How about all of those other fiestas you've been to?

ESMERALDA: Each one's the first one. That is the wonderful thing about gypsies' daughters!

KILROY: You can say that again!

ESMERALDA: I don't like when you're like that.

KILROY: Like what?

ESMERALDA: Cynical and sarcastic.

KILROY: I am sincere.

ESMERALDA: Lots of boys aren't sincere.

KILROY: Maybe they aren't but I am.

ESMERALDA: Everyone says he's sincere, but everyone isn't sincere. If everyone was sincere who says he's sincere there wouldn't be half so many insincere ones in the world and there

would be lots, lots, lots more really sincere ones!

KILROY: I think you have got something there. But how about gypsies' daughters?

ESMERALDA: Huh?

KILROY: Are they one hundred percent in the really sincere category?

ESMERALDA: Well, yes, and no, mostly no! But some of them are for a while if their sweethearts are gentle.

KILROY: Would you believe I am sincere and gentle?

ESMERALDA: I would believe that you believe that you are . . . For a while . . .

KILROY: Everything's for a while. For a while is the stuff that dreams are made of, Baby! Now? —Now?

ESMERALDA: Yes, now, but be gentle!—*gentle* . . .

(*He delicately lifts a corner of her veil. She utters a soft cry. He lifts it further. She cries out again. A bit further . . . He turns the spangled veil all the way up from her face.*)

KILROY: I am sincere.

ESMERALDA: I am sincere.

KILROY: I am sincere.

ESMERALDA: I am sincere.

KILROY: I am sincere.

ESMERALDA: I am sincere.

KILROY: I am sincere.

ESMERALDA: I am sincere.

(KILROY *leans back, removing his hand from her veil. She opens her eyes.*)

Is that all?

KILROY: I am tired.

ESMERALDA: —Already?

(*He rises and goes down the steps from the alcove.*)

KILROY: I am tired, and full of regret . . .

ESMERALDA: Oh!

KILROY: It wasn't much to give my golden gloves for.

ESMERALDA: You pity yourself?

KILROY: That's right, I pity myself and everybody that goes to the Gypsy's daughter. I pity the world and I pity the God who made it. (*He sits down.*)

ESMERALDA: It's always like that as soon as the veil is lifted. They're all so ashamed of having degraded themselves, and their hearts have more regret than a heart can hold!

KILROY: Even a heart that's as big as the head of a baby!

ESMERALDA: You don't even notice how pretty my face is, do you?

KILROY: You look like all gypsies' daughters, no better, no worse. But as long as you get to go to Acapulco, your cup runneth over with ordinary contentment.

ESMERALDA: —I've never been so insulted in all my life!

KILROY: Oh, yes, you have, Baby. And you'll be insulted worse if you stay in this racket. You'll be insulted so much that it will get to be like water off *a duck's back!*

(*The door slams. Curtains are drawn apart on the* GYPSY. ESMERALDA *lowers her veil hastily.* KILROY *pretends not to notice the* GYPSY's *entrance. She picks up a little bell and rings it over his head.*)

Okay, Mamacita! I am aware of your presence!

GYPSY: Ha-ha! I was followed three blocks by some awful man!

KILROY: Then you caught him.

GYPSY: Naw, he ducked into a subway! I waited fifteen minutes outside the men's room and he never came out!

KILROY: Then you went in?

GYPSY: No! I got myself a sailor!—The streets are brilliant!... Have you all been good children?

(ESMERALDA *makes a whimpering sound.*)

The pussy will play while the old mother cat is away?

KILROY: Your sense of humor is wonderful, but how about my change, Mamacita?

GYPSY: What change are you talking about?

KILROY: Are you boxed out of your mind? The change from that ten-spot you trotted over to Walgreen's?

GYPSY: Ohhhhh—

KILROY: *Oh, what?*

GYPSY (*counting on her fingers*): Five for the works, one dollar luxury tax, two for the house percentage and two more pour la service!—makes ten! Didn't I tell you?

KILROY: —What kind of a deal is this?

GYPSY (*whipping out a revolver*): A rugged one, Baby!

ESMERALDA: Mama, don't be unkind!

GYPSY: Honey, the gentleman's friends are waiting outside the door and it wouldn't be nice to detain him! Come on—Get going—Vamoose!

KILROY: Okay, Mamacita! Me voy!

(*He crosses to the beaded string curtains: turns to look back at the* GYPSY *and her* DAUGHTER. *The piping of the* STREETCLEANERS *is heard outside.*)

Sincere?—Sure! That's the wonderful thing about gypsies' daughters!

(*He goes out.* ESMERALDA *raises a wondering fingertip to one eye. Then she cries out.*)

ESMERALDA: Look, Mama! Look, Mama! A tear!

GYPSY: You have been watching television too much . . .

(*She gathers the cards and turns off the crystal ball as—*

Light fades out on the phony paradise of the GYPSY's.)

GUTMAN: Block Thirteen on the Camino Real.

(*He exits.*)

BLOCK THIRTEEN

(*In the blackout the* STREETCLEANERS *place a barrel in the center and then hide in the Pit.*

KILROY, *who enters from the right, is followed by a spot light. He sees the barrel and the menacing* STREETCLEANERS *and then runs to the closed door of the Siete Mares and rings the bell. No one answers. He backs up so he can see the balcony and calls.*)

KILROY: Mr. Gutman! Just gimme a cot in the lobby. I'll do odd jobs in the morning. I'll be the Patsy again. I'll light my nose sixty times a minute. I'll take prat-falls and assume the position for anybody that drops a dime on the street . . . Have a heart! Have just a LITTLE heart. Please!

(*There is no response from* GUTMAN's *balcony.* JACQUES *enters. He pounds his cane once on the pavement.*)

JACQUES: Gutman! Open the door!—*GUTMAN! GUTMAN!*

(EVA, *a beautiful woman, apparently nude, appears on the balcony.*)

GUTMAN (*from inside*): Eva darling, you're exposing yourself!

(*He appears on the balcony with a portmanteau.*)

JACQUES: What are you doing with my portmanteau?

GUTMAN: Haven't you come for your luggage?

JACQUES: Certainly not! I haven't checked out of here!

GUTMAN: Very few do . . . but residences are frequently terminated.

JACQUES: Open the door!

GUTMAN: Open the letter with the remittance check in it!

JACQUES: In the morning!

GUTMAN: Tonight!

JACQUES: Upstairs in my room!

GUTMAN: Downstairs at the entrance!

JACQUES: I won't be intimidated!

GUTMAN (*raising the portmanteau over his head*): What?!

JACQUES: Wait!—

(*He takes the letter out of his pocket.*)

Give me some light.

(KILROY *strikes a match and holds it over* JACQUES' *shoulder.*)

Thank you. What does it say?

GUTMAN: —Remittances?

KILROY (*reading the letter over* JACQUES' *shoulder*): —discontinued . . .

(GUTMAN *raises the portmanteau again.*)

JACQUES: Careful, I have—

(*The portmanteau lands with a crash. The* BUM *comes to the window at the crash.* A. RATT *comes out to his doorway at the same time.*)

—fragile—mementoes . . .

(*He crosses slowly down to the portmanteau and kneels as* GUTMAN *laughs and slams the balcony door.* JACQUES *turns to* KILROY. *He smiles at the young adventurer.*)

—"And so at last it has come, the distinguished thing!"

(A. RATT *speaks as* JACQUES *touches the portmanteau.*)

A. RATT: Hey, Dad—Vacancy here! A bed at the "Ritz Men Only." A little white ship to sail the dangerous night in.

JACQUES: Single or double?

A. RATT: There's only singles in this pad.

JACQUES (*to* KILROY): Match you for it.

KILROY: What the hell, we're buddies, we can sleep spoons! If we can't sleep, we'll push the wash stand against the door and sing old popular songs till the crack of dawn! . . . "Heart of my heart, I love that melody!". . . You bet your life I do.

(JACQUES *takes out a pocket handkerchief and starts to grasp the portmanteau handle.*)

—It looks to me like you could use a Redcap and my rates are non-union!

(*He picks up the portmanteau and starts to cross towards the "Ritz Men Only." He stops at right center.*)

Sorry, buddy. Can't make it! The altitude on this block has affected my ticker! And in the distance which is nearer than further, I hear—the Streetcleaners'—piping!

(*Piping is heard.*)

JACQUES: COME ALONG!

(*He lifts the portmanteau and starts on.*)

KILROY: NO. Tonight! I prefer! To sleep! Out! Under! The stars!

JACQUES (*gently*): I understand, Brother!

KILROY (*to* JACQUES *as he continues toward the "Ritz Men Only"*): Bon Voyage! I hope that you sail the dangerous night to the sweet golden port of morning!

JACQUES (*exiting*): Thanks, Brother!

KILROY: Excuse the *corn!* I'm sincere!

BUM: Show me the way to go home! . . .

GUTMAN (*appearing on the balcony with white parakeet*): Block Fourteen on the Camino Real.

BLOCK FOURTEEN

(*At opening, the* BUM *is still at the window. The* STREETCLEANERS' *piping continues a little louder.* KILROY *climbs, breathing heavily, to the top of the stairs and stands looking out at Terra Incognita as* MARGUERITE *enters the plaza through alleyway at right. She is accompanied by a silent* YOUNG MAN *who wears a domino.*)

MARGUERITE: Don't come any further with me. I'll have to wake the night porter. Thank you for giving me safe conduct through the Medina.

(*She has offered her hand. He grips it with a tightness that makes her wince.*)

Ohhhh . . . I'm not sure which is more provocative in you, your ominous silence or your glittering smile or—

(*He's looking at her purse.*)

What do you want? . . . Oh!

(*She starts to open the purse. He snatches it. She gasps as he suddenly strips her cloak off her. Then he snatches off her pearl necklace. With each successive despoilment, she gasps and retreats but makes no resistance. Her eyes are closed. He continues to smile. Finally, he rips her dress and runs his hand over her body as if to see if she had anything else of value concealed on her.*)

—What else do I have that you want?

THE YOUNG MAN (*contemptuously*): Nothing.

(*The* YOUNG MAN *exits through the cantina, examining his loot. The* BUM *leans out his window, draws a deep breath and says.*)

BUM: Lonely.

MARGUERITE (*to herself*): Lonely . . .

KILROY (*on the steps*): Lonely . . .

(*The* STREETCLEANERS' *piping is heard.* MARGUERITE *runs to the Siete Mares and rings the bell. Nobody answers. She crosses to the terrace.* KILROY, *meanwhile, has descended the stairs.*)

MARGUERITE: Jacques!

(*Piping is heard.*)

KILROY: Lady?

MARGUERITE: What?

KILROY: —*I'm*—*safe* . . .

MARGUERITE: I wasn't expecting that music tonight, were you?

(*Piping.*)

KILROY: It's them Streetcleaners.

MARGUERITE: I know.

(*Piping.*)

KILROY: You better go on in, lady.

MARGUERITE: No.

KILROY: GO ON IN!

MARGUERITE: NO! I want to stay out here and I do what I want to do!

(KILROY *looks at her for the first time.*)

Sit down with me please.

KILROY: They're coming for me. The Gypsy told me I'm on top of their list. Thanks for. Taking my. Hand.

(*Piping is heard.*)

MARGUERITE: Thanks for taking mine.

(*Piping.*)

KILROY: Do me one more favor. Take out of my pocket a picture. My fingers are. Stiff.

MARGUERITE: This one?

KILROY: My one. True. Woman.

MARGUERITE: A silver-framed photo! Was she really so fair?

KILROY: She was so fair and much fairer than they could tint that picture!

MARGUERITE: Then you have been on the street when the street was royal.

KILROY: Yeah . . . when the street was royal!

(*Piping is heard.* KILROY *rises.*)

MARGUERITE: Don't get up, don't leave me!

KILROY: I want to be on my feet when the Streetcleaners come for me!

MARGUERITE: Sit back down again and tell me about your girl.

(*He sits.*)

KILROY: Y'know what it is you miss most? When you're separated. From someone. You lived. With. And loved? It's waking up in the night! With that—warmness beside you!

MARGUERITE: Yes, that *warmness* beside you!

KILROY: Once you get used to that. *Warmness!* It's a hell of a lonely feeling to wake up without it! Specially in some dollar-a-night hotel room on Skid! A hot-water bottle won't do. And a stranger. Won't do. It has to be some one you're used to. And that you. *KNOW LOVES* you!

(*Piping is heard.*)

Can you see them?

MARGUERITE: I see no one but you.

KILROY: I looked at my wife one night when she was sleeping and that was the night that the medics wouldn't okay me for no more fights . . . Well . . . My wife was sleeping with a smile like a child's. I kissed her. She didn't wake up. I took a pencil and paper. I wrote her. Good-bye!

MARGUERITE: That was the night she would have loved you the most!

KILROY: Yeah, *that* night, but what about *after* that night? Oh, Lady . . . Why should a beautiful girl tie up with a broken-down champ? —The earth still turning and her obliged to turn with it, not out—of dark into light but out of light into dark? Naw, naw, naw, naw!— Washed up!—Finished!

(*Piping.*)

. . . that ain't a word that a man can't look at . . . There ain't no words in the language a man can't look at . . . and know just what they mean. and be. And act. And *go!*

(*He turns to the waiting* STREETCLEANERS.)

Come on! ... Come on! ... COME ON, YOU SONS OF BITCHES! KILROY IS HERE! HE'S READY!

(*A gong sounds.*
KILROY *swings at the* STREETCLEANERS. *They circle about him out of reach, turning him by each of their movements. The swings grow wilder like a boxer. He falls to his knees still swinging and finally collapses flat on his face.*
The STREETCLEANERS *pounce but* LA MADRECITA *throws herself protectingly over the body and covers it with her shawl.*
Blackout.)

MARGUERITE: Jacques!

GUTMAN (*on balcony*): Block Fifteen on the Camino Real.

BLOCK FIFTEEN

(LA MADRECITA *is seated: across her knees is the body of* KILROY. *Up center, a low table on wheels bears a sheeted figure. Beside the table stands a Medical Instructor addressing* STUDENTS *and* NURSES, *all in white surgical outfits.*)

INSTRUCTOR: This is the body of an unidentified vagrant.

LA MADRECITA: This was thy son, America and now mine.

INSTRUCTOR: He was found in an alley along the Camino Real.

LA MADRECITA: Think of him, now, as he was before his luck failed him. Remember his time of greatness, when he was not faded, not frightened.

INSTRUCTOR: More light, please!

LA MADRECITA: More light!

INSTRUCTOR: Can everyone see clearly!

LA MADRECITA: Everyone must see clearly!

INSTRUCTOR: There is no external evidence of disease.

LA MADRECITA: He had clear eyes and the body of a champion boxer.

INSTRUCTOR: There are no marks of violence on the body.

LA MADRECITA: He had the soft voice of the South and a pair of golden gloves.

INSTRUCTOR: His death was apparently due to natural causes.

(*The* STUDENTS *make notes. There are keening voices.*)

LA MADRECITA: Yes, blow wind where night thins! He had many admirers!

INSTRUCTOR: There are no legal claimants.

LA MADRECITA: He stood as a planet among the moons of their longing, haughty with youth, a champion of the prize-ring!

INSTRUCTOR: No friends or relatives having identified him—

LA MADRECITA: You should have seen the lovely monogrammed robe in which he strode the aisles of the Colosseums!

INSTRUCTOR: After the elapse of a certain number of days, his body becomes the property of the State—

LA MADRECITA: Yes, blow wind where night thins—for laurel is not ever-lasting ...

INSTRUCTOR: And now is transferred to our hands for the nominal sum of five dollars.

LA MADRECITA: This way thy son,—and now mine ...

INSTRUCTOR: We will now proceed with the dissection. Knife, please!

LA MADRECITA: Blow wind!

(*Keening is heard offstage.*)

Yes, blow wind where night thins! You are his passing bell and his lamentation.

(*More keening is heard.*)

Keen for him, all maimed creatures, deformed and mutilated—his homeless ghost is your own!

INSTRUCTOR: First we will open up the chest cavity and examine the heart for evidence of coronary occlusion.

LA MADRECITA: His heart was pure gold and as big as the head of a baby.

INSTRUCTOR: We will make an incision along the vertical line.

LA MADRECITA: Rise, ghost! Go! Go bird! "Humankind cannot bear very much reality."

(*At the touch of her flowers,* KILROY *stirs and pushes himself up slowly from her lap. On his feet again, he rubs his eyes and looks around him.*)

VOICES (*crying offstage*): Olé! Olé! Olé!

KILROY: Hey! Hey, somebody! Where am I? (*He notices the dissection room and approaches.*)

INSTRUCTOR (*removing a glittering sphere from a dummy corpse*): Look at this heart. It's as big as the head of a baby.

KILROY: My heart!

INSTRUCTOR: Wash it off so we can look for the pathological lesions.

KILROY: Yes, siree, that's my heart!

GUTMAN: Block Sixteen!

(KILROY *pauses just outside the dissection area as a* STUDENT *takes the heart and dips it into a basin on the stand beside the table. The* STUDENT *suddenly cries out and holds aloft a glittering gold sphere.*)

INSTRUCTOR: Look! This heart's solid gold!

BLOCK SIXTEEN

KILROY (*rushing forward*): That's mine, you bastards!

(*He snatches the golden sphere from the* MEDICAL INSTRUCTOR. *The autopsy proceeds as if nothing had happened as the spot of light on the table fades out, but for* KILROY *a ghostly chase commences, a dreamlike re-enactment of the chase that occurred at the end of Block Six.* GUTMAN *shouts from his balcony.*)

GUTMAN: Stop, thief, stop, corpse! That gold heart is the property of the State! Catch him, catch the golden-heart robber!

(KILROY *dashes offstage into an aisle of the theatre. There is the wail of a siren: the air is filled with calls and whistles, roar of motors, screeching brakes, pistol-shots, thundering footsteps. The dimness of the auditorium is transected by searching rays of light—but there are no visible pursuers.*)

KILROY (*as he runs panting up the aisle*): This is my heart! It don't belong to no State, not even the U.S.A. Which way is out? Where's the Greyhound depot? Nobody's going to put my heart in a bottle in a museum and charge admission to support the rotten police! Where are they? Which way are they going? Or coming? Hey, somebody, help me get out of here! Which way do I—which way—which way do I—*go! go! go! go! go!*

(*He has now arrived in the balcony.*)

Gee, I'm lost! I don't know where I am! I'm all turned around, I'm *confused,* I don't understand —what's—happened, it's like a—*dream,* it's— just like a—dream . . . *Mary! Oh, Mary! Mary!*

(*He has entered the box from which he leapt in Act One. A clear shaft of light falls on him. He looks up into it, crying.*)

Mary, help a Christian!! Help a Christian, Mary!—It's like a dream . . .

(ESMERALDA *appears in a childish nightgown beside her gauze-tented bed on the* GYPSY's *roof. Her* MOTHER *appears with a cup of some sedative drink, cooing . . .*)

GYPSY: Beddy-bye, beddy-bye, darling. It's sleepy-time down South and up North, too, and also East and West!

KILROY (*softly*): Yes, it's—like a—*dream* . . .

(*He leans panting over the ledge of the box, holding his heart like a football, watching* ESMERALDA.)

GYPSY: Drink your Ovaltine, Ducks, and the sandman will come on tip-toe with a bag full of dreams . . .

ESMERALDA: I want to dream of the Chosen Hero, Mummy.

GYPSY: Which one, the one that's coming or the one that is gone?

ESMERALDA: The *only* one, *Kilroy!* He was *sincere!*

KILROY: That's *right! I was,* for a while!

GYPSY: How do you know that Kilroy was sincere?

ESMERALDA: He said so.

KILROY: That's the truth, I *was!*

GYPSY: When did he say that?

ESMERALDA: When he lifted my veil.

GYPSY: Baby, they're always sincere when they lift your veil; it's one of those natural reflexes that don't mean a thing.

KILROY (*aside*): What a cynical old bitch that Gypsy mama is!

GYPSY: And there's going to be lots of other fiestas for you, baby doll, and lots of other chosen heroes to lift your little veil when Mamacita and Nursie are out of the room.

ESMERALDA: No, Mummy, never, I mean it!

KILROY: I *believe* she means it!

GYPSY: Finish your Ovaltine and say your Now-I-Lay-Me.

(ESMERALDA *sips the drink and hands her the cup.*)

KILROY (*with a catch in his voice*): I had one true woman, which I can't go back to, but now I've found another.

(*He leaps onto the stage from the box.*)

ESMERALDA (*dropping to her knees*): Now I lay me down to sleep, I pray the Lord my soul to keep. If I should die before I wake, I pray the Lord my soul to take.

GYPSY: God bless Mummy!

ESMERALDA: And the crystal ball and the tea-leaves.

KILROY: *Pssst!*

ESMERALDA: What's that?

GYPSY: A tom-cat in the plaza.

ESMERALDA: God bless all cats without pads in the plaza tonight.

KILROY: Amen!

(*He falls to his knees in the empty plaza.*)

ESMERALDA: God bless all con men and hustlers and pitch-men who hawk their hearts on the street, all two-time losers who're likely to lose once more, the courtesan who made the mistake of love, the greatest of lovers crowned with the longest horns, the poet who wandered far from his heart's green country and possibly will and possibly won't be able to find his way back, look down with a smile tonight on the last cavaliers, the ones with the rusty armor and soiled white plumes, and visit with understanding and something that's almost tender those fading legends that come and go in this plaza like songs not clearly remembered, oh, sometime and somewhere, let there be something to mean the word *honor* again!

QUIXOTE (*hoarsely and loudly, stirring slightly among his verminous rags*): Amen!

KILROY: Amen . . .

GIPSY (*disturbed*): —That will do, now.

ESMERALDA: *And, oh, God, let me dream tonight of the Chosen Hero!*

GYPSY: Now, sleep. Fly away on the magic carpet of dreams!

(ESMERALDA *crawls into the gauze-tented cot. The* GYPSY *descends from the roof.*)

KILROY: *Esmeralda! My little Gypsy sweetheart!*

ESMERALDA (*sleepily*): Go away, cat.

(*The light behind the gauze is gradually dimming.*)

KILROY: This is no cat. This is the chosen hero of the big fiesta, Kilroy, the champion of the golden gloves with his gold heart cut from his chest and in his hands to give you!

ESMERALDA: Go away. Let me dream of the Chosen Hero.

KILROY: What a hassle! Mistook for a cat! What can I do to convince this doll I'm real?

(*Three brass balls wink brilliantly.*)

—Another transaction seems to be indicated!

(*He rushes to the* LOAN SHARK's. *The entrance immediately lights up.*)

My heart is gold! What will you give me for it?

(*Jewels, furs, sequined gowns, etc., are tossed to his feet. He throws his heart like a basketball to the* LOAN SHARK, *snatches up the loot and rushes back to the* GYPSY's.)

Doll! Behold this loot! I gave my golden heart for it!

ESMERALDA: Go away, cat . . .

(*She falls asleep.* KILROY *bangs his forehead with his fist, then rushes to the* GYPSY's *door, pounds it with both fists. The door is thrown open and the sordid contents of a large jar are thrown at him. He falls back gasping, spluttering, retching. He retreats and finally assumes an exaggerated attitude of despair.*)

KILROY: Had for a button! Stewed, screwed and tattooed on the Camino Real! Baptized finally, with the contents of a slopjar!—Did anybody say the deal was rugged?!

(QUIXOTE *stirs against the wall of Skid Row. He hawks and spits and staggers to his feet.*)

GUTMAN: Why, the old knight's awake, his dream is over!

QUIXOTE (*to* KILROY): Hello! Is that a fountain?

KILROY: —Yeah, but—

QUIXOTE: I've got a mouthful of old chicken feathers . . .

(*He approaches the fountain. It begins to flow.* KILROY *falls back in amazement as the* OLD KNIGHT *rinses his mouth and drinks and removes his jacket to bathe, handing the tattered garment to* KILROY.)

QUIXOTE (*as he bathes*): Qué pasa, mi amigo?

KILROY: The deal is rugged. D'you know what I mean?

QUIXOTE: Who knows better than I what a rugged deal is!

(*He produces a tooth brush and brushes his teeth.*)

—Will you take some advice?

KILROY: Brother, at this point on the Camino I will take anything which is offered!

QUIXOTE: *Don't! Pity! Your! Self!*

(*He takes out a pocket mirror and grooms his beard and moustache.*)

The wounds of the vanity, the many offenses our egos have to endure, being housed in bodies that age and hearts that grow tired, are better accepted with a tolerant smile—like *this!*—You *see?*

(*He cracks his face in two with an enormous grin.*)

GUTMAN: Follow-spot on the face of the ancient knight!

QUIXOTE: Otherwise what you become is a bag full of curdled cream—*leche mala*, we call it!—attractive to nobody, least of all to yourself!

(*He passes the comb and pocket mirror to* KILROY.)

Have you got any plans?

KILROY (*a bit uncertainly, wistfully*): Well, I was thinking of—going *on* from—*here!*

QUIXOTE: Good! Come with me.

KILROY (*to the audience*): Crazy old bastard. (*then to the* KNIGHT.) Donde?

QUIXOTE (*starting for the stairs*): Quien sabe!

(*The fountain is now flowing loudly and sweetly. The* STREET PEOPLE *are moving toward it with murmurs of wonder.* MARGUERITE *comes out upon the terrace.*)

KILROY: Hey, there's—!

QUIXOTE: Shhh! Listen!

(*They pause on the stairs.*)

MARGUERITE: Abdullah!

(GUTMAN *has descended to the terrace.*)

GUTMAN: Mademoiselle, allow me to deliver the message for you. It would be in bad form if I didn't take some final part in the pageant.

(*He crosses the plaza to the opposite façade and shouts "Casanova!" under the window of the "Ritz Men Only." Meanwhile* KILROY *scratches out the verb "is" and prints the correction "was" in the inscription on the ancient wall.*)

Casanova! Great Lover and King of Cuckolds on the Camino Real! The last of your ladies has guaranteed your tabs and is expecting you for breakfast on the terrace!

(CASANOVA *looks first out of the practical window of the flophouse, then emerges from its scabrous doorway, haggard, unshaven, crumpled in dress but bearing himself as erectly as ever. He blinks and glares fiercely into the brilliant morning light.*

MARGUERITE *cannot return his look, she averts her face with a look for which anguish would not be too strong a term, but at the same time she extends a pleading hand toward him. After some hesitation, he begins to move toward her, striking the pavement in measured cadence with his cane, glancing once, as he crosses, out at the audience with a wry smile that makes admissions that would be embarrassing to a vainer man than* CASANOVA *now is. When he reaches* MARGUERITE *she gropes for his hand, seizes it with a low cry and presses it spasmodically to her lips while he draws her into his arms and looks above her sobbing, dyed-golden head with the serene, clouded gaze of someone mortally ill as the mercy of a narcotic laps over his pain.*

QUIXOTE *raises his lance in a formal gesture and cries out hoarsely, powerfully from the stairs.*)

QUIXOTE: *The violets in the mountains have broken the rocks!*

(QUIXOTE *goes through the arch with* KILROY.)

GUTMAN (*to the audience*): The Curtain Line has been spoken!

(*to the wings.*)

Bring it down!

(*He bows with a fat man's grace as—*
The curtain falls.)

Arthur Miller: *A View from the Bridge* (1955)

Like the protagonists in *A View from the Bridge,* Arthur Miller once lived in Brooklyn. He was born in Harlem but his family moved to Brooklyn, where he was a star football player in high school. He has reminisced often about what a poor student he was and how he had little or no interest in reading significant books. His parents were relatively "comfortable" until the early years of the Depression when his father's business (manufacturing women's clothing) suffered the same setbacks most businesses did. For a time he worked for his father, then got a job in an auto-parts warehouse, where, interestingly enough, he began to read. Partly because of boredom and partly because he no longer had the distraction of high school athletics, Miller found himself reading serious novels, the most important of which seems to have been Dostoevsky's *The Brothers Karamazov.* This novel inspired Miller to try writing.

First, however, he felt he should go to college. He was attracted to the University of Michigan because of its great football team, but he had also read a book written by a Michigan drama professor on the art of playwriting and determined that he had to study with him. When he was rejected on the basis of his "miserable academic record," he wrote a powerful letter to the university's president promising to prove himself in the first year or leave. He was admitted on a probationary basis and succeeded almost immediately. Miller won numerous prizes for his earliest efforts at writing plays and one prize—the Avery Hopwood Award—gave him over $1200, a colossal amount of money in 1935. He met his first wife at Michigan and graduated to join the Federal Theater Project in 1938. By the early 1940s he was writing for the radio and working part-time in the Brooklyn Navy Yard.

His first produced play was by no means a success. *The Man Who Had All the Luck* (1944) lasted only four performances and has been omitted from his *Collected Plays,* yet the experience made him aware that he was indeed a serious playwright and that he could actually reach Broadway. Instead of sulking, he went on to write his next play, *All My Sons* (1947), about a man who manufactures defective parts for the United States Army Air Force and who manages to put the blame for their delivery on his business partner. When his son finds out the truth, the manufacturer realizes he has lost the boy's love and that those flyers whose planes were defective were also, in a sense, "all my sons." The play was a complete success, ran for 300 performances, and won the New York Critics' Circle Award. His next play, *Death of a Salesman* (1949), written in only six weeks, was destined to have him proclaimed the leading playwright of his time, and it ran for an incredible 742 performances. Its theme concerned Willy Loman's willingness to "buy" an outworn ideal, viewing his success as a person in his success as a businessman. It has been read as an attack on the "commercialization of society" and the confusion of human and monetary values. The play also laid claim to being the only tragedy written by a contemporary dramatist, and the controversy it spawned in these terms was vigorous. The question of whether a man of low estate (Loman) could qualify for being a tragic hero was argued throughout the 1950s. This play established Miller as a major dramatist.

The Crucible (1953) was a kind of morality play, a story of the Salem witch trials of 1692, but clearly indicting the McCarthy Committee hearings of the 1950s. Its first performances were very uncertain in their reception, partly because of an inappropriate stage setting, but after Miller restaged it himself it played well to thoughtful audiences. It has been successfully revived both here and in Europe. *A View from the Bridge* (1955) began as a one-act play, but early audiences were so caught up in its tense dramatic action that Miller had to lengthen it, break in into two acts, and offer it alone (it was originally played with another one-acter).

The story of Eddie Carbone and his family was built on a perception Miller had about Greek drama, which often linked families and fate. His preoccupation with families in all his plays found a new outlet in this one, which linked people by blood and ambition. Alfieri, the spokesman-lawyer, plays the same role as the chorus in a Greek tragedy: he comments on the action, advises the hero, and acts as intermediary with the audience. Even the motif of incest, such a strong influence in Greek tragedy, is present in Eddie's overprotection of Catherine, and the scenes near the end of the play when he becomes overtly sexual toward her are gripping. The power of his unexpressed psychological needs—his actual desire for Catherine—lead him to betray his own family. In this environment, family has some of the same meaning it had for the Greeks—it is part of one's fate. The "submarines" he hides are his wife's relatives; Catherine is his wife's niece. The Mafia, that more ominous family, has brought over the "submarines," and Eddie can hardly expect to get away with turning in the illegal aliens who live under his own roof; even his wife cannot believe what he did. The forces that drove him to do what he did are dark, terrifying, and overwhelming.

Miller felt the play was not properly appreciated or understood. He saw it as being deeply mythic and symbolic, speaking with a voice that was akin to that of the Greek plays using a universal language. But many critics and viewers perceived it as a slice of life, a realistic drama of the Brooklyn tenements. For nine years after, Miller worked on plays that would speak more clearly to his audience. In that time, he found himself under terrible pressure from the McCarthy House Committee on Un-American Activities to testify against people he had known. When he refused, he was cited for contempt and fought the charges in court. In 1956 he married the dazzling actress Marilyn Monroe. In 1958 he was cleared of charges. He wrote only one important dramatic piece during his marriage to Marilyn Monroe—the film script, *The Misfits* (1960), in which she starred.

After his divorce he struggled to produce a play, and, after many attempts, wrote *After the Fall* (1964), about a divorced writer trying to write and attempting to decide on a third marriage only after getting his priorities straight. Most critics and audiences saw the play as thoroughly and achingly autobiographical, despite Miller's protest, and it did not give him the satisfaction he had hoped for. A second play produced in 1964, *Incident at Vichy*, was set in France in 1942, with anti-semitism as part of its theme. It was well received. Later plays, *The Price* (1967) and *The Creation of the World and Other Business* (1972), have also been well-received, but no recent work has truly challenged his early plays' popularity with theatergoers. Audiences in Europe have probably been Miller's most enthusiastic recent supporters, but there is no question that Miller is the "big kid on the block" in contemporary American drama.

Selected Readings

Corrigan, Robert W. *Arthur Miller: A Collection of Critical Essays*. Englewood Cliffs: Prentice-Hall, 1969.

Hayahashi, Tetsumaro. *An Index to Arthur Miller Criticism*, 2d ed. Metuchen: Scarecrow Press, 1976.

Hayman, Ronald. *Arthur Miller*. New York: Ungar, 1972.

Huffel, Sheila. *Arthur Miller: The Burning Glass*. New York: Citadel, 1965.

Martin, Robert A., ed. *The Theatre Essays of Arthur Miller*. New York: Penguin, 1978.

Miller, Arthur. *Collected Plays*. New York: Viking, 1957.

———. *After the Fall*. New York: Viking, 1964.

———. *The Misfits*. New York: Viking, 1961.

———. *Incident at Vichy*. New York: Viking, 1965.

———. *The Price*. New York: Viking, 1968.

———. *The Creation of the World and Other Business*. New York: Viking, 1973.

Moss, Leonard. *Arthur Miller*. New York: Twayne, 1967.

Murray, Edward. *Arthur Miller, Dramatist*. New York: Ungar, 1967.

Nelson, Benjamin. *Arthur Miller: Portrait of a Playwright*. New York: McKay, 1970.

A View from the Bridge

Arthur Miller

CHARACTERS

LOUIS	TONY
MIKE	RODOLPHO
ALFIERI	FIRST IMMIGRATION OFFICER
EDDIE	SECOND IMMIGRATION OFFICER
CATHERINE	MR. LIPARI
BEATRICE	MRS. LIPARI
MARCO	TWO "SUBMARINES"

(*A tenement house and the street before it.*

Like the play, the set is stripped of everything but its essential elements. The main acting area is EDDIE CARBONE'S *living-dining room, furnished with a round table, a few chairs, a rocker, and a phonograph.*

This room is slightly elevated from the stage floor and is shaped in a free form designed to contain the acting space required, and that is all. At its back is an opaque wall-like shape, around whose right and left sides respectively entrances are made to an unseen kitchen and bedrooms.

Downstage, still in this room, and to the left, are two columnar shapes ending in air, and indicating the house front and entrance. Suspended over the entire front is an architectural element indicating a pediment over the columns, as well as the facing of a tenement building. Through this entrance a stairway is seen, beginning at floor level of the living-dining room, then curving upstage and around the back to the second-floor landing overhead.

Downstage center is the street. At the right, against the proscenium are a desk and chair belonging to MR. ALFIERI, *whose office this is, and a coat hook or rack. Near the office, but separated from it, is a low iron railing such as might form a barrier on a street to guard a basement stair. Later in the play a coin telephone will appear against the proscenium at the left.*

The intention is to make concrete the ancient element of this tale through the unmitigated forms of the commonest life of the big-city present, the one playing against the other to form a new world on the stage.

As the curtain rises, LOUIS *and* MIKE, *longshoremen, are pitching coins against the building at left.*

A distant foghorn blows.

Enter ALFIERI, *a lawyer in his fifties, turning gray, portly, good-humored, and thoughtful. The two pitchers nod to him as he passes; he crosses the stage to his desk and removes his hat and coat, hangs them, then turns to the audience.*)

ALFIERI: I am smiling because they nod so uneasily to me.
That's because I am a lawyer, and in this neighborhood a lawyer's like a priest—
They only think of us when disaster comes. So we're unlucky.
Good evening. Welcome to the theater.
My name is Alfieri. I'll come directly to the point, even though I am a lawyer. I am getting on. And I share the weakness of so many of my profession—I believe I have had some amazingly interesting cases.
When one is still young the more improbable vagaries of life only make one impatient. One looks for logic.
But when one is old, facts become precious; in facts I find all the poetry, all the wonder, all the amazement of spring. And spring is especially beautiful after fifty-five. I love what happened, instead of what might or ought to have happened.
My wife has warned me, so have my friends: they tell me the people in this neighborhood lack elegance, glamour. After all, who have I dealt with in my life? Longshoremen and their wives and fathers and grandfathers—compensation cases, evictions, family squabbles—the petty troubles of the poor—and yet . . .

When the tide is right,
And the wind blows the sea air against these houses,
I sit here in my office,
Thinking it is all so timeless here.
I think of Sicily, from where these people came,
The Roman rocks of Calabria,
Siracusa on the cliff, where Carthaginian and Greek
Fought such bloody fights. I think of Hannibal,
Who slew the fathers of these people; Caesar,
Whipping them on in Latin.

Which is all, of course, ridiculous.

Al Capone learned his trade on these pavements,
And Frankie Yale was cut in half
On the corner of Union Street and President,
Where so many were so justly shot,
By unjust men.

It's different now, of course.
I no longer keep a pistol in my filing cabinet;
We are quite American, quite civilized—
Now we settle for half. And I like it better.

And yet, when the tide is right,
And the green smell of the sea
Floats through my window,
I must look up at the circling pigeons of the poor,
And I see falcons there,
The hunting eagles of the olden time,
Fierce above Italian forests. . . .

This is Red Hook, a slum that faces the bay,
Seaward from Brooklyn Bridge.

(*Enter* EDDIE *along the street. He joins the penny-pitchers.*)

Once in every few years there is a case,
And as the parties tell me what the trouble is,
I see cobwebs tearing, Adriatic ruins rebuilding themselves; Calabria;
The eyes of the plaintiff seem suddenly carved,
His voice booming toward me over many fallen stones.

This one's name was Eddie Carbone,
A longshoreman working the docks
From Brooklyn Bridge to the breakwater. . . .

(EDDIE *picks up pennies.*)

EDDIE: Well, I'll see ya, fellas.
LOUIS: You workin' tomorrow?
EDDIE: Yeah, there's another day yet on that ship. See ya, Louis. (EDDIE *goes into the house, climbs the stairs, as light rises in the apartment.* EDDIE *is forty, a husky, slightly overweight longshoreman.*)

(CATHERINE, *his niece, is discovered standing at the window of the apartment, waving down at* LOUIS, *who now sees her and waves back up. She is seventeen and is now holding dishes in her hand, preparatory to laying out the dinner on the table.* EDDIE *enters, and she immediately proceeds to lay the table. The lights go out on* ALFIERI *and the street.*)

CATHERINE (*she has a suppressed excitement on her*): Hi, Eddie.
EDDIE (*with a trace of wryness*): What's the shoes for?

CATHERINE: I didn't go outside with them.

EDDIE (*removing his zipper jacket and hat*): Do me a favour, heh?

CATHERINE: Why can't I wear them in the house?

EDDIE: Take them off, will you please? You're beautiful enough without the shoes.

CATHERINE: I'm only trying them out.

EDDIE: When I'm home I'm not in the movies,
I don't wanna see young girls
Walking around in spike-heel shoes.

CATHERINE: Oh, brother.

(*Enter* BEATRICE, EDDIE'S *wife; she is his age.*)

BEATRICE: You find out anything?

EDDIE (*sitting in a rocker*): The ship came in. They probably get off anytime now.

BEATRICE (*softly clapping her hands together, half in prayer, half in joy*): Oh, boy. You find Tony?

EDDIE (*preoccupied*): Yeah, I talked to him. They're gonna let the crew off tonight. So they'll be here any time, he says.

CATHERINE: Boy, they must be shakin'.

EDDIE: Naa, they'll get off all right. They got regular seamen papers; they walk off with the crew. (*To* BEATRICE.) I just hope they know where they're going to sleep, heh?

BEATRICE: I told them in the letter we got no room.

CATHERINE: You didn't meet them, though, heh? You didn't see them?

EDDIE: They're still on board. I only met Tony on the pier. What are you all hopped up about?

CATHERINE: I'm not hopped up.

BEATRICE (*in an ameliorative tone*): It's something new in the house, she's excited.

EDDIE (*to* CATHERINE): 'Cause they ain't comin' here for parties, they're only comin' here to work.

CATHERINE (*blushing, even enjoying his ribbing*): Who's lookin' for parties?

EDDIE: Why don't you wear them nice shoes you got? (*He indicates her shoes.*) Those are for an actress. Go ahead.

CATHERINE: Don't tell nothin' till I come back. (*She hurries out, kicking off her shoes.*)

EDDIE (*as* BEATRICE *comes toward him*): Why do you let her wear stuff like that? That ain't her type. (BEATRICE *bends and kisses his cheek.*) What's that for?

BEATRICE: For bein' so nice about it.

EDDIE: As long as they know we got nothin', B.; that's all I'm worried about.

BEATRICE: They're gonna pay for everything; I told them in the letter.

EDDIE: Because this ain't gonna end up with you on the floor, like when your mother's house burned down.

BEATRICE: Eddie, I told them in the letter we got no room.

(CATHERINE *enters in low-heeled shoes.*)

EDDIE: Because as soon as you see a relative I turn around you're on the floor.

BEATRICE (*half amused, half serious*): All right, stop it already. You want a beer? The sauce is gotta cook a little more.

EDDIE (*to* BEATRICE): No, it's too cold. (*To* CATHERINE.) You do your lessons today, Garbo?

CATHERINE: Yeah; I'm way ahead anyway. I just gotta practice from now on.

BEATRICE: She could take it down almost as fast as you could talk already. She's terrific. Read something to her later, you'll be surprised.

EDDIE: That's the way, Katie. You're gonna be all right, kid, you'll see.

CATHERINE (*proudly*): I could get a job right now, Eddie. I'm not even afraid.

EDDIE: You got time. Wait'll you're eighteen. We'll look up the ads—find a nice company, or maybe a lawyer's office or somethin' like that.

CATHERINE: Oh, boy! I could go to work now, my teacher said.

EDDIE: Be eighteen first. I want you to have a little more head on your shoulders. You're still dizzy yet. (*To* BEATRICE.) Where's the kids? They still outside?

BEATRICE: I put them with my mother for tonight. They'd never go to sleep otherwise. So what kinda cargo you have today?

EDDIE: Coffee. It was nice.

BEATRICE: I thought all day I smelled coffee here!

EDDIE: Yeah, Brazil. That's one time, boy, to be a longshoreman is a pleasure. The whole ship smelled from coffee. It was like flowers. We'll bust a bag tomorrow; I'll bring you some. Well, let's eat, heh?

BEATRICE: Two minutes. I want the sauce to cook a little more.

(EDDIE *goes to a bowl of grapes.*)

CATHERINE: How come he's not married, Beatrice, if he's so old? The younger one.

BEATRICE (*to* EDDIE): Twenty-five is old!

EDDIE (*to* CATHERINE): Is that all you got on your mind?

CATHERINE (*wryly*): What else should I have on my mind?

EDDIE: There's plenty a things.

CATHERINE: Like what?

EDDIE: What the hell are you askin' me? I shoulda been struck by lightning when I promised your mother I would take care of you.

CATHERINE: You and me both.

EDDIE (*laughing*): Boy, God bless you, you got a tongue in your mouth like the Devil's wife. You oughta be on the television.

CATHERINE: Oh, I wish!

EDDIE: You wish! You'd be scared to death.

CATHERINE: Yeah? Try me.

EDDIE: Listen, by the way, Garbo, what'd I tell you about wavin' from the window?

CATHERINE: I was wavin' to Louis!

EDDIE: Listen, I could tell you things about Louis which you wouldn't wave to him no more.

CATHERINE (*to* BEATRICE, *who is grinning*): Boy, I wish I could find one guy that he couldn't tell me things about!

EDDIE (*going to her, cupping her cheek*): Now look, Catherine, don't joke with me.
I'm responsible for you, kid.
I promised your mother on her deathbed.
So don't joke with me. I mean it.
I don't like the sound of them high heels on the sidewalk,
I don't like that clack, clack, clack,
I don't like the looks they're givin' you.

BEATRICE: How can she help it if they look at her?

EDDIE: She don't walk right. (*To* CATHERINE.) Don't walk so wavy like that.

(BEATRICE *goes out into the kitchen.*)

CATHERINE: Who's walkin' wavy?

EDDIE: Now don't aggravate me, Katie, you are walkin' wavy!

CATHERINE: Those guys look at all the girls, you know that.

EDDIE: They got mothers and fathers. You gotta be more careful.

(BEATRICE *enters with a tureen.*)

CATHERINE: Oh, Jesus! (*She goes out into the kitchen.*)

EDDIE (*calling after her*): Hey, lay off the language, heh?

BEATRICE (*alone with him, loading the plates—she is riding lightly over a slightly sore issue*): What do you want from her all the time?

EDDIE: Boy, she grew up! Your sister should see her now. I'm tellin' you, it's like a miracle

—one day she's a baby; you turn around and she's—(*Enter* CATHERINE *with knives and forks.*) Y'know? When she sets a table she looks like a Madonna. (BEATRICE *wipes a strand of hair off* CATHERINE's *face. To* CATHERINE.) You're the Madonna type. That's why you shouldn't be flashy, Kate. For you it ain't beautiful. You're more the Madonna type. And anyway, it ain't nice in an office. They don't go for that in an office. (*He sits at the table.*)

BEATRICE (*sitting to eat*): Sit down, Katie-baby. (CATHERINE *sits. They eat.*)

EDDIE: Geez, how quiet it is here without the kids!

CATHERINE: What happens? How they gonna find the house here?

EDDIE: Tony'll take them from the ship and bring them here.

BEATRICE: That Tony must be makin' a nice dollar off this.

EDDIE: Naa, the syndicate's takin' the heavy cream.

CATHERINE: What happens when the ship pulls out and they ain't on it, though?

EDDIE: Don't worry; captain's pieced-off.

CATHERINE: Even the captain?

EDDIE: Why, the captain don't have to live? Captain gets a piece, maybe one of the mates, a piece for the guy in Italy who fixed the papers for them—(*To* BEATRICE.) They're gonna have to work six months for that syndicate before they keep a dime for theirselfs; they know that, I hope.

BEATRICE: Yeah, but Tony'll fix jobs for them, won't he?

EDDIE: Sure, as long as they owe him money he'll fix jobs; it's after the pay-off—they're gonna have to scramble like the rest of us. I just hope they know that.

BEATRICE: Oh, they must know. Boy, they must've been starvin' there. To go through all this just to make a couple a dollars. I'm tellin' ya, it could make you cry.

EDDIE: By the way, what are you going to tell the people in the house? If somebody asks what they're doin' here?

BEATRICE: Well, I'll tell 'em—Well, who's gonna ask? They probably know anyway.

EDDIE: What do you mean, they know? Listen, Beatrice, the Immigration Bureau's got stool pigeons all over the neighborhood.

BEATRICE: Yeah, but not in this house—?

EDDIE: How do you know, not in this house? Listen, both a yiz. If anybody asks you, they're your cousins visitin' here from Philadelphia.

CATHERINE: Yeah, but what would they know about Philadelphia? I mean if somebody asks them—

EDDIE: Well—they don't talk much, that's all. But don't get confidential with nobody, you hear me? Because there's a lotta guys do anything for a couple a dollars, and the Immigration pays good for that kinda news.

CATHERINE: I could teach them about Philadelphia.

EDDIE: Do me a favor, baby, will ya? Don't teach them, and don't mix in with them. Because with that blabbermouth the less you know the better off we're all gonna be. They're gonna work, and they're gonna come home here and go to sleep, and I don't want you payin' no attention to them. This is a serious business; this is the United States Government. So you don't know they're alive. I mean don't get dizzy with your friends about it. It's nobody's business. (*Slight pause.*) Where's the salt?

(*Pause.*)

CATHERINE: It's gettin' dark.

EDDIE: Yeah, gonna snow tomorrow, I think.

(*Pause.*)

BEATRICE (*she is frightened*): Geez, remember that Vinny Bolzano years ago? Remember him?

EDDIE: That funny? I was just thinkin' about him before.

CATHERINE: Who's he?

BEATRICE: You were a baby then. But there was a kid, Vinny, about sixteen. Lived over there on Sackett Street. And he snitched on somebody to the Immigration. He had five brothers, and the old man. And they grabbed him in the kitchen, and they pulled him down three flights, his head was bouncin' like a coconut—we lived in the next house. And they spit on him in the street, his own father and his brothers. It was so terrible.

CATHERINE: So what happened to him?

BEATRICE: He went away, I think. (*To* EDDIE.) Did you ever see him again?

EDDIE: Him? Naa, you'll never see him no more. A guy do a thing like that—how could he show his face again? There's too much salt in here.

BEATRICE: So what'd you put salt for?

(EDDIE *lays the spoon down, leaves the table.*)

EDDIE: Geez, I'm gettin' nervous, y'know?

BEATRICE: What's the difference; they'll only sleep here; you won't hardly see them. Go ahead, eat. (*He looks at her, disturbed.*) What could I do? They're my cousins. (*He returns to her and clasps her face admiringly as the lights fade on them and rise on Alfieri.*)

ALFIERI: I only know that they had two children;
He was as good a man as he had to be
In a life that was hard and even.
He worked on the piers when there was work,
He brought home his pay, and he lived.
And toward ten o'clock of that night,
After they had eaten, the cousins came.

(*While he is speaking* EDDIE *goes to the window and looks out.* CATHERINE *and* BEATRICE *clear the dishes.* EDDIE *sits down and reads the paper. Enter* TONY, *escorting* MARCO *and* RODOLPHO, *each with a valise.* TONY *halts, indicates the house. They stand for a moment, looking at it.*)

MARCO (*he is a square-built peasant of thirty-two, suspicious and quiet-voiced*): Thank you.

TONY: You're on your own now. Just be careful, that's all. Ground floor.

MARCO: Thank you.

TONY: I'll see you on the pier tomorrow. You'll go to work.

(MARCO *nods.* TONY *continues on, walking down the street.* RODOLPHO *is in his early twenties, an eager boy, one moment a gamin, the next a brooding adult. His hair is startlingly blond.*)

RODOLPHO: This will be the first house I ever walked into in America!

MARCO: Sssh! Come. (*They mount the stoop.*)

RODOLPHO: Imagine! She said they were poor!

MARCO: Ssh!

(*They pass between the columns. Light rises inside the apartment.* EDDIE, CATHERINE, BEATRICE *hear and raise their heads toward the door.* MARCO *knocks.* BEATRICE *and* CATHERINE *look to* EDDIE, *who rises and goes and opens the door. Enter* MARCO *and* RODOLPHO, *removing their caps.*)

EDDIE: You Marco?

(MARCO *nods, looks to the women, and fixes on* BEATRICE.)

MARCO: Are you my cousin?

BEATRICE (*touching her chest with her hand*): Beatrice. This is my husband, Eddie. (*All nod.*) Catherine, my sister Nancy's daughter. (*The brothers nod.*)

MARCO (*indicating* RODOLPHO): My brother. Rodolpho. (RODOLPHO *nods.* MARCO *comes with a certain formal stiffness to* EDDIE.) I want to tell you now, Eddie—when you say go, we will go.

EDDIE: Oh, no—

MARCO: I see it's a small house, but soon, maybe, we can have our own house.

EDDIE: You're welcome, Marco, we got plenty of room here. Katie, give them supper, heh?

CATHERINE: Come here, sit down. I'll get you some soup.

(*They go to the table.*)

MARCO: We ate on the ship. Thank you. (*To* EDDIE.) Thank you.

BEATRICE: Get some coffee. We'll all have coffee. Come sit down.

CATHERINE: How come he's so dark and you're so light, Rodolpho?

RODOLPHO: I don't know. A thousand years ago, they say, the Danes invaded Sicily. (*He laughs.*)

CATHERINE (*to* BEATRICE): He's practically blond!

EDDIE: How's the coffee doin'?

CATHERINE (*brought up short*): I'm gettin' it. (*She hurries out.*)

EDDIE: Yiz have a nice trip?

MARCO: The ocean is always rough in the winter. But we are good sailors.

EDDIE: No trouble gettin' here?

MARCO: No. The man brought us. Very nice man.

RODOLPHO: He says we start to work tomorrow. Is he honest?

EDDIE: No. But as long as you owe them money they'll get you plenty of work. (*To* MARCO.) Yiz ever work on the piers in Italy?

MARCO: Piers? Ts! No.

RODOLPHO (*smiling at the smallness of his town*): In our town there are no piers, Only the beach, and little fishing boats.

BEATRICE: So what kinda work did yiz do?

MARCO (*shrugging shyly, even embarrassed*): Whatever there is, anything.

RODOLPHO: Sometimes they build a house, Or if they fix the bridge— Marco is a mason, And I bring him the cement.

(*He laughs.*)

In harvest time we work in the fields— If there is work. Anything.

EDDIE: Still bad there, heh?

MARCO: Bad, yes.

RODOLPHO: It's terrible. We stand around all day in the piazza, Listening to the fountain like birds.

(*He laughs.*)

Everybody waits only for the train.

BEATRICE: What's on the train?

RODOLPHO: Nothing. But if there are many passengers And you're lucky you make a few lire To push the taxi up the hill.

(*Enter* CATHERINE, *who sits, listens.*)

BEATRICE: You gotta push a taxi?

RODOLPHO (*with a laugh*): Oh, sure! It's a feature in our town. The horses in our town are skinnier than goats. So if there are too many passengers We help to push the carriages up to the hotel.

(*He laughs again.*)

In our town the horses are only for the show.

CATHERINE: Why don't they have automobile taxis?

RODOLPHO: There is one—we push that too.

(*They laugh.*)

Everything in our town, you gotta push.

BEATRICE (*to* EDDIE, *sorrowfully*): How do you like that—

EDDIE (*to* MARCO): So what're you wanna do, you gonna stay here in this country or you wanna go back?

MARCO (*surprised*): Go back?

EDDIE: Well, you're married, ain't you?

MARCO: Yes. I have three children.

BEATRICE: Three! I thought only one.

MARCO: Oh, no. I have three now. Four years, five years, six years.

BEATRICE: Ah, I bet they're cryin' for you already, heh?

MARCO: What can I do? The older one is sick in his chest; My wife she feeds them from her own mouth. I tell you the truth, If I stay there they will never grow up. They eat the sunshine.

BEATRICE: My God. So how long you want to stay?

MARCO: With your permission, we will stay maybe a—

EDDIE: She don't mean in this house, she means in the country.

MARCO: Oh. Maybe four, five, six years, I think.

RODOLPHO (*smiling*): He trusts his wife.

BEATRICE: Yeah, but maybe you'll get enough,

You'll be able to go back quicker.

MARCO: I hope. I don't know. (*To* EDDIE.) I understand it's not so good here either.

EDDIE: Oh, you guys'll be all right—till you pay them off, anyway. After that, you'll have to scramble, that's all. But you'll make better here than you could there.

RODOLPHO: How much? We hear all kinds of figures.
How much can a man make? We work hard,
We'll work all day, all night . . .

EDDIE (*he is coming more and more to address* MARCO *only*): On the average a whole year? Maybe —well, it's hard to say, see. Sometimes we lay off, there's no ships three-four weeks.

MARCO: Three, four weeks! Ts!

EDDIE: But I think you could probably— Thirty, forty a week over the whole twelve months of the year.

MARCO: Dollars.

EDDIE: Sure dollars.

MARCO (*looking happily at* RODOLPHO): If we can stay here a few months, Beatrice—

BEATRICE: Listen, you're welcome, Marco—

MARCO: Because I could send them a little more if I stay here—

BEATRICE: As long as you want; we got plenty a room—

MARCO (*his eyes showing tears*): My wife—my wife . . . I want to send right away maybe twenty dollars.

EDDIE: You could send them something next week already.

MARCO (*near tears*): Eduardo—

EDDIE: Don't thank me. Listen, what the hell, it's no skin off me. (*To* CATHERINE.) What happened to the coffee?

CATHERINE: I got it on. (*To* RODOLPHO.) You married too? No.

RODOLPHO: Oh, no.

BEATRICE: I told you he—

CATHERINE (*to her*): I know, I just thought maybe he got married recently.

RODOLPHO: I have no money to get married. I have a nice face, but no money. (*He laughs.*)

CATHERINE (*to* BEATRICE): He's a real blond!

BEATRICE (*to* RODOLPHO): You want to stay here too, heh? For good?

RODOLPHO: Me? Yes, forever! Me, I want to be an American.
And then I want to go back to Italy
When I am rich. And I will buy a motorcycle.
(*He smiles.*)

CATHERINE: A motorcycle!

RODOLPHO: With a motorcycle in Italy you will never starve any more.

BEATRICE: I'll get you coffee. (*She exits.*)

EDDIE: What're you do with a motorcycle?

MARCO: He dreams, he dreams.

RODOLPHO: Why? Messages! The rich people in the hotel
Always need someone who will carry a message.
But quickly, and with a great noise.
With a blue motorcycle I would station myself
In the courtyard of the hotel,
And in a little while I would have messages.

MARCO: When you have no wife you have dreams.

EDDIE: Why can't you just walk, or take a trolley or sump'm?

(*Enter* BEATRICE *with coffee.*)

RODOLPHO: Oh, no, the machine, the machine is necessary.
A man comes into a great hotel and says,
"I am a messenger." Who is this man?
He disappears walking, there is no noise, nothing—
Maybe he will never come back,
Maybe he will never deliver the message.
But a man who rides up on a great machine,
This man is responsible, this man exists.
He will be given messages.
I am also a singer, though.

EDDIE: You mean a regular—?

RODOLPHO: Oh, yes. One night last year
Andreola got sick. Baritone.
And I took his place in the garden of the hotel.
Three arias I sang without a mistake;
Thousand-lire notes they threw from the tables,
Money was falling like a storm in the treasury;
It was magnificent.
We lived six months on that night, eh, Marco?

(MARCO *nods doubtfully.*)

MARCO: Two months.

BEATRICE: Can't you get a job in that place?

RODOLPHO: Andreola got better.
He's a baritone, very strong; otherwise I—

MARCO (*to* BEATRICE): He sang too loud.

RODOLPHO: Why too loud!

MARCO: Too loud. The guests in that hotel are all Englishmen. They don't like too loud.

RODOLPHO: Then why did they throw so much money?

MARCO: They pay for your courage. (*To* EDDIE.) The English like courage, but once is enough.

RODOLPHO (*to all but* MARCO.): I never heard anybody say it was too loud.

CATHERINE: Did you ever hear of jazz?

RODOLPHO: Oh, sure! I sing jazz.

CATHERINE: You could sing jazz?

RODOLPHO: Oh, I sing Napolidan, jazz, bel canto——

I sing "Paper Doll"; you like "Paper Doll"?

CATHERINE: Oh, sure, I'm crazy for "Paper Doll." Go ahead, sing it.

RODOLPHO (*he takes his stance, and with a high tenor voice*):

"I'll tell you boys it's tough to be alone,
And it's tough to love a doll that's not your own.
I'm through with all of them,
I'll never fall again,
Hey, boy, what you gonna do—

I'm goin' to buy a paper doll that I can call my own,
A doll that other fellows cannot steal,
And then the flirty, flirty guys
With their flirty, flirty eyes
Will have to flirt with dollies that are real.
When I come home at night she will be waiting.
She'll be the truest doll in all this world—"

EDDIE (*he has been slowly moving in agitation*): Hey, kid—hey, wait a minute—

CATHERINE (*enthralled*): Leave him finish. It's beautiful! (*To* BEATRICE.) He's terrific! It's terrific, Rodolpho!

EDDIE: Look, kid; you don't want to be picked up, do ya?

MARCO: No-no!

EDDIE (*indicating the rest of the building*): Because we never had no singers here—and all of a sudden there's a singer in the house, y'know what I mean?

MARCO: Yes, yes. You will be quiet, Rodolpho.

EDDIE (*flushed*): They got guys all over the place, Marco. I mean.

MARCO: Yes. He will be quiet. (*To* RODOLPHO.) Quiet.

EDDIE (*with iron control, even a smile*): You got the shoes again, Garbo?

CATHERINE: I figured for tonight—

EDDIE: Do me a favor, will you? (*He indicates the bedroom.*) Go ahead.

(*Embarrassed now, angered,* CATHERINE *goes out into the bedroom.* BEATRICE *watches her go and gets up, and, in passing, gives* EDDIE *a cold look, restrained only by the strangers, and goes to the table to pour coffee.*)

EDDIE (*to* MARCO, *but directed as much to* BEATRICE): All actresses they want to be around here.

(*He goes to draw a shade down.*)

RODOLPHO (*happy about it*): In Italy too! All the girls.

EDDIE (*sizing up* RODOLPHO—*there is a concealed suspicion*): Yeah, heh?

RODOLPHO: Yes! (*He laughs, indicating* CATHERINE *with his head—her bedroom.*) Especially when they are so beautiful!

(CATHERINE *emerges from the bedroom in low-heeled shoes, comes to the table.* RODOLPHO *is lifting a cup.*)

CATHERINE: You like sugar?

RODOLPHO: Sugar? Yes! I like sugar very much!

(EDDIE *is downstage, watching, as she pours a spoonful of sugar into* RODOLPHO's *cup.* EDDIE *turns and draws a shade, his face puffed with trouble, and the room dies. Light rises on* ALFIERI.)

ALFIERI: Who can ever know what will be discovered?

(*Sunlight rises on the street and house.*)

Eddie Carbone had never expected to have a destiny.

(EDDIE *comes slowly, ambling, down the stairs into the street.*)

A man works, raises his family, goes bowling,
Eats, gets old, and then he dies.
Now, as the weeks passed, there was a future,
There was a trouble that would not go away.

(BEATRICE *appears with a shopping bag. Seeing her,* EDDIE *meets her at the stoop.*)

EDDIE: It's after four.

BEATRICE: Well, it's a long show at the Paramount.

EDDIE: They must've seen every picture in Brooklyn by now.
He's supposed to stay in the house when he ain't workin'.
He ain't supposed to go advertising himself.

BEATRICE: So what am I gonna do?

EDDIE: Last night they went to the park.
You know that? Louis seen them in the park.

BEATRICE: She's goin' on eighteen, what's so terrible?

EDDIE: I'm responsible for her.

BEATRICE: I just wish once in a while you'd be responsible for me, you know that?

EDDIE: What're you beefin'?

BEATRICE: You don't know why I'm beefin'? (*He turns away, making as though to scan the street, his jaws clamped.*) What's eatin' you? You're gonna bust your teeth, you grind them so much in bed, you know that? It's like a factory all night. (*He doesn't answer, looks peeved.*) What's the matter, Eddie?

EDDIE: It's all right with you? You don't mind this?

BEATRICE: Well what you want, keep her in the house a little baby all her life? What do you want, Eddie?

EDDIE: That's what I brung her up for? For that character?

BEATRICE: Why? He's a nice fella. Hard-workin', he's a good-lookin'

EDDIE: That's good-lookin'?

BEATRICE: He's handsome, for God's sake.

EDDIE: He gives me the heeby-jeebies. I don't like his whole way.

BEATRICE (*smiling*): You're jealous, that's all.

EDDIE: Of *him?* Boy, you don't think much of me.

BEATRICE (*going to him*): What are you worried about? She knows how to take care of herself.

EDDIE: She don't know nothin'. He's got her rollin'; you see the way she looks at him? The house could burn down she wouldn't know.

BEATRICE: Well, she's got a boy-friend finally, so she's excited. So?

EDDIE: He sings on the ships, didja know that?

BEATRICE (*mystified*): What do you mean, he sings?

EDDIE: He sings. Right on the deck, all of a sudden—a whole song. They're callin' him Paper Doll, now. Canary. He's like a weird. Soon as he comes onto the pier it's a regular free show.

BEATRICE: Well, he's a kid; he don't know how to behave himself yet.

EDDIE: And with that wacky hair; he's like a chorus girl or sump'm.

BEATRICE: So he's blond, so—

EDDIE (*not looking at her*): I just hope that's his regular hair, that's all I hope.

BEATRICE (*alarmed*): You crazy or sump'm?

EDDIE (*only glancing at her*): What's so crazy? You know what I heard them call him on Friday? I was on line for my check, somebody calls out, "Blondie!" I turn around, they're callin' *him!* Blondie now!

BEATRICE: You never seen a blond guy in your life? What about Whitey Balso?

EDDIE: Sure, but Whitey don't sing; he don't do like that on the ships—

BEATRICE: Well, maybe that's the way they do in Italy.

EDDIE: Then why don't his brother sing?

Marco goes around like a man; nobody kids Marco. (*He shifts, with a glance at her.*) I don't like him, B. And I'm tellin' you now, I'm not gonna stand for it. For that character I didn't bring her up.

BEATRICE: All right—well, go tell her, then.

EDDIE: How am I gonna tell her? She won't listen to me, she can't even see me. I come home, she's in a dream. Look how thin she got, she could walk through a wall—

BEATRICE: All right, listen—

EDDIE: It's eatin' me out, B. I can't stand to look at his face. And what happened to the stenography? She don't practice no more, does she?

BEATRICE: All right, listen. I want you to lay off, you hear me? Don't work yourself up. You hear? This is her business.

EDDIE: B., he's takin' her for a ride!

BEATRICE: All right, that's her ride. It's time already; let her be somebody else's Madonna now. Come on, come in the house, you got your own to worry about. (*She glances around.*) She ain't gonna come any quicker if you stand on the street, Eddie. It ain't nice.

EDDIE: I'll be up right away. I want to take a walk. (*He walks away.*)

BEATRICE: Come on, look at the kids for once.

EDDIE: I'll be up right away. Go ahead.

BEATRICE (*with a shielded tone*): Don't stand around, please. It ain't nice. I mean it.

(*She goes into the house. He reaches the upstage right extremity, stares at nothing for a moment; then, seeing someone coming, he goes to the railing downstage and sits, as* LOUIS *and* MIKE *enter and join him.*)

LOUIS: Wanna go bowlin' tonight?

EDDIE: I'm too tired. Goin' to sleep.

LOUIS: How's your two submarines?

EDDIE: They're okay.

LOUIS: I see they're gettin' work allatime.

EDDIE: Oh yeah, they're doin' all right.

MIKE: That's what we oughta do. We oughta leave the country and come in under the water. Then we get work.

EDDIE: You ain't kiddin'.

LOUIS: Well, what the hell. Y'know?

EDDIE: Sure.

LOUIS: Believe me, Eddie, you got a lotta credit comin' to you.

EDDIE: Aah, they don't bother me, don't cost me nutt'n.

MIKE: That older one, boy, he's a regular bull. I seen him the other day liftin' coffee bags over the Matson Line. They leave him alone he woulda load the whole ship by himself.

EDDIE: Yeah, he's a strong guy, that guy. My Frankie takes after him, I think. Their father was a regular giant, supposed to be.

LOUIS: Yeah, you could see. He's a regular slave.

MIKE: That blond one, though—(EDDIE *looks at him.*) He's got a sense a humor.

EDDIE (*searchingly*): Yeah. He's funny—

MIKE (*laughing through his speech*): Well, he ain't ezackly funny, but he's always like makin' remarks, like, y'know? He comes around, everybody's laughin'.

EDDIE (*uncomfortably*): Yeah, well—he's got a sense a humor.

MIKE: Yeah, I mean, he's always makin' like remarks, like, y'know? (LOUIS *is quietly laughing with him.*)

EDDIE: Yeah, I know. But he's a kid yet, y'know? He—he's just a kid, that's all.

MIKE: I know. You take one look at him—everybody's happy. I worked one day with him last week over the Moore-MacCormack, I'm tellin' you they was all hysterical.

EDDIE: Why? What'd he do?

MIKE: I don't know—he was just humorous. You never can remember what he says, y'know? But it's the way he says it. I mean he gives you a look sometimes and you start laughin'!

EDDIE: Yeah. (*Troubled.*) He's got a sense a humor.

MIKE (*laughing*): Yeah.

LOUIS: Well, we'll see ya, Eddie.

EDDIE: Take it easy.

LOUIS: Yeah. See ya.

MIKE: If you wanna come bowlin' later we're goin' Flatbush Avenue.

(*They go.* EDDIE, *in troubled thought, stares after them; they arrive at the left extremity, and their laughter, untroubled and friendly, rises as they see* RODOLPHO, *who is entering with* CATHERINE *on his arm. The longshoremen exit.* RODOLPHO *waves a greeting to them.*)

CATHERINE: Hey, Eddie, what a picture we saw! Did we laugh!

EDDIE (*he can't help smiling at sight of her*): Where'd you go?

CATHERINE: Paramount. It was with those two guys, y'know? That—

EDDIE: Brooklyn Paramount?

CATHERINE (*with an edge of anger, embarrassed before* RODOLPHO): Sure the Brooklyn Paramount. I told you we wasn't goin' to New York.

EDDIE (*retreating before the threat of her anger*): All right, I only asked you. (*To* RODOLPHO.) I just don't want her hangin' around Times Square, see; it's full of tramps over there.

RODOLPHO: I would like to go to Broadway once, Eddie.
I would like to walk with her once
Where the theaters are, and the opera;
Since I was a boy I see pictures of those lights—

EDDIE (*his little patience waning*): I want to talk to her a minute, Rodolpho; go upstairs, will you?

RODOLPHO: Eddie, we only walk together in the streets,
She teaches me—

CATHERINE: You know what he can't get over?
That there's no fountains in Brooklyn!

EDDIE (*smiling unwillingly, to* RODOLPHO): Fountains?

(RODOLPHO *smiles at his own naïveté.*)

CATHERINE: In Italy, he says, every town's got fountains,
And they meet there. And you know what?
They got oranges on the trees where he comes from,
And lemons. Imagine? On the trees?
I mean it's interesting. But he's crazy for New York!

RODOLPHO (*attempting familiarity*): Eddie, why can't we go once to Broadway?

EDDIE: Look, I gotta tell her something—

(RODOLPHO *nods, goes to the stoop.*)

RODOLPHO: Maybe you can come too.
I want to see all those lights . . .

(*He sees no response in* EDDIE's *face. He glances at* CATHERINE *and goes into the house.*)

CATHERINE: Why don't you talk to him, Eddie? He blesses you, and you don't talk to him hardly.

EDDIE (*enveloping her with his eyes*): I bless you, and you don't talk to me. (*He tries to smile.*)

CATHERINE: I don't talk to you? (*She hits his arm.*) What do you mean!

EDDIE: I don't see you no more. I come home you're runnin' around someplace—

(CATHERINE *takes his arm, and they walk a little.*)

CATHERINE: Well, he wants to see everything, that's all, so we go. You mad at me?

EDDIE: No. (*He is smiling sadly, almost moony.*) It's just I used to come home, you was always there. Now, I turn around, you're a big girl. I don't know how to talk to you.

CATHERINE: Why!

EDDIE: I don't know, you're runnin', you're runnin', Katie. I don't think you listening any more to me.

CATHERINE: Ah, Eddie, sure I am. What's the matter? You don't like him?

(*Slight pause.*)

EDDIE: *You* like him, Katie?

CATHERINE (*with a blush, but holding her ground*): Yeah. I like him.

EDDIE (*his smile goes*): You like him.

CATHERINE (*looking down*): Yeah. (*Now she looks at him for the consequences, smiling but tense. He looks at her like a lost boy.*) What're you got against him? I don't understand. He only blesses you.

EDDIE: He don't bless me, Katie.

CATHERINE: He does! You're like a father to him!

EDDIE: Katie.

CATHERINE: What, Eddie?

EDDIE: You gonna marry him?

CATHERINE: I don't know. We just been—goin' around, that's all.

EDDIE: He don't respect you, Katie.

CATHERINE: Why!

EDDIE: Katie, if you wasn't an orphan, wouldn't he ask your father permission before he run around with you like this?

CATHERINE: Oh, well, he didn't think you'd mind.

EDDIE: He knows I mind, but it don't bother him if I mind, don't you see that?

CATHERINE: No, Eddie, he's got all kinds of respect for me. And you too! We walk across the street, he takes my arm—he almost bows to me! You got him all wrong, Eddie; I mean it, you—

EDDIE: Katie, he's only bowin' to his passport.

CATHERINE: His passport!

EDDIE: That's right. He marries you he's got the right to be an American citizen. That's what's goin' on here. (*She is puzzled and surprised.*) You understand what I'm tellin' you? The guy is lookin' for his break, that's all he's lookin' for.

CATHERINE (*pained*): Oh, no, Eddie, I don't think so.

EDDIE: You don't think so! Katie, you're gonna make me cry here. Is that a workin' man? What does he do with his first money? A snappy new jacket he buys, records, a pointy pair new shoes, and his brother's kids are starvin' with tuberculosis over there? That's a hit-and-run guy, baby; he's got bright lights in his head, Broadway—them guys don't think of nobody but theirself! You marry him and the next time you see him it'll be for the divorce!

CATHERINE: Eddie, he never said a word about his papers or—

EDDIE: You mean he's supposed to tell you that?

CATHERINE: I don't think he's even thinking about it.

EDDIE: What's better for him to think about? He could be picked up any day here and he's back pushin' taxis up the hill!

CATHERINE: No, I don't believe it.

EDDIE (*grabbing her hand*): Katie, don't break my heart, listen to me—

CATHERINE: I don't want to hear it. Lemme go.

EDDIE (*holding her*): Katie, listen—

CATHERINE: He loves me!

EDDIE (*with deep alarm*): Don't say that, for God's sake! This is the oldest racket in the country.

CATHERINE (*desperately, as though he had made his imprint*): I don't believe it!

EDDIE: They been pullin' this since the immigration law was put in! They grab a green kid that don't know nothin' and they—

CATHERINE: I don't believe it and I wish 'to hell you'd stop it!

(*She rushes, sobbing, into the house.*)

EDDIE: Katie!

(*He starts in after her, but halts as though realizing he has no force over her. From within, music is heard now, radio jazz. He glances up and down the street, then moves off, his chest beginning to rise and fall in anger. Light rises on* ALFIERI, *seated behind his desk.*)

ALFIERI: It was at this time that he first came to me.

I had represented his father in an accident case some years before,

And I was acquainted with the family in a casual way.

I remember him now as he walked through my doorway—

His eyes were like tunnels;

My first thought was that he had committed a crime,

(EDDIE *enters, sits beside the desk, cap in hand, looking out.*)

But soon I saw it was only a passion
That had moved into his body, like a stranger.

(ALFIERI *pauses, looks down at his desk, then to* EDDIE, *as though he were continuing a conversation with him.*)

I don't quite understand what I can do for you. Is there a question of law somewhere?

EDDIE: That's what I want to ask you.

ALFIERI: Because there's nothing illegal about a girl falling in love with an immigrant.

EDDIE: Yeah, but what about if the only reason for it is to get his papers?

ALFIERI: First of all, you don't know that—

EDDIE: I see it in his eyes; he's laughin' at her and he's laughin' at me.

ALFIERI: Eddie, I'm a lawyer; I can only deal in what's provable. You understand that, don't you? Can you prove that?

EDDIE: I know what's in his mind, Mr. Alfieri!

ALFIERI: Eddie, even if you could prove that—

EDDIE: Listen—Will you listen to me a minute? My father always said you was a smart man. I want you to listen to me.

ALFIERI: I'm only a lawyer, Eddie—

EDDIE: Will you listen a minute? I'm talkin' about the law. Lemme just bring out what I mean. A man, which he comes into the country illegal, don't it stand to reason he's gonna take every penny and put it in the sock? Because they don't know from one day to the nother, right?

ALFIERI: All right.

EDDIE: He's spendin'. Records he buys now. Shoes. Jackets. Y'understand me? This guy ain't worried. This guy is *here*. So it must be that he's got it all laid out in his mind already—he's stayin'. Right?

ALFIERI: Well? What about it?

EDDIE: All right. (*He glances over his shoulder as though for intruders, then back to* ALFIERI, *then down to the floor.*) I'm talkin' to you confidential, ain't I?

ALFIERI: Certainly.

EDDIE: I mean it don't go no place but here. Because I don't like to say this about anybody. Even to my wife I didn't exactly say this.

ALFIERI: What is it?

EDDIE (*he takes a breath*): The guy ain't right. Mr. Alfieri.

ALFIERI: What do you mean?

EDDIE (*glancing over his shoulder again*): I mean he ain't right.

ALFIERI: I don't get you.

EDDIE (*he shifts to another position in the chair*): Dja ever get a look at him?

ALFIERI: Not that I know of, no.

EDDIE: He's a blond guy. Like—platinum. You know what I mean?

ALFIERI: No.

EDDIE: I mean if you close the paper fast—you could blow him over.

ALFIERI: Well, that doesn't mean—

EDDIE: Wait a minute, I'm tellin' you sump'm. He sings, see. Which is—I mean it's all right, but sometimes he hits a note, see. I turn around. I mean—high. You know what I mean?

ALFIERI: Well, that's a tenor.

EDDIE: I know a tenor. Mr. Alfieri. This ain't no tenor. I mean if you came in the house and you didn't know who was singin', you wouldn't be lookin' for him, you'd be lookin' for her.

ALFIERI: Yes, but that's not—

EDDIE: I'm tellin' you sump'm, wait a minute; please, Mr. Alfieri. I'm tryin' to bring out my thoughts here. Couple a nights ago my niece brings out a dress, which it's too small for her because she shot up like a light this last year. He takes the dress, lays it on the table, he cuts it up; one-two-three, he makes a new dress. I mean he looked so sweet there, like an angel—you could kiss him he was so sweet.

ALFIERI: Now, look, Eddie—

EDDIE: Mr. Alfieri, they're laughin' at him on the piers. I'm ashamed. Paper Doll, they call him. Blondie now. His brother thinks it's because he's got a sense a humor, see—which he's got—but that ain't what they're laughin'. Which they're not goin' to come out with it because they know he's my relative, which they have to see me if they make a crack, y'know? But I know what they're laughin' at, and when I think of that guy layin' his hands on her I could—I mean it's eatin' me out, Mr. Alfieri, because I struggled for that girl. And now he comes in my house—

ALFIERI: Eddie, look. I have my own children, I understand you. But the law is very specific. The law does not—

EDDIE (*with a fuller flow of indignation*): You mean to tell me that there's no law that a guy which he ain't right can go to work and marry a girl and—?

ALFIERI: You have no recourse in the law, Eddie.

EDDIE: Yeah, but if he ain't right, Mr. Alfieri, you mean to tell me—

ALFIERI: There is nothing you can do, Eddie, believe me.

EDDIE: Nothin'.

ALFIERI: Nothing at all. There's only one legal question here.

EDDIE: What?

ALFIERI: The manner in which they entered the country. But I don't think you want to do anything about that, do you?

EDDIE: You mean—?

ALFIERI: Well, they entered illegally.

EDDIE: Oh, Jesus, no, I wouldn't do nothin' about that. I mean—

ALFIERI: All right, then, let me talk now, eh?

EDDIE: Mr. Alfieri, I can't believe what you tell me. I mean there must be some kinda law which—

ALFIERI: Eddie, I want you to listen to me.

(Pause.)

You know, sometimes God mixes up the people.
We all love somebody, the wife, the kids—
Every man's got somebody that he loves, heh?
But sometimes—there's too much. You know?
There's too much, and it goes where it mustn't.
A man works hard, he brings up a child,
Sometimes it's a niece, sometimes even a
      daughter,
And he never realizes it, but through the years—
There is too much love for the daughter,
There is too much love for the niece.
Do you understand what I'm saying to you?

EDDIE (sardonically): What do you mean, I shouldn't look out for her good?

ALFIERI: Yes, but these things have to end, Eddie, that's all.
The child has to grow up and go away,
And the man has to learn how to forget.
Because after all, Eddie—
What other way can it end?

(Pause.)

Let her go. That's my advice. You did your job,
Now it's her life; wish her luck,
And let her go.

(Pause.)

Will you do that? Because there's no law, Eddie;
Make up your mind to it; the law is not interested in this.

EDDIE: You mean to tell me, even if he's a punk? If he's—

ALFIERI: There's nothing you can do.

(EDDIE sits almost grinding his jaws. He stands, wipes one eye.)

EDDIE: Well, all right, thanks. Thanks very much.

ALFIERI: What are you going to do?

EDDIE (with a helpless but ironic gesture): What can I do? I'm a patsy, what can a patsy do? I worked like a dog twenty years so a punk could have her, so that's what I done. I mean, in the worst times, in the worst, when there wasn't a ship comin' in the harbor, I didn't stand around lookin' for relief—I hustled. When there was empty piers in Brooklyn I went to Hoboken, Staten Island, the West Side, Jersey, all over—because I made a promise. I took out of my own kids' mouths to give to her. I took out of my mouth. I walked hungry plenty days in this city! (It begins to break through.) And now I gotta sit in my own house and look at a son-of-a-bitch punk like that!—which he came out of nowhere! I give him my house to sleep! I take the blankets off my bed for him, and he takes and puts his dirty filthy hands on her like a goddam thief!

ALFIERI: But Eddie, she's a woman now—

EDDIE: He's stealin' from me!

ALFIERI: She wants to get married, Eddie. She can't marry you, can she?

EDDIE (furiously): What're you talkin' about, marry me! I don't know what the hell you're talkin' about!

(Pause.)

ALFIERI: I gave you my advice, Eddie. That's it.

(EDDIE gathers himself. A pause.)

EDDIE: Well, thanks. Thanks very much. It just—it's breakin' my heart, y'know. I—

ALFIERI: I understand. Put it out of your mind. Can you do that?

EDDIE: I'm—(He feels the threat of sobs, and with a helpless wave.) I'll see you around. (He goes out.)

ALFIERI: There are times when you want to
      spread an alarm,
But nothing has happened. I knew, I knew then
      and there—
I could have finished the whole story that
      afternoon.
It wasn't as though there were a mystery to
      unravel.
I could see every step coming, step after step,
Like a dark figure walking down a hall toward a
      certain door.
I knew where he was heading for;
I knew where he was going to end.
And I sat here many afternoons,

Asking myself why, being an intelligent man,
I was so powerless to stop it.
I even went to a certain old lady in the
neighborhood,
A very wise old woman, and I told her,
And she only nodded, and said,
"Pray for him."
And so I—(*he sits*)—waited here.

(*As the light goes out on* ALFIERI *it rises in the apartment, where all are finishing dinner. There is silence, but for the clink of a dish. Now* CATHERINE *looks up.*)

CATHERINE: You know where they went?

BEATRICE: Where?

CATHERINE: They went to Africa once. On a fishing boat. (EDDIE *glances at her.*) It's true, Eddie.

EDDIE: I didn't say nothin'. (*He finishes his coffee and leaves the table.*)

CATHERINE: And I was never even in Staten Island.

EDDIE (*sitting with a paper in his rocker*): You didn't miss nothin'. (*Pause.* CATHERINE *takes dishes out;* BEATRICE *and* RODOLPHO *stack the others.*) How long that take you, Marco—to get to Africa?

MARCO: Oh—two days. We go all over.

RODOLPHO: Once we went to Yugoslavia.

EDDIE (*to* MARCO): They pay all right on them boats?

MARCO: If they catch fish they pay all right.

RODOLPHO: They're family boats, though. And nobody in our family owned one. So we only worked when one of the families was sick.

(CATHERINE *re-enters.*)

BEATRICE: Y'know, Marco, what I don't understand—there's an ocean full of fish and yiz are all starvin'.

EDDIE: They gotta have boats, nets, you need money.

BEATRICE: Yeah, but couldn't they like fish from the beach? You see them down Coney Island—

MARCO: Sardines.

EDDIE: Sure. How you gonna catch sardines on a hook?

BEATRICE: Oh, I didn't know they're sardines. (*To* CATHERINE.) They're sardines!

CATHERINE: Yeah, they follow them all over the ocean—Africa, Greece, Yugoslavia . . .

BEATRICE (*to* EDDIE): It's funny, y'know? You never think of it, that sardines are swimming in the ocean!

CATHERINE: I know. It's like oranges and lemons on a tree. (*To* EDDIE.) I mean you ever think of oranges and lemons on a tree?

EDDIE: Yeah, I know. It's funny. (*To* MARCO.) I heard that they paint the oranges to make them look orange.

MARCO: Paint?

EDDIE: Yeah, I heard that they grow like green—

MARCO: No, in Italy the oranges are orange.

RODOLPHO: Lemons are green.

EDDIE (*resenting his instruction*): I know lemons are green, for Christ's sake, you see them in the store they're green sometimes. I said oranges they paint, I didn't say nothin' about lemons.

BEATRICE (*diverting their attention*): Your wife is gettin' the money all right, Marco?

MARCO: Oh, yes. She bought medicine for my boy.

BEATRICE: That's wonderful. You feel better, heh?

MARCO: Oh, yes! But I'm lonesome.

BEATRICE: I just hope you ain't gonna do like some of them around here. They're here twenty-five years, some men, and they didn't get enough together to go back twice.

MARCO: Oh, I know. We have many families in our town, the children never saw the father. But I will go home. Three, four years, I think.

BEATRICE: Maybe you should keep more here, no? Because maybe she thinks it comes so easy you'll never get ahead of yourself.

MARCO: Oh, no, she saves. I send everything. My wife is very lonesome. (*He smiles shyly.*)

BEATRICE: She must be nice. She pretty? I bet, heh?

MARCO (*blushing*): No, but she understands everything.

RODOLPHO: Oh, he's got a clever wife!

EDDIE: I betcha there's plenty surprises sometimes when those guys get back there, heh?

MARCO: Surprises?

EDDIE: I mean, you know—they count the kids and there's a couple extra than when they left?

MARCO: No—no. The women wait, Eddie. Most. Most. Very few surprises.

RODOLPHO: It's more strict in our town. (EDDIE *looks at him now.*) It's not so free.

EDDIE: It ain't so free here either, Rodolpho, like you think. I seen greenhorns sometimes get in trouble that way—they think just because a girl don't go around with a shawl over her head that she ain't strict, y'know? Girl don't have to wear black dress to be strict. Know what I mean?

RODOLPHO: Well, I always have respect—

EDDIE: I know, but in your town you wouldn't just drag off some girl without permission, I mean. (*He turns.*) You know what I mean, Marco? It ain't that much different here.

MARCO (*cautiously*): Yes.

EDDIE (*to* RODOLPHO): I mean I seen some a yiz get the wrong idea sometimes. I mean it might be a little more free here but it's just as strict.

RODOLPHO: I have respect for her, Eddie. I do anything wrong?

EDDIE: Look, kid, I ain't her father, I'm only her uncle—

MARCO: No, Eddie, if he does wrong you must tell him. What does he do wrong?

EDDIE: Well, Marco, till he came here she was never out on the street twelve o'clock at night.

MARCO (*to* RODOLPHO): You come home early now.

CATHERINE: Well, the movie ended late.

EDDIE: I'm just sayin'—he thinks you always stayed out like that. I mean he don't understand, honey, see?

MARCO: You come home early now, Rodolpho.

RODOLPHO (*embarrassed*): All right, sure.

EDDIE: It's not only for her, Marco. (*To* CATHERINE.) I mean it, kid, he's gettin' careless. The more he runs around like that the more chance he's takin'. (*To* RODOLPHO.) I mean suppose you get hit by a car or sump'm, where's your papers, who are you? Know what I mean?

RODOLPHO: But I can't stay in the house all the time, I—

BEATRICE: Listen, he's gotta go out sometime—

EDDIE: Well, listen, it depends, Beatrice. If he's here to work, then he should work; if he's here for a good time, then he could fool around! (*To* MARCO.) But I understood, Marco, that you was both comin' to make a livin' for your family. You understand me, don't you, Marco?

MARCO (*he sees it nearly in the open now, and with reserve*): I beg your pardon, Eddie.

EDDIE: I mean that's what I understood in the first place, see?

MARCO: Yes. That's why we came.

EDDIE: Well, that's all I'm askin'.

(*There is a pause, an awkwardness. Now* CATHERINE *gets up and puts a record on the phonograph. Music.*)

CATHERINE (*flushed with revolt*): You wanna dance, Rodolpho?

RODOLPHO (*in deference to* EDDIE): No, I—I'm tired.

CATHERINE: Ah, come on. He plays a beautiful piano, that guy. Come. (*She has taken his hand, and he stiffly rises, feeling* EDDIE'S *eyes on his back, and they dance.*)

EDDIE (*to* CATHERINE): What's that, a new record?

CATHERINE: It's the same one. We bought it the other day.

BEATRICE (*to* EDDIE): They only bought three records. (*She watches them dance;* EDDIE *turns his head away.* MARCO *just sits there, waiting. Now* BEATRICE *turns to* EDDIE.) Must be nice to go all over in one of them fishin' boats. I would like that myself. See all them other countries?

EDDIE: Yeah.

BEATRICE (*to* MARCO): But the women don't go along, I bet.

MARCO: No, not on the boats. Hard work.

BEATRICE: What're you got, a regular kitchen and everything?

MARCO: Yes, we eat very good on the boats—especially when Rodolpho comes along; everybody gets fat.

BEATRICE: Oh, he cooks?

MARCO: Sure, very good cook. Rice, pasta, fish, everything.

EDDIE: He's a cook too! (*He looks at* RODOLPHO.) He sings, he cooks . . .

(RODOLPHO *smiles thankfully.*)

BEATRICE: Well, it's good; he could always make a living.

EDDIE: It's wonderful. He sings, he cooks, he could make dresses . . .

CATHERINE: They get some high pay, them guys. The head chefs in all the big hotels are men. You read about them.

EDDIE: That's what I'm sayin'.

(CATHERINE *and* RODOLPHO *continue dancing.*)

CATHERINE: Yeah, well, I mean.

EDDIE (*to* BEATRICE): He's lucky, believe me. (*A slight pause; he looks away, then back to* BEATRICE.) That's why the waterfront is no place for him. I mean, like me—I can't cook, I can't sing, I can't make dresses, so I'm on the waterfront. But if I could cook, if I could sing, if I could makes dresses, I wouldn't be on the waterfront. (*They are all regarding him now; he senses he is exposing the issue, but he is driven on.*) I would be someplace else. I would be like in a dress store. (*He suddenly gets up and pulls his pants up over his belly.*) What do you say, Marco, we go to the bouts next Saturday night? You never seen a fight, did you?

MARCO (*uneasily*): Only in the moving pictures.

EDDIE: I'll treat yiz. What do you say, Danish? You wanna come along? I'll buy the tickets.

RODOLPHO: Sure. I like to go.

CATHERINE (*nervously happy now*): I'll make some coffee, all right?

EDDIE: Go ahead, make some! (*He draws her near him.*) Make it nice and strong. (*Mystified, she smiles and goes out. He is weirdly elated; he is rubbing his fists into his palms.*) You wait, Marco, you see some real fights here. You ever do any boxing?

MARCO: No, I never.

EDDIE (*to* RODOLPHO): Betcha you done some, heh?

RODOLPHO: No.

EDDIE: Well, get up, come on, I'll teach you.

BEATRICE: What's he got to learn that for?

EDDIE: Ya can't tell, one a these days somebody's liable to step on his foot, or sump'm. Come on, Rodolpho, I show you a couple a passes.

BEATRICE (*unwillingly, carefully*): Go ahead, Rodolpho. He's a good boxer; he could teach you.

RODOLPHO (*embarrassed*): Well, I don't know how to—

EDDIE: Just put your hands up. Like this, see? That's right. That's very good, keep your left up, because you lead with the left, see, like this. (*He gently moves his left into* RODOLPHO's *face.*) See? Now what you gotta do is you gotta block me, so when I come in like that you— (RODOLPHO *parries his left.*) Hey, that's very good! (RODOLPHO *laughs.*) All right, now come into me. Come on.

RODOLPHO: I don't want to hit you, Eddie.

EDDIE: Don't pity me, come on. Throw it; I'll show you how to block it. (RODOLPHO *jabs at him, laughing.*) 'At's it. Come on, again. For the jaw, right here. (RODOLPHO *jabs with more assurance.*) Very good!

BEATRICE (*to* MARCO): He's very good!

EDDIE: Sure, he's great! Come on, kid, put sump'm behind it; you can't hurt me. (RODOLPHO, *more seriously, jabs at* EDDIE's *jaw and grazes it.*) Attaboy. Now I'm gonna hit you, so block me, see?

(CATHERINE *comes from the kitchen, watches.*)

CATHERINE (*with beginning alarm*): What are they doin'?

(*They are lightly boxing now.*)

BEATRICE (*she senses only the comradeship in it now*): He's teachin' him; he's very good!

EDDIE: Sure, he's terrific! Look at him go! (RODOLPHO *lands a blow.*) 'At's it! Now watch out, here I come, Danish! (*He feints with his left hand and lands with his right. It mildly staggers* RODOLPHO.)

CATHERINE (*rushing to* RODOLPHO): Eddie!

EDDIE: Why? I didn't hurt him. (*Going to help the dizzy* RODOLPHO.) Did I hurt you, kid?

RODOLPHO: No, no, he didn't hurt me. (*To* EDDIE, *with a certain gleam and a smile.*) I was only surprised.

BEATRICE: That's enough, Eddie; he did pretty good, though.

EDDIE: Yeah. (*He rubs his fists together.*) He could be very good, Marco. I'll teach him again.

(MARCO *nods at him dubiously.*)

RODOLPHO (*as a new song comes on the radio, his voice betraying a new note of command*): Dance, Catherine. Come.

(RODOLPHO *takes her in his arms. They dance.* EDDIE, *in thought, sits in his chair, and* MARCO *rises and comes downstage to a chair and looks down at it.* BEATRICE *and* EDDIE *watch him.*

MARCO: Can you lift this chair?

EDDIE: What do you mean?

MARCO: From here. (*He gets on one knee with one hand behind his back, and grasps the bottom of one of the chair legs but does not raise it.*)

EDDIE: Sure, why not? (*He comes to the chair, kneels, grasps the leg, raises the chair one inch, but it leans over to the floor.*) Gee, that's hard, I never knew that. (*He tries again, and again fails.*) It's on an angle, that's why, heh?

MARCO: Here. (*He kneels, grasps, and with strain slowly raises the chair higher and higher, getting to his feet now.*)

(*And* RODOLPHO *and* CATHERINE *have stopped dancing as* MARCO *raises the chair over his head.*

He is face to face with EDDIE, *a strained tension gripping his eyes and jaw, his neck stiff, the chair raised like a weapon—and he transforms what might appear like a glare of warning into a smile of triumph, and* EDDIE's *grin vanishes as he absorbs the look; as the lights go down.*

The stage remains dark for a moment. Ships' horns are heard. Light rises on ALFIERI *at his desk. He is discovered in dejection, his face bent to the desk, on which his arms rest. Now he looks up and front.*)

ALFIERI: On the twenty-third of that December

A case of Scotch whisky slipped from a net
While being unloaded—as a case of Scotch
  whisky
Is inclined to do on the twenty-third of
  December
On Pier Forty-one. There was no snow, but it
  was cold.
His wife was out shopping.
Marco was still at work.
The boy had not been hired that day;
Catherine told me later that this was the first
  time
They had been alone together in the house.

(*Light is rising on* CATHERINE, *who is ironing in
the apartment. Music is playing.* RODOLPHO *is in*
EDDIE's *rocker, his head leaning back. A piano jazz
cadenza begins. Luxuriously he turns his head to her
and smiles, and she smiles at him, then continues ironing. He comes to the table and sits beside her.*)

CATHERINE: You hungry?
RODOLPHO: Not for anything to eat. (*He leans
his chin on the back of his hand on the table, watch-
ing her iron.*) I have nearly three hundred dollars.
(*He looks up at her.*) Catherine?
CATHERINE: I heard you.

(RODOLPHO *reaches out and takes her hand and
kisses it, then lets it go. She resumes ironing. He rests
his head again on the back of his hand.*)

RODOLPHO: You don't like to talk about it
any more?
CATHERINE: Sure, I don't mind talkin' about
it.
RODOLPHO: What worries you, Catherine?

(CATHERINE *continues ironing. He now reaches out
and takes her hand off the iron, and she sits back in
her chair, not looking directly at him.*)

CATHERINE: I been wantin' to ask you about
something. Could I?
RODOLPHO: All the answers are in my eyes,
Catherine. But you don't look in my eyes lately.
You're full of secrets. (*She looks at him. He presses
her hand against his cheek. She seems withdrawn.*)
What is the question?
CATHERINE: Suppose I wanted to live in Italy.
RODOLPHO (*smiling at the incongruity*): You
going to marry somebody rich?
CATHERINE: No, I mean live there—you and
me.
RODOLPHO (*his smile is vanishing*): When?
CATHERINE: Well—when we get married.
RODOLPHO (*astonished*): You want to be an
Italian?

CATHERINE: No, but I could live there with-
out being Italian. Americans live there.
RODOLPHO: Forever?
CATHERINE: Yeah.
RODOLPHO: You're fooling.
CATHERINE: No, I mean it.
RODOLPHO: Where do you get such an idea?
CATHERINE: Well, you're always saying it's so
beautiful there, with the mountains and the
ocean and all the—
RODOLPHO: You're fooling me.
CATHERINE: I mean it.
RODOLPHO: Catherine, if I ever brought you
  home
With no money, no business, nothing,
They would call the priest and the doctor
And they would say Rodolpho is crazy.
CATHERINE: I know, but I think we would be
happier there.
RODOLPHO: Happier! What would you eat?
You can't cook the view!
CATHERINE: Maybe you could be a singer,
like in Rome or—
RODOLPHO: Rome! Rome is full of singers.
CATHERINE: Well, I could work then.
RODOLPHO: Where?
CATHERINE: God, there must be jobs some-
where!
RODOLPHO: There's nothing! Nothing,
  nothing,
Nothing. Now tell me what you're talking
  about.
How can I bring you from a rich country
To suffer in a poor country?
What are you talking about?

(*She searches for words.*)

I would be a criminal stealing your face;
In two years you would have an old, hungry face.
When my brother's babies cry they give them
  water,
Water that boiled a bone.
Don't you believe that?

CATHERINE (*quietly*): I'm afraid of Eddie here.

(*A slight pause.*)

RODOLPHO: We wouldn't live here.
Once I am a citizen I could work anywhere,
And I would find better jobs,
And we would have a house, Catherine.
If I were not afraid to be arrested
I would start to be something wonderful here!
CATHERINE (*steeling herself*): Tell me some-
thing. I mean just tell me, Rodolpho. Would

you still want to do it if it turned out we had to go live in Italy? I mean just if it turned out that way.

RODOLPHO: This is your question or his question?

CATHERINE: I would like to know, Rodolpho. I mean it.

RODOLPHO: To go there with nothing?

CATHERINE: Yeah.

RODOLPHO: No. (*She looks at him wide-eyed.*) No.

CATHERINE: You wouldn't?

RODOLPHO: No; I will not marry you to live in Italy.
I want you to be my wife
And I want to be a citizen.
Tell him that, or I will. Yes.

(*He moves about angrily.*)

And tell him also, and tell yourself, please,
That I am not a beggar,
And you are not a horse, a gift,
A favor for a poor immigrant.

CATHERINE: Well, don't get mad!

RODOLPHO: I am furious!
Do you think I am so desperate?
My brother is desperate, not me.
You think I would carry on my back
The rest of my life a woman I didn't love
Just to be an American? It's so wonderful?
You think we have no tall buildings in Italy?
Electric lights? No wide streets? No flags?
No automobiles? Only work we don't have.
I want to be an American so I can work,
That is the only wonder here—work!
How can you insult me, Catherine?

CATHERINE: I didn't mean that—

RODOLPHO: My heart dies to look at you.
Why are you so afraid of him?

CATHERINE (*near tears*): I don't know!

(RODOLPHO *turns her to him.*)

RODOLPHO: Do you trust me, Catherine? You?

CATHERINE: It's only that I—
He was good to me, Rodolpho.
You don't know him; he was always the sweetest guy to me.
Good. He razzes me all the time,
But he don't mean it. I know.
I would—just feel ashamed if I made him sad.
'Cause I always dreamt that when I got married
He would be happy at the wedding, and laughin'.
And now he's—mad all the time, and nasty.

(*She is weeping.*)

Tell him you'd live in Italy—just tell him,
And maybe he would start to trust you a little, see?
Because I want him to be happy; I mean—
I like him, Rodolpho—and I can't stand it!

(*She weeps, and he holds her.*)

RODOLPHO: Catherine—oh, little girl—

CATHERINE: I love you, Rodolpho, I love you.

RODOLPHO: I think that's what you have to tell him, eh?
Can't you tell him?

CATHERINE: I'm ascared, I'm so scared.

RODOLPHO: Ssssh. Listen, now. Tonight when he comes home
We will both sit down after supper
And we will tell him—you and I.

(*He sees her fear rising.*)

But you must believe me yourself, Catherine.
It's true—you have very much to give me;
A whole country! Sure, I hold America when I hold you.
But if you were not my love,
If every day I did not smile so many times
When I think of you,
I could never kiss you, not for a hundred Americas.
Tonight I'll tell him,
And you will not be frightened any more, eh?
And then in two, three months I'll have enough,
We will go to the church, and we'll come back to our own—

(*He breaks off, seeing the conquered longing in her eyes, her smile.*)

Catherine—

CATHERINE: Now. There's nobody here.

RODOLPHO: Oh, my little girl. Oh God!

CATHERINE (*kissing his face*): Now!

(*He turns her upstage. They walk embraced, her head on his shoulder, and he sings to her softly. They go into a bedroom.*

A pause. Ships' horns sound in the distance. EDDIE *enters on the street. He is unsteady, drunk. He mounts the stairs. The sounds continue. He enters the apartment, looks around, takes out a bottle from one pocket, puts it on the table; then another bottle from another pocket; and a third from an inside pocket. He sees the iron, goes over to it and touches it, pulls his hand quickly back, turns toward upstage.*)

EDDIE: Beatrice? (*He goes to the open kitchen door*

and looks in. He turns to a bedroom door.) Beatrice? (*He starts for this door; it opens, and* CATHERINE *is standing there; under his gaze she adjusts her dress.*)

CATHERINE: You got home early.

EDDIE (*trying to unravel what he senses*): Knocked off for Christmas early. (*She goes past him to the ironing board. Indicating the iron.*) You start a fire that way.

CATHERINE: I only left it for a minute.

(RODOLPHO *appears in the bedroom doorway.* EDDIE *sees him, and his arm jerks slightly in shock.* RODOLPHO *nods to him testingly.* EDDIE *looks to* CATHERINE, *who is looking down at the ironing as she works.*)

RODOLPHO: Beatrice went to buy shoes for the children.

EDDIE: Pack it up. Go ahead. Get your stuff and get outa here. (CATHERINE *puts down the iron and walks toward the bedroom, and* EDDIE *grabs her arm.*) Where you goin'?

CATHERINE: Don't bother me, Eddie. I'm goin' with him.

EDDIE: You goin' with him. You goin' with him, heh? (*He grabs her face in the vise of his two hands.*) You goin' with him!

(*He kisses her on the mouth as she pulls at his arms; he will not let go, keeps his face pressed against hers.* RODOLPHO *comes to them now.*)

RODOLPHO (*tentatively at first*): Eddie! No, Eddie! (*He now pulls full force on* EDDIE's *arms to break his grip.*) Don't! No!

(CATHERINE *breaks free, and* EDDIE *is spun around by* RODOLPHO's *force, to face him.*)

EDDIE: You want something?

RODOLPHO: She'll be my wife.

EDDIE: But what're you gonna be? That's what I wanna know! What're you gonna be!

RODOLPHO (*with tears of rage*): Don't say that to me!

(RODOLPHO *flies at him in attack.* EDDIE *pins his arms, laughing, and suddenly kisses him.*)

CATHERINE: Eddie! Let go, ya hear me! I'll kill you! Leggo of him!

(*She tears at* EDDIE's *face, and* EDDIE *releases* RODOLPHO *and stands there, tears rolling down his face as he laughs mockingly at* RODOLPHO. *She is staring at him in horror, her breasts heaving.* RODOLPHO *is rigid; they are like animals that have torn at each other and broken up without a decision, each waiting for the other's mood.*)

EDDIE: I give you till tomorrow, kid. Get outa here. Alone. You hear me? Alone.

CATHERINE: I'm goin' with him, Eddie.

EDDIE (*indicating* RODOLPHO *with his head*): Not with that. (*He sits, still panting for breath, and they watch him helplessly as he leans his head back on the chair and, striving to catch his breath, closes his eyes.*) Don't make me do nuttin', Catherine.

(*The lights go down on* EDDIE's *apartment and rise on* ALFIERI.)

ALFIERI: On December twenty-seventh I saw him next.
I normally go home well before six,
But that day I sat around,
Looking out my window at the bay,
And when I saw him walking through my doorway
I knew why I had waited.
And if I seem to tell this like a dream,
It was that way. Several moments arrived
In the course of the two talks we had
When it occurred to me how—almost transfixed
I had come to feel. I had lost my strength somewhere.

(EDDIE *enters, removing his cap, sits in the chair, looks thoughtfully out.*)

I looked in his eyes more than I listened—
In fact, I can hardly remember the conversation.
But I will never forget how dark the room became
When he looked at me; his eyes were like tunnels.
I kept wanting to call the police,
But nothing had happened.
Nothing at all had really happened.

(*He breaks off and looks down at the desk. Then he turns to* EDDIE.)

So in other words, he won't leave?

EDDIE: My wife is talkin' about renting a room upstairs for them.
An old lady on the top floor is got an empty room.

ALFIERI: What does Marco say?

EDDIE: He just sits there. Marco don't say much.

ALFIERI: I guess they didn't tell him, heh? What happened?

EDDIE: I don't know; Marco don't say much.

ALFIERI: What does your wife say?

EDDIE (*unwilling to pursue this*): Nobody's talkin' much in the house. So what about that?

ALFIERI: But you didn't prove anything about him.

EDDIE: Mr. Alfieri, I'm tellin' you—

ALFIERI: You're not telling me anything, Eddie;
It sounds like he just wasn't strong enough to break your grip.

EDDIE: I'm tellin' you I know—he ain't right.
Somebody that don't want it can break it.
Even a mouse, if you catch a teeny mouse
And you hold it in your hand, that mouse
Can give you the right kind of fight,
And he didn't give me the right kind of fight.
I know it, Mr. Alfieri, the guy ain't right.

ALFIERI: What did you do that for, Eddie?

EDDIE: To show her what he is! So she would see, once and for all! Her mother'll turn over in the grave! (*He gathers himself almost peremptorily.*) So what do I gotta do now? Tell me what to do.

ALFIERI: She actually said she's marrying him?

EDDIE: She told me, yeah. So what do I do?

(*A slight pause.*)

ALFIERI: This is my last word, Eddie,
Take it or not, that's your business.
Morally and legally you have no rights;
You cannot stop it; she is a free agent.

EDDIE (*angering*): Didn't you hear what I told you?

ALFIERI (*with a tougher tone*): I heard what you told me,
And I'm telling you what the answer is.
I'm not only telling you now, I'm warning you—
The law is nature.
The law is only a word for what has a right to happen.
When the law is wrong it's because it's unnatural,
But in this case it is natural,
And a river will drown you
If you buck it now.
Let her go. And bless her.

(*As he speaks, a phone begins to glow on the opposite side of the stage, a faint, lonely blue.* EDDIE *stands up, jaws clenched.*)

Somebody had to come for her, Eddie, sooner or later.

(EDDIE *starts to turn to go, and* ALFIERI *rises with new anxiety.*)

You won't have a friend in the world, Eddie!
Even those who understand will turn against you,
Even the ones who feel the same will despise you!

(EDDIE *moves off quickly.*)

Put it out of your mind! Eddie!

(*The light goes out on* ALFIERI. EDDIE *has at the same time appeared beside the phone, and he lifts it.*)

EDDIE: I want to report something. Illegal immigrants. Two of them. That's right. Four-forty-one Saxon Street, Brooklyn, yeah. Ground floor. Heh? (*With greater difficulty.*) I'm just around the neighborhood, that's all. Heh?

(*Evidently he is being questioned further, and he slowly hangs up. He comes out of the booth just as* LOUIS *and* MIKE *come down the street. They are privately laughing at some private joke.*)

LOUIS: Go bowlin', Eddie?

EDDIE: No, I'm due home.

LOUIS: Well, take it easy.

EDDIE: I'll see yiz.

(*They leave him, and he watches them go. They resume their evidently amusing conversation. He glances about, then goes up into the house, and, as he enters, the lights go on in the apartment.* BEATRICE *is seated, sewing a pair of child's pants.*)

BEATRICE: Where you been so late?

EDDIE: I took a walk, I told you. (*He gets out of his zipper jacket, picks up a paper that is lying in a chair, prepares to sit.*) Kids sleepin'?

BEATRICE: Yeah, they're all sleepin'.

(*Pause.* EDDIE *looks out the window.*)

EDDIE: Where's Marco?

BEATRICE: They decided to move upstairs with Mrs. Dondero.

EDDIE (*turning to her*): They're up there now?

BEATRICE: They moved all their stuff. Catherine decided. It's better, Eddie, they'll be outa your way. They're happy and we'll be happy.

EDDIE: Catherine's up there too?

BEATRICE: She just went up to bring pillow cases. She'll be down right away.

EDDIE (*nodding*): Well, they're better off up there; the whole house knows they were here anyway, so there's nothin' to hide no more.

BEATRICE: That's what I figured. And besides, with the other ones up there maybe it'll look like they're just boarders too, or sump'm. You want eat?

EDDIE: What other ones?

BEATRICE: The two guys she rented the other room to. She's rentin' two rooms. She bought beds and everything; I told you.

EDDIE: When'd you tell me?

BEATRICE: I don't know; I think we were talkin' about it last week, even. She is startin' like a little boarding house up there. Only she's got no pillow cases yet.

EDDIE: I didn't hear nothin' about no boarding house.

BEATRICE: Sure, I loaned her my big fryin' pan beginning of the week. I told you. (*She smiles and goes to him.*) You gotta come to yourself, kid; you're in another world all the time. (*He is silent, peering; she touches his head.*) I wanna tell you, Eddie; it was my fault, and I'm sorry. No kiddin'. I shoulda put them up there in the first place.

EDDIE: Dja ever see these guys?

BEATRICE: I see them on the stairs every couple a days. They're kinda young guys. You look terrible, y'know?

EDDIE: They longshoremen?

BEATRICE: I don't know; they never said only hello, and she don't say nothin', so I don't ask, but they look like nice guys. (EDDIE, *silent, stares.*) What's the matter? I thought you would like it.

EDDIE: I'm just wonderin'—where they come from? She's got no sign outside; she don't know nobody. How's she find boarders all of a sudden?

BEATRICE: What's the difference? She—

EDDIE: The difference is they could be cops, that's all.

BEATRICE: Oh, no, I don't think so.

EDDIE: It's all right with me, I don't care. Except for this kinda work they don't wear badges, y'know. I mean you gotta face it, they could be cops. And Rodolpho'll start to shoot his mouth off up there, and they got him.

BEATRICE: I don't think so. You want some coffee?

EDDIE: No. I don't want nothin'.

BEATRICE: You gettin' sick or sump'm?

EDDIE: Me—no, I'm all right. (*Mystified.*) When did you tell me she had boarders?

BEATRICE: Couple a times.

EDDIE: Geez, I don't even remember. I thought she had the one room. (*He touches his forehead, alarmed.*)

BEATRICE: Sure, we was all talkin' about it

last week. I loaned her my big fryin' pan. I told you.

EDDIE: I must be dizzy or sump'm.

BEATRICE: I think you'll come to yourself now, Eddie. I mean it, we shoulda put them up there in the first place. You can never bring strangers in a house. (*Pause. They are seated.*) You know what?

EDDIE: What?

BEATRICE: Why don't you tell her you'll go to her it's all right—Katie? Give her a break. A wedding should be happy.

EDDIE: I don't care. Let her do what she wants to do.

BEATRICE: Why don't you tell her you'll go to the wedding? It's terrible, there wouldn't be no father there. She's broken-hearted.

EDDIE: They made up the date already?

BEATRICE: She wants him to have like six, seven hundred. I told her, I says, "If you start off with a little bit you never gonna get ahead of yourself," I says. So they're gonna wait yet. I think maybe the end of the summer. But if you would tell them you'll be at the wedding—I mean, it would be nice, they would both be happy. I mean live and let live, Eddie, I mean?

EDDIE (*as though he doesn't care*): All right, I'll go to the wedding. (CATHERINE *is descending the stairs from above.*)

BEATRICE (*darting a glance toward the sound*): You want me to tell her?

EDDIE (*he thinks, then turns to her with a certain deliberativeness*): If you want, go ahead.

(CATHERINE *enters, sees him, and starts for the bedroom door.*)

BEATRICE: Come here, Katie. (CATHERINE *looks doubtfully at her.*) Come here, honey. (CATHERINE *comes to her, and* BEATRICE *puts an arm around her.* EDDIE *looks off.*) He's gonna come to the wedding.

CATHERINE: What do I care if he comes? (*She starts upstage, but* BEATRICE *holds her.*)

BEATRICE: Ah, Katie, don't be that way. I want you to make up with him; come on over here. You're his baby! (*She tries to draw* CATHERINE *near* EDDIE.)

CATHERINE: I got nothin' to make up with him, he's got somethin' to make up with me.

EDDIE: Leave her alone, Beatrice, she knows what she wants to do. (*Now, however, he turns for a second to* CATHERINE.) But if I was you I would watch out for those boarders up there.

BEATRICE: He's worried maybe they're cops.

CATHERINE: Oh, no, they ain't cops. Mr.

Lipari from the butcher store—they're his nephews; they just come over last week.

EDDIE (*coming alive*): They're submarines?

CATHERINE: Yeah, they come from around Bari. They ain't cops.

(*She walks to her bedroom.* EDDIE *tries to keep silent, and when he speaks it has an unwilling sharpness of anxiety.*)

EDDIE: Catherine. (*She turns to him. He is getting to his feet in a high but subdued terror.*) You think that's a good idea?

CATHERINE: What?

EDDIE: How do you know what enemies Lipari's got? Which they would love to stab him in the back? I mean you never do that, Catherine, put in two strange pairs like that together. They track one, they'll catch 'em all. I ain't tryin' to advise you, kid, but that ain't smart. Anybody tell you that. I mean you just takin' a double chance, y'understand?

CATHERINE: Well, what'll I do with them?

EDDIE: What do you mean? The neighborhood's full of rooms. Can't you stand to live a couple a blocks away from him? He's got a big family, Lipari—these guys get picked up he's liable to blame you or me, and we got his whole family on our head. That's no joke, kid. They got a temper, that family.

CATHERINE: Well, maybe tomorrow I'll find some other place—

EDDIE: Kid, I'm not tellin' you nothin' no more because I'm just an ignorant jerk. I know that; but if I was you I would get them outa this house tonight, see?

CATHERINE: How'm I gonna find a place tonight?

EDDIE (*his temper rising*): Catherine, don't mix yourself with somebody else's family, Catherine.

(*Two men in overcoats and felt hats appear on the street, start into the house.*)

EDDIE: You want to do yourself a favor? Go up and get them out of the house, kid.

CATHERINE: Yeah, but they been in the house so long already—

EDDIE: You think I'm always tryin' to fool you or sump'm? What's the matter with you? Don't you believe I could think of your good? (*He is breaking into tears.*) Didn't I work like a horse keepin' you? You think I got no feelin's? I never told you nothin' in my life that wasn't for your good. Nothin'! And look at the way you talk to me! Like I was an enemy! Like I—(*There*

is a knock on the door. His head swerves. They all stand motionless. Another knock. EDDIE *firmly draws* CATHERINE *to him. And, in a whisper, pointing upstage.*) Go out the back up the fire escape; get them out over the back fence.

FIRST OFFICER (*in the hall*): Open up in there! immigration!

EDDIE: Go, go. Hurry up! (*He suddenly pushes her upstage, and she stands a moment, staring at him in a realized horror.*) Well what're you lookin' at?

FIRST OFFICER: Open up!

EDDIE: Who's that there?

FIRST OFFICER: Immigration. Open up.

(*With a sob of fury and that glance,* CATHERINE *streaks into a bedroom.* EDDIE *looks at* BEATRICE, *who sinks into a chair, turning her face from him.*)

EDDIE: All right, take it easy, take it easy. (*He goes and opens the door. The officers step inside.*) What's all this?

FIRST OFFICER: Where are they?

EDDIE: Where's who?

FIRST OFFICER: Come on, come on, where are they?

EDDIE: Who? We got nobody here. (*The first officer opens the door and exits into a bedroom. Second officer goes and opens the other bedroom door and exits through it.* BEATRICE *now turns her head to look at* EDDIE. *He goes to her, reaches for her, and involuntarily she withdraws herself. Then, pugnaciously, furious.*) What's the matter with you?

(*The* FIRST OFFICER *enters from the bedroom, calls quietly into the other bedroom.*)

FIRST OFFICER: Dominick?

(*Enter* SECOND OFFICER *from bedroom.*)

SECOND OFFICER: Maybe it's a different apartment.

FIRST OFFICER: There's only two more floors up there. I'll take the front, you go up the fire escape. I'll let you in. Watch your step up there.

SECOND OFFICER: Okay, right, Charley. (*He reenters the bedroom. The first officer goes to the apartment door, turns to* EDDIE.)

FIRST OFFICER: This is Four-forty-one, isn't it?

EDDIE: That's right.

(*The officer goes out into the hall, closing the door, and climbs up out of sight.* BEATRICE *slowly sits at the table.* EDDIE *goes to the closed door and listens. Knocking is heard from above, voices.* EDDIE *turns to* BEATRICE. *She looks at him now and sees his terror, and, weakened with fear, she leans her head on the table.*)

BEATRICE: Oh, Jesus, Eddie.

EDDIE: What's the matter with *you?* (*He starts toward her, but she swiftly rises, pressing her palms against her face, and walks away from him.*)

BEATRICE: Oh, my God, my God.

EDDIE: What're you, accusin' me?

BEATRICE (*her final thrust is to turn toward him instead of running from him*): My God, what did you do!

(*Many steps on the outer stair draw his attention. We see the* FIRST OFFICER *descending with Marco, behind him* RODOLPHO, *and* CATHERINE *and two strange men, followed by* SECOND OFFICER. BEATRICE *hurries and opens the door.*)

CATHERINE (*as they appear on the stairs*): What do yiz want from them? They work, that's all. They're boarders upstairs, they work on the piers.

BEATRICE (*now appearing in the hall, to* FIRST OFFICER): Ah, mister, what do you want from them? Who do they hurt?

CATHERINE (*pointing to* RODOLPHO): They ain't no submarines; he was born in Philadelphia.

FIRST OFFICER: Step aside, lady.

CATHERINE: What do you mean? You can't just come in a house and—

FIRST OFFICER: All right, take it easy. (*To* RODOLPHO.) What street were you born in Philadelphia?

CATHERINE: What do you mean, what street? Could you tell me what street you were born?

FIRST OFFICER: Sure. Four blocks away, One-eleven Union Street. Let's go, fellas.

CATHERINE (*fending him off* RODOLPHO): No, you can't! Now, get outa here!

FIRST OFFICER (*moving her into the apartment*): Look, girlie, if they're all right they'll be back tomorrow. If they're illegal they go back where they came from. If you want, get yourself a lawyer, although I'm tellin' you now you're wasting your money. (*He goes back to the group in the hall.*) Let's get them in the car, Dom. (*To the men.*) Andiamo, andiamo, let's go.

(*The men start out toward the street—but* MARCO *hangs back, letting them pass.*)

BEATRICE: Who're they hurtin', for God's sake? What do you want from them? They're starvin' over there, what do you want!

(MARCO *suddenly breaks from the group and dashes into the room and faces* EDDIE, *and* BEATRICE *and the first officer rush in as* MARCO *spits into* EDDIE's *face.* CATHERINE *has arrived at the door and sees it.* EDDIE, *with an enraged cry, lunges for* MARCO.)

EDDIE: Oh, you mother's—!

(*The first officer quickly intercedes and pushes* EDDIE *from* MARCO, *who stands there accusingly.*)

FIRST OFFICER (*pushing* EDDIE *from* MARCO): Cut it out!

EDDIE (*over the* FIRST OFFICER's *shoulder to* MARCO): I'll kill you for that, you son of a bitch!

FIRST OFFICER: Hey! (*He shakes* EDDIE.) Stay in here now, don't come down, don't bother him. You hear me? Don't come down, fella.

(*For an instant there is silence. Then the* FIRST OFFICER *turns and takes* MARCO's *arm and then gives a last, informative look at* EDDIE; *and as he and* MARCO *are going out into the hall* EDDIE *erupts.*)

EDDIE: I don't forget that, Marco! You hear what I'm sayin'?

(*Out in the hall, the* FIRST OFFICER *and* MARCO *go down the stairs.* CATHERINE *rushes out of the room and past them toward* RODOLPHO, *who, with the* SECOND OFFICER *and the two strange men, is emerging into the street. Now, in the street,* LOUIS, MIKE, *and several neighbors, including the butcher,* LIPARI, *a stout, intense, middle-aged man are gathering around the stoop.* EDDIE *follows* CATHERINE *and calls down after* MARCO. BEATRICE *watches him from within the room, her hands clasped together in fear and prayer.*)

EDDIE: That's the thanks I get? Which I took the blanket off my bed for yiz? (*He hurries down the stairs, shouting.* BEATRICE *descends behind him, ineffectually trying to hold him back.*) You gonna apologize to me, Marco! *Marco!*

(EDDIE *appears on the stoop and sees the little crowd looking up at him, and falls silent, expectant.* LIPARI, *the butcher, walks over to the two strange men, and he kisses them. His wife, keening, goes and kisses their hands.*)

FIRST OFFICER: All right, lady, let them go. Get in the car, fellas, it's right over there.

(*The* SECOND OFFICER *begins moving off with the two strange men and* RODOLPHO. CATHERINE *rushes to the* FIRST OFFICER, *who is drawing* MARCO *off now.*)

CATHERINE: He was born in Philadelphia! What do you want from him?

FIRST OFFICER: Step aside, lady, come on now—

MARCO (*suddenly, taking advantage of the* FIRST OFFICER's *being occupied with* CATHERINE, *freeing himself and pointing up at* EDDIE): That one! I accuse that one!

FIRST OFFICER (*grabbing him and moving him quickly off*): Come on!

MARCO (*as he is taken off, pointing back and up the stoop at* EDDIE): That one! He killed my children! That one stole the food from my children!

(MARCO *is gone. The crowd has turned to* EDDIE.)

EDDIE: He's crazy. I give them the blankets off my bed. Six months I kept them like my own brothers! (LIPARI, *the butcher, turns and starts off with his wife behind him.*) Lipari! (EDDIE *comes down and reaches* LIPARI *and turns him about.*) For Christ's sake, I kept them, I give them the blankets off my bed! (LIPARI *turns away in disgust and anger and walks off with his keening wife. The crowd is now moving away.* EDDIE *calls.*) Louis! (LOUIS *barely turns, then walks away with* MIKE.) LOUIS! (*Only* BEATRICE *is left on the stoop—and* CATHERINE *now returns, blank-eyed, from offstage and the car.* EDDIE *turns to* CATHERINE.) He's gonna take that back. He's gonna take that back or I'll kill him! (*He faces all the buildings, the street down which the crowd has vanished.*) You hear me? I'll kill him!

(*Blackout. There is a pause in darkness before the lights rise. On the left—opposite where the desk stands—is a backless wooden bench. Seated on it are* RODOLPHO *and* MARCO. *There are two wooden chairs. It is a room in the jail.* CATHERINE *and* ALFIERI *are seated on the chairs.*)

ALFIERI: I'm waiting, Marco. What do you say? (MARCO *glances at him, then shrugs.*) That's not enough; I want an answer from you.

RODOLPHO: Marco never hurt anybody.

ALFIERI: I can bail you out until your hearing comes up.
But I'm not going to do it—you understand me?—
Unless I have your promise. You're an honorable man,
I will believe your promise. Now what do you say?

MARCO: In my country he would be dead now.
He would not live this long.

ALFIERI: All right, Rodolpho, you come with me now. (*He rises.*)

RODOLPHO: No! Please, mister. Marco—
Promise the man. Please, I want you to watch the wedding.
How can I be married and you're in here?
Please, you're not going to do anything; you know you're not—

(MARCO *is silent.*)

CATHERINE: Marco, don't you understand? He can't bail you out if you're gonna do something bad. To hell with Eddie. Nobody is gonna talk to him again if he lives to a hundred. Everybody knows you spit in his face, that's enough, isn't it? Give me the satisfaction—I want you at the wedding. You got a wife and kids, Marco—you could be workin' till the hearing comes up, instead of layin' around here. You're just giving him satisfaction layin' here.

MARCO (*after a slight pause, to* ALFIERI): How long you say before the hearing?

ALFIERI: I'll try to stretch it out, but it wouldn't be more than five or six weeks.

CATHERINE: So you could make a couple of dollars in the meantime, y'see?

MARCO (*to* ALFIERI): I have no chance?

ALFIERI: No, Marco. You're going back. The hearing is a formality, that's all.

MARCO: But him? There is a chance, eh?

ALFIERI: When she marries him he can start to become an American. They permit that, if the wife is born here.

MARCO (*looking at* RODOLPHO): Well—we did something. (*He lays a palm on* RODOLPHO's *cheek, then lowers his hand.*)

RODOLPHO: Marco, tell the man.

MARCO: What will I tell him? (*He looks at* ALFIERI.) He knows such a promise is dishonorable.

ALFIERI: To promise not to kill is not dishonorable.

MARCO: No?

ALFIERI: No.

MARCO (*gesturing with his head—this is a new idea*): Then what is done with such a man?

ALFIERI: Nothing. If he obeys the law, he lives. That's all.

MARCO: The law? All the law is not in a book.

ALFIERI: Yes. In a book. There is no other law.

MARCO (*his anger rising*): He degraded my brother—my blood. He robbed my children, he mocks my work. I work to come here, mister!

ALFIERI: I know, Marco—

MARCO: There is no law for that? Where is the law for that?

ALFIERI: There is none.

MARCO (*shaking his head*): I don't understand this country. (*Pause. He stands staring his fury.*)

ALFIERI: Well? What is your answer? You have five or six weeks you could work. Or else you sit here. What do you say to me?

(MARCO *lowers his eyes. It almost seems he is ashamed.*)

MARCO: All right.

ALFIERI: You won't touch him. This is your promise.

(*Slight pause.*)

MARCO: Maybe he wants to apologize to me.

ALFIERI (*taking one of his hands*): This is not God, Marco. You hear? Only God makes justice.

(MARCO *withdraws his hand and covers it with the other.*)

MARCO: All right.

ALFIERI: Is your uncle going to the wedding?

CATHERINE: No. But he wouldn't do nothin' anyway. He just keeps talkin' so people will think he's in the right, that's all. He talks. I'll take them to the church, and they could wait for me there.

ALFIERI: Why, where are you going?

CATHERINE: Well, I gotta get Beatrice.

ALFIERI: I'd rather you didn't go home.

CATHERINE: Oh, no, for my wedding I gotta get Beatrice. Don't worry, he just talks big, he ain't gonna do nothin', Mr. Alfieri. I could go home.

ALFIERI (*nodding, not with assurance*): All right, then—let's go. (MARCO *rises.* RODOLPHO *suddenly embraces him.* MARCO *pats him on the back, his mind engrossed.* RODOLPHO *goes to* CATHERINE, *kisses her hand. She pulls his head to her shoulder, and they go out.* MARCO *faces* ALFIERI.) Only God, Marco.

(MARCO *turns and walks out.* ALFIERI, *with a certain processional tread, leaves the stage. The lights dim out.*

Light rises in the apartment. EDDIE *is alone in the rocker, rocking back and forth in little surges. Pause. Now* BEATRICE *emerges from a bedroom, then* CATHERINE. *Both are in their best clothes, wearing hats.*)

BEATRICE (*with fear*): I'll be back in about an hour, Eddie. All right?

EDDIE: What, have I been talkin' to myself?

BEATRICE: Eddie, for God's sake, it's her wedding.

EDDIE: Didn't you hear what I told you? You walk out that door to that wedding you ain't comin' back here, Beatrice.

BEATRICE: Why? What do you want?

EDDIE: I want my respect. Didn't you ever hear of that? From my wife?

CATHERINE: It's after three; we're supposed to be there already, Beatrice. The priest won't wait.

BEATRICE: Eddie. It's her wedding. There'll be nobody there from her family. For my sister let me go. I'm goin' for my sister.

EDDIE: Look, I been arguin' with you all day already, Beatrice, and I said what I'm gonna say. He's gonna come here and apologize to me or nobody from this house is goin' into that church today. Now if that's more to you than I am, then go. But don't come back. You be on my side or on their side, that's all.

CATHERINE (*suddenly*): Who the hell do you think you are?

BEATRICE: Sssh!

CATHERINE: You got no more right to tell nobody nothin'! Nobody! The rest of your life, nobody!

BEATRICE: Shut up, Katie!

CATHERINE (*pulling* BEATRICE *by the arm*): You're gonna come with me!

BEATRICE: I can't, Katie, I can't—

CATHERINE: How can you listen to him? This rat!

(EDDIE *gets up.*)

BEATRICE (*to* CATHERINE, *in terror at sight of his face*): Go, go—I'm not goin'—

CATHERINE: What're you scared of? He's a rat! He belongs in the sewer! In the garbage he belongs! (*She is addressing him.*) He's a rat from under the piers! He bites people when they sleep! He comes when nobody's lookin' and he poisons decent people!

(EDDIE *rushes at her with his hand raised, and* BEATRICE *struggles with him.* RODOLPHO *appears, hurrying along the street, and runs up the stairs.*)

BEATRICE (*screaming*): Get out of here, Katie! (*To* EDDIE.) Please, Eddie, Eddie, please!

EDDIE (*trying to free himself of* BEATRICE): Don't bother me!

(RODOLPHO *enters the apartment. A pause.*)

EDDIE: Get outa here.

RODOLPHO: Marco is coming, Eddie. (*Pause.* BEATRICE *raises her hands.*) He's praying in the church. You understand?

(*Pause.*)

BEATRICE (*in terror*): Eddie. Eddie, get out.

EDDIE: What do you mean, get out?

BEATRICE: Eddie, you got kids, go 'way, go 'way from here! Get outa the house!

EDDIE: Me get outa the house? *Me* get outa the house? What did I do that I gotta get outa the house?

That I wanted a girl not to turn into a tramp?
That I made a promise and I kept my promise
She should be sump'm in her life?

(CATHERINE *goes trembling to him.*)

CATHERINE: Eddie—
EDDIE: What do *you* want?
CATHERINE: Please, Eddie, go away. He's comin' for you.
EDDIE: What do you care? What do you care he's comin' for me?
CATHERINE (*weeping, she embraces him*): I never meant to do nothin' bad to you in my life, Eddie!
EDDIE (*with tears in his eyes*): Then who meant somethin' bad? How'd it get bad?
CATHERINE: I don't know, I don't know!
EDDIE (*pointing to* RODOLPHO *with the new confidence of the embrace*): They made it bad! This one and his brother made it bad which they came like thieves to rob, to rob!

(*He grabs her arm and swings her behind him so that he is between her and* RODOLPHO, *who is alone at the door.*)

You go tell him to come and come quick.
You go tell him I'm waitin' here for him to apologize
For what he said to me in front of the neighborhood!
Now get goin'!
RODOLPHO (*starting around* EDDIE *toward* CATHERINE): Come, Catherine, we—
EDDIE (*nearly throwing* RODOLPHO *out the door*): Get away from her!
RODOLPHO (*starting back in*): Catherine!
EDDIE (*turning on* CATHERINE): Tell him to get out! (*She stands paralyzed before him.*) Katie! I'll do somethin' if he don't get outa here!
BEATRICE (*rushing to him, her open hands pressed together before him as though in prayer*): Eddie, it's her husband, it's her husband! Let her go, it's her husband!

(CATHERINE, *moaning, breaks for the door, and she and* RODOLPHO *start down the stairs;* EDDIE *lunges and catches her; he holds her, and she weeps up into his face. And he kisses her on the lips.*)

EDDIE (*like a lover, out of his madness*): It's me, ain't it?
BEATRICE (*hitting his body*): Eddie! God, Eddie!
EDDIE: Katie, it's me, ain't it? You know it's me!

CATHERINE: Please, please, Eddie, lemme go. Heh? Please?

(*She moves to go.* MARCO *appears on the street.*)

EDDIE (*to* RODOLPHO): Punk! Tell her what you are! You know what you are, you punk!
CATHERINE (*pulling* RODOLPHO *out the doorway*): Come on!

(EDDIE *rushes after them to the doorway.*)

EDDIE: Make him tell you what he is! Tell her, punk! (*He is on the stairway, calling down.*) Why don't he answer me! Punk, answer me! (*He rushes down the stairs,* BEATRICE *after him.*)
BEATRICE: Eddie, come back!

(*Outside,* RODOLPHO *sees* MARCO *and cries out,* "No, Marco. Marco, go away, go away!" *But* MARCO *nears the stoop, looking up at the descending* EDDIE.)

EDDIE (*emerging from the house*): Punk, what are you gonna do with a girl! I'm waitin' for your answer, punk. Where's your—answer!

(*He sees* MARCO. *Two other neighbors appear on the street, stand and watch.* BEATRICE *now comes in front of him.*)

BEATRICE: Go in the house, Eddie!
EDDIE (*pushing her aside, coming out challengingly on the stoop, and glaring down at* MARCO): What do you mean, go in the house? Maybe he came to apologize to me. (*To the people.*)
Which I took the blankets off my bed for them;
Which I brought up a girl, she wasn't even my daughter,
And I took from my own kids to give to her—
And they took her like you take from a stable,
Like you go in and rob from your own family!
And never a word to me!
And now accusations in the bargain?
Makin' my name like a dirty rag?

(*He faces* MARCO *now, and moves toward him.*)

You gonna take that back?
BEATRICE: Eddie! Eddie!
EDDIE: I want my good name, Marco! You took my name!

(BEATRICE *rushes past him to* MARCO *and tries to push him away.*)

BEATRICE: Go, go!
MARCO: Animal! You go on your knees to me!

(*He strikes* EDDIE *powerfully on the side of the*

head. EDDIE *falls back and draws a knife.* MARCO
*springs to a position of defense, both men circling each
other.* EDDIE *lunges, and* MIKE, LOUIS, *and all the
neighbors move in to stop them, and they fight up the
steps of the stoop, and there is a wild scream
—*BEATRICE's*—and they all spread out, some of them
running off.*

MARCO *is standing over* EDDIE, *who is on his knees,
a bleeding knife in his hands.* EDDIE *falls forward on
his hands and knees, and he crawls a yard to*
CATHERINE. *She raises her face away—but she does not
move as he reaches over and grasps her leg, and,
looking up at her, he seems puzzled, questioning,
betrayed.*)

EDDIE: Catherine—why—?

(*He falls forward and dies.* CATHERINE *covers her
face and weeps. She sinks down beside the weeping*
BEATRICE. *The lights fade, and* ALFIERI *is illuminated
in his office.*)

ALFIERI: Most of the time now we settle for
half,

And I like it better.
And yet, when the tide is right
And the green smell of the sea
Floats in through my window,
The waves of this bay
Are the waves against Siracusa,
And I see a face that suddenly seems carved;
The eyes look like tunnels
Leading back toward some ancestral beach
Where all of us once lived.

And I wonder at those times
How much of all of us
Really lives there yet,
And when we will truly have moved on,
On and away from that dark place,
That world that has fallen to stones?

This is the end of the story. Good night.

THE CURTAIN FALLS

Lorraine Hansberry: *A Raisin in the Sun* (1959)

One of the greatest losses to American theater was Lorraine Hansberry's death from cancer at the age of thirty-four. Anyone who sees or reads *A Raisin in the Sun,* (even now, more than twenty years after its first performance) knows almost immediately that the play is a masterpiece. It was the first play by a black woman to be produced on Broadway and the first play by a black American to win the New York Drama Critics Circle Award for the best play of the year. It was Lorraine Hansberry's first work; she died the day her second play, *The Sign in Sidney Brustein's Window* (1965), closed.

She was born in Chicago in 1930. Her father, a successful real estate man with considerable ambitions for his family, helped found one of the first banks for blacks in Chicago. However, he lost hope that America might be the kind of place where he could raise his family the way he wanted, with freedom and dignity, and died in Mexico in 1945 while searching for the perfect place. Lorraine Hansberry graduated from high school in 1948 and went to the University of Wisconsin, then, thinking she might have a future as an artist, she attended the Art Institute of Chicago as well as a number of other schools. She gave this idea up in 1950 and moved to New York City. Theater groups held some fascination for her and she began to write plays but never finished them. After she married playwright Robert Nemiroff, she began to write *A Raisin in the Sun* and read part of it after a dinner party in their apartment, when she discovered that the play had "a life of its own." She and her friends struggled for more than a year to raise money to produce the play, which finally opened with a black director, Lloyd Richards, and the now famous Sidney Poitier playing Walter Lee Younger. It was an overwhelming success.

The play was forward-looking in many ways. It preceded both the black activism of the 1960s and the revived interest in Africanism. It uses the term Negro instead of the more militant black. There are no references to riots and precious little mention of revolution, and some audiences, perhaps expecting these issues to be present, are disappointed. They see the play as a record of the ambitions of a family aspiring to the bourgeois suburbs, to the consumerism that marked the aspirations of most of America. Yet, nothing of this sort was ever envisioned by Lorraine Hansberry. One critic was cruel enough to claim the play was about investing in real estate. But, as Julius Lester points out, even Malcolm X had put a down payment on a house in the Chicago suburbs, for the same reasons that compel Mama: to have enough room for everybody, to get some sunshine, to have a garden, and to have the feeling that the boards beneath one's feet are one's own. The wish is simple enough; it has been acted on by Americans of all races and in all times.

When Hansberry wrote about the play, she took note of the criticism that saw the play as chronicling the desire for more money, a big TV, fancy clothes, and a new house. She explains that she feels people have a right to basic material comforts, but also believes that this ambition can be totally distorted. As she says, "the distortion of this aspiration surrounds us in the form of an almost maniacal lusting for 'acquisitions.' It seems to have absorbed the national mentality and Negroes, to be sure, have certainly been affected by it. The young man in the play, Walter Lee, is meant to symbolize their number. Consequently, in the beginning, he dreams not so much of being comfortable and imparting the most meaningful gifts to his son (education in depth, humanist values, a worship of dignity) but merely of being what it seems to him the 'successful' portion of mankind is—'rich'."

When Walter Lee stands up for himself at the end of the play, he is asserting his manhood, his black manhood. His decision to follow through on his mother's wishes for the family is not made because he lusts after a big house or any material gain. It is made because not making it would be admitting to the Clybourne Park Improvement Association that he and his family are inferior. His pride is too strong for him to do that, and we have the feeling at the end of the play that Walter Lee Younger has a future and that the future, despite the setbacks of the past, is a good one; it is built on the strengths and goodness of the Younger family.

Lorraine Hansberry's second play, about the intellectual Sidney Brustein, was not on a black theme. It recounts the loss of idealism and commitment on the part of a Greenwich Village intellectual. The play demonstrated what Miss Hansberry had said all along—she wrote not only about blacks, but about people. Some of them, as she said, "happened to be black."

After her death, Robert Nemiroff put together a third play from her notes, letters, and writings. It was *To Be Young, Gifted, and Black* (1969), and it became an off-Broadway hit that year and has since been produced countless times in schools, colleges, and communities. Her last play, worked on while she was in the final phases of her illness, *Les Blancs* (1970), treated a black African intellectual, Tshembe, and his uneasy cultural relationship with Europe and Africa. He ponders the meaning of freedom, thinking for a while that he might be able to live outside his own history, yet that is no more possible for him than for Sidney Brustein. Miss Hansberry thought this play might be her most important work, and although it was given serious critical evaluation when it was produced, it has not rivalled her other plays in their constant appeal to American dramatic audiences.

Lorraine Hansberry was a true and serious revolutionary who felt that the basic structure of American society had to be altered before the condition of the American black could be changed. Yet, for all her zeal, she made her dramas deep human revelations, not political tracts.

Selected Readings

Brown, Lloyd W. "Lorraine Hansberry as Ironist: A Reappraisal of *A Raisin in the Sun*." *Journal of Black Studies*, 4, pp. 237–247.

Hansberry, Lorraine, *The Sign in Sidney Brustein's Window*. New York: Random House, 1965.

————. *To Be Young, Gifted, and Black*. Englewood Cliffs: Prentice-Hall, 1969.

————. *Les Blancs: The Collected Last Plays of Lorraine Hansberry*. New York: Random House, 1972.

A Raisin in the Sun

Lorraine Hansberry

CHARACTERS

RUTH YOUNGER	JOSEPH ASAGAI
TRAVIS YOUNGER	GEORGE MURCHISON
WALTER LEE YOUNGER (*Brother*)	KARL LINDNER
BENEATHA YOUNGER	BOBO
LENA YOUNGER (*Mama*)	MOVING MEN

The action of the play is set in Chicago's Southside, sometime between World War II and the present.

ACT I

SCENE 1: Friday morning.
SCENE 2: The following morning.

ACT II

SCENE 1: Later, the same day.
SCENE 2: Friday night, a few weeks later.
SCENE 3: Moving day, one week later.

ACT III

An hour later.

What happens to a dream deferred?
Does it dry up
Like a raisin in the sun?
Or fester like a sore—
And then run?
Does it stink like rotten meat?
Or crust and sugar over—
Like a syrupy sweet?

Maybe it just sags
Like a heavy load.

Or does it explode?

—LANGSTON HUGHES

ACT I

SCENE 1

(*The* YOUNGER *living room would be a comfortable and well-ordered room if it were not for a number of indestructible contradictions to this state of being. Its furnishings are typical and undistinguished and their primary feature now is that they have clearly had to accommodate the living of too many people for too many years—and they are tired. Still, we can see that at some time, a time probably no longer remembered by the family* [*except perhaps for* MAMA], *the furnishings of this room were actually selected with care and love and even hope—and brought to this apartment and arranged with taste and pride.*

That was a long time ago. Now the once loved pattern of the couch upholstery has to fight to show itself from under acres of crocheted doilies and couch covers which have themselves finally come to be more important than the upholstery. And here a table or a chair has been moved to disguise the worn places in the carpet; but the carpet has fought back by showing its weariness, with depressing uniformity, elsewhere on its surface.

Weariness has, in fact, won in this room. Everything has been polished, washed, sat on, used, scrubbed too often. All pretenses but living itself have long since vanished from the very atmosphere of this room.

Moreover, a section of this room, for it is not really a room unto itself, though the landlord's lease would make it seem so, slopes backward to provide a small kitchen area, where the family prepares the meals that are eaten in the living room proper, which must also serve as dining room. The single window that has been provided for these "two" rooms is located in this kitchen area. The sole natural light the family may enjoy in the course of a day is only that which fights its way through this little window.

At left, a door leads to a bedroom which is shared by MAMA *and her daughter,* BENEATHA. *At right, opposite, is a second room (which in the beginning of the life of this apartment was probably a breakfast room) which serves as a bedroom for* WALTER *and his wife,* RUTH.

Time: Sometime between World War II and the present.

Place: Chicago's Southside.

At Rise: It is morning dark in the living room. TRAVIS *is asleep on the make-down bed at center. An alarm clock sounds from within the bedroom at right, and presently* RUTH *enters from that room and closes the door behind her. She crosses sleepily toward the window. As she passes her sleeping son she reaches down and shakes him a little. At the window she raises the shade and a dusky Southside morning light comes in feebly. She fills a pot with water and puts it on to boil. She calls to the boy between yawns, in a slightly muffled voice.*

RUTH *is about thirty. We can see that she was a pretty girl, even exceptionally so, but now it is apparent that life has been little that she expected, and disappointment has already begun to hang in her face. In a few years, before thirty-five even, she will be known among her people as a "settled woman."*

She crosses to her son and gives him a good, final, rousing shake.)

RUTH: Come on now, boy, it's seven thirty! (*Her son sits up at last, in a stupor of sleepiness.*) I say hurry up, Travis! You ain't the only person in the world got to use a bathroom! (*The child, a sturdy, handsome little boy of ten or eleven, drags himself out of the bed and almost blindly takes his towels and "today's clothes" from drawers and a closet and goes out to the bathroom, which is in an outside hall and which is shared by another family or families on the same floor.* RUTH *crosses to the bedroom door at right and opens it and calls in to her husband.*) Walter Lee! . . . It's after seven thirty! Lemme see you do some waking up in there now! (*She waits.*) You better get up from there, man! It's after seven thirty I tell you. (*She waits again.*) All right, you just go ahead and lay there and next thing you know Travis be finished and Mr. Johnson'll be in there and you'll be fussing and cussing round here like a mad man! And be late too! (*She waits, at the end of patience.*) Walter Lee—it's time for you to get up!

(*She waits another second and then starts to go into the bedroom, but is apparently satisfied that her husband has begun to get up. She stops, pulls the door to, and returns to the kitchen area. She wipes her face with a moist cloth and runs her fingers through her sleep-disheveled hair in a vain effort and ties an apron around her housecoat. The bedroom door at right opens and her husband stands in the doorway in his pajamas, which are rumpled and mismated. He is a lean, intense young man in his middle thirties, inclined to quick nervous movements and erratic speech habits—and always in his voice there is a quality of indictment.*)

WALTER: Is he out yet?

RUTH: What you mean *out?* He ain't hardly got in there good yet.

WALTER (*wandering in, still more oriented to sleep than to a new day*): Well, what was you doing all that yelling for if I can't even get in there yet?

(*Stopping and thinking.*) Check coming today?

RUTH: They *said* Saturday and this is just Friday and I hopes to God you ain't going to get up here first thing this morning and start talking to me 'bout no money—'cause I 'bout don't want to hear it.

WALTER: Something the matter with you this morning?

RUTH: No—I'm just sleepy as the devil. What kind of eggs you want?

WALTER: Not scrambled. (RUTH *starts to scramble eggs.*) Paper come? (RUTH *points impatiently to the rolled up* Tribune *on the table, and he gets it and spreads it out and vaguely reads the front page.*) Set off another bomb yesterday.

RUTH (*maximum indifference*): Did they?

WALTER (*looking up*): What's the matter with you?

RUTH: Ain't nothing the matter with me. And don't keep asking me that this morning.

WALTER: Ain't nobody bothering you. (*Reading the news of the day absently again.*) Say Colonel McCormick is sick.

RUTH (*affecting tea-party interest*): Is he now? Poor thing.

WALTER (*sighing and looking at his watch*): Oh, me. (*He waits.*) Now what is that boy doing in that bathroom all this time? He just going to have to start getting up earlier. I can't be being late to work on account of him fooling around in there.

RUTH (*turning on him*): Oh, no he ain't going to be getting up no earlier no such thing! It ain't his fault that he can't get to bed no earlier nights 'cause he got a bunch of crazy good-for-nothing clowns sitting up running their mouths in what is supposed to be his bedroom after ten o'clock at night . . .

WALTER: That's what you mad about, ain't it? The things I want to talk about with my friends just couldn't be important in your mind, could they?

(*He rises and finds a cigarette in her handbag on the table and crosses to the little window and looks out, smoking and deeply enjoying this first one.*)

RUTH (*almost matter of factly, a complaint too automatic to deserve emphasis*): Why you always got to smoke before you eat in the morning?

WALTER (*at the window*): Just look at 'em down there . . . Running and racing to work . . . (*He turns and faces his wife and watches her a moment at the stove, and then, suddenly.*) You look young this morning, baby.

RUTH (*indifferently*): Yeah?

WALTER: Just for a second—stirring them eggs. It's gone now—just for a second it was —you looked real young again. (*Then, drily.*) It's gone now—you look like yourself again.

RUTH: Man, if you don't shut up and leave me alone.

WALTER (*looking out to the street again*): First thing a man ought to learn in life is not to make love to no colored woman first thing in the morning. You all some evil people at eight o'clock in the morning.

(TRAVIS *appears in the hall doorway, almost fully dressed and quite wide awake now, his towels and pajamas across his shoulders. He opens the door and signals for his father to make the bathroom in a hurry.*)

TRAVIS (*watching the bathroom*): Daddy, come on!

(WALTER *gets his bathroom utensils and flies out to the bathroom.*)

RUTH: Sit down and have your breakfast, Travis.

TRAVIS: Mama, this is Friday. (*Gleefully.*) Check coming tomorrow, huh?

RUTH: You get your mind off money and eat your breakfast.

TRAVIS (*eating*): This is the morning we supposed to bring the fifty cents to school.

RUTH: Well, I ain't got no fifty cents this morning.

TRAVIS: Teacher say we have to.

RUTH: I don't care what teacher say. I ain't got it. Eat your breakfast, Travis.

TRAVIS: I *am* eating.

RUTH: Hush up now and just eat!

(*The boy gives her an exasperated look for her lack of understanding, and eats grudgingly.*)

TRAVIS: You think Grandmama would have it?

RUTH: No! And I want you to stop asking your grandmother for money, you hear me?

TRAVIS (*outraged*): Gaaaleee! I don't ask her, she just gimme it sometimes!

RUTH: Travis Willard Younger—I got too much on me this morning to be—

TRAVIS: Maybe Daddy—

RUTH: *Travis!*

(*The boy hushes abruptly. They are both quiet and tense for several seconds.*)

TRAVIS (*presently*): Could I maybe go carry some groceries in front of the supermarket for a little while after school then?

RUTH: Just hush, I said. (TRAVIS *jabs his spoon into his cereal bowl viciously, and rests his head in anger upon his fists.*) If you through eating, you can get over there and make up your bed.

(*The boy obeys stiffly and crosses the room, almost mechanically, to the bed and more or less carefully folds the covering. He carries the bedding into his mother's room and returns with his books and cap.*)

TRAVIS (*sulking and standing apart from her unnaturally*): I'm gone.

RUTH (*looking up from the stove to inspect him automatically*): Come here. (*He crosses to her and she studies his head.*) If you don't take this comb and fix this here head, you better! (TRAVIS *puts down his books with a great sigh of oppression, and crosses to the mirror. His mother mutters under her breath about his "slubbornness".*) 'Bout to march out of here with that head looking just like chickens slept in it! I just don't know where you get your slubborn ways . . . And get your jacket, too. Looks chilly out this morning.

TRAVIS (*with conspicuously brushed hair and jacket*): I'm gone.

RUTH: Get carfare and milk money—(*Waving one finger.*)—and not a single penny for no caps, you hear me?

TRAVIS (*with sullen politeness*): Yes'm.

(*He turns in outrage to leave. His mother watches after him as in his frustration he approaches the door almost comically. When she speaks to him, her voice has become a very gentle tease.*)

RUTH (*mocking; as she thinks he would say it*). Oh, Mama makes me so mad sometimes, I don't know what to do! (*She waits and continues to his back as he stands stock-still in front of the door.*) I wouldn't kiss that woman good-bye for nothing in this world this morning! (*The boy finally turns around and rolls his eyes at her, knowing the mood has changed and he is vindicated; he does not, however, move toward her yet.*) Not for nothing in this world! (*She finally laughs aloud at him and holds out her arms to him and we see that it is a way between them, very old and practiced. He crosses to her and allows her to embrace him warmly but keeps his face fixed with masculine rigidity. She holds him back from her presently and looks at him and runs her fingers over the features of his face. With utter gentleness—.*) Now—whose little old angry man are you?

TRAVIS (*the masculinity and gruffness start to fade at last*): Aw gaalee—Mama . . .

RUTH (*mimicking*): Aw—gaaaaalleeeee, Mama! (*She pushes him, with rough playfulness and finality, toward the door.*) Get on out of here or you going to be late.

TRAVIS (*in the face of love, new aggressiveness*): Mama, could I *please* go carry groceries?

RUTH: Honey, it's starting to get so cold evenings.

WALTER (*coming in from the bathroom and drawing a make-believe gun from a make-believe holster and shooting at his son*): What is it he wants to do?

RUTH: Go carry groceries after school at the supermarket.

WALTER: Well, let him go . . .

TRAVIS (*quickly, to the ally*): I *have* to—she won't gimme the fifty cents . . .

WALTER (*to his wife only*): Why not?

RUTH (*simply, and with flavor*): 'Cause we don't have it.

WALTER (*to RUTH only*): What you tell the boy things like that for? (*Reaching down into his pants with a rather important gesture.*) Here, son—

(*He hands the boy the coin, but his eyes are directed to his wife's. TRAVIS takes the money happily.*)

TRAVIS: Thanks, Daddy.

(*He starts out. RUTH watches both of them with murder in her eyes. WALTER stands and stares back at her with defiance, and suddenly reaches into his pocket again on an afterthought.*)

WALTER (*without even looking at his son, still staring hard at his wife*): In fact, here's another fifty cents . . . Buy yourself some fruit today—or take a taxi cab to school or something!

TRAVIS: Whoopee—

(*He leaps up and clasps his father around the middle with his legs, and they face each other in mutual appreciation; slowly WALTER LEE peeks around the boy to catch the violent rays from his wife's eyes and draws his head back as if shot.*)

WALTER: You better get down now—and get to school, man.

TRAVIS (*at the door*): O.K. Good-bye. (*He exits.*)

WALTER (*after him, pointing with pride*): That's my boy. (*She looks at him in disgust and turns back to her work.*) You know what I was thinking 'bout in the bathroom this morning?

RUTH: No.

WALTER: How come you always try to be so pleasant!

RUTH: What is there to be pleasant 'bout!

WALTER: You want to know what I was thinking 'bout in the bathroom or not!

RUTH: I know what you was thinking 'bout.

WALTER (*ignoring her*): 'Bout what me and Willy Harris was talking about last night.

RUTH (*immediately—a refrain*): Willy Harris is a good-for-nothing loud mouth.

WALTER: Anybody who talks to me has got to be a good-for-nothing loud mouth, ain't he? And what you know about who is just a good-for-nothing loud mouth? Charlie Atkins was just a "good-for-nothing loud mouth" too, wasn't he! When he wanted me to go in the dry-cleaning business with him. And now—he's grossing a hundred thousand a year. A hundred thousand dollars a year! You still call *him* a loud mouth!

RUTH (*bitterly*): Oh, Walter Lee . . .

(*She folds her head on her arms over on the table.*)

WALTER (*rising and coming to her and standing over her*): You tired, ain't you? Tired of everything. Me, the boy, the way we live—this beat-up hole—everything. Ain't you? (*She doesn't look up, doesn't answer.*) So tired—moaning and groaning all the time, but you wouldn't do nothing to help, would you? You couldn't be on my side that long for nothing, could you?

RUTH: Walter, please leave me alone.

WALTER: A man needs for a woman to back him up . . .

RUTH: Walter—

WALTER: Mama would listen to you. You know she listen to you more than she do me and Bennie. She think more of you. All you have to do is just sit down with her when you drinking your coffee one morning and talking 'bout things like you do and—(*He sits down beside her and demonstrates graphically what he thinks her methods and tone should be.*)—you just sip your coffee, see, and say easy like that you been thinking 'bout that deal Walter Lee is so interested in, 'bout the store and all, and sip some more coffee, like what you saying ain't really that important to you—And the next thing you know, she be listening good and asking you questions and when I come home—I can tell her the details. This ain't no fly-by-night proposition, baby. I mean we figured it out, me and Willy and Bobo.

RUTH (*with a frown*): Bobo?

WALTER: Yeah. You see, this little liquor store we got in mind cost seventy-five thousand and we figured the initial investment on the place be 'bout thirty thousand, see. That be ten thousand each. Course, there's a couple of hundred you got to pay so's you don't spend your life just waiting for them clowns to let your license get approved—

RUTH: You mean graft?

WALTER (*frowning impatiently*): Don't call it that. See there, that just goes to show you what women understand about the world. Baby, don't *nothing* happen for you in this world 'less you pay somebody off!

RUTH: Walter, leave me alone! (*She raises her head and stares at him vigorously—then says, more quietly.*) Eat your eggs, they gonna be cold.

WALTER (*straightening up from her and looking off*): That's it. There you are. Man say to his woman: I got me a dream. His woman say: Eat your eggs. (*Sadly, but gaining in power.*) Man say: I got to take hold of this here world, baby! And a woman will say: Eat your eggs and go to work. (*Passionately now.*) Man say: I got to change my life, I'm choking to death, baby! And his woman say—(*In utter anguish as he brings his fists down on his thighs.*)—Your eggs is getting cold!

RUTH (*softly*): Walter, that ain't none of our money.

WALTER (*not listening at all or even looking at her*): This morning, I was lookin' in the mirror and thinking about it . . . I'm thirty-five years old; I been married eleven years and I got a boy who sleeps in the living room—(*Very, very quietly.*)—and all I got to give him is stories about how rich white people live . . .

RUTH: Eat your eggs, Walter.

WALTER: *Damn my eggs . . . damn all the eggs that ever was!*

RUTH: Then go to work.

WALTER (*looking up at her*): See—I'm trying to talk to you 'bout myself—(*Shaking his head with the repetition.*)—and all you can say is eat them eggs and go to work.

RUTH (*wearily*): Honey, you never say nothing new. I listen to you every day, every night and every morning and you never say nothing new. (*Shrugging.*) So you would rather *be* Mr. Arnold than be his chauffeur. So—I would *rather* be living in Buckingham Palace.

WALTER: That is just what is wrong with the colored woman in this world . . . Don't understand about building their men up and making 'em feel like they somebody. Like they can do something.

RUTH (*drily, but to hurt*): There *are* colored men who do things.

WALTER: No thanks to the colored woman.

RUTH: Well, being a colored woman, I guess I can't help myself none.

(*She rises and gets the ironing board and sets it up and attacks a huge pile of rough-dried clothes, sprin-*

*kling them in preparation for the ironing and then roll-
ing them into tight fat balls.*)

WALTER (*mumbling*): We one group of men
tied to a race of women with small minds.

(*His sister* BENEATHA *enters. She is about twenty,
as slim and intense as her brother. She is not as pretty
as her sister-in-law, but her lean, almost intellectual
face has a handsomeness of its own. She wears a
bright-red flannel nightie, and her thick hair stands
wildly about her head. Her speech is a mixture of
many things; it is different from the rest of the family's
insofar as education has permeated her sense of English
—and perhaps the Midwest rather than the South
has finally—at last—won out in her inflection; but
not altogether, because over all of it is a soft slurring
and transformed use of vowels which is the decided
influence of the Southside. She passes through the room
without looking at either* RUTH *or* WALTER *and goes to
the outside door and looks, a little blindly, out to the
bathroom. She sees that it has been lost to the Johnsons.
She closes the door with a sleepy vengeance and crosses
to the table and sits down a little defeated.*)

BENEATHA: I am going to start timing those
people.

WALTER: You should get up earlier.

BENEATHA (*her face in her hands. She is still
fighting the urge to go back to bed*): Really—would
you suggest dawn? Where's the paper?

WALTER (*pushing the paper across the table to her
as he studies her almost clinically, as though he has
never seen her before*): You a horrible-looking chick
at this hour.

BENEATHA (*drily*): Good morning everybody.

WALTER (*senselessly*): How is school coming?

BENEATHA (*in the same spirit*): Lovely. Lovely.
And you know, biology is the greatest. (*Looking
up at him.*) I dissected something that looked just
like you yesterday.

WALTER: I just wondered if you've made up
your mind and everything.

BENEATHA (*gaining in sharpness and impatience*): And what did I answer yesterday morning—and the day before that?

RUTH (*from the ironing board, like someone disinterested and old*): Don't be so nasty, Bennie.

BENEATHA (*still to her brother*): And the day
before that and the day before that!

WALTER (*defensively*): I'm interested in you.
Something wrong with that? Ain't many girls
who decide—

WALTER *and* BENEATHA (*in unison*): —"to be a
doctor."

(*Silence.*)

WALTER: Have we figured out yet just exactly
how much medical school is going to cost?

RUTH: Walter Lee, why don't you leave that
girl alone and get out of here to work?

BENEATHA (*exits to the bathroom and bangs on the
door*): Come on out of there, please! (*She comes
back into the room.*)

WALTER (*looking at his sister intently*): You
know the check is coming tomorrow.

BENEATHA (*turning on him with a sharpness all
her own*): That money belongs to Mama, Walter,
and it's for her to decide how she wants to use it.
I don't care if she wants to buy a house or a
rocket ship or just nail it up somewhere and look
at it. It's hers. Not ours—*hers.*

WALTER (*bitterly*): Now ain't that fine! You
just got your mother's interest at heart, ain't
you, girl? You such a nice girl—but if Mama
got that money she can always take a few
thousand and help you through school too—
can't she?

BENEATHA: I have never asked anyone around
here to do anything for me!

WALTER: No! And the line between asking
and just accepting when the time comes is big
and wide—ain't it!

BENEATHA (*with fury*): What do you want
from me, Brother—that I quit school or just
drop dead, which!

WALTER: I don't want nothing but for you to
stop acting holy 'round here. Me and Ruth done
made some sacrifices for you—why can't you do
something for the family?

RUTH: Walter, don't be dragging me in it.

WALTER: You are in it—Don't you get up
and go work in somebody's kitchen for the last
three years to help put clothes on her back?

RUTH: Oh, Walter—that's not fair . . .

WALTER: It ain't that nobody expects you to
get on your knees and say thank you, Brother;
thank you, Ruth; thank you Mama—and thank
you, Travis, for wearing the same pair of shoes
for two semesters—

BENEATHA (*dropping to her knees*): Well—I *do*
—all right?—thank everybody . . . and forgive
me for ever wanting to be anything at all . . .
forgive me, forgive me!

RUTH: Please stop it! Your mama'll hear you.

WALTER: Who the hell told you you had to
be a doctor? If you so crazy 'bout messing 'round
with sick people—then go be a nurse like other
women—or just get married and be quiet . . .

BENEATHA: Well—you finally got it said . . .

It took you three years but you finally got it said. Walter, give up; leave me alone—it's Mama's money.

WALTER: *He was my father, too!*

BENEATHA: So what? He was mine, too—and Travis' grandfather—but the insurance money belongs to Mama. Picking on me is not going to make her give it to you to invest in any liquor stores—(*Underbreath, dropping into a chair.*)—and I for one say, God bless Mama for that!

WALTER (*to* RUTH): See—did you hear? Did you hear!

RUTH: Honey, please go to work.

WALTER: Nobody in this house is ever going to understand me.

BENEATHA: Because you're a nut.

WALTER: Who's a nut?

BENEATHA: You—you are a nut. Thee is mad, boy.

WALTER (*looking at his wife and his sister from the door, very sadly*): The world's most backward race of people, and that's a fact.

BENEATHA (*turning slowly in her chair.*): And then there are all those prophets who would lead us out of the wilderness—(WALTER *slams out of the house.*)—into the swamps!

RUTH: Bennie, why you always gotta be pickin' on your brother? Can't you be a little sweeter sometimes? (*Door opens.* WALTER *walks in.*)

WALTER (*to* RUTH): I need some money for carfare.

RUTH (*looks at him, then warms; teasing, but tenderly*): Fifty cents? (*She goes to her bag and gets money.*) Here, take a taxi.

(WALTER *exits.* MAMA *enters. She is a woman in her early sixties, full-bodied and strong. She is one of those women of a certain grace and beauty who wear it so unobstrusively that it takes a while to notice. Her dark-brown face is surrounded by the total whiteness of her hair, and, being a woman who has adjusted to many things in life and overcome many more, her face is full of strength. She has, we can see, wit and faith of a kind that keep her eyes lit and full of interest and expectancy. She is, in a word, a beautiful woman. Her bearing is perhaps most like the noble bearing of the women of the Hereros of Southwest Africa—rather as if she imagines that as she walks she still bears a basket or a vessel upon her head. Her speech, on the other hand, is as careless as her carriage is precise—she is inclined to slur everything—but her voice is perhaps not so much quiet as simply soft.*)

MAMA: Who that 'round here slamming doors at this hour?

(*She crosses through the room, goes to the window, opens it, and brings in a feeble little plant growing doggedly in a small pot on the window sill. She feels the dirt and puts it back out.*)

RUTH: That was Walter Lee. He and Bennie was at it again.

MAMA: My children and they tempers. Lord, if this little old plant don't get more sun than it's been getting it ain't never going to see spring again. (*She turns from the window.*) What's the matter with you this morning, Ruth? You looks right peaked. You aiming to iron all them things? Leave some for me. I'll get to 'em this afternoon. Bennie honey, it's too drafty for you to be sitting 'round half dressed. Where's your robe?

BENEATHA: In the cleaners.

MAMA: Well, go get mine and put it on.

BENEATHA: I'm not cold, Mama, honest.

MAMA: I know—but you so thin . . .

BENEATHA (*irritably*): Mama, I'm not cold.

MAMA (*seeing the make-down bed as* TRAVIS *has left it*): Lord have mercy, look at that poor bed. Bless his heart—he tries, don't he? (*She moves to the bed* TRAVIS *has sloppily made up.*)

RUTH: No—he don't half try at all 'cause he knows you going to come along behind him and fix everything. That's just how come he don't know how to do nothing right now—you done spoiled that boy so.

MAMA: Well—he's a little boy. Ain't supposed to know 'bout housekeeping. My baby, that's what he is. What you fix for his breakfast this morning?

RUTH (*angrily*): I feed my son, Lena!

MAMA: I ain't meddling—(*Underbreath; busybodyish.*) I just noticed all last week he had cold cereal, and when it starts getting this chilly in the fall a child ought to have some hot grits or something when he goes out in the cold—

RUTH (*furious*): I gave him hot oats—is that all right!

MAMA: I ain't meddling. (*Pause.*) Put a lot of nice butter on it? (RUTH *shoots her an angry look and does not reply.*) He likes lots of butter.

RUTH (*exasperated*): Lena—

MAMA (*to* BENEATHA. MAMA *is inclined to wander conversationally sometimes*): What was you and your brother fussing 'bout this morning?

BENEATHA: It's not important, Mama. (*She gets up and goes to look out at the bathroom, which is apparently free, and she picks up her towels and rushes out.*)

MAMA: What was they fighting about?

RUTH: Now you know as well as I do.

MAMA (*shaking her head*): Brother still worrying hisself sick about that money?

RUTH: You know he is.

MAMA: You had breakfast?

RUTH: Some coffee.

MAMA: Girl, you better start eating and looking after yourself better. You almost thin as Travis.

RUTH: Lena—

MAMA: Uh-hunh?

RUTH: What are you going to do with it?

MAMA: Now don't you start, child. It's too early in the morning to be talking about money. It ain't Christian.

RUTH: It's just that he got his heart set on that store—

MAMA: You mean that liquor store that Willy Harris want him to invest in?

RUTH: Yes—

MAMA: We ain't no business people, Ruth. We just plain working folks.

RUTH: Ain't nobody business people till they go into business. Walter Lee say colored people ain't never going to start getting ahead till they start gambling on some different kinds of things in the world—investments and things.

MAMA: What done got into you, girl? Walter Lee done finally sold you on investing.

RUTH: No. Mama, something is happening between Walter and me. I don't know what it is—but he needs something—something I can't give him any more. He needs this chance, Lena.

MAMA (*frowning deeply*): But liquor, honey—

RUTH: Well—like Walter say—I spec people going to always be drinking themselves some liquor.

MAMA: Well—whether they drinks it or not ain't none of my business. But whether I go into business selling it to 'em *is,* and I don't want that on my ledger this late in life. (*Stopping suddenly and studying her daughter-in-law.*) Ruth Younger, what's the matter with you today? You look like you could fall over right there.

RUTH: I'm tired.

MAMA: Then you better stay home from work today.

RUTH: I can't stay home. She'd be calling up the agency and screaming at them, "My girl didn't come in today—send me somebody! My girl didn't come in!" Oh, she just have a fit . . .

MAMA: Well, let her have it. I'll just call her up and say you got the flu—

RUTH (*laughing*): Why the flu?

MAMA: 'Cause it sounds respectable to 'em. Something white people get, too. They know 'bout the flu. Otherwise they think you been cut up or something when you tell 'em you sick.

RUTH: I got to go in. We need the money.

MAMA: Somebody would of thought my children done all but starved to death the way they talk about money here late. Child, we got a great big old check coming tomorrow.

RUTH (*sincerely, but also self-righteously*): Now that's your money. It ain't got nothing to do with me. We all feel like that—Walter and Bennie and me—even Travis.

MAMA (*thoughtfully, and suddenly very far away*): Ten thousand dollars—

RUTH: Sure is wonderful.

MAMA: Ten thousand dollars.

RUTH: You know what you should do, Miss Lena? You should take yourself a trip somewhere. To Europe or South America or someplace—

MAMA (*throwing up her hands at the thought*): Oh child!

RUTH: I'm serious. Just pack up and leave! Go on away and enjoy yourself some. Forget about the family and have yourself a ball for once in your life—

MAMA (*drily*): You sound like I'm just about ready to die. Who'd go with me? What I look like wandering 'round Europe by myself?

RUTH: Shoot—these here rich white women do it all the time. They don't think nothing of packing up they suitcases and piling on one of them big steamships and—swoosh!—they gone, child.

MAMA: Something always told me I wasn't no rich white woman.

RUTH: Well—what are you going to do with it then?

MAMA: I ain't rightly decided. (*Thinking. She speaks now with emphasis.*) Some of it got to be put away for Beneatha and her schoolin'—and ain't nothing going to touch that part of it. Nothing. (*She waits several seconds, trying to make up her mind about something, and looks at* RUTH *a little tentatively before going on.*) Been thinking that we maybe could meet the notes on a little old two-story somewhere, with a yard where Travis could play in the summertime, if we use part of the insurance for a down payment and everybody kind of pitch in. I could maybe take on a little day work again, few days a week—

RUTH (*studying her mother-in-law furtively and concentrating on her ironing, anxious to encourage without seeming to*): Well, Lord knows, we've put enough rent into this here rat trap to pay for four houses by now . . .

MAMA (*looking up at the words "rat trap" and then looking around and leaning back and sighing—in a suddenly reflective mood—*): "Rat trap"—yes, that's all it is. (*Smiling.*) I remember just as well the day me and Big Walter moved in here. Hadn't been married but two weeks and wasn't planning on living here no more than a year. (*She shakes her head at the dissolved dream.*) We was going to set away, little by little, don't you know, and buy a little place out in Morgan Park. We had even picked out the house. (*Chuckling a little.*) Looks right dumpy today. But Lord, child, you should know all the dreams I had 'bout buying that house and fixing it up and making me a little garden in the back—(*She waits and stops smiling.*) And didn't none of it happen. (*Dropping her hands in a futile gesture.*)

RUTH (*keeps her head down, ironing*): Yes, life can be a barrel of disappointments, sometimes.

MAMA: Honey, Big Walter would come in here some nights back then and slump down on that couch there and just look at the rug, and look at me and look at the rug and then back at me—and I'd know he was down then . . . really down. (*After a second very long and thoughtful pause; she is seeing back to times that only she can see.*) And then, Lord, when I lost that baby—little Claude—I almost thought I was going to lose Big Walter too. Oh, that man grieved hisself! He was one man to love his children.

RUTH: Ain't nothin' can tear at you like losin' your baby.

MAMA: I guess that's how come that man finally worked hisself to death like he done. Like he was fighting his own war with this here world that took his baby from him.

RUTH: He sure was a fine man, all right. I always liked Mr. Younger.

MAMA: Crazy 'bout his children! God knows there was plenty wrong with Walter Younger—hard-headed, mean, kind of wild with women—plenty wrong with him. But he sure loved his children. Always wanted them to have something—be something. That's where Brother gets all these notions, I reckon. Big Walter used to say, he'd get right wet in the eyes sometimes, lean his head back with the water standing in his eyes and say, "Seem like God didn't see fit to give the black man nothing but dreams—but He did give us children to make them dreams seem worth while." (*She smiles.*) He could talk like that, don't you know.

RUTH: Yes, he sure could. He was a good man, Mr. Younger.

MAMA: Yes, a fine man—just couldn't never catch up with his dreams, that's all.

(BENEATHA *comes in, brushing her hair and looking up to the ceiling, where the sound of a vacuum cleaner has started up.*)

BENEATHA: What could be so dirty on that woman's rugs that she has to vacuum them every single day?

RUTH: I wish certain young women 'round here who I could name would take inspiration about certain rugs in a certain apartment I could also mention.

BENEATHA (*shrugging*): How much cleaning can a house need, for Christ's sakes.

MAMA (*not liking the Lord's name used thus*): Bennie!

RUTH: Just listen to her—just listen!

BENEATHA: Oh, God!

MAMA: If you use the Lord's name just one more time—

BENEATHA (*a bit of a whine*): Oh, Mama—

RUTH: Fresh—just fresh as salt, this girl!

BENEATHA (*drily*): Well—if the salt loses its savor—

MAMA: Now that will do. I just ain't going to have you 'round here reciting the scriptures in vain—you hear me?

BENEATHA: How did I manage to get on everybody's wrong side by just walking into a room?

RUTH: If you weren't so fresh—

BENEATHA: Ruth, I'm twenty years old.

MAMA: What time you be home from school today?

BENEATHA: Kind of late. (*With enthusiasm.*) Madeline is going to start my guitar lessons today.

(MAMA *and* RUTH *look up with the same expression.*)

MAMA: Your *what* kind of lessons?

BENEATHA: Guitar.

RUTH: Oh, Father!

MAMA: How come you done taken it in your mind to learn to play the guitar?

BENEATHA: I just want to, that's all.

MAMA (*smiling*): Lord, child, don't you know what to do with yourself? How long it going to be before you get tired of this now—like you got tired of that little play-acting group you joined last year? (*Looking at* RUTH.) And what was it the year before that?

RUTH: The horseback-riding club for which she bought that fifty-five-dollar riding habit that's been hanging in the closet ever since!

MAMA (*to* BENEATHA): Why you got to flit so from one thing to another, baby?

BENEATHA (*sharply*): I just want to learn to play the guitar. Is there anything wrong with that?

MAMA: Ain't nobody trying to stop you. I just wonders sometimes why you has to flit so from one thing to another all the time. You ain't never done nothing with all that camera equipment you brought home—

BENEATHA: I don't flit! I—I experiment with different forms of expression—

RUTH: Like riding a horse?

BENEATHA: —People have to express themselves one way or another.

MAMA: What is it you want to express?

BENEATHA (*angrily*): Me! (MAMA *and* RUTH *look at each other and burst into raucous laughter.*) Don't worry—I don't expect you to understand.

MAMA (*to change the subject*): Who you going out with tomorrow night?

BENEATHA (*with displeasure*): George Murchison again.

MAMA (*pleased*): Oh—you getting a little sweet on him?

RUTH: You ask me, this child ain't sweet on nobody but herself—(*Underbreath.*) Express herself!

(*They laugh.*)

BENEATHA: Oh—I like George all right, Mama. I mean I like him enough to go out with him and stuff, but—

RUTH (*for devilment*): What does *and stuff* mean?

BENEATHA: Mind your own business.

MAMA: Stop picking at her now, Ruth. (*A thoughtful pause, and then a suspicious sudden look at her daughter as she turns in her chair for emphasis.*) What *does* it mean?

BENEATHA (*wearily*): Oh, I just mean I couldn't ever really be serious about George. He's—he's so shallow.

RUTH: Shallow—what do you mean he's shallow? He's *Rich!*

MAMA: Hush, Ruth.

BENEATHA: I know he's rich. He knows he's rich, too.

RUTH: Well—what other qualities a man got to have to satisfy you, little girl?

BENEATHA: You wouldn't even begin to understand. Anybody who married Walter could not possibly understand.

MAMA (*outraged*): What kind of way is that to talk about your brother?

BENEATHA: Brother is a flip—let's face it.

MAMA (*to* RUTH, *helplessly*): What's a flip?

RUTH (*glad to add kindling*): She's saying he's crazy.

BENEATHA: Not crazy. Brother isn't really crazy yet—he—he's an elaborate neurotic.

MAMA: Hush your mouth!

BENEATHA: As for George. Well. George looks good—he's got a beautiful car and he takes me to nice places and, as my sister-in-law says, he is probably the richest boy I will ever get to know and I even like him sometimes—but if the Youngers are sitting around waiting to see if their little Bennie is going to tie up the family with the Murchisons, they are wasting their time.

RUTH: You mean you wouldn't marry George Murchison if he asked you someday? That pretty, rich thing? Honey, I knew you was odd—

BENEATHA: No I would not marry him if all I felt for him was what I feel now. Besides, George's family wouldn't really like it.

MAMA: Why not?

BENEATHA: Oh, Mama—the Murchisons are honest-to-God-real-*live*-rich colored people, and the only people in the world who are more snobbish than rich white people are rich colored people. I thought everybody knew that. I've met Mrs. Murchison. She's a scene!

MAMA: You must not dislike people 'cause they well off, honey.

BENEATHA: Why not? It makes just as much sense as disliking people 'cause they are poor, and lots of people do that.

RUTH (*a wisdom-of-the-ages manner. To* MAMA): Well, she'll get over some of this—

BENEATHA: Get over it? What are you talking about, Ruth? Listen, I'm going to be a doctor. I'm not worried about who I'm going to marry yet—if I ever get married.

MAMA *and* RUTH: *If!*

MAMA: Now, Bennie—

BENEATHA: Oh, I probably will . . . but first I'm going to be a doctor, and George, for one, still thinks that's pretty funny. I couldn't be bothered with that. I am going to be a doctor and everybody around here better understand that!

MAMA (*kindly*): 'Course you going to be a doctor, honey, God willing.

BENEATHA (*drily*): God hasn't got a thing to do with it.

MAMA: Beneatha—that just wasn't necessary.

BENEATHA: Well—neither is God. I get sick of hearing about God.

MAMA: Beneatha!

BENEATHA: I mean it! I'm just tired of hearing about God all the time. What has He got to do with anything? Does he pay tuition?

MAMA: You 'bout to get your fresh little jaw slapped!

RUTH: That's just what she needs, all right!

BENEATHA: Why? Why can't I say what I want to around here, like everybody else?

MAMA: It don't sound nice for a young girl to say things like that—you wasn't brought up that way. Me and your father went to trouble to get you and Brother to church every Sunday.

BENEATHA: Mama, you don't understand. It's all a matter of ideas, and God is just one idea I don't accept. It's not important. I am not going out and be immoral or commit crimes because I don't believe in God. I don't even think about it. It's just that I get tired of Him getting credit for all the things the human race achieves through its own stubborn effort. There simply is no blasted God—there is only man and it is he who makes miracles!

(MAMA *absorbs this speech, studies her daughter and rises slowly and crosses to* BENEATHA *and slaps her powerfully across the face. After, there is only silence and the daughter drops her eyes from her mother's face, and* MAMA *is very tall before her.*)

MAMA: Now—you say after me, in my mother's house there is still God. (*There is a long pause and* BENEATHA *stares at the floor wordlessly.* MAMA *repeats the phrase with precision and cool emotion.*) In my mother's house there is still God.

BENEATHA: In my mother's house there is still God. (*A long pause.*)

MAMA (*walking away from* BENEATHA, *too disturbed for triumphant posture. Stopping and turning back to her daughter*): There are some ideas we ain't going to have in this house. Not long as I am at the head of this family.

BENEATHA: Yes, ma'am.

(MAMA *walks out of the room.*)

RUTH (*almost gently, with profound understanding*): You think you a woman, Bennie —but you still a little girl. What you did was childish—so you got treated like a child.

BENEATHA: I see. (*Quietly.*) I also see that everybody thinks it's all right for Mama to be a tyrant. But all the tyranny in the world will never put a God in the heavens!

(*She picks up her books and goes out.*)

RUTH (*goes to* MAMA's *door*): She said she was sorry.

MAMA (*coming out, going to her plant*): They frightens me, Ruth. My children.

RUTH: You got good children, Lena. They just a little off sometimes—but they're good.

MAMA: No—there's something come down between me and them that don't let us understand each other and I don't know what it is. One done almost lost his mind thinking 'bout money all the time and the other done commence to talk about things I can't seem to understand in no form or fashion. What is it that's changing, Ruth?

RUTH (*soothingly, older than her years*): Now . . . you taking it all too seriously. You just got strong-willed children and it takes a strong woman like you to keep 'em in hand.

MAMA (*looking at her plant and sprinkling a little water on it*): They spirited all right, my children. Got to admit they got spirit—Bennie and Walter. Like this little old plant that ain't never had enough sunshine or nothing—and look at it . . .

(*She has her back to* RUTH, *who has had to stop ironing and lean against something and put the back of her hand to her forehead.*)

RUTH (*trying to keep* MAMA *from noticing*): You . . . sure . . . loves that little old thing, don't you? . . .

MAMA: Well, I always wanted me a garden like I used to see sometimes at the back of the houses down home. This plant is close as I ever got to having one. (*She looks out of the window as she replaces the plant.*) Lord, ain't nothing as dreary as the view from this window on a dreary day, is there? Why ain't you singing this morning, Ruth? Sing that "No Ways Tired." That song always lifts me up so—(*She turns at last to see that* RUTH *has slipped quietly into a chair, in a state of semiconsciousness.*) Ruth! Ruth honey— what's the matter with you . . . Ruth!

SCENE 2

(*It is the following morning; a Saturday morning, and house cleaning is in progress at the* YOUNGERS.

Furniture has been shoved hither and yon and MAMA *is giving the kitchen-area walls a washing down.* BENEATHA, *in dungarees, with a handkerchief tied around her face, is spraying insecticide into the cracks in the walls. As they work, the radio is on and a Southside disk-jockey program is inappropriately filling the house with a rather exotic saxophone blues.* TRAVIS, *the sole idle one, is leaning on his arms, looking out of the window.)*

TRAVIS: Grandmama, that stuff Bennie is using smells awful. Can I go downstairs, please?

MAMA: Did you get all them chores done already? I ain't seen you doing much.

TRAVIS: Yes'm—finished early. Where did Mama go this morning?

MAMA (*looking at* BENEATHA): She had to go on a little errand.

TRAVIS: Where?

MAMA: To tend to her business.

TRAVIS: Can I go outside then?

MAMA: Oh, I guess so. You better stay right in front of the house, though . . . and keep a good lookout for the postman.

TRAVIS: Yes'm (*He starts out and decides to give his* AUNT BENEATHA *a good swat on the legs as he passes her.*) Leave them poor little old cockroaches alone, they ain't bothering you none.

(*He runs as she swings the spray gun at him both viciously and playfully.* WALTER *enters from the bedroom and goes to the phone.*)

MAMA: Look out there, girl, before you be spilling some of that stuff on that child!

TRAVIS (*teasing*): That's right—look out now!

(*He exits.*)

BENEATHA (*drily*): I can't imagine that it would hurt him—it has never hurt the roaches.

MAMA: Well, little boys' hides ain't as tough as Southside roaches.

WALTER (*into phone*): Hello—Let me talk to Willy Harris.

MAMA: You better get over there behind the bureau. I seen one marching out of there like Napoleon yesterday.

WALTER: Hello, Willy? It ain't come yet. It'll be here in a few minutes. Did the lawyer give you the papers?

BENEATHA: There's really only one way to get rid of them, Mama—

MAMA: How?

BENEATHA: Set fire to this building.

WALTER: Good. Good. I'll be right over.

BENEATHA: Where did Ruth go, Walter?

WALTER: I don't know. (*He exits abruptly.*)

BENEATHA: Mama, where did Ruth go?

MAMA (*looking at her with meaning*): To the doctor, I think.

BENEATHA: The doctor? What's the matter. (*They exchange glances.*) You don't think—

MAMA (*with her sense of drama*): Now I ain't saying what I think. But I ain't never been wrong 'bout a woman neither.

(*The phone rings.*)

BENEATHA (*at the phone*): Hay-lo . . . (*Pause, and a moment of recognition.*) Well—when did you get back! . . . And how was it? . . . Of course I've missed you—in my way . . . This morning? No . . . house cleaning and all that and Mama hates it if I let people come over when the house is like this . . . You *have?* Well, that's different . . . What is it—Oh, what the hell, come on over . . . Right, see you then. (*She hangs up.*)

MAMA (*who has listened vigorously, as is her habit*): Who is that you inviting over here with this house looking like this? You ain't got the pride you was born with!

BENEATHA: Asagai doesn't care how houses look, Mama—he's an intellectual.

MAMA: *Who?*

BENEATHA: Asagai—Joseph Asagai. He's an African boy I met on campus. He's been studying in Canada all summer.

MAMA: What's his name?

BENEATHA: Asagai, Joseph. Ah-sah-guy . . . He's from Nigeria.

MAMA: Oh, that's the little country that was founded by slaves way back . . .

BENEATHA: No, Mama—that's Liberia.

MAMA: I don't think I never met no African before.

BENEATHA: Well, do me a favor and don't ask him a whole lot of ignorant questions about Africans. I mean, do they wear clothes and all that—

MAMA: Well, now, I guess if you think we so ignorant 'round here maybe you shouldn't bring your friends here—

BENEATHA: It's just that people ask such crazy things. All anyone seems to know about when it comes to Africa is Tarzan—

MAMA (*indignantly*): Why should I know anything about Africa?

BENEATHA: Why do you give money at church for the missionary work.

MAMA: Well, that's to help save people.

BENEATHA: You mean save them from *heathenism*—

MAMA (*innocently*): Yes.

BENEATHA: I'm afraid they need more salvation from the British and the French.

(RUTH *comes in forlornly and pulls off her coat with dejection. They both turn to look at her.*)

RUTH (*dispiritedly*): Well, I guess from all the happy faces—everybody knows.

BENEATHA: You pregnant?

MAMA: Lord have mercy, I sure hope it's a little old girl. Travis ought to have a sister.

(BENEATHA *and* RUTH *give her a hopeless look for this grandmotherly enthusiasm.*)

BENEATHA: How far along are you?

RUTH: Two months.

BENEATHA: Did you mean to? I mean did you plan it or was it an accident?

MAMA: What do you know about planning or not planning?

BENEATHA: Oh, Mama.

RUTH (*wearily*): She's twenty years old, Lena.

BENEATHA: Did you plan it, Ruth?

RUTH: Mind your own business.

BENEATHA: It is my business—where is he going to live, on the *roof?* (*There is silence following the remark as the three women react to the sense of it.*) Gee—I didn't mean that, Ruth, honest. Gee, I don't feel like that at all. I—I think it is wonderful.

RUTH (*dully*): Wonderful.

BENEATHA: Yes—really.

MAMA (*looking at* RUTH, *worried*): Doctor say everything going to be all right?

RUTH (*far away*): Yes—she says everything is going to be fine . . .

MAMA (*immediately suspicious*): "She"—What doctor you went to?

(RUTH *folds over, near hysteria.*)

MAMA (*worriedly hovering over* RUTH): Ruth honey—what's the matter with you—you sick?

(RUTH *has her fists clenched on her thighs and is fighting hard to suppress a scream that seems to be rising in her.*)

BENEATHA: What's the matter with her, Mama?

MAMA (*working her fingers in* RUTH's *shoulder to relax her*): She be all right. Women gets right depressed sometimes when they get her way. (*Speaking softly, expertly, rapidly.*) Now you just relax. That's right . . . just lean back, don't think 'bout nothing at all . . . nothing at all—

RUTH: I'm all right . . .

(*The glassy-eyed look melts and then she collapses into a fit of heavy sobbing. The bell rings.*)

BENEATHA: Oh, my God—that must be Asagai.

MAMA (*To* RUTH): Come on now, honey. You need to lie down and rest awhile . . . then have some nice hot food.

(*They exit,* RUTH's *weight on her mother-in-law.* BENEATHA, *herself profoundly disturbed, opens the door to admit a rather dramatic-looking young man with a large package.*)

ASAGAI: Hello, Alaiyo—

BENEATHA (*holding the door open and regarding him with pleasure*): Hello . . . (*Long pause.*) Well—come in. And please excuse everything. My mother was very upset about my letting anyone come here with the place like this.

ASAGAI (*coming into the room*): You look disturbed too . . . Is something wrong?

BENEATHA (*still at the door, absently*): Yes . . . we've all got acute ghetto-itus. (*She smiles and comes toward him, finding a cigarette and sitting.*) So—sit down! How was Canada?

ASAGAI (*a sophisticate*): Canadian.

BENEATHA (*looking at him*): I'm very glad you are back.

ASAGAI (*looking back at her in turn*): Are you really?

BENEATHA: Yes—very.

ASAGAI: Why—you were quite glad when I went away. What happened?

BENEATHA: You went away.

ASAGAI: Ahhhhhhhh.

BENEATHA: Before—you wanted to be so serious before there was time.

ASAGAI: How much time must there be before one knows what one feels?

BENEATHA (*stalling this particular conversation; her hands pressed together, in a deliberately childish gesture*): What did you bring me?

ASAGAI (*handing her the package*): Open it and see.

BENEATHA (*eagerly opening the package and drawing out some records and the colorful robes of a Nigerian woman*): Oh, Asagai! . . . You got them for me! . . . How beautiful . . . and the records too! (*She lifts out the robes and runs to the mirror with them and holds the drapery up in front of herself.*)

ASAGAI (*coming to her at the mirror*): I shall have to teach you how to drape it properly. (*He flings the material about her for the moment and stands back to look at her.*) Ah—Oh-pay-gay-day, *oh-gbah-mu-shay.* (*A Yoruba exclamation for admiration.*) You wear it well . . . very well . . . mutilated hair and all.

BENEATHA (*turning suddenly*): My hair—what's wrong with my hair?

ASAGAI (*shrugging*): Were you born with it like that?

BENEATHA (*reaching up to touch it*): No . . . of course not. (*She looks back to the mirror, disturbed.*)

ASAGAI (*smiling*): How then?

BENEATHA: You know perfectly well how . . . as crinkly as yours . . . that's how.

ASAGAI: And it is ugly to you that way?

BENEATHA (*quickly*): Oh, no—not ugly . . . (*More slowly, apologetically.*) But it's so hard to manage when it's well—raw.

ASAGAI: And so to accommodate that—you mutilate it every week?

BENEATHA: It's not mutilation!

ASAGAI (*laughing aloud at her seriousness*): Oh . . . please! I am only teasing you because you are so very serious about these things. (*He stands back from her and folds his arms across his chest as he watches her pulling at her hair and frowning in the mirror.*) Do you remember the first time you met me at school? . . . (*He laughs.*) You came up to me and you said—and I thought you were the most serious little thing I had ever seen—you said: (*He imitates her.*) "Mr. Asagai—I want very much to talk with you. About Africa. You see, Mr. Asagai, I am looking for my *identity!*" (*He laughs.*)

BENEATHA (*turning to him, not laughing*): Yes —(*Her face is quizzical, profoundly disturbed.*)

ASAGAI (*still teasing and reaching out and taking her face in his hands and turning her profile to him*): Well . . . it is true that this is not so much a profile of a Hollywood queen as perhaps a queen of the Nile—(*A mock dismissal of the importance of the question.*) But what does it matter? Assimilationism is so popular in your country.

BENEATHA (*wheeling, passionately, sharply*): I am not an assimilationist!

ASAGAI (*the protest hangs in the room for a moment and ASAGAI studies her, his laughter fading*): Such a serious one. (*There is a pause.*) So—you like the robes? You must take excellent care of them— they are from my sister's personal wardrobe.

BENEATHA (*with incredulity*): You—you sent all the way home—for me?

ASAGAI (*with charm*): For you—I would do much more . . . Well, that is what I came for. I must go.

BENEATHA: Will you call me Monday?

ASAGAI: Yes . . . We have a great deal to talk about. I mean about identity and time and all that.

BENEATHA: Time?

ASAGAI: Yes. About how much time one needs to know what one feels.

BENEATHA: You never understood that there is more than one kind of feeling which can exist between a man and a woman—or, at least, there should be.

ASAGAI (*shaking his head negatively but gently*): No. Between a man and a woman there need be only one kind of feeling. I have that for you . . . Now even . . . right this moment . . .

BENEATHA: I know—and by itself—it won't do. I can find that anywhere.

ASAGAI: For a woman it should be enough.

BENEATHA: I know—because that's what it says in all the novels that men write. But it isn't. Go ahead and laugh—but I'm not interested in being someone's little episode in America or—(*With feminine vengeance.*)—one of them! (ASAGAI *has burst into laughter again.*) That's funny as hell, huh!

ASAGAI: It's just that every American girl I have known has said that to me. White—black —in this you are all the same. And the same speech, too!

BENEATHA (*angrily*): Yuk, yuk, yuk!

ASAGAI: It's how you can be sure that the world's most liberated women are not liberated at all. You all talk about it too much!

(MAMA *enters and is immediately all social charm because of the presence of a guest.*)

BENEATHA: Oh—Mama—this is Mr. Asagai.

MAMA: How do you do?

ASAGAI (*total politeness to an elder*): How do you do, Mrs. Younger. Please forgive me for coming at such an outrageous hour on a Saturday.

MAMA: Well, you are quite welcome. I just hope you understand that our house don't always look like this. (*Chatterish.*) You must come again. I would love to hear all about—(*Not sure of the name.*)—your country. I think it's so sad the way our American Negroes don't know nothing about Africa 'cept Tarzan and all that. And all that money they pour into these churches when they ought to be helping you people over there drive out them French and Englishmen done taken away your land. (*The mother flashes a slightly superior look at her daughter upon completion of the recitation.*)

ASAGAI (*taken aback by this sudden and acutely unrelated expression of sympathy*): Yes . . . yes . . .

MAMA (*smiling at him suddenly and relaxing and looking him over*): How many miles is it from here to where you come from?

ASAGAI: Many thousands.

MAMA (*looking at him as she would* WALTER): I bet you don't half look after yourself, being away from your mama either. I spec you better come 'round here from time to time and get yourself some decent home-cooked meals . . .

ASAGAI (*moved*): Thank you. Thank you very much. (*They are all quiet, then—.*) Well . . . I must go. I will call you Monday, Alaiyo.

MAMA: What's that he call you?

ASAGAI: Oh—"Alaiyo." I hope you don't mind. It is what you would call a nickname, I think. It is a Yoruba word. I am a Yoruba.

MAMA (*looking at* BENEATHA): I—I thought he was from—

ASAGAI (*understanding*): Nigeria is my country. Yoruba is my tribal origin—

BENEATHA: You didn't tell us what Alaiyo means . . . for all I know, you might be calling me Little Idiot or something . . .

ASAGAI: Well . . . let me see . . . I do not know how just to explain it . . . The sense of a thing can be so different when it changes languages.

BENEATHA: You're evading.

ASAGAI: No—really it is difficult . . . (*Thinking.*) It means . . . it means One for Whom Bread—Food—Is Not Enough. (*He looks at her.*) Is that all right?

BENEATHA (*understanding, softly*): Thank you.

MAMA (*looking from one to the other and not understanding any of it*): Well . . . that's nice . . . You must come see us again—Mr.—

ASAGAI: Ah-sah-guy . . .

MAMA: Yes . . . Do come again.

ASAGAI: Good-bye. (*He exits.*)

MAMA (*after him*): Lord, that's a pretty thing just went out here! (*Insinuatingly, to her daughter.*) Yes, I guess I see why we done commence to get so interested in Africa 'round here. Missionaries my aunt Jenny! (*She exits.*)

BENEATHA: Oh, Mama! . . . (*She picks up the Nigerian dress and holds it up to her in front of the mirror again. She sets the headdress on haphazardly and then notices her hair again and clutches at it and then replaces the headdress and frowns at herself. Then she starts to wriggle in front of the mirror as she thinks a Nigerian woman might.* TRAVIS *enters and regards her.*)

TRAVIS: You cracking up?

BENEATHA: Shut up. (*She pulls the headdress off and looks at herself in the mirror and clutches at her*

hair again and squinches her eyes as if trying to imagine something. Then, suddenly, she gets her raincoat and kerchief and hurriedly prepares for going out.*)

MAMA (*coming back into the room*): She's resting now. Travis, baby, run next door and ask Miss Johnson to please let me have a little kitchen cleanser. This here can is empty as Jacob's kettle.

TRAVIS: I just came in.

MAMA: Do as you told. (*He exits and she looks at her daughter.*) Where you going?

BENEATHA (*halting at the door*): To become a queen of the Nile! (*She exits in a breathless blaze of glory.* RUTH *appears in the bedroom doorway.*)

MAMA: Who told you to get up?

RUTH: Ain't nothing wrong with me to be lying in no bed for. Where did Bennie go?

MAMA (*drumming her fingers*): Far as I could make out—to Egypt. (RUTH *just looks at her.*) What time is it getting to?

RUTH: Ten twenty. And the mailman going to ring that bell this morning just like he done every morning for the last umpteen years.

(TRAVIS *comes in with the cleanser can.*)

TRAVIS: She say to tell you that she don't have much.

MAMA (*angrily*): Lord, some people I could name sure is tight-fisted! (*Directing her grandson.*) Mark two cans of cleanser down on the list there. If she that hard up for kitchen cleanser, I sure don't want to forget to get her none!

RUTH: Lena—maybe the woman is just short on cleanser—

MAMA (*not listening*): —Much baking powder as she done borrowed from me all these years, she could of done gone into the baking business!

(*The bell sounds suddenly and sharply and all three are stunned—serious and silent—mid-speech. In spite of all the other conversations and distractions of the morning, this is what they have been waiting for, even* TRAVIS, *who looks helplessly from his mother to his grandmother.* RUTH *is the first to come to life again.*)

RUTH (*to* TRAVIS): *Get down them steps, boy!*

(TRAVIS *snaps to life and flies out to get the mail.*)

MAMA (*her eyes wide, her hand to her breast*): You mean it done really come?

RUTH (*excited*): Oh, Miss Lena!

MAMA (*collecting herself*): Well . . . I don't know what we all so excited about 'round here for. We known it was coming for months.

RUTH: That's a whole lot different from having it come and being able to hold it in your hands . . . a piece of paper worth ten thousand dollars . . . (TRAVIS *bursts back into the room. He holds the envelope high above his head, like a little dancer, his face is radiant and he is breathless. He moves to his grandmother with sudden slow ceremony and puts the envelope into her hands. She accepts it, and then merely holds it and looks at it.*) Come on! Open it . . . Lord have mercy, I wish Walter Lee was here!

TRAVIS: Open it, Grandmama!

MAMA (*staring at it*): Now you all be quiet. It's just a check.

RUTH: Open it . . .

MAMA (*still staring at it*): Now don't act silly . . . We ain't never been no people to act silly 'bout no money—

RUTH (*swiftly*): We ain't never had none before— *open it!*

(MAMA *finally makes a good strong tear and pulls out the thin blue slice of paper and inspects it closely. The boy and his mother study it raptly over* MAMA's *shoulders.*)

MAMA: *Travis!* (*She is counting off with doubt.*) Is that the right number of zeros?

TRAVIS: Yes'm . . . ten thousand dollars. Gaalee, Grandmama, you rich.

MAMA (*she holds the check away from her, still looking at it; slowly her face sobers into a mask of unhappiness*): Ten thousand dollars. (*She hands it to* RUTH.) Put it away somewhere, Ruth. (*She does not look at* RUTH; *her eyes seem to be seeing something somewhere very far off.*) Ten thousand dollars they give you. Ten thousand dollars.

TRAVIS (*to his mother, sincerely*): What's the matter with Grandmama—don't she want to be rich?

RUTH (*distractedly*): You go on out and play now, baby. (TRAVIS *exits.* MAMA *starts wiping dishes absently, humming intently to herself.* RUTH *turns to her, with kind exasperation.*) You've gone and got yourself upset.

MAMA (*not looking at her*): I spec if it wasn't for you all . . . I would just put that money away or give it to the church or something.

RUTH: Now what kind of talk is that. Mr. Younger would just be plain mad if he could hear you talking foolish like that.

MAMA (*stopping and staring off*): Yes . . . he sure would. (*Sighing.*) We got enough to do with that money, all right. (*She halts then, and turns and looks at her daughter-in-law hard;* RUTH *avoids her eyes and* MAMA *wipes her hands with finality and starts to speak firmly to* RUTH.) Where did you go today, girl?

RUTH: To the doctor.

MAMA (*impatiently*): Now, Ruth . . . you know better than that. Old Doctor Jones is strange enough in his way but there ain't nothing 'bout him make somebody slip and call him "she"—like you done this morning.

RUTH: Well, that's what happened—my tongue slipped.

MAMA: You went to see that woman, didn't you?

RUTH (*defensively, giving herself away*): What woman you talking about?

MAMA (*angrily*): That woman who—

(WALTER *enters in great excitement.*)

WALTER: Did it come?

MAMA (*quietly*): Can't you give people a Christian greeting before you start asking about money?

WALTER (*to* RUTH): Did it come? (RUTH *unfolds the check and lays it quietly before him, watching him intently with thoughts of her own.* WALTER *sits down and grasps it close and counts off the zeros.*) Ten thousand dollars—(*He turns suddenly, frantically to his mother and draws some papers out of his breast pocket.*) Mama—look. Old Willy Harris put everything on paper—

MAMA: Son—I think you ought to talk to your wife . . . I'll go on out and leave you alone if you want—

WALTER: I can talk to her later—Mama, look—

MAMA: Son—

WALTER: WILL SOMEBODY PLEASE LISTEN TO ME TODAY!

MAMA (*quietly*): I don't 'low no yellin' in this house, Walter Lee, and you know it—(WALTER *stares at them in frustration and starts to speak several times.*) And there ain't going to be no investing in no liquor stores. I don't aim to have to speak on that again.

(*A long pause.*)

WALTER: Oh—so you don't aim to have to speak on that again? So *you* have decided . . . (*Crumpling his papers.*) Well, *you* tell that to my boy tonight when you put him to sleep on the living-room couch . . . (*Turning to* MAMA *and speaking directly to her.*) Yeah—and tell it to my wife, Mama, tomorrow when she has to go out of here to look after somebody else's kids. And tell it to *me*, Mama, every time we need a new pair of curtains and I have to watch *you* go out and work in somebody's kitchen. Yeah, you tell me then! (WALTER *starts out.*)

RUTH: Where you going?

WALTER: I'm going out!

RUTH: Where?

WALTER: Just out of this house somewhere—

RUTH (*getting her coat*): I'll come too.

WALTER: I don't want you to come!

RUTH: I got something to talk to you about, Walter.

WALTER: That's too bad.

MAMA (*still quietly*): Walter Lee—(*She waits and he finally turns and looks at her.*) Sit down.

WALTER: I'm a grown man, Mama.

MAMA: Ain't nobody said you wasn't grown. But you still in my house and my presence. And as long as you are—you'll talk to your wife civil. Now sit down.

RUTH (*suddenly*): Oh, let him go on out and drink himself to death! He makes me sick to my stomach! (*She flings her coat against him.*)

WALTER (*violently*): And you turn mine too, baby! (RUTH *goes into their bedroom and slams the door behind her.*) That was my greatest mistake—

MAMA (*still quietly*): Walter, what is the matter with you?

WALTER: Matter with me? Ain't nothing the matter with *me!*

MAMA: Yes there is. Something eating you up like a crazy man. Something more than me not giving you this money. The past few years I been watching it happen to you. You get all nervous acting and kind of wild in the eyes—(WALTER *jumps up impatiently at her words.*) I said sit there now, I'm talking to you!

WALTER: Mama—I don't need no nagging at me today.

MAMA: Seem like you getting to a place where you always tied up in some kind of knot about something. But if anybody ask you 'bout it you just yell at 'em and bust out the house and go out and drink somewheres. Walter Lee, people can't live with that. Ruth's a good, patient girl in her way—but you getting to be too much. Boy, don't make the mistake of driving that girl away from you.

WALTER: Why—what she do for me?

MAMA: She loves you.

WALTER: Mama—I'm going out. I want to go off somewhere and be by myself for a while.

MAMA: I'm sorry 'bout your liquor store, son. It just wasn't the thing for us to do. That's what I want to tell you about—

WALTER: I got to go out, Mama—(*He rises.*)

MAMA: It's dangerous, son.

WALTER: What's dangerous?

MAMA: When a man goes outside his home to look for peace.

WALTER (*beseechingly*): Then why can't there never be no peace in this house then?

MAMA: You done found it in some other house?

WALTER: No—there ain't no woman! Why do women always think there's a woman somewhere when a man gets restless. (*Coming to her.*) Mama—Mama—I want so many things . . .

MAMA: Yes, son—

WALTER: I want so many things that they are driving me kind of crazy . . . Mama—look at me.

MAMA: I'm looking at you. You a good-looking boy. You got a job, a nice wife, a fine boy and—

WALTER: A job. (*Looks at her.*) Mama, a job? I open and close car doors all day long. I drive a man around in his limousine and I say, "Yes, sir; no, sir; very good, sir; shall I take the Drive, sir?" Mama, that ain't no kind of job . . . that ain't nothing at all. (*Very quietly.*) Mama, I don't know if I can make you understand.

MAMA: Understand what, baby?

WALTER (*quietly*): Sometimes it's like I can see the future stretched out in front of me—just plain as day. The future, Mama. Hanging over there at the edge of my days. Just waiting for me—a big, looming blank space—full of *nothing.* Just waiting for *me.* (*Pause.*) Mama—sometimes when I'm downtown and I pass them cool, quiet-looking restaurants where them white boys are sitting back and talking 'bout things . . . sitting there turning deals worth millions of dollars . . . sometimes I see guys don't look much older than me—

MAMA: Son—how come you talk so much 'bout money?

WALTER (*with immense passion*): Because it is life, Mama!

MAMA (*quietly*): Oh—(*Very quietly.*) So now it's life. Money is life. Once upon a time freedom used to be life—now it's money. I guess the world really do change . . .

WALTER: No—it was always money, Mama. We just didn't know about it.

MAMA: No. . . . something has changed. (*She looks at him.*) You something new, boy. In my time we was worried about not being lynched and getting to the North if we could and how to stay alive and still have a pinch of dignity too . . . Now here come you and Beneatha—talking 'bout things we ain't never even thought about hardly, me and your daddy. You ain't satisfied or proud of nothing we done. I mean that you had a home; that we kept you out of trouble till you was grown; that you don't have to ride to work on the back of nobody's streetcar—You my children—but how different we done become.

WALTER: You just don't understand, Mama, you just don't understand.

MAMA: Son—do you know your wife is expecting another baby? (WALTER *stands, stunned, and absorbs what his mother has said.*) That's what she wanted to talk to you about. (WALTER *sinks down into a chair.*) This ain't for me to be telling —but you ought to know. (*She waits.*) I think Ruth is thinking 'bout getting rid of that child.

WALTER (*slowly understanding*): No—no— Ruth wouldn't do that.

MAMA: When the world gets ugly enough—a woman will do anything for her family. *The part that's already living.*

WALTER: You don't know Ruth, Mama, if you think she would do that.

(RUTH *opens the bedroom door and stands there a little limp.*)

RUTH (*beaten*): Yes I would too, Walter. (*Pause.*) I gave her a five-dollar down payment.

(*There is total silence as the man stares at his wife and the mother stares at her son.*)

MAMA (*presently*): Well—(*Tightly.*) Well— son, I'm waiting to hear you say something . . . I'm waiting to hear how you be your father's son. Be the man he was . . . (*Pause.*) Your wife say she going to destroy your child. And I'm waiting to hear you talk like him and say we a people who give children life, not who destroys them—(*She rises.*) I'm waiting to see you stand up and look like your daddy and say we done give up one baby to poverty and that we ain't going to give up nary another one . . . I'm waiting.

WALTER: Ruth—

MAMA: If you a son of mine, tell her! (WALTER *turns, looks at her and can say nothing. She continues, bitterly.*) You . . . you are a disgrace to your father's memory. Somebody get me my hat.

ACT II

SCENE 1

(*Time: Later the same day.*
At rise: RUTH *is ironing again. She has the radio going. Presently* BENEATHA'S *bedroom door opens and*

RUTH'S *mouth falls and she puts down the iron in fascination.*)

RUTH: What have we got on tonight!

BENEATHA (*emerging grandly from the doorway so that we can see her thoroughly robed in the costume Asagai brought*): You are looking at what a well-dressed Nigerian woman wears—(*She parades for* RUTH, *her hair completely hidden by the headdress; she is coquettishly fanning herself with an ornate oriental fan, mistakenly more like Butterfly than any Nigerian that ever was.*) Isn't it beautiful? (*She promenades to the radio and, with an arrogant flourish, turns off the good loud blues that is playing.*) Enough of this assimilationist junk! (RUTH *follows her with her eyes as she goes to the phonograph and puts on a record and turns and waits ceremoniously for the music to come up. Then, with a shout—*) OCOMOGOSIAY!

(RUTH *jumps. The music comes up, a lovely Nigerian melody.* BENEATHA *listens, enraptured, her eyes far away—"back to the past." She begins to dance.* RUTH *is dumfounded.*)

RUTH: What kind of dance is that?

BENEATHA: A folk dance.

RUTH (*Pearl Bailey*): What kind of folks do that, honey?

BENEATHA: It's from Nigeria. It's a dance of welcome.

RUTH: Who you welcoming?

BENEATHA: The men back to the village.

RUTH: Where they been?

BENEATHA: How should I know—out hunting or something. Anyway, they are coming back now . . .

RUTH: Well, that's good.

BENEATHA (*with the record*):
Alundi, alundi
Alundi alunya
Jop pu a jeepua
Ang gu soooooooooo

Ai yai yae . . .
Ayehaye—alundi . . .

(WALTER *comes in during this performance; he has obviously been drinking. He leans against the door heavily and watches his sister, at first with distaste. Then his eyes look off—"back to the past"—as he lifts both his fists to the roof, screaming.*)

WALTER: YEAH . . . AND ETHIOPIA STRETCH FORTH HER HANDS AGAIN! . . .

RUTH (*drily, looking at him*): Yes—and Africa sure is claiming her own tonight. (*She gives them both up and starts ironing again.*)

WALTER (*all in a drunken, dramatic shout*): Shut up! . . . I'm digging them drums . . . them drums move me! . . . (*He makes his weaving way to his wife's face and leans in close to her.*) In my *heart of hearts*—(*He thumps his chest.*)—I am much warrior!

RUTH (*without even looking up*): In your heart of hearts you are much drunkard.

WALTER (*coming away from her and starting to wander around the room, shouting*): Me and Jomo . . . (*Intently, in his sister's face. She has stopped dancing to watch him in this unknown mood.*) That's my man, Kenyatta. (*Shouting and thumping his chest.*) FLAMING SPEAR! HOT DAMN! (*He is suddenly in possession of an imaginary spear and actively spearing enemies all over the room.*) OCOMOGOSIAY . . . THE LION IS WAKING . . . OWIMOWEH! (*He pulls his shirt open and leaps up on a table and gestures with his spear. The bell rings.* RUTH *goes to answer.*)

BENEATHA (*to encourage* WALTER, *thoroughly caught up with this side of him*): OCOMOGOSIAY, FLAMING SPEAR!

WALTER (*on the table, very far gone, his eyes pure glass sheets. He sees what we cannot, that he is a leader of his people, a great chief, a descendant of Chaka, and that the hour to march has come*): Listen, my black brothers—

BENEATHA: OCOMOGOSIAY!

WALTER: —Do you hear the waters rushing against the shores of the coastlands—

BENEATHA: OCOMOGOSIAY!

WALTER: —Do you hear the screeching of the cocks in yonder hills beyond where the chiefs meet in council for the coming of the mighty war—

BENEATHA: OCOMOGOSIAY!

WALTER: —Do you hear the beating of the wings of the birds flying low over the mountains and the low places of our land—

(RUTH *opens the door.* GEORGE MURCHISON *enters.*)

BENEATHA: OCOMOGOSIAY!

WALTER: —Do you hear the singing of the women, singing the war songs of our fathers to the babies in the great houses . . . singing the sweet war songs? OH, DO YOU HEAR, MY BLACK BROTHERS!

BENEATHA (*completely gone*): We hear you, Flaming Spear—

WALTER: Telling us to prepare for the greatness of the time—(*To* GEORGE.) Black Brother! (*He extends his hand for the fraternal clasp.*)

GEORGE: Black Brother, hell!

RUTH (*having had enough, and embarrassed for the family*): Beneatha, you got company—what's the matter with you? Walter Lee Younger, get down off that table and stop acting like a fool . . .

(WALTER *comes down off the table suddenly and makes a quick exit to the bathroom.*)

RUTH: He's had a little to drink . . . I don't know what her excuse is.

GEORGE (*to* BENEATHA): Look honey, we're going *to* the theatre—we're not going to be *in* it . . . so go change, huh?

RUTH: You expect this boy to go out with you looking like that?

BENEATHA (*looking at* GEORGE): That's up to George. If he's ashamed of his heritage—

GEORGE: Oh, don't be so proud of yourself, Bennie—just because you look eccentric.

BENEATHA: How can something that's natural be eccentric?

GEORGE: That's what being eccentric means —being natural. Get dressed.

BENEATHA: I don't like that, George.

RUTH: Why must you and your brother make an argument out of everything people say?

BENEATHA: Because I hate assimilationist Negroes!

RUTH: Will somebody please tell me what assimila-whoever means!

GEORGE: Oh, it's just a college girl's way of calling people Uncle Toms—but that isn't what it means at all.

RUTH: Well, what does it mean?

BENEATHA (*cutting* GEORGE *off and staring at him as she replies to* RUTH): It means someone who is willing to give up his own culture and submerge himself completely in the dominant, and in this case, *oppressive* culture!

GEORGE: Oh, dear, dear, dear! Here we go! A lecture on the African past! On our Great West African Heritage! In one second we will hear all about the great Ashanti empires; the great Songhay civilizations; and the great sculpture of Bénin —and then some poetry in the Bantu—and the whole monologue will end with the word *heritage!* (*Nastily*) Let's face it, baby, your heritage is nothing but a bunch of raggedy-assed spirituals and some grass huts!

BENEATHA: *Grass huts!* (RUTH *crosses to her and forcibly pushes her toward the bedroom.*) See there . . . you are standing there in your splendid ignorance talking about people who were the first to smelt iron on the face of the earth! (RUTH *is pushing her through the door.*) The Ashanti were performing surgical operations when the English

—(RUTH *pulls the door to, with* BENEATHA *on the other side, and smiles graciously at* GEORGE. BENEATHA *opens the door and shouts the end of the sentence defiantly at* GEORGE.)—were still tatooing themselves with blue dragons . . . (*She goes back inside.*)

RUTH: Have a seat, George. (*They both sit.* RUTH *folds her hands rather primly on her lap, determined to demonstrate the civilization of the family.*) Warm, ain't it? I mean for September. (*Pause.*) Just like they always say about Chicago weather: If it's too hot or cold for you, just wait a minute and it'll change. (*She smiles happily at this cliché of clichés.*) Everybody say it's got to do with them bombs and things they keep setting off. (*Pause.*) Would you like a nice cold beer?

GEORGE: No, thank you. I don't care for beer. (*He looks at his watch.*) I hope she hurries up.

RUTH: What time is the show?

GEORGE: It's an eight-thirty curtain. That's just Chicago though. In New York standard curtain time is eight forty. (*He is rather proud of this knowledge.*)

RUTH (*properly appreciating it*): You get to New York a lot?

GEORGE (*offhand*): Few times a year.

RUTH: Oh—that's nice. I've never been to New York.

(WALTER *enters. We feel he has relieved himself, but the edge of unreality is still with him.*)

WALTER: New York ain't got nothing Chicago ain't. Just a bunch of hustling people all squeezed up together—being "Eastern." (*He turns his face into a screw of displeasure.*)

GEORGE: Oh—you've been?

WALTER: *Plenty* of times.

RUTH (*shocked at the lie*): Walter Lee Younger!

WALTER (*staring her down*): Plenty! (*Pause.*) What we got to drink in this house? Why don't you offer this man some refreshment. (*To* GEORGE.) They don't know how to entertain people in this house, man.

GEORGE: Thank you—I don't really care for anything.

WALTER (*feeling his head; sobriety coming*): Where's Mama?

RUTH: She ain't come back yet.

WALTER (*looking* MURCHISON *over from head to toe, scrutinizing his carefully casual tweed sports jacket over cashmere V-neck sweater over soft eyelet shirt and tie, and soft slacks, finished off with white buckskin shoes*): Why all you college boys wear them fairyish-looking white shoes?

RUTH: Walter Lee!

(GEORGE MURCHISON *ignores the remark.*)

WALTER (*to* RUTH): Well, they look crazy as hell—white shoes, cold as it is.

RUTH (*crushed*): You have to excuse him—

WALTER: No he don't! Excuse me for what? What you always excusing me for! I'll excuse myself when I needs to be excused! (*A pause.*) They look as funny as them black knee socks Beneatha wears out of here all the time.

RUTH: It's the college *style*, Walter.

WALTER: Style, hell. She looks like she got burnt legs or something!

RUTH: Oh, Walter—

WALTER (*an irritable mimic*): Oh, Walter! Oh, Walter! (*To* MURCHISON.) How's your old man making out? I understand you all going to buy that big hotel on the Drive? (*He finds a beer in the refrigerator, wanders over to* MURCHISON, *sipping and wiping his lips with the back of his hand, and straddling a chair backwards to talk to the other man.*) Shrewd move. Your old man is all right, man. (*Tapping his head and half winking for emphasis.*) I mean he knows how to operate. I mean he thinks *big*, you know what I mean, I mean for a *home*, you know? But I think he's kind of running out of ideas now. I'd like to talk to him. Listen, man, I got some plans that could turn this city upside down. I mean I think like he does. *Big.* Invest big, gamble big, hell, lose *big* if you have to, you know what I mean. It's hard to find a man on this whole Southside who understands my kind of thinking—you dig? (*He scrutinizes* MURCHISON *again, drinks his beer, squints his eyes and leans in close, confidential, man to man.*) Me and you ought to sit down and talk sometimes, man. Man, I got me some ideas . . .

MURCHISON (*with boredom*): Yeah—sometimes we'll have to do that, Walter.

WALTER (*understanding the indifference, and offended*): Yeah—well, when you get the time, man. I know you a busy little boy.

RUTH: Walter, please—

WALTER (*bitterly, hurt*): I know ain't nothing in this world as busy as you colored college boys with your fraternity pins and white shoes . . .

RUTH (*covering her face with humiliation*): Oh, Walter Lee—

WALTER: I see you all all the time—with the books tucked under your arms—going to your (*British A—a mimic.*) "clahsses." And for what! What the hell you learning over there? Filling up your heads—(*Counting off on his fingers.*)—with the sociology and the psychology—but they teaching you how to be a man? How to take over and run the world? They teaching you how to run a rubber plantation or a steel mill? Naw—just to talk proper and read books and wear white shoes . . .

GEORGE (*looking at him with distaste, a little above it all*): You're all wacked up with bitterness, man.

WALTER (*intently, almost quietly, between the teeth, glaring at the boy*): And you—ain't you bitter, man? Ain't you just about had it yet? Don't you see no stars gleaming that you can't reach out and grab? You happy?—you contented son-of-a-bitch—you happy? You got it made? Bitter? Man, I'm a volcano. Bitter? Here I am a giant—surrounded by ants! Ants who can't even understand what it is the giant is talking about.

RUTH (*passionately and suddenly*): Oh, Walter—ain't you with nobody!

WALTER (*violently*): No! 'Cause ain't nobody with me! Not even my own mother!

RUTH: Walter, that's a terrible thing to say!

(BENEATHA *enters, dressed for the evening in a cocktail dress and earrings.*)

GEORGE: Well—hey, you look great.

BENEATHA: Let's go, George. See you all later.

RUTH: Have a nice time.

GEORGE: Thanks. Good night. (*To* WALTER, *sarcastically.*) Good night, *Prometheus.*

(BENEATHA *and* GEORGE *exit.*)

WALTER (*to* RUTH): Who is Prometheus?

RUTH: I don't know. Don't worry about it.

WALTER (*in fury, pointing after* GEORGE): See there—they get to a point where they can't insult you man to man—they got to go talk about something ain't nobody never heard of!

RUTH: How you know it was an insult? (*To humor him.*) Maybe Prometheus is a nice fellow.

WALTER: Prometheus! I bet there ain't even no such thing! I bet that simple-minded clown—

RUTH: Walter—(*She stops what she is doing and looks at him.*)

WALTER (*yelling*): Don't start!

RUTH: Start what?

WALTER: Your nagging! Where was I? Who was I with? How much money did I spend?

RUTH (*plaintively*): Walter Lee—why don't we just try to talk about it . . .

WALTER (*not listening*): I been out talking with people who understand me. People who care about the things I got on my mind.

RUTH (*wearily*): I guess that means people like Willy Harris.

WALTER: Yes, people like Willy Harris.

RUTH (*with a sudden flash of impatience*): Why don't you all just hurry up and go into the banking business and stop talking about it!

WALTER: Why? You want to know why? 'Cause we all tied up in a race of people that don't know how to do nothing but moan, pray and have babies! (*The line is too bitter even for him and he looks at her and sits down.*)

RUTH: Oh, Walter . . . (*Softly.*) Honey, why can't you stop fighting me?

WALTER (*without thinking*): Who's fighting you? Who even cares about you? (*This line begins the retardation of his mood.*)

RUTH: Well—(*She waits a long time, and then with resignation starts to put away her things.*) I guess I might as well go on to bed . . . (*More or less to herself.*) I don't know where we lost it . . . but we have . . . (*Then, to him.*) I—I'm sorry about this new baby, Walter. I guess maybe I better go on and do what I started . . . I guess I just didn't realize how bad things was with us . . . I guess I just didn't really realize—(*She starts out to the bedroom and stops.*) You want some hot milk?

WALTER: Hot milk?

RUTH: Yes—hot milk.

WALTER: Why hot milk?

RUTH: 'Cause after all that liquor you come home with you ought to have something hot in your stomach.

WALTER: I don't want no milk.

RUTH: You want some coffee then?

WALTER: No, I don't want no coffee. I don't want nothing hot to drink. (*Almost plaintively.*) Why you always trying to give me something to eat?

RUTH (*standing and looking at him helplessly*): What else can I give you, Walter Lee Younger?

(*She stands and looks at him and presently turns to go out again. He lifts his head and watches her going away from him in a new mood which began to emerge when he asked her "Who cares about you?"*)

WALTER: It's been rough, ain't it, baby? (*She hears and stops but does not turn around and he continues to her back.*) I guess between two people there ain't never as much understood as folks generally thinks there is. I mean like between me and you—(*She turns to face him.*) How we gets to the place where we scared to talk softness to each other. (*He waits, thinking hard himself.*) Why you think it got to be like that? (*He is thoughtful, almost as a child would be.*) Ruth, what is it gets into people ought to be close?

RUTH: I don't know, honey. I think about it a lot.

WALTER: On account of you and me, you mean? The way things are with us. The way something done come down between us.

RUTH: There ain't so much between us, Walter . . . Not when you come to me and try to talk to me. Try to be with me . . . a little even.

WALTER (*total honesty*): Sometimes . . . sometimes . . . I don't even know how to try.

RUTH: Walter—

WALTER: Yes?

RUTH (*coming to him, gently and with misgiving, but coming to him*): Honey . . . life don't have to be like this. I mean sometimes people can do things so that things are better . . . You remember how we used to talk when Travis was born . . . about the way we were going to live . . . the kind of house . . . (*She is stroking his head.*) Well, it's all starting to slip away from us . . .

(MAMA *enters, and* WALTER *jumps up and shouts at her.*)

WALTER: Mama, where have you been?

MAMA: My—them steps is longer than they used to be. Whew! (*She sits down and ignores him.*) How you feeling this evening, Ruth?

(RUTH *shrugs, disturbed some at having been prematurely interrupted and watching her husband knowingly.*)

WALTER: Mama, where have you been all day?

MAMA (*still ignoring him and leaning on the table and changing to more comfortable shoes*): Where's Travis?

RUTH: I let him go out earlier and he ain't come back yet. Boy, is he going to get it!

WALTER: Mama!

MAMA (*as if she has heard for the first time*): Yes, son?

WALTER: Where did you go this afternoon?

MAMA: I went down town to tend to some business that I had to tend to.

WALTER: What kind of business?

MAMA: You know better than to question me like a child, Brother.

WALTER (*rising and bending over the table*): Where were you, Mama? (*Bringing his fists down and shouting.*) Mama, you didn't go do something with that insurance money, something crazy?

(*The front door opens slowly, interrupting him, and* TRAVIS *peeks his head in, less than hopefully.*)

TRAVIS (*to his mother*): Mama, I—

RUTH: "Mama I" nothing! You're going to get it, boy! Get on in that bedroom and get yourself ready!

TRAVIS: But I—

MAMA: Why don't you all never let the child explain hisself.

RUTH: Keep out of it now, Lena.

(MAMA *clamps her lips together, and* RUTH *advances toward her son menacingly.*)

RUTH: A thousand times I have told you not to go off like that—

MAMA (*holding out her arms to her grandson*): Well—at least let me tell him something. I want him to be the first one to hear . . . Come here, Travis. (*The boy obeys, gladly.*) Travis—(*She takes him by the shoulders and looks into his face.*)—you know that money we got in the mail this morning?

TRAVIS: Yes'm—

MAMA: Well—what you think your grandmama gone and done with that money?

TRAVIS: I don't know, Grandmama.

MAMA (*putting her finger on his nose for emphasis*): She went out and she bought you a house! (*The explosion comes from* WALTER *at the end of the revelation and he jumps up and turns away from all of them in a fury.* MAMA *continues, to* TRAVIS.) You glad about the house? It's going to be yours when you get to be a man.

TRAVIS: Yeah—I always wanted to live in a house.

MAMA: All right, gimme some sugar then— (TRAVIS *puts his arms around her neck as she watches her son over the boy's shoulder. Then, to* TRAVIS, *after the embrace.*) Now when you say your prayers tonight, you thank God and your grandfather— 'cause it was him who give you the house—in his way.

RUTH (*taking the boy from* MAMA *and pushing him toward the bedroom*): Now you get out of here and get ready for your beating.

TRAVIS: Aw, Mama—

RUTH: Get on in there—(*Closing the door behind him and turning radiantly to her mother-in-law.*) So you went and did it!

MAMA (*quietly, loooking at her son with pain*): Yes, I did.

RUTH (*raising both arms classically*): *Praise God!* (*Looks at* WALTER *a moment, who says nothing. She crosses rapidly to her husband.*) Please, honey —let me be glad . . . you be glad too. (*She has laid her hands on his shoulders, but he shakes himself free of her roughly, without turning to face her.*) Oh, Walter . . . a home . . . *a home.* (*She comes back to* MAMA.) Well—where is it? How big is it? How much it going to cost?

MAMA: Well—

RUTH: When we moving?

MAMA (*smiling at her*): First of the month.

RUTH (*throwing back her head with jubilance*): *Praise God!*

MAMA (*tentatively, still looking at her son's back turned against her and* RUTH): It's—it's a nice house too . . . (*She cannot help speaking directly to him. An imploring quality in her voice, her manner, makes her almost like a girl now.*) Three bedrooms —nice big one for you and Ruth. . . . Me and Beneatha still have to share our room, but Travis have one of his own—and—(*With difficulty.*) I figures if the—new baby—is a boy, we could get one of them double-decker outfits . . . And there's a yard with a little patch of dirt where I could maybe get to grow me a few flowers . . . And a nice big basement . . .

RUTH: Walter honey, be glad—

MAMA (*still to his back, fingering things on the table*): 'Course I don't want to make it sound fancier than it is . . . It's just a plain little old house—but it's made good and solid—and it will be *ours.* Walter Lee—it makes a difference in a man when he can walk on floors that belong to *him* . . .

RUTH: Where is it?

MAMA (*frightened at this telling*): Well—well —it's out there in Clybourne Park—

(RUTH's *radiance fades abruptly, and* WALTER *finally turns slowly to face his mother with incredulity and hostility.*)

RUTH: Where?

MAMA (*matter-of-factly*): Four o six Clybourne Street, Clybourne Park.

RUTH: Clybourne Park? Mama, there ain't no colored people living in Clybourne Park.

MAMA (*almost idiotically*): Well, I guess there's going to be some now.

WALTER (*bitterly*): So that's the peace and comfort you went out and bought for us today!

MAMA (*raising her eyes to meet his finally*): Son —I just tried to find the nicest place for the least amount of money for my family.

RUTH (*trying to recover from the shock*): Well—

well—'course I ain't one never been 'fraid of no crackers, mind you—but—well, wasn't there no other houses nowhere?

MAMA: Them houses they put up for colored in them areas way out all seem to cost twice as much as other houses. I did the best I could.

RUTH (*struck senseless with the news, in its various degrees of goodness and trouble, she sits a moment, her fists propping her chin in thought, and then she starts to rise, bringing her fists down with vigor, the radiance spreading from cheek to cheek again*): Well—well!—All I can say is—if this is my time in life—*my time*—to say good-bye —(*and she builds with momentum as she starts to circle the room with an exuberant, almost tearfully happy release*)—to these God-damned cracking walls!—(*she pounds the walls*)—and these marching roaches!—(*she wipes at an imaginary army of marching roaches*)—and this cramped little closet which ain't now or never was no kitchen! . . . then I say it loud and good, *Hallelujah! and good-bye misery . . . I don't never want to see your ugly face again!* (*She laughs joyously, having practically destroyed the apartment, and flings her arms up and lets them come down happily, slowly, reflectively, over her abdomen, aware for the first time perhaps that the life therein pulses with happiness and not despair.*) Lena?

MAMA (*moved, watching her happiness*): Yes, honey?

RUTH (*looking off*): Is there—is there a whole lot of sunlight?

MAMA (*understanding*): Yes, child, there's a whole lot of sunlight.

(*Long pause.*)

RUTH (*collecting herself and going to the door of the room* TRAVIS *is in*): Well—I guess I better see 'bout Travis. (*To* MAMA.) Lord, I sure don't feel like whipping nobody today! (*She exits.*)

MAMA (*the mother and son are left alone now and the mother waits a long time, considering deeply, before she speaks*): Son—you—you understand what I done, don't you? (WALTER *is silent and sullen.*) I— I just seen my family falling apart today . . . just falling to pieces in front of my eyes . . . We couldn't of gone on like we was today. We was going backwards 'stead of forwards—talking 'bout killing babies and wishing each other was dead . . . When it gets like that in life—you just got to do something different, push on out and do something bigger . . . (*She waits.*) I wish you say something, son . . . I wish you'd say how deep inside you you think I done the right thing—

WALTER (*crossing slowly to his bedroom door and*

finally turning there and speaking measuredly): What you need me to say you done right for? *You* the head of this family. You run our lives like you want to. It was your money and you did what you wanted with it. So what you need for me to say it was all right for? *(Bitterly, to hurt her as deeply as he knows is possible.)* So you butchered up a dream of mine—you—who always talking 'bout your children's dreams . . .

MAMA: Walter Lee—

(He just closes the door behind him. MAMA *sits alone, thinking heavily.)*

SCENE 2

(Time: Friday night. A few weeks later.

At rise: Packing crates mark the intention of the family to move. BENEATHA *and* GEORGE *come in, presumably from an evening out again.)*

GEORGE: O.K. . . . O.K., whatever you say . . . *(They both sit on the couch. He tries to kiss her. She moves away.).* Look, we've had a nice evening; let's not spoil it, huh? . . .

(He again turns her head and tries to nuzzle in and she turns away from him, not with distaste but with momentary lack of interest; in a mood to pursue what they were talking about.)

BENEATHA: I'm *trying* to talk to you

GEORGE: We always talk.

BENEATHA: Yes—and I love to talk.

GEORGE *(exasperated; rising)*: I know it and I don't mind it sometimes . . . I want you to cut it out, see—The moody stuff, I mean. I don't like it. You're a nice-looking girl . . . all over. That's all you need, honey, forget the atmosphere. Guys aren't going to go for the atmosphere—they're going to go for what they see. Be glad for that. Drop the Garbo routine. It doesn't go with you. As for myself, I want a nice—*(Groping.)*—simple—*(Thoughtfully.)*—sophisticated girl . . . not a poet—O.K.?

(She rebuffs him again and he starts to leave.)

BENEATHA: Why are you angry?

GEORGE: Because this is stupid! I don't go out with you to discuss the nature of "quiet desperation" or to hear all about your thoughts—because the world will go on thinking what it thinks regardless—

BENEATHA: Then why read books? Why go to school?

GEORGE *(with artificial patience, counting on his fingers)*: It's simple. You read books—to learn facts—to get grades—to pass the course—to get a degree. That's all—it has nothing to do with thoughts.

(A long pause.)

BENEATHA: I see. *(A longer pause as she looks at him.)* Good night, George.

*(*GEORGE *looks at her a little oddly, and starts to exit. He meets* MAMA *coming in.)*

GEORGE: Oh—hello, Mrs. Younger.

MAMA: Hello, George, how you feeling?

GEORGE: Fine—fine, how are you?

MAMA: Oh, a little tired. You know them steps can get you after a day's work. You all have a nice time tonight?

GEORGE: Yes—a fine time. Well, good night.

MAMA: Good night. *(He exits.* MAMA *closes the door behind her.)* Hello, honey. What you sitting like that for?

BENEATHA: I'm just sitting.

MAMA: Didn't you have a nice time?

BENEATHA: No.

MAMA: No? What's the matter?

BENEATHA: Mama, George is a fool—honest. *(She rises.)*

MAMA *(hustling around unloading the packages she has entered with; she stops)*: Is he, baby?

BENEATHA: Yes. *(*BENEATHA *makes up* TRAVIS' *bed as she talks.)*

MAMA: You sure?

BENEATHA: Yes.

MAMA: Well—I guess you better not waste your time with no fools.

*(*BENEATHA *looks up at her mother, watching her put groceries in the refrigerator. Finally she gathers up her things and starts into the bedroom. At the door she stops and looks back at her mother.)*

BENEATHA: Mama—

MAMA: Yes, baby—

BENEATHA: Thank you.

MAMA: For what?

BENEATHA: For understanding me this time. *(She exits quickly and the mother stands, smiling a little, looking at the place where* BENEATHA *just stood.* RUTH *enters.)*

RUTH: Now don't you fool with any of this stuff, Lena—

MAMA: Oh, I just thought I'd sort a few things out.

(*The phone rings.* RUTH *answers.*)

RUTH (*at the phone*): Hello—Just a minute. (*Goes to door.*) Walter, it's Mrs. Arnold. (*Waits. Goes back to the phone. Tense.*) Hello. Yes, this is his wife speaking . . . He's lying down now. Yes . . . well, he'll be in tomorrow. He's been very sick. Yes—I know we should have called, but we were so sure he'd be able to come in today. Yes—yes, I'm very sorry. Yes . . . Thank you very much. (*She hangs up.* WALTER *is standing in the doorway of the bedroom behind her.*) That was Mrs. Arnold.

WALTER (*indifferently*): Was it?

RUTH: She said if you don't come in tomorrow that they are getting a new man . . .

WALTER: Ain't that sad—ain't that crying sad.

RUTH: She said Mr. Arnold has had to take a cab for three days . . . Walter, you ain't been to work for three days! (*This is a revelation to her.*) Where you been, Walter Lee Younger? (WALTER *looks at her and starts to laugh.*) You're going to lose your job.

WALTER: That's right . . .

RUTH: Oh, Walter, and with your mother working like a dog every day—

WALTER: That's sad too—Everything is sad.

MAMA: What you been doing for these three days, son?

WALTER: Mama—you don't know all the things a man what got leisure can find to do in this city . . . What's this—Friday night? Well—Wednesday I borrowed Willy Harris' car and I went for a drive . . . just me and myself and I drove and drove . . . Way out . . . way past South Chicago, and I parked the car and I sat and looked at the steel mills all day long. I just sat in the car and looked at them big black chimneys for hours. Then I drove back and I went to the Green Hat. (*Pause.*) And Thursday—Thursday I borrowed the car again and I got in it and I pointed it the other way and I drove the other way—for hours—way, way up to Wisconsin, and I looked at the farms. I just drove and looked at the farms. Then I drove back and I went to the Green Hat. (*Pause.*) And today—today I didn't get the car. Today I just walked. All over the Southside. And I looked at the Negroes and they looked at me and finally I just sat down on the curb at Thirty-ninth and South Parkway and I just sat there and watched the Negroes go by. And then I went to the Green Hat. You all sad? You all depressed? And you know where I am going right now—

(RUTH *goes out quietly.*)

MAMA: Oh, Big Walter, is this the harvest of our days?

WALTER: You know what I like about the Green Hat? (*He turns the radio on and a steamy, deep blues pours into the room.*) I like this little cat they got there who blows a sax . . . He blows. He talks to me. He ain't but 'bout five feet tall and he's got a conked head and his eyes is always closed and he's all music—

MAMA (*rising and getting some papers out of her handbag*): Walter—

WALTER: And there's this other guy who plays the piano . . . and they got a sound. I mean they can work on some music . . . They got the best little combo in the world in the Green Hat . . . You can just sit there and drink and listen to them three men play and you realize that don't nothing matter worth a damn, but just being there—

MAMA: I've helped do it to you, haven't I, son? Walter, I been wrong.

WALTER: Naw—you ain't never been wrong about nothing, Mama.

MAMA: Listen to me, now. I say I been wrong, son. That I been doing to you what the rest of the world been doing to you. (*She stops and he looks up slowly at her and she meets his eyes pleadingly.*) Walter—what you ain't never understood is that I ain't got nothing, don't own nothing, ain't never really wanted nothing that wasn't for you. There ain't nothing as precious to me . . . There ain't nothing worth holding on to, money, dreams, nothing else—if it means—if it means it's going to destroy my boy. (*She puts her papers in front of him and he watches her without speaking or moving.*) I paid the man thirty-five hundred dollars down on the house. That leaves sixty-five hundred dollars. Monday morning I want you to take this money and take three thousand dollars and put it in a savings account for Beneatha's medical schooling. The rest you put in a checking account—with your name on it. And from now on any penny that come out of it or that go in it is for you to look after. For you to decide. (*She drops her hands a little helplessly.*) It ain't much, but it's all I got in the world and I'm putting in your hands. I'm telling you to be the head of this family from now on like you supposed to be.

WALTER (*stares at the money*): You trust me like that, Mama?

MAMA: I ain't never stop trusting you. Like I ain't never stop loving you.

(*She goes out, and* WALTER *sits looking at the money on the table as the music continues in its idiom, pulsing in the room. Finally, in a decisive gesture, he gets up, and, in mingled joy and desperation, picks up the money. At the same moment,* TRAVIS *enters for bed.*)

TRAVIS: What's the matter, Daddy? You drunk?

WALTER (*sweetly, more sweetly than we have ever known him*): No, Daddy ain't drunk. Daddy ain't going to never be drunk again. . . .

TRAVIS: Well, good night, Daddy.

(*The* FATHER *has come from behind the couch and leans over, embracing his son.*)

WALTER: Son, I feel like talking to you tonight.

TRAVIS: About what?

WALTER: Oh, about a lot of things. About you and what kind of man you going to be when you grow up. . . . Son—son, what do you want to be when you grow up?

TRAVIS: A bus driver.

WALTER (*laughing a little*): A what? Man, that ain't nothing to want to be!

TRAVIS: Why not?

WALTER: 'Cause, man—it ain't big enough—you know what I mean.

TRAVIS: I don't know then. I can't make up my mind. Sometimes Mama asks me that too. And sometimes when I tell you I just want to be like you—she says she don't want me to be like that and sometimes she says she does. . . .

WALTER (*gathering him up in his arms*): You know what, Travis? In seven years you going to be seventeen years old. And things is going to be very different with us in seven years, Travis. . . . One day when you are seventeen I'll come home—home from my office downtown somewhere—

TRAVIS: You don't work in no office, Daddy.

WALTER: No—but after tonight. After what your daddy gonna do tonight, there's going to be offices—a whole lot of offices. . . .

TRAVIS: What you gonna do tonight, Daddy?

WALTER: You wouldn't understand yet, son, but your daddy's gonna make a transaction . . . a business transaction that's going to change our lives. . . . That's how come one day when you 'bout seventeen years old I'll come home and I'll be pretty tired, you know what I mean, after a day of conferences and secretaries getting things wrong the way they do . . . 'cause an executive's life is hell, man—(*The more he talks the farther away he gets.*) And I'll pull the car up on the driveway . . . just a plain black Chrysler, I think, with white walls—no—black tires. More elegant. Rich people don't have to be flashy . . . though I'll have to get something a little sportier for Ruth—maybe a Cadillac convertible to do her shopping in. . . . And I'll come up the steps to the house and the gardener will be clipping away at the hedges and he'll say, "Good evening, Mr. Younger." And I'll say, "Hello, Jefferson, how are you this evening?" And I'll go inside and Ruth will come downstairs and meet me at the door and we'll kiss each other and she'll take my arm and we'll go up to your room to see you sitting on the floor with the catalogues of all the great schools in America around you. . . . All the great schools in the world! And—and I'll say, all right son—it's your seventeenth birthday, what is it you've decided? . . . Just tell me where you want to go to school and you'll *go*. Just tell me, what it is you want to be—and you'll *be* it. . . . Whatever you want to be—Yessir! (*He holds his arms open for* TRAVIS.) You just name it, son . . . (TRAVIS *leaps into them.*) and I hand you the world! (WALTER's *voice has risen in pitch and hysterical promise and on the last line he lifts* TRAVIS *high.*)

SCENE 3

(*Time: Saturday, moving day, one week later.*

Before the curtain rises, RUTH's *voice, a strident, dramatic church alto, cuts through the silence.*

It is, in the darkness, a triumphant surge, a penetrating statement of expectation: "Oh, Lord, I don't feel no ways tired! Children, oh, glory hallelujah!"

As the curtain rises we see that RUTH *is alone in the living room, finishing up the family's packing. It is moving day. She is nailing crates and tying cartons.* BENEATHA *enters, carrying a guitar case, and watches her exuberant sister-in-law.*)

RUTH: Hey!

BENEATHA (*putting away the case*): Hi.

RUTH (*pointing at a package*): Honey—look in that package there and see what I found on sale this morning at the South Center. (RUTH *gets up and moves to the package and draws out some curtains.*) Lookahere—hand-turned hems!

BENEATHA: How do you know the window size out there?

RUTH (*who hadn't thought of that*): Oh—Well, they bound to fit something in the whole house. Anyhow, they was too good a bargain to pass us. (RUTH *slaps her head, suddenly remembering something.*) Oh, Bennie—I meant to put a special note on that carton over there. That's your mama's good china and she wants 'em to be very careful with it.

BENEATHA: I'll do it. (BENEATHA *finds a piece of paper and starts to draw large letters on it.*)

RUTH: You know what I'm going to do soon as I get in that new house?

BENEATHA: What?

RUTH: Honey—I'm going to run me a tub of water up to here . . . (*With her fingers practically up to her nostrils.*) And I'm going to get in it —and I am going to sit . . . and sit . . . and sit in that hot water and the first person who knocks to tell *me* to hurry up and come out—

BENEATHA: Gets shot at sunrise.

RUTH (*laughing happily*): You said it, sister! (*Noticing how large* BENEATHA *is absent-mindedly making the note.*) Honey, they ain't going to read that from no airplane.

BENEATHA (*laughing herself*): I guess I always think things have more emphasis if they are big, somehow.

RUTH (*looking up at her and smiling*): You and your brother seem to have that as a philosophy of life. Lord, that man—done changed so 'round here. You know—you know what we did last night? Me and Walter Lee?

BENEATHA: What?

RUTH (*smiling to herself*): We went to the movies. (*Looking at* BENEATHA *to see if she understands.*) We went to the movies. You know the last time me and Walter went to the movies together?

BENEATHA: No.

RUTH: Me neither. That's how long it been. (*Smiling again.*) But we went last night. The picture wasn't much good, but that didn't seem to matter. We went—and we held hands.

BENEATHA: Oh, Lord!

RUTH: We held hands—and you know what?

BENEATHA: What?

RUTH: When we come out of the show it was late and dark and all the stores and things was closed up . . . and it was kind of chilly and there wasn't many people on the streets . . . and we was still holding hands, me and Walter.

BENEATHA: You're killing me.

(WALTER *enters with a large package. His happiness is deep in him; he cannot keep still with his new-found exuberance. He is singing and wiggling and snapping his fingers. He puts his package in a corner and puts a phonograph record, which he has brought*

in with him, on the record player. As the music comes up he dances over to RUTH and tries to get her to dance with him. She gives in at last to his raunchiness and in a fit of giggling allows herself to be drawn into his mood and together they deliberately burlesque an old social dance of their youth.)

BENEATHA (*regarding them a long time as they dance, then drawing in her breath for a deeply exaggerated comment which she does not particularly mean*): Talk about—olddddddddddd-fashioned-dddddd—Negroes!

WALTER (*stopping momentarily*): What kind of Negroes?

(*He says this in fun. He is not angry with her today, nor with anyone. He starts to dance with his wife again.*)

BENEATHA: Old-fashioned.

WALTER (*as he dances with* RUTH): You know, when these *New Negroes* have their convention— (*pointing at his sister*)—that is going to be the chairman of the Committee on Unending Agitation. (*He goes on dancing, then stops.*) Race, race, race! . . . Girl, I do believe you are the first person in the history of the entire human race to successfully brainwash yourself. (BENEATHA *breaks up and he goes on dancing. He stops again, enjoying his tease.*) Damn, even the N double A C P takes a holiday sometimes! (BENEATHA *and* RUTH *laugh. He dances with* RUTH *some more and starts to laugh and stops and pantomimes someone over an operating table.*) I can just see that chick someday looking down at some poor cat on an operating table before she starts to slice him, saying . . . (*Pulling his sleeves back maliciously.*) "By the way, what are your views on civil rights down there? . . ." (*He laughs at her again and starts to dance happily. The bell sounds.*)

BENEATHA: Sticks and stones may break my bones but . . . words will never hurt me! (BENEATHA *goes to the door and opens it as* WALTER *and* RUTH *go on with the clowning.* BENEATHA *is somewhat surprised to see a quiet-looking middle-aged white man in a business suit holding his hat and a briefcase in his hand and consulting a small piece of paper.*)

MAN: Uh—how do you do, miss. I am looking for a Mrs.—(*He looks at the slip of paper.*) Mrs. Lena Younger?

BENEATHA (*smoothing her hair with slight embarrassment*): Oh—yes, that's my mother. Excuse me. (*She closes the door and turns to quiet the other two.*) Ruth! Brother! Somebody's here. (*Then she opens the door. The man casts a curious quick glance at all of them.*) Uh—come in please.

MAN (*coming in*): Thank you.

BENEATHA: My mother isn't here just now. Is it business?

MAN: Yes . . . well, of a sort.

WALTER (*freely, the Man of the House*): Have a seat. I'm Mrs. Younger's son. I look after most of her business matters.

(RUTH *and* BENEATHA *exchange amused glances.*)

MAN (*regarding* WALTER, *and sitting*): Well—My name is Karl Lindner . . .

WALTER (*stretching out his hand*): Walter Younger. This is my wife—(RUTH *nods politely.*) —and my sister.

LINDNER: How do you do.

WALTER (*amiably, as he sits himself easily on a chair, leaning with interest forward on his knees and looking expectantly into the newcomer's face*): What can we do for you, Mr. Lindner!

LINDNER (*some minor shuffling of the hat and briefcase on his knees*): Well—I am a representative of the Clybourne Park Improvement Association—

WALTER (*pointing*): Why don't you sit your things on the floor?

LINDNER: Oh—yes. Thank you. (*He slides the briefcase and hat under the chair.*) And as I was saying—I am from the Clybourne Park Improvement Association and we have had it brought to our attention at the last meeting that you people —or at least your mother—has bought a piece of residential property at—(*He digs for the slip of paper again.*)—four o six Clybourne Street . . .

WALTER: That's right. Care for something to drink? Ruth, get Mr. Lindner a beer.

LINDNER (*upset for some reason*): Oh—no, really. I mean thank you very much, but no thank you.

RUTH (*innocently*): Some coffee?

LINDNER: Thank you, nothing at all.

(BENEATHA *is watching the man carefully.*)

LINDNER: Well, I don't know how much you folks know about our organization. (*He is a gentle man; thoughtful and somewhat labored in his manner.*) It is one of these community organizations set up to look after—oh, you know, things like block upkeep and special projects and we also have what we call our New Neighbors Orientation Committee . . .

BENEATHA (*drily*): Yes—and what do they do?

LINDNER (*turning a little to her and then returning the main force to* WALTER): Well—it's what you might call a sort of welcoming committee, I guess. I mean they, we, I'm the chairman of the committee—go around and see the new people who move into the neighborhood and sort of give them the lowdown on the way we do things out in Clybourne Park.

BENEATHA (*with appreciation of the two meanings, which escape* RUTH *and* WALTER): Un-huh.

LINDNER: And we also have the category of what the association calls—(*He looks elsewhere.*)— uh—special community problems . . .

BENEATHA: Yes—and what are some of those?

WALTER: Girl, let the man talk.

LINDNER (*with understated relief*): Thank you. I would sort of like to explain this thing in my own way. I mean I want to explain to you in a certain way.

WALTER: Go ahead.

LINDNER: Yes. Well. I'm going to try to get right to the point. I'm sure we'll all appreciate that in the long run.

BENEATHA: Yes.

WALTER: Be still now!

LINDNER: Well—

RUTH (*still innocently*): Would you like another chair—you don't look comfortable.

LINDNER (*more frustrated than annoyed*): No, thank you very much. Please. Well—to get right to the point I—(*A great breath, and he is off at last.*) I am sure you people must be aware of some of the incidents which have happened in various parts of the city when colored people have moved into certain areas—(BENEATHA *exhales heavily and starts tossing a piece of fruit up and down in the air.*) Well—because we have what I think is going to be a unique type of organization in American community life—not only do we deplore that kind of thing—but we are trying to do something about it. (BENEATHA *stops tossing and turns with a new and quizzical interest to the man.*) We feel—(*Gaining confidence in his mission because of the interest in the faces of the people he is talking to.*) —we feel that most of the trouble in this world, when you come right down to it—(*He hits his knee for emphasis.*)—most of the trouble exists because people just don't sit down and talk to each other.

RUTH (*nodding as she might in church, pleased with the remark*): You can say that again, mister.

LINDNER (*more encouraged by such affirmation*): That we don't try hard enough in this world to understand the other fellow's problem. The other guy's point of view.

RUTH: Now that's right.

(BENEATHA *and* WALTER *merely watch and listen with genuine interest.*)

LINDNER: Yes—that's the way we feel out in Clybourne Park. And that's why I was elected to come here this afternoon and talk to you people. Friendly like, you know, the way people should talk to each other and see if we couldn't find some way to work this thing out. As I say, the whole business is a matter of *caring* about the other fellow. Anybody can see that you are a nice family of folks, hard working and honest I'm sure. (BENEATHA *frowns slightly, quizzically, her head tilted regarding him.*) Today everybody knows what it means to be on the outside of *something*. And of course, there is always somebody who is out to take the advantage of people who don't always understand.

WALTER: What do you mean?

LINDNER: Well—you see our community is made up of people who've worked hard as the dickens for years to build up that little community. They're not rich and fancy people; just hardworking, honest people who don't really have much but those little homes and a dream of the kind of community they want to raise their children in. Now, I don't say we are perfect and there is a lot wrong in some of the things they want. But you've got to admit that a man, right or wrong, has the right to want to have the neighborhood he lives in a certain kind of way. And at the moment the overwhelming majority of our people out there feel that people get along better, take more of a common interest in the life of the community, when they share a common background. I want you to believe me when I tell you that race prejudice simply doesn't enter into it. It is a matter of the people of Clybourne Park believing, rightly or wrongly, as I say, that for the happiness of all concerned that our Negro families are happier when they live in their *own* communities.

BENEATHA (*with a grand and bitter gesture*): This, friends, is the Welcoming Committee!

WALTER (*dumfounded, looking at* LINDNER): Is this what you came marching all the way over here to tell us?

LINDNER: Well, now we've been having a fine conversation. I hope you'll hear me all the way through.

WALTER (*tightly*): Go ahead, man.

LINDNER: You see—in the face of all things I have said, we are prepared to make your family a very generous offer . . .

BENEATHA: Thirty pieces and not a coin less!

WALTER: Yeah?

LINDNER (*putting on his glasses and drawing a form out of the briefcase*): Our association is pre-pared, through the collective effort of our people, to buy the house from you at a financial gain to your family.

RUTH: Lord have mercy, ain't this the living gall!

WALTER: All right, you through?

LINDNER: Well, I want to give you the exact terms of the financial arrangement—

WALTER: We don't want to hear no exact terms of no arrangements. I want to know if you got any more to tell us 'bout getting together?

LINDNER (*taking off his glasses*): Well—I don't suppose that you feel . . .

WALTER: Never mind how I feel—you got any more to say 'bout how people ought to sit down and talk to each other? . . . Get out of my house, man. (*He turns his back and walks to the door.*)

LINDNER (*looking around at the hostile faces and reaching and assembling his hat and briefcase*): Well —I don't understand why you people are reacting this way. What do you think you are going to gain by moving into a neighborhood where you just aren't wanted and where some elements —well—people can get awful worked up when they feel that their whole way of life and everything they've ever worked for is threatened.

WALTER: Get out.

LINDNER (*at the door, holding a small card*): Well—I'm sorry it went like this.

WALTER: Get out.

LINDNER (*almost sadly regarding* WALTER): You just can't force people to change their hearts, son. (*He turns and puts his card on a table and exits.* WALTER *pushes the door to with stinging hatred, and stands looking at it.* RUTH *just sits and* BENEATHA *just stands. They say nothing.* MAMA *and* TRAVIS *enter.*)

MAMA: Well—this all the packing got done since I left out of here this morning. I testify before God that my children got all the energy of the dead. What time the moving men due?

BENEATHA: Four o'clock. You had a caller, Mama. (*She is smiling, teasingly.*)

MAMA: Sure enough—who?

BENEATHA (*her arms folded saucily*): The Welcoming Committee.

(WALTER *and* RUTH *giggle.*)

MAMA (*innocently*): Who?

BENEATHA: The Welcoming Committee. They said they're sure going to be glad to see you when you get there.

WALTER (*devilishly*): Yeah, they said they can't hardly wait to see your face.

(*Laughter.*)

MAMA (*sensing their facetiousness*): What's the matter with you all?

WALTER: Ain't nothing the matter with us. We just telling you 'bout the gentleman who came to see you this afternoon. From the Clybourne Park Improvement Association.

MAMA: What he want?

RUTH (*in the same mood as* BENEATHA *and* WALTER): To welcome you, honey.

WALTER: He said they can't hardly wait. He said the one thing they don't have, that they just *dying* to have out there is a fine family of colored people! (*To* RUTH *and* BENEATHA.) Ain't that right!

RUTH *and* BENEATHA (*mockingly*): Yeah! He left his card in case—(*They indicate the card, and* MAMA *picks it up and throws it on the floor— understanding and looking off as she draws her chair up to the table on which she has put her plant and some sticks and some cord.*)

MAMA: Father, give us strength. (*Knowingly —and without fun.*) Did he threaten us?

BENEATHA: Oh—Mama—they don't do it like that any more. He talked Brotherhood. He said everybody ought learn how to sit down and hate each other with good Christian fellowship.

(*She and* WALTER *shake hands to ridicule the remark.*)

MAMA (*sadly*): Lord, protect us . . .

RUTH: You should hear the money those folks raised to buy the house from us. All we paid and then some.

BENEATHA: What they think we going to do —eat 'em?

RUTH: No, honey, marry 'em.

MAMA (*shaking her head*): Lord, Lord, Lord . . .

RUTH: Well—that's the way the crackers crumble. Joke.

BENEATHA (*laughingly noticing what her mother is doing*): Mama, what are you doing?

MAMA: Fixing my plant so it won't get hurt none on the way . . .

BENEATHA: Mama, you going to take *that* to the new house?

MAMA: Un-huh—

BENEATHA: That raggedy-looking old thing?

MAMA (*stopping and looking at her*): It expresses me.

RUTH (*with delight, to* BENEATHA): So, there, Miss Thing!

(WALTER *comes to* MAMA *suddenly and bends down behind her and squeezes her in his arms with all his*

strength. *She is overwhelmed by the suddenness of it and, though delighted, her manner is like that of* RUTH *with* TRAVIS.)

MAMA: Look out now, boy! You make me mess up my thing here!

WALTER (*his face lit, he slips down on his knees beside her, his arms still about her*): Mama . . . you know what it means to climb up in the chariot?

MAMA (*gruffly, very happy*): Get on away from me now . . .

RUTH (*near the gift-wrapped package, trying to catch* WALTER's *eye*): Psst—

WALTER: What the old song say, Mama . . .

RUTH: Walter—Now? (*She is pointing at the package.*)

WALTER (*speaking the lines, sweetly, playfully, in his mother's face*):

I got wings . . . you got wings . . .
All God's children got wings . . .

MAMA: Boy—get out of my face and do some work . . .

WALTER:

When I get to heaven gonna put on my wings,
Gonna fly all over God's heaven . . .

BENEATHA (*teasingly, from across the room*): Everybody talking 'bout heaven ain't going there!

WALTER (*to* RUTH, *who is carrying the box across to them*): I don't know, you think we ought to give her that . . . Seems to me she ain't been very appreciative around here.

MAMA (*eyeing the box, which is obviously a gift*): What is that?

WALTER (*taking it from* RUTH *and putting it on the table in front of* MAMA): Well—what you all think. Should we give it to her?

RUTH: Oh—she was pretty good today.

MAMA: I'll good you—(*She turns her eyes to the box again.*)

BENEATHA: Open it, Mama.

(*She stands up, looks at it, turns and looks at all of them, and then presses her hands together and does not open the package.*)

WALTER (*sweetly*): Open it, Mama. It's for you. (MAMA *looks in his eyes. It is the first present in her life without its being Christmas. Slowly she opens her package and lifts out, one by one, a brand-new sparkling set of gardening tools.* WALTER *continues, prodding.*) Ruth made up the note—read it . . .

MAMA (*picking up the card and adjusting her glasses*): "To our own Mrs. Miniver—Love from Brother, Ruth and Beneatha." Ain't that lovely . . .

TRAVIS (*tugging at his father's sleeve*): Daddy, can I give her mine now?

WALTER: All right, son. (TRAVIS *flies to get his gift.*) Travis didn't want to go in with the rest of us, Mama. He got his own. (*Somewhat amused.*) We don't know what it is . . .

TRAVIS (*racing back in the room with a large hat-box and putting it in front of his grand-mother*): Here!

MAMA: Lord have mercy, baby. You done gone and bought your grandmother a hat?

TRAVIS (*very proud*): Open it!

(*She does and lifts out an elaborate, but very elabo-rate, wide gardening hat, and all the adults break up at the sight of it.*)

RUTH: Travis, honey, what is that?

TRAVIS (*who thinks it is beautiful and appropriate*): It's a gardening hat! Like the ladies always have on in the magazines when they work in their gardens.

BENEATHA (*giggling fiercely*): Travis—we were trying to make Mama Mrs. Miniver—not Scar-lett O'Hara!

MAMA (*indignantly*): What's the matter with you all! This here is a beautiful hat! (*Absurdly.*) I always wanted me one just like it! (*She pops it on her head to prove it to her grandson, and the hat is ludicrous and considerably oversized.*)

RUTH: Hot dog! Go, Mama!

WALTER (*doubled over with laughter*): I'm sorry, Mama—but you look like you ready to go out and chop you some cotton sure enough!

(*They all laugh except* MAMA, *out of deference to* TRAVIS' *feelings.*)

MAMA (*gathering the boy up to her*): Bless your heart—this is the prettiest hat I ever owned— (WALTER, RUTH *and* BENEATHA *chime in—noisily, festively and insincerely congratulating* TRAVIS *on his gift.*) What are we all standing around here for? We ain't finished packin' yet. Bennie, you ain't packed one book.

(*The bell rings.*)

BENEATHA: That couldn't be the movers . . . it's not hardly two good yet—

(BENEATHA *goes into her room.* MAMA *starts for door.*)

WALTER (*turning, stiffening*): Wait—wait— I'll get it. (*He stands and looks at the door.*)

MAMA: You expecting company, son?

WALTER (*just looking at the door*): Yeah— yeah . . .

(MAMA *looks at* RUTH, *and they exchange innocent and unfrightened glances.*)

MAMA (*not understanding*): Well, let them in, son.

BENEATHA (*from her room*): We need some more string.

MAMA: Travis—you run to the hardware and get me some string cord.

(MAMA *goes out and* WALTER *turns and looks at* RUTH. TRAVIS *goes to a dish for money.*)

RUTH: Why don't you answer the door, man?

WALTER (*suddenly bounding across the floor to her*): 'Cause sometimes it hard to let the future begin! (*Stooping down in her face.*)
I got wings! You got wings!
All God's children got wings!

(*He crosses to the door and throws it open. Standing there is a very slight little man in a not too prosperous business suit and with haunted frightened eyes and a hat pulled down tightly, brim up, around his fore-head.* TRAVIS *passes between the men and exits.* WAL-TER *leans deep in the man's face, still in his jubi-lance.*)

When I get to heaven gonna put on my wings,
Gonna fly all over God's heaven . . .

(*The little man just stares at him.*)

Heaven—
(*Suddenly he stops and looks past the little man into the empty hallway.*) Where's Willy, man?

BOBO: He ain't with me.

WALTER (*not disturbed*): Oh—come on in. You know my wife.

BOBO (*dumbly, taking off his hat*): Yes—h'you, Miss Ruth.

RUTH (*quietly, a mood apart from her husband already, seeing* BOBO): Hello, Bobo.

WALTER: You right on time today . . . Right on time. That's the way! (*He slaps* BOBO *on his back.*) Sit down . . . lemme hear.

(RUTH *stands stiffly and quietly in back of them, as though somehow she senses death, her eyes fixed on her husband.*)

BOBO (*his frightened eyes on the floor, his hat in his hands*): Could I please get a drink a water, before I tell you about it, Walter Lee?

(WALTER *does not take his eyes off the man,* RUTH *goes blindly to the tap and gets a glass of water and brings it to* BOBO.)

WALTER: There ain't nothing wrong, is there?

BOBO: Lemme tell you—

WALTER: Man—didn't nothing go wrong?

BOBO: Lemme tell you—Walter Lee. (*Looking at* RUTH *and talking to her more than to* WALTER.) You know how it was. I got to tell you how it was. I mean first I got to tell you how it was all the way . . . I mean about the money I put in, Walter Lee . . .

WALTER (*with taut agitation now*): What about the money you put in?

BOBO: Well—it wasn't much as we told you—me and Willy—(*He stops.*) I'm sorry, Walter. I got a bad feeling about it. I got a real bad feeling about it . . .

WALTER: Man, what you telling me about all this for? . . . Tell me what happened in Springfield . . .

BOBO: Springfield.

RUTH (*like a dead woman*): What was supposed to happen in Springfield?

BOBO (*to her*): This deal that me and Walter went into with Willy—Me and Willy was going to go down to Springfield and spread some money 'round so's we wouldn't have to wait so long for the liquor license . . . That's what we were going to do. Everybody said that was the way you had to do, you understand, Miss Ruth?

WALTER: Man—what happened down there?

BOBO (*a pitiful man, near tears*): I'm trying to tell you, Walter.

WALTER (*screaming at him suddenly*): THEN TELL ME, GODDAMNIT . . . WHAT'S THE MATTER WITH YOU?

BOBO: Man . . . I didn't go to no Springfield, yesterday.

WALTER (*halted, life hanging in the moment*): Why not?

BOBO (*the long way, the hard way to tell*): 'Cause I didn't have no reasons to . . .

WALTER: Man, what are you talking about!

BOBO: I'm talking about the fact that when I got to the train station yesterday morning —eight o'clock like we planned . . . Man —*Willy didn't never show up*

WALTER: Why . . . where was he . . . where is he?

BOBO: That's what I'm trying to tell you . . . I don't know . . . I waited six hours . . . I called his house . . . and I waited . . . six hours . . . I waited in that train station six hours . . . (*Breaking into tears.*) That was all the extra money I had in the world . . . (*Looking up at* WALTER *with the tears running down his face.*) Man, *Willy is gone.*

WALTER: Gone, what you mean Willy is gone? Gone where? You mean he went by

himself. You mean he went off to Springfield by himself—to take care of getting the license —(*Turns and looks anxiously at* RUTH.) You mean maybe he didn't want too many people in on the business down there? (*Looks to* RUTH *again, as before.*) You know Willy got his own ways. (*Looks back to* BOBO.) Maybe you was late yesterday and he just went on down there without you. Maybe—maybe—he's been callin' you at home tryin' to tell you what happened or something. Maybe—maybe—he just got sick. He's somewhere—he's got to be somewhere. We just got to find him—me and you got to find him. (*Grabs* BOBO *senselessly by the collar and starts to shake him.*) We got to!

BOBO (*in sudden angry, frightened agony*): What's the matter with you, Walter! *When a cat take off with your money he don't leave you no maps!*

WALTER (*turning madly, as though he is looking for* WILLY *in the very room*): Willy! . . . Willy . . . don't do it . . . Please don't do it . . . Man, not with that money . . . Man, please, not with that money . . . Oh, God . . . Don't let it be true . . . (*He is wandering around, crying out for Willy and looking for him or perhaps for help from God.*) Man . . . I trusted you . . . Man, I put my life in your hands . . . (*He starts to crumple down on the floor as* RUTH *just covers her face in horror.* MAMA *opens the door and comes into the room, with* BENEATHA *behind her.*) Man . . . (*He starts to pound the floor with his fists, sobbing wildly.*) That money is made out of my father's flesh . . .

BOBO (*standing over him helplessly*): I'm sorry, Walter . . . (*Only* WALTER's *sobs reply.* BOBO *puts on his hat.*) I had my life staked on this deal, too . . . (*He exits.*)

MAMA (*to* WALTER): Son—(*She goes to him, bends down to him, talks to his bent head.*) Son . . . Is it gone? Son, I gave you sixty-five hundred dollars. Is it gone? All of it? Beneatha's money too?

WALTER (*lifting his head slowly*): Mama . . . I never . . . went to the bank at all . . .

MAMA (*not wanting to believe him*): You mean . . . your sister's school money . . . you used that too . . . Walter? . . .

WALTER: Yessss! . . . All of it . . . It's all gone . . .

(*There is total silence.* RUTH *stands with her face covered with her hands;* BENEATHA *leans forlornly against a wall, fingering a piece of red ribbon from the mother's gift.* MAMA *stops and looks at her son without recognition and then, quite without thinking about it, starts to beat him senselessly in the face.* BENEATHA *goes to them and stops it.*)

BENEATHA: Mama!

(MAMA *stops and looks at both of her children and rises slowly and wanders vaguely, aimlessly away from them.*)

MAMA: I seen . . . him . . . night after night . . . come in . . . and look at that rug . . . and then look at me . . . the red showing in his eyes . . . the veins moving in his head . . . I seen him grow thin and old before he was forty . . . working and working and working like some-body's old horse . . . killing himself . . . and you—you give it all away in a day . . .

BENEATHA: Mama—

MAMA: Oh, God . . . (*She looks up to Him.*) Look down here—and show me the strength.

BENEATHA: Mama—

MAMA (*folding over*): Strength . . .

BENEATHA (*plaintively*): Mama . . .

MAMA: Strength!

ACT III

(*An hour later.*

At curtain, there is a sullen light of gloom in the living room, gray light not unlike that which began the first scene of Act One. At left we can see WALTER *within his room, alone with himself. He is stretched out on the bed, his shirt out and open, his arms under his head. He does not smoke, he does not cry out, he merely lies there, looking up at the ceiling, much as if he were alone in the world.*

In the living room BENEATHA *sits at the table, still surrounded by the now almost ominous packing crates. She sits looking off. We feel that this is a mood struck perhaps an hour before, and it lingers now, full of the empty sound of profound disappointment. We see on a line from her brother's bedroom the sameness of their attitudes. Presently the bell rings and* BENEATHA *rises without ambition or interest in answering. It is* ASA-GAI, *smiling broadly, striding into the room with energy and happy expectation and conversation.*)

ASAGAI: I came over . . . I had some free time. I thought I might help with the packing. Ah, I like the look of packing crates! A house-hold in preparation for a journey! It depresses some people . . . but for me . . . it is another feeling. Something full of the flow of life, do you understand? Movement, progress . . . It makes me think of Africa.

BENEATHA: Africa!

ASAGAI: What kind of a mood is this? Have I told you how deeply you move me?

BENEATHA: He gave away the money, Asagai . . .

ASAGAI: Who gave away what money?

BENEATHA: The insurance money. My brother gave it away.

ASAGAI: Gave it away?

BENEATHA: He made an investment! With a man even Travis wouldn't have trusted.

ASAGAI: And it's gone?

BENEATHA: Gone!

ASAGAI: I'm very sorry . . . And you, now?

BENEATHA: Me? . . . Me? . . . Me I'm nothing . . . Me. When I was very small . . . we used to take our sleds out in the wintertime and the only hills we had were the ice-covered stone steps of some houses down the street. And we used to fill them in with snow and make them smooth and slide down them all day . . . and it was very dangerous you know . . . far too steep . . . and sure enough one day a kid named Rufus came down too fast and hit the sidewalk . . . and we saw his face just split open right there in front of us . . . And I remember standing there looking at his bloody open face thinking that was the end of Rufus. But the ambulance came and they took him to the hospital and they fixed the broken bones and they sewed it all up . . . and the next time I saw Rufus he just had a little line down the middle of his face . . . I never got over that . . .

ASAGAI: What?

BENEATHA: That that was what one person could do for another, fix him up—sew up the problem, make him all right again. That was the most marvelous thing in the world . . . I wanted to do that. I always thought it was the one con-crete thing in the world that a human being could do. Fix up the sick, you know—and make them whole again. This was truly being God. . . .

ASAGAI: You wanted to be God?

BENEATHA: No—I wanted to cure. It used to be so important to me. I wanted to cure. It used to matter. I used to care. I mean about people and how their bodies hurt . . .

ASAGAI: And you've stopped caring?

BENEATHA: Yes—I think so.

ASAGAI: Why?

(WALTER *rises, goes to the door of his room and is about to open it, then stops and stands listening, lean-ing on the door jamb.*)

BENEATHA: Because it doesn't seem deep enough, close enough to what ails mankind—I mean this thing of sewing up bodies or administering drugs. Don't you understand? It was a child's reaction to the world. I thought that doctors had the secret to all the hurts. . . . That's the way a child sees things—or an idealist.

ASAGAI: Children see things very well sometimes—and idealists even better.

BENEATHA: I know that's what you think. Because you are still where I left off—you still care. This is what you see for the world, for Africa. You with the dreams of the future will patch up all Africa—you are going to cure the Great Sore of colonialism with Independence—

ASAGAI: Yes!

BENEATHA: Yes—and you think that one word is the penicillin of the human spirit: "Independence!" But then what?

ASAGAI: That will be the problem for another time. First we must get there.

BENEATHA: And where does it end?

ASAGAI: End? Who even spoke of an end? To life? To living?

BENEATHA: An end to misery!

ASAGAI (smiling): You sound like a French intellectual.

BENEATHA: No! I sound like a human being who just had her future taken right out of her hands! While I was sleeping in my bed in there, things were happening in this world that directly concerned me—and nobody asked me, consulted me—they just went out and did things—and changed my life. Don't you see there isn't any real progress, Asagai, there is only one large circle that we march in, around and around, each of us with our own little picture—in front of us—our own little mirage that we think is the future.

ASAGAI: That is the mistake.

BENEATHA: What?

ASAGAI: What you just said—about the circle. It isn't a circle—it is simply a long line—as in geometry, you know, one that reaches into infinity. And because we cannot see the end—we also cannot see how it changes. And it is very odd but those who see the changes are called "idealists"—and those who cannot, or refuse to think, they are the "realists." It is very strange, and amusing too, I think.

BENEATHA: You—you are almost religious.

ASAGAI: Yes . . . I think I have the religion of doing what is necessary in the world—and of worshipping man—because he is so marvelous, you see.

BENEATHA: Man is foul! And the human race deserves its misery!

ASAGAI: You see: *you* have become the religious one in the old sense. Already, and after such a small defeat, you are worshipping despair.

BENEATHA: From now on, I worship the truth—and the truth is that people are puny, small and selfish. . . .

ASAGAI: Truth? Why is it that you despairing ones always think that only you have the truth? I never thought to see *you* like that. Your brother made a stupid, childish mistake—and you are grateful to him. So that now you can give up the ailing human race on account of it. You talk about what good is struggle; what good is anything? Where are we all going? And why are we bothering?

BENEATHA: *And you cannot answer it!* All your talk and dreams about Africa and Independence. Independence and then what? What about all the crooks and petty thieves and just plain idiots who will come into power to steal and plunder the same as before—only now they will be black and do it in the name of the new Independence—You cannot answer that.

ASAGAI (shouting over her): I live the answer! (Pause.) In my village at home it is the exceptional man who can even read a newspaper . . . or who ever *sees* a book at all. I will go home and much of what I will have to say will seem strange to the people of my village . . . But I will teach and work and things will happen, slowly and swiftly. At times it will seem that nothing changes at all . . . and then again . . . the sudden dramatic events which make history leap into the future. And then quiet again. Retrogression even. Guns, murder, revolution. And I even will have moments when I wonder if the quiet was not better than all that death and hatred. But I will look about my village at the illiteracy and disease and ignorance and I will not wonder long. And perhaps . . . perhaps I will be a great man . . . I mean perhaps I will hold on to the substance of truth and find my way always with the right course . . . and perhaps for it I will be butchered in my bed some night by the servants of empire . . .

BENEATHA: *The martyr!*

ASAGAI: . . . or perhaps I shall live to be a very old man respected and esteemed in my new nation . . . And perhaps I shall hold office and this is what I'm trying to tell you, Alaiyo; perhaps the things I believe now for my country will be wrong and outmoded, and I will not understand and do terrible things to have things my way or merely to keep my power. Don't you see that there will be young men and women, not British soldiers then, but my own black countrymen . . . to step out of the shadows some evening and slit my then useless throat? Don't you see they have always been there . . . that they always will be. And that such a thing as my own death will be an advance? They who might kill me even . . . actually replenish me!

BENEATHA: Oh, Asagai, I know all that.

ASAGAI: Good! Then stop moaning and groaning and tell me what you plan to do.

BENEATHA: Do?

ASAGAI: I have a bit of a suggestion.

BENEATHA: What?

ASAGAI (*rather quietly for him*): That when it is all over—that you come home with me—

BENEATHA (*slapping herself on the forehead with exasperation born of misunderstanding*): Oh—Asagai—at this moment you decide to be romantic!

ASAGAI (*quickly understanding the misunderstanding*): My dear, young creature of the New World—I do not mean across the city—I mean across the ocean; home—to Africa.

BENEATHA (*slowly understanding and turning to him with murmured amazement*): To—to Nigeria?

ASAGAI: Yes! . . . (*Smiling and lifting his arms playfully.*) Three hundred years later the African Prince rose up out of the seas and swept the maiden back across the middle passage over which her ancestors had come—

BENEATHA (*unable to play*): Nigeria?

ASAGAI: Nigeria. Home. (*Coming to her with genuine romantic flippancy.*) I will show you our mountains and our stars; and give you cool drinks from gourds and teach you the old songs and the ways of our people—and, in time, we will pretend that—(*Very softly.*)—you have only been away for a day—

(*She turns her back to him, thinking. He swings her around and takes her full in his arms in a long embrace which proceeds to passion.*)

BENEATHA (*pulling away*): You're getting me all mixed up—

ASAGAI: Why?

BENEATHA: Too many things—too many things have happened today. I must sit down and think. I don't know what I feel about anything right this minute. (*She promptly sits down and props her chin on her fist.*)

ASAGAI (*charmed*): All right, I shall leave you. No—don't get up. (*Touching her, gently sweetly.*) Just sit awhile and think . . . Never be afraid to sit awhile and think. (*He goes to door and looks at her.*) How often I have looked at you and said,

"Ah—so this is what the New World hath finally wrought . . ."

(*He exits.* BENEATHA *sits on alone. Presently* WALTER *enters from his room and starts to rummage through things, feverishly looking for something. She looks up and turns in her seat.*)

BENEATHA (*hissingly*): Yes—just look at what the New World hath wrought! . . . Just look! (*She gestures with bitter disgust.*) There he is! *Monsieur le petit bourgeois noir*—himself! There he is—Symbol of a Rising Class! Entrepreneur! Titan of the system! (WALTER *ignores her completely and continues frantically and destructively looking for something and hurling things to floor and tearing things out of their place in his search.* BENEATHA *ignores the eccentricity of his actions and goes on with the monologue of insult.*) Did you dream of yachts on Lake Michigan, Brother? Did you see yourself on that Great Day sitting down at the Conference Table, surrounded by all the mighty bald-headed men in America? All halted, waiting, breathless, waiting for your pronouncements on industry? Waiting for you—Chairman of the Board? (WALTER *finds what he is looking for—a small piece of white paper—and pushes it in his pocket and puts on his coat and rushes out without ever having looked at her. She shouts after him.*) I look at you and I see the final triumph of stupidity in the world!

(*The door slams and she returns to just sitting again.* RUTH *comes quickly out of* MAMA's *room.*)

RUTH: Who was that?

BENEATHA: Your husband.

RUTH: Where did he go?

BENEATHA: Who knows—maybe he has an appointment at U.S. Steel.

RUTH (*anxiously, with frightened eyes*): You didn't say nothing bad to him, did you?

BENEATHA: Bad? Say anything bad to him? No—I told him he was a sweet boy and full of dreams and everything is strictly peachy keen, as the ofay kids say!

(MAMA *enters from her bedroom. She is lost, vague, trying to catch hold, to make some sense of her former command of the world, but it still eludes her. A sense of waste overwhelms her gait; a measure of apology rides on her shoulders. She goes to her plant, which has remained on the table, looks at it, picks it up and takes it to the window sill and sits it outside, and she stands and looks at it a long moment. Then she closes the window, straightens her body with effort and turns around to her children.*)

MAMA: Well—ain't it a mess in here, though? (*A false cheerfulness, a beginning of something.*) I guess we all better stop moping around and get some work done. All this unpacking and everything we got to do. (RUTH *raises her head slowly in response to the sense of the line; and* BENEATHA *in similar manner turns very slowly to look at her mother.*) One of you all better call the moving people and tell 'em not to come.

RUTH: Tell 'em not to come?

MAMA: Of course, baby. Ain't no need in 'em coming all the way here and having to go back. They charges for that too. (*She sits down, fingers to her brow, thinking.*) Lord, ever since I was a little girl, I always remembers people saying, "Lena—Lena Eggleston, you aims too high all the time. You needs to slow down and see life a little more like it is. Just slow down some." That's what they always used to say down home—"Lord, that Lena Eggleston is a high-minded thing. She'll get her due one day!"

RUTH: No, Lena . . .

MAMA: Me and Big Walter just didn't never learn right.

RUTH: Lena, no! We gotta go. Bennie—tell her . . . (*She rises and crosses to* BENEATHA *with her arms outstretched.* BENEATHA *doesn't respond.*) Tell her we can still move . . . the notes ain't but a hundred and twenty five a month. We got four grown people in this house—we can work . . .

MAMA (*to herself*): Just aimed too high all the time—

RUTH (*turning and going to* MAMA *fast the words pouring out with urgency and desperation*): Lena—I'll work . . . I'll work twenty hours a day in all the kitchens in Chicago . . . I'll strap my baby on my back if I have to and scrub all the floors in America and wash all the sheets in America if I have to—but we got to move . . . We got to get out of here.

(MAMA *reaches out absently and pats* RUTH'S *hand.*)

MAMA: No—I sees things differently now. Been thinking 'bout some of the things we could do to fix this place up some. I seen a second-hand bureau over on Maxwell Street just the other day that could fit right there. (*She points to where the new furniture might go.* RUTH *wanders away from her.*) Would need some new handles on it and then a little varnish and then it look like something brand-new. And—we can put up them new curtains in the kitchen . . . Why this place be looking fine. Cheer us all up so that we forget trouble ever came . . . (*To* RUTH.) And you could get some nice screens to put up in your room round the baby's basinet . . . (*She looks at both of them, pleadingly.*) Sometimes you just got to know when to give up some things . . . and hold on to what you got.

(WALTER *enters from the outside, looking spent and leaning against the door, his coat hanging from him.*)

MAMA: Where you been, son?

WALTER (*breathing hard*): Made a call.

MAMA: To who, son?

WALTER: To The Man.

MAMA: What man, baby?

WALTER: The Man, Mama. Don't you know who The Man is?

RUTH: Walter Lee?

WALTER: *The Man.* Like the guys in the streets say—The Man. Captain Boss—Mistuh Charley . . . Old Captain Please Mr. Bossman . . .

BENEATHA (*suddenly*): Lindner!

WALTER: That's right! That's good. I told him to come right over.

BENEATHA (*fiercely, understanding*): For what? What do you want to see him for!

WALTER (*looking at his sister*): We going to do business with him.

MAMA: What you talking 'bout, son?

WALTER: Talking 'bout life, Mama. You all always telling me to see life like it is. Well—I laid in there on my back today . . . and I figured it out. Life just like it is. Who gets and who don't get. (*He sits down with his coat on and laughs.*) Mama, you know it's all divided up. Life is. Sure enough. Between the takers and the "tooken." (*He laughs.*) I've figured it out finally. (*He looks around at them.*) Yeah. Some of us always getting "tooken." (*He laughs.*) People like Willy Harris, they don't never get "tooken." And you know why the rest of us do? 'Cause we all mixed up. Mixed up bad. We get to looking 'round for the right and the wrong; and we worry about it and cry about it and stay up nights trying to figure out 'bout the wrong and the right of things all the time . . . And all the time, man, them takers is out there operating, just taking and taking. Willy Harris? Shoot—Willy Harris don't even count. He don't even count in the big scheme of things. But I'll say one thing for old Willy Harris . . . he's taught me something. He's taught me to keep my eye on what counts in this world. Yeah—(*Shouting out a little.*) Thanks, Willy!

RUTH: What did you call that man for, Walter Lee?

WALTER: Called him to tell him to come on over to the show. Gonna put on a show for the man. Just what he wants to see. You see, Mama, the man came here today and he told us that them people out there where you want us to move—well they so upset they willing to pay us not to move out there. (*He laughs again.*) And —and oh, Mama—you would of been proud of the way me and Ruth and Bennie acted. We told him to get out . . . Lord have mercy! We told the man to get out. Oh, we was some proud folks this afternoon, yeah. (*He lights a cigarette.*) We were still full of that old-time stuff . . .

RUTH (*coming toward him slowly*): You talking 'bout taking them people's money to keep us from moving in that house?

WALTER: I ain't just talking 'bout it, baby— I'm telling you that's what's going to happen.

BENEATHA: Oh, God! Where is the bottom! Where is the real honest-to-God bottom so he can't go any farther!

WALTER: See—that's the old stuff. You and that boy that was here today. You all want everybody to carry a flag and a spear and sing some marching songs, huh? You wanna spend your life looking into things and trying to find the right and the wrong part, huh? Yeah. You know what's going to happen to that boy someday— he'll find himself sitting in a dungeon, locked in forever—and the takers will have the key! Forget it, baby! There ain't no causes—there ain't nothing but taking in this world, and he who takes most is smartest—and it don't make a damn bit of difference *how*.

MAMA: You making something inside me cry, son. Some awful pain inside me.

WALTER: Don't cry, Mama. Understand. That white man is going to walk in that door able to write checks for more money than we ever had. It's important to him and I'm going to help him . . . I'm going to put on the show, Mama.

MAMA: Son—I come from five generations of people who was slaves and sharecroppers—but ain't nobody in my family never let nobody pay 'em no money that was a way of telling us we wasn't fit to walk the earth. We ain't never been that poor. (*Raising her eyes and looking at him.*) We ain't never been that dead inside.

BENEATHA: Well—we are dead now. All the talk about dreams and sunlight that goes on in this house. All dead.

WALTER: What's the matter with you all! I didn't make this world! It was give to me this way! Hell, yes, I want me some yachts someday!

Yes, I want to hang some real pearls 'round my wife's neck. Ain't she supposed to wear no pearls? Somebody tell me—tell me, who decides which women is suppose to wear pearls in this world. I tell you I am a *man*—and I think my wife should wear some pearls in this world!

(*This last line hangs a good while and* WALTER *begins to move about the room. The word "Man" has penetrated his consciousness; he mumbles it to himself repeatedly between strange agitated pauses as he moves about.*)

MAMA: Baby, how you going to feel on the inside?

WALTER: Fine! . . . Going to feel fine . . . a man . . .

MAMA: You won't have nothing left then, Walter Lee.

WALTER (*coming to her*): I'm going to feel fine, Mama. I'm going to look that son-of-a-bitch in the eyes and say—(*He falters.*)—and say, "All right, Mr. Lindner—(*He falters even more.*)—that's your neighborhood out there. You got the right to keep it like you want. You got the right to have it like you want. Just write the check and —the house is yours." And, and I am going to say—(*His voice almost breaks.*) And you—you people just put the money in my hand and you won't have to live next to this bunch of stinking niggers! . . . (*He straightens up and moves away from his mother, walking around the room.*) Maybe —maybe I'll just get down on my black knees . . . (*He does so;* RUTH *and* BENNIE *and* MAMA *watch him in frozen horror.*) Captain, Mistuh, Bossman. (*He starts crying.*) A-hee-hee-hee! (*Wringing his hands in profoundly anguished imitation.*) Yassssssuh! Great White Father, just gi' ussen de money, fo' God's sake, and we's ain't gwine come out deh and dirty up yo' white folks neighborhood . . . (*He breaks down completely, then gets up and goes into the bedroom.*)

BENEATHA: That is not a man. That is nothing but a toothless rat.

MAMA: Yes—death done come in this here house. (*She is nodding, slowly, reflectively.*) Done come walking in my house. On the lips of my children. You what supposed to be my beginning again. You—what supposed to be my harvest. (*To* BENEATHA.) You—you mourning your brother?

BENEATHA: He's no brother of mine.

MAMA: What you say?

BENEATHA: I said that that individual in that room is no brother of mine.

MAMA: That's what I thought you said. You

feeling like you better than he is today? (BE-NEATHA *does not answer.*) Yes? What you tell him a minute ago? That he wasn't a man? Yes? You give him up for me? You done wrote his epitaph too—like the rest of the world? Well, who give you the privilege?

BENEATHA: Be on my side for once! You saw what he just did, Mama! You saw him—down on his knees. Wasn't it you who taught me—to despise any man who would do that. Do what he's going to do.

MAMA: Yes—I taught you that. Me and your daddy. But I thought I taught you something else too . . . I thought I taught you to love him.

BENEATHA: Love him? There is nothing left to love.

MAMA: There is always something left to love. And if you ain't learned that, you ain't learned nothing. (*Looking at her.*) Have you cried for that boy today? I don't mean for yourself and for the family 'cause we lost the money. I mean for him; what he been through and what it done to him. Child, when do you think is the time to love somebody the most; when they done good and made things easy for everybody? Well then, you ain't through learning—because that ain't the time at all. It's when he's at his lowest and can't believe in hisself 'cause the world done whipped him so. When you starts measuring somebody, measure him right, child, measure him right. Make sure you done taken into account what hills and valleys he come through before he got to wherever he is.

(TRAVIS *bursts into the room at the end of the speech, leaving the door open.*)

TRAVIS: Grandmama—the moving men are downstairs! The truck just pulled up.

MAMA (*turning and looking at him*): Are they, baby? They downstairs?

(*She sighs and sits. Lindner appears in the doorway. He peers in and knocks lightly, to gain attention, and comes in. All turn to look at him.*)

LINDNER (*hat and briefcase in hand*): Uh—hello . . .

(RUTH *crosses mechanically to the bedroom door and opens it and lets it swing open freely and slowly as the lights come up on WALTER within, still in his coat, sitting at the far corner of the room. He looks up and out through the room to LINDNER.*)

RUTH: He's here.

(*A long minute passes and WALTER slowly gets up.*)

LINDNER (*coming to the table with efficiency, putting his briefcase on the table and starting to unfold papers and unscrew fountain pens*): Well, I certainly was glad to hear from you people. (WALTER *has begun the trek out of the room, slowly and awkwardly, rather like a small boy, passing the back of his sleeve across his mouth from time to time.*) Life can really be so much simpler than people let it be most of the time. Well—with whom do I negotiate? You, Mrs. Younger, or your son here? (MAMA *sits with her hands folded on her lap and her eyes closed as* WALTER *advances.* TRAVIS *goes close to* LINDNER *and looks at the papers curiously.*) Just some official papers, sonny.

RUTH: Travis, you go downstairs.

MAMA (*opening her eyes and looking into* WALTER's): No. Travis, you stay right here. And you make him understand what you doing, Walter Lee. You teach him good. Like Willy Harris taught you. You show where our five generations done come to. Go ahead, son—

WALTER (*looks down into his boy's eyes.* TRAVIS *grins at him merrily and* WALTER *draws him beside him with his arm lightly around his shoulder*): Well, Mr. Lindner. (BENEATHA *turns away.*) We called you—(*There is a profound, simple groping quality in his speech.*)—because, well, me and my family (*He looks around and shifts from one foot to the other.*) Well—we are very plain people . . .

LINDNER: Yes—

WALTER: I mean—I have worked as a chauffeur most of my life—and my wife here, she does domestic work in people's kitchens. So does my mother. I mean—we are plain people . . .

LINDNER: Yes, Mr. Younger—

WALTER (*really like a small boy, looking down at his shoes and then up at the man*): And—uh—well, my father, well, he was a laborer most of his life.

LINDNER (*absolutely confused*): Uh, yes—

WALTER (*looking down at his toes once again*): My father almost beat a man to death once because this man called him a bad name or something, you know what I mean?

LINDNER: No, I'm afraid I don't.

WALTER (*finally straightening up*): Well, what I mean is that we come from people who had a lot of pride. I mean—we are very proud people. And that's my sister over there and she's going to be a doctor—and we are very proud—

LINDNER: Well—I am sure that is very nice, but—

WALTER (*starting to cry and facing the man eye to eye*): What I am telling you is that we called you over here to tell you that we are very proud and that this is—this is my son, who makes the sixth generation of our family in this country, and that we have all thought about your offer and we have decided to move into our house because my father—my father—he earned it. (MAMA *has her eyes closed and is rocking back and forth as though she were in church, with her head nodding the amen yes.*) We don't want to make no trouble for nobody or fight no causes—but we will try to be good neighbors. That's all we got to say. (*He looks the man absolutely in the eyes.*) We don't want your money. (*He turns and walks away from the man.*)

LINDNER (*looking around at all of them*): I take it then that you have decided to occupy.

BENEATHA: That's what the man said.

LINDNER (*to* MAMA *in her reverie*): Then I would like to appeal to you, Mrs. Younger. You are older and wiser and understand things better I am sure . . .

MAMA (*rising*): I am afraid you don't understand. My son said we was going to move and there ain't nothing left for me to say. (*Shaking her head with double meaning.*) You know how these young folks is nowadays, mister. Can't do a thing with 'em. Good-bye.

LINDNER (*folding up his materials*): Well—if you are that final about it . . . There is nothing left for me to say. (*He finishes. He is almost ignored by the family, who are concentrating on* WALTER LEE. *At the door* LINDNER *halts and looks around.*) I sure hope you people know what you're doing. (*He shakes his head and exits.*)

RUTH (*looking around and coming to life*): Well, for God's sake—if the moving men are here— LET'S GET THE HELL OUT OF HERE!

MAMA (*into action*): Ain't it the truth! Look at all this here mess. Ruth put Travis' good jacket on him . . . Walter Lee, fix your tie and tuck your shirt in, you look just like somebody's hoodlum. Lord have mercy, where is my plant? (*She flies to get it amid the general bustling of the family, who are deliberately trying to ignore the nobility of the past moment.*) You all start on down . . . Travis child, don't go empty-handed . . . Ruth, where did I put that box with my skillets in it? I want to be in charge of it myself . . . I'm going to make us the biggest dinner we ever ate tonight . . . Beneatha, what's the matter with them stockings? Pull them things up, girl . . .

(*The family starts to file out as two moving men appear and begin to carry out the heavier pieces of furniture, bumping into the family as they move about.*)

BENEATHA: Mama, Asagai—asked me to marry him today and go to Africa—

MAMA (*in the middle of her getting-ready activity*): He did? You ain't old enough to marry nobody—(*Seeing the moving men lifting one of her chairs precariously.*) Darling, that ain't no bale of cotton, please handle it so we can sit in it again. I had that chair twenty-five years . . .

(*The movers sigh with exasperation and go on with their work.*)

BENEATHA (*girlishly and unreasonably trying to pursue the conversation*): To go to Africa, Mama—be a doctor in Africa . . .

MAMA (*distracted*): Yes, baby—

WALTER: Africa! What he want you to go to Africa for?

BENEATHA: To practice there . . .

WALTER: Girl, if you don't get all them silly ideas out your head! You better marry yourself a man with some loot . . .

BENEATHA (*angrily, precisely as in the first scene of the play*): What have you got to do with who I marry!

WALTER: Plenty. Now I think George murchison—

(*He and* BENEATHA *go out yelling at each other vigorously;* BENEATHA *is heard saying that she would not marry* GEORGE MURCHISON *if he were Adam and she were Eve, etc. The anger is loud and real till their voices diminish.* RUTH *stands at the door and turns to* MAMA *and smiles knowingly.*)

MAMA (*fixing her hat at last*): Yeah—they something all right, my children . . .

RUTH: Yeah—they're something. Let's go, Lena.

MAMA (*stalling, starting to look around at the house*): Yes—I'm coming. Ruth—

RUTH: Yes?

MAMA (*quietly, woman to woman*): He finally come into his manhood today, didn't he? Kind of like a rainbow after the rain . . .

RUTH (*biting her lip lest her own pride explode in front of* MAMA): Yes, Lena.

(WALTER's *voice calls for them raucously.*)

MAMA (*waving* RUTH *out vaguely*): All right, honey—go on down. I be down directly.

(RUTH *hesitates, then exits.* MAMA *stands, at last alone in the living room, her plant on the table before her as the lights start to come down. She looks around at all the walls and ceilings and suddenly, despite herself, while the children call below, a great heaving thing rises in her and she puts her fist to her mouth, takes a final desperate look, pulls her coat about her, pats her hat and goes out. The lights dim down. The door opens and she comes back in, grabs her plant, and goes out for the last time.)*

CURTAIN

Jean–Claude van Itallie: *TV* (1965)

Born in Brussels, in 1936, van Itallie came to America when he was four and was naturalized as a citizen in 1952. Most of his life has centered around New York City, although he has also spent time on a farm in New England for part of each year. He received his bachelor's degree from Harvard in 1958 and has taught playwrighting at the New School for Social Research, Princeton, and Yale. Most of his working experience is related to theater and broadcasting; his writing has been done for the off-Broadway and off-off-Broadway stage as well as for television and films.

TV is one of three one-act plays—along with *Interview* and *Motel*—that were played together as *America Hurrah*. The plays all represent a general criticism of American life, from the world of business and work in *Interview,* to the world of television and its intrusions into our lives, in *TV,* and to the values of bourgeois family life as revealed in the brutal *Motel.* The plays were stunning in performance, but it was clear that Broadway audiences would not find these plays entertaining in the usual sense. With the beginning of the 1960s and the polarization of the American people—a result in part of the Vietnam War —the Broadway stage became in large measure a haven for long-running musicals, plays with already established "big names," and generally light entertainment in some ways almost indistinguishable from television situation comedies. It was a period in which plays were aimed at the "tired businessman" and his family or client, interested mainly in relief from the everyday world and its daily problems.

Van Itallie's work has never had a place in this kind of theatrical environment. He has been actively pacifistic in his views on war and anarchistic in his views on government. *TV,* like most of his work, is openly critical of middle-class life and of middle-class politics, whether liberal or conservative. Perhaps its most damning criticism is in its final moments, when the world of TV becomes almost indistinguishable from the world of Hal, Susan, and George. Their views, feelings, and problems are echoed by the television screen so exactly that the clichéd sit-com, "My Favorite Teenager," becomes a gloss on the lives of those watching it. In fact, it virtually absorbs their lives.

This is one of the points of the drama, but other aspects are also important. One concerns the way in which the television screen reflects the world we live in. The headnote to the play, from the writings of Marshall McLuhan, talks about Narcissus, the Greek youth who remained staring at himself in a pool, thoroughly fascinated, totally uninterested in any world beyond himself and his own reflection. The way in which this play is printed, in two half-columns, as well as the way in which it was staged, emphasizes the implications of such a "closed circuit." What Susan and Hal and George know about the world seems to have been pre-selected by television. The coverage of the Vietnam War, of politics in terms of the president and his family—not to mention the "literature" in the form of old feature films—is presented in a curious way. We have the feeling that the three viewers of the television set live lives of immense vapidity and that they no longer have the capacity to react strongly to what they see. The war does not interest them. The incredible threats the president utters do not interest them. The dramatizations of history do not interest them. The commercials interest them slightly; the mindless idiocy of the TV teenage sit-com—totally absurd in terms of any genuine adolescent experiences—is the one thing that totally absorbs their attention, from Susan in her twenties to George in his forties.

TV, like the other plays in *America Hurrah,* does not read as well as it plays. The surrealist presentation of the plays made them tremendously involving and profoundly intense. *TV* still survives well as a reading play, but *Motel* is almost totally lost because of its dependence on intense sound effects, automobiles and sirens, as well as remarkable costumes and oversize dummies. In the off-Broadway production most of the dialogue was on tape and the speed of the drama was frenetic and almost hysterical. The entire production was closer to a "happening" than to conventional theater if only because it would be difficult to imagine the plays touring or being performed outside New York.

Van Itallie has written many one-act plays: *It's Almost Like Being There (Tulane Drama Review,* 1965), *Where is de Queen?* (1966), *Collision Course* (a group of one-acters) (1968), *The Serpent: A Ceremony* (1968), and several others. *Mystery Play,* a two-act drama, was staged in 1973. Generally, these plays have been performed in regional and university theaters as well as in the little theatres of lower New York, such as Café La Mama and Café au Go Go. Several of his plays have been performed recently on educational television.

Suggested readings

Jean-Claude van Itallie, *America Hurrah* (New York: Coward, McCann, 1967).
Robert Brustein, *The Third Theatre* (New York: Simon and Schuster, 1970).
The Serif. Kent, Ohio: 1971. Special issue with critical essays.

TV

Jean-Claude van Itallie

The youth Narcissus mistook his own reflection in the water for another person . . . He was numb. He had adapted to his extension of himself and had become a closed system.

MARSHALL McLUHAN

CHARACTERS

HAL

SUSAN

GEORGE

HELEN FARGIS, *the* PRESIDENT'S WIFE, *a UGP researcher, a member of the rock and roll group, a peace marcher,* LILY HEAVEN, *the headache sufferer, a singer in the evangelist choir, and* MOTHER *in "My Favorite Teenager"*

HARRY FARGIS, FIRST NEWS ANNOUNCER, STEVE, *the* PRESIDENT, *UGP researcher, a member of the rock and roll group,* WEATHER ANNOUNCER, HE *in the Billion Dollar Movie,* EVANGELIST, *and* FATHER *in "My Favorite Teenager"*

WONDERBOY, SECOND NEWS ANNOUNCER, *the man in the cigarette commercial,* BILL, *UGP Announcer, a member of the rock and roll group, one young man from New York City, Lily Heaven's Announcer, Ron Campbell, Johnny Holland, and a singer in the evangelist choir*

The woman in the cigarette commercial, the President's older daughter, a UGP researcher, a member of the rock and roll group, a peace marcher, Famous Television Personality, CAROL, SHE *in the Billion Dollar Movie, and a singer in the evangelist choir*

SALLY, *the* PRESIDENT'S YOUNGER DAUGHTER, *the Spanish teacher, a UGP researcher, a member of the rock and roll group,* ANNIE KAPPELHOFF, LADY ANNOUNCER, LUCI, *a singer in the evangelist choir, and* DAUGHTER *in "My Favorite Teenager"*

Original design for printed script: Sharon Thie

The set is white and impersonal. There are two doors on the stage right wall: one leads to the rest rooms, the other to the hall.

Downstage right is the control console in a television viewing room. It faces the audience.

Above the console, also facing the audience, is a screen. Projected on it, from the rear, is the logo of a television station.

Downstage left is a water cooler, a closet for coats, and a telephone. Downstage right is a bulletin board. Upstage center is a table with a coffee maker on it.

HAL and SUSAN are seated at the console, Susan in the middle chair. They are both in their twenties. HAL is playing, as he often will, with his penknife: whittling pencils, paring his nails, or throwing it at the bulletin board. SUSAN is involved with the papers on the console, with sharpening pencils, and so forth.

At the back of the stage, on the left, are the five actors who will portray what will appear on television. For the moment they have no light on them and their backs are to the audience.

To indicate the correlation of the events and dialogue on television with those which occur in the viewing room, the play is printed in two columns.

HAL
So what do you say?

SUSAN
I don't know.

HAL
That doesn't get us very far, does it?

SUSAN
Well it's such a surprise, your asking. I was planning to work on my apartment.

HAL
I'll help you, after the movie.

SUSAN
That's too late. One thing I have to have is eight hours' sleep. I really have to have that.

(GEORGE *enters; he is older than* HAL *and* SUSAN, *and is in charge of the viewing room.*)

HAL

Hi, George.

SUSAN

Hello, George.

GEORGE (*to* SUSAN)

Is that a new dress?

SUSAN (*nodding toward* HAL)

HE didn't even notice.

(GEORGE *puts his coat and jacket in the closet and puts on a cardigan sweater.*)

GEORGE

How many check marks have you made, Hal?

HAL

I don't know, George. I don't count.

SUSAN

I got it on Fourteenth Street. I love going into places like that because they're so cheap.

GEORGE

If you don't make at least a hundred check marks, they'll dock you. That's what the totals count column is for.

SUSAN (*looking at herself in a mirror*)

Have I lost any weight?

GEORGE

Where would you lose it from?

HAL

George, how come they haven't asked us for a detailed report in nearly three weeks?

GEORGE

How should I know?

HAL

Think they're forgetting about us, George?

SUSAN

I was trying to tell in the Ladies, but the fluorescent light in there just burns your eyes.

HAL

I've never been to the Ladies. You think I'd like it?

GEORGE

This viewing room is the backbone of the rating system.

HAL

He said that to you LAST month, George. Things move fast.

GEORGE

Are you trying to make me nervous?

HAL

Maybe.

GEORGE

Well don't, because my stomach is not very good this morning.

SUSAN

I want to know seriously, and I mean seriously, do you think I've lost any weight?

GEORGE

Where from?

HAL

Why don't you let yourself go?

SUSAN

What do you mean?

HAL

Just let nature take its course.

SUSAN

What if nature wants you to be a big
fat slob?

HAL

Then be a big fat slob.

SUSAN

Thanks.

(HAL, SUSAN, *and* GEORGE *sit down and get ready for the day's work.* GEORGE *turns a dial on the console which turns on TV. Two of the* PEOPLE ON TELEVISION *turn around to play* HELEN *and* HARRY FARGIS.*

All of the PEOPLE ON TELEVISION *are dressed in shades of gray. They make no costume changes and use no real props. Their faces are made up with thin horizontal black lines to suggest the way they might appear to a viewer. They are playing television images. Their style of acting is cool, not pushy. As television characters, they have only a few facial masks, such as "cute," "charming," or "serious," which they use infallibly, like signals, in the course of each television segment.*

After each television segment, the PEOPLE *involved in it will freeze where they are until it is time for them to become another character.*

As the play progresses, the PEOPLE ON TELEVISION *will use more and more of the stage. The impression should be that of a slow invasion of the viewing room.* HAL, SUSAN, *and* GEORGE *will simply move around the* PEOPLE ON TELEVISION *when that becomes necessary. Ultimately, the control console itself will be taken over by television characters, so that the distinction between what is on television and what is occurring in the viewing room will be lost completely.*

The attention of the audience should be focused not on a parody of television, but on the relationship of the life that appears on television to the life that goes on in the viewing room.

All of the actors will need to be constantly aware of what is happening on all parts of the stage, in order to give and take the attention of the audience to and from each other, and also in order to demonstrate the influence of the style of certain television segments on the behavior of HAL, SUSAN *and* GEORGE.)

(*Slide on screen:* WONDERBOY'S *face.*)

HAL

Why try to look like somebody else?

(HELEN *and* HARRY FARGIS *are at home.* HELEN *is baking cookies.*)

HELEN

Harry, what are you working on in the
garage?

SUSAN

I'm trying to look like myself, thin.
Very thin.

HARRY

If I succeed in my experiments, nobody
in the world will be hungry for love.
Ever again.

HAL (*offering him one*)
Want a cigarette, George?

GEORGE
No, thanks.

HELEN
Hungry for love? Harry, you make me nervous.

HAL
Just one?

HELEN
You really do.

GEORGE
No.

HARRY
Men will put down their arms.

SUSAN
Hal, why don't you try to help George instead of being so cruel?

HELEN
You haven't been to work for a week now. You'll lose your job.

HAL
I'm just offering him a cigarette.

HARRY
You don't understand. This is more important.

HELEN
Oh, Harry. I don't understand you at all any more. I really don't.

GEORGE (*as* HAL *takes the cigarette away*)
Give me one.

SUSAN
Hal, that's utter torture for George.

(HARRY *goes to the garage.* HELEN *mumbles to herself as she cleans up the kitchen.*)

HELEN
I don't know.

GEORGE
Give me one.

HELEN
I just don't know. He used to be so docile.

SUSAN
Don't, George. He's just playing cat and mouse.

HELEN
And now I just don't know—

HARRY (*calling from garage*)
Helen!

HELEN
Harry?

HAL
That's right, George. Don't have one.
I'm just playing cat and mouse. (*Lights a
cigarette.*)

HARRY
Helen, my experiments.

HELEN
Harry, what?

GEORGE
Just give it to me, will you?

HARRY
A terrible mistake.

SUSAN
Try to control yourself for just another
half hour, George.

HELEN
Harry, your voice—

GEORGE
No.

HARRY (*his voice getting lower and gruffer*)
For the love of heaven, Helen, keep
away from me.

SUSAN
Why not?

GEORGE
Because I don't wanna control myself for
just another half hour.

HELEN
What happened?

HAL
Whatever you want, George.
(*Hands a cigarette to* GEORGE.)

HARRY
I can't restrain myself anymore. I'm
coming through the garage door.
(*Comes through the garage door, wearing
a monster mask; his voice is now very
deep and gruff.*)
I'm irresistibly attracted to you, Helen,
irresistibly.

HELEN
Eeeeeeeeeeeeeeeeeeeeek!

HARRY (*stepping toward her*)
Helen, I love you.
(*Goes to embrace her.*)

HELEN
Harry, you're hideous. Eeeeek! Eeeeee-
eeeeeeek! Eeeeeeeeeeeek!

(*As* HELEN *screams,* WONDERBOY *is discovered, in mufti, doing his homework.*)

SUSAN
What was the point of that, Hal?

HAL
No point.

WONDERBOY
Two superquantums plus five uranium
neutrons, and I've got the mini-sub fuel.
Hooray. Boy, will my friends in the
U.S. Navy be pleased. Hey, what's that?
Better use my wonder-vision. Helen
Fargis seems to be in trouble. Better
change to Wonderboy.
(*As if throwing open his shirt.*)
And fly over there in a flash.
(*Jumping as if flying.*)
I guess I'm in the nick of time.
(*With one super-powerful punch in the
jaw he subdues* HARRY, *the monster.*)

HELEN
Oh, Wonderboy, what would have happened if you hadn't come? But what will
happen to IT?

WONDERBOY
I'll fly him to a distant zoo where they'll
take good care of him.

HELEN
Oh, Wonderboy, how can I ever repay
you?

WONDERBOY
Are those home-baked cookies I smell?

SUSAN
The president of the company has an
Eames chair.

(HELEN *smiles at* WONDERBOY *through
her tears; he puts his arm around her
shoulders.*)

WONDERBOY

Tune in tomorrow, boys and girls, when I'll subdue a whole country full of monsters.

(*Slide: "Winners Eat Wondrex."*)

GEORGE

How do you know that?

WONDERBOY

And in the meantime, remember: winners eat Wondrex. (*Smiles and jumps in the air, as if flying away.*)

SUSAN

Jennifer showed it to me.

(*Slide: little girls with shopping bags.*)

GEORGE

You asked to see it?

FIRST NEWS ANNOUNCER

Little girls with big shopping bags means back to school season is here again. Among the many shoppers in downtown New York were DARLENE, nine, LILA, four, and LUCY GLADDEN, seven, of Lynbrook, Long Island.

SUSAN

Don't worry George. He wasn't there. I just had this crazy wild impulse as I was passing his office. I wanted to see what it looked like. Isn't that wild?

(*Slide: the Vice President.*)

FIRST NEWS ANNOUNCER

In Washington, D.C., as he left John Foster Dulles Airport, as President Johnson's favorite

(*Slide: second view of the Vice President.*)

HAL

Did you sit in it?

SUSAN

I didn't dare. What would I have said if he'd come in?

FIRST NEWS ANNOUNCER

representative, the Vice President said he was bursting with confidence.

(GEORGE *goes to the rest room.*)

(*Slide: first view of Vietnamese mourners.*)

HAL

I love you, Mr. President of my great big company, and that's why I'm sitting in your nice warm leather arm chair.

SUSAN

You're perverted. I don't want to be a person working in a company who's never seen her president.

SECOND NEWS ANNOUNCER

U.S. spokesmen in Saigon said families would be given adequate shelter and compensation. Our planes are under strict orders not to return to base with any bombs. The United States regrets that a friendly village was hit. The native toll was estimated at sixty.

SUSAN (*to* HAL, *who has gotten up*)
While you're up—

(Slide: second view of Vietnamese mourners.)

HAL
What?

SUSAN
You know. Get me a Coke. (*Titters at her own joke.*)

(HAL *goes out through the hall door.* GEORGE *returns from the rest room.*)

SECOND NEWS ANNOUNCER

This was high, explained spokesmen, in answer to questions, because of the type of bomb dropped. These are known as Lazy Dogs, Each Lazy Dog bomb contains ten thousand slivers of razor-sharp steel.

(Slide: third view of Vietnamese mourners.)

GEORGE (*turning TV sound off*)
Can I come over tonight?

(Volume off.)

(Slide: a pack of Longford cigarettes superimposed on a lake.)

SUSAN
Not tonight.
(*Goes to bulletin board.*)

(TWO PEOPLE ON TELEVISION *do a silent commercial for Longford cigarettes: a man lights a woman's cigarette and she looks pleased.*)

GEORGE (*following her*)
Why not tonight?

SUSAN
Because I don't feel like it.

GEORGE
You have a date?

SUSAN

What business is that of yours? Don't think because—

GEORGE

Who with?

SUSAN

None of your business.

GEORGE

What about late, after you get back, like one o'clock?

SUSAN

That's too late. I need lots of sleep.

GEORGE

I'll call first.

SUSAN

You'd better.

(*Whenever* HAL, SUSAN, *and* GEORGE *have nothing else to do, they stare straight ahead, as if at a television screen.* GEORGE *and* SUSAN *do this now.* HAL *comes back with two Cokes.* GEORGE *goes to the telephone and dials it.*)

(*Slide on the screen: "The Endless Frontier."*)

GEORGE

Hello, dear. Yes, I'm here. Listen, I'm afraid I have to take the midnight to three shift.

(*SALLY and* BILL *are two characters in the Western.*)

(HAL *turns TV volume on.*)

SALLY

Don't go, Bill.

BILL

I've got to.

GEORGE

I've got to. The night supervisor is out.

SALLY

Oh, Bill.

GEORGE

And I've already said I would.

(BILL *leaves.*)

GEORGE

Listen, let's talk about it over dinner, huh? I'll be out after you go to sleep and in before you wake up so what's the difference? Listen, let's talk about it over dinner, I said. Listen, I love you. Goodbye.

(*Hangs up.*)

HAL (*watching TV intently but talking to* GEORGE)

You have to take the midnight to three shift, George? That's really too bad.

HAL

Got a call while I was out?

GEORGE (*snapping TV volume off*)

Do either of you want to take on some evening overtime this week?

SUSAN

Which?

GEORGE

Five to midnight Tuesday and Thursday.

HAL

Thursday.

SUSAN

Oh, all right, I'll take Tuesday.

HAL

Did you want Thursday?

SUSAN

I'd like to get the apartment finished.

HAL

Then give me Tuesday.

SALLY

Oh, Bill.

(SALLY *fixes her hair in the mirror.*)

(SALLY *is surprised by* STEVE, *the villain, who has just been waiting for* BILL *to ride off.*)

SALLY

Steve!

STEVE

Bill's dead, Sally.

SALLY

I don't believe you.

(*Volume off.*)

(STEVE *tries to embrace* SALLY. *She slaps him hard as he approaches her. He tries it again. She slaps him again. He tries it a third time. She gets him a third time. Then he grabs and kisses her despite her terrible struggling.*)

SUSAN
'Not if you HAVE something on Thursday.

HAL
No sweat.

SUSAN
Oh, I know. It was that talk with that man.

(HAL *turns TV volume on.*)

GEORGE (*snapping TV volume off*)
What talk with what man?

SUSAN
A man he has to talk to.

GEORGE
About a job?

HAL
I probably won't even see him.

GEORGE
What kind of job?

HAL
For the government. I tell you I probably won't see him.

GEORGE
If you quit, Hal, I'll need three weeks' notice. If you care about severance pay.

HAL (*turning TV volume on*)
I haven't seen him yet, even.

GEORGE
Or about me.

HAL
I wasn't going to mention it.

SUSAN
I'm sorry. It was my fault.

(BILL, *his arm wounded, appears again. Seeing* STEVE *with* SALLY, *he draws and aims.*)

BILL
Sally, duck!

(*Volume off.*)

(SALLY *ducks.* BILL *shoots* STEVE, *then goes to* SALLY *to make sure she's all right.* STEVE, *however, is not badly wounded and he reaches for* BILL's *gun. The gun falls to the floor and they fight.* SALLY *tries to get into the fight but is pushed away.*)

(BILL *is losing his fight with* STEVE *because of his wounded arm. Steve is about to get the gun.*)

SALLY (*warningly*)
Bill!

GEORGE (*turning volume off*)

Just don't spring anything on me. If you don't like the job, leave. But don't spring anything on me because I can't take it, you know that.

HAL

George, I'm NOT quitting.

SUSAN

He likes this job too much, George.

HAL

I love it more than my own life. I wouldn't leave it for all the world. Honest Injun, George.
   (*Turns volume on.*)

GEORGE

Can you imagine what I'd have to go through to train another person? Can you?

(*Volume off.*)

(*In the nick of time,* SALLY *shoots* STEVE *in the back with a rifle. As he falls he makes a mute appeal to her. He is dead now and she is appalled at what she's done.*)

SALLY (*embracing* BILL)

Oh, Bill!

BILL

I love you, Sally.

SALLY (*touched*)

Oh, Bill.

BILL

Let's move to another town.

SALLY (*delighted*)

Oh Bill.

(BILL *and* SALLY *ride off together into the dusk.*)

SUSAN

Listen, I just remembered a joke. There's this writing on the subway. "I love grills" it says on the wall. So somebody crosses out "grills" and writes in "girls." "I love girls" it says now. And then somebody else writes in, "What about us grills?"
   (*Laughs and laughs over this.*)

(*Slide: the President and his family.*)

SUSAN

What abut us grills? Isn't that fantastic?

SECOND NEWS ANNOUNCER
The President is accompanied by his wife, Lady Bird Johnson, and by his two daughters, Lynda Bird Johnson and Luci Baines Johnson Nugent, who lives in nearby Austin with her husband Patrick Nugent, President Johnson's son-in-law.

(*Slide: second view of the President and his family.*)

HAL
What's the matter with you?

(*The President appears at a podium reading a speech. He is indeed accompanied by his wife and daughters.*)

(*Slide: the President alone.*)

SUSAN (*still laughing*)
I think that's the funniest thing I ever heard.

HAL
Shhhh.

PRESIDENT
We will stamp out aggression wherever and whenever.

(SUSAN *continues laughing.*)

HAL
Shhhhh. Stop it.

SUSAN
I can't.

PRESIDENT
We will tighten our defenses and fight, to guarantee the peace of our children, our children's children, and their children.

SUSAN
I can't stop. Get the water.

(GEORGE *gets up to get some water.* HAL *wants to watch TV and can't hear it at all because of* SUSAN's *laughter.*)

PRESIDENT
That all men are not well-intentioned or well-informed or even basically good, is unfortunate.

HAL
This is easier.
(*Slaps* SUSAN *very hard on the face.*)

SUSAN
Ow!

PRESIDENT
But these people will not be indulged.

(Applause by the President's family. No sound in this play need be put on tape; all of it can be provided by the People On Television.)

SUSAN
Just who do you think you are!

HAL
Are you finished?

SUSAN
I couldn't help it.

PRESIDENT
Those who are our friends will declare themselves publicly. The others, we will not tolerate.

(Slide: second view of the President alone.)

SUSAN
Sadist.

PRESIDENT
Belief in American success and victory is the cornerstone of our faith.

SUSAN
Why didn't anyone get water?

GEORGE
Don't look at me.

PRESIDENT
Whatever else may chance to happen on far-off shores, nothing, I repeat nothing, will be allowed to disturb the serenity of our cities and suburbs, and when we fight we fight for a safer and more comfortable America, now and in years to come. Thank you.

(Slide: third view of the President and his family.)

SUSAN
You don't slap people because they're sick.

HAL
Every day we go through the same thing. You laugh. We bring you water. You spill the water all over everybody, and half an hour later you stop.

SECOND NEWS ANNOUNCER
The President and his family will now be cheered by the cadet corps.

SUSAN

Give me the water, George. I'm going to take a pill.

GEORGE

What makes you laugh like that?

(HAL *lowers the volume but does not turn it off.*)

SUSAN

I'm a hysteric. I mean I'm not constantly hysterical but sometimes I get that way. I react that way, through my body. You're a compulsive, Hal, a nasty little compulsive.

HAL (*turning volume off*)

How do you know?

SUSAN

I've discussed it with my analyst. Hysterics react through their bodies. Compulsives react compulsively.

GEORGE

What does he say about me?

SUSAN

He doesn't.

GEORGE

Hmph.

HAL

How long have you been going now? Twenty-seven years?

SUSAN

A year, wise guy.

HAL

How long do you expect to be going?

SUSAN

It might take another two or three years.

(*The President and his family respond to cheers like mechanical dolls. Turning his back, the Second News Announcer provides us with one hummed bar of "So Hello Lyndon."*)

(*A Spanish Teacher appears.*)

(*Slide: the Spanish Teacher's face.*)

(*Volume low.*)

SPANISH TEACHER

Buenos dias muchachos and muchachas. Hello, boys and girls. Muchachos. Boys. Muchachas. Girls. Aqui es la casa. Here is the house. Casa. House.

(*Volume off.*)

(*The Spanish Teacher finishes the lesson.*)

(*Efficient researchers walk back and forth across the stage, checking things, nodding at each other curtly, and so on.*)

(*Slide: the efficient researchers.*)

GEORGE

    I know people who have gone for ten or twelve years.

HAL

    Don't you think that's a lot?

GEORGE

    If you need it, you need it. It's a sickness like any other sickness. It's got to be looked after.

HAL

    What did they do in the old days?

GEORGE (*turning volume up*)
    They stayed sick.

                        (*Volume up.*)

              UGP ANNOUNCER

                  Who are they? They are a community of devotion.

                  (*Slide: "UGP" in very Germanic lettering.*)

              UGP ANNOUNCER

                  Men and women whose lives are dedicated to the researching of more perfect products for you. Get the benefit of a community of devotion. Look for the letters UGP whenever you by a car, radio, television set, or any of a thousand other products. Their tool: devotion. Their goal: perfection.

                  (*Slide: a civil rights demonstration.*)

SUSAN

    My analyst has been going to HIS analyst for twenty-five years.

HAL

    How do you know?

SUSAN

    He told me.

              FIRST NEWS ANNOUNCER

                  Three men were critically injured during a civil rights demonstration in Montgomery, Alabama today.

GEORGE

    Can you feel the tranquilizer working?

SUSAN
A little bit. I think so.

GEORGE
Maybe I should have one too.

SUSAN (*turning volume off.*)
Are you upset?

GEORGE
I can feel my stomach.

SUSAN (*reaching into her bag to give him a pill*)
Here.

GEORGE
I'd like some coffee.

HAL
I'd like some lunch.

SUSAN
Lunch! I'll get it. (*Dashes into her coat and is almost out the door.*)

HAL
Hey!

SUSAN
Rare with onion and a danish. I know. So long, you guys.

HAL (*throwing his penknife into the bulletin board*)
Think she's all right?

GEORGE
People wouldn't say this was a crazy office or anything like that.

(*Slide: the Vice President.*)

FIRST NEWS ANNOUNCER
This afternoon the Vice President arrived in Honolulu. As he stepped off the plane he told newsmen things are looking up.

(*Slide: a map of China.*)

FIRST NEWS ANNOUNCER
The Defense Department today conceded that United States aircraft may have mistakenly flown over Chinese territory last month. It regrets the incident.

(*Volume off.*)

(*Slide: a rock and roll group.*)

(*A rock and roll group is seen singing and playing.*)

HAL
   Nope.

GEORGE
   She's really a nice girl, isn't she?

HAL (*doing calisthenics*)
   Yup.

GEORGE
   You like her, don't you?

HAL
   Yup.

GEORGE
   I mean you don't just think she's a good
   lay, do you?

HAL
   What makes you think I lay her?

GEORGE
   Well, don't you?

HAL
   George, that's an old trick.

GEORGE
   I'm just trying to find out if you really
   like her.

HAL
   Why do you care?

GEORGE
   I feel protective.

HAL
   That's right. She's half your age, isn't
   she?

GEORGE
   Not exactly half.

HAL
   How old are you, George, exactly?

GEORGE
   Forty-three.

HAL (*crossing to water cooler*)
  Humph.

GEORGE
  What's that mean?

HAL
  I was just wondering what it was like to
  be forty-three.

GEORGE
  It stinks.

HAL
  That's what I thought.

GEORGE
  You'll be forty-three sooner than you
  think.

HAL
  I'll never be forty-three.

GEORGE
  Why not?

HAL   (*The rock and roll group bows.*)
  I don't intend to live that long.

GEORGE   (*Slide: a group of peace marchers.*)
  You have something?

HAL   (*A group of peace marchers appears.*)
  No. I just don't intend to live that long.
  (*Returns to console and turns volume on.*)

                                       FIRST NEWS ANNOUNCER
                                         A group of so-called peaceniks marched
                                         down the center mall of the capital to-
                                         day, singing:

GEORGE (*sits*)   (*The peace marchers sing "We Shall
  You're probably a socialist.   Overcome."*)

HAL
  A socialist?

GEORGE

A socialist at twenty and a Republican at forty. Everybody goes through that cycle.

FIRST NEWS ANNOUNCER

One young man from New York City predicted:

ONE YOUNG MAN FROM NEW YORK CITY

The Washington Monument's going to burst into bloom and—

(*It is as if the sound were cut off on the word he was going to say, but we can read "Fuck" on his lips.*)

(*Slide: Annie Kappelhoff.*)

GEORGE

It's healthy.

FIRST NEWS ANNOUNCER

A little girl, Annie Kappelhoff, had her own opinion:

ANNIE (*as if leading a cheer*)

Burn yourselves, not your draft cards, burn yourselves, not your draft cards—

(*The sound is cut off on* ANNIE, *too, as she continues the same cheer.*)

FIRST NEWS ANNOUNCER

Later in the day Annie was the star of her own parade. She's head-cheer-leader of Wilumet High School in Maryland. Today Annie cheered her team on to victory, thirty to nothing, over neighboring South Dearing. Annie is also an ardent supporter of the young American Nazi party, and hopes to become a model. And now, a message.

(*Slide: a jar of K-F soap-cream.*)

HAL

Are you a Republican, George?

FAMOUS TV PERSONALITY

Are you one of those lucky women who has all the time in the world?

GEORGE

That's right.

HAL

You know I have a lot of friends who won't even speak to Republicans.

GEORGE
I'd rather not discuss politics.

HAL
Why not?

GEORGE
Because we probably don't see eye to eye.

HAL
So?

GEORGE
So I'd rather not discuss it. And my stomach's upset.

FAMOUS TV PERSONALITY
Or are you like most of us: busy, busy, busy all day long with home or job so that when evening comes you hardly have time to wash your face, much less transform yourself into the living doll he loves.

FAMOUS TV PERSONALITY
Well then, K-F is for you. More than a soap. More than a cream. It's a soap-cream. You apply it in less time than it takes to wash your face and it leaves your skin tingling with loveliness. Try it. And for an extra super thrill, use it in the shower.

(*Slide: Lily Heaven.*)

LILY HEAVEN'S ANNOUNCER
The Lily Heaven Show, ladies and gentlemen, starring that great star of stage, screen, and television: Lily Heaven.

(*Out through imaginary curtains comes LILY HEAVEN, very starlike. She greets her audience in her own inimitable way. She sings a line from a popular American love song.*)

(*There is a special knock on the viewing room door.*)

HAL
What's that?

GEORGE
Nothing.

(GEORGE *turns volume off.*)

(*Volume off.*)

HAL
What do you mean, nothing?

(*Slide: a second view of Lily Heaven.*)

GEORGE (*calling*)
One minute.

HAL (*getting panicky*)
One minute until what?

> (GEORGE *turns out the lights in the viewing room.*)

HAL
I knew it. What's going on?

GEORGE (*calling*)
Okay.

HAL
Okay what? What? What?

SUSAN (*coming through the door with a cake with lighted candles on it*)
Okay this, stupid.

SUSAN *and* GEORGE
One, two, three.
  (*Singing*)
Happy Birthday to you,
Happy Birthday to you,
Happy Birthday dear Ha-al,
Happy Birthday to you.

> (SUSAN *kisses* HAL *on the lips.*)

SUSAN
Happy Birthday. You had no idea, did you?

HAL
No.

GEORGE
Happy Birthday.

HAL
Thanks a lot.

SUSAN
Make a wish and blow.

> (HAL *blows on the candles but doesn't get them all.*)

SUSAN
Well, almost.

(GEORGE *turns the viewing room lights on
again, and* SUSAN *gets two presents from
the closet.*)

SUSAN

People thought I was crazy walking
down the hall with this cake and this
lunch in a paper bag. And I was petrified
one of you would swing the door open
while I was waiting in the corridor and
knock me down and the cake and everything. I was almost sure you'd guessed,
Hal, when I put the presents in my locker this morning.

HAL

I hadn't.

SUSAN

I love birthdays. I know it's childish but
I really do. Look at the card on George's.

HAL

It's cute.

SUSAN

Open it.

(HAL *opens the package. It's a tie.*)

HAL

Well thanks, George. I can use this.
(*Makes a mock noose of it around his
neck.*)

GEORGE

You're welcome.

SUSAN (*looking at the label as if she hadn't seen
it before*)
It's a good tie.

GEORGE

What'd you expect?

(GEORGE *is biting into an egg salad sandwich.* HAL *starts to open the second present.*)

SUSAN (*stopping* HAL)
Save mine for when we eat the cake, so
the birthday will last longer.

HAL
George, there's egg salad all over the
dials.

GEORGE (*turning volume on*)
Sorry.

SUSAN
Here's a napkin. I'll make some coffee.

GEORGE
Good.

(LILY HEAVEN *finishes singing and bows.*)

LILY HEAVEN
So long, everybody.

LILY HEAVEN
This is Lily Heaven saying so long.

(*Applause from part of Lily Heaven's audience, played by the People On Television, who stand behind her.*)

LILY HEAVEN (*as if each sentence were her last*)
Here's wishing you a good week before
we meet again. From all of us here to all
of you out there: so long. Thanks a lot
and God bless you. This is Lily signing
off. I only hope that you enjoyed watching us as much as we enjoyed being
here. So long. It's been wonderful being
with you. Really grand, and I hope
you'll invite us into your living room
again next week. I only wish we could
go on but I'm afraid it's time to say so
long, so from the actors and myself,
from the staff here, I want to wish you
all a very very good week. This is your

(GEORGE *and* HAL *are mesmerized by* LILY
HEAVEN. SUSAN *is paying no attention
but is fussing with the coffee things and
putting paper bags, as party hats, on* HAL
and GEORGE.)

Lily saying so long to you. So long. So
long. So long. So long. Have a happy,
and so long. Till next week. Bye. So
long. Bye. So long.

GEORGE
Give me another of those tranquilizers,
please. The first one doesn't seem to
have done a thing.

(*Slide: a weather map.*)

WEATHER ANNOUNCER
And now, the weather.

(HAL *turns the volume off.* SUSAN *has plugged in the hot plate and coffee maker. She also has some real coffee and a jar of dried cream, some sugar and sugar substitute in little bags stolen from a luncheonette, napkins and little wooden stick-stirrers.*)

HAL (*who has been opening his present*)
Say, this is nice.

SUSAN
It's an art book.

HAL
I can see that.

GEORGE
Hal especially interested in art?

SUSAN
A person doesn't have to be especially interested in art to like it.

HAL
It must have cost a lot, Susan. Here, George.
(*Passes* GEORGE *a piece of cake.*)

SUSAN
Well, as a matter of fact, I got it on sale at Marboro.

HAL
If I had a place for it everything would be fine. Cake, Susan?

SUSAN (*to* GEORGE)
Hal still doesn't have a place.

GEORGE
What kind of place are you looking for?

HAL
I'd like to find an apartment with more than one small room for under a hundred dollars.

SUSAN
Do you want to live in the Village?

(*Volume off.*)

(*Slide: Miracle Headache Pills.*)

(*Still without volume, an advertisement for Miracle Headache Pills: a woman is seen before and after taking the pills.*)

HAL

Makes no difference.

GEORGE

Don't live down there.

SUSAN

Why not?

GEORGE

It's too crowded.

SUSAN

It's not so crowded, and in the Village you can see a lot of wonderful faces.

GEORGE

Yes, well frankly I've been working for a living for twenty-one years and I resent having to support a lot of bums on relief.

SUSAN

That's not the Village. That's the Bowery.

(LADY ANNOUNCER *begins to speak, still without volume.*)

(*Slide: First Federal Savings Bank.*)

GEORGE

Let's not talk about it.

SUSAN

Why not?

GEORGE

I already told Hal that people with differing points of view shouldn't talk about politics. And I shouldn't be eating this cake either.

(*Snaps volume on.*)

LADY ANNOUNCER

And now First Federal Savings and Kennel-Heart Dog Food present Luncheon With Carol, a program especially designed for the up-to-date woman. Our topic for today: I Quit. And here's Carol.

(*Slide: Carol and Ron Campbell.*)

CAROL

Hello, ladies. This is Carol. I have as my guest today Mr. Ron Campbell just back from an eighteen month tour of duty in Vietnam. Mr. Campbell was a member of the famed Green Berets. He is a holder of the Bronze Star and the South Vietnamese Order of Merit; he has been nominated for the U.S. Silver Star. A few weeks ago he was offered a field commission as captain. But instead of accepting, what did you do, Ron?

RON

I quit.

CAROL

That's right, you quit. Tell us why you quit, Ron, when you were obviously doing so well.

RON

I didn't like being there.

CAROL

You didn't?

RON

No.

CAROL (*cheerfully*)

I see.

RON

We're committing mass murder.

CAROL (*interested*)

Yes?

RON

We're trying to take over a people that don't want to be taken over by anybody.

CAROL

Now, Ron, American boys are out there dying so somebody must be doing something wrong somewhere.

RON

Whoever in Hanoi or Peking or Washington is sending men out to be killed, THEY'RE doing something wrong.

CAROL (*interested in his opinion, tolerant*)

I see.

RON

You do? Well I was there for a year and a half and every day I saw things that would make you sick. Heads broken, babies smashed against walls—

CAROL (*deeply sympathetic*)

I KNOW.

RON

You know?

CAROL

War is horrible.

RON

Listen—

CAROL

Thank you, Ron. We've been talking this afternoon, ladies, with Ron Campbell, war hero.

RON

Will you let me say something, please?

CAROL (*tolerating him, kindly*)

And a fascinating talk it's been, Ron, but I'm afraid our time is up.

RON

One—

CAROL (*with her special smile for the ladies*)

Ladies, see you all tomorrow.

SUSAN (*dreamily*)

I think I'm floating further and further left.

GEORGE

You don't know a thing about it.

SUSAN

I was listening to Norman Thomas last night—

LADY ANNOUNCER

This program was brought to you by First Federal Savings and Kennel-Heart Dog Food. The opinions expressed on this program are not necessarily those of anyone connected with it. A dog in the home means a dog with a heart.

(Slide: Kennel-Heart Dog Food.)

GEORGE

I'm going to the Men's Room.

LADY ANNOUNCER

Kennel-Heart. Bow-wow. Wow.

SUSAN

Poor George.

(Slide: "Billion Dollar Movie.")

HAL

You still haven't told me about tonight.

(A very English man and a very English woman appear in the movie.)

HE

Sarah.

SUSAN

Told you what about tonight?

SHE

Yes, Richard.

HAL.

Are we going to the movies or are we not going to the movies?

HE

Our old apartment.

SUSAN

I don't know. I can't make up my mind.

SHE

Yes, Richard. It's still here.

HAL

That's just fine.

HE

It seems very small to me.

SHE

It does to me, too.

SUSAN

I want to work on my apartment.

HAL

Okay.

HE

Do you think we can live in it again?

SHE

Not in the old way.

SUSAN

I should really get it done.

HE

In a better way.

HAL

You're right.

SHE

You've changed too, Richard, for the better.

HE

So have you, darling, for the better.

SUSAN

Suppose I let you know by the end of the afternoon?

HAL

Suppose we forget I ever suggested it.

SHE

I've learned a lot.

HE

Maybe that's what war is for.

(*The People On Television hum "White Cliffs of Dover" under the following.*)

SHE

The brick wall in front of the window is gone.

HE

We'll rebuild for the future.

SUSAN

Oh, all right, I'll go. Happy?

HAL

I'm so happy I could put a bullet through my brain.

SHE

I hope there is never any more war. Ever, ever again.

HE

Amen.

(Slide: "The End.")

(The People On Television sing, meaningfully, the last line of "White Cliffs of Dover": "Tomorrow, just you wait and see.")

SUSAN
Sugar?

HAL
You're like my grandmother.

(First News Announcer appears.)

SUSAN
How?

HAL
She asked me if I took sugar every day we lived together. It was very comforting.

(Slide: baseball player.)

FIRST NEWS ANNOUNCER
Baseball's Greg Pironelli, fifty-six, died today of a heart attack in St. Petersburg, Florida. He hit a total of four hundred and eighty home runs and had a lifetime batting average of three forty-one.

HAL
Hal, she used to say to me, my grandmother, you're going to be a big man.

(Slide: a baseball game.)

HAL
Everybody's going to love you. She used to sing that song to me: "Poppa's gonna buy you a dog named Rover, and if that dog don't bark, Poppa's gonna buy you a looking glass, and if that looking glass should break, you're still the sweetest little boy in town."

FIRST NEWS ANNOUNCER
In 1963, the year he was elected to baseball's hall of fame in Cooperstown, New York, Pironelli suffered his first stroke. Pironelli owned a Florida-wide chain of laundries.

(Slide: "Johnny Holland Show.")

JOHNNY
We're back.

SUSAN
That's nice.

(Slide: Johnny and Luci.)

JOHNNY
That's a very pretty dress you've got on, Luci.

(GEORGE enters and goes directly to telephone.)

LUCI
Thank you, Johnny.

GEORGE

Hello, darling? Listen, I've gotten out of it. Isn't that good news? The midnight shift.

JOHNNY

How does it feel living in Austin after all the excitement of the big wedding?

LUCI

It feels fine.

GEORGE

I'm looking forward to being home nice and comfy with you.

JOHNNY

Do you miss your father?

GEORGE

You know my stomach is killing me. Sure I will. Wait a minute.

LUCI

Oh sure, I miss him.

(GEORGE *takes out a pencil.*)

GEORGE

Toothpaste. Cauliflower. That's a good idea.

JOHNNY (*awkward pause*)

I guess your heart belongs to Daddy, huh?

GEORGE

Large face cream. Why large? No, I don't care. I was just asking.

LUCI

That's right.

JOHNNY (*awkward pause*)

Is your father hard to get along with?

GEORGE

Okay. Listen, I'm really looking forward to seeing you.

LUCI

Oh, no. When I want something I just march right in, cuddle up in his lap, and give him a great big kiss.

(*Slide: a second view of Johnny and Luci.*)

JOHNNY (*awkward pause*)

So you'd say your father is affectionate?

LUCI

Very affectionate.

GEORGE
No, I haven't been drinking, and it's rotten of you to ask.

GEORGE
Okay, okay. Bye.
(*Hangs up telephone.*)

SUSAN
Have a little coffee, George.

GEORGE
No, thanks.

HAL
Oh, come on, George, have a little coffee.

GEORGE
A sip.

'SUSAN
Sugar or superine?

GEORGE
Sugar.

SUSAN
George.

JOHNNY (*awkward pause*)
Does he ever ask your advice about important matters?

LUCI
Well, one day I told him what I thought, good and proper, about all those nervous nellies interfering with my Daddy's war.

(JOHNNY *does a double take of scandalized amusement to the audience.*)

(*Slide: Johnny doing double take.*)

JOHNNY
And what did he say?

LUCI
He laughed.

JOHNNY
It's lovely talking to you, Luci.

LUCI
It's nice talking to you too, Johnny.

JOHNNY
We'll be back.

(*Slide: "Johnny Holland Show."*)

GEORGE
Don't take care of me. I said sugar.

SUSAN
Whatever you want, George.

(An Evangelist appears with his choir, which is singing "Onward Christian Soldiers.")

(Slide: the Evangelist.)

EVANGELIST
If we could look through the ceiling of this wonderful new air-conditioned stadium we could see the stars. Nonetheless I have heard them in faraway countries, I have heard them criticize, criticize us and the leaders we know and love.

SUSAN
George, what are you eating now?

GEORGE
Chicken sandwich.

SUSAN
Give me a bite.

(HAL plays with his penknife. SUSAN eats another piece of cake. GEORGE eats his chicken sandwich.)

EVANGELIST
Why? Well I will tell you why. They criticize us because we are rich, as if money itself were evil. Money, the Bible says, is the root of evil, not evil itself. I have seen a roomful of men and women, powerful Hollywood celebrities at four o'clock A.M. in the morning, listening to me with tears streaming down their faces crying out to me that they had lost touch with God.

(GEORGE starts to cough.)

EVANGELIST
"In God We Trust" is on our coins, ladies and gentlemen—

SUSAN
What's the matter, George?

(Slide: a second view of the Evangelist.)

(GEORGE motions her away and continues to cough.)

(The evangelist choir sings "Onward Christian Soldiers.")

HAL *(turning volume off)*
Spit it out, George.

SUSAN
Hal, leave him alone.

(Volume off.)

HAL

> George, spit it out.
> *(Thumps* GEORGE *on the back.)*

SUSAN

> Hal! George, is it epilepsy?

HAL

> It's something in his throat.

SUSAN

> Try to tell us what it is, George.

HAL *and* GEORGE

> Chicken!

HAL

> He has a chicken bone stuck in his throat.

SUSAN

> Oh my God. Well give him some water.

> (GEORGE's *choking is getting worse.)*

HAL

> Water will wash right by it. Let me
> look.
> *(Holds* GEORGE's *head and looks into his
> mouth.)*
> Don't move, George. I want to take a
> look.
> *(Looks in* GEORGE's *mouth.)*
> There it is.

SUSAN *(also looking)*

> Ugh, it's stuck in his throat. I'll get
> some water.

> (HAL *and* SUSAN *let go of* GEORGE, *who
> falls to the floor.)*

HAL

> Not water.

SUSAN

> Why not?

HAL

> Because water will wash right past the thing. It needs something to push it out.

SUSAN

> Like what?

HAL

> Like bread.

SUSAN

> Bread? Bread will get stuck on the bone and he'll choke.

HAL

> You're wrong.

SUSAN

> I'm right.

HAL

> Bread will push it right down.

SUSAN

> Water will do that.

HAL

> You're wrong.

SUSAN

> It's you that's wrong and won't admit it.

HAL

> I'm going to give him some bread.

SUSAN

> I won't allow it.

HAL

> You won't allow it?

SUSAN

> It'll kill him.

HAL

> He's choking right now and I'm going to give him some of this bread.

SUSAN
>Give him water.

HAL
>I said bread.

SUSAN (*starting to walk past* HAL)
>And I said water.

HAL (*grabbing her arm*)
>Bread.

SUSAN
>Water. Ow, you're hurting me.

>>(GEORGE *is having a very bad time.* HAL *and* SUSAN *turn to look at him, speaking softly.*)

SUSAN
>Let's call the operator.

HAL
>It would take too long.

SUSAN
>And he wouldn't like anyone to see him.

HAL
>Why not?

SUSAN
>I don't know.

>>(At this point GEORGE *finally coughs the thing up, and his cough subsides into an animal pant.*)

SUSAN (*going to him, putting him*)
>Poor George.

HAL
>It's over.

SUSAN
>No thanks to you.

HAL
>Nor you.

SUSAN (*putting* GEORGE's *head on her breast*)
He might have choked. Poor George.

GEORGE (*pushing her away*)
Fuck!

(GEORGE *lurches against the console on his way to the bathroom, accidentally turning on the volume.*)

EVANGELIST CHOIR (*still singing* "*Onward Christian Soldiers.*")
"With the cross of Jesus—"

(HAL *changes channels from the Evangelist's meeting to* "My Favorite Teenager.")

(*Slide: Mother, Father, and Daughter in* "My Favorite Teenager.")

SUSAN (*sitting in her chair*)
Poor George.

MOTHER
Why aren't you going?

DAUGHTER (*sitting in* GEORGE's *chair at the control console*)
Because I told Harold Sternpepper he could take me.

MOTHER
Yes, and—

DAUGHTER
Well, Harold Sternpepper is a creep. Everybody knows that.

(*The remaining People On Television make the sound of canned laughter.*)

HAL (*sitting in his chair*)
What movie are we going to?

MOTHER
So, why—

DAUGHTER
Oh, because I was mad at Gail.

(*Canned laughter.*)

SUSAN
I don't know.

MOTHER
What about Johnny Beaumont?

HAL
What about George?

SUSAN
What about him?

HAL
Well, I guess it's none of my business.

GEORGE (*returning*)
What's the matter?

SUSAN
Nothing.

GEORGE
Going somewhere?

SUSAN
We're going to the movies.

(HAL *and* SUSAN *and* GEORGE *are slowing down because they are mesmerized by* "My Favorite Teenager.")

GEORGE
What movie are you going to?

GEORGE
Mind if I come along?

SUSAN
Oh, George, you don't really want to.

DAUGHTER
What about him?

MOTHER
Well, I guess it's none of my business.

FATHER
What's the matter?

(*Slide: second view of Mother, Father, and Daughter in* "My Favorite Teenager.")

DAUGHTER
Nothing.

FATHER
Why aren't you dressed for the prom?

DAUGHTER
I'm not going to the prom.

FATHER
Why not? Why isn't she going, Grace?

MOTHER
Don't ask me. I just live here.

(*Canned laughter.*)

FATHER
Why doesn't anybody tell me anything around here?

(*Canned laughter.*)

DAUGHTER (*getting up from* GEORGE's *chair*)
Oh, why don't you two leave me alone? I'm not going because nobody's taking me.

FATHER (*sitting in* GEORGE's *chair*)
Nobody's taking my little girl to the junior prom? I'll take her myself.

DAUGHTER (*stifling a yelp of horror*)
Oh no, Daddy, don't bother. I mean how would it look, I mean—

GEORGE
I'd be pleased as punch.

SUSAN
Hal, say something.

HAL (*to* GEORGE)
You look bushed to me, George.

GEORGE
Who's bushed?

(GEORGE *sits in his chair.*)

(HAL, SUSAN, *and* GEORGE *are completely mesmerized by the TV show.*)

FATHER
I'd be pleased as punch.

DAUGHTER (*aside to* MOTHER)
Help.

(*Canned laughter.*)

MOTHER (*to* FATHER)
Now, dear, don't you think for your age—

(*Canned laughter.*)

FATHER
My age?

(*Canned laughter.*)

FATHER (*standing and doing a two-step*)
I'd like to see anybody laugh at my two-step.

(*Canned laughter.*)

DAUGHTER (*in despair*)
Oh, Daddy. Mother, DO something.

(*Canned laughter.*)

MOTHER (*putting her arm around* GEORGE's *shoulders*)
I think it's a very nice idea. And maybe I'll go with Harold Sternpepper.

(*Canned laughter.*)

DAUGHTER (*loudly, sitting on* HAL's *knee*)
Oh, Mother, oh, Daddy, oh no!

(*The canned laughter mounts. Music.*)

(*Slide: "My Favorite Teenager."*)

(*Now they all speak like situation-comedy characters.*)

HAL
What movie shall we go to?

GEORGE

Let's talk about it over dinner.

HAL

Who said anything about dinner?

(*All of the People On Television do canned laughter now. They are crowded around the control console.*)

SUSAN

Isn't anybody going to ask me what I want to do?

(*Canned laughter.*)

GEORGE

Sure, what do you want, Susan?

HAL

It's up to you.

(*Slide:* HAL, SUSAN, *and* GEORGE *with the same facial expressions they now have on the stage.*)

SUSAN

Well, have I got a surprise for you two. I'M going home to fix up my apartment and you two can have dinner toGETHER.

(HAL, SUSAN, *and* GEORGE *join in the canned laughter. Then, lights off. Slide off. Curtain call: all are in the same position, silent, their faces frozen into laughing masks.*)

Ed Bullins: *Clara's Ole Man* (1965)

Ed Bullins was born in 1935 and raised in "a South Philadelphia slum," where many of his plays are set. His background is a bit like that of Jack in *Clara's Ole Man:* he didn't finish high school, but joined the Navy for three years. When he got out, he realized how much he needed an education, so he returned to Philadelphia to take a college preparatory program. He went to Los Angeles City College and then to San Francisco State College, where he began writing plays. In the early 1960s, he became the Cultural Minister for the Black Panthers in San Francisco, but he quit in 1967 over the question of whether culture was to be subservient to political ideologies.

Bullins' reputation as a playwright was growing steadily in the black community and it spread into the larger community in 1968 when *Clara's Ole Man* and *The Electronic Nigger* were performed at the American Place Theater, off Broadway. Critics sometimes found Bullins' language coarse and obscene, just as they also found his dramas somewhat shapeless. His plays seemed more like direct observations of life instead of shaped, plotted dramas. Many white theatergoers, because they did not share the experience he portrayed, felt as if they were "white interlopers." There is no sense of middle-class longing in Bullins' plays and, in contrasting his work with that of Lorraine Hansberry, one can understand better how her plays could be thought of as being more in the mainstream of middle-class drama. Bullins has denied that he is even a working-class playwright; like Jean Genet (who wrote *The Blacks*), he claims to be part of the criminal class. He points out that many of the men in his family have been in prison, and he is not only the only man to have attended college—he is the only one to have gone to high school.

Clara's Ole Man is truly a play about the loss of innocence, but it is not the loss of Clara's innocence; it is the loss of Jack's innocence. It is the loss of the innocence of a traveled, educationally ambitious ex-marine. He is also an ex Jet Cobra (the street gang Bullins himself belonged to), so his loss of innocence, intensified by his beating at the end of the drama, is all the more unexpected. And, to perhaps a larger extent, the audience itself suffers a loss of innocence. Most typical American theatergoers are white and middle class; they do not expect to see some of the things Bullins insists they face. They are not used to watching people such as Stooge, Bama, and Hoss treated as ordinary folks. The fact that they are on the run from the police is of little or no concern to Big Girl. The play in no way condemns them, nor does it suggest that we should think of them badly. They are wiser than Jack, tougher than he is, and probably better suited to survive in this environment.

The constant drinking in the play is another interesting assault on the mores of the American middle class. Usually, heavy drinking is condemned explicitly or implicitly in the theater, but there is no effort to do so in this play. Big Girl condemns Miss Famie and Aunt Touhy, but mainly because she sees very little of the gin that goes upstairs. Big Girl insists that everyone should drink the "rot gut" she has in considerable abundance; no excuses are made for drinking, as they are in *Come Back, Little Sheba* and *A Raisin in the Sun*. Drinking is what people do in this place. The audiences, even in the mid-1960s, found these qualities hard to accept, but they came to find the final premise of the play—Big Girl's lesbian relationship with Clara—the premise that Jack himself never even guessed, the most difficult of all. That shock is the final loss of innocence for Jack, whose international sexual experiences make him an unusually well-informed man. Loss of innocence always implies an education, a learning. The most interesting question about this play is: who is learning and what is being learned?

Bullins is a prolific writer. He is now engaged in a series of twenty plays, a cycle of dramas relating the black experience. Several have already been performed: *In the Wine Time* (1968); *The Corner* (1969); *The Duplex* (1970), *In New England Winter* (1971); *The Fabulous Miss Marie* (1971); *Home Boy* (1976). Many of Bullins' plays written outside this cycle have been very successful. *Goin' a Buffalo* (1972) and *The Taking of Miss Janie* (1975) have been particularly well-received, with the latter winning the New York Drama Critics' Circle best play award for its season. *Daddy* and *Sepia Star* were both performed in New York in 1977.

Still a very young playwright, Bullins is likely to become one of the most influential American dramatists. He is already moving beyond the influence of the dramatist who inspired him when he was first writing: Imamu Amiri Baraka (formerly Le

Roi Jones), whose play, *The Dutchman,* showed him a way in which he could treat his own themes.

Selected Readings

Bullins, Ed. *Five Plays.* Indianapolis: Bobbs-Merrill, 1969.
————. *The Duplex; A Black Love Fable in Four Movements.* New York: Morrow, 1971.
————. *The Theme is Blackness: The Corner, and Other Plays.* New York: Morrow, 1972.
————. *Four Dynamite Plays.* New York: Morrow, 1972.
————. *The Hungered One: Early Writings.* New York: Morrow, 1971.
Evans, Don. "The Theater of Confrontation: Ed Bullins, Up Against the Wall." *Black World,* 23, vi, pp. 14–18.
Hay, Samuel A. "What Shape Shapes Shapelessness?: Structural Elements in Ed Bullins' Plays." *Black World,* 23, vi, pp. 20–26.
Tener, Robert L. "Pandora's Box: A Study of Ed Bullins' Dramas." *College Language Association Journal,* 19, pp. 533–544.

Clara's Ole Man

A PLAY OF LOST INNOCENCE

Ed Bullins

CHARACTERS

CLARA, *a light brown girl of 18, well built with long, dark hair. A blond streak runs down the middle of her head, and she affects a pony tail. She is pensive, slow in speech but feline. Her eyes are heavy-lidded and brown; she smiles—rather, blushes—often.*

BIG GIRL, *a stocky woman wearing jeans and tennis shoes and a tight-fitting blouse which accents her prominent breasts. She is of an indeterminable age, due partly to her lack of makeup and plain hair style. She is anywhere from 25 to 40, and is loud and jolly, frequently breaking out in laughter from her own jokes.*

JACK, *20 years old, wears a corduroy Ivy League suit and vest. At first, JACK's speech is modulated and too eloquent for the surroundings, but as he drinks his words become slurred and mumbled.*

BABY GIRL, BIG GIRL's *mentally retarded teenage sister. The girl has the exact hairdo as CLARA. Her face is made up with mascara and eye shadow, and she has black arching eyebrows penciled darkly, the same as CLARA.*

MISS FAMIE, *a drunken neighbor.*

STOOGIE, *a local streetfighter and gang leader. His hair is processed.*

BAMA, *one of STOOGIE's boys.*

HOSS, *another of STOOGIE's boys.*

C.C., *a young wino.*

TIME

Early spring, the mid-1950s.

SCENE

A slum kitchen on a rainy afternoon in South Philadelphia. The room is very clean, wax glosses the linoleum and old wooden furniture; a cheap but clean red checkered oilcloth covers the table. If the room could speak it would say, "I'm cheap but clean."

A cheap AM radio plays rhythm 'n' blues music throughout the play. The furniture is made up of a wide kitchen table where a gallon jug of red wine sits. Also upon the table is an oatmeal box, cups, mugs, plates and spoons, ashtrays, and packs of cigarettes. Four chairs circle the table, and two sit against the wall at the back of the stage. An old-fashioned wood- and coal-burning stove takes up a corner of the room and a gas range of 1935 vintage is at the back next to the door to the yard. A large, smoking frying pan is on one of the burners.

(JACK *and* BIG GIRL *are seated at opposite ends of the table;* CLARA *stands at the store fanning the fumes toward the door.* BABY GIRL *plays upon the floor with a homemade toy.*)

CLARA (*fans fumes*): Uummm uummm ... well, there goes the lunch. I wonder how I was dumb enough to burn the bacon?

BIG GIRL: Just comes natural with you, honey, all looks and no brains ... Now with me and my looks, anybody in South Philly can tell I'm a person that naturally takes care of business ... hee hee ... ain't that right, Clara?

CLARA: Awww, girl, go on. You's the worst messer-upper I knows. You didn't even go to work this mornin'. What kind of business is that?

BIG GIRL: It's all part of my master plan, baby. Don't you worry none ... Big Girl knows what she's doin'. You better believe that!

CLARA: Yeah, you may know what you're doin', but I'm the one who's got to call in for you and lie that you're sick.

BIG GIRL: Well, it ain't a lie. You know I got this cough and stopped-up feeling. (*Looking at* JACK.) You believe that, don't you, young-blood?

JACK: Most certainly. You could very well have a respiratory condition and also have all the appearances of an extremely capable person.

BIG GIRL (*slapping table*): Hee hee. ... *See,* Clara? ... *See?* Listen ta that, Clara. I told you anybody could tell it. Even ole hot lips here can tell.

CLARA (*pours out grease and wipes stove*): Awww ... he just says that to be nice. ... He's always sayin' things like that.

BIG GIRL: Is that how he talked when he met you the other day out to your aunt's house?

CLARA (*hesitating*): Nawh ... nawh he didn't talk like that.

BIG GIRL: Well, how did he talk, huh?

CLARA: Awww ... Big Girl. I don't know.

BIG GIRL: Well, who else does? You know what kind of line a guy gives ya. You been pitched at enough times, haven't ya? By the looks of him I bet he gave ya the ole smooth college-boy approach. ... (*To* JACK.) C'mon, man, drink up. We got a whole lot mo' to kill. Don't you know this is my day off and I'm celebratin'?

JACK (*takes a drink*): Thanks ... this is certainly nice of you to go to all this trouble for me. I never expected it.

BIG GIRL: What did you expect, youngblood?

JACK (*takes another sip*): Ohhh, well ... I ...

CLARA (*to* BABY GIRL *on floor*): *Don't put that dirty thing in your mouf, gal!* (*She walks around the table to* BABY GIRL *and tugs her arm.*) Now, keep that out of your mouf!

BABY GIRL (*holds to toy sullenly*): No!

CLARA: You keep quiet, you hear, gal!

BABY GIRL: *No!!!*

CLARA: If you keep tellin' me no, I'm goin' ta take you upstairs ta Aunt Toohey.

BABY GIRL (*throws back head and drums feet on floor*): NO! NO! SHIT! DAMN! SHIT! NO!

CLARA (*disturbed*): *Now stop that!* We got company.

BIG GIRL (*laughs hard and leans elbows upon table*): *Haw Haw Haw* ... I guess she told you, Clara. Hee hee ... that little dirty-mouf bitch (*Pointing to* BABY GIRL *and becoming choked.*) ... that little ... cough cough ... hoooeee, boy!

CLARA: You shouldn't have taught her all

them nasty words, Big Girl. Now we can't do anything with her. (*Turns to* JACK.) What do you think of that?

JACK: Yes, it does seem a problem. But with proper guidance she'll more than likely be conditioned out of it when she gets into a learning situation among her peer group.

BIG GIRL (*takes a drink and scowls*): Bullshit!

CLARA: Awww . . . B.G.

JACK: I beg your pardon, Miss?

BIG GIRL: I said bullshit! Whatta ya mean with proper guidance . . . (*Points.*) I taught that little bitch myself . . . the best cuss words I know before she ever climbed out of her crib. . . . Whatta ya mean when she gets among her "peer group"?

JACK: I didn't exactly say that. I said when . . .

BIG GIRL (*cuts him off*): Don't tell me what you said, boy! I got ears. I know all them big horseshit doctor words. . . . Tell him, Clara . . . tell him what I do. Where do I work, Clara?

CLARA: Awww . . . B.G., please.

BIG GIRL: DO LIKE I SAY! DO LIKE BIG WANTS YOU TO!

CLARA (*surrenders*): She works out at the state nut farm.

BIG GIRL (*triumphant*): And tell Mister Smart and Proper what I do.

CLARA (*automatically*): She's a technician.

JACK: Oh, that's nice. I didn't mean to suggest there was anything wrong with how you raised your sister.

BIG GIRL (*jolly again*): Haw haw haw . . . Nawh, ya didn't. I know you didn't even know what you were sayin', youngblood. Do you know why I taught her to cuss?

JACK: Why no, I have no idea. Why did you?

BIG GIRL: Well, it was to give her freedom, ya know? (JACK *shakes his head.*) Ya see workin' in the hospital with all the nuts and fruits and crazies and weirdos I get ideas 'bout things. I saw how when they get these kids in who have cracked up and even with older people who come in out of their skulls they all mostly cuss. Mostly all of them, all the time they out of their heads, they cuss all the time and do other wild things, and boy, do some of them really get into it and let out all of that filthy shit that's been stored up all them years. But when the docs start shockin' them and puttin' them on insulin they quiets down, that's when the docs think they're gettin' better, but really they ain't. They're just learn'n'

like before to hold it in . . . just like before, that's one reason most of them come back or are always on the verge afterwards of goin' psycho again.

JACK (*enthusiastic*): Wow, I never thought of that! That ritual action of purging and catharsis can open up new avenues of therapy and in learning theory and conditioning subjects . . .

BIG GIRL: Saaay whaaa . . .? What did you have for breakfast, man?

CLARA (*struck*): That sounds so wonderful. . . .

JACK (*still excited*): But I agree with you. You have an intuitive grasp of very abstract concepts!

BIG GIRL (*beaming*): Yeah, yeah . . . I got a lot of it figured out. . . . (*To* JACK.) Here, fill up your glass again, man.

JACK (*to* CLARA): Aren't you drinking with us?

CLARA: Later. Big Girl doesn't allow me to start in drinking too early.

JACK (*confused*): She doesn't?

BIG GIRL (*cuts in*): Well, in Baby Girl's case I said to myself that I'm teach'n' her how in front and lettin' her use what she knows whenever it builds up inside. And it's really good for her, gives her spirit and everything.

CLARA: That's probably what warped her brain.

BIG GIRL: Hush up! You know it was dat fuckin' disease. All the doctors said so.

CLARA: You don't believe no doctors 'bout nothin' else!

BIG GIRL (*glares at* CLARA): Are you showin' out, Clara? Are you showin' out to your little boyfriend?

CLARA: He ain't mah boyfriend.

JACK (*interrupts*): How do you know she might not have spirit if she wasn't allowed to curse?

BIG GIRL (*sullen*): I don't know anything, youngblood. But I can take a look at myself and see the two of us. Look at me! (*Stares at* JACK.) LOOK AT ME!

JACK: Yes, yes, I'm looking.

BIG GIRL: Well, what do you see?

CLARA: B.G. . . . *please!*

BIG GIRL (*ignores*): Well, what do you see?

JACK (*worried*): Well, I don't really know . . . I . . .

BIG GIRL: Well, let me tell you what you see. You see a fat bitch who's twenty pounds overweight and looks ten years older than she is. You want to know how I got this way and been this way most of my life and would be worse off if I didn't let off steam some drinkin' this rotgut and speakin' my mind?

JACK (*to* BIG GIRL, *who doesn't listen but drinks*): Yes, I would like to hear.

(CLARA *finishes the stove and takes a seat between the two.* BABY GIRL *goes to the yard door but does not go out into the rain; she sits down and looks out through the door at an angle.*)

BIG GIRL: Ya see, when I was a little runt of a kid my mother found out that she couldn't keep me or Baby Girl any longer cause she had T.B., so I got shipped out somewheres and Baby Girl got shipped out somewheres else. People that Baby Girl went to exposed her to the disease. She was lucky. I ended up with some fuckin' Christians. . . .

CLARA: Ohhh, B.G., you shouldn't say that!

BIG GIRL: Well, I sho as hell just did! . . . Damned kristers! I spent twelve years with those people, can you imagine? A dozen years in hell. Christians . . . *haaa* . . . always preachin' 'bout some heaven over yonder and building a bigger hell here den any devil have imagination for.

CLARA: You shouldn't go round sayin' things like dat.

BIG GIRL: I shouldn't! Well, what did your Christian mammy and pot-gutted pappy teach you? When I met you you didn't even know how to take a douche.

CLARA: YOU GOT NO RIGHT!!! (*She momentarily rises as if she's going to launch herself on* BIG GIRL.)

BIG GIRL (*condescending*): Awww . . . forget it, sweetie. . . . Don't make no never mind, but you remember how you us'ta smell when you got ready fo bed . . . like a dead hoss or a baby skunk. . . . (*To* JACK, *explaining.*) That damned Christian mamma and pappa of hers didn't tell her a thing 'bout herself . . . ha ha ha . . . thought if she ever found out her little things was used fo' anything else 'cept squattin' she'd fall backwards right up in it . . . ZaaaBOOM . . . STRAIGHT TA HELL . . . ha ha . . . Didn't know that li'l Clara had already found her heaven, and on the same trail.

CLARA (*ashamed*): Sometimes . . . sometimes . . . I just want to die for bein' here.

BIG GIRL (*enjoying herself*): Ha ha ha . . . that wouldn't do no good. Would it? Just remember what shape you were in when I met you, kid. Ha ha ha. (To JACK.) Hey, boy, can you imagine this pretty little trick here had her stomach seven months in the wind, waitin' on a dead baby who died from the same disease that Baby Girl had? . . .

CLARA: He didn't have any nasty disease like Baby Girl!

BABY GIRL (*hears her name but looks out door*): NO! NO! SHIT! DAMN! SHIT! SHIT!

BIG GIRL: *Haw haw haw* . . . Now we got her started . . . (*She laughs for over a minute;* JACK *waits patiently, sipping;* CLARA *is grim.* BABY GIRL *has quieted.*) She . . . she . . . ha ha . . . was walkin' round with a dead baby in her and had no place to go.

CLARA (*fills a glass*): I just can't understand you, B.G. You know my baby died after he was born. Some days you just get besides yourself.

BIG GIRL: I'm only helpin' ya entertain your guest.

CLARA: Awww . . . B.G. It wasn't his fault. I invited him.

JACK (*dismayed*): Well, I asked really. If there's anything wrong I can go.

BIG GIRL: Take it easy, youngblood. I'm just havin' a little fun. Now let's get back to the Clara Saga . . . ya hear that word, junior? S-A-G-A, SUCKER! You college boys don't know it all. Yeah, her folks had kicked her out and the little punk she was big for what had tried to put her out on the block and when that didn't work out . . . (*Mocking and making pretended blushes.*) because our sweet little thing was soooo modest and sedate . . . the nigger split! . . . HAW HAW HAW. . . . HE MADE IT TO NEW YORK! (*She goes into a laughing, choking and crying fit.* BABY GIRL *rushes over to her and on tiptoe pats her back.*)

BABY GIRL: Big Girl! Big Girl! Big Girl!

(*A knocking sounds and* CLARA *exits to answer the door.*)

BIG GIRL (*catches her breath*): Whatcha want, little sister?

BABY GIRL: The cat! The cat! It's got some-kittens! The cat got some kittens!

BIG GIRL (*still coughing and choking*): Awww, go on. You know there ain't no cats under there with no kittens. (*To* JACK.) She's been makin' that story up for two months now about how some cat crawls up under the steps and has kittens. She can't fool me none. She just wants a cat but I ain't gonna get none.

JACK: Why not? Cats aren't so bad. My mother has one and he's quite a pleasure to her.

BIG GIRL: For your mammy maybe, but all they mean round here (*Singsong.*) is fleas and mo' mouths to feed. With an invalid aunt upstairs we don't need any mo' expenses.

JACK (*gestures toward* BABY GIRL): It shows that

she has a very vivid imagination to make up that story about the kittens.

BIG GIRL: Yeah, her big sister ain't the biggest liar in the family.

(CLARA *returns with* MISS FAMIE *staggering behind her, a thin middle-aged woman in long seaman's raincoat, dripping wet, and wearing house slippers that are soaked and squish water about the kitchen floor.*)

BIG GIRL: Hi, Miss Famie. I see you're dressed in your rainy glad rags today.

MISS FAMIE (*slurred speech of the drunk*): Hello, B.G. Yeah, I couldn't pass up seein' Aunt Toohey, so I put on my weather coat. You know that don't a day pass that I don't stop up to see her.

BIG GIRL: Yeah, I know, Miss Famie. Every day you go up there with that quart of gin under your dress and you two ole lushes put it away.

MISS FAMIE: Why, B.G. You should know better than that.

CLARA (*reseated*): B.G., you shouldn't say that. . . .

BIG GIRL: Why shouldn't I? I'm payin' for over half of that juice and I don't git to see none of it 'cept the empty bottles.

BABY GIRL: CAT! CAT! CAT!

MISS FAMIE: Oh, the baby still sees them there cats.

CLARA: You should be ashamed to talk to Miss Famie like that.

BIG GIRL (*to* JACK): Why you so quiet? Can't you speak to folks when they come in?

JACK: I'm sorry. (*To* MISS FAMIE.) Hello, ma'am.

MISS FAMIE: Why howdie, son.

CLARA: Would you like a glass of wine, Miss Famie?

MISS FAMIE: Don't mind if I do, sister.

BIG GIRL: Better watch it, Miss Famie. Wine and gin will rust your gizzard.

CLARA: Ohhh . . . (*Pours a glass of wine.*) . . . Here, Miss Famie.

BABY GIRL: CAT! CAT!

BIG GIRL (*singsong, lifting her glass*): Mus' I tell' . . . muscatel . . . jittterbug champagne. (*Reminisces.*) Remember, Clara, the first time I got you to take a drink? (*To* MISS FAMIE.) You should of seen her. Some of this same cheap rotgut here. She'd never had a drink before but she wanted to show me how game she was. She was a bright little smart thing, just out of high school and didn't know her butt from a doorknob.

MISS FAMIE: Yes, indeed, that was Clara all right.

BIG GIRL: She drank three waterglasses down and got so damned sick I had to put my finger down her throat and make her heave it up. . . . HAW HAW. . . . Babbled her fool head off all night . . . said she'd be my friend always . . . that we'd always be together . . .

MISS FAMIE (*gulps down her drink*): Wine will make you do that the first time you get good 'n' high on it.

JACK (*takes a drink*): I don't know. You know . . . I've never really been wasted and I've been drinkin' for quite some time now.

BIG GIRL: Quite some time, huh? How long? Six months?

JACK: Nawh. My mother used to let me drink at home. I've been drinkin' since fifteen. And I drank all the time I was in the service.

BIG GIRL: Just because you been slippin' some drinks out of ya mammy's bottle and you slipped a few under ya belt with the punks in the barracks don't make ya a drinker, boy!

CLARA: B.G. . . . do you have to?

(MISS FAMIE *finishes her second drink as* BIG GIRL *and* CLARA *stare at each other.*)

MISS FAMIE: Well, I guess I better get up and see Aunt Toohey. (*She leaves.*)

BIG GIRL (*before* MISS FAMIE *reaches top of stairs*): That ole ginhead tracked water all over your floor, Clara.

CLARA: Makes no never mind to me. This place stays so clean I like when someone comes so it gets a little messy so I have somethin' 'ta do.

BIG GIRL: Is that why Jackie boy is here? So he can do some messin' 'round?

CLARA: Nawh, B.G.

JACK (*stands*): Well, I'll be going. I see that . . .

BIG GIRL (*rises and tugs his sleeve*): Sit down an' drink up, youngblood. (*Pushes him back into his seat.*) There's wine here . . . (*Slow and suggestive.*) . . . there's a pretty girl here . . . you go for that, don't you?

JACK: It's not that . . .

BIG GIRL: You go for fine little Clara, don't you?

JACK: Well, yes, I do . . .

BIG GIRL: HAW HAW HAW . . . (*Slams the table and sloshes wine.*) . . . HAW HAW HAW . . . (*Slow and suggestive.*) . . . What I tell ya, Clara? You're a winner. First time I laid eyes on you I said to myself that you's a winner.

CLARA (*takes a drink*): Drink up, B.G.

BIG GIRL (*to* JACK): You sho you like what you see, youndblood?

JACK (*becomes bold*): Why, sure. Do you think I'd come out on a day like this for anybody?

BIG GIRL: HAW HAW HAW ... (*Peals of laughter and more coughs.*)

JACK (*to* CLARA): I was going to ask you to go to the matinee 'round Pep's, but I guess it's too late now.

CLARA (*hesitates*): I never been.

BIG GIRL (*sobers*): That's right. You never been to Pep's and it's only 'round the corner. What you mean it's too late, youngblood? It don't start getting good till 'round four.

JACK: I thought she might have ta start gettin' supper.

BIG GIRL: She'd only burn it the fuck up too if she did. (*To* CLARA.) I'm goin' ta take you to Pep's this afternoon.

CLARA: You don't have ta, B.G.

BIG GIRL: It's my day off, ain't it?

CLARA: But it costs so much, don't it?

BIG GIRL: Nawh, not much. ... You'll like it. Soon as C.C. comes over to watch Baby Girl we can go.

CLARA (*brightens*): Okay!

JACK: I don't know who's there now, but they always have a good show. Sometimes Ahmad Jamal ...

BABY GIRL (*cuts speech*): CAT! CAT! CAT!

BIG GIRL: Let's toast to that. ... (*Raising her glass.*) ... To Pep's on a rainy day!

JACK: HERE HERE! (*He drains his glass.*)

(*A tumbling sound is heard from the backyard as they drink and* BABY GIRL *claps hands as* STOOGIE, BAMA, *and* HOSS *appear in yard doorway. The three boys are no more than sixteen. They are soaked but wear only thin jackets, caps and pants. Under* STOOGIE's *cap he wears a bandanna to keep his processed hair dry.*)

BIG GIRL: What the hell is this?

STOOGIE (*goes to* BIG GIRL *and pats her shoulder*): The heat, B.G. The man was on our asses so we had to come on in out of the rain, baby, dig?

BIG GIRL: Well, tell me somethin' I don't know, baby. Why you got to pick mah back door? I ain't never ready for any more heat than I gets already.

STOOGIE: It just happened that way, B.G. We didn't have any choice.

BAMA: That's right, Big Girl. You know we ain't lame 'nuf to be usin' yo pad fo no highway.

HOSS: Yeah, baby, you know how it is when the man is there.

BIG GIRL: Well, what makes a difference ...

(*Smiles.*) ... Hey, what'cha standin' there with your faces hangin' out for? Get yourselves a drink.

(HOSS *goes to the sink to get glasses for the trio;* STOOGIE *looks* JACK *over and nods to* BAMA, *then turns to* CLARA.)

STOOGIE: How ya doin', Clara? Ya lookin' fine as ever.

CLARA: I'm okay, Stoogie. I don't have to ask 'bout you none. Bad news sho' travels fast.

STOOGIE (*holds arms apart in innocence*): What'cha mean, baby? What'cha been hearin' 'bout poppa Stoogie?

CLARA: Just the regular. That your gang's fightin' the Peaceful Valley guys up in North Philly.

STOOGIE: Awww ... dat's old stuff. Sheeet ... you way behind, baby.

BAMA: Yeah, sweetcake, dat's over.

CLARA: Already?

HOSS: Yeah, we just finished sign'n' a peace treaty with Peaceful Valley.

BAMA: Yeah, we out ta cool the War Lords now from ov'va on Powelton Avenue.

HOSS: Ole Stoogie here is settin' up the war council now; we got a pact with Peaceful Valley and man, when we come down on those punk War Lords ... baby ... it's just gonna be all ov'va.

BIG GIRL: Yeah, it's always one thing ta another with you punks.

STOOGIE: Hey, B.G., cool it! We can't help it if people always spreadin' rumors 'bout us. Things just happen an' people talk and don' understand and get it all wrong, dat's all.

BIG GIRL: Yeah, all of it just happens, huh? It's just natural ... you's growin' boys.

STOOGIE: That's what's happen'n', baby. Now take for instance Peaceful Valley. Las' week we went up there ... ya know, only five of us in Crook's Buick.

CLARA: I guess ya was just looking at the scenery?

STOOGIE: Yeah, baby, dat's it. We was lookin' ... lookin' fo' some jive half-ass niggers. (*The boys laugh and giggle as* STOOGIE *enacts the story.*) Yeah, we spot Specs from offa Jefferson and Gratz walkin' with them bad foots down Master ... ha ha ha ...

BAMA: Tell them what happened to Specs, man.

HOSS: Awww, man, ya ain't gonna drag mah man Bama again?

(They laugh more, slapping and punching each other, taking off their caps and cracking each other with them, gulping their wine and performing for the girls and JACK. STOOGIE *has his hair exposed.)*

STOOGIE: Bama here . . . ha ha ha . . . Bama burnt dat four-eyed mathafukker in the leg.

HOSS: Baby, you shoulda seen it!

CLARA: Yeah, that's what I heard.

STOOGIE: Yeah, but listen, baby. *(Points to* BAMA.) He was holding the only heat we had . . . ha ho ho . . . and dis jive sucker was aimin' at Specs' bad foots . . . ha ha . . . while that blind mathafukker was blastin' from 'round the corner straight through the car window. . . .

(They become nearly hysterical with laughter and stagger and stumble around the table.)

HOSS: Yeah . . . ha ha . . . mathafukkin' glass was flyin' all over us . . . ha ha . . . we almost got sliced ta death and dis stupid mathafukker was shootin' at the man's bad foots . . . ha ha . . .

BAMA *(scratching his head)*: Well, man. Well, man . . . I didn't know what kind of rumble we was in.

(CLARA and BIG GIRL *laughs as they refill their glasses, nearly emptying the jug.* BIG GIRL *gets up and from out of the refrigerator pulls another gallon as laughter subsides.)*

BIG GIRL *(sits down)*: What's the heat doin' after ya?

STOOGIE: Nothin'.

CLARA: I bet!

STOOGIE *(sneer)*: That's right, baby. They just singled us out to make examples of. *(This gets a laugh from his friends.)*

BIG GIRL: What did you get?

HOSS: Get?

BIG GIRL *(turns on him)*: You tryin' ta get wise, punk?

STOOGIE *(patronizing)*: Awww, B.G. You not goin' ta take us serious, are ya? *(Silence.)* Well, ya, see. We were walkin' down Broad Street by the State Store, see? And we see this old rum-dum come out and stagger down the street carryin' this heavy package. . . .

CLARA: And? . . .

STOOGIE: And he's stumblin', see. Like he's gonna fall. So good ole Hoss here says, "Why don't we help that pore man out?" So Bama walks up and helps the man carry his package, and do you know what?

BIG GIRL: Yeah, the mathafukker "slips" down and screams and some cops think you some

wrongdoin' studs. . . . Yeah, I know. . . . Of course you didn't have time to explain.

STOOGIE: That's right, B.G. So to get our breath so we could tell our side of it we just stepped in here, dig?

BIG GIRL: Yeah, I dig. *(Menacing.)* Where is it?

HOSS: Where's what?

(Silence)

STOOGIE: If you had just give me another minute, B.G. *(Pulls out a quart of vodka.)* Well, no use savin' it anyway. Who wants some hundred proof tiger piss?

BAMA *(to* STOOGIE): Hey, man, how much was in dat mathafukker's wallet?

STOOGIE *(nods toward* JACK): Cool it, sucker.

HOSS *(to* STOOGIE): But, man, you holdin' the watch and ring too!

STOOGIE *(advancing on them)*: What's wrong with you jive-ass mathafukkers?

BIG GIRL: Okay, cool it! There's only one person gets out of hand 'round here, ya understand?

STOOGIE: Okay, B.G. Let it slide. . . .

BABY GIRL: CAT! CAT! CAT!

STOOGIE *(to* JACK): Drink up, man. Not every day ya get dis stuff.

*(*BAMA *picks up the beat of the music and begins a shuffling dance.* BABY GIRL *begins bouncing in time to the music.)*

HOSS: C'mon, Baby Girl; let me see ya do the slide.

BABY GIRL: NO! NO! *(She claps and bounces.)*

HOSS *(demonstrates his steps, trying to outdance* BAMA): C'mon, Baby Girl, shake that thing!

CLARA: No, stop that, Hoss. She don't know what she's doin'.

BIG GIRL: That's okay, Clara. Go on, Baby Girl, do the thing.

*(*STOOGIE *grabs salt from the table and shakes it upon the floor, under the feet of the dancers.)*

STOOGIE: DO THE SLIDE, MAN! SLIDE!

*(*BABY GIRL *lumbers up and begins a grotesque maneuver while grunting out strained sounds.)*

BABY GIRL: Uuuhhhhh . . . sheeeee . . . waaaa . . . uuhhh . . .

BIG GIRL *(standing, toasting)*: DO THE THING, BABY!!!!

CLARA: Awww . . . B.G. Why don' you stop all dat?

STOOGIE *(to* JACK·): C'mon, man, git with it.

(JACK *shakes his head and* STOOGIE *goes over to* CLARA *and holds out his hand.*)

STOOGIE: Let's go, baby.

CLARA: Nawh . . . I don't dance no mo'. . . .

STOOGIE: C'mon, pretty mamma . . . watch this step. . . . (*He cuts a fancy step.*)

BIG GIRL: Go on and dance, sister.

(STOOGIE *moves off and the three boys dance.*)

CLARA: Nawh . . . B.G., you know I don't go for that kind of stuff no mo'.

BIG GIRL: Go on, baby!

CLARA: No!

BIG GIRL: I want you to dance, Clara.

CLARA: Nawh . . . I just can't.

BIG GIRL: DO LIKE I SAY! DO LIKE BIG WANTS!

(*The dancers stop momentarily but begin again when* CLARA *joins them.* BABY GIRL *halts and resumes her place upon the floor, fondling her toy. The others dance until the record stops.*)

STOOGIE (*to* JACK): Where you from, man?

JACK: Oh, I live over in West Philly now, but I come from up around Master.

STOOGIE: Oh? Do you know Hector?

JACK (*trying to capture an old voice and mannerism*): Yeah, man. I know the cat.

STOOGIE: What's your name, man?

JACK: Jack, man. Maybe you know me by Tookie.

STOOGIE (*ritually*): Tookie . . . Tookie . . . yeah, man, I think I heard about you. You us'ta be in the ole Jet Cobras!

JACK: Well, I us'ta know some of the guys then. I been away for a while.

BAMA (*matter-of-factly*): Where you been, man? Jail?

JACK: I was in the Marines for three years.

STOOGIE: Hey, man. That must'a been a gas.

JACK: It was okay, I seen a lot . . . went a lot of places.

BIG GIRL: Yeah, you must'a seen it all.

STOOGIE: Did you get to go anywhere overseas, man?

JACK: Yeah, I was aboard ship most of the time.

HOSS: Wow, man. That sounds cool.

BAMA: You really was overseas, man?

JACK: Yeah. I went to Europe and North Africa and the Caribbean.

STOOGIE: What kind of boat were you on, man?

JACK: A ship.

BIG GIRL: A boat!

JACK: No, a ship.

STOOGIE (*rising,* BAMA *and* HOSS *surrounding* JACK): Yeah, man, dat's what she said . . . a boat!

CLARA: STOP IT!!!

BABY GIRL: NO! NO! NO! SHIT! SHIT! SHIT! DAMN! SHIT!

MISS FAMIE'S VOICE (*from upstairs*): Your aunt don't like all that noise.

BIG GIRL: You and my aunt better mind ya fukkin' ginhead business or I'll come up there and ram those empty bottles up where it counts!

BAMA (*sniggling*): Oh, baby. We forgot your aunt was up dere sick.

STOOGIE: Yeah, baby. Have another drink. (*He fills all glasses except* CLARA'S; *she pulls hers away.*)

CLARA: Nawh, I don't want any more. Me and Big Girl are goin' out after a while.

BAMA: Can I go, too?

BIG GIRL: There's always have ta be one wise mathafukker.

BAMA: I didn't mean nuttin', B.G., honest.

STOOGIE (*to* JACK): What did you do in the army, man?

JACK (*feigns a dialect*): Ohhh, man, I told you already I was in the marines!

HOSS (*to* CLARA): Where you goin?

CLARA: B.G.'s takin' me to Pep's.

BAMA: Wow . . . dat's nice, baby.

BIG GIRL (*gesturing toward* JACK): Ole smoothie here suggested takin' Clara but it seems he backed out, so I thought we might step around there anyway.

JACK (*annoyed*): I didn't back out!

STOOGIE (*to* JACK): Did you screw any of them foreign bitches when you were in Japan, man?

JACK: Yeah man. I couldn't help it. They were all over, ya know?

BIG GIRL: He couldn't beat them off.

STOOGIE: Yeah, man. I dig.

JACK: Especially in France and Italy. 'Course, the Spanish girls are the best, but the ones in France and Italy ain't so bad either.

HOSS: You mean those French girls ain't as good as those Spanish girls?

JACK: Nawh, man, the Spanish girls are the best.

BAMA: I never did dig no Mexican nor Rican spic bitches too tough, man.

JACK: They ain't Mexican or Puerto Rican. They Spanish . . . from Spain . . . Spanish is different from Mexican. In Spain . . .

STOOGIE: Whatcha do now, man?

JACK: Ohhh . . . I'm goin' ta college prep on the G.I. Bill now . . . and workin' a little.

STOOGIE: Is that why you sound like you got a load of shit in your mouth?

JACK: What do you mean!

STOOGIE: I thought you talked like you had shit in your mouth because you been ta college, man.

JACK: I don't understand what you're trying ta say, man.

STOOGIE: It's nothin', man. You just talk funny sometimes . . . ya know what I mean. Hey, man, where do you work?

JACK (*visibly feeling his drinks*): Nawh, man, I don't know what ya mean, and I don't go to college, man, it's college prep.

STOOGIE: Thanks, man.

JACK: And I work at the P.O.

BAMA: Pee-who?

JACK: The Post Office, man.

STOOGIE: Thanks, George. I always like to know things I don't know anything about. (*He turns his back on* JACK.)

JACK (*to* BIG GIRL): Hey, what time ya goin' 'round to Pep's?

BIG GIRL: Soon . . . are you in a hurry, young-blood? You don't have to wait for us.

JACK (*now drunk*): That's okay . . . It's just gettin' late, ya know, man . . . and I was wonderin' what time Clara's ole man gets home . . .

BIG GIRL: Clara's ole man? . . . What do you mean, man? . . .

(*The trio begins snickering, holding their laughter back;* JACK *is too drunk to notice.*)

JACK: Well, Clara said for me to come by to-day in the afternoon when her ole man would be at work . . . and I was wonderin' what time he got home. . . .

(BIG GIRL *stands, tilting over her chair to crash backwards on the floor. Her bust juts out; she is controlled but furious.*)

BIG GIRL: Clara's ole man is home now. . . .

(*A noise is heard outside as* C.C. *comes in the front door. The trio are laughing louder but with restraint;* CLARA *looks stunned.*)

JACK (*starts up and feels drunk for the first time*): Wha . . . you mean he's been upstairs all this time?

BIG GIRL (*staring*): Nawh, man, I don't mean that!

JACK (*looks at* BIG GIRL, *then at the laughing boys and finally to* CLARA): Ohhh . . . jeezus! (*He staggers to the backyard door, past* BABY GIRL, *and becomes sick.*)

BIG GIRL: Didn't you tell him? Didn't you tell him a fukkin' thing?

(C.C. *comes in. He is drunk and weaves and says nothing. He sees the wine, searches for a glass, bumps into one of the boys, is shoved into another, and gets booted in the rear before he reaches wine and seat.*)

BIG GIRL: Didn't you tell him?

CLARA: I only wanted to talk, B.G. I only wanted to talk to somebody. I don't have anybody to talk to . . . (*Crying.*) . . . I don't have anyone . . .

BIG GIRL: It's time for the matinee. (*To* STOOGIE.) Before you go, escort my friend out, will ya?

CLARA: Ohhh . . . B.G. I'll do anything but please . . . ohhh Big . . . I won't forget my promise.

BIG GIRL: Let's go. We don't want to miss the show, do we?

CLARA: Please, B.G., please. Not that. It's not his fault! Please!

BIG GIRL: DO LIKE I SAY! DO LIKE I WANT YOU TO DO!

(CLARA *drops her head and rises and exits stage right followed by* BIG GIRL. STOOGIE *and his boys finish their drinks, stalk and swagger about.* BAMA *opens the refrigerator and* HOSS *takes one long last guzzle.*)

BAMA: Hey, Stoogie babe, what about the split?

STOOGIE (*drunk*): Later, you square-ass, lame-ass mathafukker!

(HOSS *giggles.*)

BABY GIRL: CAT! CAT! CAT!

C.C. (*seated, drinking*): Shut up, Baby Girl. Ain't no cats out dere.

(MISS FAMIE *staggers from upstairs.*)

MISS FAMIE (*calling back*): GOOD NIGHT, TOOHEY. See ya tomorrow.

(*With a nod from* STOOGIE, BAMA *and* HOSS *take* JACK's *arms and wrestle him into the yard. The sound of* JACK's *beating is heard.* MISS FAMIE *wanders to the yard door, looks out but staggers back from what she sees and continues sprawling toward the exit, stage right.*)

BABY GIRL: CAT! CAT! CAT!

C.C.: SHUT UP! SHUT ON UP, BABY GIRL! I TOLE YA...DERE AIN'T NO CATS OUT DERE!!!

BABY GIRL: NO! DAMN! SHIT! SHIT! DAMN! NO! NO!

(STOOGIE *looks over the scene and downs his drink, then saunters outside. Lights dim out until there is a single soft spot on* BABY GIRL'S *head, turned wistfully toward the yard; then blackness.*)

Arthur Kopit: *Indians* (1969)

Arthur Kopit, born in 1937 in New York City, was already rumored to be an important writer when he was an undergraduate at Harvard. Not only did he graduate *cum laude* with a Phi Beta Kappa key in 1959, but he had written a number of interesting plays, some of which were produced. When he graduated, he won a fellowship that permitted him to travel in Europe and study the contemporary stage in some detail. He worked on his first nationally known play there and sent it back to Harvard in 1959, where it won a prize. New York producers heard that there was a young man coming down from Harvard with a very funny play that had the longest title in American drama: *Oh Dad, Poor Dad, Mamma's Hung You in the Closet and I'm Feelin' So Sad*. It was produced off Broadway in 1962, then moved to Broadway where it won several important awards and started Kopit off on a career noted for burlesque and absurdist farce in the service of very serious purposes.

Many critics, beginning with those who viewed *Oh Dad*, saw Kopit as part of the tradition of absurdist dramatists, those that broke with the conventions of the standard, realistic "well-made" play, but who did not simply turn to fantasy or surrealism. The absurdist drama simply ignores the realistic conventions, using them when convenient, but not hesitating to do such things as Kopit has done: feature a woman who travels with the corpse of her husband, whose pet is a cat-eating piranha, whose house plants are Venus's fly-traps. Such details amuse Kopit, and setting them into a vehicle that is, to a large degree, a farce permits them to work well. Yet Kopit has denied any symbolic or allegoric meaning to such things, and has refused to be connected with absurdist theatre. Very recent work tends to bear him out since he has moved from the realm of farce into a serious, but by no means realistic, form of drama.

Indians is Kopit's second full-length drama to reach Broadway. Its reception was very warm, and it stimulated an enormous amount of controversy regarding not only the play itself, but its subject. The play arrived at a time when the nation was doing a great deal of soul-searching. The Vietnam war was raging in its worst years and the nation was suffering tremendous internal disturbances. Many were aimed at protesting not only what America was doing, but what it had done in the past. Kopit's play was an attack on the nation's self-image.

Indians is certainly an invitation for an analysis of our national character. Particularly interesting is how it presents the material of boyhood dreams, the stuff that supported generations of moviemakers and dime novelists, the material that is singularly American: the American Wild West hero. The wonderful paradox of Buffalo Bill, Sitting Bull, and Chief Joseph playing in a vaudeville sideshow for whites in the Midwest and the East is absurd in itself. Yet it was quite true and needed little or no embellishment from Kopit. Like many such figures, Cody was best remembered for imitating himself, and the scene in the play that shows Ned Buntline's play-within-a-play performed before the President and the First Family is particularly telling when Wild Bill Hickok gets fed up with all the nonsense and really tries to seduce the beautiful "Indian" princess (truly played by an Italian actress in the White House). Cody studied Hickok in that scene and later told him that he realized Hickok really knew who he was and wouldn't put up any longer with the make-believe. But, alas, Hickok had already developed his own show, figuring to replicate as many Buffalo Bills as would be needed to populate the showplaces of North and South America.

The destruction of the buffalo, which Cody was instrumental in achieving, was catastrophic to the American Indian. The most conservative estimates suggest there were 25,000,000 buffalo when the white man came; they supported the life of all the Plains Indians and would have supplied their needs for all time. By 1904 there were no buffalo left on the plains. The few that survived were maintained in Mexico and Canada, otherwise we would have none today. The destruction of the buffalo was only a prelude to the destruction of the Indians themselves. They were massacred, as the play indicates, in a manner similar to the massacre of the animals.

The play emphasizes some terrible aspects of the entire experience of settling the country. Cody himself tries to do what he thinks is right. Even the Wild West sideshow was something that he, at least in the play, thinks might be vaguely educational. Killing the buffalo was a mistake, he realizes, but he didn't know it at the time. He brings a delegation from Washington to Sitting Bull; however, the interpretation of treaties and the questions of decorum make it a failure. Kopit is examining the basis of our civilization when he examines the laws that the nation insists it lives by. The question of law and justice for the Indian is brought clearly to bear in this drama and the detail of how the money paid for the Black Hills should stay in a bank in Washington until the Indians prove they can handle it is particularly interesting.

One of the most poignant aspects of the drama is the question of how people understand one another. The whites and the Indians do not see things the same way. They even realize there is a difference in how they value basic aspects of life, and when Sitting Bull outlines the needs of his people if they are to adopt the white man's ways, the entire conference breaks down. Both Sitting Bull and Cody come together near the end of the drama and express their innermost fears. Sitting Bull fears that not only will the Indians' destruction be a product of the white man, but that the white man would also, in the character of the gun and the pony, provide the materials for the Indians' glory. Cody's greatest fear is that he might die with his makeup on, a make-believe Buffalo Bill.

Kopit's latest play, *Wings,* won the Pulitzer Prize for 1979. It is a very different play, concentrating on the psychology of a mental patient, a woman who once flew her own plane. Kopit promises to be one of the more important playwrights of the current generation of young writers.

Selected Readings

Kopit, Arthur. *Oh, Dad, Poor Dad, Mamma's Hung You in the Closet and I'm Foolin' So Sad: A Pseudoclassical Tragifarce in a Bastard French Tradition.* New York: Hill and Wang, 1960.
———. *The Day the Whores Came Out to Play Tennis and Other Plays.* New York: Hill and Wang, 1965.
———. *Wings: A Play.* New York: Hill and Wang, 1978.

Indians
Arthur Kopit

CHARACTERS

BUFFALO BILL
SITTING BULL
SENATOR LOGAN
SENATOR DAWES
SENATOR MORGAN
TRIAL SOLDIERS
JOHN GRASS
SPOTTED TAIL
GRAND DUKE ALEXIS
INTERPRETER
NED BUNTLINE
GERONIMO
WHITE HOUSE USHER
OL' TIME PRESIDENT
FIRST LADY

WILD BILL HICKOK
TESKANJAVILA
UNCAS
VALETS
ANNIE OAKLEY
CHIEF JOSEPH
JESSE JAMES
BILLY THE KID
PONCHO
COLONEL FORSYTH
LIEUTENANT
REPORTERS
SOLDIERS
VARIOUS INDIANS

CHRONOLOGY FOR A DREAMER

1846   William F. Cody born in Le Claire, Iowa, on February 26.

1866   Geronimo surrenders.

1868   William Cody accepts employment to provide food for railroad workers; kills 4,280 buffaloes. Receives nickname "Buffalo Bill."

1869   *Buffalo Bill, the King of the Border Men,* a dime novel by Ned Buntline, makes Buffalo Bill a national hero.

1872   Expedition west in honor of Grand Duke Alexis of Russia, Buffalo Bill as guide.

1876   Battle at the Little Big Horn; Custer killed.

1877   Chief Joseph surrenders.

1878   Buffalo Bill plays himself in *Scouts of the Plains,* a play by Ned Buntline.

1879   Wild Bill Hickok joins Buffalo Bill on the stage.

1883   Sitting Bull surrenders, is sent to Standing Rock Reservation.

1883   "Buffalo Bill's Wild West Show" gives first performance, is great success.

1885   Sitting Bull allowed to join Wild West Show, tours with company for a year.

1886   United States Commission visits Standing Rock Reservation to investigate Indian grievances.

1890   Sitting Bull assassinated, December 15.

1890   Wounded Knee Massacre, December 25.

The play derives, in part, from this chronology but does not strictly adhere to it.—A.K.

SCENE 1

(*Audience enters to stage with no curtain. House lights dim.*

On stage: three large glass cases, one holding a larger-than-life-size effigy of Buffalo Bill in fancy embroidered buckskin. One, an effigy of Sitting Bull dressed in simple buckskin or cloth, no headdress, little if any ornamentation. The last case contains some artifacts: a buffalo skull, a bloodstained Indian shirt, and an old rifle. The surrounding stage is dark. The cases are lit by spotlights from above.

Strange music coming from all about. Sense of dislocation.

The house lights fade to dark.

Music up.

Lights on the cases slowly dim.

Sound of wind, soft at first.

The cases glide into the shadowy distance and disappear.

Eerie light now on stage; dim spotlights sweep the floor as if trying to locate something in space.

Brief, distorted strains of Western American music.

A VOICE *reverberates from all about the theatre.*)

VOICE: *Cody . . . Cody . . . Cody! . . . CODY!*

(*One of the spotlights passes something: a man on a horse. The spotlight slowly retraces itself, picks up the horse and rider. They are in a far corner of the stage; they move in slow motion.*

The other spotlights now move toward them, until all converge. At first, the light is dim. As they come toward us, it gets brighter.

The man is BUFFALO BILL, *dressed as in the museum case. The horse is a glorious white artificial stallion with wild, glowing eyes.*

They approach slowly; their slow motion gradually becoming normal speed.

Vague sound of cheering heard. Music becoming rodeolike. More identifiable.

Then, slowly, from the floor, an open-framed oval fence rises and encloses them.

The horse shies.

Tiny lights, strung beneath the top bar of the fence, glitter faintly. The spotlights—multi-colored—begin to crisscross about the oval.

Ghostly-pale Wild West Show banners slowly descend.

Then! It's a WILD WEST SHOW!

Loud, brassy music!

Lights blazing everywhere!

The horse rears. His rider whispers a few words, calms him.

Then, a great smile on his face, BUFFALO BILL *begins to tour the ring, one hand lightly gripping the reins, the other proudly waving his big Stetson to the unseen surrounding crowd. Surely it is a great sight; the horse prances, struts, canters, dances to the music, leaps softly through the light,* BUFFALO BILL *effortlessly in control of the whole world, the universe; eternity.*)

BUFFALO BILL: Yessir, BACK AGAIN! That triumphant brassy music, those familiar savage drums! Should o' known I couldn't stay away! Should o' known here's where I belong! The heat o' that ol' spotlight on my face. Yessir . . . Should o' known here's where I belong. . . .

(*He takes a deep breath, closes his eyes, savors the air. A pause.*)

Reminded o' somethin' tol' me once by General Custer. You remember him—one o' the great dumb-ass men in history. Not fer nothin' that he graduated last in his class at West Point! Anyways, we was out on the plains one day, when he turned t' me, with a kind o' far-off look in his eye, an' said, "Bill! If there is one thing a man must never fear, it's makin' a personal comeback."

(*He chuckles.*)

Naturally, I——
    VOICE (*softly*): And now, to start . . .
    BUFFALO BILL (*startled*): Hm?
    VOICE: *And now to start.*
    BUFFALO BILL: But I . . . just . . . got up here.
    VOICE: I'm sorry; it's time to start.
    BUFFALO BILL: Can't you *wait a second?* WHAT'S THE RUSH? *WAIT A SECOND!*

(*Silence. He takes a deep breath; quiets his horse down.*)

I'm sorry. But if I seem a trifle edgy to you, it's only 'cause I've just come from a truly harrowing engagement; seems my ... manager, a ... rather *ancient* gentleman, made a terrible *mistake* an' booked me int' what turned out t' be a ghost town! Well! I dunno what you folks know 'bout show business, but le' me tell you, there is nothin' more depressin' than playin' two-a-day in a goddam ghost town!

(*He chuckles.* INDIANS *appear around the outside of the ring. The horse senses their presence and shies;* BUFFALO BILL, *as if realizing what it means, turns in terror.*)

> VOICE: Bill.
> BUFFALO BILL: But ——
> VOICE: It's *time*.

(*Pause.*)

> BUFFALO BILL: Be—before we start, I'd ... just like to say——
> VOICE: Bill!

(*The* INDIANS *slowly approach.*)

> BUFFALO BILL: ——*to say* that ... I am a fine man. And anyone who says otherwise is *WRONG!*
> VOICE (*softly*): Bill, *it's time*.
> BUFFALO BILL: My life is an open book; I'm not *ashamed* of its bein' looked at!
> VOICE (*coaxing tone*): Bill ...
> BUFFALO BILL: I'm sorry, this is very ... hard ... for me t' say. But I believe I ... am a ... hero ... *A GODDAM HERO!*

(*Indian music. His horse rears wildly. Lights change for next scene.*)

SCENE 2

(*Light up on* SITTIN̈G BULL. *He is dressed simply— no feathered headdress. It is winter.*)

SITTING BULL: I am Sitting Bull! ... In the moon of the first snow-falling, in the year half my people died from hunger, the Great Father sent three wise men ... to investigate the conditions of our reservation, though we'd been promised he would come himself.

(*Lights up on* SENATORS LOGAN, MORGAN, *and* DAWES; *they are flanked by armed* SOLDIERS. *Opposite them, in a semicircle, are* SITTING BULL's *people, all huddling in tattered blankets from the cold.*)

SENATOR LOGAN: Indians! Please be assured that this committee has not come to punish you or take away any of your land but only to hear your grievances, determine if they are just. And if so, remedy them. For we, like the Great Father, wish only the best for our Indian children.

(*The* SENATORS *spread out various legal documents.*)

SITTING BULL: They were accompanied by ... my friend, William Cody——

(*Enter* BUFFALO BILL, *collar of his overcoat turned up for the wind.*)

in whose Wild West Show I'd once appeared ...

(BUFFALO BILL *greets a number of the* INDIANS.)

in exchange for some food, a little clothing. And a beautiful horse that could do tricks.

SENATOR MORGAN: Colonel Cody has asked if he might say a few words before testimony begins.

SENATOR LOGAN: We would be honored.

BUFFALO BILL (*to the* INDIANS): My ... brothers.

(*Pause.*)

I know how disappointed you all must be that the Great Father isn't here; I apologize for having said I thought I ... could bring him.

(*Pause.*)

However! The three men I *have* brought are by far his most trusted personal representatives. And I promise that talking to them will be the same as ...

(*Pause. Softly.*)

... talking to him.

(*Long pause; he rubs his eyes as if to soothe a headache.*)

To ... Sitting Bull, then ...

(*He stares at* SITTING BULL.)

... I would like to say that I hope you can overlook your ... disappointment. And remember what is at *stake* here. And not get angry ... or too impatient.

(*Pause.*)

Also, I hope you will ask your people to speak with open hearts when talking to these men. And treat them with the same great respect I have always . . . shown . . . to you, for these men have come to *help* you and your people. And I am afraid they may be the only ones left, now, who can.

SITTING BULL: And though there were many among us who wanted to speak first: men like Red Cloud! And Little Hawk! And He-Who-Hears-Thunder! And Crazy Horse! Men who were great warriors, and had counted many coups! And been with us at the Little Big Horn when we *KILLED CUSTER!* . . .

(*Pause.*)

I would not let them speak. . . . For they were like me, and tended to get angry, easily.

(*Pause.*)

Instead, I asked the *young* man, John Grass, who had never fought at all, but had been to the white man's school at Carlisle. And *thought* he understood . . . something . . . of their ways.

BUFFALO BILL: Sitting Bull would like John Grass to speak first.

LOGAN: Call John Grass.

BUFFALO BILL: John Grass! Come forward.

(*Enter* JOHN GRASS *in a black cutaway many sizes too small for him. He wears an Indian shirt. Around his neck is a medal.*)

JOHN GRASS: *Brothers!* I am going to talk about what the Great Father told us a long time ago. He told us to give up hunting and start farming. So we did as he said, and our people grew hungry. For the land was suited to grazing not farming, and even if we'd been farmers, nothing could have grown. So the Great Father said he would send us food and clothing, but nothing came of it. So we asked him for the money he had promised us when we sold him the Black Hills, thinking, with this money we could *buy* food and clothing. But nothing came of it. So we grew ill and sad. . . . So to help us from this sadness, he sent Bishop Marty, to teach us to be Christians. But when we told him we did not wish to be Christians but wished to be like our fathers, and dance the sundance, and fight bravely against the Shawnee and the Crow! And pray to the Great Spirits who made the four winds, and the earth, and made man from the dust of this earth, Bishop Marty hit us! . . . So we said to the Great Father that we thought we would like to go *back* to hunting, because to live, we needed food. But we found that while we had been learning to farm, the buffalo had gone

away. And the plains were filled now only with their bones. . . . Before we give you any more of our land, or move from here where the people we loved are growing white in their coffins, we want you to tell the Great Father to give us, who still live, what he promised he would! *No more than that.*

SITTING BULL: I prayed for the return of the buffalo!

(*Lights fade to black on everyone but* BUFFALO BILL.)

(*Distant gunshot heard offstage.*)

(*Pause.*)

(*Two more gunshots.*)

(*Lights to black on* BUFFALO BILL.)

SCENE 3

(*Light up on* SPOTTED TAIL, *standing on a ledge above the plains.*

It is night, and he is lit by a pale moon.

The air is hot. No wind.

A rifle shot is heard offstage, of much greater presence than the previous shots.

SPOTTED TAIL *peers in its direction.*

Sound, offstage, of wounded bulls.

Enter an INDIAN *dressed as a buffalo, wounded in the eye and bellowing with pain.*

He circles the stage.

Enter two more buffaloes, also wounded in the eyes. The first buffalo dies.

The two other buffaloes stagger over to his side and die beside him; another buffalo [missing an eye] enters, staggers in a circle, senses the location of the dead buffaloes and heads dizzily toward them—dying en route, halfway there. SPOTTED TAIL *crouches and gazes down at them. Then he stares up at the sky.*

Night creatures screech in the dark.

A pause.)

BUFFALO BILL (*offstage but coming closer*): Ninety-three, ninety-four, ninety-five . . . ninety-*six! I DID IT!*

(*Enter, running, a much younger* BUFFALO BILL, *rifle in hand, followed shortly by* MEMBERS OF THE U.S. CAVALRY *bearing torches, and the* GRAND DUKE'S INTERPRETER.)

I did it, I did it! No one believed I could, but I *did it!* One hundred buffalo—one hundred shots! "You jus' gimme some torches," I said. "I *know* there's buffalo around us. *Here.* Put yer ear t' the ground. Feel it tremblin'? Well. You wanna see somethin' fantastic, you get me some torches. I'll shoot the reflections in their eyes. I'll shoot 'em like they was so many shiny nickels!"

INTERPRETER: I'll tell the Grand Duke you did what you said. I know he'll be pleased.

BUFFALO BILL: Well he oughta be! I don' give exhibitions like this fer just anybody!

(*Exit the* INTERPRETER.)

'Specially as these critters're gettin' so damn hard t' find.

(*To the* SOLDIERS.)

Not like the ol' days when I was huntin' 'em fer the railroads.

(*He laughs, gazes down at one of the buffaloes. Pause. He looks away; squints as if in pain.*)

A SOLDIER: Are you all right, sir?
BUFFALO BILL: Uh . . . yes. Fine.

(*Exit the* SOLDIERS.
BUFFALO BILL *rubs his head.*
SPOTTED TAIL *hops down from his perch and walks up behind* CODY *unnoticed; stares at him.*
Pause.
BUFFALO BILL *senses the Indian's presence and turns, cocking his rifle. The Indian makes no move.*
BUFFALO BILL *stares at the Indian.*
Pause.)

BUFFALO BILL: *Spotted Tail!* My God. I haven't seen you in years. How . . . ya been?

(*Slight laugh.*)

SPOTTED TAIL: *What are you doing here?*

(*Pause.*)

BUFFALO BILL: Well, well, what . . . are *you* doing here? This isn't Sioux territory!
SPOTTED TAIL: It isn't *your* territory either.

(*Pause.*)

BUFFALO BILL: Well I'm with . . . these *people.* I'm scoutin' for 'em.
SPOTTED TAIL: *These people* . . . must be very hungry.
BUFFALO BILL: Hm?
SPOTTED TAIL: To need so many buffalo.
BUFFALO BILL: Ah! Of course! You were following the buffal*o also!* . . . Well listen, I'm sure my friends won't mind you takin' some. 'Tween

us, my friends don't 'specially care for the *taste* o' buffalo meat.

(*He laughs.*)

My God, but it's good t' see you again!
SPOTTED TAIL: *Your friends:* I have been studying them from the hills. They are very strange. They seem neither men, nor women.
BUFFALO BILL: Well! Actually, they're sort of a new *breed* o' people. Called dudes.

(*He chuckles.*)

SPOTTED TAIL: You *like* them?
BUFFALO BILL: Well . . . sure. Why not?

(*Pause.*)

I mean, obviously, they ain't the sort I've been used to. But then, things're changin' out here. An' these men are the ones who're changin' 'em. So, if you wanna be *part* o' these things, an' not left behind somewhere, you jus' plain hafta get *used* to 'em. You—uh—follow . . . what I mean?

(*Silence.*)

I mean . . . you've got to *adjust.* To the times. Make a *plan* fer yerself. I have one. You sould have one, too. Fer yer own good. Believe me.

(*Long pause.*)

SPOTTED TAIL: *What is your plan?*
BUFFALO BILL: Well, my plan is t' help people. Like you, ferinstance. Or these people I'm with. More . . . even . . . than that, maybe. And, and, whatever . . . it is I *do* t' help, for it, these people may someday jus' possibly name streets after me. Cities. Counties. States! I'll . . . be as famous as Dan'l Boone! . . . An' somewhere, on top of a beautiful mountain that overlooks more plains 'n rivers than any other mountain, there might even be a statue of me sittin' on a great white horse, a-wavin' my hat t' everyone down below, thankin' 'em, fer thankin' me, fer havin' done . . . whatever . . . it is I'm gonna . . . *do* fer 'em all. How . . . come you got such a weird look on yer face?
BUNTLINE (*offstage*): HEY, CODY! *STAY WHERE YA ARE!*
BUFFALO BILL: DON' WORRY! I AIN'T BUDGIN'!

(*To* SPOTTED TAIL.)

That's Mister Ned Buntline, the well-known newspaper reporter. I think he's gonna do an *article* on me! General Custer, who's in charge, an' I think is pushin' fer an article on *himself,* says this may well be the most important western expedition since Lewis 'n Clark.

BUNTLINE (*offstage*): BY THE WAY, *WHERE ARE YA?*

BUFFALO BILL: I ... AIN'T SURE! JUST HEAD FOR THE LIGHTS!

(*He laughs to himself.*)

SPOTTED TAIL: Tell me. Who is the man everyone always bows to?

BUFFALO BILL: Oh! The Gran' Duke! He's from a place called Russia. This whole shindig's in his honor. I'm sure he'd love t' meet you. He's never seen a real Indian.

SPOTTED TAIL: There are no Indians in Russia?

(BUFFALO BILL *shakes his head.*)

Then I will study him even more carefully than the others. Maybe if he takes me back to Russia with him, I will not end like my people will ... end.

BUFFALO BILL (*startled*): *What?*

SPOTTED TAIL: I mean, like these fools here, on the ground.

(*He stares at the buffalo.*)

BUFFALO BILL: *Ah* ... Well, if ya don' mind my sayin', I think you're bein' a bit pessimistic. But you do what ya like. Jus' remember: these people you're studying'—some folk think *they're* the fools.

SPOTTED TAIL: Oh, no! They are not fools! *No one who is a white man can be a fool.*

(*He smiles coldly at* BUFFALO BILL; *heraldic Russian fanfare offstage.*

Enter RUSSIAN TORCHBEARERS *and* TRUMPETEERS.

BUFFALO BILL *and* SPOTTED TAIL, *in awe, back away.*

Enter with much pomp and ceremony GRAND DUKE ALEXIS *on a splendid litter carved like a horse. He is accompanied by his* INTERPRETER, *who points out the four buffaloes to the* GRAND DUKE *as he majestically circles the clearing. He is followed by* NED BUNTLINE, *who carries a camera and tripod.*)

BUFFALO BILL: My God, but that is a beautiful sight!

(*The* GRAND DUKE *comes to a halt. Majestic sweep of his arms to those around him.*)

GRAND DUKE: (*Makes a regal Russian speech.*)

INTERPRETER: His Excellency the Grand Duke wishes to express his heartfelt admiration of Buffalo Bill ...

(*Music up.*)

... for having done what he has done tonight.

(*The* GRAND DUKE *gestures majestically. The* INTERPRETER *opens a small velvet box. Airy music. The* INTERPRETER *walks toward* BUFFALO BILL.)

GRAND DUKE (*gesturing for* BUFFALO BILL *to come forward*): Boofilo Beel!

(BUFFALO BILL *walks solemnly forward. The* INTERPRETER *takes out a medal.* BUFFALO BILL, *deeply moved, looks around, embarrassed.*

The INTERPRETER *smiles and holds up the medal, gestures warmly for* BUFFALO BILL *to kneel. He does so.*

The INTERPRETER *places the medal, which is on a bright ribbon, around his neck.*

Flashgun goes off.)

BUNTLINE: Great picture, Cody! FRONT PAGE! My God, what a night! *What a story!* Uh ... sorry, yer Highness. Didn't mean t' distoib ya.

(*He backs meekly away. Sets up his camera for another shot. The* GRAND DUKE *regains his composure.*)

GRAND DUKE: (*Russian speech.*)

INTERPRETER: His Excellency wonders how Buffalo Bill became such a deadly shot.

BUFFALO BILL: Oh, well, you know, just ... practice.

(*Embarrassed laugh.*)

GRAND DUKE: (*Russian speech.*)

INTERPRETER: His Excellency says he wishes that his stupid army knew how to practice.

GRAND DUKE: (*Russian speech.*)

INTERPRETER: Better yet, he wishes you would come back with him to his palace and protect him yourself.

BUFFALO BILL: Oh.

(*Slight laugh.*)

Well, I'm sure the Grand Duke's in excellent hands.

(*The* INTERPRETER *whispers what* BUFFALO BILL *has just said.*)

GRAND DUKE: Da! *Hands.*

(*He holds out his hands, then turns them and puts them around his throat.*)

BUFFALO BILL: I think His Majesty's exaggeratin'. I can't believe he's not *surrounded* by friends.

GRAND DUKE: FRIENDS!

(*He cackles and draws his sword, slashes the air.*)

Friends! Friends! . . . *Friends!*

(*He fights them off.*)

BUFFALO BILL (*to* BUNTLINE): I think he's worried 'bout somethin'.

BUNTLINE: Very strange behavior.

GRAND DUKE: (*Nervous Russian speech.*)

INTERPRETER: His Excellency wonders if Buffalo Bill has ever been afraid.

BUFFALO BILL: . . . Afraid?

GRAND DUKE: (*Russian word.*)

INTERPRETER: Outnumbered.

BUFFALO BILL: Ah.

(*Slight laugh.*)

Well, uh——

BUNTLINE: Go on, tell 'm. It'll help what I'm plannin' t' write.

BUFFALO BILL (*delighted*): It *will?*

BUNTLINE: Absolutely. Look: de West is changin'—right? Well, people wanna know about it. Wanna feel . . . *part* o' things. I think *you're* what dey need. Someone t' listen to, observe, *identify* wid. No, no, really! I been studyin' you.

BUFFALO BILL: . . . You have?

BUNTLINE: I think you could be de inspiration o' dis land.

BUFFALO BILL: Now I *know* you're foolin'!

BUNTLINE: Not at all . . . Well go on. Tell 'm what he wants t' hear. T'rough my magic pen, others will hear also. . . . Donmentionit. De nation needs men like me, too.

(*He pats* CODY *on the shoulder and shoves him off toward the* GRAND DUKE; CODY *gathers his courage.*)

BUFFALO BILL (*to the* GRAND DUKE): Well, uh . . . where can I begin? Certainly it's true that I've been outnumbered. And—uh—many times. Yes.

BUNTLINE: That's the way.

BUFFALO BILL: More times, in fact, than I can count.

BUNTLINE: Terrific.

BUFFALO BILL (*warming to the occasion*): An' believe me, I can count pretty high!

BUNTLINE: SENSATIONAL!

BUFFALO BILL: Mind you, 'gainst *me,* twelve's

normally an even battle—long's I got my two six-shooters that is.

BUNTLINE: Keep it up, keep it up!

BUFFALO BILL: THIRTEEN! If one of 'em's thin enough for a bullet t' go clean through. Fourteen if I got a huntin' knife. Fifteen if there's a hard surface off o' which I can ricochet a few shots.

BUNTLINE: *Go on!*

BUFFALO BILL: Um twenty . . . if I got a stick o' dynamite. HUNDRED! IF THERE'S ROCKS T' START A AVALANCHE!

(BUNTLINE *applauds.*)

What I mean is, with *me* it's never say die! Why . . . I remember once I was ridin' for the Pony Express 'tween Laramie 'n Tombstone. Suddenly, jus' past the Pecos, fifty drunk Comanches attack. Noise like a barroom whoop-di-do, arrows fallin' like hailstones! I mean, they come on me so fast they don' have time t' see my face, notice who I am, realize I'm in fact a very good *friend* o' theirs!

GRAND DUKE: FRIEND! FRIEND!

BUNTLINE (*sotto voce*): Get off de subject!

BUFFALO BILL: Well, there was no alternative but t' fire back. Well I'd knocked off 'bout thirty o' their number when I realized I was *out* o' bullets. Just at that moment, a arrow whizzed past my head. Thinkin' fast, I reached out an' caught it. Then, usin' it like a fly swatter, I knocked away the other nineteen arrows that were headin' fer my heart. Whereupon, I stood up in the stirrups, hurled the arrow sixty yards. . . . . An' killed their chief.

(*Pause.*)

Which . . . *depressed* . . . the remainin' Indians.

(*Pause.*)

And sent 'em scurryin' home. Well! That's sort o' what ya might call a typical day!

(*Bravos from everyone except the* GRAND DUKE.)

GRAND DUKE: (*Russian speech, quite angry.*)

INTERPRETER: His Excellency says he would like to kill a Comanche also.

BUFFALO BILL: Hm?

GRAND DUKE (*with obvious jealousy*): Like Boofilo Beel!

INTERPRETER: Like Buffalo Bill!

GRAND DUKE: (*Excited Russian speech.*)

INTERPRETER: He will *prove* he cannot be intimidated!

GRAND DUKE: Rifle, rifle, rifle!

BUFFALO BILL (*to* BUNTLINE): I think my story may've worked a bit too well.

BUNTLINE: Nonsense! This is *terrific!*

(*They duck as the* GRAND DUKE, *cackling madly, scans the surrounding darkness over his rifle sight.*)

Shows you've won the Grand Duke's heart.

GRAND DUKE (*pounding his chest*): Boofilo Beel! ... I am *BOOFILO BEEL!*

(*He laughs demonically.*)

BUNTLINE: I think you'd better find 'm a Comanche.

BUFFALO BILL: Right! *Well.* Um ...

(*Slight laugh.*)

That *could* be a ... problem.

GRAND DUKE: Comanche! *Comanche!*

BUFFALO BILL: Ya see, fer one thing, the Comanches live in Texas. And we're in Missouri.

GRAND DUKE: COMANCHE! *COMANCHE!*

BUFFALO BILL: Fer another, I ain't 'xactly sure what they look like.

GRAND DUKE: Ah!

(*He fires into the darkness.*

SPOTTED TAIL *stumbles out, collapses and dies. The* GRAND DUKE *and his* INTERPRETER *delirious with joy.* BUNTLINE *dumbfounded.* BUFFALO BILL *stunned, but for vastly different reasons.*)

BUNTLINE (*approaching the body cautiously*): My God, will you look at that? Fate must be smiling!

(*He laughs weakly, stares up at the heavens in awe.*

BUFFALO BILL, *almost in a trance, walks over to the body; stares down at it.*

Weird music heard.

The lights change color, grow vague.

All movement arrested.

SPOTTED TAIL *rises slowly and moves just as slowly toward the* GRAND DUKE; *stops.*)

SPOTTED TAIL: My name is Spotted Tail. My father was a Sioux; my mother, part Cherokee, part Crow. No matter how you look at it, I'm just not a Comanche.

(*He sinks back to the ground.*

Lights return to normal, the music ends.)

GRAND DUKE: (*Baffled Russian speech.*)

INTERPRETER: His Excellency would like to know what the man he just shot has said.

(*Long pause.* BUFFALO BILL *looks around, as if for help; all eyes upon him.*)

BUFFALO BILL (*softly*): He said ...

(*Pause.*)

"I ...

(*Pause.*)

should have ...

(*He looks at* BUNTLINE, *takes a deep breath.*)

stayed at home in ... Texas with the rest of my ... Comanche tribe."

BUNTLINE: Fabulous!

(*He takes* SPOTTED TAIL's *picture; the night sky glows from the flash.*)

Absolutely fabulous!

(*The scene fades around* BUFFALO BILL, *who stands in the center, dizzily gripping his head.*)

SCENE 4

(*Dimly we see the* SENATORS *and* SITTING BULL's INDIANS *glide back into view.*)

BUFFALO BILL: If it *please* the honorable senators ... there is something I would like to say to *them*, as well.

(*Pause.*)

I wish to say ... that there is far more at stake here, today, than the discovery of Indian grievances.

(*Pause.*)

At stake are these people's lives.

(*Pause.*)

In *some* ways, more than even that. For these are not just *any* Indians. These are *Sitting Bull's* Indians. ... The last to surrender.

(*Pause.*)

The last of a kind.

(*Long pause.*)

So, in that way, you see, they are ... perhaps more *important* for us than ... any others.

(*Pause.*)

For it is we, alone, who have put them on this strip of arid land. And what becomes of them is . . . our responsibility.

(BUFFALO BILL *stares helplessly as the scene about him fades to black.*)

VOICE: And now, for your *pleasure,* BUFFA-LO BILL'S WILD WEST SHOW *PROUDLY* PRESENTS . . .

(*Lights to black.*
Drum roll.)

SCENE 5

(*Stage dark; drum roll continues. Weirdly colored spotlights begin to crisscross on the empty stage.*)

VOICE: THE MOST FEROCIOUS INDIAN ALIVE! . . .

(*The bars of a large round cage slowly emerge from the floor of the stage; then, around the bars, the Wild West Show fence seen earlier.*)

THE FORMER SCOURGE OF THE SOUTH-WEST! . . .

(*The lights on the fence begin to glow; eerie, fantastical atmosphere.*
A tunnel-cage roll out from the wings and connects with the large central cage.
Sound of an iron grate opening offstage.
Rodeo music up.)

The one'n only . . . *GERONIMO!*

(*Enter* GERONIMO, *crawling through the tunnel; as soon as he is in sight, he stops, lifts his head, takes in his surroundings.*
Enter two COWBOY ROUSTABOUTS *with prods. They are enormous men—much larger than life-size. Their muscles bulge against their gaudy clothes. Their faces seem frozen in a sneer. Even their gun belts are over-sized.*
They prod GERONIMO *along, raise the gate to the center cage and coax him in, closing it behind him. Then they, move away.*
GERONIMO *paces about, testing the bars with his hands.*)

GERONIMO: I AM GERONIMO! WAR CHIEF OF THE GREAT CHIRICAHUA APACHES!

(*He stalks about.*)

Around my neck is a string of white men's genitals! MEN I HAVE KILLED! . . . Around my waist, the scalplocks of white women's geni-tals! WOMEN I RAPED AND KILLED! . . . *No Indian has ever killed or raped more than I!* Even the Great Spirits cannot count the number! . . . My body is painted with blood! I am red from white men's BLOOD! . . . NO ONE LIVES WHO HAS KILLED MORE WHITE MEN THAN *I*!

(BUFFALO BILL, *in his fancy buckskin, enters un-noticed by* GERONIMO; *drum roll. He opens the cage door and walks inside.*
Once inside, he closes the door and stands still.
GERONIMO *senses his presence and stops moving. Lifts up his head as if to hear better. Sniffs. Turns. Stares at* BUFFALO BILL.
Slowly, BUFFALO BILL *walks toward him. He stops just short of the Indian. Then defiantly turns his back.*
GERONIMO *practically frothing.*
Long pause. GERONIMO *does nothing.*
BUFFALO BILL *walks calmly away, opens the cage door, and exits. Disappears into the shadows.*
GERONIMO *stands trembling with frenzy.*
Lights fade to black.)

SCENE 6

(*Lights up on the Senate Committee* SITTING BULL'S INDIANS, *and* BUFFALO BILL.)

SENATOR LOGAN: Mister Grass, I wonder if you could be a bit more *specific* and tell us *exactly* what you think the Great Father has promised which he has not given.

JOHN GRASS: He promised to give us *as much as we would need, for as long as we would need it!*

SENATOR DAWES: Where did he promise you *that?*

JOHN GRASS: In a treaty.

SENATOR LOGAN: *What* treaty?

JOHN GRASS: A treaty signed some years ago, maybe five or six.

SENATOR LOGAN: Mister Grass, many treaties were signed five or six years ago. But frankly, I've never heard of an arrangement quite like that one.

JOHN GRASS: You took the Black Hills from us in this treaty!

SENATOR DAWES: You mean we *bought* the Black Hills in it!

(LOGAN *glares at* DAWES.)

JOHN GRASS: I have nothing else to say.

(*He turns and starts to walk away.*)

SENATOR LOGAN: Mister Grass! The . . . Senator . . . *apologizes* for his . . . tone.

(*Pause.* JOHN GRASS *returns.*)

JOHN GRASS: If you *bought* the Black Hills from us, where is our money?
SENATOR LOGAN: The money is in trust.
JOHN GRASS: *Trust?*
SENATOR MORGAN: He means, it's in a bank. Being *held* for you in a . . . bank. In *Washington!* Very . . . fine bank.
JOHN GRASS: Well, we would rather hold it ourselves.
SENATOR DAWES: The Great Father is worried that you've not been educated enough to spend it *wisely*. When he feels you have, you will receive every last penny of it. *Plus interest.*

(JOHN GRASS *turns in fury;* LOGAN *totally exasperated with* DAWES.)

BUFFALO BILL: Mister Grass, *please!* These men have come to *help* you! But their ways are *different* from yours; you must be *patient* with them.
JOHN GRASS: You said you would bring us the Great Father.
BUFFALO BILL: I *tried!* I told you! But he wouldn't come; *what else could I do?*
JOHN GRASS: You told us he was your *friend.*
BUFFALO BILL: HE *IS* MY FRIEND! *Look, don't you understand?* These men are your *only* hope. If you turn away from them, it's like . . . *committing suicide.*

(*Pause.*)

JOHN GRASS (*to the* SENATORS): At Fort Laramie, Fort Lyon, and Fort Rice we signed treaties, parts of which have never been fulfilled.
SENATOR DAWES: *Which* parts have never been fulfilled?
JOHN GRASS: At Fort Rice the Government advised us to be at *peace,* and said that *if we did so,* we would receive a span of horses, five bulls, ten chickens, and a wagon!
SENATOR LOGAN: You . . . really believe . . . these things were in the treaty?
JOHN GRASS: We were told they were.
SENATOR LOGAN: You . . . saw them written?
JOHN GRASS: We cannot read very well, but we were *told* they were!

(*The* SENATORS *glance sadly at one another.* JOHN GRASS *grows confused. Pause.*)

We were also . . . promised a STEAMBOAT!
SENATOR MORGAN: A *steamboat?*
SENATOR DAWES: What in God's name were you supposed to do with a steamboat in the middle of the plains?

(*He laughs.*)

JOHN GRASS: I don't know.

(*He turns in confusion and stares at* BUFFALO BILL; BUFFALO BILL *turns helplessly to the* SENATORS. *As* ——
Lights begin to fade.)

SITTING BULL: Where is the Great Father, Cody? . . . The one you said would help us. . . . The one you said you knew *so well.*

(*As lights go to black, a Mozart minuet is heard.*)

SCENE 7

(*Lights up on White House Ballroom, in the center of which is a makeshift stage. The front drop of this stage is a melodramatic western-heroic poster with* "Scouts of the Plains, *by NED BUNTLINE"* painted over it.
The Mozart stops as*——
A Negro USHER *enters.*)

USHER: This way, Mister President.
OL' TIME PRESIDENT (*offstage*): Thank you, George.

(*Enter the* OL' TIME PRESIDENT *in white tie and tails, cigar in mouth, brandy glass in hand.*)

This way, dear. They're about to start.

(*Enter the* FIRST LADY *in a formal gown.*)

FIRST LADY: Oh, this *is* exciting! Our *first real cowboys!*

(*The* USHER *leads them toward a pair of Louis XIV chairs set facing the stage. Drum roll.*)

OL' TIME PRESIDENT: Sssh. Here we go.

(*They sit.
Enter, from behind the canvas drop,* NED BUNTLINE. *He wears an exaggerated version of plainsman's outfit.*)

NED BUNTLINE: Mister President, hon'rable First Lady,
Before you stands a character most shady,

A knave whose presence darkens this bright
    earth,
More than does the moon's eclipsing girth.
What's that you say, I'm rude to filth espouse,
When I'm the guest of such a clean, white
    house?
Fear not, there's somethin' I didn't mention:
Recently, I found redemption.
Ah, forgive me, I'm sorry, Ned Buntline's the
    name,
It's me who's brought Bill Cody fame.
Wrote twenty-seven books with him the hero.
Made 'm better known than Nero.
And though we sold 'em cheap, one for a dime,
The two of us was rich in no time.
As for my soul's redemption, it came thus:
I saw the nation profit more than us.
For with each one o' my excitin' stories,
Cody grew t' represent its glories.
Also helped relieve its conscience,
By showing pessimism's nonsense.
Later, when people asked t' see 'm,
I wrote a play for him to be in;
A scene of which we now perform for you,
As you've so graciously implored us to.
Cody, of course, impersonates himself,
As does Yours Truly.
The Crow Maiden is Italian actress
Paula Monduli.
Our evil Pawnee Chief, the great German actor
Gunther Hookman.
Our other Indians, I'm afraid,
Come from Brooklyn.
However, as a special treat tonight,
A visitor is here,
And I've added some new dialogue,
So he might appear.
Realize though, this man's come as Cody's friend,
He's not an actor.
Though of course in *my* play, who men *are*
Is the real factor.
So get set then for anything,
May the script be damned,
An' let's give Cody an' Wild Bill Hickok
A ROUSING HAND!

(*The* FIRST LADY *and the* OL' TIME PRESIDENT *applaud enthusiastically.* BUNTLINE *exits.*

The canvas drop is rolled up to reveal another canvas drop—a painted forest of the worst melodramatic order.

On stage, wooden as only the worst amateur actors can be, stand CODY *and* HICKOK, *the latter with long, glorious hair, fancy buckskin leggings, two large guns and a knife in his belt.*)

BUFFALO BILL: God pray we're in time. Those Pawnee devils will do anything.

(*Silence.*)

BUNTLINE (*prompting from offstage*): Especially . . .

(*Silence.*)

BUFFALO BILL: Think that's your line, Bill.
WILD BILL HICKOK: Oh, hell's thunder.

(*To* BUNTLINE.)

Better give it-a-me agin.
    BUNTLINE: Especially . . .
    HICKOK: Especially.
    BUNTLINE: . . . at their . . .
    HICKOK: At their.
    BUFFALO BILL (*sotto voce*): . . . dreadful annual . . .
    HICKOK: Dreadful. Annual.
    BUNTLINE: . . . Festival of the Moon.
    HICKOK: Festival of the Moon. Which is . . . 'bout t' happen. As it does every . . .

(*Silence.*)

    BUFFALO BILL: . . . year.
    HICKOK: Year.
    BUNTLINE: Very good.
    HICKOK: Very good.
    BUNTLINE: No!
    HICKOK: Whose line's that?
    BUFFALO BILL: No one's. He was jus' congratulatin' you.
    HICKOK: Oh, Will, fer pity's sake, le' me out o' this.
    BUNTLINE: *Ad lib!*
    BUFFALO BILL: Yes! Pray God we're in time to stop the Pawnee's dreadful Festival of the Moon so that I, the great Buffalo Bill, can once again

———

    HICKOK: Will, stop it! A man may need money, but no man needs it this bad.

(*Enter* BUNTLINE, *tap-dancing the sound of horse's hooves.*)

BUFFALO BILL: Hark! Ned Buntline approaches! One o' the finest sharpshooters o' the West!

    HICKOK (*under his breath*): Couldn't hit a cow in the ass from two paces.

BUFFALO BILL: Who knows? Maybe *he* can help us in our dire strait.

    HICKOK: Mister and Missus President, if you're still out there, believe me, I'm as plumb embarrassed by this dude-written sissyshit as you.

BUNTLINE: HAIL, BUFFALO BILL! Hail— uh—Wild Bill Hickok. What brings you to this unlikely place?

HICKOK: Good fuckin' question.

BUNTLINE: Could it be that you seek, as I do, the camp of Uncas, evil Pawnee chief?

BUFFALO BILL: Yes, verily. We seek his camp so that I, the great Buffalo Bill, can, once again, save someone in distress.

(HICKOK *groans*.)

This time, specifically, a virgin maiden——

HICKOK: You gotta be jokin'.

BUFFALO BILL: *Will you shut up!* Named Tes-kanjavila! Who, 'less I save her, faces torture, sacrifice, and certain violations.

BUNTLINE: This bein' so, *let us join forces!*

HICKOK: Boy, where's your *self-respect?*

BUNTLINE (*weakly*): And save this virgin together.

BUFFALO BILL (*to* HICKOK): Will you leave me alone!

HICKOK: This ain't a *proper place* for a man t' be!

BUFFALO BILL: Well, I THINK IT *IS!* I think I'm doin' a lot o' good up here! Entertainin' people! Makin' 'em *happy!* Showin' 'em the West! Givin' 'em somethin' t' be *proud* of! *You* go spend your life in Dodge City if you want! I got *bigger* things in mind!

(*Stunned pause*.)

BUNTLINE (*very sheepishly*): To repeat: let us join forces and save this virgin together.

HICKOK: Buntline, if these guns were loaded, I'd——

BUNTLINE (*cueing the actors offstage*): HARK! The maiden's name is called!

NUMEROUS VOICES (*offstage*): Teskanjavila!

BUNTLINE: We must be near the camp of Uncas.

BUFFALO BILL: Evil Pawnee chief.

HICKOK: I'm gettin' sick.

BUNTLINE: Let us, therefore, approach with caution.

BUFFALO BILL: Guns ready.

BUNTLINE: Ears open.

BUFFALO BILL (*to* HICKOK): Mouths shut!

BUNTLINE: Eyes alert.

BUFFALO BILL: So that I, Buffalo Bill, may once aga——

(HICKOK *has walked over and is staring into his face.*)

Just *what are you doin'?*

HICKOK: What're *you* doin'?

BUFFALO BILL: I'm doin' what I'm doin', *that's* what I'm doin'!

HICKOK (*to* BUNTLINE): Always was intelligent.

BUFFALO BILL: I am doin' what my country *wants!* WHAT MY BELOVED COUNTRY *WANTS!*

HICKOK (*to the first family*): *This* . . . is . . . what you want?

FIRST LADY: Absolutely!

OL' TIME PRESIDENT: Best play I've seen in years!

(HICKOK, *staggered, sits down on the stage.*)

BUFFALO BILL: When a man has a talent, a *God*-given talent, I think it's his godly duty t' make the most of it.

(*Applause from the First Family.* BUFFALO BILL *nods acknowledgment. To* HICKOK.)

Ya see, Bill, what you fail to understand is that I'm not being false to what I *was*. I'm simply *drawin'* on what I was . . . and raisin' it to a higher level.

(*He takes a conscious pause.*)

Now. On with the show!

(*He points to* BUNTLINE, *cueing him to give the next line.*)

BUNTLINE: AVAST, AHOY! Above yon trees see the pale moon rising!

(A *cardboard moon is pulled upwards.*)

Feel the black night envelope us like a dark dream.

(BUNTLINE *and* CODY *shiver.*)

Sounds of the savage forest and heard. . . . We approach on tiptoes.

BUFFALO BILL (*to the First Family*): God pray we're in time.

(*They drop to their bellies as the canvas drop is raised to reveal the camp of* UNCAS. *Tied to a totem pole is* TESKANJAVILA, *writhing sensually.*

Clearly phony INDIANS *dance around her to the beat of drums. The heroes crawl slowly forward.* HICKOK, *eyeing the girl lustfully, joins in.*)

FIRST LADY: That Hickok's rather handsome, isn't he?

OL' TIME PRESIDENT: I'm watching the girl. Note her legs. How white they are. For an Indian. One can almost see the soft inner flesh of her thighs.

FIRST LADY: *This play excites me!*

OL' TIME PRESIDENT: We really should have more things like this at the White House.

(*The drums grow wilder. The* INDIANS *scream;* BUNTLINE, CODY, *and* HICKOK *invade the Indian camp site. Gunshots.* INDIANS *fall dead.*)

TESKANJAVILA (*Italian accent*): Saved! A maiden's prayers are answered! And may I say, not a bit too soon! Already, my soft thighs had been pried open; my budding breasts pricked by the hot tip of an Indian spear. Yet, through it all, my maidenhead stayed secure. Here. In this pouch. Kept in this secret pocket. Where no one thought to look. Thus is innocence preserved! May Nazuma, God of Thunder, grant me happiness!

(*Thunder heard.*)

HICKOK: Buntline write that speech?

BUFFALO BILL: I think she changed it a little.

(UNCAS *rises from the dead.*)

UNCAS (*German accent*): I am Uncas, Chief of the Pawnee Indians, recently killed for my lustful ways. Yet, before the white men came and did me in, I had this vision: the white man is great, the red man nothing. So, if a white man kills a red man, we must forgive him, for God intended man to be as great as possible, and by eliminating the inferior, the great man carries on God's work. Thus, the Indian is in no way wronged by being murdered. Indeed, quite the opposite: being murdered is his purpose in life. This was my recent vision. Which has brought light to the darkness of my otherwise useless soul. . . . And now, I die again.

(*He collapses.*)

HICKOK: Buntline write that?

BUFFALO BILL: Think Hookman changed it also. They all do it. It's our style. I dunno, people seem to like it.

HICKOK: Yeah? Well then, guess it mus' be my turn!

(*He pulls out his bowie knife.*)

BUFFALO BILL: HEY!

HICKOK: Make one false move an' I'll rip you 'part, friend or no.

BUNTLINE: Bill, look——

HICKOK: As for you, Buntline, you fangless lizard, you harmless bull, you ball of——

BUNTLINE: BRING DOWN THE CURTAIN!

HICKOK: First one touches that curtain, I cuts int' mincemeat an' eats fer dinner, *raw!*

FIRST LADY: I'm trembling all over.

HICKOK: Okay, Buntline. Now we're gonna settle up the score.

BUNTLINE: Score?

HICKOK: Men jus' don' humiliate Wil' Bill Hickok.

BUNTLINE: *Hu—humiliate?*

HICKOK: Or leastways don' do it twice, bein' dead shortly after the first occasion.

BUNTLINE: Wh—what . . . 're you talkin' about?

HICKOK: 'Bout havin' to impersonate myself. 'Bout the humiliation o' havin' to impersonate my *own personal self!*

BUNTLINE: Oh.

FIRST LADY: *Fantastic!*

BUNTLINE: Well, I dunno what t' say.

HICKOK: It weren't in the deal!

BUNTLINE: Deal?

HICKOK: You said if I came here, I could play Bat Masterson!

BUNTLINE: Ah, *that!*

(*He chuckles.*)

Well, . . . if you recall, I said *maybe* you could play Bat Masterson. First, we had t' see how good you did as Hickok.

HICKOK: As *Hickok?* Chrissake, I AM Hickok!

BUNTLINE: Right.

HICKOK: Well, why in hell should I play *him* then?

BUNTLINE: Well, there's audience appeal.

FIRST LADY: There sure is!

BUNTLINE: BILL! Now—now, wait-a-second! Let's talk this over. Like gentlemen.

BUFFALO BILL: Yeah. Right. Let's . . . not get too . . . carried away. After all——

HICKOK: If you don' stay out o' this, I'm gonna slit yer stuffin' gizzard an' extract, inch by inch, what's guts in most folks, but in you is thorou' garbage.

BUFFALO BILL: Now wait-a-minute! Hold on! You—you think I'm jus' gonna stand here an'——

HICKOK: Oh, shut up! Dumb, dudelickin' FRAUD!

BUFFALO BILL: *What?*

HICKOK: If I gotta play Hickok, I'm gonna play Hickok the way Hickok shoul' *played!*

BUNTLINE: *Put that knife a⸺* . . . For godsakes. Cody, *HELP ⸺*

(BUNTLINE *falls, a knife in his back. He crawls off the front of the stage; collapses.*)

FIRST LADY: He looks kind o' dead.

(BUFFALO BILL *heads for the body, stunned.*)

HICKOK: Sorry, Will. Guess I just ain't used to show business yet.

(*He chuckles and turns his attention to* TESKANJAVILA. BUFFALO BILL *is feeling for* BUNTLINE's *pulse.*)

TESKANJAVILA: O, *Sancta Maria*, I don't like this gleam in his eye.

HICKOK (*striking a pose*):
Hail, sweet cookie, tart of tempting flavors,
Why've I been denied your spicy favors?

TESKANJAVILA: AH! *What're you doing?* HELP!

(HICKOK *unties her from the pole, at the same time unhooking his gun belt. He works rapidly.*
BUFFALO BILL *lets* BUNTLINE's *limp arm drop. He stares back at the stage stunned.*)

FIRST LADY: Ooooh, look what he's doing now!

(*The First Family climb on the stage, the Negro* USHERS *bringing their chairs for them so they can have a more comfortable view.*)

Really, we must invite this theatre crowd more often.

(HICKOK *is now standing above* TESKANJAVILA, *who lies helpless at his feet.* BUFFALO BILL *watches from off stage, outside the ring. Also helpless.*)

HICKOK: Hickok, fastest shooter in the West, 'cept for Billy the Kid, who ain't as accurate, Hickok, deadliest shooter in the West, 'cept for Doc Holliday, who wields a sawed-off shotgun, which ain't fair; Hickok, shootinest shooter in the West, 'cept for Jesse James, who's absolutely indiscriminate; this Hickok, strong as an eagle, tall as a mountain, swift as the wind, fierce as a rattlesnake—a legend in his own time, or any other—this Hickok stands now above an Indian maiden——

TESKANJAVILA: I'm not an Indian and I'm not a maiden!

HICKOK: Who's not an Indian and not a maiden, but looks pretty good anyhow—an' asks those o' you watchin' t' note carefully the basic goodness of his very generous intentions, since otherwise . . .

(*He starts to finger her clothing.*)

. . . they might be mistaken for . . .

(*He rips open her buckskin dress.*)

. . . LUST!

(*She is left in a frilly Merry Widow corset.*)

TESKANJAVILA: Eh, bambino. If you don' mind, I'd like a little privacy.

(*To the First Family.*)

After all, I've not rehearsed this.

(HICKOK *pulls the cord, lowering the curtain.*)

OL' TIME PRESIDENT: Good show, Cody! *Good show!*

(BUFFALO BILL, *in a daze, walks to the stage and opens the curtain.*
"Scouts of the Plains" *drop seen. He stares at it. Pulls it down.*
NO ONE THERE.
Mozart minuet heard.
He looks around in total confusion.
The stage and all the White House furniture begin to disappear.
Lights fade to black, BUFFALO BILL *spinning dizzily in the middle.*
Music fades.)

SCENE 8

(*Lights up again on the Senate Committee.*)

SENATOR LOGAN: Mister Grass. Let's leave aside the question of the steamboat. You mentioned the treaty at Fort Lyon and said that parts of that treaty had never been fulfilled. Well, I happen to be quite familiar with that particular treaty and happen to know that it is the Indians who did not fulfill its terms, not us.

JOHN GRASS: We did not *want* the cows you sent!

SENATOR LOGAN: You signed the treaty.

JOHN GRASS: We did not understand that we were to give up part of our reservation in exchange for these cows.

SENATOR DAWES: Why'd you think we were giving you twenty-five thousand cows?

JOHN GRASS: We were hungry. We thought it was for food.

SENATOR LOGAN: It wasn't explained that *only* if you gave us part of your reservation would you receive these cows?

JOHN GRASS: Yes. That was explained.

SENATOR LOGAN: And yet, you thought it was a gift.

JOHN GRASS: Yes.

SENATOR LOGAN: In other words, you thought you could have both the cows and the land?

JOHN GRASS: Yes.

SENATOR DAWES: Even though it was explained that you couldn't.

JOHN GRASS: Yes.

SENATOR MORGAN: This is quite hard to follow.

SENATOR LOGAN: Mister Grass, tell me, which would you prefer, cows or land?

JOHN GRASS: We prefer them both.

SENATOR LOGAN: Well, what if you can't have them both?

JOHN GRASS: We prefer the land.

SENATOR LOGAN: Well then, if you knew you had to give up some land to get these cows, why did you sign the treaty?

JOHN GRASS: The white men made our heads dizzy, and the signing was an accident.

SENATOR LOGAN: An accident?

JOHN GRASS: They talked in a threatening way, and whenever we asked questions, shouted and said we were stupid. Suddenly, the Indians around me rushed up and signed the paper. They were like men stumbling in the dark. I could not catch them.

SENATOR LOGAN: But you signed it, too.

(Long pause.)

SENATOR DAWES: Mister Grass. Tell me. Do the Indians really expect to keep all this land and yet do nothing toward supporting themselves?

JOHN GRASS: We do not have to support ourselves. The Great Father promised to give us everything we ever needed; for that, we gave him the Black Hills.

SENATOR LOGAN: Mister Grass. Which do you prefer—to be self-sufficient or to be given things?

JOHN GRASS: We prefer them both.

SENATOR DAWES: Well, you can't *have* them both!

BUFFALO BILL: *Please!*

JOHN GRASS: I only know what we were promised.

SENATOR DAWES: That's *not* what you were promised!

JOHN GRASS: We believe it is.

BUFFALO BILL: *What's going on here?*

SENATOR MORGAN: Mister Grass. Wouldn't you and your people like to live like the white man?

JOHN GRASS: We are happy like the Indian!

SENATOR LOGAN: He means, you wouldn't like to see your people made *greater*, let's say?

JOHN GRASS: That is not possible! The Cheyenne and the Sioux are as great as people can be, already.

SENATOR MORGAN: Extraordinary, really.

BUFFALO BILL: Mister Grass. Surely . . . *surely* . . . your people would like to *improve their condition!*

JOHN GRASS: We would like what is owed us! If the white men want to give us more, that is fine also.

SENATOR LOGAN: Well, we'll see what we can do.

SENATOR MORGAN: Let's call the next. This is getting us nowhere.

JOHN GRASS: We would especially like the money the Great Father says he is holding for us!

SENATOR DAWES: I'm afraid that may be difficult, since, in the past, we've found that when an Indian's been given money, he's spent it all on liquor.

JOHN GRASS: When he's been given money, it's been so little there's been little else he could buy.

SENATOR MORGAN: Whatever, the Great Father does not like his Indian children getting drunk!

JOHN GRASS: Then tell the Great Father, who says he wishes us to live like white men, that when an Indian gets drunk, he is merely imitating the white men he's observed!

(Laughter from the INDIANS. LOGAN *raps his gavel.)*

SENATOR DAWES: STOP IT!

(No effect. LOGAN *raps more.)*

What in God's name do they think we're doing here? STOP IT!

(Over the INDIAN's *noise, the noise of a Wild West Show is heard; lights fade to black.)*

SCENE 9

(Wild West Show music and crisscrossing multicolored spotlights. The rodeo ring rises from the stage, its lights glittering. Wild West Show banners descend above the ring.)

VOICE: And now, ladies and gentlemen, let's hear it for Buffalo Bill's fantastic company of

authentic western heroes ... the fabulous
ROUGHRIDERS OF THE WORLD!

(*Enter, on heroically artificial horses, the*
ROUGHRIDERS—*themselves heroically over-sized.*

*They gallop about the ring in majestic, intricate
formation, whoopin' and shootin' as they do.*)

With the ever-lovely ... ANNIE OAKLEY!

(ANNIE OAKLEY *performs some startling trick shots
as the others ride in circles about her.*)

And now, once again, here he is—the star of
our show, the Ol' Scout himself; I mean the
indestructible and ever-popular——

(*Drum roll.*)

——BUFFALO BILL!

(*Enter, on horseback,* BUFFALO BILL. *He is in his
Wild West Finery.*

He tours the ring in triumph while his
ROUGHRIDERS *ride after him, finally exiting to leave
him in the center, alone.*)

BUFFALO BILL: THANK YOU, THANK
YOU! A *GREAT* show lined up tonight! With
all-time favorite Johnny Baker, Texas Jack and
his twelve-string guitar, the Dancin' Cava-
naughs, Sheriff Brad and the Deadwood Mail
Coach, Harry Philamee's Trained Prairie Dogs,
the Abilene County Girls' School Trick Roping
and Lasso Society, Pecos Pete and the ——
VOICE: *Bill.*
BUFFALO BILL (*startled*): Hm?
VOICE: Bring on the Indians.
BUFFALO BILL: What?
VOICE: The *Indians.*
BUFFALO BILL: Ah.

(BUFFALO BILL *looks uneasily toward the wings as
his company of* INDIANS *enters solemnly and in
ceremonial warpaint; they carry the Sun Dance pole.
At its summit is a buffalo skull.*)

And now, while my fabulous company of
authentic ... American Indians go through the
ceremonial preparations of the Sun Dance, which
they will re-create in all its death-defying
goriness—let's give a warm welcome back to a
courageous warrior, the magnificent Chief
Joseph——

(*Some* COWBOY ROUSTABOUTS *set up an inverted
tub; music for* CHIEF JOSEPH'S *entrance.*)

——who will recite his ... celebrated speech.
CHIEF JOSEPH!

(*Enter* CHIEF JOSEPH, *old and hardly able to
walk.*)

CHIEF JOSEPH: In the moon of the cherries
blossoming, in the year of our surrender, I, Chief
Joseph, and what remained of my people, the
Nez Perces, were sent to a prison in Oklahoma,
though General Howard had promised we could
return to Idaho, where we'd always lived. In the
moon of the leaves falling, still in the year of our
surrender, William Cody came to see me. He
was a nice man. With eyes that seemed ...
frightened; I ... don't know why. He told me I
was courageous and said he admired me. Then he
explained all about his Wild West Show, in
which the great Sitting Bull appeared, and said
if I agreed to join, he would have me released
from prison, and see that my people received
food. I asked what I could do, as I was not a very
good rider or marksman. And he looked away
and said, "Just repeat, twice a day, three times
on Sundays, what you said that afternoon when
our army caught you at the Canadian border,
where you'd been heading, and where you and
your people would have all been safe." So I
agreed. For the benefit of my people ... And for
the next year, twice a day, three times on
Sundays, said this to those sitting around me in
the dark, where I could not see them, a light
shining so brightly in my eyes!

(*Pause.*
He climbs up on the tub.
*Accompanied by exaggerated and inappropriate
gestures.*)

"Tell General Howard I know his heart. I am
tired of fighting. Our chiefs have been killed.
Looking Glass is dead. The old men are all dead.
It is cold and we have no blankets. The children
are freezing. My people, some of them, have fled
to the hills and have no food or warm clothing.
No one knows where they are—perhaps frozen. I
want to have time to look for my children and
see how many of them I can find. Maybe I shall
find them among the dead. Hear me, my chiefs.
I am tired. My heart is sick and sad. From where
the sun now stands, I will fight no more
forever. ..."

(*He climbs down from the tub.*)

After which, the audience always applauded
me.

(*Exit* CHIEF JOSEPH. *Pause.*)

BUFFALO BILL: The Sun Dance ... was the one

religious ceremony common to all the tribes of the plains. The Sioux, the Crow, the Blackfeet, the Kiowa, the Blood, the Cree, the Chippewa, the Arapaho, the Pawnee, the Cheyenne. It was *their* way of proving they were . . . real Indians.

(*Pause.*)

The bravest would take the ends of long leather thongs and hook them through their chest muscles, then, pull till they'd ripped them out. The greater the pain they could endure, the greater they felt the Spirits would favor them. Give them what they needed. . . . Grant them . . . salvation.

(*Pause.*)

Since the Government has officially outlawed this ritual, we will merely imitate it.

(*Pause.*)

And no one . . . will be hurt.

(*He steps back.*
The dance begins. The INDIANS *take the barbed ends of long leather thongs that dangle from the top of the Sun Dance pole and hook them through plainly visible chest harnesses. Then they pull back against the center and dance about it, flailing their arms and moaning as if in great pain.*
Suddenly JOHN GRASS *enters. A* ROUSTABOUT *tries to stop him.*
The INDIANS *are astonished to see this intruder;* BUFFALO BILL *stunned.*
JOHN GRASS *pulls the* INDIANS *out of their harnesses, rips open his shirt, and sticks the barbs through his chest muscles.*
He chants and dances. The other INDIANS, *realizing what he's doing, blow on reed whistles, urge him on. Finally he collapses, blood pouring from his chest.*
The INDIANS *gather around him in awe.*
BUFFALO BILL *walks slowly toward* JOHN GRASS; *stares down at him.*
The INDIANS *remove the Sun Dance pole and trappings.*
BUFFALO BILL *crouches and cradles* JOHN GRASS *in his arms.*
As lights fade to black.)

SCENE 10

(*Light up on* WHITE HOUSE USHER.)

USHER: The President is exercising in the gym, sir. This way.

(*Enter* BUFFALO BILL.)

BUFFALO BILL: You're sure it's all right?

USHER: Yes, sir. He said to show you right in. Very pleased you're here.

(*The* USHER *gestures for* CODY *to pass. When he does, the* USHER *bows, turns, and leaves.*
BUFFALO BILL *stops.*
Gym noise heard.
Lights up on the OL' TIME PRESIDENT, *dressed like* HICKOK *and astride a mechanical horse pushed by another* USHER. *Near him sits an old Victrola; "On the Old Chisholm Trail" is playing.*
The OL' TIME PRESIDENT *spurs his horse onwards.*
Nearby hangs a punching bag.
BUFFALO BILL *stares at the scene, stupefied; walks cautiously forward.*)

BUFFALO BILL: Uh———

OL' TIME PRESIDENT: *Cody!* My ol' buddy! Welcome back! Long time no see!

BUFFALO BILL: Yes, sir. Long time . . . no see.

OL' TIME PRESIDENT: Wha'd'ya think o' this thing? Latest in athletic equipment. Just got it yesterday.

BUFFALO BILL: It's a . . . nice imitation.

OL' TIME PRESIDENT: More power.

USHER: Pardon?

OL' TIME PRESIDENT: *Little more power.*

(*The* USHER *nods; the mechanical horse bounces faster.*)

Good for the figure, this bronco riding. GIDDYAP! You orn'ry sonofabitch.

(*He laughs; whips his horse furiously.*)

BUFFALO BILL: Sir. What I've come t' talk t' you about is very important.

OL' TIME PRESIDENT: Can't hear ya. Speak up!

BUFFALO BILL (*pointing to the phonograph*): May I turn this down?

OL' TIME PRESIDENT: Tell me. You think I look a little bit like Hickok?

BUFFALO BILL: Mr. President, would you *please stop this?*

OL' TIME PRESIDENT: What?

BUFFALO BILL: *STOP THIS!!!*

OL' TIME PRESIDENT: Whoa, Nellie.

USHER: Pardon?

OL' TIME PRESIDENT: WHOA, NELLIE!

(*The* USHER *stops the horse; shuts off the phonograph.*
Cold tone.)

All right. What is it?

BUFFALO BILL: Well sir, I'm here t' ask if you'd come with me t' Sitting Bull's reservation.

OL' TIME PRESIDENT: *Whose* reservation?

BUFFALO BILL: Sitting Bull's. He was in my Wild West Show for a time. And naturally, I feel a sort o' . . . obligation.

(*Pause.*)

Personal . . . obligation.

OL' TIME PRESIDENT: I see.

BUFFALO BILL: *I* figure you're just about the only one left now who can really help him. His people are in a desperate way.

OL' TIME PRESIDENT: Tell me; this—uh—Sitting Bull. Isn't he the one who wiped out Custer?

BUFFALO BILL: Uh, well, yes, he . . . is, but it was, ya know, nothin—uh—personal.

(*Weak laugh.*)

OL' TIME PRESIDENT: Can't help.

BUFFALO BILL: What?

OL' TIME PRESIDENT: I'm sorry, but I can't help.

BUFFALO BILL: *You don't understand the situation!*

OL' TIME PRESIDENT: I *don't?* All right, let's say I *want* to help. *What do I do for 'em?* Do I give 'em back their land? Do I resurrect the buffalo?

BUFFALO BILL: You can do *other* things!

OL' TIME PRESIDENT: No, Cody. *Other* people can do other things, *I* . . . must do magic. Well, I can't *do* magic for *them;* it's too late.

BUFFALO BILL: I promised Sitting Bull you'd come.

OL' TIME PRESIDENT: Then you're a fool.

BUFFALO BILL: They're going to *die.*

(*Long pause.*)

OL' TIME PRESIDENT: Tell ya what. 'Cause I'm so *grateful* to you. . . . For your Wild West Show. For what it's *done.* For this country's *pride,* its *glory.*

(*Pause.*)

I'll do you a favor; I'll send a committee in my place.

BUFFALO BILL: A committee *won't be able to help!*

OL' TIME PRESIDENT: Oh, I think the gesture will mean something.

BUFFALO BILL: *To WHOM?*

(*Silence.*)

OL' TIME PRESIDENT: Being a great President,

Cody, is like being a great eagle. A great . . . *hunted* eagle. I mean, you've got to know . . . when t' stay put.

(*He smiles.*)

On your way out, Bill, tell the guards, no more visitors today, hm?

(*He nods to the* USHER, *who starts to rock him again.*
As BUFFALO BILL *slowly leaves.*
Music back up.
Lights fade to black.)

SCENE 11

(*Lights up on reservation, as when last seen.*
The INDIANS *are laughing; the* SENATORS, *rapping for silence.*)

SENATOR DAWES: *What in God's name do they think we're doing here?*

BUFFALO BILL (*to* SITTING BULL): Please! You must tell them to stop this *noise!*

SITTING BULL: You told us you would bring the Great Father.

BUFFALO BILL: I told you! He couldn't come! It's not my fault! Besides, these men are the Great Father's representatives! Talking to them is like talking to him!

SITTING BULL: If the Great Father wants us to believe he is wise, why does he send us men who are *stupid?*

BUFFALO BILL: They're *not* stupid! They just don't see things the way *you* do!

SITTING BULL: Yes. Because they are stupid.

BUFFALO BILL: They're *not stupid!*

SITTING BULL: Then they must be blind. It is the only other explanation.

BUFFALO BILL: All right. Tell me. Do *you* understand them?

SITTING BULL: Why should I want to understand men who are stupid?

BUFFALO BILL: Because if you *don't,* your people will *starve to death.*

(*Long pause.*)

All right. . . . Now. Let me try to explain some . . . *basics.*

(*To the* SENATORS.)

Well, as you've just seen, the Indian can be hard t' figure. What's one thing t' us is another t' him. For example, farmin'. Now the *real* problem here is not poor soil. The real problem's plowin'. Ya see, the Indian believes the earth is sacred and sees plowin' as a sacrilegious act. Well, if ya can't get 'em t' plow, how can ya teach 'em farmin'? Impossible. Fertile land's another problem. There just ain't much of it, an' what there is, the Indians prefer to use for pony racin'. Naturally, it's been explained to 'em how people can race ponies anywhere, but they *prefer* the fertile land. They say, if their ancestors raced ponies there, that's where *they* must race. . . . Another difficult problem is land itself. The majority of 'em, ya see, don't understand how land can be owned, since they believe the land was made by the Great Spirits for the benefit of everyone. So, when we do buy land from 'em, they think it's just some kind o' temporary loan, an' figure we're kind o' foolish fer payin' good money for it, much as someone 'ud seem downright foolish t' us who paid money fer the sky, say, or the ocean. Which . . . causes problems.

(*Pause.*)

Well, what I'm gettin' at is *this:* if *their* way o' seein' is hard fer *us* t' follow, ours is just as hard fer *them*. . . . There's an old Indian legend that when the first white man arrived, he asked some Indians for enough land t' put his blanket down onto fer the night. So they said yes. An' next thing they knew, he'd unraveled this blanket till it was one long piece o' thread. Then he laid out the thread, an' when he was done, he'd roped off a couple o' square miles. Well, the Indian finds that sort o' behavior hard t' understand. That's all I have t' say. Maybe, if you think about it, some good'll finally come from all this. I dunno.

SENATOR MORGAN: Thank you. We *shall* think about it. And hope the Indians think about it, too. And cause no more disturbances like the one just now. . . . Ask Sitting Bull if he has anything to say.

BUFFALO BILL: Sitting Bull.

SITTING BULL: Of course I will speak if they desire me to. I suppose it is only such men as they desire who may say anything.

SENATOR MORGAN: Anyone here may speak. If you have something to say, we will listen. Otherwise, sit down.

SITTING BULL: Tell me, do you know who I am, that you talk as you do?

BUFFALO BILL: SITTING BULL, PLEASE!

(*Long pause.*)

SITTING BULL: I wish to say that I fear I spoke hastily just now. In calling you . . . stupid. For my friend William Cody tells me you are here with good intentions. So I ask forgiveness for my unthinking words, which might have caused you to wreak vengeance on my people for what was not their doing, but *mine, alone*.

SENATOR LOGAN: We are pleased you speak so . . . sensibly. You are . . . forgiven.

SITTING BULL: I shall tell you, then, what I want you to say to the Great Father for me. And I shall tell you everything that is in my heart. For I know the Great Spirits are looking down on me today and want me to tell you everything that is in my heart. For you are the only people now who can help us.

(*Pause.*)

My children . . . are dying. They have no warm clothes, and their food is gone. The old way is gone. No longer can they follow the buffalo and live where they wish. I have prayed to the Great Spirits to send us back the buffalo, but I have not yet seen any buffalo returning. So I know the old way is gone. I think . . . my children must learn a *new* way if they are to live. Therefore, tell the Great Father that if he wishes us to live like white men, we will do so.

(*Stunned reaction from his Indians. He silences them with a wave of his hand.*)

For I know that if that pleases him, we will benefit. I am looking always to the benefit of my children, and so, want only to please the Great Father. . . . Therefore, tell him for me that I have never yet seen a white man starving, so he should send us food so we can live like the white man, as he wants. Tell him, also, we'd like some healthy cattle to butcher—I wish to kill three hundred head at a time. For that is the way the white man lives, and we want to please the Great Father and live the same way. Also, ask him to send us each six teams of mules, because that is the way the white men make a living, and I want my children to make as good a living. I ask for these things only because I was advised to follow your ways. I do not ask for anything that is not needed. Therefore, tell him to send to each person here a horse and buggy. And four yokes of oxen and a wagon to haul wood in, since I have never yet seen a white man dragging wood by hand. Also, hogs, male and female, and male and female sheep for my children to raise from. If I leave anything out in the way of animals that the white men have, it is a mistake, for I want every one of them! For we are great Indians, and therefore should be no less great as white men. . . . Furthermore, tell him to send us warm clothing. And glass for the windows. And toilets. And clean water. And beds, and blankets, and pillows. And fur coats, and gloves. And hats. And *pretty silk ties.* As you see, I do not ask for anything that is not needed. For the Great Father has advised us to live like white men, so clearly, this is how we should live. For it is your doing that we are here on this reservation, and it is not right for us to live in poverty. And be treated like beasts. . . . That is all I have to say.

SENATOR LOGAN: I want to say something to that man before he sits down, and I want all the Indians to listen very carefully to what I'm going to tell him. . . . Sitting Bull, this committee invited you to come here for a friendly talk. When you talked, however, you insulted them. I understand this is not the first time you have been guilty of such an offense.

SITTING BULL: Do you know who I am that you talk the way you do?

SENATOR LOGAN: I know you are Sitting Bull.

SITTING BULL: Do you really not recognize me? Do you really not know who I am?

SENATOR LOGAN: *I said, I know you are Sitting Bull!*

SITTING BULL: You know I am Sitting Bull. But do you know what *position* I hold?

SENATOR DAWES: We do not recognize any difference between you and other Indians.

SITTING BULL: Then I will tell you the difference. So you will never ever make this mistake again. I am here by the will of the Great Spirits, and by their will I am a chief. My heart is red and sweet, and I know it is sweet, for whatever I pass near tries to touch me with its tongue, as the bear tastes honey and the green leaves lick the sky. If the Great Spirits have chosen anyone to be leader of their country, know that it is not the Great Father; *it is myself.*

SENATOR DAWES: WHO IS THIS CREATURE?

SITTING BULL: I will show you.

(*He raises his hand. The* INDIANS *turn and start to leave.*)

SENATOR LOGAN: Just a minute, Sitting Bull!

(SITTING BULL *stops.*)

Let's get something straight. You said to this committee that you were chief of all the people of this country and that you were appointed chief by the Great Spirits. Well, I want to say that you were *not* appointed by the Great Spirits. Appointments are not made that way. Furthermore, I want to say that you are arrogant and stupidly proud, for you are not a great chief of this country or any other; that you have no following, no power, no control, and no right to any control.

SITTING BULL: I wish to say a word about my not being a chief, having no authority, being proud———

SENATOR LOGAN: You are on an Indian reservation merely at the sufferance of the Government. You are fed by the Government, clothed by the Government; your children are educated by the Government, and all you have and are today is because of the Government. I merely say these things to notify you that you cannot insult the people of the United States of America or its committees. And I want to say to the rest of you that you must learn that you are the equals of other men and must not let this one man lead you astray. You must stand up to him and not permit him to insult people who have come all this way just to help you. . . . That is all I have to say.

SITTING BULL: I wish to say a word about my not being a chief, having no authority, being proud, and considering myself a great man in general.

SENATOR LOGAN: We do not care to talk with you any more today.

SENATOR DAWES: Next Indian.

SITTING BULL: I said, I wish to speak about my having no authority, being not a chief, and———

SENATOR LOGAN: I said, we've heard enough of you today!

(SITTING BULL *raises his hand; the* INDIANS *leave.* SITTING BULL *stares at* CODY.)

SITTING BULL: If a man is the chief of a great people, and has lived only for those people, and has done many great things for them, *of course he should be proud!*

(*He exits.*
Lights fade to black.)

SCENE 12

(*Guitar heard:* "Chisholm Trail."
Lights up on saloon. Most of it is in shadows.
Only a poker table is well lit.
A bar is in the distance.

Swinging doors.
Various COWBOYS *slouch about.*)

JESSE JAMES (*sings*):
Walkin' down the street in ol' Dodge City,
Wherever I look things look pretty shitty.
  Coma ti yi youpy, youpy yea, youpy yea,
  Coma ti yi youpy, youpy yea.
An' the very worst thing that I can see,
Is a dead man walkin' straight toward me.
  Coma ti yi youpy, youpy yea, youpy yea,
  Coma ti yi youpy, youpy yea.
This dead man clearly ain't feelin' well,
If you ask me I think he's just found hell.
  Coma ti yi youpy, youpy yea, youpy yea,
  Coma ti yi youpy you——

(*Enter* BUFFALO BILL *in an overcoat flecked with snow. Gloves. A warm scarf.*)

BUFFALO BILL: Where's Hickok? I'm told Hickok's here. . . . *Where's Hickok?*
BILLY THE KID: Hey, uh . . . stranger.

(*He chuckles.*
Before he can draw, BUFFALO BILL *gets the drop on him.*)

BUFFALO BILL: Who're you?
PONCHO: He . . . is the original . . . Billy the Kid.

(JESSE JAMES *makes a move and* BUFFALO BILL *draws his other gun; gets the drop on him as well.*)

And *he* is the original Jesse James. The original Doc Holliday is, I'm afraid, out to lunch.

(*The* COWBOYS *move to encircle* BUFFALO BILL.)

Who're *you?*
BUFFALO BILL: Buffalo Bill.
PONCHO: Really?

(PONCHO *laughs. Enter* HICKOK.)

HICKOK: Cody! My ol' buddy!

(*They embrace.*)

Oh, great balls o' fire! What a surprise! Why jus' this mornin' I was . . . was . . . (*Pause.*) *picturin'* you.
BUFFALO BILL: You were?
HICKOK: So how ya been? C'mon. Tell me.
BUFFALO BILL: Oh, I been . . . fine.
HICKOK: Great!
BUFFALO BILL: An' you?
HICKOK: Never better. *Never better!*

BUFFALO BILL: Mus' say, you've sure got some . . . famous . . . people here.

(*Slight laugh.*)

HICKOK: Well, ya know, it's . . . that kind o' place.

(*He laughs, too; slaps* CODY *on the back. He leads him to a table.*)

So! . . . Whatcha doin' here? Great honor. *Great honor!*
BUFFALO BILL: I hafta . . . *talk* . . . t' you.
HICKOK: Sure thing.

(*He waves the* COWBOYS *away; they sit at the table in privacy.*)

BUFFALO BILL: I've just come from Sitting Bull's reservation.
HICKOK: Oh?

(*Slight laugh.*)

That reservation's a far piece from here.
BUFFALO BILL: I need your help! Sitting Bull is . . .

(*Pause.*)

HICKOK: What?

(*Long silence.*)

BUFFALO BILL: I'm scared . . . I dunno what's happenin' anymore . . . Things have gotten . . . *beyond* me.

(*He takes a drink.*)

I see them *everywhere.*

(*Weak smile; almost a laugh.*
Music.
INDIANS *appear in the shadows beyond the saloon.*)

In the grass. The rocks. The branches of dead trees.

(*Pause.*)

Took a drink from a river yesterday an' they were even there, beneath the water, their hands reachin' up, I dunno whether beggin', or t' . . . drag me under.

(*Pause.*)

I wiped out their food, ya see. . . . Didn't *mean* to, o' course.

(*He laughs to himself.*)

I mean IT WASN'T MY FAULT! The railroad men needed food. They *hired* me t' *find* 'em food! Well. How was *I* t' know the goddam buffalo reproduced so slowly? *How was I to know that?* NO ONE KNEW THAT!

(*Pause.*
The INDIANS *slowly disappear.*)

Now, Sitting Bull is . . .

(*Long pause.*)

HICKOK: *What?*
BUFFALO BILL: The . . . hearing was a shambles. I brought these Senators, you see. To Sitting Bull's reservation. It . . . was a shambles. (*Pause.*) So we left. He . . . *insulted* them. (*Pause.*) Then I saw the letter.

(*Silence.*)

HICKOK: What letter?
BUFFALO BILL: The letter to McLaughlin. The letter ordering . . . it to be . . . done.

(*Pause.*)

So I rode back. Rode all night. Figuring, maybe . . . if I can just *warn* him. . . . But the reservation soldiers stopped me and . . . made me . . . drink with them. And by the time I got there, he . . . was dead. The greatest Indian who'd ever lived. Shot. By order of the Government. Shot with a Gatling gun.

(*Pause.*)

While the . . . wonderful, gray horse I'd given him for . . . appearing in my show danced his repertory of tricks in the background. Since a gunshot was his cue to perform.

(*He laughs.*
Stops.
Long silence.)

HICKOK: Well now. In exactly what way did you imagine *I* could . . . *help* this . . . situation?
BUFFALO BILL: You have what I *need* . . . now.
HICKOK (*smiling slightly*): Oh?
BUFFALO BILL: I'm *scared*, you see.

(*Pause.*)

Scared . . . not . . . so much of *dyin'*, but . . . dyin' *wrong*.

(*Slight laugh.*)

Dyin' . . . in the center of my arena with . . . makeup on.

(*Long pause.*)

Then I thought of you. . . . . Remembered that night in the White House. Remembered thinking, "My God! Look at Hickok. Hickok *knows just who he is!*"

(*Pause.*)

"Hickok has the answer," I said . . . Hickok knows who he *is*.

(*Pause.*)

I must see Hickok again.

(*Long silence.*)

HICKOK: Well I'm glad you came. Yes. Glad . . . to be able to . . . help.

(*Pause.*)

Funny. That night, in the White House, I remember thinking: "My God, it's *Cody* who's got the answer!"
BUFFALO BILL: . . . What?
HICKOK: Poncho!
PONCHO: *Si, señor.*
HICKOK: Bring in our . . . um . . .
PONCHO: Ah! *Si, senor! Ahorita.*

(*Exit* PONCHO.)

HICKOK: Naturally, at first, you may be a bit startled. Put off. Not . . . exactly . . . what you *had in mind.* Yet! I'm sure that once you *think* about it, you'll agree *it's the only way.* Just like Jesse has. Billy. Doc Holliday. The boys.
BUFFALO BILL: *What are you talkin' about?*
HICKOK: Why, takin' what you were and raisin' it to a . . . higher level.

(*He laughs.*)

Naturally, for my services, I get a small fee. Percentage. You get 50 per cent right off the top. Of course, if at any time you aren't happy, you can leave. Take your business elsewhere. That's written in. Keeps us on our toes. Mind you, this . . . *enterprise* . . . is still in its infancy. The *potential*, though . . . is unlimited. For example, think of this. The *great national good* . . . that could come from this: some of you, let's say, would concentrate strictly on theatrics. MEANWHILE! *Others* of you would concentrate on purely humanitarian affairs. Save . . . well, not Sitting Bull, but . . . some Indian down in Florida. Another up in Michigan. Perhaps expand into Canada. Mexico. Central America. SOUTH AMERICA! My God, there must be literally *millions* of people who could benefit by your presence! Your . . . *simultaneous presence!*

PONCHO: Here they are, *señor!*

(*Enter a group of men dressed as* BUFFALO BILL. *Their faces are covered by masks of his face. They wear his florid buckskin clothes—if anything, even more elaborately designed.*)

HICKOK: Naturally, we've still got a few wrinkles to iron out. Color of hair. Color of eyes. That sort of thing. But with *you* here, exercising artistic control, why, we could go on like this *forever!*

(BUFFALO BILL, *stunned by the sight, fires his guns at the duplicate Codys. They fall and immediately rise again.*
    They slowly surround him.
    He screams as he shoots.
    They disappear.
    The saloon fades to black.
    BUFFALO BILL *alone on stage.*)

BUFFALO BILL: AND NOT TO CLOSE! AND *NOW TO CLOSE!*

VOICE: Not *yet.*

(*Pause.*)

They also killed the rest of his tribe.

(*Music.*
    INDIANS *enter mournfully. They carry a large white sheet.*
    Sound of wind.
    BUFFALO BILL *watches, then moves slowly away; exits.*)

SCENE 13

(*The* INDIANS *cover the center area with the huge white sheet, then lie down upon it in piles.*
    Enter COLONEL FORSYTH, *a* LIEUTENANT, *and two* REPORTERS, *their coat collars turned up for the wind.* CODY *is with them; he carries a satchel.*)

FIRST REPORTER: Fine time of year you men picked for this thing.

COLONEL FORSYTH: They're heathens; they don't celebrate Christmas.

FIRST REPORTER: I don't mean the date, I mean the weather.

COLONEL: Uncomfortable?

FIRST REPORTER: Aren't you?

COLONEL: One gets used to it.

SECOND REPORTER: Colonel, I gather we lost twenty-nine men, thirty-three wounded. How many Indians were killed?

COLONEL: We wiped them out.

SECOND REPORTER: Yes, I know. But how many *is* that?

COLONEL: We haven't counted.

LIEUTENANT: The snow has made it difficult. It started falling right after the battle. The bodies were covered almost at once. By night they were frozen.

COLONEL: We more than made up for Custer, though, I can tell you that.

SECOND REPORTER: But Custer was killed fifteen years ago!

COLONEL: So what?

LIEUTENANT: If there are no more questions, we'll take you to———

FIRST REPORTER: I have one! Colonel Forsyth, some people are referring to your victory yesterday as a massacre. How do you feel about that?

COLONEL: One can always find someone who'll call an overwhelming victory a massacre. I suppose they'd prefer it if we'd let more of our own boys get shot!

FIRST REPORTER: Then you don't think the step you took was harsh?

COLONEL: Of course it was harsh. And I don't like it any more than you. But had we shirked our responsibility, skirmishes ·would have gone on for years, costing our country millions, as well as untold lives. Of course innocent people have been killed. In war they always are. And of course our hearts go out to the innocent victims of this. But war is not a game. It's tough. And demands tough decisions. In the long run I believe what happened here at this reservation yesterday will be justified.

FIRST REPORTER: Are you implying that the Indian Wars are finally over?

COLONEL: Yes, I believe they're finally over. This ludicrous buffalo religion of Sitting Bull's people was their last straw.

SECOND REPORTER: And now?

COLONEL: The difficult job of rehabilitating begins. But that's more up General Howard's line.

LIEUTENANT: Why don't we go and talk with him? He's in the temporary barracks.

COLONEL: He can tell you about our future plans.

(*They start to leave.*)

BUFFALO BILL: You said you'd———

LIEUTENANT: Ah, yes, it's that one.

(*He points to a body.*)

BUFFALO BILL: Thank you.

(*He stays. The others leave; he stares at the grave.* SITTING BULL *has entered, unnoticed.* BUFFALO BILL *takes a sprig of pine from the satchel and is about to put it on the grave.*)

SITTING BULL: Wrong grave. I'm over here... As you see, the dead can be buried, but not so easily gotten rid of.

BUFFALO BILL: Why didn't you listen to me? I *warned* you what would happen! Why didn't you *listen?*

(*Long silence.*)

SITTING BULL: We had land. ... You wanted it; you took it. That ... I understand perfectly. What I cannot understand ... is why you did all this, *and at the same time* ... professed your love.

(*Pause.*)

BUFFALO BILL: Well ... well, what ... about *your* mistakes? Hm? For, for example: you were very unrealistic ... about things. For ... example: did you *really* believe the buffalo would return? *Magically* return?

SITTING BULL: It seemed no less likely than Christ's returning, and a great deal more useful. Though when I think of their reception here, I can't see why either would really want to come back.

BUFFALO BILL: Oh, God. Imagine. For awhile, I actually thought my Wild West Show would *help.* I could give you money. Food. Clothing. And also make people *understand* things ... better.

(*He laughs to himself.*)

That was my reasoning. Or, anyway, *part* ...

(*Pause.*)

of my reasoning.

SITTING BULL (*slight smile*): Your show was very popular

(*Pause.*)

BUFFALO BILL: We had ... *fun,* though, you and I.

(*Pause.*)

Didn't we?

SITTING BULL: Oh, yes. And that's the terrible thing. We had all surrendered. We were on reservations. We could not fight, or hunt. We could do nothing. Then you came and allowed us to imitate our glory. ... It was humiliating! For sometimes, we could almost imagine it was *real.*

BUFFALO BILL: Guess it wasn't so authentic, was it?

(*He laughs slightly to himself.*)

SITTING BULL: How could it have been? You'd have killed all your performers in one afternoon.

(*Pause.*)

BUFFALO BILL: You know what worried me most? ... The fear that I might die, in the middle of the arena, with all my ... makeup on. *That* ... is what ... worried me most.

SITTING BULL: What worried *me* most ... was something I'd said the year before. Without thinking.

BUFFALO BILL (*softly*): What?

SITTING BULL: I'd agreed to go onto the reservation. I was standing in front of my tribe, the soldiers leading us into the fort. And as we walked, I turned to my son, who was beside me. "Now," I said, "you will never know what it is to be an Indian, for you will never again have a gun or pony. ..." Only later did I *realize* what I'd said. These things, the gun and the pony—they came with you. And then I thought, ah, how terrible it would be if we finally owe to the white man not only our destruction, but also our glory. ... Farewell, Cody. You were my friend. And, indeed, you still are. ... I never killed you ... because I *knew it would not matter.*

(*He starts to leave.*)

BUFFALO BILL: If only I could have saved *your* life!

(SITTING BULL *stops and stares at him coldly; turns and leaves.*

Long pause.)

BUFFALO BILL: Well! This is it!

(*He forces a weak laugh.*)

Naturally, I've been thinking 'bout this moment for quite some time now. As any performer would.

VOICE: And now to close!

BUFFALO BILL: NOT YET! ... I would ... first ... like to ... say a few words in defense of my country's Indian policy, which seems, in certain circles, to be meeting with considerable disapproval.

(*He smiles weakly, clears his throat, reaches into his pocket, draws out some notes, and puts on a pair of eyeglasses.*)

The—uh—State of Georgia, anxious to solidify its boundaries and acquire certain valuable mineral rights, hitherto held accidentally by the Cherokee Indians, and anxious, furthermore, to end the seemingly inevitable hostilities between its residents and these Indians on the question of land ownership, initiated, last year, the forced removal of the Cherokee nation, resettling them in a lovely and relatively unsettled area west of the Mississippi, known as the Mojave Desert. Given proper irrigation, this spacious place should soon be blooming. Reports that the Cherokees were unhappy at their removal are decidedly untrue. And though many, naturally, died while marching from Georgia to the Mojave Desert, the ones who did, I'm told, were rather ill already, and nothing short of medication could have saved them. Indeed, in all ways, our vast country is speedily being opened for settlement. The shipment of smallpox-infested blankets, sent by the Red Cross to the Mandan Indians, has, I'm pleased to say, worked wonders, and the Mandans are no more. Also, the Government policy of exterminating the buffalo, a policy with which I myself was intimately connected, has practically reached fruition. Almost no buffalo are now left, and soon the Indians will be hungry enough to begin farming in earnest, a step we believe necessary if they are ever to leave their barbaric ways and enter civilization. Indeed, it is for this very reason that we have begun giving rifles to the Indians as part of each treaty with them, for without armaments they could not hope to wage war with us, and the process of civilizing them would be seriously hampered in every way. Another aspect of our benevolent attitude toward these savages is shown by the Government's policy of having its official interpreters translate everything incorrectly when interpreting for the Indians, thereby angering the Indians and forcing them to learn English for themselves. Which, of course, is the first step in civilizing people. I'm reminded here of a story told me by a munitions manufacturer. It seems, by *accident,* he sent a shipment of blank bullets to the Kickapoo Indians, and . . .

(He looks around.)

Well, I won't tell it. It's too involved. I would just like to say that I am sick and tired of these sentimental humanitarians who take no account of the difficulties under which this Government has labored in its efforts to deal fairly with the Indian, nor of the countless lives we have lost and atrocities endured at their savage hands. I quote General Sheridan:——

(The INDIANS *have begun to rise from their graves; for a while they stand in silence behind* BUFFALO BILL, *where they are joined, at intervals, by the rest of the* INDIAN *company.)*

——"I do not know how far these so-called humanitarians should be excused on account of their political ignorance; but surely it is the only excuse that can give a shadow of justification for their aiding and abetting such horrid crimes as the Indians have perpetrated on our people."

BUFFALO BILL: The excuse that the Indian way of life is vastly different from ours, and that what seem like atrocities to us do not to them, does not hold water, I'm afraid! For the truth is, the Indian never had any real title to the soil of this country. We had that title. By *right of discovery!* And all the Indians were, were the *temporary occupants* of the land. They *had* to be vanquished by us! It was, in fact, our *moral obligation!*

For the earth was given to mankind to support the greatest number of which it is capable; and no tribe or people have a *right* to withhold from the wants of others! For example——

——in the case of Lone Wolf versus Hitchcock, 1902, the Supreme Court of the United States ruled that the power exists to abrogate the provisions of *any* Indian treaty if the *interests of the country demand!*

SITTING BULL: *(very softly.):* I am Sitting Bull——

(Almost inaudible.) ——and I am—*dying!*

BLACK HAWK: Black Hawk *is dying.*

TECUMSEH: Tecumseh *is dying.*

CRAZY HORSE: Crazy Horse . . . is dying.

RED CLOUD: Red Cloud *is dying.*

SPOTTED TAIL: *Spotted Tail* . . . is dying again.

SATANTA: Satanta *is dying.*

KIOKUK: Kiokuk *is dying.*

Here's another one: in the case of the Seneca Indians versus the Pennsylvania Power Authority, the courts ruled that the Seneca Treaty was invalid since perpetuity was legally a vague phrase. *Vague phrase!* Yes. Ah. Here's one, even better. In the——

GERONIMO: Geronimo . . . *is dying!*

OLD TAZA: Old Taza *is dying!*

JOHN GRASS: *John Grass is dying.*

(*Long pause.*)

No. Wait. Got it. The one I've been looking for. In the case of Sitting Bull versus Buffalo Bill, the Supreme Court ruled that the *inadvertent* slaughter of . . . buffalo by . . . I'm sorry, I'm . . . reminded here of an amusing story told me by General Custer. You remember him——one o' the great dumbass . . .

(*The* INDIANS *begin a soft and mournful moaning.*)

(*Pause.*)

BUFFALO BILL: Think I'd better close. I . . . just want to say that anyone who thinks we have done something wrong is *wrong!* And that I have here, in this bag, some——

(*He goes and picks up his satchel; he looks up and sees the* INDIANS *staring at him; he turns quickly away.*)

——Indian trinkets. Some . . . examples of their excellent workmanship. Moccasins. Beads. Feathered headdresses for your children.

(*He has begun to unpack these trinkets and place them, for display, on a small camp stool he has set across the front edge of the center ring.*)

Pretty picture postcards. Tiny Navaho dolls. The money from the sale of these few trifling trinkets will go to help them help themselves. Encourage them a bit. You know, *raise their*

spirits. . . . Ah! Wait. No, sorry, that's a—uh —buffalo skin.

(*He shoves it back in the satchel.*)

Yes. Here it is! Look, just look . . . at this handsome replica of an . . . Indian. Made of genuine wood.

(*He puts the carved head of an Indian on the camp stool so that it overlooks all the other trinkets.*
The lights now slowly begin to fade on him; he sits by the trinkets, trembling.)

CHIEF JOSEPH: Tell General Howard I know his heart. I am tired of fighting. Our chiefs have been killed. Looking Glass is dead. The old men are all dead. It is cold and we have no blankets. The children are freezing. My people, some of them, have fled to the hills and have no food or warm clothing. No one knows where they are—perhaps frozen. I want to have time to look for my children and see how many of them I can find. Maybe I shall find them among the dead.

(*Almost all the lights are now gone;* CHIEF JOSEPH *can hardly be seen;* BUFFALO BILL *is but a shadow. Only the trinkets are clear in a pinspot of light, and that light, too, is fading.*)

Hear me, my chiefs, I am tired. My heart is sick and sad! From where the sun now stands, I will fight no more, forever.

(*And then, very slowly, even the light on the trinkets fades. And the stage is completely dark.*
Then, suddenly, all lights blazing!
Rodeo ring up.
Rodeo music.
Enter, on horseback, the ROUGHRIDERS OF THE WORLD. *They tour the ring triumphantly, then form a line to greet* BUFFALO BILL, *who enters on his white stallion. He tours the ring, a glassy smile on his face.*
The ROUGHRIDERS *exit.*
BUFFALO BILL *alone, on his horse. He waves his big Stetson to the unseen crowd.*
Then, INDIANS *appear from the shadows outside the ring; they approach him slowly.*
Lights fade to black.
Pause.
Lights return to the way they were at the top of the show, when the audience was entering.
The three glass cases are back in place.
No curtain.)

Charles Gordone: *No Place To Be Somebody* (1969)

Born in 1925 in Cleveland, Ohio, Charles Gordone has been an actor and director for many years. *No Place To Be Somebody* was his first produced play, staged by the Joseph Papp New York Shakespeare Theater after Gordone spent three years trying to get a production. Unlike many American playwrights who had far less trouble getting their early work produced, Gordone was rewarded with the Pulitzer Prize for Drama for 1970. He is the first black playwright to win that honor. Considering the play's humble beginnings—in a 190-seat experimental "other stage,"—Gordone's success was especially remarkable.

The play was produced at a time of considerable racial tension in America. Watts, Newark, Chicago, Harlem and many, many smaller communities throughout the nation had erupted with mass destruction. Burnings, lootings, murder, violence of all sorts were followed by invasions of the National Guard in armored cars to restore order. In a sense, the disturbances in black communities were so extensive that many commentators felt it was more reasonable to describe them as the stagings of a revolution. The ongoing Vietnam War, in which a high proportion of blacks fought and died, added to the general racial pressures in the nation.

No Place To Be Somebody is about trying to be a man. Johnny, the protagonist, has long waited for his surrogate father to come out of prison and lead them both to taking "a piece of the action" away from the white mob, represented in this play by Mafucci. The hatred that has virtually eaten him up is directed at the white establishment; Johnny can relate to individual whites when he needs to, but his general antagonism is so powerful that even when he is given an opportunity to live independently he will not use it. Sweets Crane lectures him on the illness that consumes him, tells him that instead of imitating the worst qualities of "Mr. Charlie," he should be developing the best qualities of himself. As long as Johnny has "Charlie fever," he's going to be basically self-destructive.

Gabe represents another part of Johnny's character, a part that has somehow thrown off "Charlie fever" and sees people more for their individual qualities. Gabe is a more balanced Johnny and, as such, he contrasts with Machine Dog—who really *is* in Johnny's imagination—and who continues to express a position filled with hatred. Critics of the play generally found it striking, powerful, and significant. They did not feel the device of Machine Dog worked well, and some subsequent productions omitted it without a loss in the power of the drama.

One of the play's strengths is its study of the varieties of white/black characterizations and relationships. However, some of these tend toward the stereotypical. For instance, the weakest characterizations are probably those of Mary Lou Bolton and her father, Judge Bolton, which come dangerously close to being one-dimensional cut-outs of the evil WASP lawyer and the naive WASP civil rights worker. As the would-be black, Shanty, is another character who barely misses being stereotyped, although he is on stage longer and is clarified by Cora's need for him and by his own ambitions to be a drummer; however, he does appear as a more believable person than the Boltons. Another flaw in the play concerns the relationship between Johnny and Mike Mafucci, who were once "like brothers." This, too, is a cliché, and an undeveloped one at that. We are never permitted to feel the meaning of their closeness, since the play only expresses the differences in their loyal ties and needs. Yet, as performed, the play was able to work completely despite such defects.

The critics were generally enthusiastic about *No Place To Be Somebody,* and compared Gordone favorably with Edward Albee. One critic described Gordone as something of a conservative among black playwrights, partly because he dealt with material that is quite interracial. Audiences agreed that the play was speaking equally to whites and blacks and that it was a huge popular success.

Following up a Pulitzer Prize drama is never easy, and many playwrights have suffered setbacks after an initial victory on the stage. Gordone, who lives in New York City, has been working with budding playwrights in a Bordentown, New Jersey, reformatory, and elsewhere. He wrote three plays that were produced for the 1970–71 season, *Little More Light Around the Place, Baba Chops,* and *A Stage Western,* as well as *Gordone Is a Mutha.* They did not enjoy the success of *No Place To Be Somebody.*

Selected Readings

Walcott, Ronald. "Ellison, Gordone, and Tolson: Some Notes on the Blues, Style and Space." *Black World*, Dec. 1972, pp. 4–29.

No Place To Be Somebody

Charles Gordone

CHARACTERS

GABE GABRIEL, *a young fairskinned Negro*
SHANTY MULLIGAN, *a young white man*
JOHNNY WILLIAMS, *a young Negro*
DEE JACOBSON, *a young white woman*
EVIE AMES, *a young Negro woman*
CORA BEASELY, *a young Negro woman*
MELVIN SMELTZ, *a young Negro man*
MARY LOU BOLTON, *a white girl*
ELLEN, *a white girl*
SWEETS CRANE, *an elderly Negro*

MIKE MAFFUCCI, *a young white man*
TRUCK DRIVER, *a young white man*
JUDGE BOLTON, *a middle aged white man, father of Mary Lou*
MACHINE DOG, *a young Negro (in Johnny's imagination)*
SERGEANT CAPPALETTI, *a young white man*
HARRY, *a Negro detective*
LOUIE, *a young white man*

ACT I

SCENE 1

(Time: The past fifteen years
Place: New York City
Setting: Johnny's Bar
At rise: GABE sits near jukebox, typing. Rips page from typewriter. Balls it up, flings it angrily at audience.)

GABE: Excuse me. Forgot you were out there. My name is Gabe. Gabe Gabriel, to be exact. I'm a writer. Didn't mean to lose my temper. Something I've been working on all my life. Not losing my temper. *(Takes out marihuana cigarette. Lights it. Inhales it. Holds smoke in.)* Right now I'm working on a play. They say if you wanna be a writer you gotta go out an' live. I don't believe that no more. Take my play for instance. Might not believe it but I'm gonna make it all up in my head as I go along. Before I prove it to you, wanna warn you not to be thinkin' I'm tellin' you a bunch'a barefaced lies. An' no matter how far out I git, don't want you goin' out'a here with the idea what you see happenin' is all a figment of my grassy imagination. 'Cause it ain't! *(He picks up Bible from table. Raises it above his head. Without looking turns pages.)* "And I heard a Voice between the banks of the U'Lai. And it called, Gabriel! Gabriel! Make this man understand the vision! So He came near where I stood! And when He came, I was frightened and fell upon my face!"

(He closes Bible. As he exits, lights dim out, then come up on SHANTY, *at jukebox. Jazz is playing.* SHANTY *takes out his drumsticks. Begins to rap on bar.* JOHNNY *enters. Hangs up raincoat and umbrella.)*

JOHNNY: Cool it, Shanty.

SHANTY: Man, I'm practicing.

JOHNNY: Damned if that bar's anyplace for it. Git on that floor there.

SHANTY *(puts drumsticks away. Takes broom)*: Ever tell you 'bout the time I went to this jam session? Max Roach was there. Lemme sit in for him.

JOHNNY: Said you played jus' like a spade.

SHANTY: What's wrong with that? Ol' Red Taylor said wasn't nobody could hold a beat an' steady cook it like me. Said I had "the thing"! Member one time we played "Saints." For three hours, we played it.

JOHNNY: Had to git a bucket'a col' water an' throw it on you to git you to quit, huh?

SHANTY: One these days I'm gonna have me a boss set'a skins for my comeback. Me an' Cora was diggin' a set up on "Four-Six Street." Sump'm else ag'in. Bass drum, dis'pearin' spurs, snares, tom-toms . . .

JOHNNY: Gon' steal 'em?

SHANTY: I been savin' up. Gonna git me them drums. Know what I'm gonna do then? I'm gonna quit you flat. Go for that. Sheee! I ain't no lifetime apron. That's for damned sure.

JOHNNY: Yeah, well meantime how 'bout finishin' up on that floor? Time to open the store.

(DEE and EVIE enter. Hang coats up.)

You broads let them two ripe apples git away from you, huh?

DEE: Don't look at me.

EVIE: Aw, later for you an' your rich Texas trade.

DEE: Just gettin' too damned sensitive.

EVIE: Sensitive my black behin'! Excuse me, I mean black ass. *(Goes to jukebox. Punches up number.)*

DEE: Last night we bring those two johns up to her pad. An' like, Jack? One with the cowboy hat? Stoned? Like out of his skull. And like out of nowhere he starts cryin'.

EVIE: All weekend it was "Nigger this an' Nigger that."

DEE: Never bothered you before. I didn't like it when he started sayin' things like "The black sons a'bitches are gettin' to be untouchables! Takin' over the country!"

EVIE: Bet he'll think twice before he says sump'm like that ag'in.

DEE: That lamp I gave her? One the senator brought me back from Russia? Evie goes an' breaks it over his head.

JOHNNY: What the hell'd you do that for?

EVIE: Sure hated to lose that lamp.

JOHNNY: Wouldn't care if they b'longed to the Ku Klux Klan long's they gimme the bread. *(He goes into* DEE's *purse.)*

SHANTY: Sure had plenty of it too! When they was in here, they kept buyin' me drinks. Thought I was the boss.

JOHNNY: Crackers cain't 'magine Niggers runnin' nothin' but elevators an' toilets.

DEE: Leave me somethin', please.

EVIE: Ain't gon' do nothin' with it nohow.

JOHNNY *(finds pair of baby shoes in* DEE's *purse)*: Thought I tole you to git rid'a these?

DEE: I forgot.

JOHNNY: Save you the trouble. *(He starts to throw them away.)*

DEE: Don't you do that, you black bastard. So help me, Johnny.

EVIE: Aw, let 'er have them things, Nigger! Wha's the big deal?

JOHNNY: 'Tend to your own business, bitch. Ain't a minute off your ass for messin' it up las' night.

EVIE: Excuse me. Didn't know you was starvin' to death.

JOHNNY *(goes for* EVIE *but quickly checks himself when she reaches for her purse. He turns back to* DEE)*: Look'a here, girl. I ain't gon' have no harness bulls knockin' down yo' door.

DEE: All of a sudden you worried about me.

JOHNNY: Jus' git rid'a that crap. Worrin' over sump'm pass, over an' done with.

(CORA enters. A wet newspaper covers her head.)

CORA: Lawd'a mercy! Now I gotta do this un'form all over ag'in. Bad as I hate to iron.

JOHNNY: Ironin' for them crackers. Cain't see why you cain't iron for yourself.

CORA: This ain't no maid's un'form as any fool kin see. I makes my livin' as a pract'cal nurse. I ain't nobody's maid.

JOHNNY: Somebody tole me they seen you wheelin' a snotty nose, blue-eyed baby th'ough Washin'ton Square the other day.

CORA: They was a Wash'ton Square lie. Onlies' baby I wheel aroun' gon' be my own.

JOHNNY: Hell! By the time you an' Shanty git aroun' to somethin' like that . . . you ain't gon' wheel nothin' roun' but a tray'a black-ass coffee.

(DEE *and* EVIE *laugh.*)

CORA: You cheap husslers don't hit the street, you gon' be sellin' yo' wares in'a home for the cripple an' infirm.

EVIE: Gon' have to bring ass to git ass.

(CORA *comes off her stool. Jerks off shoe.* EVIE *comes up with a switchblade.*)

JOHNNY: Hey! Hey! Git under the bed with that shit! (*He races around bar. Comes between them.*) What the hell's the matter with you, Cora? Cain't you take a little joke?

CORA: Don't know why every time I come in here, I gotta be insulted by you an' these here Harlows.

(EVIE *still has her knife out.*)

EVIE: Bet if that heifer messes with me, I'll carve her up like'a fat piece'a barbecue.

JOHNNY: Naw you won't neither. Not in here, you won't. Put it away! I said put it away.

(EVIE *reluctantly puts knife away.*)

DEE: Let's get out of here, Evie. She's always pickin' her nose about somethin'.

EVIE: She don't scare me none. Jus' smells bad, tha's all.

DEE (*looks at her watch*): Well, I gotta date, and you gotta see your headshrinker, don't you?

JOHNNY: Headshrinker? Damned if Evie ain't gone an' got herself a pimp.

EVIE: He don't come as expensive as some pimps I know.

DEE (*goes for the coats*): Now, don't you two start up again.

(*The two women start for the street doors.*)

JOHNNY: Make money, baby. Make that money.

DEE: That's all you ever think about. Can't you just dig me for my soul?

JOHNNY: Wrong color be talkin' 'bout soul.

DEE: Negroes. Think you gotta corner on soul.

EVIE: Us has suffahd, das why.

(DEE *and* EVIE *exit.*)

CORA: Gimme a martini, Shangy. Gotta bad taste in my mouth.

JOHNNY: Make sure she pays for that drink.

CORA: I works an' I pays. I don't ask a livin' ass for nothin'.

JOHNNY: 'Member when you did.

CORA: I was broke. Couldn't fin' no work. 'Sides I had you to take care of! Like I p'omised yo' mama I would. 'Fore she died. Till you had to go git in trouble with that Eye-tralian boy.

JOHNNY: Maybe I jus' got tired'a all them col'-cuts an' fuck-ups.

CORA: When you got out'a that 'form school, I was ready to take care you ag'in! But that bad Nigger Sweets Crane got holt you an' ruint ya.

JOHNNY: Fixed it so's I didn't have to go to that orphan-house, didn't he? Took me in, treated me like I was his own son, didn't he? Damned sight more'n you or that drunken bitch of a mama'a mine did.

CORA: Jay Cee? Might God strike you dead. Maybe I ain't yo' flesh an' blood. But yo' mama? She couldn't he'p none'a the things she did.

JOHNNY: Do me one favor, bitch. Leave my mama on the outside. 'Nother thing, if you cain't say nothin' boss 'bout Sweets Crane, you don't have to come in here yo' dam-self.

(*He slaps her on the behind and exits to the kitchen.*)

CORA: Well, fan me with a brick! Tha's one Nigro you jus' cain't be civil with. (*She sips her drink as* SHANTY *finishes sweeping floor.*) Eb'm as a chile—give him a piece'a candy, wudn't the kin' he wanted, he'd rare back an' th'ow it at you. An' he'd stan' there lookin' all slang-eyed darin' you to touch him. (*She watches* SHANTY *beat on the bar.*) Never had no papa. 'Less you call that ol' dog Sweets Crane a father. His mama was always sickly an' she did drink. Never would give it out though, who it was did it to her. Carried that to her grave! (*She downs her drink.*) I knowed her ever since I was a li'l gal down South. You know, they was always sump'm funny 'bout her. Swore Jay Cee was born with a veil over his face.

SHANTY: A what?

CORA: A veil over his face. Ev'body knows babies born with veils over they faces is s'pose to see ghostes an' raise forty-one kin's'a hell.

SHANTY: Johnny? Sheee.

CORA: If I'm lyin', I'm flyin'!

SHANTY: Cora, you're superstishus as hell.

CORA: Cain't he'p but be, li'l bit. My peoples all had fogey-isms. Where I come from ev'body had 'em. One kin' or 'nother. (MELVIN *enters, hangs up knapsack and rain jacket, takes cap off.*

Knocks the wet from his pants. His head is almost clean-shaven.) Chile! you sho' don't have to worry 'bout yo' head goin' back home!

MELVIN: My home, sweety, is in Saint Albans. You don't have to inform me as to where yours is. (*He goes into a soft-shoe dance and sings.*) "Where the people beat they feet on the Mississippi mud."

CORA: Now, ain't that jus' like you ig'orint Nigroes. If they cain't think'a nothin' to say, they start slippin' you into the dozens.

JOHNNY (*enters from kitchen*): You late, Mel.

MELVIN: Today was my dance class, remember? Anyway, who can get a cab in this weather?

JOHNNY: White folks, baby. Wheeeet folks!

MELVIN: Objectively speaking, plenty of them were passed up too. (*He begins to stretch his leg muscles.*)

JOHNNY: Dig? One these days we gon' see this on tee vee.

MELVIN: You got your people mixed. The dances they do on television is ster-ictly commercial.

JOHNNY: What hell's wrong with that? If you gon' run 'roun' wigglin' yo' tukus, mights well git paid for it.

MELVIN: I study with a great artist! He deplores that sort of thing.

JOHNNY: Whozis great artist you study with?

MELVIN: Victor Weiner! He teaches the Chenier method.

JOHNNY: This Shimmy-yay method you don't wiggle the tukus?

MELVIN: Why?

JOHNNY: Them turkeys on tee vee mus' make a whole lotta coins jus' for wigglin' they tukeruseys.

MELVIN: Prostitutes. All of them.

JOHNNY: Pros'tutes, huh? (*He goes to jukebox. Punches up number. Classical music comes on.*) Go with a little sample what you jokers is puttin' down.

MELVIN: Nothing doing. To appreciate true art, one must first be familiar with it.

CORA: Talk that talk, Mel. What do Jay Cee know 'bout bein' artistic?

JOHNNY (*rejects the music*): This Wineberg you study with? He's a Jew, ain't he?

MELVIN: So what?

JOHNNY: Gotta give it to him. Connin' spades into thinkin' they gotta be taught how to dance.

MELVIN: You're just prejudiced, Johnny. That's why you have no appreciation.

JOHNNY: When you start teachin' him, maybe I'll git me some pre-she-a-shun.

(*A loud voice is heard offstage.*)

VOICE: Inn keeper!

GABE (*bursts in clad in army raincoat and Sou'wester; he brandishes an umbrella and briefcase*): Cock-a-doodle-doo!

(JOHNNY *paws the floor with his feet.*)

"I am a ringtailed squeeler. I am that very infant that refused his milk before his eyes was opened an' called out for a bottle of old rye."

(*They circle each other.*)

JOHNNY: "This is me! Johnny Earthquake. I rassle with light'nin', put a cap on thunder. Set every mammy-jammer in the graveyard on a wonder."

GABE: "I grapple with lions! Put knots in they tails! Sleep on broken glass an' for breakfast, eat nails. I'm a ba-a-a-d mother-for-ya."

(JOHNNY *goes behind the bar and takes down a bottle of whisky as* GABE *spies* CORA.)

Eeeeeow! I fell like swallowin' a nappy-headed woman whole!

CORA (*pushes him away playfully*): Better stay out'a my face, fool.

(JOHNNY *moves around bar to center. Theatrically pours a waterglass half-full of whisky. Sets glass before* GABE *on table.* GABE *removes coat and hat. Hands them to* CORA. *He eyes the whisky. Sniffs. Picks up the glass.*)

A-Lawd! Gabe you ain't. . . . (GABE *puts the glass to his lips and begins to drink.*) Ooooo! (GABE *is emptying the glass.*) Ooooo! (*He finishes. Eyes crossed. Sets the glass down. Grimaces. Shakes his head.* JOHNNY *and* SHANTY *laugh.*) I swear! Y'all is sho' crazy. Ain't neither one'a ya got good sense.

GABE: Needed that. Needed that one bad. Gimme another one.

(SHANTY *reaches for the bottle.*)

CORA: Don't you do it, Shangy. Let that fool kill hisse'f. Ain't no call for you to he'p him.

JOHNNY: Dam, Gabe! You ain't done gone an' got alcoholic on us?

GABE: Don't you worry yo' li'l happy head 'bout me, sir. Matter fact, I'm cuttin' myself right out'a the herd.

JOHNNY: Tell me sump'm, baby? Is this herd

pink? An' got snoots an' grea' big ears?

GABE: No they ain't. In color, they're black with big, thick, lip-pussys.

JOHNNY: Man! Them ain't elephants you been hangin' out with, them's hippo-bottom'a-the-pot'a-muses!

(JOHNNY *and* GABE *give each other some skin.*)

CORA: Lawd! What in the devil an' Tom Walker you Nigros talkin' 'bout now?

JOHNNY: Keep her in the dark, Gabe. Keep that mulyan in the black.

MELVIN: They're talking about Gabe's audition, Cora. Gabe had an audition today.

GABE: I said it was a herd call, Melvino Rex!

MELVIN: Lots of actors there, huh?

GABE: Actors? Actors did you say? Well, yes! Every damned black actor in town.

CORA: Well, why didn't you say so in the first place? Lawd, chile! You ought'a lean up off this stuff.

(GABE *tries to put his arm around her.*)

An' take yo' arm out from 'roun' my neck.

MELVIN: How'd you make out at that audition, Gabe?

GABE: Dig this. It was a musical! A musical about slavery.

MELVIN: Slavery? Well! It's about time.

JOHNNY: Gabe's gon' play'a ha'f-white house Nigger! An' they ain't no whiter, ha'f-white house Nigger in New Yawk than Gabe is, I'll bet'a fat man.

GABE: You jus'a-got-dat-wrong, John. Stage manager calls me over. Whispers they're auditionin' the white actors tomorrow. Baby! I refuse to see anything musical at all about slavery.

(*Everyone breaks up laughing.*)

CORA: Say, Gabe? How about doin' one o' them crazy po'ms'a your'n? Ain't heard none in a long time.

SHANTY: Yeah, Gabe! How 'bout it?

MELVIN: Might make you feel better.

JOHNNY: Git under the bed with that shit! Ain't runnin' no cabaret. Fixin' to git me a summons!

GABE: What you wanna hear?

CORA: Anythin'.

JOHNNY: If you jus' gotta. Knowin' you, you always jus' gotta. Make it sump'm you know.

GABE: Dig this one.

(*All except* JOHNNY *eagerly takes seats.*)

They met on the banks of the Potomac, the rich, the great and the small!

It's impossible to tell you, should'a been there an' seen it all!

They came by train, by plane, by bus an' by car!

Bicycle an' tricycle from near an' very far!

On mule an' on horseback!

With greasy bag an' kroker sack!

Buckboard an' clapboard an' goats pullin' wagons!

Tin lizzies an' buggies an' trucks so weighted down with people, you could see the backends saggin'!

Carts with motors, an' trams!

Wheelchairs an' wheelbarrels an' women pushin' prams!

Little boys on scooters! Little girls on skates!

Beatnicks, hippies an' hoboes, most of them had come by freights!

We had walked in light-footed an' barefooted, had walked all out'a our shoes! Some hopped it on crutches for days!

An' then we got the news, some black power agitators was arrested along the way!

'Course they was a lotta Cadillacs an' Buicks, rich people showin' off! I didn't pay that no min',

I jus' took comfort in the thought we needed people of every kin'!

An' if all America had been there or seen it on tee vee, They would'a knowed we all meant business in gittin' our e-kwa-le-tee!

Well, we moved to the square with the pool in the middle!

While we waited, some strange young folk from New Yawk played a flute an' a fiddle!

Then somebody pro nounced that reb'm somebody would pray!

An' by the settin' sun, we knelt in the dust'a that day!

Somebody else got up with a great loud voice!

Said they had on han' the speaker of our choice!

Said this black man was a black man of black deeds an' black fame!

(I'll be damned to hell, I disremember his name!)

Then a hush fell on all them people that night,

'Cause we was there for one thing, our civil right!

This black man, he rizzed up an' walked to the stan'!

I could tell at a glance that he was the man!

An' he boomed out over that mickey-phone an' called for all black folk to unite an' not roam to other orguzashuns who jus' wanted to fight white people an' git what they can in a country that would soon give liberty an' 'quality to every man!

If we worked long an' hard, he admitted it'd be rough!

But he said, black unity an' solidarity would be enough!

Then he rizzed up his arms an' bobbled his head!
Best as I kin I'll try to remember what he said!

(GABE *pretends he is skinning a team of mules.*)

Hya!
You, Afro-Americans!
Hya!
You, American Afros!
Hya!
You Muslims an' nay-cee-pees!
Hya!
You so-called Negroes!
Tan liberals!
Black radicals!
Hya!
You respec-rabble black boorwahzeees!
Hya!
Black Demos an' 'Publicans,
Git back on the track!
You Nash-na-lissys and Marx-a-sissies
Who all been pin-pointin' black!
Hya!
You half-white pro-fesh-nals!
Hya!
Civil rights pro-sesh-nals!
Hya!
You cursed sons-a-ham!
Don't rock no boat!
Don't cut ne'r th'oat!
Be a beacon for some black magazeen!
Come doctor!
Come lawyer!
Come teacher!
Black employer!
An' keepers of white latrines!
On Donner!
On Blitzen!
You black nick-surd-rich-ins!
On! On! With the soul kweezeen!
You inter-urbans!
Satisfied suburbans!
To you, I gotta say whoa!
What's needed to save us
Is not Some-a-Davus!
Or even Benjammer O.!
Giddy-up! Yippeee-ay! Or Kidney Poteeay!
They already got they dough!
Now, here are the bare facks,
Grab yo' selves by the bootblacks!
Leave Heroin Manderson on the side!
An' all you take notice,
You'll all git yo' lettuce!
You'll own the post office yet!
Off-springs off mixed couples
Who're more than a han'fu,

You'll make the cover of Jet!
We'll have invented a machine that delivers
A cream to make crackers pay the debt!
Now junkies don't dilly
You husslers don't dally!
Don't waste yo' time smokin' pot
In some park or some alley,
'Cause Cholly is watchin' you!"

Well, he would a'went that'a way
To this very day but his th'oat
It got too hoarse!
When he sat down wasn't a clap ner a soun',
Couldn't tell if he'd got to the end!
A cracker preacher there, then said a prayer!
Said civil rights you could not fo'ce!
By this time I was so confused my head was in a spin!
Somebody else got up with a grinnin' face!
Said to leave that place like we found it!
Tha's when I reached in my pocket an' pulled out my
*   packet an' before everybody took a sip'a my wine!*
Then we lef' that place without ne'r trace!
An' we didn't leave ne'r chit'lin' behin'!

(*Everyone laughs and claps his hands.*)

JOHNNY: If you ask me it's all a big-ass waste'a time an' energy. Jus' how long you gon' keep this up? Ought'a be in some office makin'a white man's pay.

GABE: Sheee! Think I'd rather be hawkin' neckbones on a Hundred an' Twenty-Fifth Street.

CORA: Uh-aw! Better git out'a here 'fore you two start goin' at it agin. (*She gets newspaper and peers out of window.*) An' 'fore it starts up rainin' ag'in! Lawd knows I ain't prepared for neither one. (*She moves to* MELVIN *who is stirring something in a skillet. She sniffs.*) Shanty! If you want sump'm 'sides Mel's warmed-over chili better see you for supper.

GABE: Better watch it, Shanty. She's thinkin' the way to a man's heart is through his stomach.

CORA (*moves to street doors*): Sho' ain't no way to stay there.

(*She exits.* MELVIN *exits to kitchen.* SHANTY *busies himself.* GABE *sits. Looks thoughtful.* JOHNNY *tosses him some bills.*)

GABE: What's this?
JOHNNY: Aw, take the bread, nigger.

(GABE *does not pick up the money.*)

Look'a here, Gabe. I know you think I'm all up 'side the wall. You hip to the books an' all like'a that. But ser-us-ly! Why ain't they doin' you no good?

GABE: Let's jus' say I ain't in no big rush.

JOHNNY: It's Charlie, ain't it?

GABE: What about Charlie?

JOHNNY: It's wrote all over you! Might be foolin' some people. Cock-a-doodle-dooin' an' comin' on with yo' funky po'try. . . .

GABE: When you git me some answers other than the one's you been handin' me, I'll git in the bed with you.

JOHNNY: One thing Sweets says to me, 'fore he got his time. He says. . . .

GABE: Screw it, John. When you start bringin' Sweets into the picture, I know exactly what's comin' next. The answer is still negative.

JOHNNY: Still wanna believe you kin sell papers an' become President, huh? Snowballs in Egypt.

GABE: I ain't lookin' to break no law.

JOHNNY: They ain't no law. They kill you an' me in the name'a the law. You an' me wouldn't be where we at, if it wasn't for the law. Even the laws they write for us makes us worse off.

GABE: From the git-go, they don't operate like Sweets anymore. Harlem's all caught up.

JOHNNY: Who's operatin' in Harlem?

GABE: You cain't be thinkin' about down here! It was branchin' out'a Harlem got Sweets where he's at right now.

JOHNNY: Man, what you think I been doin' the ten years Sweets been in the joint? I tell you the scheme is together. Me an' him gon' git us a piece'a this town.

GABE: An' end up on the bottom'a the East River with it tied aroun' your necks.

JOHNNY: Bet we'll have us a box'a crackers under each armpit if we do!

GABE: Well, I don't dig crackers that much.

JOHNNY: Okay, Hollywood! Keep knockin' on doors with yo' jeans at half-mast. Sellin' yo'self like some cheap-ass whore. If I know one thing about you, you ain't that good'a actor. Whitey knows right away you cain't even stan' to look at him.

(GABE *grins, picks money up. Pockets it. Blackout.*)

SCENE 2

(*Time: A week later*
Place: The same
Setting: The same
At rise: GABE *stands at center.*)

GABE: When I'm by myself like this, for days, weeks, even months at a time, it sort'a gets to me! I mean deep down inside things begin to happen. Lemme confess, sometimes I git to feelin'—like I get so vicious, I wanna go out an' commit mass murder. But don't misunderstand me. Because I call myself a black playwright, don't git the impression I'm hung up on crap like persecution an' hatred. 'Cause I ain't! I'm gonna leave that violence jazz to them cats who are better at it than me. I ain't been out of the house in over two months. Not because I been that busy, I just been too damned scared. I been imaginin' all kind'a things happenin' out there. An' they're waitin' just for me. All manner of treachery an' harm. But don't think because of it my play is about Negro self-pity. Or even that ol' "You-owe-me-whitey party line." 'Cause it ain't. In spite of what I learned in college, it did not give me that introduction to success, equality an' wealth, that to my parents were the most logical alternatives to heaven. Anyway, like I say, I'm gonna leave that social protest jive to them cats who are better equipped than me.

(*Lights dim out on* GABE *and come up on* JOHNNY, *who is asleep on the floor. One shoe is off and an empty bottle and glass lie nearby. A telegram is pushed under the door.* JOHNNY *rouses himself. Puts on his shoe and goes to the door. Picks up the telegram and studies it. Someone is heard trying the street doors. He hides the telegram and opens the door.* DEE *enters. Goes behind the bar. Makes a Bromo.* JOHNNY *takes out the telegram. Peers at it again.*)

DEE: What is it?

JOHNNY: Looks like a telegram from Sweets. (*He gives her the telegram.*) Read it.

(DEE *downs her Bromo.*)

Read it, I said.

(*She picks up the telegram.*)

DEE: It's from Sweets allright.

JOHNNY: Well, what does it say?

DEE: Says he's going to be released in three weeks.

(JOHNNY *snatches telegram.*)

Makes you pretty happy, doesn't it?

JOHNNY: Babeee! Happy ain't the word! I am dee-ler-russ! Yeeeeoowee!

DEE (*grabs her head*): Hold it down, will ya?

JOHNNY: S'matter? Rough night?

DEE: What else?

JOHNNY: Go home! Cop some zees!

DEE: Just sit here for a while! If you don't mind.

JOHNNY: Dam'dest thing. Las' night I stayed here. Burnt one on. Fell asleep right here. Had this dream. 'Bout Sweets gittin' out. Man, tha's weird! Tha's damned weird!

DEE: Today's my birthday.

JOHNNY: Dam! Forgot all about it.

DEE: Wish to hell I could.

JOHNNY: Anybody'd think you was a wrinkled up ol' mulyan. (*He takes money from her purse. Tosses her a few bills, stuffs the rest into his pocket.*) Here. Go out an' buy yourself sump'm real nice.

DEE (*flinging the bills back at him*): I don't want anything for my birthday.

JOHNNY: Now, lissen. Don't you start no shit this mornin'. I'm in too good'a humor.

DEE: Johnny. Let's you and me just take off for somewhere! For a couple of weeks.

JOHNNY: You off your wood, girl? With Sweets gittin' out?

DEE: I gotta bad feelin'

JOHNNY: I don't give'a dam what kind'a feelin' you got. Sweets was like a father to me.

DEE: So you told me. A thousand times you told me.

JOHNNY: I know. That bitch Evie's been puttin' ideas into your head.

DEE: That's not true. You lay off her, Johnny.

JOHNNY: Lissen to her, she'll have you husslin' tables at Howard Johnson's.

DEE: Might be better off.

JOHNNY: (*slaps her*): Kiss me an' tell me you sorry.

DEE (*she kisses him*): Sorry. (*She moves to street doors.*)

JOHNNY: Hey, girl. Gotta celebrate your birthday some way. Tomorrow mornin'. Bring over the Sunday papers an' a bottle'a my bes' wampole "All day, all night, Mary Ann!"

(*DEE exits. JOHNNY peers at telegram. Goes to jukebox. Punches up number. Presently CORA and SHANTY enter.*)

CORA: Jay Cee? I know it ain't none'a my business, but that woman'a yours? She's out there in the car. Jus'a cryin' her eyeballs out.

JOHNNY (*getting his jacket, moving to street doors*): Hol' down the store, Shanty. Be back in'a couple'a hours.

(*He exits. SHANTY goes to door. Locks it. Punches up number on jukebox.*)

CORA: Shangy? I been doin' some thinkin'. You heard anything from Gloria?

SHANTY: Heard what?

CORA: 'Bout yo' divorce! Tha's what.

SHANTY: Gloria ain't gonna give me no die-vo'ce.

CORA: Well, if she ain't that don't stop us from livin' together, do it?

SHANTY: What made you change your mind?

CORA: 'Nother thing. Ever since I knowed you, you been belly-achin' 'bout gittin' you some drums.

SHANTY: Gonna git 'em too!

CORA: Well, I'm willin' to do everything I kin to help you.

SHANTY: You mean—you mean, you'd help me git 'em? No jive?

CORA: Then you could quit ol' Jay Cee an' go back to playin' in them night-clubs like you said you used to.

SHANTY: You really mean it? You'd help me git my drums?

CORA: Ain't talkin' jus' to hear myse'f rattle.

SHANTY: Mama, you are the greatest. (*He hugs her.*)

CORA: Honey, hush.

SHANTY: Know what I'm gonna do, Cora? Soon's I git them drums I'm gonna bring 'em in here. Set 'em up an' play "the thing" for Johnny.

CORA: Lawd, Shangy! I wouldn't miss that for nothin' in this worl'.

(*SHANTY takes out marihuana cigarette. Wets, lights it. Smokes.*)

Lawd, Shangy! I done tole you 'bout smokin' them ol' nasty things.

(*He passes the cigarette to her. She grins.*)

Guess it won't hurt none once in a while. (*She inhales. Coughs.*)

SHANTY: I was just thinkin' about ol' Gloria. How much she hated jazz. Nigger music, she called it. Man, every time I'd set up my skins to practice, she'd take the kids an' go over to her mother's.

(*They begin to pass the cigarette back and forth.*)

Dig? One night after a gig, brought some cats over for a little game. Some spade cat grabs her between the legs when I wasn't lookin'.

CORA: Spent the bes' part'a my life on Nigros that won't no good. Had to baby an' take care all of 'em.

SHANTY: Never heard the last of it. You'd think he raped her or somethin'.

CORA: Cain't hol' no job! Take yo' money an' spen' it all on likker.

SHANTY: Got this job playin' the Borsh-Belt. My skins was shot! Had to borrow a set from Champ Jones.

CORA: Cain't make up their min's! Jus' be a man, I says.

SHANTY: Gone about a week. Come home. Shades all down. Key won't fit in the door.

CORA: Git evil. Nex' thing you know they goin' up 'side yo' head.

SHANTY: She's over at her mother's. Says she gonna sue me for desershun.

CORA: I thought you was a dif'rent kind'a Nigger. I'm gon' git me a white man, one that'll take care me. Or he'p me take care myse'f.

SHANTY: I never did nothin' to her.

CORA: Tha's when he went up 'side my head with the ash tray!

SHANTY: Said she needed some bread. Went to the bank. Cashed my check. Come back. Skins the cat loaned me are gone.

CORA: I loved him so much.

SHANTY: Grabbed a broom out'a the closet. Went to work on the bitch.

CORA: Them awful things he said to me.

SHANTY: Bitch never made a soun' or dropped a tear.

CORA: I cried sump'm ter'ble.

SHANTY: Says I'd never see my kids ag'in or the drums neither.

CORA: Wanted children so bad! Doctor said I couldn't have none.

SHANTY: Started chokin' her. Would'a killed her, if my kid hadn't jumped on my back.

CORA: Ain't hard to satisfy me. 'Cause Lawd knows I ain't never asked for much.

SHANTY: One thing I learned. Stay away from bitches like that. Just ain't got no soul. (He gets can of spray deodorant. Opens street doors and sprays the bar.)

CORA (rouses herself; wipes tears): Shangy! I sho' wanna see Jay Cee's face when he sees you play them drums.

SCENE 3

(Time: Three weeks later
Place: The same
Setting: The same
At rise: MELVIN is doing his dance exercises. JOHNNY enters with white tablecloth and slip of paper. SHANTY busies himself behind the bar.)

JOHNNY: Sure we need all this, Mel?

MELVIN: You hired me to a short order cook around here. That's exactly what that list is too. A short order.

JOHNNY: Jus' checkin'. Don't want you slippin' none'a that what-wuzzit over on me ag'in.

MELVIN: Po-tahge par-mun-teeay. Everybody else liked it.

JOHNNY: Been some chit'lin's, you'da been sayin' sump'm.

MELVIN: Chit'lin's? Sometimes I think you have the taste-buds of a slave.

(He snatches the slip of paper out of JOHNNY's hands and exits as MARY LOU BOLTON enters and goes to a table.)

JOHNNY: Sump'm I kin do for you?

MARY LOU: I'd like a daiquiri, please. . . .

JOHNNY: Got any identification?

MARY LOU: Really!

JOHNNY: Mary Lou Bo—

MARY LOU: Mary Lou Bolton.

JOHNNY: This the school you go to?

MARY LOU: Just graduated.

JOHNNY (goes behind the bar to mix drink): Buddy'a mine come out'a there. . . .

MARY LOU: Elmira is an all-woman's school.

JOHNNY: I mean the slammers up there.

MARY LOU: Beg your pardon?

JOHNNY (sets drink before her): Prison.

MARY LOU: Oh, yes! My father spent a lot of time up there.

JOHNNY: You kiddin'? Your father did?

MARY LOU (she laughs): He was a criminal lawyer.

JOHNNY: He ain't no lawyer no more?

MARY LOU: He's a judge now.

JOHNNY: Must'a been a hell of a lawyer.

MARY LOU: Oh, I suppose so. . . .

JOHNNY: What you mean, you s'pose so?

MARY LOU: I'd rather not discuss it.

JOHNNY: Sorry.

(ELLEN enters. Carries a civil rights placard.)

ELLEN: C'mon, Mary! Everyone's waitin' on you.

MARY LOU: Be there in a second, Ellen. (She looks into her purse. ELLEN exits.) What do I owe you for the drink?

JOHNNY: Ain't you gonna finish it?

MARY LOU: I really shouldn't. But this is my first time out! Kind of nervous, you know?

JOHNNY: First time out?

MARY LOU: We're picketing the construction

work up the street. The new hospital they're building.

JOHNNY: What for?

MARY LOU: Haven't you heard? The unions won't accept qualified Negroes.

JOHNNY: Why don't them qualified Nigroes do they own pickitin'?

MARY LOU: It's everyone's responsibility.

JOHNNY: You only git in the way.

MARY LOU: I'm glad all Negroes don't feel the way you do.

JOHNNY: You don't know how I feel.

MARY LOU (*puts a bill on the table and prepares to leave*): I don't think I care to find out.

JOHNNY: Jus' happen to think somebody invented this civil rights jive to git a whole lotta people runnin' in the wrong direction.

MARY LOU (*starts to move to street doors;* JOHNNY *catches her by the arm.*): Would you mind?

JOHNNY: Know what's in that daiquiri, baby?

MARY LOU: Let me go, please.

JOHNNY: Jizzum juice. A triple dose of jizmistic juice. Any minute you gonna turn into a depraved sex maniac! A teenage Jeckle an' Hide. Yo' head is gon' sprout fuzzy like somebody from the Fee-gee Eye-lan's. Yo' hot tongue'll roll out'a your mouth like'a fat snake. You'll pant like'a go-rilla in heat. Yo' buzzooms will blow up like gas balloons an' the nipples will swell an' hang like ripe purple plums. Yo' behin' will begin to work like the ol' gray mare an' you'll strut aroun' flappin' yo' wings like'a raped duck. Then you'll suck me up with one mighty slurp an' fly out'a here a screamin' vampire. They'll finally subdue an' slay you on top'a the Empire State Buildin', with ray guns where you'll be attemptin' to empale yo'self astride that giant antenna. An' nobody will ever know that you, li'l Mary Lou Bolton, who jus' graduated from Elmira College, was lookin' to lay down in front of a big, black bulldozer, to keep America safe for democracy.

MARY LOU: I think I get your point.

(ELLEN *enters.*)

ELLEN: Mary Lou! Are you coming or not? Everyone's leaving.

(MARY LOU *and* ELLEN *exit.* ELLEN *scolding.* CORA *enters.*)

CORA: Shangy! Movin' man's waitin'.

(SHANTY *takes off his apron.*)

JOHNNY: Where you think you goin'?

SHANTY: Movin' in with Cora today.

JOHNNY: Not on my time, you ain't! An' me 'spectin' Sweets any minute.

CORA: Wha's so 'portant 'bout that Crane Nigro Shangy's just gotta be here? Or maybe you 'spectin' standin' room for the 'casion?

JOHNNY: Ain't lettin' him off an' tha's it.

CORA: Jay Cee, why is you so bent'n boun' on breakin' up our li'l club?

JOHNNY: Somebody's gotta look out for Shangy if he don't.

CORA: What is you talkin' about? Shangy's free, white an' long pass twenty-one! It ain't none'a yo' business what he does outside this bucket'a blood.

JOHNNY: Well, bitch, I got news for you. I put him in here when none'a these other hunkies 'roun' here would hire him. Talkin' his up 'side the wall talk an' beatin' up they benches.

CORA: Wha's that gotta do with me?

JOHNNY: Ain't lettin' you or nobody else turn his head but so far. Jus' perteckin' my interest.

CORA: Ain't gon' let you stan' in my way, Jay Cee. Me an' Shangy took a likin' for one 'nother from the day I walked in here an' foun' you runnin' this place. Up to now they ain't been much happiness in this worl' for neither one of us. But what li'l we got comin', figger we bes' jump on it with all fo' feet.

JOHNNY: That the way you feel 'bout it, Shanty?

SHANTY: Man, she's gonna help me git my drums.

JOHNNY: She ain't gon' do nothin' but turn you into sump'm you don't wanna be.

CORA: What is you talkin' 'bout, fool?

JOHNNY: This black bitch is gon' turn you into a real white man, Shanty.

SHANTY: What??

CORA: You kin quit this nigger today, Honey. We'll manage.

JOHNNY: You wanna be a white man, Shanty?

SHANTY: Knock that stuff off, Johnny! I don't go for it.

JOHNNY: You think if you git with somebody like Cora, it'll make the whole thing complete, huh?

CORA: Hush up, Jay Cee.

JOHNNY: Well, it won't. She'll make you so damn white you won't be able to bang two spoons together.

CORA: I'm warnin' you, Jay Cee.

JOHNNY: An' play the drums? You'll never play no drums.

(CORA *rushes at* JOHNNY. *He catches her arm and throws her to the floor.* SHANTY *is shocked by* JOHNNY'*s cruelty. He makes a move to* JOHNNY.)

SHANTY: Why you—you—you mother fuck-er!

(JOHNNY *stands ready to throw a punch.* SHANTY *checks himself. Turns away.* CORA *gets to her feet and goes to him. Puts her arm around him. He shuns her. Exits, slowly.*)

CORA: Tha's alright, Jay Cee honey. Tha's all right! That day ain't long off, 'fore you gon' git yours. Honey, you gon' git a hurtin' put on you. You gon' git a hurtin' put on you in the place where you do wrong.

JOHNNY: Better wish all that hurtin' on all them Niggers that messed up yo' min'.

(CORA *exits as* GABE *enters.*)

GABE: Dam! What was all that smoke about?

JOHNNY: Them two ain't got sense nuff to pour piss out'a a boot if the directions was wrote on the heel.

GABE: You just don't wanna see anybody git any enjoyment out'a life.

JOHNNY: Bastard's movin' in with her. You dig that?

GABE: An' you tried to stop 'em, huh?

(JOHNNY *doesn't answer. Takes bottle of champagne and bucket. Sets it on a table.*)

Well, I see you're gettin' ready for the big homecomin', huh?

JOHNNY: That's right. An' I don't want you goin' into none'a yo' high'n mighty when Sweets git here. Tell you right now he don't go for none of that giddy-up-yippee-yaye shit!

GABE: Didn't come to stay. Lemme hold some coins! Lan'lord's on my tail.

JOHNNY: Good.

(JOHNNY *grins. Spreads bills over table.* GABE *picks them up.*)

GABE: You'll git it all back soon's I git me a show.

JOHNNY: You keepin' a record?

(*A black man enters.*)

On yo' way, wine.

SWEETS: S'matter, Sonny Boy? Don't you know me?

JOHNNY: Sweets? Is it really you?

SWEETS: It's me, all right.

(SWEETS *coughs.* JOHNNY *rushes forward. Embraces* SWEETS.)

JOHNNY: Lock the doors, Gabe. Don't want no innerrupshuns.

(GABE *locks the street doors.* JOHNNY *and* SWEETS *box playfully.*)

SWEETS: Minute there, was 'bout to go out an' come back in again.

JOHNNY: Reason I didn't rec'nize you at firs' was, well, I always remember you bein' 'bout as sharp as a skeeter's peter in the dead'a winter. Three hundred suits he had, Gabe. Nothin' but the fines' vines. Never seen so many kicks in one closet. Wasn't a cat in Harlem. . . .

(SWEETS *coughs violently.*)

Dam! What you doin' 'bout that cough, Sweets?

SWEETS: Little souvenir I picked up at the jute mill.

JOHNNY: Jute mill?

SWEETS: Where they make burlap bags at.

JOHNNY: Pretty rough in Fedsville, huh?

(SWEETS *coughs again.*)

Meet my man, Gabe.

(GABE *and* SWEETS *shake hands.*)

GABE: Pleased to meet you, Mister Crane.

SWEETS: Jus' call me Sweets.

JOHNNY (*brings bottle and two glasses*): Sweets, some'a Pete Zerroni's bes'.

SWEETS: Zerroni? You don't mean ol' big fat Pete from up there in the Bronx?

JOHNNY: Yeah. He's runnin' everything down here from soup to nuts! But we gon' change all that, ain't we, Sweets? (JOHNNY *struggles with cork.*)

SWEETS: Sonny Boy, we wasn't much on sendin' kites. Wha's been happenin' since I been in the joint?

JOHNNY: Jews, Irish an' the Ginees still runnin' things as usual.

SWEETS: No. I mean with you, Sonny Boy.

JOHNNY: Like you know I had a tough gaff gittin' my divorce. Whole thing started when I wanted her to do a little merchandizin' for me. Real Magdaleen, she was! One thing led to 'nother. Boom! Back to mama she went. Had a helluva time gittin' her to sign this joint over to me. Went into my act. Fell down on my duece'a benders. Gave her the ol' routine. Like how the worl' been treatin' us black folk an' everything . . . (*He pops cork. Pours. Holds his glass up. The two men clink their glasses.*) Well, look here, Sweets, here's to our li'l piece'a this town.

SWEETS (*looks into his glass; as* JOHNNY *sips*): Speakin'a husslers, Sonny Boy.

(*He coughs.* GABE *goes to bar. Gets large glass and fills it with champagne.*)

You runnin' any kind'a stable?

JOHNNY: You kiddin', Sweets? (*Gives* GABE *a dirty look.*)

SWEETS: Pushin' or bookin'?

JOHNNY: Nay, that ain't my stick.

SWEETS: Sonny Boy, when I was yo' age, I was into some'a ev'thing.

JOHNNY: Wish you wouldn't call me that, Sweets! I ain't that little boy runnin' up an' down Saint Nicklas Avenue for you no more.

SWEETS: Jus' habit, Johnny. But I sort'a was hopin' you was into sump'm on yo' own, like.

JOHNNY: Hell! I been tryin' to stay clean. Waitin' on you, man! Like we planned.

SWEETS: Well, now! Tha's—tha's what I wanna talk to you 'bout, Sonny Boy.

JOHNNY: Yes, sir! You still the boss, Sweets. Didn't think you wanted to git into it jus' yet. Figgered we'd have us a few drinks. Talk 'bout ol' times. . . .

SWEETS: Sonny Boy!

JOHNNY: Sir?

SWEETS: Firs' off! I gotta tell you I'm th'ough. . . .

JOHNNY: Whatchu say?

SWEETS: Wrappin' it all up for good. . . .

JOHNNY: Wrappin' what up?

SWEETS: The rackets.

JOHNNY: You gotta be jokin'.

SWEETS: Never been no more ser'us in all my life. . . .

JOHNNY: Sweets, you jus' tired.

SWEETS: Don't need no res'. . . .

JOHNNY: Git yo'self together. . . .

SWEETS: My min's made up.

JOHNNY: Waitin' on you this long, little more ain't gon' kill me.

SWEETS: Look, Sonny Boy, it's like this . . .

JOHNNY: Shut up with that Sonny Boy, shit! (*He tries to control himself.* GABE *laughs.*) Look, man. You ain't let the slammers psyche you out? That ain't like you. That ain't like you, at all. (*He reaches out to touch* SWEETS. SWEETS *jerks away.* JOHNNY *grabs* SWEETS *by the throat violently.*) Mother fucker! I been waitin' on you for ten long-ass years. You ain't gon' cop out on me like this.

GABE (*moves to contain* JOHNNY): Cut it out, John! Let him alone. Cain't you see the man's sick?

(JOHNNY *hits* GABE *in the stomach.* GABE *doubles over. Goes to the floor.*)

JOHNNY (*to* SWEETS): What the hell they do to you, huh?

SWEETS: What'd who do to me?

JOHNNY: In the bastille. They did sump'm to you.

SWEETS: Nothin that wasn't already done to me. (SWEETS *moves to* GABE.) You all right, young fella?

GABE: Yeah—yeah, I—I'm okay.

SWEETS (*takes wallet from* GABE's *back pocket; puts it into his own pocket*): Shouldn'ta mixed in. (*He turns back to* JOHNNY.) You got the Charlie fever, Johnny. Tha's what you got. I gave it to you. Took yo' chile's min' an' filled it with the Charlie fever. Givin' you a education or teachin' you to dinner-pail, didn't seem to me to be no way for you to grow up an' be respected like'a man. Way we was raised, husslin' an' usin' yo' biscuit to pull quickies was the only way we could feel like we was men. Couldn't copy Charlie's good points an' live like men. So we copied his bad points. That was the way it was with my daddy an' his daddy before him. We just pissed away our lives tryin' to be like bad Charlie. With all our fine clothes an' big cars. All it did was make us hate him all the more an' ourselves too. Then I tried to go horse-to-horse with 'em up there in the Bronx. An' ended up with a ten. All because'a the Charlie fever. I gave you the Charlie fever, Johnny. An' I'm sorry! Seems to me, the worse sickness'a man kin have is the Charlie fever.

JOHNNY (*glares at* SWEETS): Git out'a here, Sweets. Goddam you! Git out'a here. 'Fore I kill you.

(SWEETS *coughs and exits to the street.* JOHNNY *looks after him.*)

They did sump'm to him. White sons'a bitches. They did sump'm to him. Sweets don't give up that easy. Charlie fever. Sheeee!

GABE: Ten years is a long time. An' the man's sick. Anyone kin see that.

JOHNNY: He could be fakin'. He's into sump'm! Don't want me in on it. He used to do that to me all the time. He better be fakin'. (*Brings his arm up to look at his watch.*)

GABE: What? What the hell. . . . (*He searches frantically in his pockets.*) I'll be goddam.

JOHNNY: Hell's matter with you?

GABE: My watch! It's gone.

JOHNNY: Hell with your watch!

GABE: It's gone! An' my wallet! The bread you loaned me! It's gone, too.

(JOHNNY *begins to laugh hysterically.*)

What the hell's so goddam funny?

JOHNNY: It's Sweets? The bastard *is* fakin'. He snatched it!

ACT II

SCENE 1

(*Time: Two days later*
Place: The same
Setting: The same
At rise: GABE *sits at table. Whisky bottle before him. He is obviously drunk. He begins to sing an old Protestant hymn.*)

GABE:
"Whiter than snow, yes!
Whiter than snow!
Now, wash me, and I shall be
Whiter than snow!"

(*He chants.*)

We moved out of that dirty-black slum!
Away from those dirty-black people!
Who live in those dirty-black hovels,
Amidst all of that garbage and filth!
Away from those dirty-black people,
Who in every way,
Prove daily
They are what they are!
Just dirty-black people!

We moved to a house with a fenced-in yard!
To a clean-white neighborhood!
It had clean-white sidewalks
And clean-white sheets
That hang from clean-white clotheslines to dry!
They were clean-white people!
Who in every way
Prove daily
They are what they are!
Just clean-white people!

Now those clean-white people thought we were
Dirty-black people!
And they treated us like we were

Dirty-black people!
But we stuck it out!
We weathered the storm!
We cleansed and bathed
And tried to be and probably were
Cleaner than most of those clean-white people!

(*He sings.*)

"Break down every idol, cast out every foe!
Oh, wash me and I shall be whiter than snow!"

(*He speaks again.*)

We went to schools that had clean-white
Rooms with clean-white teachers
Who taught us and all of the clean-white
Children how to be clean and white!

(*He laughs.*)

Now, those dirty-black people across
The tracks became angry, jealous and mean!
When they saw us running or skipping or
Hopping or learning with all of those
Clean-white children!

They would catch us alone
When the clean-white children weren't there!
And kick us or slap us and spit
On our clean-white clothes!
Call us dirty-black names
And say that we wanted to be like our clean-white
Neighbors!

But in spite of the kicking, the slapping
The spitting, we were exceedingly glad!
For we knew we weren't trying to be like
Our clean-white neighbors! Most of all,
We were certain we weren't like those
Dirty-black Niggers,
Who lived in hovels, far away across the tracks!

(*He sings.*)

"Whiter than snow! Oh, whiter than snow!
Please wash me, and I shall be whiter than snow!"

(*He speaks again.*)

So we grew up clean and keen!
And all of our clean-white neighbors
Said we had earned the right to go
Out into the clean-white world
And be accepted as clean-white people!
But we soon learned,
The world was not clean and white!
With all of its powders and soaps!

And we learned too that no matter how
Much the world scrubbed,
The world was getting no cleaner!

Most of all!
We saw that no matter how much or how
Hard we scrubbed,
It was only making us blacker!
So back we came to that dirty-black slum!
To the hovels, the filth and the garbage!
Came back to those dirty-black people!
Away from those clean-white people!
That clean, white anti-septic world!
That scrubs and scrubs and scrubs!

But those dirty-black people!
Those dirty-black people!
Were still angry, jealous and mean!
They kicked us and slapped us and spit again
On our clothes!
Denied us!
Disowned us
And cast us out!
And we still were exceedingly glad!

For at last they knew
We were not like our clean-white neighbors!
Most of all! We were safe!
Assured at last!
We could never more be
Like those dirty-black Niggers!
Those filthy, dirty-black Niggers!
Who live far away!
Far away, in hovels across the tracks!

(He bursts into song.)

"Whiter than snow! Yes! Whiter than snow!"
Oh, wash me and I shall be whiter than snow!

(GABE *is on his knees. Hands stretched up to heaven. Lights slowly dim out on him, and come up on bar.* SHANTY *is behind the bar.* MIKE MAFFUCCI *stands at center, throwing darts into a dartboard.* SWEETS CRANE *enters.*)

SHANTY: Hit the wind, Mac. This ain't the place.

SWEETS: Johnny here?

SHANTY: What you want with Johnny?

SWEETS: I'm a frien'a his.

SHANTY: Yeah? Well, he ain't here.

SWEETS: Where's me a broom an' a drop pan?

SHANTY: What for?

SWEETS: Need me a bucket an' some rags too.

SHANTY: What do you want all that shit for?

SWEETS: The floor, they don't look too good an' the windas, it could stan'. . . .

SHANTY: Eighty-six, ol' timer! We ain't hirin'.

SWEETS: Ain't askin' f'no pay.

SHANTY: What'a ya? Some kind'a nut? C'mon! Out you go. Eighty-six.

SWEETS: Think you better wait till Johnny gets here. Let him put me out. (SWEETS *pushes* SHANTY *roughly aside and moves to kitchen.*) Think I'll fin' what I need back here.

SHANTY (*looks incredulous. Scratches his head and follows* SWEETS *to kitchen.* JOHNNY *enters.* SHANTY *rushes in from kitchen*): Hey, Johnny! Some ol' timer just came in an'. . . .

MAFFUCCI: How you doin', Johnny Cake?

JOHNNY (*stops short*): Only one cat usta call me that.

MAFFUCCI: Gettin' warm, Johnny Cake.

JOHNNY (*moves behind bar*): Little snotty-nose wop kid, name Mike Maffucci.

MAFFUCCI: On the nose.

(*Sends a dart in* JOHNNY's *direction.* JOHNNY *ducks. The dart buries into the wood of the back bar. Both men laugh. They shake hands.*)

Long time no see, eh, Johnny Cake?

JOHNNY: What you drinkin'?

MAFFUCCI: Little dago red. Gotta take it easy on my stomach with the hard stuff.

(JOHNNY *snaps his fingers.* SHANTY *bring bottle.*)

SHANTY: Dig, Johnny! Some ol' goat. . . .

JOHNNY: Cool it, Shanty. Can't you see I'm busy? How's your ol' man, Footch?

MAFFUCCI (*makes the sign of the cross*): My ol' man chalked out, Johnny. Heart attack. Right after you went to the nursery. You ain't sore 'bout what happened, are you, Johnny Cake?

JOHNNY: Bygones is bygones, Footch!

MAFFUCCI: Glad'a hear ya say that, Johnny. Didn't know what happened to you after that. When they tole me you was runnin' this joint, had'a come over an' see ya.

(*He looks around.* SWEETS *enters with broom and rags. Proceeds to sweep the floor.* JOHNNY *registers surprise and anger.* SHANTY *starts to say something but* JOHNNY *puts his finger to his lips.*)

How ya doin' with the place, Johnny?

JOHNNY: Stabbin' horses to steal blankets. Jay Cee ag'inst the worl'.

MAFFUCCI: Joe Carneri used to say that. You ain't never forgot that huh, Johnny?

(JOHNNY *glances angrily at* SWEETS.)

Remember the first time they busted him? There was this pitchure on the front page. Joe's standin' on the courthouse steps. Cops an' reporters all aroun'. Joe's yellin' "Jay Cee ag'inst the worl'! Jay Cee ag'inst the worl'!"

JOHNNY: He sho' was your hero all right.

MAFFUCCI: Too bad he had'a go an' git hit like that. Sittin' in a barber chair!

JOHNNY: Better'n the electric chair.

(SWEETS *is now dusting the chairs*.)

MAFFUCCI: You know, Johnny Cake, that was a groovy idea for a kid! Coppin' all that scrapiron from ol' Julio an' then sellin' it back to him. (*He breaks up laughing.*)

JOHNNY: Wasn't so pretty when I tried to tell the fuzz you was in on it with me.

MAFFUCCI: Awful sorry 'bout that, Johnny Cake.

(MAFFUCCI *puts his hand on* JOHNNY's *shoulder.* JOHNNY *knocks his hand off.* MAFFUCCI *comes down on* JOHNNY's *shoulder with a karate chop.* JOHNNY *punches* MAFFUCCI *in the stomach and shoves him away. Comes toward* MAFFUCCI *menacingly.* SWEETS *keeps sweeping.*)

JOHNNY: One thing I gotta give you Ginees credit for. Sho' know how to stick together when you wanna.

MAFFUCCI (*backs away*): He was my father, Johnny. Any father would'a done the same thing. If he had the connections.

JOHNNY: Who tole you I was runnin' this joint, Footch?

MAFFUCCI: To give you the works, Johnny, I'm one'a Pete Zerroni's local boys now.

(SWEETS *dusts near* MAFFUCCI.)

JOHNNY: No jive! Battin' in the big leagues, ain't you? Your ol' man was aroun', bet he'd be pretty proud'a you.

MAFFUCCI: Would you believe, my ol' man had ideas 'bout me bein' a lawyer or a doctor?

JOHNNY: What you doin' for Pete?

MAFFUCCI: Sort'a community relations like, Johnny.

JOHNNY (*laughs*): I'm one'a Pete's customers! What kind'a community relashuns you got for me?

MAFFUCCI: Glad you opened that, Johnny Cake. Pete says you got him a little concerned.

JOHNNY: What is he, crazy? Ain't he got more 'portant things on his min'?

MAFFUCCI: Way we got it, first thing ol' Sweets Crane did when he got out was come see you.

JOHNNY: So what? Sweets was like'a father to me.

MAFFUCCI: So I hear. But before they shut the gate on him, he let some things drop. Like, he made a few threats. What I hear 'bout him, might be crazy enough to give 'em a try.

(JOHNNY *laughs*.)

What, am I throwin' zingers or sump'm? What's the joke?

JOHNNY: Sweets came 'roun' to tell me he's all caught up.

MAFFUCCI: Wouldn't promote me, would you, Johnny Cake? For ol' time's sake, let's not you an' me go horse-to-horse 'bout nothin'.

JOHNNY: On the up an' up, Footch. Sweets has wrapped it all up for good. Matter'a fack, right now he's doin' odd gigs an' singin' the straight an' narrow.

MAFFUCCI: Wanna believe you, Johnny. But just in case you an' this Sweets are thinkin' 'bout makin' a little noise, Pete wants me to give you the six-to-five!

(SWEETS *bumps into* MAFFUCCI, *spilling the wine down the front of* MAFFUCCI's *suit*.)

Hey! Watch it there, pops!

SWEETS: Awful sorry 'bout that, mister! (*Attempts to wipe* MAFFUCCI's *suit with the rag.* MAFFUCCI *pushes him aside.*)

MAFFUCCI: That's okay, pops!

(SWEETS *continues to wipe* MAFFUCCI's *vest*.)

Okay, okay, I said!

(SWEETS *stops, and continues with his work*.)

Well, Johnny Cake. Like to stay an' rap with ya a little bit but you know how it is. Community relations.

JOHNNY: Sho' preshiate you lookin' out for me, Footch!

MAFFUCCI: Think nothin' of it, Johnny Cake. It's Pete. He don't like jigs. Says the minute they git a little somethin', they start actin' cute. You an' me, we was like brothers. Way I see it, was like you took a dive for me once. Figger I owe ya.

JOHNNY: You don't owe me a dam thing, Footch.

MAFFUCCI (*heads for the street doors; turns back*): You know, Johnny Cake, some reason I never been able to git you off my mind. After all these years. I think if you'da been a wop, you'da been a big man in the rackets.

(*Exits.* SWEETS *holds watch to ear.*)

JOHNNY: All right now, Sweets. Goddamit, wha's this game you playin'?

SHANTY: Sweets??? That's Sweets Crane?

JOHNNY: Shut up, Shanty. (*Snatches the rag out of* SWEETS' *hand. Gets broom. Gives both to* SHANTY.) Take this crap back to the kitchen.

(SHANTY *takes them to kitchen.*)

Man, you either gotta be stir-buggy or you puttin' on one helluva ack.

SWEETS (*checks the watch*): Jus' tryin' to be helpful, Sonny Boy.

JOHNNY: Don't you be kickin' no more farts at me, man. Wha's with this pil'fin stuff off'a people an' makin' like'a dam lackey? You mus' be plumb kinky.

SWEETS: Cain't see no point in watchin' George Raff on tee vee ev'a night. All my life I been into things. Always active.

JOHNNY: This what you call bein' active? An' look at you! Look like you jus' come off the Bow'ry! Ain't they no pride lef' in you?

SWEETS: Pride? Sheee. Pride, Sonny Boy, is sump'm I ain't got no mo' use for.

JOHNNY: For the las' time, ol' man. You better tell me wha's happenin' with you. Don't you make me have to kill you.

SWEETS (*produces an envelope*): I'm as good as dead right now! (*He hands* JOHNNY *the envelope.*)

JOHNNY: What the hell is it?

SWEETS: Guess you could call it my will.

JOHNNY (*turns it over*): Yo' will??

SWEETS: Open it up.

JOHNNY: Shanty!

SHANTY (*enters*): How ya doin', Sweets?

JOHNNY: Check this out, Shanty. I don't read this jive so good.

SHANTY (*reads will*): It's legal stuff. Says here you're gonna inherit interest in barbershops, meat markets, stores an' a whole lotta Harlem real estate. Dam!

JOHNNY (*snatches the papers out of* SHANTY's *hands*): You gotta be jokin'.

SWEETS: I'm leavin' it all to you, Sonny Boy. My lawyers will take care ev'thing.

JOHNNY: How come you ain't tole me nothin' 'bout this before?

SWEETS: Couldn't take no chance it gittin' out. Might'a strung me out on a tax rap too.

JOHNNY: You lookin' to take some kind'a back gate commute? Suicide?

SWEETS (*coughs*): Doctors ain't gimme but six months to ride. Didn't wanna lay it on you till they made sho'.

JOHNNY: Six months, huh?

SWEETS: Mo' or less.

JOHNNY: Goddamit, Sweets. What the hell kin I say? I sho' been a real bastard. Guess it don't help none for me to say I'm sorry.

SWEETS: Might he'p some if you was to turn all this into sump'm worth while an' good. Maybe the Lawd will f'give me f' the way I got it. (*Bursts into laughter and coughs.*)

JOHNNY: Git off it, Sweets. Jus' 'cause you s'pose to chalk out on us don't mean you gotta go an' 'brace relijun.

SWEETS: Figure it won't hurt more if I do.

JOHNNY: Shit. That good Lawd you talkin' 'bout is jus' as white as that judge who sent yo' black ass to Fedsville.

SWEETS: How you know? You ever seen him? When I was down there in that prison, I reads a lot. Mos'ly the Bible. Bible tells me, the Lawd was hard to look upon. Fack is, he was so hard to look upon that nobody eva looked at him an' lived. Well, I got to figgerin' on that. An' reasons that was so, 'cause he was so black. (*Goes into loud laughter and coughs again.*) Lawd knows! White's easy nuff to look at!

(JOHNNY *throws the will on the floor.* SWEETS *goes to his knees and clutches the will.*)

What you doin', Sonny Boy? My life is in them papers!

(*Hits* JOHNNY *with hat.* JOHNNY *reaches under the bar and comes up with a revolver. Levels it at* SWEETS.)

JOHNNY: See this, Sweets? My firs' an' only pistol. You gave it to me long time ago when I was a lookout for you when you was pullin' them owl jobs in Queens. I worshipped the groun' you walked on. I thought the sun rose an' set in yo' ass. You showed me how to make thirteen straight passes without givin' up the dice. Stood behin' me an' nudged me when to play my ace. Hipped me how to make a gapers cut. How to handle myself in a pill joint. Taught me to trust no woman over six or under sixty. Turned me on to the best horse players an' number runners. Showed me how to keep my ass-pocket full'a coins without goin' to jail. Said the wors' crime I ever committed was comin' out'a my mama screamin' black. Tole me all about white folks an' what to expect from the best of 'em. You said as long as there was a single white man on this earth, the black man only had one free choice. That was the way he died. When you went to jail for shootin' Cholly you said, "Sonny Boy, git us a plan." Well, I got us a plan. Now, you come back here nutty an' half dead, dancin' all over me about me goin' through a change'a life. An' how you want to help you git ready to meet yo' Lawd. Well, git ready, mother fucker. Tha's exactly what I'm gon' do. Help you to meet him. (JOHNNY *pulls back the hammer of the gun.* SWEETS *coughs and looks at the barrel of the gun.*)

SWEETS: You ain't gon' shoot me, Johnny. You cain't shoot me. They's a whole lotta you I ain't even touched.

(SWEETS *exits. Blackout.*)

SCENE 2

(*Time: Two weeks later*
Place: The same
Setting: The same
At rise: GABE *sits at a table. Glass of red wine before him, strumming a guitar.* MELVIN *stands next to him thumbing through a playscript.* SHANTY *is behind the bar as usual.*)

MELVIN: "The Tooth of a Red Tiger"? What part will you play, Gabe?

GABE: What you tryin' to do, Mel? Jinx me? I ain't got the part yet.

MELVIN: They gave you this script, didn't they?

GABE: The part calls for a guitar player. Cain't you hear these clinkers?

(MELVIN *puts script on table.*)

How was your recital?

MELVIN: Ugh! Don't remind me, Gabe. I have this solo in "variations and diversions." I have to do three *tour jêtes*? Well, ol' Mel fell! Would you believe it? I stumbled and fell! Victor, my teacher, he was there shaking! He was actually shaking.

GABE: What the hell, Mel. Always another recital.

MELVIN: I suppose you could look at it that way! Anyway, I was simply heartbroken. Gabe, do you like Carl Sandburg?

GABE: Ain't exactly in love with him.

MELVIN: I was thinking, since you do write poetry, maybe you'd like to go with me to hear

some of his works. Peter Demeter is reading tomorrow night. . . .

GABE: Got somethin' I gotta do.

MELVIN: Well, maybe you'd like to hear some chamber music at the Brooklyn Academy over the weekend.

GABE: Don't dig chamber music, Mel.

MELVIN: I believe an artist should learn all he can about the other forms too. (*Slaps* GABE *on his back and exits to kitchen.*)

DEE (*enters and goes to the bar*): Squeeze the bar rag out, Shanty. (*She glances at* GABE.) Full of little surprises, aren't you?

GABE: Just fakin'.

(SHANTY *pours her drink. She takes bottle and glass to a table. Suddenly she catches* GABE *staring at her.*)

DEE: What's with the fish eyes? I gotta new wrinkle or sump'm?

GABE: Sorry! Just thinkin'!

DEE (*downs drink*): You think too much! Give it a rest!

GABE: Tell me somethin', Dee . . .

DEE: What'a ya? Writin' a book or sump'm?

GABE: How'd you meet up with John in the first place?

DEE (*doesn't answer. Pours another drink. Presently gets to her feet. Goes to window. Peers out*): Got Evie to thank for that. She used to come in here a lot when the joint was really jumpin'. She'll never admit it but I think she had it for Johnny. She's never been much of a drinker but one night she got too looped to drive. Johnny brought her home. When they came in, I was in the process of having my face lifted by a boyfriend. Johnny pulled him off.

GABE: Stop me if I'm bein' a little too personal.

DEE: Oh, you be as personal as you like, Gabe.

GABE: How do chicks like you an' Evie . . .

DEE: Get into the life? Is that what you're askin? For me it was easy! Got a job as a sales girl! Rich Johns would come in propositioning the girls! One day I took one up on it, and here I am.

GABE: Was it for the money?

DEE: What cheap paperbacks you been readin', Gabe?

GABE: I get it! You hate your father.

DEE: That poor miserable bastard? That bum? He ain't worth hating.

GABE: You love John?

DEE: Johnny? Johnny's not the kind of man you love. I think I pity Johnny. Don't get me wrong. I don't mean the kind of pity you'd give to my father or some bum on the street. Somebody blindfolded him. Turned him around. Somewhere inside Johnny's got something. It just come out crooked! Comes out the wrong way. (*She takes drink and becomes theatrical.*) In a way, Johnny reminds me of a classmate of mine in high school.

GABE: Boyhood sweetheart, huh?

DEE: Got me pregnant. Nice decent boy. Only, he was black. Went to my folks. Said, "I'll marry her." The crazy bastard. They made his life miserable. I don't have to tell you.

GABE: Did you love this boy?

DEE: You mean, why didn't we run away together? We were too young and stupid.

GABE: And the baby?

DEE: Oh, they got rid of it for me. (*She almost appears to be improvising.*) Word got out somehow. My mother fled to Puerto Rico for a well needed vacation. I stayed around the house. (*She lapses into theatrical Southern dialect á la Tennessee Williams.*) For weeks I just read, listened to the radio or watched television. One night late my father came in dead drunk. Staggered into my room and got into bed with me. Week later, I came to New York. (*She giggles.*) Funny thing. When I first got into the life, I was always thinkin' about my father. He was always comin' into my mind. Like it was him I was screwin' over and over again. Like I was takin' him away from my mother and punishin' him for lettin' her rule his life.

GABE: You know? Just the way you're standin' there, you remind me of somebody?

DEE: Dame May Whitty?

GABE: Maxine.

DEE: Who?

GABE: Maxine.

DEE: Who's Maxine?

GABE: Probably every woman I've ever known.

DEE: I don't usually think of you with a woman.

GABE: Come on, Dee!

DEE: I didn't mean it like that, Gabe. I always think of you—well, sort'a like the intellectual type! For some reason people kind'a think intellectual types don't even use the toilet! So who's Maxine?

GABE: My mother.

DEE: Talking to you is like eatin' cotton candy.

GABE: She was the little girl who sat across from me.

DEE: In grade school?

GABE: I stole a quarter from her. It was in her inkwell. Teacher lined us up. Searched us. The quarter rolled out of the pocket of my hightop boots. I kin still hear them kids yellin' "Our theeefer!"

DEE: Pretty humiliatin', huh?

GABE: We sang duets together in the high school choir. Neck an' rub stomachs in dark alleys an' doorways. They kicked her out'a school when she got pregnant. Sent her away. They was sure I did it. Her mama was wild an' crazy. Turned tricks for a cat who owned a Cadillac. Didn't want me messin' aroun' with Maxine. Said I was a dirty Nigger an' jus' wanted Maxine's ass. When Maxine didn't make her period, her mama got drunk an' come lookin' for me with a razor. I hid out for a couple days. Heard later she slashed all the upholsterin' in her pimp's Cadillac. Ha! She was smart, Maxine was. An' Jewish too. Taught me social consciousness. Said I was a good lover. Said white boys got their virility in how much money they made an' the kind'a car they drove. Said I related better 'cause I was black an' had nothin' to offer but myself. So I quit my job. Used to hide in the closet when her folks came in from Connecticut. Listened to 'em degradin' her for livin' with an' supportin' a Nigger. Maxine got herself an Afro hair-do an' joined the Black Nationalists when I couldn't afford to get her hair straightened at Rose Meta's! Didn't really wanna marry me. Jus' wanted my baby so she could go on welfare. She is out there somewhere. Maxine is. She's out there, waitin' on me to come back to her, Maxine is.

DEE (*laughs*): Gabe? Gabe, are you sure you're all right?

(*He grins.*)

You really loved Maxine, didn't you? (*She puts her arms around his neck.*)

GABE: I sure wanted to . . .

JOHNNY (*enters*): What the hell's goin' on here?

GABE: You jealous?

JOHNNY: Depen's on yo' intenshuns.

(GABE *puts guitar into case. Picks up script. Prepares to leave.*)

JOHNNY: What, you done gone an' got yo'self a job an' ain't tole nobody?

GABE: It's only an audition.

DEE: Good luck, Gabe.

JOHNNY: Yeah. I'm lookin' forward to gettin' a few payments back on all them loans.

(GABE *gives a razz-berry and exits.*)

You know, Dee? I been thinking. Maybe we ought'a take that trip after all.

DEE: Well now, you don't say? Sweets Crane wouldn't have anything to do with this sudden change of mind, would he? (*She starts to pour another drink.*)

JOHNNY (*snatches bottle out of her hands*): Take it easy on that stuff, girl! Still wannna go, don't you?

DEE: Right now I got somethin' more important on my mind.

JOHNNY: Dump it on me.

DEE: I want out of the life, Johnny.

JOHNNY: Dam! You are stoned, ain't you?

DEE: I mean it, Johnny.

JOHNNY: Thought you an' me had a understandin'.

DEE: There's a hell of a lot more room for a better one.

JOHNNY: Like what, for instance?

DEE: I need some permanence.

JOHNNY: You mean git married?

DEE: Maybe.

JOHNNY: Thought you was down on all that housewife jazz.

DEE: I don't take tee vee commercials very seriously if that's what you mean.

JOHNNY: I gotta business here! Tough nuff time keepin' it perm'nant! Wasn't for the coins you bring in, I'd go under 'fore the week was out.

DEE: Let's build it back up, Johnny. Together. Together, Johnny.

JOHNNY: What the hell you know 'bout this business?

DEE: Teach me, Johnny! You could teach me.

JOHNNY: No good. Ain't no woman'a mine gon' be workin'. She b'long at home.

(*She laughs.*)

Look'a here, go on home. Git you'self together. We'll talk 'bout it later.

DEE: I'll tie a string around my finger. (*She gathers her things. Weaves to the street door.*)

JOHNNY: Hey, girl! You still ain't said where you wanna go.

DEE (*whirls*): I don't know. I hear the north pole's pretty swingin' these days.

JOHNNY: Keep it up. I'll break yo' damn chops yet.

DEE: Where thou goest, I will follow, Johnny baby.

JOHNNY: Thinkin' 'bout makin' the Bim'ni scene. Won't have to worry 'bout crackers doin' the bird with the long red neck. Split this weekend. You make res'vashuns.

DEE (*blows him a kiss; bows theatrically*): Yah suh, Boss! (*She exits.*)

JOHNNY: Bitches. Cain't please none of 'em.

SCENE 3

(*Time: A day later*
Place: The same
Setting: The same
At rise: MELVIN *is arranging chairs and straightening tablecloths.* GABE *enters.*)

MELVIN: What happened, Gabe? Did you get the part?

GABE: Nah! Wasn't the right type after all.

MELVIN: What type did they want?

GABE: Whatever it was I wasn't it.

JOHNNY (*enters from kitchen; he is munching a sandwhich*): Nigra type.

MELVIN: What type is that?

JOHNNY: Whatever it is, tha's what he ain't.

MELVIN: Doesn't talent have anything to do with it?

JOHNNY: Prop'ganda, Mel! When whitey pick one'a y'all you gotta either be a clown, a freak or a Nigra type.

GABE: They do the same thing among themselves too.

JOHNNY: 'Mongst themselves, they ain't so damn choosey.

GABE: Should'a seen the cat they did pick. Hell, I'm as black as he is.

JOHNNY: Gabe, ain't they no mirrors in yo' house?

GABE: I mean black in here!

MELVIN: You people are more preoccupied with color than white people are.

JOHNNY: They won't let us be porcupined with nothin' else.

GABE: Don't make no difference what color I am. I'm still black.

JOHNNY: Yeah! But you ain't gon' git no chance to prove it. Not on no stage, you ain't. You remin' whitey'a too many things he don't wanna take'a look at. Figgers he's got nuff problems dealin' with Niggers who jus' look black, like me.

GABE: Aw, shut the fuck up, John

JOHNNY: Who you talkin' to?

GABE: You, you bastard. I'm tellin' you to shut the fuck up. Jus' cool it with yo' shit.

JOHNNY: Jus' tryin' to tell you like it is, Gabe! You jus' don't b'lieve a hard head makes a sof' ass!

MELVIN (*pats* GABE *on the back*): Like you told me, Gabe. Always another recital.

(MELVIN *exits to kitchen.* JOHNNY *tosses* GABE *some bills.*)

GABE: No more handouts, baby.

JOHNNY: This ain't no handout! Want you to do me a favor.

GABE: Yeah?

JOHNNY: Me an' Dee goin' on a little vacation. Want you to help Shanty an' Mel with the store while we gone.

GABE: When you leavin'?

JOHNNY: End'a the week. Makin' it to Bim'ni.

(CORA *and* SHANTY *enter. Carry black drum cases.*)

CORA: Give us a han' here, Gabe? They's more out there in the cab.

(GABE *exits to the street.*)

JOHNNY: What you bringin' this junk in here for?

CORA: We bringin' this junk in here as you call it on a purpose.

JOHNNY: Be damned if tha's so. Git out'a here, an' Shanty, lets git to work.

(GABE *returns with another case.*)

CORA: Look'a here, Jay Cee. Me an' Shangy swore when we got these here drums, we was gon' bring 'em in here for you to look at an' lissen to with yo' own eyes an' ears.

JOHNNY: All of a sudden I done gone deaf an' blin'. Now, git this hazarae out'a here.

CORA: Ain't gon' do ner such thing. Not till me an' Shangy has got som'a what we's set out to do.

GABE: Sure got a pretty good start.

CORA: Shangy! What is you doin' with the broom?

(JOHNNY *reaches for one of the drum cases.*)

Take yo' nasty, stinkin', filthy black han's off them drums!

(JOHNNY *recoils.*)

MELVIN (*comes out of the kitchen*): What on earth is happening?

CORA: It ain't happenin' yet.

MELVIN: Well, I just never would have believed it. Isn't it wonderful?

CORA: 'Fore Shangy gits on these drums, they's sump'm you oughta know, Jay Cee.

JOHNNY: You runnin' the show.

CORA: Shangy is quittin' you today. Right now.

JOHNNY: Why the hell didn't you say that in the first place?

CORA: 'Cause you was so busy gittin' these drums out'a here. Tha's why.

MELVIN: You're really going to play for us, Shanty?

CORA: Tha's his intenchun, thank you. Shangy! Will you come on over here? Gabe don't know nothin' 'bout what he's doin'.

(SHANTY *hands* JOHNNY *the broom. Approaches the drums reluctantly.*)

JOHNNY: Some reason, Shangy, you don't look so happy. Now I want you to jump up there an' give ol' Jay Cee a little wham-bam-thank-ya-ma'm. Piece'a the funky nitty-gritty. Like the time they said you played like'a spade. Guess I kin risk gettin' a summons on that.

CORA: Ne' min', Jay Cee. Go 'head, honey! Git yo'se'f together. Take all the time you need.

GABE: Wail, baby.

(SHANTY *sits on the stool. Fumbles. Accidentally puts foot on pedal. Strikes pose. Taps cymbals. Moves to snares. Mixes. Pumps. Works. Gets loud.* CORA *fidgets. Anxious.* SHANTY *fakes. Can't cover up. Becomes frustrated. Louder. Stands. Begins to beat wildly. Moves around the drums banging for all he's worth.* CORA *is ashamed.* GABE *frowns.* CORA *grabs* SHANTY's *arm. He pushes her away. Becomes a windmill.*)

CORA: Stop it, Shangy! Stop it, I said!

(SHANTY *beats as if possessed.* CORA *is helpless.* JOHNNY *calmly reaches behind the bar. Gets pitcher of water. Pours it over* SHANTY's *head.*)

SHANTY: Ya-hoooo! (*Leaps into the air.*) I had it! I was on it! I was into it, babee! (*He moves around doing the pimp walk.*) Ol' Red Taylor said I had the thing. Said, "Shanty man! You got the thing!" (*Goes to* MEL.) Gimme some skin, mother fucker. (MEL *gives him some skin. Goes to* GABE.) Gimme some skin. (GABE *doesn't put his hand out.*)

Ah, fuck you, man. Didn't I hip you to my happenin's, Johnny? Didn't I show you where it's at?

JOHNNY: You burned, baby, you burned.

(SHANTY *gives* JOHNNY *some skin.*)

CORA: Shangy! I—think you better start packin' up now.

SHANTY: Git away from me, you funky black bitch.

CORA: Shangy!

SHANTY: Just stay away from me—you evil piece'a chunky.

CORA: You ain't got no call to say nothin' like that to me.

SHANTY: Oh, no? You ain't jive timin' me, you just like Gloria.

CORA: What you sayin', Shangy?

SHANTY: You don't want me to play no drums.

CORA: You wrong, Shangy.

SHANTY: Thought you'd make a fool out'a me, did you? Gittin' me to bring these drums in here. You thought I'd mess it up. Well, I showed you where it was at. I showed all'a you.

CORA: Shangy, you crazy! You the one suggestid that!

SHANTY: Bitch, call the man. Have him come git these drums.

CORA: Come git the drums? Why, Shangy? Why?

SHANTY: I don't need you to help me get my drums. I get my own drums. Dig it?

CORA: This chile done clean los' his min'.

SHANTY: You an' me are through! Dig it? We are through. We've had it. Splitsville.

(CORA *is numb.*)

Now you believe me huh, Johnny? A bucket'a cold water an' throw it on me, huh?

JOHNNY: To git you to quit. Come on, baby. Let's git some dry clothes on you. (JOHNNY *leads* SHANTY *to the kitchen.*)

SHANTY: A bucket'a cold water like the night we played "Saints" . . .

(JOHNNY *and* SHANTY *exit to kitchen. For a moment* CORA *looks up at the clock.*)

CORA: What time is it, Gabe?

GABE: My watch was stolen . . .

CORA (*points to clock above cash register*): What time do that clock say?

GABE: Quarter after three . . .

CORA: Know sump'm, Gabe? I ain't never learned how to tell time. Thirty years ol' an' I don't even know the time'a day. But when I gits up in the mornin', tha's the very firs' thing I'm gon' do. I'm gonna learn how to tell me some time. (*She exits.*)

JOHNNY (*enters from kitchen*): Go back there an' help Shanty, Mel! He don't feel so good.

(MELVIN *goes to kitchen.*)

Help me tear down this thing, Gabe.

(JOHNNY *begins to dismantle drums.*)

GABE: Do it your damned-self. I ain't feelin' so hot either. (*Exits hurriedly.*)

JOHNNY: Now, what in hell's matter with you? (*Busies himself with the drums.* MARY LOU BOLTON *enters.*)

MARY LOU: Hello . . .

JOHNNY (*his attention is still with the drums*): Sump'm I kin do for you?

MARY LOU (*moves to table; sits*): I'd like a daiquiri, please.

JOHNNY (*looks up*): Tha's one drink I ain't never been able to make right.

MARY LOU: Simple! Just go easy with the sugar.

JOHNNY (*goes behind bar. Begins to mix drink. Dumps in a lot of sugar*): Never 'spected to see you back here ag'in.

MARY LOU: Let's just say, I don't scare so easy. By the way, what were you trying to prove anyway?

JOHNNY (*comes to her table and sets the drink before her*): I was waitin' for you to ask sump'm like that.

MARY LOU: Really?

JOHNNY: You sho' didn't come back here for no drink.

MARY LOU: Pretty conceited, aren't you?

JOHNNY: Jus' hipt to yo' kin', tha's all.

MARY LOU: "My kind," huh?

JOHNNY: You don't like to be kept in the dark 'bout nothin'.

MARY LOU: That's the difference between man and beast.

JOHNNY: I kin see you ain't learned a damned thing in that college, neither.

MAFFUCCI (*enters with truck driver who carries case of whisky to kitchen*): How you doin', Johnny Cake?

JOHNNY: Okay, Gumba. What'd Pete do? Demote you? Got you ridin' the truck.

MAFFUCCI: New kind'a community relations, Johnny Cake. Ride aroun' with the boys, see if the customers are happy. You happy, Johnny Cake?

(*Truck driver comes out of kitchen, exits.*)

JOHNNY: Dee-leer-iuss.

MAFFUCCI (*spies* MARY LOU): Good, good. Makes me happy too. (*He moves to* MARY LOU.) Say! Ain't you Judge Bolton's kid?

MARY LOU: Why, yes. Yes I am.

MAFFUCCI (*Takes her' in his arms. Handles her. She resists, to no avail*): Never forget a face. Turned out to be a real nice tomata, huh? Don't mind me, kid. (*He releases her.*) Next time you see your ol' man, tell him Mike Maffucci says "Hello!" (*He pats her on the behind.*) See you aroun', Johnny Cake! (*Looks at drums. Taps them.*) Didn't know you was rhythmical.

JOHNNY (JOHNNY *reacts playfully by toying with the drum sticks*): Chow, Footch.

(MAFFUCCI *exits.*)

Okay. How does he know yo' ol' man?

MARY LOU (*visibly shaken*): They were clients of his.

JOHNNY: They? They who? You mean Footch?

MARY LOU (*nods*): Something about bribing a city official. And someone was murdered.

JOHNNY: Mary. Does the name Pete Zerroni ring a bell?

MARY LOU: Yes! He was one of the defendants. My father won the case.

JOHNNY: I don't care what nobody say. Your father was a damn good lawyer.

MARY LOU: What's your interest? You know this Pete Zerroni?

JOHNNY: Not personal.

MARY LOU: He's not a very good person to know.

JOHNNY: With Pete, sometimes you ain't got no choice.

(*She prepares to leave.*)

Here! Lemme freshen up yo' drink.

MARY LOU: No thanks. I'm getting—I'm getting a headache. (*She moves to the street doors.*) Goodbye, mister . . .

JOHNNY: Johnny. Johnny Williams.

MARY LOU: Goodbye, Johnny. . . . (*She exits, leaving her purse.*)

JOHNNY (*picks her purse up. Thinks for a moment. Goes to phone, dials*): Hey, Dee? Cancel them reservashuns. Sump'm important jus' came up. Won't be able to after all. Now don't hand me no crap. Just cancel.

ACT III

SCENE 1

(*Time: Two weeks later*
Place: The same
Setting: The same
At rise: Table at center has a folded newspaper leaning against a large Molotov cocktail. Its headline reads: "Negroes Riot!" A banner resembling the American flag dangles from a flagstand. Next to the Molotov cocktail is a plate, on which rests a large black automatic pistol. Beside the plate is a knife and fork. A toilet is heard flushing. GABE *comes on stage zipping his pants. His attitude is ceremonial.*)

GABE: "*They's mo' to bein' black than meets the Eye! Bein' black, is like the way ya walk an' Talk! It's a way'a lookin' at life!*
Bein' black, is like sayin', "Wha's happenin', Babeee!"
An' bein' understood!
Bein' black has a way'a makin' ya call some-Body a mu-tha-fuc-kah, an' really meanin' it! An' namin' eva'body broh-thah, even if you don't! Bein' black, is eatin' chit'lins an' wah-tah-Melon, an' to hell with anybody, if they don't Like it!
Bein' black has a way'a makin' ya wear bright Colors an' knowin' what a fine hat or a good Pair'a shoes look like an' then—an' then— It has a way'a makin' ya finger pop! Invent a New dance! Sing the blues! Drink good Scotch! Smoke a big seegar while pushin' a black Cadillac With white sidewall tires! Its' conkin' yo' Head! Wearin' a black rag to keep the wave! Carryin' a razor! Smokin' boo an' listenin' to Gut-bucket jazz!
Yes! They's mo' to bein' black than meets the eye! Bein' black is gittin' down loud an' wrong! Uh-huh! It's makin' love without no hangups! Uh-huh! Or Gittin' sanctified an' holy an' grabbin' a han'ful'a The sistah nex' to ya when she starts speakin' in Tongues!
Bein' black is havin' yo' palm read! Hittin' the Numbers! Workin' long an' hard an' gittin' the Short end'a the stick an' no glory! It's Knowin' they ain't no dif'rence 'tween White trash an' white quality! Uh-huh! Bein' black is huggin' a fat mama an' hav-in' her smell like ham-fat, hot biscuits An' black-eyed peas!
Yes! They's mo' to bein' black than meets The eye!
Bein' black has a way'a makin' ya mad mos'

Of the time, hurt all the time an' havin'
So many hangups, the problem'a soo-side
Don't even enter yo' min'! It's buyin'
What·you don't want, beggin' what you don't
Need! An' stealin' what is yo's by rights!
Yes! They's mo' to bein' black than meets the
Eye!
It's all the stuff that nobody wants but
Cain't live without!
It's the body that keeps us standin'! The
Soul that keeps us goin'! An' the spirit
That'll take us thooo!
Yes! They's mo' to bein' black than meets
The eye!"

(GABE *sits at table. Cuts into gun with knife and fork. Finally picks gun up. Bites into it. Chews and swallows. Takes drink from Molotov cocktail. Wipes mouth.*)

Bru-thas an' sistahs! Will ya jine me!

(*Blackout on* GABE. *Lights come up on* DEE *and* SHANTY. *She sits at table, bottle of whisky in front of her.* SHANTY *sits on stool reading copy of* Downbeat.)

DEE: Ain't like him to stay away from the joint like this. Can't reach him at his apartment either.

SHANTY: He don't come in but about once a day. Just to check things out—

DEE: It's a woman he's with, isn't it?

SHANTY: Huh?

DEE: Hello?

SHANTY: What you say? Eh, *que pasa?*

DEE: He's with a woman—it's a woman he's with . . .

SHANTY: Uh—it's uh—Mel's day off, Dee—gotta go clean up the kitchen . . .

DEE: Shanty, come here a second . . .

(*He comes to her reluctantly.*)

Thanks, huh?

(*She stuffs a bill into the pocket of his apron.*)

For nothing!

(*He shrugs. Exits to kitchen. She goes back to drinking.*)

EVIE (*Enters. Spies* DEE. *Moves to jukebox*): Hey.

DEE: Hey, yourself!

(*Music comes on.*)

How does it feel to be on your way to good citizenship?

EVIE: Yeah, huh? Imagine me doin' it to an IBM machine.

DEE: It ain't hard.

EVIE: That bottle ain't doin' you a damn bit'a good.

DEE: Tha's debatable.

EVIE: How 'bout a nice hot cup' a black coffee?

DEE: Uh-uh! Gotta stay here an' wait for Johnny.

EVIE: Pretty soon you'll be waitin' for him flat on the floor.

DEE: Drunk or sober, it doesn't matter anyway.

EVIE: Why you doin' this? Sheee! He ain't worth the powder it'd take to blow him up.

DEE: Tha's mah business.

EVIE: It's my business you was up at Jack's last night.

DEE: Where'd you hear that?

EVIE: Jack. He called me. Now, if you wanna kill yourself, or git killed—go right ahead! But I wanna warn you 'bout one thing. Stay out'a Jack's, you hear me? A lotta Niggers in there, jus' waitin' for somebody like you! 'Nother thing! Jack's my uncle—don't want'a see him lose his license—on account'a some bitch like you!

DEE: Okay, so I was up at Jack's!

EVIE: What was you lookin' for anyway? Way off yo' beat! Ain't nobody up there got your price!

DEE: I wasn't sellin'—I was buyin'.

EVIE: You was what?

DEE: The biggest blackest cat you ever saw picked me up.

EVIE: You just lookin' to git yourself hurt, girl.

DEE: Oh, he was polite. Too polite. Took me to his room. Smelled like that greasy pomade an' hair straightener you smell sometimes on those pretties in the subway. An' when he put on his silk stocking-cap—I just about cracked. Kept the light on so he could watch.

EVIE: Git yourself together, girl. Drunk as you are—you liable to tell Johnny 'bout this an' he'd have to kill you.

DEE: When it got good to him he started singin', "Black an' white together—black an' white together!" An' the toilet down the hall was flushing over and over again.

EVIE: Bitch, did you hear what I said?

DEE: No! I ain't goin' anyplace! I'm stayin' right here . . . (*She sits at table. Goes into purse. Takes out can of shoe polish.*) If I have to stage a sit-in to do it. (*She puts mirror before her. Begins to apply polish to her face.*)

EVIE: Girl, what are you doin' . . .

DEE (*knocks* EVIE's *hand away*): Take your hands off me, you stinkin' cunt! Dirty black sow!

EVIE (*slaps* DEE *viciously*): All right, you crazy, uptight, drunken whore! Sure as shit you gon' end up in Bellvue or git your ass sliced up an' thrown to the rats in some alley . . .

(JOHNNY *enters.* DEE *sing-songs him.*)

DEE: Where you been keepin' yo' se'f, Johnneee, babeee!

JOHNNY: Git that crap off your face an' git the hell out'a here!

DEE (*snaps her fingers*): I's black an' I's proud!

EVIE: Listen here, Johnny! This girl is in trouble!

JOHNNY: She's free, white an' always right!

(DEE *laughs. He goes to her, wipes the black from her face, forcing her to relent.* DEE *begins to weep. He is almost tender with her.*)

EVIE: She ain't free a'you—Dee, if you got an ounce a sense left in yo' head you'll git on up and come on out with me now.

DEE: Hit the wind, sugar! Git on back to your stupid analyst an' your fuckin' IBM machine! Hit da win', sugar.

(EVIE *shakes her head, moves quickly to the door.*)

JOHNNY: Hey! Pussy!

(*She turns angrily.*)

I know what's eatin' yo' ass. You don't like it 'cause I went for her an' not you! Tha's it, ain't it?

EVIE (*moves quickly to the two of them. Takes* DEE *by the shoulders. Pulls her up and draws her to her roughly. Plants a hard kiss upon* DEE's *mouth. She shoves* DEE *into the arms of* JOHNNY *who quickly puts* DEE *aside. He faces* EVIE *furiously.* SHANTY *enters*): Darlin', you way off base. I've known Niggers like you all my life! Think everything's a game. I wouldn't piss on you if yo' ass was on fire. Lef to me, I'd give you a needle—let you sit in a corner like little Jackie Horner, jerkin' off all by yourself!

(JOHNNY *raises his hand.* EVIE *beats him to the punch, clubs him with her forefinger between the legs. He winces and doubles over.* EVIE *exits quickly.* DEE *laughs hysterically.* MARY LOU BOLTON *enters.* DEE *is lying on the floor.*)

MARY LOU: Johnny, I . . .

JOHNNY: Stay where you at, Mary.

MARY LOU: Johnny, maybe I'd better . . .

DEE: Well, well, well. And just might who you be, Miss Baby Cakes?

MARY LOU: Johnny!

JOHNNY: I said stay where you at!

DEE (*struggles to her feet; gathers her belongings*): Baby Cakes, let me give you the best advice you ever had in your whole little life. Run away from here fast. Run for your life. (*She goes into her purse. Comes up with baby shoes. Drops them on the floor. Exits.*)

MARY LOU: Who is she, Johnny?

JOHNNY: Some chick with a problem.

MARY LOU: She—she looked . . .

JOHNNY: She was wiped out.

MARY LOU (*picks up the baby shoes*): Who do these belong to . . .

JOHNNY (*snatches them out of her hands and throws them into the waste basket*): Don't ask me! Never had no kid'a mine if tha's what you're thinkin'!

MARY LOU: I don't think you'll be seeing me anymore, Johnny.

JOHNNY: Why the hell not, Mary?

MARY LOU: Are you in any trouble, Johnny?

JOHNNY: Trouble? What kind'a trouble?

MARY LOU: My father! Someone called him about us!

JOHNNY: What about?

MARY LOU: Whoever it was said if he didn't stop me from seeing you, they would.

(*He grins.*)

Are you in some kind of trouble?

JOHNNY: That depen's, Mary. Take off, Shanty!

SHANTY: Man, I still got . . .

JOHNNY: I said, take off!

(SHANTY *takes off apron. Gets hat. Exits.* JOHNNY *locks doors behind him.*)

'Member when we was talkin' 'bout Pete Zerroni?

MARY LOU: Yes . . .

JOHNNY: Pete don't like it if a Nigger's got a place'a business in his ter'tory.

MARY LOU: You gotta be kidding.

JOHNNY: Ain't you learned nothin' from all that civil rights?

MARY LOU: What proof do you have?

JOHNNY: Baby, this ain't no ord'nary type 'scrimunashun. They give you the signal. You ignore it. Place burns down.

MARY LOU: But why don't they want to see you?

JOHNNY: Your ol' man was Zerroni's lawyer. Think maybe I might try to work you. . . .

MARY LOU: Work me?

JOHNNY: Yo' ol' man might have somethin' on Zerroni an' his boys in his records an' files.

MARY LOU: That's silly! It could never be used as any real evidence.

JOHNNY: Sho' could make it hot for a whole lotta people if the D.A. happened to get a few tips.

MARY LOU: What are you getting at?

JOHNNY: Nothin'. You wanted to know why they didn't want you to see me, didn't you? 'Les yo' ol' man's prege'dice.

MARY LOU: He knows I've dated Negroes before. (*She thinks for a moment.*) You really believe if you got this information it would keep Zerroni off your back?

JOHNNY: Well, they still don't know who killed Rep'senative Mahoney. . . .

MARY LOU: Well, you know I couldn't do anything like that. I mean take that information. My father would never forgive me.

JOHNNY: Like I say. Tha's the only reason I kin figger why they don't want you to be seein' me.

MARY LOU: Anyway, he keeps that sort of thing locked in a safe! In his office.

JOHNNY (*comes to her. Takes her by the hand and pulls her to him. He kisses her gently. She responds*): Queer, ain't it? Yo' ol' man's a judge. Sworn to uphol' justice. We cain't even go to him for help.

MARY LOU: I'll speak to him about it, Johnny.

JOHNNY: Don't you do that, Mary. Don't you do nothin' like that.

MARY LOU: But why, Johnny? He could probably help you.

JOHNNY: For all we know, he might be in with Zerroni.

MARY LOU: Don't you say that.

JOHNNY: Funny, after that rotten bunch'a Ginees got off he got to be judge right away.

MARY LOU: I think I'd better leave now.

JOHNNY: Why'd you come back here, Mary? Make like you wanted a daiquiri. Think I'd be a sucker for some white missionary pussy?

MARY LOU: That is a terrible thing to say.

JOHNNY: You don't give a dam about civil rights. What about my civil rights? Don't I git any?

MARY LOU: There are ways to stop Zerroni. There are people we can go to for help.

JOHNNY: Yeah? An' they'll go over to Zerroni's an' picket!

MARY LOU: That's not funny.

JOHNNY: You liberal-ass white people kill me! All the time know more 'bout wha's bes' for Niggers'n Niggers do.

MARY LOU: You don't have to make the world any worse.

JOHNNY: Never had no chance to make it no better neither.

(*There is pounding on street doors.* JOHNNY *unlocks them.* MARY LOU *rushes out as* GABE *hurries in.*)

GABE: Git your coat, John. Quick!

JOHNNY: What the hell for?

GABE: It's Dee! She's dead.

JOHNNY: Dead?

GABE: Can't figger how they got my number. She slit her wrists. Why'd they call me?

JOHNNY: Where is she?

GABE: The ladies' room. Hotel Theresa.

SCENE 2

(*Time: Three days later*
Place: The same
Setting: The same
At rise: Music from jukebox is going full blast.
SHANTY *is seated on a barstool. Beats on the next stool with drumsticks.*)

SHANTY: Aw, blow it, baby! Workout! Yeah! I hear ya! Swing it! Work yo' show!

(JOHNNY *and* GABE *enter dressed in suits.* GABE *as usual carries briefcase.*)

JOHNNY: Goddamit, Shanty! Git under the bed with that shit. Ain't you got no respect for the dead?

(*Pulls cord out of socket.* SHANTY *puts sticks away.* MELVIN *comes out of kitchen.*)

MELVIN: How was the funeral!

GABE: How is any funeral, Mel?

JOHNNY (*goes behind bar; mixes drinks*): Every damned whore in town showed up! Think they'd have a little respeck an' stay home!

MELVIN: Was her people there?

GABE: Only us!

SHANTY (*picks up newspaper*): Paper sure gave you hell, Johnny!

JOHNNY: Who the hell asked ya? (*He comes around bar.*) Comin' on like some bitch in'a cheap-ass movie! Writin' all that jive on the shithouse wall with lipstick!

SHANTY: I always liked Dee! Good tipper.

JOHNNY (*bangs on bar*): Anybody'd think I killed her! Blamin' me for everything! Hell, I never did nothin' to her!

GABE: Nothin' for her neither!

CORA (*enters. Dressed to kill. Wears white rose corsage*): Hello, ev'body.

GABE: Hello, Cora. . . .

CORA: Wha's ev'body lookin' so down in the mouth about? Like you jus' come from a funeral.

JOHNNY: Is that yo' idea of some kind'a damn joke?

MELVIN: Ain't you heard, Cora?

CORA: Heard what?

MELVIN: It's been in all the papers! Johnny's friend, Dee. She committed suicide a couple of days ago.

CORA: Lawd have mercy! I'm so sorry! I—I haven't exactly been keepin' up with the news lately! You see I—jus' got married this morning.

MELVIN: Married? I hope you'll be very happy, Cora.

GABE: Congratulations, Cora.

CORA: Oh, thank you! Thank you so much.

JOHNNY: Must'a been a whirlwin' co'tship.

CORA: Ack-shully, I been knowin' him f'quite some time! He's a heart speshlis' I met at the hospital.

JOHNNY: From the looks of you, he mus' be a pretty good'n.

CORA: He's jus' aroun' the corner gittin' the car checked over! It's a good distance to Kwee-beck.

GABE: Quebec?

CORA: Our honeymoon! Wants me to meet his peoples! 'Cause they's French, you know. Jay Cee? (*She goes to* JOHNNY.)

JOHNNY: What?

CORA: Awful sorry 'bout what happened.

JOHNNY: Yeah! Sure, Cora!

CORA: Sump'm ter'ble must'a happen to drive her to do a thing like. that!

JOHNNY: Good luck with the married bag, huh?

CORA: Why, thank you, Jay Cee! Thank you. You know me an' you knowed each other a lotta years. Some reason, I could never do nothin' to suit you. No matter how hard I tried. Sometimes you make me so mad I ha'f wanna kill you! But I was fool 'nuff to care sump'm 'bout you anyway. 'Cause to me you always been that li'l bad boy who was lef' all alone in the worl' with nobody to take care him!

JOHNNY: Guess it'll always be "Jay Cee ag'inst the worl'!"

CORA (*tries to touch him. He jerks away. She looks at* SHANTY): Ain't you gon' wish me good luck too, Shangy Mulligans?

(SHANTY *remains silent. Stares out of the window. She shrugs. Moves to street doors.*)

Well, o-re-vo-ree, ev'body! O-re-vo-ree! (*She giggles.*) Tha's French, you know! That means, "Bye, y'all!" (*She exits happily.*)

SHANTY: Se-la-goddam-vee.

MELVIN: She sure was happy!

GABE: Different too.

JOHNNY: Married a doctor! Ain't that a bitch? Say one thing for her! That number don't give up! She . . .

SHANTY: Shut up, man!

JOHNNY: What you say?

SHANTY: I said shut up, nigger.

JOHNNY: Now, look. I know you upset 'bout Cora, but . . .

SHANTY: Will you cool it! Big man! Mister hot daddy! Think you know everything in the whole goddam world, don't you? Well, lemme tell you somethin', man. You don't know a mu-thah-fuc-kun thing. (*He rips off his apron and flings it into* JOHNNY's *face.*) Here! Do your own dirty Nigger work! I've done all I'm gonna do! Took all I'm gonna take! (*He pulls out his drumsticks. Boldly beats on the bar.*) Stood behind this bar! Let you put me down for the last time 'cause my skin is white. (*He beats harder on the bar.*) Yeah, baby. I'm white. An' I'm proud of it. Pretty an' white. Dynamite. Eh, mothah fuckah. Know what else I got that you ain't got? I got soul. You ain't got no soul. Mothahfuck-ah's black an' ain't got no soul. If you're an example of what the white race is ag'inst, then baby, I'm gittin' with 'em. They are gonna need a cat like me. Somebody that really knows where you black sons-a-bitches are at. (*He picks up the butcher knife. Plunges it into the top of the bar.*) That's what I think of this ol' piece'a kindlin'! Take it an' stick it up you black, rusty, dusty! (*He moves quickly to the street doors. Turns. Gives* JOHNNY *the finger and exits quickly.*)

JOHNNY: Well, looks like ol' Corabelle Beasely done turned Shanty into a real white man, after all. Now, what about you, Mel?

MELVIN: Huh?

JOHNNY: Don't you wanna cuss me out an' split too?

MELVIN: I ain't got nothin' against you, Johnny.

JOHNNY: Tha's too damn bad. (*Tosses* MELVIN *some bills.*)

MELVIN: What's this for, Johnny?

JOHNNY: Cain't afford to keep the kitchen open no more. Business all aroun' ain't worth lickin' the lead on a pencil.

MELVIN: Let me stay on, Johnny, please? Shanty's gone. I can tend bar and still do whatever short orders there are. Please, Johnny, don't let me go.

JOHNNY: Dam, Mel. Didn't know you liked it aroun' here that much.

GABE: What about your dancin', Mel? You wanna work in a bar the rest of your life?

MELVIN: I— I quit my dancin', Gabe. . . .

GABE: Why'd you do that?

MELVIN: Well, I—I went to this party Victor gave at his penthouse. A lot of celebrities were there. And Gabe, you just wouldn't have believed it.

GABE: What happened?

MELVIN: I'm ashamed to tell you!

JOHNNY: Aw, go on, Mel. We big boys.

MELVIN: Well, they all got plastered! They were smoking marihuana, too! Even the women! Can you imagine? And then they started taking off their clothes.

JOHNNY: Didn't you know where these turkeys was at before you went?

MELVIN: I don't go to parties much. I don't drink. You know that.

JOHNNY: Did you take you clothes off too?

MELVIN: Are you kidding?

GABE: So you left.

MELVIN: They wouldn't let me leave. So I ran into that bathroom and locked that door. But they jimmied the door open.

JOHNNY: An' then what happened?

MELVIN: They— they held me down and took all my clothes off. It was awful. I said if that's what you gotta do to be a dancer then . . .

JOHNNY: Mel, yo' mama must'a gave you too many hot baths when you was a baby.

MARY LOU (*enters; she carries a paper bag*): Helped my father at the office yesterday. Must have watched him dial the combination to that safe at least twenty times.

(JOHNNY *snatches bag. Locks doors. Comes behind bar.* MARY LOU *follows.*)

Didn't get a chance to hear the tapes. Glanced through some of the other stuff, though. Looks pretty explosive.

JOHNNY: Don't read so good, Mary. What's this stuff say?

MARY LOU: Zerroni admits that he had Joseph Mahoney killed! Maffucci did it. And here it says that he was in on several bribes . . .

JOHNNY: Mary, this is it. This is the stuff I need!

MARY LOU: I—I thought about it a long time. There just wasn't any other solution.

(JOHNNY *stuffs papers back into bag.*)

Johnny, I—I . . . (*She peers at* GABE *and* MELVIN.)

JOHNNY: Go 'head! You kin say anything in front'a them.

MARY LOU: Well, it's not the kind of thing you would say in front of . . .

JOHNNY: Mary, I don't think it's wise for you to be seen aroun' here. I want you to lay low for a while.

MARY LOU: I can't go home, Johnny. Daddy will know I . . .

JOHNNY: Ain't they some girlfri'n you kin stay with?

MARY LOU: I—I suppose so. But I thought we . . .

GABE: What's this all about, John?

MARY LOU: It's to keep Pete Zerroni from forcing Johnny out of business. Don't you know about it?

MELVIN: First time I've heard about it.

GABE: What's your father got to do with it?

MARY LOU: He was Zerroni's lawyer.

GABE: And you stole that material from your father?

MARY LOU: Yes, I stole that material from my father. There was nothing else we could do.

GABE: Why, you stupid, naive little bitch. Don't you know what he wants that stuff for?

MARY LOU: To keep Zerroni from forcing him out of business.

GABE: That's a lie! He wants it so he kin blackmail his way into his own dirty racket.

MARY LOU: That's not true! Tell him, Johnny.

GABE: A black Mafia. That's what he wants. (GABE *laughs.*)

MARY LOU: You're crazy. Johnny, are you going to stand there and . . .

JOHNNY: I gotta right to my own game. Just like they do.

MARY LOU: What?

JOHNNY: My own game!

MARY LOU: Johnny!

GABE: What did you do it for, Mary? For love? Sheee! He hates you, you bitch. Hates everything you stand for. Nice little suffering white girl.

(MARY LOU *slaps* GABE. *He throws her into a chair. She begins to weep.*)

Lemme tell you something. Before he kin lay one hot hand on you, you gonna have to git out there on that street an' hussle your ass off. (GABE *moves to* JOHNNY.) Gimme that file, John.

(JOHNNY *reaches under bar. Comes up with revolver. Levels it at* GABE. MELVIN *gasps. Falls to floor.*)

JOHNNY: I don't wanna kill you, Gabe. This is the one break I been waitin' on. It ain't much but it's gon' have to do.
GABE: You kill me that file ain't gonna do you no good anyway. I'm tellin' you. Gimme that file.

(JOHNNY *finally lowers gun.* GABE *puts bag into briefcase. Starts to move to street doors.* MAFFUCCI *and* JUDGE BOLTON *enter.*)

BOLTON: Get in the car, Mary Lou.
MARY LOU: Daddy, I . . .
BOLTON: I said get in the car!

(MARY LOU *rushes out, followed by* MAFFUCCI.)

You know what I'm here for, Williams.
JOHNNY: Just like that, huh?
BOLTON: Just like that.

(MAFFUCCI *reenters.*)

JOHNNY: I wanna talk to Pete Zerroni.
MAFFUCCI: Pete ain't got nothin' to say to you, Johnny Cake.
BOLTON: Those notes belong to me. Not to Zerroni.
JOHNNY: I ain't budgin' till I see Pete, personal. He's got to come here an' go horse-to-horse with me. Ain't gon' wait too long neither. 'Lection's comin' up. Li'l phone call to the D.A. could make him very happy 'bout his future.

(MAFFUCCI *suddenly pulls gun on* JOHNNY.)

BOLTON: Put that away, you fool!

(MAFFUCCI *returns gun to shoulder holster.*)

JOHNNY: Footch, don't think Pete or the Judge here wanna see me git hit jus' yet.
BOLTON: What is it, Williams? Money? (*Produces an envelope.*)
JOHNNY: You ofays sho' think money's the root'a all evil, don't you, judge?
MAFFUCCI: Let's go, Frank. We're just wastin' time.
BOLTON: Williams, you'd better listen to me and listen good. You're in dangerous trouble. If

you don't hand over that material, I'm not going to be responsible for what happens to you.
JOHNNY: An' I sho' ain't gon' be responsible for what happens to you neither, Judge.

(*Both* JOHNNY *and the* JUDGE *laugh.* BOLTON *starts to exit.*)

Judge?

(BOLTON *turns.* JOHNNY *tosses him* MARY LOU'S *purse.* BOLTON *exits.*)

MAFFUCCI: Johnny Cake?
JOHNNY: What?
MAFFUCCI: Right now, your life ain't worth a plug nickel.
JOHNNY: Footch?

(*Puts his thumbnail under his upper teeth and flicks it at* MAFFUCCI. MAFFUCCI *exits.*)

JOHNNY: Gabe-ree-el. How come you didn't hand over the file?
GABE: I couldn't! When I saw those two bastards together, I just couldn't bring myself to do it!

(GABE *removes bag from briefcase. Hands it to* JOHNNY.)

JOHNNY: Mel, take this over to the drugstore. Get copies made, quick! Move!

(MELVIN *exits quickly.*)

GABE: You know they're gonna git you.
JOHNNY: Gabe, we was got the day we was born! Where you been? Jus' bein' black ain't never been no real reason for livin'.
GABE: If I thought that I'd probably go crazy or commit suicide.

SCENE 3

(*Time: A day later*
Place: The same
Setting: The same
At rise: JOHNNY *is seated on a barstool, checking his gun.* GABE *exits to kitchen.* MACHINE DOG *appears wearing a shabby military uniform.*)

MACHINE DOG: I don't work at the garage no more, brother.
JOHNNY: You jive. You don't know nothin' else.
MACHINE DOG: They's other work to be done. They's other mo' important things to be worked

on and fixed. Like my black brothers. They needs fixin' bad. Tha's when I got to thinkin'a you, Brother Williams.

JOHNNY: Yea, well you can just kick them farts at somebody else.

MACHINE DOG: On yo' feet, mothah fuckah!

(JOHNNY *comes to his feet militarily.* MACHINE DOG *presents a Nazi-like salute.*)

By the powers invested in me by the brothers I hereby deliver to you the edick!

(JOHNNY *and* MACHINE DOG *give each other some skin.* MACHINE DOG *goes back to his salute.*)

Brother Williams. The brothers have jus' sennunced an' condemned you to death. Now, repeat after me. I have been chosen to be the nex' brother to live on in the hearts an' min's'a the enemy host.

JOHNNY: I have been chosen to be the nex' brother to live on in the hearts an' min's'a the enemy host.

MACHINE DOG: My duty will be to ha'nt they cripple an' sore min's.

JOHNNY: My duty will be to haunt they cripple an' sore min's.

MACHINE DOG: I will cling to the innermos' closets'a they brains an' agonize them.

JOHNNY: I will cling to the innermos' closets'a they brains an' agonize them.

MACHINE DOG (*breaks his salute and gives an aside*): Maniacks though they is already! (*He goes back into his salute.*) The more they will try to cas' me out, the mo' they torment will be.

JOHNNY: The more they will try to cast me out, the more they torment will be!

MACHINE DOG: Se la an' ayman! (MACHINE DOG *shakes* JOHNNY's *hand.*) You will have plen'y'a he'p, Brother Williams. All them brothers that went before you an' all them tha's comin' after you.

JOHNNY: I gladly accept the condemnashun, Gen'ral Sheen. Tell the brothers I won't let 'em down. Tell 'em I look forward to meetin' 'em all in par'dise.

MACHINE DOG: Se la! An' ayman!

(*They salute each other.*)

JOHNNY: Se la an' ay-man!

(MACHINE DOG *goes into kitchen as* JUDGE BOLTON *and two plainclothesmen*, CAPPALETTI *and* HARRY, *enter.*)

BOLTON: This is the man, Al!

(CAPPALETTI *flashes his badge.*)

CAPPALETTI: Cappaletti. Vice squad.

JOHNNY: Big deal!

CAPPALETTI: Judge Bolton, here. His daughter was picked up this afternoon.

JOHNNY: So what?

CAPPALETTI: She tried to solicit this officer here.

JOHNNY: What's that got to do with me?

CAPPALETTI: Said she was workin' for you.

JOHNNY: Tha's a lie. Tha's a goddam lie. Lemme hear say that to my face.

CAPPALETTI: Plenty of time for that.

JOHNNY: What the hell you tryin' to pull, Bolton?

CAPPALETTI: Now, why would the Judge wanna pull anything on you, Johnny?

JOHNNY: He—he don't want his daughter seein' me. 'Cause I'm a Nigger. I'll lay odds she don't know nothin' about this.

CAPPALETTI: Go get Miss Bolton, Harry.

(HARRY *moves to street doors.*)

JOHNNY: Hurry, Harry!

(HARRY *grins. Exits.*)

CAPPALETTI: By the way. Ain't you the guy this girl killed herself about a few days ago? She was a call girl?

JOHNNY: Tell you like I tole them other fuzzys. What she did was her own business.

CAPPALETTI: Just the same you kin see how we kin believe Miss Bolton's story.

(HARRY *leads* MARY LOU *into bar.* CAPPALETTI *seats her.*)

Now, Miss Bolton. We'll ask you again. Who did you say you was workin' for when you was picked up?

MARY LOU: I—I . . .

CAPPALETTI: Speak up, Miss Bolton. We can't hear you.

MARY LOU: Daddy, I . . .

BOLTON: All you have to do is identify him. Is he the man?

(CAPPALETTI *puts his hand on* MARY LOU's *head.*)

Take your hands off her!

(HARRY *laughs.*)

Mary Lou! Is he or isn't he?

MARY LOU (*forces herself to face* JOHNNY): Yes! This is the man! Johnny Williams! I was working for him!

(MARY LOU *rushes from bar followed by* HARRY.)

JOHNNY: Dirty lyin' bitch.

BOLTON: Now, see here, Williams!

CAPPALETTI: You're gonna have to come with me, Johnny.

JOHNNY: What is this, a pinch? You gonna book me? I'm gonna call my lawyer!

CAPPALETTI: Shut up! You're not callin' nobody right now. Let's go.

BOLTON: Just a minute, Al. I want a few words with him before you take him down.

CAPPALETTI: Okay, Frank, but make it snappy.

BOLTON: Williams, I've worked too long and too hard to get where I am. I'm giving you one last chance to give back those notes and tape. If you don't, it's on the bottom of the woodpile for you. Even if I have to sacrifice my own daughter to do it. I want that file.

JOHNNY: Okay, Judge. Okay. You win.

(JOHNNY *goes behind bar. Brings out paper bag.* JUDGE *checks it. Nods to* CAPPALETTI *and exits.*)

CAPPALETTI: All right, Johnny. All of a sudden the Judge wants me to forget the whole thing. Lucky we didn't get you down to the precinct. Would have busted you up on general principles.

(CAPPALETTI *exits. Quickly* JOHNNY *puts his revolver into his back pocket. Goes behind the bar.*)

JOHNNY: Better split, Gabe. While the gittin's good.

GABE: Don't think so, John. I'm gonna stick aroun'.

JOHNNY: Suit yo'self!

(*Doors open.* JOHNNY *goes for his gun.* SWEETS CRANE *enters. He is practically in tatters. He carries a shopping bag. Goes to table and begins to take out various articles of food. He coughs and rubs his hands together.*)

SWEETS: I got fried chicken! Ham! Candied yams! Got me some hot chit'lin's! Blackeyed peas an' rice! Cornbread! Mustard greens an' macaroni salit! (*Coughs.*) Top ev'thing off I got me'a thermos full'a—full'a—lemme see now. How'd my gran'daddy used to call it? Chassy San'burg coffee! (*Laughs.*) An' a big chunk'a pee-kan pie. Y'all fellas is welcomed to join me.

JOHNNY: Wouldn't touch it if it was blessed by the pope!

SWEETS: Well, now tha's a dam shame. 'Member when I couldn't pull you away from my cookin'.

GABE: You don't mind if I join him, do you, John?

JOHNNY: Be my guest.

SWEETS: He'p yo'se'f, young fella. They's plen'y here. Have some'a these here chit'lin's!

GABE: Ain't never had none before.

SWEETS: Then let this be the day you start.

(GABE *takes a sniff.*)

Go 'head! Go 'head! You don't eat the smell.

GABE: Lemme ask you sump'm, Sweets.

SWEETS: Hope I kin answer it.

GABE: How come you took my watch an' wallet?

SWEETS: Son, all my life I been one kind'a thief or 'nother. It's jus' in me. 'Course I don't have to steal. But I steals for the pure enjoyment of it. Jus' the other day I stole a rat'la from a baby. (*Laughs.*) When you steals for fun it don't matter who you steals from! (*Goes into his pocket. Comes up with* GABE's *watch and wallet.*)

GABE: It's all here!

SWEETS: 'Co'se it is! Gave the baby back his rat'la too.

JOHNNY: You ain't gon' make the white man's heaven this way.

SWEETS: The Lawd died 'tween two thieves.

MAFFUCCI (*enters with* LOUIE): Wouldn't listen to me, would you, Johnny Cake?

JOHNNY: What Pete say? Give a jig a half'a chance . . .

SWEETS: This the fella work for big fat Pete, Sonny Boy?

MAFFUCCI: What's it to ya, Pops? You an' this other joker better get the hell out'a here before you catch cold.

SWEETS: I ain't never got up from a meal in my life 'fore I was finished . . .

MAFFUCCI: Look, Pops! Don't make me have to . . . (*Glances at food.*) What's that? Macaroni salad you got there?

SWEETS: Matter fack it is!

MAFFUCCI (*dips into it*): Ummm! Not bad. Who made it?

SWEETS: I did.

MAFFUCCI: No kiddin'? Knew it didn't taste like dela-ga-tes. Mama used to make macaroni salad.

SWEETS: Have'a piece'a my fried chicken to go with it.

JOHNNY: If Zerroni could see you now, Footch.

MAFFUCCI: How's that, Johnny Cake?

JOHNNY: Tha's the great Sweets Crane you eatin' with.

MAFFUCCI: Pops, here? He's Sweets Crane?

SWEETS: What's lef' of me.

MAFFUCCI: You'd'a made out better as a cook, Pops. Mama couldn't beat that macaroni salad!

SWEETS (*produces* MAFFUCCI's *watch*): I think this b'longs to you.

MAFFUCCI: My watch! I been lookin' all over for it. Pops, you copped my watch? (*Laughs.*) How come you're givin' it back? This watch is worth a lotta bread.

SWEETS: Figger you need it wors'n I do.

MAFFUCCI: Say, Johnny Cake, you sure Pops here is Sweets Crane?

JOHNNY: You don't know how much I wish he wasn't.

MAFFUCCI: Too bad Johnny didn't learn a lesson after what happened to you, Pops. Gotta give him credit though. Takes a lotta balls to try to put the bleed on Pete Zerroni.

SWEETS: You was tryin' to blackmail ol' big fat Pete, Sonny Boy?

JOHNNY: What the hell. Couldn't pull it off. Don't matter much now.

MAFFUCCI: That's where you're wrong, Johnny Cake. Matters a helluva lot to me. Pete now, he's willin' to forget the whole thing. Says the trick is not to take you jigs too serious. I can't do nothin' like that, Johnny. Don't look good on my record.

JOHNNY: What you gonna do about it, Footch?

(MAFFUCCI *quickly pulls his gun. Levels it at* JOHNNY. *Backs to street doors. Locks them. Pulls shades. Takes a large sign from his pocket. It reads,* "CLOSED." *He puts it on the bar in front of* JOHNNY.)

The sign in both hands, Johnny Cake.

(JOHNNY *slowly picks up sign.*)

Pops, you an' that other joker stay put!

(MAFFUCCI *nods to* LOUIE *who moves behind* SWEETS *and* GABE. JOHNNY *starts to tear sign.*)

Ah-ah! I want you to lick that sign an' paste it right up there on the door. Start lickin', Johnny Cake!

(JOHNNY *begins to wet sign with his tongue.*)

That's it! Wet it up a little more! That's enough! Now start walkin' real careful like!

(JOHNNY *moves to street door with sign.*)

Now, paste it up there!

(JOHNNY *does so.*)

Now, back up! Real slow!

(JOHNNY *backs up.* MAFFUCCI *seats* JOHNNY *on a barstool.*)

SWEETS: You don't have to do that, Sonny Boy. (*Goes to the door with knife he has been eating with.*) You don't have to do nothin' like that. (*He pulls the sign from the window and tears it up.*)

MAFFUCCI: What are you doin', Pops? Look, if you don't want hi-call-it to get hit . . .

JOHNNY: Keep out'a this, Sweets. This is my game.

SWEETS: Not any more, it ain't. You don't have to do nothin' like that. (*Advances to* MAFFUCCI.)

MAFFUCCI: What'a ya, crazy, Pops? Put that ax away.

JOHNNY: Lay out of it, Sweets. Lay out of it, I said!

MAFFUCCI: I'm warnin' you, Pops! Take another step an' . . .

(SWEETS *lunges at* MAFFUCCI *as* MAFFUCCI *fires. Knife penetrates* MAFFUCCI's *heart.* JOHNNY *kills* LOUIE. *Whirls and fires three shots into* MAFFUCCI. *Rushes to* SWEETS.)

JOHNNY: Goddamit, Sweets! I tole you I could handle it!

GABE: I'll call a doctor!

SWEETS: Fuck a doctor! Cain't you see I'm dead? (*Coughs. Winces in pain.*) Lissen to me, Sonny Boy! You—you gotta promise me one thing . . .

JOHNNY: What is it, Sweets?

SWEETS: The—the will! It's here in—in my pocket.

(JOHNNY *finds will.*)

If—if you git out'a this. Promise you'll git straightened out. (*He grabs* JOHNNY's *arm.*) Promise!

JOHNNY: I—I promise.

SWEETS: Swear!

JOHNNY: Yeah! Yeah! I swear, Sweets!

SWEETS: Git—git rid'a the—the Ch-Cholly fever—(SWEETS *goes limp.*)

GABE: He did it for you, John . . .

JOHNNY: Look, Gabe. We gotta git our story together. When the fuzz gits here we gotta have us a story.

GABE: We tell 'em the truth, John . . .

JOHNNY: What you say?

GABE: We tell the police the truth!

JOHNNY: Shit. The truth is I'm alive! I got a copy'a that file an' Sweets' will.

GABE: But you tole Sweets you was gonna throw them ideas out'a your head.

JOHNNY: Come on, man, you didn't think I meant that shit, did you?

GABE: With his last dyin' breath, you gave that ol' man your word. You swore.

JOHNNY: What good is anybody's word to that ol' bastard? He's dead an' cain't remember.

GABE: You are mad.

JOHNNY: I'm goin' ahead with my plans. (*He holds up will.*) An' he's still gon' help me do it.

GABE: Naw, naw! That ain't the way it's s'pose to be!

JOHNNY: You in this as deep as I am. It's our word ag'inst these dead turkeys. You gave me back that file, remember?

GABE: That's where I got off. I ain't got no stomach for this personal war you got ag'inst the white man.

JOHNNY: It's your war too, Nigger. Why can't you see that? You wanna go on believin' in the lie? We at war, Gabe! Black ag'inst white.

GABE: You're wrong, John. You're so god-dam wrong.

(JOHNNY *picks up gun. Puts it into* GABE's *hand.*)

JOHNNY: Take this gun in yo' han'. Feel that col' hard steel. Bet you ain't never held a heater in yo' han' like that in yo' life. Well, you gon' have to, Gabe. They gon' make you do it. 'Cause we at war, Gabe. Black ag'inst white.

GABE: I—I don't wanna—kill—you . . .

JOHNNY: You ain't got the guts! You wanna believe you kin sell papers an' become President! You're a coward, Gabe! A lousy, yellow, screamin' faggot coward!

(*Enraged,* GABE *fires at* JOHNNY. JOHNNY *tumbles backward and then forward into* GABE's *arms.* GABE *eases* JOHNNY *to the floor.* JOHNNY *goes limp.* MACHINE DOG *enters.*)

GABE (*startled*): Who're you? Where did you come from?

MACHINE DOG: The Brothers call me Machine Dog! It is written: "He that slays a true brother, he hisse'f shall howsomever be perished!"

GABE: He made me kill him! He . . .

(*During* MACHINE DOG's *speech,* GABE *takes gun. Wipes it off. Places it in* JOHNNY's *hand. Covers* JOHNNY *with tablecloth. Exits.*)

MACHINE DOG: Hush yo' lyin', trait-ious tongue! Ver'ly, ver'ly, I says into you! You has kilt all them li'l innusunt cherbs'a the ghetto! Them li'l rams who been hatin' 'thorty eb'm from the cradle! All them holy de-lin-cunts who been the true creators'a unsolved thef's an' killin's! You has slewn an' slaughtered them young goateed billygoats who been dedcated to that sanctified an' precious art'a lootin' the destruction'a private public poverty! You has hung an' lynched the black angels'a color who went by that high code'a rooftops an' been baptized in the stink of urine scented hallways! You has burnt an' melted down a million switchblade knives an' razors an' broke preshus bottles'a communion upon the empty white-paved streets'a the enemy host! An' lef' the brothers thirsty an' col' to bang the doors'a the guilty white Samaritan! You has crushed the very life fum black an' profane souls! Hordes'a un-re-gen-rants! An' smashed the spirit an' holy ghost fum rollers an' dancers who founded they faith on black, human sufferin'! Burnt an' tortured souls who knew th'ough the power of love that they trials an' trib'lashuns could not be leg'slated away by no co't, no congruss, not eb'm God Hisse'f! You has scortched an' scalded them black Moheekans an' stuffed them in the very stoves they cooked on! Se la! An' ay-man!

EPILOGUE

(GABE *enters dressed as a woman in mourning. A black shawl is draped over his head.*)

GABE: Like my costume? You like it? You don't like it! I know what I am by what I see in your faces. You are my mirrors. But unlike a metallic reflection, you will not hold my image for very long. Your capacity for attention is very short. Therefore, I must try to provoke you. Provoke your attention. Change my part over and over again. I am rehearsing at the moment. For tomorrow, I will go out amongst you, "The Black Lady in Mourning." I will weep, I will wail, and I will mourn. But my cries will not be heard. No one will wipe away my bitter tears. My black anguish will fall upon deaf ears. I will mourn a passing! Yes. The passing and the ending of a people dying. Of a people dying into that new life. A people whose identity could

only be measured by the struggle, the dehuma- the death of a people dying. Of a people dying
nization, the degradation they suffered. Or into that new life.
allowed themselves to suffer perhaps. I will
mourn the ending of those years. I will mourn

THE END

David Rabe: *The Basic Training of Pavlo Hummel* (1971)

David Rabe has been considered one of America's most promising young playwrights since his first productions with Joseph Papp's New York Shakespeare Festival Theatre—*Pavlo Hummel* and *Sticks and Bones* (1971). Both plays were written in 1968–69 while Rabe was at Villanova University earning a master's degree. Both were influenced by Rabe's own experiences in Vietnam. Drafted in 1965, he could have qualified for a deferment yet he chose to serve in the war. His reasons had to do with the war itself, and his personal commitment to fight. His own views have remained complex. In fact, Papp has pointed out that Rabe's plays, as violent and terrifying as they sometimes are, spoke to Americans of all sorts; they did not polarize those who supported the war against those who condemned it. Rabe's experiences in Vietnam were not involved in combat—most of his time was spent in hospitals, where he performed a wide variety of duties.

Rabe was born in 1940 in Dubuque, Iowa, where his father was a high school history teacher. Originally, Rabe wanted to be a professional football player, but gave up the idea and went to college in Dubuque, then to Villanova for a degree in theater. After dropping out in 1965, he went into the service.

Like many returning veterans, Rabe came home to find that no one seemed to understand the nature of the war. There were those who felt the Americans were cutthroat murderers and the Vietcong were innocent victims. Others saw the Vietcong as vicious killers and the Americans as the innocents. Somehow, no one could perceive the complexities of the situation in a way that made sense. Rabe was also struck by the deep-seated indifference of people he saw. Middle-class families maintained their striving for material success: bigger cars, fancier houses, new clothes—all without examining the world in which they lived. The Vietnam war seemed to have little or no meaning for them. *Sticks and Bones* is about such a family. It examines the shabbiness of their values and their willingness to sacrifice their own flesh and blood rather than wake up to the truth about their own nature.

The Basic Training of Pavlo Hummel is fascinating on many grounds. The play does not take sides on the question of whether or not the war should have been fought; it simply takes the war for granted. It is there; it must be dealt with. Pavlo Hummel is no typical, idealistic youngster going off to do battle. The question of innocence is certainly significant in the play, however, and the concept of basic training is used to educate Hummel, to help him become the kind of man he thinks he wants to be. Hummel is not a figure who can be taken symbolically or allegorically and he is definitely not modeled after Rabe himself. Making Hummel a product of Manhattan may be one way of declaring that. He is not modeled after any ideal soldier or average American boy—Hummel is weird. We are told that repeatedly in the play. He speaks a strange language that other soldiers do not like; he makes them feel uneasy. He is somewhat criminal in his behavior, bragging about a nonexistent uncle who "died" in San Quentin, boasting over the cars he's stolen. He has within him the desire to learn what he must know to succeed as a soldier and get out of basic training—even if it means he has to go off to combat and risk dying. He takes his beatings, watches the other men, and tries to learn what is entailed in earning self-respect. When he goes home after his basic training, he finds that no one understands him. He's changed too much; his home now is the Army.

Much of the remainder of the second act is spent in a brothel, where Hummel eventually dies. The language of the play throughout is the rough and brutal language of soldiers. The women in the brothel have learned to adapt, and their portrayal shows that they cannot be treated symbolically any more than Hummel or any of the soldiers can be. The play ultimately portrays individuals in an individual war. And as it does, it reveals the particular individual horrors of the entire experience. Considering this play in contrast with Bronson Howard's *Shenandoah* makes us realize the immense gap between their two visions of the world, much less between their idea of war. Less than one hundred years separate these plays. Both have romantic interests close to their core, but the differences between those interests can only make us gasp. The disparity in the portrayal of war—particularly in terms of duty, glory, valor, courage, and heroism—is so great that the plays seem products of cultures light years apart. By comparison, Bronson Howard's world appears as if it were constructed of *papier-mâché*. Ironically, Howard's play is told to us in a technique we must describe as realistic and natural, while Rabe's play uses fantasy episodes, flashback, and the notably unrealistic detail of Hummel and the mythic Ardell reviewing his life after it has been led. Yet, instead of feeling as if Howard's play "tells it as it is," we realize that Rabe's, for all his indulgence in expressionistic devices, seems closer to the truth. The contrast between these plays, and the changes in American culture that they clearly signal, should remind us of the theme of Royall Tyler's play, a theme basic to American culture: the contrast between European cunning and American innocence.

Rabe's later plays have been interesting, but not as successful as *Pavlo Hummel* or *Sticks and Bones. The Orphan* (1973) and *In the Boom Boom Room* (1973) closed after disappointing reviews and short runs. *Streamers*, 1976, is his most recent play.

Selected Readings

Asahina, Robert. "The Basic Training of American Playwrights: Theatre and the Vietnam War." *Theatre.* 9, pp. 30–37.
Rabe, David. *In the Boom Boom Room.* New York: Knopf, 1975.
———. *Streamers.* New York: Knopf, 1977.

The Basic Training of Pavlo Hummel

David Rabe

CHARACTERS

PAVLO HUMMEL	PIERCE
YEN	HENDRIX
ARDELL	MICKEY
FIRST SERGEANT TOWER	MRS. HUMMEL
CAPTAIN SAUNDERS	CORPORAL JONES
CORPORAL FERRARA	SERGEANT BRISBEY
PARKER	MAMASAN
BURNS	SERGEANT WALL
RYAN	PARHAM
HALL	LINH
GRENNEL	ZUNG
HINKLE	FARMER
KRESS	

ACT I

(Time and place: The United States Army—1965 –1967. A radio is playing American pop music in the darkness; and the lights rise immediately. PAVLO *is dressed in army fatigues. He wears sunglasses, though by the lighting it is clearly close to dusk. The music is not loud and* PAVLO *moves slightly, influenced by its rhythm. The wall that indicates the shanty is tin. Perhaps Budweiser beer labels mark a section of it. The wall is far upstage. It has a shelf of beer bottles, cans. Before it is a large barrel, military green; it is being used as a table. Beside it is a crate, also military green. Using it as a chair, a drunken G.I. sits slumped over the top of the barrel.* YEN, *a Vietnamese girl, moves about, trying to make some contact with* PAVLO. MAMASAN, *an older Vietnamese woman dressed in peasant garb, stands in the background, watching closely.* YEN, *pronounced "Ing," wears purple silk pajamas, slacks and pullover top. She sort of pursues* PAVLO, *trying to get him to take a drink of beer, trying to calm him down.)*

PAVLO *(dealing with everyone as he speaks)*: Did I do it to him? The triple-Hummel. *(A sort of shudder runs through his shoulders: he punches.)* A little shuffle and then a triple boom-boom-boom. Ain't I bad, man. Gonna eat up Cleveland. Gonna piss on Chicago. *(Banging with his palms on the side of the barrel.)*

YEN: Creezy, creezy.

PAVLO: Dinky dow!

SOLDIER *(disturbed by banging, looking up, but deeply drunk)*: Les . . . go . . . home . . .

YEN: Pavlo boucoup love. Sleep me all time. . . .

PAVLO: Did I ever tell you, whore? Thirteen months a my life ago—you listenin' to me, Stoner? *(Again, banging on the barrel.)* I had this girl Joanna Sorrentino. Little bit a guinea-woppin' bitch, and she was my girl. I lived with my mother and we had a cat, you know, so we had a kitty box, which is a place for the cat to shit. Yeh.

YEN: Talk "shit." I can talk "shit". Numba ten talk. *(Touching him.)*

618

PAVLO: Ohhhh, damn that Sorrentino, what she couldn't be taught. And that's what I'd like to do—look her up—"Your face, Sorrentino, I don't like your ugly face!" Did I ever tell you about my ole lady, Stoner? Me mudda. Did I ever speak her name?

YEN: Mudda you, huh, Pavlo? Very nice.

PAVLO: And now I'm the guy who's been with the Aussies. I HAD TEA WITH 'em. IT WAS ME THEY CALLED TO—"HUMMEL, MEDIC! (*With a fairly good Australian accent.*) The dirty little blighters blew me bloody arm off." (*Jumping about, animated.*) You see what she did, she wrote Joanna a letter. My ole lady wrote Joanna a letter callin' her a dirty little slut who should stay away from her good little son. Poor Joanna, a slut. Jesus Christ, no way. And when I found out, see, I wailed, I cried, baby, big tears, I screamed and threw kitty litter and cat shit all up in the air, screamin' over and over, "Happy Birthday, Happy Birthday," I don't know why except it seemed like I wasn't ever gonna get old. You listenin' to me, Fuckface? (*Banging the barrel. Maybe moving close to the drunken G.I., lifting his head to speak directly to him. And there is joy in this.*) She called that sweet little church-goin' girl a whore. To be seen by her now, oh, she would shit her jeans to see me now, up tight with this little odd-lookin' whore, feelin' (*Maybe moving to* YEN *now, grabbing her.*) good, and tall, ready to bed down. (*The grenade hits with a loud clump, having been thrown by a hand that merely flashed between curtains and everyone looks without moving.*) GREEEEENADE!

(*And by now* PAVLO *has moved. He has the grenade in his hand, and there comes the explosion, loud, extremely loud, and the lights go black, go red, or blue, the girl screams, the bodies fly. And a soldier,* ARDELL, *a black man in a uniform that is strangely unreal, perhaps gray in color, or perhaps khaki, but with black ribbons and medals. He wears sunglasses, bloused boots. He appears distantly, far upstage, at the center. A body detail is moving in the side at the instant he speaks, two men carrying a stretcher. They wear fatigues, helmets.*)

ARDELL: You want me, Pavlo? You callin'? Don't I hear you? Yeh, yeh, that the way it happen sometimes. Everybody hit, everybody hurtin', but the radio ain't been touched, the dog didn't feel a thing; the engine's good as new but all the people dead and the chassis a wreck, man. (*The stretchermen have come in to remove the body of the dead* G.I. *The body of the girl and of* MAMASAN *have vanished in the explosion. The radio has conti-*

nued to play until the point where ARDELL, *speaking, has turned it off.*) Yeh, yeh, some mean motherfucker, you don't even see, blow you away. Don't I hear you callin'? (*Pivoting, moving swiftly down center stage.*) Get off it. Bounce on up here. (*And* PAVLO, *leaps to his feet, runs to join* ARDELL.)

PAVLO: Pfc Pavlo Hummel, RA-74-313-226

ARDELL: We gonna get you your shit straight. No need to call me Sir.

PAVLO: Ardell . . .?

ARDELL: That's right. Now what's your unit. Now shout it out!

PAVLO: Second of the Sixteenth; First Division. BIG RED ONE.

ARDELL: Company.

PAVLO: Echo.

ARDELL: C.O.?

PAVLO: My company commander is Captain M.W. Henderson. My battalion commander is Lieutenant Colonel Roy J.S. Tully.

ARDELL: Platoon?

PAVLO: Third.

ARDELL: Squad.

PAVLO: Third.

ARDELL: Squad and platoon leaders.

PAVLO: My platoon leader is 1ST Lieutenant David R. Barnes; my squad leader is Staff Sergeant Peter T. Collins.

ARDELL: You got family?

PAVLO: No.

ARDELL: You lyin', Boy.

PAVLO: One mother; one half brother.

ARDELL: All right.

PAVLO: Yes.

ARDELL: Soldier, what you think a the war?

PAVLO: It's being fought.

ARDELL: Ain't no doubt about that.

PAVLO: No.

ARDELL: You kill anybody?

PAVLO: Yes.

ARDELL: Like it?

PAVLO: Yes.

ARDELL: Have nightmares?

PAVLO: Pardon.

ARDELL: What we talkin' about, Boy?

PAVLO: No.

ARDELL: How tall you? you lyin' motherfucker.

PAVLO: Five-ten.

ARDELL: Eyes.

PAVLO: Green.

ARDELL: Hair.

PAVLO: Red.

ARDELL: Weight.

PAVLO: 152.

ARDELL: What you get hit with?

PAVLO: Hand grenade. Fragmentation-type.

ARDELL: Where about it get you?

PAVLO (*touching himself*): Here. And here. Mostly in the abdominal and groin areas.

ARDELL: Who you talkin' to? Don't you talk that shit to me, man. Abdominal and groin areas, that shit. It hit you in the stomach, man, like a ten-ton truck and it hit you in the balls, blew 'em away. Am I lyin'?

PAVLO (*able to grin; glad to grin*): No, man.

ARDELL: Hurt you bad.

PAVLO: Killed me.

ARDELL: That right. Made you dead. You dead, man; how you feel about that?

PAVLO: Well . . .

ARDELL: DON'T YOU KNOW? I THINK YOU KNOW! I think it piss you off. I think you lyin' you say it don't. Make you wanna scream.

PAVLO: Yes.

ARDELL: You had that thing in your hand, didn't you? What was you thinkin' on, you had that thing in your hand?

PAVLO: About throwin' it. About a man I saw when I was eight years old who came through the neighborhood with a softball team called the Demons and he could do anything with a softball underhand that most big leaguers can do with a hardball overhand. He was fantastic.

ARDELL: That all?

PAVLO: Yes.

ARDELL: You ain't lyin'.

PAVLO: No. (*A whistle and figures move behind* PAVLO *and* ARDELL, *a large group of men in fatigues without markings other than their name tags and U.S. Army. There are a good number of them. And on a high drill instructor's tower, dimly lit at the moment, is a large Negro sergeant. A captain observes from the distance. A corporal prowls among them, checking buttons, etc.*) Who're they?

ARDELL: Man, don't you jive me. You know who they are. That Fort Gordon, man. They Echo Company, 8th Battalion, Third Training Regiment. They basic training, baby.

PAVLO (*removing Pfc stripes and 1st Division patch*): Am I . . . really . . . dead . . .?

ARDELL: Damn near, man; real soon. Comin' on. Eight more weeks. Got wings as big as streets. Got large, large wings.

PAVLO: It happened . . . to me . . .

ARDELL: Whatever you say, Pavlo.

PAVLO: Sure. That grenade come flyin', I caught it, held it.

ARDELL: New York, huh?

PAVLO: Manhattan. 231 East 45th.

ARDELL: Okay. Now we know who we talkin' about. Somebody say "Pavlo Hummel," we know who they mean.

SGT. TOWER: GEN'LMEN! (*As the men snap to parade rest and* PAVLO, *startled, runs to find his place among them.*) You all lookin' up here and can you see me? Can you see me well? Can you hear and comprehend my words? Can you see what is written here? Over my right tit-tee, can you read it? Tower. My name. And I am bigger than my name. And can you see what is sewn here upon the muscle of my arm? Can you see it? ANSWER!

THE MEN: No. (*The men all stand in ranks below the tower.*)

SGT. TOWER: No, what? WHAT?

THE MEN: NO, SERGEANT.

SGT. TOWER: It is also my name. It is my first name. SERGEANT. That who I am. I you Field First. And you gonna see a lot a me. You gonna see so much a me, let me tell you, you gonna think I you mother, father, sisters, brothers, aunts, uncles, nephews, nieces, and children—if you got 'em—all rolled into one big black man. Yeh, Gen'lmen. And you gonna become me. You gonna learn to stand tall and be proud and you gonna run as far and shoot as good. Or else you gonna be ashamed; I am one old man and you can't outdo no thirty-eight-year-old man, you ashamed. AM I GONNA MAKE YOU ASHAMED? WHAT DO YOU SAY?

THE MEN: Yes, Sergeant!

SGT. TOWER: NO! NO, GEN'LMEN. No, I am not gonna make you ashamed. SERGEANT, YOU ARE NOT GONNA MAKE US ASHAMED.

THE MEN: SERGEANT, YOU ARE NOT GONNA MAKE US ASHAMED.

SGT. TOWER: WE ARE GONNA DO EVERYTHING YOU CAN DO AND DO YOU ONE BETTER!

THE MEN: WE ARE GONNA DO EVERYTHING YOU CAN DO AND DO YOU ONE BETTER!

SGT. TOWER: YOU A BUNCH A LIARS. YOU A BUNCH A FOOLS! Now you listen up; you listen to me. No one does me one better. And especially no people like you. Don't you know what you are? TRAINEES! And there ain't nothin' lower on this earth except for one thing and we all know what that is, do we not, Gen'lman?

THE MEN: Yes . . . , Sergeant!

SGT. TOWER: And what is that? (*Pause.*) You told me you knew! Did you lie to me? Oh, no, nooo, I can't believe that; please, please, don't lie. Gen'lmen, did you lie?

THE MEN: Yes, Sergeant.

SGT. TOWER: No, no, please. If there something you don't know, you tell me. If I ask you something and you do not know the answer, let me know. Civilians. That the answer to my question. The only creatures in this world lower than trainees is civilians, and we hate them all. All. (*Quick pause.*) And now . . . and finally . . . and most important, do you see what is written here? Over my heart; over my left tit-tee, do you see? U.S. ARMY. Which is where I live. Which is where we all live. Can you, Gen'lmen, can you tell me you first name now, do you know it? (*Quick pause.*) Don't you know? I think you do, yes, I do, but you just too shy to say it. Like little girls watchin' that thing just get bigger and bigger for the first time, you shy. And what did I tell you to do when you don't know the answer I have asked?

THE MEN: What is our first name?

SGT. TOWER: You! . . . You there! (*Suddenly pointing into the ranks.*) You! Ugly! Yeah, you. That right. You ugly. Ain't you. You TAKE ONE BIG STEP FORWARD. (*And it is PAVLO stepping forward.*) I think I saw that you were not in harmony with the rest of these men. I think I saw that you were looking about at the air like some kinda fool and that malingering, Trainee, and that intol'able. So you drop, you hear me. You drop down on you ugly little hands and knees and lift up you butt and knees from off that beautiful Georgia clay and you give me TEN and that's pushups of which I am speaking. (*PAVLO begins the pushups; TOWER goes back to the men.*) NOW YOU ARE TRAINEES, ALL YOU PEOPLE, AND YOU LISTEN UP. I ask you WHAT IS YOUR FIRST NAMES. YOU TELL ME "TRAINEE"!

THE MEN: TRAINEE!

SGT. TOWER: TRAINEE, SERGEANT!

THE MEN: TRAINEE, SERGE—

SGT. TOWER: I CAN'T HEAR YOU!

THE MEN: *TRAINEE, SERGEANT!*

SGT. TOWER: AND WHAT IS YOUR LAST NAMES? YOU OWN LAST FUCKING NAMES?

THE MEN: (A CHORUS OF AMERICAN NAMES)

SGT. TOWER: AND YOU LIVE IN THE ARMY OF THE UNITED STATES OF AMERICA.

THE MEN: AND WE LIVE IN THE ARMY OF THE UNITED STATES OF AMERICA.

SGT. TOWER: WITH BALLS BETWEEN YOUR LEGS! YOU HAVE BALLS! NO SLITS! BUT BALLS, AND YOU—(*Having risen,* PAVLO *is getting back into ranks.*)

THE MEN: AND WE HAVE BALLS BETWEEN OUR LEGS! NO SLITS, BUT BALLS!

SGT. TOWER (*suddenly back to* PAVLO): Ugly! Now who told you to stand? Who you think you are, you standin', nobody tole you to stand. You drop. You drop, you hear me. (*And* PAVLO *goes back into the pushup position.*)

SGT. TOWER: What your name, Boy?

PAVLO: Yes, sir.

SGT. TOWER: Your name, boy!

PAVLO: Trainee Hummel, sir!

SGT. TOWER: Sergeant.

PAVLO: Yes, sir.

SGT. TOWER: *Sergeant. I AM A SERGEANT!*

PAVLO: SERGEANT! YOU ARE A SERGEANT!

SGT. TOWER: All right. That nice; all right, only in the future, you doin' pushups, I want you countin' and that countin' so loud it scare me so I think there some kinda terrible, terrible man comin' to get me, am I understood?

PAVLO: Yes, Sergeant.

SGT. TOWER: I can't hear you!

PAVLO: Yes, Sergeant! Yes, Sergeant!

SGT. TOWER: All right! You get up and fall back where you was. Gen'lmen. You are gonna fall out. By platoon. Which is how you gonna be doin' most everything from now on—by platoon and by the numbers—includin' takin' a shit. Somebody say to you, ONE, you down; TWO, you doin' it; THREE, you wipin' and you ain't finished, you cuttin' it off. I CAN'T HEAR YOU!

THE MEN: YES, SERGEANT.

SGT. TOWER: I say to you SQUAT, and you all hunkered down and got nothin' to say to anybody but HOW MUCH? and WHAT COLOR, SERGEANT?

THE MEN: Yes, Sergeant.

SGT. TOWER: You good people. You a good group. Now I gonna call you to attention and you gonna snap-to, that's heels on a line or as near it as the conformation of your body permit; head up, chin in, knees not locked; you relaxed. Am I understood?

THE MEN: Yes—

SGT. TOWER: AM I UNDERSTOOD GOD-DAMNIT, OR DO YOU WANT TO ALL DROP FOR TWENTY OR—

THE MEN: YES, SERGEANT! YES, SERGEANT!

ARDELL: PAVLO, MY MAN, YOU ON YOUR WAY.

CORPORAL: PLATOOOON! PLATOOOON!

SGT. TOWER: I GONNA DO SOME SINGIN', GEN'LMEN, I WANT IT COMIN' BACK TO ME LIKE WE IN GRAND CANYON—

CORPORAL: TEN-HUT!

ARDELL: DO IT, GET IT!

SQUAD LEADERS: RIGHT FACE!

SGT. TOWER: —AND YOU MY MOTHERFUCKIN' ECHO!

CORPORAL: FORWARD HARCH!

SGT. TOWER: LIFT YOUR HEAD AND LIFT IT HIGH!

THE MEN: —LIFT YOUR HEAD AND LIFT IT HIGH—

SGT. TOWER: ECHO COMPANY PASSIN' BY!

THE MEN: ECHO COMPANY PASSIN' BY!

ARDELL (and the men are going off in groups during this): MOTHER, MOTHER, WHAT'D I DO?

THE MEN: MOTHER, MOTHER, WHAT'D I DO?

ARDELL: THIS ARMY TREATIN' ME WORSE THAN YOU!

THE MEN: THIS ARMY TREATIN' ME WORSE THAN YOU!

SGT. TOWER: LORD HAVE MERCY I'M SO BLUE.

THE MEN: LORD HAVE MERCY I'M SO BLUE!

THE MEN: IT EIGHT MORE WEEKS TILL WE BE THROUGH! IT EIGHT MORE WEEKS TILL WE BE THROUGH! IT EIGHT MORE WEEKS TILL WE BE THROUGH!

(And all the men have marched off in lines of four or five in different directions, giving a sense of large numbers, a larger space and now, out of this movement, comes a spin-off of two men, KRESS and PARKER, coming down the center of the stage, yelling the last lines of the song, marching, stomping, then breaking and running stage left and into the furnace room. There is the hulk of the belly of the furnace, the flickering of the fire. KRESS is large, muscular, with a constant manner of small confusion as if he feels always that something is going on that he nearly, but not quite, understands. Yet there is something seemingly friendly about him. PARKER is smaller; he wears glasses.)

KRESS: I can't stand it, Parker, bein' so cold all the time and they're all insane, Parker. Wax-

in' and buffin' the floor at 5:30 in the morning is insane. And then you can't eat till you go down the monkey bars and you gotta eat in ten minutes and can't talk to nobody, and no place in Georgia is warm. I'm from Jersey. I can jump up in the air, if there's a good wind. I'll land in Fort Dix. Am I right so far? So Sam gets me. What's he do? Fort Dix? Uh-uh. Fort Gordon, Georgia. So I can be warm right? Down South, man. Daffodils and daisies. Year round. (Hollering.) But am I warm? Do you think I'm warm? Do I look like I'm warm? Jesus H! Even in the goddamn furnace room, I'm freezin' ta death!

PARKER: So, what the hell is hollerin' like a stupid ape gonna do except to let 'em know where we at?

KRESS (as PAVLO enters upstage, moving slowly in awe toward the tower, looking): Heat up my blood!

ARDELL (to PAVLO): What you doin' strollin' about like a fool, man, you gonna have people comin' down all over you, don't you know—

OFFICER (having just entered): What're you doing, walking in this company area? Don't you know you run in this company area? Hummel, you drop, you hear me. You drop!

(PAVLO goes into pushup position and starts to do the ten pushups.)

ARDELL (over him): Do 'em right, do 'em right!

KRESS: Why can't I be warm? I wanna be warm.

PARKER: Okay, man, you're warm.

KRESS: No; I'm not; I'm cold, Parker. Where's our goddamn fireman, don't he ever do nothin' but pushups? Don't he ever do nothin' but trouble!

PARKER: Don't knock that ole boy, Kress, I'm tellin' you; Hummel's gonna keep us laughin'!

KRESS: Yesterday I was laughin' so hard. I mean, I'm stupid, Parker, but Hummel's stupid. I mean, he volunteers to be fireman 'cause he thinks it means you ride in a raincoat on a big red truck and when there's nothin' to do you play cards.

PARKER: Yeah! He don't know it means you gotta baby-sit the goddamn furnace all night, every night. And end up lookin' like a stupid chimney sweep!

KRESS: Lookin' what?

PARKER (as PIERCE enters at a jog, moving across the stage toward ARDELL and PAVLO, the officer having exited after the order.): Like a goddamn chimney sweep!

PAVLO: Where you goin'?

PIERCE (*without hesitating*): Weapons room and furnace room.

PAVLO (*getting to his feet*): Can I come along?

PIERCE (*still running, without looking*): I don't give a shit. (*He exits, PAVLO following as ARDELL is drifting the opposite direction.*)

PAVLO: . . . great . . .

KRESS: Yeh? Yeh, Parker, that's good. Chimney sweeps!

PARKER: Yeh, they were these weird little men always crawlin' around, and they used to do this weird shit ta chimneys. (PIERCE *and* PAVLO *enter. They have their rifles.* PIERCE *is a trainee acting as a squad leader. He has a cloth marked with corporal stripes on his left sleeve.*)

PIERCE: At ease!

KRESS: Hey, the Chimney Shit. Hey, what's happenin', Chimney Shit.

PAVLO: How you doin', Kress?

KRESS: Where's your red hat, man?

PAVLO: What?

PARKER: Ain't you got no red fireman's hat?

PAVLO: I'm just with Pierce, that's all. He's my squad leader and I'm with him.

PARKER: Mr. Squad Leader.

PAVLO: Isn't that right, Pierce?

PARKER: Whose ass you kiss to get that job, anyway, Pierce.

PIERCE: At ease, trainees.

KRESS: He's R.A., man. Regular army. Him and Hummel. Lifer morons. Whata they gonna do to us today, anyway, Mr. Actin' Sergeant, Corporal. What's the lesson for the day: first aid or bayonet? I love this fuckin' army.

PIERCE: The schedule's posted, Kress!

KRESS: You know I don't read, man, hurts my eyes; makes 'em water.

PAVLO: When's the gas chamber, that's what I wanna know?

KRESS: For you, Chimney Shit, in about ten seconds when I fart in your face.

PAVLO: I'm all right. I do all right.

KRESS: Sure you do, except you got your head up your ass.

PAVLO: Yeh? Well maybe I'd rather have it up my ass than where you got it.

(*Slight pause: it has made no sense to KRESS at all.*)

KRESS: What?

PAVLO: You heard me, Kress.

KRESS: What'd he say, Parker? (*There is an element of frenzy in this.*) I heard him, but I don't know what he said. WHAT'D YOU SAY TO ME, HUMMEL?

PAVLO: Just never you mind, Kress.

KRESS: I DON'T KNOW WHAT YOU SAID TO ME, YOU WEIRD PERSON!

PARKER (*patting* KRESS): Easy, man, easy; be cool.

KRESS: But I don't like weird people, Parker. I don't like them. How come I gotta be around him? I don't wanna be around you, Hummel!

PAVLO: Don't you worry about it, I'm just here with Pierce. I just wanna know about the gas chamber.

KRESS: It's got gas in it! Ain't that right, Parker! It's like this goddamn giant asshole, it farts on you. THHPPBBBZZZZZZZZ! (*Silence.*)

PAVLO: When is it, Pierce?

KRESS: Ohhhhh, Jesus, I'm cold.

PAVLO: This ain't cold, Kress.

KRESS: I know if I'm cold.

PAVLO: I been colder than this. This ain't cold. I been a lot colder than—

KRESS: DON'T TELL ME IT AIN'T COLD OR I'LL KILL YOU! JESUS GOD ALMIGHTY I HATE THIS MOTHER ARMY STICKIN' ME IN WITH WEIRD PEOPLE! DIE, HUMMEL! Will you please do me that favor! Oh, God, let me close my eyes and when I open them, Hummel is dead. Please, Please. (*He squeezes his eyes shut, clenches his hands for about two seconds and then looks at PAVLO, who is grinning.*)

PAVLO: Boy, I sure do dread that gas chamber.

KRESS: He hates me, Parker. He truly hates me.

PAVLO: No, I don't.

KRESS: What'd I ever do to him, you suppose.

PARKER: I don't know, Kress.

PAVLO: I don't hate you.

PARKER: How come he's so worried about that gas chamber, that's what I wonder.

PAVLO: Well, see, I had an uncle die in San Quentin. (KRESS *screams.*) That's the truth, Kress. (KRESS *screams again.*) I don't care if you believe it. He killed four people in a fight in a bar.

PARKER: Usin' his bare hands right?

PAVLO: You know how many people are executed every damn day in San Quentin? One hell of a lot. And every one of 'em just about is somebody's uncle and one of 'em was my Uncle Roy. He killed four people in a barroom brawl usin' broken bottles and table legs and screamin', jus' screamin'. He was mean, man. He was rotten, and my folks been scared the same thing might happen to me; all their lives, they been scared. I got that same look in my eyes like him.

PARKER: What kinda look is that?

KRESS: That really rotten look, man. He got that really rotten look. Can't you see it?

PAVLO: You ever steal a car, Kress? You know how many cars I stole?

KRESS: Shut up, Hummel! You're a goddamn chimney sweep and I don't wanna talk to you because you don't talk American, you talk Hummel! Some goddamn foreign language!

PARKER: How many cars you stole?

PAVLO: Twenty-three.

KRESS: Twenty-three!

(PARKER *whistles.*)

PAVLO: That's a lotta cars, huh?

PARKER: You damn betcha, man. How long'd it take you, for chrissake? Ten years?

PAVLO: Two.

PARKER: Workin' off and on, you mean.

PAVLO: Sure. Not every night, or they'd catch you. And not always from the same part of town. Man, sometimes I'd hit lower Manhattan, and then the next night the Bronx or Queens, and sometimes I'd even cut right on outa town. One time, in fact, I went all the way to New Haven. Boy, that was some night because they almost caught me. Can you imagine that. Huh? Parker? Huh? Pierce? All the way to New Haven and cops on my tail every inch a the way, roadblocks closin' up behind me, bang, bang, and then some highway patrol-man, just as I was wheelin' into New Haven, he come roarin' outa this side road. See, they must a called ahead or somethin' and he come hot on my ass. I kicked it, man, arrrrgggggghhhhh . . . ! 82 per. Had a Porsche; he didn't know who he was after; that stupid fuzz, 82 per, straight down the gut, people jumpin' outa my way, kids and businessmen and little old ladies, all of 'em, and me kickin' ass, up to 97 now, roarin' baby sirens all around me so I cut into this alley and jump. Oh, Jesus, Christ, just lettin' the car go, I hit, roll, I'm up and runnin' down for this board fence, up and over, sirens all over now, I mean, *all over,* but I'm walkin' calm, I'm cool. Cops are goin' this way and that way. One of 'em asks me if I seen a Porsche go by real fast. Did *I* see—

KRESS: Jesus-goddamn—the furnace room's smellin' like the gas chamber! (*Rising to leave,* PARKER *following.*)

PARKER: That's right, Hummel. That's right. I mean, I liked your story about your really rotten uncle Roy better than the one about all the cars.

KRESS: Les go get our weapons, will ya?

PARKER: Defend our fuckin' selves. (*As they exit the furnace room, and* PAVLO *stands thinking.* PIERCE *is quiet.*)

PAVLO: I'll see . . . you guys later. (*Half calling, half to himself as they are gone.*) Hey, Pierce, you wanna hear my General Orders; make sure I know 'em okay? Like we're on guard mount and you're the O.D. . . . You wanna see if I'm sharp enough to be one a your boys. O.K.? (*Snapping to attention.*) Sir! My first general order is to take charge of this post and all government property in view, keeping always on the alert and . . .

PIERCE: Gimme your eighth, Hummel.

PAVLO: Eighth? No, no, lemme do 'em 1, 2, 3. You'll mess me up.

PIERCE: That's the way it's gonna be, Hummel. The man comes up to you on guard mount, he's gonna be all over you—right on top a you yellin' down your throat. You understand me? He won't be standin' back polite and pretty lettin' you run your mouth.

PAVLO: Just to practice, Pierce. I just wanna practice.

PIERCE: You don't wanna practice shit. You just wanna stand there and have me pat your goddamned head for bein' a good boy. Don't you know we stood here laughin' at you lyin' outa your ass? Don't you have any pride, man?

PAVLO: I got pride. And anyway, they didn't know I was lyin'.

PIERCE: Shit.

PAVLO: And anyway, I wasn't lyin', it was story-telling. They was just messin' with me a little, pickin' on me. My mom used to always tell my dad not to be so hard on me, but he knew.

(*Whistle blows loudly from off.*)

PIERCE: Let's go.

PAVLO: See, he did it to me, 'cause he loved me. I'm R.A. Pierce.

PIERCE: You got a R.A. prefix, man, but you ain't regular army.

PAVLO: They was just jumpin' on me a little; pickin' on me.

(*Again the whistle.*)

PIERCE: That whistle means formation, man.

PAVLO: They're just gonna draw weapons; I already got mine.

PIERCE: That ain't what I said, Jerkoff!

PAVLO: Well, I ain't goin' out there to stand around doin' nothin' when I can stay right here and put the time to good use practicin' D and D.

(*Again the whistle, the men are gathering; we hear their murmuring.*)

PIERCE: You ain't no motherin' exception to that whistle, Hummel!

PAVLO: You ain't any real corporal anyway, Pierce. So don't get so big with me just because you got that hunk a thing wrapped around you—

PIERCE: Don't you mess up my squad, Hummel! Don't you make me look bad or I'll get you your legs broken.

PAVLO (*as the whistle blows and* PIERCE *is leaving and gone*): I bet you never heard a individual initiative.

(*Whistle again as soldiers rush in to line up in formation at Parade Rest while* SGT. TOWER *climbs to stand atop the platform.*)

ARDELL: They don't know, do they? They don't know who they talkin' too.

PAVLO: No.

ARDELL: You gonna be so straight.

PAVLO: So clean.

(SGT. TOWER *notices that someone is missing from formation; he turns, descends, exits.*)

PAVLO: Port Harms! (*And he does it with only a slight and quickly corrected error.*)

ARDELL: Good, Pavlo. Good. (*Slight pause.*) Order Harms!

(PAVLO *does it. There is some skill in the move.*)

PAVLO: Okay . . .

ARDELL: RIGHT SHOULDER . . . HARMS . . .!

(*And* PAVLO *does this, but again there is the head flinch, the rifle nicking the top of his helmet. His back is toward the group and* SGT. TOWER *enters, watches for a time.*)

PAVLO: Goddamn it. Shit. (*Again the rifle back to order.*) RIGHT SHOULDER HARMS.

ARDELL: RIGHT SHOULDER . . .

PAVLO: HARMS! (*Again it is not good.*)

PAVLO: You mother rifle. You stupid fucking rifle. RIGHT SHOULDER, HARMS. (*He tries.*) Mother! Stupid mother, whatsamatter with you? I'll kill you! (*And he has it high above his head. He is looking up.*) Rifle, please. Work for me, do it for me. I know what to do, just you do it.

ARDELL: Just go easy. Man . . . just easy. It don't mean that much. What's it matter?

SGT. TOWER: What you doin', Trainee?

PAVLO (*snapping to attention*): Yes, Sir! Trainee Pavlo Hummel, sir.

SGT. TOWER: I didn't ask you you name, Boy. I asked you what you doin' in here when you supposed to be out on that formation?

PAVLO: Yes, sir.

SGT. TOWER: No, I don't have no bars on my collar, do you see any bars on my collar?

PAVLO: No . . . no . . .

SGT. TOWER: But what do you see on my sleeve at about the height a my shoulder less a little, what do you see?

PAVLO: Stripes, Sergeant. Sergeant stripes.

SGT. TOWER: So how come you call me "sir"? I ain't no sir. I don't want to be no sir. I am a sergeant. Now do we know one another?

PAVLO: Yes, Sergeant.

SGT. TOWER: That mean you can answer my question in the proper manner, do it not?

PAVLO: I was practicin' D and D, Sergeant, to make me a good soldier.

SGT. TOWER: Ohhhhhhh! I think you tryin' to jive this ole man, that what you doin'. Or else you awful stupid because all the good soldiers is out there in that formation like they supposed to when they hear that whistle. Now which?

PAVLO: Pardon, Sergeant?

SGT. TOWER: Which is it? You jivin' on me or you awful stupid, you take your pick. And lemme tell you why you can't put no jive on the ole Sarge. Because long time ago, this ole Sarge was one brand-new, baby-soft, smart-assed recruit. So I see you and I say "What that young recruit doin' in that furnace room this whole company out there bein' talked at by the CO? And the answer come to me like a blast a thunder and this voice sayin' to me in my head, "This here young recruit jerkin' off, that what he doin'," and then into my head come this picture and we ain't in no furnace room, we in that jungle catchin' hell from this one little yellow man and his automatic weapon that he chained to up on top of this hill. "Get on up that hill!" I tell my young recruit. And he tell me, "Yes, Sergeant," like he been taught, and then he start thinkin' to hisself, "What that ole Sarge talkin' about, 'run on up that hill'? Ah git my ass blown clean away. I think maybe he got hit on his head, he don't know what he's talkin' about no more— maybe I go on over behind that ole rock— practice me a little D and D." Ain't that some shit the way them young recruits wanna carry on? So what I think we do, you and me, long about 2200 hours we do a little D and D and PT and all them kinda alphabetical things. Make you a good soldier.

PAVLO: I don't think I can, Sergeant. That's

night time, Sergeant, and I'm a fireman. I got to watch the furnace.

SGT. TOWER: That don't make me no never mind. We jus' work it in between your shifts. You see? Ain't it a wonder how you let the ole Sarge do the worryin' and figurin' and he find a way. (*Turning, starting to leave.*)

PAVLO: Sergeant, I was wondering how many pushups you can do. How many you can do, that's how many I want to be able to do before I ever leave.

SGT. TOWER: Boy, don't you go sayin' no shit like that, you won't ever get out. You be an ole, bearded, blind, fuckin' man pushin' up all over Georgia.

PAVLO (*and* PAVLO, *speaking immediately and rapidly, a single rush of breath, again stops* SGT. TOWER): And I was wondering also, Sergeant Tower, and wanted to ask you—when I was leaving home, my mother wanted to come along to the train station, but I lied to her about the time. She would have wanted to hug me right in front of everybody. She would have waved a handkerchief at the train. It would have been awful. (*And* SGT. TOWER *now leaves, is gone.* PAVLO *calls.*) She would have stood there, waving. Was I wrong?

CORPORAL: TEN HUT! FORWARD HARCH!

(*The men begin to march in place.* PAVLO, *without joining them, also marches.*)

SGT. TOWER: AIN'T NO USE IN GOIN HOME.

THE MEN (*beginning to march and exit*): AIN'T NO USE IN GOIN' HOME.

SGT. TOWER (*at the side of the stage*): JODY GOT YOUR GAL AND GONE.

THE MEN: JODY HUMPIN' ON AND ON.

SGT. TOWER: AIN'T NO USE IN GOIN' BACK. (*And* PAVLO, *in his own area, is marching away.*)

THE MEN: JODY GOT OUR CADILLAC.

CORPORAL: AIN'T NO MATTER WHAT WE DO.

ALL: JODY DOIN' OUR SISTER TOO.

CORPORAL: COUNT CADENCE, DELAYED CADENCE, COUNT CADENCE COUNT!

ALL: 1—2—3—4. 1,2,3,4. 1234. *HEY!*

(*All are gone now except* PAVLO *who comes spinning out of his marching pattern to come stomping to a halt in the furnace room area while* ARDELL *drifts toward him, and toward the audience.*)

ARDELL: Oh, yeh; army train you, shape you up, teach you all kinds a good stuff. Like bayonet. It all about what you do you got no more bullets and this man after you. So you put this knife on the end a your rifle, start yellin' and carryin' on. Then there hand to hand. Hand to hand, cool. It (PAVLO *is watching, listening*) all about hittin' and kickin'. What you do when you got no gun and no knife. Then there CBR. CBR: chemical, biological and radiological warfare. What you do when some mean motherfucker hit you with some kinda chemical. You (ARDELL *mimes throwing a grenade at* PAVLO.) got green fuckin' killin' smoke all around you. What you gonna do? You gotta git on your protective mask. You ain't got it?

PAVLO (*choking*): But I'm too beautiful to die. (*Rummaging about in the furnace room.*)

ARDELL: But you the only one who believe that, Pavlo. You gotta be hollerin' loud as you know how, "GAS." And then, sweet lord almighty, little bit later, you walkin' along, somebody else hit you with some kinda biological jive. But you know your shit. Mask on.

(PAVLO, *having found a mask, is putting it on, waving his arms.*)

PAVLO: GAS! GAS! GAS!

ARDELL: You gettin' it, Pavlo. All right. Lookin' real good. But now you tired and you still walkin' and you come up on somebody bad —this boy mean—he hit you with radiation.

(PAVLO *goes into a tense, defensive posture.*)

PAVLO: Awww. (*Realizing his helplessness.*)

ARDELL: That right. You know what you do? You kinda stand there, that what you do, whimperin' and talkin' to yourself, 'cause he got you. You gotta be some kinda fool, somebody hit you with radiation, man, you put on a mask, start hollerin', "Gas." Am I lyin', Pavlo? What do you say?

PAVLO: Aww, no. . . . No, man—No, no.— I did not! No, no.

(*And there has been toward the end of the above a gathering of a group of soldiers in T shirts and underwear, T shirts and trousers in the barracks area.* PAVLO, *muttering in denial of the radiation, crosses the stage hurriedly, fleeing the radiation, running into* PARKER *who grabs him, spins him.*)

KRESS: The hell you didn't!

PARKER: You been found out, Jerkoff. (*Kneeling behind* PAVLO *to take a billfold from his pocket.*)

PAVLO: No.

KRESS: We got people saw you. Straight honest guys.

PARKER: Get that thing off your face. (*Meaning the mask.*)

BURNS: The shit I didn't see you.

PARKER: You never saw a billfold before in your life, is that what you're tryin' to say? You didn't even know what it was?

KRESS: Is that what you're tryin' to say, Hummel.

PAVLO: No.

KRESS: What are you tryin' to say?

PAVLO: I'm goin' to bed. (*Moving toward his bed but stopped by* KRESS.)

KRESS: We already had two guys lose money to some thief around here, Shitbird, and we got people sayin' they saw you with Hinkle's billfold in your pudgy little paws.

HINKLE (*deep Southern drawl, as* PARKER *hands him the billfold he found on* PAVLO): Is that right, Hummel?

PAVLO: I was just testin' you, Hinkle, to see how stupid you were leavin' your billfold layin' out like that when somebody's been stealin' right in our own platoon. What kinda army is this anyway, you're supposed to trust people with your life, you can't even trust 'em not to steal your money.

PARKER: Listen to him.

PAVLO: That's the truth, Parker. I was just makin' a little test experiment to see how long it'd be before he'd notice it was gone. I don't steal.

KRESS: What about all them cars?

PAVLO: What cars?

PARKER: The New Haven caper, Jerk-off. You know.

PAVLO: Ohhh, that was different, you guys. That was altogether different.

KRESS: Yeh, they were cars and you couldn't fit them in your pocket.

PAVLO: Those people weren't my friends.

PARKER: You don't steal from your friends. That what you're sayin'? Kress, Hummel says he don't steal from his friends.

KRESS (*jumping up on* PAVLO's *bed, standing, walking about*): Don't that make his prospects pretty damn near unlimited?

PAVLO: Hey! Kress, what're you doin'?

KRESS: What?

PAVLO: I said, "What're you up to?" You're on my bed.

KRESS: Who is?

PAVLO: You are. You are.

KRESS: Where?

PAVLO: Right here. You're on my bed. That's my bed.

KRESS: No it isn't. It's not anybody's. It's not yours, Hummel.

PAVLO: It is too.

KRESS: Did you buy it?

PAVLO: Get off my bed, Kress!

KRESS: If you didn't buy it, then how is it yours, Ugly!

PAVLO: It was given to me.

KRESS: By who?

PAVLO: You know who, Kress. The army gave it to me. Get off it.

KRESS: Are you going to take it with you when you leave here? If it's yours, you ought to be planning on taking it with you. Are you?

PAVLO: I can't do that.

KRESS: You're taking people's billfolds; you're taking their money; why can't you take this bed?

PAVLO: Because it was just loaned to me.

KRESS: Do you have any kind of papers to prove that? Do you have papers to prove that this is your bed?

PAVLO: There's proof in the orderly room; in the orderly room, or maybe the supply room and you know it. That bed's got a number on it somewhere and that number is like its name and that name is by my name on some papers somewhere in the supply room or the orderly room.

KRESS: Go get them.

PAVLO: What do you mean?

KRESS: Go get them. Bring them here.

PAVLO: I can't.

KRESS: If they're yours, you can.

PAVLO: They're not my papers, it's my bed. Get off my bed, Kress. (KRESS *now kneels down, taking a more total possession of the bed.*) Goddamn it, Kress. GODDAMN IT! (*Silence:* KRESS *has not moved, seems in fact about to lie down.*) All right. Okay. You sleep in my bed, I'm gonna sleep in yours. (*Everyone stands around watching as* PAVLO *charges off toward where* KRESS's *bed is located.*)

KRESS (*rising a little, tense, looking off, as all look in the direction* PAVLO *has gone*): No, Hummel. (*Warning in* KRESS's *voice.*)

PAVLO: The hell I ain't, Kress.

KRESS: No. No. I strongly advise against it. I do strongly so advise. Or something awful might happen. I might get up in the middle of the night to take a leak and stagger back to my old bed. Lord knows what I might think you are . . . laying there. Lord knows what I might do. (*Slight pause.*)

PAVLO (*yelling from off*): Then get out of my bed.

KRESS: You don't understand at all, do you, Shitbird! I'm sleeping here. This is where I'm going to sleep. You not going to sleep anywhere. You're going to sit up, or sleep on the floor, whatever. And in the morning, you're going to make this bed. This one. Because if you don't it'll be unmade when Sgt. Tower comes to inspect in the morning and as we've already discussed, there's papers somewhere in one room or another and they show whose bed this is.

PAVLO (*entering enough to be seen at the edge of the stage*): GODDAMN YOU, KRESS, GET OUT OF MY BED! GET OFF MY BED! GET OUT OFF IT!

(*Whistle blows and everyone scrambles to firing range. There is the popping of many rifles firing as on the back platform, at the very rear of the set, three or four of the men are in firing positions; others stand behind them at port arms until* SGT. TOWER *calls* "CEASE FIRE" *and the firing stops. The men who have been firing put their rifles on their shoulders to be cleared.* SGT. TOWER *walks behind them tapping each on the head when he has seen the weapon is clear. The men leap to their feet.* SGT. TOWER *then steps out in front of them, begins to pace up and down.*)

SGT. TOWER: GEN'LMEN! IT GETTIN' TOWARD DARK NOW AND WE GOT TO GET HOME. IT A LONG LONG WAYS TO HOME AND OUR MOTHERS GOT SUPPER READY WAITING FOR US. WHAT CAN WE DO? WE GOT TO GET HOME FAST AS WE CAN. WHAT CAN WE DO? DO ANYBODY HAVE AN IDEA? LET ME HEAR YOU SPEAK IF YOU DO. I HAVE AN IDEA. ANYBODY KNOW MY IDEA? LET ME HEAR YOU IF YOU DO.

PAVLO: Run . . .

BURNS: Run?

SGT. TOWER: WHAT?

MORE MEN: RUN!

SGT. TOWER: I CAN'T HEAR YOU.

THE MEN: WHAT?

SGT. TOWER: RUN!

THE MEN: RUN!

SGT. TOWER *and* THE MEN: RUN! RUN! RUN! RUN! RUN! PORT HARMS— WHOOO! DOUBLE TIME! WHOOO! (*They have been running in place. Now* SGT. TOWER *leads them off. They exit running, reappear, exit again, reappear, spreading out now, though* PAVLO *is fairly close behind* SGT. TOWER, *who enters once again and at a point down stage where he turns to* PAVLO *entering, staggering, leading.*)

SGT. TOWER: FALL OUT!

(PAVLO *collapses, the others struggle in, fall down.*)

PIERCE: FIVE GODDAMN MILES! (*All are in extreme pain.*)

KRESS: MOTHER-GODDAMN BITCH—I NEVER RAN NO FIVE GODDAMN MILES IN MY LIFE. YOU GOTTA BE CRAZY TO RUN FIVE GODDAMN MILES . . .

PARKER: I hurt. I hurt all over. I hurt, Kress. Oh, Christ.

PIERCE: There are guys spread from here to Range 2. You can be proud you made it, Parker. The whole company, man; they're gonna be comin' in for the next ten days.

(PARKER *yells in pain.*)

KRESS: Pierce, what's wrong with Parker?

PARKER: SHIT TOO, YOU MOTHER!

KRESS: It'll pass, Parker. Don't worry. Just stay easy. (*And a little separate from the others.* PAVLO *is about to begin doing pushups. He is very tired. It hurts him to do what he's doing.*) Oh, Hummel, no. Hummel, please. (*He is doing the pushups, breathing the count softly.*) Hummel, you're crazy. You really are. He really is, Parker. Look at him. I hate crazy people. I hate 'em. YOU ARE REALLY CRAZY, HUMMEL. STOP IT OR I'LL KILL YOU. (PAVLO, *saying the number of pushups, stopping, pivoting into a sit-up position.*) I mean, I wanna know how much money this platoon lost to that thief we got among us.

PIERCE: Three hundred and twelve dollars.

KRESS: What're you gonna do with all that money?

PAVLO: Spend it. Spend it.

KRESS: Something gonna be done to you! You hear me, Weird Face? You know what's wrong with you? You wouldn't know cunt if your nose was in it. You never had a piece a ass in your life.

(*There is a loud blast on a whistle.*)

PAVLO: Joanna Sorrentino. Joanna Sorrentino ga' me so much ass my mother called her a slut.

KRESS: YOU FUCKING IDIOT!

(*Again the whistle.*)

PIERCE: Oh, Christ . . .

PAVLO: Let's go. LET'S GO. LET'S GET IT.

KRESS: Shut up.

PAVLO: Let's GO, GO, GO—

(*Moving right all exit.*)

KRESS: SHUT YOUR MOUTH, ASS HOLE!

PAVLO: LET'S—GO, GO, GO, GO, GO,

GO, GO . . . (*Yelling, leading, yelling.*)

(*As a light goes on at the opposite side of the stage, there are two soldiers with pool cues at a pool table. There are no pool balls. The game will be pantomime. One of them is the* CORPORAL. *They use a cue ball to shoot and work with.*)

HENDRIX: You break.

CORPORAL: Naw, man, I shoot break on your say so, when I whip your ass, you'll come cryin'. You call. (*Flipping a coin as* PAVLO *comes running back to get his helmet.*)

HENDRIX: Heads.

CORPORAL: You got it.

(PAVLO, *scurrying off with his helmet, meets* SGT. TOWER *entering from opposite side.*)

SGT. TOWER: Trainee, go clean the day room. Sweep it up.

PAVLO: Pardon, Sergeant? I forgot my helmet . . .

SGT. TOWER: Go clean the day room, Trainee.

(*As at the pool game,* HENDRIX *shoots break.*)

CORPORAL: My . . . my . . . my . . . Yes, sir. You're gonna be tough all right. That was a pretty damn break all right. (*Moving now to position himself for his shot.*) Except you missed all the holes. Didn't nobody tell you you were supposed to knock the little balls in the little holes?

PAVLO (*entering*): Sergeant Tower said for me to sweep up the day room.

2ND SOLDIER: And that's what you do—you don't smile, laugh or talk, you sweep.

CORPORAL: You know what "buck a ball" means, Trainee?

PAVLO: What?

CORPORAL: Trainee's rich, Hendrix. Can't go to town, got money up the ass.

PAVLO: Sure I know what "buck a ball" means.

CORPORAL: Ohh, you hustlin' trainee motherfucker. New game. Right now. Rack 'em up!

(HENDRIX *moves as if to re-rack the balls.*)

PAVLO: You sayin' I can play?

CORPORAL: Hendrix, you keep an eye out for anybody who might not agree Trainee can relax a bit. You break, man.

PAVLO: I'll break.

CORPORAL: That's right.

PAVLO: You been to the war, huh? That's a 1st Division Patch you got there, ain't it? (*Shooting first shot, missing, not too good.*)

CORPORAL: That's right.

PAVLO: Where at?

CORPORAL: How many wars we got?

PAVLO: I mean exactly where.

CORPORAL (*lining up his shot*): Di An. Ever hear of it?

PAVLO: Sure.

CORPORAL: Not much of a place but real close to Da Nang. (*He shoots, watches, moves for the next shot.*)

PAVLO: You up there too?

CORPORAL: Where's that?

PAVLO: By Da Nang. (CORPORAL *is startled by* PAVLO *knowing this. He shoots and misses here. He stands now facing* PAVLO.) I mean, I thought Di An was more down by Saigon. D Zone. Down there. They call that D Zone, don't they?

CORPORAL: You're right, man, you know your shit. We got us here a map-readin' motherfucker, Hendrix. Yeh, I was by Saigon, Hummel.

PAVLO: I thought so.

CORPORAL: Your shot. (*He has moved off to the side and* HENDRIX, *who has a hip flask of whiskey.*)

PAVLO (*moving for his shot*): Bed Red One, man, I'd be proud wearin' that. (*And he shoots.*) Shit. (*Having missed.*)

CORPORAL (*moving again to the table*): Good outfit. Top kinda outfit. Mean bastards, all of 'em. Every place we went, man we used ta tear 'em a new asshole, you can believe me. (*Shooting, making it, he moves on.*) I'm gonna win all your damn money, man. You got your orders yet for where you go when you're finished with basic?

PAVLO: No.

CORPORAL: Maybe if you're lucky, you'll get infantry, huh? Yeh, yeh, I seen some shit, you can believe me. (*And during the following long speech, he moves about the table, shooting, shooting, running the table, as he speaks.*) But you go over there, that's what you're goin' for. To mess with them people, because they don't know nothin'. Them slopes; man they're the stupidest bunch a people anybody ever saw. It don't matter what you do to 'em or what you say, man they just look at you. They're some kinda goddamn phenomenon, man. Can of bug spray buy you all the ass you can handle in some places. Insect repellent, man. You ready for that? You give 'em can a bug spray, you can lay their 14-year-old daughter. Not that any of 'em screw worth a shit. (*Slight pause.*) You hear a lot a people talkin' Airborne, 173rd, 101st Marines, but you gotta go some to beat the 1st Division. I had a squad leader, Sergeant Tinden. He'd been there two goddamn years when I got there, so he knew the road, man; he knew his way. So we was comin' into this village once, the whole company, and it was supposed to be secure. We was Charlie Company and Alpha'd been through already, left a guard. And we was lead platoon and lead squad and comin' toward us on the path is this old man, he musta been a hundred, about three foot tall and he's got this little girl by the hand and she's maybe a half-step behind him. He's wavin' at us, "Okay, okay, G.I." Ad she's wavin', too, but she ain't sayin' nothin', but there's this funny noise you can hear, a kind of cryin' like. (*He still moves about, shooting, speaking, pausing, judging which shot to take.*) Anyway, I'm next to the Sarge and he tells this ole boy to stop, but they keep comin' like they don't understand, smilin' and wavin', so the Sarge says for 'em to stop in Vietnamese and then I can see that the kid is cryin'; she's got big tears runnin' outa her eyes, and her eyes are gettin' bigger and bigger and I can see she's tuggin' at the old man's hand to run away but he holds her and he hollers at her and I'm thinkin'. "Damn, ain't that a bitch, she's so scared of us." And Tinden, right then, man, he dropped to his knees and let go two bursts—first the old man, then the kid, cuttin' them both right across the face; man, you could see the bullets walkin'. It was somethin'. (*In silence he sets and takes his last shot. He flops the cue onto the table.*) You owe me, man; thirteen bucks. But I'm superstitious, so we'll make it twelve. (*As* PAVLO *is paying.*) That's right. My ole daddy— the last day he saw me—he tole me good— "Don't you ever run on nobody. Boy, or if you do I hope there's somebody there got sense enough to shoot you down. Or if I hear you got away, I'll kill you myself." There's folks like that runnin' loose, Hummel. My ole man. You dig it. (*And* PAVLO *is staring at him.*) What the fuck are you lookin at?

PAVLO: I don't know why he shot . . . them.

CORPORAL: Satchel charges, man. The both of them, front and back. They had enough T.N.T. on 'em to blow up this whole damn state and the kid got scared. They was wearing it under their clothes.

PAVLO: And he knew . . .

CORPORAL: That's right. Been around; so he knew. You ready, Hendrix? (*They are moving to exit.*)

HENDRIX: Ain't that some shit, Hummel. Ain't that the way to be.

(*Far across the stage,* PARKER *is crouching in dimness, peering toward where* PAVLO *is. Nearby,* KRESS *is*

with three or four other soldiers crouching among the beds.*)

PARKER: Dear Mother. It was the oddest thing last night. I sat near my bunk, half awake, half asleep . . .

CORPORAL: You keep your ear to the ground, Hummel, you're gonna be all (*Exiting.*) right. We'll see you around.

PAVLO: Just to see and to move; just to move. (*Miming with his broom or just his hands the firing of a rifle while* ARDELL *stares at him across the table and lunges suddenly backwards, rapidly hauling the table off.*)

PARKER: Yes, yes, good Mother, I could not sleep, I don't know why. And then for further reasons that I do not know, I happened to look behind me and there . . . was a space ship, yes a space ship, green and golden, good Mother, come down to the sand of our Georgia home. A space ship. (*He is referring to* KRESS *and the others as they hide. He speaks loudly, flamboyantly.* KRESS *kneels downstage with a blanket.* PAVLO *wanders nearer, nearer.*) And out of it, leaping they came, little green men no larger than pins. "Good Lord in Heaven," said I to myself. "What do they want? Sneaking among us, ever in silence, ever in stealth." Then I saw Hummel. Hummel is coming, said I. I will ask Hummel, said I to myself. Hummel is coming. (*KRESS and the others are stationed as if near a door through which* PARKER *is looking and toward which* PAVLO *is now moving as if to enter the barracks.*) THIEF!

(*And* PARKER *flicks a switch to shut off lights.* PAVLO *enters. Blanket is thrown over him. He is dragged to the floor. They beat and kick him, calling him "thief." He cries out. Squirms. A second blanket is thrown on him, a mattress. It is his own bedding they are using, and as they beat and kick him, a whistle blows. All but* PAVLO *go running out, grabbing rifles and helmets as they go to form up for bayonet practice.* SGT. TOWER *is there.*)

PAVLO (*emerging from beneath the blankets—no one is there*): Didn't I do enough pushups. How many do you have to do? Ardell!

ARDELL: You got to understand, Pavlo, it fun sometimes to get a man the way they got you. Come down on him, maybe pivot kick. Break his fuckin' spine. Do him, man. Do . . . him . . . good.

SGT. TOWER (*standing atop his platform, bayonet in hand*): You got to know this bayonet shit, Gen'lmen, else you get recycled, you be back to learn it all again. Eight more beautiful weeks in the armpit a the nation. Else you don't get recycled, you get killed. Then you wish for maybe half a second you been recycled. Do you know the spirit of the bayonet is to kill? What is the spirit of the bayonet?

THE MEN (*while* PAVLO *stirs about and* PIERCE *enters the barracks*): To kill!

SGT. TOWER: You sound like pussies. You sound like slits.

THE MEN: TO KILL!

(PAVLO *is still on the floor; does not see* PIERCE, *who is disheveled and a little drunk.*)

SGT. TOWER: You sound like pussies.

MEN: TO KILL! (*Freeze.*)

PIERCE (*to* PAVLO, *who grabs inside his footlocker for a book*): Look at you. Ohhh, you know how much beer I hada drink to get fucked up on 3.2 beer? Hummel, look at me. You think it's neat to be squad leader? It's not neat to be squad leader. (PAVLO *has been pretending to read from the little book he has gotten from his locker.*) I hear you got beat up this afternoon.

PAVLO: I got a blanket party.

PIERCE: You're in my squad and other guys in my squad beat you, man; I feel like I oughta do somethin'. I'm older, see. Been to college a little; got a wife. And I'm here to tell you, even with all I seen, sometimes you are unbelievable, Hummel.

PAVLO: I don't care. I don't care.

PIERCE: I mean, I worry about you and the shit you do, man.

PAVLO: You do what you want, Pierce.

PIERCE: I mean, that's why people are after you, Hummel. That's why they fuck with you.

PAVLO: I'm trying to study my code a conduct, Pierce, you mind. It's just not too damn long to the proficiency test. Maybe you oughta be studyin' your code a conduct too, instead a sneakin' off to drink at the PX.

PIERCE: I wanna know how you got those rocks down your rifle. It's a two-mile walk out to the rifle range, and you got rocks in your barrel when we get there. That's what I'm talkin' about.

PAVLO: I don't know how that happened.

PIERCE: And every fight you get into, you do nothin' but dance, man. Round in a circle, bobbin' and weavin' and gettin' smacked in the mouth. Man, you oughta at least try and hit somebody. Jesus Christ, Hummel, what's wrong with you? We're in the shower and I tell you to maybe throw a punch once in a while, step with

it, pivot, so you try *it* right there on that wet floor and damn near kill yourself smashin' into a wall.

PAVLO: Fuck you, Pierce.

PIERCE: Fuck you, Hummel.

PAVLO: You know somethin', Pierce. My name ain't even really Pavlo Hummel. It's Michael Hummel. I had it legally changed. I had my name changed.

PIERCE: You're puttin' me on.

PAVLO: No, no, and someday, see, my father's gonna say to me, "Michael, I'm so sorry I ran out on you," and I'm gonna say, "I'm not Michael, Asshole. I'm not Michael anymore." Pierce? You weren't with those guys who beat up on me, were you?

ARDELL: Sometimes I look at you, I don't know what I think I'm seein', but it sooo simple. You black on the inside. In there where you live, you that awful hurtin' black so you can't see yourself no way. Not up or down or in or out.

(PAVLO *begins making his bunk and bayonet begins.*)

SGT. TOWER (*having descended from the platform, moves among the men*): There ain't no army in the world got a shorter bayonet than this one we got. Maneuverability. It the only virtue. You got to get inside that big long knife that other man got. What is the spirit of the bayonet?

THE MEN: TO KILL!

SGT. TOWER: You sound like pussies.

THE MEN: TO KILL!

SGT. TOWER: You sound like slits!

THE MEN: TO KILL!

SGT. TOWER: EN GARDE!

THE MEN: AGGGH!

SGT. TOWER: LONG THRUST, PARRY LEFT . . . WHOOOOOO!

THE MEN (*they make the move; one of them stumbling, falling down, clumsy, embarrassed*): AGGGH!

SGT. TOWER: Where you think you are? You think you in the movies? This here real life, Gen'lmen. You actin' like there ain't never been a war in this world. Don't you know what I'm sayin'? You got to want to put this steel into a man. You got to want to cut him, hurt him, make him die. You got to want to feel the skin and muscle come apart with the push you give. It come to you in the wood. RECOVER AND HOLD!

THE MEN: AGGGH! (*And the men make the move. They yell and growl with each thrust. Another falls down, gets up.*)

SGT. TOWER: EN GARDE!

THE MEN: AGGGH!

SGT. TOWER: Lookin' good, lookin' good. Only you ain't mean. (Men growl.) How come you ain't mean? (Men growl again.) HORIZONTAL BUTT STROKE SERIES, WHOOO (They make the move, much more complicated this time. There is the thrust, recovery, then upper-cutting butt stroke, horizontal butt stroke and finally the downward slash. The growling and yelling is louder this time.) Look at you; look at you. Ohhh, but you men put into my mind one German I saw in the war. I got one bullet left, don't think I want to shoot it, and here come this goddamned big-assed German. "Agggghhhh," I yell to him and it a challenge and he accept. "Agggghhhh," he say to me and set hisself and I just shoot him. Boom! Ohhh, he got a look on his face like I never saw before in my life. He one baffled motherfucker, Jim.

(Without command, the men begin to march.)

ARDELL: ONCE A WEEK IT GET TO TOWN . . .

(Singing, marching, beginning immediately after "Jim.")

THE MEN: THEY SEE ME COMIN', THEY ALL LAY DOWN.

ARDELL: IF I HAD A LOWER I.Q. . . .

(All are marching now, exiting.)

THE MEN: I COULD BE A SERGEANT TOO.

SGT. TOWER: LORD HAVE MERCY, I'M SO BLUE.

THE MEN: LORD HAVE MERCY, I'M SO BLUE.

SGT. TOWER: IT SIX MORE WEEKS TILL I BE THROUGH.

(The earliest off are PIERCE, BURNS, 1ST SOLDER.)

THE MEN: IT SIX MORE WEEKS TILL WE BE THROUGH.

SGT. TOWER: SOUND OFF!

THE MEN: 1—2—

(BURNS, PIERCE, 1ST SOLDIER enter barracks area, still singing as others are still exiting, and these three men set up the crap game on a footlocker.)

SGT. TOWER: SOUND OFF.

(Other enter barracks; PAVLO, HINKLE)

THE MEN: 3—4. CADENCE COUNT. 1—2 —3—4. 1—2. 3-4. (The counting ends, new scene begins.)

PAVLO (talking to HINKLE. A crap game goes on nearby): Can you imagine that, Hinkle? Just knowin'. Seein' nothin' but bein' sure enough to gun down two people. They had T.N.T. on 'em; they was stupid slopeheads. That Sergeant Tinden saved everybody's life. I get made anything but infantry, I'm gonna fight it, man. I'm gonna fight it. You wanna go infantry with me, Hinkle. You're infantry and good at it, you're your own Man, I'm gonna wear my uniform everywhere when I'm home, Hinkle. My mother's gonna be so excited when she sees me. She's just gonna yell. I get nervous when I think about if she should hug me. You gonna hug your mother when you get home?

HINKLE: My mom's a little bitty skinny woman.

PAVLO: I don't know if I should or shouldn't.

HINKLE: What's your mom like?

PIERCE: You tellin' him about your barn house exploits, Hinkle?

HINKLE: Oh, no.

PIERCE: Hinkle says he screwed sheep. He tellin' you that, Hummel?

PARKER: How about pigs, Hinkle?

HINKLE: Oh, yeh.

KRESS: I'm tellin' you, Parker, it was too much; all that writin' and shit, and runnin' around. They ain't got no right to test you. Proficiency test, proficiency test; I don't even know what a proficiency is—goddamn people— crawlin' and writin'—I'm telling you they ain't got no right to test you. They get you here, they mess with you—(He is in a near frenzy, talking rapidly.) they let you go. Who says they gotta test you?

PIERCE (who has the dice and is laying down money): Who's back, man? I'm shootin' five.

KRESS: I got so nervous in hand-to-hand, I threw a guy against the wall. They flunked me for bein' too rough.

PIERCE: Who's back man?

KRESS: I'll take three. (Putting down money. PARKER drops a couple of ones.) I get recycled, I'll kill myself, I swear it. (As PIERCE is shaking the dice, saying over and over. "Karen loves me, Karen loves me.") I'll cut off my ear.

PIERCE (throwing the dice): Karen says I'm GOOD!

KRESS: Goddamn! Shit! How they do it again, Parker?

PARKER: Pierce, you're incredible.

KRESS: Parker!

PARKER: They add up your scores, man; your P.T. plus your rifle, plus the score they got today. Then they divide by 3. You lettin' it ride, Pierce. (*Throwing down a five.*)

PIERCE: Karen loves me.

KRESS: Where they get the 3? (*Putting in money.*)

PARKER: There's three events, man.

PIERCE (*throwing the dice*): Karen say, "I know the *road!*"

KRESS: You fucking asshole!

PARKER: Goddamn it, Pierce!

PIERCE: Who wants me? Back man's got no heart. Shootin' twenty I come for 11—double or nothin'. Whose twenty says I can't come for all out of the gate . . .

(*A soldier enters on the run.*)

GRENNEL: Tower's right behind me; he's got the scores.

(*General commotion as* SGT. TOWER *strides across the stage and enters their area.*)

PIERCE: TENHUT!

(*All come to attention before their bunks.*)

SGT. TOWER: AT EASE! (*Men to parade rest.*) Gen'lmen. It's truth and consequences time. The sad tidings and the (*handing a paper to* PIERCE *for him to post on the board*) glad tidings. You got two men in this platoon didn't make it. They Burn and Kress. They gonna have to stay here 8 more weeks and if they as dumb as it look, maybe 8 more after that and 8 fuckin' more. The rest a you people, maybe you ain't got no spectacular qualities been endowed upon my mind, but you goin' home when you figured. (*Turning and leaving.*)

PIERCE: TENHUT!

SGT. TOWER (*exiting*): Carry on.

(*The men are silent a moment:* KRESS *stands at or near the center.*)

PIERCE: Lemme holler . . . just one . . . time, lemme holler . . .

HINKLE: Mother, mother, make my bed!

A SOLDIER (*at the bulletin board*): Me! My name! Me!

PIERCE: AGGGGGGGHHHHHHHHHHHHH-HHHHHHHHHHHAAAA!

PARKER: Lemme just pack my bags!

HENDRIX (*entering with civilian clothes, shirt, trousers on a hanger, hat on his head*): Lookee lookee—

HINKLE: What're them funny clothes?

PIERCE: CIVILIAN CLOTHES! CIVILIAN—

HINKLE: CI-WHO-LIAN?

PIERCE: PEOPLE OUTSIDE, MAN! THAT'S WHY THEY AIN'T ALL FUNNY AND GREEN, BECAUSE YOU'RE OUTSIDE WHEN YOU WEAR 'EM. YOU'RE BACK ON THE BLOCK. BACK IN THE WORLD!

PAVLO: DON'T NOBODY HEAR ME CALLIN' "KRESS"? (*He has said the name a few times during the yelling. He is atop his own bed.*) I think we oughta tell him how sorry we are he didn't make it. I'm gonna. I'm gonna tell him. I'm sorry, Kress, that you're gonna be recycled and you're not goin' home. I think we're all sorry. I bet it's kinda like gettin' your head caught in a blanket, the way you feel. It's a bad feelin', I bet, and I think I understand it even if I am goin' back where there's lights and it's pretty. I feel sorry for you, Kress, I just wanna laugh, I feel so sorry—(*And* KRESS *pushes him off the bed, leaping after him.* PAVLO *staggers backward.*) Sonofabitch, what're you—SONOFABITCH! (*Swinging a wild right hand; they flail and crash about,* KRESS *grabbing* PAVLO's *wrist, snapping the arm up into a hammer lock.*)

KRESS: Down. (*Then lifting.*) Don't you hear me? Down, I'm sayin'. Don't you hear me? (*Then easing down.*) Thata boy . . . Called crawlin' . . . (PAVLO *has been thrown to the floor, while* PIERCE *has been seized by* HINKLE *and another soldier who keep him from going to* PAVLO's *aid.*) You got the hang of it . . . now . . . Crawlin' . . . Yeh. Now I'm gonna ask you something? Okay?

PAVLO: . . . Okay . . .

KRESS: What I'd like to know is who is it in this platoon steals money from his buddies? Who is it don't know how to talk decent to nobody? and don't have no goddamn friend? Who is that person? You tell me, Hummel? The name a that person passed his test today by cheatin'. (*Twisting the arm.*)

PAVLO: I don't . . . know . . . (*The whole of this is furious; both men are wild.*)

KRESS: Who? (*Working the arm.*)

PAVLO: No—(*And the arm is twisted again.*) Stop him, somebody. Pierce. You're my squad leader, Pierce. Ohhhh . . . Pierce, please . . . Aggghhhh . . . Pierce . . .

KRESS: WHO?

(*And* PAVLO *yells.*)

PIERCE: Ease off a little . . .

KRESS: I CAN'T HEAR YOU!

PIERCE: Kress, I—

PAVLO: HUMMEL!

KRESS: WHAT? WHAT?

PAVLO: HUMMEL! HUMMEL!

KRESS: WHAT?

PAVLO: HUMMEL! HUMMEL! He did 'em. All of those things. All of 'em. He cheated. He cheated. HUMMEL! HUM—

PIERCE: Kress, goddamn it. GODDAMN IT!

(*Leaping to lift* KRESS *away from* PAVLO.)

KRESS (*leaving* PAVLO, *pulling free of* PIERCE): What? What you want, Corporal? Don't mess with me, man. (*Staring at* PIERCE *who is now between him and* PAVLO.) Don't mess with Kress. Not when he's feelin' bad. He'll kill ya, honest to God. He'll pee in your dead mouth. (PAVLO *rushes at* KRESS, *howling.*)

PIERCE: Nooooooooo. (*Seizing* PAVLO.)

PAVLO: I'm all right. I'm all right. I do all right!

PIERCE: Will you listen to me, man; you're goin' home, not Kress. You got him.

PAVLO: Fucking asshole!

PIERCE: Will you listen? (*Shoving* PAVLO *back toward center stage. Scolding him, blocking his pursuit of* KRESS, *backing him up.*) You gotta learn to think, Hummel. You gotta start puttin' 2 and 2 together so they fit. You beat him; you had ole Kress beat and then you fixed it so you hadda lose. You went after him so he hadda be able to put you down.

PAVLO: I just wanted to let him know what I thought.

PIERCE: No, no!

PAVLO: He had no call to hit me like that. I was just talkin'—

PIERCE: You dared him, man.

PAVLO: You shoulda stopped him, that's the problem. You're the squad leader. That's just this whole damn army messin' with me and it ain't ever gonna end but in shit. How come you're a squad leader? Who the fuck are you? Not ever. Nothin' but shit. They're gonna mess with me—make a clerk outa me or a medic or truck driver, a goddamn moron—or a medic—a nurse—a fuckin' Wac with no tits—or a clerk, some little goddamn twerp of a guy with glasses and no guts at all. So don't gimme shit about what I done, Pierce, it's what you done and done and didn't—(*And during this whole thing.* PIERCE. *Squad leader, has moved about straightening the bunk, and footlockers disturbed by the fight, and* PAVLO, *in growing desperation, has followed him. Now* PIERCE *in disgust, starts to leave.*) That's right; keep on walkin' away from you duties, keep—

PIERCE: You're happy as a pig in shit. I don't know why I keep thinkin' you ain't.

PAVLO: I am not.

PIERCE: Up to your eyeballs!

PAVLO: I'm gonna kill myself, Pierce! (*It bursts out of him.*)

PIERCE: If you weren't in my squad, I'd spit in your face . . .

PAVLO: Fuck you, fuck you, fuck you. (*Rocking backward, bowing then forward.*) I hate you goddamn people!

ARDELL: I know.

(PAVLO's *bending carries him down to the floor.*)

PAVLO: Ardell. (*At his footlocker,* PAVLO *rummages about.*)

ARDELL. I know. I know. All you life like a river and there's no water all around—this emptiness—you gotta fill it. Gotta get water. You dive, man, you dive off a stone wall (PAVLO *sits, canteen and paper bag in his hands*) into the Hudson River waitin' down dark under you, for a second, it's all air . . . so free . . . do you know the distance you got to fall? You think you goin' up. Don't nobody fall up, man. Nobody.

PAVLO: What is it? I want to know what it is. The thing that Sergeant saw to make him know to shoot that kid and old man. I want to have it, know it, be it.

ARDELL: I know.

PAVLO: When?

ARDELL: Soon.

PAVLO: If I could be bone, Ardell; if I could be bone. In my deepest part or center, if I could just be bone. (*Taking a container from the bag, he takes pills, washes them down with water, while* SGT. TOWER, *already on the platform speaks and* PAVLO *crawls under the covers of his bunk.*)

SGT. TOWER: Now I'm gonna tell you gen'lmen how you find you way when you lost. You better listen up. What you do, you find the North Star and the North Star show you true north accurate all year round. You look for the Big Dipper and there two stars at the end a that place in the stars that look like the bowl of the dipper and they called the pointer. They them two stars at where the water could come out of the dipper if it had some water and out from them on a straight line you gonna see this big damn star and that the North Star and it show you north and once you know that, gen'lmen, you can figure the rest. You ain't lost no more.

THE MEN (*from the darkness*): YESSSS, SERGEANT!

SGT. TOWER: I hope so. I do hope so . . .

(PIERCE, PARKER, *others, set up card game on footlocker.*)

KRESS (*passing bunk where* PAVLO *is a lump beneath his blanket*): I wonder what the fuckin' chimney shittin' shit is doin' now?

(HINKLE *settles curiously on the bunk next to PAVLO.*)

PARKER: You gonna see me, Pierce? (*Talking even as they set the card game up.*)

PIERCE: And raise you.

PARKER: Ten ta one, he's under there jerking off!

HINKLE (*bending near to* PAVLO): No, no, he's got this paper bag and everything smells funny. Y'all some kind of acrobat, Hummel?

KRESS: He's got some chick's bicycle seat in a bag man.

HINKLE: And the noises he's makin'.

PIERCE: Poor pathetic motherfucker.

KRESS: He ain't pathetic.

PIERCE: He is too.

PARKER: Under there pounding his pud.

KRESS: You musta not seen many pathetic people, you think he's pathetic.

PIERCE: I seen plenty.

PARKER: Call.

PIERCE: Full boat. Jacks and threes! (*Laying down his cards.*)

PARKER: Jesus Goddamn Christ.

HINKLE: I was wonderin' can ah look in you all's bag, Hummel? (*Reaching under the blanket to pick up the bag.*)

PARKER: Jesus Goddamn Christ.

HINKLE: Ohhhh . . . it's . . . you been sniffin' airplane glue . . . (*And he laughs, "Ha, Ha, Ha," turns toward the others.*) Hummel's been sniffin' airplane glue.

KRESS (*from his bed*): ATTAWAY TO GO, HUMMEL.

HINKLE: An' where's all the aspirins . . . ? (*Holding the bottle.*)

PAVLO: Tum-tum, Pavlo.

HINKLE: You all kiddin' me.

PAVLO: No.

HINKLE: Y'all ate 'em?

PAVLO: Yeah!

HINKLE: Hey, y'all. . . . (*To* PAVLO.) Was it full?

PAVLO (*attempting to sit up, flops back down*): Tippy top.

HINKLE: Hummel just ate—(*Examining the bottle.*) 100 aspirins. Hummel just ate 'em.

KRESS: Attaway to go, Hummel.

PARKER: Nighty-night.

HINKLE (*moving toward* PIERCE): Won't it hurt him, Pierce?

KRESS: Kill him probably.

PARKER: Hopefully.

KRESS: Hinkle, ask him did he use chocolate syrup?

HINKLE: He's breathin' kinda funny, Pierce, don't you think?

KRESS: Hummel does everything funny.

PIERCE (*beginning to deal*): Five cards, gen'lmen; jacks or better.

HINKLE: Pierce.

PIERCE: Hummel, you stop worryin' that boy. Tell him no headache big enough in the world, you're gonna take a hundred aspirins. (*Slight pause:* KRESS *begins imitating* PAVLO's *odd breathing.*) How come everybody's all the time bustin' up my good luck.

BURNS: Shit, man, he took a hundred aspirins, he wouldn't be breathing period.

RYAN: Sounds like a goddamn tire pump.

BURNS: Hummel, TENHUT!

PIERCE: Hummel, you just jivin' cause you don't know what else to do or did you eat them pills?

BURNS: Tryin' to blow himself up like a balloon . . . drift away. Float outa the fort.

(PARKER *begins to imitate* KRESS *imitating* PAVLO's *breathing.*)

RYAN: He's fakin', man.

BURNS: How you know?

RYAN: They'd kill you like a bullet.

HINKLE: Get over here, Pierce!

(*Throwing down his cards,* PIERCE *goes to the bed.*)

KRESS: How come the army don't throw him out, Parker?

PARKER: Army likes weird people, Kress.

KRESS: I hate weird people.

PARKER: Sure you do.

KRESS: Weird chimney shitin' friendless, gutless cheatin'—

(PIERCE *is examining* PAVLO. PAVLO *makes a sound and then begins to cough, to sputter.*)

PIERCE (*realizing what is true*): NOOO! NOT IN MY SQUAD, YOU MOTHER. GET UP. (*He is trying to get* PAVLO *to his feet; the* 1ST SOLDIER *is helping.*) YOU SILLY SONOFABITCH. We got to walk him. (PAVLO *is feebly resisting, saying "no, no."*) Hinkle, double-time-it over the orderly room.

HINKLE (*making for the door*): Right.

PIERCE: Tell 'em we got a guy over here took a hundred aspirins, they should get an ambulance.

HINKLE (*turning to head for the door*): Right.

KRESS: Hinkle!

HINKLE (*hesitating, turning back, to face* KRESS): Yeh!

KRESS: Pick me up a coke on your way back.

(*And* HINKLE *leaves.*)

PIERCE (*working with the aid of another soldier*): Hold him steady, I think we oughta get him outside, more air.

ARDELL (*standing over near the base of the platform*): Pavlo, look at you. You gonna have ambulances and sirens and all kinds a good shit. Ain't you somethin'? It gonna be a celebration. C'mon over here (*As if his voice draws them, they lug* PAVLO *toward the tower; they lay him down, remove all clothes from him but his underwear and T shirt.*) Look at you. You got people runnin' around like a bunch a fools. That what you wanted? Yeah, that what you want! They sayin', "Move him. Lift him. Take his shirt off." They walkin' you around in the air. They all thinkin' about you, anyway. But what you doin' but cryin'. You always think you signifyin' on everybody else, but all you doin' is showin' your own fool self. You don't know nothin' about showboatin', Pavlo. You hear me? Now you get on up off that floor. You don't get up, man, I blow a motherfuckin' whistle up the side a you head. I blow it loud. YOU THINK YOU GOT A MOTHERFUCKIN' WHISTLE IN YOUR BRAIN. (PIERCE *and the other soldier have turned away, frozen.* PAVLO *has jumped. Everything he does is performed in the manner of a person alone, as if* ARDELL *is a voice in his head. The light perhaps suggests this.* KRESS, *all others, are frozen as when* HINKLE *left.*) I'm tellin' you how to be. That right. (PAVLO *slumps back down.*) Ohhh, don't act so bad; you actin', man. What you expect, you go out get you head smokin' on all kinds a shit, sniffin' that goddamn glue, then fallin' down all over yourself. Man, you lucky you alive, carryin' on like that. (PAVLO *is doubled over.*) Ain't doin' you no good you wish you dead, 'cause you ain't, man. You know you do. Get on up. (PAVLO *takes a deep breath and stands.*) You go on in the latrine now, get you a bromo, you wash off you face . . . (PAVLO *exits.*) Then get you ass right back out here. And you don't need no shave, man, you ain't got no beard no ways. (*He sees* PAVLO'*s uniform lying on the floor.*) What kinda shit this? Your poor ole Sarge see this, he sit down on the ground and he cry, man. Poor ole Sarge, he work himself like he crazy tryin' ta teach you so you can act like a man. An' what you do? (*Turning suddenly toward the door through which* PAVLO *exited.*) PAVLO! You diddlin' in there, you take this long. And you bring out you other uniform. We gonna shape you up. (PAVLO *enters carrying military dress uniform in clothing bag which he hangs on the tower.*) It daytime, man, you goin' out struttin'. You goin' out standin' tall. You tear it open. Trousers first, man. Dig 'em out. (PAVLO, *having selected the trousers, moves as if to put them on.*) NOOOO! Damnit, ain't you got no sense at all? (*He has rushed to* PAVLO, *lifted the trouser bottoms from off the floor.*) You drag 'em all over the floor like that, man, they gonna look like shit. Get up on this footlocker! (*Pulling a footlocker into place.* PAVLO, *standing on the footlocker* ARDELL *has placed before him, puts on the trousers. Now* PIERCE *and the other soldier move to help* PAVLO *dress. All is ease and grace now.*) That right, that it. Make 'em look like they got no notion at all what it like ta be* dirty. *Be clean, man. Yeh. (PIERCE *has moved before* PAVLO, *pulling down on the cuffs, pulling the crease tight.*) Now the shirt. (*It is a ritual now.* PAVLO *must exert no effort whatsoever as he is transformed. Everything is done for him.*) Lemme look you brass over. (*Soldier moves to the jacket.*) Ain't too bad. It do. Lemme just touch 'em up a little. You put on your tie. Make you a big knot. Big knot make you look tall. (*He is brushing with his handkerchief at the brass.*) Where you boots? (*Finished with the jacket,* PIERCE *and other soldier move to boots.*) Where you boots? An' you got some shades? Lemme get you some shades. (*Walking backwards.*) And tuck that tie square. Give her little loop she come off you throat high and pretty. (*As* ARDELL *exits, beginning the song,* PAVLO *sits on the footlocker, back to audience, and* PIERCE *and the other soldier each kneel to put on a boot.*)

PAVLO: HUT . . . HOO . . . HEE . . . HAW . . . IF I HAD A LOWER I.Q.

THE MEN (KRESS *and all sing*): IF I HAD A LOWER I.Q.

ARDELL: I COULD BE A SERGEANT TOO!

THE MEN: I COULD BE A SERGEANT TOO!

(*Across the back of the stage, two men march.*)

ARDELL: LORD HAVE MERCY, I'M SO BLUE.

(The two men do an intricate drill team step.)

THE MEN: IT FOUR MORE WEEKS TILL I BE THROUGH.

(The two men spin and stomp their rifles, exit.)

ARDELL: You gonna be over, man, I finish with you. *(Reentering with the sunglasses as* PAVLO *stands up, now fully dressed.)* You gonna be the fat rat, man; you eatin' cheese. (ARDELL *moves about* PAVLO, *examining him, guiding him toward the tower which* PAVLO *will climb and stand upon and then* ARDELL *will move to join him.)* OVER BABY! Ardell can make you straight; you startin' ta look good now; you finish up, you gonna be the fattest rat, man; eatin' the finest cheese. Put you in good company, you wear that uniform, you go out walkin' on the street, people know you, they say, "What that?" Somebody else say, "Man, he straight. He look good." Somebody else say, "That boy got pride." Yeh, baby, Pavlo, you gonna be over, man. You gonna be that fat fat rat, eatin' cheese, down on his knees, yeh, baby, doffin' his red cap, sayin' "yes, Massa." You lookee out there. *(They are both atop the tower,* ARDELL *a little behind* PAVLO *and gesturing outward, pointing.* PAVLO *stands. He has sunglasses on.)* Who you see in that mirror, man? Who you see? That ain't no Pavlo Hummel. Noooo, man. That somebody else. An' he somethin' else. Ohhh, you goin' out on the street, they gonna see you. Ardell tellin' you and Ardell know. You back on the block an' you goin' out struttin'. An' they gonna cry when they see you. You so pretty, baby, you gonna make 'em cry. You tell me you name, you pretty baby!

PAVLO *(snapping to attention)*: PAVLO MOTHERHUMPIN' HUMMEL!

ACT II

(CAPTAIN *and* SGT. TOWER *are upstage facing out.* PAVLO *still stands on the tower, with other soldiers in formation below.* MICKEY, PAVLO's *brother, stands downstage, looking out as if into a mirror, combing his hair.)*

CAPTAIN: As we enter now the final weeks of your basic training, I feel a certain obligation as your company commander to speak to you of the final purpose of what has gone on here. Normally this is more difficult to make clear. Pleiku, Vietnam is the purpose of what we have done here. A few nights ago, mortar and machine gun fire in a sneak attack in the highlands killed 9 Americans and wounded 140 serving at our camp there in Pleiku. In retaliation, a bombing of the North has begun and it will continue until the government of Hanoi, battered and reeling, goes back to the North.

SGT. TOWER: Company fall out.

(The TROOPS *scatter. Music starts from* MICKEY's *radio.* PAVLO *descends. Picks up duffle bag. AWOL bag.)*

PAVLO: Hey, Mickey, it's me. I'm home! (MICKEY, *in T shirt, slacks, shoes, combs hair.)* It's me. I'm home, I'm home, I'm home.

MICKEY: Whata you say, huh? Hey, hey, what happened? You took so long. You took a wrong turn, huh? Missed your stop and now you come home all dressed up like a conductor. What happened? You were down in that subway so long they put you to work? Huh? Man, you look good though; you look good. Where were you again?

PAVLO: Georgia.

MICKEY: Hot as a bitch, right?

PAVLO: No. Cold.

MICKEY: In Georgia?

PAVLO: Yeh, it was real cold; we used to hide out in the furnace room every damn chance we ever got.

MICKEY: Hey, you want a drink? Damn, that don't make much sense, does it?

PAVLO: What?

MICKEY: They send you to Georgia for the winter and it's like a witch's tit. Can you imagine that? A witch's tit? Eeeeeeggggggg. Put ice on your tongue. That ever happens to me, man, I'd turn in my tool. Ain't you gonna ask about the ole lady? How's she doin' and all that, cause she's doin' fine. Pickin' and plantin' daisies. Doin' fine. *(And* PAVLO *laughs softly, shaking his head, taking the drink* MICKEY *has made him.)* Whatsa matter? You don't believe yo-yos can be happy? Psychotics have fun, man. You oughta know that.

PAVLO: I just bet she's climbin' some kinda wall and she's pregnant again, she thinks, or you are or me or somebody.

MICKEY: Noo, man, noo, it's everybody else now. Only nonfamily.

PAVLO *(laughing, loudly)*: That's me and you! Nonfamily moutherfuckers!

MICKEY: All the dogs and women of the world!

PAVLO: Yeh, yeh, all the guys in the barracks used to think I was a little weird so I'd—

MICKEY: —you are a little weird—(*Slight pause.*)

PAVLO: Yeh, yeh, I'd tell 'em, "You think I'm weird, you oughta see my brother, Mickey. He don't give a big rat's ass for nothin' or nobody."

MICKEY: And did you tell 'em about his brains, too. And his wit and charm. The way his dick hangs to his knees—about his 18 thou a year? Did you tell 'em all that sweet shit?

PAVLO: They said they hoped you died of all you got.

MICKEY (*has been dressing throughout: shirt, tie, jacket*): How come the troops were thinkin' you weird? You doin' that weird stuff again. You say "George" and "the army." For all I know you been down town in the movies for the last three months and you bought that goddamn uniform at some junk shop.

PAVLO: I am in the Army.

MICKEY: How do I know?

PAVLO: I'm tellin' you.

MICKEY: But you're a fuckin' liar; you're a fuckin' myth maker.

PAVLO: I gotta go to Vietnam, Mickey.

MICKEY: Vietnam don't even exist.

PAVLO: I gotta go to it.

MICKEY: Arizona, man; that's where you're goin'. Wyoming.

PAVLO: Look at me! I'm different! I'm different than I was! (*This is with fury.*) I'm not the same anymore. I was an asshole. I'm not an asshole anymore. I'm not an asshole anymore! (*Slight pause.*) I came here to forgive you. I don't need you anymore.

MICKEY: You're a goddamn cartoon, you know that.

PAVLO (*rapidly, a rush of words*): I'm happier now than I ever was, I got people who respect me. Lots of 'em. There was this guy Kress in my outfit. We didn't hit it off . . . and he called me out . . . he was gonna kill me, he said. Everybody tried to stop me because this guy had hurt a lot of people already and he had this uncle who'd taught him all about fightin' and this uncle has been executed in San Quentin for killing people. We went out back of the barracks. It went on and on, hitting and kicking. It went on and on; all around the barracks. The crowd right with us. And then . . . all of a sudden . . . this look came into his eye . . . and he just stopped . . . and reached down to me and hugged me. He just hugged and hugged me. And that look was in all their eyes. All the soldiers. I don't need you anymore, Mickey. I got real brothers now.

MICKEY: You know . . . if my father hadn't died, you wouldn't even exist.

PAVLO: No big thing! We got the same mother; that's shit enough. I'm gonna shower and shave, okay? Then we can go out drinkin'.

MICKEY: All those one night stands. You ever think of that. Ghostly pricks. I used to hear 'em humpin' the ole whore. I probably had my ear against the wall the night they got you goin'. '

PAVLO (*after a slight silence*): You seen Joanna lately?

MICKEY: Joanna?

PAVLO: Joanna. My ole girl. I thought maybe she probably killed herself and it was in the papers. You know, on account of my absence. But she probably did it in secret.

MICKEY: No doubt.

PAVLO: No doubt.

MICKEY: Ain't she the one who got married? I think the ole lady tole me Joanna got married and she was gonna write you a big letter all about it. Sure she was. Anyway, since we're speaking of old girls and pregnant people, I've got to go to this little party tonight. Got a good new sweet young thing and she thinks I'm better than her daddy. I've had a run a chicks lately you wouldn't believe, Pavlo. They give away ass like Red Cross girls dealin' out donuts. I don't understand how I get half a what I get. Oh, yeh, old lady comes and goes around here. She's the same old witch.

PAVLO: I'm gonna go see Joanna. I'll call her up. Use the magic fuckin' phone to call her up.

MICKEY: I'll give you a call later on.

PAVLO: I'll be out, man. I'll be out on the street.

MICKEY: You make yourself at home. (*Exits.*)

(*Soldiers suddenly appear far upstage, marching forward as* ARDELL, *off to the side, counts cadence; other soldiers appear at various points about the stage.*)

ARDELL: HUT . . . HOO . . . HEE . . .

SGT. TOWER: SAW SOME STOCKIN'S ON THE STREET . . .

THE MEN: WISHED I WAS BETWEEN THOSE FEET.

SGT. TOWER: WISHED I WAS BETWEEN THOSE FEET. HONEY, HONEY, DON'T YOU FROWN.

THE MEN: I LOVE YOU DRUNK AND LAYIN' DOWN.

SGT. TOWER: STANDIN' TALL AND LOOKIN' GOOD. WE BELONG IN HOLLYWOOD.

(*Atop the tower as the men come to a stomping halt.*)

THE MEN: WE BELONG IN HOLLYWOOD.

SGT. TOWER: Take five, Gen'lmen, but the smoking lamp is not lit.

(PAVLO *is there, off to the side, disheveled, carrying a pint whiskey bottle. He undresses, speaking his anger, throwing his uniform down. The men are relaxing a little.*)

PAVLO: Stupid fuckin' uniform. Miserable hunk a green shit. Don't we go to good bars —why don't you work for me? And there's this really neat girl there sayin' to me how do I like bein' a robot? How do I like bein' one in a hundred million robots all marchin' in a row? Don't anybody understand about uniforms? I ain't no robot. You gotta have braid . . . ribbons and patches all about what you did. I got nothin'. What's so complicated? I look like nothin' cause I done nothin'. (*In his T shirt and underwear, he kneels now with the bottle.*)

SGT. TOWER: Gen'lmen, you best listen up real close now even though you restin'. Gonna tell you little bit about what you do you comin' through the woods, you find a man wounded in his chest. You gotta seal it off. That wound workin' like a valve, pullin' in air, makin' pressure to collapse that man's lung; you get him to breathe out and hold his breath. You apply the metal foil side a the waterproof wrapping of the first aid dressing, tie it off. Gonna hafta tie it extra; you use your poncho, his poncho, you get strips a cloth. You tear up you own damn shirt, I don't care. You let that boy have his lung. You let him breathe. AM I UNDERSTOOD?

THE MEN: YES, SERGEANT!

SGT. TOWER: FALL IN! DISMISSED!

(*The troops go; leaving* PAVLO *alone, in his underwear, near or on the bed.*)

PAVLO: I wanna get laid. . . , bed. . . . bottle. (*Pause.*) I wanna get laid! I wanna get laid, phone! You goddamn stuck-up motherin' phone. Need a piece of ass, phone, need a piece of ass. Bed. Lemme walk on over to that phone. Lemme crawl on over to that phone. Lemme get there. Gonna outflank you. Goddamn army ant. Thas right. Thas right. Hello, Joanna (*Dialing now, he has crawled to the phone.*) This is Pavlo, Joanna, hello. Certainly of course. I'd be glad to screw your thingy with my thingy. BSZZZZZZZ . . . BBBBBBBBBZZZZZZZZZZZZZZZ . . .

BBBZZZ . . .

WOMAN (*on the phone*): Hello?

PAVLO: BBBZZZZZZZZZZZZZZZZZZ . . .

WOMAN: Hello?

PAVLO: Little bitty creature . . . hello, hello. . . . .

WOMAN: Who is this?

PAVLO: Hollering . . . hollering . . . poor creature . . . locked inside, can't get out, can't—

WOMAN: Pavlo?

PAVLO: Do you know me? Yes. Yes, it is me, Pavlo. Pavlo Hummel . . . Joanna . . . And I am calling to ask how can you have lived to this day away from me?

WOMAN: Pavlo, listen.

PAVLO: Yes. I am. I do.

WOMAN: Pavlo: this isn't Joanna.

PAVLO: What?

WOMAN: This is Mrs. Sorrentino, Pavlo. Joanna isn't here.

PAVLO: What?

WOMAN: I said, "Joanna isn't here," Pavlo. This is her mother; may I have her call you?

PAVLO: What?

WOMAN: I said, "May I have her call you?" She's married, Pavlo. Or did you just call to say "hello"?

PAVLO: Who is this?

WOMAN: Pavlo, what's wrong with you?

PAVLO: Who are you? I don't know who this is. You get off the line, goddamn it, you hear me, or I'll report you to the telephone company. I'll report you to Bell Telephone. And G.E., too. And the Coke Company and General Motors. (*The* WOMAN *hangs up the phone.*) You'll be hurtin', Baby. I report you to all those people. Now you tell me where she is. Where is she?

(*Behind him a light pops on, a table lamp. His mother, a small, dark-haired woman, plump, fashionably dressed, has been there all the while, sitting in the dark and listening, visible only as a figure in a chair. She begins to speak almost at the same instant that the light goes on. At first tentative, she then gains confidence, gathers speed, tells her story as if she is simply thinking it.*)

MRS. HUMMEL: In Stratford, Connecticut, Pavlo. Pregnant more than likely. Vomiting in the morning. Yes . . . trying . . . to . . . get . . . rid of . . . it. . . . Hello, Pavlo . . . I wrote you that . . . I wrote you. (*Silence.*) Hello . . . Pavlo. I wrote you she was married. Why are you calling? Why? (*Silence.*) Pavlo? Listen, are you finished on the phone and could we talk a minute? I don't want to interrupt . . . I only have a few . . . few things to say. They won't take long. I've been working since you've been gone. Did you know? Doing quite well. Quite well indeed. In a department store. Yes. One of the smaller ones. Yes. And we had an awful, awful shock there the other day and that's what I want to tell you about. There's a woman, Sally Kelly, and Ken was her son, in the Army like you now, and he went overseas last August. Well I talked to Sally when I went in at noon and she was in the lunchroom writing a little card to Ken and she let me read it. She knew that you were in the army so she said she was sure I knew the way it was consolation to write a little note. Then about 5:45, I was working on the shoes and I saw two Army officers come up the escalator and talk to one of the other clerks. I never gave them another thought and at 6:00 o'clock Sally came through and went down the escalator and made a remark to me and laughed a little and went on down. In about fifteen more minutes, I was waiting on a lady and she said to me, "Isn't that terrible about the lady's son who works downstairs?" I said, "Who?" She said, "The lady who works at your candy department just got word her son was killed in Vietnam." Well, I was really shook when I heard that and I said, "Oh, you must be mistaken. She just went downstairs from her supper hour and I talked to her and she was fine." She said, "Well, that's what I heard on the main floor." Well, I went right to the phone and called the reception desk and they said it was true. This is what happened, this is what I want to tell you. The officers had gone to Sally's house but no one was home so they talked to the neighbors and found out Sally worked at the store. So they went up to our receptionist and asked for our manager. He wasn't in so they asked for one of the men and Tommy Bottle came and they told him, they needed his help because they had to tell one of the employees that her son was killed in Vietnam. Tommy really got shook as you can imagine and he took the officers to Mr. Brenner's office and closed the door. While they were in there, Sally came out of the lunchroom and came downstairs. Joyce, the girl who is the receptionist knew by this time and Sally laughed when she went by and said that she better get to work or something like that. Joyce said later on that she could hardly look at her. Anyway, Tommy called the floorman from first floor to come up and he told him what happened and then he had to go back down

to 1st floor and tell Sally she was wanted in Tommy's office. She said, "Oh boy, what have I done now?" By the time she got to the fourth floor, the office door was open and she saw the two Army men and said, "Oh, dear God, not Kenny." (*Pause.*) A mother . . . and her children should be as a tree and her branches . . . A mother spends . . . but she gets . . . change. You think me a fool . . . don't you. There are many who do. (*Pause.*) He joined to be a mechanic and they transferred him to Infantry and he was killed on December 1st. So you see . . . I know what to expect. I know . . . what you're trying to do.

PAVLO: Who . . . was . . . my father? Where is he?

MRS. HUMMEL: You know that.

PAVLO: No, I want you to tell me.

MRS. HUMMEL: I've already told you.

PAVLO: No, where is he now? What did he look like?

MRS. HUMMEL: I wrote it all in a letter. I put it all in an envelope, I sealed it, mailed it.

PAVLO: I never got it.

MRS. HUMMEL: I think you did.

PAVLO: No!

MRS. HUMMEL: No, you had many fathers, many men, movie men, filmdom's great—all of them, those grand old men of yesteryear, they were your father. The Fighting 76th, do you remember? Oh, I remember, little Jimmy what a tough little mite, he was and how he leaped upon that grenade, did you see? my God what a glory, what a glorious thing with his little tin hat.

PAVLO: My real father!

MRS. HUMMEL: He was like them, the ones I showed you in movies, I pointed them out.

PAVLO: What was his name?

MRS. HUMMEL: I've told you.

PAVLO: No. What was his name? I don't know what it was.

MRS. HUMMEL: Is it my fault you've forgotten?

PAVLO: You never told me.

MRS. HUMMEL: I did. I whispered it in your ear. You were three. I whispered the whole thing in your ear!

PAVLO: Lunatic!

MRS. HUMMEL: Nooooo!

PAVLO: Insane hideous person!

MRS. HUMMEL (*slight pause*): I've got to go to bed now. I have to get my rest. (*Her back is turned. She is walking.*)

PAVLO (*stopping her*): I picked this girl up in this bar tonight and when I took her home and got her to the door and kissed her, her tongue went into my mouth. I thought that meant she was going to let me in to her apartment. "Don't get hurt," she said "and get in touch when you get back, I'd love to see you." She knew I was going overseas, did you? And then the door was shut and all I wanted to say was, "What are you doing sticking your tongue in my mouth and then leaving me, you goddamn stuck-up mother-in' bitch." But I didn't say anything.

MRS. HUMMEL: Yes ... well ... I'll ... (*Pause.*) ... see you in the morning ... Pavlo ... (*And she leaves.*)

ARDELL (*who has been watching*): Oh, man, how come? You wanted to get laid, how come you didn't do like the ole Sarge told you steada gettin' all tore up with them walkin' blues? Take you a little money, the old Sarge say, roll it up long ways, put it in your fly, man, so it stickin' out. Then go on walkin' up and down the street that green stickin' right outa your fly. You get laid. You got that money stickin' outa your fly, you get laid. You get your nut! How come you didn't do that?

OFFICER (*who has been standing on rear platform at parade rest*): And the following will depart conus 12 August 1966 for the Republic of Vietnam on assignment to the 23rd Field Hospital. Thomas. Simpson. Horner. Hinkle. Hummel.

PAVLO: I don't wanna be no medic!

(*The bar music starts,* YEN *and older Vietnamese woman entering from one side of the stage,* BRISBEY *calling from the other and then entering, his bed on wheels pushed onstage by two soldiers, while* ARDELL *has hauled off the footlocker on which the phone had sat, revealing a pile of clothes,* PAVLO's *jungle fatigues which he immediately starts getting into.* YEN *is at the bar. All this happens nearly simultaneously,* BRIS-BY *calling "*PAVLO," YEN *entering, music starting.*)

YEN: Hey, G.I. cheap Charlie, you want one more beer.

JONES (*offstage*): One bomniba, one beer.

BRISBEY: Pavlo.

YEN (*as* JONES, *in a bright colored walking suit, enters*): EEEEEEaaaaaa? What you talk? One bomniba, one beer. Same—same, huh? I no stand. What you want?

JONES (*pursuing her; both are playing yet both have real anger*): You gimme boucoup now?

YEN: Boucoup what? I don't know what you want. Crazy G.I., you dinky dow.

BRISBEY: PAVLO!

PAVLO (*who is and has been dressing into jungle fatigues*): I'm in the can, Brisbey, I'll be there in a minute.

ARDELL: He be there, Brisbey.

JONES: You got lips as fat as mine, you know that, ho?

YEN: *Toi cum biet!*

JONES: Shit, you don't know.

YEN: Shit. I can say, too. I know. Shit. (*And he is reaching for her.*) No. We fini. Fini. You no talk me no more, you numba fuckin' ten. (*And she bounces away to sit on a crate and look at sheet music, as* BRISBEY *speaks to* PAVLO.)

BRISBEY: Do you know, Pavlo? I saw the metal point of that mine sticking up from the ground just under my foot—I said, "That's a mine. I'm stepping on a mine." And my foot went right on down and I felt the pin sink and heard the first small ... pop. I jumped ... like a fool. And up she came right outa the ground. I hit at it with my hand as if to push it away, it came up so slow against my hand ... Steel ... bits ... of dirt ...

PAVLO: I'm off duty, Brisbey. (*Having listened reluctantly.*)

ARDELL: Ole Brisbey got himself hit by a Bouncin' Betty. That a kind of land mine, you step on it, she jump up to about right here (*indicating his waist.*) then she blow you in half. That why she got that name. Little yellow man dug a hole, put it in, hoped he'd come around. He an old man, damn near; got seventeen years in the army; no legs no more, no balls, one arm.

(*As a small Vietnamese boy comes almost running across stage to grab* PAVLO's *hand and guide him into the whorehouse, bar area, and leave him there.*)

BOY: HEY, G.I. SHOW YOU NUMBA ONE!

PAVLO (*to* JONES *who is sitting there drinking a beer*): Hey, what's goin' on?

JONES: What's happenin', man?

MAMASAN (*the elderly Vietnamese woman, returning*): Hello, hello! You come my house, I am glad. Do you want a beer? I have. Do you want a girl? I have. Number one girl. Number one. You want?

PAVLO (*pointing to* MAMASAN): You?

MAMASAN: No, no I am Mamasan. But I have many girl. You see, maybe you like. Maybe you want short-time, huh? Maybe you want long-time. I don't know, you tell me. All number one. (JONES *laughs.*)

JONES: Man, don't you believe that ole lady, you just gotta get on and ride. Like her. (*Indicating* YEN.) I been. And I'm restin' to go again; an'

I don't think it any kinda numba one; but I been outa the world so *damn* long. I jus' close my eyes an' jive my own self—"That ain't no dead person," I say, "that ain't no dead Ho jus' 'cause she layin' so still. I saw her walk in here." I mean, man, they so screwed up over here. They got no nature. You understand me, Bro? They got no nature, these women. You—how long you been over here?

PAVLO: Not long; couple weeks.

JONES: You new then, huh?

PAVLO: Yeh.

JONES: You wanna go? (*Reaching out, toward* YEN *who is across the room, calling to her.*) Hey, Ho! C'mon over here!

YEN: You talk me?

JONES: Yeh, baby, you, c'mon over here. You wanna go, man?

PAVLO: What about the V.D.? (*Taking a seat.*)

JONES (*big laugh*): What about it?

YEN (*who, approaching with a beer, has heard*): I no have. I no sick. No. No, sweat, G.I. You want short-time me, no sweat.

JONES: Shit, Ho, you insides rotten. You Vietnamee, ain't you? Vietnamee same-same V.D.

YEN: No! No sick. (*As* JONES *grabs her, pulls her near, then sets her down on* PAVLO's *lap.*) What you do? No.

JONES (*holding her in place*): I'm jus' tryin' ta help you get some money, baby. I be you sportsman. Okay. (*She has stopped her struggle, is sitting nicely on* PAVLO's *lap.*) You just sit on down an' be nice on the man's lap, pretty soon, he ain't gonna be worried 'bout no V.D. If you jus' . . . sorta shift . . . (*he demonstrates*) every now and then. Okay . . . (*She is still now and he turns his attention to* PAVLO.) Now, lemme tell you 'bout it, lemme tell you how it is. It be hot, man. I come from Georgia, and it get hot in Georgia, but it ain't ever been this kinda hot, am I lyin'? An' you gonna be here one year and that 365 days, so you gonna sweat, now do you think I'm lyin'?

PAVLO (YEN *has been messing with him, rubbing under his shirt*): I ain't never sweat so much.

JONES: So that's what I'm sayin'. You gonna be here and you gonna sweat. And you gonna be here and you gonna get V.D.? You worried about sweatin'? Ahhhhh. You grinnin'. So I see I have made my meanin' clear. (YEN *has been rubbing* PAVLO's *thigh.*) How you feelin' now? She kinda nice, huh? She kinda soft and nice.

PAVLO: Where you work?

JONES (*laughs*): Don't you be askin' me where I work. That ain't what you wanna know. I gotta get you straight, gotta get outa here, buy myself some supplies. My ole mom all the time tellin me. "Don't you go near that PX. You get blown away for sure. Them V.C.'s gotta wanna get that PX."

PAVLO (*to* YEN): What's your name?

YEN: Name me Yen.

PAVLO: Name me Pavlo. Pavlo.

YEN: Paaa-blo.

PAVLO: How much?

JONES: Lord, she says his name, he loves her.

YEN: You want short-time: I ask Mamasan. (*She is getting up, but* MAMASAN *has been watching.*)

MAMASAN (*approaching*): OK. OK. Yen numba one. I am happy. 500 peas.

JONES: Two-hundred.

MAMASAN: She very beautiful.

JONES: Two-fifty.

MAMASAN: Four hundred; can do. No sweat.

JONES: Mamasan, who you think you jivin'?

MAMASAN: Yen boucoup boyfriend! She very love!

JONES: Two-fifty.

MAMASAN (*to* PAVLO): Three hundred twenty. You, huh? Three hundred twenty.

JONES: Pavlo, give her 300, tell her things is tough at home, she don't know.

MAMASAN (*as* PAVLO *hands her the money*): No, no, I talk you 320!

JONES: AND I TALK HIM 300, MAMASAN, 300.

(*Slight silence.*)

MAMASAN (*softly, whiney, to* PAVLO): G.I. You be nice, you give Mamasan 10 peas more. G.I.? Ten peas very easy you!

PAVLO (*to* JONES): How much *is* 10 peas, man?

JONES: Eight cents, or about—

PAVLO: Eight cents! Eight cents. Over 8 goddamn stupid cents I'm still standin' here!

JONES (*as* PAVLO *is giving more money to* MAMASAN): Man, no.

MAMASAN (*patting him on the back*): Okay, okay. You numba one—

YEN (*taking* PAVLO *by the hand toward the bed*): I show you.

JONES (*as he leaves*): Oh man, deliver me from these green troops; they makin' everybody fat but me. (*The whistle blows loudly, and the troops come roaring into formation for instructions; they face the tower.*)

SGT. TOWER (*his voice booming*): GEN'LMEN! (*And his voice stops* PAVLO, *who comes to attention near the bed.* YEN *has jumped onto the bed. And as*

SGT. TOWER *continues his speech, she comes around front of* PAVLO, *unbuttons his pants, unbuttons his shirt, takes his pants down, all this as* SGT. TOWER *gives instructions. He is holding up a rifle.*) This an M-16 rifle, this the best you country got, now we got to make you good enough to have it. You got to have feelin' for it, like it a good woman to you, like it you arm, like it you rib. The command is *Right Shoulder . . . HARMS!* At the command, HARMS, raise and carry the rifle diagonally across the body, at the same time grasping it at the balance with the left hand, trigger guard in the hollow of the bone. Then carry the left hand, thumb and fingers extended to the small of the stock, and cut away smartly and everything about you, Trainee, is at the position of attention. RIGHT SHOULDER. HARMS!

THE MEN (*performing it*): 1—2—3—4. (PAVLO *also yells and performs the drill in pantomime.*)

SGT. TOWER: You got to love this rifle, Gen'l-men, like it you pecker and you love to make love. You got to care about how it is and what can it do and what can it not do, what do it want and need. ORDER. HARMS!

THE MEN: 1—2—3—4.

SGT. TOWER: RIGHT SHOULDER. HARMS!

THE MEN (PAVLO *with them, yelling also*): 1—2—3—4.

CORPORAL: FORWARD HARCH!

(PAVLO *pulls up his trousers and marches.*)

SGT. TOWER: AIN'T NO USE IN GOIN' HOME . . .

THE MEN: AIN'T NO USE IN GOIN' HOME . . .

(PAVLO'S *marching is joyous.*)

SGT. TOWER: JODY GOT YOUR GAL AND GONE . . .

THE MEN: JODY HUMPIN' ON AND ON . . .

(*Something of* PAVLO'S *making love to* YEN *is in his marching.*)

SGT. TOWER: AIN'T NO USE IN GOIN' BACK . . .

THE MEN: JODY GOT OUR CADILLAC.

CORPORAL: LORD HAVE MERCY, I'M SO BLUE.

THE MEN: IT TWO MORE WEEKS TILL I BE THROUGH.

CORPORAL: Count cadence, delayed cadence, count cadence—count. (*And the men, performing delayed cadence, exit.* PAVLO *counts with them, marching away beside the bed, around the bed, leaping*

upon the bed as the counting comes to its loud end, and BRISBEY, *who has been onstage in his bed, all this while, calls to* PAVLO.*)

BRISBEY: Pavlo!

PAVLO: Just a second, Brisbey!

BRISBEY: Pavlo!

PAVLO (*crosses toward* BRISBEY): Whatta you want, Brisbey?

BRISBEY: Pavlo, can I talk to you a little?

PAVLO: Sure.

BRISBEY: You're a medic, right?

PAVLO: Yeh.

BRISBEY: But you're not a conscientious objector, are you? So you got a rifle.

PAVLO: Sure.

(*During the following,* PAVLO *busies himself with* BRISBEY'S *pulse and chart, straightening the bed, preparing the shot he must give* BRISBEY.*)

BRISBEY: I like the feel of 'em. I like to hold 'em.

PAVLO: I'm not gonna get my rifle for you, Brisbey.

BRISBEY: Just as a favor.

PAVLO: No.

BRISBEY: It's the only pleasure I got any more.

PAVLO: Lemme give you a hypo; you got a visitor; you can see him before you sleep.

BRISBEY: The egg that slept, that's what I am. You think I look like an egg with a head? (PAVLO *is preparing the needle; there is a figure off in the shadows.*) Or else I'm a stump. Some guys, they get hit, they have a stump. I am a stump.

PAVLO: What about your visitor; you wanna see him?

(*The figure steps forward.*)

BRISBEY: Henry?

SGT. WALL: It's me, Brisbey, how you doin'? (*He is middle-aged, gray-haired, chunky.*)

BRISBEY: Henry, Henry, who was the first man 'round the world, Henry? That's what I want to know. Where's the deepest pit in the ocean? You carryin'? What do you have? .45? You must have a blade. Magellan. Threw out a rope. I ever tell you that story? Gonna go sleepy-bye. Been trying to get young Pavlo Hummel to put me away, but he prefers to break needles on me. How's the unit? You tell 'em I'll be back. You tell 'em, soon as I'm well. I'll be back.

SGT. WALL: I'm off the line . . . now, Brisbey. No more boonies. I'm in Supply now.

BRISBEY: Supply? What . . . do you supply? (*Slight pause, as if bewildered, thinking, yet with bit-*

terness, with irony.) If I promise to tell you the secret of life, Henry, will you slit my throat? You can do it while I'm sleeping.

PAVLO: Don't he just go on?

BRISBEY: Young Hummel here, tell him who you love. Dean Martin. Looks at ole Dino every chance he gets. And "Combat." Vic Murrow, man. Keeps thinkin' he's gonna see himself. Dino's cool, huh. Drunk all the time.

PAVLO: That's right.

BRISBEY: You fucking asshole. Henry. Listen. You ever think to yourself, "Oh, if only it wasn't Brisbey. I'd give anything. My own legs. Or one, anyway. Arms. Balls. Prick." Ever . . . Henry?

(Silence.)

SGT. WALL: No.

BRISBEY: Good. Don't. Because I have powers I never dreamed of and I'll hear you if you do, Henry, and I'll take them. I'll rip them off you.

(Silence.)

SGT. WALL: You'll be goin' home soon. I thought . . . we could plan to get together . . .

BRISBEY: Right. Start a softball team.

SGT. WALL: Jesus Christ, Brisbey, ain't you ever gonna change? Ain't you ever gonna be serious about no—

BRISBEY: I have changed, Motherfucker. You blind or somethin' askin' me if I changed. You get the fuck outa here, hear me? (WALL *is leaving, having left a pint of whiskey.*) You take a tree, you cut off its limbs, whatta you got? You got a stump. A living feeling thinking stump.

PAVLO: You're not a tree, Brisbey.

BRISBEY: And what terrible cruelty is that? Do you know? There is responsibility. I want you to get me that rifle. To save you from the sin of cruelty, Pavlo. (*As* PAVLO *is moving with alcohol, cotton, to prepare the shot.*) You are cruel, Pavlo . . . you and God. The both of you.

PAVLO: Lemme do this, man.

BRISBEY (*as* PAVLO *gives the shot*): Do you know . . . if you were to get the rifle, Pavlo, I'd shoot you first. It's how you'll end up anyway. I'd save you time. Get you home quicker. I know you, boy.

PAVLO: Shut up, man. Relax . . .

BRISBEY: You've made me hate you.

PAVLO: I'm sorry. I didn't mean that to happen.

BRISBEY: No, no, you're not sorry. You're not. You're glad it's me, you're glad it's not you. God's always glad that way because it's nev-

er him, it's always somebody else. Except that once. The only time we was ever gonna get him, he tried to con us into thinkin' we oughta let him go. Make it somebody else again. But we got through all that shit he was talkin' and hung on and got him good—fucked him up good— nailed him up good . . . just once . . . for all the billion times he got us.

PAVLO: Brisbey, sometimes, I don't think you know what you're sayin'. (*Officer enters upstage left, carrying clip board.*) Grennel.

GRENNEL (*appearing from the back, far upstage*): Yes, sir.

CAPTAIN: Go get me Hummel. He's down with Brisbey.

BRISBEY: I keep thinkin', Pavlo, 'bout this kid got his hand blown off, and he kept crawlin' round lookin' for his fingers. Couldn't go home without 'em, he said, he'd catch hell. No fingers. (PAVLO *shakes his head, mutters, "Brisbey, Brisbey."*) I keep thinkin' about ole Magellan, sailin' round the world. Ever hear of him, Pavlo? So one day he wants to know how far under him to the bottom of the ocean. So he drops over all the rope he's got. 200 feet. It hangs down into a sea that must go down and down behind its end for miles and tons of water. He's up there in the sun. He's got this little piece of rope dangling from his fingers. He thinks because all the rope he's got can't touch bottom, he's over the deepest part of the ocean. He doesn't know the real question. How far beyond all the rope you got is the bottom?

PAVLO: Brisbey, I'm gonna tell you somethin'. I tried to kill myself once. Honest to God. And it's no good. You understand me. I don't know what I was thinkin' about. I mean, you understand it was a long time ago and I'd never been laid yet or done hardly anything, but I have since and it's fantastic. I just about blew this whore's head off, it was fantastic, but I'd killed myself, it'd never a happened. You see what I'm saying, Brisbey? Somethin' fantastic might be comin' to you, you don't know about it.

GRENNEL (*entering*): Hummel. Man, the Captain wants to see you.

PAVLO: Captain Miller? Captain Miller! (Leaving.)

BRISBEY: Pavlo!

GRENNEL (*as he wheels* BRISBEY *off*): How you doin', Brisbey?

PAVLO (*rushing up to the* CAPTAIN, *standing with his clipboard*): Sir. Pfc Hummel reporting as ordered.

CAPTAIN: Good afternoon, Hummel.

PAVLO: Good afternoon, sir.

CAPTAIN: Are you smiling, Hummel?

PAVLO: Excuse me, sir.

CAPTAIN: Your ten-forty-nine says you're not happy at all; it says you want a transfer out of this unit because you're ashamed to serve with us. I was wondering how could you be ashamed and smiling simultaneously, Hummel.

PAVLO: I don't know, sir.

CAPTAIN: That's not a very good answer.

PAVLO: No, sir.

CAPTAIN: Don't you think what you're doing here is important? You helped out with poor Brisbey, didn't you?

PAVLO: Yes, sir.

CAPTAIN: That's my point, Hummel. There are people alive who would be dead if you hadn't done your job. Those invalids you care for, you feed them when they can't. You help them urinate, defecate; simple personal things they can't do for themselves but would die without. Have you asked any one of them if they think what you are doing is important or not, or if you should be ashamed?

PAVLO: Yes, sir . . . more or less. But . . . I . . . just . . . think I'd be better off in squad duty.

(*Distant firing and yelling are heard, to which neither the* CAPTAIN *nor* PAVLO *respond. There is a quality of echo to the sounds and then there is a clattering and a young Negro Pfc appears at the opposite side of the stage in full combat gear except for his helmet which is missing. He has come a few steps onto the stage and he crouches.*)

SOLDIER: Damn, baby, why that ole Sarge gotta pick on me?

PAVLO: I'm regular army, sir; I'm going to extend my tour.

CAPTAIN: You like it here, Hummel?

SOLDIER: Damn that ole Sarge. I run across that field I get shot sure as hell. (*He breathes.*) Lemme count to five. Lemme do it on 5. (*As he tenses, preparing.*)

CAPTAIN: How many days left in your tour, Hummel?

SOLDIER: Lemme do it like track and field.

PAVLO: I enlisted because I wanted to be a soldier, sir, and I'm not a soldier here. Four nights ago on perimeter guard, I tried to set up fields of fire with the other men in the bunker —do you know what I mean, sir? Designating who would be responsible for what sector of terrain in case of an attack? And they laughed at me; they just sat on the bunker and talked all night

and they didn't stay low and they didn't hide their cigarettes when they smoked or anything.

SOLDIER: FIVE! (*And he runs, taking no more than two steps before a loud explosion hits and he goes down and bounces and rolls onto his back, slamming his fist into the ground in outrage.*) DAMN IT! I KNEW IT! I KNEW IT! I KNEW IT!

CAPTAIN: You want the V.C. to come here?

PAVLO: I want to feel, sir, that I'm with a unit Victor Charlie considers valuable enough to want to get it. And I hope I don't have to kill anyone; and I hope I don't get killed.

SOLDIER (*still trying but unable to rise*): Medic? Medic? Man, where you at? C'mon out here to me! Crawl on out here to me.

PAVLO: But maybe you can't understand what I'm saying, sir, because you're an R.O.T.C. officer and not O.C.S., sir.

CAPTAIN: You mean I'm not regular army, Hummel.

PAVLO: An R.O.T.C. officer and an O.C.S. officer are not the same thing.

CAPTAIN: Is that so, Hummel?

PAVLO: I think so, sir.

CAPTAIN: You want to get killed, don't you, Hummel?

PAVLO: No, sir. No.

CAPTAIN: And they will kill you, Hummel, if they get the chance. Do you believe that? That you will die if shot, or hit with shrapnel, that your arm can disappear into shreds, or your leg vanish, do you believe that, Hummel—that you can and will, if hit hard enough, gug and vomit and die . . . be buried and rot, do you believe yourself capable of that . . . ?

PAVLO: Yes . . . sir. I . . . do . . .

SOLDIER: Noooooooo! (*Quick pause.*) Ohhh, shit, somebody don't help me, Charlie gonna come in here, cut me up, man. He gonna do me.

CAPTAIN: All right, Hummel. (*Sitting down at the desk.*)

SOLDIER: Oh, Lord, you get me outa here, I be good, man; I be good, no shit, Lord, I'm tellin' it.

CAPTAIN: All right . . . you're transferred. I'll fix it. (CAPTAIN *salutes, pivots, exits.* PAVLO *moves to change into combat gear in darkening light. He finds the gear in a footlocker in the bar area.*)

SOLDIER: What's happenin'? I don't know what's happenin'! (*The light goes and the soldier is alone in the jungle, in a center of silver; it is night, there are sounds.*) Hummel, c'mon. It's me, man, Parham; and I ain't jivin', mister. I been shot. I been truly shot. (*He pauses, breathing, and raises his head to look down at himself.*) Ohhhh, look at me; ohhh, look at my poor stomach. Ohhhh, look at me, look at me. Oh, baby, stop it, stop bleedin', stop it, stop it; you my stomach, I'm talkin' to you, I'm tellin' you what to do, YOU STOP IT! (*His hands are pressing furiously down on his stomach. And he lies in silence for a moment: only his breathing.*) SOMEBODY GET ME A DUST-OFF! Dustoff control, do you hear me? This here Pfc Jay Charles Johnson Parham. I am coordinates X-Ray Tango Foxtrot, Lima . . . Do you hear me? I hurtin, baby; hear me. Don't know what to do for myself; can't remember; don't know what it is gone wrong . . . requesting one med-evac chopper. I am one litter patient; gunshot wounds; stomach. Area secure, c'mon hear me; this ole nigger . . . he gonna die. (*And he freezes, sensing presences behind him and he twists his head to see. They stand up, one with a rifle pointing.*)

1ST. V. C.: Hello, G.I.

SOLDIER: Oh, no. Oh, no. No.

1ST. V.C.: Okay. Okay. (*Very sing-song.*)

2ND V.C.: You number one.

SOLDIER: Get away from me! I talkin' to you, Charlie, you get away from me! You guys get away from me! MEDIC! ME—

(*They say "okay, okay." "You numba one." And at a nod from the V.C. with the weapon, his partner has jumped forward into a sitting position at the head of the soldier, one leg pinning down each shoulder, the hands, grasping under the chin, cocking the head back, stuffing a rag into the mouth. There are only the sounds of the struggle as the other V.C. crouches and holds a knife over the* SOLDIER'S *eyes. He stares at it, his feet moving slowly back and forth.*)

1ST V.C.: Numba one, you can see, G.I.? Airplane me . . . Vietnam. Have many bomb. Can do boom-boom, you stand! (*He moves the knife up and down.*) Same-same you, many friend me, fini. Where airplane now, G.I.? Where very gun? (*And he places the blade against* SOLDIER'S *chest and* SOLDIER, *behind his gag begins to howl and begins to flail his pinioned arms and beat his heels furiously upon the ground.*) Okay, okay, . . .! An di dow! (*Until the knife goes in and they rise up to stand over him as he turns onto his side and pulls himself into a knot as if to protect himself, knees tight to his chest, arms over his head. They unbuckle his pistol belt and take his flack vest and his billfold from his pocket and are working at removing his shirt when they both straighten at a sound and then seize his fallen rifle and run to disappear.* PAVLO *appears, moving low, accompanied by a second American,* RYAN.)

RYAN: Man, I'm tellin' you let's get outta here.

PAVLO (*pointing*): No, no. There (*He has a large belt hooked over his shoulder. He moves toward the body.*) Just look. (RYAN *is following.*) Hey, man . . . hey . . . Ohhhhh . . . look at him.

RYAN: It's Parham.

PAVLO: Man, he's all cut . . .

RYAN: Pavlo, let's get outta here . . .! (*And he starts to move off.*) What the hell's it matter?

PAVLO: I'll carry him.

RYAN: I ain't worried about who has to carry him, for Chrissake, I wanna get outta here. (*As* PAVLO *hands his rifle.*) I'm gonna hustle over there to the side there. (*On the move.*)

PAVLO: Nooooooo . . .

RYAN: Give you some cover.

(RYAN *is gone, leaving* PAVLO *with the body. His task is as follows: The circular belt is placed under the buttocks of the man, one length along his back, the other across his legs so that two loops are formed—one on either side of the man's hips. The carrier then lies down with his back to the dead man and he fits his arms through the two loops. He then grasps the man's left arm with his own right hand and rolls to his right so that the man rolls with him and is on his back. He then rises to one knee, keeping the body pressed tightly to his own. As* PAVLO *begins this task,* ARDELL *is there, appearing as* RYAN *departs.*)

ARDELL: How many that make?

PAVLO: What's that?

ARDELL: Whatta you think, man? Dead bodies!

PAVLO: Who the hell's countin'?

ARDELL: Loooookeeeee. Gettin' ta *beeeee bad!*

PAVLO: This one's nothin'. When they been out here a couple days, man, that's when it's interesting—you go to pick 'em up they fall apart in you hands, man. They're mud; pink mud; like turnin' over a log; all maggots and ants. You see Ryan over there hidin' in the bushes. I ain't hidin' in no bushes. And Parham's glad about that. They're all glad. Nobody wants to think he's gonna be let lay out here.

ARDELL: Ain't you somethin'.

PAVLO: I'm diggin' it, man. Blowin' people away. Cuttin' 'em down. Got two this afternoon I saw and one I didn't even see—just heard him out there jabberin' away—(*And he makes a sound mimicking a Vietnamese speaking.*) And I walked a good goddamn 20 rounds right over where it sounded like he was: he shut up his fucking face. It ain't no big things.

ARDELL: Like bringing down a deer . . . or dog.

PAVLO: Man, people's all I ever killed. Ohhhh, I feel you thinkin', "This poor boy don't know.what he's doin'; don't know what he got into." But I do. I got a dead boy in my hands. In a jungle . . . the middle a the night. I got people maybe 10 feet away, hidin'—they're gonna maybe cut me down the minute I move. And I'm gonna . . . (*During all this he has struggled to load the body like a pack on his back. Now he is rising. Is on his knees.*) . . . take this dead thing back and people are gonna look at me when I do it. They're gonna think I'm crazy and be glad I'm with 'em. I'm diggin'—(*The Vietcong comes streaking out from hiding place.*) Ryan, Ryan, Ryan! (*The Vietcong, without stopping, plunges the knife into* PAVLO's *side and flees off.* PAVLO *falls, unable, because of the body on his back, to protect himself.*) What happened?

ARDELL: The blood goin' out a hole in your guts, man, turn you water.

PAVLO: He hit me . . .

ARDELL: TURN YOU INTO WATER! Blood goin' in the brain make you think—in you heart make you move, in your prick makes you hard, makes you come. YOU LETTIN' IT DROP ALL OVER THE GROUND!

PAVLO: I won't . . . I'll . . . noooooo . . . (*Trying to free himself of the body.*) Ryan . . .

ARDELL: The knowledge comin', baby. I'm talkin' about what your kidney know, not your fuckin' fool's head. I'm talkin' about your skin and what it sayin', thin as paper. We melt; we tear and rip apart. Membrane, baby. Cellophane. Ain't that some shit.

PAVLO: I'll lift my arm. (*He can't.*)

ARDELL: AIN'T THAT SOME SHIT.

PAVLO: Noooooo . . .

ARDELL: A bullet like this finger bigger than all your fuckin' life. Ain't this finger some shit.

PAVLO: RYAN.

ARDELL: I'm tellin' you.

PAVLO: Nooooo.

ARDELL: RYAN!

PAVLO (*as* RYAN *comes running on with a second soldier*): RYAN!

ARDELL: Get on in here. (*They struggle to free* PAVLO *from the body. He flails, yelling in his panic as* SGT. TOWER *comes striding on and mounts the stairs to his tower.*)

PAVLO: Ryan, we tear. We rip apart. Ryan, we tear.

SGT. TOWER (*as they move* PAVLO *off*): You gon-na see some funny shit, Gen'lmen. You gonna see livin' breathin' people disappear. Walkin' talkin' buddies. And you gonna wanna kill and say their name. When you been in so many fights and you come out, you a survivor. It what you are and do. You survive.

(*A body detail removes* PARHAM's *body from the stage.*)

ARDELL: Thin and frail.

SGT. TOWER: Gen'lmen, can you hear me?

THE MEN (*from off. Only* ARDELL *is there below the tower, listening*): Yes, Sergeant.

SGT. TOWER: I saw this rifle one time get blown right outa this boy's hands and him start wailin' and carryin' on right there how he ain't ever goin' back on no line, he'll die for sure he don't have that one rifle in all the world. You listenin' to me, gen'lmen. I'm gonna tell you now what you do when you lost and it black black night. The North Star show you true North accurate all year round. You gonna see the big dipper and two stars on the end called the pointer and they where the water would come on outa that dipper if it had water in it, and straight out from there is this big damn star and once you know North you ain't lost no more!

(PAVLO *has appeared, rising up from the back of the set, walking slowly as in a dream, looking at* SGT. TOWER, *yelling in response to him.*)

PAVLO: YES, SERGEANT! (*An explosion hits;* PAVLO, *yelling, goes down again.*)

ARDELL: What you sayin'? YES SERGEANT. What you sayin'? (*Perhaps also having fallen with the explosion.*)

PAVLO: YES, SERGEANT! (*Struggling to rise, as distantly, downstage, drifting,* YEN *enters and moves soundlessly to a place to kneel.*)

ARDELL: Ask him what about that grenade come flyin'? How come if you so cool, if you such a fox, you don't know nothin' to do with no grenade but stand there—holdin' it—get your abdominal and groin area blown to shit.

PAVLO: I don't know what you're talking about!

ARDELL: You walkin' talkin' scar, what you think you made of?

PAVLO: I got my shit together.

ARDELL: How many times you gonna let 'em hit you?

PAVLO: As many times as they want.

ARDELL: That man up there a fool, Jim.

PAVLO: Shut up.

ARDELL: You ever seen any North Star in your life?

PAVLO: I seen a lot of people pointin'. (PAVLO *is on the move toward* YEN *now.*)

ARDELL: They a bunch a fools pointin' at the air.

PAVLO: I want her, man. I need her. (*In some way touching her.*)

ARDELL: Where you now, man? You with her? What you doin'?

PAVLO: I'm with her, man.

ARDELL: You . . . in . . . her . . .

PAVLO: . . . soon . . . (PAVLO *is taking her blouse off her.*)

ARDELL: Why you there . . .?

PAVLO: I dunno . . . jus wanna . . .

ARDELL: You jus gonna ride . . .

PAVLO: I jus' wanna . . .

ARDELL: There was one boy walkin' . . .

PAVLO: I know, don't talk no shit. (*Seizing her, embracing her.*)

ARDELL: Walkin' . . . singin' . . . soft, some song to himself, thinkin' on mosquitoes and coke and bug spray until these bushes in front of him burst in fire and his fine young legs break in half like sticks . . .

PAVLO: Leave me alone! (*Rising, trying to get off his own trousers.*)

ARDELL: At 7 his tonsils been cut out; at 12 there's appendicitis. Now he's 20 and hurtin' and screamin' at his legs, and then the gun come back. It on an fixed traversing arc to tear his yellin' fuckin' head right off.

PAVLO: Good; it's Tanner; it's Weber. It's Smith and not Pavlo. Minneti, not Pavlo. Klaus and Weber, YOU. Layin' there, lookin' at me. NOT Pavlo, not ever.

ARDELL: You get a knife wound in the ribs.

PAVLO: It misses my heart. I'm clean.

ARDELL: You get shrapnel all up and down your back.

PAVLO: It's like a dozen, 15 bee stings, all up and down my back.

ARDELL: And there's people tellin' you you can go home if you wanna. It's your second wound. They're sayin' you can go home when you been hit twice and you don't even check. You wanna go back out, you're thinkin', get you one more gook, get you one more slopehead, make him know the reason why.

PAVLO (*whirling, scooping up a rifle from the floor*): That's right. They're killin' everybody. They're fuckin' killin' everybody! (*The rifle is aimed at* ARDELL.)

ARDELL: Like it's gonna make a difference in the world, man, what you do; and somethin' made bad's gonna.be all right with this one more you're gonna kill. Poor ole Ryan get's dinged round about Tay Ninh, so two weeks later in Phu Loi you blow away this goddamn farmer . . .

FARMER (*waving in the distance*): Okay, G.I., okay. (*The farmer wears Vietnamese work clothes, conical hat.*)

ARDELL: And think you're addin somethin' up.

PAVLO: I blew him to fuckin' smithereens. He's there at 20 yards, wavin'.

FARMER: Okay, G.I., okay. (*He sways in the distance, appearing to approach.*)

PAVLO: *DUNG LYE. DUNG LYE.* (*This is "Stop" in Vietnamese.*)

ARDELL: You don't know he's got satchel charges.

PAVLO: I do.

ARDELL: You don't know what he's got under his clothes.

PAVLO: I do. He's got dynamite all under his clothes. And I shoot him. (*Gunshot, as* PAVLO, *having pushed* ARDELL *aside, fires. He will fire two more times: two more gunshots.*) I fuckin' shoot him. He's under me. I'm screaming down at him. RYAN. RYAN. And he's lookin' up at me. His eyes squinted like he knows by my face what I'm sayin' matters to me so maybe it matters to him. And then, all of a sudden, see, he starts to holler and shout like he's crazy, and he's pointin' at his foot, so I shoot it. I shoot his foot and then he's screaming and tossin' all over the ground, so I shoot into his head. I shot his head. And I get hit again. I'm standin' there over him and I get fuckin' hit again. They keep fuckin' hittin' me. (*Explosion and* PAVLO *goes flying forward.*) I don't know where I'm at. In my head . . . It's like I'm 12 . . . a kid Ardell, it's going to happen to meeeeeee? (*He is on the ground where he has been knocked, crawling.*)

ARDELL: What do you want me to do?

PAVLO: I don't want to get hit anymore.

ARDELL: What do you want me to do?

PAVLO: Tell me.

ARDELL: He was shot . . . layin' down under you, what did you see?

PAVLO: What?

ARDELL: He was squirmin' down under you in that ditch, what did you see?

PAVLO: I saw the grass . . . his head . . .

ARDELL: Nooooooooooo.

PAVLO: Help me. I saw the grass, his head. . . .

ARDELL: Don't you ever hear?

PAVLO: I want out, Ardell, I want out.

ARDELL: When you gonna hear me?

PAVLO: What are you tryin' to tell me? I saw blood . . . bits of brain . . .

ARDELL: Nooooooooooo!

PAVLO: The grass, the grass. . . .

ARDELL: When you shot into his head, you hit into your own head, fool!

PAVLO: What? Noooo.

ARDELL: IT WAS YOUR OWN.

PAVLO: NOOOOOOOOO! (*As* ARDELL *has turned to leave.*) Don't leave me you sonofabitch, I don't know what you're saying. (ARDELL *has stopped, back turned, far upstage.*) JIVE MOTHER-FUCKIN' BULLSHIT! (ARDELL *is leaving and gone.*) and I stood . . . lookin' . . . down . . . at that black, black Hudson river . . .; there was stars in it . . . I was 12 . . . I remember. . . . (*He is turning toward* YEN *who is kneeling, singing.*) I went out toward them . . . diving . . . down . . . (*He is moving toward* YEN, *crawling.*) They'd said there was no current, but I was twisted in all that water, fighting to get up . . . all my air burning out, couldn't get no more . . . (*He is moving toward* YEN.) and I was going down, fighting to get down. I was all confused, you see, fighting to get down, thinking it was up. I hit sand. I pounded the bottom. I thought the bottom was the top. Black. No air. (*As the* OFFICER *enters, striding swiftly.*)

OFFICER: YES! (*He carries a clipboard on which he writes as* PAVLO *runs up to him.* YEN, *though she remains kneeling, stops singing.* PAVLO *salutes.*)

PAVLO: Sir! I've just been released from Ward 17, gunshot wound in my side and I've been ordered back to my unit, Second of the 16th, 1st Division, and I don't think I should have to go. This is the third time I been hit. I been hit in the ribs and leg and back . . . I think there should be more trainin' in duckin' and dodgin', sir. I been hit by a knife, shrapnel and bullets.

OFFICER: Could you get to the point?

PAVLO: That is the point. I want to know about this regulation sayin' you can go home after your second wounding?

OFFICER: Pardon, Hummel?

PAVLO: I been told there's this regulation you can go home after your second wound. When you been hit twice, you can go home.

OFFICER: Hummel, wouldn't you be home if you were eligible to be home?

PAVLO: I don't know, sir; but I wanted to stay the first two times, so I don't know and I was told I had the option the second time to go home or not, but I never checked and if I passed

it by, sir, I'd like to go back and pick it up.

OFFICER: You didn't pass it by; there's no such regulation.

PAVLO: It was a sergeant who told me.

OFFICER: These orders are valid.

PAVLO: Could you check, sir?

OFFICER: I'm an expert on regulations, Hummel. These orders are valid. You've earned the Purple Heart. Now, go on back and do your job. (*Raising his hand to salute, pivots, exits as* PAVLO *is about to salute.*)

ARDELL: No! No!

PAVLO: I do my job. (SGT. WALL *enters the bar, calling to* YEN *who moves quickly to the bar area where she pets him and then moves to prepare a drink for him.*)

SGT. WALL: Come here, Pretty Piggy, we talk boucoup love; okay? Make plans go my home America.

YEN: Sow.

SGT. WALL: No lie.

SGT. TOWER (*in a kind of brooding, mournful rage atop his tower as* PAVLO *stands before him, looking up*): Gen'lmen, lemme tell you what you do, the enemy got you, he all around you. You the prisoner. You listenin', gen'lmen?

ARDELL (*all despairing sarcasm*): Yes, Sergeant

SGT. TOWER: You got to watch out for the enemy. He gonna try to make you feel alone and you got no friends but him. He gonna make you mean and afraid; then he gonna be nice. We had a case with them North Koreans, this group a American P.O.W.s, one of 'em was wounded so he cried all night. His buddies couldn't sleep. So, one night his buddies picked him up, I'm tellin' you, they carried him out the door into that North Korean winter, they set him down in the snow, they lef' him there, went on back inside. They couldn't hear him screamin' the wind was so loud. They got their sleep. You got to watch out for the enemy.

(PAVLO *pivots away from* SGT. TOWER *and into the bar, where* MAMASAN *greets him.* YEN *is with* SGT. WALL *who wears civilian clothes: flowered, short-sleeved shirt and trousers.*)

MAMASAN: Paaablooooo . . . how you-you. I give you beer, okay?

PAVLO (*unmoving, rigid*): Mamasan, Chow Ba.

SGT. WALL: ". . . so who," he says, "was the first motherfucker to sail 'round the world? Not Vasco da Gama." I don't know what he's sayin'. "Who was the first motherfucker to measure the ocean?" (*He is loud and waving his arms.*) I don't know! He wasn't even asking. MAMASAN!

MAMASAN! ONE BEER! ONE BEER, ONE SAIGON TEA! (*And he reaches now to take* YEN's *hand and tug her gently around to his side of the table, drawing her near to sit on his lap.*) Come here; sit down. No sow. Fini sow. Beaucoup love Co Yen. Beaucoup love. (*His hand on her breast, as she nibbles his ear.*)

YEN: I think you maybe papasan America. Have many babysan?

SGT. WALL: No . . . no.

YEN: I think you sow.

SGT. WALL: No lie, Yen. No wife America, no have babysan. Take you, okay?

PAVLO: Sarge! (*Slight pause as* SGT. WALL *looks up to* PAVLO.) Listen; I don't have too much time, I got to go pretty soon; how long you gonna be talkin' shit to that poor girl? I mean, see, she's the whore I usually hit on, I'm a little anxious, I'd like to interrupt you, you gonna be at her all fuckin' night. I'll bring her back in half an hour.

SERGEANT: Sorry about that. Sorry—

PAVLO: I didn't ask you was you sorry?

SERGEANT: This little girl's my girl.

PAVLO: She's a whore, man—

SERGEANT: We got a deal, see, see; and when I'm here, she stays with me.

PAVLO: You got a deal, huh?

SERGEANT: You guessed it, Pfc.

PAVLO: Well, maybe you shoulda checked with me, you shoulda conferred with me maybe before you figured that deal was sound.

SERGEANT: You have been informed.

PAVLO: But you don't understand, Sarge, she's the only whore here who move me.

SERGEANT: My baby.

PAVLO: You rear-echelon asshole!

SERGEANT (*beginning to rise*): What's that?

PAVLO: Where you think you are, the goddamn PX? This the garbage dump, man, and you don't tell me nothin' down here let alone who I can hit on, who I can't hit on, you see what I'm sayin', to you, Fuckface.

YEN: Paablo . . . no, no . . .

PAVLO: You like this ole man.

YEN (*moving to face* PAVLO *and explain*): Can be nice, Paablo . . .

PAVLO: Old man. Papasan. Can do fuck-fuck maybe one time one week. Talk, talk. Talk. No can do boom-boom. PAPASAN. NUMBA FUCKIN' TEN!

YEN: Shut up. Paablo, I do him. Fini him. Do you. Okay. (*Angry at his stupidity.*)

PAVLO: Shut up?

SERGEANT: You heard her.

PAVLO: Shut up? (*His hand twisting in her hair. She yells.*) I don't know who you think this bitch is, Sarge, but I'm gonna fuck her whoever you think she is. I'm gonna take her in behind those curtains and I'm gonna fuck her right side up and then maybe I'm gonna turn her over, get her in her asshole, you understand me? You don't like it you best come in pull me off.

SERGEANT (*switchblade popping open in his hand*): I ain't gonna have to, PUNK.

(PAVLO *kicks him squarely in the groin. The man yells, falls.*)

PAVLO: The fuck you ain't. Hey . . . were you ready for that? Were you ready for that, ole man? Called crawlin', you gettin' (*Dragging the man along the ground, shoving him.*) the hang of it, you ole man. Get up, get up. (*The man moans as* PAVLO *lifts him.*) I want you gone, you mother, you understand. I don't wanna see you no more. You gonna disappear. You are gonna vanish. (*He flings the old man.* SGT. WALL. *away.* WALL *staggers, falls, and* PAVLO *picks the knife off the floor, goes for a beer as* SGT. TOWER *begins to speak and* WALL, *grenade in hand, circles.*)

SGT. TOWER: This a grenade, Gen'lmen. M_2 fragmentation, 5.5 ounces, composition B, time fuse, 13 feet a coiled wire inside it like the inside a my fist a animal and I open it and that ANIMAL LEAP OUT TO KILL YOU. Do you know a hunk a paper flyin' fast enough cut you in half like a knife, and when this baby hit, 15 meters in all directions, ONE THOUSAND HUNKS A WIRE GOIN' FAST ENOUGH!

(ARDELL *enters, joining* PAVLO *who celebrates.*)

PAVLO: Did I do it to him, Ardell? The triple Hummel? Got to be big and bad. A little shuffle. Did I ever tell you? Thirteen months a my life ago.

YEN: Paaaabloooo, boucoup love!

PAVLO: Thirteen months a my life ago. (SGT. WALL, *pulling pin on the grenade is there in the corner, beginning to move.*) What she did my ole lady, she called Joanna a slut and I threw kitty litter, screamin'—cat shit—"happy birthday!" She called that sweet church-goin' girl a whore. To be seen by her now, up tight with this oddlookin' whore, feelin' good and tall, ready to bed down. Feelin'—

(*The grenade lands, having been thrown by* SGT. WALL *moving in a semi circle, and fleeing.* PAVLO *drops to his knees seizing the grenade, looking up in awe at* ARDELL. *The grenade is in* PAVLO's *hands in his lap. Oh Christ! The explosion is there, now loud, it is a storm going into darkness and changing light. Silence. Body detail enters as* ARDELL, *looking at* PAVLO *lying there begins to speak. The body detail will wrap* PAVLO *in a poncho, put him on a stretcher, carry him to.* ARDELL.)

ARDELL: He don't die right off. Take him 4 days, 38 minutes. And he don't say nothin' to nobody in all that time. No words; he just kinda lay up and look and when he die, he bitin' on his lower lip, I don't know why. So they take him, they put him in a blue rubber bag, zip it up tight and haul him off to the morgue in the back of a quarter-ton where he get stuck naked into the refrigerator long with the other boys killed that day and the beer and cheese and tuna and stuff the guys who work at the morgue keep in the refrigerator except when it inspection time. The bag get washed, hung out to dry on a line out back a the morgue. (*Slight pause.*) Then . . . lemme see, well, finally, he get shipped home and his mother cry a lot and his brother get so depressed he gotta go out and lay his chippie he so damn depressed about it all; and Joanna, she read his name in the paper, she let out this little gasp and say to her husband across the table, "Jesus, Jimmy, I used to go with that boy. Oh, damn that war, why can't we have peace? I think I'll call his mother." Ain't it some kinda world? (*Laughing.*) Sooooooooo . . . that about it. That about all I got to say. Am I right, Pavlo? Did I tell you true? You got anything to say? Oh, man, I know you do, you say it out. (*Slight pause as* ARDELL *moves to uncover* PAVLO.) Man, you don't say it out, I don't wanna know you. Be cool as you wanna be, Pavlo! Beee cool; leeme hear you . . . You tell it to me: what you think of the cause? What you think a gettin' your ass blown clean off a freedom's frontier? What you think a bein' R.A. regular army lifer?

PAVLO (*softly, with nearly embarrassed laughter*): Sheeeeee . . . ittttt . . . Oh, lord . . . oh . . .

ARDELL: Ain't it what happened to you? Lemme hear it.

PAVLO: . . . Shit!

ARDELL: And what you think a all the "folks back home," sayin' you a victim . . . you a animal . . . you a fool . . .

PAVLO: They shit!

ARDELL: Yeh, Baby; now I know you. It all shit.

PAVLO: It all shit!

ARDELL: You my man again.

PAVLO: It shit.

ARDELL: Lemme hear it! My *main* man.

PAVLO: SHIT!

ARDELLL: Main motherfuckin' man.

PAVLO: OH, SHIT!

ARDELL: GO!

PAVLO: SHIT!

ARDELL: GET IT! GET IT!

PAVLO: SHHHHHHHHHIIIIIIIIITTTTTTTTTT-ttttttttt!

(*As the howl continues into silence four men enter carrying the aluminum box of a coffin, while two other men go across the back of the stage doing the drill, the marching and twirling rifles that were done at the end of the first act. They go now, however, in the opposite direction, and the coffin is placed beside* PAVLO.)

ARDELL: That right. How you feel? You feel all right? You gotta get that stuff outta you, man. You body know that and you body smart; you don't get that outta you, it back up on you, man, poison you. (*The four men are placing* PAVLO *in the coffin.*)

PAVLO: But . . . I . . . am dead! (*The men turn and leave. There is no precision in anything they do. All is casual, daily work.*)

ARDELL: Real soon; got wings as big as streets; got large large wings. Comin' on. (*Slight pause.*) You want me to talk shit to you? Man, sure, we siftin' things over, ain't we. We in a bar, man, back home, we got good soft chairs, beer in our hands, go-go girls all around; one of 'em got her eye on you, 'nother one thinkin' little bit on me. You believe what I'm sayin'. You home, Pavlo. (*Pause.*) Now . . . you c'mon and you be with me . . . We gonna do a little singin'. You be with me. Saw some stockin's . . . on the street . . . (*Silence.*)

PAVLO: Saw some . . . stockin's . . . on . . . the street.

ARDELL (*slight pause*): . . . wished I was . . . between those . . . feet . . .

PAVLO: Wished I was between those feet! (*Slight pause.*)

ARDELL *and* PAVLO (*together*): Once a week, I get to town, they see me comin', they jus' lay down . . .

ARDELL: Sergeant, sergeant, can't you see . . .

PAVLO: Sergeant, sergeant, can't you see . . .

ARDELL: All this misery's killin' . . . me . . .

PAVLO: All this misery's killin' . . . (ARDELL *lets the coffin close; it thuds.*)

ARDELL:
Ain't no matter what you do . . .
Jody done it . . . all to you . . .

(*Slight pause:* ARDELL *is backing away.*)

Lift your heads and lift 'em high . . .

(ARDELL *turns, begins to walk away*.)

Pavlo Hummel . . . . passin' by . . .

(*As* ARDELL *disappears upstage, the coffin stands in real light*.)

Neil Simon: *The Sunshine Boys* (1972)

By all accounts, Neil Simon must be considered the comic prodigy of American drama. Few playwrights of any generation have dominated Broadway the way he has—at one time four of his plays ran on Broadway simultaneously. None of Simon's plays have had fewer than 100 performances; most have seen more than 500, and two have enjoyed more than 1000 performances. This record is unequaled on the American stage.

Simon was born in 1927 and raised first in the Bronx and then in Manhattan, where he still has a residence. His career as a writer began when he got out of the army in 1946 and started working in radio with his brother Danny. He moved into television relatively early (1948) and became famous as a comedy and gag writer for Sid Caesar, Phil Silvers, Garry Moore, and many others. He did some bits for shows that got on Broadway, but did not write a play of his own until 1957 or 1958, when he wrote *Come Blow Your Horn,* produced in 1961. It was based in part on his and his brother's experiences living in New York when they first went out on their own. Getting the play produced was not easy—Simon reports three years of trying and imploring eight producers before one would actually do it. He wrote the books for a number of musicals as well as screenplays for some films, but all the while he was still aiming at the legitimate stage.

His biggest hit was *Barefoot in the Park,* which ran for 1532 performances, starting in 1963. This was followed by *The Odd Couple* (1965), *Star Spangled Girl* (1966), *Plaza Suite* (1968), *The Last of the Red Hot Lovers* (1969), *The Gingerbread Lady* (1970), *Prisoner of Second Avenue* (1971), *The Good Doctor* (1973), *God's Favorite* (1974), *California Suite* (1976), *Chapter Two* (1977), and *I Ought to Be in Pictures* (1980).

Partly because he is so prolific, and partly because his comedies depend on funny lines and amusing situations, serious critics have sometimes ignored him when talking about the current developments in American drama. The fact that his work has been easily adapted to television—the long-running sit-com *The Odd Couple,* is one example—has also led some critics to devalue his work. Some of his plays have moved beyond the situation comedy genre, and in his recent *Chapter Two* he has produced an autobiographical study that is in many ways the analogue of Arthur Miller's *After the Fall.* Even *God's Favorite,* based in part on *Job,* was something of a departure, although it has proved to be his least successful play (119 performances) both in terms of its critical success and its audience appeal. As Simon once said, "When I was good, I was very, very good. When I was bad, we folded."

Simon believes his best play is *The Sunshine Boys,* yet it is one of the least likely plays to be designated as his best. It is not about young people or even the problems and foibles of middle age. Nor is it a social or satirical comedy; it does not point to the amusing sillinesses of the way we live. Because it is about very old people, it begins with an immense handicap—one rule of the theater is to write about the young, since everyone can remember being young and no one wants to think about getting old. Yet the play definitely works. Its success lies in the skillful drawing of the two main characters, Al Lewis and Willie Clark, the aging comedians who've been on the outs for eleven years. Even in their senility, they have a compelling personal dimension. By contrast, the thoughtful Ben Silverman (Willie's nephew) seems thin, brittle, and virtually uninteresting. The years of resentment and bitterness may not be very attractive in Willie's character, but they produce a flawlessly realized person on stage.

The play could easily become a diatribe on senility or an attack on aging, yet Simon moves us away from any possibility of sentimentality or melodrama. We do not feel sorry for these two old vaudevillians who, after flubbing their one-shot "comeback," are now discovering that they are condemned to an involuntary "reunion" in the Old Actors' Home in New Jersey—a reunion that will last the rest of their lives. Part of the reason we do not reach out in false sympathy for these characters and their situation is that they are too feisty. Despite their pathetic situation, they continue their own independent brawl with life, asking nothing of one another and very little of anyone else. Ben Silverman is constantly helping Willie, but it is partly out of family duty, partly out of his feeling sorry for the one-time star. Yet, Willie tells him he doesn't have to do what he's doing; he appreciates it, but it isn't necessary. The nurse's reaction in the last scene is more like ours—she does her job, but she surely does not give Willie any unnecessary pity.

Willie's a tough old guy and she is on her guard.

Characterizing these old-time comedians in this fashion preserves their dignity. True, they are sometimes very funny. And we often laugh at them, at their age, their stubbornness, their outright orneryness. But all the while we certainly do not feel sorry for them. They are a formidable pair and we know it. They have what some of Neil Simon's other characters do not have: a fullness, a roundedness, a profound third dimension that makes them seem as real as people we get to know well. Such depth of characterization is not needed for most comedies. Indeed, it sometimes hurts. But this play works well because Simon can keep us amused and yet give us the feeling that we have come to know his people very well: we would recognize them immediately if we met them on the street.

Simon's career is already amazing. It will be interesting to see how he will treat his dramatic talent in the coming years.

Suggested Readings

Edythe M. McGovern, *Neil Simon: A Critical Study* (New York: Frederick Ungar, 1979)

The Sunshine Boys

Neil Simon

CHARACTERS

WILLIE CLARK	REGISTERED NURSE
BEN SILVERMAN	VOICE FROM TV
AL LEWIS	VOICE OF TV DIRECTOR
EDDIE	VOICE OF ANNOUNCER
TV actors:	
PATIENT	
NURSE	

THE SCENE

The action takes place in New York City.

ACT I

SCENE 1: A small apartment in an old hotel on upper Broadway, in the mid-Eighties. It is an early afternoon in midwinter.

SCENE 2: The following Monday, late morning.

ACT II

SCENE 1: A Manhattan television studio.

SCENE 2: The same as Act I. It is two weeks later, late afternoon.

ACT I

SCENE 1

(*The scene is a two-room apartment in an old hotel on upper Broadway, in the mid-Eighties. It's rather a depressing place. There is a bed, a bureau, a small dining table with two chairs, an old leather chair that faces a TV set on a cheap, metal stand. There is a small kitchen to one side—partitioned off from the living room by a curtain—a small bathroom on the other. A window looks out over Broadway. It is early afternoon, midwinter.*

At rise, the TV is on, and the banal dialogue of a soap opera drones on. In the leather chair sits WILLIE CLARK, *in slippers, pajamas and an old bathrobe.* WILLIE *is in his seventies. He watches the program but is constantly dozing off, then catching himself and watching for a few more minutes at a time. The set drones on and* WILLIE *dozes off. The tea kettle on the stove in the kitchen comes to a boil and whistles.* WILLIE'S *head perks up at the sound; he reaches over and picks up the telephone.*)

WILLIE (*into the phone*): Hello? . . . Who's this?

(*The whistle continues from the kettle, and* WILLIE *looks over in that direction. He hangs up the phone and does not seem embarrassed or even aware of his own absent-mindedness. He simply crosses into the kitchen and turns off the flame under the kettle.*)

VOICE FROM TV: We'll be back with *Storm Warning* after this brief message from Lipton Tea.

WILLIE: Don't worry, I'm not going anywhere.

(*He puts a tea ball into a mug and pours the boiling water in. Then he goes over to the dining table in the living room, takes a spoon, dips into a jar of honey, and pours it into his tea. He glances over at the TV set, which has just played the Lipton Tea commercial.*)

VOICE FROM TV: And now for Part Three of today's *Storm Warning* . . .

WILLIE: What happened to Part Two? I missed Part Two? (*He drinks his tea as Part Three continues and the banal dialogue drones on.* WILLIE *listens as he shuffles toward his chair. The TV set, which is away from the wall, has an electric plug running from it, along the ground and into the wall.* WILLIE, *who never seems to look where he's going, comes up against the cord with his foot, inadvertently pulling the cord off its socket in the wall. The TV set immediately dies.* WILLIE *sits, then looks at the set. Obviously, no picture. He gets up and fiddles with the dials. How could his best friend desert him at a time like this? He hits the set on the top with his hand.*) What's the matter with you? (*He hits the set again and twists the knobs futilely, never thinking for a moment it might be something as simple as the plug. He slaps the picture tube.*) Come on, for Pete's sakes, what are you doing there? (*He stares at it in disbelief. He kicks the stand on which it rests. Then he crosses to the phone, and picks it up.*) Hello? . . . Sandy? . . . Let me have Sandy . . . Sandy? . . . My television's dead . . . My television . . . Is this Sandy? . . . My television died . . . No, not Willie. Mr. Clark to you, please . . . Never mind the jokes, wise guy, it's not funny . . . Send up somebody to fix my dead television . . . I didn't touch nothing . . . Nothing, I'm telling you . . . It's a crappy set . . . You live in a crappy hotel, you get a crappy television . . . The what? . . . The plug? . . . What plug? . . . Wait a minute. (*He lays the phone down, crosses to behind the set, bends down, picks up the plug and looks at it. He goes back to the telephone. Into the phone.*) Hello? . . . It's not the plug. It's something else. I'll fix it myself. (*He hangs up, goes over to the wall plug and plugs it in. The set goes back on.*) He tells me the plug . . . When he calls me Mr. Clark then I'll tell him it was the plug. (*He sits and picks up his cup of tea.*) The hell with all of 'em. (*There is a knock on the door.* WILLIE *looks at the wall on the*

opposite side of the room.*) Bang all you want, I'm not turning it off. I'm lucky it works.

(*There is a pause; then a knock on the front door again, this time accompanied by a male voice.*)

BEN's VOICE: Uncle Willie? It's me. Ben.

(WILLIE *turns and looks at the front door, not acknowledging that he was mistaken about the knocking on the other wall.*)

WILLIE: Who's that?
BEN's VOICE: Ben.
WILLIE: Ben? Is that you?
BEN's VOICE: Yes, Uncle Willie, it's Ben. Open the door.
WILLIE: Wait a minute. (*He rises, crosses to the door, tripping over the TV cord again, disconnecting the set. He starts to unlatch the door, but has trouble manipulating it. His fingers are not too manipulative.*) Wait a minute . . . (*He is having great difficulty with it.*) . . . Wait a minute.
BEN's VOICE: Is anything wrong?
WILLIE (*still trying*): Wait a minute. (*He tries forcing it.*)
BEN's VOICE: What's the matter?
WILLIE: I'm locked in. The lock is broken, I'm locked in. Go down and tell the boy. Sandy. Tell Sandy that Mr. Clark is locked in.
BEN's VOICE: What is it, the latch?
WILLIE: It's the latch. It's broken, I'm locked in. Go tell the boy Sandy, they'll get somebody.
BEN's VOICE: That happened last week. Don't try to force it. Just slide it out. (WILLIE *stares at the latch.*) Uncle Willie, do you hear me? Don't force it. Slide it out.
WILLIE (*fiddling with the latch*): Wait a minute. (*Carefully, he slides it open.*) It's open. Never mind, I did it myself.

(*He opens the door.* BEN SILVERMAN, *a well dressed man in his early thirties, enters. He is wearing a topcoat and carrying a shopping bag from Bloomingdale's, filled to the brim with assorted foodstuffs and a copy of the weekly* Variety.)

BEN: You probably have to oil it.
WILLIE: I don't have to oil nothing. The hell with 'em.

(BEN *hangs up his coat in the closet.*)

BEN (*crosses to the table with the shopping bag*): You feeling all right?
WILLIE: What is this, Wednesday?
BEN (*puzzled*): Certainly. Don't I always come on Wednesdays?

WILLIE: But this is Wednesday today?

BEN (*puts his bag down*): Yes, of course. Haven't you been out?

WILLIE: When?

BEN: Today. Yesterday. This week. You haven't been out all week?

WILLIE (*crossing to him*): Sunday. I was out Sunday. I went to the park Sunday.

(BEN *hands* WILLIE *the* Variety. WILLIE *tucks it under his arm and starts to look through the shopping bag.*)

BEN: What are you looking for?

WILLIE (*going through his bag*): My Variety.

BEN: I just gave it to you. It's under your arm.

WILLIE (*looks under his arm*): Why do you put it there? He puts it under my arm.

BEN (*starts taking items out of the bag*): Have you been eating properly? No corned beef sandwiches, I hope.

WILLIE (*opens to the back section*): Is this today's?

BEN: Certainly it's today's. *Variety* comes out on Wednesday, doesn't it? And today is Wednesday.

WILLIE: I'm just asking, don't get so excited. (BEN *shakes his head in consternation.*) . . . Because I already read last Wednesday's.

BEN (*takes more items out*): I got you six different kinds of soups. All low-sodium, salt-free. All very good for you . . . Are you listening?

WILLIE (*his head in the paper*): I'm listening. You got six lousy-tasting soups . . . Did you see this?

BEN: What?

WILLIE: What I'm looking at. Did you see this?

BEN: How do I know what you're looking at?

WILLIE: Two new musicals went into rehearsals today and I didn't even get an audition. Why didn't I get an audition?

BEN: Because there were no parts for you. One of them is a young rock musical and the other show is all black.

WILLIE: What's the matter, I can't do black? I did black in 1928. And when I did black, you understood the words, not like today.

BEN: I'm sorry, you're not the kind of black they're looking for. (*He shivers.*) Geez, it's cold in here. You know it's freezing in here? Don't they ever send up any heat?

WILLIE (*has turned a page*): How do you like that? Sol Burton died.

BEN: Who?

WILLIE: Sol Burton. The songwriter. Eighty-nine years old, went like that, from nothing.

BEN: Why didn't you put on a sweater?

WILLIE: I knew him very well . . . A terrible person. Mean, mean. He should rest in peace, but he was a mean person. His best friends didn't like him.

BEN (*goes to the bureau for a sweater*): Why is it so cold in here?

WILLIE: You know what kind of songs he wrote? . . . The worst. The worst songs ever written were written by Sol Burton. (*He sings.*) "Lady, Lady, be my baby . . ." Did you ever hear anything so rotten? Baby he rhymes with lady . . . No wonder he's dead. (*He turns the page.*)

BEN: This radiator is ice-cold. Look, Uncle Willie, I'm not going to let you live here any more. You've got to let me find you another place . . . I've been asking you for seven years now. You're going to get sick.

WILLIE (*still looking at* Variety): Tom Jones is gonna get a hundred thousand dollars a week in Las Vegas. When Lewis and I were headlining at the Palace, the *Palace* didn't cost a hundred thousand dollars.

BEN: That was forty years ago. And forty years ago this hotel was twenty years old. They should tear it down. They take advantage of all you people in here because they know you don't want to move.

(WILLIE *crosses to the table and looks into the shopping bag.*)

WILLIE: No cigars?

BEN (*making notes on his memo pad*): You're not supposed to have cigars.

WILLIE: Where's the cigars?

BEN: You know the doctor told you you're not supposed to smoke cigars any more. I didn't bring any.

WILLIE: Gimme the cigars.

BEN: What cigars? I just said I don't have them. Will you forget the cigars?

WILLIE: Where are they, in the bag?

BEN: On the bottom. I just brought three. It's the last time I'm doing it.

WILLIE (*takes out a bag with three cigars*): How's your family? The children all right? (*He removes one cigar.*)

BEN: Suddenly you're interested in my family? It's not going to work, Uncle Willie. I'm not bringing you any more cigars.

WILLIE: I just want to know how the children are.

BEN: The children are fine. They're wonderful, thank you.

WILLIE: Good. Next time bring the big cigars. (*He puts two cigars in the breast pocket of his bathrobe and the other one in his mouth. He crosses into the kitchen looking for a light.*)

BEN: You don't even know their names. What are the names of my children?

WILLIE: Millie and Sidney.

BEN: Amanda and Michael.

WILLIE: What's the matter, you didn't like Millie and Sidney?

BEN: I was *never* going to name them Millie and Sidney. You forgot, so you made something up. You forget everything. I'll bet you didn't drink the milk from last week. I'll bet it's still in the refrigerator. (*Crosses quickly, and opens the refrigerator and looks in.*) There's the milk from last week.

WILLIE (*comes out of the kitchen, still looking for a light*): Do they know who I am?

BEN (*looking through the refrigerator*): Who?

WILLIE: Amanda and Sidney.

BEN: Amanda and Michael. That you were a big star in vaudeville? They're three years old, Uncle Willie, you think they remember vaudeville? *I* never saw vaudeville . . . This refrigerator won't last another two days.

WILLIE: Did you tell them six times on *The Ed Sullivan Show?* (*He sits, tries a cigarette lighter. It's broken.*)

BEN: They never heard of Ed Sullivan. Uncle Willie, they're three years old. They don't follow show business. (*Comes back into the living room and sees* WILLIE *with the cigar in his mouth.*) What are you doing? You're not going to smoke that now. You promised me you'd only smoke one after dinner.

WILLIE: Am I smoking it? Do you see smoke coming from the cigar?

BEN: But you've got it in your mouth.

WILLIE: I'm rehearsing . . . After dinner I'll do the show.

BEN (*crossing back into the kitchen*)· I'm in the most aggravating business in the whole world and I never get aggravated until I come here. (*He opens the cupboards and looks in.*)

WILLIE (*looking around*): So don't come. I got Social Security.

BEN: You think that's funny? I don't think that's funny, Uncle Willie.

WILLIE (*thumbing through* Variety): If you had a sense of humor, you'd think it was funny.

BEN (*angrily, through gritted teeth*): I have a *terrific* sense of humor.

WILLIE: Like your father—he laughed once in 1932.

BEN: I can't talk to you.

WILLIE: Why, they're funny today? Tell me who you think is funny today, and I'll show you where he's not funny.

BEN: Let's not get into that, huh? I've got to get back to the office. Just promise me you'll have a decent lunch today.

WILLIE: If I were to tell a joke and got a laugh from you, I'd throw it out.

BEN: How can I laugh when I see you like this, Uncle Willie? You sit in your pajamas all day in a freezing apartment watching soap operas on a thirty-five-dollar television set that doesn't have a horizontal hold. The picture just keeps rolling from top to bottom—pretty soon your eyes are gonna roll around your head . . . You never eat anything. You never go out because you don't know how to work the lock on the door. Remember when you locked yourself in the bathroom overnight? It's a lucky thing you keep bread in there, you would have starved . . . And you wonder why I worry.

WILLIE: Calvin Coolidge, that's your kind of humor.

BEN: Look, Uncle Willie, promise me you'll eat decently.

WILLIE: I'll eat decently. I'll wear a blue suit, a white shirt and black shoes.

BEN: And if you're waiting for a laugh, you're not going to get one from me.

WILLIE: Who could live that long? Get me a job instead of a laugh.

BEN (*sighs, exasperatedly*): You know I've been trying, Uncle Willie. It's not easy. There's not much in town. Most of the work is commercials and . . . well, you know, we've had a little trouble in that area.

WILLIE: ·The potato chips? The potato chips wasn't my fault.

BEN: Forget the potato chips.

WILLIE: What about the Shick Injector? Didn't I audition funny on the Shick Injector?

BEN: You were very funny but your hand was shaking. And you can't show a man shaving with a shaky hand.

WILLIE: Why couldn't you get me on the Alka-Seltzer? That's my kind of comedy. I got a terrific face for an upset stomach.

BEN: I've submitted you twenty times.

WILLIE: What's the matter with twenty-one?

BEN: Because the word is out in the business that you can't remember the lines, and they're simply not interested.

WILLIE (*that hurt*): I couldn't remember the lines? I COULDN'T REMEMBER THE LINES? I don't remember that.

BEN: For the Frito-Lays potato chips. I sent you over to the studio, you couldn't even remember the address.

WILLIE: Don't tell me I didn't remember the lines. The lines I remembered beautifully. The name of the potato chip I couldn't remember . . . What was it?

BEN: Frito-Lays.

WILLIE: Say it again.

BEN: Frito-Lays.

WILLIE: I still can't remember it—because it's not funny. If it's funny, I remember it. Alka-Seltzer is funny. You say "Alka-Seltzer," you get a laugh. The other word is not funny. What is it?

BEN: Frito-Lays.

WILLIE: Maybe in *Mexico* that's funny, not here. Fifty-seven years I'm in this business, you learn a few things. You know what makes an audience laugh. Do you know which words are funny and which words are *not* funny?

BEN: You told me a hundred times, Uncle Willie. Words with a "K" in it are funny.

WILLIE: Words with a "K" in it are funny. You didn't know that, did you? If it doesn't have a "K", it's not funny. I'll tell you which words always get a laugh. (*He is about to count on his fingers.*)

BEN: Chicken.

WILLIE: Chicken is funny.

BEN: Pickle.

WILLIE: Pickle is funny.

BEN: Cupcake.

WILLIE: Cupcake is funny . . . Tomato is *not* funny. Roast beef is *not* funny.

BEN: But cookie is funny.

WILLIE: But cookie is funny.

BEN: Uncle Willie, you've explained that to me ever since I was a little boy.

WILLIE: Cucumber is funny.

BEN (*falling in again*): Car keys.

WILLIE: Car keys is funny.

BEN: Cleveland.

WILLIE: Cleveland is funny . . . Maryland is *not* funny.

BEN: Listen, I have to get back to the office, Uncle Willie, but there's something I'd like to talk to you about first. I got a call yesterday from C.B.S.

WILLIE: Casey Stengel, that's funny name; Robert Taylor is not funny.

BEN (*sighs exasperatedly*): Why don't you listen to me?

WILLIE: I heard. You got a call from N.B.C.

BEN: C.B.S.

WILLIE: Whatever.

BEN: C.B.S. is doing a big special next month. An hour and a half variety show. They're going to have some of the biggest names in the history of show business. They're trying to get Flip Wilson to host the show.

WILLIE: Him I like. He gives me a laugh. With the dress and the little giggle and the red wig. That's a funny boy . . . What's the boy's name again?

BEN: Flip Wilson. And it doesn't have a K.

WILLIE: But he's *black,* with a "K." You see what I mean?

BEN (*looks to heaven for help. It doesn't come*): I do, I do. The theme of this variety show—

WILLIE: What's the theme of the show?

BEN: *The theme of the show* is the history of comedy dating from the early Greek times, through the days of vaudeville, right up to today's stars.

WILLIE: Why couldn't you get me on this show?

BEN: I *got* you on the show.

WILLIE: Alone?

BEN: With Lewis.

WILLIE (*turns away*): You ain't got me on the show.

BEN: Let me finish.

WILLIE: You're finished. It's no.

BEN: Can't you wait until I'm through before you say "no"? Can't we discuss it for a minute?

WILLIE: I'm busy.

BEN: Doing what?

WILLIE: Saying "no."

BEN: You can have the courtesy of hearing me out. They begged me at C.B.S. *Begged* me.

WILLIE: Talk faster, because you're coming up to another "no."

BEN: They said to me the history of comedy in the United States would not be complete unless they included one of the greatest teams ever to come out of vaudeville, Lewis and Clark, The Sunshine Boys. The vice-president of C.B.S. said this to me on the phone.

WILLIE: The vice-president said this?

BEN: Yes. He is the greatest Lewis and Clark fan in this country. He knows by heart every one of your old routines.

WILLIE: Then let *him* go on with that bastard.

BEN: It's one shot. You would just have to do

it one night, one of the old sketches. They'll pay ten thousand dollars for the team. That's top money for these shows, I promise you. Five thousand dollars apiece. And that's more money than you've earned in two years.

WILLIE: I don't need money. I live alone. I got two nice suits, I don't have a pussycat, I'm very happy.

BEN: You're *not* happy. You're miserable.

WILLIE: *I'm happy!* I just *look* miserable!

BEN: You're dying to go to work again. You call me six times a day in the office. I can't see over my desk for all your messages.

WILLIE: Call me back sometime, you won't get so many messages.

BEN: I call you every day of the week. I'm up here every Wednesday, rain or shine, winter or summer, flu or diphtheria.

WILLIE: What are you, a mailman? You're a nephew. I don't ask you to come. You're my brother's son, you've been very nice to me. I appreciate it, but I've never asked you for anything . . . except for a job. You're a good boy but a stinking agent.

BEN: I'M A GOOD AGENT? Damn it, don't say that to me, Uncle Willie, I'm a *goddamn good agent!*

WILLIE: What are you screaming for? What is it, such a wonderful thing to be a good agent?

BEN (*holds his chest*): I'm getting chest pains. You give me chest pains, Uncle Willie.

WILLIE: It's *my* fault you get excited?

BEN: Yes, it's *your* fault! I only get chest pains on Wednesdays.

WILLIE: So come on Tuesdays.

BEN (*starts for the door*): I'm going. I don't even want to discuss this with you any more. You're impossible to talk to. FORGET THE VARIETY SHOW! (*He starts for the door.*)

WILLIE: I forgot it.

BEN (*stops*): I'm not coming back any more. I'm not bringing you your *Variety* or your cigars or your low-sodium soups—do you understand, Uncle Willie? I'm not bringing you anything any more.

WILLIE: Good. Take care of yourself. Say hello to Millie and Phyllis.

BEN (*breathing heavily*): Why won't you do this for me? I'm not asking you to be partners again. If you two don't get along, all right. But this is just for one night. One last show. Once you get an exposure like that, Alka-Seltzer will come begging to *me* to sign you up. Jesus, how is it going to look if I go back to the office and tell them I couldn't make a deal with my own uncle?

WILLIE: My personal opinion? Lousy!

BEN (*falls into a chair, exhausted*): Do you really hate Al Lewis that much?

WILLIE (*looks away*): I don't discuss Al Lewis any more.

BEN (*gets up*): We *have* to discuss him, because C.B.S. is waiting for an answer today, and if we turn them down, I want to have a pretty good reason why. You haven't seen him in—what? ten years now.

WILLIE (*takes a long time before answering*): Eleven years!

BEN (*amazed*): You mean to tell me you haven't spoken to him in eleven years?

WILLIE: I haven't *seen* him in eleven years. I haven't *spoken* to him in twelve years.

BEN: You mean you saw him for a whole year that you didn't speak to him?

WILLIE: It wasn't easy. I had to sneak around backstage a lot.

BEN: But you spoke to him onstage.

WILLIE: Not to *him*. If he played a gypsy, I spoke to the gypsy. If he played a lunatic, I spoke to the lunatic. But that bastard I didn't speak to.

BEN: I can't believe that.

WILLIE: You don't believe it? I can show you witnesses who *saw* me never speaking to him.

BEN: It's been eleven years, Uncle Willie. Hasn't time changed anything for you?

WILLIE: Yes. I hate him eleven years more.

BEN: Why?

WILLIE: Why? . . . You never met him?

BEN: Sure I met him. I was fifteen years old. I met him once at that benefit at Madison Square Garden and once backstage at some television show. He seemed nice enough to me.

WILLIE: That's only twice. You had to meet him three times to hate him.

BEN: Uncle Willie, could I make a suggestion?

WILLIE: He used to give me the finger.

BEN: The what?

WILLIE: The finger! The finger! He would poke me in the chest with the finger. (*He crosses to* BEN *and demonstrates on him by poking a finger in* BEN's *chest every time he makes a point.*) He would say, "*Listen,* Doctor." (*Pokes finger.*) "I'm *telling* you, Doctor." (*Pokes finger.*) "You know what I *mean,* Doctor." (*Pokes finger.* BEN *rubs his chest in pain.*) Hurts, doesn't it? How'd you like it for forty-three years? I got a black and blue hole in my chest. My wife to her dying day thought it was a tattoo. I haven't worked with him in eleven years, it's just beginning to fade away . . . The man had the sharpest finger in show business.

BEN: If you work with him again, I promise you I'll buy you a thick padded undershirt.

WILLIE: You think I never did that? One night I put a steel plate under my shirt. He gave me the finger, he had it in a splint for a month.

BEN: Something else must have happened you're not telling me about. You don't work with a person for forty-three years without some bond of affection remaining.

WILLIE: You wanna hear other things? He used to spit in my face. Onstage *the man would spit in my face!*

BEN: Not on purpose.

WILLIE (*turns away*): He tells me "not on purpose" . . . If there was some way I could have saved the spit, I would show it to you.

BEN: You mean he would just stand there and spit in your face?

WILLIE: What do you think, he's stupid? He worked it into the act. He would stand with his nose on top of my nose and purposely only say words that began with a "T." (*As he demonstrates, he spits.*) "Tootsie Roll." (*Spit.*) "Tinker Toy." (*Spit.*) "Typing on the *typewriter.*" (*Spits.* BEN *wipes his face.*) Some nights I thought I would drown! I don't know where he got it all from . . . I think he would drink all day and save it up for the night.

BEN: I'll put it in the contract. If he spits at you, he won't get paid.

WILLIE: If he can get another chance to spit at me, he wouldn't *want* to get paid.

BEN: Then will you answer me one question? If it was all that bad, why did you stick together for forty-three years?

WILLIE (*turns; looks at him*): Because he was terrific. There'll never be another one like him . . . Nobody could time a joke the way he could time a joke. Nobody could say a line the way he said it. I knew what he was thinking, he knew what I was thinking. One person, that's what we were . . . No, no. Al Lewis was the best. The *best!* You understand?

BEN: I understand.

WILLIE: As an actor, no one could touch him. As a human being, no one *wanted* to touch him.

BEN (*sighs*): So what do I tell C.B.S.? No deal because Al Lewis spits?

WILLIE: You know when the last time was we worked together?

BEN: Eleven years ago on *The Ed Sullivan Show.*

WILLIE: Eleven years ago on *The Ed Sullivan Show.* July twenty-seventh. He wouldn't put us on in the winter when people were watching, but never mind. We did The Doctor and the Tax Examination. You never saw that, did you?

BEN: No, but I heard it's wonderful.

WILLIE: What about a "classic"? *A classic!* A dead person watching that sketch would laugh. We did it maybe eight thousand times, it never missed . . . *That* night it missed. Something was wrong with him, he was rushing, his timing was off, his mind was someplace else. I thought he was sick. Still, we got terrific applause. Five times Ed Sullivan said, "How about that?" We got back into the dressing room, he took off his make-up, put on his clothes, and said to me, "Willie, if it's all the same to you, I'm retiring." I said, "What do you mean, retiring? It's not even nine o'clock. Let's have something to eat. He said, "I'm not retiring for the night. I'm retiring for what's left of my life." And he puts on his hat, walks out of the theater, becomes a stockbroker and I'm left with an act where I ask questions and there's no one there to answer. Never saw the man again to this day. Oh, he called me, I wouldn't answer. He wrote me, I tore it up. He sent me telegrams, they're probably still under the door.

BEN: Well, Uncle Willie, with all due respect, you really weren't getting that much work any more. Maybe he was getting tired of doing the same thing for forty-three years. I mean a man has a right to retire when he wants, doesn't he?

WILLIE: Not him. Don't forget, when he retired himself, he retired me too. And goddamn it, I wasn't ready yet. Now suddenly maybe he needs five thousand dollars, and he wants to come crawling back, the hell with him. I'm a single now . . .

BEN: I spoke to Al Lewis on the phone last night. He doesn't even care about the money. He just wants to do the show for old times' sake. For his grandchildren who never saw him.

WILLIE: Sure. He probably retired broke from the stock market. I guarantee you *those* high-class people never got a spit in the face once.

BEN: Did you know his wife died two years ago? He's living with his daughter now, somewhere in New Jersey. He doesn't do anything any more. He's got very bad arthritis, he's got asthma, he's got poor blood circulation—

WILLIE: I'll send him a pump. He'll outlive *you,* believe me.

BEN: He wants very much to do this show, Willie.

WILLIE: With arthritis? Forget it. Instead of a finger, he'll poke me with a cane.

BEN: C.B.S. wants you to do the doctor sketch. Lewis told me he could get on a stage tonight and do that sketch letter perfect. He doesn't even have to rehearse it.

WILLIE: I don't even want to discuss it ... And in the second place, I would definitely not do it without a rehearsal.

BEN: All right, then will you agree to this? Just rehearse with him one day. If it doesn't work out, we'll call it off.

WILLIE: I don't trust him. I think he's been planning this for eleven years. We rehearse all week and then he walks out on me just before the show.

BEN: Let me call him on the phone. (*Going over to the phone.*) Let me set up a rehearsal time for Monday.

WILLIE: WAIT A MINUTE! I got to think about this.

BEN: We don't have that much time. C.B.S. is waiting to hear.

WILLIE: What's their rush? What are they, going out of business?

BEN (*picks up the phone*): I'm dialing. I'm dialing him, Uncle Willie, okay?

WILLIE: Sixty-forty—I get six thousand, he gets four thousand ... What the hell can he buy in New Jersey anyway?

BEN (*holding the phone*): I can't do that, Uncle Willie ... God, I hope this works out.

WILLIE: Tell him I'm against it. I want him to know. I'll do it with an "against it."

BEN: It's ringing.

WILLIE: And he's got to come here. I'm not going there, you understand?

BEN: He's got to be home. I told him I would call about one.

WILLIE: Sure. You know what he's doing? He's practicing spitting.

BEN (*into the phone*): Hello? ... Mr. Lewis? ... Ben Silverman ... Yes, fine, thanks ... I'm here with him now.

WILLIE: Willie Clark. The one he left on *The Ed Sullivan Show.* Ask him if he remembers.

BEN: It's okay, Mr. Lewis ... Uncle Willie said yes.

WILLIE: With an "against it." Don't forget the "against it."

BEN: No, he's very anxious to do it.

WILLIE (*jumping up in anger*): WHO'S ANXIOUS? I'M AGAINST IT! TELL HIM, you lousy nephew.

BEN: Can you come here for rehearsal on Monday? ... Oh, that'll be swell ... In the morning. (*To* WILLIE.) About eleven o'clock? How long is the drive. About two hours?

WILLIE: Make it nine o'clock.

BEN: Be reasonable, Willie. (*Into the phone.*) Eleven o'clock is fine, Mr. Lewis ... Can you give me your address, please, so I can send you the contracts? (*He takes a pen out of his pocket and writes in his notebook.*) One-one-nine, South Pleasant Drive ...

WILLIE: Tell him if he starts with the spitting or poking, I'm taking him to court. I'll have a man on the show watching. Tell him.

BEN: West Davenport, New Jersey ... Oh-nine-seven-seven-oh-four ...

WILLIE: I don't want any—(*spitting*)—"Toy telephones tapping on tin turtles." Tell him. Tell him.

SCENE 2

(*It is the following Monday, a few minutes before eleven in the morning.*

The stage is empty. Suddenly the bathroom door opens and WILLIE *emerges. He is still wearing his slippers and the same pajamas, but instead of his bathrobe, he has made a concession to the occasion. He is wearing a double-breasted blue suit-jacket, buttoned, and he is putting a handkerchief in his pocket. He looks in the mirror, and brushes back his hair. He shuffles over to the window and looks out.*

There is a knock on the door. WILLIE *turns and stares at it. He doesn't move. There is another knock, and then we hear* BEN's *voice.*)

BEN'S VOICE: Uncle Willie. It's Ben.

WILLIE: Ben? Is that you?

BEN'S VOICE: Yes. Open up. (WILLIE *starts toward the door, then stops.*)

WILLIE: You're alone or he's with you?

BEN'S VOICE: I'm alone.

WILLIE (*nods*): Wait a minute. (*The latch is locked again, and again he has trouble getting it open.*) Wait a minute.

BEN'S VOICE: Slide it, don't push it.

WILLIE: Wait a minute. I'll push it.

BEN'S VOICE: *DON'T* PUSH IT! SLIDE IT!

WILLIE: Wait a minute. (*He gets the lock open and opens the door.* BEN *walks in.*) You're supposed to slide it.

BEN: I rushed like crazy. I didn't want him getting here before me. Did he call or anything?

WILLIE: Where's the *Variety?*

BEN (*taking off his coat*): It's Monday, not Wednesday. Didn't you know it was Monday?

WILLIE: I remembered, but I forgot.

BEN: What are you wearing? What is that? You look half-dressed.

WILLIE: Why, for him I should get *all* dressed?

BEN: Are you all right? Are you nervous or anything?

WILLIE: Why should *I* be nervous? *He* should be nervous. I don't get nervous.

BEN: Good.

WILLIE: Listen, I changed my mind. I'm not doing it.

BEN: *What?*

WILLIE: Don't get so upset. Everything is the same as before, except I'm not doing it.

BEN: When did you decide this?

WILLIE: I decided it when you asked me.

BEN: No, you didn't. You told me you *would* do it.

WILLIE: Well, it was a bad decision. This time I made a good one.

BEN: Well, I'm sorry, you have to do it. I've already told C.B.S. that you would be rehearsing this week and, more important, that man is on his way over here now and I'm not going to tell him that you called it off.

WILLIE: We'll leave him a note outside the door.

BEN: We're not leaving any notes. That's why I came here this morning, I was afraid you would try something like this. I'm going to stay until I think you're both acting like civilized human beings, and then when you're ready to rehearse, I'm going to leave you alone. Is that understood?

WILLIE: I'm sick. I woke up sick today.

BEN: No, you're not.

WILLIE: What are you, a doctor? You're an agent. I'm telling you I'm sick.

BEN: What's wrong?

WILLIE: I think I got hepatitis.

BEN: You don't even know what hepatitis is.

WILLIE: If you got it, what's the difference?

BEN: There's nothing wrong with you except a good case of the nerves. You're not backing out, Willie. I don't care what kind of excuse you make, you're going to go through with this. You promised me you would give it at least one day.

WILLIE: I'll pick another day.

BEN: TODAY! You're going to meet with him and rehearse with him TODAY. Now *stop* and just behave yourself.

WILLIE: What do you mean, "behave yourself"? Who do you think you're talking to, Susan and Jackie?

BEN: *Amanda* and Jackie!—Michael! I wish I were. I can reason with them. And now I'm getting chest pains on Monday.

WILLIE: Anyway, he's late. He's purposely coming late to aggravate me.

BEN (*looking out the window*): He's not late. It's two minutes after eleven.

WILLIE: So what is he, early? He's *late!*

BEN: You're *looking* to start trouble, I can tell.

WILLIE: I was up and dressed at eight o'clock, don't tell me.

BEN: Why didn't you shave?

WILLIE: Get me the Shick commercial, I'll shave. (*He looks in the mirror.*) I really think I got hepatitis. Look how green I look.

BEN: You don't get green from hepatitis. You get yellow.

WILLIE: Maybe I got a very bad case.

BEN (*looks at his watch*): Now you got me nervous. I wonder if I should call him? Maybe he's sick.

WILLIE (*glares at him*): You believe *he's* sick, but me you won't believe . . . Why don't you become *his* nephew? (*Suddenly there is a knock on the door.* WILLIE *freezes and stares at it.*)

BEN: That's him. You want me to get it—

WILLIE: Get what? I didn't hear anything.

BEN (*starts toward the door*): All right, now take it easy. Please just behave yourself and give this a chance. Promise me you'll give it a chance.

WILLIE (*starts for the kitchen*): I'll give it every possible chance in the world . . . But it's not gonna work.

BEN: Where are you going?

WILLIE: To make tea. I feel like some hot tea. (*He crosses into the kitchen and closes the curtain. Starts to fill up the kettle with water.*)

BEN (*panicky*): NOW? NOW? (BEN *looks at him, exasperated; a knock on the door again and* BEN *crosses to it and opens it.* AL LEWIS *stands there. He is also about seventy years old and is dressed in his best blue suit, hat, scarf, and carries a walking stick. He was probably quite a gay blade in his day, but time has slowed him down somewhat. Our first impression is that he is soft-spoken and pleasant—and a little nervous.*) Mr. Lewis, how do you do? I'm Ben Silverman. (BEN, *nervous, extends his hand.*)

AL: How are you? Hello. It's nice to see you. (*His eyes dart around looking for* WILLIE. *He doesn't see him yet.*) How do you do? . . . Hello . . . Hello . . . How are you?

BEN: We met before, a long time ago. My father took me backstage, I forget the theater. It must have been fifteen, twenty years ago.

AL: I remember . . . Certainly . . . It was backstage . . . Maybe fifteen, twenty years ago . . . I forget the theater.

BEN: That's right.

AL: Sure, I remember. (*He has walked into the room and shoots a glance toward the kitchen.* WILLIE *doesn't look up from his tea-making.*)

BEN: Please sit down. Uncle Willie's making some tea.

AL: Thank you very much. (*He sits on the edge of the table.*)

BEN (*trying hard to make conversation*): Er . . . Did you have any trouble getting in from Jersey?

AL: My daughter drove me in. She has a car.

BEN: Oh. That's nice.

AL: A 1972 Chrysler . . . black . . .

BEN: Yes, the Chrysler's a wonderful car.

AL: The big one . . . the Imperial.

BEN: I know. I drove it.

AL: My daughter's car?

BEN: No, the big Chrysler Imperial. I rented one in California.

AL (*nods*): No, she owns.

BEN: I understand . . . Do you come into New York often?

AL: Today's the first time in two years.

BEN: Really? Well, how did you find it?

AL: My daughter drove.

BEN: No, I mean, do you find the city different in the two years since you've been here?

AL: It's not my New York.

BEN: No, I suppose it's not. (*He shoots a glance toward the kitchen.* WILLIE *still hasn't looked in.*) Hey, listen, I'm really very excited about all this. Well, for that matter, everyone in the industry is.

AL (*nods, noncommittally*): Well, we'll see. (*He looks around the room, scrutinizing it.*)

BEN (*he calls out toward the kitchen*): Uncle Willie, how we doing? (*No answer. Embarrassed, to* AL.) I guess it's not boiling yet . . . Oh, listen, I'd like to arrange to have a car pick you up and take you home after you're through rehearsing.

AL: My daughter's going to pick me up.

BEN: Oh, I see. What time did you say? Four? Five?

AL: She's going to call me every hour.

BEN: Right . . .

(*Suddenly* WILLIE *sticks his head out of the kitchen, but looks at* BEN *and not at* AL.)

WILLIE: One tea or two teas?

BEN: Oh, here he is. Well, Uncle Willie, I guess it's been a long time since you two—

WILLIE: One tea or two teas?

BEN: Oh. Er, nothing for me, thanks. I'm just about leaving. Mr. Lewis? Some tea?

AL (*doesn't look toward* WILLIE): Tea would be nice, thank you.

BEN (*to* WILLIE): Just the one, Uncle Willie.

WILLIE: You're sure? I got two tea balls. I could dunk again.

BEN (*looks at his watch*): No, I've got to get back to the office. Honestly.

WILLIE (*nods*): Mm-hmm. One tea. (*On his way back in, he darts a look at* LEWIS, *then goes back into the kitchen. He pulls the curtain shut.*)

BEN (*to* LEWIS): Well, er . . . Do you have any questions you want to ask about the show? About the studio or rehearsals or the air date? Is there anything on your mind that I could help you with?

AL: Like what?

BEN: Like, er, the studio? Or the rehearsals? Or air date? Things like that?

AL: You got the props?

BEN: Which props are those?

AL: The props. For the doctor sketch. You gotta have props.

BEN: Oh, props. Certainly. What do you need? I'll tell them. (*Takes out a pad, writes.*)

AL: You need a desk. A telephone. A pointer. A blackboard. A piece of white chalk, a piece of red chalk. A skeleton, not too tall, a stethoscope, a thermometer, an "ahh" stick—

BEN: What's an "ahh" stick?

AL: To put in your mouth to say "ahh."

BEN: Oh, right, an "ahh" stick.

AL: A look stick, a bottle of pills—

BEN: A look stick? What's a look stick?

AL: A stick to look in the ears. With cotton on the end.

BEN: Right. A look stick.

AL: A bottle of pills. Big ones, like for a horse.

BEN (*makes a circle with his two fingers*): About this big?

AL: That's for a pony. (*Makes a circle using the fingers of both hands.*) For a horse is like this. Some bandages, cotton, an eye chart—

BEN: Wait a minute, you're going too fast.

AL (*slowly*): A-desk . . . *a*-telephone . . . *a*-pointer . . .

BEN: No, I got all that—after the cotton and eye chart.

AL: A man's suit. Size forty. Like the one I'm wearing.

BEN: Also in blue?

AL: What do I need two blue suits—Get me a brown.

BEN: A brown suit. Is that all?

AL: That's all.

WILLIE (*from the kitchen, without looking in*): A piece of liver.

AL: That's all, plus a piece of liver.

BEN: What kind of liver?

AL: Regular calves' liver. From the butcher.

BEN: Like how much? A pound?

AL: A little laugh is a pound. A big laugh is two pounds. Three pounds with a lot of blood'll bring the house down.

BEN: Is that it?

AL: That's it. And a blonde.

BEN: You mean a woman—

AL: You know a blond nurse that's a man? ... Big! As big as you can find. With a big chest—a forty-five, a fifty—and a nice bottom.

BEN: You mean a sexy girl with a full, round, rear end?

AL (*spreads hands apart*): About like this. (*Makes a smaller behind with his hands.*) This is too small. (*Makes a bigger one.*) And this is too big. (*Goes back to the original one.*) Like this is perfect.

BEN: I know what you mean.

AL: If you can bring me pictures, I'll pick out one.

BEN: There's a million girls like that around.

AL: The one we had was the best. I would call her, but she's maybe fifty-five, sixty.

BEN: No, no. I'll get a girl. Anything else?

AL: Not for me.

BEN: Uncle Willie?

WILLIE (*from the kitchen*): I wasn't listening.

BEN: Well, if either of you thinks of anything, just call me. (*Looks at his watch again.*) Eleven-fifteen—I've got to go. (*He get up.*) Uncle Willie, I'm going. (*He crosses to* LEWIS *and extends his hand.*) Mr. Lewis, I can't express to you enough how happy I am, and speaking for the millions of young people in this country who never had the opportunity of seeing Lewis and Clark work, I just want to say "thank you." To both of you. (*Calls out.*) To *both of you*, Uncle Willie.

AL (*nods*): I hope they won't be disappointed.

BEN: Oh, they won't.

AL: I know they won't. I'm just saying it.

BEN (*crosses to the kitchen*): Goodbye, Uncle Willie. I'm going.

WILLIE: I'll show you the elevator.

BEN: I *know* where it is. I'll call you tonight. I just want to say that this is a very happy moment for me. To see you both together again, reunited ... The two kings of comedy. (*Big smile.*) I'm sure it must be *very exciting* for the both of you, isn't it? (*No answer. They both just stare at him.*) Well, it looks like we're off to a great start. I'll call you later ... Goodbye.

(*He leaves and closes the door. They are alone.* WILLIE *carries the two teas to the dining table, where the sugar bowl is. He pours himself a teaspoonful of sugar.*)

WILLIE (*without looking in* AL's *direction*): Sugar?

AL (*doesn't turn*): If you got.

WILLIE (*nods*): I got sugar. (*He bangs the sugar bowl down in front of* AL, *crosses with his own tea to his leather chair and sits. And then the two drink tea ... silently and interminably. They blow, they sip, they blow, they sip and they sit. Finally.*) You like a cracker?

AL (*sips*): What kind of cracker?

WILLIE: Graham, chocolate, coconut, whatever you want.

AL: Maybe just a plain cracker.

WILLIE: I don't have plain crackers. I got graham, chocolate and coconut.

AL: All right, a graham cracker.

WILLIE (*without turning, points into the kitchen*): They're in the kitchen, in the closet.

(AL *looks over at him, a little surprised at his uncordiality. He nods in acknowledgement.*)

AL: Maybe later.

(*They both sip their tea.*)

WILLIE (*long pause*): I was sorry to hear about Lillian.

AL: Thank you.

WILLIE: She was a nice woman. I always liked Lillian.

AL: Thank you.

WILLIE: And how about you?

AL: Thank God, knock wood—(*raps knuckles on his cane*)—perfect.

WILLIE: I heard different. I heard your blood didn't circulate.

AL: Not true. My blood circulates ... I'm not saying *everywhere*, but it circulates.

WILLIE: Is that why you use the cane?

AL: It's not a cane. It's a walking stick ...

Maybe once in a great while it's a cane.

WILLIE: I've been lucky, thank God. I'm in the pink.

AL: I was looking. For a minute I thought you were having a flush.

WILLIE (sips his tea): You know Sol Burton died?

AL: Go on . . . Who's Sol Burton?

WILLIE: You don't remember Sol Burton?

AL (thinks): Oh, yes. The manager from the Belasco.

WILLIE: That was Sol Bernstein.

AL: Not Sol Bernstein. Sol Burton was the manager from the Belasco.

WILLIE: Sol Bernstein was the manager from the Belasco, and it wasn't the Belasco, it was the Morosco.

AL : Sid Weinstein was the manager from the Morosco. Sol Burton was the manager from the Belasco. Sol Bernstein I don't know who the hell was.

WILLIE: How can you remember anything if your blood doesn't circulate?

AL: It circulates in my head. It doesn't circulate in my feet. (He stomps his foot on the floor a few times.)

WILLIE: Is anything coming down?

AL: Wait a minute. Wasn't Sid Weinstein the song-writer?

WILLIE: No for chrissakes! That's SOL BUR-TON!

AL: Who wrote "Lady, lady, be my baby"?

WILLIE: That's what I'm telling you! Sol Burton, the lousy songwriter.

AL: Oh, that Sol Burton . . . He died?

WILLIE: Last week.

AL: Where?

WILLIE (points): In Variety.

AL: Sure, now I remember . . . And how is Sol Bernstein?

WILLIE: I didn't read anything.

AL: Good. I always liked Sol Bernstein. (They quietly sip their tea. AL looks around the room.) So-o-o . . . this is where you live now?

WILLIE: Didn't I always live here?

AL (looks again): Not in here. You lived in the big suite.

WILLIE: This is the big suite . . . Now it's five small suites.

(AL nods, understanding.)

AL (looks around): That's what they do today. Anything to squeeze a dollar. What do they charge now for a small suite?

WILLIE: The same as they used to charge for the big suite.

(AL nods, understanding.)

AL: I have a very nice room with my daughter in New Jersey. I have my own bathroom. They don't bother me, I don't bother them.

WILLIE: What is it, in the country?

AL: Certainly it's in the country. Where do you think New Jersey is, in the city?

WILLIE (shrugs): New Jersey is what I see from the bench on Riverside Drive. What have they got, a private house?

AL: Certainly it's a private house. It's some big place. Three quarters of an acre. They got their own trees, their own bushes, a nice little swimming pool for the kids they blow up in the summertime, a big swing in the back, a little dog house, a rock garden—

WILLIE: A what?

AL: A rock garden.

WILLIE: What do you mean, a rock garden? You mean for rocks?

AL: You never saw a rock garden?

WILLIE: And I'm not that anxious.

AL: It's beautiful. A Chinaman made it. Someday you'll take a bus and you'll come out and I'll show you.

WILLIE: I should drive all the way out to New Jersey on a bus to see a rock garden?

AL: You don't even know what I'm talking about. You have to live in the country to appreciate it. I never thought it was possible I could be so happy in the country.

WILLIE: You don't mind it's so quiet?

AL (looks at him): They got noise in New Jersey. But it's a quiet noise. Birds . . . drizzling . . . Not like here with the buses and trucks and screaming and yelling.

WILLIE: Well, it's different for you. You like the country better because you're retired. You can sit on a porch, look at a tree, watch a bush growing. You're still not active like me. You got a different temperament, you're a slow person.

AL: I'm a slow person?

WILLIE: You're here fifteen minutes, you still got a whole cup of tea. I'm finished already.

AL: That's right. You're finished, and I'm still enjoying it. That was always the difference with us.

WILLIE: You're wrong. I can get up and make a second cup of tea and enjoy it twice as much as you. I like a busy life. That's why I love the city. I gotta be near a phone. I never know when a picture's gonna come up, a musical, a commercial . . .

AL: When did you do a picture?

WILLIE: They're negotiating.

AL: When did you do a musical?

WILLIE: They're talking.

AL: When did you do a commercial?

WILLIE: All the time. I did one last week.

AL: For what?

WILLIE: For, er, for the . . . what's it, the potato chips.

AL: What potato chips?

WILLIE: The big one. The crispy potato chips . . . er . . . you know.

AL: What do I know? I don't eat potato chips.

WILLIE: Well, what's the difference what the name is?

AL: They hire you to sell potato chips and you can't remember the name?

WILLIE: Did you remember Sol Burton?

AL (shrugs): I'm not selling Sol Burton.

WILLIE: Listen, I don't want to argue with you.

AL: I didn't come from New Jersey to argue. (They sit quietly for a few seconds. AL sips his tea; WILLIE looks at his empty cup.)

WILLIE (finally): So-o-o . . . What do you think? . . . You want to do the doctor sketch?

AL (thinks): Well, listen, it's very good money. It's only a few day's work, I can be back in New Jersey. If you feel you'd like to do it, then my feeling is I'm agreeable.

WILLIE: And my feeling they told you.

AL: What?

WILLIE: They didn't tell you? My feeling is I'm against it.

AL: You're against it?

WILLIE: Right. But I'll do it if you want to.

AL: I don't want to do it if you're against it. If you're against it, don't do it.

WILLIE: What do you care if I'm against it as long as we're doing it? I just want you to know why I'm doing it.

AL: Don't do me any favors.

WILLIE: Who's doing you a favor? I'm doing my nephew a favor. It'll be good for him in the business if we do it.

AL: You're sure?

WILLIE: Certainly I'm sure. It's a big break for a kid like that to get big stars like us.

AL: That's different. In that case, I'm against it too but I'll do it.

WILLIE (nods): As long as we understand each other.

AL: And I want to be sure you know I'm not doing it for the money. The money goes to my grandchildren.

WILLIE: The whole thing?

AL: The whole thing. But not now. Only if I die. If I don't die, it'll be for my old age.

WILLIE: The same with me.

AL: You don't have grandchildren.

WILLIE: My nephew's children. Sidney and Marvin.

AL (nods): Very good.

WILLIE: Okay . . . So-o-o, you wanna rehearse?

AL: You're not against rehearsing?

WILLIE: Why should I be against rehearsing? I'm only against doing the show. Rehearsing is important.

AL: All right, let's rehearse. Why don't we move the furniture, and we'll make the set.

(They both get up and start to move the furniture around. First each one takes a single chair and moves it into a certain position. Then they both take a table and jointly move it away. Then they each take the chair the other one had moved before, and move it into a different place. Every time one moves something somewhere, the other moves it into a different spot. Finally WILLIE becomes aware that they are getting nowhere.)

WILLIE: Wait a minute, wait a minute. What the hell are we doing here?

AL: I'm fixing up the set, I don't know what you're doing.

WILLIE: You're fixing up the set?

AL: That's right.

WILLIE: You're fixing up the set for the doctor sketch?

(AL looks at him for a long time without saying a word. It suddenly becomes clear to him.)

AL: Oh, the doctor sketch?

(He then starts to pick up a chair and move it into another position. WILLIE does the same with another chair. They both move the table . . . and then they repeat what they did before. Every time one moves a chair, the other one moves the same chair to a different position. WILLIE stops and looks again.)

WILLIE: Wait a minute! Wait a minute! We're doing the same goddamn thing. Are you fixing up for the doctor sketch or are you redecorating my apartment?

AL: I'm fixing up for the doctor sketch. If you'd leave what I'm doing alone, we'd be finished.

WILLIE: We'd be finished, but we'd be wrong.

AL: Not for the doctor sketch. I know what I'm doing. I did this sketch for forty-three years.

WILLIE: And where was I all that time, taking a smoke? Who did you think did it with you for forty-three years? That was *me*, mister.

AL: Don't call me mister, you know my name. I never liked it when you called me mister.

WILLIE: It's not a dirty word.

AL: It is when you say it.

WILLIE: Forgive me, *sir*.

AL: Let's please, for Pete's sakes, fix up for the doctor sketch.

WILLIE: You think *you* know how to do it? You fix it up.

AL: It'll be my pleasure. (WILLIE *stands aside and watches with arms folded as* AL *proceeds to move table and chairs and stools until he arranges them exactly the way he wants them. Then he stands back and folds his arms the same way.*) There! *That's* the doctor sketch!

WILLIE (*smiles arrogantly*): For how much money?

AL: I don't want to bet you.

WILLIE: You're afraid to lose?

AL: I'm afraid to *win*. You don't even have enough to buy a box of plain crackers.

WILLIE: —Don't be so afraid you're gonna win—because you're gonna *lose*! That's not the doctor sketch. That's the gypsy chiropractor sketch.

AL: You're positive?

WILLIE: I'm *more* than positive. I'm *sure*.

AL: All right. Show me the doctor sketch.

WILLIE (*looks at him confidently, then goes to a chair, picks it up and moves it to the left about four inches, if that much. Then he folds his arms over his chest*): There, *that's* the doctor sketch!

AL (*looks at him*): You know what you are, Willie? You're a lapalooza.

WILLIE (*nods*): If I'm a lapalooza, you're a mister.

AL: Let's please rehearse the sketch.

WILLIE: All right, go outside. I'm in the office.

AL: You gonna do the part with the nurse first?

WILLIE: You see a nurse here? How can I rehearse with a nurse that's not here?

AL: I'm just asking a question. I'm not allowed to ask questions?

WILLIE: Ask whatever you want. But try to make them intelligent questions.

AL: I beg your pardon. I usually ask the kind of question to the kind of person I'm talking to . . . You get my drift?

WILLIE: I get it, mister.

AL: All right. Let's skip over the nurse. We'll start from where I come in.

WILLIE: All right, from where you come in. First go out.

AL (*takes a few steps toward the door, stops and turns*): All right, I'm outside. (*Pantomimes with his fist, knocking on a door.*) Knock, knock, knock! I was looking for the doctor.

WILLIE: Wait a minute. You're not outside.

AL: Certainly I'm outside.

WILLIE: If you were outside, you couldn't see me, could you?

AL: No.

WILLIE: Can you see me?

AL: Yes.

WILLIE: So you're not outside. Go *all* the way outside. What the hell kind of a rehearsal is this?

AL: It's a rehearsing rehearsal. Can't you make believe I'm all the way out in the hall?

WILLIE: I could also make believe you were still in New Jersey, but you're not. You're here. Let's have a professional rehearsal, for chrissakes. We ain't got a nurse, but we got a door. Let's use what we got.

AL (*sighs deeply*): Listen, we're not gonna stop for every little thing, are we? I don't know how many years I got left, I don't wanna spend it rehearsing.

WILLIE: We're not gonna stop for the little things. We're gonna stop for the big things . . . The door is a big thing.

AL: All right, I'll go through the door, I'll come in, and then we'll run through the sketch once or twice, and that'll be it for today. All right?

WILLIE: Right . . . Unless another big thing comes up.

AL (*glares at him*): All right, I'm going out. I'll be right back in. (*He crosses to the door, opens it, stops and turns.*) If I'm outside and my daughter calls, tell her to pick me up in an hour. (*He goes out and closes the door behind him.*)

WILLIE (*mumbles, half to himself*): She can pick you up *now* for all I care. (*He puts his hands behind his back, clasps them, and paces back and forth. He calls out.*) All right! Knock, knock, knock!

AL (*from outside*): Knock, knock, knock!

WILLIE (*screams*): *Don't say it*, for God's sakes, *do it!* (*To himself.*) He probably went *crazy* in the country.

AL (*from outside*): You ready?

WILLIE (*yells*): I'm ready. Knock, knock, knock! (AL *knocks three times on the door.*) Come in. (*We see and hear the doorknob jiggle, but it doesn't open. This is repeated.*) All right, come in already.

AL (*from outside*): It doesn't open—it's stuck.

WILLIE (*wearily*): All right, wait a minute. (*He shuffles over to the door and puts his hand on the knob and pulls. It doesn't open.*) Wait a minute. (*He tries again, to no avail.*)

AL (*from outside*): What's the matter?

WILLIE: Wait a minute.

(*He pulls harder, to no avail.*)

AL: Is it locked?

WILLIE: It's not locked. Wait a minute. (*He tries again; it doesn't open.*) It's locked. You better get somebody. Call the boy downstairs. Sandy. Tell him it's locked.

AL (*from outside*): Let me try it again.

WILLIE: What are you wasting time? Call the boy. Tell him it's locked.

(AL *tries it again, turning it in the other direction, and the door opens. They stand there face-to-face.*)

AL: I fixed it.

WILLIE (*glares at him*): You didn't fix it. You just don't know how to open a door.

AL: Did my daughter call?

WILLIE: You know, I think you went crazy in the country.

AL: You want to stand here and insult me, or do you want to rehearse the sketch?

WILLIE: I would like to do *both*, but we ain't got the time ... Let's forget the door. Stand in here and say "Knock, knock, knock."

AL (AL *comes in and closes the door. Sarcastically*): I hope I can get *out* again.

WILLIE: I hope so too. (*He places his hands behind his back and paces.*) All right. "Knock, knock, knock."

AL (*pantomimes with his fist*): Knock, knock, knock.

WILLIE (*singsong*): Enter!

AL (*stops and looks at him*): What do you mean "Enter"? (*He does it in the same singsong way.*) What happened to "Come in"?

WILLIE: It's the same thing, isn't it? "Enter" or "come in." What's the difference, as long as you're in?

AL: The difference is we've done this sketch twelve thousand times, and you've always said "Come in," and suddenly today it's "Enter." Why today, after all these years, do you suddenly change it to "Enter"?

WILLIE (*shrugs*): I'm trying to freshen up the act.

AL: Who asked you to freshen up the act? They asked for the doctor sketch, didn't they? The doctor sketch starts with "Come in," not "Enter." You wanna freshen up something, put some flowers in here.

WILLIE: It's a new generation today. This is not 1934, you know.

AL: No kidding? I didn't get today's paper.

WILLIE: What's bad about "Enter" instead of "Come in"?

AL: Because it's different. You know why we've been doing it the same way for forty-three years? Because it's good.

WILLIE: And you know why we don't do it any more? Because we've been doing it the same way for forty-three years.

AL: So, if we're not doing it any more, why are we changing it?

WILLIE: Can I make a comment, nothing personal? I think you've been sitting on a New Jersey porch too long.

AL: What does that mean?

WILLIE: That means I think you've been sitting on a New Jersey porch too long. From my window, I see everything that goes on in the world. I see old people, I see young people, nice people, bad people, I see hold-ups, drug addicts, ambulances, car crashes, jumpers from buildings—I see everything. You see a lawn mower and a milkman.

AL (*looks at him for a long moment*): And that's why you want to say "Enter" instead of "Come in"?

WILLIE: Are you listening to me?

AL (*looks around*): Why, there's someone else in the room?

WILLIE: You don't know the first thing that's going on today?

AL: All right, what's going on today?

WILLIE: Did you ever hear the expression "That's where it is"? Well, this is where it is, and that's where I am.

AL: I see ... Did you ever hear the expression "You don't know what the hell you're talking about"? It comes right in front of the *other* expression. "You *never* knew what the hell you were talking about."

WILLIE: *I* wasn't the one who retired. You know why you retired? Because you were tired.

You were getting old-fashioned. I was still new-fashioned, and I'll *always* be.

AL: I see: That's why you're in such demand. That's why you're such a "hot" property today. That's why you do movies you don't do, that's why you're in musicals you're not in, and that's why you make commercials you don't make —because you can't even remember them to *make* them.

WILLIE: You know what I *do* remember? I remember what a pain in the ass you are to work with, that's what I remember.

AL: That's right. And when you worked with this pain in the ass, you lived in a *five*-room suite. Now you live in a *one*-room suite . . . And you're still wearing the same goddamn pajamas you wore in the five-room suite. .

WILLIE: I don't have to take this crap from you.

AL: You're lucky you're getting it. No one else wants to give it to you.

WILLIE: I don't want to argue with you. After you say "Knock, knock, knock," I'm saying "Enter," and if you don't like it you don't have to come in.

AL: You can't say nothing without my permission. I own fifty percent of this act.

WILLIE: Then say *your* fifty percent. I'm saying "Enter" in my fifty percent.

AL: If you say "Enter" after "Knock, knock, knock" . . . I'm coming in all right. But not alone. I'm bringing a lawyer with me.

WILLIE: Where? From New Jersey? You're lucky if a cow comes with you.

AL: Against *you* in court, I could *win* with a cow. (*He enunciates each point by poking* WILLIE *in the chest.*)

WILLIE (*slaps his hand away*): The *finger?* You're starting with the finger again?

(*He runs into the kitchen and comes out brandishing a knife.*)

AL: I'll tell you the truth now. I didn't retire. I *escaped*.

WILLIE (*wielding the knife*): The next time you give me the finger, say goodbye to the finger.

AL (*hiding behind a chair*): Listen, I got a terrific idea. Instead of working together again, let's never work together again. You're crazy.

WILLIE: I'm crazy, heh? I'M CRAZY!

AL: Keep saying it until you believe it.

WILLIE: I may be crazy, but you're *senile!* You know what that is?

AL: I'm not giving you any straight lines.

WILLIE: Crazy is when you got a couple of parts that go wrong. Senile is when you went the hell out of business. That's you, mister. (*The phone rings.* AL *moves toward the phone.*) Get away from that phone. (*He drives the knife into the table.* AL *backs away in shock.* WILLIE *picks up the phone.*) Hello?

AL: Is that my daughter?

WILLIE: Hello . . . How are you?

AL: Is that my daughter? Is that her?

WILLIE (*to* AL): Will you shut up? Will you be quiet? Can't you see I'm talking? Don't you see me on the phone with a person? For God's sakes, behave like a human being for five seconds, will you? WILL YOU BEHAVE FOR FIVE SECONDS LIKE A HUMAN BEING? (*Into the phone.*) Hello? . . . Yes . . . Just a minute (*To* AL.) It's your daughter. (*He sits, opens up Variety.*)

AL (*takes the phone, turns his back to* WILLIE, *speaks low*): Hello . . . Hello, sweetheart . . . No . . . No . . . I can't talk now . . . I said I can't talk now . . . Because he's a crazy bedbug, that's why.

WILLIE (*jumps up*): Mister is not good but bedbug is all right?? (*Yells into the phone.*) Your father is sick! Come and get your sick father!

AL (*turns to him*): Don't you see me on the phone with a person? Will you please be quiet, for God's sakes! (*Back into the phone.*) Listen, I want you to pick me up now . . . I don't want to discuss it. Pick me up now. In front of the hotel. Don't park too close, it's filthy here . . . I *know* what I promised. Don't argue with me. I'm putting on my coat. I'll wait in the street — I'll probably get mugged . . . All right, just a minute. (*He hands the phone to* WILLIE.) She'd like to talk to you for a second.

WILLIE: Who is it?

AL (*glares at him*): Mrs. Eleanor Roosevelt . . . What do you mean, who is it? Didn't you just say it's my daughter?

WILLIE: I know it's your daughter. I forgot her name.

AL: Doris.

WILLIE: What does she want?

AL (*yells*): Am I Doris? She'll tell you.

WILLIE (*takes the phone*): Hello? . . . Hello, dear, this is Willie Clark . . . Unpleasantness? There was no unpleasantness . . . There was stupidity maybe but no unpleasantness . . .

AL: Tell her I'm getting into my coat. (*He is putting his coat on.*) Tell her I got one sleeve on.

WILLIE (*into the phone*): I was hoping it would work out too . . . I bent over backwards and forwards. He didn't even bend sideways . . .

AL: I got the other sleeve on . . . Tell her I'm up to my hat and then I'm out the door.

WILLIE: It's a question of one word, darling. "Enter"! . . . "Enter"—that's all it comes down to.

AL (*puts his hat on*): The hat is on. I'm bundled up, tell her.

WILLIE (*into the phone*): Yes . . . Yes. I will . . . I'll tell him myself. I promise . . . Goodbye, Dorothy. (*He hangs up.*) I told her we'll give it one more chance.

AL: Not if you say "Enter." "Come in," I'll stay. "Enter," I go.

WILLIE: Ask me "Knock, knock, knock."

AL: Don't fool around with me. I got enough pains in my neck. Are you going to say "Come in"?

WILLIE: Ask me "Knock, knock, knock"!

AL: I know you, you bastard!

WILLIE: ASK ME "KNOCK, KNOCK, KNOCK"!

AL: KNOCK, KNOCK, KNOCK!

WILLIE (*grinding it in*): EN-TERRR!

AL: BEDBUG! CRAZY BEDBUG! (*He starts to run out.*)

WILLIE (*big smile*): ENNN-TERRRRR!

(*The curtain starts down.*)

AL (*heading for the door*): LUNATIC BAS-TARD!

WILLIE: ENNN-TERRRR!

ACT II

SCENE 1

(*The scene is a doctor's office or, rather, an obvious stage "flat" representation of a doctor's office. It has an old desk and chair, a telephone, a cabinet filled with medicine bottles, a human skeleton hanging on a stand, a blackboard with chalk and pointer, an eye chart on the wall.*

Overhead television lights surround the top of the set. Two boom microphones extend from either end of the set over the office.

At rise, the set is not fully lit. A thin, frail man in a hat and business suit sits in the chair next to the doctor's desk, patiently waiting.)

VOICE OF TV DIRECTOR (*over the loudspeaker*): Eddie! *EDDIE!*

(EDDIE, *a young assistant TV director with headset and speaker, trailing wires and carrying a clipboard, steps out on the set. He speaks through his mike.*)

EDDIE: Yeah, Phil?

VOICE OF TV DIRECTOR: Any chance of doing this today?

EDDIE (*shrugs*): We're all set here, Phil. We're just waiting on the actors.

VOICE OF TV DIRECTOR: What the hell is happening?

EDDIE: I don't know. There's a problem with the makeup. Mr. Clark wants a Number Seven amber or something.

VOICE OF TV DIRECTOR: Well, get it for him.

EDDIE: Where? They stopped making it thirty-four years ago.

VOICE OF TV DIRECTOR: Christ!

EDDIE: And Mr. Lewis says the "ahh" sticks are too short.

VOICE OF TV DIRECTOR: The what?

EDDIE: The "ahh" sticks. Don't ask me. I'm still trying to figure out what a "look" stick is.

VOICE OF TV DIRECTOR: What the hell are we making, *Nicholas and Alexandra?* Tell them it's just a dress rehearsal. We'll worry about the props later. Let's get moving, Eddie. Christ Almighty.

(WILLIE's *nephew* BEN *appears onstage. He talks up into the overhead mike.*)

BEN: Mr. Schaefer . . . Mr. Schaefer, I'm awfully sorry about the delay. Mr. Lewis and Mr. Clark have had a few technical problems backstage.

VOICE OF TV DIRECTOR: Yeah, well, we've had it all week . . . I'm afraid we're running out of time here. I've got twelve goddamned other numbers to get through today.

BEN: I'll get them right out. There's no problem.

VOICE OF TV DIRECTOR: Tell them I want to run straight through, no stopping. They can clean up whatever they want afterwards.

BEN: Absolutely.

VOICE OF TV DIRECTOR: I haven't seen past "Knock, knock, knock"—"Come in" since Tuesday.

BEN (*looks offstage*): Right. There they are. (*Into the mike.*) We're ready, Mr. Schaefer. I'll tell them we're going to go straight through, no stopping. Thank you very much. (BEN *exits very quickly.*)

VOICE OF TV DIRECTOR: All right, Eddie, bring in the curtains.

EDDIE: What?

VOICE OF TV DIRECTOR: Bring in the curtains. Let's run it from the top with the voice over.

EDDIE (*calls up*): Let's have the curtains.

(*The curtains come in.*)

VOICE OF TV DIRECTOR: Voice over!

ANNOUNCER: The golden age of comedy reached its zenith during a fabulous and glorious era known as Vaudeville—Fanny Brice, W.C. Fields, Eddie Cantor, Ed Wynn, Will Rogers and a host of other greats fill its Hall of Fame. There are two other names that belong on this list, but they can never be listed separately. They are more than a team. They are two comic shining lights that beam as one. For, Lewis without Clark is like laughter without joy. We are privileged to present tonight, in their first public performance in over eleven years, for half a century known as "The Sunshine Boys"—Mr. Al Lewis and Mr. Willie Clark, in their beloved scene, "The Doctor Will See You Now."

(*The curtain rises, and the set is fully lit. The frail man in the hat is sitting on the chair as* WILLIE, *the doctor, dressed in a floor-length white doctor's jacket, a mirror attached to his head and a stethoscope around his neck is looking into the* PATIENT's *mouth, holding his tongue down with an "ahh" stick.*)

WILLIE: Open wider and say "Ahh."
PATIENT: Ahh.
WILLIE: Wider.
PATIENT: Ahhh!
WILLIE (*moves with his back to the audience*): A little wider.
PATIENT: Ahhh!
WILLIE (*steps away*): Your throat is all right, but you're gonna have some trouble with your stomach.
PATIENT: How come?
WILLIE: You just swallowed the stick.

(*The* PATIENT *feels his stomach.*)

PATIENT: Is that bad?
WILLIE: It's terrible. I only got two left.
PATIENT: What about getting the stick out?
WILLIE: What am I, a tree surgeon? ... All right, for another ten dollars, I'll take it out.
PATIENT: That's robbery.
WILLIE: Then forget it. Keep the stick.
PATIENT: No, no. I'll pay. Take the stick out.
WILLIE: Come back tomorrow. On Thursdays I do woodwork. (*The* PATIENT *gets up and crosses to the door, then exits.* WILLIE *calls out.*) Oh, Nurse! Nursey!

(*The* NURSE *enters. She is a tall, voluptuous and over-stacked blonde in a tight dress.*)

NURSE: Did you want me, Doctor?
WILLIE (*he looks at her, knowingly*): Why do you think I hired you? ... What's your name again?
NURSE: Miss MacKintosh. You know, like the apples.
WILLIE (*nods*): The name I forgot, the apples I remembered ... Look in my appointment book, see who's next.
NURSE: It's a Mr. Kornheiser.
WILLIE: Maybe you're wrong. Look in the book. It's better that way.

(*She crosses to the desk and bends way over as she looks through the appointment book. Her firm, round rear end faces us and* WILLIE. WILLIE *shakes his head from side to side in wonderful contemplation.*)

NURSE (*still down*): No, I was right.
WILLIE: So was I.
NURSE (*straightens up and turns around*): It's Mr. Kornheiser.
WILLIE: Are you sure? Spell it.
NURSE (*turns, bends and gives us the same wonderful view again*): K-o-r-n-h-e-i-s-e-r! (*She turns and straightens up.*)
WILLIE (*nods*): What's the first name?
NURSE (*turns, bends*): Walter.
WILLIE: Stay down for the middle name.
NURSE (*remains down*): Benjamin.
WILLIE: Don't move and give me the whole thing.
NURSE (*still rear end up, reading*): Walter Benjamin Kornheiser. (*She turns and straightens up.*)
WILLIE: Oh, boy. From now on I only want to see patients with long names.
NURSE: Is there anything else you want?
WILLIE: Yeah. Call a carpenter and have him make my desk lower.

(*The* NURSE *walks sexily right up to* WILLIE *and stands with her chest practically on his, breathing and heaving.*)

NURSE (*pouting*): Yes, Doctor.
WILLIE (*wipes his brow*): Whew, it's hot in here. Did you turn the steam on?
NURSE (*sexily*): No, Doctor.
WILLIE: In that case, take a five-dollar raise. Send in the next patient before *I'm* the next patient.
NURSE: Yes, Doctor. (*She coughs.*) Excuse me, I think I have a chest cold.

WILLIE: Looks more like an epidemic to me.

NURSE: Yes, Doctor. (*She wriggles her way to the door.*) Is there anything else you can think of?

WILLIE: I can *think* of it, but I'm not so sure I can *do* it.

NURSE: Well, If I *can* help you, Doctor, that's what the nurse is for. (*She exits and closes the door with an enticing look.*)

WILLIE: I'm glad I didn't go to law school. (*Then we hear three knocks on the door. "Knock, knock, knock."*) Aha. That must be my new patient. (*Calls out.*) Come in! (*The door starts to open.*)—and enter!

(AL *steps in and glares angrily at* WILLIE. *He is in a business suit, wears a wig, and carries a cheap attaché case.*)

AL: I'm looking for the doctor.

WILLIE: Are you sick?

AL: Are *you* the doctor?

WILLIE: Yes.

AL: I'm not *that* sick.

WILLIE: What's your name, please?

AL: Kornheiser. Walter Benjamin Kornheiser. You want me to spell it?

WILLIE: Never mind. I got a better speller than you ... (*Takes a tongue depressor from his pocket.*) Sit down and open your mouth, please.

AL: There's nothing wrong with my mouth.

WILLIE: Then just sit down.

AL: There's nothing wrong with that either.

WILLIE: Then what are you doing here?

AL: I came to examine you.

WILLIE: I think you got everything backwards.

AL: It's possible. I dressed in a hurry this morning.

WILLIE: You mean you came here for me to examine *you.*

AL: No, I came here for me to examine *you.* I'm a tax collector.

WILLIE (*nods*): That's nice. I'm a stamp collector. What do you do for a living.

AL: I find out how much money people make.

WILLIE: Oh, a busybody. Make an appointment with the nurse.

AL: I did. I'm seeing her Friday night ...

WILLIE (*jumps up and down angrily*): Don't fool around with my nurse. DON'T FOOL AROUND WITH MY NURSE! She's a nice girl. She's a *Virginian!*

AL: A what?

WILLIE: A *Virginian.* That's where she's from.

AL: Well, she ain't going *back,* I can tell you

that. (*He sits, opens the attaché case.*) I got some questions to ask you.

WILLIE: I'm too busy to answer questions. I'm a doctor. If you wanna see me, you gotta be a patient.

AL: But I'm not sick.

WILLIE: Don't worry. We'll find something.

AL: All right, you examine me and I'll examine you ... (*Takes out a tax form as* WILLIE *wields the tongue depressor.*) The first question is, How much money did you make last year?

WILLIE: Last year I made—(*He moves his lips mouthing a sum, but it's not audible.*)

AL: I didn't hear that.

WILLIE: Oh. Hard of hearing. I knew we'd find something. Did you ever have any childhood diseases?

AL: Not lately.

WILLIE: Father living or deceased?

AL: Both.

WILLIE: What do you mean, both?

AL: First he was living, now he's deceased.

WILLIE: What did your father die from?

AL: My mother ... Now it's my turn. Are you married?

WILLIE: I'm looking.

AL: Looking to get married?

WILLIE: No, looking to get out. (*He looks in* AL's *ear with a flashlight.*)

AL: What are you doing?

WILLIE: I'm examining your lower intestines.

AL: So why do you look in the ear?

WILLIE: If I got a choice of two places to look, I'll take this one.

AL (*consulting his form*): Never mind. Do you own a car?

WILLIE: Certainly I own a car. Why?

AL: If you use it for medical purposes, you can deduct it from your taxes. What kind of car do you own?

WILLIE: An ambulance.

AL: Do you own a house?

WILLIE: Can I deduct it?

AL: Only if you use it for medical purposes. Where do you live?

WILLIE: In Mount Sinai Hospital ... Open your shirt, I want to listen to your heartbeat.

AL (*unbuttons two buttons on his shirt*): Will this take long?

WILLIE: Not if I hear something. (*He puts his ear to* AL's *chest and listens.*) Uh-huh. I hear something ... You're all right.

AL: Aren't you going to listen with the stethoscope?

WILLIE: Oh, sure. I didn't know you wanted a

thorough examination. (*Puts the stethoscope to his ears and listens to* AL's *chest.*) Oh, boy. Ohhh, boyyyy! You know what you got?

AL: What?

WILLIE: A filthy undershirt.

AL: Never mind that. Am I in good health?

WILLIE: Not unless you change your undershirt.

AL: What is this, a doctor's office or a laundry? I bet you never went to medical school.

WILLIE (*jumping up and down again*): What are you talkin'? . . . WHAT ARE YOU TALKIN'? . . . I went to Columbia Medical School.

AL: Did you pass?

WILLIE: Certainly.

AL: Well, you should have gone *in!*

WILLIE: Never mind . . . I'm gonna examine your eyes now.

AL: They're perfect. I got twenty-twenty eyes.

WILLIE: That's too much. All you need is one and one. Look at that chart on the wall. Now put your left hand over your left eye and your right hand over your right eye. (AL *does so.*) Now tell me what you see.

AL: I don't see nothing.

WILLIE: Don't panic, I can cure you . . . Take your hands away. (AL *does.*) Can you see now?

AL: Certainly I can see now.

WILLIE: You know, I fixed over two thousand people like that.

AL: It's a miracle.

WILLIE: Thank you.

AL: A miracle you're not in jail . . . What do you charge for a visit?

WILLIE: A dollar.

AL: A dollar? That's very cheap for an examination.

WILLIE: It's not an examination. It's just a visit. "Hello and Goodbye" . . . "Hello and How Are You?" is ten dollars.

AL: If you ask me, you're a quack.

WILLIE: If I was a duck I would ask you . . . Now roll up your sleeve, I wanna take some blood.

AL: I can't do it.

WILLIE: Why not?

AL: If I see blood, I get sick.

WILLIE: Do what I do. Don't look.

AL: I'm sorry. I'm not giving blood. I'm anemic.

WILLIE: What's anemic?

AL: You're a doctor and you don't know what anemic means?

WILLIE: That's because I'm a specialist.

AL: What do you specialize in?

WILLIE: Everything but anemic.

AL: Listen, can I continue my examination?

WILLIE: You continue yours, and I'll continue mine. All right, cross your legs. (*He hits* AL's *knee with a small hammer.*) Does it hurt if I hit you with the hammer?

AL: Yes.

WILLIE: Good. From now on, try not to get hit with a hammer. (*He throws the hammer over his shoulder. He takes a specimen bottle from the cabinet and returns.*) You see this bottle?

AL: Yes.

WILLIE: You know what you're supposed to do with this bottle?

AL: I think so.

WILLIE: You *think* so or you *know* so? If you're not sure, let me know. The girl doesn't come in to clean today.

AL: What do you want me to do?

WILLIE: I want you to go in this bottle.

AL: I haven't got time. I have to go over your books.

WILLIE: *The hell you will!*

AL: If I don't go over your books, the *government* will come in here and go over your books.

WILLIE: Don't they have a place in Washington?

AL: Certainly, but they have to go where the books are.

WILLIE: The whole government?

AL: No, just the Treasury Department.

WILLIE: That's a relief.

AL: I'm glad you're relieved.

WILLIE: I wish *you* were before you came in here.

(*The door opens and the big-chested* NURSE *steps in.*)

NURSE: Oh, Doctor. Doctor Klockenmeyer.

WILLIE: Yes.

NURSE: Mrs. Kolodny is on the phone. She wants you to rush right over and deliver her baby.

WILLIE: I'm busy now. Tell her I'll mail it to her in the morning.

NURSE: Yes, Doctor. (*She exits and closes the door.*)

AL: Where did you find a couple of nurses like that?

WILLIE: She was standing on Forty-third and Forty-fourth Street . . . Let me see your tongue, please.

AL: I don't want to.

(WILLIE *squeezes* AL's *throat, and his tongue comes out.*)

WILLIE: Open the mouth . . . How long have you had that white coat on your tongue?

AL: Since January. In the spring I put on a gray sports jacket.

WILLIE: Now hold your tongue with your fingers and say "shish kabob."

AL (*holds his tongue with his fingers*): Thickabob.

WILLIE: Again.

AL: Thickabob.

WILLIE: I have bad news for you.

AL: What is it?

WILLIE: If you do that in a restaurant, you'll never get shish kabob.

AL (*stands with his face close to* WILLIE's): Never mind that. What about your taxes? (*On the "T,"* *he spits a little.*)

WILLIE (*wipes his face*): The what?

AL: The *t*axes. It's *t*ime *t*o pay your *t*axes to the *T*reasury.

(*All the "T's" are quite fluid.* WILLIE *wipes his face and glares angrily at* AL.)

WILLIE: I'm warning you, don't start in with me.

AL: What are you talking about?

WILLIE: You know what I'm talking about. (*Illustrates.*) "It's *t*ime *t*o pay the *t*axes." You're speaking with spitting again.

AL: I said the right line, didn't I? If it comes out juicy, I can't help that.

WILLIE (*quite angry*): It doesn't come out juicy unless you squeeze the "T's." I'm warning you, don't squeeze them on me.

(VOICE OF TV DIRECTOR *is heard over the loudspeaker.*)

VOICE OF TV DIRECTOR: Okay, let's hold it a second. Mr. Clark, I'm having trouble with the dialogue. I don't find those last few lines in the script.

WILLIE (*shouts up*): It's not in the script, it's in *his mouth.*

AL (*talking up into the mike*): I said the right line. Look in the script, you'll find it there.

WILLIE (*shouting*): You'll find the words, you won't find the spit. The spit's his own idea. He's doing it on *purpose!*

AL: I don't spit on purpose. I spit on accident. I've *always* spitted on accident. It's not possible to say that line without spitting a little.

WILLIE (*addressing all his remarks to the unseen director*): I can say it. (*He says the line with great delicacy, especially on the "T's."*) "It's time to pay your taxes to the Treasury." (*Back to his normal inflection.*) There wasn't a spit in my entire mouth. Why doesn't he say it like *that?*

AL: What am I, an Englishman? I'm talking the same as I've talked for forty-three years.

VOICE OF TV DIRECTOR: Gentlemen, can we argue this point after the dress rehearsal and go on with the sketch?

WILLIE: I'm not going to stand here and get a shower in the face. If you want me to go on, either take out the line or get me an umbrella.

VOICE OF TV DIRECTOR: Can we *please* go on? With all due respect, gentlemen, we have twelve other scenes to rehearse and we cannot spend all day on personal squabbles . . .

WILLIE: I'll go on, but I'm moving to a safer spot.

VOICE OF TV DIRECTOR: Don't worry about the moves, we'll pick you up on camera. Now, let's skip over this spot and pick it up on "I hope you don't have what Mr. Melnick had." (WILLIE *moves away from* AL.) All right, Mr. Clark, whenever you're ready.

WILLIE (*waits a minute, then goes back into the doctor character*): I hope you don't have what Mr. Melnick had.

AL: What did Mr. Melnick have?

WILLIE (*points to standing skeleton*): Ask him yourself, he's standing right there.

AL: That's Mr. Melnick?

WILLIE: It could be *Mrs.* Melnick. Without high heels, I can't tell.

AL: If he's dead, why do you leave him standing in the office?

WILLIE: He's still got one more appointment with me.

AL (*crosses to him*): You know what you are? You're a charlatan! (*As* AL *says that line, he punctuates each word by poking* WILLIE *in the chest with his finger. It does not go unnoticed by* WILLIE.) Do you know what a charlatan is? (*More pokes.*)

WILLIE: It's a city in North Carolina. And if you're gonna poke me again like that, you're gonna end up in Poughkeepsie.

VOICE OF TV DIRECTOR (*over the loudspeaker*): Hold it, hold it. Where does it say, "You're going to end up in Poughkeepsie"?

WILLIE (*furious*): Where does it say he can poke me in the chest? He's doing it on purpose. He *always* did it on purpose, just to get my goat.

AL (*looking up to the mike*): I didn't poke him, I tapped him. A light little tap, it wouldn't hurt a baby.

WILLIE: Maybe a baby elephant. I *knew* I was going to get poked. First comes the spitting, then comes the poking. I know his routine already.

AL (*to the mike*): Excuse me. I'm sorry we're holding up the rehearsal, but we have a serious problem on our hands. The man I'm working with is a lunatic.

WILLIE (*almost in a rage*): I'm a lunatic, heh? He breaks my chest and spits in my face and calls *me* a lunatic! I'm gonna tell you something now I never told you in my entire life. I hate your guts.

AL: You told it to me on Monday.

WILLIE: Then I'm telling it to you again.

VOICE OF TV DIRECTOR: Listen, gentlemen, I really don't see any point in going on with this rehearsal.

AL: I don't see any point in going on with this *show*. This man is persecuting me. For eleven years he's been waiting to get back at me, only I'm not gonna give him the chance.

(*The assistant director,* EDDIE, *walks out in an attempt to make peace.*)

WILLIE (*half-hysterical*): I knew it! I knew it! He planned it! He's been setting me up for eleven years just to walk out on me again.

EDDIE (*trying to be gentle*): All right, Mr. Clark, let's settle down. Why don't we all go into the dressing room and talk this out?

AL: I didn't want to do it in the first place.

WILLIE (*apoplectic*): *Liar! Liar!* His daughter *begged* me on the phone. She *begged* me!

(BEN *rushes out to restrain* WILLIE.)

BEN: Uncle Willie, please, that's enough. Come back to the dressing room.

EDDIE: Gentlemen, we need the stage. Can we please do this over on the side?

AL (*to the assistant director*): The man is hysterical, you can see for yourself. He's been doing this to me all week long. (*He starts taking off the wig and suit jacket.*)

WILLIE: Begged me. She begged me. His own daughter begged me.

BEN: Uncle Willie, stop it, please.

AL (*to the others*): I'm sorry we caused everyone so much trouble. I should have stayed in New Jersey in the first place. (*On his way out. To the assistant director.*) He pulled a knife on me last week. In his own apartment he pulled a knife on me. A crazy man. (*He is gone.*)

WILLIE: I don't need you. I *never* needed you. You were nothing when I found you, and that's what you are today.

BEN: Come on, Willie. (*Out front.*) I'm sorry about this, Mr. Schaefer.

WILLIE: He thinks I can't get work without him. Maybe *his* career is over, but not mine. Maybe he's finished, but not me. You hear? not me! NOT M—(*He clutches his chest.*)

BEN (*turns and sees him stagger*): Grab him, quick! (EDDIE *rushes to* WILLIE, *but it's too late*—WILLIE *falls to the floor.* BEN *rushes to his side.*) All right, take it easy, Uncle Willie, just lie there. (*To* EDDIE.) Get a doctor, please hurry.

(*A bit actor and the* NURSE *rush onstage behind* BEN.)

WILLIE (*breathing hard*): I don't need a doctor. Don't get a doctor, I don't trust them.

BEN: Don't talk, Willie, you're all right. (*To the* NURSE.) Somebody get a blanket, please.

WILLIE (*breathing fast*): Don't tell him. Don't tell him I fell down. I don't want to give him the satisfaction.

BEN: Of course, I won't tell him, Willie. There's nothing to tell. You're going to be all right.

WILLIE: Frito-Lays . . . That's the name of the potato chip . . . You see? I remembered . . . I remembered the name! Frito-Lays.

(BEN *is holding* WILLIE's *hand as the lights dim. The curtain falls on the scene. In the dark, we hear the voice of the* ANNOUNCER.)

ANNOUNCER: The golden age of comedy reached its zenith during a fabulous and glorious era known as Vaudeville—Fanny Brice, W.C. Fields, Eddie Cantor, Ed Wynn, Will Rogers and a host of other greats till its Hall of Fame. There are two other names that belong on this list, but they can never be listed separately. They are more than a team. They are two comic shining lights that beam as one. For, Lewis without Clark is like laughter without joy. When these two greats retired, a comic style disappeared from the American scene that will never see its likes again . . . Here, then, in a sketch taped nearly eleven years ago on *The Ed Sullivan Show*, are Lewis and Clark in their classic scene, "The Doctor Will See You Now."

(*We hear* WILLIE's *voice and that of the first* PATIENT.)

WILLIE: Open wider and say "Ahh."
PATIENT: Ahh.
WILLIE: Wider.
PATIENT: Ahh.

WILLIE: A little wider.

PATIENT: Ahhh!

WILLIE: Your throat is all right, but you're gonna have some trouble with your stomach.

PATIENT: How come?

WILLIE: You just swallowed the stick.

SCENE 2

(*The curtain rises. The scene is* WILLIE's *hotel room, two weeks later. It is late afternoon.* WILLIE *is in his favorite pajamas in bed, propped up on the pillows, his head hanging down, asleep.*

The television is droning away—another daytime serial. A black REGISTERED NURSE *in uniform, a sweater draped over her shoulders, and her glasses on a chain around her neck, is sitting in a chair watching the television. She is eating from a big box of chocolates. Two very large vases of flowers are on the bureau.* WILLIE's *head bobs a few times; then he opens his eyes.*)

WILLIE: What time is it?

NURSE (*turns off the TV and glances at her watch*): Ten to one.

WILLIE: Ten to one? . . . Who are you?

NURSE: Don't give me that. You know who I am.

WILLIE: You're the same nurse from yesterday?

NURSE: I'm the same nurse from every day for two weeks now. Don't play your games with me.

WILLIE: I can't even chew a piece of bread, who's gonna play games? . . . Why'd you turn off the television?

NURSE: It's either watching that or watching you sleep—either one ain't too interesting.

WILLIE: I'm sorry. I'll try to sleep more entertaining . . . What's today, Tuesday?

NURSE: Wednesday. (*She bites into a piece of chocolate.*)

WILLIE: How could this be Wednesday? I went to sleep on Monday.

NURSE: Haven't we already seen Mike Douglas twice this week?

WILLIE: Once.

NURSE: Twice.

WILLIE (*reluctantly*): All right, twice . . . I don't even remember. I was all right yesterday?

NURSE: We are doing very well.

WILLIE: We are? When did *you* get sick?

NURSE (*deadly serious, no smile*): That's funny. That is really funny, Mr. Clark. Soon as I get home tonight I'm gonna bust out laughing.

WILLIE: You keep eating my candy like that, you're gonna bust out a lot sooner.

NURSE: Well, *you* can't eat it and there's no sense throwing it out. I'm just storing up energy for the winter.

WILLIE: Maybe you'll find time in between the nougat and the peppermint to take my pulse.

NURSE: I took it. It's a little better today.

WILLIE: When did you take my pulse?

NURSE: When you were sleeping.

WILLIE: *Everybody's* pulse is good when they're sleeping. You take a pulse when a person is up. Thirty dollars a day, she takes a sleeping pulse. I'll tell you the truth, I don't think you know what you're doing . . . and I'm not a prejudiced person.

NURSE: Well, *I* am: I don't like sick people who tell registered nurses how to do their job. You want your tea now?

WILLIE: I don't want to interrupt your candy.

NURSE: And don't get fresh with me. You can get fresh with your nephew, but you can't get fresh with me. Maybe *he* has to take it, but I'm not a blood relative.

WILLIE: That's for sure.

NURSE: That's even funnier than the other one. My *whole* evening's gonna be taken up tonight with nothing but laughing.

WILLIE: I don't even eat candy. Finish the whole box. When you're through, I hope you eat the flowers too.

NURSE: You know why I don't get angry at anything you say to me?

WILLIE: I give up. Why?

NURSE: Because I have a good sense of humor. I am *known* for my good sense of humor. That's why I can take anything you say to me.

WILLIE: If you nurse as good as your sense of humor, I won't make it to Thursday . . . Who called?

NURSE: No one.

WILLIE: I thought I heard the phone.

NURSE (*gets up*): No one called. (*She crosses and puffs up his pillow.*) Did you have a nice nap?

WILLIE: It was a nap, nothing special . . . Don't puff up the pillows, please. (*He swats her hands away.*) It takes me a day and a night to get them the way I like them, and then you puff them up.

NURSE: Oh, woke up a little grouchy, didn't we?

WILLIE: Stop making yourself a partner all the time. I woke up grouchy. Don't make the bed, please. I'm still sleeping in it. Don't make a bed with a person in it.

NURSE: Can't stand to have people do things for you, can you? If you just want someone to sit here and watch you, you're better off getting a dog, Mr. Clark. I'll suggest that to your nephew.

WILLIE: Am I complaining? I'm only asking for two things. Don't take my pulse when I'm sleeping and don't make my bed when I'm in it. Do it the other way around and then we're in business.

NURSE: It doesn't bother me to do nothing as long as I'm getting paid for it. (She sits.)

WILLIE (a pause): I'm hungry.

NURSE: You want your junket?

WILLIE: Forget it. I'm not hungry. (She reads.) Tell me something, how old is a woman like you?

NURSE: That is none of your business.

WILLIE: I'm not asking for business.

NURSE: I am fifty-four years young.

WILLIE: Is that so? . . . You're married?

NURSE: My husband passed away four years ago.

WILLIE: Oh . . . You were the nurse?

NURSE: No, I was not the nurse . . . You could use some sleep and I could use some quiet. (She gets up.)

WILLIE: You know something? For a fifty-four-year-old registered widow, you're an attractive woman. (He tries to pat her. She swings at him.)

NURSE: And don't try that with me!

WILLIE: Who's trying anything?

NURSE: You are. You're getting fresh in a way I don't like.

WILLIE: What are you worried about? I can't even put on my slippers by myself.

NURSE: I'm not worried about your slippers. And don't play on my sympathy. I don't have any, and I ain't expecting any coming in, in the near future.

WILLIE: Listen, how about a nice alcohol rub?

NURSE: I just gave you one.

WILLIE: No, I'll give you one.

NURSE: I know you just say things like that to agitate me. You like to agitate people, don't you? Well, I am not an agitatable person.

WILLIE: You're right. I think I'd be better off with the dog.

NURSE: How did your poor wife stand a man like you?

WILLIE: Who told you about my poor wife?

NURSE: Your poor nephew . . . Did you ever think of getting married again? (She takes his pulse.)

WILLIE: What is this, a proposal?

NURSE (laughs): Not from me . . . I am not thinking of getting married again . . . Besides, you're just not my type.

WILLIE: Why? It's a question of religion?

NURSE: It's a question of age. You'd wear me out in no time.

WILLIE: You think I can't support you? I've got Medicare.

NURSE: You never stop, do you?

WILLIE: When I stop, I won't be here.

NURSE: Well, that's where you're gonna be unless you learn to slow up a little.

WILLIE: Slow up? I moved two inches in three weeks, she tells me slow up.

NURSE: I mean, if you're considering getting well again, you have to stop worrying about telephone calls and messages, and especially about when you're going back to work.

WILLIE: I'm an actor—I have to act. It's my profession.

NURSE: Your profession right now is being a sick person. And if you're gonna act anywhere, it's gonna be from a sick bed.

WILLIE: Maybe I can get a job on Marcus Welby.

NURSE: You can turn everything I say into a vaudeville routine if you want, but I'm gonna give you a piece of advice, Mr. Clark . . .

WILLIE: What?

NURSE: The world is full of sick people. And there just ain't enough doctors or nurses to go around to take care of all these sick people. And all the doctors and all the nurses can do just so much, Mr. Clark. But God, in His Infinite Wisdom, has said He will help those who help themselves.

WILLIE (looks at her): So? What's the advice?

NURSE: Stop bugging me!

WILLIE: All right, I'll stop bugging you . . . I don't even know what the hell it means.

NURSE: That's better. Now you're my type again.

(The doorbell rings. The NURSE crosses to the door.)

WILLIE: Here comes today's candy.

(She opens the door. BEN enters with packages.)

BEN: Hello. How is he?

NURSE: Fine. I think we're gonna get married.

BEN: Hey, Uncle Willie, you look terrific.

WILLIE: You got my Variety?

BEN (goes over to him, and hands him Variety): I also got about two hundred get-well telegrams from just about every star in show business —Lucille Ball, Milton Berle, Bob Hope, the mayor. It'll take you nine months just to answer them.

WILLIE: What about a commercial? Did you hear from Alka-Seltzer?

BEN: We have plenty of time to talk about that . . . Miss O'Neill, did you have your lunch yet?

NURSE: Not yet.

WILLIE: She just finished two pounds of appetizers.

BEN: Why don't you go out, take an hour or so? I'll be here for a while.

NURSE: Thank you. I could use some fresh air. (*Gets her coat. To* WILLIE.) Now, when I'm gone, I don't want you getting all agitated again, you hear?

WILLIE: I hear, I hear. Stop bugging me.

NURSE: And don't get up to go to the bathroom. Use the you-know-what.

WILLIE (*without looking up from his* Variety): And if not, I'll do it you-know-where.

(*The* NURSE *exits.*)

BEN (*pulling up a chair next to the bed*): Never mind, she's a very good nurse.

WILLIE (*looks in the paper*): Oh, boy, Bernie Eisenstein died.

BEN: Who?

WILLIE: Bernie Eisenstein. Remember the dance team "Ramona and Rodriguez"? Bernie Eisenstein was Rodriguez . . . He would have been seventy-eight in August.

BEN (*sighs*): Uncle Willie, could you put down Variety for a second?

WILLIE (*still reading*): Did you bring a cigar?

BEN: Uncle Willie, you realize you've had a heart attack, don't you? . . . You've been getting away with it for years—the cigars, the corned beef sandwiches, the tension, the temper tantrums. You can't do it any more, Willie. Your heart's just not going to take it.

WILLIE: This is the good news you rushed up with? For this we could have skipped a Wednesday.

BEN (*a pause*): I talked to the doctor this morning . . . and I'm going to have to be very frank and honest with you, Willie . . . You've got to retire. I mean give it up. Show business is out.

WILLIE: Until when?

BEN: Until *ever!* Your blood pressure is abnormally high, your heart is weak—if you tried to work again you would kill yourself.

WILLIE: All right, let me think it over.

BEN: *Think what over?* There's nothing to think over. You can't work any more, there's no decision to be made. Can't you understand that?

WILLIE: You decide for Ben Silverman, I'll decide for Willie Clark.

BEN: No, *I'll* decide for Willie Clark. I am your closest and *only* living relative, and I am responsible for your welfare . . . You can't live here any more, Willie. Not alone . . . And I can't afford to keep this nurse on permanently. Right now she's making more than I am. Anyway she already gave me her notice. She's leaving Monday. She's going to Buffalo to work for a very wealthy family.

WILLIE: Maybe she'll take me. I always did well in Buffalo.

BEN: Come on, Willie, face the facts. We have to do something, and we have to do it quickly.

WILLIE: I can't think about it today. I'm tired, I'm going to take a nap. (*He closes his eyes and drops his head to the side on the pillow.*)

BEN: You want to hear my suggestion?

WILLIE: I'm napping. Don't you see my eyes closed?

BEN: I'd like you to move in with me and Helen and the kids. We have the small spare room in the back, I think you would be very comfortable . . . Uncle Willie, did you hear what I said?

WILLIE: What's the second suggestion?

BEN: What's the matter with the first?

WILLIE: It's not as good as the second.

BEN: I haven't made any yet.

WILLIE: It's still better than the first. Forget it.

BEN: Why?

WILLIE: I don't like your kids. They're noisy. The little one hit me in the head with a baseball bat.

BEN: And I've also seen you talk to them for hours on end about vaudeville and had the time of your life. Right?

WILLIE: If I stopped talking, they would hit me with the bat. No offense, but I'm not living with your children. If you get rid of them, then we'll talk . . .

BEN: I know the reason you won't come. Because Al Lewis lives with his family, and you're just trying to prove some stupid point about being independent.

WILLIE: What's the second suggestion?

BEN (*a long sigh*): All right . . . Now, don't

jump when I say this, because it's not as bad as it sounds.

WILLIE: Say it.

BEN: There's the Actors' Home in New Brunswick—

WILLIE: It's as bad as it sounds.

BEN: You're wrong. I drove out there last Sunday and they showed me around the whole place. I couldn't believe how beautiful it was.

WILLIE: You went out there? You didn't have the decency to wait until I turned down living with you first?

BEN: I just went out to investigate, that's all. No commitments.

WILLIE: The Old Actors' Home: the first booking you got me in ten years.

BEN: It's on a lake, it's got twenty-five acres of beautiful grounds, it's an old converted mansion with a big porch . . .

WILLIE: I knew it. You got me on a porch in New Jersey. He put you up to this, didn't he?

BEN: You don't have to sit on the porch. There's a million activities there. They put on shows every Friday and Saturday night. I mean, it's all old actors—what could be better for you?

WILLIE: Why New Jersey? I hate New Jersey . . . I'm sorry they ever finished the George Washington Bridge.

BEN: I couldn't get over how many old actors were there that I knew and remembered. I thought they were all dead.

WILLIE: Some recommendation. A house in the swamps with forgotten people.

BEN: They're not forgotten. They're well taken care of . . . Uncle Willie, I promise you, if you spend one day there that you're not happy, you can come back and move in with me.

WILLIE: That's my choice—New Jersey or the baseball bat.

BEN: All right, I feel a lot better about everything.

WILLIE: And what about you?

BEN: What do you mean what about me?

WILLIE (a pause; looks away): I won't see you no more?

BEN: Certainly you'll see me. As often as I can . . . Did you think I wouldn't come to visit you, Uncle Willie?

WILLIE: Well, you know . . . People don't go out to New Jersey unless they have to.

BEN: Uncle Willie, I'll be there every week. With the Variety. I'll even bring Helen and the kids.

WILLIE: Don't bring the kids! Why do you think I'm going to the home for?

BEN: You know, this is the first moment since I've known you, that you've treated me like a nephew and not an agent. It's like a whole new relationship.

WILLIE: I hope this one works out better than the other one.

BEN: I've been waiting for this for fifteen years. You just wouldn't ever let me get close, Uncle Willie.

WILLIE: If you kiss me, I call off the whole thing.

BEN: No kiss, I promise . . . Now there's just one other thing I'd like you to do for me.

WILLIE: With my luck it's a benefit.

BEN: In a way it is a benefit. But not for any organization. It's for another human being.

WILLIE: What are you talking about?

BEN: Al Lewis wants to come and see you.

WILLIE: If you wanted to kill me, why didn't you bring the cigars?

BEN: He's been heartsick ever since this happened.

WILLIE: What do you think I've been? What is this, the mumps?

BEN: You know what I mean . . . He calls me twice a day to see how you are. He's worried to death.

WILLIE: Tonight tell him I'm worse.

BEN: He's not well himself, Willie. He's got diabetes, hardening of the arteries, his eyes are getting very bad . . .

WILLIE: He sees good enough to spit in my face.

BEN: He's lost seven pounds since you were in the hospital. Who do you think's been sending all the candy and flowers every day? He keeps signing the other people's names because he knows otherwise you'd throw them out.

WILLIE: They're his flowers? Throw 'em out!

BEN: Uncle Willie, I've never asked you to do a personal favor for me as long as I've known you. But this is important—for me, and for you, for Al Lewis. He won't even stay. He just wants to come up and say hello . . .

WILLIE: Hello, heh?

BEN: That's all.

WILLIE: And if he pokes me in the chest with the finger, I'm a dead man. That's murder, you know.

BEN: Come on, Willie. Give us all a break.

WILLIE: Well, if he wants to come up, I won't stop him. But I can't promise a "hello." I may be taking a nap.

BEN (starts toward the phone): I knew I could count on you, Willie. He's going to be very happy. (*He picks up the phone.*)

WILLIE: You don't have to call him from here. Why should I pay sixty cents for him to come say hello?

BEN (*he dials "O"*): It's not going to cost you sixty cents. (*To the operator.*) Hello. Would you tell the boy at the desk to send Mr. Lewis up to Mr. Clark's room, please? Thank you. (*He hangs up.*)

WILLIE (*as near to shouting as he can get*): You mean he's here now in the hotel? `

BEN: He's been with me all morning. I knew it would be all right.

WILLIE: First you commit me to the Old Man's Home, bring that bastard here and *then* you ask me?

BEN (*all smiles*): I'm sorry. I apologize. Never speak to me again . . . But just promise you'll be decent to Al Lewis.

WILLIE: I'll be wonderful to him. In my will, I'll leave him *you!* (*He starts to get out of bed.*)

BEN: What are you doing? You're not supposed to be out of bed.

WILLIE: You think I'm going to give him the satisfaction of seeing me laying in bed like a sick person? I'm gonna sit in my chair and I'm gonna look healthier than he does. (*He tries weakly to get on his slippers.*)

BEN: The doctor said you're not to get out of bed for *anything.*

WILLIE: Lewis coming to apologize to Clark is not anything. To me, this is worth another heart attack. Get my coat from the closet.

BEN (*starting for the closet*): All right, but just walk slowly, will you, please? (*He opens the closet.*)

WILLIE: And then I want you to move my chair all the way back. I want that son-of-a-bitch to have a long walk.

BEN (*takes out a bathrobe from the closet*): Here, put this on.

WILLIE: Not the bathrobe, the jacket. The blue sports jacket. This is gonna be a *formal* apology.

BEN (*puts back the bathrobe and takes out the blue sports jacket*): He's not coming to apologize. He's just coming to say hello.

WILLIE: If he doesn't apologize, I'll drop dead in the chair for spite. And you can tell him that.

(BEN *helps him into the blue sports jacket over the pajamas.*)

BEN: Now I'm sorry I started in with this.

WILLIE: That's funny. Because now I'm starting to feel good. (*Buttons the jacket.*) Push the chair back. All the way.

(BEN *picks up the chair and carries it to the far side of the room.*)

BEN: I thought I was bringing you two together.

WILLIE (*he shuffles over to the chair;* BEN *helps him to sit*): Put a pillow underneath. Make it two pillows. When I sit, I wanna look down on him.

(BEN *puts a pillow under* WILLIE.)

BEN: This is the last time. I'm never going to butt into your lives again.

WILLIE: The only thing that could have made today better is if it was raining. I would love to see him apologize dripping wet. (*And then come three knocks on the door: "Knock, knock, knock."*) Aha! This is it! . . . *This* was worth getting sick for! Come on, knock again. (*Points his finger in the air, his crowning moment.* AL *knocks again.*) En-terrr!

(BEN *crosses to the door and opens it.* AL LEWIS *timidly steps in, with his hat in his hand.* WILLIE *immediately drops his head to his side, closes his eyes and snores, feigning a nap.*)

AL (*whispers*): Oh, he's sleeping. I could come back later.

BEN (*also whispers*): No, that's all right. He must be dozing. Come on in. (AL *steps in and* BEN *closes the door.*) Can I take your hat?

AL: No, I'd like to hold on to something, if you don't mind.

(BEN *crosses over to* WILLIE, *who is still dozing. He bends over and speaks softly in* WILLIE'*s ear.*)

BEN: Uncle Willie. There's someone here to see you.

WILLIE (*opens his eyes, stirs*): Heh? What?

BEN: Look who's here to see you, Uncle Willie.

WILLIE (*squints*): I don't have my glasses. Who's that?

AL: It's me, Willie. Al . . . Al Lewis.

WILLIE (*squints harder*): Al Lewis? You're so far away . . . Walk all the way over here. (AL *sheepishly makes the trek across the room with hat in hand. He squints again.*) Oh, *that* Al Lewis.

AL: I don't want to disturb you, Willie. I know you're resting.

WILLIE: That's all right. I was just reading my telegrams from Lucille Ball and Bob Hope.

AL: Oh, that's nice . . . (*Turns, looks at the vase.*) Oh, look at the beautiful flowers.

WILLIE: I'm throwing them out. I don't like the smell. People send them to me every day with boxes of cheap candy. They mean well.

AL (*nods*): They certainly do . . . Well, I just came up to see how you're doing. I don't want to take up your time. I just wanted to say hello . . . So "hello"—and goodbye. (*He starts to put on his hat to go.*)

WILLIE: Wait a minute. You got a few minutes before my next nap. Sit down and talk for a while.

AL: You're sure it's okay?

WILLIE: I'm sure you got a lot more to say than just "hello" . . . Would you like some tea?

AL: I would love some.

WILLIE: Go in the kitchen and make it.

BEN: I've got a better idea. I'll go down and have the kitchen send up a tray. If I call room service it'll take forever. (*He starts for the door.*)

WILLIE (*to* BEN): You're going? You don't want to hear what Al has to say?

BEN: I don't think it's necessary. I'll be back in ten minutes. (*At the door.*) It's good to see you, Mr. Lewis . . . It's good to see the *both* of you.

(*He nods, then exits, closing the door. There is an awkward silence between the two men for a moment.*)

AL (*finally*): He's a nice boy.

WILLIE: He's the best . . . Not too bright, but a good boy.

AL (*nods*): You've got everything you need here?

WILLIE: What could I need here?

AL: Some books? Some magazines?

WILLIE: No, I got plenty to do. I got all my fan mail to answer.

AL: You get fan mail?

WILLIE: Don't you?

AL: I don't even get jury duty.

WILLIE: Sure, plenty of people still remember . . . (*He coughs.*) Excuse me.

AL: You're sure it's all right for you to talk like this?

WILLIE: I'm not talking. I'm just answering. *You're* talking. (*There is a long pause.*) Why? Is there something special you wanted to talk about?

AL: Like what?

WILLIE: What do I know like what? How should I know what's on your mind? Do I know why you can't sleep at night?

AL: Who said I don't sleep at night! I sleep beautifully.

WILLIE: Funny, to me you look tired. A little troubled. Like a person who had something on his conscience, what do I know?

AL: I have nothing on my conscience.

WILLIE (*a pause*): Are you sure you looked good?

AL: I have *nothing* on my conscience. The only thing I feel badly about is that you got sick.

WILLIE: Thank you. *I accept your apology!*

AL: What apology? Who apologized? I just said I'm sorry you got sick.

WILLIE: Who do you think *made* me sick?

AL: Who? *You* did, that's who! Not me. You yelled and screamed and carried on like a lunatic until you made yourself sick . . . and for that I'm sorry.

WILLIE: All right, as long as you're sorry for something.

AL: I'm also sorry that people are starving in India, but I'm not going to apologize. I didn't do it.

WILLIE: I didn't accuse you of India. I'm just saying you're responsible for making me sick, and since you've come up here to apologize, I am gentleman enough to accept it.

AL: Don't be such a gentleman, because there's nothing to accept.

WILLIE: You're the one who came up here with your hat in your hand not me.

AL: It's a twenty-five dollar hat, what was I gonna do, fold it up in my pocket?

WILLIE: If you didn't come to apologize, why did you send me the candy and flowers?

AL: I sent you candy and flowers?

WILLIE: Yes. Because it was on your conscience and *that's* why you couldn't sleep at night and *that's* why you came up here with your hat in your hand to apologize, only *this* time I'm not a gentleman any more and I *don't accept the apology!* How do you like that?

(AL *stares at* WILLIE.)

AL: I knew there was gonna be trouble when you said "Enter" instead of "Come in."

WILLIE: There's no trouble. The trouble is over. I got what I want and now I'm happy.

AL: What did you get? You got "no apology" from me, which you didn't accept.

WILLIE: I don't want to discuss it any more, I just had a heart attack.

(AL *stares at* WILLIE *silently.*)

AL (*calmly*): You know something, Willie. I don't think we get along too good.

WILLIE: Well, listen, everybody has their ups and downs.

AL: In forty-three years, we had maybe one "up" . . . To tell you the truth, I can't take the "downs" any more.

WILLIE: To be honest with you, for the first time I feel a little tired myself. In a way this heart attack was good for me. I needed the rest.

AL: So what are you going to do now?

WILLIE: Well, my nephew made me two very good offers today.

AL: Is that right?

WILLIE: I think I'm gonna take the second one.

AL: Are you in any condition to work again?

WILLIE: Well, it wouldn't be too strenuous ... Mostly take it easy, maybe do a show on Saturday night, something like that.

AL: Is that so? Where, in New York?

WILLIE: No, no. Out of town ...

AL: Isn't that wonderful.

WILLIE: Well, you know me, I gotta keep busy ... What's with you?

AL: Oh, I'm very happy. My daughter's having another baby. They're gonna need my room, and I don't want to be a burden on them ... So we talked it over, and I decided I'm gonna move to the Actors' Home in New Brunswick.

WILLIE (*he sinks back onto his pillow, his head falls over to one side, and he sighs deeply*): Ohh, God. I got the finger again.

AL: What's the matter? You all right? Why are you holding your chest? You got pains?

WILLIE: Not yet. But I'm expecting.

AL (*nervously*): Can I get you anything? Should I call the doctor?

WILLIE: It wouldn't help.

AL: It wouldn't hurt.

(*The realization that they slipped accidentally into an old vaudeville joke causes* WILLIE *to smile.*)

WILLIE: "It wouldn't hurt" ... How many times have we done that joke?

AL: It always worked ... Even from you I just got a laugh.

WILLIE: You're a funny man, Al ... You're a pain in the ass, but you're a funny man.

AL: You know what your trouble was, Willie? You always took the jokes too seriously. They were just jokes. We did comedy on the stage for forty-three years, I don't think you enjoyed it once.

WILLIE: If I was there to enjoy it, I would buy a ticket.

AL: Well, maybe now you can start enjoying it ... If you're not too busy, maybe you'll come over one day to the Actors' Home and visit me.

WILLIE: You can count on it.

AL: I feel a lot better now that I've talked to you ... Maybe you'd like to rest now, take a nap.

WILLIE: I think so ... Keep talking to me, I'll fall asleep.

AL (*looks around*): What's new in *Variety?*

WILLIE: Bernie Eisenstein died.

AL: Go on. Bernie Eisenstein? The house doctor at the Palace?

WILLIE: That was Sam Hesseltine. Bernie Eisenstein was "Ramona and Rodriguez."

AL: Jackie Aaronson was Ramona and Rodriguez. Bernie Eisenstein was the house doctor at the Palace. Sam Hesseltine was Sophie Tucker's agent.

WILLIE: Don't argue with me, I'm sick.

AL: I know. But why should I get sick too? (*The curtain starts to fall.* WILLIE *moans.*) Bernie Eisenstein was the house doctor when we played for the first time with Sophie Tucker, and that's when we met Sam Hesseltine ... Jackie Aaronson wasn't Rodriguez yet ... He was "DeMarco and Lopez" ... Lopez died, and DeMarco went into real estate, so Jackie became Rodriguez.

CURTAIN

CURTAIN CALL

AL: Don't you remember Big John McCafferey? The Irishman? He owned the Biltmore Theater in Pittsburgh? And the Adams Theater in Syracuse? Always wore a two-pound diamond ring on his finger? He was the one who used to take out Mary Donatto, the cute little Italian girl from the Follies. Well, she used to go with Abe Berkowitz who was then the booker for the Orpheum circuit and Big John hated his guts because of the time when Harry Richman ...

General Bibliography

Bibliographies and Collections

Arata, Esther. *More Black American Playwrights*. Metuchen, N.J.: Scarecrow Press, 1978.

Arata Esther, and Nicholas Rotoli. *Black American Playwrights, 1800 to the Present*. Metuchen, N.J.: Scarecrow Press, 1976.

Baker, Blanche M. *Dramatic Bibliography*. New York: Wilson, 1933.

————. *The Theatre and Allied Arts*. New York: Wilson, 1952.

Bergquist, G. William. *Three Centuries of English and American Plays*. New York: Hafner, 1963.

Hatch, James Vernon. *Black Image on the American Stage*. New York: DBS Publications, 1970.

Hill, Frank. *American Plays Printed 1714–1830*. Palo Alto, Calif.: Stanford University Press, 1934.

Long, E. Hudson. *American Drama from Its Beginnings to the Present*. New York: Appleton-Century-Crofts, 1970.

Mantle, Burns. *The Best Plays of 1919–20*. New York: Dodd, Mead, 1920. *A volume has been produced annually in this series since 1920. John Chapman has edited the series since 1948.*

Roden, Robert. *Later American Plays, 1831–1900*. New York: Burt Franklin, 1900.

Ryan, Pat. *American Drama Bibliography*. Fort Wayne, Ind.: Fort Wayne Public Library, 1969.

Stratman, Carl J. *Bibliography of the American Theatre, Excluding New York City*. Chicago: Loyola University Press, 1965.

Thompson, Lawrence. *Nineteenth and Twentieth Century Drama: A Selective Bibliography of English Language Works*. Boston: G.K. Hall, 1975.

Wegelin, Oscar. *Early American Plays, 1714–1730*. New York: Haskell House, 1968.

Weingarter, Joseph A. *Modern Playwrights, 1918–1948: A Bibliography*. New York: Privately printed, 1948.

Histories

Anderson, John. *The American Theatre*. New York: Dial, 1938.

Bernheim, Alfred. *The Business of the Theatre*. New York: Benjamin Blom, 1964.

Daly, Charles. *First Theatre in America*. New York: Dunlap Society, 1896.

Dunlap, William. *History of the American Theatre*. New York: Harper, 1832.

Flanagan, Hallie (Davis). *Arena: The History of the Federal Theatre*. New York: Benjamin Blom, 1940.

Hornblow, Arthur. *A History of the Theatre in America* (2 Vols.). 1919.

Hughes, Glen. *A History of the American Theatre, 1700–1950*. New York: Samuel French, 1951.

Mayorga, Margeret G. *A Short History of the American Drama*. New York: Dodd, Mead, 1932.

Meserve, Walter J. *An Outline History of American Drama*. Totowa, N.J.: Littlefield, Adams, 1965.

Moses, Montrose J. *The American Dramatist*. New York: Benjamin Blom, 1964.

Moses, Montrose J., and John Mason Brown. *The American Theatre as Seen by Its Critics, 1752–1934*. New York: W.W. Norton, 1934.

Quinn, Arthur Hobson. *A History of the American Drama from the Beginning to the Civil War*, Rev. Ed. New York: Crofts, 1937.

———. *A History of the American Dramas from the Civil War to the Present Day*, Rev. Ed. New York: Crofts, 1937.

Seilhamer, George. *A History of the American Theatre, 1749–1797* (3 Vols.). Philadelphia: Globe, 1891.

Taubman, Howard. *The Making of the American Theatre*. New York: Coward McCann, 1965.

Wilson, Garff B. *Three Hundred Years of American Drama and Theatre from "Ye Bare and Ye Cubb" to "Hair"*. Englewood Cliffs, N.J.: Prentice-Hall, 1973.

Specific Studies

Abramson, Doris. *Negro Playwrights in the American Theatre, 1925–1959*. New York: Columbia University Press, 1969.

Anderson, Maxwell. *The Essence of Tragedy*. Washington, D.C.: Anderson House, 1939.

Andrews, Charlton. *The Drama Today*. Philadelphia: Lippincott, 1913.

Bentley, Eric. *The Dramatic Event: An American Chronicle*. New York: Horizon Press, 1954.

———. *In Search of Theatre*. New York: Knopf, 1953.

———. *The Playwright as Thinker*. New York: Harcourt Brace, 1946.

Bonin, Jane. *Prize-Winning American Drama*. Metuchen, N.J.: Scarecrow Press, 1973.

Broussard, Louis. *American Drama: Contemporary Allegory from Eugene O'Neill to Tennessee Williams*. Norman: University of Oklahoma Press, 1962.

Brustein, Robert. *The Theatre of Revolt*. Boston: Little, Brown, 1964.

Burton, Richard. *The New American Drama*. New York: Crowell, 1913.

Clurman, Harold. *The Fervent Years*. New York: Knopf, 1945.

Dickinson, Thomas H. *Playwrights of the New American Theatre*. New York: Macmillan, 1924.

Downer, Alan. *The American Theatre Today*. New York: Basic Books, 1967.

———. *American Drama and Its Critics: A Collection of Critical Essays*. Chicago: University of Chicago Press, 1965.

———. *Fifty Years of American Drama, 1900–1950*. Chicago: Regnery, 1951.

Dusenbury, Winifred. *The Theme of Loneliness in Modern American Drama*. Gainesville: University of Florida Press, 1960.

Flexner, Eleanor. *American Playwrights 1918–1938*. New York: Simon & Schuster, 1938.

Freedman, Morris. *American Drama in Social Context*. Carbondale: Southern Illinois University Press, 1971.

Gagey, Edmond. *Revolution in American Drama*. New York: Columbia University Press, 1947.

Gardner, Rufus. *The Splintered Stage: The Decline of the American Theatre*. New York: Macmillan, 1965.

Gassner, John. *Directions in Modern Theatre and Drama*. New York: Holt, Rinehart & Winston, 1965.

———. *Theatre at the Crossroads*. New York: Holt, Rinehart & Winston, 1960.

———. *Form and Idea in Modern Theatre*. New York: Dryden, 1956.

———. *The Theatre in Our Time*. New York: Crown, 1954.

Golden, Joseph. *The Death of Tinker Bell: The American Theatre in the Twentieth Century*. Syracuse, N.J.: Syracuse University Press.

Goldstein, Malcolm. *The Political Stage: American Drama and Theatre of the Great Depression*. New York: Oxford University Press, 1974.

Gottfried, Martin. *A Theatre Divided: The Postwar American Stage*. Boston: Little, Brown, 1967.

Gould, Jean. *Modern American Playwrights*. New York: Dodd, Mead, 1966.

Krutch, Joseph Wood. *The American Drama Since 1918*, Rev. Ed. New York: Braziller, 1957.

Lewis, Allan. *American Plays and Playwrights of the Contemporary Theatre*. New York: Crown, 1965.

Mantle, Burns. *American Playwrights of Today*. New York: Dodd, Mead, 1938.

———. *Contemporary American Playwrights*. New York: Dodd, Mead, 1938.

Mersand, Joseph. *The American Drama Since 1930*. New York: Modern Chapbooks, 1951.

Merserve, Walter. *An Emerging Entertainment: The Drama of the American People to 1828*. Bloomington: Indiana University Press, 1977.

———. *Discussions of Modern American Drama*. Boston: Heath, 1965.

Moody, Richard. *America Takes the Stage: Romanticism in American Drama and Theatre*. Bloomington: University of Indiana Press, 1955.

Nathan, George Jean. *The Magic Mirror*. New York: Knopf, 1960.

———. *The Theatre in the Fifties*. New York: Knopf, 1953.

———. *The Entertainment of a Nation*. New York: Knopf, 1942.

Nolan, Paul. *Provincial Drama in America, 1870–1916*. Metuchen, N.J.: Scarecrow Press, 1967.

Phelps, William Lyon. *Essays on American Dramatists*. New York: Macmillan, 1921.

Poggi, Jack. *Theatre in America*. Ithaca, N.Y.: Cornell University Press, 1968.

Weales, Gerald. *American Drama Since World War II*. New York: Harcourt, Brace & World, 1962.

Young, Stark. *The Flower in Drama*. New York: Scribner's, 1955.

Major Plays in America

1927 *The Second Man*, S. N. Behrman
1928 *The Front Page*, Ben Hecht and Charles MacArthur
1928 *Holiday*, Philip Barry
1928 *Strange Interlude*, Eugene O'Neill
1929 *June Moon*, Ring Lardner and George S. Kaufman
1929 *Street Scene*, Elmer Rice

1930–1939

1930 *Alison's House*, Susan Glaspell
1930 *Elizabeth, the Queen*, Maxwell Anderson
1930 *The Green Pastures*, Marc Connelly
1931 *The House of Connelly*, Paul Connelly
1931 *Mourning Becomes Electra*, Eugene O'Neill
1931 *Reunion in Vienna*, Robert Sherwood
1932 *Biography*, S. N. Behrman
1933 *Ah, Wilderness*, Eugene O'Neill
1933 *Both Your Houses*, Maxwell Anderson
1933 *Men in White*, Sidney Kingsley
1933 *Tobacco Road*, Jack Kirkland (From the novel by Erskine Caldwell.)
1933 *We, the People*, Elmer Rice
1934 *The Children's Hour*, Lillian Hellman
1935 *Awake and Sing*, Clifford Odets
1935 *Dead End*, Sidney Kingsley
1935 *The Old Maid*, Zoe Akins
1935 *The Petrified Forest*, Robert Sherwood
1935 *Waiting for Lefty*, Clifford Odets
1935 *Winterset*, Maxwell Anderson
1936 *End of Summer*, S. N. Behrman
1936 *High Tor*, Maxwell Anderson
1936 *Idiot's Delight*, Robert Sherwood
1936 *The Women*, Clare Booth
1936 *You Can't Take It with You*, Moss Hart and George S. Kaufman
1937 *Golden Boy*, Clifford Odets
1937 *Of Mice and Men*, John Steinbeck
1938 *Abe Lincoln in Illinois*, Robert Sherwood
1938 *On Borrowed Time*, Paul Osborn (From the novel by Lawrence E. Watkin.)
1938 *Our Town*, Thornton Wilder
1939 *Life with Father*, Howard Lindsay and Russel Crouse
1939 *The Little Foxes*, Lillian Hellman
1939 *The Man Who Came to Dinner*, George S. Kaufman and Moss Hart
1939 *No Time for Comedy*, S. N. Behrman
1939 *The Philadelphia Story*, Philip Barry
1939 *The Time of Your Life*, William Saroyan

1940–1949

1940 *There Shall Be No Night*, Robert Sherwood
1941 *Arsenic and Old Lace*, Joseph Kesselring
1941 *Watch on the Rhine*, Lillian Hellman
1942 *The Skin of Our Teeth*, Thornton Wilder

1943 *Oklahoma*, Oscar Hammerstein II and Richard Rodgers (Musical)
1943 *The Patriots*, Sidney Kingsley
1943 *Winged Victory*, Moss Hart
1944 *A Bell for Adano*, Paul Osborn (Adapted from the novel by John Hersey.)
1944 *Harvey*, Mary Chase
1945 *Dream Girl*, Elmer Rice
1945 *The Glass Menagerie*, Tennessee Williams
1945 *Home of the Brave*, Arthur Laurents
1945 *The State of the Union*, Howard Lindsay and Russel Crouse
1946 *Born Yesterday*, Garson Kanin
1946 *The Iceman Cometh*, Eugene O'Neill
1947 *All My Sons*, Arthur Miller
1947 *Medea*, Robinson Jeffers
1947 *A Streetcar Named Desire*, Tennessee Williams
1948 *Mister Roberts*, Thomas Heggen and Joshua Logan
1948 *Summer and Smoke*, Tennessee Williams
1949 *Death of a Salesman*, Arthur Miller
1949 *South Pacific*, Richard Rodgers, Oscar Hammerstein II, and Joshua Logan (Musical)

1950–1959

1950 *Come Back, Little Sheba*, William Inge
1950 *The Country Girl*, Clifford Odets
1950 *Darkness at Noon*, Sidney Kingsley and Arthur Koestler (Based on the novel by Arthur Koestler.)
1950 *The Member of the Wedding*, Carson McCullers
1951 *The Autumn Garden*, Lillian Hellman
1951 *The Four Poster*, Jan de Hartog
1951 *I Am a Camera*, John van Druten
1951 *The Rose Tattoo*, Tennessee Williams
1952 *The Seven Year Itch*, George Axelrod
1952 *The Shrike*, Joseph Kramm
1953 *Camino Real*, Tennessee Williams
1953 *The Crucible*, Arthur Miller
1953 *Picnic*, William Inge
1953 *Tea and Sympathy*, Robert Anderson
1953 *Teahouse of the August Moon*, John Patrick (Adapted from the novel by Vern Sneider.)
1955 *Bus Stop*, William Inge
1955 *Cat on a Hot Tin Roof*, Tennessee Williams
1955 *Diary of Anne Frank*, Frances Goodrich and Albert Hackett (Based on *Anne Frank: The Diary of a Young Girl*.)
1955 *A Hatful of Rain*, Michael Gazzo
1955 *Inherit the Wind*, Jerome Lawrence and Robert E. Lee
1955 *Long Day's Journey into Night*, Eugene O'Neill
1955 *The Matchmaker*, Thornton Wilder

(Formerly *The Merchant of Yonkers.*)
1955 *A View from the Bridge*, Arthur Miller
1957 *The Dark at the Top of the Stairs*, William Inge
1957 *Look Homeward, Angel*, Ketti Frings (Based on the novel by Thomas Wolfe.)
1957 *A Moon for the Misbegotten*, Eugene O'Neill
1957 *Visit to a Small Planet*, Gore Vidal
1958 *A Touch of the Poet*, Eugene O'Neill
1958 *Two for the Seesaw*, William Gibson
1958 *The World of Suzie Wong*, Paul Osborn (Adapted from the novel by Richard Mason.)
1959 *The Connection*, Jack Gelber
1959 *The Miracle Worker*, William Gibson
1959 *A Raisin in the Sun*, Lorraine Hansberry

1960–1969

1960 *All the Way Home*, Tad Mosel
1960 *Toys in the Attic*, Lillian Hellman
1960 *The Zoo Story*, Edward Albee
1961 *The American Dream*, Edward Albee
1961 *Come Blow Your Horn*, Neil Simon
1961 *The Death of Bessie Smith*, Edward Albee
1961 *Night of the Iguana*, Tennessee Williams
1961 *Stone and Star*, Robert Ardrey (Title changed from *Shadow of Heroes*, 1958.)
1962 *Oh Dad, Poor Dad, Mamma's Hung You in the Closet and I'm Feelin' So Sad*, Arthur Kopit
1962 *A Thousand Clowns*, Herb Gardner
1962 *Who's Afraid of Virginia Woolf?*, Edward Albee
1963 *Barefoot in the Park*, Neil Simon
1963 *In White America*, Martin Duberman
1963 *One Flew over the Cuckoo's Nest*, Dale Wasserman (From the novel by Ken Kesey.)
1964 *After the Fall*, Arthur Miller
1964 *Dutchman*, LeRoi Jones
1964 *Incident at Vichy*, Arthur Miller
1964 *Slow Dance on the Killing Ground*, William Hanley
1964 *The Subject Was Roses*, Frank Gilroy
1964 *Tiny Alice*, Edward Albee
1965 *America Hurrah!*, Jean-Claude van Itallie
1965 *Clara's Ole Man*, Ed Bullins
1965 *Icarus's Mother*, Sam Shephard
1965 *The Odd Couple*, Neil Simon
1965 *TV*, Jean-Claude van Itallie
1966 *A Delicate Balance*, Edward Albee
1966 *The Lion in Winter*, James Goldman
1966 *Viet Rock*, Megan Terry
1967 *The Beard*, Michael McClure
1967 *Ceremony of Innocence*, Ronald Ribman
1967 *MacBird!*, Barbara Garson
1967 *Scuba Duba*, Bruce Jay Friedman
1968 *The Boys in the Band*, Mart Crowley
1968 *The Great White Hope*, Howard Sackler

1968 *I Never Sang for My Father*, Robert Anderson
1968 *The Indian Wants to Get to the Bronx*, Israel Horovitz
1968 *Plaza Suite*, Neil Simon
1968 *The Price*, Arthur Miller
1969 *Butterflies Are Free*, Leonard Gershe
1969 *Ceremonies in Dark Old Men*, Lonne Elder III
1969 *Indians*, Arthur Kopit
1969 *No Place To Be Somebody*, Charles Gordone

1970–1980

1970 *Child's Play*, Robert Marasco
1970 *The Effect of Gamma Rays on Man-in-the-Moon Marigolds*, Paul Zindel
1970 *The Trial of the Catonsville Nine*, Father Daniel Berrigan
1971 *The Basic Training of Pavlo Hummel*, David Rabe
1971 *The House of Blue Leaves*, John Guare
1971 *Lenny*, Julian Barry
1971 *Mad Dog Blues and Other Plays*, Sam Shephard
1971 *Moonchildren*, Michael Weller
1971 *Prisoner of Second Avenue*, Neil Simon
1971 *Sticks and Bones*, David Rabe
1971 *That Championship Season*, Jason Miller
1971 *Where Has Tommy Flowers Gone?*, Terrence McNally
1972 *The River Niger*, Joseph Walker
1972 *The Sunshine Boys*, Neil Simon
1972 *Wedding Band*, Alice Childress
1973 *Bad Habits: Ravenswood and Dunelawn*, Terrence McNally
1973 *Hot L Baltimore*, Lanford Wilson
1973 *In the Boom Boom Room*, David Rabe
1973 *When You Comin Back, Red Ryder?*, Mark Medoff
1974 *Short Eyes*, Miguel Pinero
1975 *The Shadow Box*, Michael Cristofer
1975 *The Ritz*, Terrence McNally
1975 *Same Time, Next Year*, Bernard Slade
1975 *Seascape*, Edward Albee
1975 *Sexual Perversity in Chicago*, David Mamet
1976 *American Buffalo*, David Mamet
1976 *For Colored Girls Who Have Considered Suicide When the Rainbow Is Enuf*, Ntozake Shange
1976 *Streamers*, David Rabe
1977 *The Gin Game*, D. L. Coburn
1978 *Gemini*, Albert Innaurato
1978 *Uncommon Women and Others*, Wendy Wasserstein
1978 *Wings*, Arthur Kopit
1979 *Bosoms and Neglect*, John Guare
1979 *Buried Child*, Sam Shephard
1979 *Getting Out*, Marsha Norman
1980 *Children of a Lesser God*, Mark Medoff